# The Routledge International Handbook of Criminology and Human Rights

*The Routledge International Handbook of Criminology and Human Rights* brings together a diverse body of work from around the globe and across a wide range of criminological topics and perspectives, united by its critical application of human rights law and principles. This collection explores the interdisciplinary reach of criminology and is the first of its kind to link criminology and human rights.

This text is divided into six sections, each with an introduction and an overview provided by one of the editors. The opening section makes an assessment of the current standing of human rights within the discipline. Each of the remaining sections corresponds to a substantive area of harm prevention and social control which together make up the main core of contemporary criminology, namely:

- criminal law in practice;
- transitional justice, peacemaking and community safety;
- policing in all its guises;
- traditional and emerging approaches to criminal justice; and
- penality, both within and beyond the prison.

This Handbook forms an authoritative foundation on which future teaching and research about human rights and criminology can be built. This multi-disciplinary text is an essential companion for criminologists, sociologists, legal scholars and political scientists.

**Leanne Weber** is Associate Professor and ARC Future Fellow in Internal Border Policing at Monash University, Australia, and Co-Director of the Border Crossing Observatory.

**Elaine Fishwick** is an independent research consultant currently working on a project with Sydney University Social Justice Network, Australia.

**Marinella Marmo** is Associate Professor in Criminal Justice and Associate Dean (Research) at Flinders University Law School, Australia.

This ambitious Handbook is the first major attempt to bring human rights out of the fringe and to the fore of criminological debate. This is a superb example of trans-nationalising the discipline by bringing together scholars from the global north and south. The Handbook is an essential source of original and diverse scholarship that brings criminology and human rights perspectives together. It will appeal to a broad range of scholars across a number of disciplines well beyond criminology. It is also vital reading for policy makers, legislators and human rights activists and organisations across the world. I thoroughly commend it.

**Kerry Carrington**, *Head of School of Justice, Faculty of Law, Queensland University of Technology, Australia*

For years many of us have bemoaned the lack of synergy between human rights and criminological scholarship. Happily, criminologists and human rights scholars are increasingly talking to each other and this diverse and rich collection marks an important milestone in that development. The editors and contributors are to be warmly congratulated.

**Kieran McEvoy**, *Professor of Law and Transitional Justice, Queens University Belfast, Northern Ireland*

# The Routledge International Handbook of Criminology and Human Rights

*Edited by Leanne Weber, Elaine Fishwick and Marinella Marmo*

Routledge
Taylor & Francis Group
LONDON AND NEW YORK

First published 2017
by Routledge
2 Park Square, Milton Park, Abingdon, Oxon OX14 4RN

and by Routledge
52 Vanderbilt Avenue, New York, NY 10017

First issued in paperback 2020

*Routledge is an imprint of the Taylor & Francis Group, an informa business*



*British Library Cataloguing-in-Publication Data*
A catalogue record for this book is available from the British Library

*Library of Congress Cataloging in Publication Data*
Names: Weber, Leanne, editor. | Fishwick, Elaine, editor. | Marmo, Marinella, editor.
Title: The Routledge international handbook of criminology and human rights/edited by Leanne Weber, Elaine Fishwick and Marinella Marmo.
Description: Abingdon, Oxon; New York, NY: Routledge, 2016. |
Series: Routledge international handbooks | Includes bibliographical references and index.
Identifiers: LCCN 2016003275 | ISBN 9781138931176 (hardback) |
ISBN 9781315679891 (ebook)
Subjects: LCSH: Criminology. | Human rights.
Classification: LCC HV6025 .R6974 2016 | DDC 364–dc23
LC record available at http://lccn.loc.gov/2016003275

ISBN 13: 978-0-367-58150-3 (pbk)
ISBN 13: 978-1-138-93117-6 (hbk)

Typeset in Bembo
by Sunrise Setting Ltd, Brixham, UK

# Contents

# Illustrations

## Figures



## Tables

# Contributors

**Madeline-Sophie Abbas** completed her PhD in Sociology at the University of Leeds. Her research examines the role of terror in the governance of Muslims in the 'war on terror' context. Key strands are critical race and whiteness studies, Islamophobia, postcolonial theory, and migration. Publications include 'White Terror in the "War on Terror"' (2013); for a co-edited special issue, 'New Territories in Critical Whiteness Studies' (Abbas, Burgin, Decker and Hunter, 2013), *Critical race and whiteness studies*, 9(1); and a co-edited book, *The big society: the big divide?* (Abbas and Lachman, Just West Yorkshire 2012). She is currently Research Associate for the Cambridge Migration Research Network at the University of Cambridge.

**Muradu Abdo Srur** received his undergraduate degree in law from Addis Ababa University and his LLM degree from San Francisco University. He obtained a PhD at Warwick University. His PhD thesis interrogated the theoretical and policy foundations of Ethiopia's land law. He has published articles, comments and textbooks in the areas of land law, property law, customary law and legal history. His research interest is law and development with a focus on land law and customary systems. He has edited a number of research papers. He teaches at Addis Ababa University, School of Law. He may be reached at: muradu1@yahoo.co.nz.

**Monica Aciru** is a doctoral researcher at the Leuven Institute of Criminology (KU Leuven) working on post Truth and Reconciliation Commissions and reparation for victims with a focus on the Sierra Leone TRC and Ghana NRC. She holds a degree in social sciences (BA), a master's in peace and conflict studies (MA) from Makerere University (Uganda) and a master's in governance and development from the University of Antwerp (Belgium).

**Biko Agozino** is a Professor of Sociology and Africana Studies, Virginia Tech, Blacksburg, VA. He is the author of the following books: *Today na today* (Poetry, Omala Media 2013); *The debt penalty* (Play, lulu.com ebook 2010); *ADAM: Africana drug-free alternative medicine* (lulu.com ebook 2006); *Counter-colonial criminology* (Pluto Press 2003); *Pan African issues in crime and justice* (co-edited, Taylor & Francis 2004); *Nigeria: democratising a militarised civil society* (co-authored, Centre for Democracy & Development 2001); *Theoretical and methodological issues in migration research* (edited, Ashgate 2000); and *Black women and the criminal justice system* (Avebury 1997). Also Director-Producer-Editor of *Reparative justice*, 30 minutes, colour, African Independent Television, Lagos, Nigeria, 2002; Director-Producer of *CLR James: The Black Jacobins sociology series*, 2008, NCC Television, Trinidad and Tobago; Director-Producer, *Shouters and the control freak empire*, Winner of the Best International Short Documentary, Columbia Gorge Film Festival, US, 2011. Editor-in-Chief of the *African Journal of Criminology and Justice Studies*, and Series

Editor, *Ashgate Publishers Interdisciplinary Research Series in Ethnic, Gender and Class Relations*. PhD (Edinburgh); MPhil (Cambridge); BSc First Class Hons (Calabar).

**Anthony Amatrudo** is currently Associate Professor of Criminology at Middlesex University and a Visiting Fellow at St Edmund's College, Cambridge. He is the author of *Human rights and the criminal justice system* (with Leslie Blake, Routledge 2014) and *Criminology and political theory* (Sage 2009). He has held a number of visiting posts, notably at the CEU in Budapest and the Max-Planck-Institut für ausländisches und internationales Strafrecht in Freiburg and the Max-Planck-Institut für europäische Rechtsgeschichte in Frankfurt-am-Main. In 2013 he was a senior Visiting Fellow at the Nathanson Centre on Transnational Crime, Human Rights and Security at Osgoode Hall Law School, Toronto.

**Rosemary Barberet** is Professor in the Sociology Department at John Jay College of Criminal Justice, City University of New York, US. Rosemary is also Adjunct Professor in the Faculty of Law at the Queensland University of Technology. Her research interests include crime indicators, victimization, gender and crime, and cross-cultural methodology and crime and justice in Spain. Her most recent book, *Women, crime and criminal justice: a global enquiry* (Routledge 2014) won awards from both the Division of International Criminology of the American Society of Criminology and the International Section of the Academy of Criminal Justice Sciences. Dr Barberet represents the International Sociological Association (ISA) at the United Nations and is a member of the ISA Executive Committee. She is the current editor of *Feminist Criminology*.

**Lorana Bartels** (BA LLB LLM PhD GDLP GCTE) is an Associate Professor and Head of School in the School of Law and Justice at the University of Canberra. She is also an Honorary Associate Professor at the University of Tasmania, and Life Member of Clare Hall at the University of Cambridge. Lorana is a member of the Australian Capital Territory (ACT) Government's Law Reform Advisory Council, Behavioural Law Responses Expert Reference Group, Justice Reform Advisory Group, and Justice Reinvestment Advisory Group. In addition she is a member of the ACT Law Society Criminal Law Committee and the management committee of Prisoners Aid ACT, and the ACT Editor and Sentencing Editor of the *Criminal Law Journal*. Lorana has published widely on a range of criminal justice issues. Her key research interests are sentencing, corrections, and the treatment of Indigenous people and women in the criminal justice system.

**Alan Beckley** (MSc, LLM, LLB) is studying for a PhD on the subject of policing, ethics and human rights. He served for 30 years as a police officer in the United Kingdom, where he published many articles and books on policing. Alan was on a national working party for the introduction of the *Human Rights Act 1998* to introduce the new rights-based law to the police forces of England, Wales and Northern Ireland. He was used as an expert presenter by the Council of Europe on the subject of police ethics and human rights in 13 different European countries.

**Didier Bigo** is Professor in the King's College London Department of War Studies and Research Professor of International Relations at Sciences-Po Paris/CERI. He is also Director of the Center for Study of Conflicts, Liberty and Security (CCLS) www.ccls.eu and editor of the quarterly journal *Cultures & Conflicts*, published by l'Harmattan www.conflits.org, as well as founder and previous co-editor with Rob Walker of the ISA journal *International Political Sociology*. He is currently the responsible for the KCL-WP on the professionals of security of the FP7 Source www.societalsecurity.net/partners/kcl; and the coordinator for Sc-Po of the ANR on surveillance after Snowden – UTIC. www.sciencespo.fr/ressources-numeriques/content/usage-des-technologies-liees-l-interception-des-communications.

**Jessie Blackbourn** is Lecturer in Politics and Human Rights at Kingston University, London. She is the author of *Anti-terrorism law and normalising Northern Ireland* (Routledge 2015) and has had her research on anti-terrorism laws and counter-terrorism review published in leading domestic and international journals.

**Jeremy Boland** (BA LLB (Hons) GDLP BA (Hons) MA), is Principal Consultant at Gillian Beaumont Legal and Professional Associate at the University of Canberra. Previously, he worked as Senior Manager, Workforce Development and Training at ACT Corrective Services.

**Ben Bowling** is Professor of Criminology and Criminal Justice and Deputy Dean of the Dickson Poon School of Law, King's College London. His books include *Violent racism* (OUP 1999), *Racism, crime and justice* (with Coretta Phillips, Longman 2004), *Policing the Caribbean* (OUP 2010), *Global policing* (with James Sheptycki, Sage 2012), *Stop and search: police power in global context* (with Leanne Weber, Routledge 2012) and the four-volume *Global policing and transnational law enforcement* (with James Sheptycki, Sage 2015). He has been an adviser to the UK Parliament, Foreign and Commonwealth Office, Equality and Human Rights Commission, the European Commission, Interpol and the United Nations.

**Avi Brisman** (MFA, JD, PhD) is an Associate Professor in the School of Justice Studies at Eastern Kentucky University in Richmond, Kentucky (US). He is co-editor, with Nigel South, of the *Routledge international handbook of green criminology* (Routledge 2013); co-editor, with Nigel South and Rob White, of *Environmental crime and social conflict: contemporary and emerging issues* (Ashgate 2015); and co-author, with Nigel South, of *Green cultural criminology: constructions of environmental harm, consumerism, and resistance to ecocide* (Routledge 2014).

**David Brown**, Emeritus Professor, taught criminal law and criminal justice at the University of NSW from 1974 to 2008. He is a co-author of the major and innovative *Criminal Laws* (6th edn, Federation Press 2015). He is very widely published, both in Australia and internationally. His co-authored or co-edited books include: *Justice reinvestment: winding back imprisonment* (Palgrave Macmillan 2015), *Penal culture and hyperincarceration* (Routledge 2013), *The new punitiveness* (Willan 2005), *Prisoners as citizens* (Federation Press 2002), *Rethinking law and order* (Pluto Press 1998), *Death in the hands of the state* (Redfern Legal Centre Publishing 1988), *The judgments of Lionel Murphy* (Primavera Press 1986), and *The prison struggle* (Penguin 1982), along with 35 book chapters.

**Nerida Chazal** is a Lecturer in Criminal Justice at Flinders University Law School. She previously held the position of Research Fellow with the Centre of Crime Policy and Research, South Australia. Her research examines the aims and functioning of international criminal justice in a complex and increasingly global world. She has recently published two books: *The International Criminal Court and global social control: international criminal justice in late modernity* (Routledge 2015), and *Criminal justice in international society* (co-edited with Willem De Lint and Marinello Marmo, Routledge 2014).

**Chris Cunneen** is Professor of Criminology in the School of Social Sciences, University of New South Wales, Australia, and Adjunct Professor at the Cairns Institute, James Cook

University, Australia. He has published widely on Indigenous legal issues, juvenile justice, penality and restorative justice. He is a Fellow of the Academy of Social Sciences in Australia. Recent books include *Penal culture and hyperincarceration* (with Baldry, et al., Ashgate 2013); and *Justice reinvestment: winding back imprisonment* (with Brown, et al., Palgrave Macmillan 2015).

**Louise Forde** is a PhD candidate at the School of Law, University College Cork in Ireland. She is an Irish Research Council scholar, undertaking research into children's rights and youth justice.

**Loraine Gelsthorpe** is Professor of Criminology and Criminal Justice, and Deputy Director of the Institute of Criminology, University of Cambridge. She is also Director of the Centre for Community, Gender and Social Justice and Co-founder of the Cambridge Migration Research Network, and Adjunct Professor, Crime and Justice Research Centre, QUT, Brisbane, Australia. She has written extensively on community penalties and women, crime and criminal justice. Recent publications include: 'Women and sentencing: challenges and choices' (with G. Sharpe), in *Exploring sentencing practice in England and Wales* (ed. J. Roberts, Palgrave Macmillan 2015); and 'Diversity: the voluntary sector's vision in criminal justice' (with J. Dominey) in *The voluntary sector and criminal justice* (eds A. Hucklesby and M. Corcoran, Palgrave Macmillan 2016).

**Andrew Goldsmith** is Strategic Professor of Criminology and Director of the Centre for Crime Policy and Research, Flinders University. He has been researching policing issues for more than 30 years, including Australia's involvement in police-building and peacekeeping in Timor-Leste and the Solomon Islands under a Linkage Project with the Australian Federal Police (2005–10). Between 2007 and 2012, he participated in meetings held by the United Nations Police Division related to the development of police peacekeeping doctrine. Between 2009 and 2012, he held the position of Executive Director, Centre for Transnational Crime Prevention, University of Wollongong, and rejoined Flinders in late 2012 to take up his current position. In addition to his ongoing policing research interests, he is currently conducting research on prison corruption and Internet criminality.

**Kiran Grewal** is a Senior Research Fellow with the Institute for Social Justice, Australian Catholic University. Prior to joining the institute she was the Research Manager for the Enhancing Human Rights Protection (EHRP) in the Context of Law Enforcement and Security project at the University of Sydney. She is the author of the forthcoming book, *The socio-political practice of human rights* (Ashgate 2016).

**Michael Grewcock** teaches criminal law and criminology in the Faculty of Law, University of New South Wales, Sydney, Australia. He is the author of *Border crimes: Australia's war on illicit migrants* (Federation Press 2009) and several articles and book chapters on contemporary border policing and state crime. He is co-author of David Brown et al., *Criminal laws*, 5th and 6th editions (Federation Press 2011 and 2015) and a member of the Editorial Boards of the *State Crime Journal* and the *Howard Journal of Crime and Justice*.

**Sanzhuan Guo** is a Lecturer in Law and Socio-Legal Studies at Flinders University Law School. Her research interests include international human rights law, nationality and statelessness, and international law theory. Her representative publications include a book chapter on the peacekeeping decision-making process and financing in China (2014), a book on comparative studies on the effectiveness of national human rights institutions (2013), and an article titled 'Implementation of human rights treaties by Chinese courts' in (2009) *Chinese Journal of International*

*Law*. Sanzhuan studied law in Melbourne Law School (JD), Peking University (PhD) and Northwestern in Chicago (LLM). She has been admitted to practise law in Australia, China and the United States.

**Fiona Haines** (BA (Hons), PhD) is Professor of Criminology at the University of Melbourne and Adjunct Professor at RegNet ANU. She has undertaken extensive research in white collar and corporate crime, globalization, risk and regulation, and has published widely. Her most recent book, *Regulatory transformations: rethinking economy society interactions* (Hart Publishing 2015), is co-edited with Bettina Lange (Oxford) and Dania Thomas (Glasgow). Her current work analyses economic globalization and its impact on accountability of multinational corporations for human rights abuse.

**Deena Haydon** (PhD) is an independent research consultant and a member of the Childhood, Transition and Social Justice Initiative at Queen's University Belfast in Northern Ireland. Her main research interests include parenting and family support, youth justice, and children's rights. Linking research, theory, policy and practice, her publications include: a co-authored book and numerous journal articles (in the *Journal of Law and Society*, *Youth Justice*, *The Howard Journal*, *Journal of the History of Childhood and Youth*), book chapters, research reports, resources for children and practitioners, as well as submissions to the UN Committee on the Rights of the Child. She has presented workshops, seminars and conference papers for academic and public audiences in the United Kingdom, Europe, the United States and Australia.

**Russell Hogg** is Professor in the Crime and Justice Research Centre, Faculty of Law, Queensland University of Technology. He is co-author of *Rethinking law and order* (Pluto Press 1998) and *Policing the rural crisis* (Federation Press 2006), and author of numerous articles and book chapters within the fields of criminology and criminal justice studies. His principal research interests relate to criminological theory, the politics of law and order, and punishment.

**Robyn Holder** is a Research Fellow at Griffith University, Australia, and was previously Visiting Scholar at the Regulatory Institutions Network, Australian National University where she obtained her PhD. She has over 20 years' experience in research, public policy and law reform in Australia and the United Kingdom, particularly on system reform. Her areas of research interest include victims, rights and justice; violence against women and justice responses; and the relationship between citizens and the state. More recently she has extended these research interests to explore justice for victims in conflict and post-conflict settings. Formerly, for over 15 years, she held an appointment as an independent statutory advocate for victims' rights.

**Kathryn Hollingsworth** is a Professor of Law at Newcastle University (UK). She previously held full-time academic posts at King's College London, Otago University, and Cardiff University and has been a Visiting Professor at the universities of Melbourne and New South Wales. She obtained a BA (Law) degree from Sheffield University and a PhD from Cambridge University. For the last eight years her research has focused on children's rights and youth justice, and she is co-convener (with Helen Stalford) of the AHRC-funded Children's Rights Judgments Project. She is on the Standing Committee for Youth Justice and the Steering Committee of the Youth Justice Legal Centre.

**Julia Hornberger** (PhD) is a Senior Lecturer in the Department of Anthropology, University of the Witwatersrand in Johannesburg, South Africa. She has published widely on questions of policing, violence, justice, and human rights. Her book, *Human rights and policing: the meaning of violence and justice in the everyday practice of policing in Johannesburg* was published in 2011 by Routledge. More recently, she has shifted her focus towards a project on international crime control and the circulation of fake and substandard medication, through which she explores the policing of health and intellectual property rights.

**Diete Humblet** stems from a background in both law and criminological sciences, and is affiliated to the research group Crime and Society (CRiS), research line Penality & Society, at the Vrije Universiteit Brussel (Belgium). Under the supervision of Professor Sonja Snacken, she is currently preparing a PhD on older adult prisoners in Belgium, funded by the Fonds voor Wetenschappelijk Onderzoek Vlaanderen (The Research Foundation – Flanders).

**Jill Hunter** is a Professor in the Law Faculty at the University of New South Wales. She publishes widely on criminal trial processes, evidence law, and on human rights in the criminal process. Two publications specifically combining these interests are J. Hunter and P. Roberts (eds) *Criminal evidence and human rights: reimagining common law procedural traditions* (Hart Publishing 2012) and J. Hunter et al., *Criminal process and human rights* (Federation Press 2011). Jill's most recent books are *The trial*, published by Federation Press in 2015 and J. Hunter, P. Roberts, S.N.M. Young and D. Dixon (eds), *Integrity of criminal process: from theory into practice* (Hart Publishing 2016).

**Hope Johnson** researches the intersections between trade, environment and human rights law. She is a PhD candidate, sessional academic and researcher with the Faculty of Law at Queensland University of Technology (QUT) and Institute for Future Environments. Her research examines the international governance of food production, rights-based food security, environmental justice and crimes, and the political economy of food. Hope is a member of QUT's International Law and Global Governance Group, and she teaches on Indigenous legal issues, jurisprudence and eco-crime within QUT's Faculty of Law.

**Ratna Kapur** is Global Professor of Law, Jindal Global Law School. She is also a Senior Faculty at the Institute of Global Law and Policy, Harvard Law School, and currently a Visiting Senior Research Fellow at the Graduate Institute of International and Development Studies. She is also a Visiting Professor of Law at Queen Mary University of London. She has written and published extensively on issues of feminist legal theory, postcolonial theory and human rights. Her books include *Erotic justice: law and the new politics of postcolonialism* (Cavendish Press 2005) and *Makeshift migrants: gender, belonging and postcolonial anxieties* (Routledge 2010). Her recent work has focused on the rise of the sexual security regime in international human rights law and advocacy.

**Wondwossen Demissie Kassa** is a PhD candidate in Flinders University Law School. He received his LLB from the Addis Ababa University Law School and his LLM from the University of Michigan Law School. He has a teaching position at Addis Ababa University. His teaching and research interests include human rights, security, counter-terrorism legislation and prosecution. He has published and edited books relating to Ethiopian criminal procedure and several peer-reviewed journal articles relating to counter-terrorism at the national and global levels, including their interplay. While doing his PhD he has been a research assistant for an Australian Research Council-funded project that relates to Australian counter-terrorism prosecutions.

**Ursula Kilkelly** is a Professor of Law at University College Cork in Ireland. She has been researching children's rights in juvenile justice for 20 years, publishing on youth courts and detention. She has been involved in activism throughout that time and was involved in the drafting of the Guidelines on Child-friendly Justice with the Council of Europe. Her research is available at http://research.ucc.ie/profiles/B012/ukilkelly and she is on twitter at @ukilkelly.

**Kristian Lasslett** is Senior Lecturer in Criminology at the University of Ulster and sits on the Executive Board of the International State Crime Initiative (ISCI) (www.statecrime.org). His research has featured in a range of international journals including the *British Journal of Criminology, State Crime* and *Theoretical Criminology*. Kristian's first book, *State crime on the margins of empire*, was published by Pluto Press in 2014, and his second book, *The crimes of urbanisation*, will be published by Routledge in 2017. His current research focuses on land confiscation, forced eviction and corruption, in addition to war, memory and post-conflict reconstruction. Kristian is editor of ISCI's online digital platform, the State Crime Testimony Project, and joint Editor-in-Chief of the initiative's scholarly journal *State Crime*.

**Willem de Lint** is Professor in Criminology, Flinders University. From 2007 to 2010 he was Head, Sociology, Anthropology, and Criminology at the University of Windsor, Canada. Previously, he also worked as a lecturer at the Institute of Criminology, Victoria University of Wellington, New Zealand. His areas of interest include security and policing, particularly public order policing, security intelligence, and how governance of public safety and security is accomplished by a variety of service providers, actors or agencies. Willem serves or has served on the editorial boards of the *Australian and New Zealand Journal of Criminology, Canadian Journal of Criminology and Criminal Justice, Policing and Society*, and *The Open Law Journal*.

**Randy K. Lippert** is Professor of Criminology at the University of Windsor, Canada, where he teaches in the areas of socio-legal studies, surveillance, and policing/security. He has published seven books and more than 60 refereed articles and chapters. He is currently debates editor for *Surveillance and Society* and on advisory boards of other international journals. His current book projects are *Governing practices of neo-liberalism, governmentalities, and the ethnographic imaginary* (co-edited with M. Brady, for University of Toronto Press 2016) and *National security, surveillance, and terror: Canadian and Australian sovereignty compared* (co-edited with K. Walby, I. Warren and D. Palmer, for McGill-Queens University Press 2017).

**Simon Mackenzie** is Professor of Criminology at Victoria University of Wellington in New Zealand, and Professor in the Scottish Centre for Crime and Justice Research, School of Social and Political Sciences, University of Glasgow. He works on organized, white-collar, and transnational crime, including in the Trafficking Culture research group (www.traffickingculture.org), gathering and analysing evidence on the global trade in looted cultural objects. He is a member of the editorial boards of the *British Journal of Criminology* and the *Howard Journal of Crime and Justice*, and is on the Peer Review Committee of the Arts and Humanities Research Council.

**Natasha Marhia** carried out research with Delhi Police for her doctorate on policing, gender and violence, awarded by the LSE Gender Institute in 2013. Natasha has taught masters and undergraduate-level courses at the LSE for six years, on interdisciplinary social sciences, gender theory and conflict and globalization. She has recently developed undergraduate teaching programmes on crime, race and gender, and gender inequality and intersectionality. She has conducted research for women's rights organizations in London and Delhi. Her current research interests are around gender and human security, and discourses of violence against women.

**Greg Martin** is Associate Professor of Socio-Legal Studies, School of Social and Political Sciences, University of Sydney, Australia. He has published widely in socio-legal studies, criminology, policing, and law, including in the *British Journal of Sociology, Crime Media Culture, Journal of Law and Society, Policing & Society*, and *Sydney Law Review*. Greg is author of *Understanding social movements* (Routledge 2015), and co-editor of *Secrecy, law and society* (Routledge 2015). He is an Associate Editor of *Crime Media Culture*, and a member of the Editorial Advisory Board of *Social Movement Studies*.

**Bill McClanahan** is a doctoral student in criminology in the Department of Sociology at the University of Essex in Colchester, England. He holds a Master of Science degree in Criminology from Eastern Kentucky University, and a Bachelor of Science degree in Criminal Justice and Criminology from Indiana University. His research interests include green, cultural, and visual criminologies, water justice, climate change, policing and wildlife crime. His writing on these topics can be found in *Critical Criminology, Contemporary Justice Review* and a variety of edited volumes.

**Jude McCulloch** is a Professor of Criminology at Monash University, in the School of Social Sciences. She has researched and published on the militarization of policing, police use of deadly force, counter-terrorism, state crime, crime and globalization and the politics of security and law and order. Her latest book is *Pre-crime: preemption, precaution and the future* (Routledge 2016).

**Nicola McGarrity** is a Lecturer in Criminal and Public Law in the Faculty of Law, University of New South Wales. Her research in the field of anti-terrorism law and policy has been published in leading Australian and international journals. Nicola is also the co-author of *Inside Australia's anti-terrorism laws and trials* (with Andrew Lynch and George Williams, New South Press 2015), and has co-edited *Counter-terrorism and beyond: the culture of law and justice after 9/11* (with Andrew Lynch and George Williams, Routledge 2010) and *Surveillance, counter-terrorism and comparative constitutionalism* (with Fergal Davis and George Williams, Routledge 2014).

**Des McNulty** took up this role of Deputy Director, Policy Scotland in 2012 and his role is to develop links with research users, including policy-makers, practitioners and organizations working on public policy issues and academics within the school and other colleagues in the College of Social Sciences and other colleges in the university, increase awareness and uptake of research by policy-makers, and support the professional development of staff undertaking policy-related research. Des is a sociologist and public policy specialist with 20 years' experience in the higher education sector. He has extensive experience working with policy-makers, having served at senior levels in local government, as a health board member, as a committee chair within the Scottish Parliament and as a minister. He has recently been undertaking research on education policy with colleagues from the School of Education and on media coverage of human rights with colleagues in Sociology.

**Raymond Michalowski** of Northern Arizona University has professional interest in criminological theory; international human rights; immigration and border policy; social justice; and corporate, environmental and political crime. Most of his academic career has been focused on studying the relationships between law and justice, on the one hand, and political and economic power, on the other. Professor Michalowski's current project involves continuing an inquiry begun in 2003 into the possible violations of international law associated with the invasion and occupation of Iraq. This work extends the articles on the illegality of the Iraq War that he published with my colleague Ron Kramer in *Social Justice* and the *British Journal of Criminology*.

**Sanja Milivojevic** is a Senior Lecturer in Criminology at La Trobe University. Sanja's research interests are sex trafficking and trafficking in people, migration and borders, new technologies and crime, transnational crime and victimization, organized crime, gender and victimization, and international criminal justice and human rights.

**Valsamis Mitsilegas** is Head of the Department of Law, Professor of European Criminal Law and Director of the Criminal Justice Centre at Queen Mary University of London. His interests and expertise lie in the areas of European Union (EU) law (with a particular focus on the evolution of the Union into an Area of Freedom, Security and Justice), global security governance and human rights. He has published widely in the fields of European criminal law, immigration and asylum, and security and counter-terrorism law. Professor Mitsilegas is also a regular consultant to parliaments, EU institutions and international organizations.

**Vidura Munasinghe** is an Attorney-at-Law in Sri Lanka and a researcher at the Centre for the Study of Human Rights, University of Colombo. He was the Senior Researcher for the EHRP project. Vidura holds an MA in Sociology and is currently completing a dissertation on the role of new religious movements in South Asian politics.

**Thérèse Murphy** is Professor of Law at Queen's University Belfast. Previously she worked at the University of Nottingham, where she co-founded the Economic & Social Rights Unit within the Human Rights Law Centre. She has held visiting appointments at the EUI, Toronto and Monash; she has also been a Fulbright Scholar at Harvard Law School. She is a longstanding member of the editorial board of the *Human Rights Law Review* and her own publications include *Health and human rights* (Hart Publishing 2013) and a forthcoming co-edited collection on the UN Special Procedures.

**Bronwyn Naylor** is Associate Professor of Law, and Deputy Director, Castan Centre for Human Rights Law, at Monash University, with arts, law and criminology degrees from Monash University and Cambridge University. She has been teaching, researching and publishing in criminal law, corrections, regulation, and criminal justice and gender for over 20 years. Dr Naylor has been the lead investigator on a major grant-funded project on human rights in places of detention and is a contributor to and co-editor of the Federation Press publication based on the research, *Human rights in closed environments* (Federation Press 2014).

**Stephan Parmentier** heads international relations in criminology at Leuven University, where he currently teaches sociology of crime, law, and human rights. In July 2010 and again in 2014 Stephan was appointed Secretary-General of the International Society for Criminology. He also serves on the Advisory Board of the Oxford Centre of Criminology and the International Centre for Transitional Justice (New York). Stephan is the founder and co-general editor of the international book series on transitional justice (Intersentia Publishers, Cambridge/Antwerp), and is editor of the newly established *Restorative Justice International Journal*. He co-directs the Flemish Interuniversity Network on Law and Development. He also serves as a referee to the ERC funding scheme of the European Union, and other national and international research foundations. Over the past quarter century he has been an advisor to the European Committee for the Prevention of Torture, to key Belgian government agencies and Amnesty International.

**Gregory Philo** is research director of the Glasgow University Media Group (www.gla.ac.uk/departments/sociology/media.html) and Professor of Communication and Social Change at Glasgow University. His books include *More bad news from Israel* (with M. Berry, Pluto Books 2011), *Bad news for refugees* (with E. Briant and P. Donald, Pluto Books 2013), and *New methodologies in audience research: climate change and energy security* (with C. Happer, Routledge 2014).

**Sharon Pickering** is an Australian Research Council Professorial Future Fellow and Professor of Criminology at Monash University. She is the founder and Director of the Border Crossing Observatory, an international network of scholars studying borders, security, crime and justice (www.borderobservatory.org). She researches and publishes extensively in the field of borders, migration and gender.

**Mina Rauschenbach** is a Research Fellow at the Leuven Institute of Criminology. She is currently working on survey data collected in Bosnia-Herzegovina and Serbia, analysing perceptions of non-judicial transitional justice measures and their value in terms of acknowledgment and social restoration. Holding a PhD in Social Sciences (University of Lausanne), her main research areas concern the role of responsibility and victimhood beliefs and of non-judicial justice measures in post-conflict contexts, focusing particularly on their significance in shaping justice concerns and conflict processes. She has recently published articles in peer-reviewed journals, notably *Political Psychology* and the *International Review of Victimology*.

**Diana Rodriguez-Spahia** is a student in the doctoral programme in criminal justice at the Graduate Center, City University of New York, housed at John Jay College of Criminal Justice, with a specialization in policy, oversight and administration (POA). Her research interests include gender and crime, terrorism and the intersection of policy and practice. She was the recipient of the highly competitive US Department of Homeland Security Career Pathways Scholarship and is currently an adjunct instructor in international criminal justice and public administration. She is the managing editor of *Feminist Criminology*.

**Mutuma Ruteere** is currently the UN Special Rapporteur on contemporary forms of racism, racial discrimination, xenophobia and related intolerance. He also serves as Director, Centre for Human Rights and Policy Studies, a research centre based in Nairobi, Kenya. He has most recently undertaken studies on profiling in law enforcement, glorification of Nazism and the threat of extremist movements, and Internet governance and racism among others.

**Huma Saeed** is a recipient of the Jack Kent Cooke Graduate Scholarship and a PhD candidate at the Leuven Institute of Criminology (University of Leuven), where she focuses on the intersection between the violation of socioeconomic rights and state crime in the context of transitional justice, with Afghanistan as a case study. She has an MSc in Human Rights from the London School of Economics and Political Science and a BA in Political Science from the University of Maryland, Baltimore County. She has worked with human rights and women's rights organizations in Afghanistan, Pakistan and internationally, as well as with the UN Development Programme in Afghanistan.

**Peter Scharff-Smith** is Professor in Criminology at Aalborg University and Associate Professor at Oslo University. He has published books and articles in Danish, English and German on prisons, punishment and human rights, including works on prison history, children of imprisoned parents and the use of solitary confinement in prisons. He has also published books and articles on the Waffen-SS, the Holocaust and the Nazi war of extermination at the Eastern front during World War 2. His latest book in English is *When the innocent are punished: the children of imprisoned parents* (Palgrave Macmillan 2014).

**Melanie Schwartz** is Senior Lecturer in the Faculty of Law, University of New South Wales, Australia. Her research interests focus on Indigenous legal issues, justice reinvestment and access to justice.

**David Scott** has worked at Liverpool John Moores University since August 2013. He is a qualified teacher and was awarded an MA (with distinction) in Crime, Deviance and Social Policy from Lancaster University in 1996 and a doctorate under the supervision of Professor Barbara Hudson from the University of Central Lancashire in 2006. David's main research interests include the ethical and political foundations of penal abolitionism; the connections between the emancipatory politics of abolitionism, human rights and social justice; death, suffering and ethical relationships in the prison place; critical social theory and the concept of 'crime'; and 'real utopian' alternatives to poverty, social inequalities and punishment.

**Rebecca Scott Bray** is Co-Director of the Sydney Institute of Criminology, Sydney Law School, and Senior Lecturer in Socio-Legal Studies, School of Social and Political Sciences at the University of Sydney. Her research interests lie at the intersections of criminology, law and culture, with a specific focus on issues around the dead. Research areas include medico-legal and forensic criminology; coronial law and practice, and photography, art and aesthetics as they involve the dead. She is co-editor of *Secrecy, law and society* (Routledge 2015).

**Phil Scraton** (PhD) is Professor of Criminology in the School of Law, Queen's University, Belfast, and Director of the Childhood, Transition and Social Justice Initiative. He has held visiting scholarships at Monash University, University of Melbourne and University of Sydney. In 2013 he was Karl Lowenstein Fellow at Amherst College, Massachusetts, US. Recent books include *Power, conflict and criminalisation* (Routledge 2007); *The violence of incarceration* (edited with Jude McCulloch, Routledge 2008); *Hillsborough: the truth* (Mainstream 2009); and *The incarceration of women* (with Linda Moore, Routledge 2014). Appointed by the UK Home Secretary to the Hillsborough Independent Panel, he was primary author of its ground-breaking report, *Hillsborough* (The Stationery Office 2013). Until recently he was Chair of the Board of Include Youth.

**Marie Segrave** is a Senior Lecturer in Criminology at Monash University and an ARC DECRA fellowship holder. She has researched and published widely in the area of human trafficking, migration and exploitation, including *Human trafficking* (Ashgate 2014). She leads the Trafficking and Labour Exploitation research agenda for the Border Crossing Observatory.

**Clifford Shearing** is one of the world's leading scholars in security governance and policing. Professor Clifford Shearing holds professorships at the universities of Griffith, Cape Town and Montreal. As well as his prolific academic output, Clifford has made major policy contributions to the reshaping of policing and security in Argentina, Australia, Canada, Jamaica, Northern Ireland and South Africa.

**James Sheptycki** is a Professor of Criminology at York University, Toronto, Canada. He received a PhD in Sociology from the London School of Economics in 1991 and was an ESRC post-doctoral research fellow and lecturer in the Centre for Criminology and the Social and Philosophical Study of Law at the University of Edinburgh from 1993 to 1999. He is well known for his research on policing and crime under conditions of transnationalization. His current research concerns guns, crime and social order.

**Rhona Smith** is Head of Law, Newcastle University, UK. She has taught and written on a range of human rights issues over 20 years, with a particular focus on, inter alia, the UN human rights system. Relevant publications include *Textbook on international human rights* (7th edn, OUP 2016) and a series of articles on human rights monitoring by the UN Human Rights Council.

**Sonja Snacken** is a Professor of Criminology, Penology and Sociology of Law at the Vrije Universiteit Brussel (Belgium), where she holds a Research Fellowship. Her research focuses on penality in Belgium and Europe, with a special emphasis on the integration of an empirical social scientist approach with human rights concerns. International publications include: *Principles of European prison law and policy, penology and human rights* (with D. van Zyl Smit, Oxford University Press 2009); 'Resisting punitiveness in Europe?', *Theoretical Criminology*, 14(3) (2010), 273–92; *European penology?* (with T. Daems and D. van Zyl Smit, Hart Publishing 2013); *The Routledge handbook of European criminology* (with S. Body-Gendrot, M. Hough, K. Kerezsi and R. Lévy, Routledge 2013); and 'Punishment, legitimate policies and values: penal moderation, dignity and human rights', *Punishment & Society*, 17 (2015), 397–423.

**Nigel South** is a Professor in the Department of Sociology and a member of the Human Rights Centre at the University of Essex, and also an Adjunct Professor, School of Justice, Queensland University of Technology. In 2013 he received a Lifetime Achievement Award from the American Society of Criminology, Division on Critical Criminology. With Avi Brisman, he is co-editor, *Routledge international handbook of green criminology* (Routledge 2013), co-author, *Green cultural criminology: constructions of environmental harm, consumerism, and resistance to ecocide* (Routledge 2014), and both are co-editors, with Rob White, of *Environmental crime and social conflict: contemporary and emerging issues* (Routledge 2015).

**Claire Spivakovsky** is a Lecturer in Criminology at Monash University, Australia. Her research expertise extends across the broad fields of punishment, detention and social control, and she specializes in issues of 'difference'. In practice this means that all of her research, be it an investigation of racialized approaches to punishment or an analysis of the civil detention of people with cognitive impairments and mental illness, advances criminology's understanding of the ways civil and criminal justice institutions are used to contain and control 'difference' over time. Her first book in this space, *Racialized correctional governance: the mutual constructions of race and criminal justice*, was published as part of Ashgate's *Advances in Criminology Series* in 2013.

**Elizabeth Stanley** is Reader in Criminology and Rutherford Discovery Fellow at the Institute of Criminology, Victoria University of Wellington, New Zealand. Her research has focused on state crime, human rights, institutional victimization and issues of justice, in relation to events in New Zealand, South Africa, Chile, Timor-Leste, West Papua and the United Kingdom.

**Philip Stenning** spent five years as Professor of Criminology at Keele University in the United Kingdom before going to Griffith University in 2011. Prior to that, he was Professor and Director of the Institute of Criminology at Victoria University of Wellington, New Zealand, from 2003 to 2005. He was at the Centre of Criminology at the University of Toronto, Canada, from 1968 to 2002, progressing from Research Assistant to Associate Professor. In addition to his academic work during these years, Philip has served as a consultant and adviser to a wide range of government departments and commissions of inquiry in a range of countries including Canada, New Zealand, Australia, South Africa, Venezuela and Brazil, as well as to the Council of Europe and the United Nations.

**Julie Stubbs** is a criminologist and Professor in the Faculty of Law at the University of New South Wales, Australia, where she is Director of the Criminal Justice and Criminology programme. Her research interests include justice reinvestment, restorative justice, women and criminal justice, violence against women, homicide and bail. Her publications include two new books: Brown et al., *Justice reinvestment: winding back imprisonment* (Palgrave Macmillan 2016) and Stubbs and Tomsen (eds) *Australian violence* (Federation Press forthcoming).

**Saul Takahashi** is a human rights lawyer currently located in Tokyo, where he is the Japan Representative for the Business and Human Rights Resource Centre, and also teaches human rights-related courses at Waseda and Aoyama Gakuin universities. He has worked at Amnesty International in Tokyo and in London, and from 2009 to 2014 was Deputy Head of Office of the Office of the UN High Commissioner for Human Rights in Occupied Palestine. Takahashi has an LLM from the University of Essex and is the editor of *Human rights, human security, and state security: the intersection*, a three-volume reference work (published in 2014 by Praeger Publishers) exploring the connection between the three areas.

**Juan Tauri** is an Indigenous criminologist from Aotearoa (New Zealand). A graduate from the University of Cambridge, he is a critical commentator on criminal justice matters of importance to First Nations, including state responses, policy-making, and media representation of crime and the Indigenous world. Juan has published widely and recently co-edited a special issue of the *African Journal of Criminology and Justice Studies* on 'Indigenous perspectives and counter colonial criminology'. He holds a visiting appointment at the University of Wollongong, Australia.

**Sandra Walklate** is Eleanor Rathbone Chair of Sociology at the University of Liverpool, conjoint with Professor of Criminology at Monash University and adjunct Professor at QUT. She is internationally recognized for her work in victimology, particularly around criminal victimization and the fear of crime, and gender and crime. Over the last decade this work has extended into understanding the nature and effect of 'new' terrorism, connected policy responses, and presumptions around resilience. Her recent publications include: *The contradictions of terrorism* (with Gabe Mythen, Routledge 2014), *Criminology and war: transgressing the borders* (edited collection with Ross McGarry, Routledge 2015), *Victims, trauma, testimony* (with Ross McGarry, Routledge 2015). From January 2014 she took up the role of Editor-in-Chief of the *British Journal of Criminology* and in July 2014 received the British Society of Criminology's award for outstanding achievement.

**Reece Walters** is Professor of Criminology in the Centre for Crime and Justice Research and Assistant Dean Research in the Faculty of Law at Queensland University of Technology. He has published widely on crimes of the powerful and crimes against the environment. His current research focuses on crimes against the 'essentials of life', namely food, air and water.

**Tony Ward** is Professor of Law at Northumbria University, Newcastle, England. He is both a lawyer, specializing in the law of evidence, and a criminologist, specializing in state crime.

He is Co-director of the International State Crime Initiative, one of the editors of the journal *State Crime*, and a member of the Editorial Board of the *British Journal of Criminology*. He is co-author of *State crime: governments, violence and corruption* (with Penny Green, Pluto Press 2004) and *Law and crime* (with Gerry Johnstone, Sage 2010).

**Nicholas Watson** is Chair of Disability Studies at the University of Glasgow and Director of the Glasgow Centre for Disability Research. He has written widely on disability issues including disability theory, social care provision for disabled people, disability and childhood, technologies for disabled people and media representation of disability. He is currently Director of What Works Scotland, an ESRC/Scottish Government-funded project supporting the development of effective public services in Scotland.

**Noel Whitty** is a Professor of Human Rights Law at the University of Nottingham. He is a co-author of *Civil liberties law: the Human Rights Act era* (OUP 2001) and other publications which link the development of human rights law and activism to broader political and cultural forces and sensibilities. His current research is focused on imprisonment within the UK and the dynamics of prisoners' rights and penal politics, including the legacies of different visions of prisons within the fields of law and criminology. He has been a visiting scholar at the Prisons Research Centre in the Cambridge Institute of Criminology.

**Donna Yates** is a Lecturer in Social Sciences and Arts at the University of Glasgow and a researcher on the Trafficking Culture Project. An archaeologist by training, her research broadly focuses on social aspects of antiquities trafficking, art crime, and related cultural property issues. Yates has recently held a Leverhulme Fellowship and a Core Fulbright Award to study the on-the-ground effects of high-level cultural policy in Latin America and her current work involves security for and protection of sacred art in Latin America and South Asia.

**Courtney Young** lectures in both substantive criminal law and criminal justice in the Faculty of Law, University of New South Wales (UNSW). She completed her BA LLB at UNSW, where she attained first class honours, was chosen valedictorian and was awarded the University Medal in Law. She was Associate to Her Honour Judge Flannery SC in the District Court, NSW, and in 2013–15 was the Research Associate on the Australian Research Council-funded Australian Justice Reinvestment Project. Her current research interests include pre-trial remand and narcotics. She practises as a criminal defence lawyer in a private firm in rural NSW.

# Acknowledgements

We, the editors, would like to acknowledge all the authors who have contributed chapters for this ground-breaking collection and thank them for their cooperation and willingness to accept suggestions from our team in finalizing their manuscripts.

The Centre for Crime Policy and Research in the Law School at Flinders University provided financial and administrative support for the development of the book alongside the Faculty of Education, Humanities and Law at Flinders University.

We owe a huge debt of gratitude to the two outstanding administrators based at Flinders University who helped us put such an enormous collection together: without Olivia Thomas and Deb McBratney this would have been a much more onerous job, and their assistance has made the whole enterprise run incredibly smoothly. So thank you, we really appreciate what you have done.

Once again, Julia Farrell has provided excellent editorial input with her unparalleled critical gaze. Thank you Julia. We would also like to acknowledge the administrative and financial support of the Routledge team, especially Tom Sutton who initially asked us to consider the idea of putting the Handbook together, and editorial assistants Heidi Lee and Hannah Catterall, who provided support throughout the life of the project.

Finally we would like to thank our partners and families who have provided us with an unwavering cheer squad – we salute you.

Leanne, Elaine and Marinella

# Criminology and human rights

## An introduction

*Leanne Weber, Elaine Fishwick and Marinella Marmo*

Human rights frameworks and terminology have been employed in criminological scholarship for some time, and yet there is little explicit recognition of what Stanley (2007) has referred to as a 'criminology for human rights'. The *Routledge international handbook of criminology and human rights* aims at addressing this gap in the criminological scholarship; its timely publication will enable criminologists to engage more explicitly with human rights in their research areas.

This does not mean criminologists have not dealt with human rights. In our book titled *Crime, justice and human rights* (Weber et al. 2014), we dedicated a full chapter – 'Integrating criminology and human rights' (Chapter 4) – to an exploration of existing criminological scholarship in the area of human rights. Using the work of Dembour (2014), we classified such criminological exploration into four schools of human rights' thinking within criminology: Natural, Deliberative, Protest and Discursive (see table at p. 74) to showcase how and why criminologists have addressed human rights narratives. Yet, as we recognized in the conclusion of that book, there are a number of themes that demand more criminological attention. One criticism of criminology scholarship is that, even when we engage with human rights, the terminology and the philosophical underpinning of human rights are not as explicitly addressed as is evident in other disciplines. From risk to securitization, from border control to everyday policing, from alternative forms of justice to imprisonment, environmental issues to corporate crimes, it is crucial to assess the benefits and limitations of human rights narratives by engaging critically and overtly with national and international instruments.

This is already occurring in other disciplines such as law and international studies. Most human rights resources are tailored for other disciplines but not necessarily for criminology. For example, while they are excellent resources in their own rights, there are a number of books – such as *Crime and human rights* (Parmentier and Weitekamp 2007), the *Routledge handbook of human rights* (Cushman 2014) and the *Sage handbook of human rights* (Mihr and Gibney 2014) – which are all close to our discipline but do not engage with criminological subjects, so that their arguments remain at the fringe of important criminological debates.

To date, apart from our 2014 Palgrave text and the 2014 *Human rights and the criminal justice system* co-authored by Anthony Amatrudo and Leslie Blake (Amatrudo and Blake 2014), a criminologist who wants to know more about human rights has to unpack material written in other disciplines to make sense of them. Without these resources it is hard to navigate cutting-edge criminological debates using materials from disciplines which use different theoretical and methodological approaches and are mainly adopting mainstream lenses.

The *Routledge international handbook of criminology and human rights* is therefore addressing a critical need in the criminological engagement with human rights. It aims at exploring the concern of criminologists with individual and collective social justice through a human rights lens. We have therefore asked the contributors to make human rights relevant to our discipline, rendering the discourse more than an abstract legal concept. This book has allowed contributors to engage explicitly with discussions of the benefits, pitfalls and limitations of human rights in relation to criminological activism and analysis and to look beyond the narrow confines of first- and second-generation human rights to include third- and fourth-generation human rights norms, and cognate concepts such as human security and capabilities. In this way the handbook signals a turning point for our discipline and offers an invitation to bring human rights to the forefront of the criminological debate.

The book's structure is designed to integrate human rights thinking across the discipline as a whole by breaking down pre-existing divisions between domestic and transnational criminology, between the theoretical and empirical, the particular and the universal, the legal and the socio-political, and between scholarship from the Global North and South. The handbook is divided into six parts, each with an introduction and overview provided by one of the editors. Part I makes an assessment of the current standing of human rights within the discipline, whether as an analytical and theoretical framework or as a basis for social transformation. Each of the remaining five parts corresponds to a substantive area of harm prevention and social control, which together make up the main core of the discipline, namely: criminal law in practice; transitional justice, peacemaking and community safety; policing in all its guises; traditional and emerging approaches to criminal justice; and penality, both within and beyond the prison.

Chapters in the collection cover the realization and non-realization of human rights in relation to populations around the world, including marginalized groups such as cultural, religious, political and racial minorities, Indigenous and colonized peoples, women, children in conflict with the law, LGTBI people, people with disabilities, older people, legal and irregular migrants, crime victims, people in detention, overpoliced populations, criminal and terror suspects, and both historical and modern-day slaves.

Within each part, topics have been chosen to represent a range of criminological approaches and to include both established and emerging real-world problems in transnational and domestic contexts, theoretical and situation-specific material, and authors from the Global North and South. Of the 53 chapters in the handbook, almost one-third deal with empirical studies or case material from countries beyond the mainstream criminological focus on Western European and the Anglophone countries. However, fewer than half of these chapters were written or co-written by authors originating from outside the Metropole. This indicates that there is still more to be done to forge a discipline that is truly representative of a rapidly globalizing world in which human rights might become more salient as a moral, legal and political lingua franca (McEvoy 2003).

Contributors to this handbook come from backgrounds in sociology, socio-legal studies, law, victim studies, regulatory theory, policing, penology, transitional justice, and many other branches of the diverse discipline of criminology. Many of them are world leaders within their field of specialization, others are emerging scholars doing cutting-edge empirical work in far-flung corners of the globe. For some, human rights discourse has featured in their scholarship for some time. For others, making explicit reference to human rights law and thinking is a new point of departure. And, for a small number of authors in the collection, the topic of human rights is itself an object of inquiry, which is approached with reflexivity and a critical perspective.

In our previous writing on criminology and human rights (Weber et al. 2014) we acknowledged that human rights can set out normative goals or moral standards, can be realized through the application of positive law, or can provide a powerful (and sometimes misleading) rhetoric for the articulation of political claims. In practice, human rights are often expressed across all these fields simultaneously, such as when reference is made to the agreed norms within the United Nations legal framework in order to bolster and legitimize political goals relating to equality, justice and the accountable use of coercive powers.

Our authors have drawn on all these idioms to varying degrees, using the language of human rights to make moral claims, to critique political failures to regulate power and provide positively for human welfare, and sometimes to refer to international or domestic human rights jurisprudence. Overall, their contributions range from cautiously optimistic to avowedly sceptical about the potential for human rights to live up to their liberal promise, or to improve on the analytical and political purchase of related discourses such as equality and social justice.

Another fundamental aim of this collection is to increase the range of educational resources available for those involved in teaching and studying criminology at the tertiary level. In developing our ideas for the book we surveyed current higher education courses available on criminology and human rights at universities in Europe, North and South America, Asia, the United Kingdom and the Pacific. We found many human rights courses in law, which were also available as non-compulsory options for criminology students. However, there were only a few courses in criminology that explicitly integrated the term 'human rights' as a core topic in their statements about course aims and objectives. Many individual subjects will no doubt include discussion of human rights, but we are hopeful that as the range of resources on criminology and human rights increases, it will become easier to incorporate human rights as a core topic in criminology programmes rather than as a niche subject.

Handbooks such as these not only contribute to debates and discussions about human rights but also provide practical and accessible resources for academics, students and practitioners. So, although the handbook has been grouped thematically, we have ensured that each piece can be used individually to support research, lectures, course development and practical training.

Incorporating human rights explicitly into criminological degree programmes can also make an important contribution to broader human rights education. Now, more than ever, critical human rights education needs to be at the forefront of disciplinary training. As a number of chapters in this book attest, human rights are under attack around the world and, despite the fact that human rights treaties place duties on state parties to engage in systematic human rights education, few states take up this challenge (Gerber and Pettit 2013). We hope by using this handbook readers will gain a more in-depth understanding of what human rights are, will appreciate their strengths and weaknesses, and why they are worth defending in a critical and constructive manner.

We expect that the diversity of the approaches in the *Routledge international handbook of criminology and human rights*, and the range of perspectives on human rights included, will make an important contribution to criminological research, debate and education. This edited collection not only enhances our criminological imagination (Barton et al. 2007), but also ensures that human rights become part and parcel of our criminological future.

## References

Amatrudo, A. and Blake, L., 2014. *Human rights and the criminal justice system.* Abingdon: Routledge.

Barton, A., Corteen, K., Scott, D. and Whyte, D. (eds), 2007. *Expanding the criminological imagination: critical readings in criminology.* Cullompton: Willan Publishing.

Cushman, T. (ed.), 2014. *Handbook of human rights*. Routledge International Handbooks. Abingdon: Routledge.
Dembour, M., 2014. What are human rights? Four schools of thought. *In*: T. Cushman (ed.), *Handbook of human rights*. Abingdon: Routledge, 137–45.
Gerber, P. and Pettit, A., 2013. Human rights education in the Australian curriculum. *In*: P. Gerber and M. Castan (eds), *Contemporary perspectives on human rights law in Australia*. Sydney: Thomson Reuters Lawbook Co., 531–55.
McEvoy, K., 2003. Beyond the metaphor: political violence, human rights and new peacemaking criminology. *Theoretical Criminology*, 7(3), 319–46.
Mihr, A. and Gibney, M. (eds), 2014. *Sage handbook of human rights*. London: Sage.
Parmentier, S. and Weitekamp, E. (eds), 2007. *Crime and human rights*. Series of Sociology, Crime and Deviance vol. 9. Amsterdam/Oxford: Elsevier/JAI Press.
Stanley, E., 2007. Towards a criminology for human rights. *In*: A. Barton, K. Corteen, D. Scott and D. Whyte (eds), *Expanding the criminological imagination*. Cullompton: Willan Publishing.
Weber, L., Fishwick, E. and Marmo, M., 2014. *Crime, justice and human rights*. London: Palgrave Macmillan.

# Part I

# Taking stock of human rights within criminology

This opening section of the handbook establishes a foundation for the collection. Rather than focusing on one substantive area of criminology, we have included here chapters that provide an historical overview of the application of human rights law and principles within the discipline and reflect on the impact of human rights in some key areas of criminological research. Many of the themes introduced in this opening section are explored in more depth later in the handbook. For some of the authors, human rights have played a major role in their own scholarship, either because human rights frameworks have provided a powerful rhetorical and/or legal framing for their criminological concerns, or because human rights and their relationship to crime and criminal justice are the direct object of their scholarly inquiry. For others, human rights have played a marginal role to date in their field, but may have the potential to be incorporated more fully into future scholarship.

The handbook opens with a reflexive piece from Thérèse Murphy and Noel Whitty that poses many key questions about the role played by human rights law and principles within both contemporary and historical criminology. They review four contexts in which human rights have been applied within criminology, which they identify as legal reformist, studies of state crime and genocide, socio-political approaches, and a final, less easily defined, category that advocates open minded enquiry beyond the search for human rights violations. For these authors, seeking to situate human rights within the discipline requires close engagement with past and present debates over the appropriate relationship between scholarly analysis and political/legal advocacy.

We then move beyond the disciplinary boundaries of criminology into the arena of international human rights law, in order to assess the salience of crime and criminal justice matters within human rights enforcement processes. Human rights scholar Rhona Smith provides us with an overview of United Nations treaty monitoring procedures then systematically examines a large body of documentation that assesses the human rights performance of governments. She identifies recurring themes concerning the administration of justice, the prevention of violence, and human trafficking which are also familiar topics of concern and inquiry within criminology.

Having established that there is considerable human rights terrain with which criminologists can engage, we then include a chapter from Anthony Amatrudo that reviews the contribution of three notable scholars who have elucidated the connections between human rights and criminology. Manuel Lopez-Ray is depicted as an optimistic advocate for the application of human rights principles within the criminal justice system. Stanley Cohen is portrayed as taking a somewhat bleaker view. Nevertheless, the author identifies Cohen as one of the first criminologists to champion the use of sociological analysis to illuminate human rights abuses. In relation to Lucia Zedner, the only living criminologist amongst the three, Amatrudo argues that her main contribution has been to point out actual and potential human rights violations associated with the single-minded pursuit of security by contemporary governments.

The authors of the remaining chapters discuss the relevance of human rights within specific ideological or topical strands within criminology, 'taking stock' of the relevance of human rights in their field and, conversely, of the impact of criminological research on the understanding of key human rights issues. Contributions of this type include Biko Agozino, who brings a postcolonial perspective to the task; David Scott on prisoners' rights and abolitionism; Raymond Michalowski on the study of state-corporate crime; Rosemary Barberet and Diana Rodriguez-Spahia on feminist criminology; Sandra Walklate on the study of victims; Randy K. Lippert on governmentality; and Russell Hogg on globalization.

Biko Agozino exposes the lack of recognition within historical and contemporary criminology of one of the most large-scale human rights abuses of all time: trans-Atlantic slavery. Supplementing the list of foundational thinkers provided by Amatrudo, the author argues that the nineteenth century critique of slavery by W.E.B. Du Bois represents the earliest example of a human rights perspective within criminology. The lack of mainstream recognition of the significance of this work is all the more perplexing considering that other Africana scholars subsequently expanded upon Du Bois's seminal analysis. David Scott focuses on another abolitionist cause that has arguably received wider recognition within the discipline, that of prison abolitionism. While acknowledging that human rights language has been employed by many notable abolitionists, including Stanley Cohen and Barbara Hudson, Scott recognizes widespread reticence amongst others to follow this path. He attributes this to underlying differences in understandings of the meaning of human rights, but notes that all positions are united by a focus on the vulnerability of those who are demarcated as 'other'.

The following three chapters by Rosemary Barberet and Diana Rodriguez-Spahia, Sandra Walklate and Randy K. Lippert all acknowledge, openly or tacitly, the paucity of literature in their fields that explores connections between human rights and criminological analysis. Barberet and Rodriguez-Spahia apply an historical lens in their chapter on the linkages between feminist criminology and human rights, identifying points of commonality between the many different strains of feminist criminology and human rights thinking. They note that both fields of inquiry have focused on exposing inequalities in gender relations and making the lived experience of women central, and conclude that a more active engagement would be of mutual benefit. Walklate is more circumspect about the value of human rights approaches in the study of victims. She notes that the increased recognition of crime victims that has been promoted, belatedly, through international human rights discourse and victims' rights treaties, has not been matched by a capacity to reconcile the universal normative standards they espouse with the particular circumstances of victim's lives, including fundamental needs for recognition and respect. Like Walklate, Lippert identifies the universalist claims of human rights as the main barrier to intellectual engagement with human rights by governmentality-inspired criminologists. He notes that a Foucauldian perspective cautions that rights talk may be readily deployed as a legitimizing tool of government. Lippert concludes that this scepticism, combined with the analytical toolkit provided by Foucauldian methodologies, can provide a powerful lens through which to critically assess the impacts of human rights law and discourse in practice.

The final two chapters each consider the utility of human rights for criminology within the context of neoliberal globalization. Raymond Michalowski traces the historic deployment of human rights concepts in the study of state-corporate crime, arguing that it is possible to combine an appreciation of the systemic character of actions produced by complex networks of actors with a concern for the harms that result for individual human beings. Such a perspective is needed, he claims, because of structural changes associated with neoliberal globalization that alter the relationship between corporations, states and citizens. Hogg's chapter deals with the implications of globalization for criminology as a whole, and considers the role that human rights are likely to play within a globalizing world and discipline. Adopting a wide historical lens, he sees globalization as a catalyst for an increasing convergence between human rights and criminology, notably through a broadening of the criminological gaze to recognize major crimes, often committed by states, which concern all of humanity.

All the authors adopt an aspirational and non-legalistic view of human rights as standards to be achieved through social pressure and political struggle, and as analytical tools to be deployed, where appropriate, alongside other theoretical perspectives and methodological devices. They show us that reference to human rights can bring a normative dimension to a structural analysis, or add a positive agenda to an exercise in critique that may otherwise end in a quagmire of negativity. Whatever we may think about the current standing of human rights within the world, it seems that they are likely to remain both topical and contentious within criminology.

# 1

# Turning to human rights

## Criminology past and future

*Thérèse Murphy and Noel Whitty*

---

Hope is a concept not usually associated with academic criminology. A long tradition of 'miserablism' (Brown 2013, p. 27) within the field has tended to block and undermine attempts to imagine ways forward. Ian Loader and Richard Sparks have captured this sensibility in blunt terms:

> [M]uch criminological thinking is either rather glum and fatalistic, or else excitedly apocalyptic, in content and tone. Neither of those registers are the most helpful or incisive ones with which to think about the future.
>
> *(Loader and Sparks forthcoming 2017)*

These registers, presumably, also influence how and whether criminology thinks about its past. The publication, therefore, of a *Handbook of criminology and* – and here is the novelty – *human rights* is a moment of some significance. It raises questions that we want to explore in this chapter: in particular, what does its emergence say about academic criminology,[1] both historically and looking to the future?

Should we, for instance, expect the handbook 'in content and tone' to reflect the very different criminological histories of engagement with – and, more frequently, avoidance and repudiation of – human rights? Are some (most?) perspectives likely to be contemporary in orientation, evidencing a recognition of the quotidian relevance of rights and encompassing, in some cases, enthusiasm about the potential of rights discourses in criminological contexts? Also, what sources are being drawn upon to make such assessments? In short, where is academic criminology choosing to get its human rights knowledges from, what rights knowledges is it producing itself, and to what ends are these knowledges being put?

At one time, normative approaches from law and philosophy dominated understandings of human rights: today, by contrast, a wide range of disciplinary sources and methods on rights are available for evaluation, appropriation and adaptation (Murphy and Whitty 2013, p. 580). But if it is true that the criminological field is defined by a still-reluctant relationship with its legal counterpart (Zedner 2011, p. 277), how convincing are its engagements with human rights going to be? Isn't it the case that a significant part of the story – the realities of human rights law, institutions and actors – will be left unexplored? And, if the legal field is recognized as relevant but then treated as a lumpen mass, such that the interplay between bodies of law (between, for example, international, national and local norms) is ignored, is the ability to gauge the proper place of the legal field not inevitably weakened?

Unless, of course, what is most attractive to some criminologists about rights discourses is their potential usefulness in enhancing an evidence base ('violations') and condemnatory language ('victims'), or their potential role in reinforcing theoretical and ideological positions – that is, to generate new (or boost old) forms of criminological awareness. Alternatively, is criminology across its varied terrain increasingly aligning itself with human rights advocacy (and deploying legal resources?), or is it systematically turning to human rights as an object of enquiry – all with implications for its understandings of scholar, activist and policy advisor? In other words, how much of a *Handbook of criminology and human rights* is a journey down familiar criminological pathways? And how much is a departure in focus, methodology and tone, or even an explicit breaking with (or, perhaps, a reconnecting with) aspects of criminology's past (Radzinowicz 1961)? Most interestingly of all, what is distinctive about *criminology* doing human rights?

## Present-day patterns

In addressing these questions, we start with a brief outline of what we consider to be the four principal, contemporary criminological engagements with human rights. The first of these, which we shall call legal reformist, builds upon a longstanding regard for notions of rights within criminal law and criminal justice (Morris 1958, Ashworth 1988). Today it continues across a range of contributions to criminal justice bodies and non-governmental organizations (NGOs), university teaching, political campaigning and scholarship (Morgan and Evans 2001, Finnane 2008, Zedner 2003, 2009). In recent years, the institutionalization and internationalization of human rights law has significantly affected the manner in which a range of criminal justice policies are critiqued (Brown and Wilkie 2002, Muncie 2008, van Zyl Smit and Snacken 2009). A further catalyst has been the extension, and the abuse, of state power in the aftermath of 9/11. Common cause between criminologists and lawyers is now much more apparent, with shared agendas of activism, litigation and scholarship – all motivated by the liberalizing potential of human rights (Brysk and Shafir 2007, Goold and Lazarus 2007).

The second present-day engagement flows from work on state crimes and encompasses two, very distinct, strands. The first draws on a tradition of historic distrust of state power and the alleged hegemonic nature of rights regimes. Paradoxically, however, it uses human rights reports by NGOs such as Human Rights Watch in order to better evidence the harms caused by both state and corporate power. While various theoretical positions are reflected within state crimes scholarship, a common feature is the reduction of human rights to the issue of *violations* (Stanley 2007, Green and Ward 2009, Scraton and McCulloch 2009, Welch 2009). Another feature is the belief in the power of exposure of rights violations: cultural criminology, for instance, by its focus on atrocity images, is said to put 'the 'visual human into the concept of human rights, helping to produce a moral obligation to act' (Morrison 2010, p. 193).

The second state-crimes strand, 'genocide criminology', is very different in focus and method. Its explicit aim is that the field of criminology should be extended to 'studies of international justice . . . war and international conflict' (Levi and Hagan 2011, pp. 36–7), notably for the purposes of providing genocide or war crimes statistics in criminal prosecutions. Criminology here is being closely allied with international criminal law and associated exercises of state power (which may include satellite surveillance and intervention to arrest suspects) – and a sense of urgency is pervasive: 'There is no time to lose' (Savelsberg 2010, p. 116).

The third present-day criminological engagement with human rights aims to loosen the hold of legalism. It targets the tendency of lawyers and their elite professional practices to both colonize human rights and trumpet their allegedly limitless capacity. This criminological engagement does not turn away from human rights as a global currency, with empowering potential and possible real-life benefits, but equally it insists on the limits of both law and human rights. Its insights draw in particular on the experiences of conflict and post-conflict societies (Cohen 1996, 2006, McEvoy 2007, Jefferson and Jensen 2009, Braithwaite et al. 2010, Jefferson and Gaborit 2015). A key legacy of Stanley Cohen (2001) in this regard is the recognition that no human rights form or methodology – neither words, nor images nor numbers – is immune from the negative effects of legalism or the risks of denial. Similar sensibilities about rights and law can be found in critical and feminist theoretical engagements: some of these carry forward classic critiques of legal rights (Rose 1985, Smart 1989); others, by contrast, are more optimistic, framing women's human rights for instance as 'a site of struggle for equality . . . and also a new political beginning' (Cain and Howe 2008, p. 11).

This focus on legalism characterizes two recent, and contrasting, interventions on criminology's future directions. In their work, *Public criminology?*, Ian Loader and Richard Sparks express discomfort with liberal criminology's increasing alliances with legal constitutionalism, and represent the 'legal' as overly normative and as a form of 'negative politics'. One of the costs, in their view, is that the development of 'sociological' explanation and understanding becomes sidelined (Loader and Sparks 2011, pp. 92–3). Human rights here, at least when linked with legal institutions and discourses, are a continued cause for wariness amongst criminologists (Loader 2007). In contrast, Jonathan Simon's latest book, *Mass incarceration on trial* (2014), expresses enthusiasm about the outcome of Californian prisoners' rights litigation, not just its exposure of inadequate healthcare provision within the state's prisons but – much more significantly – its acknowledgement of a link between chronic prison overcrowding and *unconstitutional* detention conditions. The historic decision of the United States (US) Supreme Court in *Brown v Plata* (2011), foregrounding the value of human dignity in the context of imprisonment, and upholding a California court order requiring a reduction of the state's prison population (to 137 per cent of its total prison capacity within two years), is characterized by Simon as a new way of 'claiming human rights for the victims of mass incarceration' (Simon 2014, p. 151). While aware of the limitations of litigation strategies and court-driven prison reform in the US context, Simon nevertheless sees the potential for dignity-based rights claims to effect a 'sea change in penal policy' (2014, p. 152). Perhaps, just as interestingly, Simon turns clearly to human rights normative frameworks (especially the work of institutions such as the European Court of Human Rights and the European Committee for the Prevention of Torture in relation to improving prison conditions) in seeking criminological inspiration. This critically informed interest in 'the European *legal* context' (2014, p. 194, our emphasis) on the part of a US penal scholar is noteworthy.

This brings us to the fourth present-day criminological engagement with human rights. We struggle to name this one; though we are clear that, in its commitment to open-minded enquiry and to a range of research methods, it draws upon a key part of criminology's heartland. Some will point out that 'genocide criminology', which is in our second category, is determined to develop new methods of data collection and statistical analysis in order to improve the chances of successful criminal prosecution of mass human rights violations. That differs however from the engagement we have in mind here, which is either less explicitly or not at all *goal-focused* in its analysis of rights. Consider, for example, the studies done on the effects of human rights inside prison systems (Piacentini 2004), or the influence of rights norms on police working-practices (Bullock and Johnson 2012, Hornberger 2011). Or, where the legal field is a focus of empirical attention, consider the analysis of the dynamics of victims' rights discourses (Rock 2004), or the study of the US death penalty as the 'story of a legal norm' (Garland 2010, p. 11). In each instance, it is theoretically grounded research methods (often ethnographical) that make the analysis of (human) rights – crucially, not reduced to the study of violations – part of a wider sociological enquiry. There is, in other words, an attachment to open-minded description of the social world as one finds it. All scholarship will of course exhibit bias, develop within certain parameters, foreground particular issues and so on; nonetheless, within this fourth category there is explicit emphasis on the object of enquiry not being allowed to predetermine, or overwhelm, the scholarly engagement.

The pivotal role that social theory can play within criminology arguably provides a major explanation for the distinctiveness of this type of engagement. Yet this in turn raises the question: what makes this sort of investigation of human rights uniquely *criminological*? Anthropology, for example, has confidently embraced human rights as a field of study, and it too draws heavily on social theory and ethnographic methods (Riles 2006). It has also entered traditionally criminological terrain, producing empirical studies of international criminal trials (Wilson 2011) and of torture as a cultural and legal category (Kelly 2012). So, if disciplinary boundaries are much more porous (McGarry et al. 2012), and theories, methods and sites of research are more likely to be shared given the prominence of human rights (law), what effects will this have on criminology's identity as 'a bridging subject' – as a subject that aims to connect 'the practical world of crime control with the academic disciplines of social science and law' (Garland 2011, p. 304)?

## Criminology going forward, going back

Interestingly, despite the increasing range of areas covered, the majority of academic criminology's contemporary engagements with human rights have demonstrated little or no interest in tracing the intellectual steps of how criminology has related to rights. How and why different branches of this academic field have moved towards, or away from, human rights – its concepts, forms, actors, institutions, cultures, practices and discourses – in particular contexts and eras remains unknown. This matters because the depth of the contestation around visions of what criminology is and what it should do (Finnane 2012, Garland 2011) – even if repressed – inevitably influences the different reasons for 'turning to' human rights, what the nature of those engagements will be and their range of effects. The 'magpie' quality of some scholarship, where human rights sources can appear mere 'add-ons' or are plucked from different (even contradictory) contexts or timeframes without discussion, is one phenomenon we have in mind here.

This dearth of historical perspective is not unique to criminology's relationship to human rights (Lawrence 2012). Paul Rock (2005, p. 475) has identified 'the methodical extinction of many ideas and authors beyond a certain age' within criminology – a phenomenon that could well accelerate as intellectual lineages, networks and practices disperse across a growing field (Loader and Sparks 2012). We believe that criminology ought to enquire into its own history with human rights. Doing so would throw new light on the variations and tensions within criminology's theories, practices and academic identities – not least in further excavating distinctive national and regional traditions, and perhaps freeing them from some legacies of 'intellectual colonization' (Doyle and Moore 2011, p. 7). A spotlight on human rights would also be useful in tracking academic criminology's patterns of change, and in particular in explaining 'the capacity of certain ideas to capture political momentum at particular junctures, at an emotional as well as an instrumental level' (Loader and Sparks 2004, pp. 18–19). Why, for example, has a *Handbook of criminology and human rights* appeared in 2016, and not earlier or later?

History also matters because, as we highlighted above, the 'unresolved relationship' between law and criminology strongly affects approaches to human rights today. Law and lawyers have always exerted a strong influence on criminology's orientations. Nonetheless, scholarship addressing the legal field – for example, legal instruments, adjudication, litigation strategies – has tended to be seen as the exclusive preserve of lawyers and law schools. What this masks however is the variation in criminology's locations and working identities, especially within different national traditions, including the multiple factors (such as education, fieldwork experiences and publication sites) that have shaped criminologists' knowledge of, and interest in, the legal field (Bosworth and Hoyle 2011). So, for example, we would nominate prisons and prisoners (both in the US and Europe) as one field where very different disciplinary affiliations and research priorities have overlapped, both in perceptions of law's relevance in general, and rights and latterly human rights in particular (Jacobs 1977, Sparks and McNeill 2009, van Zyl Smit and Snacken 2009, Murphy and Whitty 2016).

Contemporary engagements with human rights that are unable or unwilling to recognize the effects of the internationalization, and institutionalization at all levels, of human rights *law* can only ever be partial accounts (Goodale and Merry 2007). Additionally, depending on context and location, engaging the legal field today can also involve scrutiny of multi-level governance at a variety of national, regional and international sites (for example, in relation to Council of Europe prison monitoring procedures or United Nations child refugee policy). To be sure, there will always be a variety of scholarly and political agendas in engaging with rights: our point here is that serious analysis of human rights in criminological contexts (for example, prisons, policing, victims, war crimes and migration) must *inevitably* confront criminology with how (much) law frames its academic field. And this can only be convincingly done by reflecting on criminology's history.

'Genocide criminology' is a revealing example in this regard. It has consciously sought a legal legacy and turned to historical research to excavate a linkage between crime and 'atrocities'. Using archival records, a US criminological pioneer, law professor Sheldon Glueck – who advocated the prosecution of war criminals in the early 1940s – has been cast as 'criminology's ambassador to Nuremberg' (Hagan and Greer 2002, p. 234). A 'forgotten' link is thus established between the Nuremberg Trials, criminology and today's era of international criminal law (Hagan and Rymond-Richmond 2009, pp. 31–55). Moreover, invoking this history has contributed not just to a sense that criminology has a distinctive part to play in the pursuit of criminal prosecutions for mass human rights violations, but also to the growth of criminological research into the internal workings of international courts (Hagan and Levi 2005).

The point we are making is twofold: first, criminology's history generally, and in its relations with law (and human rights), is complex and diverse; and second, uncritical acceptance of particular histories, or low levels of interest in this history, will have an adverse influence on criminological engagement with human rights law today. Recent research streams in anthropology, history, law and political science may prove helpful here, in particular in broadening perspectives on rights and providing new ways of seeing the legal field. We are thinking in particular of the research that seeks critically to engage with how human rights are driving the expansion and diversification of the legal field (White and Perelman 2011, Whitty 2011, Kelly 2012, Sarfaty 2012). This research does not prejudge the nature and effects of this field; instead it engages directly with the empirical reality of human rights law, including its doctrinal technicalities and what happens both before and after court decisions.

We turn finally to the issue of appropriate 'tone' in criminological engagement about human rights. Leon Radzinowicz (1961, p. 178, see also Carlen 2011) once stated that 'criminologists should avoid crusading zeal' and Stanley Cohen, a pioneer in merging criminology and human rights into research and practical engagements, argued against any 'shouting and preaching' (cited in Taylor 2007, pp. 24–5). In an academic field as broad and non-unified as criminology, human rights will inevitably carry many meanings and aspirations. But it is particularly tempting to use them to enhance the 'apocalyptic' quality of some criminological claims. There are surely risks for criminology and human rights if the importance of reflective and engaged thought is forgotten.

## Criminology's answers and doubts

History matters for criminology. Our argument in this chapter is that there are important lessons to be learnt from deeper excavations of academic criminology's past, not least in helping to understand contemporary approaches to human rights – and possible consequences (Blackburn 2011, Alston 2013). To put that another way, academic criminology needs to be more upfront about the different ways it sees human rights – and also how it produces and uses rights knowledges. The four patterns of human rights engagement we identified all have distinctive roots in academic criminology's field, drawing on eclectic legacies, but they also have the potential to open up very different research pathways and debates about human rights and policy interventions. This is particularly true in relation to the fault line around the legal field, including the increasing legalization of rights. It is also true in relation to the question that has been an undercurrent in this chapter: what is, or should be, distinctive about criminology doing human rights?

Other options – ignoring history, closing down debates, making assumptions about human rights forms, cultures, practices and methods – have obvious dangers for academic criminology. But, perhaps, the point needs extra reinforcement in light of criminology's connection with the practical world of 'crime control', wherein human rights can be narrowed down to questions of prosecuting 'crime' (McEvoy 2007). It should be a cause for reflection therefore that it is academic *lawyers* who are expressing the strongest concerns about the tendency to collapse human rights into questions of international criminal law. (It is also surely ironic that, historically, sociological traditions in criminology and law once battled in the other direction using 'rights' to dilute the uncritical focus on 'crime'.) As Karen Engle (2015, p. 1071) points out, advocacy of international criminal prosecution as the inevitable response to human rights violations is having damaging consequences for our understanding of human rights and related concepts:

> [A]s criminal law has become the enforcement tool of choice, it has negatively affected the lens through which the human rights movement and the international law scholars who support it view human rights violations. In short, as advocates increasingly turn to international criminal law to respond to issues ranging from economic injustice to genocide, they reinforce an individualized and decontextualized understanding of the harms they aim to address, even while relying on the state and on forms of criminalization of which they have long been critical.

Unreflective analysis of 'violations', 'harms' and calls for 'punishment' is also likely to lead to the 'alignment of human rights advocates with the carceral state' (Engle 2015, p. 1126). This inevitably undercuts the potential of the human rights movement to challenge aspects of imprisonment in other contexts. It also undercuts criminology's long tradition of problematizing the nature and role of the prison in legal and political culture, including from (human) rights perspectives (Simon and Sparks 2013).

We end this chapter, therefore, by re-emphasizing its central point: the criminology and human rights relationship, in all its varied manifestations, requires more detailed, historically informed and reflective scrutiny. Unless academic criminology can engage more directly with its historical legacies, and assess their implications, it is our sense that some of the current ways of seeing and using human rights, and human rights law, may not alter much. In particular, tensions around the law–criminology relationship will continue to loom large as human rights becomes the focus of increased interest for criminology. For some, of course, it may continue to be the case that rights discourses appear useful only for the purposes of highlighting harms and misuse of power. But much more interesting questions are being raised where strands of criminology are being explicitly aligned with human rights advocacy and policy-making, sometimes in parallel with focused engagements with the legal field (for example, prisons or international criminal courts).

Perhaps though, the truly distinctive academic approaches still remain to be developed within criminology: that is, what it means to see and study human rights as inevitably multifaceted objects of enquiry in criminological settings. Or, to put that another way, it remains an open question what distinctively *criminological* accounts of a human rights field could entail. This is why we find it useful to return to Leon Radzinowicz's book, *In search of criminology* (1961), and the questions it sought to prompt about criminology's origins, disciplinary relationships and aspirations. Human rights, in a multitude of ways, are providing yet another lens through which to trace and assess academic criminology's links with its own past. Human rights are also proving to be a significant catalyst for reflections on criminology's contemporary identity and choices about future research pathways. Nevertheless, amidst the search for answers, it should not be forgotten that 'in some ways, the many doubts which criminology has prompted' could be just as important (Radzinowicz 1961, p. 181).

## Note

1 Our historical analysis draws primarily on patterns in United Kingdom academic criminology, but the chapter highlights (English language) human rights scholarship from a range of countries.

## References

Alston, P., 2013. Does the past matter? On the origins of human rights. *Harvard Law Review*, 126(7), 2043–81.

Ashworth, A., 1988. Criminal justice and the criminal process. *British Journal of Criminology*, 28(2), 111–23.

Blackburn, R., 2011. Reclaiming human rights. *New Left Review*, 69(May/June), 126–38.

Bosworth, M. and Hoyle, C. (eds), 2011. *What is criminology?* Oxford: Oxford University Press.

Braithwaite, J., Braithwaite, V., Cookson, M. and Dunn, L., 2010. *Anomie and violence: non-truth and reconciliation in Indonesian peacebuilding*. Canberra: Australian National University Press.

Brown, D., 2013. Mapping the conditions of penal hope. *International Journal for Crime, Justice and Social Democracy*, 2(3), 27–42.

Brown, D. and Wilkie, M., 2002. *Prisoners as citizens: human rights in Australian prisons*. Sydney: Federation Press.

Brysk, A. and Shafir, G. (eds), 2007. *National insecurity and human rights: democracies debate counterterrorism*. Berkeley, CA: University of California Press.

Bullock, K. and Johnson, P., 2012. The impact of the Human Rights Act 1998 on policing in England and Wales. *British Journal of Criminology*, 52(3), 630–50.

Cain, M. and Howe, A., 2008. Introduction. *In*: M. Cain and A. Howe (eds), *Women, crime and social harm: towards a criminology for the global age*. Oxford: Hart, 1–20.

Carlen, P., 2011. Against evangelism in academic criminology: for criminology as a scientific art. *In*: M. Bosworth and C. Hoyle (eds), *What is criminology?* Oxford: Oxford University Press, 95–108.

Cohen, S., 1996. Government responses to human rights reports: claims, denials and counterclaims. *Human Rights Quarterly*, 18(3), 517–43.

Cohen, S., 2001. *States of denial: knowing about atrocities and suffering*. Cambridge: Polity.

Cohen, S., 2006. Neither honesty nor hypocrisy: the legal reconstruction of torture. *In*: T. Newburn and P. Rock (eds), *The politics of crime control*. Oxford: Oxford University Press, 297–317.

Doyle, A. and Moore, D., 2011. Questions for a new generation of criminologists. *In*: A. Doyle and D. Moore (eds), *Critical criminology in Canada: new voices, new directions*. Vancouver: UBC Press, 1–24.

Engle, K., 2015. Anti-impunity and the turn to criminal law in human rights. *Cornell Law Review*, 100(5), 1069–1127.

Finnane, M., 2008. Promoting the theory and practice of criminology: the Australian and New Zealand Society of Criminology and its founding moment. *Australian & New Zealand Journal of Criminology*, 41(2), 199–215.

Finnane, M., 2012. The origins of criminology in Australia. *Australian & New Zealand Journal of Criminology*, 45(2), 157–78.

Garland, D., 2010. *Peculiar institution: America's death penalty in an age of abolition*. Oxford: Oxford University Press.

Garland, D., 2011. Criminology's place in the academic field. *In*: M. Bosworth and C. Hoyle (eds), *What is criminology?* Oxford: Oxford University Press, 298–317.

Goodale, M. and Merry, S.E. (eds), 2007. *The practice of human rights: tracking law between the global and the local*. Cambridge: Cambridge University Press.

Goold, B. and Lazarus, L. (eds), 2007. *Security and human rights*. Oxford: Hart.

Green, P. and Ward, T., 2009. The transformation of violence in Iraq. *British Journal of Criminology*, 49(5), 609–27.

Hagan, J. and Greer, S., 2002. Making war criminal. *Criminology*, 40(2), 231–64.

Hagan, J. and Levi, R., 2005. Crimes of war and the force of law. *Social Forces*, 83(4), 1499–1534.

Hagan, J. and Rymond-Richmond, W., 2009. *Darfur and the crime of genocide*. Cambridge: Cambridge University Press.

Hornberger, J., 2011. *Policing and human rights: the meaning of violence and justice in the everyday policing of Johannesburg*. London: Routledge.

Jacobs, J.B., 1977. *Stateville: a penitentiary in mass society*. Chicago: Chicago University Press.

Jefferson, A.M. and Gaborit, L.S., 2015. *Human rights in prisons: comparing institutional encounters in Kosovo, Sierra Leone and the Philippines*. London: Palgrave Macmillan.

Jefferson, A.M. and Jensen, S. (eds), 2009. *State violence and human rights*. Abingdon: Routledge-Cavendish.

Kelly, T., 2012. *This side of silence: human rights, torture and the recognition of cruelty*. Philadelphia, PA: Pennsylvania University Press.

Lawrence, P., 2012. History, criminology and the 'use' of the past. *Theoretical Criminology*, 16(3), 313–28.

Levi, R. and Hagan, J., 2011. Lawyers, humanitarian emergencies and the politics of large numbers. *In*: Y. Dezalay and B.G. Garth (eds), *Lawyers and the construction of transnational justice*. Abingdon: Routledge, 13–47.

Loader, I., 2007. The cultural lives of security and rights. *In*: B. Goold and L. Lazarus (eds), *Security and human rights*. Oxford: Hart, 27–43.

Loader, I. and Sparks, R., 2004. For a historical sociology of crime policy in England and Wales since 1968. *Critical Review of International Social and Political Philosophy*, 7(2), 5–32.

Loader, I. and Sparks, R., 2011. *Public criminology?* Abingdon: Routledge.

Loader, I. and Sparks, R., 2012. Situating criminology: on the production and consumption of knowledge about crime and justice. *In*: M. Maguire, R. Morgan and R. Reiner (eds), *The Oxford handbook of criminology*. Oxford: Oxford University Press, 3–38.

Loader, I. and Sparks, R., forthcoming 2017. Reasonable hopes: social theory, critique and reconstruction in contemporary criminology. *In*: A. Liebling, J. Shapland and J. Tankebe (eds), *Crime, justice and social order: essays in honour of A. E. Bottoms*. Oxford: Oxford University Press.

McEvoy, K., 2007. Beyond legalism: towards a thicker understanding of transitional justice. *Journal of Law and Society*, 34(4), 411–40.

McGarry, R. et al., 2012. The soldier, human rights and the military covenant: a permissible state of exception? *International Journal of Human Rights*, 16(8), 1183–95.

Morgan, R. and Evans, M., 2001. *Combating torture in Europe*. Strasbourg: Council of Europe.

Morris, N., 1958. Human rights and the criminal law in South-East Asia. *University of Tasmania Law Review*, 1(1), 68–79.

Morrison, W., 2010. A reflected gaze of humanity: cultural criminology and images of genocide. *In*: K.J. Hayward and M. Presdee (eds), *Framing crime: cultural criminology and the image*. Abingdon: Routledge, 189–207.

Muncie, J., 2008. The 'punitive' turn in juvenile justice: cultures of control and rights compliance in Western Europe and the USA. *Youth Justice*, 8(2), 107–21.

Murphy, T. and Whitty, N., 2013. Making history: academic criminology and human rights. *British Journal of Criminology*, 53(4), 568–87.

Murphy, T. and Whitty, N., 2016. Rights, justice and single-mindedness. *In*: S. Farrall, B. Goldson, I. Loader and A. Dockley (eds), *Justice and penal reform: re-shaping the penal landscape*. London: Routledge, 116–37.

Piacentini, L., 2004. *Surviving Russian prisons: punishment, economy and politics in transition*. Cullompton: Willan.

Radzinowicz, L., 1961. *In search of criminology*. London: Heinemann.

Riles, A., 2006. Anthropology, human rights, and legal knowledge: culture in the iron cage. *American Anthropologist*, 108(1), 52–65.

Rock, P., 2004. *Constructing victims' rights: the Home Office, New Labour and victims*. Oxford: Oxford University Press.

Rock, P., 2005. Chronocentrism and British criminology. *British Journal of Sociology*, 56(3), 473–91.

Rose, N., 1985. Unreasonable rights: mental illness and the limits of the law. *Journal of Law and Society*, 12(2), 199–218.

Sarfaty, G.A., 2012. *Values in translation: human rights and the culture of the World Bank*. Stanford, CA: Stanford University Press.

Savelsberg, J., 2010. *Crime and human rights*. London: Sage.

Scraton, P. and McCulloch, J. (eds), 2009. *The violence of incarceration*. Abingdon: Routledge.

Simon, J., 2014. *Mass incarceration on trial: a remarkable court decision and the future of prisons in America*. New York, NY: New Press.

Simon, J. and Sparks, R., 2013. Punishment and society: the emergence of an academic field. *In*: J. Simon and R. Sparks (eds), *The Sage handbook of punishment and society*. London: Sage, 1–20.

Smart, C., 1989. *Feminism and the power of law*. London: Routledge.

Sparks, R. and McNeill, F., 2009. *Incarceration, social control and human rights*. International Council on Human Rights Policy Working Paper. Geneva: ICHRP.

Stanley, E., 2007. Towards a criminology for human rights. *In*: A. Barton, K. Corteen, D. Scott and D. Whyte (eds), *Expanding the criminological imagination*. Cullompton: Willan, 168–97.

Taylor, L., 2007. The other side of the street: an interview with Stanley Cohen. *In*: D. Downes, P. Rock, C. Chinkin and C. Gearty (eds), *Crime, social control and human rights: from moral panics to states of denial*. Cullompton: Willan, 18–25.

van Zyl Smit, D. and Snacken, S., 2009. *Principles of European prison law and policy: penology and human rights*. Oxford: Oxford University Press.

Welch, M., 2009. Guantanamo Bay as a Foucauldian phenomenon: an analysis of penal discourse, technologies, and resistance. *The Prison Journal*, 89(1), 3–20.

White, L.E. and Perelman, J. (eds), 2011. *Stones of hope: how African activists reclaim human rights to challenge global poverty*. Stanford, CA: Stanford University Press.

Whitty, N., 2011. Human rights as risk: UK prisons and the management of risk and rights. *Punishment & Society*, 13(2), 123–48.

Wilson, R.A., 2011. *Writing history in international criminal trials*. Cambridge: Cambridge University Press.

Zedner, L., 2003. Useful knowledge? Debating the role of criminology in post-war Britain. *In*: L. Zedner and A. Ashworth (eds), *The criminological foundations of penal policy*. Oxford: Oxford University Press, 197–235.

Zedner, L., 2009. *Security*. London: Routledge.

Zedner, L., 2011. Putting crime back on the criminological agenda. *In*: M. Bosworth and C. Hoyle (eds), *What is criminology?* Oxford: Oxford University Press, 271–85.

# 2

# Criminological issues and the UN

## Key issues and trends

*Rhona Smith*

### Introduction

All states should respect, promote and protect those human rights and fundamental freedoms they have freely accepted through international human rights treaties. Accordingly by their actions, omissions, laws and policies, they should ensure adherence to international human rights standards. The normative framework is prescribed in the nine core United Nations (UN) treaties and the array of additional treaties, guidelines and rules on human rights. There is a particularly substantial body of law and guidance on the administration of justice, including provisions on policing and detention (pre and post trial). However, this is but one of a number of relevant areas on which the UN has elaborated standards and guidelines. On the international stage, a range of mechanisms are deployed to monitor and enforce international human rights standards on an ongoing basis. It is through these that a reasonably consistent set of documentation emerges which enables identification of substantial issues which appear to be of greatest concern (or simply attract most attention).

This chapter will start from a position of recognition of the UN international human rights framework as a tool for guaranteeing basic human rights and freedoms. Key treaty provisions and guidelines will be discussed though the chapter will first review the UN system, identifying which entities have greatest responsibility for monitoring human rights compliance and evaluating the documentation that emerges therefrom. This documentation will then be analysed to identify key issues of concern/interest and emergent trends. The conclusions will simply summarize the findings, indicating the key issues and trends, most of which are elaborated on in detail in discrete chapters of this book.

### The UN system: an overview

The UN system for monitoring and enforcing human rights is usually divided into two categories: those mechanisms focused on single treaties (treaty monitoring bodies); and those mechanisms which derive authority directly from the UN Charter and entities established thereunder.

Each of the nine core UN treaties (see Table 2.1) has a committee of independent experts charged under the relevant treaty with monitoring the efforts by states to comply with the treaty. These treaty monitoring bodies operate principally through a continual cycle of reports.

*Table 2.1* Expansion in high contracting parties to core UN human rights treaties

| | *Year adopted* | *Entry into force* | *No. of signatories by 1990* | *No. of signatories by 2000* | *No. of signatories by 2010* | *No. of signatories by 2015* |
|---|---|---|---|---|---|---|
| *International Convention on the Elimination of all Forms of Racial Discrimination* (ICERD) | 1965 | 1969 | 126 | 155 | 174 | 177 |
| *International Covenant on Civil and Political Rights* (ICCPR) | 1966 | 1976 | 90 | 146 | 167 | 168 |
| *International Covenant on Economic, Social and Cultural Rights* (ICESCR) | 1966 | 1976 | 94 | 142 | 160 | 164 |
| *Convention on the Elimination of all forms of Discrimination Against Women* (CEDAW) | 1979 | 1981 | 99 | 162 | 183 | 189 |
| *Convention against Torture and Other Cruel, Inhuman or Degrading Treatment or Punishment* (CAT) | 1984 | 1987 | 51 | 119 | 147 | 158 |
| *UN Convention on the Rights of the Child* (CRC) | 1989 | 1990 | 63 | 190 | 193 | 195 |
| *International Convention on the Protection of the Rights of All Migrant Workers and Members of Their Families* (CMW) | 1990 | 2003 | 0 | 17 | 45 | 48 |
| *International Convention for the Protection of All Persons from Enforced Disappearances* (CED) | 2006 | 2009 | N/A | N/A | 21 | 50 |
| *Convention on the Rights of Persons with Disabilities* (CRPD) | 2006 | 2008 | N/A | N/A | 99 | 157 |

*Note*: Data from https://treaties.un.org. Some observer states are also States Party.

The state self-reports to the UN according to a pre-specified schedule, the committee examines the report and other relevant evidence available to it, then questions the state during a process of constructive dialogue, before drafting and adopting its concluding observations on the state under review (Egan 2011, Kalin 2012). The periodicity of reports varies but is usually four or five years, although the UN system is beset by problems of backlogged reports, as well as numerous examples of non-reporting (Alston 1997, Pillay 2012, Annan 2000, Egan 2011). Each of these treaty-monitoring bodies now has competence to consider complaints brought by individuals against those states that choose to so recognize the competency of the committee. This option is not especially popular with states though there are a number of opinions of relevance to this chapter. As the nomenclature suggests, these committees are focused entirely on the rights and freedoms contained in the specific treaty establishing the committee and each committee is concerned only with states party to that treaty. All powers of the committee are outlined in the treaty itself[1] and in rules of procedure adopted thereunder. All the concluding observations adopted by the committee on each state party, the state reports, opinions on individual communications and general comments and recommendations elaborating on the committee's view on the scope and application of rights in each treaty are available online (from www.ohchr.org).

Human rights issues can also be considered by UN charter based bodies. In contrast to the treaty system outlined above, these bodies can monitor human rights in all UN Member States, irrespective of which treaties have been accepted. The UN Security Council can address any situation deemed threatening to international peace and security; the General Assembly can discuss all manner of human rights; and the work of the Economic and Social Council impacts on a range of rights and development issues.[2] Since 2006, a Human Rights Council, established under the General Assembly, has led on universal monitoring of human rights (General Assembly 2006). This Council can, and does, investigate and discuss urgent matters.[3] However, through the universal periodic review process (UPR), all UN Member States are peer reviewed (that is Member States question and comment on the reports of and on other Member States) on fulfilment of core and additional accepted standards of human rights and humanitarian law (General Assembly 2006, para. 5[e]). This process is executed in accordance with a strict timetable so all states are now reviewed every four and a half years. The Human Rights Council can also protect and promote human rights through its system of special procedures – experts who are tasked either with monitoring specific countries, or specific rights or situations impacting on rights. All special procedure reports and universal periodic review documentation is also available online (from, inter alia, www.ohchr.org).

There are many critics of the UN system and processes (Keller and Ulfstein 2012, Alston and Crawford 2000, Charlesworth and Larking 2014) but it cannot be denied that the system offers a common set of documentation for all states and is both near universal in geographical coverage and accepted by most states. Inevitably the documentation can be skewed towards the 'official' state-centric view, and perusing non-governmental organization reports often provides a starkly contrasting view of the reality in the state. Nevertheless, reviewing all the foregoing documentation, it is possible to extract evidence of areas of concern and trends that are particularly relevant within the criminal justice sphere. Moreover, these areas are acknowledged by states themselves to a greater or lesser extent. Administration of justice (including detention), violence against persons (including people held in detention), and migration and trafficking are three key issues.

## Key issues and trends

The expansion in UN membership during its 70 years and the development of human rights are notable. It is true to say that there is a trend towards acceptance of an international human rights treaty and, thereafter, a slower trend towards accepting additional UN monitoring in the form of country visits or competency of the UN entities to consider individual complaints against states. The perceived inviolability of state sovereignty takes time to reconcile with the idea of international monitoring of the national realization of human rights. With respect to special procedures, there is a trend towards the issuing of standing invitations whereby a state notionally extends an open invitation to any special procedures wishing to undertake a country visit. Both the increase in ratification of treaties and in invitations to special procedure mandate holders can be partly attributable to recommendations made during universal periodic review (Pillay 2012, p. 17).

Table 2.1 depicts the expansion in contracting parties to core treaties, especially over the past 25 years (to August 2015). Particularly notable is the increase since 2010 in ratifications to the *Convention against Torture* and the *Convention on Enforced Disappearances*. Both treaties can better be guaranteed within states by rigorous regulation of arrest and detention practices. The greater the number of parties to each treaty, the more the treaty committee obviously comments on the rights contained in the treaties. Accordingly there is more documentary evidence with relevant issues appearing to 'trend'. Torture and detention are, however, also addressed in other treaties as Table 2.2 demonstrates. Administration of justice generally is another key theme in the core UN treaties with provisions emphasizing the need for equality of treatment before courts and during detention as well as fair processes. Such overlapping treaty obligations can add weight to calls for adherence to basic principles but as Tistounet notes, can also give rise to problems (Tistounet 2000). Appointment of a special procedure mandate holder can accord greater international focus on a particular topic, sometimes indicating a key issue or even developing trends. (The appointments in 2015 of special procedures on privacy and human rights and on albinism are two examples.) Table 2.3 lists the most relevant procedures from a criminological perspective. Of course, the separate system of country mandates[4] whereby a geographical area, usually a state, is subjected to specific monitoring and annual review also focuses on criminal justice, torture, detention and violence; indeed, systematic violation of such rights often prompted the establishment of the mandate in the first instance. To identify general key issues, Table 2.4 provides examples identified by the author of the frequency with which issues are commented on during the universal periodic review process. A random selection of states is considered.[5]

Three issues have been identified: administration of justice, violence against persons and migration, refugees and trafficking. To elaborate on each matter, research on special procedures, treaty body jurisprudence and UPR documentation is drawn on.

*Table 2.2* Selected key issues in UN human rights treaties

| | *Detention* | *Criminal justice/ penalties* | *Violence against persons (individuals)* | *Prohibition on torture* |
|---|---|---|---|---|
| ICERD | Art.5(a) | Art.5(a) | Art.5(b) | Art.5(b) |
| ICCPR | Art.9; 10; 11 | Art.14; 15; 16; 6; 7; 8 | | Art.7 |
| ICESCR | | | Art.12(health) | |
| CEDAW | X | Art.15; Art.2(c+g) | Art.6 | X |
| CAT | Art.2; 11 | Art.2 (NB Art.1) | | Art.2; 4; 16 |
| CRC | Art.37 | Art.40 | Art.19 | Art.37 |
| CMW | Art.11; 16(4)–(9); 17; | Art.18; 19; 20 | Art.16(2) | Art.10 |
| CED | Art.1; 5; 17 | Art.6; 17 | | |
| CRPD | Art.14 | Art.13; | Art.16; 17 | Art.15 |

*Table 2.3* UN Special Procedure thematic mandate holders

| *Detention* | *Criminal justice* | *Violence against persons* | *Torture* |
|---|---|---|---|
| Working group on arbitrary detention | Special Rapporteur on the independence of judges and lawyers | Special Rapporteur on extrajudicial, summary or arbitrary executions | Special Rapporteur on torture and other cruel, inhuman or degrading treatment or punishment |
| Working group on enforced or involuntary disappearances | Special Rapporteur on the situation of human rights defenders | Working group on enforced or involuntary disappearances | Special Rapporteur on the promotion and protection of human rights while countering terrorism |
| Special Rapporteur on torture and other cruel, inhuman or degrading treatment or punishment | Special Rapporteur on the promotion and protection of human rights while countering terrorism | Special Rapporteur on torture and other cruel, inhuman or degrading treatment or punishment | Special Rapporteur on extrajudicial, summary or arbitrary executions |
| | | Special Rapporteur on violence against women, its causes and consequences | |

*Note*: From http://spinternet.ohchr.org/_Layouts/SpecialProceduresInternet/ViewAllCountryMandates.aspx?Type=TM.

## *Issue 1: Administration of justice*

Arrest, detention, trial and punishment bring the individual into direct contact with state authorities and state power. Any threat to the liberty and personal security of the accused/convicted individual is heightened by a potential for abuse of power and process, through arbitrariness, discrimination and corruption. Proper administration of justice arguably goes to the essence of the rule of law and is central to the functioning of a democratic state. Problems with administration of justice are raised in most concluding observations before the UN Human Rights Committee (McGoldrick 1991, Joseph and Castan 2013) and the issue is regularly flagged during universal periodic review (see Table 2.4).

Any arrest and detention must have a legal basis and respect the presumption of innocence (for example, *Wilson v The Philippines*, UN Doc CCPR/C/79/D/868/1999). Detention must be reviewed and the rights of the detained person considered. Any allegations of ill-treatment and, in particular, deaths in custody, must be promptly investigated. The trial process must be fair and impartial (for example, *Bahamonde v Equatorial Guinea*, UN Doc CCPR/C/49/D/468/1999; *Mbenge v Republic of Congo*, UN Doc CCPR/C/18/D/16/1977). Detention after conviction should be in accordance with the Basic Principles for the Treatment of Prisoners (General Assembly Resolution 45/111) and related guidelines. Spurred by the adoption of the UN *Convention on the Rights of the Child*, juvenile justice has gained prominence and the documentation studied makes frequent mention of this. A range of UN guidelines elaborate on the specific situation of children and their interactions with the justice system, including detention. Particular attention must be paid to the best interests of the child and to ensure a child understands and can participate appropriately in any court proceedings (Article 12 *Convention on*

*Table 2.4* Selected key recommendations made during working group interactive dialogue of universal periodic review

| | *HR Council regional grouping* | *Detention* | *Criminal Justice* | *Violence against persons* | *Torture* |
|---|---|---|---|---|---|
| **Afghanistan** | Asia-Pacific | 136.49, 136.83, 136.84, 136.173–176 | 136.17, 136.46, 136.47, 136.48, 136.84 | 136.21, 136.54, 136.86, 136.87, 136.111, 136.112, 136.113, 136.130–165 | 136.82, 136.83, 136.84 |
| **Albania** | Eastern Europe | 104.41; 104.42 | 104.70–79; 104.81 | 104.40; 104.43–59; 104.65–68; 105.4; 105.15–16; 105.19–22; 106.11 | 104.41–42; 105.17–18 |
| **Algeria** | African | | 129.47 | 129.39–47; 129.97–100 | 129.105–106 |
| **Andorra**** | Western European and Others | 83.22–23 | | 83.4; 83.7; 83.10–11; 83.19 | |
| **Angola** | African | 134.84; 134.118 | 134.108–113; 134.118; 134.121 | 134.37; 134.39; 134.42; 134.87–88; 134. 93–107 | 134.83; 134.114–117; 134.119–120 |
| **Antigua and Barbuda**** | Latin American | 67.17; 67.23; 68.29–30; 69.16 | 67.25–27 | 67.15; 67.18–20; 67.28; 68.28; 69.9–15 | |
| **Argentina** | Latin American | 99.33–45 | 99.68–69; 99.71 | 99.46–61; 99.66–67 | |
| **Armenia** | Eastern European | 120.95; 120.98 | 120.27–28; 120.126–134; 120.136; 120.145 | 120.24–26; 120.53; 120.72–73; 120.77; 120.99–117; 120.141 | 120.89–94; 120.96 |
| **Australia**** | Western European and Others | 86.71; 86.91; 86.126–132 | 86.88–89 | 86.47; 86.57; 86.65; 86.72–82; 86.98 | 86.136 |
| **Austria**** | Western European and Others | 92.64–65; 92.68; 92.70; 92.76; 93.46; 93.48 | 92.77 | 92.15; 92.23; 92.71–72 | 92.3; 92.8; 92.56–63 |
| **Azerbaijan** | Eastern European | 109.72; 109.76; 109.94–95 | 109.38; 109.41–43; 109.96–99 | 109.60–61; 109.66; 109.80–83; 109.89; 109.93; 109.97 | 109.71–78 |

*Note*: Data from second cycle other than for states marked** which are first cycle (second cycle pending), numbers are paragraphs of current published reports, available from www.ohchr.org/EN/HRBodies/UPR/Pages/Documentation.aspx.

*the Rights of the Child*; *T v UK*; *V v UK*, Applications 24724/94 + 24888/94, European Court of Human Rights [ECtHR]). Of course, in the event of a wrongful conviction or detention, appropriate remedies must be available to the victim.

Article 17 of the *Convention for the Protection of All Persons from Enforced Disappearances* makes clear that no one should be held in secret detention. It further makes provision for states to adequately legislate for deprivation of liberty, ensuring appropriate guarantees against arbitrary detention, determination of status, and official registers of detainees. These provisions echo other guidelines and standards such as the *Standard Minimum Rules for the Treatment of Prisoners* (approved by the Economic and Social Council by its resolutions 663 C [XXIV] of 31 July 1957 and 2076 [LXII], 13 May 1977, part I) and the *Body of Principles for the Protection of All Persons under Any Form of Detention or Imprisonment* (adopted by General Assembly resolution 43/173, 9 December 1988). Adequate detention facilities, including maintenance of accurate records, separation of detained juveniles and adults and the separation of those detained before (thus legally innocent) and after conviction are accepted evidence of compliance with international standards and are central to the protection against arbitrary detention and against maltreatment during detention as well as disappearances (ICCPR 2014).

Preventing arbitrary arrest and detention and ensuring a full and fair trial process for those appearing before courts and tribunals are especially important to fulfilling human rights obligations.

## *Issue 2: Violence against persons*

Violence against persons is a major issue of concern to the UN and is an area of law that brings specific challenges.[6] When the state is complicit in physical or mental maltreatment or punishment of an individual, the relationship and the abuse of trust is most prominent. Most human rights treaties seek to grant individuals protection against state actors (see Table 2.2). Thus, for example, the prohibition against torture, inhuman and degrading treatment limits the use of force which police officers can use when arresting or questioning a suspect. It can also be invoked to ensure both detention facilities and any judicially ordered punishment respect the dignity of the detainee/convict. As Rodley and Pollard note, '[t]he methods [of torture] are as infinite as the inventiveness of the dark side of the human imagination' (Rodley and Pollard 2009, p. 11). The prohibition on torture arguably has the force of customary international law, thus binds states irrespective of whether they have ratified salient human rights treaties (Rodley and Pollard 2009, p. 69, Parry 2010, p. 18).

The *Convention against Torture* is particularly strong on investigations of allegations of torture (Articles 12–13) and protection of victims, including provision of adequate compensation (Article 14), as well as the need for training of law enforcement officials (Article 10). Prevention is key with appropriate training supported by systematic reviews of interrogation rules and methods (Article 11). However, given that preventing torture is the central focus of that treaty, it is not surprising.[7] The *Convention against Torture* (Article 1) and the *Arab Charter* (Article 13) both explicitly include mental suffering within the definition of torture. Jurisprudence also supports the growing recognition of the mental component of torture and related practices. In *Selcuk and Asker v Turkey* Vol 1998-II, No.71, the ECtHR found a violation of Article 3 of the European Convention due to inhuman treatment occasioned by the victims having to watch their homes and personal property being burned by security forces. Across the human rights system, cruel and inhuman treatment was upheld in respect of family members of individuals who disappeared (for example, *Zohra Madoui v Algeria* UN Doc CCPR/C/94/C/1495/2006: para. 7.5). There are also findings of a range of violations in respect of the disappeared persons (*Velásquez Rodriguez*,

Inter-American Court of Human Rights 1988 Series C, No 4), though of course the *Convention for Protection of All Persons from Enforced Disappearances* now addresses this in more detail and makes extensive provisions for investigations of alleged disappearances (Article 12).

Given the seriousness with which the international community views acts of torture and related treatment, and the difficulty/impossibility of ensuring adequate reparation and compensation for torture, the primary emphasis is on prevention. As the law evolved, there is more emphasis on prevention when the torture may occur beyond their territorial boundaries. Although initially focused on 'death row phenomenon' with violations caused by the length of time convicted persons spend on death row awaiting death used to challenge extradition requests on human rights grounds (for example, *Soering v UK*, Ser A, No.161 [1989] ECtHR; *Ng v Canada*, UN Doc CCPR/C/49/D/469/1991), the same arguments are increasingly used for other deportation cases. Thus, when an individual runs a serious risk of torture or related treatment when deported, deportation orders should not be executed (for example, the protracted case of *Othman [Abu Qatada] v United Kingdom*, Application 8139/09 [2012] ECtHR).

One of the ultimate examples of lawful state violence against the person is the death penalty. Although completely abolished within the Council of Europe (Protocols 6 and 13 to the *European Convention on Human Rights*), it is not proscribed per se by human rights treaties. The Second Optional Protocol to the *International Covenant on Civil and Political Rights* does abolish it for contracting states. Where the death penalty remains, however, its use is regulated (for example, Article 6[4+5] ICCPR; Articles 6 and 7 *Arab Charter on Human Rights*). The universal periodic review process has brought the issue to the fore. Those states which retain the death penalty are regularly encouraged to introduce or maintain moratoriums on its use and to proceed with abolition. For example, the recommendation to Algeria on commutation of the death penalty sentences to prison sentences (HRC 2012, 129.91, or HRC 2011 re. Antigua and Barbuda, 69.3–8). However, some states make recommendations in support of the death penalty – for example, during the periodic review of Afghanistan, Egypt recommended the country '[c]ontinue using its sovereign right to apply the death penalty as a tool of criminal justice in accordance with proper safeguards specified under International Human Rights Law' (HRC 2014, 136.118). Whilst the UN trend is towards abolition, it remains politically charged.

More challenging to conceptualize, perhaps, is the responsibility of the state for violence committed by one private individual against another, that is an act of violence (such as an assault) not directly involving state actors. In such situations, the state is considered responsible because adequate criminal law should be in place to deter offenders and protect possible victims (*A.T. v Hungary*, UN Doc A/60/38 [Part I] Annex III). As with the deportation cases (above) the state has a positive obligation to fulfil in preventing torture and violence. Violence against women and children is a key issue before the UN. Although prevalent in all societies, it is a common subject for recommendations during universal periodic review (see Table 2.4). Indeed, it is the most frequently discussed topic of the four issues extracted in Table 2.4. More generally, the UN Secretary-General launched a campaign in 2008 to end violence against women (http://endviolence.un.org/). UN Women is also actively campaigning and working on this (www.unwomen.org/en/what-we-do/ending-violence-against-women). From a human rights perspective, violence against women infringes a range of human rights (Committee on Discrimination Against Women, General recommendation 19[1992]). It should be noted that some issues raised in the documentation are specific to certain countries – in Angola's universal periodic review, for example, several recommendations accepted by Angola related to protecting children accused of witchcraft and sorcery (HRC 2014, 134.89–91). Combatting all physical and mental violence and suffering remains a principal preoccupation of the UN human rights system.

### *Issue 3: Migration, refugees and trafficking*

Movement of humans is nothing new. However, in 2015, there are record numbers of refugees and increasing monitoring and investigation of trafficking and human migration. Trafficking in human beings is increasingly being considered not only a crime under the treaties prohibiting trafficking but also a violation of human rights. Human rights are increasingly being used as a tool when developing policies to combat trafficking. Thus, in *Rantsev v Cyprus and Russia* (Application 25965/04 [2010]) the ECtHR determined that the prohibition on slavery in Article 4 of the European Convention could be extended to trafficking in persons when considering the plight of a woman who was trafficked from Russia to Cyprus under an 'artiste' visa scheme. Looking at the universal periodic review documentation, Albania accepted a range of recommendations on combatting trafficking including adequately protecting and treating victims (HRC 2014, 104.60–65). Treatment of so-called irregular immigrants and asylum seekers was raised by many countries during Australia's first universal periodic review (HRC 2011, 86.38 [Jordan]; 86.121–134 from a range of states on issues including refoulement and detention) and with the establishment of offshore processing centres and a number of critical official reports (UN and Australian), the Australian government is unlikely to avoid this topic in its second review. Austria, too, is likely to be questioned on refugees and migration when its interactive dialogue begins, given the 2015 refugee crisis in Europe.

The treatment of migrant workers is another emerging trend – the *International Convention on the Protection of the Rights of All Migrant Workers and Members of their Families* makes extensive provision for migrant workers, including non-documented and irregular migrants (Article 5, Part III). In Southeast Asia, the position of non-documented migrants and their regular maltreatment in 'host' states regularly gives rise to concern. International (including regional) responses are necessary with a more globalized workforce regularly crossing borders for permanent or temporary contracts, or even in search of work.

Although the position outlined above in Australia in particular links to 'non-refoulement' in refugee law, a key issue in the early twenty-first century is addressing growing numbers of both refugees and migrants crossing multiple borders in search of sanctuary (in the case of refugees) or (for migrants) a better life in Europe or Asia-Pacific regions. Strengthening respect for human rights globally should better protect all individuals within and outwith their state of origin.

## *The trend towards a holistic approach*

Criminological work often examines the wider societal impact of crime and the sociological conditions related to patterns of criminal activity, rehabilitation, recidivism and such like. As international human rights have evolved as a system, there is increasing recognition of the need for holistic responses to human rights violations. Human rights are interdependent and indivisible thus there is an implicit understanding that rights cannot be singled out or stand alone when discussing protection or violation. Rather, engaging one right automatically engages additional rights. Violence against women (and children) is one obvious example, as the application of the prohibition on torture to the eradication of violence against women and children illustrates. In such a situation, the state is indirectly involved through its legal system: the state should ensure its criminal law is adequate to protect against domestic violence and that there are adequate policies in place, including education, to guarantee the inviolability of the individual against attacks by other individuals. In other words, a state can be found in breach of international human rights if it does not protect people against domestic violence through: education combatting violence; appropriate investigation of alleged violence; adequate protection of victims from future attacks; sensitive treatment of victims during investigation and trial; criminal law measures deterring would-be perpetrators and adequately punishing those convicted. The recommendations accepted by Afghanistan during its second UPR dialogue is an example – multiple states made recommendations on effectively implementing the new law on the elimination of violence against women (HRC 2014, 136.130–165).

Undoubtedly as the international system has evolved, there has been growing awareness of how different human rights interact, bringing into focus the need for a more holistic approach to both human rights protection and prevention of violations. The original pervasive principle was non-discrimination. More than 70 years since the UN recognized the equality of men and women and the prohibition on discrimination in recognition, promotion and protection of rights, challenges remain. More grounds of discrimination have been elaborated though some, such as sexual orientation, are controversial.[8] Realization of international human rights remains predicated on the need for equal treatment of all people, irrespective of their age, religion, language, race, colour, nationality and so on. There is extensive literature on profiling those subjected to police stop and search powers (particularly in Europe); those 'randomly' detained at airports on suspected drug offences (for example, in South America); those dying in custody. An intersectional analysis of many issues reveals the mesh of human rights that characterize many human rights situations.

Corruption is a newer pervasive principle underpinning work in the UN. There is an increasing emphasis on combatting corruption as corruption is identified as undermining both equality and human rights, given that it introduces arbitrariness and non-merit-based decisions. Corrupt judges, prison officers, police and government officials bias the criminal justice system and skew its operation. Those aligned with high level government officials may go unpunished; those able and willing to pay bribes can be treated differently from those who do not pay.

There are a number of other trends emerging but the need to view violations holistically and take a broader holistic approach to solutions is a modern characteristic. Eradicating corruption, combatting violence against women and children, addressing the challenges of migration, trafficking and refugees – all demand a holistic response, not simply creation of laws, but also examining the root causes, the lived experiences of victims and the varied possibilities for solutions.

## Conclusion

Given the nature of human rights, it is unsurprising that there is clear evidence of continuing interest in criminological issues before the UN human rights monitoring systems. The three key issues addressed in this chapter engage a range of human rights and fundamental freedoms. It is evident that there is no simple resolution to many of the challenges posed. More than legislation, strategic plans and policies are required. Adequate administration of justice does require a comprehensive legal basis for a state's justice system. Consideration must be given to the establishment, appointment and functioning of the judiciary and the regulation of detention. However, training and education is also required to ensure that law enforcement officers, for example, are aware of the necessity to refrain from using unnecessary force as well as the rules on arrest and detention. Movement of people, whether through regular or irregular routes, is securing a higher media profile at the time of writing. This demands a global response as several states are involved in each instance. Violence against individuals requires a strong legal framework to criminalize torture and related treatment, but this must be supported by provisions and systems for investigating allegations of torture and related mistreatment. Changing the culture of silence and acceptance of violence against women is a goal of the current UN campaigns. States can also ensure that they offer sensitive opportunities for victims to bring complaints to the legal authorities, and that victims are protected. Education, awareness raising and empowerment are essential so those with responsibility can guarantee protection of rights and those potential victims can seek redress.

The international human rights system has many detractors but as this chapter shows, it does offer possibilities for analysing a snapshot of comparable documentation addressing states around the world. What remains to be seen is what those states will do to improve their record of respecting, protecting and promoting human rights within and beyond their jurisdiction.

## Notes

1 Note that the Committee on Economic, Social and Cultural Rights, which monitors the Covenant of the same name, is the exception. It was established by the Economic and Social Council. In all other respects, it functions the same as the other eight committees.
2 Recourse should be had to the Charter of the United Nations for information on the powers and responsibilities of these organs – see also www.un.org.
3 For example, terrorist attacks and human rights abuses committed by the terrorist group Boko Haram, considered April 2015; the situation in Iraq following abuses committed by the Islamic State in Iraq and the Levant, considered September 2014.
4 Fourteen areas have such a mandate in 2015.
5 To ensure a random selection, all UN Member States beginning with the letter 'A' were examined. This selection includes states from each UN Human Rights Council regional grouping as well as a range of sizes, stages of development and geographical formation (small island developing, landlocked, developed and so on). Other regional analyses of the process suggest the findings using this sample are representative (Smith 2012a, 2012b, 2013, 2014; McMahon and Ascherio 2012; Charlesworth and Larking 2014).
6 As the laws of armed conflict and humanitarian law are not of direct relevance to the work of many criminologists, this area of law is excluded.
7 Article 16 extends the obligation to preventing other acts of cruel, inhuman or degrading treatment or punishment which falls short of torture as defined in Article 1 of the treaty.
8 HRC, 2015: Armenia accepted recommendations 120.52 and 120.81-86, various countries; compare with Uganda which did not accept recommendations on decriminalizing same-sex relationships during its review (UN Doc A/HRC/19/16; 113.1–16).

## References


General Assembly. 2006. *General Assembly resolution 60/251 Human Rights Council*, UN Doc A/RES/60/251.

ICCPR. 2014. *Human Rights Committee General Comment 35 Article 9 (Liberty and security of person)*, UN Doc CCPR/C/GC/35.

HRC. 2011. *Report of the Working Group on the Universal Periodic Review Antigua and Barbuda*, UN Doc A/HRC/19/5.

HRC. 2011. *Report of the Working Group on the Universal Periodic Review Austria*, UN Doc A/HRC/17/8.

HRC. 2011. *Report of the Working Group on the Universal Periodic Review Andorra*, UN Doc A/HRC/16/8.

HRC. 2011. *Report of the Working Group on the Universal Periodic Review Australia*, UN Doc A/HRC/17/10.

HRC. 2012. *Report of the Working Group on the Universal Periodic Review Algeria*, UN Doc A/HRC/21/13.

HRC. 2012. *Report of the Working Group on the Universal Periodic Review Argentina*, UN Doc A/HRC/22/4.

HRC. 2013. *Report of the Working Group on the Universal Periodic Review Azerbaijan*, UN Doc A/HRC/24/13.

HRC. 2014. *Report of the Working Group on the Universal Periodic Review Albania*, UN Doc A/HRC/27/4.

HRC. 2014. *Report of the Working Group on the Universal Periodic Review Angola*, UN Doc A/HRC/28/11.

HRC. 2014. *Report of the Working Group on the Universal Periodic Review Afghanistan*, UN Doc A/HRC/26/4.

HRC. 2015. *Report of the Working Group on the Universal Periodic Review Armenia*, UN Doc A/HRC/29/11.

Alston, P., 1997. *Effective functioning of bodies established pursuant to United Nations human rights instruments: final report on enhancing the long-term effectiveness of the United Nations human rights treaty system*. UN Doc E/CN.4/1997/74.

Alston, P. and Crawford, J. (eds), 2000. *The future of UN human rights treaty monitoring*. Cambridge: Cambridge University Press.

Annan, K., 2000. *Effective functioning of human rights mechanisms: treaty bodies – report of the Secretary-General on the consultations conducted in respect of the report of the independent expert on enhancing the long-term effectiveness of the United Nations human rights treaty system*. UN Doc E/CN.4/2000/98.

Charlesworth, H. and Larking, E. (eds), 2014. *Human rights and the universal periodic review: rituals and ritualism*. Cambridge: Cambridge University Press.

Egan, S., 2011. *The UN human rights treaty system: law and procedure*. London: Bloomsbury Press.

Joseph, S. and Castan, M., 2013. *The International Covenant on Civil and Political Rights: cases, materials and commentary*, 3rd edn. Oxford: Oxford University Press.

Kalin, W., 2012. Examination of state reports. *In*: H. Keller and G. Ulfstein (eds), *United Nations human rights treaty bodies: law and legitimacy*. Cambridge: Cambridge University Press, 16–72.

Keller, H. and Ulfstein, G. (eds), 2012. *United Nations human rights treaty bodies: law and legitimacy*. Cambridge: Cambridge University Press.

McGoldrick, D., 1991. *The human rights committee*. Oxford: Oxford University Press.

McMahon, E. and Ascherio, M., 2012. A step ahead in promoting human rights? The universal periodic review of the UN Human Rights Council. *Global Governance*, 231–48.

Parry, J., 2010. *Understanding torture: law, violence, and political identity*. Ann Arbor, MI: University of Michigan Press.

Pillay, N., 2012. *Strengthening the United Nations human rights treaty body system: a report by the United Nations High Commissioner for Human Rights*. Retrieved on 28 March 2016 from: www2.ohchr.org/english/bodies/HRTD/docs/HCReportTBStrengthening.pdf.

Rodley, N. and Pollard, M., 2009. *The treatment of prisoners under international law*, 3rd edn. Oxford: Oxford University Press.

Smith, R., 2012a. Towards the rule of law's human rights requirements in Commonwealth states: selected observations. *The Round Table: Commonwealth Journal of International Affairs*, 101(4), 303–22.

Smith, R., 2012b. The Pacific Island states: themes emerging from the UN Human Rights Council's inaugural universal periodic review? *Melbourne Journal of International Law*, 13(1), 569–94.

Smith, R., 2013. 'To see themselves as others see them': the five permanent members of the Security Council and the Human Rights Council's universal periodic review. *Human Rights Quarterly*, 35(1), 1–32.

Smith, R., 2014. A review of African states in the first cycle of the UN Human Rights Council's universal periodic review. *African Human Rights Law Journal*, 14(2), 346–65.

Tistounet, E., 2000. The problem of overlapping among different treaty bodies. *In*: P. Alston and J. Crawford (eds), *The future of UN human rights treaty monitoring*. Cambridge: Cambridge University Press, 383–402.

# 3

# Thinking about human rights from within criminology

*Anthony Amatrudo*

---

Human rights are amongst of the most important issues for contemporary criminology and there have been a number of attempts to incorporate human rights into the criminological canon. We shall look at three writers, all of whom furnish very useful accounts. These three thinkers are Manuel Lopez-Ray, Stan Cohen and Lucia Zedner. Lopez-Ray was taken with the practical issues that public policy throws up, such as devising agreed standards of treatment for prisoners and young offenders and using the law to secure human rights for those subject to the criminal justice system. He saw a focus upon human rights within academic criminology as enabling it to do international and comparative work, notably around the measurement of indices of good practice. Stan Cohen is a colossal figure in the Social Sciences and left an immense legacy of work. In regard to human rights his contribution spanned both practical activism as well as a deal of published literature and he had an impact upon the development of international relations as a discipline. In terms of criminology his contribution is undoubted, though complex, and we shall focus on the way he conceived of the state and the way it executes its crime control function. Lucia Zedner has explored the ways in which ethical problems have arisen in relation to the day-to-day operation of the criminal justice system; notably she has explored the ways in which the individual's ability to go about his or her business is often compromised by meta-risk considerations that undermine personal privacy and compromise civil liberties. These thinkers are representative of three broad approaches to the treatment of human rights within criminology – Lopez-Ray's with a focus on practical social policy, Zedner's with an emphasis upon deliberative democracy as a bulwark against the likelihood of a diminution in the rights and civil liberties resulting from actuarial policies of predictive risk, and Cohen's with its deeper philosophical concerns about social control and how we should live in late modernity. Interestingly both Zedner and Cohen approach human rights with one eye on social control. For them the extent, and form, of social control has definite human rights concerns for the citizenry. They are less interested with the human rights of criminals than they are with curtailment of the freedom and autonomy of the mass of citizens who are law-abiding. Therefore the form, and extent, of state social control in late modernity is the major concern. Moreover, because state social control tends to be focused on definite groups the bulk of the population typically remains unconcerned that social control is being extended in any case (Cohen 2001).

## Manuel Lopez-Ray

Manuel Lopez-Ray was a senior United Nations (UN) official and an academic, notably at the University of Madrid and the Institute of Criminology at the University of Cambridge. In the post-war era he was a key figure serving, at various times, as a lawyer and as national delegate at various international forums where international policy was determined. For example, he ensured that criminological research was used in the considerations of the UN Seminar on the Institutional Treatment of Juvenile Offenders in 1954. He saw the importance of criminological research in giving the UN a rigorous evidence base for its work, notably in arriving at agreed international standards of treatment for prisoners and young offenders. He was the author of a UN Report in 1953 *International cooperation by the UN in the prevention of crime and the treatment of offenders* which argued for the internationalization of standards of treatment for persons who are subject to the criminal law. He had witnessed the excesses of World War 2 and the dreadful results of allowing countries to set their own standards of judicial treatment outside of the international system of regulation around core issues of human rights. He understood the UN as promoting human rights within nation states through a regime of standard setting and in dealing with breaches of human rights through either the use of international law, or the incorporation of international legal standards within national legal frameworks (Lopez-Ray 1957, pp. 526–38). He knew that the most important issue, in the aftermath of the excesses of Nazism in Europe and Japanese militarism in Asia, was gaining agreement on, and then enforcing, these new post-war legally defined standards of treatment that equate to human rights. Lopez-Ray stands out as a major figure in this endeavour for he represents the template of the criminologist working collaboratively with lawyers and public policy experts and harnessing empirical research and quantitative data to develop what would become the post-war settlement around human rights enforcement, notably in regard to the criminal justice systems of sovereign nations. In his linking of the local nature of criminal justice with the broader international legal framework he was a pioneer in fostering the widest possible context, and dissemination, for criminological research (Lopez-Ray 1982, pp. 12–17). Moreover, by including state crime, and genocide, as part of the purview of criminological study he was a championing a broad treatment of crime (Lopez-Ray 1970).

Lopez-Ray understood human rights primarily as an issue for social policy and he saw the universal nature of human rights as best promoted by international agreement involving the UN. He also understood that members of the medical profession and those interested in economic development, as well as lawyers and criminologists, should contribute to the development of this new post-war infrastructure of human rights. He took up the role of Chief of the Social Defense of the UN in 1952 and saw it as his task to work with a range of non-government organizations in order to broaden the policy and research base for the UN around the treatment of offenders, including young offenders, and crime prevention. He was essentially a practical person and he ensured that his role as Chief of the Social Defense soon became associated with a form of leadership that supported those persons working locally, at the nation state level, with technical assistance, notably around the development of an enlightened criminal justice, including such matters as the practical management of prisons and the dissemination of criminological research. He believed that good practice within the criminal justice system always requires a solid research base (Lopez-Ray 1957, p. 528, 1982, p. 14).

In 1955 he chaired a UN Congress in Geneva and included representatives from 61 countries along with delegates from the International Labour Organization (ILO), the Council of Europe and the World Health Organization. It was a practical affair and the three main items on the agenda were the development of standards for the treatment of offenders, the institution of prison labour, which had been especially abused in Germany, and how to prevent young people embarking on a life of crime. It established the rehabilitative principle within local criminal justice systems. The ILO was worried that prison labour could undercut regular production and reduce wages in the general population. The ILO was also concerned with the levels of remuneration that prisoners received and also their safety in terms of the operation of machinery, including the appropriate levels of training. The Congress was judged a success and importantly in regard to prison life it argued prisons should aim: '[To] minimize the differences between prison life and life at liberty which tend to lessen the responsibility of prisoners or the respect due to their dignity as human beings' (Lopez-Ray 1957, p. 530, 1955). The Congress promoted the notion that the prisoner should continue their relationship with the wider community, not be excluded from it. This was a radical communitarian view of prison life and it is testament to Lopez-Ray's tenacity that he was able to enshrine it, not only in the 1955 Congress Report, but later in UN policy where he continually stressed the individual nature of prisoner's lives and their ongoing connection to family and community outside of the prison. It was Lopez-Ray's view, and that of the Congress, that prisons are institutions founded for rehabilitation. They should be humane places. The Congress stipulated that prisons should be small, no more than 500 inmates in Point 63 of its proceedings. The number of 500 was based on the number of prisoners a governor might reasonably be expected to know in a system that valued personal knowledge. The 1955 Congress stressed *prison welfare* as key to rehabilitation and noted it as an important and measureable indicator in the management of the prison estate. Moreover, the Congress Report is clear that all matters relating to prison welfare are enshrined in law in order that they can be challenged where breached. The purpose of the UN was understood as ensuring binding minimum standards upon nation states. Lopez-Ray saw criminological research as providing the necessary research base required for the enactment of legislation around the acceptable levels of provision prisoners should expect and the development of the expertise required to undertake such an assessment (Lopez-Ray 1982, p. 17).

The direct linkage of criminal justice policy with broader notions of human rights and a benevolent political community is established in the work and writing of Lopez-Ray. He begins a tradition of criminological research and policy analysis that seeks to work at the national and the international level to ensure that justice is advanced in all criminal justice systems; and that the work of national criminal justice systems coheres to the highest standards of treatment and human rights, as opposed to focusing narrowly upon law enforcement. He begins a tradition of measuring and monitoring the ways in which the criminal justice system operates in order to uphold these higher standards of treatment and human rights at the level of best international practice.

## Stan Cohen

Unlike Lopez-Ray, Cohen was not centrally concerned about statistical data or even criminological research, as such, but rather he was concerned with deeper political themes relating to the structures we all inhabit and their role in controlling people, especially in relation to the role of the state and its ideological capacity (Nelken 1985, p. 247). Cohen's work on human rights is extensive and he wrote a great deal about Israel and South Africa. However, it is his *Visions of social control: crime, punishment and classification* (Cohen 1985) that has had the most impact in terms of his work on social control and the ways in which political and cultural forces can exclude individuals, and groups, from the normal practices of social and political life. He argued that far from such exclusion being imposed it would be welcomed by the bulk of the population.

*Visions of social control* has an initial chapter on what Cohen terms master patterns. He sets out four transformations that occurred between the beginning of the nineteenth century and end of the twentieth century. First, he shows how the state became more and more involved in the processes of social control supplanting the established, though less formal arrangements, with more centralized and rationalized arrangements that tended to focus upon the apparatuses of control and punishment targeted at crime and delinquency, as well as the treatment of other types of deviants. Second, there then grew up an increasing differentiation, and categorization, of deviants and their arrangement into various classification systems all of with their own forms of knowledge and bodies of experts. Third, this developed into: '(an) increased segregation of deviants into "asylums" – penitentiaries, prisons, mental hospitals, reformatories and other closed purpose-built institutions' (Cohen 1985, p. 12). At this stage prison becomes the dominant mode of punishment and rehabilitation. And finally, Cohen notes a change in the practice of punishment away from an emphasis upon the body to an emphasis upon the mind. He notes how: 'The mind replaces the body as the object of penal repression and positivist theories emerge to justify concentrating on the individual offender and not the general offence' (Cohen 1985, p. 13). This four-stage scheme is not entirely novel and it certainly builds upon earlier work such as Rothman's *The discovery of the asylum* (1971); Foucault's *Discipline and punish: the birth of the prison* (1977) and Rusche and Kirchheimer's *Punishment and social structure* (2003). Cohen is keen to maintain that these developments were, at least initially, motivated by the best intentions of European post-Enlightenment thought. However, as with Rothman's writing in *The discovery of the asylum*, he holds that the reformers of the nineteenth century, though humane, were inexpert and unable to obtain the outcomes they desired. So with the case of rehabilitation the sheer numbers of incarcerated persons worked against it as a procedure. Moreover, as the nineteenth century got underway the new capitalist class demanded harsher and harsher social control and, indeed, this control became more and more focused upon the working classes. The prison: 'renders docile the recalcitrant members of the working class. It deters others, it teaches habits of discipline and order, and it reproduces the lost hierarchy. It repairs defective humans to compete in the market place' (Cohen 1985, p. 23). This being the complete opposite of the 1955 Congress the aim of which was the minimalization of the differences between the life of the prison and the life of the community outside.

Cohen was aware that the transformation he set out met with a deal of opposition in the nineteenth century and he wrote of the 'destructuring impulse' of those in positions of power (Cohen 1985, p. 31, 1993). He set out four areas that this 'destructuring impulse' concentrated upon. First, there is a movement away from the state towards a more decentralized system of community-based agencies of control. Second, there is a movement away from expert knowledge. Third, there is a movement away from institutions towards a greater emphasis upon community treatment and reintegration. Lastly, there is a movement away from the mind and back to justice (Cohen 1985, p. 31). Cohen maintained that during the latter half of the twentieth century the calls to destructure took hold and, wrongly as it turned out, advocates thought that this destructuring was synonymous with increased freedom. This destructuring resulted in a state wherein: 'the original structures have become stronger; far from any decrease, the reach and intensity of state control have been increased' (Cohen 1985, p. 37). Moreover, that: 'the system enlarges itself and becomes more intrusive, subjecting more and newer groups of deviants to the power of the state and increasing the intensity of control directed at former deviants' (Cohen 1985, p. 38). What Cohen sets out is a historically driven meta-narrative of social control. His main point being that the: 'likeliest future of social control . . . is a future of decisive and deepening bifurcation; on the soft side there is definite inclusion, on the hard side, rigid exclusion' (Cohen 1985, p. 37). Cohen has in mind a range of behaviour and states of being that count as *soft*, such as mental health and minor delinquent episodes. The deeper point he is making is in relation to the development of new forms of social inclusion that co-exist with exclusionary practices and that these would be deemed to be a risk: such inclusionary strategies would run the gamut of diagnostic, predictive and preventive measures and that such things as leisure activity, the family and the management of human sexuality would all be co-opted as part of the mechanism of social control. Furthermore, that in parallel with this surveillance will come to completely saturate our public spaces and that the urban environment we live and work in: 'will become sites for behavioural control' (Cohen 1985, p. 232). He saw observation as a form of panopticon control (Cohen 1985, p. 221). In using the term *hard* he was referring to the usual criminal breaches which would still be dealt with by incarceration and segregation in a Durkheimian fashion in regard to: 'boundary maintenance, rule classification, social solidarity' (Cohen 1985, p. 233).

The importance of Cohen's work is in his understanding late modernity as being characterized by both inclusionary and exclusionary mechanisms. The new forms of social control would not overturn the old mechanisms of social control only lead to the populace seeing their public space as increasingly a threatening place from which they need protection, including an emphasis upon surveillance. He follows Orwell in understanding these new exclusionary mechanisms will be increasingly *built in* to our daily lives and not only at the level of regulating public space but in terms of the workings of our minds (Cohen 1985, pp. 197–235). After the publication of *Visions of social control: crime, punishment and classification* it does seem that our world has indeed developed in the terms Cohen predicted and that it is true to say that it is easy to find evidence of *net widening and mesh thinning*. The prison estate has grown out of all proportion, notably in the United Kingdom and United States, and we can readily list the inclusionary systems that permeate our ordinary lives. Of course, technology has made this possible and, as he predicted, there have been calls for more and more surveillance of our public spaces, monitoring of the Internet and collection of our phone records, notably after 9/11 and 7/7. We all now accept monitoring and surveillance and now consider it part of normal life. What Cohen noted as a worrying *vision of social control* is conceived of as part of the routine job of crime control and prevention, or indeed of other things such as Islamic extremism, terrorism, the sexual exploitation of minors or immigration status. It is fair to say that Cohen's work on the increased use of inclusionary mechanisms is underscored by his earlier work around moral panic (Cohen 1972).

The richness, and usefulness, of Cohen's work lies in his noting of profound moral concerns about how we should live; notably in relation to arguments surrounding our human rights, arguments about the rightful goals of politics and even about the nature of our private lives. He wants us all to think carefully about the implications of social control in late modernity and its potential to extend itself, bit by bit, and for the net to widen and the mesh thin until we are all subject to it. The meta-point Cohen set out was a political one about the choices we make as citizens. He noted that the: 'choice between exclusion and inclusion is, above all else, a political decision determined by the nature of the state. Nevertheless, different as the actual governing criterion is, the dimensions of choice at each stage of the system are the same. At the macro-level, do we construct exclusive or inclusive systems? At the micro-level, do we exclude or include this particular individual?' (Cohen 1985, p. 271).

In *States of denial* Cohen grapples with the knotty issue of how in the face of increased social control there is, by and large, moral passivity. Why, he asks, are people so unconcerned by the unpalatable realities of our world and largely unmoved by the suffering of other people? There is awareness of human rights breaches and a plethora of other dreadful things yet Cohen argues that people are not always even aware they are switching off to these dreadful things. He argues that there is a culture of denial wherein it is: 'neither a matter of telling the truth nor intentionally telling a lie. . . . There seem to be states of mind, or even whole cultures, in which we know and don't know at the same time' (Cohen 2001, pp. 4–5). Cohen sets out three forms of psychosocial denial, which he terms literal, interpretative and implicatory. The literal form denies basic facts or knowledge; for example, the fact that prisoners at Guantanamo Bay have been treated badly. In the interpretative form the denial is not about the facts but instead the meaning is altered – for example, 'they were moved on not ethnically cleansed'. This interpretative form gives a more palatable form to the facts (Cohen 2001, p. 7). Finally, there is the implicatory form of denial which, though it does not deny the event or even the accepted interpretation of the event, nonetheless denies the 'psychological, political or moral implications' of it (Cohen 2001, p. 8). Cohen shows how such states of psychological denial are a routine form of coping mechanism. Moreover, that these three strategies are: 'learnt by ordinary cultural transmission, and are drawn from a well-established collectively available pool. . . . Socialization teaches us which motives are acceptable for which action' (Cohen 2001, p. 59). Such denials, moreover, not only allow people to live lives untroubled by the nastier side of modern life they also allow the state, and state actors, to go about their business without too much public concern; a point also made by van Dijk in relation to racism (1993).

## Lucia Zedner

Zedner has developed an argument around the concept of risk in which risk, and the language of risk, is used by the public authorities to undermine the language, and practice, of human rights. She follows Cohen in rooting her work in deeper moral and political arguments about the nature, and extent, of our civil liberties and human rights. She sets out how our language of rights, including human rights, is increasingly juxtaposed with the language of risk, and risk management by the public authorities and how this is echoed in the media (Zedner 2006, pp. 423–5). The challenge for human rights discourse is that it is progressively set alongside a form of risk assessment, such as terrorism or serious organized crime. Moreover, notions of individual rights and personal sovereignty are weighed against the safety and wellbeing of the community and the discussion is set in utilitarian terms. The media, and our elected politicians, often use a censorious and declamatory language in advocating the safety of the many over the rights of certain targeted individuals. The arguments advanced for the protection of the individual against the overwhelming power of the state tend to lose out in times of crisis, such as following 9/11. Similar arguments are advanced in the prosecution of so-called serious crime as opposed to ordinary crime (Amatrudo 2009, pp. 109–10). Zedner's point being that whether it is through the use of risk or seriousness language the outcome is often to dismantle the protections that citizens enjoy under the Common Law and she notes that this is tolerated because only minority groups are popularly understood as the target (Zedner 2009).

In 'Neither safe nor sound? The perils and possibilities of risk', Zedner (2006) set out the dangers to our civil liberties from a risk-based public policy; in terms of how a risk-based analysis can, and will, undermine our most basic legal values and sense of the importance of individual human rights. She maintains that unless the public authorities employ a rigorous moral sense of the worth of universal individual rights, and uphold that as an ethical principle, then the likely calls for more and more risk assessments and intrusions into our normal lives are likely to proceed unchecked. She sets out how risk itself is a pretty imprecise and general term whose original use was in engineering and science. In the field of engineering and science notions of risk and probability are typically related back to readily assessable, and usually mathematically determined, criteria in natural science methodology and to engineering practice. Her point being that the facts surrounding crime and terrorism are entirely different in nature, especially in terms of their causality, to the extent that they can never be straightforwardly determined. Moreover, that: 'human risks are necessarily reactive and call for reflexive strategies' (Zedner 2006, p. 423). She develops a working distinction between risk assessment and risk management and this distinction plays the major part in her critique of risk. She determines how since the 1990s there has been a change in how security is treated in terms of a marked shift towards risk-based approaches and away from rule-based approaches, such as respect for universal human rights. Indeed, she argues that risk-based approaches have become a 'central tool in the management of crime and terrorism' (Zedner 2006, p. 424). Historically, risk-based approaches to crime and terrorism have been set out in terms of legal rules and precedent. Whereas, where risk is prioritized, as with the contemporary treatment of crime and terrorism, there is tendency to play down the existing legal framework. She sets out the issues in relation to risk-based treatments in terms of proportionality and transparency, though her main criticism is in terms of what is and what is not knowable. She details how a supposedly scientific approach to risk masks both deeper political considerations and an unrealistic determination of the ability of the public authorities to calculate risk with any sort of precision. The focus upon immanent risk not only masks political considerations but tends to underestimate that risk itself is concerned with a form of prediction in which the risk itself is always weighed against the norms and values of a society, norms and values which themselves fluctuate (Amatrudo 2009, p. 76). There are real risks of not delineating the processes used for determining risk, which Zedner calls *quasi-scientific*, from those political processes of developing the concept of risk, in public policy terms, which are a political construction. Risk assessment being concerned with those elements of risk that are based on credible and objective data: whereas the management of risk is a far broader concept that concerns the actual decision-making processes that are coloured by political considerations. The point here is not to make too much of this distinction, which is open to the charge of over-determination, but instead to highlight the political considerations that are at play when dealing with risk. For example, determining the level of risk in the context of offender profiling necessarily involves a great deal of value judgement and, in any case, is tied to pre-existing categories. Moreover, there is a crudity in using simple utilitarian criteria when assessing the general welfare, which does not equate to science, and which often has disproportionately bad outcomes for certain groups and individuals, which are not only unscientific but which are unjust. In any case the public authorities often assess and re-assess some groups whilst others are left alone for a plethora of reasons. Her main point is that risk assessment and the management of risk are closely allied activities and it is mistaken to presume otherwise.

Zedner advocates a discussion about risk set in the broad terms of deliberative democracy rather than confining it too narrowly in terms of the criminal justice system; and here she follows contemporary political science (Dryzek 1997). It is at the level of political discourse that claims about risk need to be assessed. Where risk is cut off from broader political considerations a false science can grow up as was the case in determining weapons of mass destruction in Iraq (Zedner 2006, p. 431). In advocating deliberative democracy she follows Sparks in noting the importance of the social and cultural aspects of the entire risk determination process (Sparks 2001). In the process of deliberative democracy there is an ongoing negotiation between citizens and between citizens and elected officials. This sort of deliberative process allows citizens to take part in, for example, the level of counter-terrorism measures employed in city centres. She understands the sheer level of imprecision in determining risks and the dangers of allowing decisions about risk to be made narrowly by criminal justice actors, and increasingly the military and other experts; preferring instead to broaden the determination though deliberative democracy.

Zedner argued that historically crime has been treated in terms of notions of right and wrong and in terms of assessing past events. The crime always pre-dates the trial. However, following her earlier work on risk she noted an emerging focus around pre-crime; and more particularly, a pre-crime fashioned around risk or, if you like, potential risk. This emerging focus on pre-crime tends to advocate pre-emptive action by the state against *risky* individuals and groups. It also tends to see security as a purchasable commodity. Interestingly, this line of reasoning has a deal of overlap with the work of the modernist novelist Philip K. Dick, notably his 1956 short story *Minority report* (Dick 2002). Whilst she is alive to the dangers of this new emphasis upon pre-crime and security she is not altogether averse to the some of the ideas it throws up. She argues:

> A coincidental facet of the temporal shift to pre-crime is that responsibility for security against risk falls not only to the State but extends to individuals, communal and private agents. The shift is therefore not only temporal but also sectorial; spreading out from the State to embrace pre-emptive endeavours only remotely related to crime.
>
> *(Zedner 2007, p. 261)*

The implications for human rights relate to such issues as freedom of expression and religion, notably the Muslim faith, which have come under state scrutiny following 9/11 (Zedner 2014, pp. 99–105).

She determines that using the category of pre-crime greatly widens the scope of criminology; opening it up to look not only at the police and public authorities but also to the whole industry of private security and community safety more generally. It opens up the nature of public and private provision and the place of civil as well as criminal measures in dealing with crime: and, as Loader has noted, the extent to which the state delegates its prosecutorial role (Loader 1997). None of this is to suggest that policing was never focused upon preventive measures or that the police have always had a monopoly of crime control; however, it is to suggest that the emphasis has definitely altered towards a pre-crime approach, as Jones and Newburn have shown (Jones and Newburn 2002). The shift towards a pre-crime approach relates directly to the perceived threats following 9/11 and 7/7 which changed the ways in which people thought about risk and how the public authorities felt they had to adapt to these new circumstances. In such circumstances, of real existential threat, a preventive security strategy seems appropriate. However, such a strategy itself needs to battle against the pre-existing demands of regular policing in terms of obtaining resources. There is a tendency to play up this existential risk and for a pre-crime strategy to displace regular policing activity over time. The shift towards a pre-crime rationale often entails: 'earlier and earlier interventions, to reduce opportunity, to target harden and to increase surveillance even before the commission of crime is a distant prospect' (Zedner 2007, p. 265). It can lead to increased levels of incarceration as more and more persons are deemed dangerous. More concerning still is that, over time, the criminal justice system can become detached from crime and concern itself increasingly with matters of security: indeed as security itself becomes commoditized the tendency is to diminish the role of the policing in public space.

The point Zedner takes from the shift towards a pre-crime focus centre upon our everyday notions about civil liberties with its demands for protections of our private lives and beyond that our broader sense of what is rightful and fair treatment for the generality of citizens. She demands that criminologists take part in normative theory, notably around: 'the political and economic interests underlying the present pursuit of security as well as the intellectual assumptions upon which security policies are based' (Zedner 2007, p. 266). She argues that criminology will need to open to a whole new range of ideas, drawn from philosophy and contemporary political theory in order to establish: 'the values, principles and human rights that are to be defended in its (security) pursuit' (Zedner 2007, p. 275). She is alive also to the danger of a pre-crime rationale as a threat to criminology itself in a policy world where traditional ideas about crime are marginalized as there is a greater and greater, focus on pre-crime, security and the assessment of risk.

## Conclusion

Human rights have established themselves as part of the criminological corpus, notably in criminological theory. The work of Lopez-Ray, Cohen and Zedner does more than offer us a high order of scholarship: it offers us a range of approaches to the treatment of human rights within the criminal justice system. Lopez-Ray furnishes us with a very practical, and optimistic, methodology that establishes an esteemed place for criminological research. In noting how an engagement, by criminologists, with the system of governance and law can deliver results in terms of the practical realization of human rights, he saw how by embedding a notion of universal human rights within the criminal justice system, notably with regard to the prison, that we are able to recast the criminal justice system in terms of the highest ideals of human rights; and how this also represents an overall improvement for the community as a whole. On the other hand both Cohen and Zedner are less optimistic and tend to see human rights as under threat in late modernity. What Zedner highlights is the paranoia around risk which she sees as a constant companion to late modern governance though she beckons us to engage in a form of deliberative democracy as a challenge to it. Cohen's view is the bleakest of all. He demonstrates how, over time, there are incremental diminutions to all our freedoms. The state widens its net and narrows its mesh and more and more of us become subject to state surveillance, regulation and control. The creeping totalitarianism he outlines has echoes of Orwell and also of the Nazi state, which systematically profiled its citizens in the run up to World War 2 (Cohen 1996). All of these thinkers develop themes of perennial interest to criminologists, mindful of the importance of human rights to the criminal justice system: and each of them offers a guide to systematically negotiating human rights and the criminal justice system.

## References


Amatrudo, A., 2009. *Criminology and political theory*. London: Sage.

Cohen, S., 1972. *Folk devils and moral panics*. London: Routledge.

Cohen, S., 1985. *Visions of social control: crime, punishment and classification*. Cambridge: Polity Press.

Cohen, S., 1993. Human rights and crimes of the state: the culture of denial. *Australian and New Zealand Journal of Criminology*, 26(2), 97–115.

Cohen, S., 1996. Government responses to human rights reports: claims, denials and counterclaims. *Human Rights Quarterly*, 18(3), 517–543.

Cohen, S., 2001. *States of denial: knowing about atrocities and suffering*. Cambridge: Polity Press.

Dick, P.K., 2002. *Minority report*. London: Gollancz.

Dryzek, J., 1997. *The politics of the earth: environmental discourses*. Oxford: Oxford University Press.

Foucault, M., 1977. *Discipline and punish: the birth of the prison*. New York, NY: Pantheon Press.

Jones, T. and Newburn, T., 2002. The transformation of policing? Understanding current trends in policing systems. *British Journal of Criminology*, 42(1), 129–46.

Loader, I., 1997. Thinking normatively about private security. *Journal of Law and Society*, 24(5), 377–94.

Lopez-Ray, M., 1953. *International cooperation by the UN in the prevention of crime and the treatment of offenders*. New York, NY: United Nations.

Lopez-Ray, M., 1955. L'Ensemble des règles minima pour le traitement des détenus. *Revue International de Criminologie et de Police Technique*, 9(3), 1–75.

Lopez-Ray., 1957. The first UN congress on the prevention of crime and treatment of offenders. *Journal of Criminal Law, Criminology, and Police Science*, 47(5), 526–38.

Lopez-Ray., 1970. *Crime*. London: Routledge.
Lopez-Ray., 1982. Crime, criminal justice and criminology: an inventory. *Federal Probation*, 46(2), 12–17.
Nelken, D., 1985. Community involvement in crime control. *In*: *XXX Current Legal Problems*. Oxford: Oxford University Press, 239–67.
Rothman, D.J., 1971. *The discovery of the asylum*. New Brunswick, NJ: Transaction Press.
Rusche, G. and Kirchheimer, O., 2003. *Punishment and social structure*. New Brunswick, NJ: Transaction Press.
Sparks, R., 2001. Degrees of estrangement: the cultural theory of risk and comparative penology. *Theoretical Criminology*, 5, 159–76.
van Dijk, T.A., 1993. *Elite discourse and racism*. London: Sage.
Zedner, L., 2006. Neither safe nor sound? The perils and possibilities of risk. *The Canadian Journal of Criminology and Criminal Justice*, 48(3), 423–34.
Zedner, L., 2007. Pre-crime and post-criminology? *Theoretical Criminology*, 11(2), 261–81.
Zedner, L., 2009. *Security: key ideas in criminology*. London: Routledge.
Zedner, L., 2014. Terrorizing criminal law. *Criminal Law and Philosophy*, 8(1), 99–121.

# 4

# The Africana paradigm

## W.E.B. Du Bois as a founding father of human rights criminology

*Biko Agozino*

Human rights discourse is distorted by the imperialist assumptions of Occidentalism or the claim that such a discourse originated in the west and is therefore alien to the supposedly despotic Orient to the extent that human rights are presumed to be gifts to the rest of the world from a humanitarian western world. This papyrus (my preferred term for scholarly papers in honour of ancient Africans who invented writing and whose corpus continues to be referred to as such) departs from such criminological imperialist hubris to situate human rights discourse squarely within the Africana paradigm of struggles and achievements in thoughts and deeds by people of African descent (and their allies) who have been subjected by the west to the most heinous crimes ever known to humanity and yet remained committed to the struggle for social justice and human rights for all in a way that human rights discourse would be empty rhetoric if purged of all traces of Africana contents. An overview of what is without doubt the founding text of human rights criminology or the very first book of criminological research devoted to this theme, *The suppression of the African slave-trade* by W.E.B. Du Bois (1904), will support the choice here to make Africa central in the development of a critical and scholar-activist paradigm in human rights criminology. This papyrus surveys the spread of the benefits of the Africana struggles and theories of human rights to other oppressed communities for the benefit of all whose interests are strategically articulated with those of Africana communities. Finally, the papyrus concludes by highlighting the Africana paradigm of reparative justice as the most suitable response to human rights wrongs in contrast with the imperialist reason of 'control-freak criminology' that tends to abandon the fetishistic punitive obsession which it directs towards the relatively powerless when dealing with the enormous crimes of the powerful against humanity.

### Introduction

In a previous papyrus (Agozino 2014), I argued that Eurocentric scholarship on human rights sociology conveniently ignores the rich contributions of Africana scholars to the subject. Such ignorance about Africana contributions serves to stunt the growth of scholarship by suggesting that human rights is a western concept and concern. Yet, even western sociologists confess that not a lot of effort has been made to theorize human rights discourse in sociology, and by sociology here is meant a narrow focus on western sociology. Given the peculiar history of people of African descent who had been hunted as prey for hundreds of years, I suggest that no theory of human rights would ever be complete without situating the contributions of Africans at the centre of the discourse.

It is common to see assertions of western exceptionalism and essentialism that represent human rights as being of European origin and as remaining a European practice that respects individualism and the rule of law (Turner 1993). Many non-European scholars have adopted this stance uncritically by conceding that human rights issues are western ideas that must not be imposed on the developing countries which are still struggling with the attainment of Maslowian basic needs before they supposedly become ripe to pursue the higher needs of human rights (Taiwo 2010, Ake 1987). For instance, it has been suggested that the dictatorial regimes of Asia were able to grow their economies by being repressive and dismissive of human rights issues especially when labour interests conflict with the interest of capital in a presumably free market economy. In response, many scholars insist that human rights concerns were developed by Europeans long before the era of mass production and mass consumption came to suggest that Europe having attained basic needs, could now afford to emphasize human rights protection in domestic and international policies. Other scholars also warn that many African countries have gone through years of being repressed by blood-thirsty dictatorships but without producing the level of economic growth seen among Asian Tiger economies. In other words, the rights to the basic needs of Maslow appear restrictive if the conception of basic needs does not include the 'universal' declaration of human rights as a basic requirement of all human beings irrespective of their levels of economic development.

European sociologists tend to hold up the Magna Carta of 1215 as the earliest declaration of the principles of human rights but most ignore the fact on display at the British Library exhibition in 2015 that King John had no intention of implementing the Magna Carta and had signed a treaty with the Pope to ignore the document and rely on each other's armies to suppress any opposition to absolutist monarchical rule. Although the evil alliance against the Magna Carta did not succeed under the common law tradition, the record of the British around the world as a leading enslaver, conqueror, exploiter, and colonizer of others disqualifies the British from any claim to being the founders of human rights discourse. Ditto for the United States (US) with the Bill of Rights or the first 10 amendments to the constitution which reflect the influence of the Magna Carta because despite those amendments to the constitution, America continued to dehumanize American Indian Natives and African-Americans, women in general, and the poor to make it difficult for the US to pose as a beacon of human rights or civil rights protection. The same is true of Germany and Russia with records of shameless abuses of human rights even while philosophizing about the enlightenment and even while rallying to the cry of liberty, fraternity and egalitarianism.

This papyrus suggests that we should look to Africa as a land that has suffered the most egregious human rights violations much longer than any other land and we will see indelible evidence of the development of the discourse on human dignity dating further back than the Magna Carta (Agozino 2014). In the book, *Formations of modernity*, Stuart Hall et al. (1992) warn us against the oppressive foundations of the fetishes of western modernism as a reminder that we need to look beyond the west in our search for theories of human rights in a field like criminology which I suggested elsewhere remains the discipline that served colonialism more directly than most as the technology designed for the control of others (Agozino 2003). Without rehashing the evidence that forced Frantz Fanon (1963) to call on Africa and all colonized people to avoid trying to become like the west and instead find a third way for the Third World with emphasis on the education of the masses, the mobilization of the countryside, and the prevention of the rise of a phantom bourgeoisie with the ambition to replace the colonial authorities as the privileged users of the repressive fetishes of modernity, this papyrus demonstrates that knowledge itself is not served well when Eurocentrism seduces scholars into ignoring powerful contributions from outside Europe and North America.

## The foundational work of Du Bois

*The suppression of the African slave-trade* was a study of original sources – 'national, state and colonial statutes, Congressional records, reports of societies, persona; narratives, etc.' – completed by W.E.B. Du Bois (1904) while a Rogers Memorial Fellow at Harvard University and it resulted in his doctoral dissertation which was published as the founding issue of the Harvard University Historical Studies Series in 1896. It was not only the first book by Du Bois but also the first book on the criminology of human rights broadly conceived. Yet, most criminology students may not be familiar with the book while most human rights scholars may never have heard of it. In fact, an excellent article on the contributions of Du Bois to human rights scholarship and activism made a convincing argument that almost everything that Du Bois wrote and did is relevant to the topic but Elias, the author, managed to never even cite this foundational text (Elias 2009). For these reasons, I will devote a large portion of this papyrus to the reintroduction of the text to human rights scholars and to criminologists as a background to my hypothesis that the peculiar history of people of African descent has placed them at the centre of human rights and criminological discourse to be ignored at the peril of the relevant disciplines. As Du Bois put it in the preface to the book: 'the question of the suppression of the slave-trade is so intimately connected [to criminological and human rights scholarship] that it is difficult to isolate it [the suppression] and at the same time to avoid superficiality on the one hand, and unscientific narrowness of view on the other' (Du Bois 1904, p. v).

Contrary to misconceptions that continue to be held today by some communities of scholarship suggesting that slavery was a legitimate business that was supported by the values of the time, Du Bois revealed that there were legal efforts to limit or suppress the trafficking and sale of Africans right from the early colonial days in America, reflecting attitudes to the trade in England and among colonial planters in America and culminating in the final abolition of slavery in the US during the American Civil War in which over 600,000 people were killed trying to extend slavery or fighting to end slavery in America in the interest of global human rights.

Du Bois situated the criminology of human rights as a discourse that was founded on the attitudes of the English royalty which honoured human traffickers with knighthoods from 1562 and granted royal charters to corporations that specialized in kidnapping and selling millions of Africans as chattels for centuries. In other words, Du Bois was analysing the slave trade as a major form of crimes of the powerful that conventional criminology completely ignored in preference for superficial and unscientifically narrow focus on pickpockets, vagrants, sex workers, and non-violent drug offenders even today. In 1698 the effort to restrict the trade was made by William and Mary with Statutes 9 and 10 which imposed a 10 per cent duty on the importation of Africans to America whereas there were goods that did not have any import duties imposed on them and the slave traders protested that similar duties should be imposed on all goods to make for a level playing field in a laissez faire economy. This is an indication that the attitude of the English was not completely in support of the expansion of the evil and inhumane trade but by using an import duty to try to suppress it, there was enough room left for the powerful to continue committing crimes against humanity for many more centuries as a 'great benefit to the Kingdom and to the plantations and to the colonies' (Du Bois 1904, pp. 2–3).

The organized crime of kidnapping African women, men and children in their millions and selling them for profit was protected by English law as a monopoly for British traders by trying to exclude other nations from participating in the abominable crimes against humanity. With the defeat of the Spanish by the British and the signing of the Assiento Treaty in 1713, Britain acquired a virtual monopoly in the human rights crimes of trafficking and selling Africans unjustly for centuries. Spain also benefitted by charging England a duty of 33 per cent for each slave imported to the Spanish colonies of South America under the treaty. But the charging of duties could be a fiscal measure to limit the trade or suppress it to some extent to avoid being swamped by the import of too many Africans in an unscrupulous scramble for profits by a Royal African Company that was eventually bankrupted despite ninety thousand pounds a year in grants from the British government to keep it afloat. According to Du Bois, slavery was the basis of the colonial economy and without it that economy would collapse, raising questions as to why duties were imposed on the importation of enslaved people at all. As Du Bois put it, the slave trade was unquestionably central to the life of the colonies and by 1700 this centrality was regarded as an 'axiom in British practical economics'. This was supported by the colonists who declared that enslaved people were 'the strength and sinews of this western world,' and the lack of them 'the grand obstruction' here, as the settlements 'cannot subsist without supplies of them.' For these clamours in favour of slavery at home and abroad, there was a consensus in England that the country must officially encourage the slave trade. The argument was officially extended to say that if the slave trade was advantageous to Barbados and Jamaica, then it could not be injurious to Carolina, Virginia or New York. The colonial governors in America were instructed to 'give all due encouragement and invitation to merchants and others' and especially to the 'royal African company of England' by disallowing all duties laid on importers and frowning upon 'all acts in any way restricting the trade' (Du Bois 1904, p. 4).

The governor of North Carolina expressed the interests of the merchants by opposing the imposition of duties on the importation of Africans because such duties imposed by some of the states were seen as discouraging the merchants. However, the main reason given for the restrictions on the importation of Africans was that they were prone to insurrection given that they were not used to the 'docility' that had been imposed on the Africans born on the plantations who were used to being disciplined and controlled whereas the newly imported Africans were more likely to resist those who tried to keep them in slavery with cruel and unusual punishments. As Du Bois put it, 'The docility to which long years of bondage and strict discipline gave rise was absent, and insurrections and acts of violence were of frequent occurrence' (Du Bois 1904, p. 6). This dread of uprisings among the enslaved resulted in more severe laws, stronger police systems, and supported all earlier efforts to stop further importation of enslaved people.

Strangely, criminologists and human rights scholars have almost completely ignored this foundational theory of Du Bois at the expense of their intersectional disciplinary concerns. Rare exceptions include Jenny Martinez (2012), who made a passing reference to the doctoral dissertation of Du Bois and his testimony at the League of Nations as contributions to the origin of international human rights law but Martinez failed to spell Du Bois's name correctly, as two words, preferring 'DuBois' for some reason.

Du Bois followed the introductory chapter with chapters devoted to the geopolitical regions of America to demonstrate that all the states had laws restricting the slave trade including the Southern states that could arguably be said to have had historically specific and climatically favourable conditions that favour the institution of slavery. This demonstrates that there was no value-consensus in support of slavery even though the restrictive legislations were not eagerly enforced and even if the restrictions were less punitive and more in the form of duties imposed to discourage mass importation of slavery out of fear of insurrections. It was not long before the revolutionary government started entertaining resolutions that opposed slavery on moral grounds and not simply out of fear that the enslaved might rise up against their oppressors. One such draft resolution that was not passed but which prompted restrictions on the importation of Africans stated as follows with specific reference to human rights criminology:

> That the selling and enslaving [sic] the human species is a direct violation of the natural rights alike vested in all men by their Creator, and utterly inconsistent with the avowed principles on which this, and the other United States, have carried their struggle for liberty even to the last appeal.
>
> *(Du Bois 1904, p. 32)*

Similar efforts were made more successfully in Providence, Long Island, when the human rights of Africans was used as the basis for banning the importation of enslaved Africans into the colony in 1774. The preamble to the Act stated clearly that since the residents of America try to preserve their own rights and liberties, greatest of which were personal freedoms that they enjoy themselves, they 'should be willing to extend personal liberty to others' (Du Bois 1904, p. 36).

Du Bois conceded that some of the new found belief in human rights in the revolutionary era may have helped to advance the abolitionist cause by making even the 'dullest' to realize that the call for human freedom was not consistent with the institution of slavery. But Du Bois insisted that slavery was a failure as an economic system, prompting more people to oppose it on economic grounds. In addition, the imminence of war with Britain over the declaration of independence fed the genuine fear that Britain may try to mobilize the enslaved to help fight against the revolutionaries with a promise of freedom.

Moreover, the slave market was flooded with supplies and so the price paid was reduced unless the supply was suppressed to increase the value of enslaved people. Finally, more Americans saw the slave trade as an advantage to British merchants and so if Americans restricted and suppressed the trade, they would be dealing a serious blow to the economy of their enemy, Britain (Du Bois 1904, pp. 41–2). The punishment for violating the suppression of the slave trade was often informal censure in the form of a boycott of the business of the offending parties as the following quotation by Du Bois indicates with emphasis on the rights of the colonists rather than the rights of the enslaved Africans:

> In Virginia the vigilance committee of Norfolk 'hold up for your just indignation Mr. John Brown, Merchant, of this place,' who has several times imported slaves from Jamaica; and he is thus publicly censured 'to the end that all such foes to the rights of British America may be publickly known . . . as the enemies of American Liberty, and that every person may henceforth break off all dealings with him'.
>
> *(Du Bois 1904, p. 47)*

The ruin of the business of Mr John Brown may have enraged him enough to push him into trying to kill those who held enslaved people in order to level the playing field for himself. The interests of white Americans were emphasized all right but the rights of the enslaved Africans were also highlighted if only as propaganda against the British king who was waging war against the people of America who had the inalienable right to choose their own system of government and who opposed the 'execrable commerce' as was stated in the declaration of independence in which:

> The king was charged with waging 'cruel war against human nature itself, violating its most sacred rights of life and liberty in the persons of a distant people who never offended

> him, captivating and carrying them into slavery in another hemisphere, or to incur miserable death in their transportation thither. This piratical warfare, the opprobrium of infidel powers, is the warfare of the Christian king of Great Britain. Determined to keep open a market where men should be bought and sold, he has prostituted his negative for suppressing every legislative attempt to prohibit or to restrain this execrable commerce.
>
> *(Du Bois 1904, p. 48)*

The rights argument was also exploited by some in the form of the States' Rights to suggest that every state had the right to decide whether to continue supporting slavery or to suppress the slave trade but in reality, it was the slave states that tried to impose their attitudes to slavery on the states that did not want to continue being associated with the trade. Eventually, Congress decided that the federal government had the authority to regulate interstate commerce, including the slave trade, leading to a flood of petitions from some states denouncing the slave trade in strong human rights terms:

> In some of these slavery was denounced as 'an outrageous violation of one of the most essential rights of human nature,' and the slave-trade as a traffic 'degrading to the rights of man' and 'repugnant to reason'.
>
> *(Du Bois 1904, p. 80)*

The enforcement of the laws suppressing the slave trade was not always enthusiastic and the economic argument against the slave trade appeared more prominent but there remained a discourse of human rights criminology in the abolitionist movement that criminologists and human rights scholars should not continue to ignore. Thomas Jefferson was quoted by Du Bois as trying to pacify the opponents of slavery and slave holders by asserting that his fellow citizens should be congratulated for using constitutional authority to ban US citizens from 'further participation in those violations of human rights which have been so long continued on the unoffending inhabitants of Africa, and which the morality, the reputation, and the best interests of our country, have long been eager to proscribe' (Du Bois 1904, p. 95).

As a major enslaver himself who even sold his own children born by the enslaved African women he had raped all his life, Jefferson may have been trying to speak from both sides of his mouth at the same time but he still managed to identify slavery as the violation of 'human rights' while calling for the delay of the implementation of the abolitionist laws that would have impacted his own property rights over children that he fathered with enslaved women.

Criminologists will be particularly interested in the discussion by Du Bois of the proposals for the punishment of those who violated the laws that suppressed the slave trade. There were two sets of opinions and attitudes to the suitable punishment: On the one hand, it was suggested that the slave trade was one of the most serious crimes ever committed by human beings and so it should be punished with the death penalty. Whereas advocates of more severe punishment focused on the 'enormity of the offence', the punishment of murder with death under the law of God, the premeditated nature of the crime, that many will prefer death to being victimized with enslavement, and that lesser crimes were punishable by death:

> whereas the importation of slaves, a crime committed against the liberty of man, and inferior only to murder or treason, is accounted nothing but a misdemeanor. Here, indeed, lies the remedy for the evil of freeing illegally imported Negroes, – in making the penalty so severe that none will be brought in.
>
> *(Du Bois 1904, p. 102)*

Others saw the violations as misdemeanours to be punished only with a fine. They argued that the death penalty was too severe for such a violation given that slavery remained legal in the southern states in conditions 'worse than the slave trade'. It was also suggested that a severe punishment for the crime of slave trade may make members of the public sympathetic to the accused, thereby increasing crime by those who may refuse to inform on the offenders:

> John Randolph argued against even fine and imprisonment, 'on the ground that such an excessive penalty could not, in such case, be constitutionally imposed by a Government possessed of the limited powers of the Government of the United States'.
>
> *(Du Bois 1904, pp. 103–4)*

In case readers are wondering which side carried the argument and what the Bill passed was allowed to prescribe as punishment, Du Bois documents that various fines were prescribed and the forfeitures of slave ships were allowed in the Bill although another Bill, the one that Thomas Jefferson asked to be delayed in implementation, actually prescribed the death penalty for the 'felony' of illegally importing people of African descent to be enslaved. Yet, the implementation revealed that no one was hanged for the crime of importing people to be enslaved, very few people were ever fined and hardly any ship was forfeited, reminding us of the painting, *The Slave Ship*, by Turner, in which hardly any ship is visible on the canvas despite the heavy trafficking that took place for hundreds of years, after which Britain paid out huge sums of compensation to the people who violated the human rights of Africans for centuries, before the abolition of slavery. The refusal to apply the death penalty would not have displeased Du Bois given his own opposition to the death penalty especially because it was applied to innocent African-Americans in arbitrary and discriminatory ways in violation of their human rights. Western criminology cut itself short by ignoring these seminal contributions from Du Bois and many other people of African descent due to the continuing influence of racism on otherwise objective scholarship. The internalization of such racism is probably part of the reason why African and Caribbean countries along with the federal government and many states in the US continue to retain the death penalty; long after the Europeans who imposed the policy during colonialism have abolished it in their own countries as barbaric and ineffective (Greenberg and Agozino 2013).

The successful struggles by people of African descent and their allies to end slavery did not benefit only Africans but also benefitted other communities of oppressed people such as European workers who won the right to a 40-hour week only after the abolition of slavery, for obvious reasons. Similarly, European men who did not own property and women in general did not win the right to vote until such a right was extended to the former enslaved Africans. Therefore, a focus on the contributions of people of African descent to criminology of human rights will benefit not only Africans, but also the discipline as a whole.

## Conclusion

This papyrus concludes by emphasizing that Du Bois was not alone in his human rights scholar activism because his paradigm is widely shared among Africana scholars as I argued elsewhere (Agozino 2014). Although this papyrus is focused narrowly on the first book of Du Bois, interested readers will find that the theme of human rights remained the focus of all his work throughout his life, demonstrating a:

> visionary passion for justice . . . in every book . . . Du Bois rose above particularisms to deliver the same solution to Arkansas pogroms and Compers's American Federation

> of Labor, as to South African land acts and systematic brutality by cartels in Belgian Congo.
>
> (*Lewis 2000, p. 39*)

The conviction of Du Bois that 'the absolute equality of races . . . is the founding stone of world peace' (quoted in Lewis 2000, p. 39) was demonstrated not only in his scholar activism but can also be found in every page of such books as *The Philadelphia negro* (Du Bois 1898) in which he critiqued the racial profiling of former enslaved African-Americans and called for them to be given the freedom of movement to visit the parks without being arrested by the police in a country that avoided including the freedom of movement in its Bill of Rights. He also called for an end to the convict lease system that incriminated innocent African-Americans for profit. He demanded that the criminal justice system should pay attention to what is now known as white-collar crime and he called for an end to the political clubs that used thugs to intimidate and disenfranchise African-American voters. In his famous book, *The souls of black folk* (1903), Du Bois continued this theme of Human Rights Criminology advocacy by condemning lynching and segregation while advancing education as a human rights issue. In his magnum opus, *Black reconstruction in America* (Du Bois 1935), and also in his book, *Darkwater* (Du Bois 1920), Du Bois advised the white proletariat against being used as storm troopers to attack their black allies, the black proletariat, with whom they could unite to elect leaders who would be more responsive to the needs of poor Americans who were being divided under the ideology of white supremacy that benefitted the white bourgeoisie primarily.

The work of C.L.R. James (1938) and Eric Williams (1944) directly followed Du Bois by focusing on the violation of the human rights of enslaved Africans and demonstrating that the interconnectivity of human life means that the oppression of one group hurts all others directly and indirectly. Walter Rodney (1972) equally observed that the kidnapping and selling of Africans should not be called a trade at all because it was more like pillaging and warfare. This theme is evident in the work of Ida B. Wells (1972) who risked her life to campaign against lynching in America. Also contributing to what could be called a Du Boisian Human Rights Criminology, Angela Davis (1983) cautioned western feminists to avoid being recruited by white-supremacist patriarchy and used to socially construct African-American men as essentialist rapists given that the majority of rape allegations were by white men who were interested in protecting their property rights to white women's bodies and given that between 1936 and 1976 nearly 90 per cent of the men executed for rape in the US were African-American men, forcing the US Supreme Court to abolish the death penalty for rape.

Samora Machel (1975) is also on record for stating that colonialism is extremely contra humanity because there is no such thing as a humane colonialism and no such thing as a democratic colonialism. The work of Walter Rodney (1972), Amilcar Cabral (1979) and Frantz Fanon (1963) all represent major contributions to human rights criminology as does the work of Azikiwe (1960, 1937), Mandela (1994), Ekwe-Ekwe (2006), Madunagu (2006), Achebe (2012), Soyinka (2012), Tutu (1998) and Martin Luther King Jr. (1968), to mention but a few. What the papyrus indicates is the need to go beyond Eurocentrism in the search for new knowledge to advance the theory of human rights in criminology by recognizing the heroic struggles and theoretical contributions by people of African descent and Indigenous scholars who are deliberately marginalized in the discourse of human rights generally and in criminology particularly (Tauri and Porou 2014).

The focus on people of African descent is also capable of bringing innovation to the field of criminology by encouraging more explorations of the African philosophy of non-violence with emphasis on what is to be done to heal the wounds inflicted on society by human rights violators rather than obsess on making the punishment for human rights violations fit the crime since no punishment would ever be proportional to the crime. Rather, criminologists should explore the theory of reparative justice and support the campaign by people of African descent for reparations to be paid to the survivors of the African Holocaust home and abroad (Bauman 1989, Agozino 2004). Caribbean nations have recently made demands for reparations while the survivors of the British repression of the Mau Mau land and freedom army in Kenya won token reparations for the crimes against human rights committed by British colonial officials (Riri 2013).

Therefore, when Schwendinger and Schwendinger (1970) called for human rights crimes to be treated as crimes and not simply as civil wrongs or misdemeanors to be responded to with mere fines, they were not suggesting a wholesale adoption of the repressive or punitive approach. Stan Cohen (2001) made the non-violent policy options clearer by denouncing criminology as a made for export policy fabrication that ignores human rights violations while pushing to developing countries the very same policies that have failed woefully in western countries with rising crime rates and exploding prison populations. What is needed in the criminology of human rights wrongs is liberation criminology similar to what Joe Feagin and colleagues (2014) have identified as 'liberation sociology', profiling the works of Karl Marx, Du Bois and my own, among many others, as exemplars.

## References

Achebe, C., 2012. *There was a country: a personal history of Biafra*. New York, NY: Penguin.

Agozino, B., 2003. *Counter-colonial criminology: a critique of imperialist reason*. London: Pluto Press.

Agozino, B., 2004. Reparative justice: a pan African criminology primer. *In*: A. Kalunta-Crumpton and B. Agozino (eds), *Pan African issues in crime and justice*. Aldershot: Ashgate, 228–48.

Agozino, B., 2014. Contributions of Africana scholars to the theory of human rights in sociology. *Theoria and Praxis*, 2(1). *The Idea of Human Rights*. Retrieved on 1 April 2016 from http://pi.library.yorku.ca/ojs/index.php/theoriandpraxis/article/view/39370.

Ake, C., 1987. The African context of human rights. *Africa Today*, 1(2), 5–12.

Azikiwe, N., 1937. *Renascent African*. New York, NY: Negro University Press.

Azikiwe, N., 1960. *Respect for human dignity: an inaugural address*. Enugu: Government Press.

Bauman, Z., 1989. *Modernity and the Holocaust*. Cambridge: Polity.

Cabral, A., 1979. *Unity and struggle*. New York, NY: Monthly Review Press.

Cohen, S., 2001. *States of denial: knowing about atrocities and suffering*. Cambridge: Polity Press.

Davis, A., 1983. *Women, race and class*. New York, NY: Vintage.

Du Bois, W.E.B., 1898. *The Philadelphia negro*. Philadelphia, PA: University of Pennsylvania.

Du Bois, W.E.B., 1903. *The souls of black folk*. Chicago, IL: A.C. McClurg & Co.

Du Bois, W.E.B., 1904. *The suppression of the African slave-trade to the United States of America: 1638–1870*. Harvard Historical Studies, Vol. 1. Harvard University.

Du Bois, W.E.B., 1920. *Darkwater: voices from within the veil*. New York, NY: Harcourt, Brace & Co.

Du Bois, W.E.B., 1935 (1995). *Black reconstruction in America, 1860–1880*. New York, NY: Free Press.

Ekwe-Ekwe, H., 2006. *Biafra revisited*. Dakar: African Renaissance Press.

Elias, S., 2009. W.E.B. Du Bois, race and human rights. *Societies without borders*, 4(3), 273–94.

Fanon, F., 1963. *The wretched of the earth*. New York, NY: Grove Press.

Feagin, J., Hernan, V. and Kimberley, D., 2014. *Liberation sociology*, 3rd edn. Boulder, CO: Paradigm Publishers.

Greenberg, D. and Agozino, B., 2013. Executions, imprisonment and crime in Trinidad and Tobago. *In*: Peter Hodgkinson (ed.), *International Library of Essays on Capital Punishment*, Vol. 3, Aldershot: Ashgate, 123–50 (a reprint of the 2012 paper in *British Journal of Criminology*, 52, 113–40).

Hall, S. et al., 1992. *Formations of modernity: understanding modernity*. Milton Keynes: Open University Press.

James, C.L.R., 1938. *The black Jacobins*. London: Secker and Warbug.

King, Jr., M.L., 1968. *Where do we go from here: chaos or community?* Boston, MA: Beacon Press.

Lewis, D.L., 2000. *W.E.B. Du Bois: the fight for equality and the American century, 1919–1963*. New York, NY: Henry Holt.

Machel, S., 1975. *Samora Machel: The Beira Speech. In*: African Yearbook of Rhetoric 2(3), 2011. Retrieved on 1 April 2016 from www.africanrhetoric.org/pdf/Q%20%20%20Machel%20-%20Beira%20English.pdf.

Madunagu, E., 2006. *Understanding Nigeria and the new imperialism: essays 2000–2006*. Edited by Biodun Jeyifo, Bene Madunagu, Kayode Komolafe and Chido Onuma. Calabar: Clear Lines Publication.

Mandela, N., 1994. *A long walk to freedom: the autobiography of Nelson Mandela*. New York, NY: Back Bay Books.

Martinez, J.S., 2012. *The slave trade and the origin of international human rights law*. Oxford: Oxford University Press.

Riri, D., 2013. *Justice for freedom fighters: Mau Mau justice network*. London: Liberation.

Rodney, W., 1972. *How Europe underdeveloped Africa*. London: Bogle l'Ouverture.

Schwendinger, H. and Schwendinger, J., 1970. Defenders of order or guardians of human rights? *Issues in Criminology*, 5(2), 123–57.

Soyinka, W., 2012. *Of Africa*. New Haven, CT: Yale University Press.

Taiwo, O., 2010. *How colonialism preempted modernity in Africa*. Bloomington, IN: University of Indiana Press.

Tauri, J.M. and Porou, N., 2014. Criminal justice as a colonial project in contemporary settler colonialism. *African Journal of Criminology and Justice Studies*, 8(1).

Turner, B.S., 1993. Outline of a theory of human rights. *Sociology*, 27, 489–512.

Tutu, D., 1998. *Truth and reconciliation commission report*. Government of South Africa.

Wells, Ida B., 1972. Alfreda M. Duster. ed. *Crusade for justice: the autobiography of Ida B. Wells*. Chicago, IL: University of Chicago Press.

Williams, E., 1944. *Capitalism and slavery*. Richmond, NC: University of North Carolina Press.

# 5

# Regarding rights *for* the Other

## Abolitionism and human rights from below

*David Scott*

## A question of foundations

The language of human rights is a commonplace one for those actively engaged in emancipatory struggles against inequality, domination and state power, and it has a long association with penal abolitionism. Penal abolitionists question the moral and political legitimacy of the current application of the penal rationale (punishment) and call for alternative ways of handling interpersonal conflicts within a fairer and more egalitarian society. The language of rights has been championed by a number of penal abolitionists, most notably Stanley Cohen and Barbara Hudson. For Stanley Cohen (1994) human rights are a defensive strategy creating legal safeguards and protections against violations of dignity whilst at the same time facilitating a progressive utopian vision of social transformation. For Barbara Hudson (2003) human rights are absolutely necessary to protect the common humanity of those people whose behaviour we find repugnant or are unable to empathize with. Not all penal abolitionists share such enthusiasm for human rights, especially legal rights, and this chapter explores the commitment to rights in four 'abolitionist human rights schools' (Dembour 2006, Weber et al. 2014).

Each of the 'abolitionist schools' have a different way of understanding the foundations of human rights and I name the four schools *foundationalism*, *anti-foundationalism*, *neo-foundationalism* and *non-foundationalism*. Abolitionist thinkers, however, do not fit easily into such neat categories. As certain continuities cut across each school and the oeuvres of abolitionist thinkers inevitably reflect different concerns, priorities, or aspects of the debate at different times of writing, the schools are not necessarily mutually exclusive. Abolitionists have contributed to different schools and Stanley Cohen and Barbara Hudson have arguably left their mark on all four. What is clear though is that penal abolitionists have long advocated a bottom up, emancipatory praxis that actively promotes human rights *for* the Other.

## Foundationalism: dignity, need and mutuality

For foundational abolitionists human rights are natural, universal and inviolable moral values revealed through our use of reason (Hudson 2001). Although the basis of human rights differs amongst such abolitionist thinkers, dignity, need and mutuality are generally considered most essential. Foundational abolitionism takes inspiration from the deontological ethics of the German philosopher Immanuel Kant (1785), albeit severed from his notorious defence of punishment. For Kant, dignity is understood as a moral property inherent to all humans. Dignity cannot be earned and nor can it ever be lost, although it can be violated. Each human has equal moral worth and is deserving of corresponding respect and recognition. Everyone, by virtue of being human, has equivalent status and value and should be treated as an end in themselves. Dignity flourishes when people exercise their moral conscience free from discrimination, domination or authoritarian controls. To meet the requirements of dignity, basic human needs and material necessities must be adequately addressed. The material conditions underscoring existence must allow full participation in community life and be favourable to the realization of human potential. Indeed, for Norwegian peace theorist Johan Galtung (1994, p. 2) the 'link to basic human needs' makes 'human rights applicable to human beings everywhere'.

The Russian philosopher Peter Kropotkin (1924) is one of the earliest and most influential foundational abolitionists. Writing 'in the spirit' of Kant, Kropotkin maintains that mutual aid, cooperation, support and care for fellow humans are natural human dispositions. Mutual aid '*is the predominant fact of nature*' (Kropotkin 1924, p. 14, emphasis in original) and as humans are social beings our 'social instinct' is to create caring and mutually reciprocating relations in an inclusionary moral society. As dignity is a relational concept, respect and recognition for one's own dignity is intimately tied to respect and recognition for the dignity of others. To deny the dignity of the other is also to deny the dignity of the self. People have a natural 'mutual sympathy' for fellow humans resulting in an inborn tendency to help another person meet their needs. Human rights then are both for the self and *for* the other.

Abolitionists have attempted to uncover the natural foundations of human rights in two ways. The first, as illustrated above, is a 'positive approach' deducing the basis of rights from moral principles and values. Yet, whilst normative ethics clearly have an important place in the abolitionist tradition, the perspective is also closely aligned with a 'negative approach' which explores the meanings and content of human rights through a focus on their violation (Kauffmann et al. 2011). By drawing attention to what happens in immoral environments characterized by degradation, humiliation, shame, instrumentalization, non-recognition and disrespect, abolitionists shine a light upon what is most essential to the human condition. In other words, we learn what underscores our common humanity through a focus on its denial (Cohen 2001). Indeed, the very term 'abolish' indicates that abolitionism is a social movement aiming to end a given state of affairs. Drawing upon the 1948 *Universal Declaration of Human Rights*, Polish victimologist Lech Falandsyz (1991, p. 18) believes abolitionism is 'a particular version of [the] human rights movement and philosophy'. For Falandsyz abolitionism is part of 'a long struggle for human rights in the history of mankind' with the never-ending goal of 'abolishing the restrictions on human freedom, equality and dignity'.

Fellow Pole Michal Porowski (1991) similarly argues that the prison place undermines our 'inborn human dignity'. Consequently:

> dignity will always be liable to suffer a certain damage as a result of deprivation of physical liberty, the overall humiliating atmosphere of prison, and the impossibility of eliminating coercion, supervision, lack of privacy, and the fact and symbols of subjugation.
>
> *(Porowski 1991, p. 100)*

Prison presents a clear danger to our common humanity, desecrating identity and sense of worth. Prisons are steeped in morally questionable actions that violate dignity: isolation, lack of recognition and respect, monotonous daily routines, restrictions of liberty and movement, instrumentalization and unwarranted physical force. As such prisons structurally deprive prisoners of even the 'most elementary' of human needs and undermine any sense of solidarity or 'brotherhood' (ibid.). The prison is 'a space and situation where violence reigns indivisibly' (Porowski 1991, p. 94). Drawing parallels with Johan Galtung's (1969) conception of 'structural violence', Porowski (1991, p. 94) highlights the insidious and largely invisible nature of violence, which he defines as 'something which could be avoided but which hinders human self-realisation'. For foundational abolitionists prisons are hierarchical and authoritarian spaces of exploitation, domination, harm and 'institutionally-structured violence' (Scott 2015a) that can break the human spirit.

Prisons threaten personhood leaving those confined feeling helpless, overwhelmed and powerless. Through its daily operations the prison place destroys the natural flow of time, melding together past, present and future perceptions of time. This reshaped sense of time consciousness immerses the prisoner within acutely painful 'now time' awareness. The empty, monotonous, boring and wasteful 'prison time' gnaws away at the sense of self, resulting in feelings of loss, loneliness and despair (Cohen and Taylor 1981, p. 101). Quite frankly, the prison is structured to exhaust meaningful space and relationships, becoming a tomb for the living and a graveyard for those unable to cope with prison time (Scott 2015a). But prisons do not only lead to corporeal death [death of the body]. Systematically undermining forms of mutual aid, respect and recognition on the inside, the prison breaks connections with people on the outside and the ability of prisoners to build new relationships when released. For foundational abolitionists prison is a place of suffering and death. It is the negation of the fulfilled life. It is a place that generates *corporeal, civil* and *social death* (Kropotkin 1924, Porowski 1991, Scott 2015a).

The foundational abolitionist school of human rights is of course not without its critics. There are five main concerns: foundational human rights are often defined from above through legal instruments and covenants rather than directly by people in all their diversity; focus on human suffering can lead to a downplaying of radical politics and praxis; the meaning of dignity is vague, essentially contestable and often abstracted from peoples' lived reality; human needs can be reduced to lists of basic needs that do not address the full meaning of common humanity; and focus on mutuality may reduce ethical relationships to conditional reciprocity only. These concerns are further highlighted below.

## Anti-foundationalism: what is wrong with existing legal rights?

As the name indicates, *anti*-foundationalist abolitionists question the alleged foundations of human rights.[1] Anti-foundationalism, however, is not necessarily *against human rights*. Instead, the concern is often that current rights agendas do not sufficiently encompass the values underscoring emancipatory moral visions of human rights. The critique of rights by anti-foundationalists has thus focused on the *concept* of human rights and the current *content* of legal rights.

Conceptual critiques have focused on two interrelated issues – the problems of the 'rights of the self' and 'universal legal rights imposed from above'. The criticism that 'rights of the self' lead to egoism and selfishness, and undermine solidarity, has been long espoused in Marxist political theory and remains a genuine bone of contention (Douzinas 2000). Instead of promoting mutualism and the reciprocity of respect and recognition, a litigious use of legal rights results in a more self-centred and individualized society that naturalizes structural inequalities. The American penal abolitionist Dean Spade (2011) forcefully critiques the manner in which legal rights can individualize social problems. Spade (2011) argues that the interpretive framework of legal rights reconstructs the harms, discrimination and violence generated by structural inequalities as individual troubles that can only be addressed if 'bad people' with deliberately 'bad intentions' are identified as perpetrators. 'Structural violence' is therefore neglected through the human rights lens. For Spade (2011, p. 79) legal rights 'cast as private potentially political contests about distribution of resources . . . [and] converts social problems into matters of individualised, de-historicised injury and entitlement'. Further, whilst legal reforms cannot effectively address structural violence, legal rights can legitimate the status quo as they 'tinker with systems to make them look more inclusive while leaving their most violent operations in tact' (Spade 2011, p. 91).

The second main conceptual problem is that of 'universal rights imposed from above'. The concern is that claims of universal and eternal rights 'from above' are abstracted from people's lived realities. Consequently rights become an ahistorical, apolitical and acontextual idiom obscuring rather than accurately reflecting real life. The 'abstraction' of legal rights, often referred to as 'reification', is a cause of significant uneasiness, and some decades ago Norwegian abolitionist Nils Christie highlighted how the specialist jargon, reasoning and procedures of legal professions 'steal' the interpersonal conflicts and troubles of ordinary people and prevent their participation in resolution (Christie 1977). Legal rights 'from above' then are neither flexible nor negotiable. Rather than encouraging help, aid and assistance for the powerless they are instead used to consolidate professional power in the 'crime control industry'. More broadly, there is growing concern that a 'human rights industry' (Allen 2013, p. 4) has grown up around universal legal rights covenants, treaties and declarations resulting not only the creation of human rights professionals disconnected from the people, but a language of rights corrupted in the interests of personal gain and financial profit.

Fears of ineffectiveness, corruption and a bias towards the powerful are not the only believed costs associated with the ascendancy of human rights language. There is more than a little evidence indicating that the hegemony of human rights has supplanted emancipatory socialist politics with nothing but individualized humanitarian moralizing and an apolitical minimal utopianism reflecting the interests of western liberal democracies (Moyn 2010, Allen 2013). According to British Foucauldian Feminist Carol Smart (1989, p. 138) using law to forward emancipatory goals is 'hazardous' as law constitutes an 'institutionalised and formalised site of power'. Smart (1989, p. 139) maintains that rights rhetoric is now 'exhausted' and despite the historical links between legal rights and grass roots activism their advocation today may even be 'detrimental' to radical causes. The language of rights is too easily appropriated by the powerful and rights claims of the powerless effectively countered by resort to competing rights reflecting the interests of those in power.

For French abolitionist Michel Foucault (1977) legal rights are also closely bound together with existing relations of power. Whilst rights in their 'juridical form' provide formal equality and guarantee certain liberties at the same time they mask 'non-egalitarian and asymmetrical' forms of bourgeois political power. In other words, rights are paradoxical. Whilst the people benefit from the legal establishment of certain rights, at the same time such legal rights ignore antagonistic class relations, mystify structural inequalities and conceal political domination by the powerful in advanced capitalist societies. Despite their promise, legal rights are more a form of legitimating state governance than a means of effectively challenging state power, inequality or domination (Douzinas 2000, Spade 2011, Allen 2013).

Anti-foundational abolitionists have also raised concerns regarding the *content* of human rights laws. Of greatest concern is the manner in which minimalistic legal rights treaties 'imposed from above' legitimate state power and neutralize critique (Scott 2010). The enforcement of articles of rights conventions is dependent upon judicial interpretation. This is a far from neutral process, and legal rights are merely the reflections of the beliefs of certain judges. Unsurprisingly then, the legal rights of prisoners in the UK are primarily procedural rights and progressive judicial rhetoric has emerged only in cases regarding prisoners where fundamental principles of legality are in question, such as confidential correspondence and access to legal advice. The judiciary are unlikely to provide a sustained or progressive critique of those institutions that uphold the status quo. Existing legal rights 'from above' place serious restrictions upon the meaning and scope of human rights, reducing universal human rights to specific issues, determined by their historical and political context. In so doing human rights covenants and articles become static and easily negotiable by those in power. They lose their critical edge, become relatively predictable and can be co-opted by the state to demonstrate a clean bill of health when undertaking human rights audits (Scott 2013). In a further tragic twist of fate, in the United States legal victories by prisoners in the courts since the 1970s have been subverted through the building of human rights compliant super-max prisons. Despite clearly infringing upon dignity, denying human needs and undermining mutuality such prisons have been built with the explicit purpose of being human rights law proof (Guenther 2013).

Despite the considerable scepticism of the anti-foundational abolitionist school about the value of legal rights this does not necessarily mean that the abolitionist critique of currently existing legal rights entails a complete rejection of the idea of human rights. Even critics as staunch as Michel Foucault (1977) do not entirely dismiss human rights. However, any abolitionist rights agenda must be able to connect with the lived experiences of the common people and have the ability to challenge power rather than consolidate it.

## Neo-foundationalism: hearing the voice of the Other?

Neo-foundational abolitionists aim to address a number of the limitations of existing legal rights through new rights created by the 'forceless force' of rational debate (Benhabib 2004). Inspired by the discourse ethics of the neo-Kantian German philosopher Jürgen Habermas (2012), neo-foundationalism has a strong 'positive approach' to human rights. Respect for, and protection of, inviolable human dignity underscores a formal process through which the content and principles of legal rights are agreed (Benhabib 2004). In these 'special argumentation situations' (ibid., p. 13) all people capable of the speech act are allowed to participate in the moral conversation. All participants are equal conversation partners and each participant in the dialogue is allowed to ask questions and initiate new discussions as well as contribute answers. 'Discourse ethics' provide a moral normative framework for regulating conflicts through meaningful and reciprocal dialogue and reaching a decision acceptable to all who participate (Hudson 2003). By closely following procedure new valid and agreed universal human rights can be created.

Identifying the 'rules of the engagement' and privileging equality, respect and recognition, the neo-foundational school is focused on processes rather than the outcomes and has significant application to legal accountability and procedural justice. For the Dutch criminologist Rene van Swaaningen (1997) abolitionism must be grounded in a human rights discourse that promotes both legal guarantees as a defensive measure and advocates the development of concrete alternatives that challenge the penal rationale. Abolitionist visions should act as a 'replacement discourse' (ibid., p. 2) to 'create an open space for alternative scenarios' (ibid., p. 9). In a period dominated by authoritarian populism and exclusionary social policies, abolitionists must look first to the 'protective side of the law' (ibid., p. 106) so that the 'dignity and integrity of the individual' can be 'procedurally guaranteed' (ibid., p. 46).

In its 'positive approach' to dignity and human rights, the neo-foundational abolitionist school advocates respectful and reciprocal dialogue through radical alternatives such as 'informal justice', mediation and restorative justice. Though abolitionism and restorative justice in practice have had a rather ambiguous relationship, the focus on placing the victim at the centre of analysis; providing a voice to all parties, including the voice of the offender; downplaying or removing coercive solutions; placing relationships at the heart of the response to a given problematic or troublesome act; focusing on constructive *agreements* and emphasizing fixing, compensating, repairing or restoring balance, are all connected at least in part to themes raised by abolitionists such as Nils Christie (1977). They also strongly connect with the Habermasian inspired notion of 'redress' advocated by the Dutch abolitionist Willem de Haan (1990).

The abolitionist visions of redress and restorative justice are grounded in communication and openness. The British abolitionist Barbara Hudson (2003) believed that justice must have a discursive element that never allowed for a complete closure in terms of setting the boundaries and meanings of justice, and this sense of 'ethical openness' is something which will be returned to later. Although dialogue, discursiveness and negotiation has somewhat disappeared in contemporary restorative justice practice, the ideals remain central for the neo-foundational abolitionist. What restorative justice still does though is to help draw attention to the 'why punish?' question. For Hudson (2003, p. 29) this allowed space for the following key question to be raised: 'Why punishment and not reparation? Why is a stern lecture from a judge not sufficient?'

Neo-foundational abolitionist schools have attempted to address the problem of abstraction through the acknowledgment of what the Turkish-American critical theorist Seyla Benhabib (2004) calls the generalized and concrete other. When acknowledging another person as the 'generalized other' focus must be on their common humanity and relations 'governed by the norms of *formal equality and reciprocity*', whereas when a person is acknowledged as 'concrete other' they should be considered as an individual with their own unique biographical histories and relations 'governed by the norms of equity and complementary reciprocity' (Benhabib 2011, p. 69). Here the recognition of difference and diversity becomes entwined with notions of dignity, universal rights and complex equality.

For Barbara Hudson (2003) human rights can create a common language that makes it easier for people to be comprehensible to each other and facilitates a greater understanding of difference and diversity. Hudson (2001, p. 165) also points out how denial or repression is often used to contain and regulate difference. She argues that as the law has traditionally been grounded in universal notions of 'sameness', current constructions of the law fail to adequately accommodate those who fall outside such categories. However, there is room for manoeuvre and reconstruction in the realm of the law. Hudson (2001, p. 166) believed that the grounding of law in human rights covenants turns the law into a more open and transformative agent. Rights covenants become 'starting points' for a jurisprudence that can provide alternative formulations of rights 'predicated on difference, on conflicts of rights that will be generated by individual cases'. Thus rights jurisprudence could be the site for progressive change and the acknowledgment and respect for those defined as 'different'. Importantly the promotion of human rights law must go beyond merely 'technical provisions' and encourage a 'vibrant culture of rights, and a non-repressive respect for difference' (ibid., pp. 162, 168).

The neo-foundational school also pays close attention to the voice of the other. All people should be allowed to engage in open reciprocal and meaningful dialogue, no matter who they are or what they may have done. For Benhabib (2004, 2011) the 'right to have rights' means listening to the voice of the other, recognizing their diversity and facilitating the right for the other to define their own rights. To speak is to have an opinion heard – to count as a fellow but unique human being. For penal abolitionists the prisoner voice should not be disqualified out of hand but prisoners should be recognized as equal conversational partners. Subjugated knowledge should be emancipated (Foucault 1977). The prisoner voice should be heard and listened to and, where appropriate after rational debate, acted upon (Scott 2015b).

The neo-foundational school also draws attention to the conditions that undermine or devalue the voice of the other. Those who are silenced are denied their dignity and the refusal of voice is undoubtedly painful, if not a form of violence in itself (Cohen 2001, Couldry 2010). Yet, whilst the voice of the other can be interpreted as a cry of pain, or as a means of diminishing pain, it is pain and suffering which present one of the greatest threats to voice. Suffering destroys our capacity to speak and ability to relate with others. For the American literary scholar Elaine Scarry (1985, p. 4):

> Physical pain does not simply resist language but actively destroys it, bringing about an immediate reversion to a state anterior to language, to the sounds and cries a human being makes before language is learned.

For Scarry human suffering can be 'unsharable'. At times it cannot be spoken. The sufferer can be silenced, made invisible and denied full participation in the human community (ibid.). This denial of voice also presents a number of questions to the abolitionist neo-foundational school which they may be hard pressed to answer (Hudson 2003). Are lawbreakers prevented from participation because of the context of conversations or access to spaces set aside for dialogue with debating partners? Are prisoner protest and individual resistance recognized as speech acts or excluded from the meaning of speech acts? Can the voice of the estranged Other be heard, and if not, can/should their standpoint be articulated by another person in a different idiom? (Scott 2015b). To consider these points further we must turn to our fourth school.

## Non-foundationalism: a human rights agenda *for* the Other from below

Non-foundational abolitionists are influenced by the writings of Lithuanian phenomenologist Emmanuel Levinas and Argentinian liberation philosopher Enrique Dussel. Rather than searching for foundations, non-foundational abolitionists assert that certain human rights should exist. Instead of being backward looking, non-foundationalism is future orientated. The language of human rights is to be used to help realize inclusionary visions of social justice. The primary focus is thus on aspirations and emancipatory goals *still to come* (Cohen 1994, van Swaaningen 1997, Hudson 2003).

Whilst existing legal rights have been criticized for undermining communal sociality, the non-foundational school founds human rights in an individual's interconnectedness with others. The intersubjective self is formed within a social world shared with other people. As interrelated beings, humans require open intimate inter-corporeal ties with others to prosper. The prison, however, impacts upon human identity formation as it undermines 'mutually constitutive' relationships. The prisoner is estranged from family, friends and loved ones in the community and in practice prisons are places of mutual suspicion and mistrust (Guenther 2013). Indeed, confinement within the prison place oscillates between enforced isolation and what the American abolitionist Lisa Guenther (2013) calls 'forced relationality'. In an argument somewhat reminiscent of the writings of Kropotkin, Guenther (2013) notes how the prison disrupts our natural desire to choose our own company and as such prisoners are either denied human contact or forced to engage in coerced relations with others. Prisons prevent the presence of relational intimacy *and* the capacity for privacy and withdrawal (ibid.). They destroy human togetherness and as such prisoners can become isolated ghost-like figures haunted by past memories on a monotonous road to nowhere.

The ethical relationship, that is those to whom we owe responsibility, arises through a face-to-face encounter with the 'exterior being' of another person. In the encounter the face of the other speaks to us through words, expressions or actions and we then choose whether to engage in a 'non-violent' dialogue with them. For Levinas (1969, p. 39) the 'absolute other is the Other . . . the Stranger' and the strongest moral claims upon us arise from encounters with the Other. The stranger is a relatively powerless outsider beyond our normal social circle. They are someone in enormous need. The greater the asymmetry in our relation to the Other, the greater our responsibility.

To fulfil our ethical obligations we must attempt to meet the needs of the less powerful Other. Significantly, as this means helping the powerless, moral rights cannot be appropriated by the powerful for their own interests. For non-foundational penal abolitionists the prisoner stranger is an *enforced stranger* – the *estranged Other.* Prisons are profoundly hierarchical institutions that set asymmetrical relations in stone. Prisons are immersed in human suffering, structural denials of needs and violations of dignity. Consequently, whilst the ethical demand for responsibility in the prison place is immense, at the same time prisons structurally deny the possibility of an ethical encounter with the estranged Other. Neither fellow prisoners nor members of staff are in a position to affirm their responsibilities *for* the estranged Other as the prison place undermines care, kindness and other actions derived from our moral conscience. The moral demands of the estranged Other cannot be met. Thus, imprisonment is inevitably a place of immoral performance.

The absolute necessity of *exterior beings* in the creation of *the interior self* means that, unlike Kantian inspired foundational abolitionism, human rights are not the properties of autonomous persons. Human rights must exist with and *for* the Other, rather than the self (Douzinas 2000). Thus, instead of searching for universal laws based upon rationalized abstractions, in the non-foundational school human rights derive from concrete relations with the Other in situated contexts (Hudson 2003). The forging of the rights *for* the Other in such a way ensures that human rights are flexible and cannot be tied down into specific lists or legal covenants. Human rights cannot be grasped and codified but are aspired and fought for. They are contingent humanizing agents linked directly to the authentic needs and concrete realities of other humans, especially those under the yoke of repression, domination or authoritarianism. Further, there is no expectation that the respect and recognition called forth in an encounter with the Other will be mutually reciprocated. Human rights reflect our responsibilities for the inherent dignity of both our neighbours and those from far beyond our neighbourhood (Douzinas 2000, Dussel 2013).

The estranged Other must not be forced to suffer in silence (Dussel 2013, Scott 2015b). The voice of the estranged Other must be heard, even if they do not or cannot speak the 'language of the system'. Their voice must not be constrained by existing dominant discourses: the prisoner must be allowed to speak their own language (Hudson 2003). If the estranged Other does not speak the idiom of penal authorities, then abolitionists should respond by offering an interpretation of their voice, presence or actions. This may mean reading and translating the 'unsayable' suffering that is expressed through the face. The mere presence of the estranged Other is sufficient for a dialogue to begin.

When the estranged Other does speak we must patiently listen. Their voice must not be disqualified from democratic dialogue but heard as the cry of oppressed creatures demanding recognition. Prisoners must therefore have the opportunity to play a part in defining their own rights and indeed there are strong historical connections between assertions of dignity and the struggles of prisoner social movements. To be sure, non-foundational rights must always come *from below* rather than be imposed from above (Douzinas 2000, Scott 2003, 2009).

For Dussel (2013, p. 55) the 'moral formal principle' of rational intersubjective dialogue is directly connected with the 'material principle' of ensuring that the needs of the Other are met. The demands of the Other ultimately require social welfare or other forms of collective provision to meet their needs rather than individual philanthropy. Ethics must lead to politics. For Dussel (2013) the face of the [estranged] Other enjoins us to actively partake in an emancipatory struggle against injustice, domination and asymmetrical power. Dussel (2013) rightly acknowledges that asymmetrical relationships are inevitable given human diversity: equality cannot mean treating all the same and the 'boundaries of justice' must be informed by an 'ethical openness' that can accommodate difference in all its variety (Hudson 2001, 2003). Further, as a relational concept, power will always be in some ways unequally distributed across the social body (Foucault 1977). Yet for non-foundational abolitionists many existing structured hierarchies of power can and should be levelled. Non-foundational rights are underscored by a transformative political agenda from below seeking to abolish social and economic inequalities and structural violence (Dussel 2013). Thus, whilst we should 'acknowledge differences' we must also assert the 'common humanity' of the Other irrespective of a person's actions and social background (Cohen 2001, p. 297, Hudson 2003, Scott 2012).

Human rights grounded in non-reciprocation are urgent in societies where there exist great differentials in the exercise of power and distribution of the social product. Emancipatory praxis resulting in greater symmetry may though allow for the possibility of founding new ethical relations with others who have the resources to reciprocate, and this must be an abolitionist aspiration. More egalitarian societies would bring us closer to the socialist ethic of mutuality, but in our times rights *for* the Other must be based on non-reciprocation. Humans will always continue to have needs and the transformative ethics of Dussel (2013) in the end sound not so dissimilar to the socialist slogan 'from each according to their ability, to each according to their needs'.

## Beyond foundations: abolitionist praxis

Abolitionist human rights are a language of social protest directed against domination, authoritarianism and violence. Human rights first and foremost must highlight the present excesses of the punitive rationale and be a medium for articulating resistance, critique and dissent. Human rights provide a language that common people understand. Whilst this is not the only language through which to express the principles of dignity, need and mutuality, rights are the ethico-political language of our times. Irrespective of their limitations, abolitionists should promote human rights as part of their counter-hegemonic strategy.

An abolitionist rights agenda will always be 'unfinished' for it must be forged through emancipatory struggle and acts of defiance. An abolitionist human rights agenda will continuously evolve and should be focused on making more visible the institutionally structured violence of incarceration. Abolitionist critiques must reveal the ideological closure of the existing foundations of legal rights and reignite their more emancipatory potential. Abolitionist rights have to move beyond a merely humanitarian approach reflecting the content of international covenants and grounded in the amelioration of suffering. Theirs must be a human rights agenda that reflects the struggles of the powerless and contributes towards emancipatory and transformative abolitionist praxis. The aspiration must be for freedom from domination and the removal of the causes of human suffering.

Human rights from below should be *for* the Other rather than the self. To protect human rights society should learn to hear the voice of the estranged Other, recognize their inherent dignity, and meet them with non-violence. This means envisioning radical alternatives to the penal rationale that can be adopted in the here and now. Society should find new (or return to older) ways of handling human conflicts and troubles that do not systematically violate human dignity. Radical alternatives should be historically immanent, in place of an existing sanction and not be grounded in authoritarian forms of domination. They should reflect the normative frameworks of human rights, democratic accountability and social justice. Only time will tell if an abolitionist human rights agenda from below can provide an adequate language to reinvigorate a commitment to socialist ethics and politics and transform current ways of responding to the estranged Other.

## Note

1 I have focused here primarily on the 'negative approach' of the anti-foundational school to existing legal rights.

## References

Allen, L., 2013. *The rise and fall of human rights*. Stanford, CA: Stanford University Press.
Benhabib, S., 2004. *The rights of others*. Cambridge: Cambridge University Press.
Benhabib, S., 2011. *Dignity in adversity*. Cambridge: Polity Press.
Christie, N., 1977. Conflicts as property. *British Journal of Criminology*, 17(1), 1–15.
Cohen, S., 1994. Social control and the politics of reconstruction. *In*: D. Nelken (ed.), *The futures of criminology*. London: Sage, 63–88.
Cohen, S. 2001. *States of denial*. Cambridge: Polity Press.
Cohen, S. and Taylor, L., 1981. *Psychological survival*. London: Penguin.
Couldry, N., 2010. *Why voice matters*. London: Sage.
de Haan, W., 1990. *The politics of redress*. London: Sage.
Dembour, M.B., 2006. *Who believes in human rights?* Cambridge: Cambridge University Press.
Douzinas, C., 2000. *The end of human rights*. Oxford: Hart Publishing.
Dussel, E., 2013. *Ethics of liberation*. Durham, NC: Duke University Press.
Falandsyz, L., 1991. Abolitionism: between necessity and utopia. *In*: Z. Lasocik, M. Platek, and I. Rzeplinska (eds), *Abolitionism in history*. Warsaw: University of Warsaw, 16–20.
Foucault, M., 1977. *Discipline and punish*. London: Penguin.
Galtung, J., 1969. Violence, peace, and peace research. *Journal of Peace Research*, 6(3), 167–191.
Galtung, J., 1994. *Human rights in another key*. Cambridge: Polity Press.
Guenther, L., 2013. *Solitary confinement: social death and its afterlives*. London: University of Minnesota Press.
Habermas, J., 2012. The concept of human dignity and the realistic utopia of human rights. *In*: C. Corradetti (ed.), *Philosophical dimensions of human rights*. London: Springer, 63–80.
Hudson, B.A., 2001. Punishment, rights and difference: defending justice in the risk society. *In*: K. Stenson and R.R. Sullivan (eds), *Crime, risk and justice*. Cullompton: Willan, 144–72.
Hudson, B.A., 2003. *Justice in the risk society*. London: Sage.
Kant, I., 1785. *The metaphysics of morals*. Cambridge: Cambridge University Press.
Kauffmann, P., Kuch, H., Neuhauser, C. and Webster, E., 2011. Human dignity violated: a negative approach. *In*: P. Kauffmann, H. Kuch, C. Neuhauser and E. Webster (eds), *Humiliation, degradation, dehumanisation*. London: Springer, 1–6.
Kropotkin, P., 1924. *Ethics*. New York, NY: The Dial Press.
Levinas, E., 1969. *Totality and infinity*. Pittsburgh, PA: Duquesne University Press.
Moyn, S., 2010. *The last utopia*. Harvard, CT: Harvard University Press.
Porowski, M., 1991. Human rights of prisoners. *In*: Z. Lasocik, M. Platek and I. Rzeplinska (eds), *Abolitionism in history*. Warsaw: University of Warsaw, 91–104.
Scarry, E., 1985. *The body in pain*. Oxford: Oxford University Press.
Scott, D., 2003. Abolitionism and prisoner rights in Britain. *Strangeways*, October, 6(2), 5–8.
Scott, D., 2009. Resistance as reform: direct action through prisoner movements, legal activism and the radical penal lobby. *Criminal Justice Matters*, September, 77, 20–1.
Scott, D., 2010. Why didn't prisoner rights come home? *Criminal Justice Matters*, December, 82, 36–7.
Scott, D., 2012. Sympathy for the devil: human rights and the empathetic construction of sufferers. *Criminal Justice Matters*, May, 88, 8–9.
Scott, D., 2013. The politics of prisoner legal rights. *Howard Journal of Criminal Justice*, 52(3), 233–50.

Scott, D., 2015a. Eating your insides out: cultural, physical and institutionally-structured violence and the prison place. *Prison Service Journal*, September.
Scott, D., 2015b. Hearing the voice of the estranged Other. Paper presented at *Hearing the Voice of Prisoners Symposium*, Dundee, Scotland, 23 October 2015.
Smart, C., 1989. *Feminism and the power of law*. London: Routledge.
Spade, D., 2011. *Normal life*. Brooklyn, NY: South End Press.
van Swaaningen, R., 1997. *Critical criminology*. London: Sage.
Weber, L., Fishwick, E. and Marmo, M., 2014. *Crime, justice and human rights*. London: Palgrave.

# 6

# Feminist criminology and human rights

*Rosemary Barberet and Diana Rodriguez-Spahia*

## Introduction

Feminist criminology as a body of scholarship has emerged over the past 30 years, largely a development of the Anglo-American scholarly community and spurred by the feminist movement of the 1960s and 1970s. There is no unified feminist criminology, yet there are commonalities among various strands of feminist criminology: the first commonality is the emphasis on showing that women 'exist' and matter as offenders, victims, and criminal justice professionals. Much like feminist awakenings in other social sciences (such as political science and economics) feminist criminologists recognize how women have been excluded, marginalized or silenced and strive to rectify this in their work. Rendering women visible means explaining their presence (or absence, as the case may be), and recognizing the explanatory power of gender and patriarchy. The second commonality among feminist criminologists is that gender is not a variable but a system of oppression. Patriarchy – the subordination of women to men – intersects with other kinds of racial, class, and ethnic oppression and must be exposed and resisted though research and practice. Gendered power relations are foremost, then, in the construction of crime, its modus operandi, how crimes are detected and adjudicated, as well as how victims are defined and treated. Gendered power relations are also present in police work, the courtroom, and in penal policy and practice. Traditional masculinity – that which emphasizes aggression, risk taking, dominance, physical strength and ambition, is criminogenic. Violence against women is a serious crime that needs in-depth analysis, and it should be understood from a gendered, power relations perspective. Feminist criminologists believe that research subjects should be understood in context, valued, worked with collaboratively, and empowered. Research should expose injustice and spur social change (Barberet 2014, Chesney-Lind and Morash 2011, Renzetti 2013).

The links between feminist criminology and human rights are underexplored. Only a handful of scholars have explored the connections between human rights and feminist criminology (Carrington 2015, Barberet 2014, Chesney-Lind and Morash 2013, Van Gundy and Bauman-Grau 2013, Silvestri and Crowther-Dowey 2008, Pickering and Lambert 2004) such that we cannot speak of a corpus of literature. Yet, as we will see in this chapter, many of these links are inherent and reflect common interests (for example, the rule of law, non-discrimination, human dignity) and others as potentially new links would be mutually beneficial to both fields of study. For example, the human rights principles of universality and state obligation would expand the breadth of feminist criminology, while the empirically grounded, theoretically driven work of feminist criminology as a social science would benefit the more deductive, legal field of human rights. This chapter will look at these connections, including a critique of international law and human rights principles by feminist legal scholars.

## Feminism critique of international human rights law

International human rights law has made great strides in protecting and promoting the rights of women; feminist legal scholars have over time, contributed to international human rights law by identifying its biases and limitations and pushing for its reformulation. They have been aided in this task by activists who have raised public awareness, brought cases forth for consideration at international human rights bodies, or lobbied for legal reform.

Historically, international human rights law emanated from eighteenth century philosophy and the natural rights of man: a purely masculine product, based on liberal individualism, the same tradition from which liberal feminism has its roots. Equality of the sexes, as understood in formative international human rights law such as the *Universal Declaration of Human Rights* (UDHR), is based on the idea of formal equality and equality of opportunity. This individualistic view of human beings as rights bearers obscures the more sociological perspective that gender inequality is a longstanding and embedded social pattern and thus outside the realm of individual choice and action. The *Convention on Elimination of All Forms of Discrimination Against Women* (CEDAW), the modern cornerstone of international women's human rights law, which we will examine later in this chapter, is a product of liberal feminism but with transformative potential. It conceptualizes women's rights as those that should be equal to men's, but also recognizes that women's subordination is multifaceted, intertwined with culture, related to other aspects of identity, and must be combatted in both the public and private spheres.

International legal instruments are the product of the historical and societal moment in which they were conceptualized. The wording of the UDHR is very suggestive of existing social structures, and by referring directly to them, and from the perspective of the masculine sex, serves to limit the range of freedoms and protections afforded to women. Article 23 of the UDHR for example, states that: 'Everyone who works has the right to just and favourable remuneration ensuring for himself and his family' (UN 1948). As many feminist scholars have argued, this is suggestive of men's traditional breadwinner role, with that of women to engage in home-making and raising a family (Aolain 2009). Even at the time the Declaration was drafted, gender roles were quickly changing as more women were needed to work the jobs that men, out fighting World War 2, typically held. However, rather than writing to specifically include provisions for both men and women, much international human rights law is written in the masculine perspective, with the expectation that rights are applicable to both men and women.

One of the major general problems with gendering international law is trying to balance the idea of equality, or sameness, which does not allow for discrimination based on sex and yet needing to provide clear gendered protections that are often biological or anatomical in nature (Barrow 2010). We will examine this more closely in the case of the Bangkok Rules at the end of this chapter which aim to instruct states how to respond to the specific needs of women offenders and prisoners. In international law, not all language can remain neutral and there need to be specific provisions that target issues that are unique to women. However, feminist scholars have problematized the consequences of gender-specific international human rights law, pointing out that women (and men) can be stereotyped through this process.

Feminist activists and scholars started to question the exclusion of women from human rights discourse in the 1990s (Edwards 2011), culminating in the reaffirmation of the inclusion of women's rights as human rights at the 1993 World Conference on Human Rights in Vienna and the 1995 World Conference on Women in Beijing. The explosion in research on violence against women, as well as the landmark cases condemning wartime sexual violence of the International Tribunal for the Former Yugoslavia, spurred this movement. As Bunch (2006) argues, international human rights traditionally have usually only been applicable to the male subject, were narrowly construed ignoring violations of women's rights or failing to include women's particular experience of human rights violations (as prisoners of sexual torture, for example), and failed to conceptualize and include the private sphere as one in which women's rights were frequently violated (at the hands of non-state actors), along with the public sphere.

## International human rights principles: a feminist critique

As a direct response to the atrocities that occurred in World War 2, in December 1948, the United Nations (UN) General Assembly adopted the UDHR. For the first time, the most basic of human values were collected and agreed upon in an authoritative document that is still used today and has served many times over as precedent for many other international laws. Its core values, found in its 30 articles are: rule of law, inherent human dignity, non-discrimination, equality and fairness, and universality that should apply to all human beings, everywhere in the world (UN 2008). These international human rights principles are at the base of international human rights legal instruments drafted from then on. We now turn to discuss these principles, especially as they have been applied to women on a global level and also critiqued by feminist scholars. We will also look at state obligations and the statist nature of international human rights law to examine to what extent this shift of responsibility for the perpetration of violations away from the offender and towards the state can benefit the goals of feminist criminology.

### *Rule of law*

In its most basic form, rule of law can be defined as a uniform set of rules that all people within a nation, including the leader or president of a country, and lawmakers themselves, are subject to. It is meant to serve as a control on behaviour – particularly to protect citizens from individual government officials that may want to impose arbitrary laws that they themselves will not abide by. Many scholars agree that laws should be affirmed publicly, must be able to be applied clearly, and must be general, equal, and certain (Stephenson 2005). Rule of law also applies on an international level. When a state becomes a signatory to an international law, it must abide by the document it has signed, as per the preamble to the Charter of the UN. One of the objectives of the UN is 'to establish conditions under which justice and respect for the obligations arising from treaties and other sources of international law can be maintained'. The preamble to the UDHR of 1948 recognizes that 'it is essential, if man is not to be compelled to have recourse, as a last resort, to rebellion against tyranny and oppression, that human rights should be protected by the rule of law'.

The UN Secretary-General defines the rule of law as:

> a principle of governance in which all persons, institutions and entities, public and private, including the State itself, are accountable to laws that are publicly promulgated, equally enforced and independently adjudicated, and which are consistent with international human rights norms and standards. It requires, as well, measures to ensure adherence to the

> principles of supremacy of law, equality before the law, accountability to the law, fairness in the application of the law, separation of powers, participation in decision-making, legal certainty, avoidance of arbitrariness and procedural and legal transparency.
>
> *(UN 2004)*

Feminist scholarship has criticized the conceptualization of the rule of law in terms of coherence and consistency, because that tends to legitimate the status quo, institutionalize existing power relationships and prevent positive social change. Law in general reflects power relationships, and certain laws (not all) serve to reaffirm or institutionalize oppressive social practices; feminist legal scholarship has also been sceptical of the manner in which law works in practice, which can often contradict its well-intentioned aspirations. Traditionally, feminists have been wary of legal institutions as patriarchal creations, where objectivity and cold rationality take precedence over a more feminized ethic of care (Binion 2006). Similarly, much of feminist criminology is critical of the subtle and not so subtle ways in which criminal justice institutions (police, courts and prisons) serve to reinforce gender inequality and oppress women (Charlesworth and Robertson 2012, Natarajan 2014, Heidensohn 2011, Rackley 2008, Ashdown and James 2010).

## *Human dignity*

Historically, the idea of human dignity can be traced back to being afforded status, respect, or privilege. During the Middle Ages, dignity became the most significant difference between humanity and other creatures, with the ability to reason being the centre of these ideas (McCrudden 2008). The dignity of the human person is not only a fundamental right in itself, but serves as the basis of fundamental rights in international law, as per the preamble to the 1948 UDHR: 'recognition of the inherent dignity and of the equal and inalienable rights of all members of the human family is the foundation of freedom, justice and peace in the world'. The first Article of the UDHR reaffirms that 'All human beings are born free and equal in dignity and rights. They are endowed with reason and conscience and should act towards one another in a spirit of brotherhood' (United Nations 1948). Human dignity thus must be respected and protected.

Human dignity is another human rights principle based on individualistic liberal thinking, but it fits easily within feminist discourse and has great relevance for both the human rights of prisoners at the hands of the state as well as the human rights of crime victims. For example, the Bangkok Rules require that search procedures must also respect a woman's dignity, and the 1993 UN *Declaration on the Elimination of Violence Against Women* references human dignity in its opening statement.

## *Non-discrimination*

The principle of non-discrimination asserts that there are no inherent or physical characteristics within any human being that should be used as a basis for unequal treatment. The UN Charter was the first international agreement to establish non-discrimination on the basis of sex as a basic right. Article 2 of the UDHR states that 'Everyone is entitled to all the rights and freedoms set forth in this Declaration, without distinction of any kind, such as race, colour, *sex*, language, religion, political or other opinion, national or social origin, property, birth or other status' (emphasis added). Feminist scholars have long struggled with the issue of equality. First, they question the yardstick – equal to what? Most international human rights instruments conceptualize women's quest for equality as the same as the outcome for men. Second, they interrogate the differences between men and women and what equality means in the face of those differences. So, for example, they argue that the implications of women's ability to be mothers has been vastly exaggerated throughout the history of lawmaking and led to differences that stereotype or debilitate women as well as discriminating against women who choose not to be, or cannot be mothers. Third, they question the relevance of formal equality, based in liberal feminism, asking whether achieving non-discrimination is sufficient to achieve equality or whether more must be done to root out patriarchal traditions.

### *Universality*

The principle of universality is closely linked to the concepts of rule of law, human dignity, and non-discrimination and has been called by the UN the cornerstone of international human rights law. States have the responsibility to uphold and protect human rights no matter what their political, economic, or cultural system (UN 2015).

The principle of universality has often been critiqued by feminist scholars as ignoring differences among women around the globe and thus de facto, imposing 'rights' or customs of the Western world on the rest of humanity (Mohanty 2003). Yet another camp of feminists in the current relativist debate on violence against women argues that the cultural defence is a mask for patriarchal power. A misguided respect for other cultures has often been used as an excuse or mask for what are now termed by the UN 'harmful cultural practices' – female genital mutilation, child marriage, or other harmful practices to women and girls.

### *State obligation*

The essential difference between a criminal justice response and a human rights response resides in the different bodies of law and their accompanying institutional frameworks, and the focus on perpetrator responsibility as opposed to state accountability. Thus, the criminal justice system holds the perpetrator responsible for crime. The international human rights framework holds the State as ultimately responsible for violations of human rights.

Because the international human rights framework is statist, criminal justice scholars have been less trained in analysing its operations or conceiving how such a perspective could enrich our discipline. However, criminal justice scholars are increasingly examining the human rights framework. In particular, feminist legal scholars are interested in the human rights framework because it opens up another avenue for intervention – the role of the state in taking responsibility for injustice that occurs within its territory. Both human rights activists and criminal justice reformers need each other. In the long run, those who implement State reforms, or are called upon by States to advise or work more effectively in criminal justice, are typically agents of the criminal justice system (police, judiciary and prisons). For international criminal justice scholars, international human rights are a potent common 'language' of justice precisely because of their universality. Although not all violations of human rights are crimes, many are social harms, or structural or institutional violence, and thus related to crime causation.

## Convention on the Elimination of all forms of Discrimination Against Women (CEDAW)

Often proclaimed as the women's international bill of rights, CEDAW was adopted in 1979 by the UN General Assembly and entered into force in 1981. CEDAW endeavours to ensure equality of women and men in political, public, and private life and, as a human rights instrument, its value comes from encasing all of women's human rights, dispersed within international law, into one treaty. Its 30 articles are sectioned into six parts. The first part discusses the issues of non-discrimination, sex stereotypes, and sex trafficking. The second part describes women's right in the public realm, while the third part focuses on economic and social rights. Part 4 details women's equality in marriage. The fifth part establishes a Committee to oversee the Elimination of Discrimination Against Women and the last part describes the effects of CEDAW on other treaties. CEDAW is also unique in that it seeks to protect and promote the reproductive rights unique to women, and directly holds accountable tradition and culture for shaping and instituting gender roles, being the only international treaty to do this (UN 2009). CEDAW is closely aligned with the human rights principles previously discussed.

At a minimum of every four years, states that have signed the Convention are required to submit a compliance report to the Committee detailing what measures they have taken to ensure they are meeting CEDAW standards. When a state signs the Convention, they are legally bound by its terms unless they have specified reservations. A reservation is a notation by the state signatory that they are reluctant to accept, or be bound by certain sections of the Convention. The ability to have reservations can be seen as both a benefit and a pitfall of international law. On the one hand, it can be argued that more states that would have otherwise not signed the Convention do sign, and abide by at least some of what has been written. This is building on the principle that a small victory is better than no victory. On the other hand, one could also say that being able to pick and choose what is easy or what is already being implemented does not advance human rights, including the rights of women. Currently, CEDAW has 189 states parties (out of 194), but it is the Convention with the largest number of reservations on record (Cook 1990). To date, there are only five UN Member States (out of 194) that have not signed the Convention, the United States (US) being one of them, and one non-Member State, the Holy Vatican. This has been viewed as both surprising and disappointing, as the US is also the only Western country to not have signed it, and can be perceived as indicating its lack of commitment to women's rights. Although the compliance reports are required, there are no serious consequences for nations that have signed and not followed its provisions, indicating a huge gap between the treaty and its implementation. It has been noted that even countries that have signed CEDAW routinely fail to meet its standards (Lazarus-Black and Merry 2003). In 1999, following momentum from the Vienna World Conference on Human Rights, an Optional Protocol was adopted by the General Assembly which went into force in 2000 that allows the CEDAW Committee to hear individual complaints. This procedure has been underutilized, but its generation of case law holds great promise for the future of women's human rights (Hodson 2014).

As implied by its title, CEDAW is predominantly concerned with non-discrimination in relation to women. The criticism it has received in its methods of eliminating discrimination centre around the debate about whether it is best to take away the obstacles that are preventing women from being treated in the same way as men, as CEDAW does, versus acknowledging that discrimination is not only indicative of difference, but of exclusion and disadvantage (Cook 1994). It has also been noted that CEDAW targets laws and cultural conventions that aim to selectively exclude and disempower women, but it makes the assumption that the most effective way to do this is to make women and men legally equal in a marriage, promote changes in gender roles, and equal ability to receive healthcare and an education (Merry 2003).

CEDAW does not include in its articles any mention of violence against women, because at the time of its drafting there was not the awareness of violence against women that came to the fore in later years. However, the CEDAW Committee has clearly upheld in two of is general recommendations in 1989 and 1992 that violence against women is discriminatory against women. This was significant in establishing that the principle of non-discrimination could be applied to the case of violence against women. However, conceptualizing violence against women as discriminatory can be argued to limit or exclude consideration of harmful masculinities, placing too much emphasis on women as victims and not enough on men as perpetrators.

In addition, this treaty contains several articles that go much further than the discrimination discourse (Merry 2003). Article 6 incorporates specific provisions to protect women against human trafficking and prostitution, and Article 15 implements equality before the law; other articles, such as 10 (Education) and 11 (Equality) are of great importance in assisting women to become educated in order to be eligible to compete with men in the field of criminal justice such as in law and the judiciary, and the equality provision helps to ensure that women are not discriminated against when applying to such positions, such as in policing. Article 12 (Health) is also an important measure, especially for women who are incarcerated and need special healthcare services. McNeilly (2014) argues that the principle of non-discrimination in the CEDAW Committee's work is flexible and elastic and can be stretched beyond the sex binary.

It has also been noted that gender roles, which are direct and significant contributors of discrimination and inequality, are the most persistent and difficult to change (Merry 2003). Within the realm of criminal justice among countries that have ratified CEDAW, it is clear to see how ideas about gender roles are entrenched in societal norms and beliefs, and how this affects women in the criminal justice professions. In many countries, women entered the police force to work solely on matters pertaining to women and juveniles (Heidensohn 1998). In several ways, they were seen more as social workers than law enforcers, and this is still true today, with perceptions that women are 'unfit' for that line of work, or that they can only handle certain tasks (Natarajan 2014). Women in the judiciary face a similar problem. Though a more diverse judiciary helps to ensure a wide range of perspectives to help interpret the law and is more representative of the society as a whole, female judges are met with resistance and are indeed viewed as 'women in a man's world'. A woman on the bench is deemed a threat and disruption to the established masculinity that is the realm of law (Rackley 2008).

Women in the criminal justice profession have an interesting dualistic problem that is centred on gender roles. For example, part-time policing is viewed as key in retaining women on the police force. However, many police departments are loathe to hire part-time, to promote part-time employees, or provide them access to training and workshops (Charlesworth and Robertson 2012). Women who need to change their schedule to accommodate family obligations are often met with resistance, a negative response, and retaliation from superiors as this is seen as favourable treatment of women (Garcia 2003). In conclusion, though CEDAW has incorporated provisions to reduce inequality in the workplace, the criminal justice field has not advanced as far as it should have in promoting and protecting the equality of women in the workplace.

## The Bangkok Rules

We contrast CEDAW as an international human rights treaty with norm setting, or the establishment of soft law standards and guidelines, another universal yet less binding type of international human rights law. A relevant example of norm setting for feminist criminology is the recent adoption of the Bangkok Rules in 2010 by the UN General Assembly and the UN Commission on Crime Prevention and Criminal Justice in 2010. These rules drew upon precedent (the 1955 UN Standard Minimum Rules for the Treatment of Prisoners, or SMRs) but also recent research in criminal justice – particularly in feminist criminology. There was substantial civil society involvement as well as expert involvement in the drafting of these rules and their current implementation.

How do these rules intersect with feminist criminology? Part of the feminist criminological project has been to render women in prison visible and ensure they benefit from gender-sensitive prison policies and programmes. Women are incarcerated less than men, making up between 2 and 9 per cent of the total prison population in around 80 per cent of prison systems in the world. They are 6.5 per cent of the global prison population (Walmsley 2012). The problems specific to women in prison are largely related to the fact that prisons have historically been designed by and for men. Women, as the minority in prisons, have been largely ignored and remotely situated, unclassified or over-classified (that is, held too punitively), and as a consequence, receiving fewer services and programmes. Traditional gender roles are mirrored or amplified in prison: namely marginalization, domesticity, and medicalization. Mothering in prison poses a multitude of problems. As concerns mental and physical health, women are prone to victimization inside/outside. When they are used for protection and crimes of immorality, prisons are highly stigmatizing to women. Alternatives to incarceration are non-existent in many countries.

Gender-sensitive prisons, according to existing research (Bloom et al. 2003, 2006), feature gender-specific programmes, the facilitation of family contact, appropriate classification, realistic job training, mother and baby programmes, attention to mental and physical health (self-harm, substance abuse, nutritional needs, reproductive healthcare), treatment and prevention of women's victimization, alternatives when prisons are used for victimization/crimes of immorality and 'excarceration' as the preferred option.

The UN Bangkok Rules total 70 and relate to admissions, classification, prison regime, segregation, security, healthcare, pregnancy, breastfeeding, mothering, oversight, visits, programmes and services, alternatives, aftercare, needs of minorities and Indigenous peoples, training of staff, research and awareness raising. These rules supplement and complement the SMRs. The justification for these rules is that providing for women's needs, as different from those of men, will comply with the principle of non-discrimination in the SMRs – thus, increase gender equality. This is indeed a significant advancement in international human rights law: needs justify rights.

Although the rules are based on research evidence, as a final product of consensual decision-making they can nevertheless also be critiqued. They remain narrow in scope and do little to counter the causes of incarceration (including both the causes of women's offending but also punitive sentencing policies). They reify the vulnerability of women offenders and do not, for example, respond to the situation of women who are political offenders/prisoners; the rules use words like 'vulnerable', 'support' or 'needs' more than 'rights' or 'empowerment'. They include the timeworn association of 'women and children'. The rules place emphasis on sex over gender (that is, much emphasis on women's biological make-up and reproductive/caretaking role).

As a global effort to respond to women in prison, at the end of the day the rules are seen as radical in some countries and reformist in others. They are evidence based and draw on a continuum of women-centred research in the social and behavioural sciences; they acknowledge differences and similarities between women and men, and differences among women. They are humanist (and idealist) in that they assume prisons should be oriented towards rehabilitation and humane treatment. But the response of the rules to much of the existing research can be seen as tending to disempower women offenders and prisoners rather than empowering them (Barberet 2014, Hannah-Moffat 2010). As such, research input to international decision-making must always be problematized within the political context in which input is solicited, incorporated and reflected.

## Conclusion

What are the intersections, then, between international human rights and feminist criminology? Both have served to make women visible and to expose gendered power relations. Both are concerned with the lived experiences of women and both value the empowerment of women and the progressive hope for social change.

International human rights broaden and globalize feminist criminology by introducing concepts and principles that go beyond offenders, victims, and criminal justice actors within a given state. Feminist criminology, like most criminology, is mainly a domestic enterprise that is national in scope, but linking it to universal human rights means the inevitable internationalization of the discipline. Similarly, introducing the state as another party responsible (if only by ignorance or neglect) for injustice against women broadens feminist criminology's scope of enquiry. The linking of typical criminal justice topics to wider concerns for women's human rights in CEDAW connects feminist criminologists with the global feminist movement. The use of human dignity as a principle in human rights, and in the Bangkok Rules, stimulates feminist criminologists to reconceptualize penal policy for women – and men.

What can feminist criminology add to international human rights? As a social science, feminist criminology can be an evidence base for the development of international human rights, much as it served as an evidence base of women's needs that came to justify rights, in the Bangkok Rules. Because international human rights can serve to reify inequality as well as question it (male pronouns, images of family life, images of vulnerable powerless women prisoners) it must constantly be updated with the empiricism of feminist criminology. Similarly, as a social science, feminist criminology can serve to aid in the implementation of human rights norms, which tend to be abstract and translate poorly to practice. Finally, human rights activists as well as feminist criminological activists can be powerful partners in the normative and practical realms of social change for women.

## References


Aolain, F., 2009. Gendering the declaration. *Maryland Journal of International Law*, 24, 335–45.

Ashdown, J. and James, M. 2010. Women in detention. *International Review of the Red Cross*, 92, 123–41.

Barberet, R., 2014. *Women, crime and criminal justice: a global enquiry*. London: Routledge.

Barrow, A., 2010. UN Security Council Resolutions 1325 and 1820: Constructing gender in armed conflict and international humanitarian law. *International Review of the Red Cross*, 92, 221–34.

Binion, G., 2006. Human rights: a feminist perspective. *In*: B.B. Lockwood (ed.), *Women's rights: a human rights quarterly reader*. Baltimore, MD: Johns Hopkins University Press, 70–86.

Bloom, B., Owen, B. and Covington, S., 2003. *Gender responsive strategies: research, practice and guiding principles for women offenders*. Washington, DC: National Institute of Corrections, US Department of Justice.

Bloom, B., Owen, B. and Covington, S., 2006. *A summary of research, practice and guiding principles for women offenders. The gender-responsive strategies project: approach and findings*. Washington, DC: National Institute of Corrections, retrieved on 1 April 2016 from http://nicic.org/library/020418.

Bunch, C., 2006. Women's rights as human rights: toward a re-vision of human rights. *In*: B.B. Lockwood (ed.), *Women's rights: a human rights quarterly reader*. Baltimore, MD: Johns Hopkins University Press, 57–69.

Carrington, K. 2015. *Feminism and global justice*. London: Routledge.

Charlesworth, S. and Robertson, D., 2012. Policing, gender, and working time: an Australian case study. *Police Practice and Research*, 13, 241–53.

Chesney-Lind, M. and Morash, M., 2011. Introduction. *In*: M. Chesney-Lind and M. Morash (eds), *Feminist theories of crime*. Aldershot: Ashgate, xi–xxx.

Chesney-Lind, M. and Morash, M., 2013. Transformative feminist criminology: a critical re-thinking of a discipline. *Critical Criminology*, 21, 287–304.

Cook, R.J., 1990. Reservations to the Convention on the Elimination of all Forms of Discrimination Against Women. *Virginia Journal of International Law*, 30, 643–716.

Cook, R.J., 1994. Women's international human rights law: the way forward. *In*: R.J. Cook (ed.), *Human rights of women: national and international perspectives*. Philadelphia, PA: University of Pennsylvania Press, 3–36.

Edwards, A., 2011. *Violence against women under international human rights law*. Cambridge: Cambridge University Press.

Garcia, V., 2003. Difference in the police department: women, policing and 'doing gender.' *Journal of Contemporary Criminal Justice*, 19, 330–44.

Hannah-Moffat, K., 2010. Sacrosanct or flawed: risk, accountability and gender-responsive penal politics. *Current Issues in Criminal Justice*, 22(2), 193–215.

Heidensohn, F., 1998. Comparative models of policing and the role of women officers. *International Journal of Police Science & Management*, 1, 215–26.

Heidensohn, F., 2011. Gender and policing. *In*: F. Heidensohn (ed.), *Handbook of policing*. New York, NY: Taylor & Francis, 642–65.

Hodson, L., 2014. Women's rights and the periphery: CEDAW's optional protocol. *European Journal of International Law*, 25, 561–78.

Lazarus-Black, M. and Merry, S., 2003. The politics of gender violence: law reform in local and global places. *Law & Social Inquiry*, 28, 931–9.

McCrudden, C., 2008. Human dignity and judicial interpretation of human rights. *European Journal of International Law*, 19, 655–724.

McNeilly, K., 2014. Gendered violence and international human rights: thinking non-discrimination beyond the sex binary. *Feminist Legal Studies*, 22, 263–83.

Merry, S., 2003. Constructing a global law-violence against women and human rights system. *Law and Social Inquiry*, 3, 941–77.

Mohanty, C.T., 2003. *Feminism without borders: decolonizing theory, practicing solidarity*. Durham, NC and London: Duke University Press.

Natarajan, M., 2014. Police culture and the integration of women officers in India. *International Journal of Police Science & Management*, 16, 124–39.

Pickering, S. and Lambert, C. (eds), 2004. *Global issues, women, and justice*. Sydney: Sydney Institute of Criminology.

Rackley, E., 2008. What a difference difference makes: gendered harms and judicial diversity. *International Journal of the Legal Profession*, 15, 37–56.

Renzetti, C.M., 2013. *Feminist criminology*. London: Routledge.

Silvestri, M. and Crowther-Dowey, C., 2008. *Gender and crime*. Los Angeles, CA: Sage Publications.

Stephenson, M., 2005. *Rule of law as a goal of development policy*. New York, NY: World Bank.

United Nations, 1945. *Charter of the United Nations*, New York, NY: United Nations.

United Nations, 1948. *Universal Declaration of Human Rights* (217 A (III)). New York, NY: UN General Assembly.

United Nations, 1979. *Convention on the Elimination of All Forms of Discrimination Against Women* (A/34/46). New York, NY: UN General Assembly.

United Nations, 2004. *Report of the Secretary-General: The rule of law and transitional justice in conflict and post-conflict societies*. New York, NY: United Nations.

United Nations, 2008. *Dignity and justice for all of us: the Universal Declaration of Human Rights*. New York, NY: UN General Assembly.

United Nations, 2009. *CEDAW*. UN Women. Retrieved on 1 April 2016 from: www.un.org/womenwatch/daw/cedaw/.

United Nations, 2015. *What are human rights?* New York, NY: Office of the High Commissioner for Human Rights.

Van Gundy, A. and Bauman-Grau, A., 2013. *Women, incarceration, and human rights violations: feminist criminology and corrections*. Aldershot: Ashgate.

Walmsley, R., 2012. *World female imprisonment list*, 2nd edn. London: International Centre for Prison Studies.

# 7

# Victims

## Needs, rights and justice

*Sandra Walklate*

### Introduction

It is now 30 years since the United Nations (UN) Declaration of Basic Principles of Justice for Victims of Crime and Abuse of Power 40/34 29 November 1985 (henceforth the UN Declaration). That declaration 'advocates compassionate and respectful treatment of victims by the police, prosecutors, and courts, with emphasis placed on providing victims with information, assistance and compensation' (Mawby and Walklate 1994, p. 89). This declaration marked the culmination of pressure from the World Society of Victimology and key players within the UN (for a more detailed account of the processes underlying this declaration, see Joutsen 1987). Taken alongside further recommendations from the Council of Europe, the mid-1980s marked a significant moment in the recognition of the impact of crime. Since then demand for recognizing this impact has grown apace. This demand has made its presence increasingly felt as the human rights discourse has tightened its grip in both international and domestic arenas. Consequently, opportunities for the recognition of victims' voices have been afforded in not only domestic and regional criminal justice settings but also internationally. These range from the adoption of victim impact statements in a number of different jurisdictions to the development of, for example, the International Criminal Court, Truth and Reconciliation Commissions, and strategies embracing notions of transitional justice in which victim recognition is claimed to be a key feature of their rationale. Yet, as we shall see, what comprises such recognition is contested with the distance between victims' lived experiences and the political and policy rhetoric about such recognition remaining stubbornly persistent.

Lack of space inhibits discussing the availability and/or efficacy of the recognition of victims' needs or rights in all of the different justice arenas mentioned above. Neither can this chapter fully explicate the implied tensions between universalism and relativism that addressing this question also assumes (but see inter alia Donnelly 2008 for a flavour of this debate). In this light this chapter will focus on two basic questions: do victims (of crime) have needs or rights, and if they have rights per se as victims, what might those rights look like? This discussion assumes that, however each of these questions might be answered, those answers must ensure that the delivery of justice in any setting is in the collective interest rather than in the interests of victims, offenders, or any other partisan constituency (qua Waldron 1993). If this position is accepted then the question of victim recognition suggests some different thinking about how to achieve this. That thinking moves away from a debate about victims' needs and/or victims' rights to perhaps becoming reframed in terms of victim responsiveness. This chapter will conclude with some observations concerning such possibilities. However, responses to victims, in whatever form, imply that they are assigned victim status in the first instance. This, in itself, is contentious.

## Victim: a contested concept

As Christie (1986) observed some time ago conceptions of victimhood are often understood according to the extent to which the individual or the group (see van Wijk 2013) meets with the notions of the 'ideal victim'. This concept, informed as it is by notions of legitimacy and (un)deserving, points to the fact that not all victims are recognized as such. Indeed, Strobl (2010, p. 6) suggests four analytical possibilities in the construction of victimhood: the actual victim (someone seen by themselves and others as a victim), the non-victim (not recognized as a victim by themselves or others), the rejected victim (seen by themselves as a victim but not by others), and the designated victim (regarded by others as a victim but not by themselves). These categories in themselves become hotly contested in post-conflict situations as Lawther (2015) reminds us. In these circumstances, who constitutes a victim/offender/bystander is neither simple nor straightforward. These concepts, frequently used as though they were binary terms standing in opposition to one another, when used in this way, do not resonate with social reality. The terms victim, offender, and bystander are far more elastic both analytically and experientially. If we add to this elasticity the complexities associated with recognizing women's rights (that also imply rights within any justice system, see UN 2014), and the recognition of the legal rights of minority groups in general, all of which would fit within the rubric of human rights, it is easy to discern that victim claims to needs, rights, and for whom, is a difficult terrain to negotiate. It is against this backcloth that the discussion that follows is situated.

## Do victims have needs or rights?

Since the UN Declaration, debates have ensued concerning the question of victims' needs/rights and how to best address these issues. There is without doubt a complex relationship between the harm done by crime to an individual and the extent to which that harm can be, or even should be, responded to by any justice system. First, it is evidently the case that some people can transcend such harm as a result of their own coping strategies and/or with the support of friends and family. It is also the case that some do not. Indeed, as Christie (2008) observed, intervention intended to support victims can also do more harm than good. Second, for adversarial justice systems in particular, such harm done is translated into harm done to the state rather than to the individual (McBarnett 1988). Though again this is not necessarily the case in non-adversarial systems (see Shapland 2010, for a fuller discussion of these tensions). Neither of these observations is intended to imply that criminal victimization does not take its toll on people. It does. Drawing on a wide range of studies, Hall and Shapland (2007) list the direct impacts of crime as follows: shock, and a loss of trust/faith in society, guilt often associated with feelings of anger and/or fear, physical injury; minor to severe, financial losses, fear, anger, depression, changes to lifestyle induced by perceptions of the likelihood of future victimization. Of course, such wide-ranging consequences of criminal victimization can vary in their severity according to the particular circumstances of the individual. Maguire and Bennett (1982) reported some time ago that victimization is likely to have a greater effect on individuals who are also going through some other stressful event in their lives like a divorce or bereavement. Such findings are also replicated for those victimized by less 'conventional' crimes, as in the case of corporate crime (see, for example, Spalek and King 2007) or indeed genocide (see, for example, Hagan and Rymond-Richmond 2009). Moreover, if concerns with secondary victimization and indirect victimization are added to those of direct victimization, discussing victims' needs or rights in any generic or universalistic fashion (as implied by the UN Declaration) is indeed fraught with difficulties.

There are a number of issues underpinning the observations made above. One concerns the presumptions of vulnerability embedded within the question of the kind of harm done (by crime) and to whom. For example, it is assumed that the harm done to a child as a result of criminal victimization has a greater impact on them because of their inherent vulnerabilities associated with their age, physical immaturity, cognitive development, and so on. Consequently it is assumed that their needs, as individuals and as a group, from any justice system look somewhat different to those of adults. Indeed, much work across a range of jurisdictions has been done to offer children better protection as vulnerable victims and witnesses. However, even within this group their vulnerability, and hence their needs, are not necessarily fixed entities. So it is possible to infer that identifying and responding to victims' needs, even when their presumed vulnerability is obvious, is neither simple nor straightforward. Nonetheless, there appears to be a consensus on what the generic needs of victims might comprise. Goodey (2005, pp. 122–6) offers an excellent overview of them. These include: reassurance and counselling; medical assistance; financial and practical assistance to secure property; information about case progress; guidance about what to expect in court; the chance to express how the crime has affected them; assistance with filling out a form for State compensation; and information about the release date of their offender (Goodey 2005, pp. 121–2).

Of course, who fulfils and/or responds to these needs will not only vary according to the individual victim; it will also vary according to what is made available to them in the particular jurisdiction in which they live. For example, medical assistance is available through the National Health Service in the UK but is not available in the same way in the United States (US) or elsewhere. The opportunity to express how the crime has affected a victim as part of a justice process also takes a different shape and form in different jurisdictions within countries as well as between countries, some of which will be profoundly different in the 'Global South' or within jurisdictions informed by religious laws for example. Moreover, some of the needs listed above may be differently attended to by either voluntary or statutory agencies working within any particular justice system. Despite these difficulties, and taking a lead from the UN Declaration and alongside more local and/or regional declarations like those emanating from Europe, many jurisdictions have endeavoured to introduce varieties of victims' charters and codes of practice to ensure that criminal justice systems have a greater awareness of the impact of crime. Such codes of practice are intended at a minimum to ensure more sensitive and responsive recognition by criminal justice professionals of the kinds of victims' needs highlighted above. In addition there have also been moves to offer victims a greater opportunity to voice their concerns about what has happened to them as a part of the criminal justice process. These efforts range from re-orienting the role of professionals within the criminal justice system (see Garland 2001, for example, on the role of the probation service) to the increasingly extensive efforts to introduce victim impact statements into court proceedings, though the efficacy of these are somewhat in doubt (see inter alia Rock 2010, Booth 2012). However, it is also evident that moves towards good practice and making space for victims' voices do not necessarily guarantee the delivery of either in practice. Against the failures of service delivery to address victims' needs, it is possible to discern the growing presence of an argument in favour of victims' rights.

Ginsberg (2014) has argued, particularly in relation to the US, that claims to victims' rights, as opposed to needs, have increasingly made their presence felt as the commitment to a liberal state has become transposed into a neoliberal one. Indeed, the shift from an emphasis on needs to one on rights can be discerned across a range of jurisdictions, but particularly those in the Anglo-speaking world, where the embrace of a neoliberal position on the relationship between the citizen and the state has been particularly marked. In England and Wales, for example, these moves have culminated in the *Domestic Violence, Crime and Victims Act* in 2004. This piece of legislation introduced surcharges on fines and fixed penalties for motoring offences to fund a new Victims Fund; it allowed the Criminal Injuries Compensation Authority to recover payments made to victims from their offenders; it widened the opportunities for victims to be given and to provide information in cases where their offender received a prison sentence; it provided for a Commissioner for Victims and Witnesses and set out a Code of Practice for Victims with opportunities for redress for the victim should the code not be adhered to. This flagship legislation constituted a key platform from which the then government, and those that have followed, have consistently made claims for the 'rebalancing' of the criminal justice system towards the victim. Hence it is claimed that this Code of Practice afforded a space for the emergence of victims' rights. It is a moot point concerning the extent to which such a claim has been realized. However it does illustrate one way in which claims for victims' rights have been operationalized. So what might victims' rights, as opposed to victims' needs look like?

Goodey (2005, p. 130), in reviewing a range of international jurisdictions that claim to be victim-centred (some within the legal framework, others not), identifies what she calls a 'checklist of core rights'. These include compassion and respect, information on proceedings and rights, presentation of victims' views, legal aid, swift case processing, protection of privacy and identity, protection from retaliation and intimidation, compensation from the offender and the State, and recognition of victims with special needs. In a more recent intervention on the question of victims' rights, Waller (2010, Chapter 8) argues for what he sees to be the 'inalienable' rights for victims of crime. These he lists as rights to recognition (victims are people not states), rights to information, rights to assistance (counselling and other forms of assistance), rights to reparation, rights to be protected from the accused, rights to participation and representation (a voice effectively heard), rights to effective policies to reduce victimization, and rights to the effective implementation of victim-centred policies.

Both of these lists are interesting and arguably contentious for different reasons. First, it is important to note that both focus primarily on those victims whose case, and therefore capacity to be heard, has been processed by the criminal justice system. This is itself self-evidently problematic since the victim constituency is, across all jurisdictions, comprised of a much larger group than this. So these claims to rights are circumscribed for a particular group of victims; those more usually referred to as complainants. Second, many of these claims to rights within any particular jurisdiction are clearly supportive of a range of UN and Council of Europe declarations and statements of intent. However, again it is a moot point whether or not any particular jurisdiction enshrines all of the above list as victims' rights per se, that is, as rights claimable in law. Indeed, the Victims Code of Practice in England and Wales, whilst touching upon a number of the 'core rights' listed above, in its very title suggests an ambivalent relationship with the idea of constructing rights that are claimable in law (qua Rock 2004). Thus, despite political and campaign claims making claims to rights (that is rights in law, though there are notable exceptions to this, for example protection of identity for female victims of rape) the claims for victims' rights appears to be as patchy as the claims for meeting victims' needs. If the messy boundaries between victim, offender, and bystander are added to the mix here (as can be highlighted in post-conflict societies), alongside the difficulties associated with universal declarations qua the UN Declaration, then the picture of victims' needs/rights becomes very blurred indeed. Indeed when the claims to rights are matched with claims to needs it becomes evident that there is a significant conflation between these two issues in much of the literature and many of the campaigning voices speaking on behalf of victims of crime. This is perhaps not surprising if claims to rights are deployed to ensure basic human needs. However, what can be taken from these claims to rights and/or needs as articulated here is, perhaps, a common concern with the question of victim recognition. It is to this issue we shall now turn.

## Neither needs nor rights but recognition?

Given the pointed conflation of needs and rights within contemporary debates about victims and the criminal justice system it is possible to suggest that this victim focus is encapsulated more effectively by focusing on victim recognition. Yet, as de Greiff (2010) suggests, 'recognition' is itself a complex process. To be recognized means acknowledging that victims are both subjects and objects. In other words, as individuals they have agency (are subjects and can make choices) but as victims they have been made into objects (denied choices) as a result of the actions of others. It is this latter aspect of their experiences that victims want to have recognized, the fact that they have been intentionally harmed by others. This kind of recognition demands more than being given a voice in the criminal justice system or receiving appropriate support. Resonant with the work of Danieli (2006), this kind of recognition demands a reinstatement of equal citizenship: a focus that might usefully return us to the question of human rights. However, this version of recognition desires to reconstitute the victim as they were before being harmed. This is a position that neatly sidesteps its implied human rights potential. Here de Greiff (2010) is pointing to the need for a holistic rather than a partial understanding of recognition: a holistic recognition that places the victim at its heart. Nonetheless, how this might be achieved remains tricky since the same questions remain as those discussed above: who is this victim, how are they constituted, and in addition here, what kind of recognition do they seek? Moreover there is some empirical evidence that points to both the complexity of which de Greiff (2010) speaks, and the associated difficulties in the delivery of such recognition.

For example, Cairns and Mallett (2003) produce some interesting findings on the disjunction between the extent to which people in Northern Ireland perceived themselves to be 'victims' of 'the troubles' and the nature of the policies designed to respond to their (assumed) victimhood and thereby to offer them 'recognition'. In another study, Robins (2012) pointed to the limitations of the strategies of victim recognition put in place as a part of transitional justice work in Timor-Leste. His investigation revealed that for 61 per cent of the families who took part in this initiative, their greatest need was for economic support. The loss of a breadwinner during the conflict clearly made poor families poorer. Whilst this was the most commonly understood form of recognition, he also reported that when pressed, 69 per cent wanted some kind of memorial to those who were missing or dead. This form of recognition was also commonly expressed by the respondents in the study by Cairns and Mallett (2003). Robins (2012, p. 96) goes on to say that, '[f]or most families, justice was perceived as recognition and compensation, or receiving an answer regarding the fate of a loved one and the return of remains'. Both of these examples point to both similarities and differences in the claims for recognition on the part of 'victim' constituencies. Moreover, they also point to the importance of a recognition agenda that matches with those constituent claims. This adds a further layer to the complexity of translating a notion of universalistic rights (qua the UN Declaration) into a specific context. In the absence of such understandings, the 'victims' in the work reported by Robins (2012) engaged in their own processes of memorialization in tune with their local traditions. Indeed, such practices characterized by victim-led responses have also been observed elsewhere (see inter alia, Simic and Daly 2011).

Both of the studies referred to above happen to be situated in understanding the processes of repair and reconciliation in post conflict societies. Processes that more often than not claim to centre victim recognition. It is possible, however, to discern similar tensions to those alluded to above, in other arenas also claiming to recognize the victim. The studied indifference of the court in listening to victim impact statements in domestic criminal justice settings (Rock 2010, Booth 2012), and the failures of the International Criminal Court to respond to and deal with cases of sexual assault (de Brouwer 2009, see also Rothe 2014 on the more general shortcomings of the ICC capabilities of delivering victim rights) despite having been assessed as affording the perfect model for victim recognition (Groenhuijsen 2014), all point to the persistent presence of the same questions. Who is the victim? How are they constituted? What kind of recognition do they seek? Finally and importantly, how are these issues translated into policies and practice? Underpinning these questions, and the political desire for victim recognition along with the desire to translate this into practices that are meaningful for victims, suggests their realization may well be contingent on the kind of recognition being sought and the associated sociocultural and economic circumstances in which it is being sought.

Krever (2014) has observed, addressing slightly different issues, the failure to deal with victim recognition appropriately represents a political sleight of hand in the moves towards global justice in which some victims are recognized and others not. This point is well made by Nicolic-Ristanovic (2006) in commenting on the processes of victim recognition in Serbia. Her analysis centred the importance of understanding the socioeconomic and historical context of the Serbian sense of victimization which for many individuals includes the destruction caused by the North Atlantic Treaty Organization and the economic impact of sanctions imposed by the UN. Against this backcloth she goes on to say, 'among the population of Serbia there are both victims and perpetrators of crimes/gross violations of human rights, with these groups overlapping' (Nicolic-Ristanovic 2006, p. 373). To recognize this level of complexity in victim recognition, and importantly the source of that victimhood in order for it to be recognized, puts to the fore wide-ranging sources of victimization including those committed by Serbs on other Serbs. The capacity for this to happen is arguably limited given the implications of what might follow (see also Cohen 2001). It is at this juncture that the tensions underpinning the desire to centre the victim in terms of recognition surface in rather profound ways. As Nicolic-Ristanovic (2006) states, the ease with which hierarchies of victimization were constructed, particularly in public discourses in Serbia, was remarkable.

This latter point is taken up by McEvoy and McConnachie (2012). They cite examples from Northern Ireland, Argentina, and South Africa in which a hierarchy of victimhood that implicitly distinguishes between 'good' and 'bad' victims 'often maps into both subjective views on the "justifiability" of the suffering that was visited upon such victims and the strategies and tactics deployed by such victims in the transition and their attitudes to dealing with the past' (McEvoy and McConnachie 2012, p. 532). Since 'good' victims are often presumed also to be 'innocent', they go on to observe that '[d]esignation of deserving victimhood become an easy shorthand for blaming those deemed responsible for past horrors as well as absolving those deemed blameless' (McEvoy and McConnachie 2012, p. 533). This has led Verdoolaege (2008), in her analysis of truth and reconciliation commissions, to note the presence of competent witnesses who are listened to and those deemed incompetent who are not listened to, adding some weight to the view that there exists a 'regime of reconciliation' promoting 'good' victims (those recognized) and neglecting the 'bad' (those not recognized). Further to this, Madlingozi (2014, p. 185) goes on to observe the presence of entrepreneurs who make claims on behalf of the victims and whose 'entry point [is] towards reconstituting victims as hapless, disempowered, and lacking in any rational thought or action'. These '"entrepreneurs" theorize the field; set the agenda . . . and ultimately not only represent and speak for victims but also "produce" the victim'. Thus we are reminded not only of the contested nature of victimhood discussed earlier, but also the extent to which this contestation, in relation to victim recognition, is embedded in notions of the 'ideal victim' (Christie 1986) in which, following Quinney (1972), conceptions of who counts as the victim may not only be given by those in power, they may also be arbitrary.

To summarize: this brief overview points to some of the problems inherent in those initiatives that sidestep the question of victims' needs/rights and direct their concerns towards victim recognition. Many of these initiatives are top down in their nature and either fail to resonate with the victim, or miss the mark entirely, for the victim who is constituted by them. In the space afforded by such top down processes, inclusionary and exclusionary understandings of the victim can create a hierarchy of victimhood recognition infused with concepts of innocence, blame and legitimacy which in turn can fuel the politics of victimhood. In this way victim recognition becomes the means by which the problems associated with the needs/rights debate are reconstituted albeit in another form. Embedded in all of these different narratives, whether focused on needs, rights or recognition is a presumption that the category 'victim' is uniform and unifying. At this juncture the problematic connections between claims for victim rights and claims for human rights become evident.

## Conclusion: human rights and victim responsiveness

The UN report of 2014 quite rightly carries the title, 'Women's Rights are Human Rights' (UN 2014). This title, in and of itself, presumes that as human beings we are all entitled to access to the same fundamental facilities and access to resources in order to live our lives with dignity. These rights include access to justice: to be treated fairly and with dignity whether or not we find ourselves in that justice system as victims/complainants, witnesses, offenders, or indeed as criminal justice professionals. Such goals are, of course, aspirational. What has been documented in this brief overview are the difficulties in translating such ideals into practice whether or not the concern is to translate them into practice through the lens of needs, rights or recognition, returning us neatly to the question of whether rights are universal or relative. This overview has also observed the ways in which each of these discourses have become conflated with each other assuming that the category 'victim' is both uniform and one that unites campaigning voices with politicians and policy-makers. Arguably such conflations contribute to the fuzzy thinking in constructing policies and the debates that ensue. The question remains as to how it might be possible to be responsive to the difficulties faced by some victims of crime and simultaneously not fall into the policy pitfalls outlined above. One way in which this might be achieved is by centring a responsive approach to criminal victimization in all of its forms. Such an approach, as I have argued elsewhere (Walklate 2007) might be informed by the concept of respect.

Some time ago Harre (1979) argued that, personal circumstances notwithstanding, the maintenance of respect and the avoidance of contempt were crucial to individuals' sense of wellbeing. If this constitutes a reasonable starting point for understanding a central feature of people's lives, it follows that treating individuals with respect is an important contribution to their sense of themselves and their dignity as human beings. To be clear, this position takes as given the fact that people are individuals with human agency: they can, and do, make choices. Thus, whatever happens to them, they are able to make use of their own resources, and those of others, to make sense of what has happened in their lives (qua Christie 2008). There are a number of implications from this starting position. First, it challenges any presumed 'special' status associated with being a victim of crime. Victims are not necessarily good and offenders bad. Real-life experiences fundamentally challenge this kind of binary and simplistic thinking. So whilst crime does impact upon people's lives, victims of crime are people too and come in all shapes and sizes. Consequently, it makes little sense to talk of people as victims or offenders, or indeed victims or survivors. They are people. This view thus lends itself to a human rights position but one that is qualified (qua Donnelly 2008). From this point of view, whether male or female, whether a member of an ethnic minority, whether old or young, the maintenance of respect and the avoidance of contempt sustains a sense of wellbeing (Harre 1979). Importantly, justice systems can enhance or diminish that sense of wellbeing. In other words, justice systems can offer the opportunity for delivery of substance in terms of their practices to victims of crime.

As has been shown in some of the studies cited here, 'victims' can and do achieve their own resolution to what has happened whether that be an act of harm on them as an individual or an act of harm directed towards them as a collective as in the case of genocide. At this level, a responsive position would be one that would afford the space for such individual and collective resolutions to occur in their own time and to accord such processes the appropriate respect, that is, without interference from 'entrepreneurs' of any persuasion. A responsive approach would appreciate the importance of culturally situated responses rather than necessarily imposing a uniform model of recognition (although there may be some lessons in justice delivery that can and do travel between different contexts). Though it is important to note that, as Krever (2014) has observed, endeavours to construct 'global justice' that assume the appropriateness of some uniformity in victim recognition, can lack a sense of difference and diversity which would ensure that victims of crime, wherever they found themselves, were treated with respect. Thus, in this 'politics of pain' (Barker 2007) there is space for a different narrative. A narrative not of needs, rights, or recognition, but one that is situated in recognition, focused on the maintenance of respect and avoidance of contempt, that might avoid the associated disappointment and disillusionment with policies that have flowed from differently motivated agendas.

## References

Barker, V., 2007. The politics of pain: a political institutionalist analysis of crime victims' moral protests. *Law and Society*, 41(3), 619–63.

Booth, T., 2012. 'Cooling out' victims of crime: managing victims' participation in the sentencing process in a superior sentencing court. *Australian and New Zealand Journal of Criminology*, 445(2), 214–30.

Cairns, E. and Mallett, J., 2003. *Who are the victims? Self-assessed victimhood and the Northern Irish conflict.* Northern Ireland Office Research & Statistical Series: Report No. 7.

Christie, N., 1986. The ideal victim. *In*: E.A. Fattah (ed.), *From crime policy to victim policy*. London: Macmillan, 17–30.

Christie, N., 2008. Fertile Ground for Victim-Movements. Keynote Speech at the Third Nordic Conference of Victimology and Victim Support, Conference Report. Helsinki, March.

Cohen, S., 2001. *States of denial*. Cambridge: Cambridge University Press.

Danieli, Y., 2006. Essential elements of healing after massive trauma: complex needs voiced by victims/survivors. *In*: D. Sullivan and L. Tift (eds), *Routledge Handbook of Restorative Justice*. London: Routledge, 343–54.

de Brouwer, A.-M., 2009. What the International Criminal Court has achieved and can achieve for victims/survivors of sexual violence. *International Review of Victimology*, 16, 183–209.

de Greiff, P., 2010. Theorising transitional justice. *In*: S.M. Williams, R. Nagy and J. Esler (eds), *Transitional justice*. New York, NY: New York University Press, 31–77.

Donnelly, J., 2008. Human rights: both universal and relative (a reply to Michael Goodhart). *Human Rights Quarterly*, 30(1), 194–204.

Garland, D., 2001. *The culture of control*. Oxford: Polity.

Ginsberg, R., 2014. Mighty crime victims: victims' rights and neoliberalism in the American conjuncture. *Cultural Studies*, 28(5–6), 911–46.

Goodey, J., 2005. *Victims and victimology*. London: Longmans.

Groenhuijsen, M., 2014. The development of international policy in relation to victims of crime. *International Review of Victimology*, 20(1), 31–48.

Hagan, J. and Rymond-Richmond, W., 2009. *Dafur and the crime of genocide*. Cambridge: Cambridge University Press.

Hall, M. and Shapland, J., 2007. What do we know about the effects of crime on victims? *International Review of Victimology*, 14, 175–217.

Harre, R., 1979. *Social being*. London: Basil Blackwell.

Joutsen, M., 1987. *The role of the victim of crime in European criminal justice systems*. Helsinki: HEUNI.

Krever, T., 2014. Dispensing global justice. *New Left Review*, 85 January–February, 67–97.

Lawther, C., 2015. The construction and politicisation of victimhood. *In*: O. Lynch and J. Argomaniz (eds), *Victims of terrorism: a comparative and interdisciplinary study*. London: Routledge, 10–30.

Madlingozi, T., 2014. On transitional justice entrepreneurs and the production of victims. *In*: D. Buss, J. Lebert, B. Rutherford, D. Sharkey, and O. Aginam (eds), *Sexual violence in conflict and post-conflict societies: international agendas and African contexts*. London: Routledge, 169–92.

Maguire, M. with Bennett, T., 1982. *Burglary in a dwelling*. London: Heinemann.

Mawby, R. and Walklate, S., 1994. *Critical victimology*. London: Sage.

McBarnett, D., 1988. Victim in the witness box: confronting victimology's stereotype. *Contemporary Crises*, 7, 279–303.

McEvoy, K. and McConnachie, K., 2012. Victimology in transitional justice: victimhood, innocence and hierarchy. *European Journal of Criminology*, 9(5), 527–38.

Nicolic-Ristanovic, V., 2006. Truth and reconciliation in Serbia. *In*: D. Sullivan and L. Tift (eds), *Routledge Handbook of Restorative Justice*. London: Routledge, 369–86.

Quinney, R., 1972. Who is the victim? *Criminology*, November, 309–29.

Robins, S., 2012. Challenging the therapeutic ethic: a victim-centred evaluation of transitional justice process in Timor-Leste. *International Journal of Transitional Justice*, 6(1), 83–105.

Rock, P., 2004. *Constructing victims' rights: the Home Office, New Labour, and victims*. Oxford: Clarendon.

Rock, P., 2010. 'Hearing the victim': the delivery of impact statements as ritual behaviour in four London trials for murder and manslaughter. *In*: A. Bottoms and J.V. Roberts (eds), *Hearing the victim: adversarial justice, crime victims, and the state*. Cullompton: Willan Publishing, 232–54.

Rothe, D., 2014. Can an international criminal justice system address victims' needs? *In*: D. Rothe and D. Kauzlarich (eds), *Towards a victimology of state crime*. London: Routledge, 238–49.

Shapland, J., 2010. Victims and criminal justice in Europe. *In*: S.G. Shoham, P. Knepper and M. Kett (eds), *International handbook of victimology*. Boca Raton, FL: CRC Press, 347–72.

Simic, O. and Daly, K., 2011. 'One pair of shoes, one life': steps towards accountability for genocide in Srebrenica. *The International Journal of Transitional Justice*, 5(10), 1–15.

Spalek, B. and King, S., 2007. *Farepak victims speak out*. London: Centre for Crime and Justice Studies.

Strobl, R., 2010. Becoming a victim. *In*: S.G. Shoham, P. Knepper, and M. Kett (eds), *International handbook of victimology*. Boca Raton, FL: CRC Press, 1–26.

United Nations (UN). 2014. *Women's rights are human rights*. United Nations HR/PUB/14/2.

van Wijk, P., 2013. Who is the 'little old lady' of international crimes? Nils Christie's concept of the ideal victim re-interpreted. *International Review of Victimology*, 19(2), 159–79.

Verdoolaege, A., 2008. *Reconciliation discourse: the case of the Truth and Reconciliation Commission*. Amsterdam: John Benjamins Publishing Company.

Waldron, J., 1993. *Liberal rights: collected papers 1981–91*. Cambridge: Cambridge University Press.

Walklate, S., 2007. *Imagining the victim of crime*. Maidenhead: Open University Press.

Waller, I., 2010. *Rights for victims of crime*. Blue Ridge Summit, PA: Rowman and Littlefield.

# 8

# Governmentality analytics and human rights in criminology

*Randy K. Lippert*

## Introduction

Already by the mid-1990s governmentality concepts and themes were actively informing critically oriented criminological inquiries, especially in Australia, Canada and the United Kingdom (see, for example, Hunt and Wickham 1994, O'Malley 1992, Stenson 1993, Garland 1997). French philosopher and historian Michel Foucault was not a criminologist (he certainly would have resisted the moniker), but his ideas about 'governmentality' (or governing mentalities) (Foucault 1991) nonetheless were to profoundly influence criminology. This occurred largely independently of his famous historical account of the prison and the corresponding rise of discipline (Foucault 1979). Elements of this governmentality analytic continue to be deployed to render aspects of criminal justice, crime control, and penal domains more intelligible (see, for example, Gilling 2010). But those criminologists embracing the governmentality analytic as it developed rarely have engaged with human rights. Such engagement in this perspective is either absent or at best oblique, leaving any connections between these bodies of ideas undeveloped.

The neglect of rights is not limited to the governmentality analytic and exists in criminology more broadly, of course, as Murphy and Whitty (2013, p. 573) reveal in a recent 'history' of criminological engagement with human rights, noting rights are 'nearly always placed outside, against or as an antidote to criminology, rarely as having had a presence or influence *inside* criminology'. But one reason for governmentality scholars' particularly limited consideration of rights may be a perceived ill-fit between the universalism of human rights and the governmentality analytic's poststructuralist (or postmodernist) assumptions and insistence on placing empirical focus on governmental discourse in localized contexts, rather than on grand (or grandiose) societal or global scales. Regardless of the factors involved this limited engagement is unfortunate since the governmentality analytic promises to unearth aspects of human rights regimes and their interface with state crime and control that may lend themselves to strategic progressive intervention.

This chapter seeks to take stock of this situation. The governmentality conceptual toolkit is first revisited to take inventory, discover what is missing or misconceived, and evaluate tools and themes that might be usefully deployed to research human rights regimes. These points are illustrated or considered by drawing on existing governmentality research in and outside criminology in Canadian and international contexts, including in relation to less attended to refugee and privacy rights enshrined in domestic and international law. Rather than an exhaustive account, what follows has a 'where are we?' and 'where might we go from here?' flavour. It is directed at critically oriented criminologists hungry for strategic ways to illuminate the growing realms of human rights, and who possess an appetite for novel approaches, but who have presumed governmentality's conceptual cupboard is bare or its themes are normatively unpalatable. The primary concern here is with the current state and promise of governmentality scholarship that Foucault's writings and lectures inspired, and which have since evolved, rather than Foucault's work itself. There is not space here for another re-reading of Foucault's own engagement with human rights, which was relatively limited but nonetheless compelling and unique. From Ben Golder, the scholar writing most trenchantly on this issue, it can be noted that for Foucault:

> [R]ights are both political tools for the contestation and alteration of mechanisms of power and simultaneously mechanisms of inscription . . . which work to conduct those who rely upon them. Far from being an unproblematic tool for the protection of the subject's freedom, rights emerge in this account as conflicted and ambivalent mechanisms.
>
> *(Golder 2012, pp. 5–6)*

Foucault's take on rights, as *conflicted and ambivalent mechanisms*, as well as *emergent*, has much potential in relation to understanding governmentality. Consistent with this, early governmentality scholars Rose and Valverde (1998, p. 543) had remarked, somewhat obliquely, that 'the discourse of rights . . . has been deployed both to extend and to contest normalizing political strategies'. The notion that rights discourses *extend* governmental efforts suggests the possibility that particular populations are governed *through* rights. This theme is returned to below though it does not exhaust actual or potential engagements via a governmentality analytic within criminology. Governmentality analyses found in other disciplines and sub-disciplines, such as sociology, socio-legal studies, and geography, while not centrally focused on human rights, nonetheless provide insights or themes that critically oriented criminology could emulate to investigate human rights regimes too. Whether this analytic's elements are used effectively going forward may well depend on how and whether criminologists look beyond their own discipline and past preconceived notions about governmentality to more fully engage with human rights.

The remainder of this chapter unfolds as follows. It first elaborates the contemporary governmentality conceptual toolkit and themes with an eye to discerning omissions or misconceptions. The focus on neoliberal mentalities within criminology in particular has been enlightening in relation to criminal justice institutions, but it does not exhaust possibilities to provide better understanding of human rights regimes in relation to state crime and crime control. Thus, I argue that Foucault's concepts of pastoral power and sovereign power may be pertinent too. Within this analytic another key concept deserving of greater attention in relation to rights is technologies of government and how they articulate with governing mentalities (Lippert 2010). Another theme, not considered enough in or in relation to criminology, is the role of knowledge in governance (Hunt and Wickham 1994) and this implies a particular function for some forms of criminology in relation to human rights. A final misconception may well be the governmentality literature's neglect of reality, and thus the notion that human rights are incompatible with the associated postmodern epistemology, which lends itself to seeing governmentality tools as solely diagnostic. Through this stocktaking the current state of the governmentality tool crib and its value in understanding human rights regimes should become illuminated.

## Revisiting governmentality's conceptual tool crib

Understanding and overcoming misconceptions or omissions about the Foucault-inspired governmentality analytic is essential. It is crucial to recognize too that for Foucault 'government' (hereinafter governance) means the 'conduct of conduct' (Gordon 1991, p. 2), or efforts to guide, direct, or shape behaviour, as an orchestra conductor guides her musicians to play their instruments in unison. Governance is thus about how actions are directed while remaining mindful of a goal, such as reducing a type of crime in a given space. Conduct is assumed to be shaped via a set of norms implanted, approved, and reproduced by state and non-state authorities (Dean 1999). Governance includes myriad governmental programmes of states (for example, that target the population's security, welfare, and health); of comparable international state-funded or sanctioned bodies like the United Nations (UN) (Lippert 1999, Lindroth 2014); of countless international and domestic private authorities and non-governmental organizations (such as commercial corporations, non-governmental organizations, churches, sports clubs, and so on); and of those entities that do not easily fit public or private categories. Governance also encompasses rational and systematic self-governance or reflection and action on one's own behaviour.

It should be noted from the outset too that governmentality as an empirical *analytic* or *perspective* was never intended and should not be construed as a *theory* of society, governance, power, and certainly not of human rights. Thus, expecting to generate a universal theory of human rights via this analytic is doomed. Governmental analyses seek to avoid totalizing ambitions and reducing empirical findings to general theories about capitalist society, patriarchal society, risk society, information society, postmodernity and the like (Garland 1997). In this way criminologists using governmentality concepts and themes tend to differ from scholars who have traditionally used crime and crime control as sites to ground their theorizing about society or similar abstractions. Instead, the governmentality analytic in criminology and elsewhere calls for detailed analyses of specific phenomena to – simply – make the functioning of these domains and/or how they came to be more understandable (Rose et al. 2006).

### *Liberal mentalities and governing through rights*

A key concept in this analytic is mentality (sometimes called a 'governmentality', 'logic' or 'rationality'), which is 'any systematic way of thinking about government' (Dean 1999, pp. 210–11). Mentalities include questions about how to govern and about existing governmental arrangements. They justify how conduct is conducted and are based upon 'problematizing' conduct (that is, deeming particular forms of conduct, including state crime and human rights violations, as a problem) in order to curtail or otherwise change that conduct in some manner. Mentalities are translated into programmes that seek to address problems of governance (Dean 1999, p. 16) and create a language in which to think about and elaborate governance. A major focus in this analytic, then, is governmental discourse, uncovered in what are called programmatic texts (policy statements, standard operating manuals, agency mission statements, and so on). These discourses, consistent with poststructural assumptions, tend to be viewed not as representing reality, nor as obscuring reality as a form of ideology. Rather, language here is performative and constitutive; it makes practices of governing agencies and agents possible and constitutes their reality.

Governmentality scholars' attention to liberal mentalities occasionally brush up against law, but not necessarily rights. The link between the governmentality analytic and rights at first glance is most evident instead in the fact the liberal freely choosing subject that featured so prominently in early governmentality work, is rights-bearing and is therefore to be protected from state oppression and unwarranted intervention. In a classic statement in the literature, Rose (1996, p. 45) explained that liberal mentalities' 'subjects are individuals whose . . . rights are to be respected by drawing certain limits to the legitimate scope of political or legal regulation'.

Key features of neoliberal mentalities that have been identified in criminology include 'responsibilization' (Garland 1997) or movement of responsibility for governance of problematized forms of conduct to more local levels. This resonates strongly with crime prevention programmes that have arisen over the past 40 years in western countries (O'Malley 1992, Lippert 2002). Rights may well have become implicated in some of this responsibilization, though this has yet to be explored. Thus, Murphy and Whitty's (2013, p. 574) history, noted above, remarks upon Carol Smart's early work as:

> an early forerunner of the governmentality perspective on human rights ... used today. More broadly, the change from welfare to neo-liberal government which started in the 1970s could be used as a pathway to trace how rights ... began their ascent into political vernaculars and eventual formal legal status.

While it is doubtful there is, as yet, a crystallized 'governmentality perspective on human rights' on offer, the way rights are considered here in relation to neoliberal mentalities is a potentially fruitful line of inquiry to be followed in criminology. Governmentality work outside criminology is therefore vital to contemplate in this regard.

Outside accounts are worth considering because they contain lessons about rights, especially for more critically oriented criminology, and may well bear fruit. In this regard two recent accounts are illustrative, both adopting an international perspective drawing on governmentality. First, Lindroth (2014) asserts that rights are being used as a neoliberal governmental tactic directed at Indigenous peoples. She argues that governing *through* rights and expertise permits governing aboriginal people in various nations more cost effectively, a hallmark of neoliberal mentalities (Lindroth 2014, p. 342). Lindroth is not suggesting, however, that rights-claiming is necessarily always disadvantageous to aboriginal peoples (their traditional claims to a right to self-determination would be a primary example). This is a nuanced view of rights that warrants adopting. Second, Sokhi-Bulley (2011) focuses on the increasing inclusion of statistics in human rights discourse in the European Union (EU). Here rights become an element of governmental discourse and a means of governing conduct, aiding the effort to govern *through* rights. Correspondingly, she understands statistics produced by the EU regarding, for example, 'Racist violence and crime', including levels of 'racism and xenophobia' in particular EU countries, as governmental technologies. The way the EU deploys these statistics permits speaking of rights using 'apolitical language of governance' (Sokhi-Bulley 2011, p. 142). Consistent with Foucault's assumption about the open and evolving content of rights here is the notion that statistics identify 'whose rights are protected [and], by whom' while simultaneously 'concealing governmentality' (Sokhi-Bulley 2011, p. 150). This attention to technologies of government is welcome in seeking to understand human rights in criminology, which has seen previous governmentality-related work on crime statistics (Haggerty 2001).

Other governmentality work that has explored different types of human rights – refugee and privacy rights – is illustrative too as both types of rights plainly interface with state crime and crime control. Unlike some other human rights that are historically newer, however, refugee and privacy rights have longstanding formal bodies and adjudication procedures underpinning them internationally and domestically – respectively – in western nations. These two types underscore the sheer variety of rights that have emerged over the past century as a consequence and as part of political contestation consistent with Foucault's assertions about the contested and emergent nature of rights, especially in relation to western states and international governing arrangements.

Refugee rights are enshrined in the UN *Convention Relating to the Status of Refugees* developed in the aftermath of World War 2 (Lippert 1999). These rights have since been recognized in domestic legislation of western countries and are determined through procedures in the face of state persecution of populations the world over. Yet, a governmentality analytic points to the potential that, far from being a universally recognized right in practice, as current events in Europe demonstrate (*New York Times* 2015), deployment of 'refugeeness', or governing *through* refugee rights, is sometimes selectively applied and can become a moral-political tactic used to advantage powerful states over the less powerful (see Lippert 1999). Thus, some persecuted subpopulations and victims of state crime are deemed refugees, thereby highlighting the practices of enemy states that are persecuting their own populations during the current War on Terror, while other states go unrecognized or are barely responded to in practice. This could not be more obvious than in relation to the pithy effort of some western nations of recognizing and resettling populations fleeing a murderous Syrian state (rather than specifically fleeing ISIS) and those populations fleeing Africa to Europe as refugees requiring protection since they do not easily fit the logic of the War on Terror. This contrasts sharply with Cold War examples revealing the ease with which western nations recognize those fleeing the Soviet Bloc (see Lippert 1999). Instead sovereign authoritarian measures aimed at halting the movement of contemporary refugee populations ranging from turning back boats, as in Australia, to police raids to tear gas to fences in Europe are deployed instead. Sovereign power may be evident in the exceptional use of these rights; in sudden neglect or sudden recognition of refugee rights when convenient, a point returned to below.

Privacy rights are also recognized internationally and in numerous legislative acts at the domestic level (Lippert and Walby 2013a). Thus, in Canada there are federal and lower level provincial statutes governing privacy and bodies (commissions) established to oversee them. Yet, so weak are these commissions that evident here too has been the notion of governing *through* privacy rights (Lippert and Walby 2013a). Thus, obvious compliance with these provisions, for example, through the use of signage for CCTV surveillance of public space consistent with 'fair information practices' has justified and made possible state implementation and spread of surveillance technologies to watch disadvantaged or 'risky' urban populations (Lippert and Walby 2013a). Privacy is regulated through privacy rights and the emergence of 'Privacy by Design' technologies (that seek to build privacy into surveillance mechanisms, such as by automatically blocking or blurring part of a publicly owned and operated CCTV surveillance camera's field of view when directed at private spaces) that are deemed consistent with them (see Lippert and Walby 2013a). Thus, the right to privacy may be counterproductive in practice. This raises the possibility that governing *through* rights is sometimes less than progressive and may further authoritarian efforts to criminalize behaviour (see Lippert and Walby 2013a), or perhaps give way to forms of sovereign power as discussed below.

Both kinds of rights are notoriously inconsistently recognized in relation to state crimes or authoritarian measures unleashed by states. One need only ask Edward Snowden about his startling revelations about the illegal obliteration of citizens' privacy due to state surveillance and what happened to his claim to refugee status that was launched in a desperate effort to receive protection from state persecution in the aftermath. The convergence of these two failures of rights is captured nicely by the title of Greenwald's (2014) account of these events: *No place to hide*. But none of this is to suggest refugee rights or privacy rights are hollow, always ineffective, or merely a form of pure ideology in the service of capitalist exploitation or western or state domination. Undoubtedly those in a position to make rights claims in the face of state crime entailing persecution or privacy-demolishing invasive mass surveillance can gain protection or relief. But governmentality analytics remind us of the possibility their uses in any instance are decidedly political, and force us to become less sanguine about how they are deployed.

Elaboration of neoliberal mentalities that have reshaped criminal justice, crime control, and penal domains has been illuminating within criminology, and beyond this discipline, it raises the possibility of 'governing through rights', the governmentality toolkit allows for diagnoses of other mentalities too. In human rights regimes, other forms of power (and accompanying technologies) may be present to render human rights protection possible (or impossible) as the case may be.

## *Missing mentalities and powers*

As implied in previous sections, liberalism is not the only mentality or form of power relevant to criminology or human rights. Human rights discourse is potentially about more than liberalism. One overlooked mentality is pastoralism, which is a logic of intimate care of obedient subjects, which Foucault described as targeting an individual's salvation and needs laid bare through intimate knowledge of their souls (see Lippert 2005). Pastoralism is an analytically separate, if paternalistic rationality. Regarding illegal sanctuary provided to migrants facing deportation from Canada by community and church activists (Lippert 2005), and 'legal aid' provision for other legal subjects unable to afford legal representation for criminal and other human rights proceedings (Park and Lippert 2008), pastoralism is revealed to focus on needs and in this way operates alongside forms of liberal governmentality in these two realms. For example, in the former volunteers provided sanctuary's protection to migrants and in the latter some legal representation of low income people was similarly provided by lawyers *pro bono* where state provision of this right was lacking or had been dramatically cut (Park and Lippert 2008). In both sites perceived *needs* were responded to voluntarily rather than entirely due to a legal mandate to ensure rights of disadvantaged persons were respected. This sometimes had a major impact on outcomes for those whose needs were provided for, in relation to refugee and constitutional rights. This raises the broader possibility that pastoralism[1] may be present in human rights regimes alongside liberalism, that legal representation or other strategies that target needs of those who make rights-claims are not so much liberal as pastoral, paternalistic, and intimate. This has implications for how rights adjudication works and whether, for example, service provision can be withdrawn from those who claim rights because that provision is voluntary or gift-like. The broader point is that pastoralism may be present within some human rights regimes but has thus far been overlooked due to an overemphasis on forms of liberalism (Lippert 2005).

Sovereign power in domestic and international domains in relation to human rights is also pertinent. Foucault provides a genealogy of the development of varied forms of rule beginning in the sixteenth and seventeenth centuries, when sovereign power, or the monarchy, typified rule. In *Discipline and punish*, Foucault (1979) showed the exercise of sovereign power had an affinity for spectacles of which public punishment was an exemplar. He detailed the horrific dismembering as the 'spectacle of the scaffold' during which the monarch's power was literally inscribed onto the offender's body for all to witness. Yet, Foucault remarked too that publicly visible was the monarch's occasional *withholding of* the power to punish via last minute pardons of the condemned (see Foucault 1979, see also Lippert 2005, p. 68). Sovereign power is best described thus not as a monopoly to punish but as a monopoly to decide the exception (Lippert 2005, p. 69). Neglected by most governmentality scholars working within criminology is closer scrutiny of sovereign power (but see Stenson 1998), not as a return to a grand, archaic form of rule, but instead in relation to contemporary programmes, including those pertaining to human rights protection (Lippert 2005). The question of how the sovereign exception is enacted as arbitrary exclusion from human rights protection or the equally unjustified sudden provision of protection to some groups needs decidedly more attention.

With respect to refugee rights this is plainly evident in sovereign interventions by Australian and Canadian states to interdict refugees en route from travelling to distant refugee status determination processes. But sovereign power is also evident in decisions to suddenly grant refugee status outside of determination processes, as with the Indo-Chinese refugee movement to Australia, Canada and other western nations (see Lippert 1998), and recently with the new European refugee crisis with nations suddenly and seemingly arbitrarily deciding to grant resettlement to thousands more persons due to horrific scenes of their plight in mass media, not necessarily because governments recognize they have a right to have their claims of persecution heard and adjudicated.

## *Missing technologies*

A tool belonging to the governmentality analytic's toolkit that has gone missing is technologies (see Rose and Miller 1992). Technologies are methodical and material ways of allowing forms of governance to operate. While featured as a key concept in seminal statements about the governmentality analytic (see, for example, Miller and Rose 2008) that preceded its embrace by criminologists, since then technologies have received comparatively less attention than mentalities (Lippert 2010). The devices that render governmental practices possible have been neglected. If mentalities such as liberalism are about making realities of crime and human rights violations and responses amenable to methodical thought, technologies function to translate that thought within programmes, into the 'domain of reality' (Miller and Rose 2008, p. 33). Technologies advance and become arranged within specific programmes by mentalities. Governance is reliant on the use of multiple technologies informed by prevailing mentalities and translated into programmes (Rose and Miller 1992). Attending to technologies means shifting attention to what is often overlooked. They are often material features of governance that allow mentalities to settle into place and take hold and make programmes effective more broadly. When tethered to specific mentalities, they can accomplish different purposes.

In relation to human rights the way technologies are deployed matter. Focusing on technologies in this analytic entails criminologists paying attention to myriad devices of human rights regimes: hearing procedures, human rights training regimens, legal niceties, interviewing techniques, rights-claiming and adjudicating forms and databases, and physical spaces of hearings and claims of one kind of right or other. It also demands focusing on the more familiar side of the coin, that is, myriad technologies of government deployed in crime control measures that raise human rights issues. These many technologies include, for example, new forms of urban surveillance permitting on-the-spot summary justice practices like banning and dispersal of unwanted youth, working class men, and/or homeless persons in major Australian (Palmer and Warren 2013) and Canadian cities (see Sleiman and Lippert 2010, Walby and Lippert 2011) that constitute or contribute to rights violations, including their 'Right to the City' (Lippert and Walby 2013b).

Technologies relevant to human rights and crime control are infinite. However, a key aspect is that they do not appear exactly as imagined and or as originally programmed (Dean 1999). This creates the constant need for reflexivity and experimentation with new technologies and programmes. Statistics and 'privacy by design' tools were noted above. Surveillance technologies are particularly relevant here too (see Murphy and Whitty 2013); human rights enforcement has become highly dependent on such technologies. Surveillance is not necessarily intimately linked to or limited to discipline and instead can merely be installed to monitor human rights violations in particular spaces to generate statistics. A related technology is maps (see Kindynis 2014) and these would be particularly fruitful to investigate in relation to human rights within criminology. In adjudicating refugee rights, for example, the technology of maps has been crucial; they are inscription devices that bring spatial realities of human rights violations into being. Yet, they are themselves political since they represent borders in convenient ways, eliminate ambiguities, and bring the spatial distribution of human rights violations into the realm of adjudication whether by human rights tribunals of one kind or other or more specific entities, as noted above, such as a privacy commission offices or refugee determination boards of western nations.

## *Criminological knowledge?*

A key feature of the governmentality analytic is the presumption that the exercise of governmental power (or governance) always emerges with forms of knowledge (Rose and Miller 1992). Formal knowledges, including criminology, but also medicine, geography, psychology, public administration, and so on (Dean 1999) inform governing mentalities. Through these knowledges assumptions are created about what is proper, moral, ideal, appropriate, or responsible conduct (Rose and Miller 1992, p. 179). In this way governmentality-informed criminology reflexively identifies forms of criminology themselves as knowledge used to govern populations in particular ways. For example, some criminologies have come to inform individuals about how to act upon themselves and others in relation to crime risks or in pursuit of security (see Garland 1997). Though potentially in proportion to threats revealed by criminological profiling, and perhaps well intentioned, such arrangements can morph into what Simon (2007, p. 4) aptly calls 'governing through crime' whereby institutions and individuals 'deploy the category of crime to legitimate interventions that have other motivations', and which mirrors the notion of 'governing through rights' above. Simon (2007) argues this practice is evident in an array of institutions including the workplace, the school, or family, which he suggests are treated more and more as flash points for suspicions about crime (Simon 2007, p. 9). This raises the question of how criminology becomes implicated in human rights regimes too. Interestingly, a governmentality analytic's focus on knowledge also raises the vital question of why there is growing interest in human rights from within criminology at this juncture (see, for example, this collection, Murphy and Whitty [2013], and Weber et al. [2014]), suggesting that human rights and criminology may be being increasingly enlisted together in new governmental projects. Certainly there is increasing demand for 'human rights knowledge' that permits the adjudication of human rights violations that often constitute criminal acts and in which criminology is playing a role. It would seem this link is necessarily empirically studied in any 'history' of criminological engagement with human rights.

## *Reality and rights*

One final common misconception about the governmentality analytic needs dispelling in any stocktaking exercise: that by attending to governmental discourse, that is, by focusing on the discursive realm, reality is ignored. Early critiques charged that governmentality studies neglected the real (see Lippert 2005, Garland 1997, pp. 199–201). It was asserted that real effects of programmes were overlooked due to misplaced attention to discourse found in programmatic texts. As evident from the above discussion, however, technologies in particular are often already material in form and therefore qualify as what some would understand as 'real'. But more importantly, governmentality-informed studies often reflect more a matter of emphasis than a categorical denial of 'the real'. Such studies do not so much deny real effects of governmental programmes and practices as focus on components invented to shape these domains, including new and evolving international and domestic human rights regimes. In the most sympathetic and well-articulated critique to date involving criminologists, O'Malley et al. (1997, p. 512) noted too that 'many programmes exist only in the process of messy implementation', thereby suggesting there is no clear division between discursive and real, between what is imagined and what is activated. Nor is such a division plainly evident in actual governmentality-informed studies within criminology, with scholars often making assertions or assumptions about 'the real' in their accounts (see Lippert and Stenson 2010). Moreover, governmentality scholars, including within criminology, have called for greater attention to 'real effects', which can be strategic (see Stenson 2005, Lippert and Stenson 2010) by revealing a particular mentality operative in generating reality.

It is true that governmentality studies tend to be more agnostic than normative and support of human rights tends to move in lockstep with the latter. Yet, governmentality-informed criminology can reveal the detailed workings of human rights claims-making and adjudication of related forms of crime, how they are changing, and how they are made possible by new strains of criminological knowledge, mentalities, and technologies, thus rendering their workings amenable to progressive intervention and reform.

## Conclusion

The governmentality analytic has had a profound influence on criminology (Lippert and Stenson 2010), but so far not in relation to human rights. There remains a need to more closely consider human rights from within criminology and how the tether between them ought to be approached. Certainly the notion that rights can extend and are implicated in governance, that they can be 'governed through', opens the way for empirical research into their not always progressive role in various sites and, indeed, the incredible diversity of rights currently in play in relation to state crime in particular. Refugee rights and privacy rights are only two kinds that brush up against, or are increasingly of interest within, criminology due to their close tether to state control and surveillance. The foregoing revisit of this analytic's toolkit to see what might be missing and what can be used yields four questions in relation to human rights regimes: What mentalities are evident, including but also beyond forms of liberalism, and how do they conflict with or complement one another or identify sites for progressive intervention? How do sovereign powers work against recognition of rights and responses to human rights violations? What technologies are present that make operation and entrenchment of these varied mentalities possible? Perhaps most fundamentally, concerning the role of knowledge, how is criminology being enlisted in governmental projects that seek to govern state crime and other forms of conduct *through* rights and why might the interest in human rights from within the discipline be emerging now? Answering these questions can aid understanding of human rights regimes and issues amongst critically oriented criminologists. If put to good use governmentality concepts and themes can potentially reveal where progressive intervention in existing human rights domains is possible while avoiding ill-conceived totalizing endeavours doomed to fail. If 'rights are now generating new positions on method, activism and policy roles in criminology – positions that speak to the contours and future directions of the field' (Murphy and Whitty 2013, p. 575) then the need for a governmentality analytic to empirically study these arrangements and corresponding subjectivities is greater than ever. It goes without saying that restocking the tool crib along the lines above, that is, overcoming misconceptions and using the full complement of analytical tools in the growing fields of human rights could well reinvigorate the use of this analytic in critically oriented criminology too.

## Note

1 The genealogies and elements of pastoralism and humanitarianism have some similarities but possess even more significant differences, too numerous to explicate in the space available.

## References


Dean, M., 1999. *Governmentality: power and rule in modern society*. London: Sage.

Foucault, M., 1979. *Discipline and punish: the birth of the prison*. New York, NY: Random House.

Foucault, M., 1991. Governmentality. *In*: G. Burchell, C. Gordon and P. Miller (eds), *The Foucault effect: studies in governmentality*. Chicago, IL: The University of Chicago Press, 87–104.

Garland, D., 1997. Governmentality and the problem of crime: Foucault, criminology, sociology. *Theoretical Criminology*, 2(1), 173–214.

Gilling, D., 2010. Crime control and due process in confidence-building strategies: a governmentality perspective. *British Journal of Criminology*, 50, 1136–54.

Golder, B., 2012. Foucault, rights and freedom. *International Journal for the Semiotics of Law*, 26(1), 5–21.

Gordon, C., 1991. Governmental rationality: an introduction. *In*: G. Burchell, C. Gordon and P. Miller (eds), *The Foucault effect: studies in governmentality*. Chicago, IL: The University of Chicago Press, 1–51.

Greenwald, G., 2014. *No place to hide: Edward Snowden, the NSA and the US Surveillance State*. London: Signal Books.

Haggerty, K., 2001. *Making crime count*. Toronto: University of Toronto Press.

Hunt, A. and Wickham, G., 1994. *Foucault and law: towards a sociology of law as governance*. London: Pluto Press.

Kindynis, T., 2014. Ripping up the map: criminology and cartography reconsidered. *British Journal of Criminology*, 54, 222–43.

Lindroth, M., 2014. Indigenous rights as tactics of neo-liberal governance: practices of expertise in the United Nations. *Social and Legal Studies*, 23(3), 341–60.

Lippert, R., 1998. Rationalities and refugee resettlement. *Economy and Society*, 27, 380–406.

Lippert, R., 1999. Governing refugees: the relevance of governmentality to understanding the international refugee regime. *Alternatives*, 24, 295–328.

Lippert, R., 2002. Policing property and moral risk through promotions, anonymization and rewards: crime stoppers revisited. *Social and Legal Studies*, 11, 475–502.

Lippert, R., 2005. *Sanctuary, sovereignty, sacrifice: Canadian sanctuary incidents, power, and law*. Vancouver: University of British Columbia Press.

Lippert, R., 2010. Mundane and mutant devices of power: urban business improvement districts and sanctuaries. *European Journal of Cultural Studies*, 13, 477–94.

Lippert, R. and Stenson, K., 2010. Advancing governmentality studies: lessons from social constructionism. *Theoretical Criminology*, 14, 473–94.

Lippert, R. and Walby, K., 2013a. Governing through privacy: authoritarian liberalism, privacy law, and privacy knowledge. *Law, Culture, and the Humanities*, 9(3), early online version.

Lippert, R. and Walby, K. (eds), 2013b. *Policing cities: urban securitization and regulation in a twenty-first century world*. London: Routledge.

Miller, P. and Rose, N., 2008. Governing economic life. *In*: P. Miller and N. Rose (eds), *Governing the present*. London: Polity, 26–52.

Murphy, T. and Whitty, N., 2013. Making history: academic criminology and human rights. *British Journal of Criminology*, 53, 568–87.

*New York Times*, 2015. Europe must reform its deadly asylum policies. Editorial, 31 August. Retrieved on 1 September 2015 from: www.nytimes.com/2015/09/01/opinion/europe-must-reform-its-deadly-asylum-policies.html.

O'Malley, P. (1992). Risk, power and crime prevention. *Economy and Society*, 21(3), 252–75.

O'Malley, P., Weir, L. and Shearing, C., 1997. Governmentality, criticism, politics. *Economy and Society*, 26(4), 501–17.

Palmer, D. and Warren, I., 2013. Zonal banning and public order in urban Australia. *In*: R. Lippert and K. Walby (eds), *Policing cities: urban securitization and regulation in a twenty-first century world*. London: Routledge, 79–98.

Park, G. and Lippert, R., 2008. Legal aid's logics. *Studies in Law, Politics, and Society*, 45, 177–201.

Rose, N., 1996. Governing 'advanced liberal' democracies. *In*: A. Barry, T. Osborne, and N. Rose (eds), *Foucault and political reason*. New York, NY: Routledge, 37–64.

Rose, N. and Miller, P., 1992. Political power beyond the state: problematics of government. *British Journal of Sociology*, 43, 173–205.

Rose, N. and Valverde, M., 1998. Governed by law? *Social and Legal Studies*, 7, 541–51.

Rose, N., O'Malley, P. and Valverde, M., 2006. Governmentality. *Annual Review of Law and Social Sciences*, 2, 1–22.

Simon, J., 2007. *Governing through crime: how the war on crime transformed American democracy and created a culture of fear*. New York, NY: Oxford University Press.

Sleiman, M. and Lippert, R. 2010. Downtown ambassadors, police relations and 'clean and safe' security. *Policing and Society*, 20, 316–35.

Sokhi-Bulley, B., 2011. Governing (through) rights: statistics as technologies of governmentality. *Social and Legal Studies*, 20, 139–55.

Stenson, K., 1993. Community policing as a governmental technology. *Economy and Society*, 22, 373–89.

Stenson, K., 1998. Beyond histories of the present. *Economy and Society*, 27, 333–52.

Stenson, K., 2005. Sovereignty, biopolitics and local government of crime in Britain. *Theoretical Criminology*, 9, 265–87.

Walby, K. and Lippert, R., 2011. Spatial regulation, dispersal, and the aesthetics of the city: conservation officers policing of homeless people in Ottawa, Canada. *Antipode*, 44, 1015–33.

Weber, L., Marmo, M. and Fishwick, E., 2014. *Crime, justice, and human rights*. New York, NY: Palgrave Macmillan.

# 9

# Conceptualizing human rights in state–corporate crime research

*Raymond Michalowski*

This chapter explores the role of human rights in the conceptualization and application of the state–corporate model for studying crimes of the powerful. The integrated model of state–corporate crime grew out of the proposition that in capitalist societies many corporate crimes are either instigated or made possible by one or more components of political states, and that most state crimes involve either instigation by corporate sector interests or some degree of reliance on the capacity of corporations to provide the material, labour, or knowledge needed to achieve state goals (Michalowski and Kramer 2006a).

## State–Corporate crime defined

Kramer and Michalowski (1990, p. 3) initially defined state–corporate as 'illegal or socially injurious actions that occur when one or more institutions of political governance pursue a goal in direct cooperation with one or more institutions of economic production and distribution'. The definition's emphasis on 'direct cooperation' was best suited to analyses of specific instances of state–corporate engagement such as the production of nuclear weapons (Kauzlarich and Kramer 2010) or military drones (Kramer and Smith 2013). It was less applicable to situations in which crimes or harms resulted from structural rather than direct intersections of corporate and government entities. In order to broaden the understanding of harms at the structural intersections of business and government, Aulette and Michalowski (1993, p. 175) redefined state–corporate crimes as:

> Illegal or socially injurious actions that result from a mutually reinforcing interaction between (1) policies and/or practices in pursuit of the goals of one or more institutions of political governance and (2) policies and/or practices in pursuit of the goals of one or more institutions of economic production and/or distribution.

This revised definition focused greater attention on the way *structural intersections* among sectors of concentrated power are generative of social harms.[1] Table 9.1 provides an illustrative taxonomy of the forces at play in the two cases of state–corporate crime (the killing fire at the Imperial chicken processing plant in North Carolina and the explosion of the space shuttle

*Table 9.1* An integrated theoretical model of state–corporate crime

| | *Catalysts for action* | | |
|---|---|---|---|
| *Levels of analysis* | *Motivation* | *Opportunity* | *Control* |
| *Societal* | Culture of competition<br>Economic pressures<br>Organizational goals<br>Performance emphasis | Availability of legal means<br>Obstacles and constraints<br>Blocked goals/strain<br>Availability of illegal means<br>Access to resources | International reaction<br>Political pressure<br>Legal sanctions<br>Media scrutiny<br>Public opinion<br>Social movements |
| *Organizational* | Corporate culture<br>Operative goals<br>Subunit goals<br>Managerial pressures | Instrumental rationality<br>Internal constraints<br>Defective SOPs<br>Creation of illegal means<br>Task segregations<br>Role specialization<br>Communications technology<br>Normalization of deviance | Culture of compliance<br>Cultures of resistance<br>Codes of conduct<br>Reward structure<br>Safety/quality control<br>Transparency |
| *Interactional* | Socialization<br>Social meaning<br>Individual goals<br>Competitive individualism<br>Material success emphasized | Definitions of situations<br>Perceived of means availability<br>Attractiveness of illegal means | Personal morality<br>Neutralization<br>Diffuse responsibility<br>Obedience to authority<br>Remote consequences<br>Groupthink |

Note: Adapted from Kramer and Michalowski 2006. The original formulation. *In:* R. Michalowski and R. Kramer (eds), *State–corporate crime: wrongdoing at the intersection of business and government*. New Brunswick, NJ: Rutgers University Press, 25.

*Challenger*) that were the initial subjects of this model. The specific social relations that would be salient in each of the cells shown in Table 9.1 would necessarily vary depending on the harm being analysed and the social, economic and political conjuncture within which it took place.

## Criminology, human rights and state–corporate crime

Since its inception, state–corporate crime research has been shaped by the debate within criminology over the definition of 'crime', and the challenges to state-centric criminology posed by a human rights approach. During the first half of the twentieth century, a number of prominent criminologists recognized the limitations of a law-based approach to the definition of crime (Parmalee 1918, Sutherland 1924, 1939, Sellin 1938, Haynes 1930, Tannenbaum 1938, Taft 1942). Despite this recognition, the lack of any standard beyond state law by which to judge behaviour as wrongful ensured that criminological inquiry remained largely tethered to state definitions of crime.

The United States (US) began the second half of the twentieth century in the fog of post-World War 2 triumphalism coupled to McCarthyite anti-communism that silenced critiques of the dominant political-economic order (Aronowitz 2014). These forces were conducive to the continuation of criminological inquiry largely devoid of analyses into the role of political-economic interests in shaping law and crime control policy. However, the establishment of the United Nations and the passage of the *Universal Declaration of Human Rights* at the end of World War 2 laid the foundation for the eventual emergence of alternatives to state-centric criminology in two ways. First, they established a set of standards by which to judge behaviour independent of the definition given to that behaviour by any specific state. Second, the human rights violations that these treaties sought to eliminate were most often committed by political and economic elites, not by the subordinate classes who are the normal subjects of criminological inquiry. These factors contributed to the emergence of a more radical vision of criminology in the 1970s that embraced the emerging international definitions of human rights as a foundation for defining the subject matter of criminology.

One of the most influential early expressions of this search for a post-juridical criminology was Herman Schwendinger and Julia Schwendinger's (1970) 'Defenders of order or guardians of human rights', in which they called for a new criminology explicitly focused on violations of basic human rights. They argued that reliance on legal definitions of crime, while it appeared to ensure precision in selecting subject matter for study, was actually devoid of scientific validity insofar as it leaves criminological inquiry 'determined by the same political conditions that gave rise to the legal definitions in use' (Schwendinger and Schwendinger 1970, p. 138).[2] From their perspective, claims that limiting criminological inquiry to the boundaries defined by state law guaranteed 'value free' scientific inquiry were wilfully ignorant of the political nature of law. As an alternative the Schwendingers proposed that the definition of crime should include any action that deprives people of their basic human rights. They further define their vision of human rights, not as abstract, natural or 'God-given' principles, but as the rights to full human development as these have evolved through human struggles for liberation over the long course of modern history.

While the Schwendingers argued for an explicitly human rights basis for criminology, other radical criminologists in the 1970s began documenting how state definitions of crime are deeply influenced by the interests of the powerful. The underlying proposition was that the two most powerful meta-institutions shaping state law are those engaged in the accumulation of capital and those exercising the political power of what Gramsci (1959) termed the 'extended' state. According to this approach, political and economic elites, often working in concert, minimize the likelihood that most direct and collateral harms resulting from corporate pursuit of profit and the political acquisition and use of state power will be defined as violations of law (Chambliss and Seidman 1971, Platt 1974, Quinney 1974, Pearce 1976, Renee 1979, Turk 1982, Michalowski 1985). The concept of state–corporate crime emerged as a blend of these early movements to build a non-juridical criminology, particularly the search for a human rights basis for criminological inquiry.

## Studying state–corporate crimes

As noted above, the concept of state–corporate crime traces its roots to the foundational concern of US radical criminology with advancing human rights. Specific applications of the state–corporate crime model, however, vary in the degree to which they focus *explicitly* on violation of human rights. In many state-corporate crime studies, the concern for protecting and advancing human rights operates more as a foundational proposition than as specific subject matter.

State–corporate analyses can be divided into two broad groups, those that examine *acute events* and those concerned with *destructive conditions*, with the latter subdivided into *relatively bounded destructive conditions*, and *unbounded destructive conditions*.

## Acute events

Acute events are state–corporate crimes that take place within an identifiable, brief timeframe, are geographically circumscribed, and whose consequences are (usually) limited to immediate victims. The two foundational state–corporate crime studies, Kramer's (1992) study of the *Challenger* explosion and Aulette and Michalowski's (1993) study of the fire in Hamlet, North Carolina, were both studies of acute events. These were followed by other analyses of acute state–corporate crime events such as the crash of ValuJet flight 592 (Matthews and Kauzlarich 2000), rollover accidents resulting from Bridgestone-Firestone tyre failures (Mullins 2006), and the murderous release of toxic gases from the Union-Carbide plant in Bhopal, India (Walters 2009).

## Destructive conditions

Destructive conditions differ from acute events in that the harms involved are often ongoing rather than limited to the immediate consequences of a singular catastrophic moment. These can be further subdivided into *relatively bounded* and *relatively unbounded* conditions.

Relatively bounded destructive conditions are the result of some *event* whose consequences radiate outward to a wider, but identifiable, range of people and life forms than were harmed in the initial catastrophic moment, much like waves radiating outward from a stone dropped in a pond. The characteristic relatively bounded destructive condition in the state–corporate crime literature is an environmental disaster whose reach, while wider than that of acute events, can nevertheless be approximately identified, and whose consequences can be approximately ameliorated or compensated. State–corporate crime studies of relatively bounded destructive conditions include the *Exxon Valdez* oil spill (Cruciotti and Matthews 2006), the *Deepwater Horizon* blowout and subsequent pollution of the Gulf Coast of Louisiana and Mississippi (Bradshaw 2012), and the environmental harm due to oil extraction from tar sands (Smandych and Kueneman 2010). In cases such as these, specific events initiate a chain of harmful consequences that reach beyond the time and place of the original pollution. Even though it is possible to map the temporal and geographical scope of these events, I consider these events as only *relatively* bounded because their effects may ultimately reach further than is understood at the time of analysis. For instance, it will be many decades before we can fully calculate the environmental and human toll of the despoliation of the shore and offshore waters of the Gulf of Mexico by the *Deepwater Horizon* blowout (Mole 2015, Plaisance and McGill 2014).

## Harmful conditions and liberal rights

Despite its early foundation in socialist visions of human rights, state–corporate crime analyses of acute events and relatively bounded destructive conditions are more often linked to classical liberal notions of human rights. By this I mean a 'negative' approach in which rights are construed as prerogatives of individual citizen-subjects that must be protected from violation by political states (Berlin 1969). In contemporary political practices and most 'western constitutions, these are recognized as a minimal right to existence and the logocentric rights to freedom of speech, religion, press, due process, and political participation' (Michalowski 1993, p. 255; see also Agamben 2005).

From a human rights perspective, analyses of acute events and relatively bounded dangerous conditions typically focus on crimes of commission or omission by the *state*. One set of studies focuses on cases where state actors are *directly* responsible for the wrongful event or conditions studied, although with recognition that the corporate actors have supported, assisted, or even instigated the wrongful state action. Kramer and Michalowski's (2005) analysis of the invasion and occupation of Iraq by the 'coalition of the willing' and Mullins and Rothe's (2008) examination of human rights crimes in Africa, are examples of analyses of proactive state violations of human rights with the assistance, support, and sometimes urging of corporate actors.

Another group of studies reflecting a liberal approach to rights are those in which the initial wrongful actions resulted from the corporate pursuit of capital accumulation, but which implicitly or explicitly identify regulatory failure on the part of the state as facilitating violation of the basic rights to life and bodily wellbeing. Examples of this approach are found in the Aulette and Michalowski (1993) analysis of the Imperial plant fire, Harper and Israel's (1999) inquiry into environmental pollution in Papua, New Guinea, Matthews and Kauzlarich's (2000) analysis of the ValuJet crash, Bradshaw's (2012) study of the *Deepwater Horizon* well blowout, and Lasslett's analysis of the crimes of Rio Tinto in Bougainville (2014).

Both approaches are based on a distinctive construction of the *is* and the *ought* of political states as compared to the is and ought of capitalist corporations. These studies typically view capitalist corporations as if they are *what they must be*, accumulation-seeking organizations that will inevitably cause social harm unless curtailed by state regulation. In this view, there is little distinction between the practice and the potential of the corporation. By contrast, these studies frequently find that the state *is* guilty of direct harm or harm-enabling regulatory failure when it *ought* to have restrained the depredations of the corporation(s) involved and/or its own operatives.

By accepting that corporations are inevitable predators while presuming that states ought to – and can be – the ultimate defenders of human rights, this approach to state–corporate crime studies locates the burden for the protection of human rights in the state. In doing so, it reifies the distinction between the public and the private sector and forecloses discussion about transforming the corporation, that is, creating a new *ought* for corporations.

The surface appearance of both acute events and relatively bounded destructive conditions can often make them seem as if they are self-contained happenings. However, one of the core findings of the accumulating body of state–corporate crime studies is that these singularly appearing events typically result from *systemic patterns and practices* that increase the likelihood of repeated occurrences of substantively similar events, patterns that Bradshaw (2015) terms 'criminogenic industry structures'. Thus, while the specific harms studied may be relatively contained, the wider social arrangements in which they are generated are ongoing, and involve systematic patterns of wrongful behaviour. This recognition that state–corporate crimes, even those of limited reach, are symptoms of systemic forces that increase the likelihood of repeated violations of the right to life, health, and self-determination rather than discrete wrongdoings by economic and political organizations became the foundation for inquiry into unbounded destructive conditions by state–corporate crime analysts.

### *Unbounded destructive conditions*

State–corporate crime studies of acute events and relatively bounded destructive conditions differ from routine criminological studies in their focus on organizational interaction rather than individual miscreants. Nevertheless, these inquiries fit within a general investigative framework that begins with asking 'who did what to whom, when did they do it, and why?' even if the 'who' may be an aggregate of organizational actors. By contrast, analyses of relatively *unbounded* destructive conditions move beyond the specific organizations involved in the production of crimes and social harms by interrogating how the *social systems* in which these organizations are created and operate magnify, and often *necessitate*, that these organizations engage in actions that will result in blameworthy social harm.

During the 20-year US war against Vietnam (1955–74) there was a popular anti-war poster drawn as if by a young child with a box of crayons. It pictured a flower and the words 'War is not healthy for children and other living things'. In their immediacy, wars are undeniable human disasters, but ones that seem to come to an end. However, as Epstein (1997) observes, 'while it is axiomatic that war involves killing . . . war also leaves wounds, infections, and suffering lingering for years, poisoning relationships, psyches, soils, forests, and underground water systems'. Once a war begins the human, animal and environmental health consequences will radiate outward for generations to come (Blimes and Stiglitz 2008). Moreover, while all wars necessitate the participation of political and corporate actors, to label any specific actor or set of actors as having *caused* the war overlooks the reality that every war is the result of a specific historical conjuncture of multiple forces. They are the products of political-economic systems within which specific war-making apparatus operate.

What is true about war is true about other unbounded destructive conditions that harm humans and 'other living things'. We have long known that economic and social inequality kills, injures, sickens and deforms social relations (Therborn 2013), that racism is destructive to human health (Jones 2000), and that environmental pollution not only kills and sickens humans, but damages whole ecosystems (WHO 2014). The strong consensus among climate scientists is that our carbon-dependent, global economic system has placed the world well along the path toward systemic changes that will have devastating impacts not just on 'the weather', but on the long term wellbeing of humans and other species unless there is a collective global effort to reduce carbon emissions (Kolbert 2014, Klein 2014). In many parts of the world, the effects of climate change and associated desertification are already causing starvation, disease, death, and war. Meanwhile wealthier and, as yet, less-affected populations have begun pursuing what Parenti (2011) terms 'the politics of the armed lifeboat' that will continue to shift the most devastating consequences of climate change onto poorer nations and populations.

Although the study of state–corporate crime began with a focus on dramatic events, the search for intersections of economic and political relations in the production of crime and social harm also directed attention to the ways in which the behaviours of specific organizations were very much shaped by the larger systemic arrangements that they constitute (Hillyard et al. 2004, Presser 2013). This recognition is embedded in the integrated model of state–corporate crime through the inclusion of societal level forces as one of the three levels of analysis essential to state–corporate crime inquiry. Two early analyses of the neoliberal transformation of the global economy, Wonders and Danner's (2002) 'Globalization, state–corporate crime and women' and Michalowski's (2002) 'Beyond Enron: exclusions, inclusions and the ethics of corporate responsibility' specifically examined the criminogenic and rights-violating character of larger social systems rather than focusing on specific events or organizations. Wonders and Danner (2002, p. 102) detail four criminogenic areas of globalizations with particular impact on the rights of women: (1) economic displacement as a result of the privatization and corporate control of land in developing countries, (2) unfair labour practices and unsafe working conditions for women who must now work at waged labour in order to survive, (3) environmental harm, and (4) militarism. Applying a state–corporate crime perspective, they analyse these harms as substantive violations of human rights, giving particular attention to the work of human rights non-government organizations in fighting against them.

Michalowski (2002) examined how, in both ideology and law, neoliberalism reconstituted the moral responsibility of corporations in ways that weakened or eliminated many of the gains made by labour and human rights movements in the first three-quarters of the twentieth century.

Specifically, he notes that the neoliberal corporation has rehabilitated and obtained state authorization for 'a set of highly exclusionary nineteenth-century laws and practices that limited the moral community of corporations to the "owners", that is to their stockholders'. This re-embrace of nineteenth century corporate practices has enabled the neoliberal corporation, in concert with emergent supra-national economic entities such as the World Bank, the International Monetary Fund (IMF), and the World Trade Organization (WTO), to globalize capital accumulation through practices that violate a multitude of human rights by freeing corporations from legal responsibility, and in the minds of many, from moral responsibility, to protect those who might otherwise be harmed by the global pursuit of capital accumulation.

As the key components of 'globalization' – that is, neoliberalism, transnationalized investment, and supra-national regulatory systems such as the WTO and the IMF – became the dominant framework for state–corporate intersections, analyses of state–corporate crimes began to encompass, not only the specific harms and violations of human rights resulting from neoliberal globalism, but also analyses that viewed the global political-economic system, qua system, as criminogenic. Reflecting this view, David Whyte (2014, p. 237) characterizes earlier state–corporate crime theorizing as limited by its focus on the state–corporate relations as institutional phenomena that become observable during what he terms 'moments of rupture'. He proposes instead that analysts of the crimes of corporations and states should examine the 'deeper structural relation' between capital and the state as 'the material foundations of a criminogenic and profoundly harmful system of capital accumulation'. Whyte (2014, p. 240) goes on to challenge the image of state–corporate crimes as the consequence of regulatory failure by noting:

> Because regulatory agencies hold out the possibility of challenging corporate power, they typically dissipate – or even replace – conflicts between workers or publics and organized capital. By offering concrete routes to address corporate harms, regulatory agencies thus offer state-controlled solutions to problems over which the state had previously lost control ... regulatory agencies are ultimately unable to resolve conflicts and crises, but can merely repackage them in ways that allow governments to, temporarily at least, retain some control over the amelioration of corporate harms.

Whyte (2014) and Tombs and Whyte (2015) recognize the state–corporate nexus as a symbiotic network of relations necessary for the facilitation of capital accumulation within social systems that are able to garner sufficient legitimacy to avoid revolt and maintain a modicum of social peace.

Bernal et al. (2014) analyse the economic and social crisis that engulfed much of the Spanish population after the 2008 onset of the Great Recession from a perspective similar to Whyte's (2014) image of states as 'regimes of permission' that legalize harmful state–corporate violations of rights. Specifically, they note that the economic devastation resulting from transnational financial speculation in the Spanish housing and bond markets resulted 'directly from state tolerance, absolving the international financial institutions from accountability for their decisions and allowing private enterprises to act freely, without being sanctioned for breaking the law' (Bernal et al. 2014, p. 224). The wider implication of their work is not simply detailing a case of state corruption, but rather an indictment of the entire global financial system as a breeding ground for state–corporate violations of human rights.

In a similar vein, Barak (2012) and Friedrichs and Rothe (2014) argue that criminologists should focus greater attention on 'crimes of globalization', particularly the kinds of financial speculations that triggered the 2008 collapse of global financial markets. These writers propose that the intensifying intersections and overlaps involving transnational corporations, government sponsored enterprises (for example, state-supported or -insured mortgage funds, sovereign wealth funds), and state-sponsored international financial institutions (such as the IMF, World Bank) make it increasingly difficult to draw any kind of bright line between states and corporations. The implication is again that political states and capital-accumulating corporations are wholly blended into a unitary criminogenic system.

## Beyond the liberal vision

As Soederberg (2014) details in *Debtfare states and the poverty industry*, the blurring of once *seemingly* clearer boundaries between corporations as engines of capital accumulation and states as systems of social control has become profound in the twenty-first century. This poses new challenges and creates new opportunities for state–corporate crime analyses of violations of human rights, particularly as it becomes increasingly evident that these violations are rooted in evolving globalized regimes of capital accumulation.

Social harms such as wars, economic exploitation, gender, racial and ethnic inequality, resistance to limiting climate-altering greenhouse gasses, loss of access to water, food shortages resulting from market speculation and land grabs, profitable production and intense marketing of health-harming products (for example, tobacco and high fat, high sugared foods), continued international pressures to weaken national regulations limiting air, soil and water pollution, and increasingly effective efforts to eviscerate social safety nets for billions of people worldwide have become *routine and legal activities* with devastating consequences for the wellbeing of people and the planet (Robinson and Harris 2000).

These threats to basic human rights generated by neoliberal globalization are not natural phenomena. They are the proximate results of decisions and actions undertaken within economic and political networks. Neoliberal globalization has also made it apparent that the relationship between capital and state is not one between separate, though often colluding actors, but rather a relationship among many nodes within global networks of economic and political power that create and condition one another in multiple ways. That is, capital and political states are mutually constitutive, or 'symbiotic' networks, to use the term favoured by Tombs (2012).

The state–corporate crime model discussed here can contribute to the struggle to advance human rights in the face of the many challenges to these rights faced under neoliberal globalization. To do so, however, will require two steps. The first is to fully appreciate the dash in state–corporate crime. We wrote the term in this manner, rather than as 'state corporate crime' (as my friend and eminent criminologist Piers Beirne argues we should have) to emphasize what we saw as the unity of the state–corporate entity. Recent analyses of systemic forms of state corporate crime discussed above are positive moves in this direction. The second task is to give greater attention to processes of corporate capital accumulation, not just as the cause of crime and social harm, but also as the target for social change.

To date, state–corporate crime research has given more attention to failures of state regulation than to how the corporate functions of producing and distributing social products can and should be reconstituted in ways that are less generative of crime and social harm. In an effort to address this limitation, Michalowski and Kramer (2006b, p. 174) argued that: 'Insofar as corporations control nearly all production and distribution, they must become responsible for maximizing societal wellbeing, not just for generating private profit'. They follow this with a five-point strategy for democratizing the corporation by: (1) replacing stockholder corporations with stakeholder corporations, (2) reconstituting corporate boards of directors such that 50 per cent of their members are elected by stakeholders, (3) making board memberships full-time, paid positions and disallowing interlocking directorate memberships, (4) requiring complete openness and transparency of all corporate board decisions, and (5) expanding the scope of legal standing under which citizens can sue corporations for harms they cause beyond the currently highly restrictive legal avenues through which citizens can challenge corporate wrongdoing (Michalowski and Kramer 2006b, p. 183). I would add an additional sub-requirement to item (2). Appointments and elections to corporate boards of directors should be proportional to the populations in those countries where corporations operate.

These steps would not eliminate the threats state–corporate crimes pose to human rights around the globe, although they would help. Nor are these steps likely to happen in any near-term dominated by the current ideology and practice of neoliberalism. However, the time has come to shift from asking how states can better regulate corporations to exploring how the existing state–corporate nexus can be rendered less threatening to the fundamental right of human beings to live dignified lives in peace and security.

## Notes

1 See, inter alia, *State Crime Journal*, Vol. 3, No. 2, State–corporate Crime (Autumn 2014) and Tombs (2012) for further elaboration of these intersections.

2 Rafael Garofalo (1885/1914, p. 59) made a very similar observation at the end of the nineteenth century when he observed that 'The attempt to show us what the law views as crime ends in our being told that crime, in the eyes of the law, is the doing of that which the law itself forbade'.

## References


Agamben, G., 2005. *State of exception*. Chicago, IL: University of Chicago Press.

Aronowitz, S., 2014. *Taking it big: C. Wright Mills and the making of political intellectuals*. New York: Columbia University Press.

Aulette, J. and Michalowski, R., 1993. Fire in Hamlet: a case study of a state–corporate crime. *In*: K.D. Tunnell (ed.), *Political crime in contemporary America: a critical approach*. New York: Garland, 171–206.

Barak, G., 2012. *Theft of a nation: Wall Street looting and federal regulatory colluding*. Lanham, MD: Rowman and Littlefield.

Berlin, I., 1969. *Four essays on liberty*. Oxford: Clarendon Press.

Bernal, C., Forero, A. and Rivera, I., 2014. State–corporate crime and social harm in the Spanish crisis. *State Crime Journal*, 3(2), State–corporate Crime (Autumn), 220–36.

Blimes, L. and Stiglitz, J., 2008. *The three trillion dollar war: the true cost of the Iraq conflict*. New York: W.W. Norton.

Bradshaw, E., 2012. *Deepwater, deep ties, deep trouble: a state–corporate environmental crime analysis of the 2010 Gulf of Mexico oil spill*. Thesis (PhD). Western Michigan University. Retrieved on 20 May 2015 from: http://scholarworks.wmich.edu/cgi/viewcontent.cgi?article=1078&context=dissertations.

Bradshaw, E., 2015. State–corporate environmental cover-up: the response to the 2010 Gulf of Mexico oil spill. *State Crime Journal*, Special issue on state corporate crime (Steve Tombs ed.), 3(2), 163–81.

Chambliss, W. and Seidman, R., 1971. *Law, order and power*. New York: Addison-Wesley Publishing Co.

Cruciotti, T. and Matthews, R., 2006. The *Exxon Valdez* Oil Spill. *In*: R. Michalowski and R. Kramer (eds), *State–corporate crime: wrongdoing at the intersection of business and politics*. New Brunswick, NJ: Rutgers University Press, 116–33.

Epstein, P., 1997. War and public health. *Journal of the American Medical Association*, 277(18), 1479–80.

Friedrichs, D. and Rothe, D., 2014. State–corporate crime and major financial institutions: interrogating an absence. *State Crime Journal*, 3(2), State–corporate Crime (Autumn), 146–62.

Garofalo, R., 1885/1914. *Criminologia: studio sul delitto, sulle sue cause e sui mezzi di repressione*. Torino, IT: Fratelli Bocca.

Gramsci, A., 1959. *Modern prince and other essays*. New York: International Publishers.

Harper, A. and Israel, M., 1999. *The killing of the fly: state–corporate victimization in Papua New Guinea.* Australian National University, Working/Technical Paper. Retrieved on 20 May 2015 from: https://digitalcollections.anu.edu.au/handle/1885/40949.

Haynes, F., 1930. *Criminology.* New York: McGraw-Hill.

Hillyard, P., Pantazis, C., Gordon, D., Tombs, S. and Dorling, D., 2004. *Beyond criminology: taking harm seriously.* London: Pluto Press.

Jones, C., 2000. Levels of racism: a theoretic framework and a gardener's tale. *American Journal of Public Health*, 90(8), 1212–15.

Kauzlarich, D. and Kramer, R., 2010. *Crimes of the American nuclear state, at home and abroad.* Boston, MA: Northeastern University Press.

Klein, N., 2014. *This changes everything: capitalism vs. the climate.* New York, NY: Simon & Schuster.

Kolbert, E., 2014. *The sixth extinction: an unnatural history.* New York, NY: Henry Holt.

Kramer, R., 1992. Space shuttle *Challenger* explosion: a case study of state–corporate crime. *In*: Weisburd and Schlegel (eds), *White-collar crime reconsidered.* Boston: Northeastern University Press, 213–43.

Kramer, R. and Michalowski, R., 1990. Toward an integrated model of state–corporate crime. Paper presented at the Society for the Study of Social Problems.

Kramer, R. and Michalowski, R., 2005. War, aggression and state crime: a criminological analysis of the invasion and occupation of Iraq. *British Journal of Criminology*, 45(4), 446–69.

Kramer, R. and Smith, A., 2013. Death flies down: the bombing of civilians and the paradox of international law. *In*: D. Kauzlarich and D. Rothe (eds), *Towards a victimology of state crime.* New York, NY: Routledge, 110–30.

Lasslett, K., 2014. *State crime on the margins of empire: Rio Tinto, the war on Bougainville and resistance to mining.* London: Pluto Press.

Matthews, R. and Kauzlarich, D., 2000. The crash of Valujet flight 592: a case of study in state–corporate crime. *Sociological Focus*, 3(3), 281–98.

Michalowski, R., 1985. *Order, law and crime.* New York: Random House.

Michalowski, R., 1993. Eurocentrism, logocentrism, and law: the rhetorical construction of human rights in Cuba and the United States. *Humanity & Society*, 17(3), 251–65.

Michalowski, R., 2002. Beyond Enron: exclusions, inclusions and the ethics of corporate responsibility. Paper presented at the Center for the Study of Ethics, Western Michigan University.

Michalowski, R. and Kramer, R. (eds), 2006a. *State–corporate crime: wrongdoing at the intersection of business and politics.* New Brunswick, NJ: Rutgers University Press.

Michalowski, R. and Kramer, R., 2006b. Enron era economics versus economic democracy. *In*: R. Michalowski and R. Kramer (eds), *State–corporate crime: wrongdoing at the intersection of business and politics.* New Brunswick, NJ: Rutgers University, 172–85.

Mole, B., 2015. Five years on, Deepwater Horizon oil spill's impact lingers. *Science News.* Retrieved on 6 June 2015 from: www.sciencenews.org/article/five-years-deepwater-horizon-oil-spills-impact-lingers.

Mullins, C., 2006. Bridgestone-Firestone, Ford and the NHTSA. *In*: R. Michalowski and R. Kramer (eds), *State–corporate crime: wrongdoing at the intersection of business and politics.* New Brunswick, NJ: Rutgers University Press, 134–48.

Mullins, C. and Rothe, D., 2008. *Blood, power and bedlam: violations of international criminal law in post-colonial Africa.* New York, NY: Peter Lang.

Parenti, C., 2011. *Tropic of chaos: climate change and the new geography of violence.* New York, NY: Nation Books.

Parmalee, M., 1918. *Criminology.* New York, NY: The MacMillan Company.

Pearce, F., 1976. *Crimes of the powerful: Marxism, crime, and deviance.* London: Pluto Press.

Plaisance, S. and McGill, K., 2014. Nearly four years after the BP oil spill, long-term health impacts remain unclear. *Huffington Post.*

Platt, T., 1974. Prospects for a radical criminology in the United States. *Crime and Social Justice*, 1(Spring–Summer), 2–10.

Presser, L., 2013. *Why we harm.* New Brunswick, NJ: Rutgers University Press.

Quinney, R., 1974. *Critique of legal order: crime control in capitalist society.* Boston, MA: Little, Brown.

Renee, Y., 1979. *The search for criminal man.* Boston, MA: Sage.

Robinson, W.I. and Harris, J., 2000. Towards a global ruling class? Globalization and the transnational capitalist class. *Science & Society*, 64(1) (Spring), 11–54.

Schwendinger, H. and Schwendinger, J., 1970. Defenders of order or guardians of human rights. *Issues in Criminology*, 5(2), 123–57.

Sellin, T., 1938. *Culture conflict and crime*. New York, NY: Social Science Research Council.

Smandych, R. and Kueneman, R., 2010. The Canadian-Alberta tar sands: a case study of state–corporate environmental crime. *In*: R. White (ed.), *Global environmental harm: criminological perspectives*. New York, NY: Routledge, 87–109.

Soederberg, S., 2014. *Debtfare states and the poverty industry*. New York, NY: Routledge.

Sutherland, E., 1924. *Criminology*. Philadelphia, PA: J.B. Lippincott.

Sutherland, E., 1939. *Principles of criminology*, 3rd edn. Philadelphia, PA: J.B. Lippincott.

Taft, D., 1942. *Criminology: an attempt at a synthetic interpretation with a cultural emphasis*. New York, NY: Macmillan.

Tannenbaum, F., 1938. *Crime and the community*. New York, NY: Columbia University Press.

Therborn, G., 2013. *The killing fields of inequality*. London: Polity Press.

Tombs, S., 2012. State–corporate symbiosis in the production of crime and harm. *State Crime*, 1(2), 170–95.

Tombs, S. and Whyte, D., 2015. *The criminal corporation*. London: Routledge.

Turk, A., 1982. *Political criminality: the defiance and defense of authority*. Thousand Oaks, CA: Sage.

Walters, R., 2009. Bhopal, corporate crime and harms of the powerful. *Global Social Policy*, 9(3), 324–7.

Whyte, D., 2014. Regimes of permission and state–corporate crime. *State Crime Journal*, 3(2), State–corporate Crime (Autumn), 237–46.

Wonders, N. and Danner, M., 2002. Globalization, state–corporate crime and women. *In*: R. Michalowski and R. Kramer (eds), *State–corporate crime: wrongdoing at the intersection of business and politics*. New Brunswick, NJ: Rutgers University, 98–115.

World Health Organization (WHO), 2014. 7 million premature deaths annually linked to air pollution. Retrieved on 6 July 2015 from: www.who.int/mediacentre/news/releases/2014/air-pollution/en/.

# 10

# Criminology, globalization and human rights

*Russell Hogg*

## Introduction

Criminology throughout its short history has been overwhelmingly concerned with domestic crime and criminal justice within the internal life of liberal democratic societies. It is only relatively recently that any concerted attention has been paid to the most lethal and atrocious of crimes, those involving gross abuses of human rights. But this oversight also stems from the global context that shaped the emergence and concerns of criminology. This chapter will explore that context, and consider how contemporary globalizing forces have influenced criminology's belated engagement with questions of human rights and the challenges these forces pose for both criminology and the human rights movement.

## Criminology and human rights: the historical disconnect

Criminology's past substantial indifference to the 'crimes' and gross human rights abuses perpetrated by states has to do with the status and power of nation-states in the modern world system, what might be regarded as a Hobbesian international order after the seventeenth century English theorist of sovereignty, Thomas Hobbes (Hogg 2002). The sovereignty of states, and its corollary – the principle of non-interference in the affairs of other states – dated from the Treaty of Westphalia (1648) that brought to a close the bloody confessional wars of the European Reformation. The exclusive authority of the state to rule within its own borders (including to determine what constituted punishable conduct) was designed to contain religious loyalties that traversed borders and thus threatened other states (Hirst 2001). It effectively conferred impunity on states for any action directed against their own peoples, what at the end of the day amounted to a 'right of genocide' (Kuper 1989).

Criminology developed within this shell: European states that were by the nineteenth century internally liberal in character and by the twentieth century also mostly democratic (with notable exceptions). Doubtless this fortified its deference to state definitions of crime and state-directed criminal justice practices. Criminology accepted without demurrer the claims of the liberal democratic state to be sovereign in defining the meanings of justice and injustice within its territorial boundaries. For much of its short history the theoretical and research agendas of criminology were consequently confined to the pacified space of the European liberal democratic state and its offshoots around the world, and this remains the case to a considerable extent.

Criminology devoted most of its attention to crimes that disturbed the domestic peace of the liberal democratic societies that nurtured its development. It conceived its principal mission to be enhancing the capacities of the local criminal justice systems of these societies to manage domestic crimes and punish, treat and control the socially marginal individuals and groups responsible for committing them.

This had the effect of extruding from the remit of criminology those atrocities, war crimes and human rights abuses perpetrated by states, leaving it mute in the face of the most violent atrocities in history. In the space of little more than 30 years in the first half of the twentieth century two European wars and other related forms of state-sponsored violence left more than 50 million people dead. Many millions more died in wars, genocides and other armed conflicts flowing from the break-up of empires and other seismic repercussions of the two world wars. The Nazi regime slaughtered between 5 and 6 million Jews and tens of thousands of others, gypsies, communists, trade unionists, mentally ill, and anyone they deemed socially unfit or dangerous to the state. European and Japanese cities were subject to indiscriminate saturation bombing by the allied powers as World War 2 came to a close and atomic bombs were dropped on Hiroshima and Nagasaki.

State sovereignty and liberal democracy had been principles nourished within and confined to the world of western modernity. They had no necessary application to non-European peoples, who were regarded as not having attained the level of civilization required to exercise sovereign power. This legitimized their colonization and subjugation by European imperial powers, which reached its apogee in the nineteenth century. Even that most liberal (and, on matters of the limits of criminal law and state power, most widely cited) of nineteenth century liberal thinkers, John Stuart Mill, was clear that the liberty principle, limiting the exercise of state compulsion to the prevention of harm to others, only applied to members of a 'civilized community'. 'Despotism [he said] is a legitimate mode of government in dealing with barbarians, provided the end be their improvement' (Mill 1993 [1859], pp. 78–9). Accepting this inherited framework of assumptions, criminology also declined any critical interest in what imperial European states did in their colonial domains where their actions frequently made no pretence to observe liberal norms. At its worst, positivist criminology that melded racial science with biological theories of criminality actually provided legitimation for systematic state abuses of human rights against non-European peoples and other minorities. Categories and classifications of pathology invented or borrowed by criminology (atavism, mental deficiency, feeblemindedness, the habitual criminal) actually provided a scientific warrant for abuses.

World War 2 and the atrocities of the Nazi regime did, however, catalyse a turning point in the advance of human rights. Alongside the *Universal Declaration of Human Rights* and the establishment of the United Nations (UN), the Nuremberg and Tokyo war trials also planted the seeds of a system of international criminal law. But the Cold War quickly stymied any further development for the next 40 years. In the absence of any effective supra-national mechanism of enforcement, participation in the developing UN framework of international human rights (involving state ratification of the *International Covenant on Civil and Political Rights* and other instruments) reflected commitments that were often more rhetorical than real. Certainly rulers remained comfortably beyond the reach of justice for crimes perpetrated against their citizens or for the deaths inflicted in proxy wars, conflicts and coups conducted or sponsored by the superpowers.

The political and cultural ferment of the 1960s and 1970s led some radical criminologists to turn their attention outward from the traditional concerns of the discipline. Joining a debate initiated by Edwin Sutherland in the 1940s in the context of the criminological neglect of white collar crime, a landmark article by Herman and Julia Schwendinger (1975) in the 1970s argued that criminological research agendas should, in place of the state definitions of crime to which they had always deferred, adopt a definition reflecting established international human rights standards. State human rights violations, no less than the crimes of individuals, would thereby attract the gaze of criminology. Whilst these concerns inspired work in developing radical and critical currents within criminology, the mainstream remained largely untouched by them. More interest would begin to be shown only when the end of the Cold War and new patterns of global conflict produced further developments in international criminal law.

Criminology has been very slow in coming to the study of the worst of crimes – war crimes, genocide, torture, and other crimes against humanity and gross human rights abuses – and in key respects this engagement remains tentative (Green and Ward 2004, Savelsberg 2010). It is also the case that even as global events – the end of the Cold War, the increasing globalization of the economy, communications and culture – have led criminology to a greater engagement with the crimes of states, new and different patterns of violent conflict have appeared to challenge both criminology and the human rights movement.

## Globalization and new powers to help and to harm

The history of European imperialism underlines the fact that whilst the term globalization may have only achieved widespread currency in academic, political and popular lexicon in the last three decades (Giddens 2002), the phenomenon of globalization has been around much longer. Western capitalist modernity was global from the beginning (Beckert 2014), and the historical legacy of its reach and impact resonates in many of the conflicts, troubles and human rights controversies of the contemporary world, from armed conflicts arising from contested borders artificially imposed by European map-makers (for example, in the Middle East, South Asia and Africa) to the excessive criminalization of Indigenous or formerly enslaved peoples in settler states like the United States (US), Canada and Australia.

What has changed in recent times is not the fact of global interconnectedness but its character. This is important for understanding, not only the past disconnect between criminology and human rights, but also the more recent attempts to draw them closer together and the serious challenges the present global era presents for criminology and human rights advocates.

### *What is different about contemporary globalization?*

Contemporary globalization has seen rapid acceleration in the mobility of people, goods, capital and ideas across national borders and the growing interconnectedness of economic and political systems. Importantly, new communications technologies have also empowered individuals and non-state groups to organize themselves and to act without reference to national borders and outside the purview of states. As Rodin observes, it has 'enabled us *to harm and to help* others in ways that our forebears could not have imagined' (Rodin 2012, p. 33, emphasis added). So it has fostered both optimistic and pessimistic prognoses for the future.

The optimistic view sees these profound transformational forces as fostering a 'great convergence' in the global human condition, 'a new global civilization' characterized by increasing cooperation in place of war and conflict; rising living standards for the vast bulk of the world's population; the spread of democracy and the rule of law as universal values; and increased access to education and growing respect for rights, reason and science across the globe (see Mahbubani 2013). Although obstacles aplenty are acknowledged, the optimists argue that 'the revolution in communications has created a global audience' that provides 'the material basis for a new ethic that will serve the interests of all those who live on the planet in a way that, despite much rhetoric, no previous ethic has ever done' (Singer 2002, pp. 13–14). For some the 'universal core' of this new global ethic is 'articulated most powerfully by the idea of human rights' (Rodin 2012, pp. 33–4). For these thinkers globalization creates a highly favourable climate for the advance of human rights as the effective basis of a new global morality.

We do not need to look far for evidence of this in relation to state crimes. The key turning points occurred in the 1990s within years of the implosion of the Soviet Union and the close of the Cold War. In 1998 erstwhile Chilean military dictator, Augusto Pinochet, was arrested in London whilst visiting for medical treatment. His arrest was under warrant relating to crimes committed by his regime, for which, it may be safely assumed, he believed he enjoyed impregnable sovereign immunity. The arrest breached, for the first time, that edifice, which had to this point seemed so solid. As one of the judges in the case, Lord Millet, described the shift:

> The way in which a state treated its own citizens within its own borders has become a matter of legitimate concern to the international community. . . . Large scale and systematic use of torture and murder by state authorities for political ends has come to be regarded as an attack upon the international order.[1]

In the same decade an international ad hoc tribunal was established to try the perpetrators of crimes against humanity in the former Yugoslavia, including the former Yugoslav leader Slobodan Milosevic and many of his lieutenants. A similar tribunal was established for Rwanda where genocidal violence directed against the Tutsi minority (and Hutus who opposed the violence) resulted in the slaughter of 800,000 people in the space of a few months in 1994 whilst the international community looked on. In 1998 the adoption of the Rome Statute by 120 nations saw the establishment of a standing International Criminal Court with powers to prosecute crimes against humanity (on these and other pivotal developments set against the long-term struggle to establish an international system of criminal justice, see Robertson 2006).

Alongside these hopeful signs of advancing global justice, there is another, less optimistic view of contemporary globalization. As Rodin acknowledges, globalizing forces increase the capacity to harm as well as to help. New technologies enable individuals and non-state groups to organize themselves economically and politically outside the purview and regulation of states and unrestricted by geography. They make violent power, as well as economic power, 'cheaply available' to non-state groups whilst eroding the capacity of states to regulate, tax, police and protect their citizens (Davidson and Rees-Mogg 1998, p. 5). Consider here the metastasizing forms of contemporary Islamic terrorism, and in particular the sudden appearance of Islamic State (as if from nowhere), the power it has rapidly accrued and its global recruiting success. In the rapidly changing global environment states may come to resemble just another form of association competing with other non-state authorities for allegiance and resources, what Bobbitt depicts as the transition in the constitutional order of states from the form of the 'nation-state' to that of the 'market state' (Bobbitt 2003, 2008).

Human rights advocates who share the traditional focus on state abuses of power, might see a weakened state as a less dangerous state. On the other hand, there is the risk (and growing evidence) that non-state actors are becoming major sources of contemporary conflict, violence, atrocities and other gross human rights abuses in many parts of the world. This led Robert Cooper to suggest that 'where the state is too weak to be dangerous, non-state actors might become too strong' (Cooper 2004, p. 18). Terrorist groups, drug cartels, warlords, criminal gangs, rapacious mining corporations and financial institutions variously evade and corrupt the rule of weakened state institutions. Contemporary civil (or more accurately, uncivil) conflicts and violence shade into, are sustained by, or have as their core purpose, various forms of crime: terror, corruption, trafficking in drugs, arms, people, sex, diamonds, and so on (Cooper 2004). Stan Cohen reached the rather prophetic conclusion in the 1990s that what was happening in many strife-torn parts of the world was the growing 'criminalization of political conflict', a case of crime taking over, or threatening to take over, politics (Cohen 1996).

This gives crime a novel geopolitical salience and strategic interest, especially as the impacts in the global era readily flow across borders, threatening neighbouring states and even faraway places. Crime ceases to be merely a domestic legal problem and becomes a regional and global security problem. The asymmetry between state and non-state control of the means of violence upon which the conventional international political order rested in the twentieth century no longer pertains. The point is underlined by the fact that the major international conflict opening the twenty-first century involved the most powerful state on earth responding to a terrorist attack on its own soil by going to war against a small, non-state network with no stable territorial base or army. Moreover, the upshot of these campaigns has been to foment further chaos in zones of conflict in the Middle East and South Asia and increase the global appeal of the non-state groups involved, so that the real and phantom impacts are being felt in polities across the globe.

This presents major challenges for human rights norms and discourse shaped within and by the twentieth century international order of states. These new actors are even less amenable to any sort of human rights appeals and mechanisms than traditional nation-states. Nor, as is clear, can they be readily controlled or defeated by conventional military campaigns, as events in Afghanistan, Iraq and Syria demonstrate. At the same time, the counter-terrorist models and measures promoted by the US and its allies – that have involved torture, rendition, detention without trial, assassinations, support for warlords or other irregular forces – violate international law and human rights norms, even if they command widespread popular political support. Novel domestic counter-terrorist regimes also impinge fundamental human rights. What we see, following the logic of the market state order described by Bobbitt (2008), is the blurring of the boundaries between criminal justice administration at home and the deployment of force abroad for military and security purposes, with the latter increasingly taking the form of 'police' actions and the former subject to ever more exceptions to rule of law principles that normally pertain to government in the domestic sphere (in relation to terrorism obviously, but the logic is also infecting responses to drugs and gangs, the militarization of border control, intensified domestic surveillance and so on). Martial and national security ends, on the one hand, and civilian law enforcement, on the other, become confused: is the aim to defeat an enemy or to restore order and bring offenders to justice? The former objective is little concerned with moral legitimacy as distinct from victory; the latter risks being self-defeating if it cannot maintain its legitimacy.

The tendency of governments to adopt a strategy of enforcement against novel threats is fuelled by other consequences of globalization, notably the weakened capacity of states to manage the volatile economic, financial, social and political forces unleashed by globalization and to respond effectively to the 'vertiginous' anxieties (Young 2007) these forces have unleashed in large sectors of the population. Bauman pinpoints the way in which complex, remote, uncontrollable sources of popular insecurity and uncertainty are all too readily collapsed into an obsession with the issue of personal safety. This in turn prompts the adoption of tough law and order measures as a palpable sign of political resolution in the protection of public safety and a salve for political impotence in the face of the deeply disruptive effects on everyday economic and social life (Bauman 1998, Chapter 5). Capturing the general mood pervading the new law and order politics Cohen referred to the rise of 'a cult of personal insecurity which links the hazards of predatory crime with other nameless risks' (Cohen 1996, p. 10). This encourages a harsh and punitive attitude, not only to crime, but also towards anybody and anything experienced as threatening the values of the 'silent majority': welfare recipients, foreign immigrants, minority rights and so on.

Gearty worries that the basis of the authority claimed by human rights and the means of their effective enforcement have been destabilized by these developments, and even that human rights is being, or may be, politically co-opted to support the very measures that threaten human rights (Gearty 2006, p. 14, Chapter 4). Where contemporary global conflict is depicted as an existential struggle between 'good' and 'evil' (as it has been in the rhetoric of many political leaders and academic commentators, such as Huntington, 1998, Ignatieff, 2004), the defence of civilization against the advance of barbarism (a 'death cult' 'coming to get us', in the words of a recent Australian prime minister), Gearty's concerns appear wholly warranted.

The more pessimistic assessments carry lessons and warnings it would be foolish to ignore. At the same time, they risk inadvertently fuelling the very political tendencies they criticize by paying insufficient attention to the evidence of a more positive kind, suggesting a long-term decline in the incidence of violence and the worst human rights abuses. The pattern of global conflict and violence has altered quite dramatically since the 1960s, with an overall and significant drop in the death toll from armed conflicts that, in part, has stemmed from a decline in the incidence of the most lethal sources of violence, wars and armed conflicts involving states. And while the end of the Cold War saw some bloody civil wars around the world, the pattern this century appears to be one of declining global incidence of political violence. Civil war and armed conflicts involving parties contending for political power has given way to the growing significance of organized criminal violence of drug cartels, terrorist groups and other non-state actors as sources of global violent death and mayhem. The violence is gruesome in its scale and character, but pales in overall lethality alongside the armed conflicts of the past (Human Security Report Project 2013, Geneva Declaration Secretariat 2015).

As the earlier analysis suggests, prevailing global conditions are volatile and it is not possible to confidently predict a continuation of these more positive trends in the overall state of global violence. It remains to be seen whether, and if so, how far, the rise of Islamic State and other violent Islamic insurgencies will affect this pattern in the future. There is also the risk that environmental catastrophe, notably the impacts of climate change, could trigger future wars and violent conflicts. For the present, however, it is significant that criminal violence (including homicide, gendered violence and the role of factors like the small arms trade, whether or not linked to armed conflicts) is being increasingly regarded as a global problem of human security that is integrally related to the challenges of economic and social development, the quality of governance and the pursuit of global justice (World Bank 2011, and see the Geneva Declaration on Armed Violence and Development).

Interestingly, these changes draw debates around global justice onto terrain more familiar to criminologists. Indeed, surveying the emerging global disorders in the 1990s, Cohen wondered whether 'for grasping today's political barbarism, the language of the sociology of crime may be uncomfortably more useful than we would like to think' (Cohen 1996, p. 18). The case is strengthened, therefore, for broadening the criminological vision beyond the borders of the nation-state to engage with issues of global security and justice (see Roberts and McMillan 2003, Aas 2012, Carrington 2015).

In the final section of this chapter I will briefly consider three related challenges this poses for a criminology of human rights in light of the dynamics of contemporary globalization.

## Criminology, human rights and globalization

> [T]he essential challenge of global ethics: how to accommodate the tension between our universal and particular natures.
>
> *(Rodin 2012, p. 33)*

Here Rodin correctly names one of the core challenges. While there is evidence suggestive of a long-term global decline in tolerance for war, armed violence, torture and other forms of cruel treatment (towards animals as well as people) – what Singer described as an 'expanding circle' of moral concern towards all sentient creatures (Singer 2011) – it is necessary to recognize the historical contingency, specificity and reversibility of any such apparent trend towards a universal humanism. It does not represent the progressive realization of some set of self-evident truths, the triumph of our universal over our particular natures (as Rodin implies), but is conditional upon the shaping of particular moral sensibilities by determinate cultural practices according to changing historical, political and economic circumstance (Bourke 2013, Hunt 2007).

Presently, a common response to the insecurities and uncertainties created by globalization has been a retreat into and a hardening of bellicose local identities and fundamentalisms, be they nationalist, racial, ethnic, religious or other. At the same time, global media and communications technologies ensure that such identities and the actions they promote are not territorially bounded. Appeals to the abstract universalism of human rights struggle to contend with the robust solidarities rooted in tradition and community, especially in times of uprooting change and pervasive uncertainty. The latter provides fertile ground for moral panics around national security (and other threats), as noted earlier. Criminology has an important role to play in analysing these dynamics and intervening in policy debates to moderate their dangerous effects.

Second, there is the related fact that norms that attract general assent in the abstract admit all manner of exceptions according to the particulars of the situation in which they are to apply and the standpoint of parties involved.

In what was a significant contribution to both criminological and human rights analyses of state crimes and atrocities, Stan Cohen (2001) examined practices of denial with respect to atrocities and other human rights abuses engaged in by governments and others, often with the implicit support of their wider communities (for an application to discourses of denial around civilian casualties in the global War on Terror see Hogg 2012). Cohen drew on Sykes and Matza's (1957) work on the techniques of neutralization that juvenile delinquents employed to deflect blame for their acts without repudiating the legal norms they had violated and on George Orwell's observations on nationalism. In his essay, 'Notes on Nationalism', Orwell explored the 'habits of mind' and emotions that are commonly generated by a tribal attachment to a group or idea. As he makes clear, his usage of the term 'nationalism' is not confined to the ordinary sense of the word but is intended to encompass other forms of extreme group identification (such as religious, racial and ideological). It involves, he argued, 'the habit of identifying oneself with a single nation or other unit, placing it beyond good and evil and recognizing no other duty than that of advancing its interests'. According to Orwell (1984 [1945], pp. 306, 307): 'Every nationalist is capable of the most flagrant dishonesty, but he is also – since he is conscious of serving something bigger than himself – unshakably certain of being in the right.' The cultural disposition of the nationalist involved a particular way of seeing the world and apprehending/framing social reality such that only certain things could be 'known' and other inconvenient events might be rendered invisible.

This disposition is served by the inevitable uncertainty concerning 'the facts'. The 'whole texture of facts in which we spend our daily life' is, as Hannah Arendt pointed out, 'vulnerable'. She noted that: 'Facts need testimony to be remembered and trustworthy witnesses to be established in order to find a secure dwelling place in the domain of human affairs' (Arendt 1973, p. 11). If this is true for everyday life it is more obviously so in the context of violent conflict, undertaken across a global canvas and in extreme conditions that are generally not conducive to gathering reliable testimonies. So as Orwell observed:

> All nationalists have the power of not seeing resemblances between similar sets of facts. . . . Actions are held to be good or bad, not on their own merits but according to who does them, and there is almost no kind of outrage – torture, the use of hostages, forced labour, mass deportations, imprisonment without trial, forgery, assassination, the bombing of civilians – which does not change its moral colour when it is committed by 'our' side. . . . The nationalist not only does not disapprove of atrocities committed by his own side, but has a remarkable capacity for not even hearing about them.
>
> *(Orwell 1984 [1945], p. 313)*

Orwell, Cohen and others leave us with a powerful sense of the precariousness of civilized norms and the importance of situated cultural dispositions in framing how violence and suffering are understood and responded to in different communities and contexts.

Finally, rights talk is inevitably entangled with legalism. This is perhaps unsurprising given the understandable desire to give human rights the force of law, to secure them as non-negotiable norms and thus (as much as possible) entrench them outside and above politics. As Gearty points out, however, this carries a range of pitfalls (2006, Chapter 3). The narrow end of entrenching certain (often vaguely defined and not always readily enforceable) rights as individualized entitlements risks sacrificing the radical potential of human rights as an emancipatory political project. Questions of power and of the forms of governance and collective provision needed to achieve human security in a limited sense, let alone economic redistribution and social justice, are simply avoided.

Cohen (2001) also questioned the role of legalism because, he argued, it is particularly amenable to strategies of interpretive denial. Controversy is readily drawn into abstruse, technical, hair-splitting disputes over words and events in which meaning and substance are erased or obscured. The torture memos of the Bush Administration during the War on Terror provide a case in point. Laden with euphemism, technical jargon and a pronounced reliance on nouns over verbs – like 'enhanced interrogation techniques', 'force multipliers', 'sleep adjustments' – they were calculated to mask and divert, until the confronting images from Abu Ghraib blew the pettifogging legalisms away (Hogg 2012, pp. 101–4). This is a yet further reminder that effective responses to human rights abuses require an understanding of the 'cultural lives' of law, rights and security (Loader 2007).

## Concluding comments

Human rights, as rights accorded all people by virtue simply of their status as human, are rights that do not depend upon formal membership of a political community: being a citizen of a state. Yet, in the absence of a global community and sovereign capable of enforcing such rights, states remain the pivotal actors in the legislation and administration of all rights. This may serve to further underline the arguments above as to the limitations of viewing human rights through a narrow legal lens. Gearty reminds us that the objective of the human rights movement is 'the proper achievement of human rights' (2006, p. 4), that is certain conditions of life rather than the passage of treaties, declarations, bills of rights and laws which, at best, provide merely some of the means. Modern human rights are vitally concerned to prevent the wanton infliction of suffering – genocide, torture, slavery, killing, cruelty, humiliation and discrimination – and, more positively, to promote human flourishing and betterment in the lives of all (Gearty 2006, pp. 5–7). The two sets of rights are closely related insofar as conditions of economic and social injustice commonly provide the context in which abuses of the first kind are most prevalent. Although acknowledging this interrelatedness in the different generations of human rights (and the relevance of criminology to illuminating the connections), my focus has been on the contemporary challenges that globalization and its impact on patterns of crime and violent conflict pose for human rights and criminology at the present time.

The right to a life free from violence is the most fundamental of human rights and an essential pre-condition for the realization of others. The recent trend to approach the threat of violence in all its various forms – armed conflicts, abuses by states, organized criminal violence, homicide and violence against women – as a global human security issue represents a significant shift in thinking, reflecting the novelty of challenges posed by globalization. It may also encourage a growing convergence of the traditional concerns of the human rights movement with the research interests, theories and methods of criminology. At the same time as they draw lessons from each other, they would also do well to look outward for the constant intellectual and political renewal needed to meet the proliferating challenges of the present.

## Note

1 (*R v Bartle and the Commissioner of Police for the Metropolis; ex parte Pinochet (No 2)*)(1999) 1 All ER 577.

## References


Aas, F., 2012. 'The earth is one but the world is not': criminological theory and its geopolitical divisions. *Theoretical Criminology*, 16(1), 5–20.

Arendt, H., 1973. Lying in politics. *In*: H. Arendt, *Crises of the republic*. London: Penguin, 9–42.

Bauman, Z., 1998. *Globalization: the human consequences*. Cambridge: Polity Press.

Beckert, S., 2014. *Empire of cotton: a new history of global capitalism*. London: Allen Lane.

Bobbitt, P., 2003. *The shield of Achilles: war, peace and the course of history*. London: Penguin.

Bobbitt, P., 2008. *Terror and consent: the wars for the twenty-first century*. London: Allen Lane.

Bourke, J., 2013. *What it means to be human: reflections from 1791 to the present*. London: Virago.

Carrington, K., 2015. *Feminism and global justice*. London: Routledge.

Cohen, S., 1996. Crime and politics: spot the difference. *British Journal of Sociology*, 47(1), 1–21.

Cohen, S. 2001. *States of denial*. Cambridge: Polity.

Cooper, R., 2004. *The breaking of nations: order and chaos in the twenty first century*. London: Atlantic Books.

Davidson, J. and Rees-Mogg, W., 1998. *The sovereign individual*. London: Pan Books.

Gearty, C., 2006. *Can human rights survive?* Cambridge: Cambridge University Press.

Geneva Declaration on Armed Violence and Development. Retrieved on 2 April 2016 from: www.genevadeclaration.org/.

Geneva Declaration Secretariat, 2015. *Global burden of armed violence 2015: every body counts*. Retrieved on 2 April 2016 from: www.genevadeclaration.org/measurability/global-burden-of-armed-violence/global-burden-of-armed-violence-2015.html.

Giddens, A., 2002. *Runaway world: how globalisation is reshaping our lives*. London: Profile Books.

Green, P. and Ward, T., 2004. *State crime: governments, violence and corruption*. London: Pluto Press.

Hirst, P., 2001. *War and power in the 21st century*. London: Polity.

Hogg, R., 2002. Criminology beyond the nation state: global conflicts, human rights and the 'new global disorder'. *In*: K. Carrington and R. Hogg (eds), *Critical criminology*. Cullompton: Willan, 185–217.

Hogg, R., 2012. Law, death and denial in the 'Global War on Terror'. *In*: S. Bronitt, M. Gani and S. Hufnagel (eds), *Shooting to kill: socio-legal perspectives on the use of lethal force*. Oxford: Hart, 83–104.
Human Security Report Project, 2013. *Human security report 2013: the decline in global violence: evidence, explanation, and contestation*. Vancouver: Human Security Press. Retrieved on 2 April 2016 from: www.hsrgroup.org/docs/Publications/HSR2013/HSRP_Report_2013_140226_Web.pdf.
Hunt, L., 2007. *Inventing human rights: a history*. New York, NY: W.W. Norton and Co.
Huntington, S., 1998. *The clash of civilizations and the remaking of world order*. London: Touchstone Books.
Ignatieff, M., 2004. *The lesser evil: political ethics in an age of terror*. Edinburgh: University of Edinburgh Press.
Kuper, L., 1989. The sovereign territorial state: the right to genocide. *In*: R. Claude and B. Weston (eds), *Human rights in the world community*. Philadelphia, PA: University of Pennsylvania Press, 56–64.
Loader, I., 2007. The cultural lives of security and rights. *In*: B. Goold and L. Lazarus (eds), *Security and human rights*. Oxford: Hart Publishing, 27–44.
Mahbubani, K., 2013. *The great convergence: Asia, the west, and the logic of one world*. New York, NY: Public Affairs.
Mill, J.S., 1993 [1859]. *On liberty*. *In*: G. Williams (ed.), *Utilitarianism, on liberty, considerations on representative government*. London: Everyman, 69–185.
Orwell, G., 1984 [1945]. Notes on nationalism. *The Penguin essays of George Orwell*. London: Penguin Books, 306–23. *Notes on Nationalism by George Orwell (Copyright © George Orwell, 1945)*. Reprinted by permission of Bill Hamilton as the Literary Executor of the Estate of the Late Sonia Brownell Orwell.
Roberts, P. and McMillan, N., 2003. For criminology in international criminal justice. *Journal of International Criminal Justice*, 1, 315–338.
Robertson, G., 2006. *Crimes against humanity: the struggle for global justice*, 3rd edn. London: Penguin.
Rodin, D., 2012. Toward a global ethic. *Ethics and International Affairs*, 26(1), 33–42.
Savelsberg, J., 2010. *Crime and human rights*. London: Sage.
Schwendinger, H. and Schwendinger, J., 1975. Defenders of order or guardians of human rights? *In*: I. Taylor, P. Walton and J. Young (eds), *Critical criminology*. London: Routledge & Kegan Paul, 113–46.
Singer, P., 2002. *One world: the ethics of globalisation*. Melbourne: Text Publishing.
Singer, P., 2011. *The expanding circle: ethics, evolution, and moral progress*. Princeton, NJ: Princeton University Press.
Sykes, G. and Matza, D., 1957. Techniques of neutralization: a theory of delinquency. *American Sociological Review*, 22, 664–70.
Young, J., 2007. *The vertigo of late modernity*. London: Sage.
World Bank, 2011. *World development report 2011: conflict, security, and development, overview*. Washington, DC: World Bank.

# Part II

# Law, regulation and governance through a human rights lens

Human rights have become a key concept through which to unpack the law at international and domestic level. The 'shield' function and the 'sword' function of human rights in the application of criminal law are often cited. This refers to the ability of human rights to empower law to function better (sword) or to limit or stop the law from causing damage (shield). Yet, is this binary function of human rights having such an impact on law and governance?

The readings in this section engage, albeit implicitly, with this question. The defensive-offensive role of human rights in relation to criminal law is discussed more as an ideal than a reality. Through the various chapters in this section, we note a common theme emerging. Many authors reflect on how the state has used its legislative powers with sophistication to advance its own agenda of expansion and dominance. This occurs to the detriment of human rights and yet the state covers its action or omission while also engaging with a human rights narrative.

The section opens with a chapter by Valsamis Mitsilegas on the recent development of criminal law and human rights in the European Union (EU). This discussion gives us an opportunity to reflect on the transnationalism and versatility of human rights in a system of states, which are fairly different from each other, albeit with some historical similarities. An emerging point is a reflection on how the introduction of a Charter of Human Rights at the EU level contributes to the strengthening of the supranational body over national states 'through the normalisation – and thus enhancement – of the powers of the European Commission and of the Court of Justice to monitor the implementation of EU criminal law by Member States' (Mitsilegas, Chapter 11 this volume).

This is followed by a discussion on digital surveillance by Didier Bigo, on anti-terrorism legislation by Nicola McGarrity and Jessie Blackbourn, followed by a shift to an examination of the secrecy of local coronial inquests by Rebecca Scott-Bray and an analysis of state crime by Michael Grewcock. These chapters discuss the law and governance of cyber security, military operations, terrorism, secrecy and border security in the context of human rights. Here, the binary shield/sword model of human rights shows its weaknesses, given the 'destabilisation' of basic human rights principles on 'everyday democracy' (Bigo), the normalization of secrecy and investigatory powers in the case of anti-terrorist legislation (McGarrity and Blackbourn) and death investigation (Scott-Bray), and through the state violation of international human rights obligations by imprisoning children in offshore immigration detention centres (Grewcock).

The next two chapters focus on corruption, multinational corporations and state crimes. Common to these discussions is the theme of harm to citizens and non-citizens which it is argued ought to be of high interest from a human rights perspective concerned with law and governance. The analysis by Tony Ward on state organizational deviance and perception of corruption sheds lights on neoliberal ideals of good governance, which build an invisible barrier to a better understanding and appreciation of harms. Along the same lines, Fiona Haines reflects on the challenges posed by the strong support for capitalist industrialization even with existing human rights obligations of multinational enterprises.

The treatment of children and cognitively impaired people by the law is discussed in the next two chapters. Kathryn Hollingsworth discusses children's rights and the importance of ensuring that they are legally enforceable. Claire Spivakovsky reflects on how human rights 'logics' can be exploited to favour the state interest in the case of cognitive impairment and mental illness. These chapters select two of many categories of people whose human rights have been historically violated or undermined by the law as a way of offering an example of a current vigorous debate on the binary function of human rights and the arduous road ahead.

The two chapters that follow offer a macro-reflection on human rights, legal practices, social and cultural and 'green' identity through a discussion on safeguarding the environment (Johnson, South and Walters) and international cultural heritage (Mackenzie and Yates). In both cases, it is evident that a new way is emerging to consider how to balance existing legislation on human-centric entitlements, property rights, self-determination and protections against harm through adopting a criminological and human rights lens.

Arising from the above chapters is a healthy debate on how much the human rights regime has influenced practices of law and governance; and yet how much more can be done in each of the selected topics to allow the full potential of human rights, law and discourse to be realized. The danger, highlighted by some, is the misuse of the human rights narrative to serve other interests.

# 11

# The European Union, criminal law and human rights

*Valsamis Mitsilegas*

## Introduction

The past 15 years have witnessed a remarkable rise of European Union (EU) criminal law as a distinct legal, policy and academic field. The proliferation of EU measures in the field, many of which were adopted in response to major security incidents including 9/11 and the London and Madrid bombings, have resulted in a legal landscape focused heavily on security, and with limited emphasis on the protection of human rights. The entry into force of the Treaty of Lisbon in 2009 had the potential to change this landscape in three ways: by the introduction of specific, high-level commitments by the EU to uphold human rights – most notably via the constitutionalization of the EU Charter of Fundamental Rights and the commitment for the Union to accede to the *European Convention on Human Rights* (ECHR); by granting the EU, for the first time in the history of European integration, of express competence to legislate on human rights, by embarking on a minimum harmonization of Member State legislation in the field of criminal procedure, including the rights of the suspect and the accused in criminal proceedings; and by strengthening the institutional framework in the field of EU criminal law, through the normalization – and thus enhancement – of the powers of the European Commission and of the Court of Justice to monitor the implementation of EU criminal law by Member States. This chapter will examine the impact of the entry into force of the Treaty of Lisbon on human rights protection in the context of European integration in criminal matters. It will start by analysing the impact of the constitutionalization of the Charter of Fundamental Rights on EU criminal law; it will continue by explaining the application of the principle of mutual recognition in the field of criminal justice, and evaluate the place of human rights in a system which is largely based on a high level of trust between national authorities based on the presumption that the systems of all EU Member States are compliant with their human rights obligations save in exceptional circumstances. The chapter will continue by evaluating the impact of new EU legislation on defence rights on the operation of mutual recognition, and will highlight the transformative impact of not only these measures, but also of the enhanced monitoring powers of EU institutions, for the protection of human rights in the field of EU criminal justice after Lisbon.

## The impact of the charter of fundamental rights

A key development in the protection of human rights in the field of EU criminal law post-Lisbon has been the constitutionalization of the Charter of Fundamental Rights, which has the same legal value as the Treaties (Article 6[1] of the TEU; see Craig 2010, p. 200) and has been seen as contributing to reinforcing the centrality of fundamental rights in the EU legal order (Sanchez 2012, p. 1582). The Charter contains a separate Title, Title VI, on Justice. Title VI enshrines key rights and principles for the development of EU criminal law including the right to an effective remedy and to a fair trial [Article 47], the presumption of innocence and right of defence [Article 48], the principles of legality and proportionality of criminal offences and penalties [Article 49] and the right not to be tried or punished twice in criminal proceedings for the same criminal offence [Article 50]. Further Charter rights which are relevant to EU criminal law include rights and principles enshrined in Title I of the Charter on dignity (including the provisions on human dignity [Article 1], the right to life [Article 2], the right to the integrity of the person [Article 3] and the prohibition of torture and inhuman or degrading treatment or punishment [Article 4]), in Title II on freedoms (including the provisions on the right to liberty and security [Article 6], the respect for private and family life [Article 7] and the protection of personal data [Article 8] as well as the provisions on freedom of expression and information [Article 11], freedom of assembly and association [Article 12], right to property [Article 17] and protection in the event of removal, expulsion or extradition [Article 18]), in Title III on Equality (most notably the provisions on equality before the law [Article 20], non-discrimination [Article 23] and the rights of the child [Article 24]) and in Title V on citizens' rights (including the right to good administration [Article 41], the right of access to documents [Article 42] and freedom of movement and of residence [Article 45]). A wide range of Articles thus, the majority of the Charter provisions, are relevant and applicable in the implementation of EU criminal law. The impact of the Charter in this context will be analysed in detail throughout this volume. Linked to the protection by the Charter is the emphasis of the Lisbon Treaty on other sources of rights. Fundamental rights as guaranteed by the ECHR and as they result from the constitutional traditions common to the Member States constitute general principles of the Union's law (Article 6[3] of the TEU). The Treaty also calls for the Union's accession to the ECHR (Article 6[2] of the TEU).

The influence of the Charter in the development of EU criminal law after Lisbon is not limited to the interpretation of the content of EU criminal law in conformity with the Charter. It is also crucial when determining the scope of application and interpretation of rights and the level of protection provided by the Charter – aspects which are addressed in the final, horizontal provisions of the Charter.[1] These provisions aim to regulate the relationship between the Charter and national law on the one hand, and the relationship between the Charter and other sources of human rights protection (including the ECHR) on the other. The Court of Justice has thus far intervened on both aspects. In the seminal ruling in *Melloni*, the Court found that EU law which is found to be in compliance with the Charter has primacy over national constitutional law which provides a higher level of protection.[2] While this ruling may be seen as lowering the protection of fundamental rights in certain jurisdictions, the Court has compensated for this potential outcome (which was explained by the need to ensure the primacy, unity and effectiveness of Union law) by adopting a broad interpretation of what constitutes the implementation of Union law which triggers the application of the Charter under Article 51(1) of the Charter. In the case of *Fransson*,[3] the Court of Justice adopted a broad interpretation of the application of the Charter, including in cases where national legislation does not implement expressly or directly an EU criminal law instrument. The Court found that domestic law on

VAT fraud does fall within EU law since there is a direct link between the collection of VAT revenue in compliance with the EU law applicable and the availability to the EU budget of the corresponding VAT resources (para. 26). The Court of Justice developed its approach on the applicability of the Charter in *Siragusa*[4] where it ruled that the concept of 'implementing Union law', as referred to in Article 51 of the Charter, requires a certain degree of connection above and beyond the matters covered being closely related or one of those matters having an indirect impact on the other (para. 24). As will be seen in the section on implementation below, the Court's approach has the effect of including a wide range of national legislation and measures related to national criminal justice systems within the scope of the Charter. This view is reinforced by the Court's finding in *Siragusa* that it is important to consider the objective of protecting fundamental rights in EU law, which is to ensure that those rights are not infringed in areas of EU activity, whether through action at EU level or through the implementation of EU law by the Member States (para. 31).

## Mutual recognition, mutual trust and human rights

A key testing ground for the relationship between EU criminal law and the protection of human rights has been the application of the principle of mutual recognition in criminal matters.[5] The construction of the Area of Freedom, Security and Justice as an area without internal frontiers has intensified and justified automaticity in inter-state cooperation (Mitsilegas 2012). Automaticity in inter-state cooperation means that a *national* decision will be enforced beyond the territory of the issuing Member State by authorities in other EU Member States across the Area of Freedom, Security and Justice without many questions being asked and with the requested authority having at its disposal extremely limited – if any at all – grounds to refuse the request for cooperation. The method chosen to secure such automaticity has been the application of the principle of mutual recognition in the fields of judicial cooperation in criminal matters. Mutual recognition is attractive to Member States resisting further harmonization or unification in European criminal law as mutual recognition is thought to enhance inter-state cooperation in criminal matters without Member States having to change their national laws to comply with EU harmonization requirements (Mitsilegas 2006). Mutual recognition creates extraterritoriality (Nicolaïdis and Shaffer 2005): in a borderless Area of Freedom, Security and Justice, the will of an authority in one Member State can be enforced beyond its territorial legal borders and across this area. The acceptance of such extraterritoriality requires a high level of mutual trust between the authorities which take part in the system premised upon the acceptance that membership of the EU means that all EU Member States are fully compliant with fundamental rights norms. It is the acceptance of the high level of integration among EU Member States which has justified automaticity in inter-state cooperation and has led to the adoption of a series of EU instruments which in this context go beyond pre-existing, traditional forms of cooperation set out under public international law, which have afforded a greater degree of scrutiny to requests for cooperation. Membership of the EU *presumes* the full respect of fundamental rights by all Member States, which creates mutual trust which in turn forms the basis of automaticity in inter-state cooperation in Europe's area of criminal justice. The best example of mutual recognition in these terms is the system introduced by the Framework Decision on the European Arrest Warrant.[6] Automaticity and speed are coupled with the inclusion of only limited grounds of refusal to recognize and execute a Warrant. The Framework Decision includes only three, in their majority procedural, mandatory grounds for refusal (Article 3) which are complemented by a series of optional grounds for refusal (Article 4) and provisions on guarantees underpinning the surrender process (Articles 5, 27 and 28). Non-compliance with fundamental rights is not, however, included as a ground to refuse to execute a European Arrest Warrant. This legislative choice reflects the view that cooperation can take place on the basis of a high level of mutual trust in the criminal justice systems of Member States, premised upon the presumption that fundamental rights are in principle respected fully across the EU.

In a consistent line of case law starting before the entry into force of the Lisbon Treaty, the Court of Justice has adopted a broad approach to mutual recognition, embracing a teleological interpretation and stressing the need to achieve the effectiveness of the Framework Decision by ensuring that in principle mutual recognition takes place in a speedy and simplified manner.[7] The entry into force of the Treaty of Lisbon has added a further dimension to the question the extent to which fundamental rights concerns should be taken into account and form grounds of refusal in a system of mutual recognition based on mutual trust. The Lisbon Treaty has signified the constitutionalization of the EU Charter of Fundamental Rights and it was a matter of time before the Court of Justice would be asked to examine the compatibility of the system of mutual recognition with the Charter. The first major case in this context was the case of *Radu*,[8] in which the Court of Justice was asked for the first time in such a direct manner by a national court on whether mutual recognition could be refused on fundamental rights grounds. In the present case, the Court answered in the negative. The Court reaffirmed the adoption of a teleological interpretation reiterating the purpose of establishing a simplified and more effective system of surrender based on mutual recognition (paras 33 and 34). Such system will contribute to the Union's objective of becoming an area of freedom, security and justice by basing itself on the high degree of confidence which should exist between the Member States (para. 34). On the basis of this presumption of mutual trust, the Court found that the observance of Articles 47 and 48 of the Charter does not require that a judicial authority of a Member State should be able to refuse to execute a European arrest warrant issued for the purposes of conducting a criminal prosecution on the ground that the requested person was not heard by the issuing judicial authorities before that warrant was issued (para. 39). Once again the Court placed effectiveness considerations at the forefront of its reasoning. It pointed out that such an obligation would inevitably lead to the failure of the very system of surrender (para. 40) and added that in any event, the right to be heard will be observed in the executing Member State in such a way as not to compromise the effectiveness of the European arrest warrant system (para. 41). *Radu* thus follows the Court's earlier case law in two respects: it confirms that it is satisfied with the provision of fundamental rights protection in one of the two states which take part in the cooperative mutual recognition system – here, it is the executing state which is under the duty to uphold the right to be heard; and it places the protection of fundamental rights within a clear framework of effectiveness of the enforcement cooperation system which is established by the Framework Decision on the European Arrest Warrant. Too extensive a protection of fundamental rights (in both the issuing and the executing state) would undermine the effectiveness of law enforcement cooperation in this context.

The focus on the effective operation of mutual recognition was reiterated by the Court of Justice in the case of *Melloni*.[9] In *Melloni*, the Court effectively confirmed the primacy of third pillar law (the European Arrest Warrant Framework Decision as amended by the Framework Decision on judgements in absentia, interpreted in the light of the Charter) has primacy over national constitutional law providing a higher level of fundamental rights protection. In order to reach this far-reaching conclusion, the Court followed a three-step approach. The first step for the Court was to demarcate the scope of the Framework Decision on the European Arrest Warrant as amended by the Framework Decision on judgements in absentia (and in particular Article 4a[1] thereof) in order to establish the extent of the limits of mutual recognition in such cases. The Court reiterated its reasoning in *Radu* in adopting a teleological interpretation of the

European Arrest Warrant Framework Decision and stressing that under the latter Member States are in principle obliged to act upon a European Arrest Warrant (paras 36–8). In the light of these findings, the Court adopted a literal interpretation of Article 4a(1), confirming that that provision restricts the opportunities for refusing to execute a European Arrest Warrant (para. 41). That interpretation is confirmed by the mutual recognition objectives of EU law (para. 43). The second step was to examine the compatibility of the above system with fundamental rights and in particular the right to an effective judicial remedy and the right to fair trial set out in Articles 47 and 48(2) of the Charter. The Court of Justice found that the right of an accused person to appear in person at his trial is not absolute but can be waived (para. 49). The Court further stated that the objective of the Framework Decision on judgements in absentia was to enhance procedural rights whilst improving mutual recognition of judicial decisions between Member States (para. 51) and found Article 4a(1) compatible with the Charter.

Having asserted the compatibility of the relevant provision with the Charter, the third step for the Court was to rule on the relationship between secondary EU law in question with national constitutional law which provided a higher level of protection. The Court rejected an interpretation of Article 53 of the Charter as giving general authorization to a Member State to apply the standard of protection of fundamental rights guaranteed by its constitution when that standard is higher than that deriving from the Charter and, where necessary, to give it priority over the application of provisions of EU law (paras 56–7). That interpretation of Article 53 would undermine the principle of the primacy of EU law inasmuch as it would allow a Member State to disapply EU legal rules which are fully in compliance with the Charter where they infringe the fundamental rights guaranteed by that State's constitution (para. 58). Article 53 of the Charter provides freedom to national authorities to apply national human rights standards provided that the level of protection provided for by the Charter, as interpreted by the Court, and the primacy, unity and effectiveness of EU law are not thereby compromised (para. 60). In the present case, Article 4a(1) of Framework Decision 2002/584 does not allow Member States to refuse to execute a European arrest warrant when the person concerned is in one of the situations provided for therein (para. 61). The Framework Decision on judgements in absentia is intended to remedy the difficulties associated with the mutual recognition of decisions rendered in the absence of the person concerned at his trial arising from the differences as among the Member States in the protection of fundamental rights and reflects the consensus reached by all the Member States regarding the scope to be given under EU law to the procedural rights enjoyed by persons convicted in absentia who are the subject of a European arrest warrant (para. 62). Consequently, allowing a Member State to avail itself of Article 53 of the Charter to make the surrender of a person convicted in absentia conditional upon the conviction being open to review in the issuing Member State in order to avoid an adverse effect on the right to a fair trial and the rights of the defence guaranteed by the constitution of the executing Member State, by casting doubt on the uniformity of the standard of protection of fundamental rights as defined in that framework decision, would undermine the principles of mutual trust and recognition which that decision purports to uphold and would, therefore, compromise the efficacy of that framework decision (para. 63).

The Court's emphasis on the centrality of mutual trust as a factor privileging the achievement of law enforcement objectives via mutual recognition over the protection of fundamental rights has been reiterated beyond EU criminal law in the broader context of the accession of the EU to the ECHR. Opinion 2/13 has included a specific part dealing with mutual trust in EU law. The Court has distilled its current thinking on mutual trust stating that:

> it should be noted that the principle of mutual trust between the Member States is of fundamental importance in EU law, given that it allows an area without internal borders to

> be created and maintained. That principle requires, particularly with regard to the area of freedom, security and justice, each of those states, save in exceptional circumstances, to consider all the other Member States to be complying with EU law and particularly with the fundamental rights recognized by EU law.

and adding that:

> when implementing EU law, the Member States may, under EU law, be required to presume that fundamental rights have been observed by the other Member States, so that not only may they not demand a higher level of national protection of fundamental rights from another Member State than that provided by EU law, but, save in exceptional cases, they may not check whether that other Member State has actually, in a specific case, observed the fundamental rights guaranteed by the EU.
>
> *(Opinion 2/13, paras 191–2)*

From the perspective of the relationship between EU criminal law and fundamental rights, this passage is striking. The passage follows a series of comments on the role of Article 53 of the Charter in preserving the autonomy of EU law, with the Court citing the *Melloni* requirement for upholding the primacy, unity and effectiveness of EU law (para. 188). The Court then puts forward a rather extreme view of presumed mutual trust leading to automatic mutual recognition. It thus represents a significant challenge to our understanding of the EU constitutional order as a legal order underpinned by the protection of fundamental rights. The Court deifies mutual trust and endorses a system whereby the protection of fundamental rights must be subsumed to the abstract requirements of upholding mutual trust, instead of endorsing a model of a Union whereby cooperation on the basis of mutual trust must be underpinned by an effective protection of fundamental rights. The Court asserts boldly that mutual trust is not only a principle, but also a principle of fundamental importance in EU law. However, this assertion seems to disregard the inherently subjective nature of trust and the difficulties in providing an objective definition that meets the requirements of legal certainty. It is further clear that, although mutual trust is viewed by the Court as inextricably linked with the establishment of an area without internal borders (at the heart of whose is the free movement principle and the rights of EU citizens), the Court perceives mutual trust as limited to trust 'between the Member States' – the citizen or affected individual by the exercise of state enforcement power under mutual recognition is markedly absent from the Court's reasoning. This approach leads to the uncritical acceptance of presumed trust across the EU: not only are Member States not allowed to demand a higher national protection of fundamental rights than the one provided by EU law (thus echoing *Melloni*), but also, and remarkably, Member States are not allowed to check (save in exceptional circumstances) whether fundamental rights have been observed in other Member States in *specific* cases. This finding is striking as it disregards a number of developments in secondary EU criminal law aiming to grant executing authorities the opportunity to check whether execution of a judicial decision by authorities of another Member State would comply with fundamental rights.[10] It also represents a fundamental philosophical and substantive difference in the protection of fundamental rights between the Luxembourg and Strasbourg Courts.[11]

## Legislating for human rights: the rights of the defendant

For the first time, the Lisbon Treaty confers upon the EU express competence to adopt minimum rules on the rights of individuals in criminal procedure in Article 82(2) TFEU. On the basis of this provision, a number of measures on the rights of the individual in criminal procedure have been adopted. These are thus far a Directive on the right to interpretation and translation;[12] a Directive on the right to information;[13] and a Directive on the right to access to a lawyer.[14] The Commission has also published a Green Paper on the application of EU criminal justice legislation in the field of detention[15] and tabled, in November 2013, a number of draft Directives on legal aid,[16] procedural safeguards for children[17] and the presumption of innocence.[18] These proposals have been accompanied by Commission Recommendations on the right to legal aid[19] and on procedural safeguards for vulnerable persons.[20] The adoption of EU measures harmonizing national law on the rights of the individual in criminal proceedings has a transformative effect (Mitsilegas 2016a). It signals a paradigm shift from a system focused primarily – if not solely – on promoting the interests of the state and of law enforcement under rules of quasi-automatic mutual recognition to a system where the rights of individuals affected by such rules are brought into the fore, protected by and enforced in EU law. There are four main ways in which the Directives on procedural rights in criminal procedure will enhance the protection of fundamental rights in EU Member States. First of all, a number of key provisions conferring rights in the Directives have direct effect. This means that, in a system of decentralized enforcement of EU law, individuals can evoke and claim rights directly before their national courts if the EU Directives have not been implemented or have been inadequately implemented. Direct effect means in practice that a suspect or accused person can derive a number of key rights – such as the right to an interpreter or the right to access to a lawyer – directly from EU law if national legislation has not made appropriate provision in conformity with EU law. Second, this avenue of decentralized enforcement is coupled with the high level of centralized enforcement of EU criminal law which has been 'normalized' after the entry into force of the Lisbon Treaty. The European Commission now has full powers to monitor the implementation of these Directives by Member States and has the power to introduce infringement proceedings before the Court of Justice when it considers that the Directives have not been implemented adequately. Third, national criminal procedural law must be applied and interpreted in compliance and conformity with the Directives. The procedural standards set out in the Directives will have an impact on a wide range of acts under national criminal procedure.[21] Fourth, the implementation of the Directives must take place in compliance with the Charter of Fundamental Rights. The Charter will apply not only to national legislation which specifically implements the EU Directives on procedural rights, but also to all other elements of domestic criminal procedure which have a connection with EU law on procedural rights in criminal proceedings (see Mitsilegas 2015, upon which this section is based).

## Monitoring human rights: evaluation and implementation

A central feature of the development of EU criminal law after Lisbon is the emphasis on the monitoring of the implementation of Member States' commitments in the field. On a political level, this emphasis can be explained on the one hand by the need to achieve the smooth transition from the intergovernmental third pillar to the largely supranational Lisbon reality by ensuring in particular the full implementation of pre-Lisbon third pillar law, while on the other hand it may mask the reluctance of Member States to proceed to the adoption of a new raft of new EU legislation in EU criminal law. This approach has been reflected in the European Council Conclusions which followed up the end of the Stockholm Programme, according to which building on the past programmes, the overall priority now is to consistently transpose, effectively implement and consolidate the legal instruments and policy measures in place.[22] Irrespective of whether this approach will have the effect of stifling the Union's legislative ambition in the field, the emphasis on implementation and transposition is key in ensuring the effectiveness of EU law in the field and may have far-reaching consequences for national criminal justice systems which will have to be increasingly scrutinized to ensure their conformity with EU law, including the Charter. As seen above, the Commission has assumed post-Lisbon its full powers as guardian of the treaties to monitor implementation of Title V law (and, from 1 December 2014, also third pillar law) and introduce infringement proceedings in cases where national implementation is deemed to be defective. These supranational powers of the Commission are coupled in the Lisbon Treaty with a more intergovernmental level of evaluation established by Article 70 TFEU. The latter establishes a legal basis for the adoption of a system whereby, without prejudice to the infringement powers of the Commission and the Court of Justice, Member States, in collaboration with the Commission, conduct objective and impartial evaluation of the implementation of the Union policies referred to in Title V by Member States' authorities, in particular in order to facilitate full application of the principle of mutual recognition. The European Parliament and national parliaments will be informed of the content and results of the evaluation. The Treaty provides thus two parallel mechanisms of monitoring of the implementation of EU criminal law by Member States, although Article 70 TFEU has not been used extensively since the entry into force of the Lisbon Treaty. What is key in this context is also *what* is going to be evaluated. It is submitted that the Court's case law on the applicability of the Charter combined with the EU law requirement for Member States to ensure the effectiveness of EU law generate the requirement that the scrutiny of implementation of EU criminal law by Member States is not limited to the scrutiny of the implementation of specific provisions set out in Directives and Framework Decisions, but also includes a holistic scrutiny of domestic criminal justice systems to the extent that elements of the latter have a degree of connection with the implementation of EU criminal law along the lines of the Court's approach in *Siragusa*. To give two concrete examples of where such degree of connection may exist: in the case of mutual recognition, the monitoring of the implementation of measures such as the Framework Decisions on the European Arrest Warrant or on the Transfer of Sentenced Persons cannot be complete without monitoring of prison conditions at EU level. Similarly in the case of the European Arrest Warrant scrutiny of implementation must include scrutiny of pre-trial detention length and conditions in Member States, as well as scrutiny of the duration of pre-trial periods. The second example involves the implementation of the rights of the defendant in criminal proceedings. It is submitted that effective implementation of the relevant Directives will only be ensured if national criminal justice systems are scrutinized holistically from the police station to trial and if scrutiny also covers the levels of resources Member States commit towards the effective implementation of EU law (Mitsilegas 2016b). The emphasis on implementation in this manner has the potential to have – along with the content of EU law – a transformative effect on national criminal justice systems.

## Conclusion

The entry into force of the Lisbon Treaty has already triggered significant changes in the relationship between EU criminal law and the protection of human rights. The constitutionalization of the Charter of Fundamental Rights has placed both EU institutions and Member States under enhanced obligations to comply with human rights. Compliance with the Charter is not limited to cases where Member States have implemented specific provisions of secondary EU criminal legislation, but extends to national measures that have a connection with the implementation of EU measures as per the case law of the Court of Justice. To take the example of the European arrest warrant: this means in practice that Member States are under an obligation to comply with the Charter not only when they implement specific provisions of the Framework Decision on the European Arrest Warrant, but also when they operate aspects of their criminal justice systems (such as pre-trial detention) for individuals subject to the European arrest warrant procedure. This holistic approach strengthens and extends the powers of the Commission and the Court of Justice to monitor compliance by Member States with human rights in the field of EU criminal law. In terms of the actual operation of EU secondary legislation in the field of criminal law, mutual recognition is still based on a high level of presumed trust, with the Court of Justice being reluctant to give meaningful space to the examination of human rights claims by the courts of the executing Member State. This approach is strikingly at odds with the approach taken by the European Court of Human Rights, which has emphasized the need for a case-by-case examination of the human rights consequences of action by Member States and has not adopted the high threshold of mutual trust put forward by the Court of Justice. It remains to be seen whether and to what extent there is space for convergence of the positions of the two courts on the protection of human rights in the field of criminal justice. In the meantime, the adoption of specific EU secondary law on the rights of the defence has a transformative potential, in enhancing the protection of human rights on the ground across the EU.

## Notes

1 See, in particular, Articles 51–3 of the Charter. For commentaries see, inter alia, Lenaerts 2012, Sarmiento 2013, and Fontanelli 2014.
2 Case C-399/11, *Melloni*, judgement of 26 February 2013. For an analysis see Chapter 5 on mutual recognition.
3 Case C-617/10, *Åklagaren v Hans Åkerberg Fransson*, judgement of 26 February 2013.
4 Case C-206/13, *Siragusa*, judgement of 6 March 2014.
5 For a recent analysis, see Mitsilegas 2015, upon which this section is based.
6 Framework Decision 2002/584/JHA of 13 June 2002 on the European Arrest Warrant [2002] OJ L 190/1.
7 See, inter alia, Case C-303/05 *Advocaten voor de Wereld* [2007] ECR I-3633 para. 28; Case C-388/08 PPU, *Leymann and Pustovarov*, para. 42; Case C-192/12 PPU, *Melvin West*, para. 56; Case C-168/13 PPU, *Jeremy F.*, para. 35.
8 Case C-396/11, *Radu*, judgement of 29 January 2013.
9 Case C-399/11, *Melloni*, judgement of 26 February 2013.
10 The post-Lisbon Directive on the European Investigation Order has introduced an optional ground for non-recognition or non-execution: where there are substantial grounds to believe that the execution of the investigative measure indicated in the EIO would be incompatible with the executing State's obligations in accordance with Article 6 TEU and the Charter (Article 11[1][f]). Directive 2014/41/EU of the European Parliament and of the Council of 3 April 2014 regarding the European Investigation Order in criminal matters, OJ L130, 1.5.2014, p. 1.
11 See, in particular, the case of *Tarakhel v Switzerland*, Application No. 29217/12. For a full analysis, see Mitsilegas 2016b.
12 Directive 2010/64/EU on the right to interpretation and translation in criminal proceedings, OJ L280, 26.10.2010, p. 1.
13 Directive 2012/13/EU on the right to information in criminal proceedings, OJ L142, 1.6.2012, p. 1.
14 Directive 2013/48/EU on the right of access to a lawyer in criminal proceedings and in European arrest warrant proceedings, and on the right to have a third party informed upon deprivation of liberty and to communicate with third persons and with consular authorities while deprived of liberty, OJ L294, 6.11.2013, p. 1.
15 COM (2011) 327 final, Brussels, 14.6.2011.
16 COM (2013) 824 final, Brussels, 27.11.2013.
17 COM (2013) 822 final, Brussels, 27.11.2013.
18 COM (2013) 821 final, Brussels, 27.11.2013.
19 OJ C 378/11, 24.12.2013.

20 OJ C 378/8, 24.12.2013.
21 See Opinion of AG Bot above, in particular paras 105–6.
22 European Council Conclusions, 26–27 June 2014, Brussels, 27 June 2014, EUCO 79/14, para. 3.

## References

Craig, P., 2010. *The Lisbon Treaty: law, politics, and treaty reform*. Oxford: Oxford University Press.

Fontanelli, F., 2014. Implementation of EU law through domestic measures after Fransson: the Court of Justice buys time and 'non-preclusion' troubles loom large. *European Law Review*, 39, 682–700.

Lenaerts, K., 2012. Exploring the limits of the EU Charter of Fundamental Rights. *European Constitutional Law Review*, 8, 375–403.

Mitsilegas, V., 2006. The constitutional implications of mutual recognition in criminal matters in the EU. *Common Market Law Review*, 43, 1277–311.

Mitsilegas, V., 2012. The limits of mutual trust in Europe's area of freedom, security and justice: from automatic inter-state cooperation to the slow emergence of the individual. *Yearbook of European Law 2012*, 31, 319–72.

Mitsilegas, V., 2015. The symbiotic relationship between mutual trust and fundamental rights in Europe's area of criminal justice. *New Journal of European Criminal Law*, 6(4), 460–85.

Mitsilegas, V., forthcoming 2016a. Legislating for human rights after Lisbon: the transformative effect of EU measures on the rights of the individual in criminal procedure. *In*: M. Fletcher, E. Herlin-Karnell and C. Matera (eds), *The European Union as an area of freedom, security and justice*. London: Routledge.

Mitsilegas, V., forthcoming 2016b. *EU criminal law after Lisbon: rights, trust and the transformation of justice in Europe*. London: Hart Publishing.

Nicolaïdis, K. and Shaffer, G., 2005. Transnational mutual recognition regimes: governance without global government. *Law and Contemporary Problems*, 68, 263–317.

Sanchez, S.I., 2012. The Court and the Charter: the impact of the entry into force of the Lisbon Treaty on the ECJ's approach to fundamental rights. *Common Market Law Review*, 49, 1565–612.

Sarmiento, D., 2013. Who's afraid of the Charter? The Court of Justice, national courts and the new framework of fundamental rights protection in Europe. *Common Market Law Review*, 50, 1267–304.

# 12

# Digital surveillance and everyday democracy

*Didier Bigo*

Allen Dulles, a decade before the most important reform of the American intelligence services, wrote that 'our government in its very nature, and our open society in all its instinct, under the Constitution and the Bill of Rights automatically outlaws intelligence organizations of the kind that have developed in police states' (Dulles 1963).

Digitization has transformed the relation between surveillance and everyday democracy in western countries. It is now possible to trace almost all of the online activities that an Internet user undertakes during the day: what they read on the web or purchase on Amazon, what they send to colleagues and family members via email, what sort of holidays they take and whether they travel abroad, and what kind of online payment system they use. The open society is more open than ever before in terms of opportunities, but also in terms of surveillance in the name of the protection of society or the state. The capacity to act at distance has increased the traceability of data; the possibility of data retention; the capacity to build software that enables complex relations between databases, and to deduct from these data emerging trends, statistical categories of behaviours or individuals; and the belief that these emergent and minority trends give intelligence services an advantage in conducting their various activities such as espionage, economic intelligence, and the struggle against terrorism and crime. All of these elements have structured a new political imagination that has radicalized the fear of global terrorism and the necessity of a maximum and global security regime to counter terrorism on the one side, and on the other has produced a fear of an Orwellian world in the making, in which citizens are systematically spied upon in their everyday practices. The possibility of doing something is nevertheless different from the reality of doing it. The driver is never inherent to the technology itself but rather the legitimization to use this technology, and whether or not to use it moderately. It is in this context that the controversy about the practices of intelligence services in a democracy must be situated. The organizations in charge of intelligence activities insist that they only engage in targeted surveillance of specific people – those invariably deemed guilty of the preparation of a crime – and that their 'bulk collection' of data does not equate to the mass surveillance seen in police states. They claim to use such data to protect the people and the state, and insist that people must recognize their role as safeguarding democracy, and even to love and admire intelligence organizations if they are real patriots. Unfortunately for them, their adversaries often come from within the services, like most of the whistle-blowers, and they contend this vision. They know the secret practices and agree in fact with the human rights lawyers who consider that such organizations infringe the rule of law and are sometimes even proud to work in full illegality and without respecting human rights principles. The non-governmental organizations (NGOs) representing human rights or Internet user activists have almost always mobilized in favour of the whistle-blowers, and they have joined activist lawyers in their lawsuits. Such groups consider that intelligence organizations are carrying out illegitimate forms of surveillance, through the mass of data and metadata collected on profiles that are most often based on prejudice rather than statistical knowledge, and by the way this surveillance operates as an intrusion that destroys anonymity by connecting all the details of an individual's life, in order to cast out anyone who is too original or deviant.

The emerging controversy surrounding these matters, evident in the Edward Snowden leaks of information concerning the United States (US) National Security Agency (NSA) and the other services exchanging information transnationally, is nevertheless far from new. It is more the revival of a permanent struggle about the legitimacy of the secret actions of intelligence services and the right of the citizen in a democracy to know what the executive is doing in their name. This old story of the limits of secret actions in a democracy, where nobody believes anymore like during the period of Allen Dulles that they exist 'naturally', is nevertheless now more acute subsequent to the heightened use of these technologies of surveillance in the name of prevention and prediction claimed to be necessary to counter terrorism efficiently.

## Technology of interception of communication for intelligence purposes: an old story

In the mid-1960s, the idea that the state could spend its resources monitoring and spying on its own citizens or even on large groups of citizens of another state seemed bizarre to Dulles, despite the McCarthy era which had come to an end just 10 years prior. The notion of the 'police state', in the context of the Cold War, was associated with the kinds of practices in which the countries of the Eastern Bloc would indulge while the foundational texts of American democracy were supposed to prevent the government from taking the path of these police states. A little more than a decade later, the revelation by Seymour Hersh of vast governmental programmes designed to collect information and build files on the political activities of American citizens shocked the nation, and was followed immediately by the creation of the Church Committee,[1] assembled to investigate these allegations and offer policy recommendations. The revelation of such practices received a considerable echo among the American public opinion and led to the adoption of severe reforms in 1976, which extended the limits imposed by Congress on the powers of the Executive branch. However, since the 1980s, the struggle by the US Executive and the White House to 'regain' their power has taken centre stage in the political arena, with each subsequent Republican president systematically seeking to enlarge such powers, from Ronald Reagan, to George Bush senior, and George Bush junior after 11 September 2001, with his declaration of the War on Terror. But this story would have been quite different if the development of electronic and digital communications had been less vivid, as it is at this very specific intersection between the political will and the development of technologies of digitization of surveillance that emerges the key question of the scale of surveillance for intelligence purposes and its impact on civil liberties.

Digitization has not been a product of the Internet alone. A number of studies have documented in detail the pre-Internet period of the different Signal-Intelligence (or SIGINT) agencies at the transatlantic scale, including how they were set up, their technological capabilities in terms of interception of communication, and their purpose both during the Cold War and since the 1990s (Campbell 2000, Schmid 2001). As soon as it was possible to transmit electronic signals, as early as the Boers wars, armies were putting in place means of interceptions. After World War 2, the United Kingdom Government Communications Headquarters (GCHQ) and the US NSA established a secret agreement to exchange information. Australia, Canada and New Zealand joined the agreement to form the club of the 'Five Eyes' (as it was known) in the 1960s, although a formal (and secret) agreement was not signed until 1971. The central objective was to cover the exchange of communications coming from and directed to the Union of Soviet Socialist Republics and the Eastern Bloc. However, the collaborative network of technologies of interception was not restricted to military intelligence operations and also served the purposes of industrial espionage.

In 1988, Duncan Campbell (as well as Gerard Schmid and the European Parliament in its enquiry of 2000) discovered that under the code name of Echelon for software linking the different computer networks of the Five Eyes, the Anglo-American services were spying on the rest of the world, including their allies, to the benefit of their own companies. The Echelon scandal developed after the report of the European Parliament was released to the press, and was, at the time, quite important, even if too easily overshadowed by the current Snowden revelations presented too quickly as 'unprecedented'. The controversy around the Five Eyes, which broke out with Echelon, implied that the collaboration in terms of exchange of information was engaged in an illegitimate form of large-scale surveillance, yet this did not majorly transform intergovernmental transatlantic relations.

In a foreshadowing of today, the European governments did not follow the recommendations of the LIBE Committee of the European Parliament and were complacent about the activities of the US intelligence services. The NSA and Central Intelligence Agency (CIA) kept silent during the inquiry, but the former CIA director, after waiting a year to see in what direction the scandal was evolving, wrote a piece in *The Wall Street Journal* in answer to the diverse criticisms, entitled 'Why we spy on our allies' (Woolsey 2000). The prevalence of irony and cynicism in this piece was a sign that, for these Five Eyes services, the idea that democracies must have rules between them forbidding economic espionage and theft of private correspondence was dismissed. Intelligence and spying were considered normal activities of the state, covered by secrecy, under national security and an enlarged vision of the 'reason of state' (*raison d'état*).

Interestingly, at the time the argument put by the journalists close to the Five Eyes SIGINT services was that their surveillance was not a question concerning citizens, as they were not involved in the game of spying. They were not the target, but rather the group to be protected. The practice and even the imaginary of identifying everybody travelling or communicating internationally, and checking this against a watch list of suspicious individuals that may be terrorists, criminals or illegal, was not yet on the map.

Of course, the complexity of putting large groups of people under surveillance was significant, and it was difficult to imagine a reason for capturing so much data, if it was impossible to effectively follow the movement of the suspected individuals. The traditional idea that you need two or three people to follow one suspect in order to gather evidence was still in currency at the time of these scandals of Echelon.

However, by 2000, the structure of the game had changed. Email traffic was rapidly expanding as was navigation on the Internet, and, more importantly for intelligence services, the traces left on the Internet were being captured by private providers for commercial purposes. To use this 'gold mine' of data haunted some technicians, especially when the ability to capture, store and trace back the circulation of data greatly increased. In the 2000s, the number of people connected to the Internet rose exponentially, and became a normal part of everyday life in most western democracies. And with this, the possibility to put under surveillance phone calls and correspondence, via a couple of clicks of a mouse by the surveillor, was seen as a dream come true.

At the same time, in everyday life, using emails instead of traditional correspondence, undertaking research via the net and search instruments like Google, and communicating via social media became activities transversal to work and leisure, to the interest about local places and remote ones. This created a sense that 'Internet users' were highly diverse, but nevertheless seen as one category, even a community with a sense of solidarity. The argument underpinning the development of the digital economy at the turn of the millennium was that it was a way to revive growth in decline and to avoid economic crisis. Nobody would have dared to block the trend, or to insist on its 'dark side'. Policing the Internet had to be done 'quietly', and even if the idea of cybercrime emerged, it was certainly not in the media, except when some (in)security managers created fear about the turn of the millennium and what might happen for global computer systems on 1 January 2000. The lack of impact of this so-called crisis went against the rhetoric of the inherent danger of the Internet (Bohlin 2004).

## Using big data analytics for the surveillance of suspects not yet known: a science or an astrological tale?

By the late 1990s, SIGINT services had begun to develop software to achieve large-scale surveillance and to maximize data retention, following the rise of the commercial and banking activities, but for their own purposes. With the development of the first 'giants of the net', such as Yahoo, eBay, Amazon, Netscape and AOL, the everyday life of millions of people became traceable and their travels, communications, activities could be monitored, not on an individual base, but at least statistically, using their metadata and statistical software specifically designed for what has been called 'big data analytics'. This raised the question: was it possible to be sure that online activities would remain anonymous? The debates surrounding encryption and decryption, and the right to maintain one's anonymity on the web, emerged, and are still raging today (Hillstrom 2005).

The fight between the computer analysts and the lawyers working inside these SIGINT agencies began, especially in the US, during this period preceding 2001. And it is important to remember this fact as most of the current-day rhetoric by both the promoters and critics of the large-scale surveillance of the Internet has all too quickly combined the arguments for the War on Terrorism with those supporting the development of large-scale surveillance. However, in our view, this is an error of judgement. Clearly, the Bill Clinton Administration, while of course keen to have more efficient counter-terrorist policies, was reluctant to develop technologies of intrusive and large-scale surveillance that threatened privacy. The White House still remembered the recommendations of the 1975 Frank Church Committee regarding intelligence services, encapsulated by the statement that 'rogue elephants need to be under strict supervision'.[2] The government was therefore considering that it was important to have a warrant for each case; that the Federal Bureau of Investigation needed to have an exclusive right of surveillance of US citizens, excluding the CIA and NSA; and that it was necessary that the Foreign Intelligence Surveillance Court (FISC), created in 1978, conduct a review of the NSA. Bill Clinton was notoriously not a fan of meetings with the intelligence services, and if his Administration was certainly interested in the fact that anyone using the net could be easily traced, when it asked the agencies – in particular the NSA – to add this Internet monitoring activity to their political and economic espionage, they insisted that such monitoring was an experimental phase to be monitored. The first results of this 'experiment' did not convince the government at all, because of the poor quality of the software used, and the limited capacity to 'discover' things and persons by statistical correlation alone. They did not believe in the use of big data analytics as a revolution of thought.

Nevertheless, these setbacks did not prevent the NSA from developing, more or less in secret, a programme to 'catch it all' – code-named 'the bag', even if its method of collecting data was clearly breaking the rules of interception of communication, and particularly when directed at citizens. The NSA lobbied the Clinton Administration to change or relax the laws governing their activities, and especially to change the rules of its own oversight body, the FISC[3] (Harris 2010) – but without success.

In a series of interviews, Admiral Poindexter claims that he was among the first, in the mid-1990s, to foresee the value of 'connecting all the dots' on the Internet via specific data-mining and profiling software. He actively lobbied the government and industry to create a platform of interrelated software that would permit, in theory at least, the creation of a full archive of the past and the (real-time) present, and to run profiling software in order to predict the future of specific behaviours of individuals still unknown by the police. He explained the philosophy underpinning this platform as the tools enabling a 'Total Information Awareness'.[4]

## Justifying the preventive logic and the War on Terror via a techno-scientific narrative based on the capability of digital surveillance

When the Bush Administration gained power in 2001, it called Poindexter back into the Administration, and after September 11, he worked with the NSA, the CIA and the military before finally moving into private enterprise to develop the full scale of his ambitious programme, supported by Booz Allen Hamilton firm (Harris 2010). As Poindexter explains in a very explicit way, September 11 gave him the opportunity to develop his programme. This general preventive logic, by its systematic and global reach, he argued, was one of the most useful tools of counter-terrorism 'detection' and 'prevention', but also for intelligence in general, including economic and political espionage and future trends analysis. And this discourse was particularly in tune with the ideas of Dick Cheney and the Secretary of Defence Donald Rumsfeld. These individuals all shared the idea that one cannot wait for the next bombing, as emergency services do; rather, one must seek to discover, through low-intensity signals transmitted by profiling software, 'things' before they happen.

Rumsfeld theorized, or more precisely 'theologized', this narrative of prevention as a struggle against various forms of 'unknown' and described prevention as acting before the enemy through the capacity to imagine and detect the risk before it manifests. Known as the '1 per cent doctrine', Rumsfeld's approach was developed in order to change the rules of the game of global counter-terrorism and national security by anticipating the threats and risks, even if this meant that 99 per cent of potential innocents had to be monitored in order to catch the 1 per cent who are potentially guilty (Dillon 2007, Bigo and Guittet 2011).

Digital surveillance, by its ease of application, has modified the conditions under which intelligence operates. It has led to a form of large-scale harvesting of data, including personal data and data communication (metadata) coming from all electronic means of communication (including Internet, social networks and smart phones), not because of the ineluctable progress of a technology, but because of its association with a suspicious and preventive logic encapsulated in a philosophy of speculation about the limits of the political imagination of the ones who govern and the inventiveness of the violent dissidents (Aradau and Munster 2011, De Goede 2014).

Therefore, the argument that monitoring the Internet by intercepting large-scale data (personal and non-personal) is necessary in the struggle against terrorism and organized crime does not stand. It is not up to the law to adjust to technology, regarding the progress of the later one. It is always the use of technology for some political purposes that creates the rhetoric that the law must be amended accordingly, rather than vice versa. The discourse about a 'state of exception' that has been popularized in the literature does not describe the practices of the Bush Administration, but, on the contrary, its strategy of legitimization, masking the arbitrariness of the logic of expanding presidential power and secrecy in matters of foreign affairs, and convincing the population to accept this via a form of patriotism and paranoid politics that legitimates a heightened intrusive surveillance of all kinds. In turn this is based on the belief that the technology of profiling and predicting software can bare the truth and distinguish among a very large number of suspects who is guilty and who is not.

In this regard, it could be argued that September 11 has been used as a strong justification for a policy that was already well established, and was not the key factor driving the development of surveillance by SIGINT agencies. Indeed, it is becoming increasingly clear that this modality of surveillance is not even useful in the struggle against terrorist organizations and can in fact multiply false positives (see below).

The War on Terror was said to begin a couple of days after September 11, with the belief that predicting the future via technology was the solution to the struggle against clandestine transnational violence, but was certainly not a necessity answering to a 'new era'. This 'war' has been an ideological choice and the engine that has accelerated and justified the large-scale surveillance of the Internet, masking the fact that this form of surveillance was reinforcing obedience to the presidential power.

It is this specific move that has allowed intelligence services to intercept without warrant all sorts of communications, and to extract information from these communications, by collecting millions and millions of data every day, even if, at the end of the process of selection, the list of suspicious activities, computers and/or persons was reduced to a couple of thousand.

The suspicion-preventive-predictive triptych that articulates the strategy of a technologizing security via the connection of different means of surveillance to generate intelligence has been directed theoretically against global counter-terrorism, but was never limited to it, and has continued to be applied also to traditional forms of spying. It has destabilized the limits of what is acceptable behaviour by intelligence services in a democracy and has created a push in favour of a 'maximum security' discourse, without considering that the ambition to have maximum security, when applied, destroys liberties and the principle of innocence, and generates new forms of insecurities.

It has imposed the view – which has become the common sense of the political class since 2004 and 2007, in the US and Europe, respectively – that the strict respect of Fundamental Rights, in particular of the different articles of the *European Convention on Human Rights* (Article 6 – Right to a Fair Trial, Article 7 – Right to privacy, Article 8 – Right to data protection and even Article 3 – Protection against torture), hampered security instead of regulating it by allowing suspects to know that they are under surveillance and blocking the possibility of clandestine governmental surveillance (Bigo et al. 2014). Many western politicians have argued that the law is always 'late' and is an ineffective tool against terror, fanatics, radicals or even 'pre-radicals'. Therefore, the rule of law and fundamental rights, including those on *jus cogens*, had to adjust to the advances of the latest technologies of surveillance, as they are the only solution to transnational violence.

In this reasoning, the main concern is no longer about respect for the presumption of innocence in the face of large-scale suspicion, or the right to privacy and data protection; it is even not a way to have careful derogations for security purposes covered by judicial warrants. Rather, the focus is on a technological escalation, whereby the government needs to have, at any price, the higher hand against its clandestine virtual enemies. But, as has been reported many times, the technology that enables the maximum speed of a car does not justify using the car on the road at that maximum speed; the law is there to impose strong limits on technology. This applies to the allowed speed of a car, the potential use of a nuclear bomb, and so to the surveillance of the Internet. It is not because large-scale surveillance is possible and 'convenient' that it is necessary and justified. Unchecked and unbalanced forms of intrusive surveillance destroy what they claim to defend: democracy.

However, the counter-arguments to the use of large-scale surveillance, despite their logical strength, have been marginalized because of the success of the association between this use of digital surveillance technology and the purported predictive value of this technology regarding terrorism. The controversy before Snowden intervened with his leaks of data has been restricted to a discussion where security and the rise of surveillance have been amalgamated as if the latter were inextricably connected to the former, and as if freedom and presumption of innocence against suspicion can be reduced to a question of 'data protection'. This framing of a collective security threatened by a permanent risk of catastrophic terrorism, which has to be balanced against individual data protection rights, has been accepted, including by the fiercest critics who wanted to valorize data protection and privacy.

Many lawyers have accepted this initial framing of collective security versus individual freedom, but have been hopeful that the courts would defend data protection. So they have been disappointed when some of the courts immediately accepted the reasoning of the governments in place, regarding the priority of secrecy over privacy. It obliged them to revise their strategies when they went to superior courts, arguing that they had to protect, not only data protection and privacy, but also freedom and democracy; yet time played in favour of the Administration.

This has been more or less the nature of the debate for the past 10 years. Security has trumped privacy, because the discourse of preventive counter-terrorism implying large-scale surveillance of suspects without evidence and based only on profiling extracting from metadata so-called behavioural prediction has been accepted as an absolute necessity to safeguard the population from catastrophes. The fight in favour of privacy has been unequal because of this degree of acceptance that a preventive logic assorted to a predictive technology can work. The fight against global terrorism and maximum security has turned into a dominant paradigm, which has only recently been challenged. Jef Huysmans has warned: security has become 'unbound' (2014).

The Obama Administration was very tactical in 2008 in criticizing the methods of the CIA's extraordinary rendition programme and its use of torture, while at the same time developing the NSA programme of extraction of information. Instead of torturing the bodies of individuals, the doctrine has been to carry out data-mining extraction and profiling in order to connect the so-called predictive capacities of the software with the use of drones to kill actual and future enemies that appear on the integrated list of suspects compiled by the agencies – an approach previously adopted by the Israeli services.[5]

The SIGINT services, including the NSA, were not the first to be criticized for their activities against human rights and violations of privacy; the CIA was first in line, with the accusation of torture and/or complicity of torture via the programme of extraordinary rendition. Before the emergence of the evidence from Edward Snowden concerning the NSA and the Feinstein report concerning the CIA, both agencies were insisting on justifying their actions that the imperatives of national security were a response to the globalization of crime via the Internet and implied the necessity of collaboration between national agencies. They were disputing the academics by declaring that they had only very limited transnational exchanges with other SIGINT agencies, due to the national security imperatives of their tasks. They were also insisting on the specificities of their mandates in terms of counter-terrorism and serious crime, and on the fact that they were not using data at random, because profiling was a scientific process. They were claiming that their predictions and discoveries of plots, before they become operational, were highly efficient and that their capacity to disrupt terrorism and even radicalism from the very first signs of their appearance was due to the success of these preventive tools. But almost all of these claims and assumptions are today subject to caution after the leak of more than 200,000 documents (including top secret ones) by Edward Snowden in June 2013 and their careful analysis by investigative journalists.

## The Snowden impact: evidence concerning the scale of the 'Five Eyes plus' surveillance and the discovery of a transnational collaboration for extracting information worldwide

From the Echelon scandal to the Five Eyes scandal, from David Campbell to Edward Snowden, we have a continuous line of resistance by people who have understood how the rhetoric of counter-terrorism, which posits the web as a place of danger, has succeeded in transforming the central question of democratic politics and transnational clandestine violence into a shadow theatre opposing collective security with individual data protection. Data protection, which is also collective – linked as it is to privacy and functioning as a key element for freedom in a democracy – has thus been depicted as a standalone issue, defended by a 'lobby group' of lawyers.

By chance, against this frame that justified any increased measure of surveillance, some investigative journalists and academic books have been central (Bauman et al. 2014, Lyon 2014, Greenwald et al. 2013). Coming from different disciplines, they have sought to raise a number of issues. First, they have asked why the question of the role of surveillance in a democracy has been reduced to the one about the limits of the rights to data protection and privacy. Second, they question why the discussion around the balance of power has been reframed as one about the exaggerated power of the courts, especially the regional and international courts that can more readily challenge the legitimacy of presidential powers. And third, they ask why the question of secrecy in a democracy has been silenced, limited to a question of transparency, leaving aside the rights of persons accused of crimes based only on accumulated suspicions, and caricatured by the discourse that real innocents have nothing to fear if they have nothing to hide from the police.

It is impossible to provide here a detailed account of the debates that emerged following the discovery of the transnational collaboration between the western services known as the 'Five Eyes plus'.[6] But, in contrast to the Echelon scandal, this time the debate is more intense because the private Internet companies do not want to appear complicit with intelligence services and challenge them in front of tribunals, and NGOs and human rights lawyers are able to show that the scale and intrusiveness of the practices of data mining and extraction of profiles are touching thousands of people. In addition, some states believe that they have been victims of this intrusive surveillance and are complaining in international arenas like the UN in order to defend the integrity of the Internet and its value for our freedom. If some western governments are now in an ambiguous position in claiming that they have been victims of surveillance while also participating in collaborative efforts towards digital surveillance, their parliaments and courts are still motivated to limit the intrusiveness of the techniques applied by the intelligence services and to identify the ways in which information is extracted at the world level.

As far as we know now, two of the most interesting features of the SIGINT collaboration are that, first, collaboration is no longer organized strictly nationally and, second, that these agencies have difficult relations with their own national counter-terrorist services. SIGINT agencies like NSA-GCHQ are in many cases in fierce competition with the counter-terrorist agencies like CIA-FBI or MI5 – competition which, paradoxically, has been reinforced by the efforts of politicians to integrate them all together into 'national security councils'. And this competition has obstructed the transmission of intelligence information and its transformation into evidence in front of a judge that might lead to prosecution and criminal trials, and exacerbated the difference between the logic of the penal system and the preventive and suspicious logic.

In addition, it has become clear that extracting information is done at the world scale by a transnational alliance of western agencies whose core is an Anglo-American grouping, in existence since the Cold War, and which, by its recent extension to other services, is positioned at key intersections of the world Internet terrestrial and submarine cable network. This has been undertaken by specific agencies and often without the knowledge or against the will of other national organizations participating in counter-terrorism (Moraes 2014).

To establish a reinforced network, these agencies have acted as a guild of professionals developing a specific craft (in this case, data analytics), and have recruited many analysts from the private sector, including banking, telecommunications and major internet companies (Bigo 2013). Some agencies have worked closely with private companies on data processing and integrated their activities into the chain of the intelligence process. Others have been more reluctant to work with the private sector, and have reserved for them the analytical logic while subcontracting the retention of data to private firms, and sometimes part of the collection and extraction of the data. When private companies have refused to collaborate, they have been offered incentives in the form of competitive advantages over other firms in the market place; and if they have persisted in their refusal they have been threatened with severe financial penalties and even penal sanctions.

Nevertheless, the privacy supporters may finally have some hope after so much disillusionment. If the US Supreme Court was cautious on the subject, the European Court of Justice, on 6 October 2015, was more clear on the hierarchy of values and decided in the case of Max Schrem that it was necessary to strike down the EU–US data-sharing agreement known as Safe Harbour because the US government by its methods of large-scale surveillance was 'compromising the essence of the fundamental right to respect for private life', and declared that the US authorities, by prioritizing their 'national security, public interest and law enforcement requirements of the United States over the Safe Harbour scheme, were violating Europeans' fundamental rights' – a decision that will have effect beyond the case of Safe Harbour if it is followed by the data protection authorities of the EU Member States.[7]

Digitization at the world scale has been contemporary to the phenomenon of transnationalization and hybridization of the public and private logic. These three elements have together been imbricated and provoked crucial changes in the fundamental rights regimes in the main democracies. Digitization has affected data protection of communication, privacy, but also the presumption of innocence, democratic rules, and the sense of national belonging and of solidarity within both the online and offline worlds. So, beyond the question of the balance between collective security and individual privacy, what is at stake is the nature of the relations between criminal justice and intelligence, the destabilization of the principle of innocence, and equality of arms in trial, as well as a generalization of the argument of 'legitimate' suspicion.

## Notes

1 Officially known as the *United States Senate Select Committee to Study Governmental Operations with Respect to Intelligence Activities*.

2 On 17 August 1975, Senator Frank Church appeared on NBC's 'Meet the Press', and said: 'Now, that is necessary and important to the US as we look abroad at enemies or potential enemies. We must know, at the same time, that capability at any time could be turned around on the American people, and no American would have any privacy left such is the capability to monitor everything – telephone conversations, telegrams, it doesn't matter. There would be no place to hide. . . . I know the capacity that is there to make tyranny total in America, and we must see to it that this agency and all agencies that possess this technology operate within the law and under proper supervision so that we never cross over that abyss. That is the abyss from which there is no return'.

3 But they will succeed later with the section 702 of the FISA amendments Act of 2008 which does not involve FISC oversight of individual surveillance orders. The Attorney-General and the Director of National Intelligence are allowed to 'jointly' authorize 'the targeting of persons reasonably believed to be located outside the US to acquire foreign intelligence information'. Surveillance will become warrantless de facto.

4 The Total Information Awareness programme began in the late 1990s and was based on the idea that big data analytics can discover correlations between events that the human mind cannot, by using the capacity to find 'weak signals' or small correlations between activities or individuals if the mass of data collected is sufficient and if all the data collected are interoperable and integrated into a platform. The scope of surveillance included, among other things, credit card purchases, magazine subscriptions, web browsing histories, academic grades, bank deposits, passport applications, driver's licences, toll records, judicial records, divorce records, drug prescriptions, medical records, and individual DNA. Among the rare programmes partly refused by the US senate, the programme was 'limited' to anti-terrorism purposes and was called in May 2003 Terrorism Information Awareness (TIA). Some investigative journalists, such as Tim Dowling who has access to the Snowden files, consider that the current PRISM programme is the child of the TIA.

5 See The intercept_the drone papers from 19 October 2015: https://theintercept.com/ consulted 22 October 2015.

6 The 'Five Eyes plus' is the terminology used after the analysis of the documents leaked by Snowden to describe the full network of exchange of information between SIGINT agencies. In addition to the Five Eyes themselves, other SIGINT agencies of western countries have participated regularly in these exchanges, especially the agencies of Sweden, the Netherlands, Norway, Denmark, and, on an ad hoc basis, Germany, Belgium, Italy, Spain and France.

7 Retrieved on 3 April 2016 from: http://curia.europa.eu/juris/document/document.jsf?docid=157862&doclang=en.

## References


Aradau, C. and Munster, R.V., 2011. *Politics of catastrophe: genealogies of the unknown*. London; New York: Routledge.

Bauman, Z., Bigo, D., Esteves, P., Guild, E., Jabri, V., Lyon, D. and Walker, R.B.J., 2014. After Snowden: rethinking the impact of surveillance. *International Political Sociology*, 8, 121–44.

Bigo, D., 2013. The transnational field of computerised exchange of information in police matters and its European guilds. *In*: Niilo Kauppi and Mikael Madsen, eds, *Transnational power elites: the new professionals of governance, law and security*. London: Routledge, 155–82.

Bigo, D. and Guittet, E.-P., 2011. Northern Ireland as metaphor: exception, suspicion and radicalization in the 'war on terror'. *Security Dialogue*, 42, 483–98.

Bigo, D., Carrera, S., Hernanz, N. and Scherrer, A., 2014. *National security and secret evidence in legislation and before the courts: exploring the challenges*. Justice and Home Affairs Committee of Civil Liberties. European Parliament.

Bohlin, E., 2004. *Global economy and digital society*. Amsterdam, Boston: Elsevier.

Campbell, D., 2000. *Inside Echelon: the history, structure, and function of the global surveillance system known as Echelon*. Retrieved on 3 April 2016 from http://www.heise.de/tp/artikel/6/6929/1.html.

De Goede, M., 2014. The politics of privacy in the age of preemptive security. *International Political Sociology*, 8, 100–4.

Dillon, M., 2007. Governing terror: the state of emergency of biopolitical emergence. *International Political Sociology*, 1, 7–28.

Dulles, A.W., 1963. *The craft of intelligence*. New York, NY: Harper & Row.

Greenwald, G., Macaskill, E. and Poitras, L., 2013. Edward Snowden: the whistleblower behind the NSA surveillance revelations. *The Guardian*, 9.

Harris, S., 2010. *The watchers: the rise of America's surveillance state*. New York, NY: Penguin Press.

Hillstrom, K., 2005. *Defining moments: the internet revolution*. Detroit: Omnigraphics.

Huysmans, J., 2014. *Security unbound: enacting democratic limits*. London and New York: Routledge.

Lyon, D., 2014. Surveillance, Snowden, and big data: capacities, consequences, critique. *Big Data & Society*, 1–13.

Moraes, C., 2014. *US NSA surveillance programme, surveillance bodies in various Member States and their impact on EU citizens' fundamental rights and on transatlantic cooperation in justice and home affairs*. Bruxelles, 12 March. European Parliament.

Schmid, G., 2001. *On the existence of a global system for the interception of private and commercial communications (ECHELON interception system)*. Session document; Final A5-0264/200., 11 July European Parliament.

Woolsey, R.J., 2000. Why we spy on our allies. *The Wall Street Journal*, 17 March.

# 13

# Anti-terrorism laws and human rights

*Nicola McGarrity and Jessie Blackbourn*

## Introduction

In their response to terrorism, nations have generally chosen to move away from the 'ordinary law' towards the creation of a new body of law directed specifically at this threat. For example, there was no anti-terrorism legislation at the national level in Australia prior to the 9/11 terrorist attacks in New York and Washington. However, within six months, the then Liberal-National government had introduced a package of five Bills into the federal parliament (Lynch et al. 2015, Williams 2011). The impetus for the creation of a specific body of anti-terrorism legislation in Australia and other nations was not simply domestic political pressure. United Nations *Security Council Resolution 1373* (2001) required all Member States to ensure that terrorist acts 'are established as serious criminal offences in domestic laws and regulations and that the punishment duly reflects the seriousness of such terrorist acts' (UN 2001, para. 2e). As a consequence, even those nations with a long history of anti-terrorism legislation have witnessed a steady increase in the scope of terrorism offences as well the penalties attached to these offences since 9/11.

There are two key aspects to the development of a specific body of anti-terrorism legislation. The first is driven by what might be described as an 'intelligence' mindset (Roach 2010). In addition to non-legislative measures such as the increase in human and financial resources for the identification of potential terrorist threats, this has involved domestic parliaments expanding the investigatory powers of their intelligence agencies, strengthening the veil of secrecy, and establishing new mechanisms for the incapacitation of suspects (and even non-suspects in some circumstances). The other aspect emphasized by Resolution 1373 – and upon which this chapter will concentrate – is criminal.

The gravity of the threat posed by terrorism, that is, the huge potential for loss of life and damage to critical infrastructure, and the political or religious motivation of terrorists has been relied upon by domestic parliaments to justify the creation of new and/or expanded criminal offences. In most nations, the offence of engaging in a terrorist act unsurprisingly lies at the heart of the anti-terrorism criminal regime. Such an offence is relatively uncontroversial. Putting to one side questions about how an act of 'terrorism' is defined, it is generally accepted that those who engage in such acts should be subject to the full weight of the law. What is interesting, however, is that it is extremely unusual for this offence to be relied upon by law enforcement agencies and prosecutors. Instead, they have tended to rely upon *preparatory* offences. The precise nature of these offences differs from country to country but what they have in common is that they give law enforcement agencies the power to pre-empt terrorist acts before they occur. In other words, these offences do not require proof of the prior (or, in many circumstances, even the likely) commission of a terrorist act.

The criminalization of preparatory conduct is not unique to the terrorism context. For example, offences for the importation of 'precursors', that is, substances essential for the production process for illicit drugs, are common. Furthermore, the domestic criminal law generally contains some form of inchoate offence such as attempt, conspiracy or incitement to commit another offence. The difference between these and the preparatory terrorism offences lies in the *extent* to which they pre-empt criminal conduct. Preparatory offences criminalize 'activities taken before the inchoate offences are enlivened – namely acts that are merely preparatory to a completed offence' (Tulich 2012, p. 217). This creates 'pre-inchoate' liability such that the criminal law is 'enlivened prior to the risk of harm developing' (ibid.). In *Lodhi v R* [2006] NSWCCA 121, 66, Chief Justice Spigelman of the Supreme Court of New South Wales explained that:

> Preparatory acts are not often made into criminal offences. . . . A policy judgment has been made that the prevention of terrorism requires criminal responsibility to arise at an earlier stage than is usually the case for other kinds of criminal conduct, e.g. well before an agreement has been reached for a conspiracy charge.

Intervention at an 'earlier stage' is particularly obvious in prosecutions involving the combination of inchoate offences, such as conspiracy, and the preparatory terrorism offences. This has been described as 'pre-pre-inchoate liability' (Burton et al. 2012, p. 10) or 'pre-crime' (Zedner 2010). Whilst the potential for mass casualty terrorist attacks arguably justifies some level of pre-emption, it is the extent to which the criminal law does so that has been the subject of extensive criticism.

This chapter starts by examining the criminal regimes in Australia and the United Kingdom (UK) that have been enacted in response to the terrorist threat. The preparatory offences in these nations have – in light of the prior existence of inchoate offences – been criticized as unnecessary. Law enforcement agencies themselves have expressed concern about the workability and even potentially counterproductive effects of these offences. The most common criticisms that have been put forward, however, are those based on fundamental norms of human rights. This chapter will examine how the preparatory offences affect the freedoms of association, expression and religion, as well as the presumption of innocence.

## The criminal regimes

### *The UK*

The UK's anti-terrorism laws pre-date the 9/11 terrorist attacks. Starting in the mid-1970s, the UK parliament enacted an extensive regime of emergency and temporary anti-terrorism laws to combat the threat of Northern Irish terrorism (Hogan and Walker 1989, Walker 1992). In 2000, following a lengthy consultation and review process, these laws were replaced with a new permanent anti-terrorism law to deal with this ongoing – although much reduced – threat, and also to help prevent and prosecute other forms of terrorism, including 'international' terrorism

(Lloyd 1996). The *Terrorism Act 2000* (TA) was relatively unusual in that it did not criminalize the act of terrorism itself. Instead, it included a broad definition of terrorism upon which a range of preparatory offences hinged. Section 1 defined terrorism as having three key elements. The action or threat of action: involves a considerable level of harm, such as 'serious violence against a person . . . [or] property'; is 'designed to influence the government or an international governmental organisation or to intimidate the public or a section of the public'; and is done 'for the purpose of advancing a political, religious, racial or ideological cause.'

The TA prescribed a number of preparatory offences which had proven useful in Northern Ireland, such as membership of, demonstrating support for, and wearing the uniform of a proscribed organization (ss 11–13), as well as directing a terrorist organization (being 'an organisation which is concerned in the commission of acts of terrorism') (s. 56). It also set out a range of offences for preliminary activities such as weapons and explosives training (s. 54), fundraising for terrorism (ss 15–18), possessing articles 'for a purpose connected with the commission, preparation or instigation of an act of terrorism' (s. 57), and collecting 'information of a kind likely to be useful to a person committing or preparing an act of terrorism' (s. 58).

Despite the existing legislative framework, the UK parliament nevertheless enacted new legislation after the 9/11 terrorist attacks. The *Anti-Terrorism, Crime and Security Act 2001* gave precedence to the intelligence (over the criminal) approach by introducing a range of executive powers such as the indefinite detention of non-national terrorist suspects (pt 4). It was only in response to the 7 July 2005 London bombings that the UK parliament revisited the question of criminalization. The *Terrorism Act 2006* enacted a range of new preparatory offences, including engaging in 'any conduct in preparation for giving effect to' an intention to commit acts of terrorism or assist another to commit acts of terrorism (s. 5). This offence not only criminalizes conduct undertaken long in advance of the typical inchoate offences in criminal law, it also carries a severe maximum penalty of life imprisonment (s. 5[3]). Other offences in the 2006 Act included encouraging terrorism (s. 1), disseminating terrorist publications (s. 2), training for terrorism (s. 6) and attending a place used for terrorist training (s. 8). Since the mid-2000s, the UK parliament has enacted three other pieces of anti-terrorism legislation, however, for the most part, their provisions form part of the intelligence paradigm.

### Australia

The vast majority of the Australian criminal offences were enacted in the year immediately following the 9/11 terrorist attacks. It is notable that in Australia – unlike in the UK – there *is* an offence of engaging in a terrorist act in s. 101.1 of the *Criminal Code Act 1995* (Cwlth) (Criminal Code). In most major respects, the Australian definition of terrorism mirrors that in the UK. Indeed, the Bills Digest to the *Security Legislation Amendment (Terrorism) Bill 2002 [No 2] (Cwlth)* explicitly states that the Australian definition was 'largely reproduced' from s. 1 of the TA (Commonwealth Parliament 2002, p. 19). The existence of the offence of engaging in a terrorist act has not, however, made any significant difference to Australia's prosecution of individual terrorists and terrorist groups. All of the prosecutions to date have concentrated upon the various other preparatory terrorism offences.

The first category of preparatory offences consists of activities, such as training, possessing a thing and collecting or making a document, that are connected with preparation for, the engagement of a person in, or assistance in a terrorist act (*Criminal Code Act 1995* [Cwlth] Div. 1). The most frequently used of these is the catch-all offence in s. 101.6 of doing 'any act in preparation for a terrorist act'. It is notable that – as with the offence of actually engaging in a terrorist act – this offence carries a maximum penalty of life imprisonment.

The terrorist organization offences in Division 102 of the Criminal Code represent the second category of offences. The fundamental purpose of these is to restrict the flow of human and financial resources to terrorist organizations. They criminalize directing the activities of, being a member of, recruiting for, providing training to or receiving training from, providing funding to or receiving funding from, providing support or resources to and associating with a member of a terrorist organization. The third category of offences are the terrorist financing offences (*Criminal Code Act 1995* [Cwlth] Div. 103; *Charter of the United Nations Act 1945* [Cwlth] ss 20–21), such as providing funds to another person being reckless as to whether they will be used to facilitate or engage in a terrorist act (*Criminal Code Act 1995* (Cwlth) s. 103.1[1]).

Despite the lapse of nearly 12 years since these categories of offences were enacted, very few changes of any real significance to the criminal law were made until 2014. In that year, the federal parliament introduced several pieces of legislation in response to the problem of Australians travelling overseas to fight with terrorist organizations in Syria and Iraq and subsequently attempting to return home. The most substantial change insofar as Australia's criminal response to terrorism is concerned was the introduction of what is commonly known as a declared zone offence by the *Counter-Terrorism Legislation Amendment (Foreign Fighters) Act 2014* (Cwlth). Under section 119.2 of the Criminal Code, the Minister for Foreign Affairs may now declare an area in a foreign country if he or she is satisfied that a listed terrorist organization is engaging in a hostile activity there. The consequence of such a declaration is to make it an offence to intentionally enter, or remain in, that area. To date, two areas – the Mosul district in Iraq and the al-Raqqa province in Syria – have been declared by the Minister (*Criminal Code (Foreign Incursions and Recruitment – Declared Areas) Declaration 2014 – Al-Raqqa Province, Syria*; *Criminal Code (Foreign Incursions and Recruitment – Declared Areas) Declaration 2015 – Mosul District, Ninewa Province, Iraq*).

## Freedom of association

One of the offences that has been most heavily relied upon in terrorism prosecutions in Australia, although slightly less so in the UK, is that of membership of a terrorist organization. Both jurisdictions establish a process by which an organization may be listed as a terrorist organization. In the UK, the Secretary of State may list an organization if he or she believes that it is 'concerned in terrorism' (*Terrorism Act 2000* s. 3[4]), namely, it commits or participates, promotes or encourages, or 'is otherwise concerned in terrorism' (*Terrorism Act 2000* s. 3[5]). The Australian Governor-General may – on the advice of the federal Attorney-General – list an organization if satisfied on reasonable grounds that it 'is directly or indirectly engaged in, preparing, planning, assisting in or fostering the doing of a terrorist act' or 'advocates the doing of a terrorist act' (*Criminal Code Act 1995* [Cwlth] s. 102.1[2]). The most significant difference between the terrorist organization provisions in the two nations is that, in Australia, it is also possible for a *court* to conclude that an unlisted organization is a terrorist organization if it satisfies the first of these tests (*Criminal Code Act 1995* [Cwlth] s. 102.1[1]).

The consequence of characterization as a terrorist organization is that certain offences – including that of membership – are enlivened. There are two aspects to the membership offence in section 11 of the TA. First, it criminalizes belonging to a terrorist organization. 'Belonging' includes not only persons who actively engage in the activities of a terrorist organization but also those who are passive members. This is similar to how membership has been defined in Australia. It includes 'informal' membership or even the situation where a person has 'taken steps to become a member of the organisation' (*Criminal Code Act 1995* [Cwlth] s. 102.1[1]). In both nations, there is the distinct possibility that a person with only a tangential association with an organization, for example, who has attended a meeting or subscribed to a newsletter, may be convicted of the membership offence.

The UK offence – unlike that in Australia – also captures the situation where a person 'professes' to belong to a proscribed organization. This is not defined in the TA. However, in one case, a prosecution was brought against a person who simply stated: 'I am Hamas' (*Sheldrake v Director of Public Prosecutions; Attorney General's Reference (No 4 of 2002)* [2004] UKHL 43, para. 48). The defendant was ultimately acquitted because the witnesses were unsure as to whether he was serious when making this statement. Nevertheless, the House of Lords described the offence of membership as 'a provision of extraordinary breadth' (para. 47) that could capture 'a person who is innocent of any blameworthy or properly criminal conduct' (para. 51).

It is notable that the federal parliament in Australia has chosen to go further than its UK counterpart by not only criminalizing membership of a terrorist organization but also 'associating' with a member of a terrorist organization on two or more occasions (*Criminal Code Act 1995* [Cwlth] s. 102.8). There are three categories of association that are excluded from the scope of this offence. These include association with a 'close family member' or in 'a place being used for public religious worship' or that which is protected by the implied constitutional guarantee that political communication should remain free (*Criminal Code Act 1995* [Cwlth] s. 102.8[4]). However, in each case, the defendant bears the evidential burden of establishing that his or her communication falls within the exception. The human rights concerns regarding a reversed burden of proof are discussed below. Even though this offence has not been relied upon in any prosecutions to date, it nevertheless remains one of the most controversial aspects of Australia's anti-terrorism regime. In 2006, the Security Legislation Review Committee criticized the emphasis upon 'association' as problematic because it targeted civil liberties rather than concentrating upon those who provide material support to terrorist organizations. For this reason, it recommended that the association offence should be repealed (SLRC 2006, p. 133).

## Freedom of expression

In 2006, the UK parliament made the 'encouragement of terrorism' an offence (*Terrorism Act 2006* s. 1). This applies wherever the speaker glorifies terrorist acts – 'whether in the past, in the future or generally' – and a reasonable audience would infer that the glorified conduct should be emulated. Glorification 'includes any form of praise or celebration' (*Terrorism Act 2006* s. 20[2]). The enactment of this offence was a direct response to the concern that the perpetrators of the London bombings in July 2005 had been incited by others (Home Office 2006). However, at the same time, many Members of Parliament were concerned that the provisions would have a chilling effect on the freedom of speech and, in particular, might capture those who had supported the overthrow of repressive regimes in the past, such as the apartheid regime in South Africa (HC Deb 26 October 2005 cc 326; 368; 375). This is because the UK's definition of terrorism – like that in Australia – provides no exceptions for legitimate acts of liberation or for resistance against dictatorship or other forms of oppression (Anderson 2014). The glorification offence could, for example, apply to a person who expresses support for fighters opposing the Assad regime in Syria and/or encourages further resistance by these groups.

More recently, Australia has followed in the UK's footsteps by enacting a new offence of 'advocating terrorism' (*Counter-Terrorism Legislation Amendment (Foreign Fighters) Act 2014* [Cwlth] s. 61). This applies wherever a person counsels, promotes, encourages or urges the doing of a terrorist act or the commission of a terrorism offence. The advocating offence is considerably broader than the traditional offence of inciting a criminal offence because it merely requires that the defendant be *reckless* as to whether – rather than requiring an *intention* to urge – another person commits a terrorism offence. The same concerns outlined above about the UK glorification offence also apply to its Australian equivalent.

This is not the only part of the Australian criminal regime that makes reference to 'advocacy'. As mentioned above, one of the grounds upon which an organization may be listed as a terrorist organization is that it 'advocates' terrorism (*Criminal Code Act 1995* [Cwlth] s. 102.1[2]). This term is extremely broadly defined. As enacted in 2002, it included directly or indirectly urging, counselling or providing instruction on the doing of a terrorist act or even if the organization 'directly praises the doing of a terrorist act in circumstances where there is a risk that such praise might have the effect of leading a person (regardless of his or her age or any mental impairment that the person might suffer) to engage in a terrorist act' (*Criminal Code Act 1995* [Cwlth] s. 102.1[1A]). This was expanded in 2014 to include the direct or indirect 'promotion' or 'encouragement' of terrorism (*Counter-Terrorism Legislation Amendment (Foreign Fighters) Act 2014* [Cwlth] s. 64). The purpose of this amendment was explained by the then Prime Minister Tony Abbott as being to enable the listing of organizations such as Hizb ut-Tahrir that engage in hate speech. He said that this is 'an organisation that campaigns against Australian values, that campaigns against Australian interests. They are a thoroughly objectionable organisation' (cited in Lynch et al. 2015, p. 55).

However, the most problematic aspect of the advocacy ground for listing remains the original reference to *praising* terrorism. An organization may be listed as a terrorist organization – with the result that the wide-ranging terrorist organization offences are enlivened – if a member praises past liberation struggles in East Timor or against a colonial power, or current battles in West Papua, the Middle East and parts of Africa. The fact that no organization has yet been listed on the ground of advocacy demonstrates executive restraint. However, this does not mean that the provision should not be of concern; it still has the potential to chill the willingness of people to express their political and other views.

## Freedom of religion

The definitions of terrorism in Australia and the UK have at their heart a motive requirement. This is different from the traditional elements of a criminal offence in that it requires the prosecution to not only prove that an act was committed intentionally, recklessly or negligently but also the underlying purpose. Whilst controversial, such a requirement has a long history as part of the legislative response to terrorism in the UK. The *Prevention of Terrorism (Temporary Provisions) Act 1974*, for example, defined terrorism as 'the use of violence for political ends, and includes any use of violence for the purpose of putting the public, or any section of the public in fear' (s. 9). The limitation of the concept of terrorism to 'political ends' only is explained by the fact that the primary threat of terrorism was perceived to come from Northern Irish nationalism (Lloyd 1996, p. 1). However, the report prepared by Lord Lloyd of Berwick in 1996 recommended that the definition be expanded because, 'being limited to political ends, it might be said not to apply to acts of terrorism perpetrated by single issue or religious fanatics' (p. 25). The TA therefore defined terrorism so as to require that the act had the 'purpose of advancing a political, religious or ideological cause' (*Terrorism Act 2000* s. 1). Very similar wording is used in the Australian definition of a terrorist act. It requires that the action or threat of action had the 'intention of advancing a political, religious or ideological cause' (*Criminal Code Act 1995* [Cwlth] s. 100.1).

In 2007, the UK Independent Reviewer of Terrorism Legislation recommended that the definition should be expanded to apply to 'a political, *philosophical*, ideological, racial, *ethnic*, religious *or other similar cause*' (emphasis added) (Carlile 2007, p. 37). However, the primary issue raised by the Reviewer was to 'cement into the law clarity that terrorism includes campaigns of terrorist violence motivated by racism' (ibid.). The *Counter-Terrorism Act 2008* therefore adopted the Reviewer's recommendation in part by adding a new category of 'racial' cause to the motive element in the definition of terrorism (s. 75[1]). No equivalent amendment has been made in Australia.

The inclusion of a motive requirement has been the subject of considerable controversy. Saul usefully summarizes the human rights arguments put forward by opponents of the requirement (although he ultimately concludes that it is a useful part of the definition of terrorism) as being:

> that investigative and prosecutorial scrutiny would inevitably focus on political, religious and ideological beliefs, opinions and expressions; freedoms and consequently democratic life would be chilled; and suspicion and anger would fall on anyone belonging to a religious, political or ideological group that is connected with terrorist acts.
>
> *(Saul 2007, p. 34)*

These arguments are particularly pertinent given that virtually all of the terrorism prosecutions in Australia and the UK have identified the motive for the action or threat of action as being to advance some kind of Islamic cause, for example, to force the adoption of Sharia law by the government or to convince western forces to withdraw from Islamic lands.

It is not, however, the motive element in isolation that poses the greatest threat to the freedom of religion. Rather, it is the interaction between this element and the preparatory offences upon which all of the terrorism prosecutions in Australia and the UK have relied. Such offences – by definition – do not involve the commission of a substantive act of terrorism; the action may be something as abstract as asking a question about the permissibility of terrorism under Islam or as ambiguous as buying garden fertilizer. In the former example, it is evidence of an extremist religious or political motivation that provides the connection between the speech and the existence of a genuine plan to engage in a terrorist act. And, in the latter, it is that same evidence which differentiates between a person who purchases large quantities of fertilizer for the purposes of gardening and as a preliminary step towards the making of an explosive device.

A general principle of criminal procedure in Australia and the UK is that evidence should not be admitted if its probative value is outweighed by its prejudicial effect. This would normally result in the exclusion of any evidence of the extremist religious views of a criminal defendant. This is because such evidence bears little relevance to the elements of traditional criminal offences. Furthermore – and more relevantly for present purposes – such evidence has the potential to prejudice the fair trial of the defendant by undermining the juror impartiality. It runs the risk that jurors will prejudge the case by giving greater emphasis to who the defendant is – in the sense of his or her religious orientation – rather than what he or she has done.

The anti-terrorism legislation represents a significant deviation from this traditional approach. The combined effect of the motive requirement and the preparatory nature of the offences is to render such evidence of critical importance. The courts have therefore admitted into evidence a broad range of evidence to establish the willingness of the defendant in a terrorism trial to use violence to advance their religion. Most controversially, in several Australian and UK trials, the courts have permitted evidence that the defendants downloaded graphic videos of the beheading of hostages by mujahedeen fighters in the Middle East (*R v Benbrika (Ruling No 15)* [2007] VSC 545 para. 8); *R (Cwlth) v Elomar* (2010) 264 ALR 759 paras 48-49; *R v Ibrahim and Ors*, Woolwich Crown Court, 11 January 2007, unreported). In some cases, such videos have even been shown to the jury in whole or in part. It is difficult to doubt – given its gruesome nature and the manner in which it plays upon stereotypical images of Islamic terrorism – the great potential that this evidence has to undermine the impartiality of jurors in a terrorism trial.

## Presumption of innocence

The presumption of innocence is a cornerstone of the right to a fair trial. In practical terms, it means that the burden is upon the prosecution to prove all of the physical and mental elements of a criminal offence beyond a reasonable doubt. The anti-terrorism legislation in both Australia and the UK undermines this presumption by placing the burden of disproving certain elements of the preparatory offences upon the defendant. This is especially problematic because, in many cases, these elements are critical to what makes conduct of the defendant worthy of criminalization.

In the UK, a number of offences include such a reversal of proof (Walker 2011). An example is the membership offence. Where the prosecution has adduced evidence beyond a reasonable doubt that the defendant belongs or professes to belong to a listed organization, the defendant may escape liability by establishing:

> (a) that the organisation was not proscribed on the last (or only) occasion on which he became a member or began to profess to be a member, and (b) that he has not taken part in the activities of the organisation at any time while it was proscribed.
>
> *(Terrorism Act 2000, s. 11[2])*

The House of Lords has mitigated the unfairness of this provision by holding that (b) imposes only an evidential – rather than a legal – burden on the defendant (*Sheldrake v Director of Public Prosecutions*, paras 51–2). In other words, the defendant need only point to the existence of a reasonable possibility that this element is established before the burden reverts back to the prosecution to disprove the defence beyond a reasonable doubt. The Lords felt that whilst a defendant might easily be able to establish the first element of the defence on the balance of probabilities, it would be all 'but impossible for him to show that he had not taken part in the activities of the organisation at any time while it was proscribed' (*Sheldrake v Director of Public Prosecutions*, para. 51). However, the Lords' conclusion does not leave the presumption of innocence unaffected. The fact that the defendant effectively has to present evidence of his or her innocence is a significant departure from the accepted notion in UK criminal procedure that a defendant is presumed to be innocent.

In Australia, the Criminal Code imposes a reverse burden of proof on the defendant for many of the preparatory offences. For example, it is a defence, with an evidential burden placed on the defendant, if 'the possession of the thing' or 'the collection or making of the document' was not 'intended to facilitate preparation for, the engagement of a person in, or assistance in a terrorist act' (*Criminal Code Act 1995* [Cwlth] s. 101.5[5]). And, in sharp contrast to the situation in the UK after *Sheldrake v Director of Public Prosecutions*, the Criminal Code explicitly provides that it is only a defence to the offence of membership of a terrorist organization if the defendant is able to prove on the balance of probabilities that 'he or she took all reasonable steps to cease to be a member of the organisation as soon as practicable after the person knew that the organisation was a terrorist organisation' (*Criminal Code Act 1995* [Cwlth] s. 102.3[2]).

Arguably, the most problematic reversal of the burden of proof in either jurisdiction lies in the new Australian declared zone offence. Section 119.2 of the Criminal Code simply requires the prosecution to prove that the defendant entered into or remained in a declared zone. There is no requirement to show that he or she did so for a wrongful purpose, such as engaging in hostile activity against a foreign government. The purpose is only relevant to the establishment of a defence. The defendant bears the evidential burden of establishing that the purpose of travel was a legitimate one, namely, one of the very narrow list of purposes contained in section 119.2(3) of the Criminal Code. These include humanitarian aid, appearing before a court or tribunal, making a bona fide visit to family, making a news report and performing an official duty.

The way this defence operates is highly objectionable. First, from a practical perspective, the defendant is likely to be placed in the difficult position of proving a negative. He or she may be required to adduce evidence not only that the purpose of travel was a legitimate one but also that this was his or her *sole* purpose. Second, and even more critically, it is not acceptable in a liberal democracy that a person should be gaoled simply for travelling to an area designated by the executive branch of government as a no-go zone. It is only the fact that a person travels to that area for an illegitimate purpose that makes it worthy of criminalization. For that reason, the burden should be upon the prosecution to prove beyond a reasonable doubt that the defendant travelled for such a purpose.

## Conclusion

This chapter has examined some of the key ways in which the preparatory terrorism offences in Australia and the UK burden fundamental human rights. It is, of course, a truism that these rights are not absolutes; they must in some circumstances give way to protect other rights. All nation states have a basic responsibility to ensure the security of their people (for example, against the threat of terrorism) and it may therefore prove necessary to restrict the freedoms of association, expression and religion, as well as the presumption of innocence. Given this, the basic tenet of the ongoing critique of anti-terrorism legislation in Australia and the UK has been that the measures contained therein are *disproportionate* to this threat. The effect of the preparatory terrorism offences is to target people on the basis of their extremist associations, speech and beliefs. They undermine the presumption of innocence by assuming that a person in this category poses a serious danger to society. No allowances are made for the fact that he or she may not in fact have a genuine plan to commit a terrorist act, may never take any concrete steps towards the commission of a terrorist act or even that he or she may have a change of heart at some point prior to the commission of that act. In short, the preparatory terrorism offences subvert the basic principle that it is better that 10 guilty persons escape than that one innocent suffer.

## References

Anderson, D., 2014. *The Terrorism Acts in 2013* [online]. London, Independent Reviewer of Terrorism Legislation. Retrieved on 17 September 2015 from: https://terrorismlegislationreviewer.independent.gov.uk/wp-content/uploads/2014/07/Independent-Review-of-Terrorism-Report-2014-print2.pdf.

Burton, L., Davis, F., Lynch, A., McGarrity, N., Tulich, T., Welsh, R. and Williams, G., 2012. *Submission to COAG Review of Counter-Terrorism* [online]. Sydney, Gilbert + Tobin Centre of Public Law. Retrieved on 17 September 2015 from: www.gtcentre.unsw.edu.au/sites/gtcentre.unsw.edu.au/files/coag_counter-terrorism_review.pdf.

Carlile, Lord, 2007. *The Definition of Terrorism – A Report by Lord Carlile of Berriew QC Independent Review of Terrorism Legislation* (Cm 7052). London: The Stationery Office.

Commonwealth Parliament, 2002. *Security Legislation Amendment (Terrorism) Bill 2002 [No 2] [Cwlth]* (Bills Digest, No 126 of 2001–2002). Canberra: Department of the Parliamentary Library.

Hogan, G. and Walker, C., 1989. *Political violence and the law in Ireland.* Manchester: Manchester University Press.

Home Office, 2006. *Countering international terrorism: the United Kingdom's strategy* (Cm 6888). London: The Stationery Office.
Lloyd, Lord, 1996. *Inquiry into legislation against terrorism* (Cm 3420). London: The Stationery Office.
Lynch, A., McGarrity, N. and Williams, G., 2015. *Inside Australia's anti-terrorism laws and trials*. Sydney: NewSouth.
Roach, K., 2010. The eroding distinction between intelligence and evidence in terrorism investigations. *In*: N. McGarrity, A. Lynch and G. Williams (eds) *Counter-terrorism and beyond: the culture of law and justice after 9/11*. London and New York: Routledge, 48–68.
Saul, B., 2007. The curious element of motive in definitions of terrorism: essential ingredient or criminalising thought? *In*: A. Lynch, E. MacDonald and G. Williams (eds) *Law and liberty in the war on terror*. Sydney: Federation Press, 28–38.
Security Legislation Review Committee [SLRC], 2006. *Report of the Security Legislation Review Committee*. Canberra: Commonwealth of Australia.
Tulich, T., 2012. A view inside the preventive state: reflections on a decade of anti-terror law. *Griffith Law Review*, 21(1), 209–44.
UN, 2001. *United Nations Security Council Resolution 1373* (UN Doc S/RES/1373 28 September 2001).
Walker, C., 1992. *The prevention of terrorism in British law*. Manchester: Manchester University Press.
Walker, C., 2011. *Terrorism and the law*. Oxford: Oxford University Press.
Williams, G., 2011. A decade of Australian anti-terror laws. *Melbourne University Law Review*, 35(3), 1136–76.
Zedner, L., 2010. Pre-crime and pre-punishment: a health warning. *Criminal Justice Matters*, 81(1), 24–5.

## Cases

*Lodhi v R* [2006] NSWCCA 121.
*R (Cwlth) v Elomar* [2010] 264 ALR 759.
*R v Benbrika (Ruling No 15)* [2007] VSC 545.
*R v Faraz* [2012] EWCA Crim 2820.
*R v Ibrahim and Ors*, Woolwich Crown Court, 11 January 2007, unreported.
*R v K* [2008] EWCA Crim 185.
*R v G, R v J* [2009] UKHL 13.
*Sheldrake v Director of Public Prosecutions; Attorney General's Reference (No 4 of 2002)* [2003] EWCA Crim 762.

## Australian legislation

*Charter of the United Nations Act 1945* (Cwlth).
*Counter-Terrorism Legislation Amendment (Foreign Fighters) Act 2014* (Cwlth).
*Criminal Code Act 1995* (Cwlth).
*Criminal Code (Foreign Incursions and Recruitment – Declared Areas) Declaration 2014 – Al-Raqqa Province, Syria.*
*Criminal Code (Foreign Incursions and Recruitment – Declared Areas) Declaration 2015 – Mosul District, Ninewa Province, Iraq.*

## UK legislation

*Anti-Terrorism, Crime and Security Act 2001* (c. 24).
*Counter-Terrorism Act 2008.*
*Prevention of Terrorism (Temporary Provisions) Act 1974* (c. 56).
*Terrorism Act 2000* (c. 11).
*Terrorism Act 2006* (c. 11).

# 14

# Death investigation, coroners' inquests and human rights

*Rebecca Scott Bray*

## Introduction

> For victims, the bereaved and survivors, death reflects no hierarchy. Whether victims of state violence, of institutionalized brutality or negligence, the 'pain' of death is evenly distributed; it does not discriminate.
>
> *(Scraton 1999, p. 296)*

The nexus between human rights and death investigations is often discussed in the context of human rights abuses perpetrated in war and conflict, where death investigation is framed in terms of its role in, and value to, any subsequent restorative mechanisms. Literature on death investigations in these circumstances has emerged from the forensic sciences, wrestling with the practical and ethical issues of dealing with the dead, and international law scholars, querying the normative work of these exceptional investigations. Comparatively little attention is placed upon the role of human rights in local death investigations, such as coronial inquests, with a handful of legal scholars canvassing rights in the context of coronial work (see, for example, Hunyor 2008, 2009, McIntosh 2012, Freckelton and McGregor 2014). Despite the growing jurisprudence in this area, there remains a general dearth of theoretical literature, and a paucity of sustained attention from a criminological viewpoint. Yet, the expanding role of human rights vis-à-vis coronial work, both in countries with and without an established human rights framework, invites comment. Litigation is clarifying the coronial role apace, while a number of jurisdictions such as the United Kingdom (UK), Australia and New Zealand, have implemented considerable legislative reform.

In some jurisdictions, including Europe and the UK, human rights jurisprudence has exerted a powerful influence upon death investigation law and practice, exhibiting the degree to which a human rights perspective has emerged as 'an important yardstick' in terms of contemporary expectations and requirements (Freckelton and McGregor 2014, p. 584). In other jurisdictions, such as Australia, which does not have an overarching legislative human rights framework, rights issues are nonetheless raised at inquest, testifying to the coronial protection of human rights (Hunyor 2008, p. 71). In Australian inquests, human rights intermittently concern coroners because interested parties (such as human rights agencies and community legal centres) are increasingly raising human rights concerns derived from Strasbourg decisions, thus commenting on state obligations and requirements of 'a human-rights compliant death investigation' (Freckelton and McGregor 2014, p. 585). Given these developments, this chapter elucidates the human rights facets of coronial death investigations in the UK and Australia and possible futures of criminologically inclined death studies.

The focus of this chapter is on inquests, which are inquisitorial, public, fact-finding hearings directed towards ascertaining the identity of the deceased, the place, and the cause and circumstances of death; often referred to as the 'who, where, what and how'. Where previously this task was interpreted narrowly, the modern coroner augments this fact-finding mission with an eye to the preventability of avoidable death, possessing statutory powers to make recommendations so as to communicate the lessons of death to the community, including government agencies and policy-makers. This preventive function has been steadily legislated for throughout Australia, and is finding greater purchase in the UK as a result of human rights litigation, yet these jurisdictions are fundamentally distinct in their 'legal architecture' around human rights (Freckelton and McGregor 2014, p. 586). This chapter now turns to consider the hitherto contribution of criminology to death investigation study, before addressing those key jurisdictional differences.

## Criminology and the coroner

Save few exceptions, criminological scholarship is found largely wanting on any wholesale attention to theorizing death investigation. As a research focus, death investigations are typically brought into the field of criminology by virtue of methodological questions (see, for example, Pelfrey and White Covington 2007) or where coronial processes and documents (coronial findings, inquest proceedings and transcripts) form the basis for case study research (see, for example, Prenzler 2010). Until recently, case-based research has comprised the most significant body of criminological consideration of death investigation practices and systems, and has centred on controversial deaths, with a predominant focus on deaths in custody and policing-related deaths, but extending to deaths in disasters and other scenarios (see, for example, Warwick Inquest Group 1985, Scraton and Chadwick 1987, Hogan et al. 1988, Scraton 1999).

Criminological research is typified by the signal work of Phil Scraton who has queried inquests since the 1980s (see, for example, Scraton and Chadwick 1987). Scraton identifies that the:

> expanding case-based literature demonstrates that deaths in controversial circumstances ... are increasingly contested. They comprise a broad range of individual and collective cases in which the working practices of powerful political-economic institutions, from state agencies to major corporations, are placed under public scrutiny in the context of criminal and civil liability.
>
> *(Scraton 2002, p. 109)*

This research has scrutinized not only working practices, such as policing, but also official responses to deaths in certain contexts. In a damning indictment, it has highlighted how official discourses on death, including coroners' inquests, are shot through with 'powerful political-economic interests' shaping the material conditions of life and death (Scraton 2002, p. 110). The delivery of coronial justice has been critiqued for being 'sustained by ideologies which are expressions of structural inequalities. The structural relations of production (class) reproduction (patriarchy), neocolonialism ('race') and age (childhood) are powerful determining contexts'

(Scraton 2002, p. 110). Correspondingly, through case-based research, inquests have been analysed to reveal a litany of deficiencies that ultimately compromise their value as a truth-seeking exercise, leaving researchers underwhelmed, the truth degraded and the bereaved denied justice (Scraton 1999, p. 273, Scraton 2002, Warwick Inquest Group 1985).

Save these exceptions and promising theoretical beginnings, criminologists still neglect the coronial jurisdiction and do not afford it steady theorizing across its jurisdictional idiosyncrasies. Research into coronial law and practice has been left to disciplines such as medicine, law, sociology, social work and psychology, with the latter's expertise in grief, bereavement and death studies. Yet given coronial law mandates a response to the broad genre of deaths, it exposes a wide-ranging set of issues worthy of sustained criminological examination, including matters such as inquest scope, evidence, and coronial verdicts and findings. These matters become particularly germane when coupled with questions about police powers, or national security, to name but a few. In response, recent scholarship has begun to reignite criminological attention to the coronial jurisdiction, tackling myriad issues such as Indigenous deaths (Finnane and Richards 2004, Scott Bray 2008, Razack 2015), policing (Martin and Scott Bray 2013) and immigration custodial deaths (Powell et al. 2015), medical and legal epistemologies (Kramar 2006, Carpenter and Tait 2010), autopsies and cultural concerns (Carpenter et al. 2011, 2015), coronial fact finding (Scott Bray 2010) and inquests in a new media age (Scott Bray 2013).

Despite this renewed attention to coroners, human rights considerations emerge in only a handful of criminological and criminal justice contributions (see, for example, Scraton 1999, Martynowicz 2011). With his emphasis on truth-seeking and acknowledgment of the marginalized 'view from below', Phil Scraton has notably promoted a human rights agenda to address the shortcomings of official discourses around death (Scraton 1999, p. 297). For example, he has comprehensively observed the failings of official responses to the 15 April 1989 Hillsborough Stadium disaster, when 96 people died as a result of the fatal crush at the stadium (see, for example, Scraton et al. 1995). Despite the extensive range of public investigations, reviews and inquiries, the Hillsborough Independent Panel, of which Scraton was a part, paradoxically remarked that 'many bereaved families and survivors considered that the true context, circumstances and aftermath of Hillsborough had not been adequately made public' (Hillsborough Independent Panel 2012, p. 4). Revealing a catalogue of official failings, including the inadequacy of the inquest process, the Panel dismantled the official 'truth' of the disaster; subsequent to which the Attorney-General successfully applied to the High Court to quash the original 'accidental death' inquest verdicts, and new inquests were ordered. Turning to a human rights framework, Phil Scraton has worked with the Hillsborough families and examined official processes to outline how 'deep political and ideological assumptions, coupled with professional self-interest and survival, combined to demonize the victims, to deny their 'truth', to disqualify their experiences, and to undermine justice' (Scraton 1999, p. 296). Calling for more attention to the capacities of human rights approaches, Scraton notes that '[f]or too long, the witnessing and acknowledgement of the "truth", through alternative accounts formally presented and recorded, have been considered appropriate only after the overthrow of terror-based state regimes. Yet there is a case for wider application' (Scraton 1999, p. 280).

Notwithstanding this call, it is clear that human rights concerns have strongly impacted normative coronial practice. The UK is bound by the *European Convention on Human Rights* (ECHR) obligations through the implementation of the *Human Rights Act 1998* (UK) (HRA), which affects coroners, from the shape of their inquiries to the form of coronial findings. Australia has no federal bill of rights, with only two jurisdictions, Victoria and the Australian Capital Territory (ACT), enacting human rights legislation. Despite this, coronial law displays a uniquely rights-attuned focus, making Australia a distinctively principled coronial jurisdiction.

As such, coronial practice in the UK and Australia differentially highlights the prevalence of human rights law *and* principles in death investigation. This chapter now turns to discuss the UK approach, with its fuller rights-based statutory mandate.

## Death investigation and human rights in the UK

### Spotlighting human rights

The impact of human rights on UK coronial death investigation was thrown into sharp relief in 2008 when the government proposed holding closed, juryless inquests into deaths where the inquest would involve sensitive material, including material that should not be made public in the interests of national security (Scott Bray 2012). The 'secret' inquests clauses were introduced in the context of counter-terrorism, ushering in a three-year period in which successive governments repeatedly sought to pass legislation that prescribed holding closed inquests (Martin and Scott Bray 2013).

The proposals were precipitated by a legal impasse around inadmissible intercept evidence at the inquest into the death of Azelle Rodney, who was shot dead during a police operation in London in 2005. The coroner acknowledged the tensions between his obligation to hold a jury inquest, an Article 2 compliant inquest – which included 'the disclosure of core documents' (Walker 2007, p. 3) – and the prohibition on the material's disclosure. With his hands tied, the coroner adjourned the inquest into Rodney's death. The paramount importance of human rights considerations to these events spotlighted rights in the context of coronial death investigation. After all, the government asserted that the proposals for closed inquests would ameliorate the bind it was in to satisfy the state's obligations under Article 2 in circumstances where sensitive material could not be disclosed (Scott Bray 2012, pp. 576–7). Despite these claims, it was widely argued that Article 2 obligations would be further frustrated, not advanced, by a lack of public scrutiny, independence, transparency and accountability (Scott Bray 2012, p. 579). This chapter now moves to discuss those obligations in greater depth, for, arguably, it is Article 2 that has had the most impact on UK coronial law and practice.

### Article 2 and death investigations

Human rights litigation has transformed the field of UK death investigation, clarifying the coronial role in the context of ECHR obligations, which is augmented by recent statutory law reform. Arguably, the most significant influence has come from the impact of Article 2, the right to life. Since the passage of the *Human Rights Act 1998* (UK) which incorporated the ECHR into domestic law, UK coronial law is necessarily contextualized by Article 2, which provides that 'everyone's right to life shall be protected by law'.

The right to life infers two substantive obligations on the state: a negative obligation to refrain from taking life without justification, and a positive obligation to protect it by establishing a framework of laws, precautions, procedures and means of enforcement (see *R (Middleton) v HM Coroner for West Somerset*, para. 2). The positive duty inferred includes a duty to investigate unnatural death, including, but not restricted to, deaths involving state agents (*Edwards v United Kingdom*; *McCann v United Kingdom*). This general obligation to provide a legal system that independently and effectively investigates *any* death provides a benchmark standard to which all inquests need comply. Resulting inquests are now commonly termed '*Jamieson*' inquests, following the decision of *R v Coroner for North Humberside and Scunthorpe; Ex parte Jamieson*, which elucidated the statutory fact-finding role of the coroner. *Jamieson* determined that the coronial obligation to find 'how' the deceased died was construed narrowly to refer to 'by what means' the deceased came about their death, that is, the immediate means of death (and not the broader circumstances), thereby limiting the scope of available verdicts.

In addition to these substantive obligations on the state, an autonomous procedural, or investigative, duty is triggered following a breach of a substantive Article 2 obligation, where the state may be responsible for the death or where it fails to prevent a death (*R (Middleton) v HM Coroner for West Somerset*, para. 19). The duty is triggered automatically in certain categories of cases, including killings by state agents and deaths in custody (Thomas et al. 2014, p. 409). The automatic duty to investigate deaths in such circumstances is due to the fact that such individuals are vulnerable, under the care and control of the state, and because the events in issue lie within the knowledge of the authorities (Thomas et al. 2014, p. 409, *Jordan v United Kingdom*, para. 103, *R (Sacker) v HM Coroner for West Yorkshire*, para. 11, *McCann v United Kingdom*, para. 191). As stated in *McCann v United Kingdom*, an effective system of investigation is vital in such cases because '[a] general legal prohibition of arbitrary killing by state authorities would be rendered nugatory if, in practice, there was no mechanism for reviewing the action of the state agents' (para. 191).

The importance of Article 2 for UK coronial law lies in the expectation that the inquest is usually the means by which the state discharges the investigative duty (*R (Middleton) v HM Coroner for West Somerset*). The essential purpose of an Article 2 death investigation is 'to secure the effective implementation of the domestic laws which protect the right to life and, in those cases involving State agents or bodies, to ensure their accountability for deaths occurring under their responsibility' (*Jordan v United Kingdom*, para. 105, *R (Amin) v Secretary of State for the Home Department*: para. 20[5]). Furthermore, as stated in *Amin*, the purposes of the investigation are:

> to ensure so far as possible that the full facts are brought to light; that culpable and discreditable conduct is exposed and brought to public notice; that suspicion of deliberate wrongdoing (if unjustified) is allayed; that dangerous practices and procedures are rectified; and that those who have lost their relative may at least have the satisfaction of knowing that lessons learned from his death may save the lives of others.
>
> *(Para. 31)*

To satisfy Article 2, the investigation must be on the state's initiative (that is, not next of kin); independent – requiring investigators to be independent from those implicated in events, both institutionally and in practice; effective – so that the investigation is capable of leading to a determination of whether state action was justified, and identification and punishment of those responsible; reasonably prompt; transparent – by allowing for sufficient public scrutiny to ensure accountability; and allow the next of kin to participate to the extent necessary to safeguard their interests (see *Jordan v United Kingdom*, paras 105–9, *R (Amin) v Secretary of State for the Home Department*; *Edwards v United Kingdom*, paras 69–73).

Litigation has clarified Article 2 obligations, highlighting a number of different scenarios in which substantive and procedural obligations have been breached. The European Court of Human Rights has found breaches in cases involving use of force by state agents, delays in arrest, a failure to appropriately support operations, a failure to prosecute, inadequate staff training, a failure to protect certain individuals at risk (such as prisoners), failure or a delay in carrying out appropriate forensic tests, and a failure to take witness statements (see Thomas et al. 2014, Chapter 18). Such cases demonstrate the degree to which human rights litigation scrutinizes not only human rights breaches but death investigation processes themselves.

In the UK, those inquests required to satisfy the Article 2 procedural duty are referred to as 'Article 2', 'enhanced' or '*Middleton*' inquests after key litigation that sought to establish whether domestic UK coronial law was compatible with ECHR obligations. *R (Middleton) v HM Coroner for West Somerset* considered what the ECHR required by way of verdict, judgment, findings or recommendations of an Article 2 investigation, whether UK coronial legislation met those requirements and, if not, whether and how the regime governing the conduct of inquests might be revised to meet ECHR obligations (para. 4). The death in custody case of *Middleton* determined that, to satisfy the procedural duty, coroners and juries were to take a broad approach to the question of 'how' the deceased died, interpreting it as not strictly confined to 'by what means' (as in *Jamieson*) but 'by what means and in what circumstances'. This broader consideration of the background or surrounding circumstances of a death is now shored up by s 5(2) of the *Coroners and Justice Act 2009* (UK). Correspondingly, in some cases, the jury's conclusions on surrounding issues could not be sufficiently accommodated in a traditional short form verdict. Instead, this change of approach to the interpretation of how the deceased came by their death could require the coroner to invite a narrative verdict (para. 35), which may be more informative than short verdicts such as 'misadventure', giving greater scope to appreciate the surrounding circumstances of a death, such as the instructions, training and supervision of officials (*R (Ali Zaki Mousa) v Secretary of State for Defence (No 2)*, paras 148–9, 221).

The change brought about by *Middleton* was 'of real consequence', ushering in 'an era of more probing investigation of the overall context and issues that give rise to deaths' with a concomitant focus on whether they are preventable (Freckelton and McGregor 2014, p. 588). Consequently, human rights jurisprudence has steered contemporary coronial law and practice towards a more preventive promise. Cases such as *Amin*, with its emphasis on *lessons learned* from death, have encouraged the preventive role (Freckelton and McGregor 2014, p. 590). The *Coroners and Justice Act 2009* (UK) similarly reflects this evolving ethos by upgrading prevention of future deaths reports from a rule to part of the substantive Act, and securing a coroner's duty to make a report where a concern is identified. Human rights considerations have therefore clarified what is expected in the conduct of inquests and their outcomes. In this way, such rights-based accountability illustrates how these rights operate in the context of coronial work itself. Correspondingly, the rich field of Strasbourg jurisprudence and consequent coronial change highlights a jurisdiction more deserving of critical criminological reflection.

In respect of inquest investigation scope and purpose, the UK approach is broadly consistent with Australian coronial evolution, which demonstrates a preventive ethos. Arguably, Article 2 has greatly flavoured UK coronial rigour, whereas Australia, despite not being influenced by human rights in quite the same way, still displays a uniquely rights-attuned focus. This chapter now moves to consider human rights and death investigation in this latter context.

## Human rights in Australian death investigation

Australia is a signatory to a number of human rights treaties, including the *International Covenant on Civil and Political Rights* (ICCPR) and the *International Covenant on Economic, Social and Cultural Rights* (ICESCR). However, international obligations under these conventions do not provide for domestically enforceable rights in the absence of legislation incorporaing those rights in local laws, although aggrieved individuals can, for example, communicate their claim in respect of a breach of the ICCPR to the United Nations Human Rights Committee (UNHRC). Both Victoria, by way of its *Charter of Human Rights and Responsibilities Act 2006* (Vic) (Charter), and the ACT by virtue of its *Human Rights Act 2004* (ACT) (HRA), give some effect to human rights in the local context, providing for rights-protecting legislative scrutiny and the requirement that public authorities act consistently with human rights. Yet these latter instruments do not have the 'array of teeth' as the ECHR does in the UK in terms of compensatory remedies (Freckelton and McGregor 2014, p. 587). In effect, there remains a weakness with respect to enforcing right to life obligations and addressing any possible breach.

This is not to say that Australia disregards the protection of human rights in the coronial context. As with the UK, Australia has undergone a considerable amount of coronial reform in recent decades that reflects the degree to which its coronial law and practice is practically 'fashioned and influenced by considerations that are respectful of human rights' (Freckelton and McGregor 2014, p. 599). The coroner's jurisdiction has moved from a strictly reactive to a more proactive assessment of deaths, as demonstrated by coroners' recommendatory functions, which 'represent the distillation of the preventive potential of the coronial process' (Halstead 1998, p. 187). This development has, as outlined by Hunyor, 'recognised the potential for a coroner to have a role in preventing future deaths, rather than simply reporting on past incidents' (Hunyor 2008, p. 65). Coroners in all Australian jurisdictions have the power to make recommendations, however, mandatory responses are required in only some jurisdictions, leading commentators to question the ultimate impact of coronial insight, and signaling the devastating amount of coronial expertise that is stockpiling without consequence throughout Australia (Scott Bray 2008, p. 36). Some jurisdictions have gone further, to statutorily express the preventive principle (see, for example, *Coroners Act 2008* [Vic] s. 1[c]). This focus on prevention is considered faithful to right to life obligations, which demand an independent inquiry into deaths and the facility to learn lessons to prevent avoidable deaths (Australian Inquest Alliance 2011, p. 16).

Arguably, Australian coronial evolution owes much to the impetus of the Royal Commission into Aboriginal Deaths in Custody (RCIADIC), which was established in 1987 to investigate the high number of Aboriginal custodial deaths. The focus on the coronial recommendatory function was loudest following the release of the RCIADIC's 1991 *National Report*, which revealed 'the pervasive and troubling failure' of the coronial system in every State and Territory to uncover the circumstances of Aboriginal deaths in custody and to make appropriate recommendations (Watterson et al. 2008, p. 6). It recognized the vital role of the coroner, producing 34 recommendations to modernize the system and enhance its preventive potential, which have been variously implemented (see Amnesty International 2015). It has been argued that the clause-by-clause nature of post-RCIADIC coronial reforms, including the ad hoc changes throughout jurisdictions regarding coronial recommendations and responses, demonstrates a capricious level of reform that potentially forfeits the preventive power of the coroner (Scott Bray 2008, p. 30).

A broadly principled approach to rights is evident in other reforms. Throughout Australia, coronial law reform has focused on a range of issues that highlight the management of the deceased; post-mortem examination practices; the rights and role of families in the coronial process; and inquest scope. These reforms provide a rich statutory mandate giving regard to cultural concerns around, for example, postmortem practices, matters that are not comparatively legislated for in UK coronial law. Such reforms quite practically give life to rights such as the right to privacy, family and cultural life (Article 8 of the ECHR, Articles 17, 23, 27 of the ICCPR) and the right to freedom of religion (Article 9 of the ECHR, Article 18 of the ICCPR).

Furthermore, despite not being preoccupied wholesale by the same Article 2 enunciations that find purchase in *Middleton*, Australian coronial fact-finding has nevertheless echoed the *Middleton* approach, with *Atkinson v Morrow* determining that the expression 'how the death occurred' should be given the broad construction of 'by what means and in what circumstances the death occurred'. Correspondingly, the narrative form of coronial findings has long been a strong feature of Australian coronial practice. Coroners routinely declare their findings of fact through discursive statements of circumstances. And while the structure of findings varies from jurisdiction to jurisdiction, the robust narration of findings is a common feature and arguably significantly more contextually discursive than even the most fulsome UK narrative verdicts. This approach has been known to frustrate the courts, who have castigated Australian coroners for prolix findings (*Keown v Kahn*).

Ostensibly, the fact-finding task of the coroner appears uncontroversial, yet criminological scholars have unpacked this task to highlight how death's 'facts' have an extra-legal life, so that the call for coronial justice is weighted with particular histories. This is especially notable in deaths in custody, including Indigenous deaths, which can 'petition distinct socio-legal legacies', such as social injustice and the historical tenor of policing practices (Scott Bray 2013, p. 464, 2010). Correspondingly, it is by stretching back through Australian social and legal history that the external facts, such as policing of Indigenous people, come to make sense of contemporary death, and coronial processes involve a circuit whereby deaths simultaneously 'represent and reinforce the issues between Indigenous people and authorities' (Scott Bray 2010, p. 587). When the facts of death freight specific histories of Indigenous life, coronial inquiries have implications well beyond 'mere' fact-finding in individual deaths.

In terms of the coronial task, human rights are finding effect via human rights interveners in inquests, such as the (then) Australian Human Rights and Equal Opportunity Commission's (HREOC) submissions to the inquest into the death in custody of Mulrunji Doomadgee in 2004 on Palm Island, Queensland, the inquest into the death of Elder Ward during prison transportation in Western Australia in 2008, and the Human Rights Law Centre (HRLC) submissions to the inquest into the death of 15-year-old Tyler Cassidy, who was shot dead by police in Victoria in 2008. Commonly, interveners are granted leave to appear as interested parties to assist the coroner with identifying human rights issues, understanding the interplay between those rights and the circumstances of death, and understanding state obligations with respect to the implementation and protection of those rights. In practice, this means making submissions on matters such as inquest scope, and coroner's comments and recommendations. These contributions are often effective. For example, the HREOCs final submission to the Mulrunji Doomadgee inquest detailed 40 recommendations across four main areas (including arrest and policing) that it saw as necessary to the protection of human rights. The coroner accepted the HREOC submission and adopted all recommendations, demonstrating that human rights interveners can have very material impacts at inquest (Hunyor 2008, pp. 70–1).

In some cases, the situation is more controversial. A case highlighting the impetus for change around Australian right to life obligations in the coronial context is the death of Tyler Cassidy. Cassidy was 15 years old when he was shot dead by Victoria Police in Melbourne. In 2013, the HRLC submitted a communication to the UNHRC on behalf of Tyler's mother, Shani Cassidy. It contended that Australia breached Article 6(1) (right to life) of the ICCPR by not providing an independent and effective investigation into Tyler's death, as Victoria Police investigated a death at the hands of its own officers; and that Article 2 of the ICCPR (effective remedy) was also breached, as the state did not ensure an effective remedy via the inquest process itself, nor via its recommendations (HRLC 2013, pp. 54–7). For example, a key coronial recommendation to ensure independent oversight of interviews with police in all police-related deaths was not implemented (see Freckelton and McGregor 2014, pp. 598–9), highlighting the bugbear around coronial recommendations which are just that: solely recommendatory, with coroners possessing no power to make enforceable orders. Thus, despite the not incompatible nature of the Australian coronial jurisdiction with human rights principles, read at its worst, the Cassidy communication has spotlighted the Australian coronial system 'in an international forum where Australia is increasingly out of step with jurisprudential developments' (Freckelton and McGregor 2014, p. 585).

## Conclusion: towards a more exacting law and critique?

In 2011 the Australian government released its draft Baseline Study for consultation as part of the process of implementing a National Human Rights Action Plan. In their submission, the advocacy group Australian Inquest Alliance (AIA) outlined the relevance of the coronial system to Australia's human rights obligations. The AIA documented a number of areas that highlight the coronial capacity to protect human rights, in addition to the limitations that frustrate and potentially breach these rights, such as inquest delays, lack of resources for coroners, and limitations with respect to coronial recommendations. Whether a federal Australian bill of rights, enshrining human rights obligations in local laws, would ameliorate these thorny coronial matters remains to be seen.

Writing on UK inquest law, Thomas et al. have noted that while there are a number of domestic UK cases prior to the HRA that have emphasized 'the need for full and fearless inquiries . . . the requirements of the ECHR are more exacting than domestic law was' (Thomas et al. 2014, p. 380). Arguably, however, despite recent reform and judicial comment, UK coronial legislation is paradoxically less rights-attuned than its Australian counterpart, not containing, for example, comparative statutory provisions around objections to post-mortems (*R (Rotsztein) v HM Senior Coroner for Inner London North*). Notably, in 2000, Australia established the National Coronial Information System, a database of coronial information, and States and Territories coroner's offices regularly publish coronial findings on their websites, demonstrating an accessibility and openness to coronial process not found in the UK. In many ways, Australia already has progressive coronial law and practice, with the result that 'the exigencies which have generated some of the human rights litigation in respect of United Kingdom death investigation law and practice are not replicated in Australia' (Freckelton and McGregor 2014, p. 601). Still, would greater recognition of human rights obligations in Australian law have the potential to enhance key coronial functions, such as the recommendatory function considered so vital to protecting human rights through its preventive ethos? In this area, despite their distinct legal architectures around rights, both the UK and Australia have some way to go until coronial recommendations reach their preventive promise, including resources for informed recommendations and any enforceability.

Whatever the argument, it seems at a minimum that robust rights-attuned coronial legislation is beneficial. Legislative scrutiny on recent UK coronial reform commented on it as a 'human rights enhancing measure' (UK Joint Committee on Human Rights 2009, p. 25). All told, Australia statutory and appellate coronial law demonstrates an affinity with human rights considerations that is not incompatible with the European approach. It is becoming clear that Australian coroners cannot, and in fact, do not ignore human rights considerations in discharging their investigative duty. Thus, while national human rights legislation might further hone the human rights considerations of Australian coroners, coroners themselves are already operating under the influence of international jurisprudence in working towards a more exacting law. This work would be matched beneficially by critical assessments from criminologists, who, despite being alive to the numerous criminal justice contexts in which deaths occur, tend to overlook the coronial jurisdiction. Given the recent surge in international coronial law reform and its tenor of human rights, criminologists may exact much more from this jurisdiction than hitherto they have. Deaths that are subject to this type of investigation surely demand it.

## References

Amnesty International, 2015. *Review of the implementation of the recommendations of the RCIADIC Recommendations.* Chapter 3 The Adequacy of Post Death Investigations (Recommendations 6-40) [online]. Retrieved on 14 November 2015 from: https://changetherecord.org.au/review-of-the-implementation-of-rciadic-may-2015.

Australian Inquest Alliance, 2011. *Submission to the National Human Rights Action Plan Baseline Study Consultation* [online]. Victorian Aboriginal Legal Service. Retrieved on 14 August 2015 from: www.vals.org.au/assets/2015/06/Australian-Inquest-Alliance-submission-to-the-National-Human-Rights-Action-Plan-Draft-Baseline-Study-Consultation.pdf.

Carpenter, B. and Tait, G., 2010. The autopsy imperative: medicine, law, and the coronial investigation. *Journal of Medical Humanities*, 31(3), 205–21.

Carpenter, B., Tait, G., Adkins, G., Barnes, M., Naylor, C. and Begum, N., 2011. Communicating with the coroner: how religion, culture, and family concerns may influence autopsy decision making. *Death Studies*, 35(4), 316–37.

Carpenter, B., Tait, G., Quadrelli, C. and Drayton, J., 2015. Scrutinising the other: incapacity, suspicion and manipulation in a death investigation. *Journal of Intercultural Studies*, 36(2), 113–28.

Finnane, M. and Richards, J. 2004. 'You'll get nothing out of it'? The inquest, police and Aboriginal deaths in colonial Queensland. *Australian Historical Studies*, 123(35), 84–105.

Freckelton, I. and McGregor, S., 2014. Coronial law and practice: a human rights perspective. *Journal of Law and Medicine*, 21(3), 584–601.

Halstead, B., 1998. Coroners' recommendations following deaths in custody. *In*: H. Selby (ed.), *The inquest handbook*. Leichhardt, NSW: Federation Press, 186–205.

Hillsborough Independent Panel, 2012. *Hillsborough: the report of the Hillsborough Independent Panel*. London: Stationery Office.

Hogan, M., Brown, D. and Hogg, R. (eds), 1988. *Deaths in the hands of the state*. Redfern: Redfern Legal Centre Publishing.

Human Rights Law Centre, 2013. *Individual communication to the United Nations Human Rights Committee by Shani Cassidy*. 29 May 2013 [online]. Human Rights Law Centre. Retrieved on 14 August 2015 from: www.hrlc.org.au/wp-content/uploads/2013/05/UN_Communication_regarding_TylerCassidy_May2013.pdf.

Hunyor, J., 2008. Human rights in coronial inquests. *Australian Indigenous Law Review*, 12(SE2), 64–74.

Hunyor, J., 2009. Disgrace: the death of Mr Ward. *Indigenous Law Bulletin*, 7(15), 3–8.

Kramar, K., 2006. Coroners' interested advocacy: understanding wrongful accusations and convictions. *Canadian Journal of Criminology and Criminal Justice*, 48(5), 803–22.

Martin, G., and Scott Bray, R., 2013. Discolouring democracy? Policing, sensitive evidence, and contentious deaths in the United Kingdom. *Journal of Law and Society*, 40(4), 624–56.

Martynowicz, A., 2011. Oversight of prison conditions and investigations of deaths in custody: international human rights standards and the practice in Ireland. *The Prison Journal*, 91(1), 81–102.

McIntosh, S., 2012. Fulfilling their purpose? Inquests, Article 2 and next of kin. *Public Law*, 3, 407–15.

Pelfrey, W. and White Covington, M., 2007. Deaths in custody: the utility of data collected from county coroners. *Criminal Justice Studies*, 20(1), 65–78.

Powell, R., Weber, L. and Pickering, S., 2015. Every death counts: an argument for counting deaths in immigration custody in the national deaths in custody collection. *Current Issues in Criminal Justice*, 27(1), 113–21.

Prenzler, T., 2010. Learning from police deaths on duty: a case study. *Policing: A Journal of Policy and Practice*, 4(4), 421–31.

Razack, S., 2015. *Dying from improvement: inquests and inquiries into indigenous deaths in custody*. Toronto: University of Toronto Press.

Scott Bray, R., 2008. Why this law?: vagaries of jurisdiction in coronial reform and indigenous death prevention. *Australian Indigenous Law Review*, 12(SE 2), 27–44.

Scott Bray, R., 2010. Death scene jurisprudence: the social life of coronial facts. *Griffith Law Review*, 19(3), 567–92.

Scott Bray, R., 2012. Executive impunity and parallel justice? The United Kingdom debate on secret inquests and inquiries. *Journal of Law and Medicine*, 19(3), 569–92.

Scott Bray, R., 2013. Paradoxical justice: the case of Ian Tomlinson. *Journal of Law and Medicine*, 21(2), 447–72.

Scraton, P., 1999. Policing with contempt: the degrading of truth and denial of justice in the aftermath of the Hillsborough disaster. *Journal of Law and Society*, 26(3), 273–97.
Scraton, P., 2002. Lost lives, hidden voices: 'truth' and controversial deaths. *Race & Class*, 44(1), 107–18.
Scraton, P. and Chadwick, K., 1987. *In the arms of the law: coroners' inquests and deaths in custody*. London: Pluto Press.
Scraton, P., Jemphrey, A. and Coleman, S., 1995. *No last rights: the denial of justice and the promotion of myth in the aftermath of the Hillsborough disaster*. Liverpool: Liverpool City Council.
Thomas, L. et al., 2014. *Inquests: a practitioner's guide*. London: Legal Action Group.
UK Joint Committee on Human Rights, House of Lords, 2009. *Legislative scrutiny: coroners and Justice Bill*. Eighth Report of Session 2008-09, HC 362 HL Paper 57.
Walker, A., 2007. *In the matter touching the death of Azelle Rodney: reasons for the ruling made August 2 2007*.
Warwick Inquest Group, 1985. The inquest as a theatre for police tragedy: the Davey case. *Journal of Law and Society*, 12(1), 35–61.
Watterson, R., Brown, P. and McKenzie, J., 2008. Coronial reform and the prevention of indigenous death. *Australian Indigenous Law Review*, 12(SE2), 4–26.

## Cases

*Atkinson v Morrow* [2005] QCA 353.
*Atkinson v Morrow* [2005] QSC 92.
*Edwards v United Kingdom* (2002) 35 EHRR 19.
*Jordan v United Kingdom* (2003) 37 EHRR 2.
*Keown v Kahn* [1999] 1 VR 69.
*McCann v United Kingdom* (1996) 21 EHRR 97.
*R (Ali Zaki Mousa) v Secretary of State for Defence (No 2)* [2013] EWHC 1412 (Admin).
*R (Amin) v Secretary of State for the Home Department* [2004] 1 AC 653.
*R (Middleton) v HM Coroner for West Somerset* [2004] 2 AC 182.
*R v Coroner for North Humberside and Scunthorpe; Ex parte Jamieson* [1995] QB 1.
*R (Rotsztein) v HM Senior Coroner for Inner London North* [2015] EWHC 2764 (Admin).
*R (Sacker) v HM Coroner for West Yorkshire* [2004] UKHL 11.

## Legislation

*Coroners and Justice Act 2009* (UK).
*European Convention on Human Rights*.
*International Covenant on Civil and Political Rights*.
*International Covenant on Economic, Social and Cultural Rights*.
*Charter of Human Rights and Responsibilities Act 2006* (Vic).
*Human Rights Act 2004* (ACT).
*Human Rights Act 1998* (UK).

# 15

# Australian border policing, the detention of children and state crime

*Michael Grewcock*

## Introduction

> Australia has undertaken international obligations to take all appropriate legislative, administrative, social and educational measures to protect children from sexual abuse and other forms of abuse, including measures for the prevention, identification, reporting, referral, investigation, treatment and follow up of incidents of child abuse.
>
> *(Terms of Reference, Royal Commission into Institutional Responses to Child Sexual Abuse January 2013)*

> Data from the Department of Immigration and Border Protection describes numerous incidents of assault, sexual assault and self-harm in detention environments. . . . [T]he prolonged, mandatory detention of asylum seeker children causes them significant mental and physical illness and developmental delays, in breach of Australia's international obligations.
>
> *(Australian Human Rights Commission [AHRC] December 2014)*

> I saw a six year old girl who tried to hang herself with a fence tie and had marks around her neck. I've never seen a child self-harm of that age before. . . . After five days I went home and had nightmares. . . . It's child abuse. Putting children in detention is child abuse.
>
> *(Paediatrician, Dr David Isaacs, reflecting on his visit to Nauru Regional Processing Centre August 2015)*

This chapter discusses the systemic abuse of children within Australia's immigration detention regime identified by the AHRC National Inquiry into Children in Immigration Detention (AHRC 2014); the review of allegations of sexual assault and other misconduct by staff employed at the Australian funded Regional Processing Centre on Nauru (Moss 2015); and the Australian Senate's Select Committee Inquiry into the Nauru Regional Processing Centre in 2015.[1]

Australia is a signatory to the main international human rights instruments relevant to refugees, including the Refugee Convention, the *International Covenant on Civil and Political Rights*, the *Convention Against Torture* and the *Convention on the Rights of the Child*. Yet, since 1992, when a unique system of mandatory detention was introduced to target refugees arriving by boat without a visa, the Australian government has undermined or openly breached its formal human rights commitments to refugees and sought where possible to deny them access to Australian jurisdiction for the purpose of claiming protection. Australian government policies have been condemned repeatedly by United Nations (UN) human rights bodies, international non-government organizations and the AHRC. However, these criticisms have been rejected or ignored, largely on the basis that unauthorized migration by refugees represents a more fundamental existential threat (Grewcock 2009, 2015). Within the dominant paradigm of Australian border policing, the right to inflict levels of institutional harm that would be considered grossly deviant, if not criminal, in other circumstances is at best rationalized as an unfortunate necessity; at worst, as a measure of government competence and resolve to 'protect' the borders.

The Australian government's commitment to a criminogenic immigration detention underscores a deep contradiction at the heart of Australian public policy. When she announced the establishment of a Royal Commission into Institutional Child Abuse in November 2012, the Labor Prime Minister reflected the bipartisan parliamentary rhetoric that any form of child abuse is unacceptable, by declaring: 'I believe we must do everything we can to make sure that what has happened in the past is never allowed to happen again' (Cullen 2012).

However, the concerns animating the government's decision to establish the Royal Commission do not extend to child refugees. In 2012–13, the numbers of children detained in immigration detention centres spiked to a near-record 1992 by July 2013 (AHRC 2014, p. 11). By the time the AHRC established its Inquiry into Children in Immigration Detention in February 2014, there were 'over 1,000 children in detention . . . for longer periods than in the past with no pathway to resettlement' (AHRC 2014, p. 11). Most of these children were detained on Christmas Island or in centres on the Australian mainland. However, over 170 were also being held on Nauru following the Labor government's re-introduction of offshore processing in August 2012, a policy that revived the Liberal-National Party Coalition's Pacific Solution of 2001–07. Under the revived policy, unauthorized arrivals became liable to forced transfer to Nauru or Manus Island (PNG) and any refugee attempting unauthorized entry after July 2013, was rendered ineligible for re-settlement in Australia (Grewcock 2014).

## History repeating itself: children in immigration detention

In 2004, the Human Rights and Equal Opportunities Commission[2] conducted an inquiry into the detention of 2,184 children detained between July 1999 and June 2003 (HREOC 2004, p. 9). The inquiry found that the detention system was 'fundamentally inconsistent with the Convention on the Rights of the Child' (HREOC 2004, pp. 5–6) and its recommendations included the release with their parents of all children in immigration detention centres and residential housing projects within four weeks and urgent amendments to Australia's immigration laws to ensure compliance with the *Convention on the Rights of the Child* (HREOC 2004, pp. 2–3). Ultimately, some policy changes were made to the detention regime by the then Coalition government but the basic legal framework mandating detention remained intact, enabling the return to the mass incarceration of children, once unauthorized refugee arrivals increased after 2012 (Grewcock 2009, pp. 224–30).

The AHRC Inquiry into Children in Immigration Detention was conducted between February and October 2014. The Inquiry teams visited 11 Australian detention centres but did not have jurisdiction to visit the Offshore Processing Centre on Nauru (AHRC 2014, p. 12). The Commission's report detailed multiple breaches of the *Convention on the Rights of the Child* and other human rights treaties. Its main recommendations included: the release of all children and their families into community detention or the community on bridging visas with a right to work; legislation to ensure that children may be detained for only so long as is necessary for health, identity and security checks; no child be sent offshore for processing unless it is clear their human rights will be respected; the appointment of an independent guardian for unaccompanied children seeking asylum in Australia; legislation to give direct effect to the *Convention on the Rights of the Child* under Australian law; and the establishment of a Royal Commission similar to the current Royal Commission into Institutional Child Abuse (AHRC 2014, pp. 14–15).

The Children in Detention Inquiry enabled detained children to exercise a degree of agency otherwise denied them by the nature and circumstances of their detention. The children's voices in the form of surveys, direct testimony, letters and drawings bore a stark similarity to those recorded by the 2004 report and provided a detailed narrative of the stress and harm caused by detention:

> Living here is hard. The tension in here and the tension from home. . . . Many people here are hurting themselves. Boys cutting hands, arms . . . I was thinking about that.
>
> *(Unaccompanied child, Christmas Island, 4 March 2014)*
>
> It affects the people's mind and the children too. They have 10 months on the detention that means they get crazier and upset.
>
> *(Unaccompanied child, Nauru Detention Centre, May 2014)*
>
> My hope finished now. I don't have any hope. I feel I will die in detention.
>
> *(Unaccompanied 17-year-old, Phosphate Hill Detention Centre, Christmas Island, 4 March 2014).*
>
> *(AHRC 2014, pp. 61–2, 71)*

The Inquiry detailed the systemic developmental impairment of children in detention and the significant impacts on their emotional and mental health. A survey of parents of detained pre-school children found that '25 percent were always sad and crying' (AHRC 2014, p. 117). A child and family psychiatrist who visited Christmas Island noted:

> The distress of even very young children was evident in many of those we met, with tearfulness or anxiety, delayed or absent speech and parental reports of children crying themselves to sleep at night, nightmares and regression such as bedwetting ...
>
> Children who are prevented from playing and learning, are frightened or frustrated can develop difficult behaviours such as emotional outbursts/tantrums, sleep disturbance, nightmares, nail biting, head banging, poor concentration, walking around in an agitated state, failure to listen to parents' requests and playing out their distress in their games ... This was evident in many of the children we saw.
>
> *(AHRC 2014, p. 118)*

The impacts were more severe in relation to primary school age children. Eighty seven percent of primary school age children 'identified changes to their emotional or mental health' (AHRC 2014, p. 123). Moreover:

> Forty percent of children said that they felt sad and were crying all the time. Twenty-five percent said that they were always worried; 13 percent had problems with eating or weight

> loss; nine percent reported nightmares; and seven percent were frightened to be apart from their parents.
>
> *(AHRC 2014, p. 123)*

Amongst teenagers, there was 'a high level of self-reported emotional and mental ill-health' and 'high levels of self-harm' (AHRC 2014, p. 139) far exceeding the norm for this age group. Between January 2013 and March 2014, '125 teenagers aged 13 to 17 years old engaged in actual self-harm, and 153 teenagers engaged in threatened self-harm' (AHRC 2014, p. 139). The circumstances in which teenagers engaged in self-harm included:

> - A 14 year old boy self-harmed seven times, six of which were in a one month period. On one occasion this involved putting his head through a glass window.
> - A 17 year old boy self-harmed ten times during a 15 month period . . . The methods of harm for this individual included attempting to jump off a building, punching through a window, and cutting himself.
> - A 16 year old girl was witnessed hitting herself in the face and banging her head against the wall on separate occasions.
> - A 16 year old boy on Christmas Island told a welfare officer that he would 'cut myself every day until I am released into community detention'.
>
> *(AHRC 2014, p. 140, bullet points in original)*

The Inquiry was particularly concerned about the impact of detention on unaccompanied children. The child psychiatrist who visited the Christmas Island and Darwin detention centres wrote:

> Many [unaccompanied] boys had symptoms consistent with major depression, PTSD and generalised anxiety disorder. One or two appeared potentially psychotic with confused and bizarre mood or presentation. There is an intense shared anxiety about transfer to the adult compound or to Manus Island, and of concern is a sense of loss for peers who have been 'extracted' and transferred. For some of the boys, this anxiety and despair includes suicidal ideation.
>
> *(AHRC 2014, p. 155)*

The Inquiry highlighted the obvious conflict of interest between the Immigration Minister's responsibilities as the guardian of these children[3] and the Minister's role as administrator of the immigration detention regime. The government rejected concerns about this conflict, emphasizing that guardianship powers are delegated to senior Immigration Department officers and that independent advice and assistance is provided to those exercising the delegated powers (AHRC 2014, p. 167). Such sophistry denies the reality that there is no guardianship power capable of being exercised to prevent mandatory detention, a legal position reinforced by legislative amendments in 2012 specifying that the Minister or delegated guardian can only exercise the 'same rights, powers, duties, obligations and liabilities as a natural guardian' and cannot affect the performance or exercise of any function under migration law.[4]

## Narratives of denial

In any other circumstances where the state has primary responsibility for the care of children, a policy that so plainly results in multiple harms to even newborn babies would be rejected as deviating from acceptable social norms. A policy that has generated extensive documentation of institutional abuse over a 15-year period, condemnation by all major human rights agencies and opposition from Australia's peak medical professional and social welfare organizations would be politically untenable. Nevertheless, immigration detention has been legitimized repeatedly by the two major political parties; it has been declared lawful by the High Court of Australia;[5] and enforced vigorously by the Immigration Department.[6] As part of the wider strategy of force directed against unauthorized refugees, sections of the Australian navy, Customs and the Australian Federal Police have been engaged in interdiction and forced transfer operations and a new Australian Border Force was created in 2015.[7]

Maintaining the political consensus and unity of practice within the highest levels of the Australian state requires that the indisputably abusive dimensions to the detention policy are reframed publicly as falling within an acceptable moral code, rather than a breach of values (such as the protection of children) the government supposedly is committed to uphold. Criminologist Stanley Cohen's elaboration of Sykes and Mata's 'Techniques of Neutralization' (Cohen 2001, pp. 58–64) provides a useful explanatory framework for understanding the methods consciously deployed by the Australian political establishment to legitimize actions that it knows would be condemned in other circumstances. Drawing on the earlier work of Sykes and Matza (1957), Cohen outlines five mechanisms of denial that enable perpetrators of human rights abuses to 'prepare the ground for the offence to take place' (Cohen 2001, p. 61).

The first is *denial of responsibility*. The political rationale advanced by Australian governments for their detention policies and the means by which detention is administered and organized enables blame for its deleterious impacts to be shifted on to a number of different parties. Principal amongst these are the refugees themselves who, regardless of the lack of alternatives, are deemed to have made a wrong 'choice' if they attempt to enter Australia without authorization, usually with the assistance of smugglers. The offshore detention regime also means that notwithstanding the Australian government's direct political and economic responsibilities, formal responsibility and legal jurisdiction rests with the governments of Papua New Guinea and Nauru. Moreover, private companies are responsible for the operation of both the offshore centres and Australian centres such as those on Christmas Island. Many parts of these operations are further subcontracted; medical care is the responsibility of a private company; and non-government organizations such as the Salvation Army and Save the Children have provided welfare and other key services. All of these arrangements are underpinned by administrative decision-making practices that normalize indefinite incarceration and forced transfers. This results in complex chains of command, opaque contractual arrangements protected by commercial confidentiality and an absence of direct political accountability.

The Coalition government also attributed specific political blame for the numbers of children in detention to the previous Labor governments and maintained that the circumstances referred to in the report were 'of historical interest only'.[8] By the time the Commission's report was eventually tabled in parliament, the number of children detained in Australia had declined to 196 and most had been removed from Christmas Island. However, this decline is neither guaranteed in the longer term nor achieved on the basis of enhancing the capacity of refugees to seek Australia's protection. As a result of Labor government policy, any refugee arriving without visa after July 2013 has been transferred offshore and in December 2014, the Coalition government tied the release of children from Christmas Island to the re-introduction of temporary protection visas that deny refugees rights to permanent residency and family reunion.[9]

The Coalition government also sought to deny or dismiss the AHRC's findings. Asked if he felt any guilt over the Children in Detention report, Prime Minister Abbott replied: 'None whatsoever' (Whyte and Browne 2015). The government's dismissive attitude towards criticisms of detention exemplified Cohen's second and third techniques, *denial of injury* and *denial of the victim*. At one level, this involved complete denial, with the Attorney-General claiming that '[a]ll people in immigration detention . . . are provided with appropriate care [and] treated with dignity and respect' and that 'the best interests of the child are appropriately considered, consistent with international law'.[10] It also involved denial of the seriousness of the situation as typified by Prime Minister Abbott's comment that: 'Occasionally . . . things happen' when referring to subsequent evidence of sexual assault on Nauru during the term of his government (Hurst 2015, Moss 2015).

By itself, such an approach could not succeed given the detailed accounts of harm arising from immigration detention over a number of years. Consistent with Cohen's fourth technique, the government's main tactic for dismissing the detailed medical and other evidence was to *condemn the condemner*. The President of the AHRC, Professor Gillian Triggs, was subjected to a series of public criticisms by government ministers, who claimed the report was politically biased (Ireland 2015). The Prime Minister described the report as 'a transparent stitch-up'[11] and the Chair of the Senate Estimates Committee that discussed the report declared he had 'not bothered' to read it because it was 'too partisan'.[12] The Attorney-General declared he had 'lost confidence' in Professor Triggs and acknowledged he had asked to her to resign (Whyte 2015). Sections of the media also mounted a campaign against Professor Triggs that included personal attacks for her decision many years earlier to place her severely disabled daughter in care (Akerman 2015). The sustained nature of these attacks prompted a formal rebuke from the UN special rapporteur on human rights defenders (Gordon 2015) but the government's complaints about the AHRC reflected a generalized condemnation of human rights organizations, typified by Prime Minister Abbott's claim that: 'Australians are sick of being lectured to by the United Nations' (Kozaki 2015).

As he had done with the AHRC report, the Prime Minister went on to argue that the government should instead be congratulated by human rights organizations for 'stopping the boats' (Whyte and Browne 2015, Kozaki 2015). This *appeal to higher loyalties*, Cohen's fifth technique, re-stated the essential legitimating imperative of Australian border policing – that preventing unauthorized refugee movement and the integrity of national borders is vital to the national interest and takes priority over any human rights obligations. The conventional political wisdom in Australia is that this is an electorally popular stance but the ideology of border policing that dominates within the political establishment is far from hegemonic. Thus, while the government is determined to maintain the established narratives of denial, it is also using increasingly authoritarian measures to stifle criticism of its detention practices and prevent disclosure of human rights abuses.

## Nauru and the culture of secrecy

The conditions at the Nauru and Manus Island Regional Processing Centres generated numerous concerns during the course of the AHRC Inquiry. In September 2014, Greens Senator Sarah Hanson-Young raised with the Immigration Minister allegations from Nauru that: women had been forced to expose themselves to sexual exploitation in exchange for access to showers and other amenities; access to cigarettes was being traded for sexual favours involving children and young girls; children as young as 8 years old were lip-stitching and engaging in other forms of self-harm; young female detainees were being threatened with rape; Nauruan guards were trading marijuana with detainees in exchange for sexual favours; and that a guard previously employed at the centre had been accused of forcing 'children to engage in sexual activity in front of him' (Moss 2015, p. 14).

The Immigration Minister responded a couple of days later by announcing that the authority to work of 10 staff employed by Save the Children, who were contracted by the Immigration Department to provide welfare services to detainees on Nauru, had been revoked following allegations they had facilitated protest activity; coached and encouraged self-harm; fabricated allegations in order 'to undermine' the offshore processing policy; and engaged in the 'misuse and unauthorised disclosure of sensitive and confidential information' (Moss 2015, p. 15). The government then established a review into both the Hanson-Young allegations and the dismissal of the Save the Children staff (Moss 2015).

The Moss Review made no conclusive findings regarding the various cases of detainee abuse. Its conclusion 'that many transferees are apprehensive about their personal safety and have concerns about their privacy at the Centre' (Moss 2015, p. 43) typified the understated bureaucratic language that permeated the report. The Review did acknowledge 'several cases of inappropriate sexual behaviour by minors' (Moss 2015, p. 39) and highlighted the absence of local child protection procedures (Moss 2015, p. 51). However, this was presented as a shortcoming that could be resolved by the development of 'best practice' and 'a robust child protection framework' (Moss 2015, p. 51) rather than the cessation of detention.

The Review also failed to find any 'conclusive information' that Save the Children staff were involved in organizing protests, coaching self-harm or disclosing confidential information (Moss 2015, pp. 69–70). The government played down this finding, having used the allegations against staff to distract attention from the issue of detainee abuse, to stifle information and to intimidate others working in the centre. Save the Children staff told the Review of their concern 'about reporting incidents and information they've been given because they are concerned that this is what led to the removal of those staff' (quoted, Moss 2015, p. 68). One former Save the Children employee later told a journalist that her colleagues were 'treated like criminals':

> They were taken to the hotel, banished from the centre, and told they were being taken back to Australia. It seemed so random – there was nothing connecting these people. It's also crazy that anyone here would have confected claims of abuse because we had personally witnessed so much of it. There is literally no reason to invent anything.
>
> As for coaching refugees to harm, it was frustrating because Save the Children were the only ones who cared. It was a low blow. And this from the department that told us not to include certain incriminating things in our reports. They asked us to change our reports.
>
> *(Quoted in McKenzie-Murray 2015)*

The decision to dismiss the 10 staff was based on a secret intelligence report compiled by Wilson Security, who were contracted to enforce security at the centre. Immigration Department officials made the decision to have the staff removed from Nauru without undertaking any follow-up investigation or providing any opportunity for staff to see or respond to the allegations. The Department maintained this approach during the Moss Review, claiming that: 'any requirement for procedural fairness . . . when making decisions under a commercial contract . . . has potentially serious implications for our contract management and our obligations to service providers and their staff' (quoted in Moss 2015, p. 71).

The intimidation of staff prepared to criticize the regime on Nauru was an undercurrent running through the both AHRC and Moss inquiries. The government's priorities became apparent when the Australian Federal Police were directed to investigate Save the Children staff after they provided documentary evidence supporting their claims of child abuse to the AHRC (Doherty 2015). The former Director of Mental Health Services for the detention health contractor, International Health Medical Services (IHMS), also told the subsequent Senate Inquiry that Immigration Department officials had warned against detention centre staff making submissions to the Commission's inquiry and had vetoed 'IHMS proposed recruitment of child psychiatrists who had publicly expressed opinions that immigration detention was damaging to mental health'.[13] He also gave evidence that the Immigration Department was slow to react to reported incidents of sexual abuse involving children on Nauru, had resisted medical recommendations that children be removed from the detention environment, and that:

> [T]here would be these statements that it was just unacceptable to make reports which showed that people had been harmed. There were instructions not to present the data in relation to this or to show that there were these effects over time ... I also recall us being told ... that if you are making recommendations that people could not be treated effectively in the detention setting it was an admission of failure on the part of IHMS and that that was really unacceptable.[14]

The Senate Inquiry was initiated by Senator Sarah Hanson-Young in March 2015 to ascertain whether the Australian government was fulfilling its responsibilities relating to the management and operation of the Nauru Regional Processing Centre. One of the main purposes of the Inquiry was to enable staff who had worked on Nauru, many of whom had not been interviewed for the Moss Review, to give evidence protected by the legal privilege afforded a Senate inquiry. The Inquiry received 101 submissions containing many new allegations of abuse, sexual assault and neglect of children and other detainees.[15] These included assaults on children by security staff, ranging from an eight-year-old boy being handcuffed as 'a joke' to a four-year-old girl being knocked to the ground after being hit on the head by an adult male guard. One of the social workers employed by Save the Children, who was removed from Nauru, detailed 32 cases of sexual and other abuse based on incident reports she lodged while at the centre, many of which were made known to the Immigration Department at least one year prior to any formal acknowledgement or action being taken.[16]

The Senate Select Committee published its report on 31 August 2015. Its recommendations included: the removal of children and their families from Nauru; a full audit of allegations of sexual abuse, child abuse and other criminal conduct; mandatory reporting provisions regarding such matters; and a further Senate Inquiry into the operation of the Nauru Centre (The Senate 2015, pp. ix–xii). One of the key themes of the report was the lack of transparency about the Nauru operations, especially given the AHRC's exclusion from the island. The atmosphere of hostility to scrutiny was reflected by evidence to the Committee from a former Wilson Security staff member that Senator Hanson-Young was the subject of extensive, clandestine surveillance by the Wilson Security Emergency Response Team when she visited Nauru in December 2013.[17] Both Wilson Security and the Prime Minister dismissed these allegations (Main 2015) but the government's desire to restrict public disclosure of abuse and silence whistle-blower critics of detention was made clear by the introduction of the *Australian Border Force Act* on 1 July 2015.

This legislation, which creates a new border policing agency, the Australian Border Force, within the Immigration Department, includes provisions that criminalize medical professionals, social workers and other 'entrusted persons' who record or disclose 'protected information', such as a detainee's medical condition or experiences of abuse, without the permission of the Secretary of the Immigration Department.[18] This legislation has been condemned by virtually all the peak bodies, including the Australian and World Medical Associations, the Australian College of Nursing and the Australasian College of Physicians, with members who are affected

(Farrell 2015, Talley 2015). On the day the legislation was enacted, 40 current and former staff at Nauru and Manus Island reflected the depth of opposition by publishing an open letter that challenged the government to prosecute them:

> We have advocated and will continue to advocate for the health of those for whom we have a duty of care, despite the threats of imprisonment, because standing by and watching sub-standard and harmful care, child abuse and gross violations of human rights is not ethically viable . . .
>
> There are currently many issues which constitute a serious threat to the health of those in detention for whom we have a duty of care. The Department of Immigration and Border Protection is aware of these problems and has for years failed to address them adequately.
>
> We are aware that in publishing this letter we may be prosecuted . . . and we challenge the department to prosecute so that these issues may be discussed in open court and in the full view of the Australian public.[19]

The Immigration Minister offered assurances the *Australian Border Force Act* will not be used to prosecute those who air 'general claims about conditions in immigration detention facilities' (Morris 2015) but the government refused specifically to exclude doctors and similar employees from the legislation,[20] leaving the open letter signatories and others vulnerable to prosecution should the government decide such a move would be politically viable.

## Systemic abuse and state crime

The evidence of child abuse in immigration detention discussed in this chapter adds to the extensively documented abuses associated with Australian border policing since the introduction of mandatory detention in 1992. In this context, the deviance and criminality associated with Australian border policing arises from state policy and practice, rather than the often desperate attempts by refugees to attempt unauthorized entry into Australia.

The deliberate use of detention with full knowledge of its adverse effects makes the mandatory detention of children a form of state crime (Grewcock 2009, 2015). State crime occurs when governments engage in goal-driven, organized and abusive practices that contravene social rules accepted as legitimate within civil society (Green and Ward 2004). Australian border policing involves not only multiple breaches of formal commitments under international human rights law but also the normalization of practices such as arbitrary detention that would be unacceptable in virtually any other circumstance. Moreover, while immigration detention exposes all detainees to serious harm, the additional vulnerabilities of children make the detention policy particularly egregious and perversely at odds with current government and wider public concerns about institutional child abuse.

These policies have not gone unchallenged. Since the first major human rights inquiry into mandatory detention (HREOC 1998), opposition has taken a variety of forms, including: public protests and forums; protests and escapes by detainees; reports by human rights bodies; condemnation by medical professionals and others working in the centres; repeated legal challenges; investigative journalism; and a diverse network of support and advocacy groups. The impact this has had on mainstream political debate has varied but there is a critical mass of people within civil society willing to challenge and sanction what the government is doing. No Australian government has framed the detention of children as a deliberate exercise in child abuse. Rather, the official responses to the Children in Detention Report and the exposure of practices on Nauru demonstrate the range of ideological techniques and restrictive legal measures that have been deployed to neutralize opposition and legitimize an inherently criminogenic border policing strategy.

## Conclusion

Refugees typically are unable to access authorized means of transport to secure safety and protection. At the time of writing, appalling images of a young child refugee washed up on a beach in Turkey (*The Independent* 2015) reflect the risks many are forced to take and are emblematic of forced migration from conflict zones such as Syria. The reception to these refugees within individual European Union states has varied but the outpouring of popular sympathy that followed the publication of the dead boy's photo demonstrated the possibility of constructing an official response to refugees not characterized primarily by forced exclusion and separation from the wider community. Australia's policies of mandatory detention and offshore processing should not operate as a model in these circumstances. Such measures do not make safer the necessary journeys of refugees; instead, they narrow the flight options, increase the risks of being stranded in conflict and transit zones and further punish those, such as children, most in need of protection. The organized abuse of children in Australia's immigration detention network compounds the harm from which they are fleeing. A policy that reflected the spirit of Australia's formal human rights commitments would facilitate entry to refugees, enable them to live in the community while their claims for protection are considered, address health and other personal needs, and operate in the best interests of the child.

## Notes

1 Retrieved on 4 April 2016 from: www.aph.gov.au/Parliamentary_Business/Committees/Senate/Regional_processing_Nauru.
2 The Human Rights and Equal Opportunities Commission was renamed the AHRC in 2008.
3 s.6 *Immigration (Guardianship of Children) Act* 1946.
4 s.8(2) *Immigration (Guardianship of Children) Act* 1946.
5 *Al-Kateb v Godwin* (2004) 208 ALR 124; *Re Woolley, Ex parte Applicants M276/2003 by their next friend GS* [2004] HCA 49.
6 Here, I use the generic term 'Immigration Department'. The department has undergone many name changes, reflecting wider debates about migration policy. The present government renamed it the Department for Immigration and Border Protection in 2013.
7 *Australian Border Force Act* 2015.
8 Statement by the Attorney-General, Senator George Brandis, 11 February 2015.
9 Refer Second Reading speeches, Migration and Maritime Powers Legislation (Resolving the Asylum Legacy Caseload) Bill 2014, *Hansard*, Senate, 4 December 2014.
10 Statement by the Attorney-General, Senator George Brandis, 11 February 2015.
11 *Hansard*, House of Representatives, 12 February 2015, p. 714.
12 *Hansard*, Senate Estimates Hearing, 23 February 2015.
13 Submission 65, Select Committee on the recent allegations relating to conditions and circumstances at the Nauru Regional Processing Centre (Senate Select Committee).
14 Evidence of Dr Peter Young to Senate Select Committee, 9 June 2015.
15 Retrieved on 4 April 2016 from: www.aph.gov.au/Parliamentary_Business/Committees/Senate/Regional_processing_Nauru/Regional_processing_Nauru/Submissions.
16 Submission 63, Senate Select Committee.
17 Submission 62, Senate Select Committee.
18 Sections 41–51, *Australian Border Force Act* 2015. Under s42, the maximum penalty for disclosing protected information is 2 years imprisonment.

19 Retrieved on 1 September 2015 from: www.theguardian.com/australia-news/2015/jul/01/open-letter-on-the-border-force-act-we-challenge-the-department-to-prosecute.

20 See also *Public Interest Disclosure Act* 2013. This legislation provides limited protection to whistle-blowers but only in situations where they have exhausted internal reporting options.

## References


Akerman, P., 2015. The rights and wrongs of a Labor luvvie. *Daily Telegraph*. Retrieved on 1 September 2015 from: http://blogs.news.com.au/dailytelegraph/piersakerman/index.php/dailytelegraph/comments/the_rights_and_wrongs_of_a_labor_luvvie/.

Australian Human Rights Commission [AHRC], 2014. *The Forgotten Children: National Inquiry into Children in Immigration Detention*. Retrieved on 1 September 2015 from: www.humanrights.gov.au/our-work/asylum-seekers-and-refugees/publications/forgotten-children-national-inquiry-children.

Cohen, S., 2001. *States of denial: knowing about atrocities and suffering*. Cambridge: Polity Press.

Cullen, S., 2012. Gillard launches royal commission into child abuse. *ABC News*. Retrieved on 1 September 2015 from: www.abc.net.au/news/2012-11-12/gillard-launches-royal-commission-into-child-abuse/4367364.

Doherty, B., 2015. Police investigate Save the Children whistleblowers over Nauru abuse report. *The Guardian*. Retrieved on 1 September 2015 from: www.theguardian.com/australia-news/2015/mar/04/police-investigate-save-the-children-whistleblowers-over-nauru-abuse-report.

Farrell, P., 2015. Australian detention centre secrecy laws condemned by world medical body. *The Guardian*. Retrieved on 1 September 2015 from: www.theguardian.com/australia-news/2015/jul/03/australian-detention-centre-secrecy-laws-condemned-by-world-medical-body.

Gordon, M., 2015. Revealed: how the UN told the Abbott government to back off on Gillian Triggs. *The Sydney Morning Herald*. Retrieved on 1 September 2015 from: www.smh.com.au/federal-politics/political-news/revealed-how-the-un-told-abbott-government-to-back-off-on-gillian-triggs-20150609-ghk224.html.

Green, P. and Ward, T., 2004. *State crime: governments, violence and corruption*. London: Pluto Press.

Grewcock, M., 2009. *Border crimes: Australia's war on illicit migrants*. Sydney: Institute of Criminology Press.

Grewcock, M., 2014. Back to the future: Australian border policing under Labor, 2007–2013. *State Crime*, 3(1), 102–25.

Grewcock, M., 2015. Australian border policing and the production of state harm. *In*: G. Barak (ed.), *The Routledge international handbook of the crimes of the powerful*. Abingdon: Routledge, 331–47.

Human Rights and Equal Opportunities Commission [HREOC], 1998. *Those who've come across the seas: detention of unauthorised arrivals*. Retrieved on 1 September 2015 from: www.humanrights.gov.au/our-work/asylum-seekers-and-refugees/publications/those-whove-come-across-seas-detention.

Human Rights and Equal Opportunities Commission [HREOC], 2004. *A last resort? Report of the National Inquiry into Children in Immigration Detention*. Retrieved on 1 September 2015 from: www.humanrights.gov.au/our-work/asylum-seekers-and-refugees/projects/last-resort-report-national-inquiry-children.

Hurst, D., 2015. 'Things happen': Tony Abbott on sexual assault allegations in offshore detention. *The Guardian*. Retrieved on 1 April 2015 from: www.theguardian.com/australia-news/2015/mar/20/things-happen-tony-abbott-on-sexual-assault-allegations-in-offshore-detention.

Ireland, J., 2015. Immigration Minister Peter Dutton ups pressure on Gillian Triggs to quit. *Sydney Morning Herald*. Retrieved on 1 September 2015 from: www.smh.com.au/federal-politics/political-news/immigration-minister-peter-dutton-ups-pressure-on-gillian-triggs-to-quit-20150607-ghighd.html.

Kozaki, D., 2015. Abbott says Australians 'sick of being lectured to by UN' after scathing report on asylum policies. *ABC News*. Retrieved on 1 September 2015 from: www.abc.net.au/news/2015-03-09/tony-abbott-hits-out-united-nations-asylum-report/6289892.

Main, L., 2015. Sarah Hanson-Young says 'women don't like to be watched' after PM's comments on Nauru spy claims. *ABC News*. Retrieved on 1 September 2015 from: www.abc.net.au/news/2015-06-05/greens-senator-sarah-hanson-young-nauru-spying-claims/6524430.

McKenzie-Murray, M., 2015. Nauru abuse goes further than the Moss review. *The Saturday Paper*. Retrieved on 1 September 2015 from: www.thesaturdaypaper.com.au/news/politics/2015/03/28/nauru-abuse-goes-further-than-the-moss-review/14274612001684.

Morris, S., 2015. Detention centre doctors stare down prosecution. *The Saturday Paper*. Retrieved on 1 September 2015 from: www.thesaturdaypaper.com.au/news/health/2015/08/15/detention-centre-doctors-stare-down-prosecution/14395608002246.

Moss, P., 2015. *Review into recent allegations relating to conditions and circumstances at the Regional Processing Centre in Nauru*. Retrieved on 1 September 2015 from: www.border.gov.au/ReportsandPublications/Documents/reviews-and-inquiries/review-conditions-circumstances-nauru.pdf.

Sykes, G. and Matza, D., 1957. Techniques of neutralization: a theory of delinquency. *American Sociological Review*, 22, 664–70.

Talley, N., 2015. Doctors must be allowed to speak freely on poor detention centre conditions. *The Age*. Retrieved on 1 September 2015 from: www.theage.com.au/comment/doctors-must-be-allowed-to-speak-freely-on-poor-detention-centre-conditions-20150607-ghih50.html.

*The Independent*, 2015. If these extraordinarily powerful images of a dead Syrian child washed up on a beach don't change Europe's attitudes to refugees, what will? Retrieved on 7 September 2015 from: www.independent.co.uk/news/world/europe/if-these-extraordinarily-powerful-images-of-a-dead-syrian-child-washed-up-on-a-beach-dont-change-europes-attitude-to-refugees-what-will-10482757.html.

The Senate, 2015. *Report of the Select Committee on the recent allegations relating to conditions and circumstances at the Regional Processing Centre in Nauru*. Retrieved on 1 September 2015 from: www.aph.gov.au/Parliamentary_Business/Committees/Senate/Regional_processing_Nauru/Regional_processing_Nauru/Final_Report.

Whyte, S., 2015. 'A fatal perception of bias': George Brandis admits he asked Gillian Triggs to resign. *The Sydney Morning Herald*. Retrieved on 1 September 2015 from: http://www.smh.com.au/federal-politics/political-news/a-fatal-perception-of-bias-george-brandis-admits-he-asked-gillian-triggs-to-resign-20150224-13n59y.html.

Whyte, S. and Browne, R., 2015. Human Rights Commission should congratulate Scott Morrison: Tony Abbott responds to report on children in immigration detention. *The Sydney Morning Herald*. Retrieved on 1 September 2015 from: www.smh.com.au/federal-politics/political-news/human-rights-commission-should-congratulate-scott-morrison-tony-abbott-responds-to-report-on-children-in-immigration-detention-20150211-13ci2j.html.

# 16

# Civil society perspectives on corruption and human rights

## The case of Papua New Guinea

*Tony Ward*

### Introduction

> Let us be clear. Corruption kills. The money stolen through corruption every year is enough to feed the world's hungry 80 times over. Nearly 870 million people go to bed hungry every night, many of them children; corruption denies them their right to food, and, in some cases, their right to life. A human rights-based approach to anti-corruption responds to the people's resounding call for a social, political and economic order that delivers on the promises of 'freedom from fear and want'.
>
> *(UN 2013, p. 3)*

Navi Pillay's speech in her then role as UN High Commissioner for Human Rights sums up a central dilemma of the politics of anti-corruption. It is hardly controversial to say that 'corruption is an enormous obstacle to the realisation of all human rights' (ibid., p. 8); but to create 'a social and political and economic order that delivers . . . freedom from fear and want' would require wide-ranging and fundamental changes in countries where corruption is rife. In linking anti-corruption with human rights and recognizing 'a strong and engaged civil society' as a key protagonist in fighting corruption (ibid., p. 5), the UN appears to have recognized that the limitations of a strategy of legal reforms specifically targeting corruption. Since narrowly based reform strategies have achieved little demonstrable success in reducing corruption, an approach that links anti-corruption to wider popular movements for rights and accountability offers an appealing alternative (Beyerle 2014, Johnstone 2014). But in this wider perspective, the 'enormous obstacle' constituted by corruption is only part of the even bigger obstacle of unaccountable political and corporate power.

This chapter illustrates the relation between corruption and human rights by drawing on research on civil society and state crime in Papua New Guinea (PNG). The research was part of the International State Crime Initiative (ISCI)'s project 'State Crime and Resistance: A Comparative Study of Civil Society', and concerned the ways in which civil society organizations (CSOs) in countries with high levels of state violence and corruption defined and resist state crime.[1]

In PNG, even more than in the other countries in the study (Colombia, Tunisia, Kenya, Turkey and Burma/Myanmar), corruption is central to patterns of state crime, which following Green and Ward (2004), we define as state organizational deviance involving the violation of human rights. As many commentators on PNG have noted, the misappropriation of state assets occurs on a massive scale, is barely concealed, and is regularly exposed by official inquiries and a relatively free press. It was to be expected, therefore, that many interviewees would mention corruption as one of the main problems they faced. What is perhaps more surprising is that the interviewees did not dwell on glaring and well-documented examples of bribery and embezzlement. On the contrary, their references to corruption are nearly always marked by ambiguity. They concern the 'grey area' between corruption and legitimate economic and political behaviour.

This feature of our data from PNG illustrates an important point about corruption and its relationship to human rights. It is not just that corruption is an inherently ambiguous concept, though it clearly is. There is a core of behaviour that almost anyone would recognize as corrupt, but the boundaries of corruption are vague and contested. More importantly, the main threat to human rights in PNG, as in many other areas, comes not from simple and visible acts of bribery and theft, but from systemic features of the state: its close and collusive relationships with business, and the pervasiveness of clientelistic networks in which political support is exchanged for political benefits. These systemic features elude any attempt to draw bright-line distinctions between corrupt and non-corrupt transactions. Indeed any such bright-line division is politically suspect; it legitimizes too many transactions that undermine democracy and harm the interests of citizens. This point links to a criticism that is often made of mainstream anti-corruption organizations like Transparency International (TI) (see, for example, Hindess 2009, de Sousa 2009): that their single-issue focus and strategy of 'coalition building' tends to ally them to neoliberal ideas of 'good governance' rather than a politics even mildly critical of capitalism.

My colleague Kristian Lasslett carried out 34 interviews in 2013 with members, staff and lawyers from various organizations in PNG, most of which represented people whose interests were under threat by corporations and the government. A particularly important category of threatened interests are those of 'landowners', which in PNG usually means the members of clans who collectively own land under what the PNG legal system recognizes as customary law. This chapter draws mainly on interviews with groups promoting some combination of environmentalism and protection of landowner/community rights: the Madang Indigenous People's Forum, Bismarck Ramu Group, Eco-Forestry Forum and CELCOR (Center for Environmental Law and Community Rights). It also draws on interviews conducted by Lasslett in 2010 and 2012 with senior figures in Transparency International PNG.

The next two sections of the chapter discuss the definition of corruption and its relationship with human rights, illustrating the argument with examples from PNG. I then look more closely at the specific forms that corruption takes in PNG before turning to two forms of opposition to it: the global anti-corruption 'industry' and its PNG representatives, and that of the CSOs in our own study.

## Defining corruption

The once standard definition of corruption as 'the abuse of public office for private gain' has now been largely superseded by the definition that TI adopted in 2000, 'the abuse of *entrusted power* for private gain' (Hindess 2009). This definition recognizes that corruption can occur in the corporate and NGO sectors without necessarily involving public officials. The concept of 'abuse' is vague, but in relation to 'entrusted power' it appears to cover not only illegal behaviour but conduct that violates the informal norms on which relations of trust are based. The main limitation of this definition is the emphasis on *private* gain; this does not easily fit *institutional* corruption, which benefits officials in their capacity as officials, politicians, or corporate executives, rather than in a private capacity (Philp 1997). A good example of institutional violation of informal norms of trust was provided by a PNG civil society worker reflecting on his former career as an official of PNG's Department of Environment and Conservation:

> Government gives you a duty, says ok, you go out to this particular community and you get these people to sign these agreements. . . . And, and the way I see it is also, there is a level of corruption, it's not explaining to people, and getting people to sign agreements which are not – they don't understand. And I see, I've seen that very much in the Department of Environment.
>
> *(Interview, John Chitoa, Bismarck Ramu Group, 13 August 2013)*

In a narrow sense, this was not corrupt at all: officials were simply doing their 'duty' to secure the agreements with logging companies necessary for the government's development policy. But it could reasonably be defined as corrupt in the sense that it violated the expectations of citizens that they would receive honest and impartial advice, and did so for purposes of gain on the part of the state and the logging industry. Chitoa also noted the difficulty of distinguishing between regulatory failures due to corruption and those that resulted from simple 'laziness' – a reluctance to make one's life difficult by challenging logging company activities. In a similar vein, two interviewees (Kenn Mondiai of Eco-Forestry Forum and Rosa Koiann of Bismarck Ramu Group) pointed to the importance of food in building excessively cosy relationships between the regulators and the regulated.

In an important recent study, Beyerle (2014, p. 25) suggests the following definition of corruption:

> [A] system of abuse of entrusted power for private, collective or political gain – often involving a complex, intertwined set of relationships, some obvious, others hidden, with established vested interests, that can operate vertically within an institution or horizontally across political, economic and social spheres in a society or transnationally.

Both in its inclusion of collective or political gain and in its emphasis on systemic behaviours and relationships, this definition does better than the standard one in capturing the kinds of corruption that concerned our respondents in PNG. The difficult question is what distinguishes *abuse* of entrusted power from the alliances of vested interests that are a feature of politics in any capitalist democracy. Beyerle goes some way to answering this by writing that corruption 'can also be defined from a human rights framework – through the eyes and experiences of regular people'; it is 'a form of oppression and loss of freedom' (Beyerle 2014, pp. 25–6). It is unlikely that many *systems* of abuse falling within her definition fail to violate human rights; but 'a human rights framework' and 'the eyes and experiences of regular people' are not synonymous.

Walton (2015) explored 'regular people's' views of corruption in discussions with focus groups of PNG citizens. He found that some residents in the poorer villages did not perceive the widespread practice of buying votes to be necessarily corrupt. It is common for politicians to use 'slush funds' to distribute money in their constituencies (Dinnen 2001). So long as it was done openly, this did not violate the norms of PNG's patrimonial form of politics, as these were understood in remote rural areas. The hypothetical case of a woman drinking home-brewed alcohol and selling sex, on the other hand, was widely seen as corrupt by Walton's respondents.

She was not 'abusing entrusted power', but she transgressed the norms governing her role in community life for economic gain.

The general approach to state crime adopted in our study implies that we must take account *both* of human rights norms *and* of informal social definitions of deviance (Green and Ward 2004). To count as 'state crime' in our sense, corruption must be a systemic part of the way state agencies operate, and it must cause the kind of harm to basic human interests that we would class as violating human rights. Other forms of corruption may not be systemic (there can be isolated instances of bribe-taking in generally honest agencies), and may not violate human rights (officials can breach the trust placed in them by their superiors in ways that are harmless or benign from the standpoint of ordinary citizens). Corruption is a form of deviance, so it must violate the social norms of at least some important audience in the relevant society – as the distribution of 'slush funds' does, however acceptable it may be to the recipients. There is no completely 'objective' definition of corruption – in defining corruption, civil society also defines the norms that corruption violates. 'Civil society' includes criminological research: ISCI is not merely a passive observer or corruption in PNG but actively intervenes in the debate (see, for example, ISCI 2014).

## Corruption and human rights

In speaking of human rights, we adopt a normative framework which assumes that there are certain basic human interests that any legitimate government must protect. Treating human rights as an ethical/political rather than a legal construct, we can identify three kinds of rights that corruption may violate. First, there are the basic civil and political liberties: the right to life, bodily integrity, freedom of expression, etc. Second, there are economic, social and cultural rights, including a right to be free from 'severe poverty', which seriously limits the capacities of human agents (Pogge 2007), and a right to preserve the cultural frameworks within which human lives are meaningful. Third, and of particular significance in relation to corruption, there is a right to political participation (Steiner 1988) – the right to make some contribution to political decisions that affect one's vital interests. The case of PNG illustrates how corruption leads to violations of all three kinds of rights.

In defending their corrupt interests, states often violate basic rights such as bodily integrity and freedom of expression. Lasslett (2012) provides an example in his study of the demolition of the Paga Hill settlement near the PNG capital Port Moresby. The land on which the settlement of 3,000 people stood had been publicly owned and formed part of a national park. Its sale to developers and the subsequent failure to reverse this unlawful transaction was described by the parliamentary Public Accounts Committee as:

> a good illustration of the failings and corrupt conduct of the Department of Lands and Physical Planning ... the continued acquiescence of the Department in corrupt dealings and ... the extent to which private interests control the Department at the expense of the State and the citizens of Papua New Guinea.
>
> *(PAC 2006, ss 3.35–3.36)*

After the developers apparently bribed two residents to sign a spurious 'consent order', purportedly on behalf of the community, the police attempted to evict the residents and demolish the settlement. Their methods included beating and cutting residents with sticks, metal bars and machetes, firing on unarmed protestors (fortunately without causing injury) and assaulting a senior opposition politician (Lasslett 2012).

There is little doubt that corruption plays a major part in perpetuating chronic severe poverty in PNG. The 1990s and early 2000s saw PNG's Gross National Product increase while poverty increased and public services declined disastrously, leaving many citizens with little access to roads, education or health care (Cammack 2008). The head of Task-Force Sweep, the anti-corruption agency whose government funding was cut off in 2014 after it obtained an arrest warrant against the Prime Minister, estimated that 'at least 40 per cent of our national budget is lost through corruption, wastage and mismanagement annually' (quoted by Bonjui 2013).

Another major assault on economic and cultural rights has been the theft of land from its customary owners and the Special Agricultural Business Lease scheme. This allows the state to lease land from its customary owners then lease it out to businesses, ostensibly for agricultural development but in practice usually for the clear-felling of timber. An official inquiry (Numapo 2013) found that most of these leases were unlawful for lack of informed consent from the landowners. The officials who were supposed to investigate the leases received 'allowances' from the companies concerned – justified on the ground that there was inadequate public funding to pay for their investigations – and invariably decided in the companies' favour. Though some form of consent was usually obtained it was often from individuals who had no right to give it, and the first many residents knew of the deal was when the bulldozers arrived (Lawson 2014). The campaign against these leases was probably the most successful activity of the CSOs in our study, although at the time of writing the PNG government is stalling on its commitment to revoke the leases (PNGexposed 2015).

PNG has been a parliamentary democracy since independence in 1975, but governments have been weak and unstable owing to the tendency of MPs and parties to shift allegiances for political and personal advantage. Elections, including the most recent general election in 2012, have been characterized by 'inaccurate voter rolls, electoral fraud and malpractice, bribery and coercion of voters in some parts of the country, and election-related violence' (May 2013, p. 168). Observers have expressed concern about the growth of 'money politics', with 'reports of candidates boasting about the millions of kina they had to hand out, and of amounts as high as PGK 3,000 [about US$1,000] being handed to individual voters for their loyalty' (Commonwealth Observer Group 2012, p. 19). Elections attract large numbers of candidates who are drawn to politics as one of the few opportunity structures that afford access to wealth and status in PNG society:

> In the absence of alternative sources of material advancement, political office becomes key to gaining access to public and private resources. Resources acquired in this way can be used to promote the interests of individual leaders and their small voting base. This environment encourages candidates and their supporters to engage in both vote-buying and intimidation.
>
> *(Dinnen 2001, p. 174)*

This emphasis on short-term gain and local patronage networks undermines any meaningful right to political participation in the formulation of policy goals. It also undermines principles of equality and non-discrimination that are central to international human rights law (Kumar 2011, pp. 46–8).

## Bribes and scams in PNG

The most unequivocal forms of corruption in state agencies are bribery and the embezzlement of public assets. Both appear widespread in PNG. In the latest (2013) edition of Transparency International's 'Corruption Barometer', 37 per cent of PNG respondents reported that they or someone in their household had paid a bribe to the police in the last 12 months, and 20 per cent to 'the judiciary', which may mean court clerks rather than judges. Lawrence Stephens of TI PNG said that while it was 'just taken for granted in the law firms' that 'you have to pay bribes in court in order to get your paperwork processed', he had previously had confidence in the professionalism of the judges themselves; but he added that 'in the last few years, that's been more and more problematic' and he suspected that some 'scatty' judicial decisions might have been paid for (Interview, 29 July 2012). Needless to say, this would negate the right to a fair trial.

Larger-scale bribery is harder to document. One major example is the bribery of officials in the Department of Health by medical suppliers. This had grave human rights implications because hospitals were starved of supplies so as to create an 'emergency' that allowed officials to bypass the normal tendering process. According to local media, 'all health centres and aid posts in the six districts of Madang Province had run out of drugs, forcing patients to go to pharmacies in town to buy their medicines, with three children dying as a result' (IRIN 2011).

As Walton (2013, p. 152) observes, despite widespread rumours of grand corruption in the mining sector, very little is known about any corrupt practices. Mining interests were clearly implicated in the worst episode of systematic human rights abuse in PNG's history, the armed conflict in Bougainville between 1988 and 1997 (Lasslett 2014). While there is ample evidence that the Rio Tinto subsidiary which ran the huge Panguna mine on the island had a close working relationship with the government and subsidized the security forces' operations, this relationship did not depend on anything so crude as bribery. As Rose-Ackerman (1999, p. 122) points out, where a country is heavily dependent on a multinational firm, and the firm is in a strong position to make demands on the government, 'One may not see much overt corruption . . . but the harm to ordinary citizens may nevertheless be severe'.

The other major form of unequivocally corrupt behaviour is the siphoning-off of government resources through various forms of fraud. Such scams are facilitated by the clientelistic networks known as *wantoks*, made up of people who share 'one talk', a common Indigenous language among the 850 or so spoken in PNG (Lasslett 2014, p. 39). Two of the main types of scam are payments to 'shell' companies for fictitious services, and spurious legal claims which are settled out of court by the government (Sharman 2012). Some of these claims concern matters which, if true, would be serious human rights violations, such as a police raid in 1995 alleged to have resulted in a death, two rapes and 10 serious assaults, as well as extensive damage to property (Commission of Inquiry 2009, p. 226). Whatever the truth of this particular matter, which was settled for PGK 1.7m (over US$600,000) it is a salutary reminder of the 'commodification of victimhood' which can distort outwardly worthy actions against state and corporate crime (MacManus 2014).

If a proportion of *legitimate* state revenues will find its way into the pockets of senior politicians and officials, they may have corrupt incentives to reach lucrative bargains with corporations even if no direct kickback is on offer. The PNG government has been criticized for negotiating a deal with ExxonMobil and other corporations (including one owned by the PNG state) for the construction of a liquid natural gas pipeline that was unduly advantageous to the corporations and placed too many risks of the project on the shoulders of the state and its citizens (Jubilee Australia 2012). Some ministers have spoken of being under such pressure that they had 'no alternative but to conform to the will of the developer' (quoted ibid., p. 29). As Jubilee Australia's (2012) report implies, given the PNG state's track record it would be surprising if a substantial proportion of the revenues from this major project did not end up being stolen. There is also every likelihood that it will lead to more of the same human rights violations we have already noted: failure to deliver health and education services, loss of Indigenous people's land rights, and the risk of further violent conflict between dissident landowners and the state–corporate complex. Even in the absence of corruption, however, same results might follow from the state's need for revenue to balance its books. The boundary between corrupt and non-corrupt forms of corporate power is difficult to identify.

## The politics of anti-corruption

Corporations that do not rely on bribery to influence states may well find it useful to present a 'clean' image by supporting anti-corruption campaigns such as Transparency International (TI). TI operates a 'franchising' system with a secretariat based in Berlin and numerous national chapters (de Sousa 2009), including one in PNG. Like other TI chapters, TI PNG 'focuses primarily on building coalitions', embracing government departments, the private sector and NGOs (Peter Aitsi, interview, 28 July 2010). Critics of TI (see, for example, Hindess 2009, de Sousa 2009) see it as an ally of a neoliberal politics of 'good governance' and privatization – which Peter Aitsi saw as one way to tackle the 'criminality' of the public sector, though he acknowledged its 'cost aspect' (Interview, 28 July 2010). Walton (2013) found that TI PNG was dependent on funding from local businesses, which secured its independence from the state and enabled it to campaign quite effectively against measures such as a proposal to increase the discretionary 'slush funds' available to individual MPs, but which Walton suggests explains the organization's lack of criticism of corporate involvement in corruption. He makes similar points about the (now defunct) Australian aid organization AUSAID, and argues that both organizations were broadly supportive of a neoliberal agenda.

While TI epitomises what Sampson (2010) calls the 'anti-corruption industry', the CSOs in our study were more akin to what he characterizes as a 'craft':

> Craftsmen work with a limited set of tools, are sensitive to local variation and adapt their work to local conditions. A crafted product lasts longer and feels more authentic than an imposed, standardised industrial product. Craftsmen pass on their knowledge in a traditional, practice-oriented form, improvising as they go along. ... They figure things out locally, in their context.
>
> *(Sampson 2010, p. 277)*

Groups such as MELSOL (Melanesian Solidarity) and the Bismarck Ramu Group see their struggle as rooted in customary law and more broadly in Melanesian culture with its strong sense of collective attachment to the land. In contrast to Transparency and AUSAID, and also to some local environmentalist NGOs, activists in these groups expressed vehement opposition to the encroachment of corporate power, particularly that of foreign corporations seeking to exploit PNG's resources:

> They are thinking that they own this province or this country or what. So they go on their own way. And you have to – even our government have to come and submit to them. That is – that is why I hate them. I really hate them.
>
> *(Interview, Alfred Kaket, Chair of the Madang Indigenous People's Forum, 1 August 2013)*

Interviewees from these groups struggled, however, with the concept of 'corruption', recognizing the definitional difficulties it involved. Tony Fofoe of MELSOL said that he did not know the 'real meaning' of 'corruption', but the biggest problem facing PNG society was 'how the wealth is going away' that was supposed to bring services to the people (Interview, 28 July 2013).

One effect of this lack of services, as Wina Kayonga of Bismarck Ramu Group pointed out, is to increase the dependence of local communities on exploitative corporations:

> These corporations are coming in and trying to exploit these people because of corruption. These people are desperate for health services, education, the basic health services. That, that's why they will have to allow logging companies to build roads. If there wasn't corruption, the government would have provided roads. . . . It's because of corruption. People have no choice. They have been forced into that corner that they will have to make such decision. It is because of corruption that there is no medicine. People are dying of curable diseases. So this is the consequences. People making decisions that they shouldn't make, just because of corruption.
>
> *(Interview, 5 August 2013)*

When civil society activists talk about state–corporate relations they do not always distinguish clearly between corruption (in a narrow sense) and the common interests of political and business elites. Frank Don Jnr of Madang Indigenous People's Forum thought that:

> the most corrupt government in the – possible, you could find in PNG. Because, you know, instead of people getting . . . basic services such as school, health, water supply and power and the other things, I mean, those basic government services, yeah – instead of [that] they fly in and out of Moresby to other countries in [the] west. Stole mining from the people and all this.
>
> *(Interview, 8 August 2013)*

Although corruption in a narrow sense is undoubtedly a factor in the lack of services he describes, what he condemns is the cosy and mutually beneficial relationship between the political elite and foreign businesses. In another interview, a trade union organizer commented that 'the money's flowing in, the senior civil servants are pocketing it and they have no interest, therefore, to act as an independent arbitrator' (Group interview, Alfred, Joe and Julius, 31 July 2013). This could be an allegation of embezzlement but in the context of the discussion it more likely means simply that legitimate corporate revenues benefit the national government bureaucracy rather than local people – although part of that benefit is the creation of opportunities for embezzlement.

Some respondents bemoaned the lack of clarity in norms about state and corporate behaviour. Wina Kayonga of Bismarck Ramu Group said that people rarely spoke of state or corporate 'crimes' because:

> [what] I would say is that, it is an acceptable frame. Framed by the model of development to accept that, so what I would [say] is that the people that are faced up with these challenges see it as normal. Acceptable.
>
> *(Interview, 9 August 2013)*

Alfred Kaket of the Madang Indigenous People's Forum thought that police corruption and subservience to corporate interests could be defeated if communities were able to present a united front, and appeal to values that the police shared as men who also had land rights under customary law (Interview, 1 August 2013). Asked what he saw as the main threats to his group, Kaket replied:

> I see my threat is that I don't want my members to be bribed. That's how I see. That's my only threat. Being bribed and then just, just leave all their awareness and everything and they go away. Because since we don't have the money to do that, that's how my threat is. They will use a lot of money to do bribe.

Kenn Mondiai of the Eco-Forestry Forum and Partners for Melanesia spoke of being offered a very large amount of money to abandon his defence of the Indigenous residents' land rights, and one NGO, the Environmental Law Center, have become 'consultants' to ExxonMobil. A major problem for the environmentalist/landowner groups was how to dissuade customary landowners from literally selling out to logging, mining or other corporations. For the Bismarck Ramu Group, this could only be accomplished by cultivating a sense of pride in Indigenous culture, with its strong sense of connection to the land: as the Group's slogan puts it, 'Land is Life' (Barry Lalley, interview, 11 August 2013).

While customary rights formed much of the basis for resistance to state and corporate power in PNG, activists did not always connect these customary norms to more universalistic ideas of legality and human rights. Two interviewees referred explicitly to human rights as an emerging new discourse that they needed to learn to employ:

> But slowly we're becoming – we're starting to realise that those rights of those Indigenous people are actually breaches of human rights. And are breaches by the state, you know. Slowly, even the NGOs are coming to realise that. Not all of them are ... it's probably just the legal NGOs now.
>
> *(Interview, Mary Boni, Eco-Forestry Forum, 13 July 2013)*

Marjorie Wairo Santo of CELCOR, the Center for Environmental Law and Community Rights, said that her organization had recently started a project to identify the human rights implications of violations of local communities' property rights, and that 'being exposed to like, generally, the human rights values and all that stuff, kinda opens your mind' (Interview, 16 July 2013).

This is linked to the point made in the quotation from Wina Kayonga above. The pressure on individuals and communities to 'sell out', to succumb to what others might interpret as bribery, is increased if they are desperate to see the economic development and public services which the state, due largely to corruption, is failing to provide.

## Conclusion

Though it could be said that civil society in PNG has not been very sophisticated in its efforts to conceptualize the relations between corruption, human rights violations and corporate power, the ambiguity of the activists' view of corruption reflects their accurate sense that there is no clear distinction between corruption and the ordinary influence of economic interests over the political process. Both pose threats to human rights: to economic, social and cultural rights, as economic development damages land rights, the environment and traditional cultures; to civil and political rights as state repression is mobilized to protect corporate interests; and to political participation as economic power undermines democracy. From a human rights perspective, the task for both civil society and criminology is to identify the threats to human rights from the interweaving of economic and political power, and to seek to define those threats as unacceptable and in that sense corrupt.

## Note

1 Kristian Lasslett carried out the field research in Papua New Guinea, and made very helpful comments on a draft of this chapter. The Economic and Social Research Council funded the research by grant no. ES/I030816/1. Thanks also to Kavita Desai, Fatima Kanji and Orlando Goodall, who transcribed the interviews. The usual disclaimer applies.

## References

Beyerle, S., 2014. *Curbing corruption: people power for accountability and justice.* Boulder, CO: Lynne Rienner.

Bonjui, P., 2013. PNG loses billions to government corruption. Retrieved on 22 July 2015 from: www.abc.net.au/news/2013-08-27/an-png-billions-lost/4916656.

Cammack, D., 2008. Chronic poverty in Papua New Guinea. Retrieved on 22 July 2015 from: www.chronicpoverty.org.

Commission of Inquiry Generally into Government Finance, 2009. Final Report. Retrieved on 22 July 2015 from: https://pngexposed.wordpress.com/2010/08/17/the-full-finance-department-commission-of-inquiry-report/.

Commonwealth Observer Group, 2012. Papua New Guinea national elections 2012. Retrieved on 22 July 2015 from: http://thecommonwealth.org/sites/default/files/news-items/documents/COGPNG 2012Final.pdf.

de Sousa, L., 2009. TI in search of a constituency. *In*: L. de Sousa, P. Larmour and B. Hindess (eds), *Governments, NGOs and anti-corruption: the new integrity warriors.* London: Routledge, 186–208.

Dinnen, S., 2001. *Law and order in a weak state: crime and politics in Papua New Guinea.* Honolulu, HI: University of Hawai'i Press.

Green, P. and Ward, T., 2004. *State crime: governments, violence and corruption.* London: Pluto Press.

Hindess, B., 2009. International anti-corruption as a programme of normalization. *In*: L. de Sousa, P. Larmour and B. Hindess (eds), *Governments, NGOs and anti-corruption: the new integrity warriors.* London: Routledge, 19–32.

International State Crime Initiative [ISCI], 2014. ISCI condemns demolition exercise at Paga Hill. Retrieved on 22 July 2015 from: http://statecrime.org/state-crime-research/isci-condemns-demolition-exercise-at-paga-hill/.

IRIN, 2011. Papua New Guinea: moves to tackle health kickback scam. Retrieved on 22 July 2015 from: www.irinnews.org/report/92202/papua-new-guinea-moves-to-tackle-health-kickback-scam.

Johnstone, M., 2014. *Corruption, contention and reform: the power of deep democratization.* Cambridge: Cambridge University Press.

Jubilee Australia, 2012. Pipe dreams: the PNG LNG project and the hopes of a nation. Retrieved on 30 July 2015 from: www.jubileeaustralia.org/page/work/pipe-dreams-report.

Kumar, C.R., 2011. *Corruption and human rights in India: comparative perspectives on transparency and good governance.* Oxford: Oxford University Press.

Lasslett, K., 2012. The demolition of Paga Hill: A report by the International State Crime Initiative. Retrieved on 17 June 2015 from: www.statecrime.org/testimonyproject/pagahill.

Lasslett, K., 2014. *State crime on the margins of empire: Rio Tinto, the war on Bougainville, and resistance to mining.* London: Pluto Press.

Lawson, S., 2014. *Illegal logging in Papua New Guinea.* London: Chatham House.

MacManus, T., 2014. Civil society and state-corporate crime: a case study of Ivory Coast. *State Crime*, 3(2), 200–19.

May, R.J., 2013. Papua New Guinea: from coup to reconciliation. *Journal of Democracy*, 24(1), 165–71.

Numapo, J., 2013. *Commission of Inquiry into the Special Agricultural and Business Lease (SABL). Final report.* Retrieved on 23 July 2015 from: https://pngexposed.files.wordpress.com/2013/12/numapo-sabl-final-report.pdf.

Philp, M., 1997. Defining political corruption. *Political Studies*, 45, 436–62.

PNGexposed Blog, 2015. O'Neill's illegal logging: 756 days and counting. . . . 20 July. Retrieved on 22 July 2015 from: https://pngexposed.wordpress.com/.

Pogge, T., 2007. Severe poverty as a human rights violation. *In*: T. Pogge (ed.), *Freedom from poverty as a human right*. Oxford: Oxford University Press, 11–54.

Public Accounts Committee [PAC], 2006. *Inquiry into the Department of Lands and Physical Planning: report to the National Parliament*. Port Moresby: author.

Rose-Ackerman, S., 1999. *Corruption and government: causes, consequences and reform*. Cambridge: Cambridge University Press.

Sampson, S., 2010. The anti-corruption industry: from movement to institution. *Global Crime*, 11(2), 261–78.

Sharman, J., 2012. Chasing kleptocrats' loot: narrowing the effectiveness gap. Retrieved on 23 July 2015 from: www.u4.no/publications/chasing-kleptocrats-loot-narrowing-the-effectiveness-gap/.

Steiner, H. J., 1988. Political participation as a human right. *Harvard Human Rights Yearbook*, 1, 77–134.

Transparency International, 2013. Global corruption barometer 2013. Retrieved on 22 July 2015 from: www.transparency.org/gcb2013.

UN, 2013. The human rights case against corruption. Retrieved on 1 October 2015 from: www.ohchr.org/Documents/Issues/Development/GoodGovernance/Corruption/HRCaseAgainstCorruption.pdf.

Walton, G.W., 2013. The limitations of neoliberal logic in the anti-corruption industry: lessons from Papua New Guinea. *Crime, Law & Social Change*, 60, 147–64.

Walton, G.W., 2015. Defining corruption where the state is weak: the case of Papua New Guinea. *Journal of Development Studies*, 51(1), 1–31.

# 17

# Human rights and multinational enterprises

## A criminological analysis of non-judicial mechanisms of redress

*Fiona Haines*

Multinational enterprises (MNEs) are now recognized by the United Nations as having human rights responsibilities. The United Nations (UN) Guiding Principles on Business and Human Rights states that businesses must respect human rights and provide redress when they fail in doing so. These guiding principles draw strength from the concept of 'enlightened self-interest' which understands there is a confluence of interest between international business interests and local communities. For some, they are a sign of significant progress whilst others point to their weaknesses in holding MNEs to account. This chapter analyses these debates and briefly outlines the substance of the guiding principles before turning to research that looks at the capacity of the guiding principles, as realized through non-judicial mechanisms, to provide redress. The research reveals the diverse nature of the grievances and shows that limited redress is possible for some individuals and communities, but a basic philosophy of support for capitalist industrialization means that significant problems remain.

### Introduction

Activists and academics highlight the significant harms perpetrated by MNEs, abuses that range from forced displacement from land, intimidation and violence, child and forced labour, environmental devastation, inhumane working conditions to repression against the formation of independent trade unions. In the context of economic globalization, increases in international trade have seen MNEs grow in size and reach, developing global supply chains supported by disparate sources of international finance. Multiple actors are involved in these chains, with business actors complicit in human rights abuse either acting alone or with state actors at local, regional, national and international levels. Identifying which actors are involved in these harms and where they are finding sources of financial support for their activities can be difficult. Even where they can be identified, finding ways to bring actors to account is hard. Ultimately, complexity in causation coupled with a lack of robust sources of leverage means that holding MNEs to account for the harms they cause remains challenging.

Despite this, a human rights orientation to dealing with the harms caused by MNEs appears to hold promise. The UN Guiding Principles on Business and Human Rights (hereafter guiding principles) are now in place, developed from the work of John Ruggie and his role as the UN special representative on business and human rights (Ruggie 2007, 2008). Under the guidelines MNEs are seen as responsible for respecting human rights and are no longer able to divert sole responsibility to states. The guiding principles are framed around three pillars: the state's responsibility to protect human rights, business responsibility to respect human rights and the joint responsibility to provide redress. The guiding principles now frame a plethora of initiatives aimed to improve the standards of MNEs that include: the UN Global Compact, the Organisation for Economic Co-operation and Development (OECD) Guidelines for Multinational Enterprises, industry codes such as the International Council on Mining and Minerals, the Equator Principles for financial institutions, multiple corporate codes of conduct and multi-stakeholder initiatives (Addo 2014).

The focus of this chapter is on the capacity of these approaches to provide redress for those affected by the activities of MNEs. This redress element is given effect through internal business grievance processes complemented by non-judicial grievance mechanisms set up in a broad array of institutional settings, often associated with the initiatives above, where accountability and justice is delivered through mediation and problem-solving approaches and, where these fail, public condemnation through findings of malfeasance. A critique of redress requires attention to context which is explored in the first section below. Redress is shaped by contested terrain not only about the proper form of accountability (voluntary or mandatory) but also whether the activities of MNEs and their supply chains are primarily beneficial or whether fundamental problems are an intrinsic element of current forms of industrialization. The second part of the chapter reviews the emergence of non-judicial avenues for redress, processes which are associated with diverse institutional settings but which all share an emphasis on practical forms of redress that can make a difference to the lives of those who are affected. Whilst some mechanisms have achieved redress, for some there remains a significant gap between the aspirations of these mechanisms and their actual impact on the ground.

## Business and human rights: a brief contextualization

The responsibilities of MNEs in respecting human rights has a complex history, comprised of tensions between individual and collective rights as well as different views of the specific obligations that MNEs should assume. The public framing of the responsibilities of multinational business as one anchored in human rights is considered to be of recent origin, specifically the 1990s. During this decade, a number of non-government organizations (NGOs) highlighted abuses perpetrated by multinational enterprises with a particular focus on high profile cases, such as the high levels of pollution caused by the Shell oil company in Nigeria. Protests against Shell ultimately resulted in the execution of the representatives of those most affected by the activities of Shell, Ken Saro-Wiwa and eight other Ogoni people. These events cemented in the public sphere the connection between business and the perpetration of human rights abuses (Cragg et al. 2012) galvanizing civil society which ultimately led to the development of the guiding principles.

This was not a straightforward process. The guiding principles resulted from a complex and contested process where a number of countries and civil society actors wanted a more binding treaty approach. The Ruggie process itself emerged from the failure of an earlier 2003 report, which argued that businesses should be brought directly under the ambit of human rights law, to gain endorsement by the UN (Cragg et al. 2012). The focus on guiding principles as opposed to binding treaty and strict legal forms of accountability remains a source of contention. At the international level there remains no credible or legitimate authority that might allow for criminal sanctions to be laid against MNEs. Examinations of the way that international forms of criminal accountability might be bought to fruition, for example through the International Criminal Court (Sundell 2011) remain unrealized.

For many the development of the guiding principles as a voluntary system is a sign of failure rather than success. Within criminology, for example, a human rights approach to framing crime and criminality has long been on the agenda (Schwendinger and Schwendinger 1975). However, a human rights approach that can move beyond traditional conceptions of what is, and what is not, criminal behaviour to include the crimes and harms of the powerful does not equate with the need for a voluntary approach in reducing such harm. Indeed, a non-judicial approach stands in some contrast to calls within criminology for greater powers to criminalize and sanction business, and corporate executives, for this abuse (see, for example, Bittle and Snider 2013). The complicity between states and business that results in corporate harm and impunity, what some criminologists term state–corporate crime (Kramer et al. 2002), needs to be counted by a more rigorous approach to sanctioning at the international level (Bittle and Snider 2013). Beyond criminology, the push for a tougher approach continues. Both civil society and some countries continue to advocate for a more binding treaty framework to govern the activities of multinational enterprises. Their demand has seen a UN Intergovernmental Working Group recently set up to explore the possibilities of a legally binding treaty (for a discussion see Business & Human Rights Resource Centre n.d.).

A focus on the guiding principles and a push for a more binding treaty, however, should not overlook an earlier history of protest and organizing centred on labour rights. The connection between the responsibilities of business and labour rights has been institutionalized through the work of the International Labour Organisation (ILO) since 1919. The separate trajectory of the development of business responsibilities for human rights compared with the need to engender labour rights reveals a tension in views concerning the responsibility of MNEs for collective, democratic and participatory rights and not just individual rights or (often) more passively understood collective rights, such as the right to health. In the increased emphasis on the UN guiding principles it is possible to see a marginalization of core ILO standards as being centrally relevant to a business' human rights (Bellace 2014).

To understand the tension in views regarding the responsibilities of MNEs and the proper boundaries to their accountability, it is helpful to place these debates within divergent views of the process of economic globalization itself. Contestation around the precise nature of human rights obligations of business and whether a failure to meet those obligations should, or should not, be subject to legal sanction reflects competing views of the significance that should be placed on harm perpetrated by MNEs and the benefits, or otherwise, that accrue from MNEs and their global supply chains. For proponents of economic globalization instances of human rights abuse by MNEs arise from aberrant business practice. Despite specific instances of harm, proponents argue, economic globalization remains the primary means by which economic growth is secured, growth that underpins dramatic declines in global poverty (see, for example, Bhagwati 2004, Department for International Development 2008). Grievances can and should be managed. Nonetheless, addressing grievance should not derail the process of economic globalization itself nor undermine the benefits MNEs and their supply chains bring. The past three or more decades' emphasis on international trade, trade underpinned by ideas of a level playing field, should be maintained even as grievances are addressed. For critics of economic globalization (at least in its current manifestation), the same grievances arise not from abnormal business practice but as an inevitable consequence of the process itself. Economic globalization based on capitalist expansion has not only unleashed growing inequalities in wealth (Piketty 2014, Stiglitz 2001) but also inequalities in the experience of risk leading to a reduction in lifespan, increased rates of disease, and heightened conflict (Gilbert and Russell 2002, Marmot et al. 2008, Idemudia 2009, Kröger 2012).

These contrasting views not only affect the activities of those who work within global institutions but also the experiences of local communities and workers in countries that host the activities of MNEs. Diverging views on the benefits of and experiences with economic globalization fundamentally affect local communities, individuals and workers and shape their demands for redress. The redistribution process of both wealth and risk itself can generate significant conflict which in turn leads to multiple grievance claims (Halifax Initiative 2004, Rosenblum 2004). What is demanded in the form of redress for a specific grievance varies significantly between places and over time. Some communities demand a fairer share of the benefits of industrialization spurred by the processes of economic globalization, some greater protection from the risks, yet others wish to retain their current forms of livelihood with a demand for the removal of a particular project (such as a mine) even as others within the same community may desire the wealth promised by the same project.

## Grievance and non-judicial processes

The discussion below draws from research undertaken by myself and my colleagues[1] into the effectiveness of non-judicial redress mechanisms that have emerged since the development of the guiding principles. Our focus is on the adequacy of redress provided by these mechanisms for grievances against MNEs. This research has been undertaken in India and Indonesia in agribusiness, mining and the textile, clothing and footwear industries. In all, we have undertaken 10 case studies of grievance and redress in the two countries: four in agribusiness (two in each country), three in mining (two in India and one in Indonesia) and three in textile, clothing and footwear (two in India and one in Indonesia). In general, grievances emerged at two particular junctures. The first set of grievances arose from projects with the potential to fundamentally re-orientate communities away from subsistence and traditional livelihoods to the wage economy. With successful completion of the project, self-sufficiency in terms of livelihood, albeit often one of considerable poverty, would be transformed into dependency on a cash economy where securing employment was essential. The second set of grievances centred on the conditions of work. The right to free association, living wages and a healthy and safe workplace form the centrepiece here.

The institutional settings of the non-judicial mechanisms are diverse. An important non-judicial redress mechanism studied in the research was the mechanism of the International Finance Corporation, the primary intergovernmental financier of the private sector, named the Compliance Advisor Ombudsman (hereafter IFC CAO). This mechanism forms the primary focus of the discussion below. But it is important to recognize a number of other mechanisms. In our research, these other mechanisms included the National Contact Point (hereafter NCP) arrangement associated with the OECD Guidelines for Multinational Enterprises. NCPs are designed specifically to hear the grievances of those affected by MNEs headquartered in the specific OECD Member State jurisdiction. There is a voluntary recommendation for all OECD members to set up a NCP. There are currently 47 NCPs within the OECD. NCPs in the United Kingdom (UK), Holland, Norway and Korea were all represented in the research. Finally, are grievance mechanisms associated with multi-stakeholder initiatives (MSIs). MSIs are voluntary member-based schemes set up to improve standards across global supply chains in different industries. Examples of MSIs included in our research were the Ethical Trading Initiative based in the UK, the Roundtable on Sustainable Palm Oil (RSPO) aiming to raise standards in the palm oil industry and the Rainforest Alliance (our focus here was specifically on the tea sector). MSIs are seen as a desirable alternative to industry-based schemes since their governance structure includes civil society as well as industry members. This structure is argued to enhance the independence of the scheme and its capacity to respond to the concerns of local communities (for a critical discussion see Fransen and Kolk 2007, Utting 2002).

The size of our research project means that it is impossible to give a comprehensive account of the findings. Nonetheless, in only two of the 10 cases were there material forms of redress forthcoming and in a further case a finding of non-compliance did support local legal efforts to halt a mine. As Utting (2005) noted a decade ago soft law, non-judicial redress mechanisms, then, are likely to form only one element of a broad array of processes needed to ensure MNEs are accountable for the harm they perpetrate. The discussion below on grievances in the context of the shift away from subsistence teases out some of the elements for this lack of success.

## Grievances in the context of the shift away from subsistence

The most common scenario in the case of grievances arising in the context of subsistence is loss of land either for dwellings or livelihood or for both. In five of the 10 case studies the grievances concerned loss of land; three in Indonesia and two in India. In Indonesia, one of the cases concerned loss of forest land for conversion into palm oil plantations (Wilmar), one case concerned forest conservation (through the REDD+ project aimed at reducing carbon emissions) with potential loss of access to land for food and the third concerned loss of land for subsistence due to the development of a nickel mine (PT Weda Bay). In India, both cases concerned mining and associated refining complexes one in aluminium (Vedanta) and the other in steel (POSCO). The grievance mechanisms used were the IFC CAO in the Wilmar case and in the case of PT Weda Bay; the Korean, Dutch and Norwegian NCP in the case of POSCO and the UK NCP in the case of Vedanta. The RSPO was also involved in the Wilmar case. In the REDD+ case, the successful development of local project-based grievance processes on the ground prior to the inauguration of the REDD+ project, together with the stalling of the project itself, has seen no formal claim laid by the local communities in this case. This was despite considerable public debate in the international media about grievances arising from REDD+ projects.

At least in terms of the IFC CAO significant redress for some communities could be achieved. In the Wilmar case, two of the locations, Sambas (involving two communities) and Riau, both in Western Kalimantan, mediation resulted in financial compensation, return of cleared land and some planted with oil palm and a commitment to end land clearing (for a more detailed discussion of the case see Balaton-Chrimes and Haines 2015, Balaton-Chrimes and Macdonald 2015). The success of this outcome can be understood to flow from several contextual features of the case. The first is the presence of considerable civil society advocacy at all levels from the most local to the global. This attention to destruction of forest for oil palm plantations led the World Bank group (which includes the IFC) to withdraw all funding from the industry in September 2009. Funding resumed with enhanced safeguards in April 2011. Attention to this industry generated considerable motivation to generate successful outcomes from the grievance claims. Finally, the IFC CAO was the best resourced of all the non-judicial mechanisms studied. It has a high degree of institutional independence from the IFC itself, it engages in significant capacity-building at the local community level and has a philosophy for local empowerment in mediation and decision-making. The resources it provides in terms of money, expertise and capacity-building were important to the outcomes.

The beneficial outcomes in Western Kalimantan can be contrasted with a failure of mediation in Sambas, Sumatra. This was despite considerable efforts to conclude mediation by local communities, local advocacy groups and the IFC CAO. The grievance in this case involved a Wilmar subsidiary, PT Asiatic Persada. Before the completion of mediation, Wilmar sold PT Asiatic Persada. In doing so, the IFC CAO no longer had jurisdiction to hear the grievance. The new owners of the subsidiary had neither funding from the IFC nor guarantees through the Multilateral Investment Guarantee Agency (MIGA) no did they belong to the RSPO which could have provided an alternative venue for claiming particular grievance. In the case of non-judicial mechanisms, as in the case of the law, there are questions of jurisdiction in terms of who can press a grievance claim and where. In the case of the IFC CAO, it can only hear a grievance when funding or guarantees are provided by the IFC or MIGA. The sale put the grievance outside of the relevant jurisdiction. The IFC CAO offered to continue mediation, but the new owners of PT Asiatic Persada refused. The land was cleared and our interviewees reported the villages destroyed. In their final report on the case, the IFC CAO were damning in their condemnation of Wilmar's conduct.

Even in the cases where mediation was successful, caution is needed in interpreting its impact and significance. Most of the land was cleared, so that local peoples now are dependent on a wage economy. Whilst they have the potential to realize a significant income through the sale of palm fruit on their planted land, this requires a considerable change in lifestyle. What was allowed in the case of these two mediations was a franchise like arrangement with the plots of palm (named plasma) involved. That is, at least for a period of time, the palm fruit had a guaranteed market with Wilmar. However, there have been some difficulties in local people developing the necessary skills in maintaining the plantations and in harvesting the fruit. Further, the demand of activists for a wholesale reorientation of the palm oil industry in a more sustainable direction has not been realized. The IFC CAO did not proceed with a sector wide response to grievances in the industry as a whole but selected three specific locations to respond to specific grievances. The reasons for this failure are multiple. Clearly, there are considerable interests at stake in terms of both the Indonesian federal and regional governments. Land tenure and land ownership laws are extremely complex with multiple interests at play. Malaysia, too, has a particular dependence on the palm oil industry in Indonesia (Varkkey 2013). The pressures on advocacy groups and the resources demanded for successful mediation, let alone sustained advocacy, too, are considerable. But there is also the philosophical orientation of the IFC CAO itself that needs to be understood. Ultimately, the IFC CAO sees projects such as palm oil as beneficial. Capitalist forms of industrialization are seen as the primary method by which levels of poverty will be reduced. Ultimately, the IFC CAO considers as a success projects which are completed without significant levels of grievance and with the inevitable problems that arise being dealt with at the local level in a fair and equitable manner.

This orientation of the IFC CAO means that it is primarily effective in how a project proceeds not in preventing a project from continuing (or beginning) where there is sustained local resistance to the project. This orientation is evident in its resistance to conduct an audit of PT Weda Bay's operations in Weda Bay, Halmahera province (another of our case studies) following the failure of mediation initiated in response to a complaint bought by three local NGOs. The project is designed to exploit a large deposit of laterite nickel, the largest undeveloped known deposit of the mineral. There are a number of villages affected, but our research focused on three villages in particular (for a more detailed analysis of the case see Marshall et al. 2013). The loss of livelihood is a major issue in this case. That is, a number of communities may not need to physically relocate but they will lose access to land that they use to grow food, most of which used is by the household and a minor portion traded. The current experience with the cash economy is that money is a *supplement* to livelihood not as the major element sustaining it. The experience with a cash economy, then, is limited. The mine has not yet started operation (it was in its feasibility phase during the period of our research), but building has begun for a processing plant. There has been acquisition of land with compensation offered. A number of communities accepted compensation and were waiting for the mine to begin to access the jobs and economic benefits that have been promised. There was some evidence that those who accepted compensation felt that they had little option to refuse. Other households had rejected compensation. The level of compensation offered did not represent a full evaluation of the ongoing livelihood value of the land itself: it represented only the purchase price of the land (IDR 8000). This purchase price was extremely low, equivalent to each hectare of land yielding less than the cost of a basic meal.

A complaint was made to the IFC CAO in 2010 based on the potential for widespread environmental and social consequences of the project that had not been fully investigated or managed. Further, the NGOs claimed that the displacement of remote Indigenous peoples, the Tobelo Dalam, had not been addressed. The IFC CAO visited the region three times in 2010 and 2011 in order to try to set up mediation. However, in an environment of considerable tension where there were fears for personal safety, those affected were not willing to reveal their identity in order to take part in mediation. Mediation failed to eventuate and so the case was passed on to the Compliance function, where an assessment could be made of whether breaches of IFC performance standards had occurred by MIGA in their support of PT Weda Bay. The basis for investigation by the IFC CAO is not that the MNE has perpetrated some human rights abuse, but that the IFC or MIGA has breached one or more of the eight IFC performance standards in its support of the project. These performance standards cover environmental and social risks, labour and working conditions, resource efficiency and pollution prevention, community health safety and security, land acquisition and involuntary resettlement, biodiversity and sustainability, Indigenous peoples and cultural heritage (International Finance Corporation 2012). In essence, a breach of the standards involves a failure of due diligence by the IFC or MIGA in ensuring that companies involved in projects supported by the IFC or MIGA have undertaken sufficient assessment of the social, environmental and related risks as outlined in the standards and have the capacity to ensure its operations will not breach those standards. The compliance unit within the IFC CAO declined to audit a potential breach of standards stating that because it was too early in the life history of the project for an audit to be conducted.

This case reinforces the findings of the Wilmar case that the IFC CAO has greatest potential to shape how the project proceeds not whether it does so. When this is understood, it is difficult to see how a grievance process, even one as well resourced as the IFC CAO, can have a lasting impact on those most marginalized and most at risk from major projects. The tension and conflict that surrounded the Weda Bay project was a finding common across our case studies involving the transition from subsistence to wage labour, a finding that reflects literature in the area (for a review in the context of mining see Owen and Kemp 2015). The development of a major project such as a mine or a processing plant is sold to local communities as a potential means for them to improve their livelihoods. Local subsistence communities often do not have the skills often required for ongoing employment in a particular project. They are most likely to be employed during the construction phase and after this phase is complete may be left with little or no income having lost access to land to enable them to grow their own food. Ultimately, the risk for many in a project affected area is displacement and extreme poverty on the one hand (Satiroglu and Choi 2015) and, for those who stay, a gradual erosion of social and environmental conditions on the other (Owen and Kemp 2015).

Given this situation, it is not surprising that a number of grievances arise in contexts where a project has not yet begun operation and where some in the community reject the promises made by project proponents. Of the five case studies we examined only one of the grievances had occurred where land had been forcibly acquired (Wilmar). In the case of PT Weda Bay the mine was not yet in operation in part because of ongoing protests but also because of a decline in the price of nickel and also legislative changes within Indonesia that changed the profitability of the investment (Marshall et al. 2013). Conflict and protest could be intensified where current livelihoods had either economic or cultural significance (or both). This was the situation in two of our case studies: Vedanta and POSCO. In the case of Vedanta, the project threatened the sacred sites and livelihood of local tribal people, the Dongria Kondh. In the case of POSCO the cultivation of betel leaf generated significant income. Destruction through the project development in both cases promised little compared to the social, economic and cultural benefits of existing livelihoods. In the case of Vedanta, a complaint to the UK NCP that resulted in significant condemnation of the company provided some support for local court action within India eventually halting the project. The tension and conflict in the POSCO case is significant and ongoing, despite POSCO stating it was suspending operations in July 2015. In each case significant promises are held out to those affected by both governments and the MNEs themselves which reflects considerable national and international support for particular projects. This was certainly the case here. In the case of POSCO, for example, the project represents the largest foreign direct investment by any country in India.

## Conclusion

To date the most prominent debates around MNE responsibilities in terms of human rights abuse relates to the specific nature of accountability for MNEs and human rights abuse. Yet the nature of accountability needs to be placed squarely in the context of competing views on the processes of economic globalization and its current form, views which are represented not only in global debates but also in the views of those on the ground regarding what form of redress they seek. Divergent expectations, and in a number of cases significant conflict, are present in communities affected by MNE activities. In this context non-judicial grievance mechanisms can generate some benefits, but these benefits are heavily circumscribed by a firm belief in the benefits of capitalist industrialization.

Current abuses perpetrated by MNEs are enmeshed in current dynamics of industrialization, at least as they are expressed in the shift from subsistence to wage labour. The challenges to a just outcome are considerable. Global poverty remains a significant challenge and industrial projects promise a brighter future for many. When viewed in this way, accountability through a grievance approach which does not hinder such industrialization seems logical. However, this research suggests that those most affected by capitalist industrialization risk being further marginalized through such projects even where a grievance mechanism is available. It is not clear from this research, though, that criminal accountability would resolve such deep seated tensions. A criminological account of the intersection between business and human rights and the need for more binding forms of accountability may need to be tempered by some humility in terms of possible outcomes from such a shift. The analysis above suggests that a focus on accountability needs to be accompanied by a more rigorous examination of what capitalist industrialization can achieve and what forms of redress will be permitted by those convinced of its benefits.

## Note

1 Kate Macdonald, University of Melbourne, Shelley Marshall, Monash University, Samantha Balaton-Chrimes, Deakin University, Tim Connor, Newcastle University, and Annie Delaney, RMIT University.

## References

Addo, M.K., 2014. The reality of the United Nations Guiding Principles on Business and Human Rights. *Human Rights Law Review*, 14(1), 133–47.

Balaton-Chrimes, S. and Haines, F., 2015. The depoliticisation of accountability processes for land-based grievances, and the IFC CAO. *Global Policy*, 6(4), 446–54.

Balaton-Chrimes, S. and Macdonald, K., 2015. *Wilmar*. Unpublished Report, copy on file with author.

Bellace, J.R., 2014. Hoisted on their own petard? Business and human rights. *Journal of Industrial Relations*, 56(3), 442–57.

Bhagwati, J., 2004. Corporations: predatory or beneficial? *In*: *In defense of globalization*. New York, NY: Oxford University Press, 162–95.

Bittle, S. and Snider, L., 2013. Examining the Ruggie Report: can voluntary guidelines tame global capitalism? *Critical Criminology*, (2), 177.

Business & Human Rights Resource Centre, n.d. *Binding Treaty*. Retrieved on 6 June 2015 from: http://business-humanrights.org/en/binding-treaty.

Cragg, W., Arnold, D.G. and Muchlinski, P., 2012. Human rights and business. *Business Ethics Quarterly*, 22(1), 1–7.

Department for International Development, 2008. *Growth: building jobs and prosperity in developing countries*. Great Britain: Department for International Development.

Fransen, L.W. and Kolk, A., 2007. Global rule-setting for business: a critical analysis of multi-stakeholder standards. *Organization*, 14(5), 667–84.

Gilbert, M.J. and Russell, S., 2002. Globalization of criminal justice in the corporate context. *Crime, Law & Social Change*, 38(3), 211–38.

Halifax Initiative, 2004. *Risk responsibility and human rights: assessing the human rights impacts of trade and project finance*. Ottawa Canada: Halifax Initiative. Retrieved on 6 June 2015 from: www.halifaxinitiative.org/updir/HR_final_report.pdf.

Idemudia, U., 2009. Oil extraction and poverty reduction in the Niger Delta: a critical examination of partnership initiatives. *Journal of Business Ethics*, 90, 91–116.

International Finance Corporation, 2012. *Performance standards on environmental and social sustainability*. Retrieved on 6 June 2015 from: www.ifc.org/wps/wcm/connect/topics_ext_content/ifc_external_corporate_site/ifc+sustainability/our+approach/risk+management/performance+standards/environmental+and+social+performance+standards+and+guidance+notes.

Kramer, R.C., Michalowski, R.J. and Kauzlarich, D., 2002. The origins and development of the concept and theory of state-corporate crime. *Crime & Delinquency*, 48(2), 263–82.

Kröger, M., 2012. The expansion of industrial tree plantations and dispossession in Brazil. *Development & Change*, 43(4), 947–73.

Marmot, M. , Friel, S., Bell, R., Houweling, T.A.J. and Taylor, S., 2008. Closing the gap in a generation: health equity through action on the social determinants of health. *The Lancet*, 372(9650), 1661–9.

Marshall, S., Balaton-Chrimes, S. and Pidani, O., 2013. *Access to Justice for Communities Affected by the PT Weda Bay Nickel Mine: Interim Report*. Retrieved on 24 September 2015 from: http://business-humanrights.org/sites/default/files/media/weda-bay-public-report-oct2013.pdf.

Owen, J.R. and Kemp, D., 2015. Mining-induced displacement and resettlement: a critical appraisal. *Journal of Cleaner Production*, 87, 478–88.

Piketty, T., 2014. *Capital in the twenty-first century*. Cambridge, MA: The Belknap Press of Harvard University Press.

Rosenblum, P., 2004. Human rights and trade financing: Chad Cameroon Pipeline. *In*: The Halifax Initiative, *Risk, responsibility and human rights: assessing the human rights impacts of trade and project finance*. Final Report for a panel discussion and expert meeting on developing a human rights impact assessment framework, 7–9. Retrieved on 15 April 2016 from www.halifaxinitiative.org/updir/HR_final_report.pdf.

Ruggie, J., 2007. *Report of the Special Representative of the Secretary-General on the issue of human rights and transnational corporations and other business enterprises: business and human rights – mapping international standards of responsibility and accountability for corporate acts*. United Nations General Assembly, A/HRC/4/35.

Ruggie, J., 2008. *Promotion and protection of all human rights, civil, political, economic, social and cultural rights, including the right to development: protect, respect and remedy – a framework for business and human rights*. United Nations, A/HRC/8/5.

Satiroglu, I. and Choi, N., 2015. *Development-induced displacement and resettlement: new perspectives on persisting problems*. Hoboken, NJ: Taylor & Francis.

Schwendinger, H. and Schwendinger, J., 1975. Defenders of order or guardians of human rights? *In*: I. Taylor, P. Walton and J. Young (eds), *Critical criminology*. London: Routledge and Kegan Paul, 113–46.

Stiglitz, J., 2001. Foreword. *In*: K. Polanyi (ed.), *The great transformation: the political and economic origins of our time with a new introduction by Fred Block*. Boston, MA: Beacon Press, vii–xvii.

Sundell, J., 2011. Ill-gotten gains: the case for international corporate criminal liability. *Minnesota Journal of International Law*, 20(2), 648–680.

Utting, P., 2002. The global compact and civil society. *Development in Practice*, 12(5), 644–7.

Utting, P., 2005. *Rethinking business regulation: from self-regulation to social control*. United Nations Research Institute for Social Development.

Varkkey, H., 2013. Malaysian investors in the Indonesian oil palm plantation sector: home state facilitation and transboundary haze. *Asia Pacific Business Review*, 19(3), 381–401.

# 18

# The utility and futility of international standards for children in conflict with the law

## The case of England

*Kathryn Hollingsworth*[1]

Over the past 30 years, international instruments have emerged across a number of legal regimes that impose on states binding and non-binding obligations relating to children in conflict with the law (Hespel et al. 2012). The rights-based standards contained in these measures cover all elements of youth justice from prevention to detention. Using England as an example, this chapter examines the utility *and* futility of international standards in affecting change in domestic youth justice systems and in providing legally enforceable remedies. I focus on two legal regimes: the United Nations (UN) and the Council of Europe (CoE).[2] Considered individually, neither system provides the perfect vehicle for securing the rights of children in conflict with the law. The UN has detailed, comprehensive and child-specific standards but an historically weak method of enforcement; the CoE has the European Court of Human Rights (ECtHR) to which individuals can bring complaints for breach of the *European Convention on Human Rights* (ECHR), but this is a general rights treaty the substantive content of which is not tailored to children's interests.[3] Both regimes have, however, recently sought to address their respective weaknesses: at the UN level, a system of individual complaint was adopted in 2014 (the Third Optional Protocol, or 'OP3'); and in 2010, the CoE published child-friendly justice guidelines. This chapter considers both of these developments but the primary focus is on what Kilkelly (2001) has described as the 'best of both worlds': the use of UN standards to interpret the ECHR in order to secure legally enforceable *children's* rights.

### The UN and the rights of children in conflict with the law

The most comprehensive source of international standards for children, both generally and for those in conflict with the law, is the UN and in particular the *Convention on the Rights of the Child* (CRC). The CRC was not the first international children's rights instrument but its emergence marked an important conceptual shift in the image of the child from object of concern to legal subject (Verhellen 1992). Accordingly, the Convention includes many autonomy-based rights (including civil and political rights and rights of participation) as well as interests deriving from children's physical, developmental, economic, and legal dependencies: thus helping to 'mediate the tensions' (Cipriani 2009) between the justice and welfare models of youth justice. Of the CRC's 54 Articles, two have specific relevance to children in conflict with the law. Article 37 prohibits cruel, inhuman and degrading treatment and punishment, specifically proscribing the death penalty and life imprisonment without parole. It also includes the child-specific requirement that detention should be used only as a last resort and for the shortest possible time. Article 40 sets out many of the procedural rights for minors. These go beyond the usual fair trial rights to also include the desirability of reintegration, diversion and non-custodial responses; the requirement to set a minimum age of criminal responsibility (MACR); protection of privacy; and the child's right to be supported by her parents and by legal or other assistance. All of the other substantive rights – for example to education, access to health care, parental contact – extend to (putative) child offenders but apart from the four general principles (best interests, the right to be heard, non-discrimination, and the right to life, survival and development) their utility remains largely underexplored in the criminal justice context.

The breadth of the CRC's content, together with its jurisdictional reach (all UN members except the United States have ratified or are in the process of ratification), underlie its strengths *and* its weaknesses: securing almost universal agreement from vastly different states for a legally binding treaty that contains over 40 substantive provisions meant that, in order to be politically feasible, the rights were widely drafted (sometimes vague) and the enforcement mechanisms weak (Kilkelly 1996, p. 117). However, neither of these shortcomings necessarily limits the Convention's utility. First, the CRC is supplemented by a range of ambitious, comprehensive, and detailed (non-binding) soft law measures that raise standards through their persuasive force, their use in advocacy and campaigning, and by aiding the interpretation of the Convention and other legally binding instruments (see below). These include, in the context of juvenile justice, the Beijing Rules, the Havana Rules, and the Riyadh Guidelines and secondary sources that derive from the jurisprudence of the UN Committee on the Rights of the Child (hereafter, UN Committee).[4] Soft law fleshes out the Convention, providing detailed requirements such as a MACR over the age of 12 (UN Committee 2007, para. 32) and consent prior to the use of diversion (Beijing Rules 1985, Rule 11.3). Second, enforcement of the CRC has been strengthened by two developments: the adoption of OP3 and the Convention's use as an aid to interpretation by domestic and regional courts. Initially, monitoring and enforcement of the CRC was limited to a five-yearly periodic reporting process, overseen by the UN Committee. The concluding observations of the Committee that follow each report contain non-binding recommendations, compliance with which depends on diplomacy and political pressure rather than legal sanction (Kilkelly 1996, 2001, Woll 2000). Through this process the United Kingdom (UK) has been criticized (in relation to England) for its MACR, high custody figures (especially remand), the use of adult courts, inadequate protection of privacy, and conditions in detention. Subsequent reforms to law, policy and practice have addressed some of the Committee's recommendations (HM Government 2014) but compliance has been piecemeal. On issues about which the government is resolute, or which would be politically unpopular – for example, the MACR or anti-social behaviour measures – the monitoring process can appear futile. Further, even where the government *has* reported progress on its compliance with previous recommendations, this has usually been partial (thus appearing tokenistic[5]) and/or attributable to other factors.[6] Nonetheless, although non-binding, concluding observations play an important role within domestic political accountability processes (House of Lords House of Commons Joint Committee on Human Rights 2014) and – as the UN Committee's jurisprudence – provide the definitive interpretation of the CRC (Hespel et al. 2012). Though infrequent, there are examples of the English courts giving indirect legal effect to concluding observations with which the government had previously failed to comply.[7] However, the ability of the courts to do so is highly circumscribed (see below).

As noted above, the CRC's enforcement mechanisms have been strengthened by the adoption in 2012 of OP3. The Protocol brings the CRC into line with all the other UN human rights treaties by (inter alia) introducing a system of individual complaints for alleged infringements of children's rights. Buck and Wabwile (2013) suggest that OP3 has two key benefits. First, it fills an institutional gap by providing a child-specific complaints mechanism which represents 'an emblem of relevant values, norms and principles that prompts awareness of children's rights' that can 'drive states to review and reform their domestic human rights policies and practices' (Buck and Wabwile 2013, p. 226). Second, it reduces the knowledge gap by providing a concrete and context-specific arena for the development of the UN Committee's jurisprudence. However, OP3 has been criticized for failing to include a collective complaints process (Grover 2015) and for being insufficiently 'child-friendly', with little to differentiate it from the complaints processes of other human rights treaties (Egan 2014). Furthermore, complaints can only be made against states that have ratified the Protocol itself (Article 1[3]). The UK has not ratified and is unlikely to do so soon (House of Lords House of Commons Joint Committee on Human Rights 2014, para. 35). Therefore, for children in England and Wales the utility of OP3 is indirect only, via its contribution to the Committee's jurisprudence (which domestic and intra-national courts may draw on).

## Child-friendly justice in the Council of Europe

In 2012, the Council of Europe published its Strategy for the Rights of the Child, designed to achieve 'effective implementation of existing children's rights standards (Committee of Ministers of the Council of Europe 2012). As part of the predecessor programme to the Strategy (Building a Europe for and with Children programme) the Guidelines on Child Friendly Justice (hereafter 'Guidelines') were produced (Committee of Ministers of the Council of Europe 2010). The Guidelines do not create *new* standards; rather they collate international rights to provide practical guidance for Member States to design their judicial and non-judicial systems in a child-specific way. The Guidelines emphasize general norms including dignity and the rule of law (due process, presumption of innocence, legality, proportionality, the right to a fair trial and so on), and child-specific principles drawn from the CRC (participation, best interests and non-discrimination). The more specific standards broadly replicate UN measures; however, the involvement of children and young people in the drafting process led to greater emphasis on confidentiality, the importance of support from family and friends, the provision of feedback on decisions, the right to gain access to independent support and complaint mechanisms, and the right to be informed and heard (Kilkelly 2010a, p. 40). As a non-binding instrument, the effectiveness of the Guidelines depends on political commitment, professional awareness, and their value as a judicial interpretative tool. The EU has committed to taking the Guidelines into account in future legal instruments, but lack of awareness amongst professionals in the UK (judges, police, lawyers, and social workers) diminishes their utility (EU Agency for Fundamental Rights 2015). Thus, along with other European soft law (including Council of Ministers recommendations[8]) and UN standards, the Guidelines might prove most useful if they can acquire indirect legal effect through the ECHR; however, this has not happened in any significant way to date.

## Giving (indirect) legal effect to international standards: the ECHR and the courts

Even without direct incorporation into domestic law, international standards can be used in litigation to secure immediate advances in children's rights by providing the basis for legally binding remedies for individual or groups of children and, when used strategically, systemic change (Kilkelly 2010b, p. 247). For children in England, it is the ECHR, enforced by the ECtHR and given domestic legal effect by the *Human Rights Act 1998* (HRA), that has provided the primary vehicle for the development of child-specific rights informed by other, non-enforceable measures. This is possible, says Kilkelly (2001, p. 313) because the ECHR is broadly drafted (which allows for imaginative interpretation) and because it is a 'living instrument . . . which must be interpreted in the light of present-day conditions' (*Tyrer v UK*), which for children includes taking account of developing international standards. In the field of juvenile justice, it is standards deriving from the CRC that have been most influential, primarily because of its specificity and the consensus indicated by its almost universal ratification (Forowicz 2010). This has led Kilkelly to suggest this is the 'best of both worlds', combining 'the child-specific provisions of the CRC with the ECHR's effective system of individual petition in order to maximise the potential of both instruments to advance children's rights' (Kilkelly 2015).

## The European Court of Human Rights

The ECtHR has considered complaints relating to various aspects of the youth justice system in England: the MACR (*V v United Kingdom*); trial procedures in the Crown Court (*V v United Kingdom* and *SC v United Kingdom*); sentencing (*Hussain v United Kingdom*; *V v United Kingdom*; *Bailey v United Kingdom*); procedural protections for out of court disposals (*R v United Kingdom*); retention of DNA samples and fingerprints following acquittal (*S and Marper v United Kingdom*); and the placement of vulnerable children in young offender institutions (*Bailey v United Kingdom*). In most, though not all of these cases, the Court drew on UN standards. The applicant children were at least partially successful in four of the decisions (*Hussain*, *V*, *SC* and *S*[9]) and legal and policy changes have subsequently been made to the sentence of detention during Her Majesty's pleasure (to allow periodic review and to remove the power of the Secretary of State to set the tariff period); to Crown Court procedures in order to secure effective participation and limit the child's intimidation, humiliation, or distress (see Practice Direction 2/11); and to the retention of DNA of child suspects (see *Protection of Freedoms Act 2012*).

However, the ECtHR is *not* a de facto CRC court. It has its own political, jurisdictional and operational boundaries which limit its capacity to give effect to other international norms: its authority and legitimacy – and thus the likelihood of Member States complying with its pronouncements – depends on it remaining within those boundaries (McInerney-Lankford 2012). Therefore, although children's rights constitute an area where the ECtHR has been receptive to international law (Forowicz 2010), the court nonetheless operates under a number of constraints.

The first constraint relates to the ECHR's substantive content: the ECtHR 'will not stretch an existing European Convention right to meet the global standard if it means creating a new right' (van Bueren 2007, p. 19). In *R v United Kingdom*, for example, the ECtHR held that Article 6 did not apply to pre-charge diversion when a 14-year-old boy received a final warning (caution) for a sexual offence, which had resulted in his placement on the sex offender's register. Without Article 6 there was no vehicle for the boy to argue that his consent to the warning was required, as per the Beijing Rules (Hollingsworth 2007).

The second limitation relates to the Court's role within the constitutional structure of the CoE, and its need to balance the development of common standards with the legitimate diversity that exists across Member States in *how* to protect those rights. The ECtHR has adopted the 'margin of appreciation' doctrine as the means of deferring to states in circumstances where they have special knowledge, particularly when there is no European consensus on the issue. McInerney-Lankford has noted that the doctrine 'operates indirectly to restrict the Court's freedom to consider other sources of international law, by restricting the Court from moving beyond the consensus binding Contracting States or exceeding its jurisdictional mandate' (McInerney-Lankford 2012, p. 613). The setting of a MACR is one area where there is little consensus and in some countries – the UK included – it is highly politicized. Unsurprisingly then, in *V v United Kingdom* the ECtHR rejected the Article 3 claim that holding criminally to account for murder two boys aged 10 constituted degrading and inhuman treatment. At the time, the relevant international norm required only that a MACR be set (Article 40[3][a] CRC), and that it not be too low, bearing in mind the facts of emotional, mental and intellectual maturity (Beijing Rule 4.1); and, although the UN Committee had earlier recommended that the MACR in England be raised, it had not specified to what age (UN Committee 1995). Since this decision, the UN Committee has stated that a MACR below the age of 12 is internationally unacceptable (UN Committee 2007). However, given that the more recent, more geographically specific, child-friendly justice Guidelines[10] replicate the vaguer Beijing Rules, the ECtHR is unlikely to regard the UN Committee's statement as the most authoritative indication of *European* consensus (Hespel et al. 2012, p. 353). This points to a larger problem with the proliferation of international norms for juvenile justice emerging from different legal regimes: they can 'overlap, place different emphasis on different aspects and, at worst, contradict each other' (Hespel et al. 2012, p. 337). Although 'non-regression' (or 'savings') clauses are included in most rights instruments (that is, that where higher standards exist in international or domestic law they should apply), the fragmentation of international law (Koskenniemi and Leino 2002) can result in 'textual variation, or even inconsistency, [which] weakens the authority of all and creates incoherence' (Chinkin 2003, p. 28). The child-friendly justice guidelines may therefore stymie (for example, with regards to the MACR or privacy[11]), as well as improve,[12] the development by the ECtHR of children's rights in juvenile justice.

The final point to make here is that where children in conflict with the law in England have been successful in their claims before the ECtHR, the government's response has been *just* sufficient to comply with the court's decision (thus acquiring legitimacy for those actions) but falls short of full compliance with international standards. This is perhaps most obvious in relation to the remedial action taken after *S and Marper v United Kingdom* where, in response to the finding that the blanket retention of suspected/offenders' DNA is unlawful, the *Protection of Freedoms Act 2012* nonetheless still allows the DNA of children convicted of more than one minor offence to be kept indefinitely (House of Lords House of Commons Joint Committee on Human Rights 2011, para. 61ff). The UN Committee also continues to criticize the use of adult Crown Courts for children despite the practice direction introduced following *V v United Kingdom* which attempted to make them more child friendly. We might, therefore, agree with van Bueren that it is an 'overgeneralisation to say that the use of the UN convention by the ECtHR is "the best of both worlds"' (van Bueren 2007, p. 23).

## *International standards in the English courts*

The English courts adopt the approach of their Strasbourg colleagues and interpret ECHR rights – given domestic legal effect by the HRA – using the CRC and associated soft law.

But, within juvenile justice, as in other contexts, engagement with international children's rights varies (Tobin 2009). In some cases, and for some judges, the CRC is invisible (no reference is made[13]); in others it is marginal (it is referred to but forms no real part of the reasoning; it may be dismissed as not relevant or it is used merely to assert that domestic law is compatible[14]); at times a superficial approach is adopted (the CRC features in the reasoning but the analysis is superficial[15]); but elsewhere, judges have adopted a 'substantive approach' (conceptualizing issues, adopting procedures, interpreting content, or reasoning in a way compatible with children's rights [Tobin 2009]).[16] It is beyond the scope of this chapter to survey all of the English case law. Instead, two cases are discussed to exemplify the ways in which the English courts have, and have not, used the CRC.

*R (HC) v Secretary of State for the Home Department* is an exemplar of judicial engagement with international juvenile justice standards. The case concerned the child-specific rights available when children are arrested, detained and questioned by the police (namely, the right to an appropriate adult and parental notification of arrest) and which extended only to those aged 16 and under. A claim was therefore brought by a 17-year-old boy that Article 8 and Article 6 ECHR, interpreted in line with the CRC (including the definition in Article 1 of a child as a person under 18), had been breached. Interestingly, the court did not base its decision on Article 6, as one might expect in a case concerning procedural rights of suspects, but on Article 8. One reason for this was that it allowed the High Court to follow the precedent of the Supreme Court in *ZH (Tanzania)* and elevate the child's best interests to a 'primary consideration' when determining whether a restriction of Article 8 was proportionate. In assessing this, the Court held that since children (that is, 17-year-olds) were treated in the same way as adults, their best interests could not have been a primary consideration: hence, the decision was unlawful. The emphasis in *HC* on the child's best interests, needs, vulnerabilities, and on his familial relationships as the source of his rights when in police detention conveys an important message about the way in which children in conflict with the law are socially – and legally – constructed, challenging the pervasive negative images of (putative) child offenders that, in England, have been dominant since the 1990s. However, as I have noted elsewhere (Hollingsworth 2014, p. 91), the specific content of children's procedural rights in police detention was left legally undefined, and so the possibility remains that legislation could be passed that limits the child suspect's rights but which, provided children are treated differently from adults, would nonetheless be compatible with the ostensibly 'substantive' children's rights approach in *HC*.

The second example, *R (JC) v Central Criminal Court*, examined the statutory provisions that restrict media reporting of Crown Court cases involving child defendants. The legal framework is broadly compliant with international children's rights norms[17] that privacy be fully respected at all stages of the proceedings (Article 40[2][vii] UNCRC; Beijing Rules, Rule 8[18]). However, in *JC* the Court of Appeal held that reporting restrictions expire upon the child's 18th birthday, reasoning that the terms 'child or young person' used in the statute unambiguously fixed their temporal reach and that the purpose of the statute was to protect children not the adults they become. Further, since this issue concerned the interests of *adults* (that is, those convicted as a child but now over 18) the CRC was afforded little significance (para. 31). One thing this case illustrates is the need for a coherent normative and theoretical basis for the rights of children in conflict with the law, against which the scope and purpose of international standards, including the CRC, can be better articulated. Elsewhere I have suggested that a rights-based youth justice system is one that is consistent with the child's autonomy: not only her autonomy in the present (the child as 'being'), but also her capacity for autonomy as a future adult (the child as 'becoming'), protected by a class of rights I call 'foundational rights' (Hollingsworth 2013). Foundational rights help to ensure that the child's capacity for autonomy *as an adult* is not permanently harmed by her childhood offending. Applied to the issue of reporting restrictions, it is clear that lifelong anonymity is not about protecting the rights of *adults*, but about protecting the *child's* capacity for future autonomy. The rights of the child as a future adult are not inseparable from her rights during childhood and as such, the CRC *should* apply, including (the rather weak) obligation towards children's reintegration in Article 40(1). It is this, as well as the child's welfare and participation during trial, which underpins the child's rights to privacy in criminal proceedings and which is secured by *lifelong* reporting restrictions.

## Concluding comments

International children's rights measures provide a detailed, comprehensive framework that can be, and have been, used to improve the treatment of children in conflict with the law in England. Despite the weaknesses in child rights-specific enforcement mechanisms, international standards have been used to secure systemic change as well as remedies for individual children when used in litigation as an interpretative aid for the ECHR. However, this is not a panacea. As the discussion above has shown, the ECHR cannot provide a vehicle for all international standards: at times the judiciary use the norms superficially; the lack of a clear normative basis can limit the scope of the rights in litigation; and the government's response is usually only *just* enough to secure compliance and shows little overall commitment to children's rights. The introduction of OP3 may also have the unintended consequence of causing a diminution in the child-specific jurisprudence of the ECtHR should children from OP3-ratifying European states take their complaints instead to the UN Committee. This could have a detrimental effect on English children whose government is unlikely to ratify and who must, therefore, rely on the ECtHR's jurisprudence as the source of their rights domestically and internationally.

However, by far the greatest limitation of the ECHR as the vehicle for English children's rights is the threat of repeal of the HRA, as proposed by the Conservative Party. Should this happen, the ECHR will no longer be domestically enforceable, and the 'hook' for CRC rights will be lost. The children's Convention will not, however, lose all domestic application. As with any international human rights treaty, the CRC can be used to interpret ambiguous legislation and to develop the common law. However, the utility of the CRC in statutory interpretation is limited only to *ambiguous* legislation and, following a line of juvenile justice-related cases, only to legislation passed *after* UK ratification in 1991 (see again *JC*; and *R [T] v Secretary of State for Justice*). The CRC cannot, therefore, be used to interpret the *Children and Young Persons Act 1933* and the *Police and Criminal Evidence Act 1984*, both of which contain provisions that are vital for children in conflict with the law. The common law holds more promise and the courts have used the CRC to develop judicial review principles for example to require adult assistance for children in parole hearings (*R [K] v Parole Board*). There are also indications that the judiciary are embedding rights in the common law rather than using the ECHR, in anticipation of HRA repeal (*R [Osborn] v Parole Board*). But none of this is sufficient to provide a child-friendly criminal justice system, one that complies fully with international standards. For that to occur, the starting point has to be domestic incorporation of the CRC.

## Notes

1 My thanks to Helen Stalford and Claire Sands for earlier comments.

2 Space precludes an examination of the European Union (EU), but – at least for now – it provides an important source of rights for children (see, for example, Article 24 of the *Charter of Fundamental Rights of the European Union* and Stalford 2012), that in the criminal justice system are strengthened by the

proposed Directive of the European Parliament and the Council on procedural safeguards for children suspected or accused in criminal proceedings (COM [2013] 822 final). The directive draws on the UN standards discussed below (Stalford 2015), and when implemented will oblige domestic compliance.

3 Other relevant CoE treaties include the European Social Charter (for children's socioeconomic) rights (Kilkelly 2015; see especially Articles 7 and 17) and the *European Convention on the Exercise of Children's Rights*. These have featured less as a source of rights for children in conflict with the law and thus, again, space precludes its full consideration.

4 Namely, General Comments (especially General Comment No 10) and concluding observations.

5 For example, 17-year-olds were removed from the adult system of remand ostensibly to comply with the UN Committee's requirement (UN Committee 2002) that there be a separate system of criminal justice for children (see Ministry of Justice 2011) yet the same government refused to extend to 17 year olds in police detention the same rights enjoyed by all other children until it was forced to do so by a legal challenge (*R [HC] v Secretary of State for the Home Department;* see further Hollingsworth 2014).

6 For example, the drop in child custody figures since 2009 are as much due to changes in managerial practices in the police which have reduced first time entrants into the youth justice system as they are any commitment to children's rights (Allen 2011).

7 In *HC* (above note 5).

8 See also Recommendations of the Council of Ministers on the European Rules for Juvenile Offenders Subject to Sanctions or Measures; and New Ways of Dealing with Juvenile Delinquency and the Role of Juvenile Justice.

9 In *V v United Kingdom* (conjoined with *T v United Kingdom)*, only the Article 6 claim (right to participate effectively in one's trial) was successful.

10 As well as the EU-proposed directive, above note 2.

11 See below note 18.

12 The guidelines have higher standards, for example, in relation to the requirement for specially trained lawyers: Rap 2013.

13 For example, *R (W) v Commissioner of Police for the Metropolis* (curfew powers).

14 For example, *D v Chief Constable of Merseyside* (strip searching of a vulnerable 14-year-old girl in the police station); *R (Y) v Aylesbury Crown Court* (reporting restrictions).

15 For example, *R (SR) v Nottingham Magistrates Court* (discrimination between boys and girls vis-à-vis remand).

16 For example, *R (R) v Durham Constabulary* (diversion)*; R (C) v Secretary of State for Justice* (restraint in secure accommodation); *R (HC) v Secretary of State for the Home Department* (rights of 17-year-olds in police stations).

17 Courts have a *duty* to impose reporting restrictions in the youth court (which can be lifted in the public interest), and *discretion* to do so when children appear as defendants in the (adult) Crown Court (*Children and Young Persons Act 1933* (CYPA), s. 49 and Youth Justice and *Criminal Evidence Act 1999* (YJCE), s. 45 respectively).

18 The guidelines on child-friendly justice are weaker, and require only that: 'The privacy and personal data of children who are or have been involved in judicial or non-judicial proceedings and other interventions should be protected in accordance with national law. This generally implies that no information or personal data may be made available or published, particularly in the media, which could reveal or indirectly enable the disclosure of the child's identity'.

## References

Allen, R., 2011. *Last resort? Exploring the reduction in child imprisonment 2008–11*. London: Prison Reform Trust.

Buck, T. and Wabwile, M., 2013. The potential and promise of communications procedures under the Third Protocol to the *Convention on the Rights of the Child. International Human Rights Law Review*, 2(2), 205–39.

Chinkin, C., 2003. Normative development in the international legal system. *In*: D. Shelton (ed.), *Commitment and compliance: the role of non-binding norms in the international legal system*. Oxford: Oxford University Press, 21–42.

Cipriani, D., 2009. *Children's rights and the minimum age of criminal responsibility*. Farnham: Ashgate.

Committee of Ministers of the Council of Europe, 2010. *Guidelines of the Committee of Ministers of the Council of Europe on child-friendly justice and their explanatory memorandum.*
Committee of Ministers of the Council of Europe 2012. *Council of Europe Strategy for the Rights of the Child (2012–2015)*, CM(2011)171 Final.
Egan, S., 2014. The new complaints mechanism for the *Convention on the Rights of the Child. International Journal of Children's Rights*, 22(1), 205–25.
European Union Agency for Fundamental Rights, 2015. *Child-friendly justice: perspectives and experiences of professionals on children's participation in civil and criminal judicial proceedings in 10 EU Member States.*
Forowicz, M. 2010. *The reception of international law in the European Court of Human Rights.* Oxford: Oxford University Press.
Grover, S., 2015. *Children defending their human rights under the CRTC communication procedure.* Berlin Heidelberg: Springer Verlag.
Hespel, S., Put, J. and Rom, M., 2012. Navigating the maze: the interrelation of international legal norms, with illustrations from international juvenile justice standards. *Human Rights and International Legal Discourse*, 6(2), 329.
HM Governmnent, 2014. *The fifth periodic report to the UN Committee on the Rights of the Child: United Kingdom.*
Hollingsworth, K., 2007. Judicial approaches to children's rights in youth crime. *Child and Family Law Quarterly*, 19(1), 42–59.
Hollingsworth, K., 2013. Theorising children's rights in youth justice: the significance of autonomy and foundational rights. *Modern Law Review*, 76(6), 1046–69.
Hollingsworth, K., 2014. Bright lines and best interests: children, age and rights in police detention: *R (HC) v Secretary of State for the Home Department. Child and Family Law Quarterly*, 26(1), 78–98.
House of Lords House of Commons Joint Committee on Human Rights, 2011. *Eighteenth report legislative scrutiny: Protection of Freedoms Bill* (HL Paper 195/HC 1490).
House of Lords House of Commons Joint Committee on Human Rights, 2014. *The UK's compliance with the UN Convention on the Rights of the Child* (HL Paper 144/HC 1016).
Kilkelly, U., 1996. The UN Committee on the Rights of the Child: an evaluation in the light of recent UK experience. *Child and Family Law Quarterly*, 8(2), 105–20.
Kilkelly, U., 2001. The best of both worlds for children's rights? Interpreting the *European Convention on Human Rights* in the light of the UN *Convention on the Rights of the Child. Human Rights Quarterly*, 23(2), 308–26.
Kilkelly, U., 2010a. *Listening to children about justice: report of the Council of Europe consultation with children on child-friendly justice.* Strasbourg: Group of Specialists on Child-Friendly Justice, Directorate General of Human Rights and Legal Affairs.
Kilkelly, U., 2010b. Protecting children's rights under the ECHR: The role of positive obligations. *Northern Ireland Legal Quarterly*, 61(3), 245–61.
Kilkelly, U., 2015. The CRC in litigation under the ECHR. *In*: T. Liefaard and J.E. Doek (eds), *Litigating the rights of the child.* Dordrecht: Springer, 193–212.
Koskenniemi, M. and Leino, P., 2002. Fragmentation of international law? Postmodern anxieties. *Leiden Journal of International Law*, 15(3), 553–79.
McInerney-Lankford, S. 2012. Fragmentation of international law redux: the case of Strasbourg. *Oxford Journal of Legal Studies*, 32(3), 609–32.
Ministry of Justice, 2011. *Breaking the cycle: the government response.*
Rap, S.E., 2013. *The participation of juvenile defendants in the youth court: a comparative study of juvenile justice procedures in Europe.* PhD Dissertation, Utrecht University. Retrieved on 17 April 2016 from: http://dspace.library.uu.nl/handle/1874/287562.
Stalford, H., 2012. *Children and the European Union: rights, welfare and accountability.* Oxford: Hart.
Stalford, H., 2015. The use of the CRC in litigation under EU law. *In*: T. Liefaard and J.E. Doek (eds), *Litigating the rights of the child.* Dordrecht: Springer, 211–230.
Tobin, J., 2009. Judging the judges: are they adopting the rights approach in matters involving children? *Melbourne University Law Review*, 33(2), 579–625.
UN Committee on the Rights of the Child, 1995. *Concluding observations of the Committee on the Rights of the Child: United Kingdom of Great Britain and Northern Ireland.*
UN Committee on the Rights of the Child, 2002. *Concluding observations of the Committee on the Rights of the Child: United Kingdom of Great Britain and Northern Ireland.*

UN Committee on the Rights of the Child, 2007. *General Comment No 10: Children's rights in juvenile justice.*
United Nations General Assembly, 1985. *Standard Minimum Rules for the Administration of Juvenile Justice* ('Beijing Rules').
United Nations General Assembly, 1990. *Guidelines for the Prevention of Juvenile Delinquency* ('Riyadh Guidelines').
United Nations General Assembly, 1990. *Rules for the Protection of Juveniles Deprived of their Liberty* ('Havana Rules').
van Bueren, G., 2007. *Child rights in Europe.* Strasbourg: Council of Europe Publishing.
Verhellen, E., 1992. Changes in the images of the child. *In*: M.D.A. Freeman and P.E. Veerman (eds), *The ideologies of children's rights.* Dordrecht: Martinus Nijhoff Publishers, 79–94.
Woll, L., 2000. Reporting to the UN Committee on the Rights of the Child: a catalyst for domestic debate and policy change. *International Journal of Children's Rights*, 8(1), 71.

## Cases

*Bailey v United Kingdom.* 2010. Application No 39953/07 (unreported).
*D v Chief Constable of Merseyside.* (2015) [2015] EWCA 114; [2015] Crim LR 539.
*Hussain v United Kingdom.* 1996. (1996) 22 EHRR 1.
*R (C) v The Secretary of State for Justice* [2008] EWCA Civ 882.
*R (HC)(a child, by his litigation friend CC) v The Secretary of State for the Home Department; The Commissioner of Police of the Metropolis.* 2013. [2013] EWHC 982 (Admin).
*R (JC) v Central Criminal Courts.* [2014] EWCA Civ 1777; [2015] 1 W.L.R. 2865.
*R (K) v Parole Board.* (2006). [2006] EWHC 2413 (Admin); [2006] All ER (D) 75.
*R (Osborn) v Parole Board* [2013] UKSC 61; [2014] AC 1115.
*R (R) v Durham Constabulary.* (2005). [2005] UKHL 21; [2005] 1 WLR 1184.
*R (SR) v Nottingham Magistrates Court.* (2001). [2001] EWHC Admin 802.
*R (T) v Secretary of State for Justice.* (2013). [2013] EWHC 1119 (Admin).
*R (W) v Commissioner of Police for the Metropolis.* (2006). [2006] EWCA Civ 458.
*R (Y) v Aylesbury Crown Court.* (2012). [2012] EWHC 1140; [2012] EMLR 26.
*R v United Kingdom.* 2007. (2007) 44 EHRR SE17.
*S and Marper v The United Kingdom* 2008. (2008) ECHR 1581.
*SC v United Kingdom.* 2004. (2004) 40 EHRR 10.
*T v Director of Public Prosecutions.* (2004) 168 JP 194.
*Tyrer v UK* (1978) 2 EHRR 1 para. 31.
*V v United Kingdom.* 1999. (1999) 30 EHRR 121.
*ZH (Tanzania) V Secretary of State for the Home Department.* (2011). [2011] UKSC 4; [2011] 2 WLR 148.

# 19

# Human rights and the governance of cognitive impairment and mental illness

*Claire Spivakovsky*

## Introduction

During the 1970s and 1980s, western countries around the world entered a process of deinstitutionalization, releasing many people with cognitive impairments and mental illness from state-run institutions and asylums. Primarily this process occurred in response to both the emergence of rights-based disability movements (see Campbell and Oliver 1996), as well as subsequent rights-based challenges, such as the *United Nations Declaration on the Rights of Disabled Persons 1975*. Unfortunately, however, this process of deinstitutionalization failed on several fronts.

Rather than being integrated into the community to enjoy the 'decent', 'normal' and 'full' life envisioned by the 1975 United Nations (UN) Declaration, many people with cognitive impairments and mental illness now reside in community-based institutional settings like group homes, boarding houses or nursing homes (Dear and Wolch 1987, Taylor et al. 1991, Hudson 1991). These community-based institutional settings enable people with cognitive impairments and mental illness to live within the community, but not amongst its citizens.

Existing in this fashion has resulted in many people with cognitive impairments and mental illness struggling to find meaningful and sustained employment, accommodation or support within the community. Some have subsequently come to the attention of the criminal justice system. Indeed, using the deinstitutionalized landscape of Australia, for example, we know that 30,000 people with cognitive impairments and mental illness are currently detained in Australian prisons (AIHW 2012, Rushworth 2011), with a further 400,000 of these individuals held in group homes, nursing homes and hospitals within the community (ABS 2013). Figures like these have prompted many disability scholars to argue that people with cognitive impairments and mental illness did not experience a process of deinstitutionalization per se, but rather a process of 'transinstitutionalization' (Oliver 1990). That is to say, people with cognitive impairments and mental illness have simply been moved from one institutionalized context to the next over the past 40 years.

In an attempt to rectify this problem, many western nations have begun to reform their mental health and disability legislation. Such reforms take place with the dual goals of better supporting the lives of people with cognitive impairments and mental illness who receive institutional services within the community, and ensuring that these individuals' human rights are protected throughout these interactions. This chapter seeks to examine the operationalization of human rights safeguards and protections within the context of recent mental health and disability law reform. In particular, it aims to explore how human rights conventions are used in relation to the contentious practices of involuntarily detaining or compulsorily treating people with cognitive impairments or mental illness under disability and mental health acts. To do this, the chapter is divided into four main parts.

First, the chapter provides a brief overview of human rights scholarship in the context of involuntary detention and compulsory treatment. Second, the chapter outlines the broader context within which these contentious practices have emerged, drawing attention to the ways that risk logics and public protection approaches dominate contemporary mental health and disability law reform processes. Third, the chapter offers a framework for understanding the operation and focus of contemporary mental health and disability law. This framework is then applied in the fourth section of the chapter, where the chapter reveals how a concerning relationship has formed between risk and rights logics in the contentious practices of involuntary detention and compulsory treatment.

## Human rights, involuntary detention and compulsory treatment

Human rights scholarship concerning the practices of involuntary detention and compulsory treatment primarily revolves around questions of compliance. That is to say, several scholars have questioned the compliance of contemporary mental health and disability law with human rights instruments, and explored the reasons for divergence. Cairns et al. (2010), for instance, note that in England and Wales, both the *Mental Health Act 2007* and the *Mental Capacity Act 2005* were recently reformed so as to better comply with the *European Convention on Human Rights*. However, as these authors explain, while these acts now appear to be human rights compliant, it is unclear how the human rights considerations articulated in these laws are operationalized in practice. Indeed, Cairns and colleagues report that when it comes to making decisions about when to employ practices of involuntary detention and compulsory treatment – two practices which deprive people of their liberty and autonomy – many practitioners lack guidance about how to enact rights-based considerations and protocols, and as a result, rely solely on their clinical judgement.

Of course the lack of practical guidance available for practitioners is only one of the barriers to human rights compliance identified in the literature. A lack of resources, negative attitudes towards individual's rights, and difficulties when trying to find a balance between conflicting human rights principle were all identified by Fistein and colleagues (2009) as key reasons why many Commonwealth countries do not adequately protect people's rights in accordance with the *Universal Declaration of Human Rights*. Yet while these barriers remain a concern, recent additions to the international human rights landscape such as the UN *Convention on the Rights of Persons with Disabilities 2008* (the CRPD), and in particular, Article 14 of the CRPD, have prompted scholars to consider a slightly different and more pressing compliance issue. That is: are contemporary mental health and disability laws compliant with human rights conventions if they include the practice of involuntary detention?

Article 14 of the CRPD proposes that 'the existence of a disability shall in no case justify a deprivation of liberty'. It further explains that if a person with a disability is to be deprived of their liberty, then this must be done 'on an equal basis with others'. Following this line of argument, if the practice of involuntary detention practices is to continue in society, then the criteria for eligibility must be open to and reflective of behaviours which are apparent within all populations in society, and applied accordingly. As such, mental health or disability legislation which continues to exclusively enable the involuntary detention of people with cognitive impairments and mental illness should be considered incompatible with human rights frameworks, and require reform. Indeed, Article 14 of the CRPD suggests that the very act of including involuntary detention practices within the exclusively applied context of mental health and disability law is incompliant with international human rights conventions.

Yet while Article 14 of the CRPD provides the clearest position on involuntary detention to date, its translation to practice is less certain. This is because, as Bartlett (2011, 2012) observes, Article 14 of the CRPD appears to be in conflict with other, more localized and better established human rights instruments currently in operation. Thus, for example, while Council of Europe countries are expected to comply with the CRPD, they are also governed by the *European Convention on Human Rights and Fundamental Freedoms*. Under the European Convention, these countries are granted limited permission to subject individuals to deprivations of liberty such as involuntary detention if the individual is found to be of 'unsound mind' (Article 5[1][e]). In these ways, it is unclear whether or not a Council of Europe country which detains a person with a disability based on their 'unsound mind' (that is, their disability) would be considered to be acting in a way that is incompatible with human rights Conventions and Declarations, given that this action is specifically permitted under the European Convention.

Given the current state of affairs, it is evident that more work needs to be done to both clarify if involuntary detention and compulsory treatment practices are permissible under mental health and disability law, and to ensure that the rights of people with cognitive impairments and mental illness are protected should they become subject to them. It is the contention of this chapter, however, that some of this work needs to take place beyond the confines of a human rights framework and human rights scholarship. That is to say, while the struggle to translate human rights principles into practice is, and should remain a key concern for human rights scholars, the reasons for this miscommunication may have more to do with the broader context within which mental health and disability laws are developed in society, and the strategies for population management currently operating within them. This chapter will now focus on these broader context issues.

## The conditions for contemporary mental health and disability law

There are two common, and somewhat interlinked conditions for the emergence and reform of most mental health and disability laws around the world. First, the majority if not all mental health and disability laws have emerged from the deinstitutionalization process outlined in the introduction to this chapter. That is to say, most took shape in response to the need to manage the lives of people with mental illness and cognitive impairments within the community after their release from large institutions. Thus, for example, Carney (2003) explains that as people with mental illness began to be released from large psychiatric facilities in Australian during the 1980s and 1990s, the Australian state of Victoria developed the *Mental Health Act 1986*. The *Mental Health Act 1986* introduced Community Treatment Orders (CTOs), a mechanism which ensures the ongoing management of people with mental illness upon their release to the community from psychiatric institutions. Specifically, CTOs enable the compulsory treatment of people with mental illness in the community.

But there is a second condition by which mental health and disability laws have also developed or been reformed around the world. As a number of scholars have shown, mental health and disability laws often take shape or undergo reform in direct response to high profile criminal cases where a person with a severe cognitive impairment or mental illness has committed a violent or serious offence against a member of the public. Indeed, Hatfield and Antcliff (2001) explain that when cases like this take place, it is typical for the media, society, and subsequently, governments, to raise questions about the 'proper' place for people with cognitive impairments and mental illness in society (that is, in society or in institutions), and the types of 'treatment' these individuals require to manage their lives and behaviour (that is, voluntary or compulsory). When this line of questioning occurs, mental health and disability laws typically undergo reform, and more often than not, become imbued with risk logics (see Glover-Thomas 2011). These logics shift the emphasis of mental health and disability legislation from a focus on how to regulate the lives of people with cognitive impairments and mental illness in the community, to how to ensure the public's protections from the range of people with cognitive impairments and mental illness now residing in the community.

Of course an infiltrating risk logic and a move towards public protection would not be new to the reader. It is well established that we live in a 'risk society' that prioritizes community safety over individual needs (Beck 1992). Yet, as Nikolas Rose (1998) contends, while the emergence and orientation of risk logics in mental health and disability law bears a 'family resemblance' to the many versions of risk-focused regulation currently operating in society, there is nothing homogenous about the ways risk logics are deployed or prioritized within society. Indeed, Rose (1998) proposes that there are particular nuances to the ways that risk logics have infiltrated mental health and disability spheres which should not be overlooked. These nuances are considered in detail below.

## A framework for understanding the operation of mental health and disability law

What is unique about the infiltration of risk logics in the context of mental health and disability law is the way by which these logics have gained traction within mental health and disability spheres. That is to say, risk logics, with their emphasis on first locating individuals on a spectrum of risk (low, medium, high), and then managing risk through graduated responses (from more to less intensive and intrusive), did not simply emerge within mental health and disability law because of a broader trend towards risk-focused regulation in society. Rather, as Rose (1998) explains, they gained traction because of an emerging and pressing need for governments to manage the lives of people with cognitive impairments and mental illness within a 'new territory': the deinstitutionalized community. Yet, as Rose further clarifies, what is of interest here is not simply that risk logics found footing within this 'new territory', but rather that these logics *replaced* a longstanding reliance on the binary logic of dangerousness, a logic which had for centuries successfully positioned people with cognitive impairments or mental illness as either dangerous, or not; as requiring intervention, or not.

This is not to suggest however, that in the 'new territory' of the deinstitutionalized community, practices that were originally introduced under the binary logic of dangerousness simply disappeared. Rather, they underwent two major transformations so as to better align with the move towards a spectrum, or graduated logic of risk and risk management. First, they shifted target. They stopped being provided for the purposes of responding to a *specific population* who were seen as wholly and definitively incapable of making a contribution to society, and started being implemented as a means by which to manage the security of a *society* that had made space within its community for (some) diversity. Second, and as a result of this first shift, practices introduced under the logic of dangerousness also shifted their temporality: they moved from being permanent to periodic. Thus, for example, keeping a specific population institutionalized for their whole life became illogical and unjustifiable in the post-deinstitutionalization era when all populations were understood as being capable of making a contribution to the community and society. However, it soon became necessary (apparently) to temporarily remove or detain certain individuals from the community if it could be shown that the only contribution they were making was harm, and that their presence in the community posed an ongoing risk to community safety that needed to be managed. Similarly, while the practice of forcing people with cognitive impairments and mental illness to be sterilized in order to stop another generation of 'incurably problematic' individuals lost its appeal with the move towards a social model of disability in the post-deinstitutionalized period, it is, at least according to some contemporary mental health and disability law (for example, the *Disability Act 2006* [Vic] – hereafter, the *Disability Act*), still necessary to subject some individuals to temporary forms of compulsory treatment such as anti-libidinal medication, in order to manage their risky and harmful behaviour. These are the nuances to the ways by which risk logics have infiltrated mental health and disability law.

Yet, while it is important to recognize that these nuances to risk-based management are unique to mental health and disability law, the risk-based management of people with cognitive impairments and mental illness more broadly is not. Indeed, this risk-based management approach can easily be located within and among the broader strategies of governance and population management operating in society. Again, the work of Nikolas Rose provides insight.

Rose (2000) argues that society is shaped by a variety of different strategies of governance. These strategies, he argues, typically operate through two key circuits: those of inclusion and those of exclusion. Circuits of inclusion address issues of security; that is to say they regulate and manage populations through logics, tactics, and mechanisms which seek to optimize individual potential and self-advancement. Circuits of exclusion, on the other hand, are concerned with problems of insecurity; they pathologize segments of the population deemed unable or unwilling to manage their conduct in desired ways, and utilize specific logics, tactics, and mechanisms which neutralize the risks these deviant populations pose to society. Accordingly, Rose and colleagues (2006) propose that any study of law and regulation must ask: who or what is being governed? What combination of logics, tactics, and mechanisms are being utilized? And, to what end (that is, does the practice ultimately address an issue of security or insecurity)? These are an important set of questions to consider in the context of people with cognitive impairments and mental illness, and the emergence of contemporary mental health and disability law.

In the case of people with cognitive impairments and mental illness, it certainly appears that *what* is being regulated through contemporary mental health and disability law is the 'problem' of managing their lives within the 'new territory' of the deinstitutionalized community. Moreover, *how* this 'problem' seems to be managed is through a combination of risk-based logics and mechanisms which prioritize public protection and temporary forms of targeted intervention that neutralize risk. In other words, it appears that the emergence and operation of contemporary mental health and disability law, and in particular, the practices of involuntary detention and compulsory treatment legislated therein, can be located within society's circuits of exclusion and a broader strategy of governance which seeks to manage issues of insecurity.

But this framework for interpretation leaves us with a very obvious and pressing set of questions. If the lives of people with cognitive impairments and mental illness are governed in these ways, how if at all are their rights considered and negotiated? What is the balance or relationship between the different logics of risk and rights within contemporary mental health and disability law? And, what does this relationship look like in the contentious context of involuntary detention and compulsory treatment practices which appear to operate exclusively within the circuits of exclusion? To answer these questions, this chapter will work through the case example of the Australian state of Victoria, and the ways by which Victoria's *Charter of Human Rights and Responsibilities 2006* operates alongside and within disability law.

## Balancing rights and risk logics: is it possible?

In Australia's human rights landscape, both the CRPD and the International Covenant on Civil and Political Rights have been ratified. The guidance provided by these instruments does not, however, form part of Australia's domestic law. Rather, Australian bodies are expected to adhere only to those Articles which have been specifically incorporated by parliament into Australian law. To encourage adherence, two Australian jurisdictions have enacted their own Charters of Human Rights, the State of Victoria and the Australian Capital Territory. This chapter is only concerned with the Victorian *Charter of Human Rights and Responsibilities 2006* (the Charter).

Under Victoria's Charter, any Bill introduced into Victoria's parliament must be accompanied by a statement of human rights compatibility. It is within this human rights landscape that Victoria's disability and mental health laws have recently undergone reform. Indeed, one of the major reasons Victoria developed the *Disability Act, Disability Amendment Act 2012,* and the more recent *Mental Health Act 2014,* was to ensure Victoria's mental health and disability laws were effectively protecting the rights of people with cognitive impairments and mental illness in accordance with Victoria's Charter. The question of concern, however, is how does this commitment to human rights compatibility operate alongside and in relationship with the risk logics and public protection approaches that are embedded within contemporary involuntary detention and compulsory treatment practices? To answer this question, the chapter will illustrate and discuss the application of a key practice in Victorian disability law which combines involuntary detention and compulsory treatment: Supervised Treatment Orders.

Supervised Treatment Orders (STOs) were introduced under Victoria's *Disability Act 2006,* and are exclusively applied to people with intellectual disabilities. In practice, STOs enable service providers to detain people with intellectual disabilities within the service provider's premises for up to 23 hours a day, locking them within the premises, and keeping them there with alarmed doors and windows. These individuals are then further subjected to some form of compulsory treatment such as anti-libidinal medication, tranquilizers, or other forms of psychotropic pharmaceuticals which manage their behaviour rather than treat an illness.

Like other contemporary forms of involuntary detention and compulsory treatment, STOs operate from a public protection approach, and are thoroughly embedded with risk logics. Thus for example, to become subject to an STO, a person with an intellectual disability must:

- have 'previously exhibited a pattern of violent or dangerous behaviour causing serious harm to another person or exposing another person to a significant risk of serious harm' (*Disability Act 2006,* Part 8, Section 191, 6a);
- pose 'a significant risk of serious harm to another person which cannot be substantially reduced by using less restrictive means'(*Disability Act 2006,* Part 8, Section 191, 6b);
- require a treatment plan that will 'substantially reduce the significant risk of serious harm to another person' (*Disability Act 2006,* Part 8, Section 191, 6c);
- be 'unable or unwilling to consent to voluntarily complying with a treatment plan to substantially reduce the significant risk of serious harm to another person' (*Disability Act 2006,* Part 8, Section 191, 6d); and
- require involuntary detention in order 'to ensure compliance with the treatment plan and prevent a significant risk of serious harm to another person'(*Disability Act 2006,* Part 8, Section 191, 6e).

The decision-making process surrounding STO Tribunal Hearings does, however, include a number of human rights protections and safeguards. Indeed, one of the core requirements placed on Tribunal Members during STO Hearings is to consider: are the rights outlined in Victoria's Charter limited when imposing an STO on a person with an intellectual disability? And if so, in what ways are these rights limited? And, are these limitations justified (for example, are Tribunal Members satisfied that there is no less restrictive means reasonably available by which to ensure the person's risk is managed)? But the question remains, how does this commitment to the Charter and its principle of least restrictive practice operate in the context of STOs? Three important observations can be made.

First, echoing Cairns et al.'s (2010) concern about the difficulty associated with operationalizing human rights expectations and protocols in practice, it must be acknowledged that in some Tribunal Hearings, the presence of the Charter appears primarily perfunctory. That is to say, in some Hearings, the task of considering the principles and protocols of the Charter appears to be something which can be simply ticked-off as part of the decision-making process. Thus, for instance, in the STO hearing of *AC (Guardianship) [2009] VCAT 753*, the Tribunal Member comments:

> In her submissions Ms. X made brief but important reference to the Charter of Human Rights and Responsibilities Act 2006 ... It has not been necessary for me to comment further about that. My decision obviously cannot involve any limitation on AC's human rights.

In Hearings like this, it is unclear exactly how this safeguard operates and has been applied. In what ways did the Member in *AC (Guardianship) [2009] VCAT 753* ensure AC's human rights were not limited by the decision?

Yet, even when Tribunal Members articulate their process of considering the Charter, certain questions remain about the capacity of this instrument to operate effectively alongside and in relationship to risk logics. Indeed, the second observation to be made about the relationship between risk and rights in contemporary disability law is that in some cases, it appears as if the logics of risk and rights merge and conflate. This phenomenon is aptly illuminated in the case of *LM (Guardianship) [2008] VCAT 2084*.

LM is a young woman with an intellectual disability. During her STO Hearing, LM's service provider argues that LM should be involuntarily detained and subjected to compulsory, behaviour-modifying treatment because LM has previously been convicted of several serious offences. It is proposed that this history of prior behaviour constitutes a pattern of violent and dangerous behaviour, and as such, LM is considered to be at high risk of causing another person harm. At the time of her Hearing, LM has not committed a new offence, and has already served the necessary time for all of her previous offences. In fact, at the time of her Hearing, LM had just been released from custody on a good behaviour bond, which implies that she had already been assessed as *not* posing a sufficient enough risk to the community to warrant a period of detention.

In compliance with the requirements of the Charter, the deciding Tribunal Member in LM's case notes that imposing an STO on these grounds would limit a number of LM's human rights. In particular, it would limit her right to equal and effective protection against discrimination, right to freedom of movement, and right to liberty and security of the person. Yet, when the Tribunal Member attempts to balance LM's rights alongside the previously outlined proposal for risk management and public protection, these considerations lose ground, or more precisely, they merge with the overriding logic of risk management, enabling LM to be detained. Indeed, the primary reason why an STO is ultimately made in the case of LM, is because the Tribunal Member argues that *this* form of involuntary detention (that is, detention in a locked service provider's premises for up to 23 hours a day for the period of a year) is going to be '*less restrictive*' than a period of incarceration which might come into play if LM proves to be as risky a subject as has been argued. In this way, it is the so-called human rights 'protection' of the least restrictive practice principle which ultimately justifies the questionable logic of risk that is being deployed in LM's case.

This conflation of risk and rights logics is concerning for a number of reasons. In particular, while LM's fundamental human rights *will* be limited as a direct result of this decision, the likelihood of LM ending up in the apparently unjustifiably more restrictive setting of the prison is purely *hypothetical*. But perhaps this is the point of the relationship between right and risk logics. That is to say, the rights-based principle of least restrictive practice provides a framework of certainty within which the otherwise intangible and predictive logic of risk can take hold.

It is hasty to suggest, however, that a concerning relationship may have formed between risk and rights logics in contemporary mental health and disability law based only on this and other STO Tribunal Hearings (see Spivakovsky 2014 for other examples of concerning STO Hearings). Accordingly, let us now consider who ultimately becomes subject to STOs and other involuntary detention or compulsory treatment orders to make a final and important observation about the relationship between risk and rights in mental health and disability law.

Contemporary involuntary detention and compulsory treatment orders are predominately applied to a particular group of people with cognitive impairments or mental illness in society. That is to say, these practices repeatedly capture a specific cohort of the population: those who deviate from society, and who are deemed unable or unwilling to manage their conduct in desired ways. Thus, returning to the example of STOs, the Office of the Public Advocate (2010) recently revealed that approximately 70 per cent of STOs are applied to people who have had previous contact with the criminal justice system, with approximately 80 per cent of this subgroup having committed sexually based offences. This profile is not entirely unique to STO recipients.

Several scholars have begun to show how contemporary compulsory treatment practices in mental health law have predominantly been applied to a very similar subgroup of people (Brophy et al. 2006, Nagel 2003, Power 1999). Indeed, in the context of mental health law, compulsory treatment practices are overwhelmingly applied to people who have been diagnosed with 'violent' forms of schizophrenia, and who do not engage in typical practices of self-advancement and community life (getting married, living with others, being employed, and so on). In other words, contemporary involuntary detention and compulsory treatment orders repeatedly capture those members of the community who fall within the purview of the circuits of exclusion previously described.

But there is another important commonality among these cohorts which can be observed here. In each of these cases of involuntary detention or compulsory treatment, the human rights of the person with the cognitive impairment or mental illness has been limited – involuntary detention and compulsory treatment cannot take place without limiting people's rights to freedom, liberty, security, autonomy, and so on. Moreover, in each of these cases, risk-based logics and public protection arguments have succeeded. That is to say, to have received an order for involuntary detention or compulsory treatment these individuals must have met the risk-focused and community safety criteria for eligibility. Thus, it is important to recognize that what is common among these cohorts of people with cognitive impairments and mental illness is that they, and their common ways of operating within the remit of the circuits of exclusion, represent the specific segment of the community for whom risk logics appear to consistently outweigh the obligations of rights. It is at this point that some final conclusions can be drawn.

## Final thoughts

The purpose of this chapter was to examine the operationalization of human rights safeguards and protections in the context of recent mental health and disability law reform, and in particular, to explore how human rights conventions have been used in relation to the contentious practices of involuntarily detaining or compulsorily treating people with cognitive impairments or mental illness within community settings. In doing this, the chapter put forward the argument that while much mental health and disability-focused human rights scholarship has focused on questions of compliance, such questions need to be repositioned within the much broader issue of the governance of people with cognitive impairments and mental illness over time, and the emergence and subsequent reliance upon risk logics and public protection approaches in mental health and disability law. Having repositioned the focus of this chapter to engage with this issue, this chapter has begun to show how human rights conventions and declarations, while aspiring to universality, may in fact play on and be used to reinforce existing social divisions within society. This occurs not as a result of the simple incompliance of a government with human rights conventions and declarations, but rather by the ways by which risk-focused governments interpret this universal conception of rights as presupposing a particular type of liberal subject who engages with concepts of mutual obligation, self-advancement and risk-free behaviour. In fact, it is through the act of *complying* with this skewed interpretation of human rights that certain people with cognitive impairments or mental illness who do not manage their behaviour in desired ways are ultimately deemed secondary citizens whose rights can be *legitimately limited* in the name of public protection and specific forms of community contribution. This is the nature of the relationship between risk and rights that has formed in the governance of people with cognitive impairments and mental illness.

## References

Australian Bureau of Statistics [ABS], 2013. *Disability, ageing and carers, Australia: summary of findings 2012*. Canberra: ABS.

Australian Institute of Health and Welfare [AIHW], 2012. *The mental health of prison entrants in Australia 2010*. Canberra: AIHW.

Bartlett, P., 2011. 'The necessity must be convincingly shown to exist': standards for compulsory treatment for mental disorder under the Mental Health Act 1983. *Medical Law Review*, 19, 514–47.

Bartlett, P., 2012. A mental disorder of a kind or degree warranting confinement: examining justifications for psychiatric detention. *The International Journal of Human Rights*, 16(6), 831–44.

Beck, U., 1992. *Risk society: towards a new modernity*. London: Sage.

Brophy, L., Reece, J. and McDermott, F., 2006. A cluster analysis of people on community treatment orders in Victoria, Australia. *International Journal of Law and Psychiatry*, 29, 469–81.

Cairns, R., Richardson, G. and Hotopf, M., 2010. Deprivation of liberty: mental capacity act safeguards versus the mental health act. *The Psychiatrist*, 34(6), 246–7.

Campbell, J. and Oliver, M., 1996. *Disability politics: understanding our past, changing our future*. London: Routledge.

Carney, T., 2003. Mental health law in post-modern society: time for new paradigms? *Psychiatry, Psychology and Law*, 10, 12–32.

Dear, M. and Wolch, J., 1987. *Landscapes of despair: from deinstitutionalization to homelessness*. Princeton, NJ: Princeton University Press.

Fistein, E., Holland, A., Clare, I. and Gunn, M., 2009. A comparison of mental health legislation from diverse Commonwealth jurisdictions. *International Journal of Law and Psychiatry*, 32(3), 147–55.

Glover-Thomas, N., 2011. The age of risk: risk perception and determination following the Mental Health Act 2007. *Medical Law Review*, 19, 581–605.

Hatfield, B. and Antcliff, V., 2001. Detention under the Mental Health Act: balancing rights, risks and needs for services. *Journal of Social Welfare and Family Law*, 23(2), 135–53.

Hudson, B., 1991. Deinstitutionalisation: what went wrong? *Disability, Handicap and Society*, 6(1), 21–36.

Nagel, T., 2003. Involuntary mental health treatment in the remote Northern Territory. *Psychiatry, Psychology and Law*, 10, 171–8.

Office of the Public Advocate, 2010. *Supervised treatment orders in practice: how are the human rights of people detained under the Disability Act 2006 protected?* Melbourne: Government Printer.

Oliver, M., 1990. *The politics of disablement*. London: Macmillan.

Power, P., 1999. Community treatment orders: the Australian experience. *Journal of Forensic Psychiatry*, 50, 27–30.

Rose, N., 1998. Governing risky individuals: the role of psychiatry in new regimes of control, *Psychiatry, Psychology and Law*, 5(2), 177–95.

Rose, N., 2000. Government and control. *British Journal of Criminology*, 40(2), 321–39.

Rose, N., O'Malley, P. and Valverde, M., 2006. Governmentality. *Annual Review of Law and Social Sciences*, 2, 83–104.

Rushworth, N., 2011. *Out of sight, out of mind: people with ABI and the criminal justice system*. Ryde: Brain Injury Australia.

Spivakovsky, C., 2014. From punishment to protection: containing and controlling the lives of people with disabilities in human rights. *Punishment & Society*, 16(5), 560–77.

Taylor, S., Bogdan, R. and Racino, J. (eds), 1991. *Life in the community: case studies of organizations supporting people with disabilities*. Baltimore, MD: Paul Brookes.

## Cases

*AC (Guardianship) [2009] VCAT 753.*
*LM (Guardianship) [2008] VCAT 2084.*

## Legislation

*Charter of Human Rights and Responsibilities 2006* (Victoria, Australia).
*Disability Act 2006* (Victoria, Australia).
*Disability Amendment Act 2012* (Victoria, Australia).
*European Convention on Human Rights 1953.*
*Mental Capacity Act 2005* (England and Wales).
*Mental Health Act 2007* (England and Wales).
*Mental Health Act 1986* (Victoria, Australia).
*Mental Health Act 2014* (Victoria, Australia).
*United Nations Convention on the Rights of Persons with Disabilities 2008.*
*United Nations Declaration on the Rights of Disabled Persons 1975.*
*United Nations Universal Declaration of Human Rights 1948.*

# 20

# Environmental crime, human rights and green criminology

*Hope Johnson, Nigel South and Reece Walters*

## Human rights and environmental issues: links and disconnections

> All human beings depend on the environment in which we live. A safe, clean, healthy and sustainable environment is integral to the full enjoyment of a wide range of human rights, including the rights to life, health, food, water and sanitation. Without a healthy environment, we are unable to fulfil our aspirations or even live at a level commensurate with minimum standards of human dignity.
>
> *(Office of the High Commissioner for Human Rights 2015)*

It is widely accepted that the environment and human rights are interdependent to the extent that environmental harms can, and often do, undermine progress towards the full realization of human rights. At the same time, progress towards achievement of human rights, for instance, improving the land rights of women in developing countries or increasing access to education, will often, in turn, improve the health of the environment. Another dimension to the interrelationship between human rights and environmental protection is the link between particular human rights such as the right to participation in decision-making and good governance concepts relating to environmental issues (Brisman 2013). In other words, in order for environmental governance to be effective, the human right to participate in governance and have access to information must be enforced (UNEP 2009, South 2015). In reflecting upon these dimensions of the relationship, Justice Weeramantry, in the *Gabčíkovo -Nagymaros* (1997) case before the International Court of Justice, spoke of the connection between human rights and environmental health as if it were undeniable. He explained:

> The protection of the environment is . . . a vital part of contemporary human rights doctrine, for its *sine qua non* [absolute necessity] for numerous human rights such as the right to health and the right to life itself. It is scarcely necessary to elaborate on this, as damage to the environment can impair and undermine all the human rights spoken of in the Universal Declaration on Human Rights and in other human rights instruments. While, therefore, all peoples have the right to initiate development projects and enjoy their

> benefits, there is likewise a duty to ensure that those projects do not significantly damage the environment.
>
> *(Gabčíkovo-Nagymaros Project Hungary/Slovakia, 1997. Judgment, 1. C. J. Reports, p. 7 paras 91–2)*

Accordingly, Justice Weeramantry sees no clear distinction between the protection of the environment and human rights. From this perspective, action that protects or rehabilitates the natural environment is a means to progress the realization of human rights.

Likewise, international environmental law instruments confirm the connection between the environment and human rights. Principle 1 of the Stockholm Declaration (1972) affirmed that humans have a 'fundamental right to freedom, equality and adequate conditions of life, in an environment of quality that permits a life of dignity and well-being'. This relationship was reaffirmed in the Rio Declaration (1992). This instrument explained that humans are 'at the centre of concerns for sustainable development. They are entitled to a healthy and productive life in harmony with nature'. Similarly, the Johannesburg Declaration, which arose from the World Summit on Sustainable Development in 2002, notes that States are committed to 'building a humane, equitable and caring global society, cognizant of the need for human dignity for all'.

Somewhat similar constructions may impliedly exist in human rights instruments where particular rights can be taken as requiring a healthy environment as a prerequisite. For instance, 'the right to life' in Article 6 of the *International Covenant on Civil and Political Rights* (ICCPR) can be used to enforce environmental protection and restoration. Clearly this is because humans cannot survive without natural resources like air, water and habitable environments. Another example comes from the *International Covenant on Economic, Social and Cultural Rights* (ICESCR) where Article 12 creates 'a right to health' that encompasses the right to 'enjoy the highest attainable standard of physical and mental health'. The right to health has been interpreted, by the United Nations Committee on Economic, Social and Cultural Rights (UNCESCR), as covering not only healthcare but also the:

> wide range of socio-economic factors that promote conditions in which people can lead a healthy life and extends to the underlying determinants of health, such as food . . . access to safe and potable water and adequate sanitation . . . and a healthy environment.
>
> *(General Comment Number 14)*

Likewise, Article 11 of the ICESCR contains 'the right of everyone to an adequate standard of living . . . including adequate food . . . and to the continuous improvement of living conditions'. Article 11 arguably implies a certain level of environmental health to the extent that the ability to produce food and other necessities is not threatened by environmental degradation. This point was incorporated by the UNESCR in General Comment 12 in relation to the right to food. Here, the committee explained that the core content of the right to food implies 'The accessibility of . . . food in ways that are sustainable and that do not interfere with the enjoyment of other human rights'. Accordingly, the interpretation of human rights is being closely linked with sustainability.

Despite the general recognition in both environmental and human rights law of the links between environmental protection and human rights, a separate, substantive human right to a healthy environment does not exist other than through the expansion of existing human rights. On this point Lewis (2012, p. 43) has extensively analysed human rights constructions related to the environment and concluded that 'it is unlikely that a right to a healthy environment currently exists in any enforcement sense at international law'. Consequently, the only way to use human rights law as a tool to enforce environmental protection and conservation is to show that an instance of environmental degradation is impacting upon a recognized human right.

To address this potential disconnect, a number of scholars have suggested that a right to a healthy environment should be included as an individual right via a multilateral treaty (Atapattu 2002, p. 69). Boyle (2010, p. 32) considered this perspective and commented that a collective human right to a healthy environment would:

> benefit society as a whole, not just individual victims. It would enable litigants and NGOs to challenge environmentally destructive or unsustainable developments. . . . It would give environmental concerns greater weight in competition with other rights.

Other scholars argue that linking human rights with the environment reinforces an anthropocentric approach where the environment is treated as something to use for economic gains (Lewis 2012, p. 41). Additionally, there is a concern that a standalone right to a healthy environment would be so broad that it would be judicially unenforceable and would dilute existing human rights (Cullet 1995, p. 34). Shelton (1991, p. 105) points out that the environment and human rights share common interests and objectives but that 'not all human rights violations are necessarily linked to environmental degradation' and therefore environmental protection and restoration will not 'always be addressed effectively within the human rights framework'. This debate and gap in governance can be addressed using a Green Criminology framework, which encompasses calls for the recognition of the intrinsic rights of nature as well as a proposal for an international law against ecocide. Green Criminology can also provide insight into why it is difficult to enforce human and environmental rights. To lay the basis for such an understanding, we first need an analysis of the relationship between law and environmental crime.

## Law and environmental crime

Within the rhetoric of international environmental law, the language of crime is rarely used. There is a significant amount of law that discusses obligations to protect the environment and much emphasis on notions of precaution, liability and responsibility – but crime does not feature (Bodansky et al. 2008). From a purely legal perspective this is best explained by the fact that environmental offences are not contained within either international or national criminal law. Rather, until recently, they have been dealt with as administrative offences and prosecuted in civil courts. This position has changed significantly during the past two decades with the increasing creation of specialist courts to deal with environmental matters. For instance, there are approximately 350 environmental courts operating across 41 countries (Walters and Westerhuis 2013). The growth of these courts has been attributed to 'continual [pressure] worldwide for effective resolution of environmental conflicts and/or expanding recognition of the need for procedural and substantive justice vis-à-vis environmental matters' (White 2013, p. 268). For others, the acceleration of specialized jurisdictions exemplifies the increasing seriousness attached to crimes against the environment (Hamman et al. 2015). Moreover, in recent years environmental crime has become attractive to organized criminal networks (Walters 2013, South 2014). As Banks et al. (2008, p. 2) explain 'environmental crime is one of the most profitable forms of criminal activity and it is no surprise that organised criminal groups are attracted to its high profit margins'.

Interpol (2011) divides environmental crime into 'pollution' and 'wildlife' which, respectively, denote the illegal disposal of waste that contaminates air, water and land; and the unlawful trade in endangered species. These two broad categories have been further expanded upon by the United Nations Interregional Crime and Justice Research Institute (UNICRI) to provide a now widely used classification scheme of 'crimes against the environment' prohibited by international law. Other organizations, including Europol, the UN Environment Programme (UNEP) and G8, also employ the following descriptors of five key areas when referring to transnational and organized environmental crime. These areas are:

i) Illegal trade in endangered species and wildlife (breach of the 1973 Washington Convention on International Trade in Endangered Species: CITES);
ii) Illegal trade in ozone-depleting substances (breach of the 1987 Montreal Protocol on Substances that Deplete the Ozone Layer);
iii) Illegal dumping, trade and transport of waste and hazardous substances (breach of the 1989 Basel Convention on the Control of Transboundary Movement of Hazardous Wastes and Other Wastes and their Disposal);
iv) Illegal, unregulated and unreported commercial fishing;
v) Illegal logging and trade in protected woodlands (CITES) (Hayman and Brack 2002, p. 5).

Other environmental offences share similar characteristics with these five main categories. These include:

i) Bio-piracy and transport of controlled biological or genetically modified material;
ii) Illegal dumping of oil and other wastes in oceans (that is, offences under the 1973 International Convention on the Prevention of Pollution from Ships (MARPOL) and the 1972 London Convention on Dumping);
iii) Violations of potential trade restrictions under the 1998 Rotterdam Convention on the Prior Informed Consent Procedure for Certain Hazardous Chemicals and Pesticides in International Trade;
iv) Fuel trafficking to evade taxes or future controls on carbon emissions (Hayman and Brack 2002, p. 5).

The UNEP estimates that organized crime syndicates earn between US$20–30 billion from environmental crimes (Clarke 2011, UNEP 2005). Such earnings come at substantial social, economic and environmental expense for communities, their livelihoods and habitats. Indeed, organized environmental crime is identified by the UN as a key factor in the impoverishment, displacement and violent conflicts of millions of people, notably in developing societies (UNODC 2009). Political unrest and armed conflict provide both the conditions and impetus for organized environmental crime that result in species decline and human dislocation (Humphreys and Smith 2011).

As Antonio Maria Costa (2008), Executive Director of the United Nations Office on Drugs and Crime has stated:

> People are profiting from the destruction of our planet, by dumping hazardous waste, illegal logging, or the theft of bio-assets. This crime not only damages the eco-system, it impoverishes so many countries where pollution, deforestation and population displacement trigger conflict and prevent them reaching the millennium development goals.

Costa's comment highlights the victims of environmental harms, which include not only the environment but also vulnerable communities.

Widespread environmental crimes and harms have led to 'environmental refugees', that is, people dislocated and forced to migrate due to loss of livelihoods (Walters 2012). For example, the impacts of climate change are being experienced by Torres Strait Islanders, a large Indigenous Islander community off Northern Australia. Torres Strait Islanders rely on their environment for cultural, social, subsistent and economic purposes. While these communities are some of the first to be affected by sea level rises that have forced some to relocate, they are also among those with the least capacity to adapt yet who have not contributed to climate change (Lewis 2009, p. 10, Green et al. 2010). At the same time, 'environmental refugees' are not addressed by either the climate change regime or refugee law (Docherty and Giannini 2009, p. 357).

Generally, an action that is considered 'legal' is legitimized because of the formal, foundational and authoritative nature of law. Subsequently, Green Criminology is uniquely placed to evaluate the issues described in this section because it moves past legal frameworks and discourses to encompass sociological notions of environmental harm (White 2010). This allows the 'legal acts' undertaken by powerful elites, such as governments and corporations, to be examined and critiqued (Spapens et al. 2014, South and Brisman 2013, Walters et al. 2013). The following section explores this further.

## Green criminology framework

The idea of a '*Green* Criminology' simply expresses the environmental concerns that are prominent in other fields of scholarship and research in a way that is relevant to criminology (South and Brisman 2013). This is a broad field of investigation and debate, concerned with the bio-physical and socioeconomic consequences of various sources of threat and damage to the environment whether pollution, resource degradation, biodiversity loss or climate change (South 1998, 2014, Lynch 1990, Sollund 2008, Walters 2010). In a core and crucial sense, this perspective emphasizes the need to defend environments in relation to acts or forces of exploitation, suppression or disregard. Unlike human rights, Green Criminology has drawn attention to the interests of other species; it raises the profile of unpopular or marginalized issues; and it offers articulation to forgotten or neglected voices. Green Criminology has developed in various ways but remains an 'open' framework that does not aim to provide a single or unified 'theory'. Nonetheless – and fundamentally – a Green Criminology is concerned with 'rights' (whether considered in terms of law, philosophy or fairness) and the need for frameworks of justice that might accommodate the broader interests and needs posed by threatened environments, a changing climate and endangered species. Accordingly, it moves beyond the anthropocentric nature of human rights and the debate regarding a right to a healthy environment.

Necessarily then, Green Criminology reflects deep concern regarding – and objections and opposition to – some of the values and assumptions that are inherent to economic systems (capitalist or other) in which nature is simply an economic asset. As described by Broswimmer (2002, p. 58, drawing on Worster 1979), this ethos takes 'Trees, wildlife, minerals, water, and the soil' to be 'commodities' in a natural world where humans are seen as 'naturally' dominant and as having '*a right*, even an obligation, to use nature and its products for constant self-advancement' (emphasis added). But, of course, this particular view of a 'right' is contestable and there are ways of approaching 'use of nature' which attempt to balance human interest with environmental sustainability. So ideas such as environmental protection, agroecology and sensitive landscape management, can all be seen as positive approaches to human engagement with nature as well as safeguarding of human rights. But this perspective still diminishes the importance of rights *for* the environment. For example, for all its significance as a statement of environmental protection, the founding declaration of UNEP (1972, para. 2) is worded in an anthropocentric way that allows for permissive interpretation:

> The protection and improvement of the human environment is a major issue which affects the well-being of peoples and economic development throughout the world; it is the urgent desire of the peoples of the whole world and the duty of all Governments.

Green Criminology has highlighted and explored the intersection between human rights and environmental crimes/harms. As illustrated in the first section of this chapter, human rights and environmental protection are entwined in principle and in politics; yet it can be difficult to bring the two together such that both can be protected from violation and destruction (Ruiz 2011, South and Brisman 2012, Brisman and South 2013). This leads to a situation where environmental harms have to be manipulated into claims of human rights breaches. Additionally, Green Criminology is particularly interested in the paradoxical ways in which human 'good intentions' (notably through the corporate extensions of science into the manipulation of the natural world), and even the assertion of 'rights' and 'justice', can have adverse outcomes (Brisman and South 2015, Walters 2010, White 2012). In fact, we can see how the push for neoliberal development, rationalized for its ability to progress human rights, has coincided with widespread destruction of culture and the environment (Gianolla 2013). Industrial agriculture provides a useful example where it is argued that, in order to achieve the right to food, agriculture needs to become more intensive and reliant on synthetic external-inputs.

A 'bio-centric' perspective regarding rights would acknowledge the intrinsic value of non-human species, which as Halsey and White (1998, p. 352) explain 'possess a moral worth and will continue to have moral worth no matter how insignificant human beings conceive their existence or "use value" to be'. This leads to the point that human rights should be considered as only one dimension of rights amongst a complex set of rights for the environment (White 2007, p. 35). Recent work in Green Criminology has explored how the 'rights' of environmental entities could be protected by law and considered proposals for an international law against a crime of ecocide (Higgins et al. 2013).

## Ecocide and international law: propositions and debates

The 1957 Treaty of Rome was a product of an era when environmental concerns were not high on the international agenda. However, the policy context of subsequent decades has meant that some legislation directed at environmental 'rights' has been required, although this arguably remains weak in scope and status compared to other major international laws or prohibitions. For example, crimes against the planet or the environment are missing from the remit of the International Criminal Court to address genocide, war crimes and crimes against humanity as offences that can be brought before it. Operating from July 2002 (following adoption of the Rome Statute in 1998) the Court might very well have also had jurisdiction over a crime of ecocide to sit alongside the crime of genocide but for the way in which a hidden history unfolded (recently re-told as part of the development of a campaign – and resulting debate – concerning the prospects for an amendment to the Rome Statute and inclusion of a crime of ecocide (Crook and Short 2014, Higgins et al. 2013).

In recent years, the UK barrister Polly Higgins has been a principal (although not the first, see, for example, Falk 1973, Gray 1996) advocate of an international law of ecocide and has made the case for such a law in the following way:

> In 1948 the United Nations created the crime of genocide in response to the mass atrocities which arose out of World War Two. . . . War Crimes prohibit mass environmental damage, yet there is no law to stop the daily destruction that has become the norm for business. Corporate law dictates that profit determines activity, regardless of the consequence to others in the earth community.
>
> *(Higgins 2012, p. 9)*

A proposal for a crime of ecocide would embrace the principle that human-caused environmental devastation and species extinction is a responsibility of governments as well as businesses – those who are policy-makers, directors or who are responsible for funding or investment, would become legally bound to ensure that any business practice that causes mass damage, destruction or loss of ecosystems is brought to an end (Higgins et al. 2013).

This proposal resonates with similar calls for extensions of international law (see, for example, DiMento 2003, Kotz 2012) although the idea of such extension is not without its critics, even if they are sympathetic to its aims. Thus Gilbert (2014, p. 552), referring specifically to global warming as a manifestation of human impact on the environment, argues that 'just because [global warming] can be made subject to criminal law in no way justifies a comprehensive application of international criminal law to global warming *per se*'. Importantly, in terms of considering the relationship between human and environmental rights, Gilbert is concerned with climate change-induced displacement of humans which he acknowledges is 'automatically to have taken an anthropocentric approach to the problem, from protecting the environment *per se* to protecting human beings dealing with the consequences of climate change' and Gilbert's purpose is to make the process of criminalization more compatible with domestic and international criminal law in general given that otherwise 'the complexity of those crimes, the issues surrounding necessary *mens rea*, causation and remoteness, suggest that successful prosecutions will be rare.' Gilbert's reticence about the proposal is primarily based on scepticism about whether a measure based on international criminal law is an appropriate way of responding to global warming or the specific consequential problem of human displacement. Gilbert points out that law requires clarity and that complexity or ambiguity can diminish the chances of successful prosecution. On this point, while the call for a law of ecocide is attracting support, its formulation may still need some clarification and it might be anticipated that interpretation 'in practice' might not be what was intended 'in theory'.

## Conclusion

We have outlined the dual importance of human rights and environmental health as expressed in international law. Gaps in the governance structure include the lack of a human right to the environment and the difficulties current legal regimes face when responding to new levels of environmental degradation. This analysis fed into a discussion on Green Criminology and the rights of the environment (Hiskes 2009, Gianolla 2013). We support the need to acknowledge the intrinsic value and rights of the environment but much still needs to be addressed and reconciled before these could be incorporated into legal frameworks. For instance, a system for harmonizing competing rights between nature, non-human species and humans would be required. Moreover, widespread social and political support is required for legal reform.

Perhaps the major challenge that existing international environmental laws and regulatory regimes face is that concerns regarding non-human species and impacts of environmental harms on human health are seen as subsidiary to the continued advancement of global trade and economic prosperity. The environment is constructed as a resource for human exploitation and for human consumption rather than something interconnected with humanity. Whilst trade continues to assert a status of international priority within the dominant narrative of global economics and fiscal prosperity, the planet and long-term economic growth suffers. Organized environmental crime, state and private exploitation of resources, as well as the public craving for consumer goods, all impose their costs and burdens. Human rights will ultimately be worth a lot less unless humanity also pays more attention to the rights – or at least the wellbeing – of the planet.

## References


Atapattu, S., 2002. Right to a healthy life or the right to die polluted: the emergence of a human right to a healthy environment under international law. *Tulane Environmental Law Journal*, 16(1), 65–126.

Banks, D. et al., 2008. *Environmental crime: a threat to our future*. London: Environmental Investigation Agency.

Bodansky, D., Brunnee, J. and Hey, E. (eds), 2008. *The Oxford handbook of international environmental law*. Oxford: Oxford University Press.

Boyle, A., 2010. *Human rights and the environment: a reassessment*. United Nations Environment Program. Retrieved on 31 August 2015 from: http://www.unep.org/environmentalgovernance/Portals/8/documents/Events/HumanRightsEnvironmentRev.pdf.

Brisman, A., 2013. The violence of silence: some reflections on access to information, public participation in decision-making, and access to justice in matters concerning the environment. *Crime, Law and Social Change*, 59(3), 291–303.

Brisman, A. and South, N., 2013. Resource wealth, power, crime and conflict. *In*: R. Walters, D. Westerhuis and T. Wyatt (eds), *Debates in green criminology: power, justice and environmental harm*. London: Palgrave, 57–71.

Brisman, A. and South, N., 2015. State–corporate environmental harms and paradoxical interventions: thoughts in honour of Stanley Cohen. *In*: R. Sollund (ed.), *Green harms and crimes: social injustice, protest and oppression*. London: Palgrave, 27–42.

Broswimmer, F., 2002. *Ecocide: a short history of the mass extinction of species*. London: Pluto Press.

Clarke, E., 2011. Environmental crime and national security. *Environmental Crime and Security Workshop*. Antigua: United Nations Environment Programme.

Costa, A., 2008. *Rule of law: a (missing) Millennium Development Goal that can help reach the other MDGs*. Vienna: United Nations Commission on Crime Prevention and Criminal Justice. Retrieved on 1 August 2015 from: www.unodc.org/unodc/en/about-unodc/speeches/2008-04-14.html.

Crook, M. and Short, D., 2014. Marx, Lemkin and the genocide–ecocide nexus. *The International Journal of Human Rights*, 18(3), 298–319.

Cullet, P., 1995. Definition of an environmental right in a human rights context. *Netherlands Quarterly of Human Rights*, 13, 25–40.

DiMento, J.F.C., 2003. *The global environment and international law*. Texas: University of Texas Press.

Docherty, B. and Giannini, T., 2009. Confronting a rising tide: a proposal for a convention on climate change refugees. *Harvard Environmental Law Review*, 33, 349–403.

Falk, R., 1973. Environmental warfare and ecocide: facts, appraisals and proposals. *Bulletin of Peace Proposals*, 4, 80–4.

*Gabčíkovo-Nagymaros Project* (Hungary/Slovakia), 1997. Judgment, 1. C. J. Reports, p. 7.

Gianolla, C., 2013. Human rights and nature: intercultural perspectives and international aspirations. *Journal of Human Rights and the Environment*, 4(1), 58–78.

Gilbert, G., 2014. International criminal law is not a panacea: why proposed climate change 'crimes' are just another passenger on an overcrowded bandwagon. *International Criminal Law Review*, 14, 551–87.

Gray, M., 1996. The international crime of ecocide. *California Western International Law Journal*, 26, 215–71.

Green, D., Alexander, L., McInnes, K., Church, L., Nicholls, N. and White, N., 2010. An assessment of climate change impacts and adaptation for the Torres Strait Islands, Australia. *Climatic Change*, 102(3), 405–33.

Halsey, M. and White, R., 1998. Crime, ecophilosophy and environmental harm. *Theoretical Criminology*, 2(3), 345–72.

Hamman, E., Maguire, R. and Walters, R., 2015. Environmental crime and specialist courts: the case for a 'one stop (judicial) shop' in Queensland. *Current Issues in Criminal Justice*, 27(1), 59–77.

Hayman, G. and Brack, D., 2002. *International environmental crime: the nature and control of environmental black markets – workshop report*. Chatham House. Retrieved on 29 August 2015 from: http://www.chathamhouse.org.uk/files/3050_riia_environmental_crime_workshop_report.pdf.

Higgins, P., 2012. *Earth is our business: changing the rules of the game*. London: Shepheard-Walwyn.

Higgins, P., Short, D. and South, N., 2013. Protecting the planet: a proposal for a law of Ecocide. *Crime, Law and Social Change*, 59(3), 251–66.

Hiskes, R., 2009. *The human right to a green future: environmental rights and intergenerational justice*. Cambridge: Cambridge University Press.

Humphreys, J. and Smith, M., 2011. Protecting endangered species. *Criminal Justice Matters*, 83(1), 6–7.

*International Covenant on Economic, Social and Cultural Rights*, opened for signature 16 December 1966, 993 UNTS 3 (entered into force 3 January 1976).

*International Covenant on Civil and Political Rights*, opened for signature 16 December 1966, General Assembly resolution 2200A (XXI) (entered into force 23 March 1976).

Interpol, 2011. *Wildlife crime*. Retrieved on 4 August 2015 from: www.interpol.int/Public/Environmental Crime/Wildlife/Default.asp.

*Johannesburg Declaration on Sustainable Development*, UN Doc, A/CONF.199/20 (4 September 2002) art 5; *Agenda 21: Programme of Action for Sustainable Development*, U.N. GAOR, 46th Sess., Agenda Item 21, UN Doc A/Conf.151/26 (14 June 1992).

Kotz, L., 2012. *Global environmental governance: law and regulation for the 21st century*. Cheltenham: Edward Elgar.

Lewis, B., 2009. Environmental rights, justice and climate change. *In*: E. Webber (ed.), *Environmental ethics: sustainability and education*. Oxfordshire, UK: Inter-Disciplinary Press, Freeland, 63–80.

Lewis, B., 2012. Environmental rights or a right to the environment? Exploring the nexus between human rights and environmental protection. *Macquarie Journal of International and Comparative Environmental Law*, 1, 36–7.

Lynch, M., 1990. The greening of criminology: a perspective for the 1990s. *Critical Criminologist*, 2, 3–12.

Office of the High Commissioner for Human Rights, 2015. *Special Rapporteur on human rights and the environment (former Independent Expert on human rights and the environment)*. Retrieved on 10 June 2015 from: www.ohchr.org/EN/Issues/Environment/SREnvironment/Pages/SRenvironmentIndex.aspx.

'Rio Declaration' 1992 *Rio Declaration on Environment and Development*, UN Doc. A/CONF.151/26 (vol. I) / 31 ILM 874 (12 August 1992).

Ruiz, D., 2011. Ecocide in the Mesopotamian marshes. *In*: G. Mesko, A. Sotlar and J. Winterdyk (eds), *Social control of unconventional deviance*. Ljubljana: University of Maribor, 139–47.

Shelton, D., 1991. Human rights, environmental rights, and the right to environment. *Stanford Journal of International Law*, 28, 103–38.

Sollund, R., 2008. Causes for speciesism: difference, distance and denial. *In*: R. Sollund (ed.), *Global harms: ecological crime and speciesism*. New York, NY: Nova Science Publishers, 109–30.

South, N., 1998. A green field for criminology? A proposal for a perspective. *Theoretical Criminology*, 2, 211–33.

South, N., 2014. Green criminology and organised environmental crimes, *ECPRSGOC Newsletter*, 11(3), 2–3. Retrieved on 10 August 2015 from: http://sgocnet.org/site/wp-content/uploads/2014/05/Sept-2014_Final2.pdf.

South, N., 2015. Environmental justice. *Scottish Justice Matters*, 3(1), 4–5.

South, N. and Brisman, A., 2012. Critical green criminology, environmental rights and crimes of exploitation. *In*: S. Winlow and R. Atkinson (eds), *New directions in crime and deviance*. London: Routledge, 99–110.

South, N. and Brisman, A. (eds), 2013. *The Routledge international handbook of green criminology*. London: Routledge.

Spapens, T., White, R. and Kluin, M. (eds), 2014. *Environmental crime and its victims: perspectives within green criminology*. Aldershot: Ashgate.

'Stockholm Declaration' *Declaration of the United Nations Conference on the Human Environment*, 21st plen mtg, ch 11, U.N. Doc. A/Conf.48/14/Rev. 1(1973) (16 June 1972).

United Nations Environment Program [UNEP], 1972. *Declaration of the United Nations Conference on the Human Environment* (Stockholm Declaration). Retrieved on 5 April 2016 from: http://www.unep.org/Documents.Multilingual/Default.asp?documentid=97&articleid=1503.

United Nations Environment Program [UNEP], 2005. *Green Customs Initiative Targets Environmental Crime.* Retrieved on 5 August 2015 from: http://new.unep.org/Documents.Multilingual/Default.asp?DocumentID=457&ArticleID=5030&l=en.

United Nations Environment Program [UNEP], 2009. *High level expert meeting on the future of human rights and environment: moving the global agenda forward.* Retrieved on 5 April 2016 from: www.unep.org/environmentalgovernance/Events/HumanRightsandEnvironmen//tabid/2046/Default.aspx.

United Nations Office on Drugs and Crime, 2009. *What does environmental crime have in common with organized crime?.* Retrieved on 18 August 2015 from: www.unodc.org/unodc/en/frontpage/what-does-environmental-crime-have-in-common.

Walters, R., 2010. *Eco crime and genetically modified food.* London: Routledge.

Walters, R., 2012. Organized crime and the environment. *In*: G. Bruinsma and D. Weisburd (eds), *Encyclopaedia of criminology and criminal justice.* New York, NY: Springer, 3368–75.

Walters, R., 2013. Eco mafia and environmental crime. *In*: K. Carrington, M. Ball, E. O'Brien and J. Tauri (eds), *Crime, justice and social democracy: international perspectives.* Basingstoke: Palgrave, 281–94.

Walters, R. and Westerhuis, D., 2013. Green crime and the role of environmental courts. *Crime, Law and Social Change*, 59(3), 279–90.

Walters, R., Westerhuis, D. and Wyatt, T. (eds), 2013. *Emerging issues in green criminology: exploring power, justice and harm.* London: Palgrave.

White, R., 2007. Green Criminology and the pursuit of social and ecological justice. *In*: P. Beirne and N. South (eds), *Issues in Green Criminology.* Cullompton: Willan Publishing, 32–54.

White, R. (ed.), 2010. *Global environmental harm: criminological perspectives.* Cullompton: Willan Publishing.

White, R., 2012. Climate change and paradoxical harm. *In*: S. Farrell, D. French and T. Ahmed (eds), *Legal and criminological consequences of climate change.* London: Hart Publishing, 63–78.

White, R., 2013. Environmental crime and problem-solving courts. *Crime, Law and Social Change*, 59(3), 267–78.

Worster, D., 1979. *Dust bowl: the Southern Plains in the 1930s.* New York, NY: Oxford University Press.

# 21
# Trafficking cultural objects and human rights

*Simon Mackenzie and Donna Yates*[1]

## Introduction

Since the end of World War 2, international cultural heritage protection law and its domestic legal components have proceeded in their development in tandem with the development of international human rights laws and norms. A core tension in human rights thinking is evident also in debates about the right to cultural property: the potential for conflict between the right to cultural self-determination by one group and attempts to develop and promulgate human rights standards with universalizing ambitions. This is reflected in cultural property ownership debates, where cultural heritage[2] may be considered by some people as the common heritage of humankind and thus to some extent owned by us all, while others would see it as more properly owned by members of a more restricted group, or perhaps communally as tangible items of a certain culture.

So there is a universalism versus particularism debate about the right to own, possess or otherwise enjoy, worship or value cultural objects just as there is the same debate on a much wider scale about universalism versus particularism in human rights in general. As with that wider debate, where universalism has been criticized for being a veil for the global transfer of western liberal capitalist values (see, for example, Woodiwiss 2005), so too in the cultural property debate the construction of the idea of 'the world's cultural heritage' has tended to represent in practice a view that favours the idea of the 'encyclopaedic' western model of the museum, thus suggesting an ideal where material cultural heritage is stored in cultural repositories around the world rather than leaving (or reinstating) it to its country of origin or to a community thought to have the closest historical, cultural or religious connection to it.

This view is fiercely opposed by those who consider this to be, in effect, an attempted justification of the forcible extraction of this particular resource from the developing world. They prefer to define and delineate cultural property rights in terms of 'the property of a culture' rather than as 'property which is cultural' insofar as the latter might represent a contemporary reflection of the values and views of the global art market rather than the communities and cultures whose heritage is at stake. In international legislation aimed at cultural property protection there is some ambivalence around these views, with the preambles of the governing conventions tending to strike a diplomatic balance between recognizing important cultural artefacts as the particular interests of cultural groups, states or 'all peoples', while also approving of some of the effects of the worldwide diffusion of cultural heritage, most of which is due to the mechanics of the art market.

Globally significant acts of cultural destruction threaten or completely eliminate people's opportunity to enjoy cultural heritage, as has been seen in acts of desecration like the destruction of the Bamiyan Buddhas in Afghanistan by the Taliban, or the reported acts of destruction by ISIS of ancient and magnificent cultural heritage sites like Nimrud in Iraq and Palmyra in Syria. These acts tend to shore up the arguments of the 'cultural internationalists' (Merryman 1986) who argue for the safekeeping of objects in world museums in developed countries. The interests of this type of internationalism are complicated by the legal regimes of many antiquities source countries which largely favour state or at least in-country ownership of cultural property, including archaeological objects that have not yet been discovered, even during times of conflict and instability. This leads to an impasse between the stated desire on the part of 'cultural internationalists' to pre-empt future destruction by storing international cultural property in cultural institutions within stable, inevitably western countries, and the desire on the part of source countries to retain cultural property. The artefacts coming out of source countries that the 'cultural internationalists' save are often therefore crossing borders illegally.

The illegal looting of cultural property from sites like tombs and temples, predominantly in the developing world, destroys the archaeological record, depleting opportunities for gathering knowledge about our past (Brodie et al. 2000). Although archaeological looting is less immediately dramatic than acts of large-scale iconoclastic destruction, it is no less important. Beyond the irrecoverable loss to our knowledge of the ancient past and, thus, to our own modern identity and social cohesion, the transnational criminal market in looted antiquities is associated with insecurity, corruption, and related serious crimes (Mackenzie and Davis 2014, Yates 2014).

The evidence suggests that, like other transnational criminal markets, the illicit antiquities trade is driven by the supply–demand effects exerted when wealthy private and institutional collectors are prepared to buy looted artefacts for their collections (Polk 2000, Renfrew 1993). Is buying an antiquity in the high end boutiques of New York or London really an act with significant albeit obscured human rights implications? This contribution will review the literature on aspects of cultural property destruction, plunder and trafficking as they relate to human rights.

## Cultural heritage crimes and human rights standards

Until recently, references to human rights in cultural heritage discourse have been more frequent than references to cultural heritage in human rights discourse:

> worldwide, cultural heritage does not figure prominently in the extensive literature on human rights, but this does not mean it is an issue of minor importance or without significant social impact ... the notion of 'world cultural heritage' may, in fact, promote tolerance ... whereas the lack of tolerance for the identity of others often leads to the repression of minority cultural expressions.
>
> *(Silverman and Ruggles 2007)*

The major treaties which have been established to engage with the international aspects of cultural property trafficking and destruction do not explicitly reference human rights, although they do hint at some relevant universalist conceptions in their preambles. The 1970 United Nations Educational, Scientific and Cultural Organization (UNESCO) *Convention on the Means of Prohibiting and Preventing the Illicit Import, Export and Transfer of Ownership of Cultural Property* broadly approaches the issue using the state as its unit of analysis, looking to states to be both protectors of their own and other countries' cultural heritage, while also supporting in somewhat imprecise language a legal trade in cultural objects; imprecise enough to keep both antiquities trade interests and cultural property protectionists onside:

> Considering that the interchange of cultural property among nations for scientific, cultural and educational purposes increases the knowledge of the civilisation of Man, enriches the cultural life of all peoples and inspires mutual respect and appreciation among nations. . . . Considering that it is incumbent upon every State to protect the cultural property existing within its territory against the dangers of theft, clandestine excavation, and illicit export; Considering that, to avert these dangers, it is essential for every State to become increasingly alive to the moral obligations to respect its own cultural heritage and that of all nations.

The 1995 UNIDROIT *Convention on Stolen or Illegally Exported Cultural Objects* also begins with a similar statement of support for the benefits of international cultural 'exchanges' and 'dissemination', which can be read as a backing for a legal commercial trade in cultural objects, while the Convention generally supplements the nation-state view of UNESCO 1970 with a raft of provisions on private personal rights to ownership of cultural property and recovery when it is stolen. The 1954 'Hague' *Convention for the Protection of Cultural Property in the Event of Armed Conflict* presents the most unambiguous statement of the universalist view: 'Being convinced that damage to cultural property belonging to any people whatsoever means damage to the cultural heritage of all mankind, since each people makes its contribution to the culture of the world'.

Explicit reference to human rights standards in UNESCO international instruments concerned with the protection of cultural property against destruction and theft began in 2001 with the *Universal Declaration on Cultural Diversity* which reaffirms in its preamble a commitment to the full implementation of human rights and fundamental freedoms contained within the *Universal Declaration of Human Rights* (UDHR) and other multilateral instruments, including the 1970 UNESCO Convention. In response to the Taliban's destruction of the Bamiyan Buddhas, UNESCO formulated its 2003 *Declaration Concerning the Intentional Destruction of Cultural Heritage* which in its preamble notes that intentional destruction 'may have adverse consequences on human dignity and human rights'. These and other examples show a trend towards the increasing insertion of references to human rights in international cultural heritage protection instruments since the turn of the millennium.

Vrdoljak (2012), a key writer on the relationship between cultural heritage and universal human rights, sees the relationship between legal protection against plunder of cultural objects and specific human rights as being based on: the right to property; the right to self-determination; the right to participate in cultural life; and minority protection. Other writers have acknowledged the wider relationship between cultural heritage and human rights, and it is helpful to consider some examples of this if we want to contextualize the place of our narrower concern with cultural heritage *crime* within the domain of human rights. That broader context of the intersection between cultural heritage and human rights includes:

> indigenous rights (which are often articulated in resistance to national identity); war and other violence (political, ethnic, religious); access to and exclusion from shared sacred sites; the impact of economic development on cultural heritage of local populations; memory/forgetting; and intellectual property rights.
>
> *(Silverman and Ruggles 2007, pp. 6–7)*

This list of possibilities shows the very wide prospective relationships between human rights and 'crimes to do with cultural heritage' including, for just one set of examples, the remembering/forgetting rights debate around the preservation of 'negative heritage' sites like concentration camps in Germany, or Ground Zero in New York, where criminal atrocities have created a legacy of sites which promote painful episodes of remembrance, but ones which affected groups may wish to maintain expressly for that purpose of never forgetting. Mindful of the very wide landscape of a debate around the relationship between crime, cultural heritage, and human rights, in this chapter we have selected to focus on the area of overlap between human rights thinking and the looting and trafficking of ancient cultural objects (antiquities) from archaeological contexts.

## Internationalism, nationalism and community interests

Perhaps the most important step represented by the development of cultural heritage protection in connection with human rights values has been a move away from thinking about cultural heritage as solely a state interest (as evident in the comments about the UNESCO 1970 Convention above), and towards affirming its primary fundamental importance as being to people and to the international community: 'Human rights law reinforces that states alone are not the only rights-holders in respect of moveable heritage . . . it is "peoples" who have the right to determine whether and how their moveable heritage is transferred' (Vrdoljak 2012, p. 139). This move away from seeing the state as the primary benefactor from and interested party in the cultural heritage which may at any time reside within its borders not only broadens and deepens the community of 'victims' who may be affected by its theft or destruction, but it also expands 'downwards' the amount and types of cultural heritage which may be seen as deserving of protection in law. As Vrdoljak puts it: 'contemporary interpretations of several human rights norms require states parties to protect and prevent illicit traffic of cultural heritage which is not only of national importance but also of significance to non-state groups, including minorities and indigenous peoples' (Vrdoljak 2012, p. 121).

This movement in the dialogue is to be welcomed: the signal importance of a human rights discourse in the approach to penal/legal and property/interest issues around trafficking antiquities is that it makes it increasingly difficult for global economic interests to ignore community-level interests in source countries. As alluded to in the introduction, those in the market who want to deal in and collect cultural heritage have famously been called, approvingly, 'cultural internationalists' by Merryman, with their interests set against those he disapprovingly calls 'cultural nationalists' or 'retentionists' (Merryman 1986, 2000). In Merryman's version of events, community and state interests in not having their heritage looted out and transmitted around the world by market forces are condemned as striking against the educative and ambassadorial dissemination value of travelling heritage, as well as concerns about preservation and restoration which are said to be better allayed by elite global ownership. This, therefore, is the legitimate academic face of the 'it belongs to all of us' approach to the right to ownership or possession of cultural property; but the inherent risk in such a view is that it may be feared to function as a veil for the continuation of a kind of resource exploitation that carries colonial undertones and reinvents them in the world of cultural appreciation and financial investment markets. The injection of a human rights ethos, or even a human rights *question*, into this debate may work at least to unravel some of the now ingrained, and perhaps therefore hard to see, assumptions about the natural supremacy of market practice and the right to property.

Meanwhile, some philosophers have developed arguments against the private right to ownership of everything, considering ideas around the 'moral limits of markets' and concluding that 'some things should not be for sale' for a variety of reasons including adverse social outcomes, but ultimately because for some things the concept of private ownership is simply morally offensive to the very essence of the category of the things in themselves (Sandel 2012, Satz 2010). Private international collection of culturally significant antiquities is seemingly under pressure from all sides.

That tangible cultural objects play an important role in the development of intangible cultural and social identity is well established in academic literature and is clearly reflected in recent human rights instruments. The UN *Declaration on the Rights of Indigenous Peoples* (UNDRIP 2007) states that 'Indigenous peoples and individuals have the right not to be subjected to forced assimilation or destruction of their culture', and that 'Indigenous peoples have the right to practice and revitalize their cultural traditions and customs. This includes the right to maintain, protect and develop the past, present and future manifestations of their cultures, such as archaeological and historical sites, artefacts, designs, ceremonies, technologies and visual and performing arts and literature'. In other words Indigenous people, who are often equated with the communities that normally 'lose' their cultural objects via looting and trafficking, have the right to not have their culture, as they define it, destroyed and they have the right to maintain that culture, which specifically includes archaeological sites and artefacts, not because of an inherent right to property, but rather an inherent right to a self-determined identity.

The original 'cultural internationalist' conception essentially rested on a constructed dichotomy between the global public (or rather a global public constructed of individuals who wish to own property) and retentionist states considered to propagate a dangerous form of nationalism by restricting the movement of cultural heritage (Merryman 1985). If that debate could ever be accepted as a reasonable reflection of facts on the ground, which is a contentious proposition to say the least, the contemporary assertion of an 'internationalist' right to property and the definition of heritage objects as property seems to run into new types of conflict with the emerging understandings that there is a human right to identity and self-definition, that cultural heritage can be an important component in that process, and that these human rights may subsist in people and collectives sitting below a level of analysis that engages with positions taken on issues of cultural heritage trade or retention by states. In human rights mechanisms, the state is not the primary unit of the right to assertion of identity, rather it is the individual or, at times, the cultural group or community. These nations, in the true sense of the word, usually do not form a political state and almost certainly lack the power to define property and ownership. Yet it is in these groups that mechanisms like UNDRIP vest control over identity-based cultural assets. Abusing or denying the right to self-determination and identity in these groups brings a new register to allegations against the market. The discussion moves beyond the trade's previous portrayals of the issue as being conflict between the legitimate claims of private individuals and the illegitimate claims of states, the latter often having been denied true 'ancientness' in the argument by a focus on fractures between past civilizations and modern groups claiming a past-based identity, therefore suggesting a sort of deficient cultural 'title and interest' to claim true ownership. An example would be the pro-trade position that modern Greek society is not really linked to ancient Greek society due to the passing of time, religious conversion, and the genetic influx of Ottoman DNA; and therefore that contemporary Greek claims to restitution of ancient Greek artefacts should be denied.

The history of the negotiation of the 1970 UNESCO Convention is instructive in helping us understand the political economy of the interests at play in the question of regulating the international trade in antiquities. An early draft of the convention's preamble referred to Article 27 UDHR (Vrdoljak 2012). The United States (US), however, pressed through a revised (by them) draft of the Convention which was the one that ultimately came to be agreed (Bator 1983), and from which reference to UDHR was deleted. The rights which the US preferred, as a significant market country for cultural property originating overseas, were pro-trade and the preamble to the 1970 Convention, mentioned above, now carries more of a flavour of cultural internationalism than the earlier more protective drafts. Seen in this context we can perhaps observe that rights-related discourse can be quite ideologically loaded towards economic interests. The particular way one incorporates rights-based thinking into the language of international law can support and promote the continuance of international trade, putting pressure on the rights of those with an original local cultural interest in the heritage at stake. In that case, what we end up with is a neoliberal version of human rights protection, which in preferring to cast cultural heritage as the subject of 'interchanges' presumed to be beneficial, promotes a capitalist model of elite global property ownership in which the right to own heritage is in principle considered most appropriately (absent the demonstration of manifest criminality in the supply chain) to be dependent on money. This capacity to 'wash' a human rights discourse about cultural heritage in one political or economic colour or another is not really surprising, especially considering the significant and now well established line of critique aimed at human rights discourse in general, that it is a contemporary veil for the evaluation of global society through the lens of US neoliberal capitalist values and norms (Woodiwiss 2005).

These debates are therefore in broad terms indicative of the inherent capacity for human rights-oriented views of cultural heritage to lead to dispute about which person or group the particular right appropriately vests in; and in narrower terms may suggest a productive new direction in developing standards to use when trying to resolve these disputes, based in rights around identity. Although the statist, and implicitly market oriented, discourse prevailed to a significant extent in the final draft of the 1970 UNESCO Convention, as we have observed there has since then been an incremental progression towards the inclusion, in UN level debates about cultural heritage, of a human rights discourse that is more sophisticated, and more willing to recognize and value the rights of 'peoples'. In its General Comment No. 21 (2009), the Committee on Economic, Social and Cultural Rights recognized the right of minorities to conserve, promote and develop their own culture, and the obligation on states to recognize, respect and protect minority cultures as an essential component of the identity of the states themselves. The UNDRIP 2007, mentioned above, in Article 12 obliges states to implement effective mechanisms of redress for cultural objects removed without free, prior and informed consent and in violation of customary law.

## Crimes of necessity?

A troublesome aspect of the debate about local people's rights to their cultural heritage comes in the question whether this extends to destroying it, or selling it after having dug, chiselled, chainsawed or otherwise removed it from its archaeological context. Some authors have proposed a 'human right to loot', but in very restricted circumstances (Hardy 2015). Effectively this has been proposed as the case only where survival demands it and the economic rewards of looting are put to use in keeping people alive, where otherwise they would likely have perished. In such a construction of the case, the right to life is set against concerns about the protection of cultural heritage, and the former would seem to trump the latter. Circumstances are rarely so clear-cut on the ground, however. While there have been anthropological and archaeological studies and reports of so-called subsistence diggers (Staley 1993, Brodie et al. 2001), including acknowledgements that 'subsistence' looting happens in the absence of other economic alternatives and in the context of a struggle for survival including 'basic living expenses and medical supplies' (Foster et al. 2005), many other reports suggest various levels of organized criminality in the looting process, and if not organized crime then local opportunism which is entrepreneurial and driven by the temptations of the illicit market rather than by a basic need for economic survival (Atwood 2004). Cultural heritage is not a sustainable (in the sense of endlessly self-reproducing) resource, so looting involves the realization only of short-term local gain at the expense of any longer term monetization of the heritage, for example through sustainable tourism in the region (Prott and Bessières 2001). Furthermore, looting enriches only the individuals involved rather than whole communities in the way other forms of monetization of the resource might do (Brodie 2010). Studies of the price escalation up the supply chain have shown that looters are paid only a fraction of the final sale prices of artefacts once they make their way to market destinations, with the biggest mark-ups and rewards going to middlemen who traffic cultural objects from source to international market (Brodie 1998). The result of all of these studies and reflections is that looting, as well as being a crime, is a short-termist and anti-communitarian economic strategy, which seems difficult to view positively in human rights propositions framed around cultural groups, since whatever survival benefits may be obtained by individuals come at the expense of other people in the region who lose access to a resource which may be both culturally and traditionally important (Udvardy et al. 2003), and potentially a useful income generator for the longer term.

For these reasons, archaeologists have tended to agree that 'it is very clear that looting destroys the contexts that give objects their meaning; it is to be condemned' (Silverman and Ruggles 2007, p. 16). However, the question of the ethics of dealing in objects that may have been previously looted is sometimes considered less unequivocally: 'But the moral implication of historic (and archaeological, artistic, etc.) objects bought by wealthy collectors from impoverished sellers is more complex' (Silverman and Ruggles 2007, p. 16). Many in the dealing and collecting community do not agree that there is much complexity to it, and argue straightforwardly and often forthrightly both for their right to acquire (Cuno 2008) and against repatriation (Cuno 2014).

## Repatriation: towards a restorative approach?

While analysis of criminal justice responses to trafficking in illicit antiquities shows that they are often weak – weakly designed and weakly implemented (see, for example, Mackenzie and Green 2008, 2009) – in some places, to the contrary, criminal sanctions for offences against cultural heritage have been extremely harsh. In 2004 the convicted looters of the ancient site of Jiroft in Iran were sentenced to death, and China has also used the death penalty in respect of cultural property looting offences. Such highly retributive state responses would seem to merit their own level of inquiry into the infringement of the human rights of offenders. Although this 'sharp end' of the relationship between justice and the antiquities market may seem the obvious place to look for human rights abuses, and of course it clearly is important to do so, the less obvious discussion is in respect of the corrupting exercise of trade power behind the scenes of the 'weak law' examples (Mackenzie and Green 2008). This can be considered pertinent to a discussion of adverse effects on the human rights of source communities by an international commercial enterprise controlled by a networked global elite of dealers, collectors, appraisers, authenticators, ethically compromised academics who wish to study illicit material (Brodie 2009), and public and private institutions which acquire and display or, in some cases, hoard antiquities (for museums, it is not unusual for items sequestered long term in basements and warehouses vastly to outnumber the objects on display).

In civil, criminal, and diplomatic cases raised in the contemporary field of looted and trafficked cultural objects, success is often seen as the repatriation, restitution or, in layman's terms, return of the artefact to its country of origin. There have been a string of recent examples of this trend towards repatriation, many of them involving multi-million dollar ancient statues. On the face of it, this may look like a process of restorative justice: reparation is made to 'the victim' (if we conceive of the state as the victim, which the repatriation mechanism tends to do), the object is returned, the state may hold a return ceremony which records among other things the legal acknowledgement of its international standing as a culturally rich political entity, and some sort of balance is restored. For various reasons including expediency and the massive cost of international litigious proceedings, however, the person or institution returning the object will often negotiate a type of 'no-fault' settlement agreement whereby they agree to surrender the offending item but without any admission of guilt (in having knowingly or negligently bought the object, for example), and sometimes with a requirement that all parties to the return agreement make explicit public statements to the effect that there is no longer any guilt alleged. Current international repatriation claims are therefore very often concluded in a way which those who study criminal justice might struggle to recognize as being much like restorative justice, other than in a surface veneer. In genuine applications of restorative justice theory to dispute resolution, a process of reintegrative shaming is a key goal, through which the offender may be brought back into the normative and moral life of the community (Braithwaite 1989). This rip in the social fabric is the thing that needs to be addressed, and respect for the community's value system, and the dislocated offender, are the things that need to be 'restored'. Apology, acceptance of guilt, a productive form of shame, attention to the social forces driving offending behaviour – these are all thought to be key elements of a restorative approach which binds societies back together when a criminal breach occurs. Simply giving back stolen goods when caught red handed with them, and with an explicit agreement that no apology will be made, looks problematic as a process of restorative justice. A wider discussion would seem useful about the human rights implications of looting and trafficking cultural heritage in the context of restorative approaches to deep historical social and cultural rifts and the legacy their economic modes of 'internationalization' have left, and continue to leave, on victimized communities in less powerful parts of the world. Those economic forces, however, work to make such an overarching restorative discussion strained.

## Conclusion

The debate about the criminalization of theft, trafficking, fencing and purchasing of antiquities stands to gain insights from human rights arguments which have the potential to open up new avenues of progress in what has become a vitriolic pitched battle between two sides. Trade interests are entrenched on one side, justifying their international buying and collecting decisions as the practice of certain kinds of property-oriented rights against an activist opposition which seeks to undermine those rights by drawing attention to their role as drivers of a culturally harmful system of enterprise. The increasing recognition of the value that should be placed on the identity rights of sub-state cultural groups brings a nuance to a debate that has often been conducted in reified and statist terms. The increasing rights-based sensitivity to cultural group identities introduces difficulties and complexities to the ethical, legal and financial positions so far adopted by protagonists in the discourse in this field. It will be interesting to see if this will be a progressive incursion of human rights ideas into a domain of thought and practice traditionally premised on principles which may have to adapt to new more culturally aware modes of 'thinking about cultural property' (Merryman 1986).

## Notes

1 The work on which this publication is based received funding from the European Research Council under the European Union's Seventh Framework Programme (FP7/2007–2013)/ERC Grant agreement n° 283873 GTICO.

2 In this chapter we use the terms 'antiquities', 'cultural heritage', 'cultural property', and 'cultural objects' relatively interchangeably – occasionally we even say 'artefacts' since that is how lay persons and newspapers often describe the objects in question. All these terms have different inflections to their meaning, however, and in the way they are interpreted by parties interested in the debate we describe in the chapter. For example, 'property' clearly has a different implication to 'heritage' as terminology to employ when it comes to arguing about who should rightfully own cultural objects, and indeed whether they should be owned in a trading-market sense at all. This being a criminology text, and our attempt being to raise awareness of these debates rather than necessarily resolve them, we have spared readers terminological partiality or impartiality here and simply mixed the terms throughout, to give a flavour of the way the objects in question can be described.

## References


Atwood, R., 2004. *Stealing history: tomb raiders, smugglers, and the looting of the ancient world*. New York, NY: St Martin's Press.

Bator, P.M., 1983. *The international trade in art*. Chicago, IL: University of Chicago Press.

Braithwaite, J., 1989. *Crime, shame and reintegration*. Cambridge: Cambridge University Press.

Brodie, N., 1998. Pity the poor middlemen. *Culture Without Context*, 3(Autumn).

Brodie, N., 2009. Consensual relations? Academic involvement in the illegal trade in ancient manuscripts. *In*: S. Mackenzie and P. Green (eds), *Criminology and archaeology: studies in looted antiquities*. Oxford: Hart, 41–58.

Brodie, N., 2010. Archaeological looting and economic justice. *In*: P.M. Messenger and G.S. Smith (eds), *Cultural heritage management, policy and issues in global perspective*. Gainsville, FL: University Press of Florida, 261–77.

Brodie, N., Doole, J. and Renfrew, C. (eds), 2001. *Trade in illicit antiquities: the destruction of the world's archaeological heritage*. Cambridge: McDonald Institute for Archaeological Research.

Brodie, N., Doole, J. and Watson, P., 2000. *Stealing history: the illicit trade in cultural material*. Cambridge: McDonald Institute for Archaeological Research.

Cuno, J., 2008. *Who owns antiquity? Museums and the battle over our ancient heritage*. Princeton, NJ: Princeton University Press.

Cuno, J., 2014. The case against repatriating museum artifacts. *Foreign Affairs*, November/December.

Foster, B., Foster, K. and Gerstenblith, P., 2005. *Iraq beyond the headlines: history, archaeology, and war*. London: World Scientific Publishing.

Hardy, S., 2015. Virtues impracticable and extremely difficult: the human rights of subsistence diggers. *In*: A. González-Ruibal and G. Moshenska (eds), *Ethics and the archaeology of violence*. New York, NY: Springer, 229–39.

Mackenzie, S. and Davis, T., 2014. Temple looting in Cambodia: anatomy of a statue trafficking network. *British Journal of Criminology*, 54(5), 722–40.

Mackenzie, S. and Green, P., 2008. Performative regulation: a case study in how powerful people avoid criminal labels. *British Journal of Criminology*, 48(2), 138–53.

Mackenzie, S. and Green, P., 2009. Criminalising the market in illicit antiquities: an evaluation of the dealing in *Cultural Objects (Offences) Act 2003* in England and Wales. *In*: S. Mackenzie and P. Green (eds), *Criminology and archaeology: studies in looted antiquities*. Oxford: Hart, 145–70.

Merryman, J.H., 1985. Thinking about the Elgin Marbles. *Michigan Law Review*, 83, 1880.

Merryman, J.H. 1986. Two ways of thinking about cultural property. *American Journal of International Law*, 80, 831.

Merryman, J.H. 2000. A licit international trade in cultural objects (originally published in (1995) *International Journal of Cultural Property*, 4, 13). *In*: J.H. Merryman (ed.), *Thinking about the Elgin Marbles: critical essays on cultural property*. Art and Law. London: Kluwer Law International, 244–93.

Polk, K., 2000. The antiquities trade viewed as a criminal market. *Hong Kong Lawyer*, September, 82–92.

Prott, L.V. and Bessières, M., 2001. The cost of looting: Indiana Jones has no future. *UNESCO Courier*, 54(4), 18–21.

Renfrew, C., 1993. Collectors are the real looters. *Archaeology*, 46(3), 16–17.

Sandel, M.J., 2012. *What money can't buy: the moral limits of markets*. London: Penguin.

Satz, D., 2010. *Why some things should not be for sale: the moral limits of markets*. New York, NY: Oxford University Press.

Silverman, H. and Ruggles, D.F. (eds), 2007. *Cultural heritage and human rights*. New York, NY: Springer.

Staley, D.P., 1993. St Lawrence Island's subsistence diggers: a new perspective on human effects on archaeological sites. *Journal of Field Archaeology*, 20, 347–55.

Udvardy, M.L., Giles, L.L. and Mitsanze, J.B., 2003. The transatlantic trade in African ancestors: Mijikenda Memorial Statues (Vigango) and the ethics of collecting and curating non-western cultural property. *American Anthropologist*, 105(3), 566–80.

UNDRIP, 2007. *United Nations Declaration on the Rights of Indigenous People*. 13 September.

Vrdoljak, A.F., 2012. Human rights and illicit trade in cultural objects. *In*: S. Borelli and F. Lenzerini (eds), *Cultural heritage, cultural rights, cultural diversity: international law perspectives*. Leiden: Martinus Nijhoff, 107–40.

Woodiwiss, A., 2005. *Human rights*. London: Routledge.

Yates, D., 2014. Church theft, insecurity and community justice: the reality of source–end regulation of the market for illicit Bolivian cultural objects. *European Journal of Crime Policy and Research*, 20, 445–57.

# Part III

# Human rights in the promotion of peace, community safety and social justice

This section of the book takes the discussion of human rights and criminology beyond the concept of first generation civil and political rights, the confines of the criminal justice systems and national boundaries to encompass an examination of the importance of second- and third-generation rights. In the tradition of peacekeeping criminology the section explores broader concepts of justice, democracy and capacity-building and incorporates discussions of transformation and transition and the relationship between human rights and social justice. The contributors in the section challenge us to think differently about crime, deviance, human rights and justice and in so doing to re-evaluate and rework our existing criminological understandings.

The section opens with a discussion by Stephan Parmentier, Monica Aciru, Huma Saeed and Mina Rauschenbach of human rights and transitional justice. Using case examples from Sierra Leone and Afghanistan, the chapter explores the four pillars of transitional justice – criminal prosecutions, truth commissions, victim reparation programmes, institutional reforms and their capacity in practice, to deal with the aftermath of serious human rights violations (including those relating to socioeconomic and cultural rights) in times of conflict. The authors suggest that there remains a missing link in criminological explanations of transitional justice and propose future avenues for criminological exploration.

The following chapter by Kristian Lasslett uses in-depth ethnographic and investigative material gathered by the author, to examine the devastating impact of state supported corporate mining interests on the Nasioi people of the South Pacific Island of Bougainville. The author argues that despite attempts to resolve conflict, the violence perpetrated by the combined corporate and state interests continues to disrupt and harm the social, cultural, gender and economic relations of local populations, and that despite attempts to redress harms the violations of human rights continue.

Deena Haydon and Phil Scraton's chapter also focuses on a post-conflict period of transition but this time in Northern Ireland. In particular, they discuss how the social, political and economic characteristics of Northern Ireland, in the shadow of the Good Friday Peace Accord, continue to shape the ways in which young people are governed through policing, diversionary programmes and sentencing. They examine the impact of human rights instruments and principles on the justice system in relation to young people and argue that, despite many progressive reforms, the full realization of children's rights in Northern Ireland is limited by the social and economic injustices that continue to exist, the legacy of inter-community conflict and violence which underpins social, cultural and institutional relations, and the continued punitive approach to young people expressed in the media and by politicians. Human rights and social justice go hand in hand.

The following chapter by Andrew Goldsmith continues the theme of transition and peace making with its exploration of the role of international police as peacekeepers in post-conflict zones. It examines the challenges facing them as they endeavour to educate local personnel and reform policing and governance in local communities, while at the same time promoting human rights principles and practices. Drawing on his own experiences and research in the field, Goldsmith argues that peacekeepers face a daunting task, especially when local police and state officials are themselves complicit in human rights abuses. Greg Martin also investigates the nexus between policing and human rights during periods of transformation with his analysis of the policing of dissent in contemporary democracies. Martin argues that the perceived threat of terrorism and discourse of risk and security have resulted in an escalation of the criminalization of dissent, a focus on de-radicalization and a concomitant dilution in human rights protections. However, he maintains that these incursions on freedoms are met with resistance from activists as they engage in digital modes of political action.

The final four chapters take the idea of transition in different directions. Sanja Milivojevic, Marie Segrave and Sharon Pickering discuss the movement of peoples across borders and the continued vulnerability of undocumented migrants to human rights abuses and exploitation in their countries of origin, transit and destination. Using comparative research material the authors argue that despite the existence of international treaties and human rights instruments, there needs to be a transformation of current human rights frameworks in order to ameliorate the situation where states have hardened border policies and as a consequence punish irregular migrants who are fleeing harm. Tight border policing, immigration detention, contracting out offshore detention and the tying of human rights protections to citizenship status, ensures that vulnerable populations are subject to continuing harms whether they are in indeterminate detention, existing on the fringes of society, or are confined to countries of transit that have the least resources.

Ratna Kapur's piece offers a critique, through a postcolonial lens, of current normative human rights discourses on sex, sexuality and gender. The chapter problematizes dominant ideas of sexual rights interventions in law and human rights, arguing that a western ontology of human rights advocacy with its focus on normalization, equal marriage and respectability prohibits the possibility of a plurality of postcolonial perspectives and lived experiences in relation to sex and sexuality. Kapur calls for a more reflexive human rights debate that engages with the diaspora of experiences in order to offer a more responsive range of principles, policy and practice options.

In the final chapter of the section, Chris Cunneen, Melanie Schwartz, Julie Stubbs, David Brown and Courtney Young discuss the relationship between justice reinvestment, social justice and human rights. They suggest that that there needs to be a fundamental shift in the way that we think about reducing crime and prison populations, towards a position that is more responsive to the needs of vulnerable and marginalized communities, especially those communities where high numbers of individuals are recycled in and out of custody. Using a comparative study of the United States and Australia, they argue that current justice reinvestment strategies that only focus on cost savings and actuarial understandings of 'smart justice' will do little to address the underlying causes of crime. It is only by adopting positive social justice and human rights informed agendas that address gendered and racialized social and public policies, that justice reinvestment can achieve its real potential.

As this section demonstrates the connections between human rights, peacemaking and social justice are not straightforward. They are complex in the sense that not only are they complicated, but they are also holistically intertwined and their articulation is shaped by global and local social, political and economic factors. The authors have also demonstrated how our criminological understanding of human rights is a work in progress especially when we move beyond the confines of civil and political rights.

# 22

# Human rights in situations of transitional justice

*Stephan Parmentier, Monica Aciru, Huma Saeed and Mina Rauschenbach*

## Introduction

Many observers consider the twentieth century as the bloodiest and cruellest in human history, at least to judge by the sheer numbers of casualties. The past couple of decades have indeed witnessed numerous situations of extreme violence that have generated massive numbers of victims and often implicated many perpetrators. The following examples of atrocities committed in the past 50 years, and by no means an exhaustive list, are engrained in human conscience: the killing fields in Cambodia, the genocides in Guatemala and Rwanda, the ethnic cleansings in the former Yugoslavia, the ethnic-religious conflicts in East Timor, the Apartheid regime in South Africa, and successive civil wars in the Democratic Republic of Congo. Each of these situations has resulted in several tens of thousands of people killed, tortured and mutilated, disappeared, and many more seeking refuge from these horrors. Going further back into the former century, two world wars have resulted in many millions killed, wounded and families shattered and relocated. The start of the twenty-first century is not likely to fundamentally change this grim picture, at least not when looking at some of the most salient ongoing war situations in Afghanistan, Iraq and Syria, as well as violent conflicts in other parts of the world.

In some cases, political regime changes have taken place and new elites have replaced the old ones, while other conflicts leave little room or imagination for change. Whatever the exact origins and routes for change, new elites and new regimes are all facing the challenge of 'transitional justice' (henceforth TJ), namely how to deal with the aftermath of serious human rights violations, international crimes and violent conflict in general. Discussing and clarifying the relationship between human rights and TJ constitutes the central objective of this chapter. This is particularly important in a volume that is composed from a criminological perspective. We will first present the core concept of TJ and then discuss its four main pillars with frequent reference to human rights. We also briefly include the two cases of Sierra Leone and Afghanistan to demonstrate how TJ is discussed and implemented in concrete contexts.

## Transitional justice: origins and aspects

Although the practice of addressing serious human rights violations of the past has some pedigree in history, the very notion of TJ started to emerge in the mid-1990s only, some years after the fall of the Berlin wall, a period of the twentieth century that drastically changed the outlook of the modern world. Just before the turn of the millennium, the 1998 Rome Statute establishing the International Criminal Court turned some of these human rights violations into crimes of an international nature. And the key report of the then Secretary-General Annan to the United Nations (UN) Security Council (2004, para. 8) coined the term transitional justice as 'the full range of processes and mechanisms associated with a society's attempts to come to terms with a legacy of large-scale past abuses, in order to ensure accountability, serve justice and achieve reconciliation'.

Teitel (2000) has been among the first to argue that TJ is commonly seen as encompassing four major pillars: (1) criminal prosecutions, (2) truth commissions, (3) victim reparation programmes, and (4) institutional reforms. In her view, each of these pillars corresponds to a specific type of justice: (1) criminal justice, (2) historical justice, (3) reparatory justice, and (4) administrative justice. What is crystal clear is that TJ mechanisms are deemed to address legacies of serious and massive human rights abuses and engage the responsibilities of states, while some of them also amount to international crimes that involve the responsibilities of individuals. According to the Secretary-General's report (2004) the ultimate aim of TJ is to let the rule of law prevail in the long run.

In the past 20 years, TJ has been developed side by side with the legal and policy framework to fight impunity for serious violations of human rights law and international humanitarian law. Rooted in the pioneering work of international experts Joinet (UN Commission 1997) and Orentlicher (UN Commission 2005), the UN Human Rights Commission (currently Human Rights Council) adopted the most recent Set of Principles to Combat Impunity in 2005. These principles include (1) the right to know – for individuals and society – about violations committed in the past, (2) the right to justice – that is, to bring the offenders before a criminal judge, and (3) the right to reparation for victims of the harm inflicted upon them. The ultimate goal of these principles is to 'assist states in strengthening their domestic capacity to combat all aspects of impunity' (UN Commission 2005, para. 4).

The following paragraphs contain a brief overview of the four main pillars of TJ, with links to human rights and criminology.

## *Criminal prosecutions*

The first pillar commonly associated with TJ is comprised of criminal prosecutions of the offenders involved in committing the crimes. For a long time, roughly until the mid-twentieth century, the dominant strategy of states for dealing with very serious human rights violations, like genocide, widespread killings, and torture, was not to do anything and move on, thus making total impunity the rule rather than the exception. After World War 2, the Nuremburg and Tokyo trials constituted the first major attempts to prosecute and sentence the crimes committed or condoned by a previous regime. The next 30 years witnessed the rapid development of international human rights standards and the corresponding monitoring bodies, including the 'duty for states to prosecute' serious human rights violations, but very little happened in practice in relation to such acts (Orentlicher 1991). A major step against impunity took place with the national criminal prosecutions of the senior personnel at the top of the Greek colonel's regime and the Argentinian military junta, in the mid-1970s and mid-1980s respectively. A second major step followed with the establishment of the two international tribunals by the UN Security Council to deal with the war crimes in ex-Yugoslavia (1993) and the genocide in Rwanda (1994). Meanwhile and mostly in the 1990s, various countries developed national criminal legislation establishing their 'universal jurisdiction' for serious crimes committed outside of their territory and by non-nationals (Slaughter 2006). TJ can thus be seen to refer to three main bodies of law – international humanitarian law, international human rights law and international criminal law. The tendencies to expand criminal justice responses demonstrate also a paradigm shift away from total impunity and towards a 'culture of accountability' for violations and crimes of an egregious nature.

Next to being heralded for reinstituting the rule of law and providing justice to victims, criminal prosecutions have also entailed many critiques (Weitekamp and Parmentier 2014). Some relate to legal issues, like the possible contradictions with the principle of non-retroactivity for crimes committed in the past, the difficulties of guaranteeing the independence and impartiality of police, judges and lawyers, and the lack of capacity of weakened criminal justice systems to deal with massive numbers of crimes, offenders and victims within a reasonable period of time. Other issues are of a political nature, including the continuing power and sometimes threats of the old political and military national elites, and the highly selective character of national and international tribunals to prosecute former enemies and losers of wars and violent conflicts. Finally, also cultural issues arise, like the strong focus on offenders at the expense of victims, and the difficult balance between the western attachment to due process rules and local needs for stability and reconciliation.

### *Truth commissions*

The second main mechanism of TJ relates to truth-seeking initiatives and most frequently refers to the work of truth commissions. These commissions are non-judicial in nature and therefore do not intend to establish the criminal or civil responsibility of individuals or states, but instead focus on highlighting the 'truth' about violations or crimes of the past and acknowledging the suffering of the victims. In terms of combatting impunity, truth commissions contribute primarily to 'the right to know' for victims and society at large, as well as to 'historical justice'. They are not directly engaged in criminal prosecutions and sentences (although they can sometimes 'name names' of responsible persons or have the power to refer cases to a prosecutorial service), nor involved in reparations for victims (although they can issue recommendations for victim reparations and sometimes provide limited reparations themselves). They are sometimes viewed as prime examples of a restorative justice approach.

In order for a body to be considered a truth commission, Hayner has argued that a number of key features need to be present. In her widely accepted definition, a truth commission: (1) is concerned with past events, not present ones; (2) investigates patterns of events, rather than individual events, over a certain period of time; (3) is engaged in a direct and broad manner with the people that are affected, and collects information about their perceptions and needs; (4) is not a permanent but a temporary body that is supposed to produce a final report; and (5) enjoys the support and/or the powers provided by the state being investigated (Hayner 2011). As a result, truth commissions are different from other truth-seeking initiatives, such as non-governmental human rights investigations, human rights commissions, human rights complaint procedures and state reports on human rights practices (Freeman 2006).

Over 40 truth commissions have been established and relate to quite diverse types of human rights violations and international crimes. Most of them were established in countries of the Global South and carried different names depending on their focus. Commissions that stand out were the Truth and Reconciliation Commission in South Africa, the Commission for Historical Clarification in Guatemala, the Truth and Reconciliation Commission in Peru, the Commission for Reception, Truth and Reconciliation in Timor Leste, and the Equity and Reconciliation Commission in Morocco (Hayner 2011). More recently, similar commissions have dealt with the human rights abuses against Indigenous peoples in Canada and the US, and racial riots in the US. The model of a truth commission is thus flexible and can easily be adapted to the concrete context at hand.

### *Reparations for victims*

The third 'pillar' of TJ relates to reparations for victims of violations of human rights and humanitarian law or international crimes. For a long time in international law only the duty of states to repair the harm to victims (physical or legal persons and states) was firmly established. With the advent of universal and regional human rights frameworks came the gradual recognition by international monitoring bodies and regional courts of the subjective and enforceable 'right to reparation' for individual victims (de Greiff 2006, de Feyter et al. 2005). In 2005, the UN General Assembly adopted the Basic Principles and Guidelines (BPG) on the Right to a Remedy and Reparation for Victims of Gross Violations of International Human Rights Law and Serious Violations of International Humanitarian Law.

These principles, although non-binding, collected for the first time all existing standards in relation to victim reparations. They also clearly list the five main categories of victim reparations (UN General Assembly 2005): (1) restitution (of property or rights) in order to bring victims back into the position *ex ante* – that is, before their rights were violated; (2) compensation – that is, financial reimbursement for all kinds of damage (physical, material, and emotional); (3) rehabilitation, including medical and psychological assistance, as well as legal and social services; (4) satisfaction, a very broad category encompassing the search for victims' remains and facilities for reburials; organizing memorial services for victims, or arranging public apologies; and even legal and administrative sanctions for those responsible for the violations. In our own work, we have explored people's perceptions in Bosnia and Serbia about these categories of victim reparations (Parmentier et al. 2009, Parmentier et al. 2014).

The fifth and last category of victim reparations relates to 'guarantees of non-repetition', the central idea of which is to avoid similar violent conflicts, violations and crimes in the future, or to provide 'administrative justice'. This category refers to institutional reforms, both of state institutions deemed responsible for the violations and crimes (including military, intelligence services, police, courts, prisons) and of other institutional settings (such as education, health, media). Because this category is part of the Basic Principles and Guidelines, it is discussed within this framework and not as a separate fourth mechanism of TJ following the most common definitions mentioned above.

## The case of Sierra Leone: striking a balance between international human rights standards and local realities

Between 1991 and 2002, Sierra Leone was caught up in a violent conflict that brought the country to its knees and the devastating effects of which were felt on all fronts. It destroyed families and communities, particularly through displacements, killings, mutilations, sexual violence, and the ruthless practice of abductions of children to use as child combatants. The war also made the country ungovernable and reinforced the already widespread poverty and other social imbalances. None of the institutions were working properly and various rebel factions and warlords engaged in combat with the government and other external forces for control (Hayner 2007).

The events leading to the cessation of hostilities, re-establishing normalcy and pursuing redress for the human rights violations in Sierra Leone reflects the complexity of upholding international human rights standards in conflict and post-conflict situations. This often involves many compromises, concessions and sometimes coercion. In Sierra Leone, a series of mechanisms were implemented to first of all bring the war to an end and get the country running, a dilemma which gave rise to the peace versus justice discourse and secondly, to ensure redress for the victims.

### Peace vs. justice: peace agreements and amnesties

While the war was still raging, a key priority for some key actors – both local and international – was to bring the war to an end and stop the various factions from engaging in further combat. The situation was even more precarious because the government forces were not militarily strong enough to suppress the rebel groups, much of the country was already under the control of rebel forces, and military support from the Economic Community of West African States Monitoring Group was under threat of being withdrawn (Hayner 2007).

In the course of nearly 20 years, three peace agreements saw the light of day. The first was drawn up in Abidjan (Ivory Coast) in 1996 and signed between the government and the Revolutionary United Front (RUF). A prominent feature of the Abidjan Peace Accord was the amnesty clause (Article 14), which ensured that 'no official or judicial action is taken against any members of RUF/SL'. It further guaranteed the full restoration of the civil and political rights and protection of former RUF/SL combatants, exiles and other persons outside the country because of reasons related to armed conflict. In addition, a clause on disarmament, demobilization and reintegration of all combatants (Article 5-8) further afforded protection for the combatants. This peace deal has been criticized as being one-sided, mainly in favour of the combatants (Bangura 1997) and involving one rebel group despite the presence of other fighters (Gberie 2000). Despite falling apart rapidly, Gberie asserts that one of the significant contributions of this accord was the recognition of human rights law and humanitarian law, which played key roles in the subsequent peace agreements. Notably Articles 19, 20 and 21 sought to observe basic civil and political rights, established a national commission on human rights and upheld to respect the principles and rules of international humanitarian law. Following a coup in 1997, a second peace agreement, the Conakry peace plan (Guinea) maintained similar principles as the previous accord and called for amnesties as well as DDR (disarmament, demobilization and reintegration) programmes for the combatants.

The most well-known agreement, the Lomé Peace Agreement (Togo) sparked the peace and justice debate. It was widely assumed that a blanket amnesty and pardon were crucial to bringing the war to an end. This, however, was met with disapproval, particularly from those seeking to uphold international standards of justice. Article IX called for blanket pardon and amnesty, as well as legislative and other measures necessary to guarantee immunity with the aim of bringing 'lasting peace to Sierra Leone'. The clause, however, did not go down well with the UN position on amnesty for serious international crimes, leading the UN Representative to add a disclaimer against amnesty for crimes of genocide, crimes against humanity, war crimes and other serious violations of international humanitarian law (UN Security Council 1999). This precarious position reinforced the notion of adherence to international human rights standards in times of transition and sent out a clear message on the intolerance of impunity for such crimes. In the end, the Lomé Peace Agreement was progressive in that it sought to capture the concerns of various stakeholders and it became an important element in the development of the practice of TJ in Sierra Leone.

### Measures for redress

Following the peace agreements several mechanisms of TJ were set up in Sierra Leone, each bearing strongly the influence of international human rights norms.

## The Special Court for Sierra Leone (SCSL)

Despite the UN disclaimer in the Lomé Peace Agreement, no real efforts towards any criminal prosecution of perpetrators were undertaken. However, the tension and unrest in the subsequent months prompted the government to make a request to the UN to establish a special court in order to try Foday Sankoh, one of the key players, as well as other individuals. The court began its operations in 2002 and only targeted those bearing the greatest responsibility, totalling 13 persons. Despite sending forth a clear message that international crimes cannot be tolerated, some of the criticisms levelled against the court are reflective of the difficulty of balancing human rights ideals and local realities in post-conflict societies. A particularly sore point has been the amount of money allocated to the Special Court against the backdrop of a situation of widespread poverty and a cash-strapped government. The special court had an estimated annual budget of about $30 million a year and the office of the prosecutor's annual budget of $4 million was more than the budget of the Sierra Leone Supreme Court (Gberie 2014). Furthermore, critiques were levelled against the offender focus of the court. Our own empirical study carried out in Freetown in 2011 and 2012 illustrated that none of the respondents disputed the significance of the SCSL, but they viewed it as not being relevant to the local needs of the moment (Aciru n.d.). Recalling the substantial DDR programmes between 1998 and 2002, they viewed it as favouring issues of perpetrators over those of victims and national development.

## The Truth and Reconciliation Commission (TRC)

Emanating from the Lomé Peace Agreement (Article XXVI), the TRC was viewed as a victim-centred approach for facilitating national reconciliation and the consolidation of peace. The commission considered itself as promoting 'the inalienable right to truth' (TRC Report 2004, Volume 1). It operated from 2002 to 2004 alongside the Special Court. In spite of the logistical, funding, staffing and scathing public opinion challenges, it produced an exhaustive report that detailed victims' testimonies, overall findings regarding the causes, development and responsibility for the war and more importantly, comprehensive recommendations for reform, redress and reconciliation. What emerged strongly from our own empirical study with regards to the truth commission body in Sierra Leone was the lack of continuity (Aciru n.d.). Respondents strongly questioned the purpose of flaunting the truth if there was to be nothing done about it. More so, this raises practical questions about the mandate of truth commissions, particularly their operational period whereby they function for a specific duration and then close up shop.

## Reparations for victims

A significant aspect of the TRC was the recommendations on reparation for victims. It not only reiterated the 'right to an effective remedy' for violations of human rights but also emphasized the position and needs of victims in post-conflict situations. These measures included proposals on health, pensions, education, skills training and micro credit, community and symbolic reparations, all issues identified by victims as important to their quality of life, but also according to the commissioners, mirroring the national development agenda. This service-oriented approach has achieved among other objectives the recontextualization of reparation and has fuelled debates on its meaning and content (Roht-Arriaza and Orlovsky 2009, Carranza 2009).

## Institutional reforms

A number of reforms in Sierra Leone were carried out prior to the truth commission recommendations. These reforms aimed at facilitating economic growth, good governance, rule of law and sustainable peace. The TRC recommendations further reinforced these reforms by specifying institutional and legal improvements in order to address the underlying causes of the conflict. A number of these recommendations were imperative, particularly those concerning fundamental rights and freedoms (TRC Report 2004, Volume 2). In principle, these reforms sought to reinforce Sierra Leone's adherence to international human rights standards.

### *Lessons learnt*

'*He who pays the piper calls the tune.*' This common idiom was often used in Sierra Leone to describe the relationship between the various actors and how the decisions taken by the government, civil society and even individuals were not pursued in isolation, but involved compromises between various actors. For instance, questions have been raised about the notion of human rights, rule of law or democratization as espoused by the international actors, and what they really mean on the ground. While the push for a truth commission has been described as an embodiment of the right to truth, empirical studies done by Shaw (2007) and Millar (2010) showed that local alternative memory initiatives were not easily identifiable within the truth commission paradigm. In contrast, the most 'successful' mechanism of TJ appears to have been the Special Court, which finished its activities in 2013 and treated 13 cases.

The case of Sierra Leone also constitutes a typical illustration of the difficulties to translate objectives into action, particularly for non-legally binding proposals. More than 10 years after the truth commission came to an end, victims are still waiting for the reparations to be carried out. In 2010, many other TRC recommendations had been stalled or had not been implemented at all. This raises the notion of the ability and willingness to effect change by the responsible actors. It has, for example, been argued that the timely implementation of the DDR programme for perpetrators, which amounted to less than half the number of victims, was due to the military and political threat the former posed to the government. Victims on the other hand remained largely harmless and their demands could therefore be deferred.

## The case of Afghanistan: an anomaly in the transitional justice discourse

A country in turmoil for almost four decades, where human rights of any shades and colours have been committed, Afghanistan remains an anomaly in the TJ discourse, which argues that TJ has become a norm in post-conflict contexts. Not so much because the country is not fit to have one or more mechanisms of TJ, but more likely due to the reluctance of political actors to launch any serious initiative(s) both from the part of national and international actors. Yet, the situation on the ground as well as empirical research (Saeed n.d.) indicate that it will be difficult for the country and its people to move forward unless it deals with its past – and current – human rights abuses, including socioeconomic rights violations considered here as a form of economic crime.

### *Decades of violent conflict . . .*

Afghanistan has been suffering from war and widespread atrocities since April 1978, when a Soviet-backed *coup d'état* ended the relative calm period of President Daud rule. Following a period of mass disappearances and killings of the opposition by the then Soviet-backed regime in Kabul, the 1979 Soviet Union invasion turned the country into a battlefield between the two superpowers of the time. Apart from the widespread Afghan resistance, the colossal support to the Islamist groups, commonly referred to as the Mujahedeen, by the US, Saudi Arabia, Pakistan, Iran and other countries, eventually turned Afghanistan into the Soviet Union's 'Vietnam'. During this period, hundreds of thousands disappeared or were killed and millions fled the country, making Afghans the largest single refugee population in the world until the recent crisis in Syria.

The 10-year long battle, that left deep physical and emotional scars on the nation, was followed by a bloody civil war in 1992 among the militias and factions (the Mujahedeen) who survived and thrived on the foreign funds during the previous conflict against the Soviet Union and the regime in Kabul led by President Najibullah. The factional war for power destroyed all but the capital city, killing over sixty thousand people and plunging its inhabitants in a reign of plunder, rape and terror. While this period further entrenched war and violence in a society already wounded, it was not the end of the game. In 1996, the oppressive regime of the Taliban came to power until their removal, through a US-led intervention, in 2001. Shortly after this period, a window of opportunity was opened, which led many Afghans to think that war and their miseries would end (Rubin 2003). However, despite the heavy presence of the international community, or some may argue because of it, the security situation has deteriorated since 2006, which has further complicated TJ efforts (Kouvo 2009).

## *... without transitional justice*

As discussed, multiple regimes, each supported by foreign powers and their proxies, have ruled Afghanistan in the past 40 years. While each government has been responsible for massive atrocities and the destruction of the country, no accountability mechanism has ever been established to address past crimes. On the contrary, during every transition, which has often involved an agreement to lead to the next phase of short term peace and stability, the question of demanding accountability and justice has been ignored, leading to the further entrenchment of a culture of impunity (Mani 2003).

As regards to TJ measures, in 2005, an Action Plan for Peace, Reconciliation and Justice was adopted by the Afghan Government, the UN Assistance Mission to Afghanistan and the Afghanistan Independent Human Rights Commission (AIHRC). The Action Plan identified five key components, including truth-seeking, symbolic measures, accountability mechanisms involving vetting procedures, institutional reform, and reconciliation. Furthermore, it emphatically rejected amnesty provisions, stating that neither Islam nor international law allows amnesty for gross violations of human rights, including crimes against humanity. Although an important document containing significant measures in theory, in practice very little, if anything at all, was achieved before the three-year timeline mandate of the Action Plan expired in March 2009 (Winterbotham 2010). This was primarily due to fierce opposition from within the Afghan parliament and important sectors of the Administration. In March 2007, the parliament passed the Amnesty Law (officially published in 2009) that ensured a blanket amnesty for all perpetrators of human rights abuses of the past regimes, thus turning impunity into law (Kouvo 2010). Moreover, while much important work of documentation has been undertaken, including an 800-page conflict mapping report by the AIHRC, nothing has officially been released for fear of retaliation from the warlords and of further escalation.

Arguably, one of the causes of a deteriorating human rights situation in Afghanistan, despite billions of dollars in international aid as well as other types of support during the past decade, has its origins in the lack of responses to its past. As a result, those accused of human rights violations continue to thrive, as does the culture of impunity. In its 2014 World Report, in the section on Afghanistan (p. 286), Human Rights Watch stated: 'Impunity for abuses was the norm for government security forces and other armed groups'. One of the consequences of an entrenched culture of impunity has been the fact that the country is plunged into endemic corruption where economic crimes of various types constitute a daily occurrence, including land grabbing briefly discussed here. It is, therefore, argued in this part that any mechanism of TJ that may be implemented sometime in the future must deal with such crimes as well.

Carranza (2008, p. 310) defines economic crimes as 'offenses committed by both state and non-state actors that may constitute violations of the human rights enumerated in the International Covenant on Economic, Social and Cultural Rights'. According to this definition, violations of the right to housing, which is included under the right to adequate standard of living in the international human rights documents, has been one of the salient features of the Afghan conflict in its various forms. A considerable number of people have lost home and property either due to bombardments, or as Internally Displaced Persons or refugees, who, upon return, could no longer access their property. During the past decade, however, a prominent feature of the economic crimes landscape has been land-grabbing, which has been facilitated by a weak and failed state with no questions of demanding accountability. Massive amounts of public and private lands have been confiscated by warlords, government officials, Members of Parliament and others in power across the country. At best, they have attempted to present forged documents to claim ownership. In many cases, however, strategic lands were grabbed by forcing the actual owner(s) to leave the property, often at gunpoint. Despite this vicious surge, thus far there has been no accountability mechanism to address this phenomenon. After all, in the absence of any TJ measures, implementing an accountability mechanism to deal with land grabbing – and other types of economic crimes – would amount to the Afghan saying 'putting rabbits in charge of carrots'.

### *And the future?*

As mentioned above, TJ has traditionally addressed civil and political rights violations. However, over decades, there has been a shift in the application, scope and goals of the field (de Greiff 2009, Sharp 2014, Teitel 2003). Teitel argues that not only has the discourse moved from the periphery to the centre, but also its scope has broadened from its historically legal approach, associated with 'extraordinary post-conflict conditions' to becoming a commonplace experience for many post-conflict transitions during recent years. Therefore, the domain of TJ application has moved from its 'original context' – societies emerging from authoritarianism – to societies coming out of conflict (de Greiff 2009, p. 30). This shift in the understanding of TJ is important for its future orientation, particularly considering the current crisis in the Middle East and elsewhere, of which Afghanistan is but one. Moreover, the context and nature of a number of these conflicts increasingly signal a need for post-conflict mechanisms that will address socioeconomic rights violations and economic crimes, and not just civil and political rights violations.

## Human rights, transitional justice and criminology: towards an interplay

The above cases make clear that the field of TJ encompasses a wide array of human rights issues. It can be argued that TJ and human rights constitute a double bind: (a) on the one hand, TJ deals with the aftermath of serious human rights violations, some of which amount to international crimes; (b) on the other hand, human rights are present throughout TJ policies and mechanisms, and particularly in criminal prosecutions, truth commissions and victim reparation systems.

It should be noted that the vast majority of TJ research has and still is focused on the violations of civil and political rights (for example, right to life, freedom from torture and enforced disappearances), or crimes against the physical and moral integrity of the person (such as murder and attempted murder, and rape). Also criminal prosecutions and victim reparations tend to be concerned with this type of rights violations, if not exclusively at least predominantly. However, the early origins of violent conflicts can frequently be traced back to situations of inequality, inadequate distribution of resources, racism, and other forms of social and political exclusion. The latter relate primarily to violations of economic, social, and cultural rights and related crimes like corruption, which have received very little attention in TJ studies (Carranza 2008). Only truth commissions, with varying degrees of insight and depth, have paid some attention to the root causes of civil unrest and violent conflict. Therefore, the paradigm of human rights, with its several 'baskets' or 'generations' of human rights, can become very inspirational to expand and enrich the field of TJ.

The relationship between TJ and criminology on the other hand is quite different. As the examples in this chapter demonstrate, although criminology can easily be considered as the discipline specializing in criminal behaviour, and the respective roles of offenders and victims, it is nearly completely absent from the area of international crimes and TJ. Some older theories in criminology include insights that can be relevant, such as anomie and rebellion (Merton), neutralization techniques (Sykes and Matza), political crimes (Turk), state crimes (Chambliss), and 'taking crime seriously' (Lea) (Parmentier and Weitekamp 2007). Overall, however, there is still a 'missing link' (Parmentier 2011) in the field, which is even more striking as international crimes are very serious in nature, tend to produce massive numbers of victims and often involve many perpetrators as well.

At the same time, many changes are underway in criminology to devote more attention to the field of international crimes. In the early years of the new millennium criminologists have advocated for a stronger place of criminology in international criminal justice, not only to analyse the establishment and operation of international criminal justice institutions, but also introduce the many insights of criminology on crimes, offenders and victims (Roberts and McMillan 2003). The past decade has witnessed the rapid emergence of a 'criminology of genocide' (Hagan et al. 2005, Woolford 2006) aimed at gaining a deeper understanding of the root causes and mechanics of genocide, but also of the modes of reaction by national and international actors. Furthermore, some criminologists have argued in favour of a 'bottom-up' approach to understanding international crimes and transitional justice (McEvoy and McGregor 2008). Finally, criminology is also host to various studies about different models of justice in transitional or post-conflict settings. Next to institutions of retributive justice, increasing attention is paid to mechanisms of restorative justice in situations of transition (Parmentier et al. 2009). And most recent reflections refer to 'transformative justice' aiming at treating causes of conflicts rather than symptoms and emphasizing the reformulation of power structures in conflict and post-conflict societies (Gready and Robins 2014). While still very tentative, these endeavours seem quite promising routes for future research, and by entering them criminology will be able to take up these challenges and resume its central role at the crossroads of disciplines.

## References

Aciru, M., n.d. *Transitional justice in practice: truth commissions and policies of victim reparations*. Leuven: Faculty of Law, Leuven Institute of Criminology (doctoral research ongoing since 2010).

Bangura, Y., 1997. Reflections on the Sierra Leone Peace Accord. *African Journal of International Affairs*, 1(1), 57–78.

Carranza, R., 2008. Plunder and pain: should transitional justice engage with corruption and economic crimes? *International Journal of Transitional Justice*, 2(3), 310–30.

Carranza, R., 2009. *The right to reparations in situations of poverty*. New York, NY: International Center for Transitional Justice.

Communiqué issued at Conakry on 23 October 1997 at the conclusion of the meeting between the Ministers of Foreign Affairs of the Committee of Five on Sierra Leone of the Economic Community of West African States and the delegation representing Major Johnny Paul Koromah. Retrieved on 10 December 2015 from: http://allafrica.com/download/resource/main/main/idatcs/00010134:fedb598070ce399032d0cecdd3ca45e8.pdf.

de Feyter, K., Parmentier, S., Bossuyt, M. and Lemmens, P. (eds), 2005. *Out of the ashes: reparation for victims of gross and systematic human rights violations*. Antwerp/Oxford: Intersentia Publishers.

de Greiff, P., 2006. *The handbook of reparations*. Oxford: Oxford University Press.

de Greiff, P., (2009) Articulating the links between transitional justice and development: justice and social integration. *In*: P. de Greiff and R. Duthie (eds), *Transitional justice and development: making connections*. New York, NY: Social Science Research Council, 28–75.

Freeman, M., 2006. *Truth commissions and procedural fairness*. Cambridge: Cambridge University Press.

Gberie, L., 2000. First stages on the road to peace: the Abidjan Process (1995–96). *In*: L. David (ed.), *Paying the price: the Sierra Leone peace process*. Conciliation Resources, September. Retrieved on 10 December 2015 from: www.c-r.org.

Gberie, L., 2014. The Special Court for Sierra Leone rests – for good. *Africa Renewal*, April. Retrieved on 10 December 2014 from: www.un.org/africarenewal/magazine/april-2014/special-court-sierra-leone-rests-%E2%80%93-good.

Gready, P. and Robins, S., 2014. From transitional to transformative justice: a new agenda for practice. *International Journal of Transitional Justice*, 8, 339–61.

Hagan, J., Rymond-Richmond, W. and Parker, P., 2005. The criminology of genocide: the death and rape of Darfur. *Criminology*, 43(3), 525–62.

Hayner, P., 2007. *Negotiating peace in Sierra Leone: confronting the justice challenge*. Geneva/New York: Centre for Humanitarian Dialogue and International Center for Transitional Justice, December 2007. Retrieved on 6 April 2016 from: http://www.hdcentre.org/uploads/tx_news/90NegotiatingpeaceinSierraLeone-ConfrontingtheJusticechallenge.pdf.

Hayner, P., 2011. *Unspeakable truths: transitional justice and the challenge of truth commissions*, 2nd edn. New York, NY: Routledge.

Human Rights Watch, 2014. *World report 2014: events of 2013*. Retrieved on 6 April 2016 from: http://www.hrw.org/sites/default/files/wr2014_web_0.pdf.

Kouvo, S., 2009. *Transitional justice in the context of ongoing conflict: the case of Afghanistan*. New York, NY: International Center for Transitional Justice.

Kouvo, S., 2010. After two years in legal limbo: a first glance at the approved 'Amnesty law'. *Afghanistan Analysts Network*. Retrieved on 29 August 2010 from: www.aan-afghanistan.org/index.asp?id=665.

Mani, R., 2003. *Ending impunity and building justice in Afghanistan*. Kabul: Afghanistan Research and Evaluation Unit.

McEvoy, K. and McGregor, L., 2008. Transitional justice from below: an agenda for research, policy and praxis. *In*: K. McEvoy and L. McGregor (eds), *Transitional justice from below: grassroots activism and the struggle for change*. London/Oxford: Hart, 1–14.

Millar, G., 2010. Assessing local experiences of truth-telling in Sierra Leone: getting to 'why' through a qualitative case study analysis. *International Journal of Transitional Justice*, 4, 477–96.

Orentlicher, D., 1991. Settling accounts: the duty to prosecute human rights violations of a prior regime. *Yale Law Journal*, 100(8), 2537–615.

Parmentier, S., 2011. The missing link: criminological perspectives on dealing with the past and transitional justice. *In*: M. Bosworth and C. Hoyle (eds), *What is criminology?* Oxford: Oxford University Press, 380–92.

Parmentier, S. and Weitekamp, E., 2007. Political crimes and serious violations of human rights: towards a criminology of international crimes. *In*: S. Parmentier and E. Weitekamp (eds), *Crime and human rights*, Series in Sociology of Crime, Law and Deviance, vol. 9. Amsterdam/Oxford: Elsevier/JAI Press, 109–44.

Parmentier, S., Rauschenbach, M. and Weitekamp, E., 2014. Repairing the harm of victims after violent conflict: empirical findings from Serbia. Special issue on celebrating the 20th anniversary, edited by J. Shapland and J. Sloan. *International Review of Victimology*, 20(1), 85–99.

Parmentier, S., Valiñas, M. and Weitekamp, E., 2009. How to repair the harm after violent conflict in Bosnia? Results of a population-based survey. *Netherlands Quarterly of Human Rights*, 27(1), 27–44.

*Peace Agreement between the Government of the Republic of Sierra Leone and the Revolutionary United Front of Sierra Leone*, signed at Abidjan on 30 November 1996. Retrieved on 10 December 2015 from: www.usip.org/publications/peace-agreements-sierra-leone.

Roberts, P. and McMillan, N., 2003. For criminology in international criminal justice. *Journal of International Criminal Justice*, 1(2), 315–38.

Roht-Arriaza, N. and Orlovsky, K., 2009. A complementary relationship: reparations and development. *In*: P. de Greiff and R. Duthie (eds), *Transitional justice and development: making connections*. New York, NY: Social Science Research Council, 170–213.

Rubin, B., 2003. Transitional justice and human rights in Afghanistan. *International Affairs*, 79(3), 567–81.

Saeed, H., n.d. *Transitional justice and criminology: making connections through the study of state crime in Afghanistan*. Leuven: Faculty of Law, Leuven Institute of Criminology (doctoral research ongoing since 2012).

Sharp, D.N., 2014. Economic violence in the practice of African truth commissions and beyond. *In*: D.N. Sharp (ed.), *Justice and economic violence in transition*. New York, NY: Springer, 79–107.

Shaw, R., 2007. Memory frictions: localizing the truth and reconciliation commission in Sierra Leone. *International Journal of Transitional Justice*, 1, 183–207.

Slaughter, A.M., 2006. Defining the limits: universal jurisdiction and the national courts. *In*: S. Ratner (ed.), *Universal jurisdiction: national courts and the prosecution of serious crimes under international law*. Philadelphia, PA: University of Pennsylvania Press, 168–92.

Teitel, R., 2000. *Transitional justice*. Oxford: Oxford University Press.

Teitel, R., 2003. Transitional justice genealogy. *Harvard Human Rights Journal*, 16, 69–95.

Truth and Reconciliation Commission of Sierra Leone, 2004. *Witness to truth: report of the Sierra Leone Truth and Reconciliation Commission*, 4 volumes. Accra: TRC. Retrieved on 10 December 2015 from: www.usip.org/publications/truth-commission-sierra-leone.

United Nations [UN] General Assembly, 2005. *Basic principles and guidelines on the right to a remedy and reparation for victims of gross violations of international human rights law and serious violations of international humanitarian law*. UN Doc. A/RES/60/147, 16 December 2005 (also known as the BPG).

UN Commission on Human Rights, 1997. *Report of the Independent Expert on the Set of Principles to Combat Impunity*. New York, NY: United Nations, Commission on Human Rights, E/CN.4/Sub.2/1997/20/Rev.1, 2 October 1997 (also known as the Joinet Report).

UN Commission on Human Rights, 2005. *Report of the Independent Expert to Update the Set of Principles to Combat Impunity*. New York, NY: United Nations, Human Rights Council, E/CN.4/2005/102, 18 February 2005 (also known as the Orentlicher Report). Retrieved on 16 April 2016 from: www.refworld.org/docid/42d66e7a0.html.

UN Security Council, 1999. *Seventh report of the Secretary-General on the United States observer mission in Sierra Leone*. S/1999/836, 30 July 1999.

UN Security Council, 2004. *The rule of law and transitional justice in conflict and post-conflict societies: report of the Secretary-General*. UN Doc. S/2004/616, 23 August 2004.

Weitekamp, E. and Parmentier, S., 2014. Restorative justice and state crime. *In*: D. Weisburd and G. Bruinsma (eds), *Encyclopedia of criminology and criminal justice*. New York, NY: Springer Verlag, 4430–46.

Winterbotham, E., 2010. *The state of transitional justice in Afghanistan: actors, approaches and challenges*. Kabul: Afghanistan Research and Evaluation Unit.

Woolford, A., 2006. Making genocide unthinkable: three guidelines for a critical criminology of genocide. *Critical Criminology*, 14(1), 87–106.

# 23

# The violence of war, the violence of peace

## Mining, conflict and social justice on Bougainville

*Kristian Lasslett*

## Introduction

The South Pacific island of Bougainville was the site of a protracted conflict that lasted from 1988 until 1997, in which time up to 20,000 lives were lost (see Lasslett 2014). An enduring end to hostilities was achieved in 2001 through the *Bougainville Peace Agreement*. This presaged a range of transitional mechanisms designed to heal community rifts, and rebuild both state and market institutions. As the island approaches a referendum over independence from Papua New Guinea, slated to take place between 2015 and 2020, the Bougainville peace process has been widely celebrated in the scholarly literature for its resounding achievements (see Braithwaite et al. 2010, Dinnen and Peake 2013, Wallis 2012).

One particular language group on Bougainville, the Nasioi have a special place of significance within the conflict and post-conflict period. It was their custodial lands that were most deeply impacted by a large-scale copper and gold mine (the Panguna mine) operated by the Rio Tinto subsidiary Bougainville Copper Limited (BCL) between 1972 and 1988 (see Ogan 1972, 1999). Furthermore, it was a Nasioi-led landowners' association which enacted a campaign of industrial sabotage against the mine that triggered a government counter-insurgency campaign.

This chapter focuses on the Nasioi experience of mining, conflict, mass atrocities and peace-making, drawing on primary data collected using both investigative and ethnographic methods. In particular, the findings presented here rest on 44 semi-structured interviews conducted with senior state-corporate personnel during 2005–06, which were triangulated with documentary research involving internal organizational records. Additionally, the author was part of an inter-cultural research team that conducted an empirical study with mine-affected communities, using biographical methods to explore personal experiences of mining and conflict. The latter research took place in 2013 and involved 82 participants from the mine-affected region of central Bougainville.

Drawing on this primary data, it will be suggested that from the vantage point of mine-affected communities, the orthodox sequencing of events on Bougainville, which distinguish between the pre-conflict (pre-1988), conflict (1988–97) and post-conflict (post-1997) periods, obscure a fundamental form of violence that spans all three. However, this violence, it will be contended, cannot be easily thought about by employing conventional categories of wrong doing focused on inter-personal harms. Rather, the violence inflicted on Nasioi communities, which is strongly linked to the Panguna mine, targets the structural content of local social systems – custom, land, spirituality, social relations, culture – which has profound consequences for their Indigenous membership who must either assimilate to alien social practices, or mount resistance.[1]

By framing violence this way, it becomes possible for transitional mechanisms with ostensibly laudable motives, to be conduits for a renewal of violence against the Nasioi, especially when antagonistic industrial vehicles are leaned upon to economically secure the peace. It will be concluded that social justice and peace-making can come into opposition in certain contexts, when the structural harms experienced by Indigenous peoples are ignored or misunderstood.

## Continuity and change for the Nasioi

The mine-affected region of central Bougainville is an expansive area, encompassing not only the mine pit itself, but also significant tracts of land directly impacted by the dumping of tailings and waste-rock, and ancillary mine infrastructure, including for instance roads, port facilities, townships, and a power station. This is a socially uneven landscape encompassing a range of different language groups with complex, differentiated histories. However, for heuristic purposes a number of generalizations can be made about Nasioi communities impacted by the mine.

First, flexible kinship networks are the principal social mechanism through which vital cultural assets are managed. Critically they provide individual community members with a social identity, attached to which are numerous fundamental rights, including to land, which is distributed on a matrilineal basis (Ogan 1972, Oliver 1991). As an agrarian based society, in possession of sophisticated farming techniques, land rights underpin social security for rural households. Mediating kinship bonds and agrarian production, is a complex system of customary norms, spiritual beliefs and ethical principles, in which the concept of motherhood has an important place (Hermkens 2007, Saovana-Spriggs 2007). Saovana-Spriggs (2007, p. 36) observes, 'women as the main custodians of the land' are 'central in many local contexts in opposing the encroachment of capitalist development and the associated ecological degradation of land and environment'.

Of course, Nasioi social structures should not be counterposed with individual members, as if two external entities which enter into relations on an accidental basis; rather, these social forms are inextricably bound together. The aforementioned structures of Nasioi society – which is the objective legacy of past generations – create the performative contexts in which new community members can realize their human potential in specific ways, facilitated by different bearers of cultural knowledge who are responsible for inducting children and young adults into society. Out of this performance based, inductive process, which is mediated by a range of practical and ceremonial duties, emerge forms of personhood marked by a profound lived connection with the land, surrounding ecosystems and clan, which are holistically bound together. This identity is also marked by a strong sense of responsibility towards custodial duties that will see the society's assets thrive for future generations.

Although a truncated summary of social structure, nonetheless, it hints at the rich, complex processes that differentiate these societies from those broadly constructed in a capitalist mould. The latter system operates through very different arrangements, out of which emerge personalities with motivations, principles and responsibilities that cannot be easily married with those prevailing in Nasioi societies. Up until the mine period these contrasting social worlds, and their agents, were not necessarily destined to enter into forms of confrontation that would presage conflict. That said, there have historically been critical forms of exchange between the two systems, with important social consequences that need to be noted.

The initiating agents for these historical exchanges are varied, ranging from missionaries through to colonial administrators and traders. Also, the impetus has not always been purely external; customary leaders and ambitious young men keen to elevate their status in rural society have appropriated social spaces created by these interfaces to accrue certain advantages (see Connell 1978, Donaldson and Good 1981, Ogan and Wesley-Smith 1992).

The changes triggered by these exchanges have proven socially significant. For example, cash cropping has expanded rapidly (albeit unevenly), across Bougainville from the 1960s onwards (Griffin 1990, Oliver 1991). As a result, land usage patterns have transformed, bringing forth relative land shortages and new competitive tensions (Mitchell 1976, Moulik 1977). The emergence of smallholder production for global markets has also cultivated a nascent bourgeoisie, who have helped to stimulate an Indigenous led process of assimilation into capitalist relations of reproduction (Connell 1978, MacWilliam 2005, Moulik 1977, Ogan 1972). Furthermore, there have been critical technical changes to the means of production and consumption, as a range of introduced technologies have been absorbed into rural life (Ogan 1999). Local customary norms too have been moulded in order to manage new processes, ambitions and tensions (see, for example, Tanis 2005).

However, for the Nasioi communities of central Bougainville, immersion into social arrangements congruent with the circulation of industrial capital has been an accelerated process, largely spearheaded by a range of powerful external actors committed to the Panguna mine, including colonial and postcolonial regimes, along with the mine operator BCL (Lasslett 2010, 2014). This rapid immersion, with the associated forms of assimilation it necessarily involves, has constituted for mine-affected Nasioi communities a profound form of structural violence that translates into feelings of alienation, dislocation and personal trauma for individual community members. In turn, such feelings have inspired resistance, which the state has countered with retributive violence. It is to this dynamic that we will now turn.

## The violence of mining

The initial impetus for large-scale mining on Bougainville can be traced back to the post-World War 2 shift in Australian colonial policy towards Papua New Guinea. Until then Australia had maintained a skeletal administration, with little investment in local infrastructure or capacity. The post-war era saw a greater urgency in Australian colonial policy with respect to state-building and market growth (Denoon 1985, Hawksley 2006). Initially, the latter aim precipitated a raft of policies and stimulus measures directed towards smallholder cash-cropping, alongside the maintenance of existing plantation estates. However, when colonial geologists noted the commercial viability of a significant low-grade copper and gold deposit in Bougainville's Crown Prince Ranges, Australian state-building efforts in Papua New Guinea vigorously turned to this prospective large-scale mining venture, which it believed could significantly increase internal revenue flows.

When the Anglo-Australian mining conglomerate, Conzinc Rio Tinto of Australia (CRA), signalled its willingness to spearhead the venture, the colonial regime pushed ahead despite widespread opposition from customary landowners (Denoon 2000). The Australian Minister for Territories, Charles Barnes, justified his government's decision, explaining 'economic development is essential to sustain political and social development. . . . The mineral resources of Bougainville provide probably the most significant single prospect of development in this field' (Barnes 1967). As local opposition grew, the Minister became more hostile. In a report featured in *The Canberra Times* (13 August 1969) Barnes warned, 'the people of the Territory had a choice of whether to drift in a primitive and backward situation depending on the generosity of the Australian taxpayer, or to advance as a modern State financed by its own resources'.

In this social context, the challenge became one of neutralizing or containing local resistance, while investing in forums that could help win consent from influential local leaders. As the Assistant District Commissioner for Bougainville noted, 'the problem is now to change the attitude of the people – for their own good' (Redmon 1966). To that end, extensive efforts were plumbed into advertising the benefits of mining to sceptical landowners. However, in the face of enduring opposition, riot squads were eventually flown to the island in 1969 to disperse and arrest resisters (Denoon 2000). Australia's Minister for Territories opined, 'in the structure of ignorance, superstition and prejudice, persuasion and explanation are not easy' (cited in *The Canberra Times* 13 August 1969).

The Panguna mine eventually opened in 1972 and operated for 17 years. When it was shut down in 1988, the mine was responsible for 24 per cent of Papua New Guinea's internal revenue (Namaliu 1995). Alongside growth in agriculture – which was underpinned by smallholder production (Lumanni 2005) – the mine also helped prompt a significant expansion of Bougainville's market economy. This opened up opportunities for a nascent capitalist class to increase its share in a range of sectors. Nasioi businessmen, in particular, could take advantage of their position at the epicentre of mining.

To that end, during the 1980s a number of prominent businessmen with land rights in the mine-affected region used the Panguna Landowners Association to lobby the mine operator for increased compensation and other economic benefits (Okole 1990). Set up in 1979, the association ostensibly acted as a formal mouthpiece for mine-affected communities. In effect, however, it became an organ for aspiring Indigenous entrepreneurs to expand the economic stake they could vie for, drawing on the power of local communities to disrupt the mine operation as leverage.

These processes, as a totality, were rapidly stimulating a range of forces deeply antagonistic to Nasioi social systems, and the people whose identity, capacities and personhood were intrinsically bound to them (see Lasslett 2014). Land shortages appeared, when it had once been plentiful. Custom was being refashioned by ambitious commercial farmers to help increase their smallholder estates, and to deny kin traditional use-rights. Women saw their status and power eroded as men began to monopolize the commercial economy and the prestige that came with it. Inward migration from the rest of Papua New Guinea was bringing into Bougainville a range of new ethnic groups, whose norms and practices chafed against local cultural systems. Urban centres began to emerge, along with rising levels of crime and the lures of consumerism.

The mine greatly intensified and amplified these processes for the Nasioi, while adding into the mix a disastrous environmental footprint as surrounding land and waterways were awash with tailings and waste-rock carved out of the mine pit. Quite literally the pillars of Nasioi society – custom, culture, land, environment, social relations, spirituality – were facing an existential threat from the vigorous metabolism the mine had triggered.

Local landowners remember a period of social devastation. A Dapera villager recalls:

> All animals, the land, our food crops and plants were destroyed. Sacred places where we don't go into were all destroyed. Have they [Rio Tinto/BCL] realized that we have endured so many problems and trauma? . . . We still live with these problems and have not recovered yet.
>
> *(Interview 18, female community leader, 2013)*

A villager from Darenai paints a similar portrait:

> The company was at Panguna, it disposed all its waste into the Kabarong river polluting the environment from Panguna all the way to the sea. Huge masses of land were destroyed . . . the fish in the river too were killed once and for all. Trees used for building were also buried.
>
> *(Interview 82, male elder, 2013)*

In addition to BCL, blame for this destruction is also apportioned to local elites. An elder from Enamira village notes, 'only a few of us were educated in their system, what the company did to this minority was it bribed them with money. Money zipped their mouths from addressing our needs' (Interview 71, male community leader, 2013).[2] As a result, new intra-community tensions emerged: 'During the operation era friends became enemies, families became divided and money became the centre of society' (Interview 35, female landowner from Guava village, 2013). The trauma these multiple tendencies generated is captured by a Dapera villager, 'we are now living like aliens; no roots' (Interview 77, male landowner, 2013).

The general experience of the Nasioi, of course, is shared by other Indigenous peoples internationally, which has precipitated a global rights movement. As a result, we now see encapsulated in international norms, growing recognition that this structural violence is deviant, and the state has a positive duty to combat it. For example, Article 8 of the *United Nations Declaration on the Rights of Indigenous People* states: 'Indigenous peoples and individuals have the right not to be subjected to forced assimilation or destruction of their culture'. Article 8 also places a positive duty on the state to uphold the integrity of Indigenous peoples by enacting mechanisms of protection and redress that buttress the core pillars of Indigenous life.

In the absence of such mechanisms on Bougainville, the destruction of Nasioi social structures prompted an increasingly militant landowner movement, which would go on to challenge the forms of assimilation and dispossession being endured. In a historical twist, this movement was led by the Panguna Landowners Association, which was the site of a democratic coup. Following a grass-roots political campaign the original, self-appointed executive was replaced by a new, radical executive led by Perpetua Serero and Francis Ona from Guava village, who were elected by members in August 1987. Enjoying support from influential customary leaders in the mine region, the association administered an expansive campaign of resistance that ultimately aimed to rejuvenate Indigenous customs, culture and sovereignty. As the mine was believed to be the central circuit board powering the expansive processes harming indigenous social systems, its closure became a core pillar of the campaign. However, landowner attempts to close Panguna would trigger a formidable military response jointly engineered by the Papua New Guinea and Australian states.

## The violence of war

For over 25 years Nasioi communities affected by the mine experienced violence in multiple forms. They endured the dispossession of their land and its contents; some villages had been forcefully displaced from their ancestral home and resettled elsewhere; protestors had been attacked and imprisoned for resisting the mine's construction; and then, perhaps most critically, indigenous communities witnessed the large-scale devastation of the surrounding ecosystems, which was experienced as a deeply spiritual and material loss. During 1988–89, the violence facing Nasioi communities transformed in character.

The initial trigger was a campaign of industrial sabotage launched by the Panguna Landowners Association in November 1988. Key installations around the mine were burnt, and electrical pylons felled. These attacks had a practical and normative component (Lasslett et al. 2014). Most immediately they stemmed the harm that the extractive operation was inflicting on local ecosystems and communities. On a symbolic level the sabotage attacks also communicated, in a dramatic fashion, mass disapproval of the damage mining had generated over the previous two decades.

However, BCL and the Papua New Guinea state were only faintly aware of the deep social and personal trauma that was inspiring events. Indeed, it was wrongly believed by both organizations that the sabotage attacks were organized by a new generation of ambitious young landowners in order to ratchet up the economic benefits being delivered to local communities. In a bid to resolve the crisis, Papua New Guinea's Prime Minister offered landowning communities a substantive settlement that would have increased levels of compensation, provided a raft of new business opportunities, in addition to an equity stake in the mine. The package was rejected by the mine-affected communities.

Compounding matters, police riot squads were attempting to quell the uprising using a range of institutionally embedded practices, including the burning of villages and brutal reprisal attacks on landowner leaders. Along with other tensions, this helped prompt the establishment of the Bougainville Revolutionary Army (BRA), a guerrilla force set up to combat state violence and pursue, through arms, a range of political objectives. At the forefront of which was independence from Papua New Guinea, a political move BRA leaders felt would help revitalize social relations, processes and cultural assets undermined during the colonial and postcolonial period (Lasslett 2014). The pursuit of independence had the advantage of rallying support from communities less affected by mining but deeply resentful of Papua New Guinea's continued sovereignty over Bougainville. Furthermore, there was an ambitious political element within Bougainville's provincial government, who believed a more equitable and muscular market economy could be facilitated by an independent Bougainville in command of mining revenues. In short, the BRA's platform fused together a range of political currents – a process that contained its own contradictions – which gradually gave the struggle pan Bougainville significance.

The BRA's growing influence brought the Papua New Guinea Defence Force (PNGDF) to the fore during 1989. Beginning in July, the PNGDF embarked on a series of increasingly more violent counter-insurgency operations designed to rout the rebels, and reopen the mine. While the theatre of armed struggle would gradually consume Bougainville in its entirety, during 1988–89 it was the mine-affected communities who bore the greatest burden.

To weaken the BRA's operational capacity around critical mine infrastructure, villages in the adjacent regions were cordoned off and assaulted from land and air, employing a heavy arsenal of weaponry supplied largely by the Australian government. Many of the displaced were put into detention camps (labelled 'care centres' by the Papua New Guinea state), where restrictions were placed on freedom of movement and communication. These camps became the site of serious physical and sexual violence, as torture assumed a critical place in the PNGDF's tactical arsenal. Furthermore, extrajudicial killings were commonplace – circumstantial evidence of BRA collaboration was enough of a precursor to prompt execution. Compounding the situation, a military blockade was placed around the island. Nothing was allowed in, even medical goods and humanitarian assistance were denied to the civilian population.

During this period, the mine continued to act as a circuit board for violence, as BCL availed its substantial logistic infrastructure to the PNGDF. The company supplied transport, communications equipment, rations and accommodation, while senior executives frequently met with the PNGDF command and state officials to discuss operational matters, including military offensives (see Lasslett 2014).

Australia was also enmeshed in the violence. Having championed itself as the guarantor of regional stability, the Australian Government was keen to prove its credentials to allies, particularly the United States, by bringing about a quick, adept resolution to the Bougainville crisis. As a result, it became one of the strongest proponents of PNGDF offensive operations, in addition to being their primary sponsor, through the provision of armaments, equipment and special advisors (see Lasslett 2012).

As the scale of the violence increased during 1990, the BRA struggled to maintain internal discipline, as numerous decentralized guerrilla units – sometimes known as skin-BRA – appropriated their new-found status to violently settle longstanding vendettas, steal consumer goods, and attack political opponents. Australia and Papua New Guinea capitalized on the BRA's disorganization by sponsoring local paramilitary units who were prepared to combat the rebel force. This set the scene for an increasingly complex war, as numerous intra-Bougainville conflicts broke out, within the context of a broader independence struggle against Papua New Guinea.

However, for Nasioi communities the war was simply a new modality of violence perpetrated by BCL, and allied state actors. A villager from Dupanta observes, 'Australia killed us, PNG killed us and the company too – all came here under the same name, the PNGDF' (Interview 54, 2013). A female landowner from Enamira village adds:

> They [westerners] teach us what is human rights and they themselves end up not respecting human rights by getting involved in this conflict. . . . Most of the machinery and supplies used by PNG came from Rio Tinto. . . . There is nothing to be denied by Rio.
>
> *(Interview 42, 2013)*

Yet many Nasioi impacted by the war also remember a contradiction that punctuated the conflict period. As the blockade and fighting took its human toll, communities revitalized ailing indigenous social systems in order to survive this tumultuous period. A leader from Darenai recalls, 'the time of isolation to me was the best time of our lives, because for survival we had to revisit our traditional way of life' (Interview 45, male community leader, 2013). A villager from Enamira also approvingly points to the environmental and social respite the community experienced, 'it is very good that the conflict started. It blocked the way for BCL to continue the destruction, destroying many lives' (Interview 46, female landowner, 2013). Other Nasioi recall with pride the way in which communities innovated using local savvy to survive the prolonged siege and blockade. Therefore, while the war certainly remains etched in people's memory as a time of immense loss and suffering, it was also a period of cultural revival and rediscovery, as the structural violence of the mine years began to dissipate.

## The violence of peace

After a decade of fighting, the conflict was ushered to a formal close with the signing of the *Bougainville Peace Agreement* in 2001. The agreement shepherded a process of demobilization, peace-making and post-conflict reconstruction. Critically, an Autonomous Bougainville Government (ABG) has been established, overseen by an elected parliament, which wields a range of devolved powers. In addition to this, a referendum over independence is slated to take place between 2015 and 2020.

Wallis (2012, p. 29) observes 'in light of the extreme scale of the destruction wrought by the war, it is somewhat surprising how successful the peace process has been'. Dinnen and Peake

(2013, p. 11) go so far as to suggest it is 'one of the world's most successful peace processes'. Yet, however success is defined in the arena of peace – which is a contested question – in Bougainville's case, it can be observed that successful peace-making does not necessarily mean the curtailment of violence. This is especially so once we move beyond immediate inter-personal models of violence, and acknowledge that violence can also occur at a structural level, with debilitating individual effects. For the mine-affected Nasioi communities, the peace process has precipitated forces that indeed threaten to buttress a new episode in structural violence. At the heart of this threat is the policy relation being established between mining and peace.

To that end, a number of Bougainvillean politicians and international scholarly commentators have framed mining as vital to economic and political stability on Bougainville. This view has received its most overt expression under the Presidency of John Momis who was elected President of the ABG in 2010 and again in 2015. President Momis maintains that political self-reliance, whether it be complete independence or autonomy, requires a rapid injection of revenues, which only the Panguna mine can provide. Speaking to *The National* in February 2011 he observed: 'We want empowerment. Political power without economic power is nothing. Bougainville copper mine must open under a new regime' (Momis cited in Nicholas 2011).

With the question of mining returning to the post-conflict agenda, Boege and Franks (2012, p. 98) have suggested Bougainville 'has the potential to become another kind of success story: one in which conflict-sensitive and conflict-relevant redevelopment of mining actually strengthens peacebuilding'. To facilitate this ambitious endeavour the World Bank has invested US$2 million to help build capacity within the ABG's Department of Mining, it has also funded devolved mining legislation, drafted by British consultants, Adam Smith International.[3]

In defence of his policy, President Momis argues that the Panguna landowners welcome BCL's return. Speaking to the media in 2014, he remarked: 'It is the landowners who specifically wanted BCL. They argued then and now that it is better to deal with the devil you know, and the devil that knows us than a completely new devil' (Momis cited in *PNG Loop* 2 January 2014). However, empirical research conducted with mine-affected communities has uncovered evidence of significant opposition to BCL's return, and large-scale mining. A landowner from Pirurari village argues:

> we do not want mining. Absolutely not! No mining means no mining . . . It has destroyed the lives of us, the landowners. . . . Whatever white men want to re-open the mine are killers. The company treated us like animal, we are not animals.
>
> *(Interview 42, female landowner, 2013)*

An Enamira landowner similarly notes, 'I for one do not want the mine to reopen because if it does it will cause a lot of destruction, like it caused in the past. I personally don't want it reopened because now everything is growing again' (Interview 46, female landowner, 2013). A neighbour adds, 'the thought of repeating history again traumatizes me. Because it will happen again' (Interview 76, male community member, 2013).

However, the ABG, BCL and international donors, remain convinced that Nasioi communities can be adequately compensated for the repercussions of mining through a more enlightened governance regime. As a result, institutional efforts have been focused on recruiting the right team of experts who can engineer social arrangements that will secure consent locally, while ensuring the ABG receives a significant new source of revenue. Although, where consent cannot be achieved, Bougainville's new mining law contains a raft of powers – including heavy custodial sanctions and the suspension of constitutional and common law rights – that allow the ABG to acquire customary land and imprison resisters using strict liability provisions.[4]

Complicating matters, this venture is not being spearheaded by a heavy-handed colonial power, rather it is led by a Bougainvillean government ostensibly striving to stabilize the peace through economic growth. However, regardless of the author this venture remains an increasingly deviant form of state practice that violates the right of indigenous peoples to 'practise and revitalize their cultural traditions and customs. This includes the right to maintain, protect and develop the past, present and future manifestations of their cultures' (Article 11, *United Nations Declaration on the Rights of Indigenous Peoples*). Early signs suggest that this structural violence will again be strongly resisted by Nasioi communities.

## Structural violence, peace-making and social justice: concluding remarks

Since the early days of mine exploration, Nasioi communities have actively censured those practices underpinning the dispossession and destruction of their heritage, through protest, direct action and arms. This, in turn, has materially impressed a social stigma on the organizational actors complicit in these processes.

Yet the structural violence being condemned by Panguna landowners cannot be easily understood applying the empiricist methods that have dominated transitional policy on Bougainville. From the vantage point of sense perception this violence is non-existent, the target after all is not a thing or a person, but a historically developed way of life and the identities that emerge from this social mode of being. As a result, addressing interpersonal forms of violence has been prioritized on Bougainville, while its roots in structural violence is left largely unexplored.

Accordingly the social justice Nasioi communities have struggled for will not necessarily be found in restorative processes designed to heal interpersonal rifts from the conflict period, although their importance should not be underplayed. Nor will it necessarily be achieved by bringing to account perpetrators of war crimes, although this lacuna is in bad need of redress. Rather, for the mine-affected communities uprooted by structural violence, it would appear social justice is being gradually secured by resisting assimilation into a rejected social paradigm, whilst revitalizing those cultural assets and processes, essential to the reproduction of indigenous social systems. It is also being pursued through the exertion of greater local regulation over interactions with market capitalism. However, with a range of powerful organizational actors looking to secure a lasting liberal peace on Bougainville, which is congruent with a broader hegemonic conception of regional stability, new threats are emerging that could inhibit Nasioi communities from enjoying the justice they have struggled for.

## Notes

1 This analysis is informed by the theoretical work of Frantz Fanon and Amilcar Cabral.
2 Note the participant is not alleging that BCL was involved in making illicit payments. Rather this comment denotes a feeling that the company strategically distributed licit compensation payments, in order to win support from those more literate in westernized forms of commerce and politics.
3 ASI is an independent offshoot of the Adam Smith Institute, a think tank that came to the fore as a policy hub for the Thatcher government in Britain.
4 The legislation contains provisions requiring landowner consent for mining operations. However, consent can be given on behalf of communities by ABG sanctioned landowner associations; and as the history of the Panguna mine demonstrates, associations are highly contentious vehicles.

## References

Barnes, C., 1967. Statement by the Minister for Territories. Contained in National Archives of Australia, 'Political situation on Bougainville'; A452, paper files and documents, 1966–67; NAA: A452, 1967/1347.

Boege, V. and Franks, D., 2012. Reopening and developing mines in post-conflict setting: the challenge of company-community relations. *In*: P. Lujala and S.A. Rustad (eds), *High-value natural resources and peacebuilding*. London: Earthscan, 87–120.

Braithwaite, J., Charlesworth, H., Reddy, P. and Dunn, L., 2010. *Reconciliation and architectures of commitment: sequencing peace in Bougainville*. Canberra: ANU E Press.

Connell, J., 1978. *Taim bilong mani: the evolution of agriculture in a Solomon Island society*. Canberra: Australian National University.

Denoon, D., 1985. Capitalism in Papua New Guinea. *The Journal of Pacific History*, 20(3), 119–34.

Denoon, D., 2000. *Getting under the skin: the Bougainville Copper Agreement and the creation of the Panguna mine*. Melbourne: Melbourne University Press.

Dinnen, S. and Peake, G., 2013. *Bougainville community policing project: independent evaluation*. Bougainville Community Policy Project. Retrieved on 31 July 2015 from: www.aid.govt.nz/sites/default/files/ Bougainville%20Commuity%20Policing%20Project%20(BCPP)%20Independent%20Evaluation%20 February%202013%20%20Public%20Version.pdf.

Donaldson, M. and Good, K., 1981. The Eastern Highlands, coffee and class. *In*: D. Denoon and C. Snowden (eds), *A time to plant and a time to uproot*. Boroko: Institute of Papua New Guinea Studies, 143–69.

Griffin, J., 1990. Bougainville is a special case. *In*: R.J. May and M. Spriggs (eds), *The Bougainville crisis*. Bathurst: Crawford House Press, 1–15.

Hawksley, C., 2006. Papua New Guinea at thirty: late decolonisation and the political economy of nation-building. *Third World Quarterly*, 27(1), 161–73.

Hermkens, A.K., 2007. Religion in war and peace. *Culture and Religion: An Interdisciplinary Journal*, 8(3), 271–89.

Lasslett, K., 2010. Winning hearts and mines: the Bougainville crisis 1988–1990. *In*: R. Jackson, E. Murphy and S. Poynting (eds), *Contemporary state terrorism: theory and practice*. Abingdon: Routledge, 141–62.

Lasslett, K., 2012. State crime by proxy: Australia and the Bougainville conflict. *British Journal of Criminology*, 52(4), 705–23.

Lasslett, K., 2014. *State crime on the margins of empire: Rio Tinto, the war on Bougainville and resistance to mining*. London: Pluto Press.

Lasslett, K., Green, P. and Stańczak, D., 2014. The barbarism of indifference: sabotage, resistance and state-corporate crime. *Theoretical Criminology*. Advance online publication. doi: 10.1177/13624806 14558866.

Lumanni, J., 2005. Post-1960s cocoa and copra production in Bougainville. *In*: A.J. Regan and H.M. Griffin (eds), *Bougainville: before the conflict*. Canberra: Pandanus Books, 239–57.

MacWilliam, S., 2005. Post-war reconstruction in Bougainville: plantations, smallholders and indigenous capital. *In*: A.J. Regan and H.M. Griffin (eds), *Bougainville: before the conflict*. Canberra: Pandanus Books, 224–38.

Mitchell, D.D., 1976. *Land and agriculture in Nagovisi, Papua New Guinea*. Boroko: Institute of Applied Social and Economic Research.

Momis, J., 2015. Speech by Chief John L. Momis on the occasion of the inauguration of the 3rd Autonomous Bougainville Government House of Representatives. Buka, Autonomous Region of Bougainville, 15 June.

Moulik, T.K., 1977. *Bougainville in transition*. Canberra: Australian National University.

Namaliu, R., 1995. Politics, business and the state in Papua New Guinea. *Pacific Economic Bulletin*, 10(2), 61–5.

Nicholas, I., 2011. Plans to reopen Bougainville copper mine. *The National*, 10 February.

Ogan, E., 1972. *Business and cargo: socioeconomic change among the Nasioi of Bougainville*. Canberra: Australian National University.

Ogan, E., 1999. The Bougainville conflict: perspectives from Nasioi. *Discussion Paper* 99/3. Canberra: Research School of Pacific and Asian Studies, Australian National University.

Ogan, E. and Wesley-Smith, T., 1992. Papua New Guinea: changing relations of production. *In*: A.B. Robillard (ed.), *Social change in the Pacific Islands*. London: Kegan Paul International, 35–64.

Okole, H., 1990. The politics of the Panguna Landowners Association. *In*: R.J. May and M. Spriggs (eds), *The Bougainville crisis*. Bathurst: Crawford House Press, 16–24.

Oliver, D. 1991. *Black islanders: a personal perspective of Bougainville 1937–1991*. Melbourne: Hyland House Publishing.

Redmon, H. J., 1966. Letter from H.J. Redmon, Assistant District Commissioner, to The District Commissioner, Bougainville District, Sohano, 28 December 1966. Contained in National Archives of Australia, 'Political Situation on Bougainville'; A452, paper files and documents, 1966–67; NAA: A452, 1967/1347.

Saovana-Spriggs, R., 2007. *Gender and peace: Bougainvillean women, matriliny, and the peace process*. Thesis (PhD). Australian National University.

Tanis, J., 2005. Nagovisi villages as a window on Bougainville in 1988. *In*: A.J. Regan and H.M. Griffin (eds), *Bougainville: before the conflict*. Canberra: Pandanus Books, 447–72.

Wallis, J., 2012. Ten years of peace: assessing Bougainville's progress and prospects. *The Round Table: The Commonwealth Journal of International Affairs*, 101(1), 29–40.

# 24

# Childhood, rights and justice in Northern Ireland

*Deena Haydon and Phil Scraton*

## Introduction

What is 'childhood'? When does it start? When does it end? Seemingly self-evident, definitions of 'childhood' are not universally shared; varying over time, between cultures, within sovereign state policies and legislation. 'Childhood' as a distinct period of human development is a relatively recent construct. Developmental theories identify discrete 'stages' in the transition from birth to adulthood, the assumption being that the latter represents the 'completed' human condition. In contrast, social constructionist analyses affirm the significance of the determining contexts of culture, religion, learning and political economy in mapping this transition. At its simplest, the distinction between these quite different approaches has been represented as the 'nature versus nurture' dichotomy. A more complex, critical analysis focuses on social and political constructions of childhood within the dominant social order, differential power relations, and consequent impacts on the lives of children and young people.

Political economies, social mores and cultural dynamics differ between and within states, manifested in institutional and interpersonal conflictual relations of class, 'race', sectarianism, gender, sexuality, ability and *age*. Thus, 'adultism becomes institutionalised and mediated through social structures and their processes and policies', with material power 'complemented by persistent ideologies of subservience and subjugation to silence and nullify the actions of young people' (Scraton 1997, p. xiii). Within advanced democratic states, to varying degrees, childhood is perceived and regulated as a period of potential; children as adults 'under construction'. This ideological representation encourages public discourses and policy formulations that 'deprive them [children] of an existence as human beings in favour of an image of them as human becomings, thus underlining the suggestion that *children are not authentic contemporaries of adults*' (Qvortrup 2005, p. 5). More than a suggestion, this assumption is central to adult hegemony evident in the use, and abuse, of adult power.

The late twentieth century was a period in which the 'rights' of children were formulated and shared internationally, culminating in the 1989 United Nations (UN) *Convention on the Rights of the Child* (UNCRC). In essence the UNCRC articulates the distinctiveness of childhood and the need to establish universally agreed principles and provisions that both *protect* and *affirm* the rights of all under the age of 18. Minimum standards in the form of Rules and

Guidelines focus on the administration of criminal justice, prevention of 'juvenile delinquency', and responses to 'anti-social' or 'offending' behaviour aimed at promoting children's wellbeing and development.[1] Regular assessment by the UN Committee on the Rights of the Child of a state's progress towards meeting the expectations contained within the Convention's Articles and related standards can be a significant lever in promoting and protecting children's rights.

What follows considers the progress made in Northern Ireland towards realization of children's rights within the broader context of the United Kingdom and the specific circumstances of a jurisdiction emerging from a century of conflict and 30 years of war. While prioritizing *criminal* justice, this analysis acknowledges the significance of *social* justice in policies and practices affecting children's lives.[2] A key focus will be on the findings and recommendations of a review of the youth justice system that followed the devolution of policing and criminal justice powers from the United Kingdom (UK) government to the Northern Ireland Assembly in 2010.

## Northern Ireland: from conflict to peace

### *The Conflict*

Contemporary Northern Ireland is a society in transition. Between the late 1960s and the mid-1990s ceasefires it endured three decades of armed, political conflict regarding its constitutional status.[3] While Nationalists/Republicans, the majority of whom were Roman Catholic, demanded a united Ireland, Unionists/Loyalists, the majority of whom were Protestant, remained dedicated to retaining the union with the British State. Communities most affected by the Conflict were those with the highest levels of deprivation and poverty (Hillyard et al. 2005). In a population of just 1.7 million people, during the Conflict 3,600 men, women and children were killed, 40 per cent of whom were aged 24 or under. Between 1969 and 2003 this included 274 children aged 17 or under and 629 young people aged 18–21. Almost three-quarters of children under the age of 18 who were killed were Catholic and a fifth were Protestant (Smyth et al. 2004).

Within Republican communities, the police and the criminal justice system were perceived 'as instruments of oppression without any legitimate mandate' (Doak and O'Mahony 2011, p. 306). In Loyalist communities, those supporting paramilitaries disengaged with the formal criminal justice system (Byrne and Monaghan 2008). Paramilitaries filled the policing void, providing protection from external threats and severe regulation of those accused of 'criminal', 'anti-social' or 'anti-community' behaviour through public humiliation, beatings, shootings and forced exiling. The largest proportion of informal punishments was inflicted on young people aged under 25 (Knox 2002).

In 1970, Northern Ireland's Unionist government passed the *Criminal Justice (Temporary Provisions) Act* as a direct riposte to the Nationalist/Republican/Catholic community demands for civil, political and economic rights. Two years later, with British troops on the streets, and following the introduction of internment without trial and the killing of 13 unarmed civilians by the Parachute Regiment in Derry, the Conflict escalated. The Northern Ireland parliament was suspended and the UK government introduced direct rule. Nearly three decades of war followed.

In 1998 negotiations between the political parties in Northern Ireland, the UK and Irish governments resulted in the Good Friday Agreement establishing the constitutional foundation for a democratically elected Northern Ireland Assembly. Committed to embedding human rights, accountability and transparency into all institutions and practices, the Agreement prioritized: sustainable economic stability and growth; equality and social inclusion; normalization of state security operations and practices; representative and accountable civil policing; review of criminal justice; disarmament of paramilitary organizations; and the early release of politically affiliated prisoners.

In December 1999 limited powers were devolved to the Assembly. Following brief periods during which the Assembly's powers were suspended, in 2002 direct rule was reintroduced. In October 2006, the St Andrews Agreement prepared the way for resumption of the Assembly. Devolution returned seven months later. In May 2007 the Northern Ireland Executive took responsibility for all law and policy matters with the exception of policing and criminal justice, later devolved following the 2010 Hillsborough Agreement.[4] This Agreement's priorities included a review of the youth justice system to ensure compliance with international obligations (see Youth Justice Review Team 2011).

## *The legacy of the Conflict*

In 2014 Northern Ireland's population was 1,840,498, of whom 24 per cent were aged under 18 (NISRA 2015). A discrete legal jurisdiction of the UK, it remains a divided society. Housing, schools, public services and leisure facilities are segregated according to religious or political allegiances (see Roche 2008, McAlister et al. 2009). Forty-two per cent of the population identify as Protestant, 41 per cent as Roman Catholic (2011 Census, NISRA n.d.). Following expansion of the European Union 'newcomers' have made a significant contribution to the labour market, but cultural diversity has resulted in a marked increase in recorded racist attacks and racially motivated crimes (PSNI 2014, p. 13).

The Conflict has left a lasting legacy, affecting the lives of contemporary children, young people, families and their communities. The Commission for Victims and Survivors estimates that 30 per cent of the population are 'victims' of the Conflict – directly affected by bereavement, physical injury or trauma (*Hansard* 17 April 2013). Transgenerational trauma, evident in educational underachievement and mental ill-health, remains a reality for many children of parents and grandparents whose childhoods were blighted by war. Segregation, reflecting entrenched sectarianism, persists; its manifestation visible in 'peace walls' and security barriers at the 'interfaces' of Nationalist and Unionist communities. Sporadic outbreaks of violence or 'disturbances' continue at interfaces. Flags, murals and symbols delineate territory, demonstrating allegiances to paramilitary organizations. Cross-community interaction is limited, consolidating negative attitudes towards the 'other' community and protection of a shared identity within people's 'own' community (Leonard 2007, McAlister et al. 2009).

Contentious marches through Nationalist/Republican communities by the Orange Order (a fraternity committed to defending Protestantism and opposed to Ireland's reunification) prompt inter-community violence. Within the reformed Police Service of Northern Ireland (PSNI), 67 per cent of officers self-identify as Protestant, 31 per cent as Catholic (PSNI 2015). In Nationalist/Republican communities, mistrust of the police persists and Loyalist working class communities remain disengaged from policing.

In this climate of 'uneasy peace', and despite a much-proclaimed commitment to human rights principles and practices, the realization of children's rights has been undermined. Children continue to suffer 'informal' regulation by community-based paramilitaries alongside formal regulation by welfare and criminal justice systems. Young people report being threatened, experiencing punishment and exiling by paramilitaries (Haydon 2009, McAlister et al. 2009, Harland 2011, McAlister and Carr 2014). Between 2008 and 2010, 47 per cent of the 272 recorded casualties from 'paramilitary style' shootings and attacks were aged under 25 (PSNI 2011).

## Implementation of international standards

The UNCRC provides 'a directional framework' for policy and practice, 'recognising the role of the state in supporting families and carers in the development, socialisation and welfare of children' (Scraton and Haydon 2002, p. 313). Ratified by the UK government of Britain and Northern Ireland in 1991, it came into force in 1992. Following periodic examination of the UK government's implementation of the Convention, the UN Committee repeatedly has raised concerns regarding the regulation of children.

### *Minimum age of criminal responsibility*

International standards do not specify a minimum age of criminal responsibility, but Beijing Rule 4 warns that it should 'not be fixed at too low an age, bearing in mind the facts of emotional, mental and intellectual maturity'. A close association between responsibility for criminal behaviour and other social responsibilities (for example, marriage, voting) is expected. The UN Committee (2007, para. 32) states that a minimum age of criminal responsibility below the age of 12 is unacceptable. In Northern Ireland it is 10. The Youth Justice Review Team (2011, p. 107) recommended raising the minimum age to 12 with immediate effect, with consideration given to raising it to 14 following a period of review. These recommendations have been rebutted because of doubts about public and political will to accept reform (CJINI 2013, p. 8).

### *The aims of youth justice*

According to the Beijing Rules, the administration of youth justice should meet the diverse needs of young offenders while protecting their basic rights. The aims of the youth justice system should prioritize the child's wellbeing, avoid punitive sanctions, and ensure that reaction is proportionate to the circumstances of the offender and the offence. While acknowledging that public safety is a legitimate aim of the criminal justice system, the UN Committee (2007, para. 14) considers this is best served by implementation of the overarching principles of juvenile justice enshrined in the UNCRC.

The *Justice (Northern Ireland) Act 2002* established that the 'principal aim of the youth justice system is to protect the public by preventing offending by children' (Part 4, Section 53[1]). In this, children should be encouraged to 'recognise the effects of crime and to take responsibility for their actions' alongside responses aimed at 'furthering their personal, social and educational development' (ss 53[2] and [3]). Consequently, a 'responsibilising' agenda with a welfare-based orientation was established, ignoring the 2000 Criminal Justice Review recommendation that the 'best interests' principle be enshrined in juvenile justice legislation. Fourteen years after this recommendation, the 'best interests' principle was incorporated into the 2014 Justice Bill.

### *Prevention of offending*

The Riyadh Guidelines establish prevention of offending as a society-wide responsibility, grounded in promoting children's development and wellbeing with sufficient resources to ensure delivery of adequate medical and mental health care, nutrition, housing and other relevant services, including drug and alcohol abuse prevention and treatment. The Guidelines state that prevention policies should facilitate the socialization and integration of children through the family, the community, peer groups, education, vocational training and employment, and voluntary organizations. Criminalizing or punishing children for behaviour that does not cause serious damage to their development or harm to others should be avoided. Non-conformity should be accepted as part of maturation, declining through transition to adulthood. Labelling children 'deviant', 'delinquent' or 'pre-delinquent' should be recognized as contributing to subsequent 'undesirable' behaviour and the 'formal agencies of social control' should only be 'utilised as a means of a last resort' (Riyadh Guideline 5). Community-based programmes and services should be voluntary, designed and implemented in collaboration with young people.

In 2008 Northern Ireland established an early intervention programme targeting 8–13-year-olds 'at risk of offending'. Prioritizing prevention of offending as a long-term objective, it emphasized the personal, social and educational development of referred children and increased access to local support for parents. Practitioners were aware that using 'criminogenic' risk factors as referral criteria deflected attention from addressing the diverse and complex needs of referred children and their families (Haydon 2014). The programme conflated welfare provision for children 'in need' with criminalizing responses by defining them as children 'at risk of offending'. Despite practitioners' concerns about focusing on children's 'problematic' behaviour rather than its underlying causes, work concentrated on helping referred children manage their behaviour at home, in school or in the community. Practitioners suggested that many referred children did not understand the meaning of 'anti-social' behaviour and had been 'under-socialised' by parents whose capacity to parent had been 'compromised' by poverty, depression, domestic violence, substance misuse, abuse, lack of support and/or social isolation. Assumed 'anti-social' behaviour of groups on the streets brought children to the attention of the police, generating regulation of behaviour that was neither harmful nor causing damage.

The Northern Ireland Policing Board (2011) acknowledges that negative stereotyping reinforces the 'demonisation' of young people 'feed[ing] perceptions of anti-social behaviour', and amplifying a regulatory spiral. This is reflected in frustrations expressed by children and young people about negative media stereotyping, being 'moved on' from public spaces, and threatened with Anti-Social Behaviour Orders (McAlister et al. 2009, Nelson et al. 2010). These civil injunctions, which can lead to a criminal offence if breached, have been served disproportionately on young people, potentially 'fast-tracking' them into the criminal justice system (CJINI 2012a). Young people have stated that police officers regularly behave disrespectfully and make wrongful allegations of misbehaviour, but they were reticent to complain formally because they assumed they would not be believed (CJINI/NICCY 2007, p. 12). Such experiences were verified by the Youth Justice Review Team's (2011, p. 39) finding that 'too many officers are still adopting a judgemental and prejudiced, even antagonistic, attitude towards some of the young people they encounter'.

In July 2010, following rioting in Ardoyne, North Belfast, the PSNI released photographs of children they wished to interview. Simultaneously, the PSNI's 'Operation Exposure' was mounted in Derry where 50 photographs of young people were released to the media, followed by a house-drop of 25,000 leaflets containing photographs of 23 young people. These interventions breached children's right to privacy, undermined the presumption of innocence and access to due process, and placed the identified children at risk of community-based punishments. Despite criticism, the PSNI claimed their initiative was in children's 'best interests' as a way of identifying those requiring help and deterring them from involvement in further disorder (Burrows 2010) – illustrating the assertion that rights violations are often presented 'as a courtesy to the child' (Goldson 2000, p. 52).

### Diversionary measures

The UNCRC, the Beijing and Tokyo Rules, articulate a commitment to dealing with young people who offend without resorting to court proceedings. Diversion to community-based services is expected to mitigate the negative effects and stigma of criminal conviction. Given that most child offenders commit minor offences, removal from criminal/juvenile justice processing and referral to alternative (social) services should be used in most cases (UN Committee 2007, p. 24).

The optimum response is non-intervention (by criminal justice or social services), especially when the family, school or other social institution has reacted constructively. If involved, it is expected that the police, prosecution or other agencies should use their discretion to dispose of juvenile cases without recourse to formal hearings. In addition to ensuring that the powers of these agencies are regulated and reviewed to protect children from discrimination, it is anticipated that care will be taken to minimize potential for children to be coerced into admitting responsibility for an alleged offence or pressured into accepting a diversionary measure to avoid criminal prosecution.

In 2002, diversionary measures were introduced via the *Justice (Northern Ireland) Act*. Decisions regarding diversion from prosecution were located within the remit of the Public Prosecution Service, which can impose police-led informed warnings or restorative cautions, or diversionary youth conferences delivered by the Youth Justice Agency. As a prerequisite, however, guilt must be admitted, the offence must not be deemed serious, and the young person must not be regarded a persistent offender. Although not a conviction, these measures are registered on the young person's criminal record for 12 months for an informed warning and two years for a restorative caution or diversionary youth conference.

A youth conference brings together the young person, their parent or appropriate adult, the victim or a representative, a police officer and a youth conference coordinator. The young person is confronted with the impact of their behaviour and is expected to acknowledge any harm done. A Conference Plan is agreed, comprising actions intended to meet the needs of the victim and prevent further offending. However, procedural safeguards afforded by the formal criminal justice process are absent. Guilt has to be admitted, rather than determined by a court, and there is limited legal representation. Concerns have also been raised concerning 'informed consent' (Haydon 2008, p. 46), particularly when a young person is eager to avoid court (Doak and O'Mahony 2011, p. 318).

Young people have described the youth conferencing process and outcomes as oppressive, punitive and shaming, with unfair emphasis on acceptance of individual responsibility. Their criticisms include being publicly lectured or berated with minimal potential for negotiation of the Conference Plan (Maruna et al. 2007). Although not classified a criminal conviction, details are disclosed through criminal record checks, potentially affecting a young person's access to education, training or employment (Carr et al. 2015). In youth conference referrals there is a significant over-representation of 'looked-after' children (that is, those in the care of the state) (CJINI 2015a, p. 20).

### Non-custodial measures

The Beijing and Tokyo Rules emphasize that prosecuted children should receive a fair trial in which proceedings recognize their best interests and enable participation. A range of disposals should be available, drawing on community support to implement non-custodial measures. In determining outcomes, a balance should be achieved between the rights of the offender, the rights of the victim and the needs of society. Conditions should be practical, precise, minimal and aimed at prevention of offending and at social integration. Prioritizing individual needs, non-custodial measures could include casework, group therapy, residential programmes and specialized treatment by appropriately trained and experienced professionals. Practical assistance (accommodation, education or vocational training and psychological, social, or material support) should be provided to facilitate rehabilitation.

A range of non-custodial disposals have been introduced in Northern Ireland for those prosecuted and found guilty of an offence by the youth court. Rather than emphasizing the rights of the young person, however, restorative justice measures delivered by the Youth Justice Agency, such as court ordered youth conferences (in which the conference plan is agreed as the basis of a youth conference order), community responsibility orders and reparation orders, tend to focus on balancing the concerns of victims and the community with reintegration of the young person into their community.

## *Custody*

International standards stress that deprivation of liberty should be used as a last resort, for the minimum necessary period, in exceptional cases (a serious, persistent or violent act for which there is no alternative response). Detention pending trial should also be a measure of last resort. Outlining the rights of those held in secure facilities, the Beijing and Havana Rules emphasize that young people should receive care, protection, education and vocational training in preparation for assuming socially constructive and productive roles post-release in addition to any assistance they require for their holistic development.

The 2002 *Justice (Northern Ireland) Act* made provision for children aged 10–13 to serve a custodial sentence in secure accommodation, but this has never been enacted. In 2007 a purpose-built Juvenile Justice Centre (JJC) was opened. Operated by the Youth Justice Agency, it accommodates up to 48 young people aged 10–17. Inappropriate use of remand is more pronounced in Northern Ireland than in other UK jurisdictions (CJINI 2011, p. 4). Many on remand are neither serious nor persistent offenders but 'troubled children' (CJINI 2008, p. vii). Given that 80 per cent are subsequently bailed and do not receive a custodial sentence, the Youth Justice Review Team (2011, p. 55) concluded that custodial remands are used inappropriately by the courts, 'as a kind of "short, sharp, shock" or more benignly to secure the young person's safety'. Further, the Review Team criticized the imposition of bail conditions that are disproportionate or impossible to fulfil, particularly given the long delays between arrest and disposition. This leads to a 'revolving door' involving the young person being remanded to custody, bailed, breaching bail, and remanded again, often for the same offence (ibid., p. 56).

The Police and Criminal Evidence (NI) Order (PACE) was amended in 1998 to include the JJC as a 'place of safety' for children awaiting a court appearance. Usually PACE admissions are held for under 24 hours, justified on the basis of 'absence of alternative accommodation when they [children] presented chronic social problems' (CJINI 2011, p. 4). Noting that the majority of PACE admissions during weekends are looked after children, the Youth Justice Review Team (2011, p. 53) questioned, 'how children, already under the protection of the state, can be in need of a place of safety'. Four years later, the Criminal Justice Inspectorate stated: 'Alternatives must be found to the Juvenile Justice Centre being used as a temporary, short term location for children who breach children's home rules' (CJINI 2015b, p. 5).

In 2014–15, just 10 per cent of the 645 transactions in the JJC related to sentenced young people, while 54 per cent related to remand and 36 per cent to PACE (O'Neill 2015, p. 5). The average daily population was one individual held under PACE, 20 on remand, and 30 sentenced (ibid., p. 2). The over-representation of children from residential care has been a 'longstanding feature of juvenile custody in Northern Ireland' (CJINI 2008, p. vii) and, in 2014–15, 39 per cent of the transactions involved young people in care (ibid., p. 7).

Many young people in custody have special educational needs and/or been excluded from school, are on the child protection register, have a diagnosed mental health disorder, a history of self-harm and attempted suicide, or have been subjected to paramilitary threats or punishments (CJINI 2012b). It is an indictment of the inadequacy of existing provision that 'in many cases courts, social services and even children themselves felt they were better off in the JJC than living at risk in the community or in residential care' (CJINI 2008, p. 5). That some young people appreciate the routine, safety and provision they receive in custody (McAlister and Carr 2014), or welcome 'a period of respite in the JJC' (CJINI 2015b, p. 7), reveals serious deficits within community-based health, education and welfare provision.

## Tensions and challenges

Tensions prevail between the dynamics of criminalization and promotion/protection of children's rights. Since the late 1990s, in legislation and policy, 'crime' has been linked to 'public disorder' and 'anti-social behaviour'. Media and political debate has focused on negative stereotypes, reinforcing assumptions that children and young people pose a 'threat' in public spaces. Yet many behaviours considered 'anti-social' are learned by children from influential adults in their families and communities. As stated previously, sectarian antagonism, contentious rituals and parades, and inter-community violence reflect the legacy of the Conflict.

While the rationale behind early intervention may be progressive, when conceptualized and delivered through a 'crime prevention' framework it can reinforce and amplify the process of criminalization. Since devolution of policing and criminal justice, in contrast to England and Wales, the Department of Justice has resisted introducing punitive, mandatory 'support' targeted at 'troublesome' young people, parents or families. Northern Ireland's Community Safety Strategy defines interventions during the early years and key transition periods as 'positive child-focused support services rather than "crime prevention" strategies', with the justice system intended to play 'a supportive role' (DoJ 2012, p. 16). This includes support for 'intergenerational programmes to build trust and positive perceptions of young people' (ibid., p. 23).

The Youth Justice Review Team (2011, p. 37) recommended cross-departmental funding for early intervention and development of a strategy to be delivered through a partnership between statutory and non-statutory agencies. Achieving this investment, however, entails overcoming legislative, administrative and cultural barriers to resource-sharing, and the processes of government in Northern Ireland inhibit cross-departmental working. Undermining the best interests of the child, restorative justice initiatives emphasize the needs of victims and communities rather than the rights of children and, as currently operated, diversionary interventions do not ensure the legal safeguards underpinning formal criminal justice processes. Most significantly, the high proportions of those detained on remand and under PACE clearly illustrate that custody is not being used as a measure of last resort.

Regarding non-discrimination, lack of gender-specific data is a matter of concern. In 2015, the Youth Justice Agency published figures showing that the majority of young people processed through the youth justice system are male. Over the five years 2010–15, the proportion of males in custody in the Juvenile Justice Centre has been consistently between 83 per cent and 89 per cent (O'Neill 2015, p. 29) and the proportion involved with Youth Justice Services under diversionary and non-custodial disposals has been between 82 per cent and 85 per cent (ibid., p. 33). While these statistics reflect established patterns, state agencies do not routinely provide disaggregated data or contextual analysis recording the administration of gender-specific youth justice (for example, in relation to policing, diversionary disposals, bail or non-custodial measures for those found guilty of an offence).

To secure children's rights principles and provisions within a hostile political and ideological context is a daunting challenge. This chapter provides a brief insight into the complexities of tackling systemic social, political and economic inequalities and the abiding tensions within communities divided by sectarianism and the legacy of war. The fledgling, fragile Northern Ireland Assembly, elected via proportional representation, is a microcosm of societal division operating against a backcloth of continuing paramilitary activity within some communities.

Of the 12 UK regions, Northern Ireland records the lowest economic growth, the highest costs of basic goods and necessities, the highest concentration of families living in persistent poverty, and restricted sustainable employment opportunities. It has the highest proportion of children leaving school with the lowest range of qualifications. Despite vibrant voluntary and community sector interventions, this combination of material factors has contributed to the marginalization of children and young people living through the out-workings of the Conflict in working class communities. Within this bleak context, the relationship between a deficit in *social* justice and the regulation of children through *criminal* justice alongside the *informal* justice of community-based punishments are powerful determinants of children's futures. For those in conflict with the law, diversion from the criminal justice system is essential, with interventions focused on addressing their needs and supporting their families. Further, to prevent criminalization and in line with other social responsibilities, the minimum age of criminal responsibility should be raised to 16.

The question we raised over a decade ago (Scraton and Haydon 2002) remains relevant: can the State's endorsement of a rights-based agenda through ratification of international standards contribute to the resolution of structural inequalities? Recognizing the 'special status' afforded to all under 18s, the UNCRC and other international human rights standards affirm a comprehensive body of entitlements which are not 'rewards' or 'privileges, nor are they dependent on acceptance of responsibilities. They specify the obligations of the State and its agencies as duty-bearers. These are useful 'auditing tools', providing a common reference point or benchmark against which law, policy and practice can be measured (Kilkelly 2008).

Implementation of policy and practice grounded in the principles of social justice and inclusion necessitates provision, throughout childhood, of universal services and additional support by mainstream health, social care, education, youth and community services. Challenging and overcoming structural inequalities cannot be achieved solely through ratification of Conventions, Guidelines and Rules. While advanced democratic states proclaim social responsibility and equal opportunity, their class systems protect and sustain the acquisition of wealth by a privileged minority. Welfare capitalism has enabled a reasonable standard of living through income redistribution. Yet a high proportion of families and their children remain trapped in systemic poverty – socially excluded, politically silenced, permanently disadvantaged. For rights on paper to become rights in practice a fundamental redistribution of power, wealth and opportunities is required to enable the personal, social, and educational development of *all* children and young people.

## Notes

1 UNCRC Article 40 focuses on the administration of youth justice, Article 37 on the rights of children deprived of their liberty; the 1985 Beijing Rules on the administration of justice; the 1990 Riyadh Guidelines on the prevention of juvenile delinquency; the 1990 Tokyo Rules on non-custodial measures; the 1990 Havana Rules on the rights of children deprived of their liberty.

2 For a detailed analysis of the implementation of children's rights in Northern Ireland, see Children's Law Centre and Save the Children NI (2015). For a comprehensive overview of contemporary trends in criminal justice in Northern Ireland, see McAlinden and Dwyer (2015).

3 The *Government of Ireland Act 1920* partitioned Ireland, establishing six of the nine northern counties of Ulster as Northern Ireland within the United Kingdom (May 1921). The Irish Free State was established as a British Commonwealth Dominion and in 1937 the creation of Ireland as a sovereign state replaced the 1922 constitution. In 1949 it secured full independence as the Republic of Ireland.
4 The UK Government retains responsibility for 'excepted' and 'reserved' matters.

## References


Burrows, J., 2010. PSNI defend releasing photographs of children. *News Letter,* 18 August.

Byrne, J. and Monaghan, L., 2008. *Policing Loyalist and Republican communities: understanding key issues for local communities and the police.* Belfast: Institute for Conflict Research.

Carr, N., Dwyer, C. and Larrauri, E., 2015. Young people, criminal records and employment barriers. Paper 1, *New directions: understanding and improving employment pathways in youth justice in Northern Ireland.* Belfast: NIACRO.

Children's Law Centre and Save the Children NI, 2015. *Northern Ireland NGO alternative report: submission to the UN Committee on the Rights of the Child for consideration during the Committee's examination of the United Kingdom of Great Britain and Northern Ireland Government Report.* Belfast: CLC/Save the Children NI.

Criminal Justice Inspection Northern Ireland [CJINI], 2008. *Inspection of Woodlands Juvenile Justice Centre.* Belfast: CJINI.

CJINI, 2011. *Announced Inspection of Woodlands Juvenile Justice Centre.* Belfast: CJINI.

CJINI, 2012a. *Anti-Social Behaviour: an inspection of the criminal justice system's approach to addressing anti-social behaviour in Northern Ireland.* Belfast: CJINI.

CJINI, 2012b. *Early youth interventions: an inspection of the contribution the criminal justice agencies in Northern Ireland make to preventing children and young people from entering the criminal justice system.* Belfast: CJINI.

CJINI, 2013. *Monitoring of progress on implementation of the Youth Justice Review recommendations.* Belfast: CJINI.

CJINI, 2015a. *The effectiveness of youth conferencing.* Belfast: CJINI.

CJINI, 2015b. *An Announced Inspection of Woodlands Juvenile Justice Centre.* Belfast: CJINI

Criminal Justice Inspection Northern Ireland and NICCY, 2007. *The handling of complaints in the criminal justice system: a review of how the main criminal justice organisations deal with complaints.* Belfast: CJINI/NICCY.

Department of Justice [DoJ], 2012. *Building safer, shared and confident communities: a community safety strategy for Northern Ireland 2012–2017.* Belfast: Department of Justice.

Doak, J. and O'Mahony, D., 2011. In search of legitimacy: restorative youth conferencing in Northern Ireland. *Legal Studies,* 31(2), 305–25.

Goldson, B., 2000. Wither diversion? Interventionism and the new youth justice. *In:* B. Goldson (ed.), *The New Youth Justice.* Lyme Regis: Russell House Publishing, 35–57.

Harland, K., 2011. Violent youth culture in Northern Ireland: young men, violence, and the challenges of peacebuilding. *Youth and Society,* 43(2), 414–32.

Haydon, D., 2008. *Northern Ireland NGO alternative report.* Belfast: Save the Children and Children's Law Centre.

Haydon, D., 2009. *Developing a manifesto for youth justice in Northern Ireland: background paper.* Belfast: Include Youth.

Haydon, D., 2014. Early intervention for the prevention of offending in Northern Ireland. *Youth Justice,* 14(3), 226–40.

Hillyard, P., Rolston, B. and Tomlinson, M., 2005. *Poverty and conflict in Ireland: an international perspective.* Dublin: Combat Poverty Agency.

Kilkelly, U., 2008. Youth justice and children's rights: measuring compliance with international standards. *Youth Justice,* 8(3), 187–92.

Knox, C., 2002. 'See no evil, hear no evil': insidious paramilitary violence in Northern Ireland. *British Journal of Criminology,* 42(1), 164–85.

Leonard, M., 2007. Trapped in space? Children's accounts of risky environments. *Children and Society,* 21(6), 431–45.

Maruna, S., Wright, S., Brown, J., Van Marle, F., Devlin, R. and Liddle, M., 2007. *Youth conferencing as shame management: results of a long-term follow-up study.* Belfast: Youth Justice Agency.

McAlinden, A.-M. and Dwyer, C. (eds), 2015. *Criminal justice in transition: the Northern Ireland context.* Oxford: Hart Publishing.

McAlister, S. and Carr, N., 2014. Experiences of youth justice: youth justice discourses and their multiple effects. *Youth Justice*, 14(3), 241–55.

McAlister, S., Scraton, P. and Haydon, D., 2009. *Childhood in transition: experiencing marginalisation and conflict in Northern Ireland*. Belfast: Queen's University Belfast/Save the Children/Princes Trust.

Nelson, E., McBride, R.-S., O'Riordan, O. and Smyth, P., 2010. *Beyond the margins: building trust in policing with young people*. Belfast: Public Achievement/Institute for Conflict Research.

NISRA, 2015. Population by sex and single year of age 1961–2014. Retrieved on 7 April 2016 from: www.nisra.gov.uk/demography/default.asp17.htm.

NISRA, n.d. Religion in Northern Ireland. Retrieved on 7 April 2016 from: www.ninis2.nisra.gov.uk/publiccensus2011analysis/religion/religioninfographic.pdf.

Northern Ireland Policing Board, 2011. *Thematic review on children and young people*. NI Policing Board Human Rights and Professional Standards Committee, Belfast: NIPB.

O'Neill, N., 2015. *Youth Justice Agency Annual Workload Statistics 2014/15, Statistical Bulletin 1/2015*. 25 September. Belfast: YJA, Statistics and Research Branch.

Police Service of Northern Ireland [PSNI], 2011. *Paramilitary style incidents*. Freedom of Information Request F-2011-00341. Retrieved on 7 April 2016 from: www.psni.police.uk/para_style_incidents.pdf.

Police Service of Northern Ireland [PSNI], 2014. *Trends in hate motivated incidents and crimes recorded by the police in Northern Ireland 2004/5 to 2013/14*. Belfast: Police Service of Northern Ireland.

Police Service of Northern Ireland [PSNI], 2015. Workforce composition statistics, 1 May. Retrieved on 7 April 2016 from: www.psni.police.uk/updates_workforce_composition_figures.

Qvortrup, J., 2005. *Studies in modern childhood: society, agency, culture*. Basingstoke: Palgrave Macmillan.

Roche, R., 2008. *Sectarianism and segregation in urban Northern Ireland: Northern Irish youth post-agreement – a report on the facts, fears and feelings project*. Belfast: Queen's University Belfast.

Scraton, P., ed., 1997. *'Childhood' in 'crisis'?* London: UCL Press.

Scraton, P. and Haydon, D., 2002. 'Challenging the criminalisation of children and young people: securing a rights-based agenda. *In*: J. Muncie, G. Hughes and E. McLaughlin (eds), *Youth justice: critical readings*. London: Sage, 311–28.

Smyth, M., Fay, M. T., Brough, E. and Hamilton, J., 2004. *The impact of political conflict on children in Northern Ireland*. Belfast: Institute for Conflict Research.

UN Committee on the Rights of the Child, 2007. *General Comment No. 10 (2007) Children's Rights in Juvenile Justice*. 2 February, CRC/C/GC/10.

Youth Justice Review Team, 2011. *A review of the youth justice system in Northern Ireland*. Belfast: Youth Justice Unit, Department of Justice.

# 25

# Keeping the peace

## Police peacekeeping and capacity development in the promotion of human rights

*Andrew Goldsmith*

### Introduction

In this chapter, I propose to examine the challenge still facing policing in many parts of the world today in terms of providing basic policing services to residents. By those basic services, I include the protection of human rights. As noted already, not only do police fail to protect in many instances, but they are often part of the problem of insecurity that ordinary people face in their daily lives. Understanding how policing can let people down, and why accountability for these failures is so often lacking, is important before we can assess the recent and current efforts to build peace and uphold human rights.

In the next section, I present some observations about the nature of the challenges to effecting improvements in policing, drawing upon a number of personal experiences and research conducted in this area. This is done principally to sensitize readers to some of the key themes that will be addressed in the balance of the chapter. Then I examine the normative and institutional moves, mainly at the international level, to bring about improvements in public safety and security and how policing has been incorporated in these efforts. This is followed by a reflection upon the impact of these programmes and policies in terms of reducing forms of policing that undermine human rights and the safety of individuals and groups. The chapter concludes by looking at the conditions that would be needed to ensure greater success in efforts in international policing to improve safety, security and respect for human rights.

### The nature of the challenge

> You would have to impress upon them [Papua New Guinea police officers] the importance of not killing anybody especially while we were there because we would get the blame and you know if you had any respect for us, you wouldn't do it and that's where that friendship and trust and that built up.
>
> *[R49]*[1]

This statement is that of an Australian police officer working in Papua New Guinea (PNG) alongside local police officers around 2005. The officer was there as part of a capacity-building mission, an arrangement (in this case) between the PNG and Australian governments to 'build capacity' through mentoring of PNG officers by Australian police officers. There are several points to be read from this particular observation that speak to the theme of this chapter – the role of international police in preventing further violence in conflict-affected areas and in building local police forces with the objectives of upholding the rule of law and protecting human rights.

One is the fact that in many parts of the world (international policing scholar, David Bayley thinks the overwhelming majority of countries, Bayley 2014) police not only don't perform well by western standards of professionalism in terms of 'keeping the peace' and upholding the Rule of Law. Quite the contrary, they are a major threat to public safety and the Rule of Law. And, in many countries, police kill people with impunity on a disturbingly regular and arbitrary basis (see, for example, Chevigny 1995, Huggins 1998). Recent events in the United States (US), such as in Ferguson, Missouri, remind us that this problem is not one confined to post-conflict societies or developing countries (Amnesty International 2015). Concerns about police use of excessive force, including killings, needless to say, has not escaped the attention of many observers. These include western governments, international governmental organizations including the United Nations (UN), and human rights bodies such as Amnesty International and Human Rights Watch. In most instances, there have been calls for significant police reform at the local level (see, for example, Amnesty International 2015).

A second point is the difficulty of effecting real police reform. The comment by the Australian police officer alludes to the strangeness of the message to recipients in that setting that it is not acceptable to routinely kill suspected perpetrators of crime. Part of the difficulty of efforts to change behaviour and attitudes in such places, where police violence is commonplace and even tolerated to some degree, is the fragility of even the best intentioned and well-resourced efforts of outsiders to bring about changes to what are often ingrained attitudes and behaviours. In this comment, feelings of personal loyalty towards their Australian mentoring officer emerge as perhaps the only significant impediment to local police dispensing arbitrary killings. Implicitly then, the formal structures of control (law, training, hierarchical oversight) were insufficient to hold the officers back from acting in otherwise blatantly illegal abuses of their authority and the law.

Another observation that can be made is the central importance of an ability to build relationships of trust between foreign police personnel *and* local police and residents (Goldsmith 2005). While, as this example makes clear, establishing trust is not a sufficient requirement to produce sustainable improvements, it is fairly clear that without it nothing positive of this kind is likely to emerge from capacity development exercises (Goldsmith and Harris 2012). That said, as I will suggest further below, police reform intended to improve human safety or respect for human rights standards depends on much more than good interpersonal relationships or the formal adoption of foreign police models by local police forces.

For more than a decade countries such as Australia, Canada, the US and various European countries have invested considerable human and other resources in nation-building efforts as well as in peacekeeping as part of the resolution of wars and other conflicts. Over the past two decades, the composition of international peacekeeping missions, particularly those led by the UN, has increasingly included policing as well as military and civil components. Whereas the UN deployed only 35 police officers in 1988, this number had risen to 13,328 by 31 July 2015 (UN 2015). Police have been engaged as peacekeepers as well as in nation-building tasks as mandated by the UN Security Council or as part of bilateral or regional arrangements between countries. They have also increasingly become a key component of governance capacity-building, either under UN Security Council or similar mandates, or under bilateral arrangement between two countries (in a similar way, historically to the provision of much overseas development assistance).

In many ways this development can be seen as overdue. Within many European countries, processes of pacification and stabilization of governance arrangements and consolidation of the modern state relied in large measure upon the establishment of regular civilian police from the late eighteenth century onwards. In the United Kingdom (UK), the modern institution of policing set up by Sir Robert Peel in the early nineteenth century drew explicitly upon a tradition of the role of the constable and the duty of constables to 'keep the peace' and to uphold the rule of law. While initially many citizens feared the loss of their freedoms as a consequence of having standing police forces, the idea of 'policing by consent' that accompanied this development meant that legitimate policing depended upon overt acts of independence and impartiality (Reiner 2010, Chapter 3). When linked to the idea of professionalism, one can see the formation of an ideology of modern policing that was committed to protecting freedoms of those who did not breach the laws or act in a disorderly fashion. This institution would seem then peculiarly suited to the aims of many contemporary or recent peacekeeping missions – to reduce violence, to restore order to enhance the personal freedoms of law-abiding persons.

It needs to be noted, however, that many of the settings in which international policing missions have recently sought or currently seek to operate have not had the same period of time to consolidate and absorb this model of policing or indeed any other model of professional policing. In reckoning with the degree of challenge faced by these missions in particular settings, it is necessary to go further by taking account of the particular colonial experiences of those settings, and particularly the ways in which colonial authorities undertook policing in those places. While generalization is difficult and experiences often varied between places, it is widely acknowledged that in parts of Africa, Asia and Latin America, colonial policing models were often more martial and openly repressive in nature that those being practiced in many parts of Europe (Anderson and Killingray 1991). Historical conditioning of local communities to such negative forms of policing looms large therefore among the difficulties faced by foreign police reformers in attempting to 'improve' policing in various ways, including the protection of human rights (Goldsmith 2002, 2005, Goldsmith and Harris 2012).

## Endangered people: a protection needs analysis

In the early 2000s, I was employed by an international non-government organization with a focus on justice reform issues to undertake a scoping exercise in terms of the need for reform of criminal justice systems, and particularly police forces, in more than twenty countries across the globe. The countries included countries in sub-Saharan Africa, the Caucasus, Central Asia, Latin America and South East Asia. The methodology I employed was to gather and read a variety of reports on each of these countries and the public order problems they were facing, whether as a consequence of recent conflict, a lack of economic and human development or the prevalence of serious crime and corruption. The sources of my information came mainly from official reports produced by international and national non-governmental organizations (for example, Amnesty International, Human Rights Watch) as well as by national governments and international bodies such as the UN.

These reports were often filled with the diligent reporting of incidents of serious abuse of human rights by state officials, not infrequently on a wholesale level. Often those officials accused of serious abuse were police officials rather than, or in addition to, military personnel. Police were accused of crimes such as torture, disappearances, and massacres. There was something fundamentally incongruous here. Those one would expect to exercise restraint against such abuses of ordinary people by offering effective prevention and deterrence mechanisms were in fact the authors of many of these abuses. Despite more than fifty years since the passing of the UN *Universal Declaration of Human Rights*, the values of international human rights protection being widely subverted by the very forces that most civilized societies hold responsible in civilian life for that protection. Unfortunately, reading a report such as HRW's *World Report 2015* today only confirms the persistent nature of the police reform challenge.

There was an additional irony here. These changes also coincided with international advocacy among police reformers of the notion of community policing (Ellison 2007). Community policing, as the name implies, requires a level of closeness and consultation between police and members of local communities. Inherent in such a notion is the idea that individuals are worthy of respect and protection by police, and that police need to work cooperatively with the communities in which they operate. How can this occur, one is forced to ask, if the police concerned are viewed as perpetrators of abuse by the very communities they are seeking to enlist in community policing programmes? It is difficult to be too hopeful for such initiatives given the *lack of public trust* in police in many of these places (see Goldsmith 2005). A definition of community policing offered to me by a senior officer in Turkey during a field visit in 2005 underlines this point: 'we go to the community and give them the questions we want answered and they tell us'.

Despite developments in human rights consciousness over the past six decades or so, many people remain vulnerable to attack or intimidation in their daily lives (see, for example, HRW 2015). The rising global number of internally displaced persons, counted at more than 38 million in 2014 (UNHCR 2014) as well as persons fleeing their home countries, another twenty million people or so (UNHCR 2014, p. 2), points to widespread social disruption and violence at a local level. The need for good policing in these environments is palpable. While the drivers of violence and disorder are often linked to civil conflicts between competing armed actors, there is also the impact of groups engaged in activities such as trafficking of drugs, arms, and persons. While not directly involved in political struggles, many crime groups seek to benefit from instability, desperation, and disorder among the population by providing protection or meeting demand for goods of different kinds.

These, fundamentally are policing problems that in large measure, paradoxically, emerge from the absence of effective policing (Goldsmith 2002). The ability to live without fear of physical attack is fundamental to the exercise of political and other kinds of rights (Przeworski 1995, p. 36, Whitehead 2002). As Patricia Morgan noted: 'Freedom lies in not having to calculate the risk to oneself on every journey outdoors' (quoted in Berki 1986, p. 20). Where there are threats to this fundamental freedom, it is clear the 'rubber' of effective policing needs to meet the 'road' of human rights protection (Goldsmith 2002).

Summing up, there is a growing global demand for, as well as obvious need for improved civilian protection and public safety. While ending wars and ensuring adequate economic and social opportunities through better governance are an essential part of any effective improvement in human security, a point I will return to in the final section of the chapter, there is a strong case within any broader strategy for improved public policing arrangements and hence for police reform. The role of policing is linked, not least of all, to what Henry Shue called the *right to physical security* – 'a right . . . not to be subjected to murder, torture, mayhem, rape, or assault' (Shue 1980, p. 20). How the role for policing has been inserted, and how that has been done, in governance, rights, and development agendas is examined in the next section. Implementation of this role and a measure of its achievements is the subject of the subsequent section.

## Protecting people: agendas and motivations

The case for police reform, including the restoration of civil peace by the participation of police peacekeepers, is one that can be grounded normatively in a number of contemporary discourses dealing with international peace and security. Indeed, as well as being a security or human rights issue, it forms part of a broader governance agenda, as well as an element of overseas development aid agendas (see, for example, World Bank 2011). What is fairly clear is that for a long time, questions of police reform tended to be viewed in isolation from many of the bigger themes – peacekeeping, foreign aid and nation-building. Even within human rights talk for many years, questions of how policing needed to change institutionally and how appropriate changes might be achieved were either ignored or only lightly touched upon (Goldsmith 2002). Policing has often been overshadowed by concerns about ending conflicts, providing aid and dealing with the crimes and abuses of military forces and militias. As crime, however, has come to be seen less as a discrete issue and more as a threat not just to improved security but also to governance and development goals over the past decade or so (World Bank 2011), attention to policing has grown.

Police reform, though implicitly required as a logical consequence of many critiques of human rights performance, has also tended to be overlooked in other crucial contexts. This observation applies to the majority of analyses of International Humanitarian law, the *Responsibility to Protect* principle and the doctrine of *Protection of Civilians* (see Wills 2009, Chappuis and Gorur 2015, Goldsmith 2006). Put bluntly, many lawyers, including human rights lawyers, did not for a long time 'get' policing or law enforcement in the way they tended to 'get' prosecution, conviction and punishment. They could not, or would not, analyse the contribution, either negative or positive, of police to the difficult and often intractable problems that concerned them. The same could be said for many working in nation-building, peacekeeping and peace-building policy and doctrine development. One struggles to find in reports or books on these topics, even recently, any substantial recognition of the centrality of good policing to improving general life opportunities and even less about how this might realistically be achieved.

A major distraction in this regard can be attributed at the international level to the War on Drugs, initiated by the US in the 1980s and which has continued albeit in modified form until the present (Kuzmarov 2009). A tendency to militarize policing and to focus on targeting 'the bad guys' at whatever cost in relation to Latin American drug trafficking (see Goldsmith and Sheptycki 2007) can also be seen to have permeated approaches to police training in Iraq and Afghanistan since 2003. A *counter-insurgency model* of policing has commonly been promulgated in countries such as Iraq, Afghanistan and Colombia by the US and other western countries, one in which, among other things, the local population is seen as a resource primarily for exploitation of intelligence. Where this intelligence is not forthcoming, too often we have seen evidence of harsh measures including torture of locals. Needless to say, such police training and professional development is in direct contradiction to human rights-based policing training (ironically, which many of these police have also received) as well as undermining of prospects for the successful operation of community policing models in these settings. This has been referred to as the 'Janus face' of police building – the furthering of humanitarian assistance (such as reform) while simultaneously advancing a strategic policy of building institutions and quiescent states that do not threaten US or western policy interests (Heiduk 2015).

A number of threads began to converge around 2000 that ensured that policing would play a larger role in these operations in the future. What we can see in general terms is the increasing articulation of security considerations with human rights issues, nation-building and economic development. By this time, a small number of police were beginning to make up a component of broader peacekeeping missions undertaken by the UN. As part of the reflection upon some of the intervention failures of the 1990s (such as Rwanda, Somalia), the UN's Panel on UN Peace Operations, head by Lakhdar Brahimi (the 'Brahimi report'), reported in 2000 on the need to devise more effective and robust peace operations. Albeit only fairly incidentally, the important role for police personnel in such missions was confirmed in that report in various ways. The need to stop violence against civilians, something that previously military peacekeepers had proven to do very poorly in many instances, required adequate police responses as well as better-trained military personnel, the Report noted (see Wills 2009, pp. 43–4). As Wills points out, from this point one can observe the UN articulating that peacekeeping was not simply about limiting threats to international peace and security at a strategic level but also included providing support for a parallel UN agenda, that of the protection of human rights (Wills 2009, p. 44).

By 2015, the situation has changed significantly. The complex linkages between different UN rights-related agendas with implications for UN police peacekeeping as well as capacity-building is evident in the UN Security Council Resolution 2185, 20 November 2014. Within the Preamble is contained a list of previous resolutions and Presidential statements considered pertinent to the Resolution at hand, one focused upon the UN policing role. This list refers to security sector reform, peacekeeping operations, protection of civilians, women and children in armed conflict, small arms and light weapons, the rule of law and post-conflict peace-building (UN Security Council 2014). The Resolution links its purposes even more broadly to conflict prevention and sustainable peace and the need to address root causes of related problems.

While these areas typically bear a peace and security framing because of the terms of the Security Council's mandate, almost all bear as well either directly or indirectly upon rights, in particular issues of human rights. For example, it is perfectly clear that the UN's longstanding interest in protecting women and children from domestic as well as conflict-related violence is premised upon respect for, and hence protection of, those rights not to be the subject of violent attacks. However recognition of the police role in a human rights context is becoming more pervasive in UN policies and doctrine. In the *Policy on UN Police in Peacekeeping Operations and Special Political Missions* (UN DPKO 2014), it is explicitly stated that '[p]romotion, protection and respect for human rights must be incorporated into every aspect of the work of United Nations police', and furthermore that UN police officers must be 'prepared to raise issues of human rights if confronted with violations' (UN DPKO 2014, p. 7).

## Protecting people: capabilities and achievements

While peacekeeping mandates tended to expand in scope and complexity after 2000 (see Durch 2014), to explicitly include respect for human rights and capacity-building, the ability to implement these mandates and to produce lasting change in terms of peace or improved policing has proven far more difficult (Murney et al. 2011). This has been the case for a number of reasons. Aspirations and expectations both among those leading and implementing the mission, as well as those subject to them, have tended not to match the achievements.

One of the perpetual challenges facing policing missions, whether engaged in peacekeeping or capacity-building, is the uncertain and inadequate nature of resources provided for these tasks. As one seasoned observer of these missions recently noted, 'for far too long, political authorities responsible for establishing UN and other peace and stability operations have had little familiarity with the actual capacities needed to enhance, let alone create, public security within a mission's area of operation' (Durch 2014, p. 17). This, Durch adds, 'has been especially true of police functions'. This has meant that money and other resources have been limited in amount and in terms of the length of time over which they are committed. The shortness of many mission terms, as well as the failure to properly resource mission activities, are two well-accepted reasons why missions so frequently fail to meet international as well as local expectations.

In addition to the amount of resources provided for these purposes, there is also the issue of resource quality and appropriateness. This is particularly true of human resources. One of the truisms of many UN policing missions is that they are often composed of police personnel from countries whose own human rights record is deeply blemished, in part by the actions of members of the same police forces that are providing personnel to UN missions. In short, many police serving on UN missions are, by reason of their backgrounds, unconvincing ambassadors for many of the UN human rights standards that form part of UN policy and doctrine.

Another difficulty in establishing effective policing programmes is the diversity of aims, and consequently methods, brought to bear in particular missions. There is the real risk that one or more aim can undermine the achievement of others. There is in short an over-ambition of mandate expectations in many cases, partly the result of perceived urgency to 'do something' and partly the consequence of planning failing to anticipate certain outcomes of their actions. While capacity-building local police forces may be one necessary task that is tackled, this task may sit alongside others such as public order policing, the investigation of atrocities arising from the previous conflict period, and the targeting of organized crime or local corruption. Human rights and community policing agendas, while often present, can get lost in practical as well as doctrinal terms, in this 'reform soup' that international missions frequently embark upon.

The mission environments in which police reforms and peacekeeping are attempted often conspire on several fronts to constrain what missions can achieve. Where there is ongoing conflict, there is a need to ensure force protection, meaning often that there is an acceptance by police personnel of military primacy, or at least an enhanced reliance upon paramilitary style policing. Even when the level of public order is less than that where armed groups are actively fighting each other, police sent to train in community policing or human rights will tend to live constrained lives on missions, subject to the security directives of others. During the crisis in Timor-Leste in 2006, many of the capacity-building programmes in which Australian police were involved had to be closed down and put on hold. During this time, many police were limited in where they could go, and police patrols depended upon military force and paramilitary units as to when they could be undertaken (Goldsmith 2009).

Another constraint on mission effectiveness is the kinds of relationships that can be achieved with local people and local officers. Typically the settings in which international police missions become engaged are structurally contrarian to many of the aims of these missions. Police reform is an essentially political exercise, so that new initiatives inevitably run afoul of existing interests and ways of doing things. Almost inevitably, existing power structures within local police forces are expected to change. Changing police leadership and altering police priorities can also threaten the balance of interests in the wider setting, undermining positions of advantage that some groups or individuals have managed to establish within the current policing arrangements. The dysfunctional consequences of the partisan policing system in Timor-Leste became very apparent in the 2006 crisis, a situation that the UN and Australian police there had failed to anticipate or correct in the course of their reform efforts up to that point (Goldsmith and Dinnen 2007).

As well as threatening local political leadership and the existing power arrangements within the local police, international police personnel also must address certain obstacles in their relationships with local police officers and members of the local community. Many locals, whether police or civilian, will exhibit suspicion towards the ends and methods of international police. For local police, many will retain loyalties to political leaders in their environment, which makes acceptance of change driven by temporary outside visitors difficult. Many will also be sceptical that the police sent to mentor them by the UN or a foreign contributing country are well-suited to provide instruction in better policing, a perception that is reinforced when foreign police are seen to be involved themselves in sexual exploitation of local women and children or other kinds of opportunistic crime (Simic 2010).

In the case of many local people, emerging from conflict or with past experiences of partisan and frequently abusive or even indifferent policing, there is little basis for trust of person assuming policing roles, even those coming from outside who cannot be linked to local patterns of political loyalty. While local reactions can vary widely, and change over time, the ambivalence that many international police encounter when attempting to keep the peace among local residents is well captured in the following quotation from an Australian police officer who had served in Timor-Leste in 2006:

> Yeah, they're quite friendly really, when they weren't throwing rocks at you.
>
> *(Respondent 35) (Goldsmith 2009, p. 122)*

The difficulties of establishing good working relationships for many police personnel is made even more difficult by short mission rotations, often a few months only or a year, and the general lack of local cultural or language appreciation. Peacekeeping or capacity-building missions that lack a ready means of communicating with local people face an immediate difficulty from their very beginning, a difficulty which is not often overcome in the life cycle of the mission, given the short-termism that characterizes so many of these missions.

So far, I have provided a series of challenges to effectiveness of policing missions in general terms. However they inevitably reflect also upon the ability of these missions to leave a lasting legacy in terms of improved human rights conditions on the ground. While assessing 'success' in these missions is difficult, in part because it is hard to isolate specific policing intervention effects from the wider conditions that impact upon those interventions (often in subtle rather than obvious ways), the overall picture, while mixed, is not a particularly hopeful one (Bayley 2014). In some places, the structures of reform exist but the evidence of deep, sustained change in behaviours and attitudes is harder to find. Experienced observers refer to this situation sometimes as *isomorphic mimicry* – the legacy left behind by international policing missions looks like something taken from functioning systems elsewhere, but in fact is only a shell or façade, and thus incapable of delivering on reform expectations. There is growing recognition that the time scale assumed in many previous missions has been unrealistically short for achieving real lasting improvements. Yet budgetary limitations, political sovereignty concerns, and reform fatigue beset even the best planned interventions and capacity-building programmes, rendering longer-term commitments less viable or acceptable to locals.

On the positive side, many police missions have contributed to consciousness-raising in areas such as domestic violence and gender relations through such measures as explicitly targeting domestic violence in the community through education as well as prosecutions, in recruiting and training women for the reformed local police forces, and in modelling different policing approaches through deployment of women police to mentoring and other field-based roles. The UN Police Division has deployed women-only public order units on some missions, thereby demonstrating that policing need not be a predominantly male preserve (see, for example, Natarajan 2008).

Even limiting violence on a temporary basis can provide relief to persons trapped in civil conflict or victimized unfairly in their communities. Sparing lives and avoiding serious injuries is one thing that peacekeeping missions can make a significant contribution to so long as their influence on the ground is maintained and sufficiently robust. In recent years, peacekeeping has grown from a purely monitoring role in the 1990s and before to formations that include more robust units that can hold ground and if necessary return fire and make arrests (Friesendorf 2012).

The message from the limited evaluation data in relation to effectiveness in situations of significant civil conflict is a positive one. Police can help to change the terms on the ground that impact upon human freedoms and rights. As a recent study observed:

> Even if violence on the battlefield is reduced by PKO [peacekeeping] troops, the sides still have reason to shape civilian loyalties through violence behind the front. Violence can be used to forcibly recruit new combatants, extract more resources, and improve a faction's relative power in preparation for renewed conflict. However, the costs to predatory factions for targeting civilians increase when UN police forces patrol civilian communities behind the frontlines. Police forces thus play an instrumental role in reducing the belligerents' opportunities to commit atrocities. Increasing UN police by just a few hundred can make a substantial difference in protecting civilian lives.
>
> *(Hultman et al. 2013, p. 888)*

This is a hopeful message. The first major problem we face however is that we lack globally the means or the will to establish police peacekeeping, or peacekeeping in general on a sufficient scale to tackle the number of conflicts currently or in the future generating human rights abuses. The situations in Syria, Libya, the Democratic Republic of Congo, Darfur and so many other places make this point about our limitations abundantly obvious. The second problem is that challenges to the Rule of Law and to human security more broadly are bigger than anything that can be resolved through police peacekeeping or institutional reform alone. This issue is examined further in the final section, in terms of what may yet be achievable.

## Conclusion: doing better in the future

More than a decade ago, the following conclusion seemed apt in terms of why police reform had only had limited impact in terms of improving the human rights' predicaments of ordinary people in many places around the world:

> We must urge upon human rights analysts and others interested in police reform the difficulty of effecting institutional reform without addressing structural and systemic factors that impact on policing. While perhaps less morally satisfying than a retributive gesture directed at guilty officials, its much greater pertinence to bringing about substantive change in practice should provide a sufficient justification to move beyond the binary judgments that have been commonplace but often lacked reform potency.
>
> *(Goldsmith 2002, p. 18)*

The need to see policing reform within a larger set of considerations (political, socioeconomic, justice system) has not altered since then (Heiduk 2015, Murney et al. 2011). Indeed, bodies such as the UN and countries such as Australia, the US and the UK have acquired a lot more experience in terms of the difficulties of reforming police and getting police to reduce violence and improve respect for human rights. From Iraq, Afghanistan and sub-Saharan Africa to the Solomon Islands and Timor-Leste, the track record of achievements is modest at best and perhaps more realistically, disappointing overall (Bayley 2014). A full accounting would probably confirm that in some places things have not only not improved but deteriorated since then. What is probably indisputable is that *international police missions are better at ending or reducing civil violence and disorder than they are at producing sustained change and improvement in local police forces.* Both conclusions have significance for human rights analysts.

There is, however, no doubt in the minds of most observers that, properly constituted and mandated, international police missions, whether engaged in peacekeeping or capacity-building or both, have and deserve to have a role, in future interventions and attempts to provide assistance to countries in need of more effective governance and controls over civil disorder. Improving human rights achievements will require a number of changes in how police are selected for international missions, how they are empowered to act in those roles, and what supportive structures and changes are needed to make change viable and sustainable. These matters have recently been the subject of detailed examination by scholars and practitioners alike. One outcome has been the production of a major statement of doctrine under the UN Strategic Guidance Framework for International Police Peacekeeping. The first statement under this Framework, the *Policy on United Nations Police in Peacekeeping Operations and Special Political Missions*, went into effect in February 2014.

The clear and present danger remaining in such efforts is the confusion around mission objectives and the mixed messages that local police and populations receive from international policing missions engaged in separate or indeed integrated and simultaneous counter-terrorism, counter-drug, community-oriented, public order, and human rights functions. This ultimately is a matter to be judged from practice and outcomes on the ground, rather than statements of principle in the form of mandates, etc. Avoiding cynicism and building trust, necessary ingredients for effective police reform, requires greater care and consideration around such matters than we have witnessed until now.

## Note

1 This and other quotes are from an interview-based study of more than 120 Australian police officers who served in international policing missions, led by the author between 2005 and 2010. The study is known as the Policing the Neighbourhood study. It was an Australian Research Council Linkage grant in partnership with the Australian Federal Police.

## References


Amnesty International, 2015. *Deadly force: police use of lethal force in the United States*. New York, NY: Amnesty International USA.

Anderson, D. and Killingray, D., 1991. Consent, coercion and colonial control: policing the Empire 1830–1940. *In*: D. Anderson and D. Killingray, *Policing the empire: government, authority and control, 1830–1940*. Manchester: Manchester University Press, 1–15.

Bayley, D., 2014. Human rights in policing: a global assessment. *Policing & Society*, 25(5), 540–7.

Berki, R.N., 1986. *Security and society: reflections on law, order and politics*. London: JM Dent.

Chappuis, F. and Gorur, A., 2015. *Reconciling security sector reform and the protection of civilians in peacekeeping contexts*. Washington, DC: Stimson Center.

Chevigny, P., 1995. *Edge of the knife: police violence in the Americas*. New York, NY: New Press.

Durch, W., 2014. *Police in UN peace operations: evolving roles and requirements*. Occasional paper 14. Oslo: International Forum for the Challenges of Peace Operations.

Ellison, G., 2007. Fostering a dependency culture: the commodification of community policing in a global marketplace. *In*: A. Goldsmith and J. Sheptycki (eds), *Crafting transnational policing*. Oxford: Hart, 203–42.

Friesendorf, C., 2012. *International intervention and the use of force: military and police roles*. Geneva: DCAF.

Goldsmith, A., 2002. Policing weak states: citizen safety and state responsibility. *Policing & Society*, 13(1), 3–21.

Goldsmith, A., 2005. Police reform and the problem of trust. *Theoretical Criminology*, 9(4), 443–70.

Goldsmith, A., 2006. Policing after conflict: peace-building and the responsibility to protect. *In*: U. Dolgopol and J. Gardam (eds), *The challenge of conflict: international law responds*. Martinus Nijhoff, 21–48.

Goldsmith, A., 2009. 'It wasn't like normal policing': voices of Australian police peacekeepers in Operation Serene, Timor-Leste 2006. *Policing & Society*, 19(2), 119–33.

Goldsmith, A. and Dinnen, S., 2007. Transnational police-building: critical lessons from Timor-Leste and Solomon Islands. *Third World Quarterly*, 28(6), 1091–109.

Goldsmith, A. and Harris, V., 2012. Trust, trustworthiness and trust-building in international policing missions. *Australian & New Zealand Journal of Criminology*, 45(2), 231–54.

Goldsmith, A. and Sheptycki, J. (eds), 2007. *Crafting transnational policing*. Oxford: Hart.

Heiduk, F., 2015. Rethinking police building. *Cooperation and Conflict*, 50(1), 69–86.

Huggins, M., 1998. *Political policing: the United States and Latin America*. Durham, NC: Duke University Press.

Hultman, L., Kathman, J. and Shannon, M., 2013. United Nations peacekeeping and civilian protection in civil war. *American Journal of Political Science*, 57(4), 875–91.

Human Rights Watch [HRW], 2015. *World report 2015*. New York, NY: HRW.

Kuzmarov, J., 2009. Modernizing repression: police training, political violence, and nation-building in the 'American century'. *Diplomatic History*, 33(2), 191–221.

Murney, T., Crawford, S. and Hider, A., 2011. Transnational policing and international development: a rule of law perspective. *Journal of International Peacekeeping*, 15, 39–71.

Natarajan, M., 2008. *Women police in a changing society: back door to equality*. Aldershot: Ashgate.

Przeworski, A., 1995. *Sustainable democracy*. Cambridge: Cambridge University Press.

Reiner, R., 2010. *The politics of the police*, 4th edn. Oxford: Oxford University Press.

Shue, H., 1980. *Basic rights*. Princeton, NJ: Princeton University Press.

Simic, O., 2010. 'Boys will be boys': human trafficking and UN peacekeeping in Bosnia and Kosovo. *In*: L. Holmes (ed.), *Trafficking and human rights: European and Asia-Pacific perspectives*. Cheltenham: Elgar, 79–94.

United Nations [UN], 2015. *UN Peacekeeping Operations Fact Sheet* 31 July 2015. Retrieved on 7 April 2016 from: www.un.org/en/peacekeeping/documents/bnote0715.pdf.

United Nations Department of Peacekeeping Operations [UN DPKO], 2014. *Policy on United Nations police in peacekeeping operations and special police missions*. New York, NY: United Nations.

United Nations High Commissioner for Refugees [UNHCR], (2014). *World at war: UNHCR global trends forced displacement 2014*. Geneva: UNHCR.

United Nations Security Council, 2014. *Resolution 2185 (2014)*. Adopted by the Security Council at its 7317th meeting on 20 November 2014.

Whitehead, L., 2002. *Democratization: theory and experience*. Oxford: Oxford University Press.

Wills, S., 2009. *Protecting civilians: the obligations of peacekeepers*. Oxford: Oxford University Press.

World Bank, 2011. *World development report 2011: conflict security and development*. Washington: World Bank.

# 26

# Criminalizing dissent

## Social movements, public order policing and the erosion of protest rights

*Greg Martin*

### Introduction

One could argue that social movements are inherently about human rights. Historically, there have been important movements against slavery, racial discrimination and gender inequality, all of which resonate with international law enshrined in the United Nations (UN) *Universal Declaration of Human Rights 1948*. In many respects, human rights reflect citizenship rights, which in the classic formulation of T.H. Marshall (1950) comprise civil, political and social rights. Social movements have been key in securing many of these rights too. In Britain, for example, early welfare movements were organized around what the 1942 Beveridge Report identified as the 'five evils' of disease, want, squalor, ignorance, and idleness. Social movement thinkers have argued that these older welfare movements paved the way for newer movements, which 'operate in and around an already established welfare state system to preserve, extend, deepen and improve service delivery' (Annetts et al. 2009, p. 10). Examples include lesbian, gay, bisexual and transgendered activism, and eco-welfare movements. However, in the current age of austerity, with dwindling welfare provision, it is questionable whether this remains the case, as many contemporary movements have emerged to protest against new forms of precarity and enduring socioeconomic inequality (Martin 2015a, pp. 78–86).

Animal rights activism demonstrates that not all social movements are about *human* rights. Moreover, the rise of neo-fascism in Europe and the emergence of the Tea Party movement in the United States (US) show how movements can be conservative, reactionary and regressive, rather than aimed at positively transforming existing power structures, which have created inequality and other kinds of disadvantage (Martin 2015a, p. 1). What is clear from the literature, however, is that most if not all social movement activity is about identifying and attempting to rectify injustice of one sort or another (Martin 2015a, pp. 56–7). And, in this regard, activists would argue they have a fundamental human 'right to protest' against perceived injustices. Before discussing the nature and scope of protest rights, some intersections of criminology, human rights and protest are explored to contextualize the issues examined in this chapter.

## Criminology, human rights and protest

Murphy and Whitty (2013) argue that if criminology is to engage with the field of human rights in the present, reflection on the history of the relationship between human rights and criminology is needed. Despite longstanding criminological engagements acknowledging the relevance of law and legal institutions in human rights (especially in the international arena), Murphy and Whitty show how some scholars are critical of the influence of the liberal legal tradition in criminology. For instance, Loader and Sparks say liberal criminology's reliance on legal rights 'is limiting because to fall back on legal discourses and institutions is a "form of negative politics", a "fencing in" of contemporary democratic forces' (Murphy and Whitty 2013, p. 577, quoting Loader and Sparks 2011, p. 93). Hence, to Loader and Sparks, 'human rights promote an unhelpful individualism and an "anti-state" oppositionalism, and lead to a liberal criminology that "throws in its lot with legal rather than political constitutionalism"' (Murphy and Whitty 2013, p. 577, quoting Loader and Sparks 2011, p. 93).

In large part, this stance is born of liberal criminologists' fear of 'state power and its potential to inflict suffering on its citizen and meddle with their legitimate rights and entitlements' (Loader and Sparks 2011, p. 93). Indeed, many of those fears have been realized since the terror attacks of 11 September 2001 (9/11), where states have moved to enhance police power, and increase generally the use of criminal law, pre-emptive crime control methods, and surveillance technologies (Martin et al. 2015). Drawing on Dembour's (2012) four ideal types of human rights thinking (natural, deliberative, protest, discursive), this liberal approach to criminological work most resembles the natural human rights school of thought, which places 'a high value on the normative power of human rights and other ethical standards', and seeks 'to preserve their protective function' in the face of penal populism, securitization, and risk society (Weber et al. 2014, p. 75).

Fear of state power or, at least, scepticism as to the motives of the political class, should cause us to reflect that '[t]he institutions which are designed to protect human beings – the state, the law, and the church in particular – are often precisely those institutions which threaten human life by the fact that they enjoy a monopoly of power' (Turner 1993, pp. 501–2). And that is why, argues Turner, '[t]he point about the concept of *human* rights is that they are extra-governmental and have been traditionally used to counteract the repressive capacity of states' (1993, pp. 498–9, emphasis in original). Thus, unlike citizenship rights, human rights cannot (and arguably should not) be tied to the nation-state (Turner 1993, p. 500).

State abuse of human rights has meant that a sizable part of criminology's historical focus has been on state crimes perpetrated by repressive regimes (Murphy and Whitty 2013, p. 570). And this is perhaps one reason why criminologists have appeared to throw in their lot with legal rather than political constitutionalism, since it is through international human rights law that most progress has been made. Moreover, it is here where social movements have had a role in forging international alliances and interacting with key supranational institutions, such as the UN, and transnational non-governmental organizations, such as Amnesty International, and Human Rights Watch (Martin 2015a, pp. 222–49). In this way, the international system provides resources and political opportunities that facilitate the global human rights movement, which is, in turn, able to exert internal pressure domestically on nation-states accused of violating human rights.

The political mobilization of 'comfort women' is an example where '[t]he relative openness of the global political system was crucial for the advancement of the comfort women movement' (Tsutsui 2006, p. 338). Comfort women were subject to systematic sex slavery by the Japanese military during World War 2. While the movement emerged in the late 1980s, it was not until 1992 that it launched its international campaign, appealing to the UN Commission on Human Rights, 'against the background of the international expansion of women's rights and the emergence of global norms about past human rights violations in the preceding decades' (Tsutsui 2006, p. 337).

Another example is in Argentina where the cause of the Mothers of the Disappeared (*Les Madres de la Plaza de Mayo*) has resonated globally and resulted, among other things, in international actors contributing 'in a concrete way to the establishment of new democratic institutions to insure human rights accountability' (Brysk 1993, p. 279). This has been described as a 'boomerang effect', which denotes 'a world-level process in which oppressed citizens use international channels to publicize human rights violations and pressure their governments and multinational corporations' (Tsutsui and Wotipka 2004, p. 595). Similarly, although the signing of the North American Free Trade Agreement represented a dark side of globalization, Muñoz (2006) argues it also drew attention to the plight of people living in the south of Mexico and the collective action of the Zapatistas, thus creating political opportunities for human rights reform within the country. Inspired by the Zapatistas, the global justice movement is another example of a movement that springs up periodically to oppose global neoliberalism at high-profile international events (Martin 2015a, pp. 236–7). Alternatively, activists conceive of themselves as part of a global movement for social justice by opposing global forces at a local level, in what is described as 'globalization from below' (Martin 2015a, p. 231).

The local–global relationship has also been regarded pertinent to relations between international human rights law and social movements, where Nash (2012) has shown how, regardless of the influence of international opportunity structures on state responses, national law remains an important means of institutionalizing human rights norms. This is because states are the ultimate guarantors of international human rights, which are interpreted by national courts. Hence, institutionalizing human rights is not an entirely top-down process, which, Nash argues, is why we need to adopt a middle way approach that brings the state back in when discussing human rights law. However, just as this approach takes issue with top-down perspectives, it is also critical of the multiplicity of social movements that demand human right 'from below', because, Nash (2012, p. 808) contends, human rights law is state-centric, 'in that it is virtually exclusively through states that international human rights law is made and enforced'. This is no less the case in respect of legal determinations about the 'right to protest', which is recognized, to varying degrees, in domestic contexts, both in the common law and in statutes.

## Right to protest

As stated earlier, all social movement activity is premised on an assumed 'right to protest'. However, whether and to what extent this right exists is the matter of some contention across common law jurisdictions. The right to protest is essentially an amalgam of the right to free speech, and the right to assemble peacefully in public. Historically, these allied rights have gained some recognition in the English common law. In the late Victorian period, *Bonnard v Perryman* contains an early expression of a right to free speech. In that case, the court considered the 'right of free speech is one which it is for the public interest that individuals should possess, and, indeed, that they should exercise without impediment, so long as no wrongful act is done'.[1] After this, according to Mead (2010, p. 4), there is a clear line of cases establishing a right of freedom of expression, culminating in 2000 in the House of Lords case of *Simms*, where Lord Steyn was of the view that, '[i]n a democracy it is the primary right: without it an effective rule of law is not possible'.[2]

The lineage of a common law right to demonstrate, protest or assemble is more complex than the right of freedom to speak. In 1936, Lord Hewart CJ stated, 'English law does not recognize any special right of public meeting for political or other purposes'.[3] However, in the 1970s, in the case of *Hubbard v Pitt*, Lord Denning MR asserted in his dissenting speech that 'the right of protest is one aspect of the right of free speech'.[4] His Lordship relied in part on a prior report by Lord Scarman, which advocated for recognition, albeit qualified, of the right to peaceful assembly and public protest (McGlone 2005, p. 276). Although Lord Denning's opinion was of limited application – as he insisted the right to demonstrate was secondary to the need for good order and passage of traffic, and that 'passage' was inconsistent with protest – it nevertheless reflected 'a growing acceptance of protesting as a normal feature of the wider political landscape' (McGlone 2005, p. 276).

In 1999, in *DPP v Jones and Lloyd*, a majority of the House of Lords recognized a right to peaceful public assembly (in the highway). However, Mead (2010, p. 5) argues the case was 'not a clear-cut ringing endorsement of a general right of protest and assembly against all-comers – though not necessarily absolute – in all places and at all times'. Indeed, it was only Lord Hutton who recognized, as a general proposition, the common law right for members of the public to assemble together to express views on matters of public concern, as 'one of the fundamental rights of citizens in a democracy'.[5]

In the United Kingdom (UK), reliance on a common law right to protest, assemble and demonstrate has now effectively been superseded by the *Human Rights Act 1998* (UK), which protects the right to peaceful protest by incorporating into domestic law Articles 10 and 11 of the *European Convention on Human Rights* (ECHR). For Mead (2010, p. 25), this amounts to a situation in the UK where 'there is now a fully-fledged right to protest [which] encompasses aspects of the rights of free speech under Article 10 and peaceful assembly contained within Article 11'. In this way, discussion of whether there is a right to protest at common law would appear redundant (Mead 2010, p. 6).

Beyond the UK, other jurisdictions have their own issues in respect of recognizing a right to protest. In the US, freedom of speech and the right to peaceable assembly are guaranteed under the First Amendment to the Constitution, although as a US federal judge recently ruled, that does not protect a right to take photos or record videos of police, unless the filming is done in the spirit of protest. This is a decision that is in line with prior proposals in California to protect citizens who record or photograph police actions, without obstructing them from performing their duties,[6] but out of step with later plans in Arizona to make it illegal to shoot close-up videos of police on the basis it would put officers in danger by distracting them while engaging with suspects.[7]

In Canada, freedom of expression and freedom of peaceful assembly are protected under Section 2 of the Charter of Rights and Freedoms, although research there has shown how protest policing, for example, has involved 'the systematic violation of constitutional protections against arbitrary arrest and detention . . . as well as protection against abusive searches' (Fortin et al. 2013: 41). Indeed, this tied to what has been observed as a marked erosion of rights and freedoms since 9/11, not only in Canada but also in the US, where commentators have argued the *USA PATRIOT Act 2001* is a source of human rights incursions and constitutional breaches, and in the UK, where the *Justice and Security Act 2013* has been regarded as one of the latest challenges to the British Constitution, civil liberties and due process rights (Martin 2014; Martin and Scott Bray 2013; Martin et al. 2015).

It is well known that Australia is the only western democracy without a national human rights statute or Bill of Rights (Charlesworth et al. 2003, p. 424), and there is only limited provision in the Australian Constitution to protect individual rights and freedoms. Some of those rights are express rights, such as freedom of religion, right to vote, and trial by jury. Other rights, such as freedom of political communication, are implied from the system of representative government provided for in the Constitution.[8] In Australia, then, while there is no right to protest at common law, the courts have accepted such a right exists as part of the democratic system of government (McGlone 2005, pp. 274–5).

The absence in Australia of a federal human rights instrument is largely the result of the fact that the drafters of the Constitution believed the doctrine of representative and responsible government would be sufficient to protect individual rights and freedoms (Martin 2014, p. 534). More recently, Victoria and the Australian Capital Territory have enacted human rights legislation protecting the right of peaceful assembly, although those human rights are not absolute, and 'are subject to such reasonable limits as can be demonstrably justified in a free and democratic society' (Gotsis 2015, p. v). Moreover, in Queensland, the *Peaceful Assembly Act 1992* (Qld) provides expressly for a statutory right to assembly, even though commentary suggests statutory rights such as this do not necessarily provide greater protection for the right to assembly (Gotsis 2015, p. 34). In New South Wales (NSW), by contrast, Part 4 of the *Summary Offences Act 1988* (NSW), which relates to public assemblies, makes no mention of the right to assembly. Nevertheless, the objective of the Act is to facilitate cooperation between police and protestors (Gotsis 2015, p. 14).

As we shall see in the next section, this approach is referred to as the 'negotiated management' of protest, which many believe is now the dominant mode of public order policing. But others disagree, arguing that current protest policing style is increasingly coercive and authoritarian. Indeed, recent events in NSW have led opposition parties to claim heavy-handed police tactics at anti-mining demonstrations have undermined the right to peaceful protest, which has, in turn, caused the state government to consider new legislation to counteract 'illegal protest activity' and safeguard business interests (Gotsis 2015, p. 1), including up to seven years in jail for protestors locking onto mine equipment (Robertson 2016). Similarly, Tasmania has introduced legislation seeking 'to "rebalance the scales" between the right to protest and the rights of business to create economic opportunities and develop the economy' (Gotsis 2015, p. 35). Likewise, Western Australia has enacted laws 'to deter environmental protestors from locking on to equipment at mining and logging sites or taking other obstructionist action' (Gotsis 2015, p. 36). These developments reinforce the importance in capitalist societies of what is considered below as the *political economy of protest*, which appears more than ever to be accompanied by an increased recourse to criminal law to deal with public protest: what is referred to later as *criminalizing dissent*.

## Policing protest

Numerous developments that have occurred since 9/11 pertaining to the intersection of criminology, human rights and protest involve the regulation and control of protest by police, who are granted power to do so at common law but are increasingly given authority in statutes. Perhaps unsurprisingly, in this context, there has been an 'increasing conflation of direct action with terrorism' (Mead 2010, p. 380). In the UK, that has resulted in police being given stop and search powers, which under Section 44 of the *Terrorism Act 2000* (UK), for example, do not require reasonable suspicion (Mead 2010, p. 380). While these powers have been used to stop and search protestors and journalists at demonstrations in London, police have also arrested and charged protestors with 'violent disorder' offences under the *Public Order Act 1986* (UK) (Gilmore 2010, p. 21).

Globally, high-profile 'mega-events' such as World Trade Organization, World Bank, G8 and G20 meetings have all been subject to increased securitization since 9/11. Although this is a process that started after the Battle of Seattle in 1999, it intensified after the terror attacks in 2001 (Martin 2011). The Asia-Pacific Economic Cooperation (APEC) meeting held in Sydney, Australia, in 2007 was an example where police were given enhanced powers to deal with public order at a one-off international event. Subsequently, however, those powers were incorporated into the *Major Events Act 2009* (NSW), which is an amalgamation of laws specially enacted for major events, such as the APEC meeting, the 2000 Olympics Games, and the 2003 Rugby World Cup (Martin 2011, p. 34). This generic piece of legislation has been seen as oppressive and trespassing on individual rights and civil liberties, since it provides that penalties will apply to the person who *is about to contravene* a provision of the Act (Martin 2010, p. 164). Laws like these have been regarded as symptomatic of the normalization of exceptional measures since 9/11, which is a process that has transformed police function from reactive to pre-emptive (Martin 2010). In the current era, this becomes the usual means of dealing not only with terrorists, dissidents, and protestors, but also organized crime gangs, and refugees; often through the use of control orders and secret procedures (Martin 2014, 2015b).

Accordingly, a feature of contemporary policing is 'exceptional consent', which subjugates citizen rights and the rule of law to the imperatives of security and a politics of privileging the rights of the state (De Lint and Hall 2009, p. 267). That not only affects everyday police practice but also protest policing style, which assumes the form of 'strategic incapacitation' to include pre-emptive arrests, the demarcation of protest-free zones, and the corralling or 'kettling' of protestors (Martin 2011, p. 28). As one of the most controversial police tactics, kettling was held to be lawful by the House of Lords in *Austin v Commissioner of the Police for the Metropolis*.[9] Subsequently, the European Court of Human Rights agreed there was no deprivation of liberty under Article 5(1) of the ECHR, although the Court limited its findings to the 'specific and exceptional facts of this case',[10] also holding that kettling should not be used 'to stifle or discourage protest, given the fundamental importance of freedom of expression and assembly in all democratic societies'.[11]

Endorsement of the technique of kettling nevertheless seems to have been perceived by police to sanction its much wider use (Mead 2010, p. 355), such as during the G20 protests in London in 2009, which resulted in the death of innocent passer-by, Ian Tomlinson, after he was assaulted by a police officer (Martin and Scott Bray 2013). Arguably, the fallout from the Tomlinson affair could explain the relatively timid police approach during the English riots of 2011, although, as Wainwright et al. (2012, pp. 32–3) say, the reverberations from the riots have influenced the attitude of courts to public order policing, forging an acceptance that kettling may be employed in limited situations.

The apparent normalization of kettling and other repressive tactics gainsays the view of those who observe a trend towards a more democratic protest policing style; a 'negotiated management' approach whereby police and protestors engage in dialogue with one another (see Martin 2011 for discussion). By contrast, it has been argued the current style of policing, particularly at international mega-events, constitutes a 'global protest policing repertoire' (Martin 2011), which tends to involve increased use of authoritarian and wholly undemocratic tactics (Gilmore 2010). Nevertheless, 'the current mode is an effective mixture of hard- and soft-line tactics, including the use of "non-lethal weapons" as well as laws, codes, regulations, and public relations strategies that attempt to control protest spaces directly and indirectly' (Fernandez 2008, p. 15).

Policing of space is linked to the increased privatization of public space in urban settings under global neoliberalism (Martin 2011). That has been illustrated most recently by Occupy, which, in London, set up physical encampments 'to identify the geography of capitalism', and to reassert 'the spatial dimensions of exclusion and inequality by forcing society to recognize that capitalist accumulation happens in certain places, and that these places can be named, located and objected to' (Pickerill and Krinsky 2012, pp. 280–1). The police's harsh treatment of Occupy also serves as another illustration of the increased securitization of society over the last decade, as well as 'an ongoing erosion of the right to dissent for much longer', which is why, say Pickerill and Krinsky (2012, p. 285), 'the very act of confronting the police has a central place in what could be called the "Occupy" repertoire'.

## Political economy of protest and criminalizing dissent

The erosion of civil liberties and human rights since 9/11 has included the attrition of protest rights, which have been impacted by two significant developments. The first pertains to what might be described as a *political economy of protest*. Particularly at high-profile international events, protest has to be contained and controlled (even nullified) to provide the appearance of 'total security' (Martin 2011, p. 29). Especially in urban space that is not privatized, demonstrations are carefully orchestrated and managed by state authorities to facilitate 'place promotion', advertising 'global cities' as safe and secure to reassure and attract tourists and corporate investment (Martin 2011, pp. 37–8). Among other things, this means restricting the freedom of movement of known activists, as well as socially and economically marginalized groups, such as the homeless, whose presence challenges sanitized images of cites as sites free from decay and danger (Martin 2011, p. 31).

Just as the political economy of protest reveals as fragile the idea that we live in free liberal democratic societies, where public dissent and peaceful assembly are assumed rights, so too does the *criminalization of dissent*, which was alluded to earlier when we looked at the provision for pre-emptive measures at protest events in New South Wales. Indeed, it has been said that the limits imposed on the right to assembly by the criminal law here are so extensive that, '[a]n analysis which referred to every possible demonstration offence would constitute a veritable summary of much of the criminal law' (Bronitt and Williams 1996, p. 315), including, among other things, offences of breach of the peace, obstruction, offensive conduct, affray, unlawful entry and damage to property (see Gotsis 2015: 22–31). Criminalizing dissent is also indicated in the propensity of authorities to conflate public protest and terrorism (mentioned above), which is especially easy to do in the post-9/11 context where a generalized culture of fear and anxiety means politicians are able to exploit public insecurity about law and order, which they can use for political advantage (Martin 2011, p. 37). The protest–terrorism nexus was highlighted recently when the Australian government published a radicalization awareness kit, which warns that violent extremism, such as radical environmentalism, can grow out of involvement in the 'alternative music scene, student politics and leftwing activism' (Australian Government 2015: 11).

An example that highlights some of these developments in protest policing was evident in Queensland, when it hosted the G20 summit in Brisbane and Cairns, 15–16 November 2014. In preparation for the event, the state government introduced the *G20 Safety and Security Act 2013* (Qld). This statute was by no means unusual, and, in many respects, it aped legislation enacted ahead of the 2007 Sydney APEC meeting. Among other things, the Queensland Act provided for: police searches, including strip searches, in security areas (ss 23–25); arrest without warrant, and detention if the person is charged with an offence under another Act (s. 79); and presumption against bail for those arrested for assault of a police officer, discharging a missile at a police officer, or generally otherwise disrupting the G20 meeting (s. 82) (Galloway and Ardill 2014, p. 6).

The G20 laws cannot be seen in isolation, however. They formed part of the broader populist agenda of the Queensland government, led by State Premier Campbell Newman, which had as its centrepiece a raft of measures designed to deal with the serious organized crime of 'bikies' (outlaw motorcycle gangs). Legislation here includes the *Vicious Lawless Association Disestablishment Act 2013* (Qld) (VLAD), Section 7(1) of which imposes:

> mandatory sentences of 15 years' imprisonment in addition to the original sentence for a declared offence on a 'vicious lawless associate', such as a bikie club member, and an extra 10 years (that is, 25 years on top of the original sentence) for a vicious lawless associate who was an office bearer of the relevant association at the time or during the commission of the offence.
>
> *(Martin 2014, p. 535)*

Although granting police extraordinary powers at large international events is not unusual, what is worrying about the situation in Queensland is the potential for those laws to interact with legislation directed at bikies:

> If for example an otherwise peaceful (and lawful) assembly turns violent, there is the possibility for people to be charged with affray, one of the offences listed as a trigger for operation of the *VLAD Act*. Carrying out such an act with three others deemed to be participants in a serious crime then renders the accused a participant in a criminal organization. This would attract the additional mandatory sentences.
>
> *(Galloway and Ardill 2014, p. 6, emphasis in original)*

Notwithstanding the fact that Queensland provides a statutory right to peaceful assembly, it has been argued that what has occurred there is an affront to the doctrine of representative and responsible government, which, as we saw earlier, is a lynchpin of Australian constitutionalism (Martin 2014). First, the idea of representativeness is something of a misnomer, given Queensland's unicameral system (where there is no upper house to act as a check on power exercised by the government and executive branch); the fact that the anti-bikie laws were rushed through, bypassing parliamentary committee and public consultation processes; and despite claims made by the state's then Attorney-General that 70 per cent of Queenslanders supported the new laws, the Newman government secured its overwhelming parliamentary majority with 49.66 per cent of the overall vote in the 2012 state election (Martin 2014, pp. 536–7). It has been argued the idea of responsible government is also inappropriate in the Queensland case, which highlights the dangers of 'overcriminalization'; that is 'an increased recourse to criminal law and penal sanctions to solve particular problems that may be better addressed through alternative means, such as increasing state resources or allocating them more efficiently' (Martin 2014, p. 537).

## Conclusion

Despite being an extreme example, the Queensland case demonstrates what we saw earlier as liberal criminologists' suspicion of the motives of politicians, and fear of state power to erode citizen rights and freedoms. However, while interest in human rights abuses has tended to focus on state coercion and violation of civil liberties, the policing of high-profile demonstrations also highlights the political economy of protest, and the private interests involved in controlling these events. Although there is an increasing convergence of private and state interests in this respect, the state will intervene to criminalize protest, whereas private corporations use civil litigation to contain resistance and prevent criticism of their activities that undermine human rights and damage the environment. An example are Strategic Lawsuits Against Public Participation or SLAPPs, which are being used across western democracies not to acquire damages but to silence protest and instil fear of civil action in the minds of activists (Anthony 2009).

It would seem then that public protest is getting hard to do in societies that profess to be democratic and support human rights. This is especially so for Muslims in the post-9/11 era, who, fearing their criticism of western governments' foreign policy might be misconstrued, and indeed that they may be subject to criminal charges under anti-terrorist legislation, are now less likely to participate in traditional modes of political activism, such as street protests (Kundnani 2014, p. 199). Indeed, this reflects arguments made by liberal criminologists writing from the natural human rights perspective (mentioned above), who say that:

> an absence of human rights protections in relation to certain security practices designated as 'preventive' is 'unsafe', particularly in a context where the burdens of these policies fall mainly on minorities who cannot necessarily expect to be protected via political processes.
> *(Weber et al. 2014, p. 75)*

However, the idea that public dissent is becoming less easy to do is also of wider concern, given populations in liberal democracies display a generalized apathy towards political participation and civic engagement, and a deep-seated suspicion of political elites (Martin 2015a, pp. 2–3). For some, social media and new digital technologies provide hope to beleaguered activists. We saw this during the Arab Spring of 2011, which spread virally through peoples' use of Facebook, Twitter and YouTube. Although some campaign organizations, such as GetUp! in Australia, are focused almost exclusively on digital activism (Vromen 2015), commentary on the Arab Spring (and Occupy) highlights the fact that protest in actual public spaces was just as important as mobilization in virtual spaces (Martin 2015a, p. 217).

Despite widespread disenchantment with traditional modes of political engagement, the state nevertheless remains a key player in many social movement struggles. Indeed, as Nash (2012) argues, nation-states and domestic courts remain important guarantors and interpreters of international human rights. However, even state actors now realize that, like activists, they need to embrace digital technologies to foster public engagement in political processes. Disillusionment with politics is particularly prevalent among young people, although they are perhaps better placed than any other cohort to take advantage of opportunities provided by digital forms of political participation (Vromen et al. 2014). Recently, this potential was recognized in UK debates over intergenerational injustice associated with the unfunded promises baby boomers have made to themselves, which young people and subsequent generations will have to pay for in taxes.

In 2012, baby boomers took advantage of a British government initiative introducing a website for registering e-petitions, which promised that those reaching 100,000 signatures would be passed to a House of Commons backbench committee. Boomers garnered enough signatures to trigger a backbench debate, calling for a Minister for Older People. Although they lost, the government initiative hinted at the potential of digital democracy for campaigns over intergenerational fairness, where, it has been suggested, Generation Y might also petition 'for their own minister to represent their long-term interests, not least to pursue mechanisms to counter baby boomers' innate talent for kicking the financial can down the road' (Johnson

2015, p. 8). This is but one example demonstrating how future campaigns over human rights and injustice will likely involve greater citizen participation via digital media.

## Notes

1 *Bonnard v Perryman* [1891] 2 Ch 269 (CA) at 284.
2 *R v Secretary of State for the Home Department; ex parte Simms* [2000] 2 AC 115 (HL) at 125.
3 *Duncan v Jones* [1936] 1 KB 218 at 222.
4 *Hubbard v Pitt* [1976] QB 142 (CA) at 178–9.
5 *Director of Public Prosecutions v Jones and Lloyd* [1999] 2 AC 240 (HL) at 287.
6 See 'California moves to protect citizens' right to record, photo police', 8 April 2015, available at: https://www.rt.com/usa/247981-california-recording-cops-reprisal-protections/.
7 See 'Arizona lawmaker introduces bill to criminalize filming police at close range', 11 January 2016, available at: https://www.rt.com/usa/328547-arizona-police-filming-bill/.
8 *Australian Capital Television v Commonwealth* (1992) 177 CLR 106; *Lange v Australian Broadcasting Corporation* (1997) 175 CLR 520.
9 *Austin v Commissioner of the Police for the Metropolis* [2009] UKHL 5.
10 *Austin v United Kingdom* ECtHR, 15 March 2012 at [68].
11 *Austin v United Kingdom* ECtHR, 15 March 2012 at [68].

## References


Annetts, J., Law, A., McNeish, W. and Mooney, G., 2009. *Understanding social welfare movements*. Bristol: Policy Press.

Anthony, T., 2009. Quantum of strategic litigation: quashing public participation. *Australian Journal of Human Rights*, 14(2), 1–38.

Australian Government (2015) *Preventing Violent Extremism and Radicalization in Australia*, available at: www.livingsafetogether.gov.au.

Bronitt, S. and Williams, G., 1996. Political freedom as an outlaw: republican theory and political protest. *Adelaide Law Review*, 18(2), 289–330.

Brysk, A., 1993. From above and below: social movements, the international system, and human rights in Argentina. *Comparative Political Studies*, 26(3), 259–85.

Charlesworth, H., Chiam, M., Hovell, D. and Williams, G., 2003. Deep anxieties: Australia and the international order. *Sydney Law Review*, 25(4), 423–65.

De Lint, W. and Hall, A., 2009. *Intelligent control: developments in public order policing in Canada*. Toronto: University of Toronto Press.

Dembour, M., 2012. What are human rights? Four schools of thought. *In*: T. Cushman (ed.), *Handbook of human rights*. Abingdon: Routledge, Chapter 13.

Fernandez, L.A., 2008. *Policing dissent: social control and the anti-globalization movement*. Brunswick, NJ: Rutgers University Press.

Fortin, V., Lemonde, L., Poisson, J. and Poisson, M. (2013) *Repression, discrimination and the student strike: testimonies and analysis*. Québec: Ligue des droits et libertés; Association des jurists progressistes; Association pour une solidarité syndicale étudiante.

Galloway, K. and Ardill, A., 2014. Queensland: a return to the moonlight state? *Alternative Law Journal*, 39(1), 3–8.

Gilmore, J., 2010. Policing protest: an authoritarian consensus. *Criminal Justice Matters*, 82(1), 21–3.

Gotsis, T., 2015. *Protests and the law in NSW*. Briefing Paper No 7/2015. Sydney: New South Wales Parliamentary Research Service.

Johnson, M., 2015. *Who will care for generation Y? The Baby Boomers' Legacy*. London: Centre for Policy Studies.

Kundnani, A., 2014. *The Muslims are coming! Islamophobia, extremism and the domestic war on terror*. London: Verso.

Loader, I. and Sparks, R., 2011. *Public criminology?* Abingdon: Routledge.

Marshall, T.H., 1950. *Citizenship and social class and other essays*. Cambridge: University of Cambridge Press.

Martin, G., 2010. No worries? Yes worries! How New South Wales is creeping towards a police state. *Alternative Law Journal*, 35(3), 163–7.

Martin, G., 2011. Showcasing security: the politics of policing space at the 2007 Sydney APEC meeting. *Policing & Society*, 21(1), 27–48.

Martin, G., 2014. Outlaw motorcycle gangs and secret evidence: reflections on the use of criminal intelligence in the control of serious organised crime in Australia. *Sydney Law Review*, 36(3), 501–39.

Martin, G., 2015a. *Understanding social movements*. London: Routledge.

Martin, G., 2015b. Stop the boats! Moral panic in Australia over asylum seekers. *Continuum: Journal of Media & Cultural Studies*, 29(3), 304–22.

Martin, G. and Scott Bray, R., 2013. Discolouring democracy? Policing, sensitive evidence and contentious deaths in the United Kingdom. *Journal of Law and Society*, 40(4), 624–56.

Martin, G., Scott Bray, R. and Kumar, M. (eds), 2015. *Secrecy, law and society*. London: Routledge.

McGlone, D., 2005. The right to protest. *Alternative Law Journal*, 30(6), 274–7.

Mead, D., 2010. *The new law of peaceful protest: rights and regulation in the Human Rights Act era*. Oxford: Hart Publishing.

Muñoz, J.A., 2006. International opportunities and domestic protest: Zapatistas, Mexico and the new world economy. *Social Movement Studies*, 5(3), 251–74.

Murphy, T. and Whitty, N., 2013. Making history: academic criminology and human rights. *British Journal of Criminology*, 53, 568–87.

Nash, K., 2012. Human rights, movements and law: on not researching legitimacy. *Sociology*, 46(5), 797–812.

Pickerill, J. and Krinsky, J., 2012. Why does Occupy matter? *Social Movement Studies*, 11(3–4), 279–87.

Robertson, J. (2016) 'Mining protestors could face seven years' jail under Baird government CSG plans', *The Sydney Morning Herald*, 11 March 2016, available at: http://www.smh.com.au/nsw/mining-protesters-face-seven-years-jail-under-baird-government-csg-plans-20160310-gnfdi8.html.

Tsutsui, K., 2006. Redressing past human rights violations: global dimensions of contemporary social movements. *Social Forces*, 85(1), 331–54.

Tsutsui, K. and Wotipka, C.M., 2004. Global civil society and the international human rights movement: citizen participation in human rights international nongovernmental organizations. *Social Forces*, 83(2), 587–620.

Turner, B.S., 1993. Outline of a theory of human rights. *Sociology*, 27(3), 489–512.

Vromen, A., 2015. Campaign entrepreneurs in online collective action: GetUp! in Australia. *Social Movement Studies*, 14(2), 195–213.

Vromen, A., Xenos, M.A. and Loader, B., 2014. Young people, social media and connective action: from organizational maintenance to everyday political talk. *Journal of Youth Studies*, 18(1), 80–100.

Wainwright, T., Morris, A., Craig, K. and Greenhill, O., 2012. *The protest handbook*. Haywards Heath: Bloomsbury.

Weber, L., Fishwick, E. and Marmo, M., 2014. *Crime, justice and human rights*. Basingstoke: Palgrave Macmillan.

# 27

# The limits of migration-related human rights

## Connecting exploitation to immobility

*Sanja Milivojevic, Marie Segrave and Sharon Pickering*

### Introduction

The increased desire for cross-border mobility in the age of globalization is well documented in contemporary social science research (see works of Pickering, Weber, Aas, Bosworth, Wonders and others). Within this context, however, the opportunities for safe and/or regulated[1] transnational mobility have been limited and largely bifurcated along lines of privilege whereby (generally) those from rich, western nations who have social and economic capital travel the most freely. Conversely, those from the least desirable nations, who have little or no social or economic capital are prevented or *discouraged* from travelling (see Bauman 1998, Adey 2009, Wolff 1993, Kaufmann 2002). As a consequence, the desire for mobility and access to regulated migration routes is no more than a mere aspiration for many (Aas 2007, Bowling and Sheptycki 2015). Nonetheless transnational mobility remains achievable, albeit via undocumented means and irregular routes.[2] Indeed it is estimated that undocumented migrants total at least 50 million of the world's 232 million international migrants (International Organization for Migration 2014, p. 4). Arguably undocumented migrants are more likely than their documented counterparts to exist at the fringes of society; marginalized, exploited, silenced and violated in countries of origin, transit and destination. This vulnerability can be attributed in large part to the role of the state in creating and sustaining conditions via law and policy, which limit regular migration opportunities and seek to punish irregular migrants. Our focus is to consider how individual harms that can be linked to the broader legal and political infrastructure, may be sustained in spite of international treaties and human rights obligations.

Human rights frameworks are often singled out as the potential lifeline for mobile bodies at risk (Satterthwaite 2005, Weber and Pickering 2011). Yet it has also been noted that there exists a 'genuine tension between international human rights law and the exercise of state sovereignty' (Crépeau et al. 2007, p. 312) when it comes to resolving complex questions of irregular migration. We examine this tension primarily via the efforts to prevent, deter and punish human trafficking, which offers a lens through which to identify the limits of human rights protection in relation to mobility and migration. In this chapter we consider how existing international human rights frameworks are deployed in addressing and preventing harm in relation to transnational mobility between the Global North and Global South, for those most vulnerable to exploitation and harm.

## The stratification of mobility and human rights protection

Transnational mobility, the simple crossing into and out of a national sovereign territory, is a human right written into the *Magna Carta Libertatum* in 1215 (Articles 41 and 42; Adey 2009, p. 105). Yet while the language of human rights in its contemporary form continues to speak to the universal (see Donnelly 2007) it is noted repeatedly that the most vulnerable across the globe are least likely to experience the full expression of their human rights and/or access the means through which to challenge the abuse of their human rights. This is absolutely evident in the area of human mobility and border control.

In an age of globalization our capacity to turn the *potential* to be mobile into actual mobility projects is deeply stratified (Wolff 1993, Kaufmann 2002). While many aspects of the nation state have been dismantled, or at least loosened in the context of globalization (cf. Sassen 1998), borders are a critical site for the assertion of sovereignty and the performance of protection (Pickering and Weber 2006, Sassen 1998, Weber and Bowling 2008). We live in a time where, arguably, equal capital is invested into both accelerating the process for desired migrants to cross national borders (for example, in relation to tourists, skilled workers) and preventing 'unwanted' migrants (including asylum seekers, minorities, women, and economic migrants from the Global South) from entering. While human rights frameworks encourage nation states to respect, protect and fulfil rights of migrants, we can consistently identify a range of practices that directly or indirectly impact undesired migrant populations negatively (Satterthwaite 2005, Khosravi 2010). When mobile bodies embark on their migratory journeys, they are subjected to a whole range of policies that seek to further regulate and immobilize. Many of these strategies adopted by nations across the globe can be characterized as practices of 'crimmigration' (Stumpf 2007, Aas 2011) involving the work of immigration and justice processes coming together within the context of the securitization of migration. The merging of security narratives in border regulation processes, combined with anti-immigration sentiment (targeted at unwanted migrant populations who are seen as a threat) across the Global North (Wickes and Sydes 2015) has justified increasingly strict limitations on the right to enter and exit a sovereign state. Despite the heavy investment in immobilizing policies, they have generally failed to achieve their intended purpose of preventing unwanted flows and managing immigration (Castles 2004). For us, what is critical, is not so much the failure to prevent or deter migration flows (and/or to detect and remove unwanted irregular migrants) but the harms that efforts to prevent, deter and detect produce and sustain, and the failure of the existing human rights regime to either delimit these harms or to effect better protection for the most vulnerable. We are able to explore some of these harms through an examination of the suite of measures implemented to address human trafficking and the overarching commitments to the rights of migrants to be mobile and protected from harm or persecution.

For the purposes of this chapter we simply note that human trafficking is understood at the international level as a crime in the traditional sense: involving victims and offenders, where offenders may be individuals or part of organized crime (see Segrave et al. 2009). This is evidenced via its location within the Human Rights and international law: which is a supplementary protocol within the UN *Convention against Transnational Organized Crime* (UNTOC).[3] The UNTOC and its two key protocols – the *Protocol to Prevent, Suppress and Punish Trafficking in Persons, especially Women and Children* (the 'Palermo Protocol') and the *Protocol against the Smuggling of Migrants by Land, Sea or Air* (the 'Smuggling Protocol') – constitute the backbone of the international framework applicable in the context of migration and mobility. Problematically, the Convention and its Protocols locates migration (through practices of human smuggling and human trafficking) in the context of transnational organized crime. An outcome of such an approach is that combatting trafficking and smuggling requires a tough law and order, 'zero tolerance' approach to both the crime itself and offenders. To combat trafficking and smuggling, nation states are required to, above all, criminalize such practices (Article 5 of the Palermo Protocol and Article 6 of the Smuggling Protocol), prosecute offenders (Article 4 of the Palermo Protocol and the Smuggling Protocol) and strengthen border controls 'as may be necessary to prevent and detect trafficking in persons/the smuggling of migrants' (Article 11 of the Palermo Protocol and the Smuggling Protocol). While criminal liability of migrants is explicitly forbidden in Article 5 of the Smuggling Protocol, the process of criminalizing undocumented migrants and even victims of trafficking is well documented in the literature (Lee 2011, Sanchez 2015). The Protocol is not located under a readily identifiable human rights convention, but rather it is a specifically crime-related treaty. This in and of itself extends the gap between human rights and the international legal framing of human trafficking.

We adopt an understanding of human trafficking that sits counter to the Palermo Protocol, recognizing human trafficking as a practice of exploitation enabled and sustained via practices of nation states (see Segrave et al. 2009, Chuang 2014). There is a significant body of work that sets out different positions on how best to understand and respond to human trafficking (cf. Segrave et al. 2009, Anti-Trafficking Review 2015), as well as detailing the process through which it came to be recognized as a concern for the international community both historically and contemporaneously (see Kempadoo et al. 2005, Agustin 2007, Lee 2011). Through understanding human trafficking as a form of exploitation that can happen to transnational migrants with limited options to move across and within borders via regularized, transparent routes we begin to recognize how various state practices can create or further entrench vulnerability and, in so doing, contribute to the vulnerability to exploitative practices including, but not limited to, human trafficking. Thus in this chapter we examine the desire to be globally mobile, the process of transnational travel and the arrival in a country of destination; specifically, we look at how the process of moving through these phases of travel (that some people will move through many times over, through both forced and unforced passages) interacts with human rights and human trafficking-related protections in place, and how they fail in various ways to protect the most vulnerable.

## Mediating mobility: border hardening

It is difficult to easily identify a right to mobility and it is broadly agreed that a right to mobility is only partially located within the international human rights frameworks (see Pécoud and de Guchteneire 2006). The UN Universal Declaration of Human Rights (UDHR) in Article 13(2) states that '[e]veryone has the right to leave any country, including his own, and to return to his country'. Similarly, the *European Convention on Human Rights* states that '[e]veryone shall be free to leave any country, including his own' (Article 2 of the Protocol No. 4 to the Convention[4]). However, the explicitly acknowledged right to emigrate does not include the right to immigrate (Pécoud and de Guchteneire 2006, Pécoud 2009), and immigration is a process that requires the balance of human rights with 'the interest of national security or public safety' (Article 2 of the Protocol No. 4 of the European Convention). Restricting the right to mobility, to emigrate but not to immigrate, impacts the global population as all transnational mobility is subject to some form of regulation and oversight.

However, the international human rights framework has largely been silent on the long (and intensifying) process of border hardening across the Global North (and increasingly, the Global South) which have resulted in these legal and administrative processes being drastically reduced for some and greatly increased for others. The dominant narrative that defines migration and mobility as a national security issue has effectively drowned out the discourse of human rights as an important priority or obligation to uphold (see Pécoud and de Guchteneire 2006, p. 73, Pickering 2011). On the one hand this process of border hardening has occurred within the context of fortifying geographical borders from the 'threat' of organized crime and 'illegal' migrants. This has justified a range of militarized interventions targeted at threats to the nation including terrorism, human trafficking, drug trafficking, and people smuggling (Wilson 2015, Segrave and Milivojevic 2015, Chacón 2010). Yet these same militarized practices can also be implemented in the name of protection. In the case of human trafficking, preventing 'potential victims' from crossing borders and/or protecting potential victims upon their arrival into a nation (see Pickering and Ham 2014, Milivojevic 2015). Strategies of immobilization range from traditional border policing measures that recently include a new fence built in the heart of Europe (along the Serbian–Hungarian border, see Womack 2015), to these more subtle so-called 'humanitarian' immobilizing strategies, driven by dubious pre-crime strategies (especially in the context of preventing potential exploitation in sex industry and human trafficking of transiting migrant women).

It is through examining responses to trafficking in people that we can begin to identify the ways in which efforts to stop exploitation have become merged with preventing and discouraging migration and mobility of those deemed to be most vulnerable (those who are also part of the population of 'undesirable' migrants from the perspective of nations in the Global North). For example, recent international sporting events such as the 2006 and 2010 FIFA World Cup and the 2012 London Olympic Games have generated a media maelstrom regarding the potential for women to be 'trafficked' to the location of the sporting event (see Ford 2012 regarding London Olympics, and Milivojevic 2008, Gould 2010 and Ham 2011 regarding the 2006 and 2010 FIFA World Cup) for the purposes of sexual exploitation. These concerns have been challenged and undermined by data on what is occurring, including women choosing to migrate to these locations for sex work in some instances (see Milivojevic and Pickering 2013, Milivojevic 2008, Ham 2011). However, what is important to note here is that in countries identified as the most at risk of 'vulnerable women' being 'tricked' into leaving the country, the response has been a commitment to making emigration processes more rigorous and strict, making it *more difficult* for women who want to migrate to do so via regulated means. In this context there is little evidence of empowering vulnerable populations, or upholding their rights, rather what we see is evidence of the reduction of the agency that 'further immobilizes women migrants' (Milivojevic 2015, p. 297). Importantly, we have noted elsewhere that the inaccessibility of legal migration routes does not actually result in immobilizing populations but instead leads them into the willing and able black market of migration service providers who charge significant funds to enable immigration. In doing so, they are often putting individuals at the risk of situations of debt bondage and/or other exploitative practices in transit or upon arrival (Segrave et al. 2009, Lee 2011, Chacón 2010).

These practices of preventing and deterring mobility, as Weber and Pickering (2011) document, also have a tangible, and countable human cost. Between 1993 and 2010, nearly 14,000 people crossed borders, many in the process of trying to enter Fortress Europe (Weber and Pickering 2011). Despite the death toll, which increases daily, it remains the case that 'virtually nothing is done to improve the situation' (Pécoud and de Guchteneire 2006, p. 74). Importantly, accountability of nation states of the Global North in failing to respect, protect and fulfil rights of migrants is sporadically, if ever, invoked. While Aas and Gundhus (2015, p. 1) have recently argued that securitization and militarization of borders are increasingly followed by the development of 'humanitarian forms of solidarity within the international and domestic governance', the finger of blame for human rights violations including migrant deaths almost exclusively points to human smugglers, traffickers, sending or transit countries, and migrants themselves (Pécoud and de Guchteneire 2006, Sanchez 2015, Sitkin 2015). Through the crime control framework that the international and national human trafficking response relies upon, restrictive migration policies are scapegoated from the problem and thus, are not attended to in the development of a holistic solution that puts first the reduction of vulnerability to exploitation (cf. Pécoud and de Guchteneire 2006). There are no calls to consider liberalization of migration regimes to disrupt trafficking in people and various exploitative practices associated with trafficking. The results, as we demonstrate elsewhere (Segrave et al. 2009), is that anti-trafficking policies can work hand-in-hand with border hardening efforts, resulting in human rights violations as tough immigration policies are often justified by the need to prevent and suppress trafficking. The process of immobilizing undocumented migrants and asylum seekers before they reach the geographical borders of the Global North is ever intensifying, as mobile bodies are increasingly denied the opportunity to leave the country of origin, or continue their migratory processes through countries of transit. What is also intensifying, as we examine below in relation to migrant labour, is the policing of internal borders to identify and deport irregular non-citizens with a similar emphasis on targeting the least desirable and most vulnerable migrant population.

## Regulating mobile bodies in the country of destination: work and regulation

The international human rights framework around migrant labour consists of three key documents: the *International Convention on the Protection of the Rights of All Migrant Workers and Members of Their Families* ('Migrant Workers Convention' or 'MWC'), the International Labour Organization (ILO) Convention 97 on Migration for Employment, and the ILO Convention 143 on migrant workers (Supplementary Provisions). Together with the UN Special Rapporteur on the human rights of migrants and the UN Committee on Migrant Workers, this framework aims to provide a platform for comprehensive protection of migrant workers, development of national migration policies and international cooperation (Office of the High Commissioner for Human Rights [OHCHR] 2015).[5]

The MWC is a UN multilateral treaty, signed on 18 December 1990. As 'one of the core UN human rights treaties' (OHCHR 2015), the MWC entered into force on 1 July 2003, stipulating standards for domestic policies and legal frameworks that acknowledge vulnerabilities of migrant workers, and calls for humane working and living conditions, as well as rights for family members of migrant workers (OHCHR 2015). While celebrated as 'a major milestone in the effort to provide human rights protections to migrant workers all over the world' (Satterthwaite 2005, p. 2), no migrant-receiving nation states in Western Europe, North America and Australia have ratified the Convention as of June 2015. This is in stark contrast to other UN Conventions, particularly the UNTOC and the Palermo Protocol, ratified by 167 parties, including the United States, United Kingdom, Australia, and the nation states of European Union.

As Pécoud (2009) notes, migrant workers as non-nationals are more vulnerable to exploitation and social exclusion. They also have fewer rights, and are exposed to racism, xenophobia and discrimination. Migrant women and men, even when documented, are resorted to job opportunities in unregulated sectors and informal job markets (Satterthwaite 2005, Pécoud 2009).

They predominantly engage in low-skilled, low-paid jobs, where exploitation is a daily routine and common experience of many. Both men and women but more particularly women migrants pay higher fees to be able to work, have limited access to justice and restricted freedom of movement, work for substandard wages or no pay, often in unregulated and hazardous conditions (see Satterthwaite 2005). Undocumented workers are vulnerable to severe exploitation and mistreatment, fearing deportation (Sitkin 2015). However, compared to exploitation in other markets, such as exploitation of women in the sex industry, these experiences are largely silenced and/or not considered as drastic as the horror stories of 'sex slaves'. The most common outcome of the exploitation is the criminalization of offenders, while the role of the state in 'fostering immigrant workers' particular susceptibility to exploitation (Sitkin 2015, p. 224) is ignored. For the purpose of this chapter, we are particularly interested in the ways in which border protection practices are enacted to target specific groups of less desirable irregular migrant populations.

Within the shifting global economy, we are witnessing changes in migration and labour patterns, the reliance on cheap labour in industrialized or high-income nations, the devaluation of certain forms of work, and a labour market that can operate outside the boundaries of regulation with an assured supply of workers willing to work without the security of being regularized labour (see Shamir 2012, Berlinsci and Squicciarini 2011, Kagan et al. 2011). As Berlinsci and Squicciarini (2011) have noted, illegal migrant labour plays an important role in host country's economies, but this is never (or rarely) acknowledged. What we are witnessing in nations across the Global North, such as Australia, is the increased emphasis on 'illegal migrant labourers' and the importance of locating and deporting this group.

Nations such as Australia are making constant commitments to protect workers (citizens and non-citizens) as well as enforcing domestic migration and labour regimes via raids to detain and deport illegal workers. In this process, however, policy responses are not attuned to the overlap between illegal migrant labour and exploitation that may include human trafficking. This is important because often those who are subject to human trafficking are also irregular migrants: due to being undocumented or utilizing false documents to enter the country and/or due to working which is a breach of their visa conditions. In Australia it is estimated that there are between 50,000 and 100,000 unlawful migrant labourers (defined by working in breach of visa conditions or working whilst having an unlawful migration status possible for a range of reasons including the expiration of their visa) (Howells 2010, p. 7). The federal government's commitment is to address the 'significant problem' posed by 'illegal work' (Howells 2010, p. 7). This national policy framework defines and responds to unlawful migrant labour as a regulatory problem – to be actively pursued via migration, criminal justice and labour regulation. Yet there is emerging evidence that internationally and nationally unlawful migrant labourers are vulnerable to criminal victimization and workplace exploitation, including human trafficking, generated by their unlawful migration status (Andrijasevic and Anderson 2008, Segrave 2009). While there have been multiple inquiries into unlawful migrant labour (Howells 2010) and exploitation experienced by lawful migrant labourers (Deegan 2008) there has been no government-led investigation into exploitation experienced by non-citizens without work rights. Little is known about their welfare or work conditions. In Australia, sanctions and enforcement efforts to target illegal work (aimed at employers and migrants) have been in place and increased over the past decade, in the absence of any evidence that this has reduced the numbers of unlawful migrant labourers.[6] It is important to note that the vulnerability of workers being employed illegally is listed as one of the drivers for increasing sanctions, with the assumption that criminalization and punishment of unlawful migrants and employers will deter other migrants working illegally. Immigration raids have been responsible for the identification of the majority of potential victims, and having the same authorities responsible for targeting illicit migrant labour and detecting human trafficking is problematic. This was recognized in the 2013 *Trafficking in persons report* which criticized the reliance on immigration compliance actions in identifying victims in Australia because of this dual role of enforcement and protection (US Department of State 2013, p. 79).

We would argue that there are two distinct approaches to illegal migrant labour and human trafficking, where the response to human trafficking is to identify victims and prosecute offenders compared to deporting illegal workers immediately. The focus in both cases is on illegality rather than exploitation (see Shamir 2012). The focus on illegality of status matters because it serves to separate unlawful non-citizens from issues of exploitative work conditions. Such focus also ensures that human trafficking remains a situation of exploitation that is most often detected and determined in the context of immigration enforcement. When a zero tolerance approach to illegal workers, not to exploitative work conditions, is the focus, systems of protection and enforcement are inevitably limited. And, unfortunately, the international community is weak in being able to respond. As there are no mechanisms for enforcement of international human rights frameworks pertinent to protection of migrants on the national level, some authors have argued that an intersectional approach should be used to create more effective mechanisms for migrant workers' protection (amongst others and in particular, human rights frameworks pertinent to women such as CEDAW, Satterthwaite 2005). The argument is that human rights mechanisms that do not specifically target migrants might be more potent in respecting, protecting and fulfilling rights of migrants, a notion that requires further exploration.

## Conclusion

Through taking the issue of human trafficking and re-examining it via the experience of vulnerable, irregular migrant labourers, we begin to identify some of the key impediments of contemporary responses to trafficking which have asserted human rights drivers but are in essence crime control responses. Our interest here is how efforts to address human trafficking, combined with irregular migration and illegal migrant labour, expose the limits of crime control in responding to the human rights of irregular migrants.

Human rights frameworks too often fail mobile bodies that rank low on the hierarchy of mobility. As such, they recognize only the right to leave the country, not the right to immigrate (Pécoud and de Guchteneire 2006). Mobility, however, is crucial for fulfilling basic human rights, such as the right to liberty and security of person (Article 3 of the UDHR), the right to seek asylum (Article 14), the right to work and free choice of employment (Article 23), the right to an adequate standard of living (Article 25), and the right to education (Article 26).

Human rights frameworks need to be redesigned and reapplied, in order to mitigate if not prevent harmful effects of border hardening policies across the Global North and Global South. As Weber and Pickering (2011, p. 204) suggest, '[t]he most obvious application of human rights standards in relation to border control is to place limits on the means employed by states to defend their borders'. While the sovereign right of nation states to protect its borders is rarely questioned, the strategies deployed at the geographical border and beyond are, and should be, thoroughly scrutinized. Such inquiry should not be limited only to border deaths; instead, it needs to capture nation states, failure to respect, protect and fulfil rights of migrants in countries of origin, transit and destination. Accountability needs to incorporate both foreseeable (Grant 2011) and the unforeseen impacts that such policies have on mobile bodies in countries of origin, transit and destination. Whether we frame it as state crime (Green and Grewcock 2002) or not, accountability must be sought. Human rights should not be reduced to citizens' rights

(Weber and Pickering 2011), nor can it be the only mechanism or framing. Also importantly, and as we argue elsewhere, the responsibility of countries of the Global North should not end at the geographical border (Segrave et al. 2009, Milivojevic and Segrave 2010). The process of 'border offshoring' or 'contracting out' (Pickering 2011) of border policing strategies to countries of the Global South has equally harmful consequences for mobile bodies in transit (see, for example, Milivojevic 2015), for which nation states that find themselves on the path of mobile bodies cannot, and should not be solely responsible.

Importantly, an effective human rights framework responsive to the realities of irregular migration under conditions of globalization is necessary. The current framework set up by the UDHR that only acknowledges the right to move freely within state borders and the right to leave needs to be reconsidered.

## Notes

1 We note that regulated border crossings are not always safe and that lawful crossing does not negate the vulnerability of migrants.
2 We note at this point, that the term undocumented irregular migration includes asylum seekers, people being smuggled, people being trafficked, people travelling via regulated processes using false means (for example, fake documentation). During this chapter we focus primarily on those who seek irregular migration opportunities who are not asylum seekers, which we indicate through the chapter.
3 Passed by the UN General Assembly in 2000 (UNODC 2000).
4 Protocol No. 4 to the *Convention for the Protection of Human Rights and Fundamental Freedoms* securing certain rights and freedoms other than those already included in the Convention and in the First Protocol thereto, 1963.
5 Given the brevity of this chapter, we focus exclusively on the main instrument of the migrant workers international human rights framework: the Migrant Workers Convention.
6 In 2012 the Migration Amendment (Reform of Employer Sanctions) Bill 2012 was introduced with the intention of increasing the provisions to both monitor and sanction those involved in employing (directly or indirectly) illegal work (Morrison in Hansard 2012, p. 14).

## References


Aas, K.F., 2007. *Globalization and crime*. London, Thousand Oaks, New Delhi and Singapore: Sage.

Aas, K.F., 2011. 'Crimmigrant' bodies and bona fide travelers: surveillance, citizenship and global governance. *Theoretical Criminology*, 15, 331–46.

Aas, K.F. and Gundhus, H., 2015. Policing humanitarian borderlands: FRONTEX, human rights and the precariousness of life. *British Journal of Criminology*, 55, 1–18.

Adey, P., 2009. *Mobility*. Abingdon and New York: Routledge.

Agustin, L., 2007. *Sex at the margins: migration, labour markets and the rescue industry*. London: Zed Books.

Andrijasevic, R. and Anderson, B., 2008. Sex, slaves and citizens: the politics of anti-trafficking. *Soundings: A Journal of Politics and Culture*, 40, 135–45.

Anti-Trafficking Review, 2015. *Special Issue: Forced Labour and Human Trafficking* (eds Nicola Piper and Marie Segrave). Issue 5, September.

Bauman, Z., 1998. *Globalization*. Cambridge: Polity Press.

Berlinsci, R. and Squicciarini, M., 2011. The political economy of illegal migration: minimum wages and migrants' cheaper labour. Ku Leuven. Retrieved on 21 February 2014 from: https://lirias.kuleuven.be/bitstream/123456789/319676/3/PB_Rux_Mar.pdf.

Bowling, B. and Sheptycki, J., 2015. Global policing, mobility and social control. *In*: S. Pickering and J. Ham (eds), *The Routledge handbook on crime and international migration*. Abingdon and New York: Routledge, 57–74.

Castles, S., 2004. Why migration policies fail. *Ethnic and Racial Studies*, 27(2), 205–27.

Chacón, J., 2010. Tensions and trade-offs: protecting trafficking victims in the era of immigration enforcement. *University of Pennsylvania Law Review*, 158(6), 1609–53.

Chuang, J., 2014. Exploitation creep and the unmaking of human trafficking law. *The American Journal of International Law*, 108(4), 609–49.
Crépeau, F., Nakache, D. and Atak, I., 2007. International migration: security concerns and human rights standards. *Transcultural Psychiatry*, 44, 311–37.
Deegan, B., 2008. *Visa subclass 457 integrity review: final report*. Department of Immigration and Citizenship, Canberra. Retrieved on 10 September 2015 from: http://www.immi.gov.au/skilled/skilledworkers/_pdf/457-integrity-review.pdf.
Donnelly, J., 2007. The relative universality of human rights. *Human Rights Quarterly*, 29(2), 281–306.
Ford, C., 2012. *Human trafficking, sporting mega events, and the London Olympics of 2012: assessing the risks, opportunities and socio-cultural legacy since Palermo*. Cambridge: Cambridge Centre for Applied Research in Human Trafficking.
Gould, C., 2010. Moral panic, human trafficking and the 2010 Soccer World Cup. *Agenda: Empowering Women for Gender Equality*, 85, 31–44.
Grant, S., 2011. Irregular migration and frontier deaths: a right to identity. *In*: M. Dembour and T. Kelly (eds), *Are human rights for migrants? Critical reflections on the status of irregular migrants in Europe and the United States*. London: Routledge, 48–70.
Green, P. and Grewcock, M., 2002. The war against illegal immigration: state crime and the construction of a European identity. *Current Issues in Criminal Justice*, 14(1), 87–101.
Ham, J., 2011. *What's the cost of a rumour? A guide to sorting out the myths and the facts about sporting events and trafficking*. Bangkok: GAATW.
Hansard, 2012. House of Representatives Official Hansard. No. 16. Retrieved on 10 September 2015 from: http://parlinfo.aph.gov.au/parlInfo/download/chamber/hansardr/a99811dc-5385-4eff-88af-aa8ad29fe367/toc_pdf/House%20of%20Representatives_2012_11_01_1478_Official.pdf;fileType=application%2Fpdf#search=%22chamber/hansardr/a99811dc-5385-4eff-88af-aa8ad29fe367/0101%22.
Howells, M., 2010. *Report of the 2010 Review of the Migration Amendment (Employer Sanctions) Act 2007*. Retrieved on 21 February 2014 from: http://www.immi.gov.au/media/publications/compliance/review-employer-sanctions/.
International Organization for Migration, 2014. *Global migration trends: an overview*. Retrieved on 10 August 2015 from: http://missingmigrants.iom.int/sites/default/files/Global-migration-trends_December-2014_final.pdf.
Kagan, C., Lo, S., Mok, L., Lawthom, R., Sham, S., Greenwood, M. and Baines, S., 2011. *Experiences of forced labour among Chinese migrant workers*. Joseph Rowntree Foundation. Retrieved on 21 February 2014 from: www.jrf.org.uk/sites/files/jrf/Chinese-migrants-forced-labour-full.pdf.
Kaufmann, V., 2002. *Re-thinking mobility: contemporary sociology*. Aldershot: Ashgate.
Kempadoo, K., Sanghera, J. and Pattanaik, B., 2005. *Trafficking and prostitution reconsidered: new perspectives on migration, sex work, and human rights*. Boulder and London: Paradigm Publishers.
Khosravi, S., 2010. *Illegal traveller: an auto-ethnography of borders*. Basingstoke: Palgrave.
Lee, M., 2011. *Trafficking and global crime control*. London, Thousand Oaks, New Delhi and Singapore: Sage.
Milivojevic, S., 2008. Football and sex: the 2006 FIFA World Cup and sex trafficking? *Temida*, 11(2), 21–48.
Milivojevic, S., 2015. Stopped in the traffic, not stopping the traffic: gender, asylum and anti-trafficking interventions in Serbia. *In*: S. Pickering and J. Ham (eds), *The Routledge handbook on crime and international migration*. Abingdon and New York: Routledge, 287–301.
Milivojevic, S. and Pickering, S., 2013. Trafficking in people twenty years on: moral panic, immobilised bodies and the global trafficking complex. *Current Issues in Criminal Justice*, 25(2), 585–604.
Milivojevic, S. and Segrave, M., 2010. Responses to sex trafficking: gender, borders and 'home'. *In*: L. Holmes (ed.), *Trafficking and human rights: European and Asia-Pacific perspectives*. Cheltenham and Northampton: Edward Elgar Publishing, 37–55.
Office of the High Commissioner for Human Rights [OHCHR], 2015. Human rights framework. Retrieved on 6 August 2015 from: www.ohchr.org/EN/Issues/Migration/Pages/HumanRights-Framework.aspx.
Pécoud, A., 2009. The UN Convention on Migrant Workers' Rights and International Migration Management. *Global Society*, 23(3), 333–50.
Pécoud, A. and de Guchteneire, P., 2006. International migration, border controls and human rights: assessing the relevance of a right to mobility. *Journal of Borderlands Studies*, 21(1), 69–86.
Pickering, S., 2011. *Women, borders and violence*. New York, NY: Springer.

Pickering, S. and Ham, J., 2014. Hot pants at the border: sorting sex work from sex trafficking. *British Journal of Criminology*, 54(1), 2–19.
Pickering, S. and Weber, L., 2006. Borders, mobility and technologies of control. *In*: S. Pickering and L. Weber (eds), *Borders, mobility and technologies of control*. Dordrecht: Springer, 1–19.
Sanchez, G., 2015. *Human smuggling and border crossings*. Abingdon and New York: Routledge.
Sassen, S., 1998. *Globalization and its discontents: essays on the new mobility of people and money*. New York, NY: The New Press.
Satterthwaite, M., 2005. Crossing borders, claiming rights: using human rights law to empower women migrant workers. *Yale Human Rights and Development Journal*, 8, 1–66.
Segrave, M., 2009. Human trafficking and human rights. *Australian Journal of Human Rights*, 14(2), 71–94.
Segrave, M. and Milivojevic, S., 2015. Human trafficking: examining global responses. *In*: G. Barak (ed.), *The Routledge international handbook of the crimes of the powerful*. London and New York: Routledge, 132–43.
Segrave, M., Milivojevic, S. and Pickering, S., 2009. *Sex trafficking: international context and response*. Devon: Willan Publishing.
Shamir, H., 2012. A labor paradigm for human trafficking. *UCLA Law Review*, 60(1), 76–136.
Sitkin, L., 2015. The state's contradictory response to the exploitation of immigrant workers. *In*: S. Pickering and J. Ham (eds), *The Routledge handbook on crime and international migration*. Abingdon and New York: Routledge, 223–36.
Stumpf, J., 2007. The crimmigration crisis: immigrants, crime, and sovereign power. *Lewis & Clark Law School Legal Research Paper Series*, 2, 1–44.
United Nations Office on Drugs and Crime, 2000. *United Nations Convention Against Transnational Organized Crime and the Protocols Thereto*. Retrieved on 10 September 2015 from: www.unodc.org/documents/treaties/UNTOC/Publications/TOC%20Convention/TOCebook-e.pdf.
United States Department of State, 2013. *Trafficking in persons report*. Retrieved on 11 September 2015 from: www.state.gov/j/tip/rls/tiprpt/2013/.
Weber, L. and Bowling, B., 2008. Valiant beggars and global vagabonds: select, eject, immobilise. *Theoretical Criminology*, 12(3), 355–75.
Weber, L. and Pickering, S., 2011. *Globalization and borders: death at the global frontier*. Basingstoke: Palgrave.
Wickes, R. and Sydes, M., 2015. Immigration and crime. *In*: S. Pickering and J. Ham (eds), *The Routledge handbook on crime and international migration*. Abingdon and New York: Routledge, 11–25.
Wilson, D., 2015. Border militarization, technology and crime control. *In*: S. Pickering and J. Ham (eds), *The Routledge handbook on crime and international migration*. Abingdon and New York: Routledge, 141–54.
Wolff, J., 1993. On the road again: metaphors of travel in cultural criticism. *Cultural Studies*, 7(2), 224–39.
Womack, H., 2015. Iron curtain: bewildered migrants confronted with new Hungary-Serbia border fence. *The Sydney Morning Herald,* 17 July. Retrieved on 11 August 2015 from: www.smh.com.au/world/iron-curtain-bewildered-migrants-confronted-with-new-hungaryserbia-border-fence-20150717-giee4q.html.

# 28

# (De)criminalizing queer lives

## Viewing through a postcolonial optic

*Ratna Kapur*

In this chapter I problematize sexual rights interventions in law and human rights advocacy through a postcolonial critically queer lens. I start with the lesbian, gay, bisexual and transgender (LGBT) advocacy in India and the legal rollercoaster ride it has gone through in recent years. The focus of the advocacy has been on curtailing the scope of section 377 in the *Indian Penal Code, 1860*, that criminalizes sodomy so that it no longer applies to adult consensual sexual relations. The provision is a remnant of British colonialism that made sodomy a crime even between consenting adults and is contrary to the *Yogyakarta Principles on the Application of International Human Rights Law in relation to Sexual Orientation and Gender Identity* (Yogyakarta Principles).[1] Today, somewhat paradoxically, section 377 is embraced as a part of Indian cultural values.

In 2009 a lower court, the Delhi High Court, upheld a Constitutional challenge to section 377 primarily on the grounds that it interfered with the privacy rights of homosexuals who were citizens of India and deserved equal protection.[2] There was jubilation in the courtroom and celebration in the streets. And in the days following the High Court's pronouncement, gays and lesbians around India openly declared their sexuality, held queer pride parades and, more interestingly, some interpreted the victory as enabling marriage. Couples began to take vows and exchange garlands in a ritual symbolizing marriage that marked their passage into acceptance and legitimacy. These gestures thus gave the judgement a vastly expanded meaning and interpretation in the public arena.

But four years later, in December 2013 the Indian Supreme Court reversed the 2009 decision of the lower Court on the grounds that it was for the parliament to decide such matters.[3] The LGBT community wept. The Court further held that in any case the matter involved only a 'miniscule' fraction of the population. The Court also held that there was no sufficient evidence on record that the provision was used to target and harass homosexuals. The decision thus withdrew the legal potential for gays to become fully legible subjects, entitled to the same rights as everybody else. Re-criminalization after a gap of nearly four years brought to a halt efforts by LGBT and human rights groups working to consolidate the triumph of the 2009 decision, which included developing advocacy in favour of same-sex marriage prior to the decision. The 2013 decision reflects the precariousness of subaltern desires as well as the fragility of sexual rights interventions.

In April 2014, somewhat unexpectedly, a separate bench of the Indian Supreme Court upheld an equality challenge brought by the transgender community and held that transgendered persons were entitled to the legal rights to health, education, marriage, and to be included in the category of 'other' on official government documents.[4] The decision was hailed as a victory amongst the LGBT community as recognizing the humanity of sexual minorities. The community celebrated again. The case reflects the struggle by the excluded subject to realize her desire for sexual rights through law given that it allows entry and access to state benefits and whatever else a legal framework has to offer, including the right to marry.

## The 'gay international'

These polarized and contradictory responses to sexual subalterns in a postcolonial context reflect the polarized responses to LGBT rights that we are witnessing within the global context. At one end, there is an increased criminalization of queer lives, where not just the sex act, but the very identity of homosexuals are criminalized, such as in Nigeria, Uganda, Kenya, Ethiopia, the Democratic Republic of Congo and Russia.[5] At the opposite end of the spectrum the struggle for rights claims has challenged the pathologizing and criminalizing of homosexuality, resulting in legal recognition in countries such as Nepal, Cambodia, Chile, South Africa, several European countries[6] and a number of American states. The ultimate culmination point of this struggle for legitimacy rests it seems in the recognition of same-sex marriages that is normatively bound,[7] rather than a broader recognition of the right to sexual freedom (Otto 2014).[8]

In the choice between criminality and legitimacy, legitimacy seems clearly preferable. The struggle for legal recognition would seem an obvious strategy given that it affords access, public standing, and legibility – all of which would appear to be the end point of struggles for justice and equality through sexual rights advocacy in the human rights arena. It may be better to have legal recognition, including the option to get married as a gay person as opposed to having an active law that persecutes not only homosexual conduct, but also the very identity of homosexuals. Who can argue with that? Well you can't. It is better not to be persecuted.

However, there are several concerns that arise through pursuing a normative agenda in the area of sexual rights. The first and most obvious is the de-radicalization of queer advocacy through human rights and the instantiation of queer desire into a linear, regulatory framework – designed to cabin and confine, rather than to liberate or emancipate. For example, shortly after the Delhi High Court 2009 decision, the public discourse on the part of many gays and lesbians not only claimed that homosexuality was not illegal, but they promptly plunged into discussions about same-sex marriage and many even married before deities, priests or through the exchange of garlands, a ritual that marks the marriage between two people. The sexual subaltern was transcending the disciplinary limits of the decision, a provocative and subversive appropriation of the decision. But such responses also provoke the question of whether the objective of sexual subalterns is primarily to acquire respectability and participate in the rituals of familial domesticity (Joshi 2012). Through 'becoming desires' do sexual subalterns want to pursue everything that straight people have in order to prove their own humanity, feel normal, and have a sense of belonging? While it is important to give greater acknowledgement to the moments of disruption that same-sex marriage produces, the slippery slopes are present. It is after all in these small moments, like marriage, adoption or consensual sex, in the minutiae of everyday life, where power is most immediately exercised and felt, where it regulates, manages and governs.

A second concern is that these normative and normalizing moves obscure the colonial legacies that have informed sexual rights advocacy in the postcolonial present. A postcolonial optic urges a deeper interrogation of the human rights interventions on sexual rights. This optic relocates the story of sexuality within the logic of the colonial encounter and contemporary economic processes, rather than a teleological, steady march towards a progressive goal that ostensibly reflects the emergence from a primitive into a civilizationally mature stage of development. Re-visiting the story of sexual rights through the experience of the colonial encounter helps in understanding the issue of homosexuality within the contemporary postcolonial context. The modern postcolonial state has its antecedents in the colonial encounter, which was not structurally designed to secure justice for the colonial subject, but to govern the subject in a specific way (Haldar 2007, pp. 1–17). Its civilizing zeal was tied to a notion of justice that was linked to the capacity to reason and civilizational maturity that complied with a Eurocentric understanding of the rational subject (Mehta 1999, Goswami 2004). In the contemporary period the tensions produced in the area of queer rights between the potentially liberating influences of the (neoliberal) market in the public arena and the continued constraints imposed by dominant cultural, sexual, and familial norms that inform the legal regulation of sexual subjectivity and are remnants of the colonial past provide a more nuanced understanding of sexual rights struggles pursued within postcolonial contexts.

A third and related point is that, if gay marriage is permissible in the United States (US) or Canada or Europe, it cannot be based on the one-dimensional reasoning that these societies are just better, more civilized, and mature than say Uganda or Nigeria. Such reasoning deflects attention from the way in which, for example, Christian evangelicals from the US have been implicated in partly producing an anti-gay, homophobic, agenda in these African nations (and elsewhere) (Kohn 2014, Gettleman 2010, Lively and Abrams 2002).[9] Christian evangelicalism from the US, not Islam, is driving an agenda that is received within a context where conservative sexual and gender norms constituted partly by the legacies of the colonial past continue to resonate in the postcolonial present. It's a toxic combination. It is unlikely that LGBT rights can be secured through the imposition of sanctions or the withdrawal of aid by the very countries from where these anti-gay fundamentalists come.

Fourth, a position that continues to associate the securing of sexual rights in the form of same-sex marriage with both justice and the west while African countries and their leaders are cast as retrogressive and barbaric, does not implicate the way in which justice operates against a normative agenda on both sides of this equation. This position obscures how there continues to exist a position across the east/west, north/south divides that abhors homosexuality and the homosexual. For example, in May 2013, France witnessed some of the largest protests ever seen in Paris since the 1960s by those opposed to the move to legalize same-sex marriages, as well as an upsurge in violence against the gay community exemplifying how precarious desires require more than just legal sanction (Heneghan 2014, Willsher 2014).[10] The Paris protests illustrate that homosexuals continue to be regarded as not fully developed subjects within the cultural and political space despite legal recognition. Dominant Catholic theological notions provide the scaffolding of the liberal subject and the frames of recognizability that determine who is entitled to recognition and who is not. Similarly, ballot initiatives and legal proposals in several US states ranging from allowing private enterprises to refuse to serve gays and lesbians to targeting them for killing are similarly indicative how abhorrence continues to circulate and justify the use of violence and advocacy of hatred, despite the recognition of same-sex marriage by the US Supreme Court.

Finally, international LGBT human rights advocacy has not necessarily challenged the cultural binary within which sexual rights are advocated and in fact continue to reproduce the binary – between us and them, north and south – through their advocacy. While international LGBT human rights groups amongst others, have condemned the Uganda laws or the 2013 Indian Supreme Court decision upholding section 377, they may do so on terms that accept the idea that homophobia is endemic to civilizationally immature countries or Islam. Such interventions have tended to operate against problematic civilizational and cultural divides that have ghosted the emergence of the 'gay international' in such advocacy. While countries such as Nepal and Cambodia clearly stand as examples that challenge this divide, the bigger point that needs to be understood is how issues of injustice are not clarified by linking them to essentialist assumptions about culture and religion and take us no further down the road towards understanding the features that produce such discriminations. LGBT human rights advocacy has not challenged the framework within which sexual rights are addressed. Their interventions have at times in fact not only inscribed a set of sexual normativities of their own, but also reproduced the binary between those who are progressive and civilized, and those societies that remain in a state of transition until the human rights of LGBT persons are secured. Puar sets out how queer can be deployed in ways that are complicit with dominant formations of sexuality (Puar 2007, p. 39). In the context of the US, queer assemblages consist of US sexual exceptionalism, which relates to the successful management of life in regard to people that is both heteronormative and homonormative. This exceptionalism operates to include some homosexuals, that is, those who conform or assimilate – the 'good homosexuals' – but not others. Part of this assimilative project is the indoctrination of the sexual subject into a belief in the superiority and exceptionalism of the US as a nation and a culture.

## Problematizing the gay international and a postcolonial optic

At one level, the critique of the gay rights movement has reduced it to a neo-colonial enterprise that erases the possibility of a postcolonial Asian perspective on sex and sexuality.[11] As Joseph Massad somewhat controversially argues, the production of a specific sexual subject in LGBT international human rights advocacy is a culturally imperialistic imposition of western ontology on Arabs (Massad 2002, 2007). He states that a certain modern western conception of sexuality and sexual identity is seen as replacing other non-western indigenous forms of sexual practices that are not hinged to 'identity' (Massad 2002, pp. 361–2). Rahman similarly argues that there are no monolithic or consistent cultural formations of Muslim or Islamic notions of sexuality, and that the 'western' version of gay sexuality is itself culturally specific (Rahman 2014). Rahman does, however, question Massad's contention that there has been a consistent trajectory of the 'gay international' in the international arena and an empirical assessment reveals that different non-government organizations and international organizations have had mixed results in their advocacy (Rahman 2014, p. 80). Rahul Rao further problematizes the critique of LGBT interventions and elaborates on the dilemma posed when evaluating the impact of western discourses of LGBT rights on third world contexts. He questions whether it is possible to find the language in which 'to criticize the hierarchies and supremacism that lurk within the cosmopolitan politics of LGBT solidarity without minimizing or ignoring the impressiveness of communitarian homophobia' (Rao 2010, p. 176). He argues that there is a danger of slipping into a communitarian authenticity that determines how sexual identities and practices ought to be expressed in a non-western context (Rao 2010, p. 177). In light of this danger, Rao asks whether the 'gay international' offers anything useful in terms of solidarity with 'traditional' sexual ontologies that are seen as problematic and exact tremendous personal costs (Rao 2010, p. 178, Rao 2014). Rao argues that contemporary gay identity needs to be in conversation with the 'global gay identity' as well as local expressions and idioms of same-sex desire.

Similarly, Gopinath resists any effort to counter the franchise of the 'gay international' emerging from within a Euro-American context through the resurrection of a third world, authentic lesbian subject (Gopinath 2005). Using what she describes as a 'scavenger' methodology to 'unearth queer diasporic lives and cultures', she disrupts homonormative imaginings and prescriptions of same-sex desire by illustrating how a postcolonial queer female subject formation is capable of migrating and pollinating other cultural spaces in ways that do not fit within a first world/third world, homosexuals/heterosexual, male/female binary, clearly stating that these translations are not always progressive or liberating (Gopinath 2005, p. 50). The arguments of Rao, Gopinath and others opens up the possibility for unpacking the ways in which postcolonial sexual subjectivities are constructed and deployed and moves us away from a thesis based exclusively on sexual repression or sexual liberation. While sexual repression has been a primary mode of characterizing the native subject and served as a justification for ostensibly liberating imperial interventions, the sexual liberation thesis based on a rights agenda does not examine how such moves reinforce the states regulatory authority and freezes sexual subjectivities.

Despite these more nuanced positions by postcolonial scholars, what remains evident is that the expression of sexuality, its features and operations, at an international level and specifically within the context of human rights advocacy continues to be presupposed and constituted against a cultural other (Shalanky 2007).[12] This in turn always assumes something about freedom and what freedom should look like – that is, 'outness' as opposed to the closet (El Menyawi 2006, Katyal 2002, Gross 2007). The 'coming out' framing of the narratives that locate the issue of sexuality within the logic of visibility and the closet, fail to capture both the dilemmas as well as the particulars of homoerotic experience and existence in postcolonial contexts articulated by Rao, Gopinath and others (Bose and Bhattacharyya 2007, Narrain and Bhan 2005). While it is problematic to represent the closet or western notions of sexuality and sexual subjectivity as nothing more than an imposition by the West on the Rest as Massad suggests, the argument nevertheless demonstrates the need to complicate our ideas of legal justice as an end goal together with the cultural assumptions that inform the faith that it has the ability to remedy, repair or restore the lives of 'others'.

The analysis compels those involved in sexual rights advocacy to interrogate their faith in human rights as a progressive project, and reflect on how such advocacy may reproduce dominant sexual, gender as well as cultural norms rather than perform any counter-hegemonic function. Such interventions can trigger coercive norms that operate to exclude other disadvantaged or discriminated groups while also reproducing cultural and civilizational divides. A similar critique has been made of women's human rights advocacy. Sexual freedom, like women's freedom, comes to be advocated partly through the restriction and exclusion of religious expression or demonizing of the cultural other. Injustice is not clarified by linking it to essentialist assumptions about culture and religion. It takes us no further along the road in understanding the features that produce such discriminations and that cannot be limited to conservative sexual morality or culture.

## Conclusion

The decriminalizing of homosexuality does not in and of itself equate with sexual justice and release one into a space of freedom and liberation. Incorporating identities once excluded by the law from the public domain brings about the reconstitution of these once excluded identities into newly inscribed regimes of governance. To paraphrase Gayatri Spivak, while sexual rights seem to be something that we cannot not want, they also cannot give us what we want (Spivak 1993, pp. 45–6). In other words they are not necessarily emancipatory. The conferment of legal recognition can move in the direction of becoming a totalized response and invite regulation of what were once radical subjectivities through the legal regulation and governance of difference. Such advocacy can operate to uphold a specific normative order, which continues to regulate, incarcerate, and discipline in and through for example the institution of marriage, and determine who counts and who does not; who is eligible and who is not. What is important to recognize is that this move, while different from one that criminalizes and outlaws, is also constraining. It is not self evident that recognition and legitimacy equate to the idea of human rights as a progressive end goal. Instead, human rights operate to uphold a specific normative order, which continue to regulate, discipline and monitor the sexual 'other'.

From a postcolonial critically queer perspective, sexual rights advocacy needs to interrogate its faith in a progressive sexual politics, which may simultaneously trigger coercive norms for example through the focus on same-sex marriage or invocation of cultural stereotypes that operate to exclude other disadvantaged or discriminated groups who do not conform to governing sexual, gender and cultural norms: the failed queer, or uncivilized queer or queerly queer as opposed to the successful queer. At the same time we need to remain attentive to the fragility of these legal victories where a criminalized sodomite one day can become a legal though not fully recognized legal subject the next day, only to become a criminalized sodomite again.

Legal recognition can bring with it a humanness, legibility and visibility – a subject that can be grieved and mourned. But such recognition can be fragile and tentative. In the course of the seismic shifts from non-recognition to recognition to de-recognition, what is significant is that precarious desires continue to be managed and policed, governed and regulated. The temporality of subversion through the process of becoming recognized subjects and unbecoming precarious desires hardly serves as a satisfactory model or recipe for freedom. Reading moments of subversion while important, become an event or process rather than about being free. And ultimately becoming respectable queers through the process of marriage, adoption or consensual sodomy becomes part of the neoliberal as well as neo-colonial politics of normalization and the desire for sameness (Joshi 2012, Richardson 2005).

## Notes

1 The Yogyakarta Principles were adopted by the International Panel of Experts in International Human Rights Law and on Sexual Orientation and Gender Identity in March 2007. This is the first non-binding set of principles to specifically address the issue of human rights issues in relation to sexual orientation and gender identity (SOGI). There are few express references to sexual freedom, or sexual life more generally in international human rights instruments. Most references are with regard to sexual violence or mainstreaming gender. Some of these include HRC, General Comment 28, Article 3 (Equality of Rights between Men and Women), HRI/GEN/1/Rev 5, March 29, 2000, para. 20, that refers specifically to the need for legal protections against rape and removing restrictions on women's rights to reproductive decision-making. See also the ICESCR Committee's Gender Comment 16, 'The equal right of men and women to the enjoyment of all economic, social and cultural rights (Art. 3 of the International Covenant on Economic, Social and Cultural Rights)', E/C.12/2005/4, 11 August 2005, para. 29, that refers to removing restrictions on women's reproductive health. Similarly the Committee on the Elimination of Racial Discrimination, General Recommendation 25, recognizes that racial discrimination may have a gendered impact in the area of sexual violence, including rape, forced sterilization and abuse of women workers: Committee on the Elimination of Racial Discrimination, General Recommendation XXV, 'Gender-Related Dimensions of Racial Discrimination', HRI/GEN/1/Rev.5, 26 April 2001, para. 2. However, none of these major human rights instruments, including the Convention on the Elimination of All Forms of Discrimination Against Women, the International Covenant on Economic Social, and Cultural Rights, nor the International Conventions on the Elimination of Racial Discrimination make any reference to sexual orientation. The Treaty of Amsterdam, 1999, elaborating the issue of citizenship and rights of individuals in the emerging European Union was the first international treaty to explicitly mention and protect sexual orientation.

2 *Naz Foundation v Govt. of NCT of Delhi* 160 Delhi Law Times 277 (Delhi High Court 2009).

3 *Suresh Kumar Kaushal v Naz Foundation and Others* Supreme Court of India: Civil Appeal No. 10972 of 2013.

4 *National Legal Services Authority (NALSA) v Union of India* available at http://supremecourtofindia.nic.in/outtoday/wc40012.pdf.

5 See Human Rights Council, Discrimination and Violence Against Individuals based on Their Sexual Orientation and Gender Identity, *Report of the Office of the United Nations High Commissioner for Human Rights,* A/HRC/29/23, 4 May 2015. An earlier 2011 study commissioned by the Human Rights Council on SOGI discrimination found that there was a pattern of 'violence and discrimination based on' SOGI in all regions of the world and that this demanded a global response: Report of the United Nations High Commissioner for Human Rights, *Discriminatory Laws and Practices and Acts of Violence Against Individuals Based on their Sexual Orientation and Gender Identity*, A/HRC/19/41, 17 November 2011.

6 See, for example, *Dudgeon v United Kingdom*, one of the first cases to be decided by the European Court of Human rights on the criminalization of male homosexual acts in England, Wales, and Northern Ireland, which held that such provisions violated the *European Convention on Human Rights* (European Court of Human Rights, 22 October 1981).

7 The current of human rights for SOGI has drifted in the direction of fitting diverse sexual and gender practices into mainstream and normative sexual and gender categories. See for example the *Yogyakarta Principles*, where the right to found a family, assumes that such a family will be a monogamous couple which will have the interests of children as its primary concern, even though it recognises a diversity of family forms: *Yogyakarta Principles*: Principle 24. This normative move is particularly evident in relation to lesbian rights where the advocacy around sexual freedom has been displaced by gender mainstreaming and a focus on sexual violence. See for example HRC, General Comment 28, Article 3 (Equality of Rights between Men and Women), HRI/GEN/1/Rev 5, 29 March 2000, paras 8, 10, 11 and 22, that condemns violence against women during armed conflict; requests that reports on the implementation of the right to life should include data on birth rates, pregnancy, and childbirth related deaths of women; on the right to be free from torture should include information about laws and practices with regards to domestic and other types of violence against women; and on the right to freedom of expression provide information on legal restrictions on the publication or dissemination of obscene and pornographic material. The International Covenant on Economic, Social and Cultural Rights Committee addresses gendered violence extensively and particularly in the context of marriage and the family: ICESCR Committee, General Comment 16, The equal right of men and women to the enjoyment of all economic, social and cultural rights (Article 3 of the *International Covenant on Economic, Social and Cultural Rights*), E/C.12/2005/4, 11 August 2005, para. 27. The Committee Against Torture, in General Comment 2 recognizes that certain people may be especially at risk of torture or ill-treatment, including because of their 'gender, sexual orientation' or 'transgender identity' and also that for women, gender is an important fact that may intersect with other identities including sexual orientation: Committee Against Torture, General Comment No.2, Implementation of Article 2 by States Parties, CAT/C/GC/2, 24 January 2008.

8 Sexuality is rarely mentioned in human rights documents, nor have gross violations of human rights relating to SOGI been seriously addressed in various committees. For example, as Otto points out, the CEDAW Committee has addressed issues relating to SOGI in only 31 of its 174 concluding observations on state reports between 2007 and 2014: id at 636.

9 Amongst those US evangelicals who have lead the anti-gay campaign in Uganda and elsewhere is Scott Lively. Lively co-authored a book, *The Pink Swastika*, in which he argued that homosexuals were the true inventors of Nazism and responsible for the Nazi atrocities (Lively and Abrams 2002).

10 LOI n° 2013-404 du 17 Mai 2013 ouvrant le mariage aux couples de personnes de même sexe, 18 May 2013.

11 Katherine Franke (2012) discusses the polarisation over gay rights between a universal human rights perspective that pursues and exposes the persecution of sexual minorities in postcolonial contexts, and those such as Massad who critique their missionary zeal that effaces the colonial past and other ways in which to perform and live sexuality in non-western contexts.

12 Shalanky further complicates the relationship between Orientalism and human rights of sexual minorities in the context of Egypt.

## References

Bose, B. and Bhattacharyya, B. (eds), 2007. *The phobic and the erotic: the politics of sexualities in contemporary India.* London, New York, Calcutta: Seagull Books.

El Menyawi, H., 2006. Activism from the closet: gay rights and strategising in Egypt. *Melbourne Journal of International Law,* 7(1), 28–51.

Franke, K., 2012. Dating the state: the moral hazards of winning gay rights. *Columbia Human Rights Law Review*, 44(1), 1–46.

Gettleman, J., 2010. Americans' role seen in Uganda anti-gay push. *New York Times*, 3 January. Retrieved on 10 December 2014 from: www.nytimes.com/2010/01/04/world/africa/04uganda.html?partner=rss&emc=rss.

Gopinath, G., 2005. *Impossible desires: queer diasporas and South Asian public cultures*. Durham, NC: Duke University Press.

Goswami, M., 2004. *Producing India: from colonial economy to national space*. Chicago, IL: University of Chicago Press.

Gross, A., 2007. Queer theory and international human rights law: does each person have a sexual orientation? *American Society of International Law Proceedings*, 101, 129–32.

Haldar, P., 2007. *Law, orientalism, and postcolonialism: jurisdiction of the lotus-eaters*. London: Routledge.

Heneghan, T., 2014. French conservatives march against government family 'phobia'. *Reuters*, 2 February. Retrieved on 10 December 2014 from: www.reuters.com/article/2014/02/02/us-france-protests-idUSBREA110AG20140202.

Joshi, Y., 2012. Respectable queerness. *Columbia Human Rights Law Review*, 43(2), 415–66.

Katyal, S., 2002. Exporting identity. *Yale Journal of Law and Feminism*, 14(1), 97–146.

Kohn, H., 2014. 'The family', and Uganda's anti-gay Christian mafia. *DailyBeast*, 25 February. Retrieved on 10 December 2014 from: http://thedailybeast.com/articles/2014/02/25/obama-the-family-and-uganda-s-anti-gay-christian-mafia.html.

Lively, S. and Abrams, K., 2002. *The pink swastika: homosexuality in the Nazi Party*, 4th edn. Sacramento: Veritas Aeterna Press.

Massad, J., 2002. Re-orienting desire: the gay international and the Arab world. *Public Culture*, 14(2), 361–85.

Massad, J. 2007. *Desiring Arabs*. Chicago, IL: University of Chicago Press.

Mehta, U., 1999. *Liberalism and empire: a study in nineteenth century British political liberal thought*. Chicago, IL: University of Chicago Press.

Narrain, A. and Bhan, G. (eds), 2005. *Because I have a voice: queer politics in India*. New Delhi: Yoda Press.

Otto, D., 2014. Between pleasure and danger: lesbian human rights. *European Human Rights Law Review*, 6, 618–28.

Puar, J., 2007. *Terrorist assemblages: homonationalism in queer times*. Durham, NC: Duke University Press.

Rahman, M., 2014. *Homosexualities, Muslim cultures and modernity*. Basingstoke: Palgrave Macmillan.

Rao, R., 2010. *Third world protest: between home and the world*. Oxford: Oxford University Press.

Rao, R., 2014. Queer questions. *International Feminist Journal of Politics*, 16(2), 199–217.

Richardson, D., 2005. Desiring sameness?: the rise of a neoliberal politics of normalisation. *Antipode*, 37(3), 515–35.

Shalanky, A., 2007. On a certain queer discomfort with orientalism. *American Society of International Law Proceedings*, 101, 125–9.

Spivak, G., 1993. *Outside in the teaching machine*. New York: Routledge.

Willsher, K., 2014. France's future at risk from 'unnatural' families say conservative protestors. *The Guardian*, 2 February. Retrieved on 10 December 2014 from: www.theguardian.com/world/2014/feb/02/france-protests-families-paris-lyon.

# 29

# Justice reinvestment as social justice

*Chris Cunneen, Melanie Schwartz, Julie Stubbs, David Brown and Courtney Young*

## Introduction

This chapter draws on the work of the Australian Justice Reinvestment Project (AJRP) (Brown et al. 2016). The AJRP has examined the development of justice reinvestment particularly in the context of its alignment with broad social justice values. We are also specifically interested in how and whether justice reinvestment can meet the needs of those social groups that have been adversely affected by mass imprisonment and hyper-incarceration, particularly racial and Indigenous minorities, women and people with mental health issues and cognitive impairment (Cunneen et al. 2013). We argue that justice reinvestment was in its early development strongly tied to civil rights, particularly with the focus on imprisonment and racialization, and social justice for communities where large numbers of residents were recycled in and out of prison.

In 2003, justice reinvestment emerged as a strategy to reduce the number of people incarcerated in the United States (US). The goal of this new strategy was to:

> redirect some portion of the $54 billion America now spends on prisons to rebuilding the human resources and physical infrastructure – the schools, healthcare facilities, parks, and public spaces – of neighborhoods devastated by high levels of incarceration.
>
> *(Tucker and Cadora 2003, p. 2)*

Citing the 'cumulative failure of three decades of "prison fundamentalism"' (ibid., p. 3), the authors argued for a holistic approach to both the systemic drivers of the prison population and to underlying issues that lead to offending. They suggested that this was best done through localism that 'seeks community level solutions to community level problems' (ibid., p. 2). Justice reinvestment was conceived as working both inside and beyond the criminal justice system to achieve reduced levels of incarceration. They proposed that savings from the corrections budget be reinvested to address the causes of reoffending in places where large numbers of residents spend time in prison.

The first element of the approach is the collection and analysis of available data about, inter alia, where prisoners come from and where they go home to and the associated costs. An analysis of the costs of criminal justice interventions goes beyond the direct costs of housing an inmate to associated costs such as policing, court costs, transporting defendants to court (if they live in more remote communities), hospital costs and other services for victims of violent crime (Brown et al. 2016, p. 56). Based on this evidence about the drivers and costs of incarceration, a package of policy options is devised. Stand-out issues, such as very high numbers of parole or probation revocations or people being remanded in custody after being refused bail, can be examined to see what might decrease detention rates without compromising public safety. The chosen policy options are implemented, and some or all of the savings realized from their enactment are (re)invested into the communities identified in the data collection phase to address the criminogenic factors particular to that place. Local stakeholders are involved in nominating the way that reinvestment happens in their community.

Justice reinvestment captured the imagination of communities, criminal justice system actors and legislators in a range of western countries. In the US, there are currently 17 local justice reinvestment initiatives and 24 at the state level in varying stages of development. Within the United Kingdom (UK), justice reinvestment has been framed within the marketization ideology of the government, largely in the form of 'payment by results' schemes. In Australia, the groundswell of support for justice reinvestment has been led by the community sector; there is a growing number of community initiated justice reinvestment pilots as well as government interest in the strategy in multiple jurisdictions.

Perhaps inevitably, justice reinvestment has taken a range of forms in practice. While its architects envisaged that it would be strongly aligned with social justice, this has not always been the focus in practice. While justice reinvestment has the potential to address important social justice issues, this objective can be nurtured, or sidestepped, as it plays out on the ground. It is our argument that the social justice imperative to justice reinvestment has the potential to reinsert social, economic and political rights in the forefront of prison reform. The extent to which justice reinvestment reforms meet the needs of the most vulnerable groups of imprisoned populations, including women, racialized minorities and people with mental illness and cognitive impairment, is a barometer of its social justice commitment.

## Characterizing justice reinvestment in public discourse

The uptake of justice reinvestment in the US and UK, and the high level of interest in it in Australia and elsewhere, is in large part a response to the fact that ever-increasing imprisonment rates are expensive at a time of fiscal stringency, and provide very little return in terms of high recidivism rates (Brown 2010). Economic arguments for penal reform may have purchase where other arguments have had limited success. As the Aboriginal and Torres Strait Islander Social Justice Commissioner [ATSISJC] stated in the 2009 *Social Justice Report*, 'framing the problem of Indigenous imprisonment as an economic issue might be more strategic than our previous attempts to address it as a human rights or social justice issue' (ATSISJC 2009, p. 10). While the ATSISJC is specifically referring to Indigenous issues, the argument has wider potential purchase. However, there is a danger of framing the problem purely in this way because it in turn delineates the terms of the solution: where the problem to be addressed is a fiscal one, concerns around human rights and social justice in proposed solutions are not likely to be given high priority, or may be conveniently forgotten.

In the US, the language around justice reinvestment has reflected the push for reduced spending following the global economic downturn. Although, arguments based on fiscal 'rationality' are a prominent feature of justice reinvestment advocacy, they do not necessarily trump emotive law and order policies that are electorally popular. Retributive public sentiments are central to long established justifications for punishment as 'deserved' and are deeply culturally embedded, such that they cannot be ignored (Brown et al. 2012, p. 101, Freiberg and Carson 2010). As Tonry (2011) asks, when the economic tide turns, and fiscal concerns no longer top political priorities, what will stop justice reinvestment from washing away with it, if this is its primary justification? Justice reinvestment rhetoric can speak both in the language of saving taxpayer dollars/increasing community safety, and of neighbourhood renewal and social justice. To be robust enough to stand the test of time, justice reinvestment needs to speak to practical concerns (including resource allocation), but also to be rooted in moral and social approaches to penality, including social justice discourses (Brown et al. 2012).

## Addressing mass incarceration

Justice reinvestment emerged from the fact that the geographies of imprisonment intersect with the geographies of poverty and race. In the US, the story of mass incarceration, as initially defined by Garland (2001), developed through the notion of hyper-incarceration by Wacquant (2010) and revitalized by Alexander (2012), is that, historically, high incarceration rates are borne most heavily by communities of colour. In December 2013, 37 per cent of incarcerated males in the US were black, translating to almost 3 per cent of the black male population being imprisoned (2,805 per 100,000). In December 2013, 22 per cent of the women in prison were black, at twice the rate for white women (Carson 2014, p. 8). Statistics such as these led Alexander (2012, p. 24) to conclude that '[t]oday mass incarceration defines the meaning of blackness in America: black people, especially black men, are criminals. That is what it means to be black'. Mass incarceration is thus squarely conceptualized as a key civil rights and social justice concern.

Similarly, justice reinvestment in Australia has emerged from a focus on Indigenous communities. As one of the original proponents of justice reinvestment, Susan Tucker, said in an interview with the AJRP:

> It's striking . . . that the places that are considering or doing Justice Reinvestment are New Zealand, Australia, the UK and the USA. . . . All places where minorities are disproportionately incarcerated. . . . I think it's a recognition that the disinvestment in these communities and their lack of political participation or involvement, is part of the problem.
>
> *(Brown et al. 2016, p. 247)*

The processes characterizing justice reinvestment, particularly the focus on local solutions and the devolution of control over those solutions to the nominated community itself, are well suited to developing social justice initiatives for various communities, including those of colour. Place-based policies address entrenched disparity that has come about through combinations of systemic failures, public policy decisions, market forces and patterns of discrimination (Cytron 2010, p. 3).

It is concerning that the commitment to localized, place-based solutions has largely fallen out of justice reinvestment initiatives in the US. Similarly, a failure to prioritize the reinvestment of savings in high-incarceration communities undermines the prospects of a social justice-oriented programme of reform. Rather, state-based justice reinvestment in the US has focused on working with the political leadership to secure the passage of legislation, and where reinvestment has occurred it has largely been within the criminal justice system rather than community-based solutions to address reoffending behaviour (Brown et al. 2016, pp. 87–91).

In a powerful critique of the trajectory of justice reinvestment in the US, Austin et al. (2013, p. 8) emphasize that an ambitious vision for criminal justice reform requires the inclusion of reform coalitions rooted in the long-term interests of the communities they are part of, especially minority leaders and elected representatives. We would add that active ownership of the project by the community, especially where its members have been historically rendered voiceless or been subject to systemic discrimination and disadvantage, is a pillar of a social justice approach to justice reinvestment.

## Justice reinvestment as a place-based approach

Justice reinvestment was originally conceptualized as a 'place-based' strategy focused on particular geographic communities. As such, justice reinvestment is connected to social and economic policies based on research showing the long term concentration of poverty and disadvantage in particular neighbourhoods and communities. As we have noted elsewhere, justice reinvestment as a place-based approach can be linked to public policy initiatives attacking social exclusion and enhancing social justice (Brown et al. 2016, p. 94). However, although justice reinvestment is defined as a place-based approach, this can have competing definitions, differing political imperatives, and contrasting priorities for policy and practice. We draw the distinction that can be made between 'top-down' and 'bottom-up' approaches to public policy development and implementation. Much of the development of justice reinvestment in the US has been largely top-down and the local participatory focus of justice reinvestment has been lost. There is also a danger in reframing basic government obligations to meet human needs around housing, health, education and employment only within a discourse of crime prevention. There are human rights obligations to meet basic needs, irrespective of whether they contribute to lowering imprisonment rates.

A key element of a bottom-up approach to justice reinvestment is that policy priorities, and service delivery models are determined through community decision-making and negotiated with different levels of government. A community development approach lies at the foundation of justice reinvestment. However, it has not received the attention it deserves. As we have suggested:

> It is perhaps easier for criminologists and lawyers working in the area of justice reinvestment to concentrate on systemic criminal justice change (through, for example, reforms to probation and parole), rather than on how local participatory and reinvestment processes can be developed in specific communities, particularly when an understanding of community development is usually outside their professional repertoire.
>
> *(Brown et al. 2016, p. 244)*

The question also remains as to the adequacy of justice reinvestment as a place-based approach in addressing the needs of those social groups who have been particularly affected by the growth in incarceration: people with mental illness and/or cognitive impairment, women, and Indigenous and racialized peoples. We argue that there are opportunities and potential for justice reinvestment strategies to change the way the criminal justice system responds to the needs of these groups. For example, the needs of homeless, criminalized and incarcerated people with a mental illness and/or cognitive impairment can be better met with integrated and more holistic support to people in the community and prior to their becoming caught within the criminal justice system. Presently, such support as exists tends to be available after criminalization and incarceration (Brown et al. 2016, pp. 115–21). The AJRP research noted the example of a local justice reinvestment project in Travis County, Texas where a broad-based coalition of government, community and business sectors were able to initiate a housing programme for homeless people who had been frequently rotating in and out of the county courts and gaol (Brown et al. 2016, pp. 120–1).

Thus far a specific focus on criminalized women has not been a significant feature of justice reinvestment in the US, Australia or the UK. There have been some guidelines proposed for justice reinvestment to meet women's specific needs in the UK, and a couple of justice reinvestment initiatives in the US have some focus on women (Brown et al. 2016, pp. 121–8). None of the justice reinvestment initiatives in Australia have a specific focus on women. Current gender-neutral justice reinvestment strategies, particularly in the US, tend to focus on back-end criminal justice measures such as parole and post-release support. However, front-end measures such as diversion, community-based sanctions, specific programmes and social support are more likely to benefit women, and these are also particularly conducive to development through a place-based social justice approach.

As noted earlier, Indigenous and other community organizations have been advocating for justice reinvestment in Australia. We have seen some particularly innovative approaches in Cowra, Bourke and Katherine where justice reinvestment is being driven by the local Indigenous communities (Brown et al. 2016, pp. 131–8). For example, in Bourke, New South Wales (NSW), a process has unfolded that stands in stark contrast to the American experience. In Bourke the Indigenous community spent 18 months building broad support for justice reinvestment and a governance structure to initiate programmes. The Bourke community then developed a plan of what justice reinvestment might look like. In an interview with AJRP, Sarah Hopkins from the Just Reinvest NSW campaign, encapsulated the importance of self-determination in the justice reinvestment process:

> The reality is, if you look at the Aboriginal experience in terms of government, their relationship with government, support from government funding . . . it's so fraught that this is the only way to do it because there's no trust there . . . I think for community leaders to actually begin to trust a process I think that's when you see that real community capacity building.
>
> *(cited in Brown et al. 2016, p. 6)*

Thus community capacity-building has been fundamental to how justice reinvestment has been envisaged at the local level. Further, the potential for democratic decision-making in justice reinvestment is a significant departure from the way that government has traditionally approached policy-making for Indigenous communities. Community capacity-building and democratic decision-making coheres with what Indigenous advocates have always said: to give programmes implemented in Indigenous communities the best chance of success, communities need to lead the direction of those strategies (ATSISJC 2009, Gooda 2010, Brown et al. 2016, p. 5). Through self-determination, well-implemented initiatives of this kind can work to redress these issues that sometimes manifest in contact with the criminal justice system.

It is also clear that the imperative for community-led programming in Indigenous communities goes beyond the question of the success or failure of a given initiative, moving into the deeper territory of self-determination which has had such a fraught track record in government programming, and where the 'rhetoric about "partnering" with communities [has] not translated into communities having genuine involvement in decision-making about the solutions to their problems' (NSW Ombudsman 2011, 2.2). As the Aboriginal and Torres Strait Islander Social Justice Commissioner said, 'what I like about Justice Reinvestment is that it provides opportunities for communities to take back local control . . . to not only take some ownership of the problem but also to own the solutions' (Gooda 2010). The challenge now is to ensure that governments understand that 'partnering' with communities is not mere rhetoric, but that communities have a genuine involvement in decision-making.

## *Evidence-led practices*

Justice reinvestment is described as 'data-driven', 'evidence-led' and rational rather than emotional. These features have strong practical and rhetorical appeal and mostly have been seen as welcome (Clear 2010). However, a great deal turns on how evidence is conceptualized and the measures that are used. These are not mere technical details. The measures that are included, and just as importantly those that are excluded, shape what counts and what is counted and set limits on the questions that can be examined, the policy options that are considered, and the capacity for evaluation and future research. These decisions have a substantial influence on the possibilities of justice reinvestment for tackling social justice issues, including who will share in any benefits, financial or otherwise, and how the problems besetting high incarceration communities such as housing, education, unemployment and illicit drug use are addressed.

The value of reliable data and an evidence base to inform policy, programme development and service delivery in criminal justice is widely recognized. Criminal justice systems commonly suffer from the absence or poor quality of data and the failure to evaluate programmes and practices. Within the US, government and philanthropic funding has provided much needed technical assistance to establish datasets and undertake the detailed data analysis that is essential to justice reinvestment. Technical assistance providers also have brought legitimacy and an independent perspective to identifying the drivers of incarceration, quantifying potential savings and developing and choosing between policy options. Without a similar programme of technical assistance, UK schemes faced significant obstacles (Wong et al. 2014). Proposals for the adoption of justice reinvestment across Australia are likely to face similar challenges.

The drivers of incarceration may differ for different groups. For instance, the rates and patterns of incarceration are very different for women, minorities and mentally ill or cognitively impaired people. This may reflect the differential effects of criminal justice practices on vulnerable groups, the criminalization of social and health issues (for example, when homeless, intoxicated or mentally ill people are charged with public order offences), social determinants of imprisonment (such as poverty, homelessness, unemployment, poor levels of education, low levels of literacy), or a combination of these factors. A social justice aligned approach requires understanding differential drivers of incarceration; this in turn depends on having data, a methodology and an analytical framework adequate for the task. Assessing the contribution of policing practices is also important, yet this is not commonly addressed within US approaches to justice reinvestment.

During fieldwork in the US, the AJRP was surprised to find that racial disparities in incarceration have been given little explicit attention in justice reinvestment schemes. Marshall Clement from the CSG Justice Center told us in an interview that state policy-makers had never asked for an analysis by race, possibly because 'people recognise that there's not clear solutions. . . . It's not clear cut in the data'. We found that little consideration had been given to questions about whether the drivers of incarceration differ for different groups, although some schemes operating at the local level had identified that mental illness and homelessness were common among 'frequent users' of jails.

Where datasets and analytical frameworks do not address these differences, they may entrench the invisibility of vulnerable groups into the future, and preclude more tailored policies and programmes. Groups that are in a minority within correctional populations may be overlooked, especially where cost cutting is prioritized, because they are seen as unlikely to yield substantial savings. For instance, within correctional systems women have often been seen as 'too few to count'. However, there are other ways of approaching savings. For instance, the costs of incarceration and its effects are not only borne by criminal justice agencies, but also by other state agencies (for example, out-of-home care of children, welfare support for families) and disproportionately by disadvantaged individuals, families and communities. Taking account of these costs would likely direct attention to the need to provide targeted interventions and support to those most affected.

Justice reinvestment in the US has shifted from an initial focus on reinvesting in high incarceration communities to reinvesting in 'high-performing public safety strategies' (Urban Institute 2013, p. 1). This may, in part, reflect the political limits on what is achievable but the emphasis on evidence-based practice (EBP) and 'what works' has encouraged a focus on criminal justice reforms and programmes to reduce recidivism over other possible objectives (Clear 2010). Evidence-based approaches have assisted legislators, policy-makers and correctional administrators to choose cost-effective policy options and programmes. Forms of cost–benefit analysis (CBA), such as developed by the Washington State Institute for Public Policy, are commonly used to select interventions likely to 'give taxpayers a good return on their crime fighting dollars' (Aos and Drake 2013, p. 1). However, this narrower focus on the delivery of programmes is in tension with visions of justice reinvestment that focus on place-based initiatives, community redevelopment (Tucker and Cadora 2003) and social justice.

Approaches to EBP differ but a common feature is the use of meta-analysis which synthesizes previous evaluative studies that meet an established threshold. Meta-analyses are seen as more rigorous and authoritative than narrative reviews, although there are ongoing debates about the merits of each approach. It is common for a hierarchy of evidence to be adopted with random control trials endorsed as 'the gold standard'. However, meta-analyses only include well-established practices that are in widespread use and that have been evaluated within a particular statistical framework (Van Voorhis 2012, p. 120) but few criminal justice programmes or practices are evaluated to these standards. The evidence base is poor concerning programmes tailored to particular groups, such as racial minorities or women. Programmes that respond to minority interests or arise from local initiatives may be less likely to be funded for evaluation or may use evaluation methodologies that are deemed unacceptable for meta-analysis and, thus, they are unlikely to be endorsed as evidence-based. Yet programmes 'may have effects on the community beyond those that can be observed within an experimental or quasi-experimental framework' (Roman 2004, p. 271).

Within justice reinvestment, EBP is strongly linked to the 'what works' framework and to 'principles of effective intervention' based on the risk-needs-responsivity approach and risk assessment (Latessa and Lowencamp 2006, pp. 521–2). The risk-needs-responsivity approach has its origins in individual psychology and focuses on predicting recidivism (Andrews and Bonta 2010), but has been challenged conceptually and empirically (Van Voorhis 2012, Hannah-Moffat 2009) especially when used with women and racialized peoples. However, it continues to be very influential within justice reinvestment and it has become common for state justice reinvestment schemes in the US to mandate the use of EBP. In 2011 alone, five US states passed legislation mandating the use of risk assessment tools and specific evidence-based programmes such as drug treatment, cognitive behavioural therapy or forms of intensive community supervision (James et al. 2012, p. 826).

The reliance on EBP, 'what works' and the risk-needs-responsivity approach may enshrine a limited range of programmes deemed to be evidence-based and stifle innovation. This possibility is greatest where other forms of knowledge and other modes of assessing effectiveness are excluded. As Clear (2010, p. 10) has argued, the 'what works' approach tells us 'which current practices deserve to be spread more widely' but justice reinvestment requires knowledge to 'enable us to imagine new and potent strategies for improving justice and public safety'. A social justice aligned justice reinvestment is likely to need different methodologies and measures that recognize family, neighbourhood, community and societal factors. Here we note some approaches that may be more congruent with a social justice vision of justice reinvestment.

As Roman (2004, p. 261) observed, EBP and CBA largely rely on indices such as recidivism to gauge success, and commonly measure outcomes at the individual level. However, he urges the use of CBA to ask different questions: '[b]ecause the de facto goal of virtually every criminal justice intervention is to improve public safety, it is critical that welfare effects are measured at the community level' (ibid., p. 271). Others have recommended measuring Social Return on Investment in recognition of a wider range of costs and benefits that accrue beyond the criminal justice system (UK House of Commons Justice Committee 2010, paras 368–75). Desistance scholars point to the inadequacy of recidivism as a measure of success; they note that programmes have a range of objectives and thus various measures of effectiveness are needed. They also note that understanding how to bring about positive change in offenders requires understanding the family and community contexts in which it is embedded (McNeill et al. 2012, p. 50). Qualitative evaluations and methodologies have a place in such approaches.

The need to develop culturally relevant indices and standards of measurement for Indigenous communities and contexts has been recognized internationally and in Australia. Work by the United Nations Permanent Forum on Indigenous Issues to promote Indigenous participation in developing such standards, and the International Center for the Prevention of Crime community safety framework for Indigenous communities, offer models that can be built upon (Willis 2010, p. 2). The Bourke justice reinvestment project uses a collective impact approach with five key elements: a common agenda, shared measurement, mutually reinforcing activities, continuous communication and a backbone of support (Just Reinvest NSW 2012).

## Conclusion

Throughout this chapter we have discussed the importance of a social justice oriented approach as a necessary component to justice reinvestment. Much of the commitment to social justice in the original vision of justice reinvestment has changed, particularly in the US, into a more practical, government-oriented programme that attempts to reduce incarceration rates through criminal justice reform. However we argue there is scope to reinsert social justice values. We suggest that human rights are a key part of the normative framework of a social justice approach. There are broad normative principles including non-discrimination and rights to participation, access and social inclusion that are fundamental, and these have special resonance for those groups who have borne the brunt of increases in imprisonment including women, people with mental illness and cognitive impairment, and Indigenous and racialized minorities. The principle of least restriction is an important protective safeguard in the support for and care of people with mental and/or cognitive disability in health and justice settings (Baldry 2014, p. 380). This principle supports the focus on developing community-based options for people who would otherwise be incarcerated. In the area of Indigenous rights, there are well-articulated norms such as respect, recognition, and specific Indigenous rights, including the right to self-determination and to free, prior and informed consent (see the *Declaration on the Rights of Indigenous Peoples*). Thus the potential of justice reinvestment policies in Australia to realize social justice outcomes is bound up with issues of community governance and empowerment, and specifically for Indigenous people, with self-determination and nation-building.

Our research indicates that justice reinvestment can be an *inspiration* for locally based community development strategies that utilize enhanced data on and identification of local community assets and current forms of service support. We need to challenge the over-emphasis on EBP and CBA where it can lead to ignoring communities of vulnerability that have high contact with the criminal justice system, and the organic solutions to problems that derive from the community itself. The development of justice reinvestment in Bourke is one such localized approach developed for Australian conditions and for a specific Indigenous community.

Justice reinvestment is a major source of policy, programme or rhetorical support for a diverse range of activities. It has served to encourage a focus on penal reduction, and provided a narrative that offers something positive in developing political strategies and programmes for change. However, we argue that the reliance only on arguments about cost savings or limited interpretations of 'smart' justice, needs to be balanced by a clear articulation of a normative position which values social justice and human rights, particularly for those social groups affected by decades of growing imprisonment rates.

## References


Aboriginal and Torres Strait Islander Social Justice Commissioner [ATSISJC], 2009. *Social justice report 2009*. Sydney: Australian Human Rights Commission.

Alexander, M., 2012. *The new Jim Crow: mass incarceration in the age of colorblindness*, revised edn. New York, NY: The New Press.

Andrews, D. and Bonta, J., 2010. *The psychology of criminal conduct*, 5th edn. Cincinnati: Anderson Publishing.

Aos, S. and Drake, E., 2013. *Prison, police, and programs: evidence-based options that reduce crime and save money*, 13-11-1901, November. Olympia: Washington State Institute for Public Policy.

Austin, J., Cadora, E., Clear, T.R., Dansky, K., Greene, J., Gupta, V., Mauer, M., Porter, N., Tucker, S. and Young, M.C., 2013. *Ending mass incarceration: charting a new justice reinvestment*. Retrieved on 1 September 2015 from: http://sentencingproject.org/doc/Charting%20a%20New%20Justice%20Reinvestment%20FINAL.pdf.

Baldry, E., 2014. Disability at the margins: the limits of the law. *Griffith Law Review*, 23(3), 370–88.

Brown, D., 2010. The limited benefit of prison in controlling crime. *Current Issues in Criminal Justice*, 22(1), 137–48.

Brown, D., Cunneen, C., Schwartz, M., Stubbs, J. and Young, C., 2016. *Justice reinvestment: winding back imprisonment*. Palgrave Macmillan.

Brown, D., Schwartz, M. and Boseley, L., 2012. The promise and pitfalls of justice reinvestment. *Alternative Law Journal*, 37(2), 96–102.

Carson, E.A., 2014. *Prisoners in 2013*. BJS Bulletin, September, Washington, DC.

Clear, T., 2010. Policy and evidence: the challenge to the American Society of Criminology – 2009 Presidential Address to the American Society of Criminology. *Criminology*, 48(1), 1–25.

Cunneen, C., Baldry, E., Brown, D., Brown, M., Schwartz, M. and Steel, A., 2013. *Penal culture and hyperincarceration*. London: Ashgate.

Cytron, N., 2010. Improving the outcomes of place-based initiatives. *Community Investments*, 22(1), 3.

Freiberg, A. and Carson, W., 2010. The limits of evidence-based policy: evidence, emotion and criminal justice. *Australian Journal of Public Administration*, 69(2), 152–64.

Garland, D., 2001. Introduction: the meaning of mass imprisonment. *In*: D. Garland (ed.), *Mass imprisonment: social causes and consequences*. Thousand Oaks: Sage, 1–3.

Gooda, M., 2010. Justice reinvestment: a new strategy to address family violence. Paper presented at the National Family Violence Prevention Forum, Mackay QLD, 19 May. Retrieved on 19 October 2015 from: www.humanrights.gov.au/news/speeches/national-family-violence-prevention-forum-aiatsis-and-cdfvr-justice-reinvestment-new.

Hannah-Moffat, K., 2009. Gridlock or mutability: reconsidering 'gender' and risk assessment. *Criminology and Public Policy*, 8(1), 209–19.

James, J., Eisem, L.-B. and Subramanian, R., 2012. A view from the States: evidence-based public safety legislation. *Journal of Criminal Law and Criminology*, 102(3), 821–50.

Just Reinvest NSW, 2012. *Do you want to pay for failure or success? Justice reinvestment and a collective impact framework*. Retrieved on 1 September 2015 from: http://justreinvest.org.au/wp-content/uploads/2012/04/About-Collective-Impact11.pdf.

Latessa, E. and Lowencamp, C., 2006. What works in reducing recidivism?, *University of St. Thomas Law Journal*, 3(3), 521–35.

McNeill, F., Farrall, S., Lightowler, C. and Maruna, S., 2012. Re-examining evidence-based practice in community corrections: beyond 'a confined view' of what works. *Justice Research and Policy*, 14(1), 35–60.

NSW Ombudsman, 2011. *Addressing Aboriginal disadvantage: the need to do things differently*. A Special Report to Parliament under s. 31 of the *Ombudsman Act 1974*. Sydney: Office of the NSW Ombudsman.

Roman, J., 2004. Can cost–benefit analysis answer criminal justice policy questions, and if so, how?, *Journal of Contemporary Criminal Justice*, 20(3), 257–75.

Tonry, M., 2011. Making peace, not a desert: penal reform should be about values not justice reinvestment. *Criminology and Public Policy*, 10(3), 637–49.

Tucker, S. and Cadora, E., 2003. Justice reinvestment. *Ideas for an Open Society*, 3(3), New York, NY: Open Society Institute.

UK House of Commons Justice Committee, 2010. *Cutting crime: the case for justice reinvestment*. London: House of Commons.

Urban Institute, 2013. *The justice reinvestment initiative: experiences from the States*. Washington, DC: Urban Institute.

Van Voorhis, P., 2012. On behalf of women offenders: women's place in the science of evidence-based practice. *Criminology and Public Policy*, 11(2), 111–45.

Wacquant, L., 2010. Class, race and hyperincarceration in revanchist America. *Daedalus*, 139(3), 74–90.

Willis, M., 2010. *Indicators used internationally to measure indigenous justice outcomes*. Indigenous Justice Clearing House Research Brief 8. Canberra: NSW Department of Justice and Attorney-General.

Wong, K., Fox, C. and Albertson, K., 2014. Justice reinvestment in an 'age of austerity': developments in the United Kingdom. *Victims and Offenders*, 9(1), 76–99.

# Part IV
# Policing and human rights

In this section of the handbook authors examine the utility of human rights in relation to policing practice, police education, legitimacy and accountability. The section features a productive mix of cutting edge theoretical analysis, rich empirical accounts, and insights drawn from direct experience. Authors go beyond the identification of core human rights norms that apply to policing, taking into account the complex socio-political and institutional context in which police do, or more often do not, adhere to human rights standards intended to regulate the use of their special powers. The chapters highlight pressing concerns about both new policing powers and emerging trends, and longstanding debates about the potential of police to both uphold and undermine the human rights of victims, suspects and wider populations.

All authors acknowledge the unique position occupied by the police as repositories of the state's coercive powers, and recognize the paradox this poses for human rights-compliant policing. The promotion of human rights at the international level relies on states to safeguard populations within their territories, while at the same time it is recognized that states are often unwilling or unable to carry out this role. The same contradiction is reflected domestically in the positioning of police as both a primary vehicle of state power and the protectors of populations from abuses of those powers. Additional practical and conceptual problems arise in the case of emerging forms of transnational and private policing, and in jurisdictions where there is not even the pretence of the separation of police from the state that is at least espoused in liberal and social democracies. The authors in this section collectively grapple with all of these themes, predictably coming to different conclusions about the possibility of achieving forms of policing that promote, or even comply with, established human rights standards.

The section starts with a review by Jude McCulloch of the police record in Anglo-American countries of both upholding and violating the rights enshrined in the *International Covenant on Civil and Political Rights* and other human rights instruments. McCulloch links a record of police abuses to a continuing history of colonialism, identifying systemic racial discrimination and the under-policing of violence against women, as long-established themes in the critical analysis of policing. Her analysis identifies both emerging challenges for human rights compliant policing and new technological developments that could improve accountability.

The next two chapters address the role of human rights in police accountability, coming to different conclusions about the potential of human rights regimes to control the exercise of police power. Focusing on racialized shootings by police in the United States (US), McClanahan and Brisman observe that civil rights protections inscribed in the US Constitution have failed spectacularly to prevent unjustified killings by police officers. Certain individuals when they encounter police are routinely viewed as threats, they argue, rather than as the bearers of rights. Drawing on critical readings of legal theory, the authors conclude that police are beyond the reach of legal regulation, both for practical reasons and at a conceptual level. In a more abstract discussion, Willem de Lint locates human rights norms as just one of many 'ideological filters' that have the potential to influence police practice, alongside the liberal tradition of policing by consent and the contemporary influence of authoritarian neoliberalism. De Lint comes to a more hopeful conclusion than the previous authors about the potential of human rights to enhance police accountability, concluding that, while human rights cannot compensate for structurally produced inequalities, their influence as a filter on police organizations continues even in the face of countervailing pressures.

In a discussion that aligns human rights with democratic governance, Alan Beckley draws on his experience as an international police educator to describe a programme of human rights training delivered to police in the United Kingdom and in emerging democracies in Eastern Europe. Beckley observes that the programme was met with varying degrees of enthusiasm amongst different groups of trainees. While the teaching methods were designed to effect deep cultural change to promote human rights observance, the author notes that there is little evidence available about the impact of such training on subsequent police practice. Filling this gap, the chapter by Kiran Grewal and Vidura Munasinghe provides a detailed empirical account of the response of Sri Lankan police to human rights training delivered during a period of post-conflict transition in that country. These authors note that points of tension with police cultural norms and wider community expectations often resulted in human rights principles being subordinated to established practice, and that lack of respect for the human rights of operational police officers themselves also served to subvert the human rights message.

The next two chapters add further empirical insight into police practice in two locations where a history of violence and human rights abuses has led to demands for policing reform. The chapter by Natasha Marhia examines the response of Delhi police to public outrage over sexual violence against women. Her detailed study reveals that prevention of gendered violence is still largely viewed as a responsibility of women, rather than as an inalienable and claimable right, so that even well-intentioned police initiatives may still operate to reinforce social norms that undermine human security for women. Julia Hornberger's account of state police in post-Apartheid Johannesburg draws on a series of ethnographic studies of operational policing in that city. She shows how policing was transformed after the dismantling of the Apartheid system as police were encouraged to play a key role in the realization of the social, economic, civil and political rights that were newly enshrined in the country's Constitution. Nevertheless, Hornberger notes that the momentum for human rights based policing has encountered an ongoing tension between inclusionary and exclusionary forms of policing, with populations sometimes using human rights claims to demand aggressive interventions that may subsequently violate the rights of others.

The final two chapters consider the human rights implications of broad structural changes in policing arising from the twin effects of neoliberalism and globalization. Ruteere, Shearing and Stenning discuss the human rights implications of plural policing, noting both a proliferation of policing agencies in recent times and shifting conceptions of what constitutes human rights compliant policing. The authors conclude that the state-centric logic of human rights is at odds with this more complex policing landscape in which both policing and governance are increasingly pursued via assemblages. They argue for new formulations that can deal with plurality if human rights are to provide an effective basis for future regulatory regimes. In a similar vein, Bowling and Sheptycki chart the increasing transnational reach of policing. They note that the reality of this largely unfettered police power is increasingly at odds with established understandings of both policing and human rights as covalent with the state. In a world that has 'gone global', they argue, there are as yet no institutions of global governance by which worldwide standards of procedural justice can be guaranteed. While finding no ready answer to the question of who will police the globalized police, the authors question recourse to the language of human rights to legitimate the transnational use of force by police, illustrating their arguments with reference to case studies of transnational policing in the Caribbean.

Collectively, these chapters set a benchmark for our understanding of the use, misuse and sometimes lack of usefulness, of human rights in a diverse and rapidly changing array of policing contexts. All the authors recognize to varying degrees the contradictions and failures of human rights to achieve accountable policing. On the one hand, Alan Beckley acknowledges the lack of evidence for the efficacy of human rights training, while at the same time advocating the need for more, and more effective, human rights education for police officers. In contrast, McClanahan and Brisman see potentially insurmountable barriers to bringing the actions of police fully under the rule of law. Other authors have adopted positions in between, demonstrating through their critical analyses how the ideals of human rights encounter the practical and conceptual complexities of the real-world environments in which policing occurs. But most retain some belief that the language and institutions of human rights are worth safeguarding, rehabilitating where necessary, and refining where needed in order to meet the ongoing challenges of policing, and of policing the police.

# 30

# Police, crime and human rights

*Jude McCulloch*

## Introduction

The police are simultaneously agents of human rights and prime actors in the violation of human rights. As gatekeepers of the criminal justice system charged with protecting and serving the community, police are critical in preventing human rights violations and providing recognition and justice for victims. As Crawshaw et al. put it:

> Police agencies and police officials are uniquely placed to prevent the barbarity of gross abuse of power; to protect the mental and physical integrity of vulnerable people; to alleviate the suffering of victims of human rights violations; and to bring to justice those responsible for such violations.
>
> *(Crawshaw et al. 2007, p. 3)*

The coercive power vested in police to protect and bring to justice, however, also provides the means by which police become violators of rights. In Anglo-American countries where the military has historically been confined to dealing with external enemies in times of war, police are the foremost agents of human rights violations domestically (Green and Ward 2004, pp. 68–85).

Police are perhaps most obviously critical to the human rights contained in the *International Covenant on Civil and Political Rights* (ICCPR). Article 7 of the ICCPR, for example, bans torture and cruel, inhuman or degrading treatment and Article 6 the arbitrary deprivation of life. Police may violate these articles where they use excessive force or engage in the unlawful or unnecessary use of lethal force, though police are also critical in protecting people from crimes of violence that may violate these rights. The ICCPR includes provisions relating to freedom of movement (Articles 12 and 13). Police may facilitate such freedom, for example, by minimizing the risk that people using or traversing public space will become the targets of random or prejudice motivated crimes. Police, however, may inhibit such freedom when they disproportionately stop, search and question minorities or use their powers to interfere with people's movement in an arbitrary or unrestrained way (see, for example, Bowling and Weber 2011). Article 10 of the ICCPR enshrines the right 'to be treated with humanity and respect for the inherent dignity of the human person'. The policing of those low on the social hierarchy may infringe upon this right where it involves harassment, provocation, brutality or the ready assumption that certain identities, particularly racialized identities, are innately suspect. Article 26 of the ICCPR prohibits discrimination and requires that all people are considered equal before the law. Policing impacts on this fundamental human right in myriad ways.

Article 2 of the United Nations (UN) *Code of Conduct for Law Enforcement Officials* states that 'in the performance of their duty, law enforcement officials shall respect and protect human dignity and maintain and uphold the human rights of all persons'. Women and children, ethnic, sexual and religious minorities, racialized groups, political dissidents, the disabled, mentally ill, and the poor are particularly vulnerable to human rights violations perpetrated by community members. Effective protection of these groups relies to a significant extent upon law enforcement. However, police are often responsible for systematic human rights violations with impunity targeted at groups low on the social hierarchy. Vast numbers of human rights reports document the involvement of police in such violations (see, for example, Human Rights Watch 2014). The violation of human rights by police is sometimes rationalized as a 'noble cause' in the service of 'doing something about bad people' where ends justify means (Caldero and Crank 2010). However, policing that does not accord with human rights is likely to undermine police effectiveness, given that police legitimacy and community support are critical to effective law enforcement (Tyler and Huo 2002). The police mission to serve and protect, investigate and prevent crimes and maintain the peace amount to a promise to enhance human rights. Policing that breaches human rights should be considered a failure of policing, whatever the short-term crime control achievements (Crawshaw et al. 2007, p. xviii).

Police are vital in shaping people's experience of law. Police are the law on the street using their discretion in ways that uphold or undermine human rights. In recognition of the significance of police decision-making, Muir refers to police as 'street corner politicians' (Muir 1979). The criminal law is typically enshrined in legislation and interpreted through the courts. Policing is less transparent than formal law but just as significant in defining the activities and people that come to be seen as crime problems and the extent to which human rights are afforded or denied to individuals and groups. This chapter looks at human rights and policing in Anglo-American countries. In particular it considers the nature and history of human rights abuses by police and links between these abuses and a continuing history of colonialism. It also briefly examines the potential of human rights bodies, instruments and ideals to recognize, prevent and address human rights violations alongside the contemporary challenges and opportunities that are likely to undermine or enhance human rights in policing.

## Police, criminology and human rights

Despite what might now appear to be the rather obvious relevance of human rights and policing to criminology it was not until the 1960s that criminology started to take policing seriously and three decades later in the early 1990s that criminologists began to take human rights seriously (Cohen 1993). The democratic policing ideal involves non-discriminatory law enforcement designed to bring offenders before the courts, where guilt or innocence is decided and punishment determined. This division between judicial and police roles is crucial to human rights aimed at protecting citizens from violent, arbitrary or discriminatory coercive state interventions. The checks on police powers afforded by the courts are underpinned by the human right to a fair trial, and due process standards such as the presumption of innocence and the criminal burden of proof (Article 14 ICCPR). Criminology was slow to recognize the significance of police as shapers of law and justice. Until the 1960s, police were widely viewed by criminologists as neutral enforcers of the law, significant primarily as a conduit for bringing suspects before the courts. With the advent of television from the late 1950s and the involvement of students and people, particularly younger people, from all social classes in social justice, civil rights and anti-war movements in the following decades, the politically partisan, racially charged, gendered and brutally repressive nature of policing was exposed and more often directly experienced by a broader range of people (see, for example, York 1987). The changing social landscape, combined with changes in communication technology, opened up space in which groups experiencing systemic human rights violations at the hands of police became more vocal and more visible. During the 1960s, for example in the US, police brutality, including the use of attack dogs, water cannon, whips, truncheons, boots and fists against African-Americans involved in civil rights marches was captured on film and broadcast on television. In 1966, African-American writer and civil rights activist James Baldwin wrote 'A report from occupied territory' for *The Nation* magazine where he declared that 'the police treat the Negro like a dog', describing the routine, gratuitous, arbitrary and sometimes-fatal violence inflicted with impunity by police upon African-American residents of Harlem.

The increased exposure and discussion of widespread police violence, brutality, misconduct, and systemic racism alongside the rise of radical politics tied to social justice ideals, led to growing recognition amongst those in positions of influence of the substantial gap between the rhetoric and the reality of policing. In Australia, for example, systematic police violation of Indigenous people's rights in the inner city Sydney suburb of Redfern, where many Indigenous people settled after being alienated from land and separated from families in policies that gave rise to 'stolen generations', led to the establishment of one of Australia's first free community legal centres. Justice Wootten, writing about his observations of police in Redfern in the 1970s, wrote of a police-imposed curfew:

> I found, as most people do, it a little hard to believe when I first heard it, but when I observed it operating with my own eyes, I was left with little doubt. The simple position was that any Aboriginal who was on the streets of Redfern at a quarter past 10 was simply put into the paddy wagon and taken to the station and charged with drunkenness and that was something that was just literally applied to every Aboriginal walking along the street, irrespective of any sign of drunkenness.
>
> *(Wootten 1974, p. 60)*

American criminologist Jerome Skolnick, writing in 1966 about policing, maintained that: 'the observer's question is . . . not whether police operate under the constraints of due process of law, but whether they operate within bounds of civilized conduct' (quoted in James and Warren 1995, p. 4). Skolnick's still influential account of the police officer's 'working personality' (Skolnick 1966) began the search within criminology for explanations as to why and how police behave contrary to their official mandate and routinely become violators of human rights.

While the discriminatory and often brutal overpolicing of groups low on the social hierarchy began to attract attention during the last half of the twentieth century, the underpolicing of gendered crimes and the impact of this on the human rights of women became a focus of second wave feminists from the 1970s. From this time feminism began to illuminate the nature, extent, and impact of sexual assault and family violence and the role of the police in the broader political, social and cultural processes that systematically excluded the majority of women and children subject to such crimes from being recognized as deserving victims (see, for example, Scutt 1983). Today the exclusion of women and children from the law's protection is increasingly couched in terms of human rights, particularly the statements made by the

UN Committee on the Elimination of Discrimination against Women and the Special Rapporteur on Violence against Women (McQuigg 2011).

Despite the ideal of police as neutral enforcers of the law there is a growing acceptance in criminology that policing entails punitive elements that usurp or overlap with the judicial function. Mona Lynch, arguing that criminologists need to expand the boundaries of what is understood as punishment, lists the punitive dimensions of policing as including:

> shame and humiliation . . . the risk of physical harm due to use of force; infringement on privacy and autonomy in heavily policed communities; financial burdens due to confiscation of property; and work and family disruptions caused by arrest and detention.
>
> *(Lynch 2012, p. 191)*

Perhaps the most significant aspect of police powers relevant to human rights is use of force. The UN Code of Conduct for Law Enforcement Officials requires that police use force 'only when strictly necessary and to the extent required for the performance of their duty'. While human rights standards require that police use only minimum force, excessive force is often used to inflict what has been dubbed 'backstage punishment' (Chan 2000). The overlapping issues of excessive use of force (Skolnick and Fyfe 1993), unnecessary police shootings (McCulloch 2001, pp. 92–115), and systematic or institutionalized racism (Scraton 1985) are core police practices that violate human rights.

The growth of critical attention to policing within criminology is tied to the growing recognition of human rights as a criminological issue and crime and justice are inherently political (Cohen 1993). The rise of the prominence of human rights within criminology is also linked to the rise of the field of state crime. State crime, to adopt Green and Ward's influential definition, is 'state organizational deviance involving the violation of human rights' (Green and Ward 2004, p. 2). Human rights are central to defining and understanding state crime. Police are understood as key agents in the commission of state crimes. Green and Ward summarize factors that contribute to 'police deviance' and the violation of human rights as 'the centrality of coercive force, the need to make rapid discretionary decisions, and the task of preserving the existing social order in a class society' (ibid., p. 69). To this list can be added police as agents of colonialism and colonial relations of power.

## Policing and (neo)colonialism

The realization of policing as a human rights consistent endeavour is founded on the ideal of non-discriminatory implementation of laws consistent with human rights principles. The police, however, are significant actors in the ongoing history of colonialism, which is characterized by (in)justice systems that assign rights according to racialized categories. Colonial relations of power distribute rights according to identity based on the view that some lives matter more than others. This is the antithesis of human rights built on respect for the inherent dignity of *all* people. Colonial policing reflects, maintains and reproduces colonial relations of power. The democratic policing ideal in Anglo-American countries assumes a civil police force. Modern styles of policing in Anglo-American countries were traditionally underpinned by a strict demarcation between the police and the military in the national constitution and in the operational philosophy and principles of police (Hocking 1993, Kraska and Kappeler 1997). The demarcation between the police and military is important for human rights because the police and military serve different roles, adhere to different operational philosophies and located themselves differently in relation to community (McCulloch 2001, pp. 15–31). Under the tenets of civil policing citizens may be suspects, against whom minimum force may be used in certain circumstances, but they are not enemies to be overcome or eliminated using overwhelming force. Police keep the peace at home while the military are used externally in times of war. The police are typically considered part of the community while the military, by way of contrast, are deployed against enemies considered a threat to the nation or community. A close association between the police and the military and the use of the military against citizens has long been associated with repressive regimes where human rights violations are commonplace. Hybrid police, military and criminal justice frameworks are, however, standard in colonial contexts (Saada 2003).

Contradicting the democratic ideal of policing, colonial powers, such as Britain, while maintaining civil police forces at home, oversaw highly militarized and repressive forces in occupied colonies (see, for example, Duschinski 2010). As England established a civil police force in the early nineteenth century, militarized styles of policing continued to dominate in the colonies. In more contemporary decades colonial styles of law and order were obvious in the highly militarized policing and hybrid police-military operations used against Catholics in Northern Ireland, particularly those involved in or supportive of the civil rights and republication movements, before a successful peace process in the early 1990s (Cunningham 2001). In the decades from the 1970s these colonial styles of policing were imported into the centre of colonial power from the territories with the result that more military styles of policing that approached some sections of the community as enemies became more fully integrated into everyday policing (see, for example, Manwaring-White 1983).

Settler countries like Australia and the United States (US) were founded on the violent dispossession of Indigenous people accomplished by armed settlers, armed and militarized police and the military proper. Indigenous populations in both Australia and the US were considered and dealt with, not as citizens with rights, but as a less than fully human threat to nation, and thus enemies and inferior peoples to be overcome, dispersed, assimilated or eliminated using a range of repressive measures including punitive raids, and lethal and overwhelming force (see, for example, Reynolds 2006). In the US, the status of slaves trafficked from Africa as property to be traded, rather than autonomous human beings with rights, was rationalized on the colonial logic of the presumed inferiority of non-whites (Fields 1990). Once slavery was abolished in the US in the mid-nineteenth century, African-Americans were no longer regarded in law as property but were treated instead as second-class citizens, and particularly in the South, subjected to a racial caste system, known as 'Jim Crow' (Alexander 2012, pp. 30–35). In the decades after slavery was abolished law enforcement participated in and was complicit with vigilante violence against African-Americans, particularly lynching in the South. Rather than protecting a vulnerable minority from human rights abuses, including violation of the right to life, the police participated in or were complicit with gross human rights violations. Skolnick and Fyfe draw a historical line between contemporary police violence against African-Americans and this history of vigilantism (Skolnick and Fyfe 1993, pp. 23–37).

The abolition of slavery in the US, and the formal recognition of indigenous people in Australia, and African-Americans and Native Americans from the mid-1950s as full citizens, signalled a new era in the colonial relations of power. The police continue to be critical in maintaining these hierarchical power relationships through to the present. Systemic or institutionalized police racism is critical to overpolicing of racialized groups that is a key driver of criminalization and mass incarceration of indigenous people in Australia (Blagg 2008, pp. 20–3, Cunneen 2001). Michelle Alexander (2012) documenting the impacts of the war on drugs in the US describes how it has led to the mass incarceration of African-Americans in particular and people of colour more generally. Alexander and others note the key role of discriminatory policing in criminalization and mass incarceration (see also Lynch 2012).

Overpolicing violates fundamental human rights pertaining to discrimination and the right to be treated with respect for the inherent dignity of the human person (Human Rights Law Centre 2011). The process of criminalization is critical to maintaining former slaves and indigenous people as second-class citizens in an age where formal equality is lauded. The past ideology of racial inferiority as a basis for differential rights has been eclipsed and replaced by the construction of non-white identities as criminal. Apart from continuing colonial relations of power into the present, police practices of criminalization also obscures historical injustice, undermining legitimate claims that Indigenous people and former slaves might have on the nation-state. As Cunneen puts it:

> The process of criminalization, the denial of human rights, marginalization and incarceration ensure that Aboriginal and Torres Strait Islander people are maintained as a dispossessed minority, rather than a people with legitimate political claims on the nation state.
>
> *(Cunneen 2001, p. 250)*

Where criminalization is linked to disenfranchisement, as it is in the US, it can also impact negatively on the right to vote, without discrimination, as set out in Article 25 the ICCPR and the *International Convention on the Elimination of All Forms of Racial Discrimination* (Article 5[c]). Writing specifically about the US, but in a comment more broadly applicable to the way criminalization and mass incarceration works to continue colonial relations of power, Michelle Alexander argues that it has created a 'new caste system', and that slavery, segregation and mass incarceration are aligned with core definitions of 'what it means to be black' in different periods – a slave, a second-class citizen, a criminal (Alexander 2012, p. 197).

The various, continuous and interlocking wars on crime, drugs and terrorism post-9/11 undermined the separation of the police and military, crystalizing and intensifying colonial relations of power. The militarization of police has continued apace under the banner of these various wars since the 1970s (Kappeler and Kraska 2015). Counter-terrorism in particular has been a vehicle for integrating the counter-insurgency tactics used by former colonial powers to repress nationalist movements into the policing and security apparatus of democratic states (Hocking 1993). In the United Kingdom (UK) contemporary counter-terrorism practices are argued to have brought home the colonial strategies formerly used in Northern Ireland to create new 'suspect communities' (Pantazis and Pemberton 2009). The response to ongoing street protests about fatal shootings and deaths in custody of African-Americans in the US since 2014 reveal new levels of militarization amongst police. In a statement indicating the extent of the integration of military hardware into policing, President Barack Obama (2015) announced that police would be barred from using 'tracked armoured vehicles, bayonets, grenade launchers and large-caliber firearms, in response to accusations that US law enforcement has become too militarised'. The wars on crime and terrorism give rise to styles of policing that classify categories of people, not simply as people who may have broken the law, but as 'presumptive enemies' (Zedner 2010, p. 391).

The increasing militarization of policing, particularly under the banner of countering terrorism is matched by laws that provide extraordinarily broad powers to police. Ericson characterizes these laws as 'counter-laws' because they 'erode or eliminate traditional principles, standards, and procedures of criminal law that get in the way of preempting imagined sources of harm' (Ericson 2008, p. 57). Another way of putting this is that these laws remove the checks and balances that help ensure that police act in accordance with human rights. Pre-emptive laws fortify the imaginary binary between those considered potential victims in need of protection and those understood to be threats (McCulloch and Wilson 2016). Such laws 'exacerbate divisions between forms of justice open to distinct citizen groups' contrary to human rights principles that mandate equal justice (Mythen 2014, pp. 395, 105). The lack of distinction between the police and the military in a context of exceptional laws that expand police powers reinvigorates colonial relations of power.

## Some challenges and opportunities for human rights consistent policing

There are a number of other contemporary trends which likewise create a context in which policing is more likely to violate human rights. Policing is more likely to lead to systematic breaches of human rights where suspects and defendants who have insufficient funds to pay for legal services are unable to rely on publicly funded schemes to challenge police charges and police behaviour. In these circumstances victims of state crimes at the hands of police are likely themselves to be branded criminals, regardless of the substantive injustice involved in such a construction. Current reductions and restrictions to publicly funded legal aid will bolster a climate of impunity surrounding human rights abuses by police (see Noone 2014 on legal aid).

The growth in transnational policing and the growing integration of national security and law enforcement provide other challenges to human rights consistent policing. Over the past decades there has been a steady increase in policing across national borders (Andreas and Nadelmann 2006). Bowling and Sheptycki (2012) describe the ways this trend increases the opacity of policing and the inability of national police management and accountability systems to effectively oversee cross border policing. In addition to this the integration of national security and law enforcement (McCulloch and True 2015), particularly in the 'War on Terror' has led to the rise of 'secret police' that combine covert intelligence functions with coercive functions (McCulloch and Tham 2005). Human rights bodies note the way that combining secrecy with coercive powers 'has the potential to allow human rights violations to go unnoticed and in a climate of impunity' (Amnesty International 2003). The International Commission of Jurists investigation of counter-terrorism states that it 'received evidence that intelligence services worldwide effectively enjoy impunity for human rights violations because of a lack of meaningful civilian oversight' (International Commission of Jurists 2009, p. 23). Beyond this, it argues that executive government may be 'accruing power and privileging intelligence over law enforcement approaches, precisely *because of* the lack of accountability to others' (ibid., p. 68, emphasis in original).

Changes in technology, by way of contrast, have the potential to increase police accountability, enhance human rights and challenge impunity. The filming of the Los Angeles Police Department beating of Rodney King in 1991 was a landmark in the rise of the 'citizen journalists'. The ubiquity of mobile devices with cameras means that acts of excessive use of force by police are far more likely to be filmed than in the past, so that outright denial of such violations becomes less tenable (Goldsmith 2010). In one recent US case, a police officer was charged with murder after mobile phone footage of him shooting an unarmed man emerged at odds with police statements about the circumstances of the shooting (Knight 2015).

Human rights standards and the shared language it creates about what is expected in policing creates a context in which violations perpetrated by police or structures in the policing organizations that support such violations are potentially made more transparent and open to redress. The European Commission of Human Rights' Rapporteur on Police Complaints, for example, sets conditions for the effective investigation of alleged human rights violations by police, including that the investigation be independent, adequate, and capable of resulting in discipline and prosecution of perpetrators, prompt, transparent and involves and protects the alleged victims (Smith 2010). These standards of investigation are typically not realized within the extant frameworks for investigating complaints against police (Hopkins 2010). In some jurisdictions, such as the UK, the European Court of Human Rights may declare certain police policy or operations contrary to human rights. In Australia, where there is no national human rights instrument the UN Human Rights Committee may make decisions which, in rare circumstances, impact on policy and practice and lead to redress for victims (Victorian Human Rights and Equal Opportunity Commission 2014). There is a danger, however, that human rights standards are used in ways that obscure human rights abuses. Integrating the language of human rights into policing, the development of human rights training and knowledge of human rights standards does not readily translate into human rights practice and may serve as a way of legitimating practices that are antithetical to human rights (Bullock and Johnson 2011).

## Conclusion

Police are front line workers when it comes to implementing human rights and at the forefront of violations. While the police mandate to keep the peace and prevent and investigate crimes promises to protect the vulnerable and enhance human rights it is widely recognized that police are key state agents in the violation of rights. Police brutality, excessive use of force, and unnecessary or unlawful shootings are major human rights concerns, particularly as such violations are most frequently perpetrated against racialized minorities and others low on the social hierarchy. Such groups are frequently treated and viewed as 'police property' (Lee 1981), making violations of human rights with impunity commonplace. While human rights is based on equal justice for all, police have had a central role in maintaining colonial relations of power that accords different levels of rights according to identity.

In the contemporary period the language of human rights and policing are more frequently coupled both in terms of critique of police practices and in promoting the role of police as a critical human rights enhancing organization. Human rights provide a language with which to characterize police abuses of power and a standard to hold police organizations accountable. Human rights discourses provide a way of illuminating state crimes committed by police while human rights bodies may, in some cases, provide an avenue for redress where police have violated rights. Tokenistic gestures towards human rights can, on the other hand, provide unwarranted legitimacy for policing fundamentally at odds with human rights.

The various and continuous wars on crime and particularly terrorism provide challenges for achieving human rights consistent policing. Folding the language, philosophy, tactics, weapons and hardware of the military into policing and coupling this with laws that undermine due process, creates a context in which policing is likely to generate human rights abuses above and beyond what might be observed in more democratic styles of civil policing. The disparity of power between police and victims of human rights abuses is exacerbated where victims are unable to access legal assistance. The merging of security and police and intelligence alongside the combining of coercive police powers with secrecy generate a climate fertile for human rights abuses. Against this backdrop, changes in technology which gave rise to 'citizen journalists' potentially bring 'back stage' punishment and human rights abuses into the open in ways that challenge police impunity.

## References

Alexander, M., 2012. *The new Jim Crow: mass incarceration in the age of colorblindness.* New York, NY: The New Press.

Amnesty International, 2003. Concerns regarding the ASIO Legislation Amendment Bill 2003. Retrieved on 22 December 2003 from: http://www.amnesty.org.au/airesources/report-03-12-03.html Amnesty International.

Andreas, P. and Nadelmann, E., 2006. *Policing the globe*. New York, NY: Oxford University Press.

Baldwin, J., 1966. A report from occupied territory. *The Nation*, 11 July. Retrieved on 20 May 2015 from: www.thenation.com/article/159618/report-occupied-territory#.

Blagg, H., 2008. *Crime, aboriginality and the decolonisation of justice*. Hawkins Press.

Bowling, B. and Sheptycki, J., 2012. *Global policing*. London: Sage.

Bowling, B. and Weber, L., 2011. Stop and search in global context: an overview. *Policing and Society*, 21(4), 480–8.

Bullock, K. and Johnson, P., 2011. The impact of the *Human Rights Act 1998* on policing in England and Wales. *British Journal of Criminology*, 52(3), 630–50.

Caldero, M.A. and Crank, J.P., 2010. *Police ethics: the corruption of noble cause*. London: Routledge.

Chan, J., 2000. Backstage punishment: police violence, occupational culture and criminal justice. *In*: T. Coady, S. James, S. Miller and M. O'Keefe (eds), *Violence and police culture*. Melbourne: Melbourne University Press, 85–108.

Cohen, S. 1993. Human rights and crimes of the state: the culture of denial. *Australian and New Zealand Journal of Criminology*, 26(2), 97–115.

Crawshaw, R., Cullen, S. and Williamson, T., 2007. *Human rights and policing*. Leiden: Martinus Nijhoff Publishers.

Cunneen, C., 2001. *Conflict, politics and crime: aboriginal communities and the police*. London: Allen and Unwin.

Cunningham, M., 2001. *British government policy in Northern Ireland, 1969–2000*. Manchester: Manchester University Press.

Duschinski, H., 2010. Reproducing regimes of impunity: fake encounters and the informalization of everyday violence in Kashmir Valley. *Cultural Studies*, 24(1), 110–32.

Ericson, R., 2008. The state of preemption: managing terrorism through counter law. *In*: L. Amoore and M. De Goede (eds), *Risk and the war on terror*. London and New York: Routledge, 57–76.

Fields, B.J., 1990. Slavery, race and ideology in the United States of America. *New Left Review*, 181(1), 95–118.

Goldsmith, A.J., 2010. Policing's new visibility. *British Journal of Criminology*, 50, 914–34.

Green, P. and Ward, T., 2004. *State crime: governments, violence and corruption*. London: Pluto Press.

Hocking, J., 1993. *Beyond terrorism: the development of the Australian security state*. London: Allen & Unwin.

Hopkins, T., 2010. *An effective system for investigating complaints against police: A study of human rights compliance in police complaint models in the US, Canada, UK, Northern Ireland and Australia*. Victoria Law Foundation.

Human Rights Law Centre, 2011. National Human Rights Action Plan. Retrieved on 20 August 2015 from: www.humanrightsactionplan.org.au/nhrap/focus-area/police.

Human Rights Watch, 2014. *Dispatches: tracking US police brutality*. Retrieved on 12 August 2015 from: www.hrw.org/news/2014/08/12/dispatches-tracking-us-police-brutality.

International Commission of Jurists, 2009. *Assessing damage, urging action. Report of the Eminent Jurists Panel on terrorism, counter-terrorism and human rights*. Retrieved on 12 August 2014 from: www.refworld.org/cgi-bin/texis/vtx/rwmain/opendocpdf.pdf?reldoc=y&docid=4a7836d62.

James, S. and Warren, I., 1995. Police culture. *In*: J. Bessant, K. Carrington and S. Cook (eds), *Cultures of crime and violence: the Australian experience*. Bundoora, Australia: La Trobe University Press in Association with the Victorian Law Foundation, 3–15.

Kappeler, V.E. and Kraska, P.B., 2015. Normalising police militarisation, living in denial. *Policing and Society*, 25(3), 268–75.

Knight, B., 2015. Cincinnati campus police officer charged with murder after shooting unarmed black motorist. 30 July 2015 *ABC News*. Retrieved on 11 August 2015 from: www.abc.net.au/news/2015-07-30/cincinnati-campus-police-officer-charged-with-murder/6658726n.

Kraska, P.B. and Kappeler, V.E., 1997. Militarizing American police: the rise and normalization of paramilitary units. *Social Problems*, 1–18.

Lee, J.A., 1981. Some structural aspects of police deviance in relations with minority groups. *In*: C. Shearing, ed., *Organizational police deviance*. Toronto: Butterworth.

Lynch, M., 2012. Theorizing the role of the 'war on drugs' in US punishment. *Theoretical Criminology*, 16(2), 175–99.

Manwaring-White, S., 1983. *The policing revolution: police technology, democracy and liberty in Britain*. London: Harvester.

McCulloch, J., 2001. *Blue army: paramilitary policing in Australia*. Melbourne: Melbourne University Press.

McCulloch, J. and Tham, J.C., 2005. Secret state, transparent subject: the Australian security intelligence organisation in the age of terror. *Australian & New Zealand Journal of Criminology*, 38(3), 400–15.
McCulloch, J. and True, J., 2015. Shifting borders. *In*: S. Pickering and J. Ham (eds), *The Routledge handbook on crime and international migration*. London: Routledge, 367.
McCulloch, J. and Wilson, D., 2016. *Pre-crime: pre-emption, precaution and the future*. London: Routledge.
McQuigg, R.J., 2011. *International human rights law and domestic violence: the effectiveness of international human rights law*. London: Taylor & Francis.
Muir, W.K., 1979. *Police: streetcorner politicians*. Chicago, IL: University of Chicago Press.
Mythen, G., 2014. *Understanding the risk society: crime, security and justice*. London: Palgrave Macmillan.
Noone, M.A., 2014. Legal aid crisis: lessons from Victoria's response. *Alternative Law Journal*, 39(1), 40–44.
Obama, B., 2015. Barack Obama moves to demilitarise US cops after Baltimore and Ferguson protests. *The Age*, 20 May. Retrieved on 20 May 2015 from: www.theage.com.au/world/-gh4v2p.html.
Pantazis, C. and Pemberton, S., 2009. From the 'old' to the 'new' suspect community examining the impacts of recent UK counter-terrorist legislation. *British Journal of Criminology*, 49(5), 646–66.
Reynolds, H., 2006. *The other side of the frontier: Aboriginal resistance to the European invasion of Australia*. New South Wales: UNSW Press.
Saada, E., 2003. The history of lessons: power and rule in imperial formations. *Items: Social Science Research Council*, 4(4), 10–17.
Scraton, P., 1985. *The state of the police*. London: Pluto Press.
Scutt, J.A., 1983. *Even in the best of homes: violence in the family*. London: Penguin Books.
Skolnick, J.H., 1966. *Justice without trial: law enforcement in democratic society*. New York, NY: Wiley.
Skolnick, J.H. and Fyfe, J.J., 1993. *Above the law: police and the excessive use of force*. New York, NY: Free Press.
Smith, G., 2010. Every complaint matters: Human Rights Commissioner's opinion concerning independent and effective determination of complaints against the police. *International Journal of Law, Crime and Justice*, 38(2), 59–74.
Tyler, T.R. and Huo, Y., 2002. *Trust in the law: encouraging public cooperation with the police and courts*. New York, NY: Russell Sage Foundation.
Victorian Human Rights and Equal Opportunity Commission, 2014. Media Statement on the UN Human Rights Committee findings on the police assault of Corinna Horvath in 1996. Retrieved on 20 August 2015 from: www.humanrightscommission.vic.gov.au/index.php/news-and-events/media-releases/item/802-media-statement-on-the-unhcr-findings-on-the-police-assault-of-corinna-h.
Wootten, H. 1974. Aboriginal legal services. *In*: G. Nettheim (ed.), *Aborigines, human rights and the law*. Sydney: Australian and New Zealand Book Company.
York, B., 1987. Baiting the tiger: police and protest during the Vietnam War. *In*: M. Finnane (ed.), *Policing in Australia: historical perspectives*. Kensington: New South Wales University Press, 170–87.
Zedner, L. 2010. Security, the state, and the citizen: the changing architecture of crime control. *New Criminal Law Review: An International and Interdisciplinary Journal*, 13(2), 379–403.

# 31

# Police violence and the failed promise of human rights

*Bill McClanahan and Avi Brisman*

## Introduction

On 9 August 2014, Darren Wilson, a uniformed and on-duty white police officer, fired 10 shots from his service weapon in Ferguson, Missouri, a suburb of St Louis. At least six of the bullets fired by Wilson hit their intended target, Michael Brown, an unarmed black youth who died on the scene (United States [US] Department of Justice 2015). In the weeks and months that followed, the residents of Ferguson – a majority black city where nearly all city officials are white (Robertson 2015) – expressed their longstanding concerns regarding the racialized enforcement strategies of the local police.[1] Vigils and protests were held nationwide; meanwhile, in Ferguson, peaceful demonstrations led to some violent clashes and moments of unrest, which were described by some as 'riots' (Bucktin 2014, Thompson 2014) and 'uprisings' (Howard and Lang 2014, Maupin 2014).

The death of Brown – and the subsequent killings of Gilbert Collar, John Crawford, Eric Garner, Freddie Gray, Akai Gurley, Tamir Rice, Walter L. Scott and countless (or, at least, *uncounted*[2]) other young men – seems to have renewed conversations in the US about racialized police violence, in general, and lethal force, in particular.[3] While even a cursory glance at the demographics of the most notable and recognized victims of fatal police violence reveals the deeply racialized nature of police homicide in the US, directly addressing the racial dimensions of the violent policing of the US is not the central goal of this chapter. Instead, our goal in this chapter is to explore briefly the relationship between police violence and human rights in the US, while remaining mindful of the inherent limitations of legalistic frameworks – including human rights frameworks – to address the intersections of police power and class-based and racialized police violence.[4]

With this in mind, we begin with a broad discussion of human rights regimes and their potential intersection(s) with police violence. Next, we turn our attention to the meaning of 'police' and how police power continues across spatial, social and historical borders beyond what is generally comprehended by criminology. Following that, we consider the central *problem* of police, interrogating how police might be – or, more significantly, might not be – constrained by law and assertions of human rights, invoking what Walter Benjamin calls the related 'spectrality' and formlessness of police and human rights. Unsurprisingly, we raise more questions than we answer, and so we conclude not with any prescription for 'fixing' the problem of police,[5] but instead with some thoughts on the relationship between human rights and the violence of police and policing.

## Conceptions and sources of human rights; police as protectors and abusers

As Weber and colleagues (2014, p. 129) explain, because the police in the modern nation-state are often armed with lethal weaponry and invested with special powers[6] – most notably, the capacity to use force and invade privacy – they possess the potential to act either as *protectors* or *abusers* of the different 'generations' of human rights (Brisman 2014).[7] For example, police can employ their power and skills to keep the peace and enforce the law, and Weber and colleagues (2014, p. 129), drawing on Crawshaw and colleagues (2007), point out that police can be vital for determining whether nation-states meet their human rights obligations towards their populations, especially with respect to the rights contained in the *International Covenant on Civil and Political Rights* (ICCPR). By the same token, however, police can become abusers of human rights by either directly misusing their power (ranging from torture and extrajudicial killings to unwarranted invasions of privacy and discriminatory treatment of ethnic, racial, religious or sexual minorities) or by providing inadequate protection for those who need their assistance (Weber et al. 2014, pp. 130, 131).

Although police are not vested with the power to determine guilt and punish offenders – at least not in liberal democracies – they are authorized to use force where necessary to apprehend a criminal suspect, prevent harm to other individuals and groups of people, or to restore order.[8] While police perform a wide range of duties and tasks (for a discussion, see, for example, Gaines and Kappeler 2015, Kappeler and Gaines 2015), it is their mandate to use force that generates the most persistent human rights concerns. Moreover, and as we argue below, the processes of essential police power so frequently and fundamentally violate those fundamental human rights (or, more accurately, disregard, as 'violate' seems to imply some form of eventual legal recognition, which can never be expected by the victims of police violence) that it begins to become clear that the police power acts as a fundamental challenge to human rights, rather than the other way around.

## What we talk about when we talk about police[9]

To adequately and accurately explore and interrogate the intersections of police and human rights, we must first be clear about what we talk about when talk about *police* and *police power*. As Neocleous (2014) explains, police power is a far more wide-reaching and historically continuous power than what is represented by the contemporary image of the uniformed police officer. Indeed, police power is not about the control of crime and the minimization of harm, as criminology has so frequently suggested, but is instead a power that exists for the production and reproduction of order and capitalism and the securing of insecurity, of which the 'fighting of crime' and 'enforcing the law' is just one small part. While a history of policing is outside the scope of this chapter (see Gaines and Kappeler [2015] for a helpful account), we note that it was not until the 1800s, with the widespread adoption of formal and uniformed police agencies (what we now think of as *the* police), that the already established police power begin to justify itself using the logics of law enforcement and crime fighting. From a genealogical vantage point, then, police is a power that runs uninterrupted – albeit changing to some extent to reflect new technologies, fads, logics, and politics – through the history of capitalism, starting with the first moments of primitive accumulation essential to industrial capitalism, and carrying on undisturbed to the contemporary moment. As such, police power is many things – air power, war power, power to securitize (Neocleous 2013, 2014), power of the visible and visual (Wall and Linnemann 2014) and on and on endlessly – but it is first and foremost and most fundamentally the power to commit violence; where and however it is exercised, police power is premised on the police monopoly on legitimate violence. When we speak, then, of police power and its relationship to human rights, we are speaking fundamentally about the violence of the state and the relationship of that violence to human rights.

With this notion of police power in mind, potential subjects of police violence, then, frequently seem to be viewed or approached not as individuals bearing *rights*, but rather in terms of *threats*. These may be threats to individual police officers, as was the case with Michael Brown, who – according to Officer Wilson – attempted to grab Wilson's gun after repeatedly punching him in the face. Threats that – again, in the view of police – warrant a lethally violent response may also be threats to economic order, as was the case in the police killing of Eric Garner, who transgressed the boundaries of acceptable capitalism by selling unlicensed and untaxed cigarettes on a New York City sidewalk. In each of these moments – along with virtually any other police encounter, violent or otherwise – police can be seen to approach members of the policed population not with regard or consideration for rights, but instead with an intense focus on the potential threat that a policed subject may pose.

The language of 'threats' pervades policing to an extent that reveals its primacy in the police logic. This was made abundantly clear in an open letter issued in the immediate wake of the police killing of Deng Manyoun on 13 June 2015. The open letter was issued five days later by Louisville, Kentucky's River City Fraternal Order of Police, a local police union seemingly fearful of a response resembling the uprisings in Ferguson, New York and Baltimore following high-profile police killings of black men. Union president David Mutchler, author of the letter, not only illustrates the fundamental police interest in 'threats', but extends that interest reciprocally to the populations subject to the Louisville Metropolitan Police Department (LMPD). Addressing the letter to 'the criminal element' (and, in an interesting conflation, also 'the public we serve'), Mutchler claims that the 'lies and hate' 'put[s] all of us [police] in danger' and that LMPD officers 'WILL stop the threat to us'. Human rights, to be clear, are of no concern to Mutchler or the police posture and logic his letter embodies; lamenting any constraints on police violence via 'weak policies' that limit police power, Mutchler promises that 'we [the police] will find a way' (Capps 2015). Mutchler's statements reveal not only the supremacy, within police logics, of the subject-as-threat position, but also the fundamental ambivalence police feel towards the same legal systems that construct and promise human rights. When Officer Wilson, as an executive agent of the state, approached Mike Brown, he approached Brown not as a rights-bearing individual, but only as a potential threat – and it is imperative that we recognize that this approach is not a distortion of police power, but exactly the normal police mandate given to police armed by the state. It is *threats*, then, and not *rights* that interest and guide police.

The 'problem' of the police power is not, though, limited to the types of domestic and departmental uniformed police described above. Rather, the problem of police – and, more importantly here, the intractable problem of the intersection of police and human rights – is as wide reaching, fundamental and global as the violent police logic itself. If, as Neocleous suggests, the police power is inseparable historically and philosophically from war power, then it follows that *police is war* and vice versa. When considering human rights and police, then, we must be mindful to include war, warfighting and state militaries in our conceptualization of 'police'.

Once this broadened (but historically and politically accurate) understanding of police is applied, policing becomes even more fundamentally at odds with human rights: few would argue that 'grave violations' of human rights stemming from 'massacres, the starvation of entire populations, and genocide' are not 'increasingly' part and parcel of war (Maiese 2003). Put simply, even if uniformed police were at this very moment to set aside what is ultimately their institutional mandate and stop disregarding the human rights of policed populations through murder, nonlethal violence, incarceration and intimidation, the violent logics of police would, all the same, remain alive and well in the exercise of military power.

## Rights and the violence of law and police

The potential for the rejection and abuse of human rights, as explored in more detail below, is present at each step of the justice system, from the initial moment of contact with the police power, through to the moments where the central powers of police – the power to hunt, seize, arrest, detain, try and punish the subjects of police power – are exercised. Why, though, do rights regimes so sacrosanct as to be unquestionable in mainstream political and social discourse not restrict police power? Why does the police power seem so unrestrained by claims of human rights? The answer, it seems, might be found in the very foundations of the relationship between law and police power. Drawing on Benjamin's 'Critique of violence' (1986), Taussig (2010, p. 176) notes that police power begins, essentially, where the law ends: 'the "law" of the police . . . is independent of the rest of law'. Taussig then questions what, exactly, police power is subject to if not law. Unsurprisingly, Taussig finds that human rights – 'the monitors of which form a cultural and bureaucratic movement across the globe' (Taussig 2010, p. 176) – presents no obstacle to or constraint on police violence whatsoever, owing to his view of the very nature of human rights as themselves part and parcel of law. For Taussig, then – and we can safely extend the attribution to Benjamin – a truly lawless police power (that is, police violence) can rarely, if ever, be limited by legal doctrines and discourses of human rights, precisely because of their place in the law.

The intersection of human rights and policing has received a substantial amount of academic attention. Scholars have, variously, considered police as both frequent violators and protectors of human rights. Extending the engagement, some have noted that individual police themselves may suffer human rights abuses as an attendant dimension of their profession.[10] What seems to be missing from contemporary academic considerations of the nexus of human rights and the police power is a radical critique of the very potential of human rights as a constraining force on the police power. Indeed, a vexing problem for anyone considering launching any critique of human rights as discursive and legal categories and frameworks is that any such criticism 'verges on the heretical' (Brogden 2009, p. 175) or is often read as 'tantamount to heresy' (Jensen and Jefferson 2009, p. 1). Despite the sanctity of human rights as a conceptual construct and the reverence with which it is treated in certain academic, activist and political circles, there has recently been increasingly critical attention given to the field of human rights (see generally Kennedy 2002, Rajagopal 2006).

As noted by Weber and colleagues (2014, p. 21), human rights are significant 'largely because they have been translated into a body of international law'. For the problem we wish to address here – the central problem of police and police violence – these authors' point is key. If – as Weber and colleagues aptly note – human rights gains its saliency and significance first and foremost from its place in codified international law, then it is in the application of legal doctrines that we would most expect to find meaningful constraints on the violence of police. Surveying the landscape of criminal law and its application, however, we instead find what adherents to the conceptual foundations of human rights could understand only as abuses and rejections of the rights of marginalized groups (classes, ethnicities and races) by police. At every turn in the processes and systems constructed to administer criminal justice, the accused, suspicious, or even furtive subject is made to suffer in a manner that surely violates his or her socially constructed humanity, if not his or her legally constructed human rights.

Part of the problem, it seems, with conceptual understandings of human rights as a realized or potential constraint on police violence is the *ex post facto* nature of the exercise of those rights. Human rights violations, that is, are addressed only after the violation takes place, with claims made in court and heard by judges (themselves a central component of the police power) – a long, costly and often painful process that requires, first, adequate legal knowledge and awareness of rights, and, second, the social and financial capital to initiate and negotiate legal proceedings. Compounding the difficulty of even making a claim of human rights abuses as part of an experience of police violence is found, it seems, in the lethal nature of so many of those moments of violence: the assertion of human rights would have not saved the lives of Michael Brown as he bled to death on the street in Ferguson, or Eric Garner as he was choked to death on a New York sidewalk. Indeed, Garner made verbal assertions of his rights in the moments immediately prior to his death, but those claims of rights seemed, in fact, to only anger his police antagonists. What good, then, would human rights do to prevent or constrain a police power that so frequently exercises the ultimate violence – the taking of a life/the eradication of a threat – without leaving any space or time for even the verbal assertion of rights? Even when the police power is *not* exercised to its full murderous potential – when 'less-than-lethal force' (Gaines and Kappeler 2015) is employed, and when those subjected to the legal terror of police are simply hunted, beaten, bitten, tasered, pepper-sprayed, or incarcerated (Blow 2015)[11] – there is little opportunity for the effective assertion of rights. This predicament is well understood by those frequently subjected to the fundamental violence of everyday policing, as illustrated in the cultural knowledge conveyed in the maxim 'you can beat the rap, but you can't beat the ride'. And lest we be dulled into accepting that 'the ride' may somehow be an unfortunate but necessary and harmless function of policing, we must recall the police killing of Freddie Gray by uniformed officers in Baltimore, Maryland, following Gray's arrest and the 'rough ride' or 'nickel ride'[12] that killed him.

Because human rights, insofar as the term is understood to refer to a legal framework or regime, are only ever made real by the state and its police power (particularly in the US, which does not have legal structures of human rights that may operate with more independence, such as the *European Convention on Human Rights*), the relationship between state violence and human rights is entirely dependent on the orientation of the state and its willingness to act as a constraining force on itself. The relationship between rights and the power of the state, according to a radical critique of rights frameworks, may be 'rendered, even where formally acknowledged, more or less ineffective' through 'social, economic and political relations of power . . . dominance and subordination' (Benton 1993, p. 165). In formulating a critique of international humanitarian law through an examination of Israeli legal experts working in the aftermath of a sustained 22-day attack in 2008–09 by Israeli forces against Palestinians in Gaza, Weizman (2009, 2010) notes that the languages and architectures of humanitarian law – a legal force intimately intertwined with discourses and legal structures of human rights – may ultimately have served Israeli power (a war/police power) in not only justifying but increasing violence against Palestinians. Weizman, also drawing on Benjamin, highlights the use of 'lawfare' as a justifying force for state violence, and here, we can return to the fundamental relationship between war and police powers to extend lawfare into the realm of policing. Put simply, it can be suggested that police power – which is at once war power – may employ the languages and architectures of law (and its attendant languages and architectures of rights) to justify and increase police violence. The power of lawfare – which, perhaps more than anything, illustrates what Benjamin calls 'the rottenness of the law' – is not, then, limited to the military battlefield, but is instead exercised by police power in all of its forms and moments of spatial instantiation.

## Conclusion: police, rights and formlessness

Young (1999, p. 130) notes that while some in criminology assert that 'crime causes problems for society rather than society causes the problem of crime', such a belief reverses causality and fails to recognize the triviality of most crime. In a discussion of the intersection of human rights and police violence, then, we might tweak Young's observation: crime *control* causes problems for society (in the form of lived human rights violations) rather than society causing the problem of crime (and human rights infringements). Crime control (or, more simply, police) is, for Benjamin, a power that not only is beyond and above the power of law, but exists explicitly to extend the power of *state violence* beyond the power of law: police, in Benjamin's conceptualization, 'marks the point at which the state . . . can no longer guarantee through the legal system the empirical ends that it desires at any price to attain' (Benjamin 1986, p. 287). Police, then, is a power that takes up the violent purposes of law – the production of order and security – at the borders of law's efficacy, deploying the material violence of the state in ways that law cannot. This is significant in many ways, but perhaps most noteworthy is that we see that the law itself recognizes its limitations, and so gives way to the police power in order to continue apace with the production of ordered space and subjects. Here, Benjamin observes again both the 'formless' and 'spectral' nature of police (ibid., p. 287) – a point that suggests that perhaps police finds what is ultimately its perfect complement and counterpart in human rights, which is also more formless and spectral than material. This is the problematic dialectic of human rights that prevents it, as a legal construct, from providing meaningful protection from moments of police violence; human rights, for the subjects of police violence, exist only in law, not in everyday life.

Adding to the difficulty of making claims of human rights abuses by the police power, at least in the US, is what Taussig notes is the difficulty in even 'imagin[ing] human rights being raised' in the spatial-legal context of the US (Taussig 2010, p. 176). Human rights, then, has so little salience and meaning in the contexts of police violence and murder mentioned at the outset of this chapter that the suggestion that the application of the human rights legal doctrine as a means of achieving justice in – or, more importantly, preventing – cases of police violence and murder seems patently laughable. Even in moments of extreme police violence in the US that are able, through some mysterious social processes (usually, though, processes involving the capture and dissemination of recorded evidence of violence), to momentarily capture the public's attention, the sort of 'after the fact' justice of law and human rights fails to constrain the police power. Here, the notorious case of Rodney King, who was beaten viciously by Los Angeles Police Department officers in 1991 in an incident following a traffic stop that was caught by an amateur video camera enthusiast, serves as an illustration of the limits of law in constraining the violence of police: the four officers involved in the assault on King were acquitted, leading not only to the Los Angeles riots but also to the eventual second acquittal, on appeal, of two of the officers. Law and rights, then, can only be understood to consistently uphold the impunity of police violence, and only rarely – if ever – act as a reliable and meaningful constraint on police power or as a force interested in upholding the human rights of policed subjects.

## Notes

1 According to an article written by two staff members of the Urban Institute, a Washington, DC-based think tank that carries out economic and social policy research, Ferguson shifted from a predominantly white population (74 per cent) in 1990 to a predominantly black one (67 per cent) in 2010 (Gordon and Gault 2015).

2 In the US, police departments are not required to release data on how often their officers use force (Apuzzo and Cohen 2015, Schmidt and Apuzzo 2015). As such, there is no precise accounting of how many citizens are killed, much less their race or ethnicity or other important details (Apuzzo and Cohen 2015, Wines and Cohen 2015). For years, data from the Federal Bureau of Investigation on police homicides understated the problem; only recently have online databases compiled by volunteers begun to paint a more accurate picture (Wines and Cohen 2015).

3 While studies show that police encounters with persons who are mentally ill are more likely to involve police use of force than those interactions with individuals who are not similarly situated or impaired (Kappeler and Gaines 2015, citing Engel et al. 2000, Garner et al. 2002, Terrill and Mastrofski 2002), here, we are speaking primarily about violence against African-Americans. For a discussion of the multifarious ways in which encounters with criminal justice bodies, such as the police, may be experienced depending on biological features (such as skin tone) country of origin, ethnic group, language and religion, see Barrett et al. (2014, pp. 197, 210); cf. Skogan (2006, p. 101), who acknowledges the lack of research on the views of and interactions with police of racial minorities other than African-Americans, but who observes that, at least in some US metropolises, such experiences and perspectives more closely resemble those of African-Americans than Caucasians.

4 While the US's diffused, local policing model bears some similarity to those found in some European countries (for example, France, Italy) and differs from the national, centralized policing model of countries like Israel, where agencies often have significant internal security responsibilities, we acknowledge that some have questioned the very idea of a homogenous police culture (see, for example, Skogan (2006) and we accept that 'every national setting has unique components' (Jonathan-Zamir and Harpaz 2014, p. 474). Moreover, because of the US federal system of government and its legacy of slavery in the south, we recognize that the relationship of police violence and human rights may differ in and between the several states. While our focus is on a consideration of the operation of police power as a guarantor and violator of human rights, rather than a case study analysis of specific incidents or localities, we are mindful of the inherent limitations of attempting to generalize from specific policing contexts. Nevertheless, we would point out that even the police forces in the (presumably more progressive) major metropolitan areas in the northern US possess violent pasts (see, for example, Editorial 2015), giving us a degree of confidence in writing broadly about the relationship of human rights and police violence in the US. Finally, we would note that although we focus on police violence in the US, we do not wish to dismiss or ignore such dynamics or phenomena elsewhere. For a brief note about Mark Duggan, a black, 29-year-old Tottenham resident, who was shot and killed by police in Tottenham, North London, England, on 4 August 2011, and whose death was seen as the proximate cause of the 2011 England riots, see Barrett et al. (2014, citing Athwal 2011); and see Treadwell et al. (2013).

5 For some provocative suggestions for bringing about police reform, see Brooks (2014); see generally Gaines and Kappeler (2015) and Kappeler and Gaines (2015).

6 See generally Kappeler and Gaines (2015, pp. 508–9) for a discussion of the historical differences between UK and US policing with respect to use of force.

7 It bears mention that under US Supreme Court jurisprudence, *Castle Rock v Gonzalez*, 545 US 748 (2005), police do not have a constitutional duty to protect an individual from harm. See Greenhouse (2005) for a discussion.

8 For a discussion of *Tennessee v Garner*, 471 US 1 (1985), and *Graham v Connor*, 490 US 386 (1989), the US Supreme Court cases setting forth the legal standards in the US regarding police use of lethal force, see, for example, Engel and Smith (2009), Gaines and Kappeler (2015), Klinger and Brunson (2009), Lab et al. (2016), Novak (2009), Terrill (2009).

9 This subheading is a reformulation of Raymond Carver's 1981 short story collection (and story) *What we talk about when we talk about love.*

10 And we are not insensitive to the stress, anxiety and other negative emotional, physical and psychological experiences that individual officers may encounter or undergo in their day-to-day operations. For a discussion, see, for example, Alpert 2009, Engel and Smith 2009, Gaines and Kappeler 2015, Klinger 2004, and Klinger and Brunson 2009.

11 According to Gaines and Kappeler (2015, p. 314), '[m]any police officers use force or coercion on nearly a daily basis. It may range from a verbal command to the use of a weapon against a suspect. It is part of their job'. 'Less-than-lethal force', they explain, refers to 'any force other than the discharge of a firearm at a suspect . . .; however, it should be remembered that less-than-lethal force could cause grave bodily harm or death' (ibid., p. 324). As such, they contend that '[t]he phrase "less-than-lethal" is somewhat misleading because almost any use of force can result in fatal consequences. A better way of understanding the concept is to note that *less-than-lethal force* is any use of force that is not intended or likely to lead to death or serious physical injury. The most common less-than-lethal force weapons include the baton, pepper spray, and conducted energy devices' (2015, pp. 328–9).

12 'Rough ride' and 'nickel ride' are each colloquialisms for the police practice of shackling detained subjects in the rear of a police vehicle so as to remove the subject's ability to steady himself or herself, and then driving erratically in order to cause injury to the subject (Vibes 2015). The practice was widely cited as the determinant factor in Gray's death, and some reports indicate that the Baltimore Police Department, in particular, has a long history of using the 'nickel ride' as a way to injure detainees (Graham 2015).

## References


Alpert, G.P., 2009. Interpreting police use of force and the construction of reality. *Criminology and Public Policy*, 8(1), 111–15.

Apuzzo, M. and Cohen, S., 2015. Data on use of force by police across US may prove almost useless. *The New York Times*, 12 August, A9.

Athwal, H., 2011. *The spotlight is back on black deaths at the hands of the police*. Institute of Race Relations. 31 August. Retrieved on 24 July 2015 from: www.irr.org.uk/2011/august/ha000019.html.

Barrett, G.A., Fletcher, S.M.G. and Patel, T.G., 2014. Black minority communities and levels of satisfaction with policing: findings from a study in the north of England. *Criminology & Criminal Justice*, 14(2), 196–215.

Benjamin, W., 1986. Critique of violence. *In*: W. Benjamin, *Reflections*. New York: Schocken Books, 277–300.

Benton, T., 1993. *Natural relations: ecology, animal rights, and social justice*. London: Verso.

Blow, C.M., 2015. Police abuse is a form of terror. *The New York Times*. 12 August. Retrieved on 8 April 2016 from: www.nytimes.com/2015/08/13/opinion/police-abuse-is-a-form-of-terror.html?_r=0.

Brisman, A., 2014. Environmental and human rights. *In*: G. Bruinsma and D. Weisburd (eds), *Encyclopedia of criminology and criminal justice*, Vol. 3. New York, NY: Springer Verlag, 1344–5.

Brogden, M., 2009. Commentary: the piggy in the middle. *In*: A. Jefferson and S. Jensen (eds), *State violence and human rights*. London: Routledge, 175–184.

Brooks, D., 2014. The union future. *The New York Times*. December 19, A35.

Bucktin, C., 2014. *Ferguson Riots: mirror man told 'leave now or you're dead' as 150 shots fired during protests*. 25 November. Retrieved on 8 April 2016 from: www.mirror.co.uk/news/world-news/ferguson-riots-mirror-man-told-4690290.

Capps, K., 2015. Did the Louisville Police Union just threaten city residents? CityLab, 19 June. Retrieved on 8 April 2016 from: www.citylab.com/crime/2015/06/did-the-louisville-police-union-just-threaten-city-residents/396350/.

Crawshaw, R., Cullen, S. and Williamson, T., 2007. *Human rights and policing*. Leiden: Martinus Nijhoff.

Editorial, 2015. The violent legacy of Chicago's police. *The New York Times*, April 21, A22.

Engel, R.S. and Smith, M.R., 2009. Perceptual distortion and reasonableness during police shootings: law, legitimacy, and future research. *Criminology and Public Policy*, 8(1), 141–51.

Engel, R.S., Sobol, J.J. and Worden, R.E., 2000. Further exploration of the demeanor hypothesis: the interaction effects of suspects' characteristics and demeanor on police behavior. *Justice Quarterly*, 17, 235–58.

Gaines, L.K. and Kappeler, V.E., 2015. *Policing in America*, 8th edn. Waltham, MA: Anderson Publishing.

Garner, J.H., Maxwell, C. and Heraux, C., 2002. Characteristics associated with the prevalence and severity of force used by police. *Justice Quarterly*, 19, 705–46.

Gordon, T. and Gault, S., 2015. Ferguson city finances: not the new normal. Urban Institute. 8 April. Retrieved on 8 April from: www.urban.org/urban-wire/ferguson-city-finances-not-new-normal.

Graham, D.A., 2015. 'Rough rides' and the challenges of improving police culture. *The Atlantic*, 27 April. Retrieved on 8 April from: www.theatlantic.com/politics/archive/2015/04/the-rough-ride-and-police-culture/391538/.

Greenhouse, L., 2005. Justices rule police do not have a constitutional duty to protect someone. *The New York Times*, 28 June.

Howard, A. and Lang, C., 2014. The Ferguson uprising through a historical lens. From an interview conducted with The Real News Network, 3 October. Retrieved on 8 April 2016 from: http://therealnews.com/t2/index.php?option=com_content&task=view&id=31&Itemid=74&jumival=12321.

Jensen, S. and Jefferson, A., 2009. Repopulating state violence and human rights. *In*: A. Jefferson and S. Jensen (eds), *State violence and human rights*. London: Routledge, 1–22.

Jonathan-Zamir, T. and Harpaz, A., 2014. Police understanding of the foundations of their legitimacy in the eyes of the public. *British Journal of Criminology*, 54(3), 468–89.

Kappeler, V.E. and Gaines, L.K., 2015. *Community policing: a contemporary perspective*, 7th edn. New York and London: Routledge.

Kennedy, D., 2002. International human rights movement: part of the problem? *Harvard Human Rights Journal*, 15, 101.

Klinger, D., 2004. *Into the kill zone: a cop's eye view of deadly force*. San Francisco, CA: Wiley.

Klinger, D.A. and Brunson, R.K., 2009. Police officers' perceptual distortions during lethal force situations: informing the reasonableness standard. *Criminology and Public Policy*, 8(1), 117–39.

Lab, S.P., Williams, M.R., Holocomb, J.E., Burek, M.W., King, W.R. and Buerger, M.E., 2016. *Criminal Justice: The Essentials*, 7th edn. New York and Oxford: Oxford University Press.

Maiese, M., 2003. Human rights violations. *In*: Guy Burgess and Heidi Burgess (eds), *Beyond intractability*. Conflict Information Consortium, University of Colorado, Boulder. Retrieved on 8 April 2016 from: www.beyondintractability.org/essay/human-rights-violations.

Maupin, C., 2014. *The global context of the Ferguson uprising*. New Eastern Outlook, 6 December. Retrieved on 8 April 2016 from: http://journal-neo.org/2014/12/06/the-global-context-of-the-ferguson-uprising/.

Neocleous, M., 2013. Air power as police power. *Environment and Planning D: Society and Space*, 31(4), 578–93.

Neocleous, M., 2014. *War power, police power*. Edinburgh: Edinburgh University Press.

Novak, K.J., 2009. Reasonable officers, public perceptions, and policy challenges. *Criminology & Public Policy*, 8(1), 153–61.

Rajagopal, B., 2006. Counter-hegemonic international law: rethinking human rights and development as a Third World strategy. *Third World Quarterly*, 27(5), 767–83.

Robertson, C., 2015. A city where policing, discrimination and raising revenue went hand in hand. *The New York Times*, 5 March, A14.

Schmidt, M.S. and Apuzzo, M., 2015. Officer is charged with murder of a black man shot in the back. *The New York Times*, 8 April, A1.

Skogan, W.G., 2006. Asymmetry in the impact of encounters with police. *Policing & Society*, 16(2), 99–126.

Taussig, M., 2010. *Walter Benjamin's grave*. Chicago, IL: University of Chicago Press.

Terrill, W., 2009. The elusive nature of reasonableness. *Criminology & Public Policy*, 8(1), 163–72.

Terrill, W. and Mastrofski, S., 2002. Situational and officer-based determinants of police coercion. *Justice Quarterly*, 19(2), 215–48.

Thompson, J., 2014. *'No justice, no respect': why the Ferguson riots are justified* [online]. The Intercept, 1 December. Retrieved on 8 April 2016 from: https://firstlook.org/theintercept/2014/12/01/justice-respect-ferguson-riots-justified/.

Treadwell, J., Briggs, D., Winlow, S. and Hall, S., 2013. Shopocalypse now: consumer culture and the English riots of 2011. *British Journal of Criminology*, 53(1), 1–17.

United States Department of Justice, 2015. *Department of justice report regarding the criminal investigation into the shooting death of Michael Brown by Ferguson, Missouri police officer Darren Wilson*. Retrieved on 8 April 2016 from: www.justice.gov/sites/default/files/opa/press-releases/attachments/2015/03/04/doj_report_on_shooting_of_michael_brown_1.pdf.

Vibes, J., 2015. Freddie Gray's death reveals a dark history of 'nickel rides' and police van torture. *Free Thought Project*, 27 April. Retrieved on 8 April 2016 from: http://thefreethoughtproject.com/freddie-grays-death-reveals-dark-history-nickel-rides-police-van-torture.

Wall, T. and Linnemann, T., 2014. Staring down the state: police power, visual economies, and the 'war on cameras'. *Crime, Media, Culture*, 10(2), 133–49.

Weber, L., Fishwick, E. and Marmo, M., 2014. *Crime, justice and human rights*. Basingstoke: Palgrave Macmillan.

Weizman, E., 2009. *Lawfare in Gaza: legislative attack*. Open Security, OpenDemocracy.com, 1 March. Retrieved on 8 April 2016 from: https://www.opendemocracy.net/article/legislative-attack.

Weizman, E., 2010, Legislative attack. *Theory, Culture & Society*, 27(6), 11–32.

Wines, M. and Cohen, S., 2015. Police killings rising slightly, data suggests. *The New York Times*, 1 May, A1.

Young, J., 1999. *The exclusive society: social exclusion, crime and difference in late modernity*. London: Sage.

# 32

# Bent to good authorities?

## Human rights, authoritarian neoliberalism and consent policing

*Willem de Lint*

Across southern Europe, there is a growing legitimacy crisis as frustrations with austerity – in particular unemployment and curtailed public services – spill out into the street. In Madrid, Barcelona, and other cities, police have sought to protect state government buildings against street protests and riots. Ada Colau, who co-founded the anti-eviction group, Platform for People Affected by Mortgages, framed the connection between human rights and policing from the point of view both of an activist who was repeatedly arrested during protests and, as of May 2015, mayor-elect of Barcelona:

> when we have unjust laws, like the ones we have now in Spain, one has to massively disobey these unjust laws to protect human rights.... In order to defend rights and to win rights, many times it has been necessary to disobey unjust laws. Of course, now, as future mayor of Barcelona, I hope the police are going to be at the service of human rights, and not of the banks.
>
> *(Colau, Democracy Now 2015)*

As in Europe, in the United States (US) growing economic disparity, unemployment and a lack of access to social services is related at a minimum to conditions that produce crime and disorder (Hagan and Albonetti 1988). Instead of addressing underlying inequalities, which have worsened since 2008 (Saez 2014), governments have sought to contain social disorders with more aggressive social control instruments (Garland 2001), including welfare surveillance (Gilliom 2001, Wacquant 2009) and policing. Evidence of the scale of that aggression is represented by deaths caused by police and the soaring cost of police settlements.[1] Police shootings of underclass visible minorities in several municipalities have sparked violent urban unrest, and a legitimacy crisis directly concerns police.

At its 110th session, the United Nations Human Rights Committee (UNHRC) issued concluding recommendations on the US focusing its questions on what was being done:

> to address racial disparities in the U.S. criminal justice system . . . and to address cases of police brutality and excessive use of force, in particular against persons belonging to racial, ethnic or national minorities . . . and to hold responsible officers accountable for such abuses.
>
> *(UNHRC 2013, p. 3)*

It also asked the US to clarify whether a national human rights institution 'with a broad human rights mandate' will be established in the US. At a follow-up review of the matter at the UNHRC in May 2015, the criticism was more pointed, putting the US on the defensive. US Assistant Attorney-General James Cadogan told the committee that the Department of Justice, as well as striking a task force on policing, was pursuing or had pursued 20 investigations of various departments (Sheriff 2015). The *Task Force on 21st Century Policing* (2015, hereafter Task Force), set up to review policing against the principle of equality under the law, noted that confidence in the police 'has remained flat' among the general population, but has declined among those that have most police contact, who believe that police are not 'acting procedurally in just ways' (President's Task Force 2015, p. 7). Whilst the UNHRC suggested the creation of a new oversight body, the Task Force sought to reinvigorate many of the principles and practices of consent policing (defined below) through reference to civil rights.

This remedy to compel a more participatory, inclusionary or iterative expression of policing comes up against neoliberalism as a strong ideological force that *bends state authority away from policing by consent*. Which brings us to a longstanding problem in policing: how is police independence, not to mention the legitimacy of the state, to be maintained under conditions that implicitly or explicitly undermine the bases of social inclusion, participation and equality? How is this to be achieved where the disenfranchised are denied access to adequate platforms of social engagement and political expression (such as protest)? Where, at the same time, increasingly authoritarian neoliberal demands of austerity push them into untenable conditions? This suggest two schisms: on the one hand, there is a disconnect between the traditional controls of police through the oversight of the lower judiciary and public or community representations (consent policing); on the other hand, social control efforts to paper over the deepening disconnect between social and economic conditions (austerity) appear to be stretched to breaking. Perceiving this dynamic tension opens up police organizational and institutional behaviour to further understanding: police behaviour is conditioned both by authorities and by what might be called ideological filters. Whilst liberal consent policing creates a host of authorities that inform police behaviour, they are each more or less persuasive depending on the work of those ideological filters. Human rights is one such filter on action inviting powerful authorities, but recently authoritarian neoliberalism is another.

## Liberal consent policing

As the historian Charles Reith noted, Sir Robert Peel's great achievement was to establish in Great Britain a modern police whose mission it was to instill not an abject fear of state power and authority, but the upholding of the rule of law on the willing consent of the public. 'Policing by consent' was devised to place police in a *plurality between executive, judicial and community or local council accountabilities* (see Figure 32.1), thereby seeking to provide some insulation from but also a means of answerability to the public at large. It may and has been argued that this vision of policing has only ever been an incomplete ideal. As Reiner (2010, p. 7, emphasis added) puts it, 'police ideology has always rested upon the *myth* of a fundamental distinction between their model of community-based policing and an alien, "Continental", state-controlled system'. As Storch argued, Peel's 'bobbies' were a response to an increasingly insistent and non-deferential working class that needed to be disciplined and controlled (Storch and Engels 1975). Fraught and weak as it may have been, consent policing was nonetheless an alignment to a political vision and rationality (that was later to be found wanting by leaders in its very pluralities). In addition, even if never fully realized, those lines of accountability presented a means of correction, as intended by visionaries of modern police and liberal democracy alike.

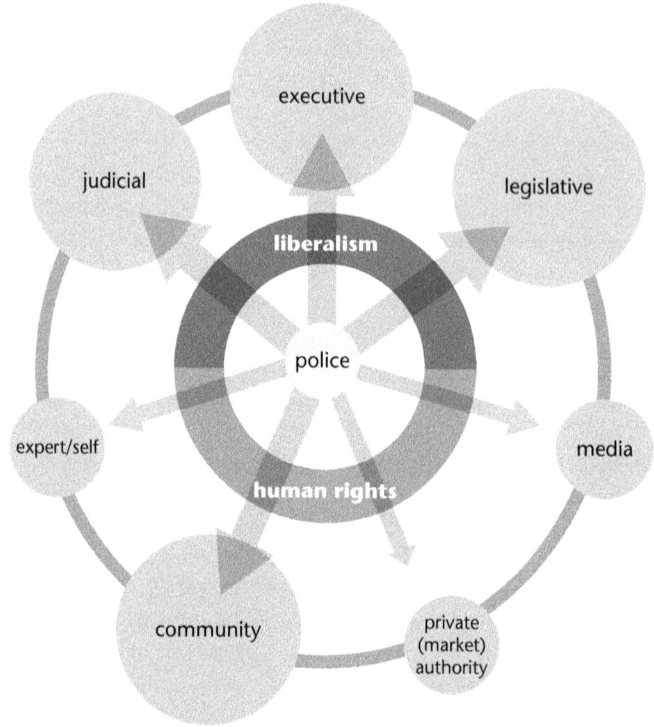


*Figure 32.1* Liberal consent pluralities

Documented in analyses by O'Malley and Palmer (1996) and Garland (2001), among many others, the dynamics and mechanics of criminal justice policy and administration in liberal democracies are adaptive and align to political rationalities or frames. Under the post-World War 2 welfare paradigm police bureaucracies, like the state itself, conceived of crime as a shared burden the mitigation of which required programmes, strategies and annual budget increases that were dedicated in some fashion to make good on the ideal of consent policing. Disenfranchised groups used the appeal to the universality of the human condition and often to human rights to claim political representation and to delegitimize police repression.

Under 'advanced' or neoliberal doctrine, the 'social' or welfare state began to be viewed, as per influential thinkers such as Friedrich Hayek, as damaging to economic growth because of its dependence on 'penal rates of taxation on private profit' that would eventually result in stagnation (Rose 1999, p. 153). As Donzelot (2008, p. 123) puts it, neoliberals sought to create a 'social reality to counter the effects of economic irrationality' and to 'nullify the social irrationality of capitalism with an economic rationality.' At bottom, the aim of this political rationality is to nurture and support not disadvantage but its opposite, the spirit of enterprise in the entrepreneur who may 'exploit his own human capital' (ibid., p. 124). The aim of social policy is not the reduction of inequalities but the maintenance of each individual within a competitive 'system of inequalities' (ibid., p. 124).

The welfare model had overstretched liberalism's true aim as a project of government minimalism; as is clear in numerous economic historical accounts (Hudson 2003) the tide had turned. The question of police institutionalization was reborn: noting the powerful influence of Hayek, analysts queried public policing as a relation between the limited capacity of government to govern, on the one hand, and the freedom of a self-supporting individual, on the other (Bayley and Shearing 2001, Johnston 1992, Loader and Walker 2001). Welfare liberalism, producing a social worker-officer hybrid, was reviewed as unjustifiable and duly trashed by neoconservatives, neoliberals and a large body of academic criminologists as an aberrant relic ripe for superseding by the emergent political rationality (cf. O'Malley and Palmer 1996).

Whilst this reading of events has been very persuasive it papers over persistent contradictions in political authority. According to Hannah Arendt, the gulf between the ideal of formal legal equality and the substantive conditions and manufacture of widening social inequalities under capitalism is a contradiction and defect in the political community of modern liberal representative democracies (Arendt 1973, p. 12). Consequently, liberalism will demonstrate a recidivist inability to resist totalitarianism (Arendt 1994, p. 282), in light of which there is hypocrisy as peace, freedom, justice (and human rights generally) are repeatedly brought to heel; the actuality of colonial expansion or development in the service of restless elites is served by extreme violence, war and impoverishment. She argues that liberalism fails to live up to its ideals and will be unable to resist totalitarianism, a failure 'that may already be counted among the historical facts of our century' (ibid., 1994, p. 282).

## Ideological filters

### *Human rights*

As an affordance to police practice, the discourse and implementation of human rights is too enormous to take on in its entirety here, nor is it necessary to rehearse all of its intersections on police conduct (see, for example, O'Rawe and Moore 1997). Suffice to say that in liberal democratic jurisdictions human rights codes are used to flag a required duty of service or care on the part of authorities that respects various individual freedoms (assembly, expression, religion, association) and legal rights (to life, security of the person [from search, seizure, detention, torture], right to counsel, silence, equal protection and non-discrimination). In the US experience, scholars speak of a period of reform in policing under the US Supreme Court Chief Justice Earl Warren.[2] As noted, for instance, by Manning (2010, p. 52) and Wilson (1978), in the post-World War 2 period and through the 1970s, American police became more engaged to exercise policing *through* a human rights filter and were understood to be generally more legalistic by, for instance, extending procedural guarantees or protections and reviewing their practices according to rule of law accountabilities.

In practice we know that police accountability to the rule of law is moderated by several other accountabilities. Legalistic policing has been frequently reviewed in policing literature, for instance, in work on discretion and due process, in international or peacekeeping police work and in community and intelligence policing, to name but a few. In this vein, it is useful to recall the revision of Packer's (1968) two metaphors as representing not only a police but also criminal justice conflict between the efficiency of crime control administration (get cases on and off the assembly line as quickly as possible) and due process (put things through an obstacle course to see which should really come out as worthy of the full process). McBarnet (1978) made the argument that due process is *for crime control*, because in looking at the daily behaviour of the lower judiciary it was clear to her that much was done in the granular decisions by magistrates to lubricate the system against or over the invocation of rights. It is also instructive that legalistic policing was criticized in the late 1960s by federal commissions (Kerner Commission 1968, US 1969, US 1970) that investigated serious public disorder. According to the National Advisory Committee on Civil Disorder (Kerner Commission 1968, p. 80), widespread American rioting in the mid-1960s was caused by reactive, mechanical policing that tended 'to aggravate the already volatile nature of the urban poor' (Platt et al. 1982, p. 128). In the United Kingdom, a similar finding was made about a decade later by Lord Scarman in his report on the Brixton 'police riots' (Scarman 1981).

In other words, public policy on policing discovered Arendt's paradox. More than 60 years after the UN Convention and long after her observations, scholars continue to query the human rights framework, particularly as it acts inconsistently to posit a rights-demanding *individual* where *social* structural conditions are known to produce systemic (counted and uncounted) violations (Brown 2004). Brown notes that in the context of liberalism's dominance of the social and political, 'rights sought by a politically defined group are conferred upon depoliticized individuals; at the moment a particular "we" succeeds in obtaining rights, it loses its "we-ness" and dissolves into individuals' (Brown 1995, p. 98). She refers to an irreconcilable conflict between:

> rights as boundary, and as access; rights as markers of power, and as masking lack; rights as claims, and as protection; rights as organization of social space, and as defense against incursion; rights as articulation, and as mystification; rights as disciplinary, and as antidisciplinary; rights as a mark of one's humanity, and as a reduction of one's humanity; rights as expression of desire, and as foreclosure of desire.
>
> *(Ibid., p. 97)*

For our purposes, it is convenient to see human rights as a relatively powerful filter, but one that is given direction and purpose and relative weight or standing in the context of state and capital interests.[3] Rights claims will be evaluated by state authorities as more or less supportive or disruptive of the purposes of the political rationality in the context of perceived economic and social imperatives. Under a strong welfare state, human rights may act powerfully to support claims by forgotten identities or groups, defend or expand social or common space and mark humanity firmly against incursions and indignities. But under authoritarian neoliberalism, human rights may be used (or suspended or ignored) to support an alternative government mission, one that advances entrepreneurial capacity and security, which is itself restricted in meaning. This is to reiterate the point made by numerous analysts – most dramatically following the R2P debates – that a human rights regime falls short as an emancipatory vehicle (Foucault 1972).

So what about the police? Whilst it may seem a revelation (as in the Task Force and by the UNHRC above), or newly discovered remedy to systemic problems, it is noteworthy that police in liberal democracies already view themselves and are widely perceived as amongst the staunchest defenders of human rights. If US police are seen by many as too unaccountable and or uncontrolled in their use of force, the cause is not so much the absence of legality. It is the interpretation of their mandate and practices in the context of a contradictory set of public and political beliefs and a variety of public bodies including courts under the US Constitution. If many European police are perceived as too quick to defend sites at which austerity encroachments against public space presents a battle line for activists, the cause is not a lack of police accountability to human rights, but rather the diminution of the play of the common 'we' of those rights under the strong and competing claim of authoritarian neoliberalism. And if authoritarian neoliberalism drives police organizational and institutional behaviour through the filter of *liberal freedom* toward outcomes that condition accountabilities, human rights is conditioned by organizational and institutional experience and behaviour to take meanings from multiple authorities and accountabilities.

## *Authoritarian neoliberalism*

As documented in Hudson (2003) neoliberalism's first 'dress rehearsal' was Chile, by which a Central Intelligence Agency-funded and University of Chicago-crafted monetarist economic blueprint provided the country's military and top business families with the incentive to lead an about-face from Allende's social democratic agenda. Accordingly, International Monetary Fund loans were approved dependent on how fully the 'shock treatment' of drastically reduced social spending, industry privatization and financial institutions' deregulation was followed (Hudson 2003). Connected to US-centred 'super imperialism', shock therapy was a disciplinary measure that was foisted on governments throughout Latin America (in the 1980s), Africa, parts of Asia, Eastern Europe (in the 1990s) and breakaway states of the former Soviet Union (Hudson 2003, Perkins 2004). As argued by Bruff (2014), not just neoliberalism but authoritarian neoliberalism emerged in an uneven, zigzagging process. As in so-called weak states, so in strong states leaders reconfigured the relations between the state and civil society to erode the legitimate means by which the pluralities of popular opinion could find expression and representation. The Chicago School, and prominently Milton Freidman, was also an inspiration on 'this side' of the imperial divide (Hudson 2003), providing ideological support to Thatcher and Reagan (both of whom 'cut their teeth' with successful attacks on organized labour) (Hall 1988).

Through monetary and fiscal policy, that is to say through spending levels, tax rates and a non-inflationary money supply, neoliberalism disciplines the state; it sets a 'deeper and longer-term recalibration of the kinds of activity that are feasible and appropriate for nonmarket institutions to engage in' (Bruff 2014, p. 116). A government of 'diminished expectations' (ibid., p. 116) turns away from class redistributions (and the Keynesian approach to growing out of debt) in favour of a lean, and now austere, approach to government. It demands the conversion of public entitlement schemes into privatized or semi-private programmes. This produces 'greater socioeconomic inequality and dislocation' (Bruff 2014, p. 115) and increasing unresponsiveness to democratic processes and opinion, subordinated only to 'constitutional and legal rules that are deemed necessary for prosperity to be achieved' (ibid., p. 116). Under neoliberalism, government agencies are disciplined to a political rationality that posits the (false) ideal that unencumbered markets are capable of sorting out almost everything regulatory.

There are variations in thinking on the uptake of authoritarianism as adjunct to neoliberalism that have been developed under various theoretical traditions, but we will have space for a synopsis of two recent treatments. As per Hall (1988) and Wacquant (2009), through coercive instruments (including public police and criminal law), authoritarian neoliberalism is a hardening of the state's response to non-traditional forums of political expression (Hall et al. 1978), in effect growing the penal arm of the state to stifle or criminalize dissent and opposition. Human 'waste' (Bauman 2013) is forcibly pushed into peripheral employment market or the 'reinforced mesh' of the penal net (Wacquant 2009, p. 14). Bruff (2014) cites forced austerity and marginalization in response to the GFC as an illustration of how authoritarian neoliberalism meets crises of delegitimation.

A similar description of the effect of authoritative neoliberalism, albeit from a different set of assumptions, comes from Dean (2002). Dean argues that as liberal governments adapt to the norms stipulating 'the substantive content of freedom' into enforcements 'by sovereign means' they may do so through dispensing with the so-called pluralist contest between political ideologies. The state enforces its provisions *through* 'governmentally contrived markets', as if the defence of freedom requires deploying the state to turn common or public domains into places of free exchange. Dean (2002, p. 47) argues that it may be 'a necessary feature of all liberalisms' that governs through freedom to 'use *authoritarian liberal rationales*' and methods, targeting coercion at those who are not deemed ready or capable of governing themselves in accordance with the content of those liberal norms (Dean 2002, pp. 45–7).

As per Hall (1988) and Bruff (2014, p. 115) authoritarianism is understood in the drive to configure power relations that *insulate government from a competition or plurality of values and interests*. This configuration includes rebuffing the instruments by which that plurality may seek to feed and inform government policy. There is repugnance for liberal democracy's separation of powers and redundant authorities, except where an idealized conception of the market is empowered to tame the state.[4] Liberal consent policing, where it still expresses itself, draws upon and implies a plurality of authorities under the rule of law, whereas police service under authoritarianism implies resort to a singular source of power.

*Authoritarian* neoliberalism now confronts policing. Authoritarianism pulls police at the level of individual-occupational behaviour, in occupation-institutional adaptations and in institutional-political rationality alignments. At the level of individual accommodation to occupational norms, it is well-understood that authoritarianism impacts against police recruits' training in ethics, as with the occupational norm that 'instructs' police not to presume to hold senior officers to account (see, for example, Wooden and Nixon 2014, Chan 1996). At the level of occupational-institutional adaptations, where disciplinary knowledge is formed, authoritarianism will push police expertise and craft knowledge against fluid and into more insular manifestations. Much of the disconnect between police use of force and community expectations in many US jurisdictions is attributable to the more defensive and insular conception of the police mission under an authoritarian pull that is supplanted by an occupational epistemic authority (that, for instance, makes 'officer safety' the prime directive).

Parenti (2000) uses the term authoritarian policing to denote the expanded 'reach and severity' of 'broken windows' style enforcements against black and working class youth. Exploitation of the tranche of available legislation on minor infringements provided tools of discretionary access to non-compliant (and superfluous) cohorts. Schneider and Amar (2003) offer an analysis of 'authoritarian security' that links 'regional tendencies in police brutality, militarization and impunity', 'border crossing policing' and the 'intensification of human rights abuses by law enforcement and security forces in the Americas'. They ask how authoritarian security has come to 'infus[e] public spheres and public spaces with violence and fear, foreclosing political options and modes of participation and undermining [those officials] who are supposed to control policing policy, monitor security practice, and provide legitimacy and stability to governance' (ibid., p. 13). Following the line offered by Bruff (2014) and Hall et al. (1978), they contend that police take their cue from crime panics that are stimulated by bipartisan 'tough on crime' electioneering. Then, through the authoritarian security practices that 'cut across democratic and authoritarian regimes' 'urban elites' try to 'manage the contradictions of [a] highly volatile neoliberal global order that constantly triggers crises, rendering elite legitimacy tenuous at best' (Schneider and Amar 2003, p. 14).

Following political practice, then, liberal policing is emerging in several domains of operations as increasingly authoritarian. Police will be deployed, as also Dean (2002), O'Malley and Palmer (1996) and Wacquant (2009) illustrate, to protect market conduits and discipline ideological outsiders. In various domains governments have developed mechanisms to cut out spaces for sovereign or exceptional practices, and in the US and other countries, national campaigns against drugs and now terrorism have provided the technical means to overcome barriers to militarization (see Figure 32.2).

## Bent consent: policing under neoliberal authorities

The relative proneness of police to authoritarian neoliberalism should be a matter of some interest. To what extent must police (I have been confining this discussion to publicly funded,

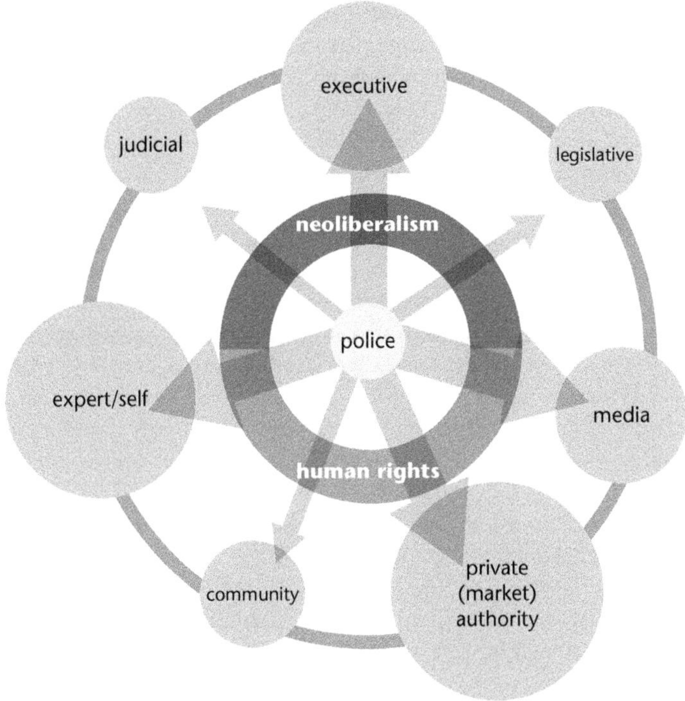


*Figure 32.2* Authoritarian neoliberal pluralities

local, state or federal police) answer to neoliberal authoritarianism? Or, in the positive, is consent policing, as a deliberately and somewhat ambiguous plurality of engagements with government and constituents, still viable where neoliberalism is the political rationality?

At various times over the past century, police reformers have attempted to go against the grain of popular and political majorities in carving out disciplinary and institutional space (Wilson 1953, Stenning 2011, Scarman 1981). They have often done so to assert against the totalitarian tendency that Arendt noted because not to do so has been rightly seen as anathema to that institutional independence and, as such, the necessary plurality of liberal authority in the proof of which police play a crucial role. Accordingly, public police have been defined against the branches of government in the terms of a dialogical relationship with the community they serve and to which they are accountable. Given that historical legacy, if there is now a large democratic deficit under authoritarian neoliberalism, police are in an unenviable position of becoming institutionally incoherent as they mind this gap.

## *Institutional incoherence?*

Let us have a look at this by way of anti-radicalization programmes, which have become a popular remedy to the risk of violent Muslim extremism. According to the first order discourse, the programmes seek to convert an intelligence problem (risk of terrorism) into the strengthening of community bonds (or 'resilience') by deploying classic community policing or consent practices (cf. Lyons 2002, Schneider and Chapman 2003, Pelfrey 2005; Greene 2011; Spalek 2010). In Britain, the application of community policing principles is advocated to 'bridge steep trade-offs between effective prevention and the social and political integration of Britain's Muslims' (Klausen 2009). In the meantime, laws against 'hate crime' and state campaigns in support of anti-radicalization are touted as appropriate measures or remedies to promote human rights. In western countries a large and apparently growing constituency (including many liberals) is defining itself in opposition to migrants and Muslims and does so claiming to *protect* the rule of law and the separation of church and state.

To turn this argument or follow the second order discourse, anti-radicalization is a moral panic (Hall et al. 1978) where state authorities are invited to assert the dominance of particular constituencies aligned to a strong ideology and politics. It attracts human rights protagonists by suggesting authoritarian state remedies are needed to protect liberal democracy. But the use of public monies to build resilience through state-funded agencies is anathema to the neoliberal view that government should not set itself the task of rehabilitating people and the police should not do social work. The vice president of the Association of Chief Police Officers, Sir Peter Fahy, said that responsibility *lay with parents* for stopping young people travelling to join extremist groups abroad:

> If there is one thing possibly we have made a mistake in Prevent,[5] it is we have created the impression that somehow that is the job of the police.

The tension between consent policing and neoliberal authoritarian policing is evident; Sir Peter appears to seek a more straightforward alignment of police with neoliberal responsibilization. However, the error in his statement is that he implies that police have a singular task. Much as we may be tempted to do so, we oversimplify the complex mandates of current public police organizations where we see them only in terms of their statutory mandates and reporting requirements. Police agencies are responsive and adaptive actor-networks that continuously branch out and blend into a *changing configuration of authorities*. Yes, they do provide protective services in risk mitigation through law enforcement and order maintenance somewhat consistent with a simplification of authoritarian neoliberalism. But they will continue to resist this restricted mandate for two reasons. As Peel rightly saw, the public requires a more comprehensive police service if it is to maintain approval, particularly among the most disenfranchised. And police persist as the primary means by which to bridge the gap between the ruthless necessities of capitalism and the ideal of social democracy. The extent to which police subtract from the republican plurality of their representation is the extent to which the political community and then also whole societies depart from the political tactics of liberal democracy (de Lint 2014). In this regard, it is not incoherence that is the worst enemy of police; it is the profound institutional self-destruction that awaits their abandonment to authoritarian neoliberalism. If police are not among the first to know this, they cannot afford to be among the last.

In the above discussion we have presented the argument that police that are aligned to neoliberalism is part and parcel of authoritarian neoliberalism. The latter is presented as a correction to how resources and services are distributed and evaluated so that the vitality of the economy and of the entrepreneurial spirit is not stultified by the state. To return to our question at the end of section one, which saw the Task Force calling for a human rights corrective, it has been contended that such a corrective cannot overcome the democracy gap. Instead, it is observed that police will and should continue to overcome the gap by continuing to respond to social and public need. As stated by Portillo (2015):

> As we consider police reform, we should not focus exclusively on police accountability, but also look broadly at how local governments oversee police and promote community

initiatives for health, poverty reduction, education and safety. . . . Police should not see their central focus as punitive, but rather as promoting public safety and the public good. They should be part of local government efforts to improve communities.

## Conclusion

In a response that has been indicative of police alignment in what is described above as 'authoritarian neoliberalism' police are compelled to enforce the law and to seek efficient methods as they carry out unpopular policies that are particularly unfriendly to disempowered youth, minorities, and those suffering from economic hardship and social and political disenfranchisement. As they do so they are caught between the aims of a democratizing movement from below and increasingly authoritarian regimes demanding compliance to the new order from above. The burden on human rights increases, but the standard of guilty conduct, by individual or group, is not absolute; it is adjudicated according to fluid cultural, social and political sensibilities. In reviewing the transition between liberal consent and authoritarian neoliberal policing configurations, we may observe a somewhat diminished role of human rights, but given the observations of Arendt and Brown among others, it would be unreasonable to expect protections on the individual to make up for the structural inequalities that unfolding capital relations produce by design.

Police play accountability to a medley of authorities and this configuration changes with adaptation to political rationalities. This is not saying anything new. What is freshly observable when we unpack these police-authority alignments (and we had space to unpack only a couple here) is that human rights is not an inalienable authority, but operates more or less robustly as a filter in modulating the character of those other authorities.

## Notes

1 See https://www.facebook.com/KilledByPolice; http://www.theguardian.com/us-news/ng-interactive/2015/jun/01/the-counted-police-killings-us-database; *New York Times*, 7 December 2014; Elinson and Frosch 2015.
2 In several landmark cases, the Warren Court exercised its claim on police oversight by curbing the police power to search (see, for example, *Mapp v Ohio*, 367 U.S. 643 [1961]), obtain confessions (see, for example, *Miranda v Arizona*, 348 U.S. 436 [1966]) and limit the right of representation through an attorney (see, for example, *Escobedo v Illinois*, 378 U.S. 478 [1964]).
3 There are a variety of forces in addition to government interests driving the character of a human rights regime, but I am focusing here only on the tension between the state and market as expressed in the political rationality (as per the above discussion).
4 Here, we need to be cognizant that in the somewhat ambiguous context in which classic liberal values compete with authoritarian neoliberalism for expression in our institutions; police authority cannot simply be equated with the latter.
5 Prevent is a £40 million anti-radicalisation strategy. Please see https://www.gov.uk/government/uploads/. . ./prevent-strategy-review.pdf

## References

Arendt, H., 1973. *The origins of totalitarianism*. Boston, MA: Houghton Mifflin Harcourt.
Arendt, H., 1994. *Essays in understanding, 1930–1954: formation, exile, and totalitarianism*. New York, NY: Schocken Books.
Bauman, Z., 2013. *Wasted lives: modernity and its outcasts*. New York, NY: John Wiley & Sons.
Bayley, D. and Shearing, C., 2001. *The new structure of policing: description, conceptualization, and research agenda*. NCJ 187083.

Brown, W., 1995. *States of injury: power and freedom in late modernity*. Princeton, NJ: Princeton University Press.
Brown, W., 2004. 'The most we can hope for . . .': human rights and the politics of fatalism. *The South Atlantic Quarterly*, 103(2), 451–63.
Bruff, I., 2014. The rise of authoritarian neoliberalism. *Rethinking Marxism: A Journal of Economics, Culture and Society*, 26(1), 113–29.
Chan, J., 1996. Changing police culture. *The British Journal of Criminology*, 109–34.
Colau, A., 2015. From occupying banks to City Hall: meet Barcelona's new mayor Ada Colau. *Democracy Now*, 5 June.
de Lint, W., 2014. Police authority in liberal consent democracies: a case for anti-authoritarian policing. *In*: M.D. Reisig and R.J. Kane (eds), *The Oxford handbook of police and policing*. New York, NY: Oxford University Press, 219–37.
Dean, M., 2002. Liberal government and authoritarianism. *Economy and Society*, 31(1), 37–61.
Donzelot, J., 2008. Michel Foucault and liberal intelligence. *Economy and Society*, 37(1), 115–34.
Elinson, Z. and Frosch, D., 2015. Cost of police-misconduct cases soars in big U.S. cities. *The Wall Street Journal*. 15 July. Retrieved on 8 April 2016 from: www.wsj.com/articles/cost-of-police-misconduct-cases-soars-in-big-u-s-cities-1437013834.
Foucault, M., 1972. On popular justice: a discussion with Maoists. *Power/knowledge: Selected interviews and other writings*, 1977, 1–36.
Garland, D., 2001. *The culture of crime control*. Chicago, IL: University of Chicago Press.
Gilliom, J., 2001. *Overseers of the poor: surveillance, resistance, and the limits of privacy*. Chicago, IL: University of Chicago Press.
Greene, J.R., 2011. Community policing and terrorism: problems and prospects for local community security. *Criminologists on terrorism and homeland security*, 208–44.
Hagan, J. and Albonetti, C., 1988. *Structural criminology*. Cambridge: Polity Press.
Hall, S., 1988. *The hard road to renewal. Thatcherism and the crisis of the left*. London: Verso.
Hall, S., Clarke, J., Critcher, C., Jefferson, T. and Roberts, B., 1978. *Policing the crisis: mugging, law and order and the state*. London: Palgrave Macmillan.
Hudson, M., 2003. *Super imperialism: the origin and fundamentals of world domination*. London: Pluto Press.
Johnston, L., 1992. *The rebirth of private policing*. London: Routledge.
Kerner Commission, 1968. National advisory commission on civil disorder. Washington, DC: US Government Printing Office.
Klausen, J., 2009. British counter-terrorism after 7/7: adapting community policing to the fight against domestic terrorism. *Journal of Ethnic and Migration Studies*, 35(3), 403–20.
Loader, I. and Walker, N., 2001. Policing as a public good: reconstituting the connections between policing and the state. *Theoretical Criminology*, 5(1), 9–35.
Lyons, W., 2002. Partnerships, information and public safety: community policing in a time of terror. *Policing: An International Journal of Police Strategies & Management*, 25(3), 530–42.
Manning, P.K., 2010. *Policing contingencies*. Chicago, IL: University of Chicago Press.
McBarnet, D.J., 1978. *The police and the state: arrest, legality and the law*. London: Croom Helm.
O'Malley, P. and Palmer, D., 1996. Post-Keynesian policing. *Economy and Society*, 25, 137–55.
O'Rawe, M. and Moore, L., 1997. *Human rights on duty: principles for better policing, international lessons for Northern Ireland*. Committee on the Administration of Justice Belfast.
Packer, H., 1968. *The limits of the criminal sanction*. Stanford, CA: Stanford University Press.
Parenti, C., 2000. *Lockdown America: police and prisons in the age of crisis*. London: Verso.
Pelfrey Jr, W.V., 2005. Parallels between community oriented policing and the war on terrorism: lessons learned. *Criminal Justice Studies*, 18(4), 335–46.
Perkins, J., 2004. *Confessions of an economic hit man*. San Francisco, CA: Berrett-Koehler Publishers.
Platt, T., Frappier, J., Gerda, R., Schauffler, R., Trujillo, L., Cooper, L., Currie, E. and Harring, S., 1982. *The iron fist and the velvet glove: an analysis of the US police*, 3rd edn. San Francisco, CA: Synthesis Publications.
Portillo, S., 2015. Stop-and-frisk policies can cause police to lose legitimacy, study finds. School of Public Affairs and Administration, University of Kansas. 3 June. Retrieved on 8 April 2016 from: http://news.ku.edu/2015/05/22/stop-and-frisk-policies-can-cause-police-lose-legitimacy-study-finds#sthash.DkEW66G7.dpuf.
President's Task Force on 21st Century Policing (Task Force), 2015. *Interim Report of the President's Task Force on 21st Century Policing*. Washington, DC: Office of Community Oriented Policing Services.

Reiner, R., 2010. *The politics of the police*. Oxford: Oxford University Press.

Rose, N., 1999. *Powers of freedom: reframing political thought*. Cambridge: Cambridge University Press.

Saez, E., 2014. *Striking it richer: the evolution of top incomes in the United States* (updated with 2014 preliminary estimates). Retrieved on 8 April 2016 from: http://eml.berkeley.edu/%7Esaez/saez-UStopincomes-2014.pdf.

Scarman, L., 1981. *The Scarman report: the Brixton disorders*. London: HM Stationery Office.

Schneider, C. and Amar, P., 2003. The rise of crime, disorder and authoritarian policing: an introductory essay. *NACLA Report on the Americas*, 38(2), 12–16.

Schneider, M.C. and Chapman, R., 2003. Community policing and terrorism. *Journal of Homeland Security*, 4–8.

Sheriff, N., 2015. US cited for police violence, racism in scathing UN review on human rights. *Al Jazeera*. 11 May. Retrieved on 8 April 2016 from: www.google.com.au/url?sa=t&rct=j&q=&esrc=s&source=web&cd=2&cad=rja&uact=8&ved=0CCMQFjABahUKEwjy9r3IuebIAhVO1WM-KHeLVCSk&url=http%3A%2F%2Famerica.aljazeera.com%2Farticles%2F2015%2F5%2F11%2Fus-faces-scathing-un-review-on-human-rights-record.html&usg=AFQjCNE-4oW3F0ITwqgWdNC9RlOMjrnqzg.

Spalek, B., 2010. Community policing, trust, and Muslim communities in relation to 'new terrorism'. *Politics & Policy*, 38(4), 789–815.

Stenning, P.C., 2011. Governance of the police: independence, accountability and interference. *Flinders Law Journal*, 13, 241.

Storch, R.D. and Engels, F., 1975. The plague of the blue locusts. *International Review of Social History*, 20(1), 61–90.

United Nations Human Rights Committee [UNHRC], 2013. List of issues to be taken up in connection with the consideration of the fourth periodic report of the United States of America (CCPR/C/USA/4), adopted by the committee at its 107th session, 11–28 March 2013. Retrieved on 8 April 2016 from: http://s3.documentcloud.org/documents/1097784/un-human-rights-final.pdf.

United States, 1969. National Commission on the Causes and Prevention of Violence. 1969. *To Establish Justice, to Insure Domestic Tranquility: Final Report of the National Commission on the Causes and Prevention of Violence*. US Government Printing Office.

United States, 1970. The President's Commission on Campus Unrest, & Scranton, W.W. *The report of the president's commission on campus unrest*. US Government Printing Office.

Wacquant, L., 2009. *Punishing the poor: the neoliberal government of social insecurity*. Durham, NC: Duke University Press.

Wilson, J.Q., 1978. *Varieties of police behavior*. Vol. 156. Cambridge, MA: Harvard University Press.

Wilson, O.W., 1953. A. Vollmer. *The Journal of Criminal Law, Criminology, and Police Science*, 91–103.

Wooden, K. and Nixon, J., 2014. The incorporation of obedience to authority into New South Wales police force recruit training. *Salus Journal*, 2(1), 43–62. Retrieved on 10 May 2015 from: http://search.informit.com.au.ezproxy.flinders.edu.au/documentSummary;dn=748235409984483;res=IELHSS> ISSN: 2202-5677.

# 33

# Human rights and police training

## Democratizing policing systems

*Alan Beckley*

### Introduction

Public police organizations are uncomfortable with discussion around human rights, mainly because they are frequently criticized in the media for lapses and errors in safeguarding the civil liberties of their citizens. This should not be the case as human rights are intrinsically incorporated in the tenets of democratic policing models which half the world purports to embrace. It has been identified that there are numerous models of policing (Emsley 2012) ranging from totalitarian to democratic policing, but many of the formats contain the ingredients of the democratic style, which according to Bayley (2006, p. 19) consists of police who: are accountable to law, protect human rights, are accountable to the public (independent oversight of police), and respond to the needs of individual citizens. This chapter will discuss the optimum methods of teaching and learning about human rights within the policing organization and also describe some case studies involving countries that have altered the style of their policing to encompass the democratic model. A simplistic description of the extremes of policing styles is that the key objective of totalitarian styles of policing is to protect the *state* from liberation of the citizens or external influences; whereas the key objective of democratic policing systems is to protect the security and freedom of all the *citizens* (Beckley 2014b). The problem, when amending a policing style from one extreme to another, is that it is necessary to change police officers' hearts, minds and attitudes in a 180-degree direction towards a new paradigm of operational policing; the international case studies will illustrate this point later in the chapter. Training is one of the means to change attitudes but this is a difficult task, especially with experienced personnel and an ingrained culture, therefore the method of training is important along with sensitivity around loyalty to pre-existing regimes and accepted practices. There is not space to debate the issues around the advantages and disadvantages of specific policing styles or models, therefore the discussion will be limited to the principles of democratic policing only.

### Importance of human rights in policing

All democratic countries respect the 'rule of law' which in essence means that no individual persons are above the law, indeed: 'All authority is subject to and constrained by law'

(Williams and Hume 2013, p. 131). Furthermore, a well-known police training manual links two major principles together: 'Democracy is linked with two ideals: rule of law; the promotion and protection of human rights' (Kalajdziev 2002, p. 9). The concept of rule of law is traceable back 800 years to Magna Carta, signed by King John of England in the year 1215 (Beckley 1997). Researchers have linked the rule of law, human rights and democratic policing to the theories of procedural justice and organizational justice which relate directly to internal and external operations in police organizations. Procedural justice in this context is the way that police officers interpret and execute criminal law powers through the use of discretion, or they decide not to use their powers; all of which have a direct impact on their day-to-day encounters with citizens external to the police organization. In addition, organizational justice, which is the way that police agencies internally treat their staff, has a direct bearing on police culture, integrity, fairness and staff morale that again might have an effect on the way that police officers treat citizens in their everyday encounters (Beckley 2014a). Of more immediate importance to the understanding of operational police officers, human rights are integral to most, if not all, policing activities as they relate directly to respecting citizens' rights and fundamental freedoms; this point is of essential significance and is crucial to emphasize in police training. The foundation of all types of police training is mainly statute law and most police powers are specified in some detail in Acts of Parliament such as the *Police and Criminal Evidence Act* in the UK or the *Law Enforcement (Powers and Responsibilities) Act 2002* in New South Wales, Australia, although some police powers remain in the common law clouded in antiquity dating from the fourteenth century. However, all police powers are cloaked in discretion and it is in this area that reference to human rights provides an ethos and guidance on how to operate coercive police powers humanely in practice. A useful example of this is the thoughtful and innovative Code of Police Ethics provided to the Police Service of Northern Ireland, the principles of which are covered by a Golden Rule: 'Police Officers to treat the public in the way they would wish an officer to treat them or their family' (NIPB 2008). Under the *Police (NI) Act 2000* (s. 32), police have the usual duties of protecting life and property, preserving order, preventing the commission of offences, bringing offenders to justice, and, in addition: *to protect human dignity and uphold human rights.*

## *Links of human rights to police statutory powers*

Upon consideration of the robust coercive powers that are given to police, in addition to the powers of other citizens to *keep the peace*, it is clear there is a need for accountability. To illustrate this one should realize the whole range of police powers that restrict fundamental rights and freedoms of citizens which include: 'move on' powers; stop; search; arrest, seizure, covert surveillance and interception of communications. These are provided in overview by legislation, regulation and codes of practice and are contained in more detail in police policies, practices and procedures. Also to consider, is the use of coercive force to execute these powers and the discretion in how, when and with what force to use the powers. These are decisions *directly* affecting the lives of citizens but there may be others of an indirect nature, such as the granting or refusal to grant licences by police organizations (such as granting/refusing firearms licences, gaming, lottery and betting licences) which affect fundamental rights and freedoms.

To provide a sound basis for interpretation of rights-based law, the *European Convention on Human Rights* (ECHR) provides some tests of compatibility for operating the law:

- Legality – Is there a statute or written law that is available to the public?
- Proportionality – Is the relationship between the aim of the action and the means used reasonable?

- Relevance/necessity – Is use of the power strictly relevant and least intrusive to the threat/problem?
- Equality of arms – Do all parties to the action have the same access to information and evidence?
- Remedy – Is there an independent public remedy or means to appeal? (Beckley 2000, p. 18).

As a paragon of good practice police powers should only be executed after applying these legal rules. A simple, practical guide follows that was used for police training in the UK after the introduction of the *Human Rights Act 1998* (HRA):

- Do I have a lawful power? – Every action must have a legal basis.
- Is what I am doing proportionate? – Is there a reasonable relationship between the aim to be achieved and the means used?
- What is my objective? – What is the proposed action intended to achieve? Is it relevant and is it necessary?
- Is there a less intrusive alternative? Consider whether the objective can be achieved with less impact on the rights of the subject and any other person likely to be affected.
- Do I need to act now? – Is the proposed action urgent or could it wait?
- Is there a record of my reasoning? – Keep a record of the basis of your decisions whenever they affect someone's rights.

Moving from consideration of local or regional rights-based law systems, it is important to transpose the discussion into human rights instruments that purport to apply globally, and certainly in democratic countries. The definitive relevant document is the United Nations (UN) *Universal Declaration of Human Rights* (UDHR), which was formulated following the peace agreements after World War 2 in 1948 (UN 1948). Many of the 30 Articles contained in this instrument are directly relevant to operational policing (Goodman-Delahunty et al. 2014, pp. 94–6).

The problem in relation to police training is that international treaties such as UDHR and other more specific guidelines such as the *Code of Conduct for Law Enforcement Officials* (UN 1979) and *Basic Principles on the Use of Force and Firearms by Law Enforcement Officials* (UN 1990), have no basis in law in most countries; therefore if an individual's rights are infringed there is no legal right of remedy against an individual or corporate public or private sector transgressor. Many national criminal justice systems, such as that in Australia, purport to reflect the principles of human rights in their legal decisions, but the only remedy for excessive use of police powers or use of force is to make a complaint against police or take a civil law action. Police officers should be aware of their responsibility and 'duty of care' for the citizens in their community and the human rights of individuals balanced against those of society as a whole (Bartkowiak-Theron and Asquith 2012, p. 14). The UN training manual for police officers states: 'Law enforcement officials are obliged to know, and to apply, international standards for human rights' (UNOHCHR 2004, p. 1).

## *Misuse of police powers and police misconduct*

The vagaries and pitfalls of accessing the police complaints system are well documented (Goodman-Delahunty et al. 2014), along with the necessity of independent oversight of police to achieve effective accountability of public police organizations (den Heyer and Beckley 2013). In Australia police corruption has been investigated by a long series of Royal Commissions (Beckley 2013) which, among many other things, has highlighted the need to inculcate police officers with a culture to respect the rights of citizens and operate to high ethical standards of behaviour. Many of the commissions concluded that the only way to introduce change to eradicate corruption and engender ethical behaviour was through effective police training; changing minds, attitudes and behaviour. Experience has identified that this objective is difficult, but not impossible, to achieve (Beckley 2012, Das and Verma 2002).

## Methods of police training in human rights

To the author's knowledge there has been intense discussion for the last forty years around the most effective teaching and learning methods to achieve optimum learning outcomes for police training (Norris 1992, Police Training Council 1985). Additionally, in recent decades, many public inquiries into police misconduct throughout the western world have identified a need to change the culture in the police organization which has been described in a negative light in many studies (Macvean and Cox 2012). Part of the problem in identifying the most appropriate form of training is the nature of policing: is it a craft? is it a profession? Although police academics and executive police officers would aspire towards a profession, therefore indicating an academic training regime and a *body of knowledge*; it appears most operational police officers would prefer a more vocational education style of training (Lauritz et al. 2012, Oliva and Compton 2010). Professionalization of the police service is attempting to address this issue by introducing mandatory continuous professional development (Neyroud 2011) for all police practitioners in England, Wales and Northern Ireland.

### *Optimum methods of teaching human rights*

It is important to establish the objective of the training and then identify the optimum method of teaching and learning to achieve that objective. What is required is that police officers should recognize and respect the human rights of citizens; they should make good decisions on the use of their powers; and they should reflect and evaluate the outcomes of their actions so that they learn from mistakes. This has been called a *culture of human rights* within the organization (O'Rawe 2005). The theories, methods and pedagogies employed in police training have been discussed in many publications and space does not permit a review here, therefore the optimum method for human rights training will be described (Beckley 1998, Elliott 1991, Norris 1992, O'Rawe 2005, Paterson 2011, Pollock and Williams 2015, Schon 1991). From many years of practical experience of delivering training to police officers at all levels of the organization the author recommends training in human rights with the use of real life case studies and/or problem-based learning (Vander Kooi and Palmer 2014, Werth 2009), then facilitation of a discussion of the issues revealed. This method allows optimum opportunities to link theory with realistic practice and the prospect of engaging practitioners in frank discussion with their peers using personal experiences to illustrate best practice operational policing that encourages reflection on observing human rights actions. In this way a positive human rights culture can be nurtured, leading to the desired ethos in the police organization, although the police organization does not exist in isolation and will reflect the climate of integrity within the wider public sector (Beckley 2012). To summarize this very simply, 'the ideal ethical police service' could be characterized as an organization with:

1 no corruption;
2 honesty;
3 restraint in the use of force;

4 no incompetence;
5 no acceptance of gratuities;
6 compliance with human rights (Neyroud and Beckley 2001, p. 194).

This was the objective in the case studies that follow in which the author was engaged by several organizations to disseminate the message of good practice in policing.

## Case studies of policing and human rights

### *Policing and human rights in England, Wales and Northern Ireland*

The *European Convention on Human Rights and Fundamental Freedoms* was adopted into law in England, Wales and Northern Ireland by the HRA. In response to suggestions that the Act would fundamentally change policing operations and activities, the Association of Chief Police Officers of England, Wales and Northern Ireland set up a working party of which the author was a member. The working party initiated research into the implications of this legislation and concluded that all laws relating to police operations and related policies, practices and procedures would have to be amended to ensure compliance with the principles of rights-based law (Beckley 2000). The working party proposed and devised new methods of police training using case studies to ensure the provisions of the Act were adopted in police practice; also an audit tool was devised so that police policies could be assessed for their compliance with human rights principles (Neyroud and Beckley 2001, pp. 205–14). At that time, the working party found that high-risk areas of policing that should be audited by all police forces were:

- child protection
- complaints and discipline
- covert policing
- custody
- domestic violence
- firearms
- hate and race crime
- major crime
- mental health
- personnel management
- personnel grievance procedure
- public order.

Advice about decision-making in day-to-day policing situations was to follow a decision-making process:

1 Is there existing policy? If so follow
2 Research facts, consult team
3 Review options
4 Is it: ethical; reasonable; proportionate; logical?
5 Record reasons for deciding on favoured option and reasons for rejecting others
6 Decide and implement (Beckley 1999, p. 13).

Subsequent studies in the UK on the effectiveness and outcomes of the training for police on human rights have reported different results. Bullock and Johnson (2012) found that, although

## Case study example 1: England and Wales

### *Human rights in-force audit course: police personnel procedures*

### Problem 1: The 'dishonest' Chief Constable

A Chief Officer of police was suspended from duty after being arrested and charged with an offence relating to dishonesty. The officer was subsequently acquitted of all criminal charges. Meanwhile the Police Authority held a meeting when the officer was not present and unanimously decided to dismiss the Chief Officer. The Chairman of the Police Authority told the Chief Constable he was dismissed with immediate effect.

*What issues were revealed in relation to disciplinary proceedings and the rules of natural justice? For the purposes of this question assume that Chief Officers are subject to the same misconduct proceedings as the Federated ranks.*

### Problem 2: The 'moonlighting' Special Constable

A Special Constable in Blankshire Constabulary was suspected of doing private security type work (which Special Constables are not allowed to do). The Assistant Chief Constable (Support) arranged for the SPC to be served with a letter of dismissal which did not contain any explanation for his dismissal, nor did the ACC speak directly to the SPC.

*What issues are revealed relating to employment law? What rights does the SPC have? Are there legal or ethical principles breached? What action would you advise the Chief Constable of Blankshire to take?*

the 20 interviews they carried out with police officers revealed the police officers perceived that the HRA had 'a very significant impact' (Bullock and Johnson 2012, p. 631), the researchers also reported that it had 'bureaucratized aspects of decision making' (ibid., p. 647). The study concluded that 'the institutionalization of the HRA by the police service cannot be seen to have succeeded' (ibid., p. 647). However, Barton and Tait (2008, p. 3) reported 'the biggest impact in the United Kingdom [UK] has been on policy development and implementation, which in general terms has led to better outcomes for the United Kingdom's increasingly diverse population' (UKDCA 2006). The author was subsequently asked to deliver human rights training to police organizations in Northern Ireland and the Republic of Ireland.

### *International work on behalf of the Council of Europe*

Between the years of 1999 and 2008, the author was privileged to work on behalf of the Council of Europe with the police services of the following countries: Armenia, Azerbaijan, Czech Republic, Republic of Georgia, Hungary, Kosovo, Macedonia, Montenegro, Poland, and Serbia. There were three drivers that combined to require that human rights should be incorporated into the operational policing of those countries:

1 Ex-Warsaw pact countries which announced independence and separation from the Soviet Union which was experiencing disintegration.

2 Countries that had formed the Former Republic of Yugoslavia (FRY) which had disintegrated through civil war and warring cultural and religious factions.
3 Newly independent countries that applied for accession to the European Union, which required, among other things, a demonstration of faith that the applicant country would introduce a democratic policing system.

The *missions* (as they were called) of the Council of Europe consisted of a head of mission from the Council and several 'expert' advisers from 'old' European countries in which democratic policing systems were installed. The countries involved were Armenia, Azerbaijan, Czech Republic, Georgia, Hungary, Kosovo, Macedonia, Montenegro, Poland and Serbia. The missions linked to the Department of the Interior or relevant Ministries in the accession countries which had policing in their portfolio. The Ministry provided contact with executive and senior police officers with whom to discuss human rights and police ethics issues. This section of the chapter will discuss as many case studies of work with countries as space allows.

### *Armenia*

The first time the author visited Armenia, there was considerable resistance to messages about improving policing operations in the country; indeed, during the first presentation on human rights and police ethics, the mission was greeted by senior police officers deliberately showing their contempt by openly reading their newspapers during the proceedings. Younger and more enlightened senior police officers apologized for this behaviour which belonged to the 'old guard' from a totalitarian policing system whose objective was protection of the state at all costs. Subsequent visits to Armenia were more productive and produced a real desire for change, although, as in many of the countries in the above list; the profession of policing was so poorly paid that low-level corruption was almost impossible to eliminate. Through the Declaration of Independence in 1991, Armenia split from the former Soviet Republic and subsequently joined the Council of Europe in 2001 thereby adopting the ECHR (Ivkovic and Haberfeld 2015). A thorough research project was completed in 2013 with a sample of 969 police officers relating to integrity which found that most police officers recognized scenarios correctly as misconduct although they assumed a 'relaxed disciplinary environment' (Ivkovic and Haberfeld 2015, p. 37). Further work was completed by Ivkovic and Khechumyan (2014) when it was discerned that 'despite identical official rules, we found consistent and large differences in the perception of the disciplinary environment prevailing in the two police agencies' (Ivkovic and Khechumyan 2014, p. 39); the comments were linked to one rural and one urban police agency within Armenia. This point reiterates the need to create a culture of human rights within the police organization which will benefit alike police officers, citizens and the wider community; in effect a 'win–win' situation (Beckley 2014a).

### *Poland*

Poland was a country most keen to integrate with Europe and adopt the rights-based approach to policing. The Polish Ministry of the Interior commissioned the highly regarded Jagiellonian University, established 1364, and noting Pope John Paul II among its alumni, to work with the Council of Europe to produce new training materials for police officers. A seminar was organized jointly by the university and the World Organisation Against Torture; delegates included staff from the Polish National Police Training School, the police commander from Krakow, the Council of Europe, Europol, civil liberty organizations, police trainers and academics

## Case study example 2: Armenia

*Armenia police ethics*

Problem 1: Heroin

A prisoner who is being interviewed for minor shoplifting offences claims that she has important information to offer which will help solve a number of serious international crimes. You have an international airport in your Division and the prisoner; Janet MacLeod is an American traveller who is a heroin addict, desperate for her next fix. She says that she will say nothing more unless she is given heroin. The investigating officers believe her.

This is a problem as the Division is going through a bad patch at the moment on detected crimes and recently, at the last quarterly policing plan review, the ACC (O) criticized the low detection rates. The Divisional Commander has asked all officers to make a special effort to detect more crime, and there is a reasonable expectation that giving MacLeod what she wants will help to achieve this. However, (as you are aware) the use of heroin is illegal and the drug cannot be obtained from a doctor. On the other hand, you know that the drug squad has recently seized a large amount of 'pure' heroin, which will not be needed as evidence.

*What are the issues here? What action will you take?*

from universities. The seminar was intended to discuss a police training strategy for Polish police officers to learn about human rights and how citizens' rights should be safeguarded by police; it also reported on a research report during which 116 Polish police officers were interviewed about the level of force used during policing incidents. The findings were that on many occasions excessive force was used unnecessarily when police officers assaulted and kicked citizens and restrained them by use of head locks. The overall interactions with Poland were a very fruitful relationship resulting in the translation to Polish of a book on policing and human rights that had been published in Britain (Beckley 2000) and several training workshops. The author has not found research relating to Poland evaluating the effect of human rights training.

## Case study example 3: used in South/Eastern European countries

*Operations Management: Worksheet*

Subject: Managing Operations

*Group 1*

You are planning to deal with a threatened incident of public disorder in Prague which will start with a 'protest march' through the streets.

1 Compile in your group the 'Intention' section of the operational order.
2 State how you would brief other police officers who have been assigned to the task of policing the event.

3 What human rights issues might be involved in an incident of this kind?
4 What ethical issues might be involved in such an incident?

### *Group 2*

Discuss in your group incidents which you have attended as a police officer and any others about which you have knowledge. Pick two incidents which the group have good knowledge of which did not achieve their objectives.

1 What was the purpose of the operational planning in the incidents?
2 Were all the stated objectives/purposes achieved in the operation?
3 Of the objectives that were not met, why was this the case?
4 How could the incidents have been planned more effectively?
5 Were any human rights or ethical issues raised during the operation?

## *Macedonia*

The author visited Macedonia several times after its split from the Former Republic of Yugoslavia. Police officers and Ministry of the Interior staff were very open to democratic policing systems although there were still many violent incidents on the country's border with Kosovo. The police were keen to identify codes of practice in operational policing and change the organizational culture towards a culture of human rights. With this objective in mind, several training programmes from the UK were contextualized and transferred to Macedonia such as the Custody Officers training and the Tutor Constable system. The author has not found an evaluation of the transition to human rights policing in Macedonia; although an excellent start was made, with an open and honest evaluation, towards progression to a democratic policing style.

### **Case study example 4: Sergeant training in Macedonia**

#### *Activity: Ethical Dilemmas – Imagine you are the Detective Sergeant*

#### Case Study 1

You are a Detective Sergeant working in the Divisional CID. Pete, as registered informer, has been supplying your colleague, DC Smith, with good class intelligence about a number of armed robberies which have been occurring throughout the Midlands. In one of these incidents, a security guard was shot and seriously injured.

Although to date the information supplied has been insufficient to make any arrests, Pete is now in a position with the robbery team where he will be able to tell DC Smith when and where the team will carry out their next offence.

You learn, however, that Pete has committed a serious assault on his wife. He is on bail for a similar offence and only last year had completed a two-year sentence for an offence of violence.

*What do you do?*

## Conclusion

The work of introducing democratic policing systems around the world has been supported by many humanitarian organizations along with police academics and commentators (Bayley 2014, Sheptycki 2000). The author can vouch for its rewarding and fulfilling nature, but the work takes time to reap its rewards and suffers setbacks on the way, because of police corruption and misconduct. It should also be noted that the police organization reflects its community; therefore the whole context of integrity should be assessed within the country to establish the level and type of corruption and misconduct that exists in the criminal justice sector, the public sector and nation as a whole. Once this initial assessment has been completed, interventions to address issues and problems can be commenced (Beckley 2012). Experience has shown that a training programme only will not result in effective change; a holistic, well-planned and executed change management programme is required with robust support, guidance and role modelling from the very top of the organization (Beckley 2012). That there is a need for human rights training for police officers is not in doubt as the author has subsequently worked in Australia, China, India and Indonesia. However, many people with knowledge of the policing and law enforcement context would agree that a commitment to best practice policing involves observing the human rights of individual citizens (including police officers) in order to maintain police legitimacy and procedural justice for all concerned, thereby enhancing trust and support in the police from the community. The optimum method of training of human rights for police officers is to utilize actual case studies of policing practice, discuss the integral issues, reflect and learn to achieve change and continuous improvement. However, to ensure success, there is a need for all police organizations to have a culture of human rights so that each police officer thinks carefully about the necessity of using coercive powers. Unless this happens, there will be many incidents resulting in regrettable outcomes for all parties concerned.

## References


Bartkowiak-Theron, I. and Asquith, N.L. (eds), 2012. *Policing vulnerability*. Sydney: Federation Press.

Barton, D. and Tait, S., 2008. *Human rights and cultural change in policing*. Paper presented at the Australasian Human Rights and Policing Conference, Melbourne 8–10 December 2008.

Bayley, D.H., 2006. *Changing the guard: developing democratic police abroad*. New York, NY: Oxford University Press.

Bayley, D., 2014. Human rights in policing: a global assessment. *Policing and Society: An International Journal of Research and Policy*, doi: 10.1080/10439463.2014.895352.

Beckley, A., 1997. *Operational policing: liabilities & entitlements*. London: Police Review Publishing Company.

Beckley, A., 1998. Learning for life: the path to job satisfaction? *Police Research & Management*, 3(1).

Beckley, A., 1999. Human rights: the key to police professionalism and better decision making. *Police Research & Management*, 3(2).

Beckley, A. 2000. *Human rights: the pocket guide for police officers and support staff*. London: The New Police Bookshop.

Beckley, A., 2012. Capacity building. *In*: P. Aepli (ed.), *Toolkit on police integrity*. Geneva: Geneva Centre for the Democratic Control of Armed Forces (DCAF), 249–85.

Beckley, A., 2013. Royal Commissions into policing: Australia. *Salus Journal*, 1(3), 33–52.

Beckley, A., 2014a. Organizational justice: is the police service ready for it? *Journal of Policing, Intelligence and Counter Terrorism*, 9(2), 176–90.

Beckley, A., 2014b. *Human rights: the route towards ethical policing or to global domination?* Paper presented at the ANZ SOC Conference, 2 October 2014, Conference Theme 14: Policing. Sydney: University of Sydney.

Bullock, K. and Johnson, P., 2012. The impact of the *Human Rights Act 1998* on policing in England and Wales. *British Journal of Criminology*, 52, 630–50.

Das, D.K. and Verma, A., 2002. Teaching police officers human rights, *The International Journal of Human Rights*, 6(2), 35–48.
den Heyer, G. and Beckley, A., 2013. Police independent oversight in Australia and New Zealand. *Police Practice and Research: An International Journal*, 14(2), 130–43.
Elliott, J., 1991. A model of professionalism and its implications for teacher education. *British Educational Research Journal*, 17(4), 309.
Emsley, C., 2012. Marketing the brand: exporting British police models 1829–1950. *Policing*. doi:10.1093/police/par061.
Goodman-Delahunty, J., Beckley, A. and Martin, M., 2014. Complaints against the New South Wales Police Force: analysis of risks and rights in reported police conduct. *Australian Journal of Human Rights*, 20(2), 81–105.
Ivkovic, K. and Haberfeld, M.R. (eds), 2015. *Measuring police integrity across the world: studies from established democracies and countries in transition*. New York, NY: Springer.
Ivkovic, K. and Khechumyan, A., 2014. Measuring police integrity among urban and rural police in Armenia: from local results to global implications. *International Journal of Comparative and Applied Criminal Justice*, 38(1), 39–61.
Kalajdziev, G. (ed.), 2002. *Police and human rights manual for police training*. Copenhagen: Danish Institute for Human Rights.
Lauritz, L.E., Astrom, E., Nyman, C. and Klingvall, M., 2012. Police students' learning preferences, suitable responses from the learning environment. *Policing*, 1–9. doi: 10.1093/police/pas009.
Macvean, A. and Cox, C., 2012. Police education in a university setting: emerging cultures and attitudes. *Policing*, 6(1), 16–25.
Neyroud, P., 2011. *Review of police leadership and training*. London: UK Government.
Neyroud, P. and Beckley, A., 2001. *Policing, ethics and human rights*. Cullompton: Willan Publishing.
Norris, N., 1992. Problems in police training. *Policing*, 8, Autumn.
Northern Ireland Policing Board [NIPB]. 2008. *PSNI Code of Ethics 2008*. Belfast: PSNI. Retrieved on 6 July 2015 from: www.nipolicingboard.org.uk/final_code_of_ethics-2.pdf.
Oliva, J.R. and Compton, M.T., 2010. What do police officers value in the classroom? *Policing: An International Journal of Police Strategies & Management*, 33(2), 321–38.
O'Rawe, M., 2005. Human rights and police training in transitional societies: exporting the lessons of Northern Ireland. *Human Rights Quarterly*, 27, 943–68.
Paterson, C., 2011. Adding value? A review of the international literature on the role of higher education in police training and education. *Police Practice and Research: An International Journal*, 12(4), August, 286–97.
Police Training Council. 1985. *Police training strategy*. London: Home Office Quarterly.
Pollock, J.M. and Williams, H.E., 2015. Using ethical dilemmas in training police. *In*: M.C. Braswell, B.R. McCarthy and B.J. McCarthy (eds), *Justice, crime and ethics*, 8th edn. Waltham, MA: Anderson Publishing, 93–112.
Schon, D.A., 1991. *The reflective practitioner: how professionals think in action*. London: Arena.
Sheptycki, J., 2000. Policing and human rights: an introduction. *Policing and Society*, 10, 1–10.
United Kingdom Department for Constitutional Affairs [UKDCA], 2006. *Review of the implementation of the Human Rights Act*. London: UK Government.
United Nations [UN], 1948. *The Universal Declaration of Human Rights*. Adopted and proclaimed by General Assembly resolution 217 A (III) of 10 December 1948. New York, NY: United Nations.
UN, 1979. *Code of Conduct for Law Enforcement Officials*. 12 December 1979. New York, NY: UN General Assembly.
UN, 1990. *Basic principles on the use of force and firearms by law enforcement officials*. Havana: UN Congress.
United Nations Office of the High Commissioner for Human Rights (UNOHCHR), 2004. *Human rights standards and practice for the police: Expanded pocket book on human rights for the police*. Professional Training Series No 5/Add 3: Geneva: United Nations.
Vander Kooi, G.P. and Palmer, L.B., 2014. Problem-based learning for police academy students: comparison of those receiving such instruction with those in traditional programs. *Journal of Criminal Justice Education*. doi: 10.1080/10511253.2014.882368.
Werth, E.P. 2009. Student perception of learning through a problem-based learning exercise: an exploratory study. *Policing: An International Journal of Police Strategies & Management*, 32(1), 21–37.
Williams, G. and Hume, D. 2013. *Human rights under the Australian Constitution*, 2nd edn. Sydney: Oxford University Press.

# 34

# Human rights and everyday practices of policing in post-war Sri Lanka

*Kiran Grewal and Vidura Munasinghe*

## Introduction

With the *Universal Declaration of Human Rights* now over 60 years old the focus of recent human rights scholarship and practice has been on implementation. Alongside the continued push for accountability and enforcement of human rights laws, since the 1990s there has been a shift towards seeing education as a crucial factor in the establishment of a human rights respecting society (Phillips and Gready 2013, Coysch 2014).

Meanwhile the traditional focus on victims of human rights violations and civil society has broadened. Following the United Nations (UN) Decade for Human Rights Education (1995–2004), the World Programme for Human Rights Education launched a second phase in which priority was given to, amongst others, human rights training for law enforcement personnel and military. The rationale for this, as a 2012 report of the Office for Security and Cooperation in Europe (OSCE) noted, was: 'the central role law enforcement officers play in human rights protection'. For this reason, the OSCE asserted, 'human rights should be a key component of [law enforcement officers'] professional development' (OSCE 2012, p. 9).

The introduction of human rights as a core competency in policing has been witnessed globally. However, it has been even more strongly promoted in post-war/post-atrocity societies. In these contexts there has been an ever-greater investment made by an array of international and local, governmental and non-governmental actors in interventions designed to promote human rights, democracy and 'Rule of Law'.[1]

So what is the impact of these human rights initiatives on the everyday practices and attitudes of police? And how effective are they in establishing respect for human rights in societies emerging from periods of intense violence, atrocity and repression? These are the questions we explore in this chapter, drawing on ethnographic research done with Sri Lankan police officers over a three-year period from 2012 to 2015.[2]

## Promoting human rights in policing: the example of Sri Lanka

Sri Lanka has been no exception as a site for initiatives aimed at promoting human rights within the law enforcement sector. As a result of efforts by local and international governmental, non-governmental and intergovernmental actors Sri Lanka has a fairly robust set of laws and policies enshrining human rights, although these have been compromised over the decades of insurgency and counter-insurgency (discussed in a moment). The *Constitution of Sri Lanka* (1978) contains a range of fundamental rights provisions, including due process, protection from arbitrary detention and torture. The criminal procedure laws also provide for basic fair trial rights and the *Evidence Ordinance* contains a number of provisions aimed at protecting suspects and reducing the incentive for police to use improper interrogation methods.

In terms of international obligations, Sri Lanka has ratified most of the major human rights conventions[3] and incorporated many of them explicitly into domestic law. Of particular significance for the police are the *Convention against Torture (CAT) Act 1994* and the *ICCPR Act 2007*. Alongside this legislation, the police are subject to regulations, departmental orders and codes of conduct that provide guidelines in line with international standards. Finally, the courts have traditionally heard fundamental rights cases and issued a number of important judgements in which state actors have been held responsible for fundamental rights violations and ordered to pay compensation.

Yet (as with many other countries) these measures, while formally enshrining human rights have not eradicated instances of abuse in practice. In fact, allegations of serious human rights violations have continued to hang over both the police and military apparatuses even since the end of the armed conflict in 2009. So how are we to understand the ongoing disconnect (even now in an apparent period of peace) between an established human rights framework and the violation of these rights in practice?

Certainly the decades of armed conflict have had a significant impact on both the formal and informal human rights framework in Sri Lanka. The introduction of emergency regulations, the *Prevention of Terrorism Act 1978* and regulations made under *Public Security Ordinance* all gave the state the ability to restrict (and in some cases violate) certain human rights for the sake of the national security. The fact that they have been in force for more than two decades means they have undermined the legal system's ability and apparent commitment to upholding basic human rights. At the same time, wartime propaganda (particularly between 2005 and 2009, during the final stages of the armed conflict with the Liberation Tigers of Tamil Ealam, or LTTE) specifically devalued human rights values by placing them in direct opposition to national security: a phenomenon we have seen in many parts of the world in the post-9/11 context of the 'War on Terror'.

Since 2009 there have been renewed efforts by both local and international actors, to (re)inscribe a commitment to human rights within the Sri Lankan police force. Human Rights and Fundamental Rights form a core topic in the basic training of all police officers with external lecturers brought in to teach this component. The UN Office of the High Commissioner for Human Rights (OHCHR) as well as local human rights centres have provided resource materials and a number of other donor agencies have funded projects aimed at building up police competency and enshrining democratic and human rights policing values.[4] Reflecting global trends, there has been an emphasis on promoting community policing models and developing police attitudes and skills in line with human rights values.

In order to explore the impact of these post-war human rights training and reform initiatives in Sri Lanka, we conducted research between February 2012 and February 2015 on the everyday attitudes and practices of police. Starting with interviews, focus group discussions and observation of training sessions in an array of different locations across the country, we finally focused on police operating in one district in the north west of Sri Lanka. In this phase of the research we conducted interviews and observations not only of the police but other community members interacting with the police in this area. In the next section of our chapter we present a few of our key findings.

## A snapshot of everyday policing in post-war Sri Lanka

To begin with, many police observers and retired senior police officers themselves spoke of the impact that Sri Lanka's colonial history and its experience of decades of armed conflict have had on the culture of the police. The structure of the police force has remained largely unchanged since the establishment by the British of the colonial police force. As a result, for the majority of the population the police have long been viewed as enforcers of the will of the rulers (originally the colonial masters and then following independence local elites). This lack of popular legitimacy is one experienced by many postcolonial police forces and affects both police attitudes and those of the broader society towards the police (Tankebe 2008, Jauregui 2010). For the police, they are (willing or reluctant) subjects of patronage, while for the general public the police are often seen as figures to be avoided or manipulated to achieve particular personal aims.

Added to this colonial history, since the 1970s Sri Lanka has experienced repeated waves of political violence. In the south of the country a Marxist-inspired movement of disaffected youth calling themselves the *Janatha Vimuthki Peramuna* staged violent insurrections in both the early 1970s and late 1980s. Meanwhile the most infamous conflict in Sri Lanka has been that between the government and the Tamil separatist movement the LTTE located in the north and east of the country. Both of these insurgency movements often targeted police and police stations, creating a culture of fear and mistrust for sections of the community (particularly Tamils) amongst police officers.

In response the government launched ever more violent counter-insurgency operations. Alongside the deployment of military, police training became increasingly focused on military rather than more 'soft' policing skills. This militarization of the police's role has been identified by older, retired police officers as having played a significant part in reducing their respect for human rights.

With these structural and historical factors in mind, we also explored the current views and experiences of police officers both to their work and to human rights. In doing so a number of important issues emerged which impact on how human rights interact with the everyday practices of police. Here we will discuss just four.

### *Knowledge of human rights*

The language of human rights has penetrated everyday police practice in Sri Lanka. A core component of basic training, all the police we spoke with knew of human rights. However they often expressed the sentiment that while they knew they should respect human rights, this was perceived as being in conflict with fulfilling their professional obligations. For example, as one female police constable explained: 'We should obey human rights. But it makes our duty more difficult. Earlier people were scared of police, now they are not. Now we have to respect even the criminals' (Interview 01). Another senior police officer explained:

> We are restricted by the article 11 of the constitution. Earlier we used to record confessions by using various means such as hanging from feet, putting testicles to a drawer and closing it, beating the soles. We know we cannot use a confession in a court case. But we used it as a weapon in order to make the suspect reveal the evidence, which we can use at the court. But with the introduction of human rights we cannot do it. We find it difficult to conduct investigations now.
>
> *(Interview 01)*

In this way he saw rights as an obstacle to be overcome rather than a professional obligation. Another police officer argued that:

> culprits are the people who have mastered human rights. When we make an arrest they start to count the time. They know we have to produce them to the courts within 24 hours. They think if they can fool us for 24 hours they can get away.

Again, human rights were perceived as a tool that could be used to undermine effective police work. This suspicion of human rights – and the perception that it was a tool that was misused by undeserving people – was further exacerbated by police officers' own experiences of disempowerment.

### *Experiences of empowerment and disempowerment*

It quickly became clear through our research that the experiences of police officers varied greatly depending on the level at which they entered the police service. While those entering at officer rank were often upwardly mobile and saw the police force as a means of furthering their social status and power, those who entered at the level of constable (PC) had very different backgrounds and expectations.

All the sergeants we interviewed were between the ages of 45 and 55 and had joined as PCs in their early 20s. In other words, during their entire career, they had only been able to move up one rank: a fact that indicates the paucity of opportunities for a person who joins at the entry level of the police force. In a highly hierarchical society like Sri Lanka where education, family background and connections are crucial to getting ahead, these police officers were by and large resigned to their position.

However they did complain extensively about their poor basic living and working conditions. Salaries of police officers are relatively low, when compared to other government and private sector employees. Junior officers live in barracks with tin roofs that leak during the rainy season. The barracks we observed have minimal facilities (bunk beds in one hall, small lockers, shared showers and toilets) and are uncomfortably hot and plagued with mosquitoes.

The officers also spoke often of the problems they experienced in getting leave even for serious family matters, their heavy workload and the lack of basic facilities to do their job. For example, many police stations have only one official police vehicle. This is generally used by the Officer-in-Charge of the station (OIC). We witnessed lower rank officers bringing in suspects on the back of their own personal bicycles and hitching rides to take suspects to court, either with local community members who had vehicles or on public transport. One female PC told us of an incident during which, while waiting for a free ride on the main road, the driver of a vehicle intentionally hit her. This incident also captures the ways in which socially influential members of the general public treat low-ranking police officers: ignoring, abusing and threatening them. Beatrice Jauregui has documented similar working conditions amongst north Indian police officers, leading her to describe them as 'subalterns of the state': 'a uniquely depoliticized labor force, whose official uniform ironically strips them of basic rights afforded to other citizens' (Jauregui 2010, p. 22).

As a result, for many low-ranking police officers, not only are human rights seen as providing protections to undeserving members of society ('criminals'), rights are also perceived as something they themselves are denied. This creates tension, leading them to feel antagonism to the very concept of human rights. In a study of junior prison wardens in Delhi's Tihar Jail, Tomas Martin (2009) made similar findings. The contrast between what the wardens perceived as the promotion of prisoner's living standards with their own poor living and working conditions made junior prison wardens both resentful of human rights and allowed them to justify the use of violence as the only way to cope.

At the same time, despite their feeling of being disrespected and devalued, police also saw their role as an important one in society. This involved not simply enforcing the law but ensuring public order and morality. For example, one sergeant we met told us of his own personal crusade against illicit liquor producers in his district: a widely accepted social ill (most of the people we interviewed in this district said that illicit liquor was the biggest social problem). This self-identification as the guardians of public morality is not unique to Sri Lankan police. However it points to the importance of a broader examination of how discipline and order are conceived within Sri Lankan society.

## *The concept of 'discipline'*

We found that a high number of respondents interviewed in villages in our selected district expressed the view that 'it is OK to be beaten by the police, if you have done something wrong'. One lawyer we interviewed about police torture laughed and said, 'it's obvious they will beat the wrongdoers' (Interview 02). Therefore, not only has violence been normalized in the post-war setting but it is also considered an essential component of maintaining law and order in the society.

In this regard it is informative to understand the role that the concept of *Lajja-baya* (shame-fear) plays in disciplining (at least Sinhalese) Sri Lankan society. The anthropologist Gananath Obeyesekere has documented this phenomenon, exploring the ways in which *Lajja-baya* is instilled from early childhood during the process of socialization. By accusing their children with admonishments like '*lajja nathdha*?' ('aren't you ashamed?') or, '*minissu monawa kiyaida*?' ('what will other people say?'), parents normalize certain types of behaviour within a broader field of power (Obeyesekere 1984, p. 505). Within this field of power, authority is vested with certain classes of people who police the normalization process: amongst them are parents, teachers and police officers. The methods used to facilitate the process often involve humiliating, threatening and punishing subjects who violate the norm of restraint and engage in *Lajja nathi-baya nathi* (shameless-fearless) acts. This is true not only of police but also the other authorized 'social policers'.

School principals and teachers we interviewed frequently adopted strategies for provoking shame and fear in their students as a means of disciplining them. One school principal described an incident where she had cut the hair of a student and explained that whenever she finds students with improper hairstyles she cuts their hair in a manner that humiliates them in front of their peers. In another school we observed the principal wandering the school premises with a cane in hand. In fact all the principals we interviewed said they used canes to punish students (despite a circular issued by the Ministry of Education in 2005 prohibiting corporal punishment). One Buddhist monk who is the principal of a Sunday (religious) school told us:

> Children are very scared of me. I beat them with a cane. I ask teachers to frighten students with the cane. Otherwise you cannot control them. We were beaten by our parents. They did it with the good intention of disciplining us. Therefore even today we respect them.
>
> *(Interview 03)*

Thus the belief that human rights might reduce the ability to maintain order and be abused by 'bad elements' was not limited to the police and their work. It was also a view held by many others within the community. Many individuals spoke of the dangers of children's rights in breaking down discipline and respect for authority. The notions of 'discipline' and 'respect' were clearly associated with a certain degree of fear and the possible use of violence. In the words of one Buddhist Monk: 'human rights is problematic. We cannot beat a child now. When we cannot beat them it's hard to control them' (Interview 03). Human rights is seen as disrupting a necessary process of socialization by prohibiting certain types of disciplining that have long been seen as essential.

When viewed in this context, the sense of disconnect many police officers expressed with human rights principles becomes more comprehensible. As members of the society (and therefore similarly socialized), they are informed by the same ideas about the necessary link between humiliation and violence and discipline and (social) order. It is therefore unsurprising that if they see this as an acceptable means of socializing children, they would be resistant to what they see as 'softer' methods being used on adults caught committing much worse wrongs. At the same time, this broader social context also explains how members of the general public, rather than inhibiting police violation of human rights, may in fact contribute to encouraging such behaviour.

## *Community expectations*

A number of police officers we interviewed saw their obligation to follow human rights principles as being compromised by their efforts to satisfy community demands. A police officer based in a regional headquarters began by stating, 'we should respect human rights'. However he went on to argue that, 'most of the police officers get into trouble by committing human rights violations by fulfilling the wishes of the people. People expect quick reactions from the police, not the due procedure' (Interview 04). This view was also expressed by a police sergeant who stated: 'People expect police to deal with their problems quickly. They do not want to waste their time in courts. They want to finish everything in police' (Interview 05).

One might argue that these types of views are offered by police as a cynical attempt at self-justification. Perhaps this is the case but we also found support for their position amongst others in the community. For example, one *Grama Niladhari*[5] stated that in his opinion it was, 'due to the harshness of the police [that] people refrain from wrongdoings'. Meanwhile an inquiry officer from the local office of the Sri Lankan Human Rights Commission told us:

> People have lost their faith on judicial process due to its delays and the other influences. And most of them are not aware of this process. So they want answers from something which is closer to them: police. That's why they want police to find, arrest and punish the culprits. They think culprits will get away during the long, delaying due process.
>
> *(Interview 06)*

To illustrate this one can look at how the villagers in one district viewed the actions of the former OIC of the police station. This OIC had adopted a method of arresting people suspected of involvement with producing or selling illicit liquor that involved shaming them in public and producing them to courts with charges that were more severe than their actual offence. None of the villagers we interviewed said anything negative about this OIC. In fact the majority praised his work highly and greatly appreciated the methods he used to 'control fearlessness'.

What the above research points to is an ongoing disconnect for many people in Sri Lanka between the values supposedly enshrined in human rights (equality, dignity, individual autonomy and freedom) and those considered important for the proper functioning of a good society. It is here that Sally Falk Moore's observations back in 1973 are useful. Writing about the relationship between formal law and the social norms within which these laws are interpreted and applied, Moore observes: 'law and the social context in which it operates must be inspected together' (Moore 1973, p. 719). A seemingly obvious observation, it is startling how infrequently it has been incorporated by those seeking to introduce human rights within different institutional contexts.

Moore points out: '[t]he law (in the sense of state enforceable law) is only one of a number of factors that affect the decisions people make, the actions they take and the relationships they have' (Moore 1973, p. 743). This is clearly evidenced within our own research in terms of how the police balance their professional duties (as they understand them), their own beliefs, community expectations and their obligations to abide by human rights standards. Current approaches to human rights education and institutional reform in Sri Lanka have yet to find a way to incorporate these understandings. We conclude this chapter with a few suggestions that might begin this process.

## Contextualizing human rights and policing

As Karp and Stenmark identify, 'what actually takes place in day-to-day police training and police work is dependent on structural and historical factors as well as on those who work in the police service' (Karp and Stenmark 2011, p. 5). In the case of Sri Lanka the legacies of the colonial policing model, the process of militarization of the society and state institutions over the course of decades, social hierarchies and established social norms regarding order, discipline and status all contribute to the ways in which human rights are received and engaged with by police in their everyday actions and attitudes.

### *The multiple cultures of the police*

The first factor that requires further consideration when planning human rights reform strategies with police is the recognition of multiple cultures within the institution. At present human rights training packages in Sri Lanka tend to be generic, presenting legal, professional and ethical obligations with little consideration for how these might apply to differently placed police officers. Not only does this fail to take into account the differential power of different ranks, it can also seem quite alien to what happens in practice.

For example, it became clear to us through our interviews that, while human rights and fundamental rights were introduced to police officers in their basic training, what they actually understood of these concepts mainly came from their interactions with colleagues and supervisors. One sergeant commented: 'When I am in charge I tell my subordinates what [they] should and what should not do. It comes from experience. If they obey my orders there will be no violation of human rights' (Interview 07). The role of 'on the job' learning in socializing police officers has been well documented by police ethnographers (Chan 1997). Yet there remains a need for steps to be taken to bridge the gap between human rights education that new recruits may receive in the academy and contradictory values they may be socialized into once they enter active service.

As Karp and Stenmark write, 'it may be difficult to achieve change in a police organization if new routines are at odds with established conceptions about police work held among police officers' (Karp and Stenmark 2011, p. 7). In the case of the Sri Lankan police, deeply held beliefs regarding the necessity of violence to both solve crimes and ensure social order will not be easily overturned through teaching human rights principles. This is even more so when these beliefs are in fact supported by many others within the community.

Training within academies and in-service training for more experienced officers also has to more explicitly deal with the 'commonsense' assumptions that police officers inevitably develop in the course of their work. For example, it was frequently suggested to us that experienced police officers can – and should – identify who in the community were 'problem characters' and who were 'good citizens'. One Inspector at a regional headquarters stated: 'A police officer should be able to identify who is a criminal and who is a good person. That comes with experience' (Interview 04). Speaking with one senior police officer in charge of a regional training academy about how to improve human rights protection within policing, he told us he was keen to prioritize teaching junior officers and community members how to 'spot a criminal'.

It is also interesting that human rights was sometimes perceived as justifying the following of one's own ethical beliefs rather than the rules. In the words of one OIC of a police station: 'Our duties cannot be carried out just according to the book. If we just follow the law and file cases some poor people will suffer more'. This discretionary power is another well-documented feature of police ethnographies (de Lint 1998, Chan 1997). On this occasion the OIC described using his discretion to protect vulnerable members of society (by letting them off with warnings rather than charging them). However, in other instances this following of one's own ethical code could justify more punitive approaches: something made evident by the example of the previous OIC's approach to illicit liquor producers.

This may be an example of Hornberger's (2010) argument that human rights policing may in fact *increase* the capacity for state violence by allowing police to play a greater role in the community. Community policing – a model of reform that has been very popular in Sri Lanka, as elsewhere – is a prime example of how this may happen. Without significant shifts in police attitudes, it is not clear how simply putting police in closer contact with the general public will achieve better and not worse human rights outcomes. So too, communal attitudes and expectations in relation to punitive forms of justice (such as those set out above) may in fact promote rather than inhibit human rights violations.

## *A universal police culture? Global divides*

There is also a need to recognize that while there are of course similarities across police forces internationally, the assumption of a 'universal police culture' may be counterproductive. Alice Hills (2009) has made a similar observation in her research on the Nigerian Police. The different histories, structural and living conditions of law enforcement officers operating in different parts of the Global South mean that their experience of, and attitude towards policing may well be quite different from those of officers coming from the Global North. In Hills's words: 'No matter how harsh life in Ohio is, it does not compare to that in, say, Nigeria where police violence is merely one manifestation of a wider acceptance of violence' (Hills 2009, p. 307; see also Jensen and Jefferson 2009, Jauregui 2010).

As discussed above, the legacies of a colonial police structure, many decades of public violence and widely accepted social norms regarding the necessity of violence to achieve 'discipline' and social order are important and often neglected factors in understanding Sri Lankan police's use of force and suspicion of human rights. So too, depending on the rank and location of different police officers in Sri Lanka their own experience of disempowerment and denial of basic rights is also a source of antagonism when they are told that they should nonetheless be respectful of, and have regard for, the rights of others, even those accused of serious crimes and/or those deemed socially deviant.

Other scholars have also observed the tension that is often at play where personnel in the Global South are instructed on the importance of rights, equality and respect for each individual even as this message is contradicted through their own treatment.[6] Of course human rights training must place emphasis on the added responsibility of police officers as representatives of the state and those authorized within society to use force and coercion. Yet to do this without a simultaneous recognition of the often disempowered position from which police may be operating undermines the effectiveness of human rights training by both appearing unrealistic and potentially antagonizing recipients.

## Conclusion

In this chapter we have sought to explore the relationship between models of human rights and security sector reform currently being promoted around the globe and the experiences, attitudes and practices of police in particular locations. In the context of Sri Lanka, the operationalization of human rights has been enacted through legal and institutional reform and the introduction of education and training aimed at ensuring law enforcement personnel are aware of these legal and professional obligations. However, without efforts to first understand particular local contexts and belief systems which might interact (positively or negatively) with human rights and then to find ways to challenge those that are antithetical to human rights the possibility of human rights being internalized remains remote.

To quote Sally Falk Moore once more:

> Innovative legislation or other attempts to direct change often fail to achieve their intended purposes; and even when they succeed wholly or partially, they frequently carry with them unplanned and unexpected consequences. This is partly because new laws are thrust upon going social arrangements in which there are complexes of binding obligations already in existence. Legislation is often passed with the intention of altering going social arrangements in specified ways. The social arrangements are often effectively stronger than the new laws.
>
> *(Moore 1973, p. 723)*

Through exploring how police officers in Sri Lanka understand and engage with the language of human rights and also how police operate within a particular local context, we have sought to show the importance of shifting our focus away from abstract normative approaches to human rights towards more situated engagements. It is only by doing this, we contend, that the aim of operationalizing human rights can possibly be achieved.

## Notes

1 See, for example, the OSCE 'Guidebook on Democratic Policing', which clearly articulates the assumed link between a model of 'democratic policing' which respects human rights and broader peace, security and development objectives. See also OHCHR (2006), Bajraktari et al. (2006) and Bayley (2015).

2 This research was made possible by a grant from the European Union for a project entitled, 'Enhancing Human Rights Protection in the Context of Law Enforcement and Security'. We would also like to acknowledge Kaushalya Ariyaratne and Thilini Chandrasekara both of whom were instrumental in conducting the research detailed in this chapter.

3 With the exception of the Second Optional Protocol to the *International Covenant on Civil and Political Rights*, the *Convention on the Non-Applicability of Statutory Limitations to War Crimes and Crimes Against Humanity* and the *Rome Statute* for the International Criminal Court.

4 For example, the Asia Foundation has an extensive community policing programme operating across Sri Lanka and has also conducted torture prevention training (http://asiafoundation.org/country/overview/sri-lanka). The Swedish National Police Board was involved in a project, funded by the Swedish government's development agency, working with the Sri Lankan police on developing its civilian policing capacity between 2005 and 2008 (Olander et al. 2007). In recent years the European Union has also funded two programmes aimed at building the respect for human rights and professional investigation skills of the police: The first is the project of which this research formed part (http://sydney.edu.au/arts/research/ehrp/about/index.shtml). The other, which is ongoing is the 'Sri Lanka: A Society that Values Human Dignity' project conducted by the Family Rehabilitation Centre in association with the Sri Lanka Foundation (www.frcsl.org/index.php/what-we-do/prevention/current-programmes).

5 A village officer: the lowest rank of the administrative structure of the country.

6 See, for example, Andrew Jefferson's (2007) study of prison guard training in Nigeria.

## References


Bajraktari, Y. et al., 2006. *The PRIME System: Measuring the Success of Post-Conflict Police Reform*. Princeton University Woodrow Wilson School of Public and International Affairs. Retrieved on 9 August 2015 from: www.princeton.edu/bobst/docs/WWS591b_FINAL_Police_Reform_Report.pdf.

Bayley, D., 2015. Human rights in policing: a global assessment. *Policing and Society: An International Journal of Research and Policy*, 25(5), 540–7.

Chan, J., 1997. *Changing police culture: policing in a multicultural society*. Cambridge: Cambridge University Press.

Coysch, J., 2014. The dominant discourse of human rights education: a critique. *Journal of Human Rights Practice*, 6(1), 89–114.

de Lint, W., 1998. Regulating autonomy: police discretion as a problem for training. *Canadian Journal of Criminology*, 40, 277–304.

Hills, A., 2009. The possibility of transnational policing. *Policing and Society: An International Journal of Research and Policy*, 19(3), 300–17.

Hornberger, J., 2010. Human rights and policing: exigency or incongruence? *The Annual Review of Law and Social Science*, 6, 259–83.

Jauregui, B., 2010. *Shadows of the state, subalterns of the state: police and 'law and order' in postcolonial India*. Thesis (PhD). University of Chicago.

Jefferson, A.M., 2007. Prison officer training and practice in Nigeria: contention, contradiction and re-imagining reform strategies. *Punishment & Society*, 9(3), 253–69.

Jensen, S. and Jefferson, A. (eds), 2009. *State violence and human rights: state officials in the south*. Oxon and New York: Routledge-Cavendish.

Karp, S. and Stenmark, H., 2011. Learning to be a police officer: tradition and change in the training and professional lives of police officers. *Police Practice and Research: An International Journal*, 12(1), 4–15.

Martin, T., 2009. Letting the snake out of the basket. *In*: S. Jensen and A. Jefferson (eds), *State violence and human rights: state officials in the south*. Oxon and New York: Routledge-Cavendish, 139–57.

Moore, S.F., 1973. Law and social change: the semi-autonomous social field as an appropriate subject of study. *Law and Society Review*, 7(4), 719–46.

Obeyesekere, G., 1984. *The cult of the goddess Pattini*. Chicago, IL: University of Chicago Press.

Office of the High Commissioner for Human Rights [OHCHR], 2006. *Rule of law tools for post-conflict states: mapping the justice sector*. New York and Geneva: United Nations.

Office for Security and Cooperation in Europe [OSCE]/ODIHR. 2012. *Guidelines on Human Rights Education: For Law Enforcement Officials*. Warsaw, Poland: OSCE/ODIHR.

Olander, K., Orjuella, C. and Edrisinha, R., 2007. *Review of development cooperation between Sri Lanka Police and Swedish National Police Board*, SIDA Evaluation 07/43. Retrieved on 9 August 2015 from: www.sida.se/publications.

Phillips, B. and Gready, P., 2013. Introduction: why a special issue on human rights education (HRE) and training? *Journal of Human Rights Practice*, 5(2), 215–19.

Tankebe, J., 2008. Colonialism, legitimation and policing in Ghana. *International Journal of Law, Crime and Justice*, 36, 67–84.

# 35

# 'Like running on one leg'

## The regulation of sexual rights through the preventative policing of sexual violence in Delhi

*Natasha Marhia*

In a dusty square in a densely populated resettlement colony in the north-western outskirts of Delhi, a large crowd has gathered inquisitively around a makeshift stage framed with giant banners advertising Delhi Police's Parivartan campaign for the safety of women in Delhi. The actors in mime artists' hyperbolic make-up, glistening in the oppressive heat of Delhi's late afternoon summer sun, have secured a captive audience in the children weaving their way nimbly to the front. The performance, *Hadsa*, is a 10-minute educative pantomime about rape. The audience knows that the suspicious neighbour who befriends the father of the teenage girl is a Bad Man, but why can't the parents *see* this patent truth? Viewers voice their disapproval and dread as the girls' parents are obliviously lured from the house so that the Bad Man can make his move on the helpless daughter. The sexual attack takes place off-stage. When the parents return, they mime their horror at their daughter's torn clothes and blood-stained legs and face. In a dramatic gesture accompanied by a drum roll, she raises her arm and publicly points the finger at her attacker. 'What should we do with him?' the show's narrator asks the excitable crowd. 'Arrest him!', 'Throw him in jail!', 'Beat him up!', they heckle. Two women police officers in khaki Delhi Police uniforms stride purposefully onto the stage. These are not actors, their faces are clean of clown like make-up. They are beat constables from Delhi Police's Parivartan Cell. They demonstratively handcuff the Bad Man and drag him offstage, miming a faux struggle, amid an uproarious frenzy of triumphant whoops, cheers and laughter from the crowd.

Street theatre was a signature feature of Delhi Police's Parivartan programme – 'Operation Change' – initiated in key violence hot spots in the city in 2005 in response to bad press vis-à-vis police handling of sexual violence. The city was dubbed the 'rape capital' by local media for several years before the horrific rape and murder of a young woman on a moving bus in December 2012, which catalysed a wave of activism and attracted international attention. Delhi's authorities were already under pressure to demonstrate their credentials to domestic and international audiences. It is perhaps unsurprising, given the 'hegemony' of rights discourse (Grewal 2005), and the framing of violence against women as an international human rights issue in recent decades (Macaulay 2000, pp. 146–7, Youngs 2003, Kelly 2005), that the promotion of women's rights has become an indicator of a state's status as modern, developed and responsible

(Marhia 2013, p. 202). A key mechanism through which states are called upon to protect women's rights is through the criminalization of violence against women, and the effective enforcement of the law by the police (Adelman et al. 2003, p. 106).

If the language of rights has been both imperative to feminist projects, and simultaneously a source of intractable paradoxes (Brown 2000), so too has embracing the police as potential upholders of women's rights. Policing has been a site for the accomplishment of certain hegemonic variants of masculinity (Marhia 2013, pp. 50–78, Messerschmidt 1993, Fielding 1994, p. 47, Silvestri 2003, p. 31, Martin and Jurik 1996, p. 64, Prokos and Padavic 2002, p. 443). In India, where the police service has never fully lived down its origins as an instrument of colonial control and repression, custodial rape has been central to feminist theorizing and activism around violence against women and its normalization (Kannabiran 2005, Gangoli 2007). While police complicity in the explicit violation of people's rights is an important topic, it is also crucial to analyse mundane, everyday police practices. This chapter draws on Foucault's (1984, p. 241) understanding of the police as agents of disciplinary power, not exclusively through the exertion of coercive force (or its threat), but through regulating the minutiae of people's lives. I consider how some of Delhi Police's preventative work on sexual violence paradoxically serves to regulate behaviours and interpersonal relationships in ways that reinforce gendered sexual norms and mores, renormalizing certain (gendered and gendering) violences.

Parivartan joined a number of existing Delhi Police initiatives addressing women's security, (Marhia 2013, pp. 91–3) and emulated established practices in the policing of violence against women in India,[1] but was distinctive in its focus on prevention. The programme combined intensive beat policing by women constables with educational activities implemented by experts in youth work, social communication and psychology, collaborating closely with the police. The decision to deploy exclusively *women* constables on the Parivartan beats was strategic, reflecting assumptions about the suitability of women for performing violence-against-women work and providing services to women complainants – assumptions which have informed similar police initiatives in India and elsewhere (Natarajan 2008, Santos 2005). The demonstrative use of women police constables in beat patrolling and in Parivartan's street theatre performances was intended to convey their availability to women in the community, to enable them to feel safe reporting violence. The deployment of women police for this work carries with it a range of implications and effects, both advantageous, and problematic, for the realization of gendered and sexual rights; the construction of gendered skills, abilities and bodies it distils have been contested (Jordan 2002), although that discussion is beyond the scope of this chapter (for a fuller discussion see Marhia 2013, pp. 233–51).

The chapter proceeds as follows: the first section discusses the beat constables' direct interventions in the community, while the remaining sections analyse safety workshops, sexual responsibility lectures and street theatre performances and scripts, respectively. These are not exhaustive of Delhi Police's violence-against-women work, but they provide useful insights into how the latter conceptualizes gendered and sexual rights, and the implications. The analysis is based on qualitative interviews and observational fieldwork with Delhi Police in 2008. All quotes appearing in the text were translated into English from the original Hindi, unless prefaced with an *asterisk which indicates material recorded in English.

## Keeping adolescent girls 'on track': informally policing elopement

Parivartan's frontline officers, the women beat constables, spent most of their beat time intervening in domestic disputes and intimate partner violence, but were not authorized to investigate rape cases – ironically, given the programme's preoccupation with addressing *sexual* violence

(Delhi Police n.d.). This preoccupation did not stem exclusively from the imperative to mitigate bad press. Feminist analyses have shown how Indian legal constructs cast sexual violence through a lens of sexual integrity (Singh 2004, Menon 2004, pp. 129–34, Gangoli 2007, pp. 62–3, Das 1996, Baxi 2005). Such concerns are also reflected in police discourse/practice, and emerge as a common strand underlying distinct aspects of Delhi Police's sexual violence prevention work. They permeated beat constables' accounts of 'elopement' cases, a significant sub-category of domestic disputes.

'Elopement' is the term used in Delhi Police to describe illicit, pre-marital (hetero)sexual relationships in which a girl typically runs away from her parents' home with her boyfriend. If the girl is below the age of consent (16[2]), charges of statutory rape can be brought. The girl's parents may file a case and seek her recovery, or a case may be filed retrospectively when the relationship ends. My interview respondents spoke about elopement when asked about violence against women, the rationale for Parivartan and their day-to-day community interventions. The theme dominated some discussions of rape. There is no clear legal distinction due to provisions against statutory rape, but this overlap also reflects the alignment of safety with sexual integrity, which renders consent less relevant to the character of the crime. In police discourses on elopement, sexual safety is equated with confining one's sexuality to marriage with an approved partner.

Accounts of elopement often construct young women and girls as vulnerable and helpless, 'not knowing any better', lured by a boyfriend's false promises. Their sexual agency is all but completely effaced and they are reified as victims, more or less *by virtue of* their sex. This is reinforced by the fact that a minor boy like an adult man can legally be charged with rape of a minor girl, irrespective of her consent. Significantly, however, when a girl's sexual agency *is* acknowledged, it is constructed as deviant and in need of containment. These two discourses are not mutually exclusive, but imbricated, and both enmeshed with notions of responsibility. A significant way in which they are imbricated is through the idea of vulnerability to temptation or transgression, a tendency to 'go out of track', attributed to teenage girls:

> The girls get attracted in a certain [age]. . . . Suppose there are boys living around and they keep looking at her and if they do it ten times, the girl may fall for it once . . . the age group is such, girls can take wrong step and run away from home.
>
> *(Woman beat constable, Parivartan Cell)*

> If from 14 to 20 years she is able to control herself, then she will face no difficulty. Girls tend to go out of track in this age, the rapes are in this age only . . . they do wrong things. If they control themselves from 14 to 18, then these rape cases will be very less.
>
> *(Male constable, Parivartan target area)*

Some girls, comments one woman Sub-Inspector (SI) who has investigated rape cases, 'are such' that they go around freely enjoying sex. This putative susceptibility to transgression is also indicated by the frequent use of the word 'wrong' (*galat*) to characterize teenage girls' behaviour and decisions. However, these 'wrong' attachments, steps and choices are produced partly by the girls' vulnerability, which in turn is produced by their lack of (moral) understanding:

> The girls belonging to the age group of 14 to 16, they don't have the thinking power of what is right or wrong . . . she might go to a boy and there is something between them, physical relation is made but it is wrong.
>
> *(Woman SI, former investigating officer for rape cases, Parivartan target area)*

This makes them particularly vulnerable to compromising their sexual integrity in ways which have devastating consequences. One male constable commented:

> These days it is like this once the boy and girl meet, two or three times they will eat together ... do some wrong things, I saw that a girl and a guy were lying naked, like in compromising condition. ... For a little greed they destroy their lives. And after falling in that they are of nowhere. They don't have anywhere to go.

After 'falling in' to the trap of doing 'some wrong things' with boys, these girls have destroyed their lives and 'are of nowhere', they have 'nowhere to go'. This evocation of space implies that such girls have ruined their marriage prospects and alienated themselves from their natal families. Having compromised their sexual integrity, there is no *space* that they can legitimately inhabit. A woman without a family is 'of nowhere' and can have no legitimate existence. Although framed in part through a discourse of lack of awareness and therefore vulnerability, these accounts underscore the burden of responsibility for managing the risk of violence – and for/through safeguarding their own sexual integrity – which police discourses place upon women and girls. They are held responsible for these 'wrong' attachments, for failing to 'control themselves', for being 'careful' in making their choices 'at the right instant . . . after reconsideration and proper thinking', to quote one male senior police official involved in Parivartan.

Both direct police interventions in (potential) cases of elopement, and aspects of the violence prevention work discussed in the following sections, have the effect of disciplining young people – especially women – to conduct themselves (gender) normatively and in accordance with prevailing sexual mores. This regulatory function exemplifies the exercise of 'disciplinary power' (Foucault 1984, p. 241) through the policing of violence/crime against women in Delhi. Women inspectors/SIs investigating rape complaints, and Parivartan beat constables, described instances of informally advising against and intervening in pre-marital relationships. One SI who had investigated rape cases in a Parivartan area described advising a girl whose parents had brought statutory rape charges against her boyfriend: 'I asked her does she understand the meaning of love and I explained to her that this was wrong for her, for the boy and for everybody.' In another example, a Parivartan beat constable reported the following:

> [A local woman] came that my daughter is going to run away, she is having an affair. I ... explained her. ... She was about to run away any time. But listening to us she stopped ... and now her mother has married her. ... She was 17 years, she would have run away, then again [a] rape case.

In some instances, this involved policing young people's use of public space, and their personal time:

> There was a park, so many couples used to come, we used to make them understand. This is not good. . . . Means just trying to protect against a mishap happening. . . . Some girl might run away with some boy, so we used to ask them how have you come, why have you come. Some . . . used to tell at home that we are going to school and used to sit there. . . . We used to make them understand that this is their age of studying.
>
> *(Woman beat constable, Parivartan Cell)*

Beat constables reported that they helped to settle some cases by arranging for the boy and girl to marry, legitimizing the relationship. Insofar as police discourses posit any *societal* responsibility for addressing violence/crime against women, this is largely expressed through the regulation of girls'/young women's sexual agency. While my research does not measure the 'success' of this regulatory function (in terms of young people's sexual behaviours or adherence to norms), this regulation serves to (violently) reproduce sexual and gender norms in ways that enable the very violences these interventions seek to ameliorate.

## 'Who makes Delhi unsafe? *We* do': safety workshops for schoolgirls

One of Parivartan's interventions was a safety workshop delivered in selected government schools by Swanchetan, an eminent not-for-profit group of psychologists who also worked with the police, providing trauma counselling to victims of violent crime. I observed the workshop and took detailed notes. Information about Parivartan was shared with schoolgirls, including helpline numbers to call in an emergency, to report abuse, and for psychological support. The content of the workshop had a strong focus on empowerment, which the psychologists and workshop leaders interviewed stressed as part of their philosophy. The workshop leader gave practical suggestions about what the girls could do to prevent assaults and protect themselves, most of which were about resisting coercion and/or manipulation. For instance: Don't be scared. If someone tells you not to tell anyone, not to shout, then *do* tell someone, *do* shout. Don't be shy. Don't be polite. If someone asks you for help, tell them to ask someone senior to help them. If someone drags you through the streets and no-one intervenes, shout 'he's not my father' or, 'he's not my brother/uncle'. Raise your voice and protest if someone teases you. If someone gets too close, blow your nose in his face. Remember that attackers may not look ferocious, they look like ordinary people, and they may do things to win your sympathy and/or gratitude, like helping you, or telling you they've lost their pet puppy.

The workshop attempts to challenge gender norms that make girls into compliant victims – feminine submissiveness and shyness, in particular, as well as other norms such as unconditional respect for elders. It seeks to actively empower girls to resist, and to believe they have both the *power* and the *right* to resist. It highlights that attackers are not monstrous or easily identifiable, and equips girls with legal knowledge about certain rights, which can enable them to resist attack by someone posing as a person in authority. The workshop thus implicitly aligns safety with empowerment, resistance and self-determination, and seeks to provide girls with tools to actualize their rights.

Importantly, the messages of the workshop counteract some of the dominant repertoires observable in interviews with police personnel, which tended to both naturalize violence as an inevitable consequence of female bodily and sexual vulnerability, and construct this essentialized vulnerability as a liability when women's and girls' bodies transgress boundaries and are 'out of place', or use public space in inappropriate ways. These belong to a wider set of discourses which place a heavy burden of responsibility on women and girls for managing the liability of their bodies and avoiding, averting and minimizing the risk of violence – including the notion expressed by one woman constable, that women have to 'save their honour',[3] and the concomitant mapping of safety onto sexual integrity. The workshop implicitly challenges the idea that female bodies and their lack of strength and/or anatomical composition make women and girls vulnerable, by proposing that vulnerability is a *transient* state which we *put ourselves into*. Girls make themselves vulnerable by blocking their senses, talking on mobile phones in public, not being vigilant, not setting boundaries, not saying no or telling someone when a boy makes unwanted advances, being shy and polite, not speaking out.

Challenging the inevitability of vulnerability can contribute to denaturalizing violence. The workshop seeks to actively promote girls' agency: to empower girls *not* to be, or think of themselves as, vulnerable. The rights that the workshop promotes include the right to freely and confidently make use of public spaces, and to exercise control over one's own body. However, this framing of rights remains ambivalently tempered by the double-edged burden of *responsibility* for managing violence and its risk, which the workshop reproduces. The safety advice dispensed encumbers adolescent girls with responsibility for anticipating and protecting themselves from attack. Not only does this responsibility deflect attention away from changing and denormalizing the behaviour of men and boys who feel entitled to act in sexually coercive ways towards women and girls across a range of spaces (public transport, the workplace, the home). There is a risk that it can also insidiously reinvigorate woman-blaming discourses. This is not intended by the workshop leaders – but, in the claim that 99 per cent of attacks can be prevented by taking certain steps to keep safe; in the constant refrains, 'What could she have done to prevent it?', 'What did she do wrong?', lies the implication that, if violence can be anticipated and is so eminently preventable (on the part of the victim), you have yourself to blame if you are attacked. We make *ourselves* vulnerable, the workshop leader tells his captive audience. 'Who makes Delhi unsafe?', he asks. 'We do', the girls chorus. This effaces the ways in which Delhi is made unsafe by the atmosphere which implicitly condones 'eve-teasing' (an Indian euphemism for street-level sexual harassment) and by gender norms which make women and girls uncomfortable when vociferously resisting it; by men who think it is normal and feel entitled to harass women and girls.

## 'Like running on one leg': regulating adolescent girls' sexual rights and responsibilities

As with the policing of elopement, a key dimension of Parivartan's sexual violence prevention work is enabling girls not only to resist attack, but to withstand 'temptation' – which invariably means transgressing sexual boundaries by getting inappropriately involved with a boy. This is illustrated by the sexual responsibility lecture delivered to teenage schoolgirls by a United Nations Population Fund consultant, which I was permitted to voice record. Like Swanchetan's safety workshop, it emphasized empowerment, resistance to violence, and challenging gender norms that produce compliance. However, its framing of rights was again ambivalently tempered by the coupling of rights with notions of responsibility, which reproduced the mapping of safety onto sexual integrity so discernible across my data.

The consultant tells the girls that they have a right to information about their bodies, which she is there to provide. Given Abraham's (2004) argument that withholding information is a key way in which families control young Indian women's sexuality, this dissemination of information is potentially empowering. It is significant, however, *which* information she provides – marriage and motherhood as women's natural, biological destiny:

> Nature has made the body of women such that she will get married, and she will become a mother, who gives birth. . . . Why are the hips of women wide? Because in future the girl will become a mother and her body develops in that way, and her body is getting ready for her to become a mother in future, when she will have a foetus in her womb.

A key message distilled in this lecture was that that heterosexual marriage is the only option for the expression of sexual rights. The consultant illustrates the problems attendant upon having a boyfriend through the metaphor of 'running on one leg': getting a boyfriend is trying to access your sexual rights without adhering to your sexual responsibilities. You run on one leg, you fall over. Some sexual rights are specified, including the rights not to be forced to do anything, or touched against one's will – important rights which delegitimize sexual control and violence – and to give birth to a child. The sexual responsibilities continually referenced are less clear, but they are implicitly tied to (gender) normative behaviours. They involve not transgressing norms about which (sexual) relationships are off limits. The consultant constructs this as not succumbing to pressure and, in addition to emphasizing the importance of not succumbing to the social pressure to get a boyfriend, gives the following examples:

> He comes to her home, does homework together and then . . . misbehaves with the girl and molests her, a friend who used to study with her in the same school but he misbehaves today since there was no-one at home. . . . What somebody is thinking . . . you cannot know about it. In most rape cases . . . the rapist is always a known person.
>
> There was a party, friends had pressured [her] to come ... there also she was misbehaved with.

The lecture posits not only having a boyfriend, but associating too freely with boys – studying with a male friend unsupervised – as risky. The longstanding feminist knowledge about rape being perpetrated by known men is mobilized, not in order to disrupt the sanctity of the family, but in order to control the sexuality and freedom of association of adolescent girls: the known person is a friendly boy whom the girl has invited home to study together. Similarly, giving in to the pressure to socialize outside of the family in contexts where there will be unrelated boys is posited as dangerous, and threatens sexual violation.

In another example, the consultant urges the girls not to give in to pressure and allow themselves to be molested by men on crowded public transport,[4] lest someone think they are enjoying it. She encourages to resist and to speak out. Thus, 'pressures' to socialize with boys at a party, or to get a boyfriend, are equated with the 'pressure' of being sexually assaulted in a cramped, crowded space. It is the girls' *responsibility* to protect their sexual integrity, by resisting both temptation *and* violation in all these circumstances, just as it is their right to speak out, name the violence and accuse the attacker: sexual responsibilities are the flipside of sexual rights. The message is that sexually responsible behaviour can protect women from violation. The blurring of the boundaries between consensual (giving in to 'temptation' with a boyfriend) and non-consensual (being assaulted on a bus) sexual encounters illustrates that a loss of sexual integrity is common to both scenarios, which both sexual rights and sexual responsibilities seek to safeguard.

The consultant intended to empower girls. In important ways her lecturing challenges gender norms such as passivity and submissiveness as feminine virtues, and silence due to the shame of sexual violation. However, her message also replicates police discourses/practices that construct safety as sexual integrity and violence/crime against women as (resulting from) sexually improper conduct. In this lecture, the 'sexually responsible' adolescent girl who is empowered and aware of her rights also knows where the proper boundaries of sexual (and social) decorum are, and has the tools at her disposal to resist temptations and pressures to transgress them. In this way she can realize her sexual rights, to self-knowledge, self-determination and motherhood, while – indeed, through – progressing towards her destiny as a (good, chaste) wife and mother. The realization of her sexual rights becomes harmonized with this destiny, while transgression of sexual mores, and weakness in the face of pressure to do so, is the path towards violation and the loss of sexual rights and integrity. This discourse reflects Kannabiran's (2005, p. 28) argument, that the articulation of women's rights in India is only possible within the normative frameworks of heterosexual marriage and kinship.

## Innocence, mishaps and temptations: Parivartan's signature street theatre performances

The intervention for which Parivartan was perhaps most renowned was the lively, free pantomime-style performances staged by social communications organization Jagran in open community spaces, to raise awareness about violence/crime against women. I attended several performances and interviewed Jagran's Managing Director, Arijit. The topic of elopement arose again. Arijit was putting together a new script on elopement, featuring a young man secretly dating a schoolgirl, who is rushed into marrying her by a wily man who promises him a job if he brings the girl to a specified place. The couple is 'saved' from their dangerous naïvety just in time by a do-gooding *chaiwallah*[5] who alerts the girl's parents. The wily man is revealed to be a scheming sex trafficker.

The title is 'Innocence', and Arijit emphasizes that the boy is not predatory, he is just as innocent as the girl: the wily man is the Bad Guy. All the danger and menace of the elopement is displaced onto this character, and *the threat of sexual violation and exploitation he represents.* Arijit did not believe trafficking to be a pervasive issue in the Parivartan target communities.[6] Its narrative function in the proposed script is to dramatize the danger of elopement without demonizing the boyfriend (because if the message is 'anti-men', it won't get through). The trafficking element serves as a tropic encapsulation of the loss of sexual integrity that attends illicit pre-/extra-marital sex.

Arijit was considering depicting the 'recovered' girl's ostracization. I asked if he wanted to challenge the norms that justify this social punishment for her illicit relationship. The point, he replied, is to show that when you are young there are all sorts of *'temptations'. The couple is 'naïve' to put 'value' into their decision, it won't be 'balanced'. The temptation, it seems, is to commit a transgression – to conduct one's sexual life outside of the norms that are supposed to contain and structure it. The narrative goes thus: when you are young you are naïve; vulnerable to the temptation to transgress, but transgression carries consequences – violation, the loss of sexual integrity. It is not the road to freedom. This is a message for young people, but also, Arijit insists, for parents. Young girls are vulnerable to predatory men – but also, implicitly, to *their own curiosity and desire.* Parents are called on to keep these vulnerable girls on the straight and narrow. The effect is to reinscribe the norm of marriage sanctioned by the family as the only legitimate form of sexual relationship, especially for women and girls – despite Arijit's acknowledged ambivalence about these norms.

*Innocence* was a script in progress, which distilled some of the themes surrounding elopement that permeated my data. *Hadsa*, or 'Mishap' – the pantomime about rape that I described in opening this chapter – was widely performed in the Parivartan target areas. Like the safety workshops and sexual responsibility lectures, these performances powerfully communicate the importance of speaking out, in an effort to give women confidence to register complaints or seek assistance from the police. In the closing scene, the rape survivor publicly points the finger at her attacker so that justice can be done. However, the script ambivalently negotiates sensitive issues relating to sexual violence, again reinscribing the home and family as the legitimate space for the realization of gendered sexual rights. Arijit explained that the senior police officer tasked with establishing and overseeing Parivartan had asked him to show that most perpetrators are known to their victims – but they both thought it inappropriate to depict sexual violence by a family member. Instead, the predatory neighbour serves as a sort of proxy. The effect is that *Hadsa*'s rape narrative fails to directly challenge the sanctity of the family. The safety of the home is breached by careless parents, and infiltrated by a dangerous outsider. The pantomime carries a message designed to educate and discipline parents to keep a close watch on their (girl) children (Arijit is explicit about this in his interview) – and reinforces the idea that threats to the safety of women and girls *come from outside (the home). Hadsa* exemplifies how the feminist knowledge that most rapes are perpetrated by known assailants is rarely mobilized to open discussion of abuse and violence *within* families.

Arijit justified the decision to make the perpetrator a neighbour as follows:

> *We, I believe, through this play actually address the lowest common denominator in society. . . . And in appealing to all, we also have to be very careful that we do the play within the prevalent norms of society. We can't come up and say something which is so inflammatory, which will actually go against being persuasive theatre.

Arijit talks explicitly about working with and within prevalent norms *in order (partly) to change them.* This captures the ambivalence of the Parivartan project as a whole – which both reproduces problematic gender (and sexual) norms at the same time as it tries to challenge, dislodge and rework some of them. It brings this ambivalence to the surface and shows how it is, at times, explicitly negotiated.

## Conclusion

Violence against women is an intractable problem for the realization of human rights, and police institutions are both complicit in it, and part of the solution. In addition to calling institutional authorities to account for explicit rights violations, it is important to look at more subtle levels of complicity and how this is unintentionally (re)produced. The way in which police work on violence contributes to regulating people's behaviours and beliefs may partly account for the intractability of gendered and sexual violence despite the efforts invested in its prevention. Police organizations are not monoliths, and in spite of internal contestation, some interesting and creative programmes have been initiated to address violence against women by Delhi Police. This work is not without value; arguably more of it is needed. However, the way in which sexual and gendered rights are discursively constructed and communicated therein matters significantly. Gendered and sexual norms that legitimate and normalize certain violences may be reproduced through work intended to address violence. Police initiatives on violence are embedded in a social context, and analyses should pay careful attention to the delicate work of negotiating prevalent norms in order to loosen and rework them. These findings underscore the importance of gender analysis in accounting for the role of police institutions as upholders of rights, as well as different levels of complicity in their violation.

## Notes

1 Established practices include deploying all-women units to work with women complainants and/or offer informal 'counselling' services to help complainants in domestic violence cases to 'reconcile' with their husbands/families and avoid criminalization. See Dave (2005) and Natarajan (2008).
2 Sections 375–6 of the Indian Penal Code on rape state that a man who has sex with a woman or girl aged under 16 commits rape, regardless of consent. However, there are inconsistencies between different legal provisions, with the *Juvenile Justice Act* fixing the age of consent at 18, and the recent Protection of Children from Sexual Offences Bill (2012) proposing the same. Police participating in this research were not always clear about whether the age of consent was 16 or 18.
3 'Honour' (*izzat*) is an important form of social capital in India; caste, clan, village or family *izzat* can be damaged by certain sexual transgressions by group members, especially women. See Chowdhury (1997), Kakar (1996) and Das (1993 [1976]).

4 Delhi's public buses are notorious for the high incidence of sexual harassment and assault against women and girls.
5 A tea-seller – someone in a position to accidentally eavesdrop on conversations.
6 I do not have data to confirm or contest the empirical accuracy of his claims about this, including that girls are trafficked *into* Delhi's red light district from Nepal and Bihar, except insofar as trafficking was not considered to be a key issue for intervention in any of my other interviews with Parivartan police staff, with the exception of isolated cases.

## References


Abraham, L., 2004. Redrawing the *Lakshman Rekha*: gender differences and cultural constructions in youth sexuality in urban India. *In*: Sanjay Srivastava (ed.), *Sexual sites, seminal attitudes: sexualities, masculinities and culture in South Asia*. New Delhi, Thousand Oaks, London: Sage, 209–41.

Adelman, M., Erez, E. and Shaloub-Kevorkian, N., 2003. Policing violence against minority women in multicultural societies: 'community' and the politics of exclusion. *Police and Society*, 7, 105–33.

Baxi, P., 2005. The medicalisation of consent and falsity: the figure of the *habitué* in Indian rape law. *In*: Kalpana Kannabiran (ed.), *The violence of normal times*. New Delhi: Women Unlimited/Kali for Women, 266–311.

Brown, W., 2000. Suffering rights as paradoxes. *Constellations*, 7(2), 208–29.

Chowdhury, P., 1997. Enforcing cultural codes: gender and violence in Northern India. *Economic and Political Weekly*, 10 May, 1019–28.

Das, V., 1993 [1976]. Masks and faces: an essay on Punjabi kinship. *In*: Patricia Uberoi (ed.), *Family, kinship and marriage in India*. New Delhi: Oxford University Press, 198–224.

Das, V., 1996. Sexual violence, discursive formations and the state. *Economic and Political Weekly*, September, 2411–22.

Dave, A., 2005. Feminist social work intervention: special cells for women and children. *In*: Kalpana Kannabiran (ed.), *The violence of normal times: essays on women's lived realities*. New Delhi: Women Unlimited/Kali for Women, 172–96.

Delhi Police, n.d. *Parivartan: a campaign for the safety of women in Delhi – the problem and the approach*. Retrieved on 18 October 2012 from: www.delhipolice.nic.in/parivartan/parivartan.htm.

Fielding, N., 1994. Cop canteen culture. *In*: Tim Newburn and Elizabeth A. Stanko (eds), *Just boys doing business? Men, masculinities and crime*. London and New York: Routledge, 46–63.

Foucault, M., 1984. *The Foucault reader*, P. Rabinow (ed.). New York, NY: Pantheon.

Gangoli, G., 2007. *Indian feminisms: law, patriarchies and violence in India*. Aldershot: Ashgate.

Grewal, I., 2005. *Transnational America: feminisms, diasporas, neoliberalisms*. Durham, NC: Duke University Press.

Jordan, J., 2002. Will any woman do?: Police, gender and rape victims. *Policing: An International Journal of Police Strategies & Management*, 25(2), 319–44.

Kakar, S., 1996. *Indian identity: three studies in psychology*. New Delhi: Penguin.

Kannabiran, K. (ed.), 2005. *The violence of normal times: essays on women's lived realities*. New Delhi: Women Unlimited/Kali for Women.

Kelly, L., 2005. Inside outsiders: mainstreaming violence against women into human rights discourse and practice. *International Feminist Journal of Politics*, 7(4), 471–95.

Macaulay, F., 2000. Tackling violence against women in Brazil: converting international principles into effective local policy. *In*: Susie Jacobs, Ruth Jacobson and Jennifer Marchbank (eds), *States of conflict: gender, violence and resistance*. London and New York: Zed Books, 144–61.

Marhia, N., 2013. *Everyday (in)security/(re)securing the everyday: gender, policing and violence against women in Delhi*. PhD thesis, London School of Economics.

Martin, S. and Jurik, N., 1996. *Doing justice, doing gender: women in law and criminal justice occupations*. Thousand Oaks, CA, London, New Delhi: Sage.

Menon, N., 2004. *Recovering subversion: feminist politics beyond the law*. Urbana, IL: Permanent Black/University of Illinois Press.

Messerschmidt, J., 1993. *Masculinities and crime: critique and reconceptualization of theory*. Lanham, MD: Rowman and Littlefield Publishers.

Natarajan, M., 2008. *Women police in a changing society: back door to equality*. Aldershot, Burlington, VT: Ashgate.

Prokos, A. and Padavic, I., 2002. 'There oughtta be a law against bitches': masculinity lessons in police academy training. *Gender, Work and Organization*, 9(4), (August), 439–59.

Santos, C., 2005. *Women's police stations: gender, violence and justice in São Paulo, Brazil.* New York and Basingstoke: Palgrave Macmillan.

Silvestri, M., 2003. *Women in charge: policing, gender and leadership.* Cullompton; Portland, OR: Willan Publishing.

Singh, K., 2004. Violence against women and the Indian law. *In*: Savitri Goonesekere (ed.), *Violence, law and women's rights in South Asia.* New Delhi: Sage, 77–147.

Youngs, G., 2003. Private pain/public peace: women's rights as human rights and Amnesty International's report on violence against women. *Signs: Journal of Women in Culture and Society*, 28(4), 1209–29.

# 36

# Human rights and policing in South Africa as a matter of in/exclusion

*Julia Hornberger*

## Introduction

It was on 16 August 2015 that I started writing this chapter. This was three years to the day after the Marikana massacre and only a few months after the report of the Commission of Inquiry into the massacre had finally been released. The Marikana massacre was an ill-conceived attempt, gone badly wrong, by the South African Police Service (SAPS) to dissolve an illegal strike of Lonmin Platinum miners demanding higher wages. The attempt to disperse the crowd resulted in 36 people being shot dead by the police. What transpires from the report, even though in a rather muted form, is that what is at stake here is a classic concern about political and civil rights being violated and people not being protected enough from the actions of the state. In the case of Marikana the infringement of rights took two forms: the first is the use of disproportionately lethal force by the police; the second is political interference that pushed the police to act in the interest of the employers (who had the ear of the government) instead of reinforcing the need to resolve the strike through negotiations (Marikana Commission of Inquiry 2015). In many ways this allows one to draw a direct line between current and apartheid times. During apartheid rule the state interest representing the white minority also superseded the respect for black people's lives. Crowd control measures were also utterly deficient, and crude force was used indiscriminately against groups whose actions were delegitimized as irrational and criminal. It seems therefore that once again and maybe even more than ever a focus on civil and political rights, to curb the powers of the police, should be at the centre of any debate regarding policing and human rights in South Africa. The only difference is that political and civil rights are enshrined now in the country's Constitution.

However, this claim that today simply mirrors the past overlooks the fact that South Africa in the meantime has undergone a particular kind of process regarding human rights and policing, and has widened the democratic responsibility of police officers. It also overlooks the fact that, when we move away from dramatic stand-offs between police and people during public gatherings into the nitty-gritty encounters between police and people in their homes around cases of everyday crime, a much messier picture emerges. While it remains a fact that those who are the poorest, and who have the least means to protect themselves – be it through status and social networks, or more materially, through a safe and protective home and workplace or private security – are also most likely to be the victims of police abuse. At the same time, however, based on many years of fieldwork, beginning in 2000, with the SAPS in Johannesburg, it has become clear to me that it is exactly these people, exactly because they have nothing else to draw on, who draw on police intervention as a way to protect themselves in often intimate but violent local conflicts.

It is important to consider that this role of the police – actively intervening in the private sphere and in socially intimate conflicts – was clearly part of the message that was impressed upon police officers by the human rights training that police received during the early transformation period. In addition, through a range of legislative changes, such as the *Domestic Violence Act 1998*, the *Children's Act 2005* and the amendments made in the light of Chapter Two (Bill of Rights) of the South African Constitution, police officers have not only been encouraged but actually legally tasked with increasingly looking after the disadvantaged and the weak in society, and protecting people against each other. Such horizontal human rights concerns, where the relationship amongst people is at stake, rather than that between state and people, have considerably increased the responsibility of police officers. And even though, many years into the new South Africa the discourse of human rights has lost much of its original imperative force, what remains are the legal and habitual traces of this development. It has redefined the possibilities of a practice of policing which potentially produces inclusion and at least complements the form of policing which victimizes and results in exclusion. How the two go together, how they are being played out against each other, and how they produce their own social forms as they constantly articulate with each other in this contradictory manner, especially at the margins of society, will be discussed through some of my own ethnographic work towards the end of this chapter.

First however, I will go back to the early 1990s, to look at how police officers were tasked with realizing the rights of the disadvantaged and vulnerable; in other words how the police were put in charge of protecting democracy rather than being a threat to it. With this I hope to throw some light on the inclusionary practices of the police, which is, I suppose, the less well-known story about human rights and policing. This history and its trajectory also connect South Africa in interesting ways to politics and policies about policing more globally.

## Bringing about democracy: the power to include

The transformation of the South African police coincided with the hegemonic politics of the time – what was then called 'the end of history' (Fukuyama 1992). A confidence reigned widely that across the world a liberal, human rights respecting, free-market democracy had become the one and only politically acceptable model. This was a short-lived period, as a new anti-Islamist security paradigm would soon take over geopolitics. With this it again became more expedient and acceptable to disregard civil and political rights within even those states that always claimed to be at the forefront of democratic practice. Still, the 'end of history' period – in which it seemed that all countries previously run by military dictators or other autocratic regimes turned towards democracy – created the temporary illusion that protection against the state was no longer necessary. Instead the focus shifted towards humanitarianism and how people's positive rights could be realized. This included the mainstreaming of social and economic rights within human rights discourse (Koch 2009). At the same time, the main worry was with conflicts internal to states, especially inter-ethnic conflicts on the one hand, and gender inequality on the other. It is in this context also that police organizations were increasingly perceived more as a crucial partner for dealing with these internal issues and positive rights, rather than a dangerous power that had to be reined in and disciplined at every end. Even an organization like Amnesty International (AI), whose reputation was built on opposition to unjust criminal justice institutions, such as police and prisons, radically changed its position. AI considered it suddenly acceptable, if not pressing, to hire a special staff member who would be in charge of dealing with the police from within, liaising and partnering with police around how police could help to protect people better (Hornberger 2011).

South Africa, with its progressive and visionary constitutional writing process, was a beacon of this development. It made sure that social and economic rights would be judiciable – meaning enforceable instead of just an aspiration. And with the dignity of the person at the centre of its Bill of Rights, it made sure that all kind of provisions for protecting women, children, the disabled, and cultural difference were being made in legally substantial ways.

It was within the climate of this particular post-Cold War human rights common sense that the South African police had to legitimize themselves – to regain the confidence of the South African population, but also of the new African National Congress (ANC) government, which was utterly suspicious of its role and its staff. The police did so through a language of community policing, crime prevention, and the advancement of human rights. They willingly submitted themselves to a partly internally driven and partly externally imposed project of human rights training, assisted in the setting up of community police forums, sent police officers on special training regarding the handling of domestic violence cases and other cases which involved minors, and adjusted some of their internal standing orders. They also got rid of their military ranks, called themselves a service, changed their insignias and symbols, and applied affirmative action criteria to their promotion policies.

The human rights training which police officers received between 1998 and 2003 had been set up with the help of a few local officials and every possible significant international human rights institution (non-government organizations, government organizations, intergovernmental organizations). It literally presented the cutting edge of police human rights training at the time. People working on it became international experts who consequently toured many of the other democratizing countries (for example, Indonesia, Russia and Brazil) to lend their newly gained experience to similar processes elsewhere. Through this the particular human rights common sense was complimented by a globally shared toolkit for translating such standards into policing practice. At the centre of promoting transformed police action stood the image of the child as helpless victim which had to be protected proactively by a socially conscious and empathetic police officer (Cronje and Venter 2000) – in other words a police officer with ample discretion which would be guided by a strict human rights ethos.

The impact of human rights training in modelling police behaviour is of course limited. Workshops often form fleeting experiences. They are more like bubbles of momentary agreement, producing insights that get crushed quickly by realities that contradict even the most basic assumptions of such training – bringing the whole structure tumbling down. For example, to stay with the image of the child, rarely are children just hapless victims. Street children, for example, clearly display a survivalist agency which for police officers can appear aggressive and bring out their defensive rather than mothering side. The same is true for questions of domestic violence. Here the histories of victimizations are not just a question of violent abusive relationships between husband and wife. Instead there exists an entire social context that combines male disempowerment with deeply ingrained, unequal gender identities which not only condone but also promote violent masculinities. All these experiences complicate an intervention on behalf of the victim (Hornberger 2011).

Also, human rights policing requires a set of skills from police officers which they do not always have available. Certain writing, communication and legal skills are contingent on a middle class education, while many police officers come from working class backgrounds. This makes them fail and feel misplaced in the light of an increased formalized accountability, involving judicial paperwork, and the role of non-violent verbal mediation. For others however, who bemoan the low status within society of the job of the police officer, a vernacular or improvised version of human rights policing promises to polish up the image of the police officer and to make it more akin to other, well respected, legal professions (Hornberger 2011).

Still, it is as part of a plethora of various measures amounting to a comprehensive 'discursive grit' (Dreyfus et al. 1983) that the human rights training had some impact. In this 'grit' the training was further joined on the one hand by the change of certain laws and on the other hand by a much more amorphous but broadly present popular human rights lingo, pervading all kinds of social and political institutions. Together this created a certain impetus for a more forthcoming, protective kind of policing that focused on the conflictual relationships *among* people who share the same social if not private space.

One could argue that this is effectively represented by the statistical drop in the high rate of murders (Gosh 2011). Many murders took place exactly in the intimate and social spaces, like local taverns, which previously, during apartheid, were no-go zones for police interventions, at least unless they were sent out to confiscate beer and close down establishments. People would get drunk and rowdy, and conflicts would quickly escalate with no one to intervene. Within the new climate police would be more compelled to go into these spaces and disperse a nasty fight before it could turn really ugly.

## Fighting crime and dissent: the power to exclude

But the seemingly omnipresent human rights common sense did not last forever. It soon lost some of its morally and politically imperative force. Once the new ANC government had taken full control of the institution that they had inherited from the previous regime the goal posts for transforming the police quickly shifted. When their own cadres had been installed in leadership positions, and political rapport between the government and its ministers and the police management had been established, the role of human rights as a means to rein in and discipline an otherwise relatively autonomous institution became less important.

Instead, with the sense of a crime wave sweeping through the country, an acceptance of – if not a popular demand for – a 'tough on crime' policing took shape. As anywhere in the world, this flattened out the concern for protection from too much state intrusion in favour of an unconstrained and trenchant police intervention – be it in the form of comprehensive surveillance or persuasive and forceful handling of criminals. For example, in order to strengthen police officers' resolve to intervene fearlessly in crime scenes, their discretion to use lethal force was considerably widened. This happened through amending a law, which had just been amended in order to exactly set the bar to use lethal force as high as possible. Such toning down of human rights standards, and regression towards what seemed familiar from apartheid times, also happened with the reintroduction of military ranks. Military ranks had been abandoned in favour of civilian ranking in the immediate post-apartheid period, just to be reintroduced at a later stage. Thus, what was once a General, but had become a Commissioner, was once again a General (Hornberger 2013).

Also, some restructuring of the organization was carried through to meet the need for crime fighting. On the one hand, heavily armed tactical crime fighting units were introduced to intercept organized crime and aggravated robberies such as cash-in-transit heists. On the other hand, other units, such as a substantial part of the Public Order Policing Unit, were being dissolved and their manpower redistributed to boost station-level capacity (Omar 2007). Yet the methods that were used to counter the 'crime wave' were other than intelligence and investigation. In fact, it was during this time that it became known that detective units were in a pitiful state as most resources had gone towards crime control units (Altbeker 1998). The main modus operandi was one of great public performance (Comaroff and Comaroff 2004) and especially stopping (black) people from moving around freely. The roadblock was the ultimate manifestation of this practice. Creating huge traffic backlogs, the actions of the police could not fail to be noticed by large numbers of people on their way from and back to work. Roadblocks also make very clear who is suspicious within society, meaning who is pulled out and searched, and who is waved on. In a similar vein, raids of entire neighbourhoods and street patrols would take place, where the police stopped and searched those people and their homes who they thought would be out of place. Steinberg (2012, p. 358), drawing inspiration from Landau (2006), argues that 'concepts such as targeted patrolling and policing for risk factors issue in the idea that public space is too full, that people, especially young men, are moving around too freely, that security resides in the never finished job of sweeping the streets'. Cities, here, with their mobile population were then by definition infinite spaces contagious with crime.

In the long run, the move to reconstruct the police organization to fight crime, would have some disastrous consequences of another kind as well. It added to the fact that the police were not just experienced as failing but progressively as a threat to society once again. At the time of the anti-crime restructuring the police management naïvely believed that questions of protest and the disruption of public order were no longer a problem in a democratic South Africa. However, just a few years later the first so-called service-delivery protests erupted. These were protests by communities that increasingly felt dissatisfied that the promises of a 'better life for all', the ANC's election slogan, were not materializing. The protests were also symptomatic of a very uneven development where some communities were provided with new amenities like water and houses, while others, which had failed to build up the right patrimonial relationships, were excluded from such developments. The protests were thus reflective of increasingly sectarian interests playing themselves out at local level (von Holdt et al. 2011).

During these conflicts the police were often called in by local authorities and would inevitably side with them against the protesters. At the same time, violence, from damage to property to physical threats against people, became one of the desperate means for protesters to attract attention and to be heard (von Holdt et al. 2011). Again, the police's first impulse would be to see this as a gross disturbance if not even as disrespect for their authority. They would respond to it with often the same unhinged means as the protesters, aiming to suppress but ultimately escalating the violence (Hornberger 2014). As this wave of protest grew across the country, the police management realized that it (no longer) had the skills nor the manpower to deal with so many dispersed protests at the same time. Often then, to fill the void, tactical crime fighting units and their war-like methods were re-employed. This is exactly what happened at Marikana, the massacre described in the beginning of this text, where an illegal strike was handled by sharp shooting units lacking experience in crowd management and de-escalating, crowd-dispersing strategies (Bruce 2012). On top of that, as two police officers had been killed brutally by the protesters in a violent clash on a previous day, police officers are suspected to have been beset with a desire for revenge that drove them to deal with the protesters in the style of gang war and summary execution.

Some people have argued that the disastrous restructuring of the SAPS was not even caused by short sightedness or by a naïve misreading of the political landscape, but in contrast, by conscious calculation. The suggestion here is that the existing Public Order Police had to be dissolved as they were too much of a soft tool. And indeed, the Public Order Police Unit had been probably the most retrained unit in the immediate post-apartheid period. Besides the basic human rights training, they had also received training from Belgian specialists in the broad range of techniques of de-escalating crowd control. Most important, these training efforts were supported by the respective police unions and therefore had a broad legitimacy among the officers. This gives the training intervention a much better chance to be absorbed and applied by its trainees (Marks 2005). But, as the allegation goes, such conciliatory policing would be useless in the suppression of serious political dissent, and so a more militarized unit would be required. From this perspective, a tactical crime unit filling the gap of public order policing is not a desperate deed but a calculated move to strengthen what Jonny Steinberg (2014), following Brodeur (1983), calls 'high policing'. What is at stake here, according to Steinberg, is that in contemporary South Africa the political order is threatened or challenged not by the dissent of an opposition party but by dissent within the ruling power. High policing as a form of political policing is directed at reining in those recalcitrant forces that mobilize the poor in their interests.

To assess if such conspiratorial assessments of the situation are accurate or maybe overestimate the strategic capacity of police management is unfortunately beyond the reach of this chapter. What should, however, be clear at this point is that the disciplining and restraining grip that human rights instruments in their immediate and more popular form had on policing originally, in the early transformation period, has increasingly been loosened. There is also a clear closing of ranks within the police, and transparency and accountability is becoming a question of political loyalty rather than popular legitimacy.

## With nothing to protect them from the police: reinforcing exclusion

Together, this development and its trickle-down effects in everyday policing and patrolling methods have driven a mode of policing which is hugely victimizing to those who have little else to protect them. The level to which young black men are targeted in roadblocks, and appear in arrest statistics for petty crimes such as loitering, drinking in public, dealing in fake DVDs and possession of marijuana, etc., is disproportional. So is the number of illegal immigrants, who though they have in the first instance not committed any other crime than not carrying the right papers and being of the wrong country, are being labelled and treated as major criminals. The recent 'Operation Fiela' – meaning Operation Clean Sweep – is a good example of how such targeting is systematically ordered (Nicolson 2015). It receives support as a way of 'purifying the nation'.

But even in a much more dispersed way such policing producing exclusion is deeply ingrained. This became clear already in my fieldwork with the SAPS Sophiatown branch in Johannesburg in 2000–1. The police officers of Sophiatown would regularly go out on night raids. The Sophiatown policing district covers a range of socioeconomically diverse neighbourhoods, from upper-class mansions to squatter camps. One of these neighbourhoods, Westbury, is an old working-class suburb which during apartheid, under the *Group Areas Act 1950*, was 'reserved' for people classified under apartheid law as 'Coloured' (meaning mixed-race). With the end of apartheid it became much more racially diverse, but still with the common denominator of being a very poor area. Close social relations often played out as both claustrophobic and violent, and yet as inescapable. Many of the police raids were particularly targeted at Westbury. Police officers on these raids normally followed a list of addresses where suspects were suspected to reside. However, as the news that the police were out for a raid travelled faster than the police could drive their cars, the chances that police officers would stumble on one of these suspects still in his sleep was slim. This put a downer on the already strenuous night shift, and potentially confronted police officers with the futility of their work. Smaller fish, like a young man smoking a joint at the back of a house police had raided, thus had to serve as substitutes for crime fighting. Without warning, police officers would pounce upon such a figure and rough him up. Then they would threaten arresting him for dealing in drugs. They would throw him in the back of the police van and drive him around over bumpy roads for a few hours. They would then release him in the middle of nowhere, since, in the end, they did not really want to deal with the paperwork that a 'real' arrest would require.

One day a police officer I was working with complained about working in one of the rich neighbourhoods. His comments brought home to me the sense, both materially and in a symbolically significant way, that the primary targets for policing were always those whose lives were already most exposed and most precarious. He was saying how terribly frustrating it was to work in these rich areas where there was no chance to get over the often two-to-three metre high walls that sheltered the well-offs and their homes. Barking dogs, electric fences and alarm systems added to the impossibility of ever simply pouncing on someone in these areas. Instead police officers had to humbly ring the doorbell and hope that somebody would open for them. The arrogance with which they were often treated by people who were much better educated than they were, and who anyway did not rely on the police but on private security for their protection, added to the humiliation. Meanwhile in Westbury the walls were low, if at all existent: just high enough to turn the jump across into a bit of a performance, but ultimately completely surmountable. And if it was not walls there were always still the doors, which could simply be kicked in. This was common practice, to the extent that police officers' reputations were built on the number of times they had ran down a door. People already knew the sound of a ramming shoulder, in the case of the most hard-boiled police officer, or another sturdy device against the door. They quickly opened it up to prevent having to replace the door afterwards. The only time police officers were deterred was when they saw people praying. But otherwise nothing would stop them. The image of innocent people just being pulled out of bed in the middle of the night was one of the strongest and most painful impressions of my work with the police. Police officers would smash through people's houses, walking over the mattresses which had been laid out in the living rooms because there were too few bedrooms, while people tried to disguise their dishevelled hair, their eyes still half closed, with children crying, dressed in flimsy clothes and hanging on to their mothers' legs. It was after all an image of complete exposure and vulnerability; nothing protected them from such intrusion and harassment in the name of crime fighting. If they would mention just the word human rights, the situation would only aggravate and police officers would use the occasion to put people even more so into their place.

## Making due: desire for the police

One would think that if this were the overwhelming reality, then people would have very little reason to still approach the police. And indeed the growth of the private security industry is a clear indicator that people expect nothing good to come from police. Yet, it is often exactly those who do not have the means to build up or hire their own private security – the fact that made them so vulnerable to the police in the first place – who actually express a strong desire for police presence in their lives. It is in realms that are bare of other sources for security and care that people involve the police in the most intimate conflicts. How else could one understand that police stations are a commonplace for extremely desperate women to abandon their babies at the doorstep. Here the police station is still the primary point of reference for the potential of some form of (state) care and protective (state) intervention. A South African police officer once told me: 'We are probably the only thing in this country which is for free. When you go to a shop, when you call an ambulance, when you want your passport renewed, you have to pay. But calling the police is for free. And so people call us with whatever there is wrong in their lives, from disciplining their children to fixing a running tap.' While this was said grudgingly, it still confirmed the sense that, despite everything, people very regularly reach out to the police as an immediate and attainable source of help.

More systematically, this is how, for example, as I have seen in my fieldwork, the *Domestic Violence Act 1998* has been taken up. The Act, which was introduced in 1998, put increased pressure on the police to intervene in domestic conflicts. People in the area of Westbury often invoked the Act when there was conflict within the familial realm, not just between partners such as husband and wife, but also for example among members of the extended family or neighbours. Often the police would arrive when the fight was still ongoing, and would take into custody the one who seemed to be the aggressor. But as the heat of the moment would cool down and the immediate threat would reside, a wife, for example, would caringly bring a jacket for the arrested husband so he would not suffer from cold in the police cells overnight. She then would come to the police station first thing in the morning, not so much to give a statement as to plead with the police officer who was now in charge of the case to allow her to withdraw the case and let her husband go. It became clear that she just wanted the police to momentarily help her manage the violence of her relationship, but not fundamentally change it by permanently removing her husband. All she wanted was *their – the police's – violence* to silence and suppress *her husband's violence*. A legal case, a formal working of the law, seemed futile in the light of wider social relations which would probably shame her for 'doing this to her husband' and the prospect of having to provide for the family alone. But she might have also feared being stripped of her husband's violence which, when not directed at her, was also what protected her. As much as police violence was a two-edged sword, so was her husband's. Here then, policing is made momentarily useful and desirable as it is remade into a familial force mirroring the means of conflict-resolution locally, in which physical violence had a high currency (Hornberger 2009).

Another incident during my fieldwork showed a similar pattern with regards to migrants living in the inner city of Johannesburg. Here a police officer interacted with some migrants from Bangladesh who were constantly harassed by other traders or even by city police when selling their goods on the street. He was quite enamoured with human rights as he was tired of the low status that police officers had in the public eye, and fancied himself to be rather like a human rights lawyer. But his efforts to put human rights into practice in a formal way were badly frustrated when the migrants he wanted to help refused to go to court. Instead, they rather sought out his personal friendship so they could call on him if they got into trouble with other forceful local actors using violence and upsetting their informal trade in the city. He had given them his personal mobile phone number in order to win their trust. But instead of following him in opening up a legal case, they called him to establish a tight network of give-and-take around him. They cherished the number as a practical means as well as a token of their connection. They wooed him by offering him food, presents, and a share in their network of traders across the country. Through this they made clear that social capital was the mode through which they were organizing their lives in the interstices of legal existence in the country; and that they saw him as a source of further social capital – a very powerful one, since he was of the state, with access to state violence and authority. Again, the connection here between people and police was built through a mode of personalizing the relationship and drawing the police into a local way of conducting affairs (Hornberger 2011). Through this, people express a strong desire for the means of the police. However they were only able to harbour these means when the exclusionary and victimizing forms of policing were transformed into a local mode over which they had some measure of control.

## Conclusion

What is at play is not a denial of the reality of a violent and exclusionary police, but a renegotiation, a making-do with a reality where the horizon of a truly public police has never been experienced and where it is hard to imagine it ever to occur. What people express then, through these actions, is that if they can make some of this violence not so much work against them but rather for them, then exclusionary policing, as they experience it every day, might actually be quite an effective policing. It is in this way that the inclusionary tendencies of the police have been taken up despite a constant experience of exclusion. The insidiousness of this is that such practice is both a critique of how things are – meaning that people make clear that they cannot just interact with the police as if they were the means for justice to be delivered – but also a confirmation if not a complicity with the exclusionary practices of the police, basically saying that the police can work for us in the same way they can work against us. In other words, people who have nothing to protect them will use the inclusionary imperatives of the police – which have particularly been brought about through the policies of the early transformation period, and which reflect global efforts to transform police institutions through horizontal human rights concerns – but by doing so they will seek a form of policing which mainly impresses not through its formal constraint but rather by its unhinged rawness.

## References


Altbeker, A., 1998. *Solving crime: the state of the SAPS Detective Service*. Vol. 31. ISS Monograph Series. Pretoria: Institute for Security Studies.

Brodeur, J.-P., 1983. High policing and low policing: remarks about the policing of political activities. *Social Problems*, 30(5), 507–20.

Bruce, D., 2012. Marikana: disastrous crowd control led to mayhem. *M&G*, 24 August. Retrieved on 8 April 2016 from: http://mg.co.za/print/2012-08-24-00-marikana-disastrous-crowd-control-led-to-mayhem.

Comaroff, J. and Comaroff, J.L., 2004. Criminal obsessions, after Foucault: postcoloniality, policing and the metaphysics of disorder. *Critical Inquiry*, 30(4), 800–24.

Cronje, P. and Venter, E., 2000. *Human rights and policing: presenters guide for law enforcement officials*. Pretoria: South African Police Service.

Dreyfus, H.L., Rabinow, P. and Foucault, M., 1983. *Michel Foucault: beyond structuralism and hermeneutics*. Chicago, IL: University of Chicago Press.

Fukuyama, F., 1992. *The end of history and the last man*. New York, NY: Free Press.

Gosh, P., 2011. South Africa: murder rate high, but dropping. *International Business Times*. Retrieved on 11 January 2016 from: http://www.ibtimes.com/south-africa-murder-rate-high-dropping-212280.

Hornberger, J., 2009. 'Ma-Slaan-Pa Dockets': negotiations at the boundary between the private and the public. *In*: G. Blundo and Pierre-Yves Le Meur (eds), *Governance of daily life in Africa*. Leiden: Brill Press, 171–204.

Hornberger, J., 2011. *Policing and human rights: the meaning of violence and justice in everyday policing in Johannesburg*. Law, Development and Globalization. London: Routledge.

Hornberger, J., 2013. From general to commissioner to general: on the popular state of policing in South Africa. *Law and Social Inquiry*, 38(3), 598–614.

Hornberger, J., 2014. We need a complicit police! Political policing then and now. *SA Crime Quarterly*, 48(June).

Koch, I.E., 2009. *Human rights as indivisible rights: the protection of socio-economic demands under the European Convention on Human Rights*. Leiden, Netherlands: Martinus Nijhoff Publishers.

Landau, L., 2006. Immigration and the state of exception: security and sovereignty in East and Southern African. *Millennium: Journal of International Studies*, 34, 325–480.

Marikana Commission of Inquiry, 2015. *Report on matters of public, national and international concern arising out of the tragic incidents at the Lonmin Mine in Marikana, in the North West Province. GG 38978, GeN 699.* Republic of South Africa: Department of Justice and Constitutional Development 10 July.

Marks, M., 2005. *Transforming the robocops: changing police in South Africa.* Scottsville: University of Kwa Zulu-Natal Press.

Nicolson, G., 2015. Operation Fiela: thousands of arrests, doubtful impact. *Daily Maverick*, 8 September. Retrieved on 8 April 2016 from: www.dailymaverick.co.za/article/2015-09-08-operation-fiela-thousands-of-arrests-doubtful-impact/#.Ve61rbc0Fo6.

Omar, B., 2007. *SAPS's costly restructuring: a review of public order policing capacity.* Vol. 138. ISS Monograph Series. Pretoria: Institute for Security Studies.

Steinberg, J., 2012. Security and disappointment: policing, freedom and xenophobia in South Africa. *British Journal of Criminology*, 52, 345–60.

Steinberg, J., 2014. Policing, state power, and the transition from apartheid to democracy: a new perspective. *African Affairs*, 113(451), 173–91.

von Holdt, K., Langa, M., Molapo, S., Mogapi, N., Ngubeni, K., Dlamini, J. and Kirsten, A., 2011. *The smoke that calls: insurgent citizenship, collective violence and the struggle for a place in the New South Africa.* CSVR and SWOP. Retrieved on 8 April 2016 from: www.csvr.org.za/docs/thesmokethatcalls.pdf.

## *Legislation*

*South Africa, Republic of (RSA) (1950) Group Areas Act.*

*South Africa, Republic of (RSA) (1998) Domestic Violence Act.*

*South Africa, Republic of (RSA) (2005) Children's Act.*

# 37

# Human rights and pluralization of policing

*Mutuma Ruteere, Clifford Shearing and Philip Stenning*

## Introduction

Calls for governments and government agencies to be 'human rights compliant' have a long history, and since they were established in Britain in the nineteenth century, the 'new police' (what we now call 'public police') have been in the sights of rights activists. What is understood by the term 'human rights', however, has evolved substantially in recent decades, and so is what is understood by the term 'policing'. Most specifically, in the latter case, the term 'policing' has come to be understood as not just what the public police do, but as a social and political function that is performed by a growing array of state and non-state providers. In this chapter, we explore the implications of human rights for the governance and accountability of policing in an increasingly pluralized policing environment, domestically, internationally and transnationally.

Our objective in this chapter is to give an account of the current 'state of play' on this topic. Given its features, however, a more critical discussion of this topic will be needed, exploring in more detail the important connections between the realities of human rights protection, neoliberalism politics, and the pluralization of policing, in the twenty-first century. That, however, will be a discussion for another time. The chapter begins with a brief review of recent developments in understandings of conceptions of 'human rights' and 'policing', including the proliferation and diversity of policing providers in the late twentieth and early twenty-first centuries. We then consider the history of calls for 'human rights compliant' policing, and how the emergence of 'plural policing' has necessitated a rethinking of what 'human rights compliant policing' means and requires, in terms of re-theorizing and reforming the governance of policing. We end by reviewing some of the recent initiatives that have been taken, or just proposed, to achieve this necessary re-theorizing and reform, and consider what is still needed to achieve a genuine human-rights-compliant policing in the twenty-first century.

## From 'natural law rights' to 'universal human rights'

Over a period of approximately 300 years, from the mid-seventeenth to the mid-twentieth centuries, the concept of human rights progressively expanded from a limited conception of natural law rights propounded particularly by Hugo Grotius (1583–1645), to a very broad listing of human rights in the *Universal Declaration of Human Rights* promulgated by the newly established United Nations (UN) General Assembly in 1948, and various subsequent more specific international covenants derived from it, that were promulgated during the1960s. In modern times, therefore, the concept of human rights embraces a wide range of civil and political rights, as well as social, economic and cultural rights (including rights such as the right to an education, the right to privacy, and freedom from human trafficking). These developments are discussed in other chapters of this handbook, so we do not need to rehearse them here. For the purposes of this chapter, it is sufficient to note that, as Steven Lukes has argued, this expansive conception of human rights is now 'accepted virtually everywhere' and 'virtually no one actually *rejects* the principle of defending human rights' (Lukes 1993, p. 20). It is this conception of universal human rights that has underpinned modern advocacy of 'human rights compliant policing'.

## Policing: from civil policing, to state policing, to 'plural' policing – shifts in the governance of security

The approximately 200 years since the establishment of modern public police services, has similarly witnessed radical changes in understandings of what 'policing' involves and who provides it. These developments have been well documented in recent policing literature (for overviews, see, for example, Jones and Newburn 2006, Abrahamsen and Williams 2011, Stenning and Shearing 2012), so we do not need to describe them in detail here. Most importantly for this chapter, in the latter half of the twentieth century academic interest in 'policing' began to focus on two key developments in policing provision – pluralization and globalization. This broadened focus began with research on the burgeoning post-World War 2 policing and security provision by the private sector, which began to be recognized as performing policing functions that are strikingly similar to those of the public police, but without the same legal authorization or government oversight (Stenning and Shearing 2012, Stenning 2000). It also became apparent that as a direct result of economic globalization during the last decades of the twentieth century, policing provision by the private sector was becoming increasingly transnational in ways and to an extent that could not be matched by more traditional state-sponsored police organizations. Abrahamsen and Williams (2009, p. 3), however, have argued more recently that this global 'security privatization' has not been primarily about the 'transfer of previously public functions to private actors', but reflects 'important developments in the relationship between security and the sovereign state, structures of political power and authority, and the operations of global capital'.

In addition to more formal private sector providers, policing is now provided and authorized by other actors some of whom do not enjoy the legitimacy that public police are assumed to have in the nation state. Bruce Baker, for instance, has suggested that policing provision in Africa is characterized by a multiplicity of actors including militias and gangs – 'offering localised protection of various levels of legality, effectiveness, availability, methods and services' (Baker 2004, p. 171, see also Baker 2010, Chapter 2).

Together these developments have radically multiplied both the auspices and the providers of security governance, so that today states constitute but one source among many of authority for, and provision of, order maintenance. Policing, referred to nowadays by many scholars as the governance of security, is now hybrid, 'plural', polycentric, and networked (Jones and Newburn 2006, Black 2002, Wood and Shearing 2007, Castells 2011).

## Plural policing and human rights

Almost all those who advocate for and write about 'human rights compliant policing' have focused exclusively on the public police. The significance or implications of the modern pluralization of policing provision for this concept have rarely been addressed. Yet these developments have had profound implications for the human rights project which to date has been almost exclusively state-centric in its philosophy, institutional arrangements and practices. In fact, it might not be amiss to think of existing human rights protections as constituting a Maginot Line that has been outflanked as a consequence of unforeseen and unimagined developments within the governance of security.

Police accountability mechanisms have largely grown out of concerns about the activities of public police. International human rights law as well as domestic laws of various countries have over the years developed fairly elaborate standards for governing the conduct of police and ensuring their accountability for human rights violations. In 1979, for instance, the UN General Assembly adopted, by resolution, a *Code of Conduct for Law Enforcement Officials*, who are defined in it as including 'all officers of the law, whether appointed or elected, who exercise police powers, especially the powers of arrest and detention'. Article 2 of the Code provided that: 'In the performance of their duty, law enforcement officials shall respect and protect human dignity and maintain and uphold the human rights of all persons.' The Code, however, neither recognized nor mentioned non-state policing personnel who do not exercise 'police powers', and would often not consider themselves to be 'law enforcement officials', but who may have just as much propensity to violate human dignity and abuse human rights in performing their policing duties. As a consequence of such exclusive focus on state police officials, human rights accountabilities do not align well with the new security governance realities.

Public police are seen as acting as agents of the state and consequently, rights claims can be made against them and the state for any violations. This connection between the acts of the police and the obligations of the state is, at least in theory if not in practice, simple and unproblematic within the state-centric framework of human rights. The problem for this framework begins with the actions of non-state policing providers against whom recourse is largely in the form of civil claims or criminal complaints that require the action of state police and prosecutors. This means that for non-state nodes within the new security assemblages, like private security, human rights claims cannot be pursued through established human rights pathways, in those countries that have them. This raises challenges given the access to coercion, including violence, available to, and often deployed by, non-state security actors.

The pluralization of policing raises a number of human rights concerns (Dinzey-Flores 2012, Kovâcs and Hegedüs 2014, Landman and Schonteich 2002). For instance, private control of public spaces such as roads can lead to violations of the rights of those who may be categorized as not 'fitting the profile' of the neighbourhood – sometimes termed 'carding'. Such individuals may be excluded from accessing some privately governed spaces or they may be subjected to discriminatory scrutiny. Privately governed spaces often have less public scrutiny, and where it is private security that is policing them, the options for their accountability with regard to human rights abuses tend to be limited to civil claims which will often be beyond the means of those who may have fallen victim to them.

Private security companies possess technologies that are often far more advanced than those of the public police and are being deployed outside the regulatory protections that are applied to the public police. Increased use of surveillance technologies by private security companies has raised significant concern with regard to privacy rights, and the potential that data collected by private companies can be used to unfairly profile individuals and increase their vulnerability to discrimination (Lazarus and Goold 2008). Historically, the concept of privacy has been developed under the assumption that the state and its agents present the most serious threat to it. The development of non-state plural policing during the past 50 years or so, however, suggests that this is probably no longer the case.

Further, private security companies, along with other non-state security actors, bring to the security governance arena immense financial muscle and that often translates into significant political and legal influence. While such power and influence does not inevitably lead to violations of human rights, it often does increase the vulnerability of the less powerful, for instance by enrolling police to respond to crime in rich areas to the disadvantage of the poor (Bayley and Shearing 1996). This influence does not lend itself to easy regulation or accountability through the familiar accountability mechanisms.

## Risk governance

One of the technologies that have been developed by non-state security providers is what has been termed 'preventive governance' (Braithwaite 2000). Based on what Feeley and Simon (1994) have referred to as 'actuarial logic', this technology enables governance actors to anticipate security risks so that they may take pre-emptive measures to prevent them before they happen. This form of risk anticipation uses computer modelling to predict those individuals most likely to commit specified offences, nowadays facilitated by the analysis of 'big data' sets by artificial intelligence mechanisms. An advantage of these technologies has been that they have enabled policing actors to move beyond technologies based on ethnic profiling, as they seek to 'repair the future' (Leman-Langlois and Shearing 2004).[1] Human rights advocates have raised concerns about the dangers that these big data technologies present, as such predictions will, by definition, encroach on the liberty of so-called false positives – innocent people who may not have acted as predicted.

Globally, the increased focus on counter-terrorism since the 2000s – nowadays as much a concern for the private sector as for states – has thrust such risk control strategies onto the centre of the policing stage. For example, prevention of terrorism laws such as the *Patriot Act* in the United States (US) and the accompanying policing practices have, to a large extent, been focused on control of individuals who may be potential terrorists even in the absence of law-violating behaviours (Lazarus and Goold 2008, Tsoukala 2008).

As a consequence, individuals face sanctions, by the private sector as well as by the state, even when they have not committed offences. For instance, in the United Kingdom (UK), football fans have pre-emptively been banned from travelling to attend football games to avoid the risk that they would engage in violence (Tsoukala 2008). Anti-Social Behaviour Orders in the UK are based on a similar pre-emptive, preventive approach. This raises serious human rights concerns. The risk management of individuals on account of their membership of 'suspect' groups runs counter to the logic of human rights that focuses on individual conduct (Tsoukala 2008).

While risk-policing strategies certainly constitute a serious challenge, they are nudging human rights advocates to explore strategies that recognize, and respond effectively, to these developments. One of the suggestions being mooted is that the logic of risk policing could indeed be extended to the application of human rights. In this approach human rights violations would be anticipated and prevented from occurring through legal, policy and programmatic interventions.

## Surveillance

Everyday policing routinely involves the use of surveillance via the watching of individuals and spaces, and surveillance is a practice that is accepted as an essential feature of policing. Indeed, the 'new police', according to Radzinowicz (1956), were established in London to provide an 'unremitting watch' over the citizenry. Surveillance technologies have proliferated dramatically, have become increasingly sophisticated in recent decades, and have assumed increasing prominence in policing by the public as well private police. Yet the practices of routine and panoptic surveillance by definition infringe the right to privacy that is found in many liberal constitutions and other state laws as well as in the *International Covenant on Civil and Political Rights*.[2] Human rights provisions, in this and other areas, seek to ensure that permitted derogations of rights are undertaken within a context of procedural safeguards.

The increased role of surveillance is another development associated with the shift to private policing, risk governance and the rise of private governments, especially in conjunction with pre-emptive technologies. A growing volume of literature has paid attention to the growth and expansion of surveillance of both public and private life (see, for instance, Galison and Minow 2005, Goold 2006, Haggerty and Ericson 2006, Deflem and Ulmer 2008).

Sociological studies have highlighted that surveillance is not a neutral watching activity but a targeted strategy of control (International Council on Human Rights Policy 2010). Surveillance is about 'social sorting' and its uses shape attitudes, behaviour and various forms of social interventions (International Council on Human Rights Policy 2010). Leman-Langlois and Shearing (2004) have pointed out that private actors are more likely to adopt new surveillance technologies than the public police. Stenning (1994) has termed this 'seduction of technology' as 'techno-domination' in policing. Increasingly the distinction between public and commercial surveillance has become blurred, with some observers speaking of the emergence of a 'Surveillance-Industrial Complex', particularly in Europe and the US (International Council on Human Rights Policy 2010, p. 57). Surveillance has also become transnational with agreements to share surveillance data such as the Schengen Agreement in Europe, and the sharing of airline passenger data.

Some have noted that 'social sorting' facilitated by surveillance carries with it the dangers of exclusion of those groups and individuals seen as dangerous or risky (Kempa 1999, International Council on Human Rights Policy 2010). Such categorizations of individuals can have consequences for their access to and enjoyment of a range of rights such as health, housing and freedom of movement. But the secrecy associated with data collection and analysis makes it difficult to accurately assess the human rights impacts of surveillance.

## Recent efforts to improve governance of policing to ensure human rights compliance

We have noted the lack of attention that the implications of the pluralization of policing (in particular, the involvement of the private sector in policing) for human rights compliance have received in the academic and policy literature to date. Certainly, since World War 2, there have been instances in which executives of private corporations have been held accountable in international tribunals (such as the Nuremberg Trials [Marrus 1997]) for their role in violations of human rights (specifically war crimes). More recently, however, some significant initiatives have been undertaken, and some recently proposed, to improve and enhance governance of policing in this respect, both domestically and internationally (Stenning 2009, Johnston and Stenning 2010). Some of the more significant recommendations domestically (albeit never fully implemented anywhere) were those of the Patten Inquiry in its report on policing in Northern Ireland (Independent Commission on Policing for Northern Ireland 1999). The commission recommended the establishment of a Policing Board which would have responsibility for governing the plural provision of policing in the province (that is, including all state and non-state policing providers within its remit), and would have a policing budget which it could allocate between the various policing providers on the basis of its assessment of their contribution to effective policing in the province, and their adherence to human rights standards (see also Berg and Nouveau 2011). Similar recommendations in Canada have so far also not led to any actual reform (see most recently Council of Canadian Academies 2014).

At the international level, two recent initiatives deserve recognition. In 2000, the UN initiated a Global Compact, described as 'a call to companies to align strategies and operations with universal principles on human rights, labour, environment and anti-corruption, and take actions that advance societal goals', and issued a document entitled 'The Ten Principles of the Global Compact'.[3] Three years later, the UN Sub-Commission on the Promotion and Protection of Human Rights, drafted a document entitled 'Norms on the Responsibilities of Transnational Corporations and Other Business Enterprises with Regard to Human Rights'. This document, which was intended to apply to transnational private security providers as well as other transnational corporations, was reviewed, but not officially adopted, by the UN Human Rights Commission in 2004. The following year, the Secretary-General of the UN appointed a Special Representative on Business and Human Rights, who subsequently drafted a document entitled *United Nations Guiding Principles on Business and Human Rights* (Office of the High Commissioner for Human Rights 2011), which was eventually endorsed by the UN Human Rights Council in 2011[4] (see also Wright 2008, Ruggie 2008).

In 2009, the Swiss government in collaboration with the International Committee of the Red Cross, after wide international consultation with government and private sector representatives, issued a document known as *The Montreux Document on pertinent international legal obligations and good practices for States related to operations of private military and security companies during armed conflict*.[5] This document outlines the legal obligations, under international humanitarian and human rights law, of states who contract with private military companies (PMCs) and private security providers (PSPs) during armed conflicts, and sets out 'good practices' which should be adopted to comply with such obligations. The document has been published in seven languages, and several national governments now insist that they will only contract with PMCs and PSPs that commit to Montreux Document compliance.

## Conclusion: rethinking contemporary policing and human rights

As we progress through the twenty-first century a key question that has arisen for liberal democratic states is how to harmonize the logics of plural policing and human rights as mechanisms of governance. We have noted various domestic and international initiatives aimed at monitoring and regulating human rights compliance by state-sponsored ('public') police. Such human rights norms and tools, however, were invented when the governance of security was seen as the exclusive domain of the state, and their 'guns' (to return to the Maginot Line metaphor) continue to point in this direction even though many of the harms they seek to ameliorate are now occurring within a territory that lies behind them. Even though human rights protocols that recognize this are being developed, the established human rights logic, with its continuing state-centric focus, is hampering these developments. The human rights project remains primarily about regulating state power. Consequently, within policing, human rights regulation continues to be focused on public police as if they were the only source of human rights violations. This means that accountability of private security, for instance, remains weak even as their numbers and role continue to grow exponentially.

The fact that policing is now governed though assemblages of providers presents significant human rights challenges as the roles of various actors are often shared and the demarcation of responsibilities of each of the actors may not be clear. In response to these challenges interesting developments are beginning to emerge domestically and internationally, such as the Patten Commission's report (Independent Commission on Policing for Northern Ireland 1999), the UN's *Guiding Principles on Human Rights and Business* (2011), and the Montreux Document (2009). While these initiatives are to be welcomed, the fact that they are all aspirational, that the kinds of initiatives recommended by the Patten Commission have not so far been implemented anywhere, and that the international initiatives rely entirely on voluntary compliance and have no regulatory 'teeth', cannot be overlooked. Much more concrete and enforceable regulatory regimes will be required to ensure human rights compliant policing, both domestically and internationally, in the future. So far, there are no signs of that happening any time soon, and academics and policy-makers need to think more about how it might be achieved.

At the conceptual level, there is need to critically revisit the security-human rights discourse within the context of plural policing and polycentric governance more generally. The emergence of terrorist threats and their policing through risk governance, surveillance and through private policing, for instance, calls for conceptual engagement beyond the arguments of balancing security with human rights values. More radically, human rights need to be seen as constitutive of security (International Council on Human Rights Policy 2010, see Goold 2016 on the extent to which this is likely to be possible). In summary, the human rights project needs to recognize the shifting realities of governance and reshape the contours of human rights thinking, its institutions and practices, accordingly. While these changes remain in their infancy, as Professor Gillian Triggs (2015), President of the Australian Human Rights Commission, noted in her opening address to Griffith University's Global Integrity Summit in October 2015, the importance of the private sector, not only as a threat to human rights but as a source of renewal for the human rights project, is being increasingly recognized. These engagements with the private sector are likely to be at the forefront of developments within the human rights project.

## Notes

1 See similar argument in Ruteere 2015.
2 Article 17 (1) of the ICCPR states: 'No one shall be subjected to arbitrary or unlawful interference with his privacy, family, home or correspondence, nor to unlawful attacks on his honour and reputation.'
3 Details on this initiative can be found online at www.unglobalcompact.org/what-is-gc, and the Ten Principles at www.unglobalcompact.org/what-is-gc/mission/principles.
4 Details on this initiative can be found online at http://business-humanrights.org/en/united-nations-sub-commission-norms-on-business-human-rights-explanatory-materials, and a copy of the Guiding Principles at www.ohchr.org/Documents/Publications/GuidingPrinciplesBusinessHR_EN.pdf.
5 This document can be accessed online at www.icrc.org/eng/assets/files/other/icrc_002_0996.pdf.

## References

Abrahamsen, R. and Williams, M., 2009. Security beyond the state: global security assemblages in international politics. *International Political Sociology*, 3(1), 1–17.
Abrahamsen, R. and Williams, M., 2011. *Security beyond the state: private security in international politics*. Cambridge: Cambridge University Press.
Baker, B., 2004. Protection from crime: What is on offer for Africans? *Journal of Contemporary African Studies*, 22(2), 165–88.
Baker, B., 2010. *Security in post-conflict Africa: the role of nonstate policing*. Boca Raton, FL: CRC Press.
Bayley, D. and Shearing, C., 1996. The future of policing. *Law & Society Review*, 30(3), 585–606.
Berg, J. and Nouveau, J.P., 2011. Towards a third phase of regulation: re-imagining private security in South Africa. *South African Crime Quarterly*, 38, 23–32.

Black, J., 2002. Critical reflections on regulation. *Australian Journal of Legal Philosophy*, 27, 1–35.
Braithwaite, J., 2000. The new regulatory state and the transformation of criminology. *British Journal of Criminology*, 40(2), 222–38.
Castells, M., 2011. *The rise of network society: the information age – economy, society and culture*. Volume I, 2nd ed. Oxford: Wiley-Blackwell.
Council of Canadian Academies, Expert Panel on the Future of Canadian Policing Models, 2014. Policing Canada in the 21st century: new policing for new challenges. Ottawa: Council of Canadian Academies.
Deflem, M. and Ulmer, J. (eds), 2008. *Surveillance and governance: crime control and beyond*. Bingley: Emerald Group Publishing.
Dinzey-Flores, Z.Z., 2012. Where rights begin and end in Puerto Rico's gated communities. *Singapore Journal of Tropical Geography*, 33(2), 198–211.
Feeley, M. and Simon, J., 1994. Actuarial justice: the emerging new criminal law. *In*: D. Nelken (ed.), *The futures of criminology*. London/Thousand Oaks, CA: Sage Publications, 173–201.
Galison, P. and Minow, M., 2005. Our privacy, ourselves in the age of technological intrusions. *In*: R. Wilson (ed.), *Human rights in the 'war on terror'*. Cambridge: Cambridge University Press, 258–94.
Goold, B., 2006. Open to all? Regulating open street CCTV and the case for 'symmetrical surveillance'. *Criminal Justice Ethics*, 25(1), 3–17.
Goold, B., 2016. Policing and rights. *In*: B. Bradford, B. Jauregui, I. Loader and J. Steinberg (eds), *Sage handbook of global policing*. London: Sage, 226–400.
Haggerty, K. and Ericson, R. (eds), 2006. *The new politics of surveillance and visibility*. Toronto: University of Toronto Press.
Independent Commission on Policing for Northern Ireland (C. Patten, Chair), 1999. *Report: a new beginning: policing in Northern Ireland*. London: HMSO.
International Council on Human Rights Policy, 2010. The widening web of control: a human rights analysis of public policy responses. Versoix, Switzerland: International Council on Human Rights Policy.
Johnston, L. and Stenning, P., 2010. Challenges of governance and accountability for transnational private policing. *In*: F. Lemieux (ed.), *International police co-operation: emerging issues, theory and practice*. Cullompton: Willan Publishing, 281–97.
Jones, T. and Newburn, T. (eds), 2006. *Plural policing: a comparative perspective*. London and New York: Routledge.
Kempa, M., 1999. A genealogical analysis of sorting practices: governance and policing. Submitted for the Masters Degree in Criminology, University of Toronto, June.
Kovâcs, Z. and Hegedüs, G., 2014. Gated communities as new forms of segregation in post-socialist Budapest. *Cities*, 36(February), 200–9.
Landman, K. and Schonteich, M., 2002. Urban fortresses: gated communities as a reaction to crime. *African Security Review*, 11(4), 71–85.
Lazarus, L. and Goold, B. (eds), 2008. *Security and human rights*. Oxford: Hart Publishing.
Leman-Langlois, S. and Shearing, C., 2004. Repairing the future: the South African Truth and Reconciliation Commission at work. *In*: G. Gilligan and J. Pratt (eds), *Crime, truth and justice: official enquiry, discourse, knowledge*. Cullompton: Willan Publishing, 222–42.
Lukes, S., 1993. Five fables about human rights. *In*: S. Shute and S. Hurley (eds), *On human rights: the Oxford Amnesty lectures 1993*. New York, NY: Basic Books, 19–40.
Marrus, M.R., 1997. *The Nuremberg war crimes trial, 1945–46: A documentary history*. London: Macmillan.
Office of the High Commissioner for Human Rights, 2011. *Guiding Principles on Human Rights and Business*. Retrieved on 8 April 2016 from: www.ohchr.org/Documents/Publications/GuidingPrinciples BusinessHR_EN.pdf.
Radzinowicz, L., 1956. *A history of English criminal law: vol. III – the reform of the police*. London: Stevens & Sons.
Ruggie, J., 2008. *Promotion and protection of all human rights, civil, political, economic, social and cultural rights, including the right to development: protect, respect and remedy: a framework for business and human rights*. Report of the Special Representative of the Secretary-General on the issue of human rights and transnational corporations and other business enterprises. Retrieved on 8 April 2016 from: http://daccess-dds-ny.un.org/doc/UNDOC/GEN/G08/128/61/PDF/G0812861.pdf?OpenElement.
Ruteere, M., 2015. *Report of the UN Special Rapporteur on contemporary forms of racism, racial discrimination, xenophobia and related intolerance*. Retrieved on 8 April 2016 from: www.ohchr.org/Documents/Issues/Racism/A-HRC-29-46.pdf.

Stenning, P., 1994. Private policing: some recent myths, developments and trends. *In*: D. Biles and J. Vernon (eds), *Proceedings of a conference held 30 November–2 December 1992*. Canberra: Australian Institute of Criminology.

Stenning, P., 2000. Powers and accountability of private police. *European Journal of Criminal Policy and Research*, 8(3), 325–52.

Stenning, P., 2009. Governance and accountability in a plural policing environment: the story so far. *Policing: A Journal of Policy & Practice*, 3(1), 22–33.

Stenning, P. and Shearing, C., 2012. The shifting boundaries of policing: globalization and its possibilities. *In*: T. Newburn and J. Peay (eds), *Policing: politics, culture and control*. Oxford: Hart Publishing, 265–84.

Triggs, G., 2015. Human rights, human security, sustainable development goals and the 'bottom billion'. Paper presented at The Global Integrity Summit, 13–14 October, Brisbane, Australia: Griffith University.

Tsoukala, A., 2008. *Security, risk and human rights: a vanishing relationship?* CEPS Special Report. Brussels: Centre for European Policy Studies.

Wood, J. and Shearing, C., 2007. *Imagining security*. Cullompton: Willan Publishing.

Wright, M., 2008. *Corporations and human rights: a survey of the scope and patterns of alleged corporate-related human rights abuse*. Corporate Social Responsibility Initiative Working Paper No. 44. Cambridge, MA: John F. Kennedy School of Government, Harvard University. Retrieved on 8 April 2016 from: www.hks.harvard.edu/m-rcbg/CSRI/publications/workingpaper_44_Wright.pdf.

# 38

# Transnational policing and the end times of human rights

*Ben Bowling and James Sheptycki*

## Introduction

Human rights theory and activism in the early twenty-first century grew acutely concerned about the possibility of the end times of human rights in the new global system (Hopgood 2013, Lettinga and van Troost 2013). Both policing and human rights are modern ideas covalent with the modern state. Policing corresponds to the political structure of which it is a part and is that instrument of governance that gives force to law. Absent of policing institutions, law – including human rights law – is nothing; but policing institutions both shape and are shaped by the laws they embody (Bowling and Sheptycki 2015). Given the power that police must possess in order to fulfil their function as upholders of law, a problem arises around how to override those powers if and when they are abused. This problem has at times led to the establishment of bodies independent of police institutions whose job it is to 'police the police'. This could entail an endless process of appeal to ever-higher powers but for the fact that police have traditionally been a department of 'the state' which has, at its apex, some theoretical point of reference to ground a final judgment. Yet, under transnational conditions, policing power has become significantly unfettered from the state. Since the global system is a polycentric power system and is not governed from a generally recognized and agreed institutional point of reference whose authority presides and to which appeals to legality may be registered, transnational police power is effectively above the law (Bowling and Sheptycki 2015).

Understanding the relationship between transnational policing and human rights involves an articulation of a very old question in social and political thought around the ontological status of law. There can be no more crucial question about global governance than this one. On one view, the answer is a simple one. Since the significance of law lies in the procedures necessary to enact and adjudicate it, there can only be positive law if there is a process of adjudication. All law is positive law since any law, in order to be law, must be justiciable. This is a popular form of argument asserted by proponents of procedural justice (Tyler 1990) which concludes that, if there are any natural rights, there is the following: the right to judgement by an independent and disinterested party according to fair and transparent procedures available to all. The practical problem is that, in a world that has 'gone global', there is no institutional set-up through which worldwide standards of procedural justice can be guaranteed. In the contemporary period, these problems are often papered over with political rhetoric about the need to enforce human rights and the rule of law. This can have paradoxical effects such that human rights can thereby become a pretext for militarized policing and war-like action which is an affront to the human dignity of all those who bear the consequences (Ignatieff 2005). Clearly there is considerable confusion about the status of transnational policing vis-à-vis human rights. Clarifying the relationship between these two concepts, in terms of how they manifest in reality and how they might be ideally, is foundational to the theory and practice of global governance.

When it comes to transnational policing, who polices the police? This question is fundamental, especially considering that, as we shall here illustrate, the primary instruments for enforcing human rights worldwide are firearms and force, in the hands of police. One major source of difficulty in answering questions like this is the disposition of the transnational system of states that comprises the global system.

## The transnational-state-system and the present predicament of human rights

It is very common to reify 'the state' when talking about global affairs. Often people discuss politics as if states were monolithic entities capable of unified and directed self-interest. There is an enormous literature (see, for example, Evans et al. 1985) on state formation that cannot be rehearsed here, but an important point of agreement is that mutual state recognition is the *sine qua non* for states to exist. In the modern period, political scientists studied states and international relations scholars studied the international system of states. With the end of the Cold War the conditions for state existence changed (Sklair 1995). With that historical turn came the hollowing out of the domestic welfare state and the creation of a 'crimefare state' – a sort of 'rump state' which retained the capacity for coercion and punishment while losing the ability to promote the general welfare of the population (Andreas 1997). At the end of the millennium, Manuel Castells's monumental study of the globalization of culture, economy and society demonstrated empirically how the emerging global networked society had overflowed the boundaries of the international system of states (Castells 1998). About the same time, political theorists recognized that states were disaggregated agglomerations of 'loosely coupled' or 'relatively autonomous' institutions, all of which acted transnationally (Slaughter 2004). The emergent configuration of power was a different kind of transnational-state-system (Sheptycki 1995, 1998, Bowling and Sheptycki 2012, pp. 29–32).

The complex polycentric power system that circumscribes world society is imaginatively held together in reaction to a catalogue of suitable enemies who are simultaneously rendered banal, absolute and ubiquitous (Bowling and Sheptycki 2012, pp. 91–4). Just as the seigneurial system of the European feudal period 'parcelized' territory with a multiplex system of justice and social control that bound peasants and serfs to the land and granted privileges to an elite social class who were in a state of permanent conflict with each other, so it is in the global system of the twenty-first century (ibid., p. 117). Under transnational conditions, social elites based in the bureaucracies of seigneurial states, corporate institutions and the transnational capitalist markets dominate a global population, not simply by 'calling the shots', because the global system is such a vast complex of institutions – some under putatively public auspices, others under private auspices – within which different interests joust for position and power in the governance of the world. A direct consequence of this set-up is the 'politics of insecurity' (Ericson 2007) which itself results in the 'security-control paradox', as general feelings of insecurity are used to justify the hardening of security measures which, in turn, intensify feelings of insecurity in an amplification spiral (Bowling and Sheptycki 2012, pp. 18–19, 98–100, 133).

The theoretical implications of this for understanding the relationship between transnational policing and human rights are evident. From top to bottom, the global system is policed. Jude McCulloch (2004) has observed a trend in policing involving a police–military fusion and the collapse of the distinction between domestic and international in the new security politics of the global War on Terror. For some, the militarization of policing and the transformation of the state system, together with the transnationalization of the politics of policing, were harbingers of the future end times of the global human rights project (Hopgood 2013). We aim to add to these discussions by making global policing more theoretically visible (Bowling and Sheptycki 2012). One of the interesting things about transnational policing practice is how human rights discourse has been articulated within it.

## Transnational policing and human rights

Conventionally speaking, there are two opposite views concerning the relationship between policing and human rights: one suggests that policing is a risk or threat to human rights, while the other suggests that it is the very basis of such rights. Crawshaw et al. (1998) articulate both positions. With respect to the latter view, they state that 'it can be convincingly argued that not only are police required to respect human rights when exercising their powers, they are required to protect human rights as one of their functions' (ibid., p. 225). On this view, policing is a protective service to society (ibid., p. 18). The opposite view, which Crawshaw et al. (1998) also describe, that policing poses a threat to human rights and civil liberties, is probably a more widely held view in the contemporary period. Chevigny's landmark study *Police power: police abuses in New York City* (1969), for example, was an examination of cases of assault, false arrest, unlawful search, summary punishment, deliberate framing of suspects and other nefarious activities by the New York Police Department. In *Edge of the knife: police violence in the Americas* he made a similar case, citing examples from cities across North America, Latin America and the Caribbean (Chevigny 1995). Both Human Rights Watch and Amnesty International have produced a catalogue of reports that empirically detail the many instances of police use of torture and extrajudicial killings. In the present period, media representations of policing overwhelmingly focus on disproportionate police use of force; crystallizing questions about the crimes of state institutions (Stanley and McCulloch 2013), and challenging the institutional basis of the global human rights regime.

Some argue that democratic policing under a broad banner of human rights is still a possibility (Bayley 1995, Policing and Society 2000, Goldsmith and Sheptycki 2007). To others the evidence seems overwhelmingly negative (Ellison and Pino 2012). And yet, the global system inevitably will require major 'international police operations' – for example, the 2004 Tsunami disaster in the Indian ocean, which was followed by a police operation involving over 3,000 police officers from 31 countries (Bowling and Sheptycki 2012, p. 34). Looked at from a transnational point of view, these big policing interventions may or may not appear antithetical to the aims of human rights advocates and global wellbeing (Hopgood 2013). But humanitarian police missions are not the whole story. There are other transnational policing phenomena, such as intelligence-led policing, that are also experienced in local jurisdictions everywhere (Bowling and Sheptycki 2012, pp. 68–71). Global policing phenomena are bundled together in a complex system of symbolic justification. However awkwardly 'transnational policing' and 'human rights' seem to fit together, they are bonded by a powerful analogy used to justify the use of force in the maintenance of human rights. In the early 1990s, former Prime Minister of Canada, Brian Mulroney, likened the policing of 'domestic violence' with the then new doctrine of R2P. Speaking publicly in the aftermath of the Rwandan crisis, he said, 'just as it is no longer acceptable for society, the police, or the courts to turn a blind eye to family violence, so it is equally unacceptable for the international community to ignore violence and repression within national borders' (quoted in Abiew 1999, p. 237). Thus transnational policing powers were conferred – but onto what or whom?

There can be no doubt as to the means of these supposed ends, given the aforementioned police–military convergence in a transnational-state-system. Transnationally networked policing undergirds the global system. History records that Hans-Dietrich Genscher, a former German Foreign Minister who had been an important broker in German reunification, spoke before the United Nations (UN) General Assembly at around the same time that Mulroney used his analogy, expressing the conviction that 'where human rights are trampled upon the family of nations cannot be confined to a role of spectator' (ibid., p. 237). Thus was fused the imagery of family violence and humanitarian crises into a fully-fledged metaphor justifying transnational policing in the global system from the micro-social level of the family unit to the macro-social level of 'countries', 'nations' and not-quite-right states. Transnational policing is the *sine qua non* of the global system partly because of the persuasive use of the trope of 'domestic violence', which was, in the 1990s and despite criticism, widely believed to be within the purview of control of professional policing (Sheptycki 1991).

## Human rights and the power of transnational policing

The ambiguities of human rights discourse constitute its allure as a political ethic for global governance because it provides legitimacy for the use of power and coercion in the name of those ultimately most affected by power and coercion. In this section, we illustrate our theoretical claims by looking at two examples. Although we treat them as two different cases they are complexly interconnected examples of global governance as enacted through transnational policing practice. The first of these concerns an example of transnational policing as 'law enforcement', the second as 'peace enforcement'. Together they help to illustrate the many contradictions inherent in human rights expressed through the power of transnational policing.

### *Transnational policing and the Dudus Affair*

In 2010, the Toronto Police Service announced the successful conclusion of Project Corral (Balkissoon 2010, DiManno 2010, Vallis 2010), which exposed a sophisticated organized crime network that smuggled guns, cocaine and other drugs into southern Ontario (Leuprecht 2014). Project Corral roughly coincided with the arrest and extradition of Christopher 'Dudus' Coke from Jamaica on a United States (US) warrant. The Jamaican government had resisted taking action against Coke who was known as the 'Godfather of Tivoli Gardens' and was described as one of the most powerful men in the country by the then Jamaican Minister for National Security, Peter Philips. When the Jamaican government bowed to heavy US pressure on the matter of his arrest and extradition, his supporters in the country attacked police stations. The paramilitary police response was swift and furious, and pitched battles were fought over a number of days, resulting in the deaths of at least 70 people (BBC 2011, *Jamaica Observer* 2009, Schwartz 2012). The arrests in Canada were part of a transnational police sweep of the Jamaican organized criminal networks. These operations were enabled by transnational police liaison arrangements of considerable strategic depth and involving police agents from several US law enforcement agencies including the Federal Bureau of Investigation, the Drug Enforcement Administration and US Customs; United Kingdom (UK) police and customs agencies; as well as several Canadian police agencies (chiefly the Toronto Police Service and the Royal Canadian Mounted Police).

The strategic depth of these relations was largely an achievement of the London Metropolitan Police operating under the rubric of Operation Trident, which began in the early 2000s (Bowling 2010). This was a police effort to investigate the routes of illicit guns and drugs used by criminal networks hidden within the trans-Atlantic communities of the West Indian diaspora. Trident brought a number of UK officers into close working relations with the Jamaican Constabulary Force (JCF), among them Mark Shields who had substantial experience working for Special Branch. Things came to a head in May 2003, when a number of JCF officers killed four people in what came to be called the Kraal Shootings (Bowling and Sheptycki 2012, pp. 79–81). UK police were instrumental in the unsuccessful prosecution of the police involved in the deaths. Local reaction was ambiguous. When officers Reneto Adams, Shane Lyons and Patrick Coke left the Kingston courthouse after being found not guilty, in spite of a wealth of forensic evidence implicating them in wrongdoing, they were met by jubilant crowds of supporters gleeful at their release while simultaneously they were condemned by human rights activists (ibid., p. 81). Shields subsequently became the Deputy Commissioner of the JCF until 2009, during which time the network of transnational police cooperation in the Caribbean was further strengthened.

By the time of Project Corral in 2010, a number of police operations against Caribbean-based criminal networks were taking place in the UK, the US and Canada. Arrests of people associated with these networks in all three countries were local crime news, while the arrest and extradition of Christopher Coke was international news (Silverman 2010). His father, Lester Lloyd Coke, was one of the prime movers of the Jamaican Shower Posse underworld, a phenomenon that was itself transnational (Gunst 1996). Jamaica established patterns of outward migration to North America and the UK from the time of its independence in 1962. The mercenary street conflicts between rival political parties in Jamaica during the 1980s incubated a 'posse underworld' that rode the coat tails of migration and was vilified in the UK as 'Yardies' and in the US as the Jamaican Shower Posse. Members of this underworld were feared and honoured for being 'harder than the rest' as they established their American turf with 'outlaw bravura and ruthlessness' (Gunst 1996). Network connections between Miami, Los Angeles, Kansas City, Chicago and New York, as well as branches in London and Toronto were eventually established. When Lester Coke was burned to death in a fire in a Kingston prison cell in 1992 the family's participation in the business continued. By this time, the centre of the network, based in Tivoli Gardens and a number of other 'garrison' neighbourhoods in Kingston, was securely financed, its economic wellspring of success being the illicit international cocaine and marijuana markets (Harriot 2008). As a result, the 'garrisons' were police 'no-go areas' connected to the Jamaican state only by subterranean patronage and vote-rigging (Sives 2010). The Dons of Tivoli Gardens and the other garrison towns ruled quasi-states, exhibiting sovereign control over their territory, symbolized by public acts of welfare and social control. Subsequent to the arrest and successful prosecution of Dudus Coke in the US, this system of patronage fragmented into myriad smaller networks and the economic business carried on as usual (Grillo 2014).

Although none of these police operations explicitly invoked a human rights mandate, such a mandate was implicit in all of the law enforcement operations against this diasporic network. Purportedly, successful law enforcement operations against serious criminals are inherently in support of human rights by virtue of the violent nature of the organized crime in question. In Toronto, the news was largely filtered through the local understanding of urban street crime, guns, gangs and cops (Powell 2010). Local academics focused on the social construction of the 'Jamaican criminal' and the social support and companionship provided by neighbourhood street gangs (see, for example, D'Arcy 2007, Wortley 2013). When police announced the results of Project Corral in Toronto in May 2010, they focused on their success in 'disrupting and dismantling' criminal networks that had 'terrorized the neighbourhoods in which they operate'. Announcements about seizures of quantities of drugs and firearms, alongside 71 arrests from the execution of 105 search warrants, were evidence of agency success. Local police watchdogs denounced police use of the 'guns and gangs issue' as a pretext for maintaining racially biased policing practices (Wortley and Owusu-Bempah 2011), suggesting that many well-placed local observers were sceptical of any implicit human rights claims made about Project Corral and similar policing operations.

In the US, authorities presented the case as a successful law enforcement operation against the famous Shower Posse that had 'invaded' cities across the country. There, critics of the police focused on the massacre that took place in Tivoli Gardens when Dudus was captured by joint teams made up of JCF police and transnational police partners. During the gun battles that ensued, 73 people died, three of whom were women and most of whom appeared to be unarmed – suggesting a police human rights violation (Schwartz 2012). Controversies in the US concerning the treatment of Jamaican criminals were filtered through American cultural tropes concerning race and national identity. Between 1997 and 2004, roughly 12,000 Jamaicans were deported from the US (Headley 2006, p. 48). The poor treatment of people in deportation parallels the treatment inside domestic penal establishments in the US (Huggins 1998, Parenti 2004, UN 2014), providing further clues concerning the relationship between transnational policing control and human rights.

In the UK, the national institutional framework for policing organized crime changed three times from the early 1990s. At the national level there was a continuous process of institutional restructuring as first the double act of the National Criminal Intelligence Service and the National Crime Squad was replaced by the Serious Organized Crime Agency (SOCA) in 2006, only to be superseded in 2013 by the National Crime Agency. At the time of Dudus Coke's arrest in 2010, SOCA was heavily emphasizing the issue of urban organized crime groups in the UK, illustrating the shifting fabric of the underworld with a new 'heat map' of 6,000 gangs with an estimated 38,000 members, relatively few of whom had specifically Jamaican roots (Clements 2010). For this agency, the governance of Jamaican organized crime was part of a bigger problem. While the national agency was in a process of more or less continuous restructuring, policing problems were manifest locally, leading to, among other things, the London Metropolitan Police's transnational venture Operation Trident (Bowling 2010). In June of 2010, UK police statistics released through a *Freedom of Information Act* request revealed a significant disproportion of violent street crime perpetrated by black men: approximately 60 per cent of violent street crimes were perpetrated by black males, but only 12 per cent of London's population fell into that ethnic category (Alderson 2010). A dominant theme in the public discourse concerning police, race and crime continued to be problems of both overpolicing and underpolicing of ethnic minority communities, and considerable ambivalence. Bowling and Phillips (2010) summed it up this way:

> There is a view that 'black on black' crime and 'Asian criminality' have been exaggerated by police and media as a means to renew police legitimacy. On the other hand, it can be argued that it is now minority ethnic communities themselves that are demanding police action to restore peace and safety. These developments underscore the central paradox of policing that, in their efforts to protect the public, the tactics most frequently used involve the use of intrusion, coercion and force against the very people crying out for protection
>
> *(Bowling and Phillips 2010, p. 23)*

They went on to add that, 'in recent years, the British police have drifted further towards a "military model" of policing that emphasizes crime fighting . . . this shift to a "law and order society" is likely to be both counterproductive and undermine fundamental human rights' (ibid., p. 24).

Scholars close to the action in the West Indies were highly critical of the tactics and strategies adopted as part of transnational policing in the region (Agozino et al. 2009). The militarized war on drugs produced documented human rights failings. The refusal of US agencies to address the flow of illicit guns from the US into the Caribbean countries was taken as evidence of hypocrisy. According to Agozino et al. (2009), the alternative policy choices to the existing misguided law enforcement practices favoured public health and social welfare approaches (see also Cukier and Sheptycki 2012). The practices of transnational law enforcement policing in the region were thus condemned on human rights grounds. According to Edwards and Sheptycki (2012, p. 385), they showed that 'the transnational-state-system is a volatile order and efforts to assert the values of cosmopolitan democracy and human rights often fall victim to geo-strategic and financial interests'.

The Dudus Affair tells us something about how transnational policing relates to human rights. It shows how local policing in Jamaica, Canada, the US and the UK can be institutionally interconnected transnationally. It shows that any implicit or explicit claims vis-à-vis transnational law enforcement policing and human rights are ambivalent. It also shows up a contradiction regarding the power of transnational policing and its implications for human rights: police are expected to uphold human rights yet are continuously suspected of undermining them (Syal 2010).

### *Transnational policing and the 2010 Haitian Earthquake*

When Port-au-Prince was levelled by an earthquake on 12 January 2010, there was an immediate global outpouring of sympathy. Worldwide, police and other emergency service providers were mustered in order to provide disaster relief and humanitarian assistance. There was a widespread public expectation that these efforts were based in the philosophy of human rights, but informed observers were deeply pessimistic about the trends in human insecurity evident in Haiti (Henley 2010). By the time of the earthquake, the historical trajectory of Haiti had combined to produce a people so poor, an infrastructure so non-existent, and a state so ineffectual that international disaster relief experts placed its vulnerability to natural disasters 'at the top of the scale'. If ever there was an opportunity for explicit claims about the power of transnational policing in terms of providing the conditions that make human rights possible, Haiti provided the most extreme test case.

When the earthquake happened, the country had already been host to an ongoing UN police peacekeeping force called *Mission des Nations Unies pour la stabilisation en Haiti* (MINUSTAH) since 2004 (Bowling and Sheptycki 2012, pp. 125–7). Indeed, foreign police interventions of one kind or another have been almost continual in Haiti since the early twentieth century. MINUSTAH started life as a UN-sponsored 'stabilization mission', its main theatre of operations was *Cité Soleil* – a notorious shantytown. Under Brazilian force command, the joint police–military mission had more than 3,000 police officers from around the world, including Canadians and Nepalese – the latter of whom brought cholera with them. Responding to the earthquake disaster, US authorities temporarily muscled MINUSTAH aside. Around the world, most people were scarcely aware of the broader historical and transnational dimensions of policing in Haiti and charitable donations poured in to help the relief effort. At this time, MINUSTAH had already come to be a well-documented failure in transnational police peacekeeping:

> Critics charged that despite one of the strongest human rights mandates in UN peacekeeping history, MINUSTAH did not effectively investigate or report human rights abuses, nor protect human rights advocates. Charged to train and reform the Haitian National Police, MINUSTAH instead provided unquestioning support to police operations resulting in warrantless arrests, detentions, unintended civilian casualties and deliberate extra-judicial killings. Rather than protecting civilians from imminent violence, MINUSTAH instead inflicted stray bullets on them.
>
> *(Bowling and Sheptycki 2012, p. 125)*

In the immediate aftermath of the earthquake, the US dispatched more than 13,000 military personnel, including the 82nd Airborne and naval hospital ships, in a high-profile international emergency response to an obvious humanitarian crisis. In the US, the domestic political concern was around a 'refugee crisis', and authorities there moved to ensure that the earthquake did not result in a flood of refugees. In a public statement directed at the Haitians, then Homeland Security Secretary, Janet Napolitano, said, 'please do not have us divert our necessary rescue and relief efforts that are going into Haiti by trying to leave at this point' (ibid., p. 125).

Six months later, the majority of the US contingent had left (Beaumont 2010), while the situation on the ground remained significantly impacted by the disaster. Still, the expected refugee flood had been contained. By the third anniversary of the earthquake, questions were being asked about the estimated $9 billion in public and private donations that seemed largely to have vanished. The amount of aid was equivalent to Haiti's gross domestic product and yet, in 2013, hundreds of thousands of people were still living in tents without access to safe drinking water (Ramachandran and Walz 2013). In 2015, during the 'FIFA scandal' – in which US authorities undertook investigative and enforcement efforts against specified senior officials allegedly responsible for large-scale corruption and white-collar crime in the world of World Cup football – the US State Department accused FIFA Vice-President Jack Warner (a Trinidadian national) of diverting funds from the Haitian relief effort into his own private accounts (Phipps 2015). The missing money is, as of this writing, still largely unaccounted for and the good works for which it was intended remain substantially incomplete.

Roughly around the fifth anniversary of the earthquake, the FIFA imbroglio briefly diverted attention from the awful human rights conditions in Haiti. According to Pierre Esperance, Executive Director of the Haitian National Human Rights Defense Network, progress had been made in restoring infrastructure, roads, housing and clean water, but overwhelming problems remained and much of the disaster relief had been mismanaged, wasted or siphoned off through corrupt means. Additionally, the UN peacekeeping mission had a bad reputation. According to Esperance:

> it costs $33 million a month but it has done nothing . . . UN soldiers [sic] have been involved in rapes and human rights violations and they brought cholera to Haiti . . . they say they're here to improve things and work on the rule of law, but there's been no impact.
>
> *(quoted in Jones 2015)*

Around the time of the fifth anniversary of the disaster, Amnesty International issued a report showing that, amidst the controversy about the missing aid money and relief funds, pervasive human misery and police brutality remained a persistent fact of life on the ground (Amnesty International 2015).

Haiti has long been a focal point for transnational policing as peacekeeping. The response to the 2010 earthquake provides further evidence concerning the contradictions of transnational policing power. While human rights discourse provides legitimacy for transnational policing practice, a good deal of the evidence suggests that the solution to the problem is itself part of the problem. Transnational policing in Haiti has largely been about suppression and containment, not building a social order based on human rights. The global system is one that is integrated economically, politically and socially and the transnational-state-system has evolved to containerize insecurity, from the micro-social level of the public housing project or urban ghetto to the macro-social level of the weak, failing or failed state. This is a basic feature of the contemporary global system and it is why transnational efforts to enforce human rights and the rule of law look more like a failed strategy to impose peace through superior firepower (Bowling and Sheptycki 2012, p. 32).

## Discussion and conclusions

The above examples were chosen to illustrate the depth and breadth of transnational policing practice. We are concerned to make global policing theoretically visible as a whole. Discussion about global human rights is confused because the global system is a maelstrom and scholarly interests are often too narrowly focused. Our theoretical view of global policing is general and expansive and we argue the phenomenon is a synecdoche of the global system (Bowling and Sheptycki 2012, pp. 3, 28). The critique of transnational policing practice is important, we believe, because the transnational connections that make up global policing are largely invisible. Too much theory is derived based upon what is readily apparent on the surface. We hope that, by linking these two examples of transnational policing activity circulating in one region of the global system, we have given a useful indication of myriad ways in which global policing is empirically manifest. Transnational policing is the sharp end of global governance and it therefore holds vital clues about the place of human rights in the global system.

Internationally, lawyers and socio-legal theorists are often content with analysis of legal texts and tend to want to believe that human rights law can somehow translate into human rights. Globally, governmental programmers often seem to believe that it is possible to enforce the rule of law and human rights. A primary justification for transnational policing resides in claims about the necessity of policing in support of human rights, but the case studies and theoretical literature reviewed here reveal considerable ambivalence and certain contradiction. The language of human rights has provided metaphorical 'moral glue' which justifies the use of force in the maintenance of human rights in the global system. Human rights discourse is alluring as a political ethic for governance because it legitimizes the use of power and coercion in the name of those ultimately most affected by power and coercion. When the primary instruments for enforcing human rights are firearms and force, it seems likely that – good intentions to the contrary – the effects will at best be contradictory. Inevitably, as the global system veers towards the end times of human rights (Hopgood 2013) the ancient question 'who will guard the guards?' is asked anew. Before beginning to answer that question it is first necessary to make transnational policing theoretically and empirically visible, and in order to do that the rhetoric of its justification needs to be summarily dismissed.

## References


Abiew, Francis Kofi, 1999. *The evolution of the doctrine of humanitarian intervention.* The Hague: Kluwer Law International.

Agozino, B., Bowling, B., Ward, E. and St. Bernard, G., 2009. Guns, crime and social order in the West Indies. *Criminology and Criminal Justice*, 9, 287–305.

Alderson, A., 2010. Violent inner-city crime, the figures and a question of race. *The Sunday Telegraph*, 26 June.

Amnesty International, 2015. *'15 minutes to leave' denial of the right to adequate housing in post-quake Haiti.* London: Amnesty International Publications.

Andreas, P., 1997. The rise of the American crimefare state. *World Policy Journal*, 14(3), 37–45.

Balkissoon, D., 2010. Deadly Shower Posse gang has deep ties to Toronto. *Toronto Star*, 25 May.

Bayley, D., 1995. *Democratizing the police abroad: what to do and how to do it.* US Department of Justice.

BBC, 2011. Profile: Christopher 'Dudus' Coke'. 1 September. Retrieved on 11 April 2016 from: www.bbc.com/news/10146172.

Beaumont, P., 2010. Haiti earthquake: six months on. *The Guardian*, Saturday 10 July.

Bowling, B., 2010. *Policing the Caribbean.* Oxford: Oxford University Press.

Bowling, B. and Phillips, C., 2010. Policing ethnic minority communities. LSE Research Online (originally published in T. Newburn, ed., *Handbook of policing.* Cullompton: Willan, 528–55. Retrieved on 11 April 2016 from: http://eprints.lse.ac.uk/9576/1/Policing_ethnic_minority_communities_%28LSERO%29.pdf.

Bowling, B. and Sheptycki, J., 2012. *Global policing.* London: Sage.

Bowling, B. and Sheptycki, J., 2015. Global policing and transnational rule with law. *Transnational Legal Theory*, 6, 1–33.

Castells, M., 1998. *End of the millennium, the information age: economy, society and culture, Vol. III.* Oxford: Blackwell.

Chevigny, P., 1969. *Police power: police abuses in New York City.* New York, NY: Pantheon Books.

Chevigny, P., 1995. *Edge of the knife: police violence in the Americas.* New York, NY: The Free Press.

Clements, J., 2010. Organised crime: mobsters' £40 billion underworld exposed . . . and 1,500 are teens climbing the criminal ladder. *The Mirror*, 31 July.

Crawshaw, R., Devlin, B. and Williamson, T., 1998. *Human rights and policing: standards for good behaviour and a strategy for change.* The Hague: Kluwer Law International.

Cukier, W. and Sheptycki, J., 2012. Globalization of gun culture: transnational reflections on pistolization and masculinity, flows and resistance. *International Journal of Law, Crime and Justice*, 40, 3–19.

D'Arcy, S., 2007. The 'Jamaican criminal' in Toronto 1994: a critical ontology. *Canadian Journal of Communication*, 32, 241–59.

DiManno, R., 2010. Raid exposes international crime group. *Toronto Star*, 4 May.

Edwards, A. and Sheptycki, J., 2012. Third wave criminology: guns, crime and social order. *Criminology and Criminal Justice*, 9(3), 379–97.

Ellison, G. and Pino, N., 2012. *Globalization, police reform and development: doing it the western way?* London: Palgrave Macmillan.

Ericson, R.V., 2007. *Crime in an insecure world.* Cambridge: Polity Press.

Evans, P.B., Rueschemeyer, D. and Skocpol, T., 1985. *Bringing the state back in.* Cambridge, MA: Harvard University Press.

Goldsmith, A. and Sheptycki, J., 2007. *Crafting transnational policing.* Oxford: Hart.

Grillo, I., 2014. Jamaican organized crime after the fall of Dudus Coke. *CTC Sentinel*, 7(1), 5–7.

Gunst, L., 1996. *Born fi' dead: a journey through the Jamaican posse underworld.* New York, NY: Henry Holt and Co.

Harriot, A., 2008. *Organized crime and politics in Jamaica: breaking the nexus.* Michigan: Canoe Press.

Headley, B., 2006. Giving critical context to the deportee phenomenon. *Social Justice*, 33(1), 40–56.

Henley, J., 2010. Haiti: a long descent to hell. *The Guardian*, 14 January.

Hopgood, S., 2013. *The endtimes of human rights.* Ithaca, NY: Cornell University Press.

Huggins, M., 1998. *Political policing: the United States and Latin America.* Durham, NC: Duke University Press.

Ignatieff, M., 2005. *The lesser evil: political ethics in an age of terror.* Princeton, NJ: Princeton University Press.

*Jamaica Observer*, 2009. The Cokes then and now. 6 September.

Jones, S., 2015. Aid, cholera and protest: life in Haiti five years after the earthquake. *The Guardian*, Monday 12 January.

Lettinga, D. and van Troost, L. (eds), 2013. *Debating the endtimes of human rights: activism and institutions in a New-Westphalian World*. Amnesty International Netherlands, Strategic Studies Project.

Leuprecht, C., 2014. Guns for hire: North America's intra-continental gun trafficking networks. *Criminology, Criminal Justice Law and Society*, 15(3), 57–74.

McCulloch, J., 2004. Blue armies, khaki police and the cavalry on the New American Frontier: critical criminology for the 21st century. *Critical Criminology*, 12, 309–26.

Parenti, C., 2004. *The soft cage: surveillance in America from slavery to the war on terror*. New York, NY: Basic Books.

Phipps, C., 2015. FIFA's Jack Warner accused of diverting funds intended for Haiti earthquake victims. *The Guardian*, Tuesday 9 June.

Policing and Society, 2000. *Special Issue on Policing and Human Rights*, 10(1). London: Routledge.

Powell, B., 2010. Street gangs still thriving despite big busts. *Toronto Star*, 5 May.

Ramachandran, V. and Walz, J., 2013. Haiti's earthquake generated a $9 billion response – where did the money go? *The Guardian*, Monday 14 January.

Schwartz, M., 2012. As Jamaican drug lord is sentenced, US still silent on massacre. *The New Yorker*, 7 June.

Sheptycki, J., 1991. Using the state to change society, the example of domestic violence. *The Journal of Human Justice*, 3(1), 47–66.

Sheptycki, J., 1995. Transnational policing and the makings of a postmodern state. *British Journal of Criminology*, 35, 613–35.

Sheptycki, J., 1998. Policing, postmodernism and transnationalisation. *British Journal of Criminology*, 38, 485–504.

Silverman, J., 2010. Jamaica violence linked to US drug market. BBC News Website, www.bbc.com/news/10173302.

Sives, A., 2010. *Elections, violence and the democratic process in Jamaica 1944–2007*. Kingston: Ian Randle Publishers.

Sklair, L., 1995. *The sociology of the global system*. Baltimore, MD: Johns Hopkins University Press.

Slaughter, A.-M., 2004. *A new world order: government networks and the disaggregated state*. Princeton, NJ: Princeton University Press.

Stanley, E. and McCulloch, J., 2013. *State crime and resistance*. London: Routledge.

Syal, R., 2010. Operation Trident may be ditched in spending cuts. *The Guardian*, Sunday 21 September.

Tyler, T., 1990. *Why people obey the law*. New Haven, CT: Yale University Press.

United Nations [UN], 2014. *Concluding observations of the fourth periodic report of the United States of America*. Human Rights Committee; International Covenant on Civil and Political Rights, Adopted by the Committee at its 110th session (10–28 March 2014) CCPR/C/USA/CO/4.

Vallis, M., 2010. Massive police raids executed across Ontario: Project Corral. *National Post*, 4 May.

Wortley, S., 2013. Respect friendship and racial injustice: justifying gang membership in a Canadian city. *In*: Frank van Gemert, Dana Peterson and Inger-Lise Lien (eds), *Street Gangs, Migration and Ethnicity*. London: Routledge, 192–210.

Wortley, S. and Owusu-Bempah, Akwasi, 2011. The usual suspects: police stop and search practices in Canada. *Policing and Society*, 21(4), 395–407.

# Part V
# Human rights and the justice process

This section investigates aspects of the criminal justice process through the lens of human rights. Accessing a fair trial and just treatment at all stages of criminal procedure are fundamental individual and collective rights that have shaped the justice system profoundly. Human rights jurisprudence has had a real capacity to influence jurisdictions at national and international level. Each chapter engages with elements of individual rights in a given context, and offers an understanding of their practical operation and their wider socio-legal and cultural dimensions, which, it is argued, may have a detrimental effect on the application of human rights to real cases. This is mainly explained by authors, either implicitly or explicitly, by identifying justice institutions as acting for the state and being in a hegemonic position, rendering powerless the end-users of such institutions, whatever role they may have (as defendant, victims, witnesses).

Although the authors in this section recognize that more can be done in their selected area, it is evident that the application of human rights in the criminal process has produced a change in the relationship between the state and the people, which in turn has brought a shift, more visible at some times than others, from the authoritarian state to the regulatory state. This is closely linked to the acceptance that human rights carry positive propositions rather than just limiting actions.

The section opens with an exploration of human rights and their application to the criminal process in various contexts, starting with a discussion on victims of crime within criminal procedure by Robyn Holder. This chapter highlights the difference between how victims' rights 'look' in a book and how they are applied to real cases, identifying a gap between the two.

The second chapter by Chris Cunneen and Juan Tauri considers the intersection between Indigenous people and human rights in the law and justice process. They argue for a decolonized criminology which can allow for a reshape or reinterpretation or a better application of human rights, depending on cases. Alternative justice models are central to this re-orientation of human rights for Indigenous justice.

The next two chapters discuss women's rights and gender equality by justice institutions. The first one by Jill Hunter considers women's rights to dignity and privacy when acting as witnesses in an adversarial court in two separate scenarios: when accessing their religious rights by wearing an Islamic veil and when testifying as victims of sexual violence. The second chapter on domestic violence by Sanzhuan Guo recounts the contradiction of those states, which aim to be seen as human rights leaders in an international arena while acting very slowly in making domestic changes to the justice system. Further, this situation is presented as being the product of sociocultural hindrances that do not allow most recent legislative changes to produce tangible effects in courts.

The following chapter by Ursula Kilkelly and Louise Forde allows us to explore the case of child defendants' rights in the criminal justice system. The authors consider international, European and a number of domestic jurisdictions, to argue that child-friendly approaches are becoming more frequent now because of a positive promotion of children's human rights in courts.

Next, we are offered a reflection on customary justice in the chapter by Wondwossen Demissie Kassa and Muradu Abdo Srur. Taking the case of the coexistence in Ethiopia between customary and state law, the authors discuss ways to settle criminal disputes and highlight how a more evolved human rights lens that considers customary laws in a non-colonized context is needed.

Further, Saul Takahashi discusses the case of pre-indictment detention for ordinary crimes in the context of the Japanese criminal justice process. During such police detention, people can be subjected to heavy interrogation that can amount to torture especially where access to a lawyer is prohibited. It was hoped that recent reviews of Japan's implementation of the *International Covenant on Civil and Political Rights* would ignite changes, and certainly the advocacy of scholars such as Takahashi is fundamental for societal transformation.

The section concludes with a review of the International Criminal Court by Nerida Chazal. This chapter offers us an opportunity to see the evolution of the 'preventive state' at international level, an ideal that sees attempts to prevent criminal behaviour through the creation and reinforcement of a judicial arm of humanitarian intervention measures.

The chapters in this section offer a broad view on human rights in the context of various aspects of the criminal justice process. Read together, they offer a positive view of how much human rights are producing change but also remind us of the importance of adopting a critical lens to examine these changes so that we can improve domestic and international criminal justice systems further.

# 39

# Seeing the state

## Human rights violations of victims of crime and abuse of power

*Robyn Holder*

There is a deeply held view within criminology that victims' rights 'movements' are to be resisted. There is equally entrenched opinion amongst victim advocates that persons accused of offences have rights including human rights but persons as victims do not.[1] Both perspectives are fixated on the relationship between victim and accused. Both fail to 'see' the state in relation to persons as victims of crime and abuse of power.[2] This chapter considers how, through the lens of human rights, it may come more clearly into view.

In post-conflict and international justice settings and using human rights arguments, advances for victims have been considerable (Bassiouni 2006). Yet in the parallel universe of domestic adversarial justice systems, rights recognition remains both ambiguous and contested. Two basic approaches to victims are identified. One places responses to victims in a service sphere; another is a containment strategy providing for circumscribed participation. This chapter argues a different approach that re-centres the state as duty bearer to both victim and accused. People are 'citizens first' before, during and after their encounters with criminal justice (Holder 2013, p. 217). The proposition rests not only on the ideal of persons as equal before the law, but also on assumptions that states are obliged to treat citizens equally. These are classical liberal promises but powerful nonetheless.

The chapter explores definitional connections between victims of crime, of abuse of power and of human rights violations. It then focuses attention on the nature of rights and what we see of the state through its agents in criminal justice. Through a composite case the chapter then asks what human rights, relevant to victims of crime within domestic adversarial criminal procedure, are 'in the books' and what these look like 'in action'. The chapter concludes with brief discussion on how the human rights of victims may be progressively realized. A brief sketch of debate about victims in criminal justice sets the scene.

### Crime victims and criminal justice

Much has been written about crime victims and criminal justice; their subsidiary even marginal role.[3] Research has particularly explored the negative experiences with justice processes of victims in general (Shapland et al. 1985), and for different groups of victims.[4] The sheer diversity of people and populations victimized in different circumstances by a wide range of offences means victims are a political subject that, chameleon-like, reflect and absorb the competing and contradictory claims of others.

As a constituency, victims are not easily united (Bumiller 1988). The categorization of and boundaries to recognition of victim status are at once narrow and broad. They are narrowly cast as those victimized by offences specified in criminal codes, or as innocent and ideal (Christie 1986). More broadly there are victims of large-scale atrocity, of environmental degradation, of consumer capitalism and authoritarianism (White 2015, Garkawe 2004). Others now argue for victim-status for the non-human and of the natural world (Nussbaum 2006).

Of interest, however, is the rhetoric with which victims are swept into service for institutional ends. They have been cast as the battering ram of 'the law and order lobby' (Simon 2007) and as the powerless in need of the state's protection (Rock 2004). In post-conflict and international justice settings, it is in the interests of victims that justice organizations stake their legitimacy and purpose (Kendall and Nouwen 2014). Across every justice domain, however, has been heard the assertion that, in comparison with the accused, victims have no rights. Some say this is as it should be (Matravers 2010). From this perspective, criminal justice is a contest between the accused and the State in which the latter wields enormous and unequal power. Others have pressed for greater victim recognition and decried a fundamental unfairness to rules that see people used as expendable evidence.[5]

In response, one approach is to create a 'victim sector' that is parallel to though linked with criminal justice. Within the victim sector are reparation, criminal injuries compensation or financial assistance schemes plus various support and therapeutic services (Dunn 2007). Some are generic to any victim of crime and others for specific categories of victim such as of homicide or sexual assault. Service responses also include access to universal medical, welfare, housing and social support schemes. Arguably this assistance falls under state obligations pursuant to the UN *Covenant on Economic, Social and Cultural Rights* (1966).[6] Through such investment governments can say that they are even-handed in the allocation of public resources between populations of victims and of offenders.[7] The constituencies are separate but equal.

A second approach locates in the juridical domain. It delineates agency standards that victims may anticipate and provides circumscribed participatory opportunities. Charter documents specify items such as access to information and respectful treatment. These are 'legitimate expectations' of citizens[8] but, in public policy discourse, are presented as 'rights'. Also in this approach is an array of legislative provisions providing protections for witnesses[9] and occasions for involvement such as victim impact statements and submissions to parole boards.[10] The containment strategy recognizes the logic of victims as essential actors to the operation of criminal justice.

The achievements contained in these approaches have been hard won. In the main they are also valued by victims (Dunn 2007). The approaches reflect both humanitarian regard for the consequences of victimization, and legal recognition (in particular circumstances) of persons *as* victims. Yet both approaches work to divert attention from claims for substantive and procedural rights and also do not unduly upset the priorities and arrangements of justice institutions themselves. How then does a rights lens reveal different arrangements?

## Special rights for victims of crime?

Some argue that the 1985 United Nations *Declaration of Basic Principles of Justice for Victims of Crime and Abuse of Power* constitute special rights for an identifiable disadvantaged group (Doak 2008, Garkawe 2005, Wemmers 2012). The instrument[11] sets out provisions for fair and respectful treatment, for access to justice and redress, to information and opportunities to put their views and have these considered, measures for protection of safety and privacy, for restitution and compensation, and for informal dispute resolution. It also specifies that there be 'proper assistance' for victims 'throughout the legal process' and for access to 'the necessary material, medical, psychological and social assistance'.

Like other similar guideline instruments of the UN, the 1985 Declaration is 'soft'.[12] To differing degrees, its provisions have been incorporated into the legal framework of nations as legislated or administrative charters. These are, however, highly contingent and not enforceable (Groenhuijsen 2014). Despite argument that victim charters impinge on fair trial rights of the accused (Sanders 2004), provisions fall largely outside trial parameters and do little than position the victim as a consumer of agency kindness (Shapland 2000). Observers point not only to the hard law gap between what victims can rely on and actionable rights of an accused, but also to a normative gap. They perceive that one carries more legitimacy, even more *value* than the other. From this perspective, it is a logical next step to strengthen and extend rights specific to the interests of victims of crime. Examples of this approach are the 2012 European Directive specifying minimum standards on the rights, support and protection of victims of crime,[13] and moves to secure binding Convention status for the 1985 Declaration (Garkawe 2009, Groenhuijsen 2014).

## Victims of abuse of power

However, victims of crime are not as marginal to human rights principles and standards as some would have us believe. The specification of victim interests has progressed in regional jurisprudence,[14] various international instruments,[15] in Articles establishing the International Criminal Court,[16] and Guidelines on the Right to a Remedy and Reparation.[17] Indeed, drafters of this latter instrument have called it 'an international bill of rights of victims' (Bassiouni 2006, p. 203).

Substantively, the connecting idea within this human rights canon is that victims are persons who have suffered not just 'harm' but 'substantial impairment of their fundamental rights'. Whether victims of crime, of violation of human rights or of 'abuse of power', this core definition is shared (McGonigle Lehy 2011, p. 232, Lamborn 1987, van Boven 2010). Often overlooked by scholars and legislators alike, the 'substantial impairment of their fundamental rights' may arise from 'violation of criminal laws' or of 'internationally recognized norms relating to human rights' (1985 Declaration, paras 3 and 18). The application of the 1985 Victims Declaration to victims of abuse of power as well as of crime binds it to human rights law; and human rights law to it.

From this perspective human rights scholar Francesca Klug writes that 'victims are at the centre of human rights thinking' (Klug 2004, p. 117). They are central, she says, by virtue of a violation of their human rights *and* their individual standing to claim in consequence. In essence, they are human before they are victim.

## Of rights and the state

Klug's assertion has been obscured by two issues. One is the nature of the rights at issue and the other is 'the state' and how we think of it in relation to rights and to victims. On the first, attention has tended to focus on victim charters – arguably second tier documents. In contrast human rights as norms and as laws are treaty based and carry enormous moral appeal. They are radical by virtue of their universality. Human rights 'by definition, apply to all people: from old to young, from rich to poor, from virtuous to corrupt, to female, male and other sexual identities' (Charlesworth 2014, p. 560). And from accused to victim. Thus, the forensic question is what human right(s) of the victim may be at issue in criminal proceedings and how these are recognized and enabled.

Second, the state has a dual role to all its citizens. It is the principal *duty bearer* and must refrain from actions that violate human rights and, for certain human rights, act positively to protect. It is also the body against which breaches of human rights are made (whether the original conduct was of a private or public actor) (Klug 2004, p. 117). The state is both 'goody' and 'baddy'.

Hidden behind a group of everyday institutions, the state in criminal justice is at its most powerful. This power is deployed for the individual and public good; *and* can be used in arbitrary and repressive ways. Thus, constraining what is most obvious of the state's power, specific protections vest in persons accused of a criminal conduct: the presumption of innocence, and rights to be heard by a competent, independent and impartial tribunal, to a public hearing, to be heard within a reasonable time, to legal representation and to interpretation.[18] These rights constitute very specific and concrete obligations. Yet the state's power over and duties to persons as victims (and witnesses) are less in view. Because, says Edwards, victims are not 'in a position of inequality vis-à-vis the state' as is the accused (Edwards 2004, p. 972). But are they?

## Agents of states

Justice institutions such as prosecution are 'agents of States' (Myjer et al. 2003, p. vii). They are also hegemonic (Sarat and Clarke 2008). For individuals seeking formal adjudication on an allegation of crime there is no way around the public prosecutor. It is a monopoly institution[19] that is substantively without review.[20] They are 'a representation of the State which has the power to interfere with the life, liberty and property of the citizen' (Refshauge 2005, p. 3). As such – as goodies – they are required to 'perform their duties fairly, consistently and expeditiously, and respect and protect human dignity and uphold human rights' (*Guidelines on the Role of Prosecutors 1990*, para. 12).[21] Under various national and state-based human rights legislation, prosecution are also 'public authorities' and must act in accordance with and 'give proper consideration' to human rights.[22]

Prosecutors assert their purpose in 'the public interest' and commonly fold the victim into a baggy notion of 'the public' or place them into a box marked 'private interests'. In either space, the victim has no autonomy from prosecution (Mouthaan 2012). This smudging of victims' independent interests fosters a perspective that they and prosecution are one and the same. They are not. Equating the interests and power of the prosecution with the member of the public fosters a notion that victims, under the prosecution cloak, have 'equality of arms' with the accused (McGonigle Lehy 2011).[23] It is convenient for the state to allow this fiction to continue; that nestled under the benevolent wing of the public prosecutor the human rights of the victim of crime are robustly or even adequately protected. By not 'seeing' the individual crime victim as a rights-bearing citizen in the same way they see the individual accused, prosecuting authorities shift to a place where routine abuse of state power becomes possible.[24]

## The human rights of crime victims

It is easy to avoid understanding the state as both goody and baddy in its various relationships to victims and witnesses. A composite case (see Box below) can illustrate the human rights of crime victims, the abuse of power (the human rights violation) and the state's duties. The case study is a rudimentary analysis of various violations (abuse) of state power and the obligations of the duty-bearing prosecution to Jane.

## A composite victim of crime case

Jane is a victim of a sexual assault and a criminal charge is brought against the alleged assailant. After a committal in the lower court, the matter is listed for trial. With numerous adjournments it takes five years for the trial to commence.[25] Over this time, Jane has commenced a new career and is afraid her colleagues will learn about her involvement with the case. She asks for a closed court and for suppression of her identity and her testimony. During the trial she is inadvertently made aware that defence have secured access to all her medical records. At trial the assailant is determined unfit to plead. At a special hearing he was found to have engaged in the conduct alleged and not acquitted and directed to be subject to the jurisdiction of the Mental Health Tribunal. The Court's judgement, including identifying information, is posted on the court website. The Mental Health Tribunal makes orders for the person.

*Table 39.1* Human rights application to victims/witnesses (Jane's case)

| *The violation of state power* | *Human Right*[1] | *Application to victim/witness* |
|---|---|---|
| Women uniquely subject to sexual victimization inadequately protected | Equality before the law and to equal protection of the law | Ensure non-discrimination, provision and implementation of effective remedies and operational measures[2] |
| Failure to mount an effective investigation and failure to provide a`n effective remedy | Life, liberty and security of person | Positive obligation to provide adequate protection / preventive measures[3]<br>Ensure provision and implementation of effective remedies<br>Exercise due diligence[4] |
| Failure to consider individual privacy and reputation rights, and failure to intervene positively to protect those rights | Right to private life/reputation | Protect privacy as a witness and as victim[5]<br>Privacy of medical records[6]<br>Special protections and provisions for victim / witnesses[7] |
| Failure to consider and intervene to protect human dignity | | Covers 'physical and moral integrity of the person'[8] |
| Failure to consider and to provide for protection of vulnerable witness | Right to fair trial | Undue delay is significant for all parties[9]<br>Organise criminal proceedings such that victim / witness human rights are 'not imperilled'[10,11] |
| Failure to employ an assessment framework for 'just and proportionate balance' in rights protection | | May exclude press and public 'if interests of private lives of parties require'[12]<br>Witness protections (screens, CCTV, pre-record evidence, closed court) not necessarily violation of 'right to confront'[13] |
| Failure to ensure that victim 'informed of their rights' | | Fair trial principles apply whether criminal, civil or other proceedings[14,15] |

*Notes:*

[1] Whether the original conduct and the violation is by public or private act. That is, human rights law is NOT solely concerned with violations by the state but also of violations by 'non-state actors' (Klug 2004: 112).

[2] Expected to be provided through criminal & domestic law. When the state fails to provide such remedies that it may be in breach of HR (*X&Y v Netherlands* 1985). Legislation is insufficient, preventive 'operational measures' may

be necessary (*Osman v UK* 1999). Inhuman and degrading treatment (*A v UK* 1998). Duty on state to respond promptly, diligently and effectively in investigations and backed by prosecutions (various Turkish cases). And Gonzales (IACHR 2011) and *Vertido v The Philippines*. See also Human Rights Committee General Comment No. 28 (2000) para. 18, General Comment 18 (1989) para. 4.

[3] Human Rights Committee General Comment 35 (2014) para. 9. *Whiteside v UK* (1992). This protection cannot necessarily be provided by civil remedies (*X&Y v Netherlands* 1985), and Gonzales (IACHR 2011).

[4] A positive standard – Velasquez Rodríguez (IACHR 1988) and Gonzales (IACHR 2011) – the latter judgement noting that the effect of US Supreme Court case law is that 'there is no constitutional or statutory remedy at the federal level' (p. 55). The Declaration on the Elimination of all Forms of Violence against Women (1993) requires governments to exercise due diligence to prevent and punish violence against women committed by state agents or private persons (Article 4c).

[5] Balanced for rape victim alongside accused right to fair trial (*Baegen v Netherlands* 1995 and *X&Y v Netherlands*) – positive obligation to protect against arbitrary interference by public authorities. And see Human Rights Committee General Comment No.16 (1988) paras 7, 8, 11. Relevant also is the discussion seeking a 'just and proportionate balance' between two fundamental rights in the Canadian Supreme Court in *R v NS* 2012 SCC 72.

[6] *Z v Finland* – ruling that medical records could be disclosed but confidential for 10 years, but named in judgement. ECtHR – breach privacy but necessary to prevent and protect others (HIV) BUT breached on website. UK HMCPSI 2013 report reviewing prosecution protections on disclosures of medical records and counselling notes.

[7] ICC Rome Statute Article 68 (exception for public hearing), Articles 67 and 69 (oral or recorded testimony). *Stubbings v UK*.

[8] *X&Y v Netherlands*.

[9] UN Human Rights Committee General Comment No.32 (2007) (replacing No. 13, 1984) paras 27, 35; and para. 6(e) 1985 Victims Declaration.

[10] *Doorson v Netherlands* (1996). Screens and other equipment to protect vulnerable witnesses (*X v UK* 1992). Not necessarily unfair to prevent cross-examination of vulnerable witnesses (*HM Advocate v Nulty* 2000). ECtHR – concerned that '*proceedings as a whole are fair*' (Klug 2004: 118) (emphasis in original).

[11] Right to information, e.g. about subpoenas for records.

[12] The Press and the public may be excluded from all or part of a trial for reasons of morals, public order (*ordre public*) or national security in a democratic society, or when the interest of the private lives of the parties so requires, or to the extent strictly necessary in the opinion of the court in special circumstances where publicity would prejudice the interests of justice.

[13] *R v Zuber* (2010 ACTSC 107) and *X v Austria* (1965) (closed court). And Convention Against Transnational Organized Crime & Convention Against Torture.

[14] Article 14(1) and in General Comment 13.

[15] The Standards of Professional Responsibility and Statement of the Essential Duties and Rights of Prosecutors (1990).

What of Jane's human rights might be engaged is drawn from case law, jurisprudence and provisions from regional and national jurisdictions (see Table 39.1). The referencing draws from Jonathan Doak's extensive analysis of decisions of the European Court of Human Rights and the human rights jurisdiction of the UK (Doak 2008).

Two issues are important to note. First, raising the human right of a victim at issue does not mean that person directs prosecution. As the European Court of Human Rights stated in *Finucane*, 'the duty to investigate under Article 2 is "not an obligation of result but of means"'.[26] Second, Jane's case reveals that different human rights for both civilian parties may be engaged – for example, her right to privacy and reputation in seeking a closed court and orders, and the accused person's right to (a public) fair trial. The point is that the state's agent, here the prosecution, must deliberately consider and seek ways to reconcile the rights. As the Canadian Supreme Court stated in considering a clash of two different human rights, the obligation is to find 'reasonably available alternative measures' that may reconcile the tension.[27]

## Progressive realization of the human rights of victims of crime

Jane's case reveals precisely this structural tension for the state's agent in 'everyday' justice processing. States are routinely confronted by different interests of different individuals and different groups. On one level, the rights claim of any given citizen is of no less or greater strength than another; and has no less or greater call on the state than another. Human rights provide an 'interest-balancing' framework through which the state's agents must work (Doak 2003, p. 32); and one through which citizens themselves assess the state's fair treatment of and between them.

The view that accused persons have human rights and victims don't has been allowed to fester in part because justice institutions have not 'seen' their obligations to the human rights of victims. But it has also been because citizens who have been victims of crime have been left to flounder without representation of their independent interests in a space where the state holds all the cards. Victim advocates have failed to bring human rights home (Bettinger-López 2008). Learning the language of human rights, building alliances, implementing due diligence audits,[28] submitting amicus briefs,[29] and speaking victims' human rights to the state form the beginning of a strategy to check abuse of power.

## Notes

1 Braithwaite and Pettit discuss their presumption that victim social movements should be resisted but then qualify this by highlighting circumstances where there might be 'power imbalance' between victims and offenders (1994, pp. 773–4). For references on debates about victims and offenders rights, see note 3.

2 James Scott was interested in the ways the state 'sees' citizens. Here I am concerned with bringing the state into the view of citizens (see Scott 1998).

3 For Australia, see O'Connell (2015), the US see Beloof (2005) and Davis and Mulford (2008), and in the United Kingdom (UK) see Hall (2009, Chapter 2).

4 For seminal texts on the experience of domestic violence victims see Buzawa and Buzawa (2003), Temkin and Krahé (2008) on sexual assault, Morgan and Zedner (1992) on child victims, Maguire and Bennett (1982) on residential burglary, and Rock (1994) on homicide. For work on crimes against minorities and hate crimes see Jacobs and Potter (2000) and Memmot et al. (2001).

5 See note 3.

6 Retrieved on 30 July 2015 from: www.ohchr.org/EN/ProfessionalInterest/Pages/CESCR.aspx.

7 Notwithstanding that there is a wide disparity between the quanta of public funds going specifically to offenders as to victims. An Australian costs of crime report estimated that direct assistance to victims of crime was $880 m/year and for adult and juvenile offenders was $1,940 m/year (Mayhew 2003, pp. 69–74).

8 The principle of 'legitimate expectations' is used in public and administrative law in order 'to strike a fair balance between the exercise of public functions and the protection of private interests' (Thomas 2000, p. 1). See also Shapland (2000, pp. 147–64).

9 See Doak (2003).

10 For an overview, see Roberts (2009).

11 Retrieved on 30 July 2015 from: www.un.org/documents/ga/res/40/a40r034.htm.

12 'Soft laws' are not legally binding on states. However, they can be said to 'reflect the intention of states [and] can be regarded as obligations of cooperation and good faith' (Myjer et al. 2003, pp. 6–7).

13 Retrieved on 30 July 2015 from: http://eur-lex.europa.eu/legal-content/EN/TXT/PDF/?uri = CELEX:32012L0029&from =EN.

14 For example, Doak (2008) and Leverick (2004) discuss case law relevant to victims of crime at the European Court of Human Rights; and Bettinger-López (2008) discusses case law and the Gonzales case at the Inter-American Court of Human Rights.

15 Notably a whole instrument for victims of human trafficking, sections within instruments on organized crime, atrocity and slavery as well as provisions within conventions on women, children, persons with a disability and so forth.

16 In particular, Articles 64 (protection of witnesses), Article 68 (information), Articles 75, 81 and 82 (assistance, reparations), and Regulations 80 and 81 (OPVC) (Greco 2007).

17 *Guidelines on the Right to a Remedy and Reparation for Victims of Gross Violations of International Human Rights Law and Serious Violations of International Humanitarian Law* (2006). However, the Preamble states that the Guidelines 'do not entail new international or domestic legal obligations but identify mechanisms, modalities, procedures and methods for the implementation of existing legal obligations under international human rights law and international humanitarian law which are complementary though

different as to their norms'. There does not appear to be a firm agreed definition of a 'gross' violation. It does not assume large-scale and can be systematic, with an element of planning and be of inhumane and degrading character (Geneva Academy 2014, p. 15). Van Boven (2010, p. 2) discusses the meaning of 'gross' as connected to the serious character of the violations and their nature.

18 *International Covenant on Civil and Political Rights* (1966) Articles 9 and 14.

19 The existence of a right to private prosecution in common law countries is tenuous at best.

20 Scope for review of prosecution decisions is extremely narrow. In Australia, see *Maxwell v R* [1996] HCA 46; (1996) 184 CLR 501 (15 March 1996). In contra for the UK, see Spencer (2010, pp. 148–51). Note also a new initiative of the UK CPS on victims' right of review, retrieved on 3 July 2015 from: www.cps.gov.uk/victims_witnesses/victims_right_to_review/index.html.

21 The *Human Rights Manual for Prosecutors* produced by the International Association of Prosecutors (IAP) (the 'Prosecutors' Human Rights Manual') specifies that 'on behalf of society' the prosecutor must observe 'the rights of the individual'. In Recommendation (2000) 19 of the Committee of Ministers on the Role of Public Prosecution in the Criminal Justice System, prosecutors 'should take or promote actions to protect their life, safety and privacy' (para. 32) (Myjer et al. 2003).

22 In Australia, s. 38 *Charter of Human Rights and Responsibilities* (Victoria 2006) stipulates that public authorities must perform their functions in a manner that is not incompatible with the charter rights. In s. 40B of the *Human Rights Act* (ACT 2004), and in the UK *Human Rights Act* 1998 (s. 6) it is unlawful for a public authority to act in a way which is incompatible with Charter rights.

23 McGonigle Lehy cites the European Court of Human Rights judgement in *Foucher v France* (1997) as providing substantive definition to the concept of 'equality of arms' (2011, p. 15). She uses the concept to argue against victim participation in international criminal proceedings (2011, pp. 354–6). In the domestic criminal jurisdiction, see also Hudson (2004, p. 126).

24 The 'Prosecutors' Human Rights Manual' does not reference or include the 1985 UN Victims Declaration. The Standards of Professional Responsibility and Statement of the Essential Duties and Rights of Prosecutors (1990) specifies that they '*shall . . . safeguard* the rights of the accused' whereas prosecutors '*shall . . . seek to ensure* that victims and witnesses are informed of their rights' (s. 4.3) (emphasis added) (Myjer et al. 2003). Sarat and Clarke claim that the exercise of prosecution discretion is 'the language of administration' disguising the logic of power (2008, p. 387).

25 Delays in a matter coming to trial are not confined to sexual offences.

26 Cited in Leverick (2004, p. 189).

27 In *R v NS* (2012 SCC 72) the Canadian Supreme Court had to decide between two sets of Charter rights – a right to religious freedom of a victim witness to wear a *niqab* while testifying and the right of those accused of sexual offences to a fair trial. The Court found in favour of the accused. The dissenting judgement of Abella J. traverses a wider set of questions of relevance to the witness as well as to the wider interests of justice. See https://scc-csc.lexum.com/scc-csc/scc-csc/en/item/12779/index.do (accessed 11 April 2016).

28 For some examples, see UK Equalities and Human Rights Commission (2014).

29 The National Crime Victim Law Institute in the United States has developed expertise in this area. Related are 'position papers' on specific rights issues. See, for example, ACT Victims of Crime Commissioner (2015).

## References

ACT Victims of Crime Commissioner, July 2015. *Protecting privacy of victims in court and tribunal proceedings of subpoenaed health information*. Canberra.

Bassiouni, M.C., 2006. International recognition of victims' rights. *Human Rights Law Review*, 6(2), 203–79.

Beloof, D.E., 2005. Third wave of crime victims' rights: standing, remedy, and review. *The Brigham Young University Law Review*, 2, 255–370.

Bettinger-López, C., 2008. Human rights at home: domestic violence as a human rights violation. *Columbia Human Rights Law Review*, 40(19), 19–77.

Braithwaite, J. and Pettit, P., 1994. Republican criminology and victim advocacy: comment. *Law and Society Review*, 28(4), 765–76.

Bumiller, K., 1988. *The civil rights society: the social construction of victims*. Baltimore, MD: The Johns Hopkins University Press.

Buzawa, E. and Buzawa, C., 2003. *Domestic violence: the criminal justice response*. Thousand Oaks: Sage.

Charlesworth, H., 2014. Two steps forward, one step back? The field of women's human rights. *European Human Rights Law Review*, 6, 560–5.

Christie, N., 1986. The ideal victim. In: E. Fattah (ed.), *From crime policy to victim policy: reorienting the justice system*. Basingstoke: Macmillan, 17–30.

Davis, R. and Mulford, C., 2008. Victim rights and new remedies: finally getting victims their due. *Journal of Contemporary Criminal Justice*, 24(2), 198–208.

Doak, J., 2003. The victim and the criminal justice process: an analysis of recent trends in regional and international tribunals. *Legal Studies*, 23(1), 1–32.

Doak, J., 2008. *Victims' rights, human rights and criminal justice: reconceiving the role of third parties*. Portland, OR: Hart Publishing.

Dunn, P., 2007. Matching service delivery to need. *In*: S. Walklate (ed.), *Handbook of victims and victimology*. Cullompton, Devon: Willan Publishing, 255–81.

Edwards, I., 2004. An ambiguous participant: the crime victim and criminal justice decision-making. *British Journal of Criminology*, 44, 967–82.

Garkawe, S., 2004. Revisiting the scope of victimology: how broad a discipline should it be? *International Review of Victimology*, 11(2–3), 275–94.

Garkawe, S., 2005. Victims' rights are human rights. Speech to the National Conference, *Peaceful Coexistence: victims' rights in a human rights context*. July 2015, Canberra.

Garkawe, S., 2009. A victims' convention: the arguments in favour and an analysis of the draft by the World Society ofVictimology/Intervict. *In*: F. Winkel, P. Friday, G. Kirchhoff and R. Letschert (eds), *Victimization in a multidisciplinary key: recent advances in victimology*. The Netherlands: Wolf Legal Publishers, 171–206.

Geneva Academy of International Humanitarian Law and Human Rights, 2014. What amounts to 'a serious violation of international human rights law'? An analysis of practice and expert opinion for the purposes of the 2013 Arms Trade Treaty. *Academy Briefing No. 6*. August, Geneva.

Greco, G., 2007. Victims' rights overview under the ICC legal framework: a jurisprudential analysis. *International Criminal Law Review*, 7(2), 531–47.

Groenhuijsen, M., 2014. The development of international policy in relation to victims of crime. *International Review of Victimology*, 20(1), 31–48.

Hall, M., 2009. *Victims of crime: policy and practice in criminal justice*. Cullompton, Devon: Willan Publishing.

Holder, R., 2013. *Just interests: victims, citizens and the potential for justice*. PhD Thesis. The Australian National University. Retrieved on 11 April 2016 from: http://hdl.handle.net/1885/11464.

Hudson, B. 2004. Balancing the rights of victims and offenders. *In*: E. Cape (ed.), *Reconcilable rights?*, 126.

Jacobs, J. and Potter, K., 2000. *Hate crimes: criminal law and identity politics*. Oxford: Oxford University Press.

Kendall, S. and Nouwen, S., 2014. Representational practices at the International Criminal Court: the gap between juridified and abstract victimhood. *Law and Contemporary Problems*, 76(3&4), 235–62.

Klug, F., 2004. Human rights and victims. *In*: E. Cape (ed.), *Reconcilable rights?* 111–24.

Lamborn, L., 1987. The UN Declaration on victims: incorporating 'abuse of power'. *Rutgers Law Journal*, 19, 59–95.

Leverick, F., 2004. What has the ECHR done for victims? A United Kingdom perspective. *International Review of Victimology*, 11, 177–200.

Maguire, M. and Bennett, T., 1982. *Burglary in a dwelling: the offence, the offender and the victim*. London: Heinemann Educational Books.

Matravers, M. 2010. The victim, the state, and civil society. *In*: A. Bottoms and J. Roberts (eds), *Hearing the victim: adversarial justice, crime victims and the state*. Cullompton: Willan Publishing, 1–16.

Mayhew, P., 2003. Counting the costs of crime in Australia. *Trends and Issues*, 247, Canberra: Australian Institute of Criminology.

McGonigle Lehy, B., 2011. *Procedural justice? Victim participation in international criminal proceedings*. Utrecht: Intersentia.

Memmott, P., Stacy, R., Chambers, C. and Keys, C., 2001. *Violence in Indigenous communities*. Full Report. Canberra: Crime Prevention Branch, Attorney-General's Department.

Morgan, J. and Zedner, L., 1992. *Child victims: crime, impact and criminal justice*. Oxford: Oxford University Press.

Mouthaan, S., 2012. Victim participation at the ICC for victims of gender-based crimes: a conflict of interest? *Cardozo Journal of International and Comparative Law*, 21, 619–51.

Myjer, E., Hancock, B. and Cowdery, N. (eds), 2003. *Human rights manual for prosecutors*. International Association of Prosecutors. The Netherlands: Wolf Publishing.

Nussbaum, M., 2006. *Frontiers of justice: disability, nationality, species membership*. Cambridge, MA: Belknap Press.

O'Connell, M., 2015. The evolution of victims' rights and services in Australia. *In*: D. Wilson and S. Ross (eds), *Crime, victims and policy: international contexts, local experiences*. London: Palgrave, 240–78.

Refshauge, R., 2005. The prosecution role in upholding the right to a fair trial and responding to victims/witnesses. Speech to the National Conference, *Peaceful Coexistence – victims' rights in a human rights context*, July 2015, Canberra.

Roberts, J., 2009. Listening to the crime victim: evaluating victim input at sentencing and parole. *Crime and Justice*, 38(1), 347–412.

Rock, P., 1994. *After homicide: practical and political responses to bereavement*. Oxford: Oxford University Press.

Rock, P., 2004. *Constructing victims' rights: the Home Office, New Labour, and victims*. Oxford: Oxford University Press.

Sanders, A., 2004. Involving victims in sentencing: a conflict with defendants' rights? *In*: E. Cape (ed.), *Reconcilable rights?* 91–110.

Sarat, A. and Clarke, C., 2008. Beyond discretion: prosecution and the logic of sovereignty, and the limits of law. *Law and Social Inquiry*, 33(2), 387–416.

Scott, J., 1998. *Seeing like a state: how certain schemes to improve the human condition have failed*. New Haven, CT: Yale University Press.

Shapland, J., 2000. Victims and criminal justice: creating responsible criminal justice agencies. *In*: A. Crawford and J. Goodey (eds), *Integrating a victim perspective within criminal justice: international debates*. Dartmouth: Ashgate, 147–64.

Shapland, J., Willmore, J. and Duff, P., 1985. *Victims in the criminal justice system*. Aldershot: Gower Publishing.

Simon, J., 2007. *Governing through crime: how the war on crime transformed American democracy and created a culture of fear*. Oxford: Oxford University Press.

Spencer, J., 2010. The victim and the prosecutor. *In*: A. Bottoms and J. Roberts (eds), *Hearing the victim: adversarial justice, crime victims and the state*. Cullompton, Devon: Willan Publishing, 141–62.

Temkin, J. and Krahé, B., 2008. *Sexual assault and the justice gap: a question of attitude*. Portland, OR: Hart Publishing.

Thomas, R. 2000. *Legitimate expectations and proportionality in administrative law*. Oxford: Hart Publishing.

United Kingdom Equalities and Human Rights Commission, 2014. *Human Rights in Action: case studies from Regulators, Inspectorates and Ombudsmen (RIOs)*. London.

United Nations, 1990. *Guidelines on the Role of Prosecutors*. Adopted by the Eighth United Nations Congress on the Prevention of Crime and the Treatment of Offenders, Havana, Cuba, 27 August–7 September 1990.

van Boven, T., 2010. *The United Nations Basic Principles and Guidelines on the Right to a Remedy and Reparation for Victims of Gross Violations of International Human Rights Law and Serious Violations of International Humanitarian Law*. United Nations Audiovisual Library of International Law. Retrieved on 1 July 2015 from: http://un.org/law/avl.

Wemmers, J., 2012. Victims' rights are human rights: the importance of recognizing victims as persons. *Temida*, June, 71–84.

White, R., 2015. Environmental victimology and ecological justice. *In*: D. Wilson and S. Ross (eds), *Crime, victims and policy*. London: Palgrave Macmillan, 33–52.

# 40

# Survival, dignity and wellbeing

## Indigenous human rights and transformative approaches to justice

*Chris Cunneen and Juan Tauri*

In considering the intersection between Indigenous people and human rights, there are potentially three broad areas of interest to criminology. These are: compliance with international human rights treaties; the question of redress for historical abuses of human rights; and, finally, the role of normative human rights principles that have emerged in the last decade and apply specifically to Indigenous peoples. The high levels of criminalization and hyper-incarceration of Indigenous people in settler colonial societies (Cunneen et al. 2013, Cunneen and Tauri forthcoming) raise fundamental compliance questions with a range of treaties including the *International Covenant on Civil and Political Rights, Convention against Torture, International Convention on the Elimination of All Forms of Racial Discrimination, Convention on the Elimination of all Forms of Discrimination Against Women, Convention on the Rights of the Child* and *Convention on the Rights of Persons with Disabilities*. The United Nations (UN) monitoring committees for these treaties regularly question the compliance of countries like Australia, Canada and the United States (US) in relation to their treatment of Indigenous peoples within criminal justice systems (Cunneen and Tauri forthcoming). The long-term effects of the policies and practices of colonization have also given rise to claims for redress for historical human rights abuses. The specific nature of these claims for redress varies between settler colonial states. However, they have included reparations for the forced removal of Indigenous children from their families and their treatment in residential schools, and various abuses of Indigenous trust funds and other state-controlled monies, including fraud, corruption and mismanagement (Cunneen 2012).

While both the failure to comply with existing human rights treaties, and the failure to adequately redress historical human rights abuses are important in their own right, this chapter will focus on the third area identified above: the role of normative human rights principles, particularly those established in the UN *Declaration on the Rights of Indigenous Peoples* (hereafter the Declaration). The framework for understanding, developing and promoting Indigenous human rights has advanced significantly since the adoption of the Declaration by the UN General Assembly in 2007. The Declaration is a normative document that establishes the 'minimum standards for the survival, dignity and wellbeing of the indigenous peoples of the world' (Article 43). It was adopted by a majority of 143 states, with four votes against and

11 abstentions. Significantly, the four states that voted against the Declaration were the Anglo settler colonial states of Australia, Canada, Aotearoa/New Zealand and the US. During the period of 2009–10, these states reversed their opposition to the Declaration, and moved to affirm and support the document. However, they also stressed that the Declaration is 'aspirational' and 'non-binding' (Lightfoot 2012), thereby hedging their support for the principles underpinning Indigenous human rights.

The purpose of this chapter is to look at the normative framework of human rights provided by the Declaration in the context of Indigenous peoples' assertions of their right to 'justice'. It is argued that the evolving Indigenous justice movement provides a decolonizing moment in challenging the operation of settler colonial criminal justice systems. It can also be argued that Indigenous justice activism, in particular their claims for a measure of jurisdictional autonomy, problematizes the normative foundations of human rights frameworks established by nation-states and supra-national bodies like the UN, frameworks that are often utilized to deny Indigenous claims of exceptionalism afforded them as the 'First Peoples'.

## The normative human rights framework established in the declaration

There are four key principles that underpin the Declaration: self-determination; participation in decision-making and free, prior and informed consent; non-discrimination and equality; and respect for and protection of culture (ATSISJC 2011, p. 18). Each of these principles provides a basis for assessing criminal justice in settler colonial states as it impacts on Indigenous peoples, and a guide to understanding Indigenous demands for reconceptualizing justice. These principles have both practical and theoretical implications. They require us to rethink the way we approach the institutional frameworks of policing, courts, sentencing, punishment and the reintegration of Indigenous offenders. They require us to move from a position inside of the taken-for-granted institutional frameworks of criminal justice, to one that is continually *questioning* whether these institutions can or do meet the requirements of Indigenous human rights norms. As argued further in this chapter, this normative position also challenges a range of theoretical, research and ethical assumptions within criminology.

The four principles noted above provide a framework for the discussion in this chapter. Put briefly, every issue concerning Indigenous peoples is implicated in the collective right of self-determination. 'Self-determination is a process. The right to self-determination is the right to make decisions' (ATSISJC 1993, p. 41). At a community or tribal level, it includes the right to exercise control over decision-making, community priorities, how communities operate and processes for resolving disputes (ATSISJC 2011, pp. 109–10). The recognition that self-determination is a process rather than a single act has important implications: it requires that there are *ongoing* processes that facilitate self-determination, and these may change over time. The right to make decisions might include Indigenous controlled and operated criminal justice processes (for example, policing), but it might also involve collective decisions to participate in non-Indigenous criminal justice processes where Indigenous people negotiate processes and outcomes. For example, the recommendations from Australia's Stolen Generations Inquiry relating to juvenile justice require that accredited Indigenous organizations play a role in decision-making when diversionary options are being considered for Indigenous young people (NISATSIC 1997, pp. 590–7).

Self-determination is closely linked to the second principle of participation. Participation in decision-making requires participation in both internal Indigenous community decision-making, as well as external decision-making processes with government, industry and non-government organizations. Decision-making must be free, prior to any activity occurring, informed of all the options and consequences, and based on Indigenous consent. As the Aboriginal and Torres Strait Islander Social Justice Commissioner explains:

> Free means no force, bullying or pressure. Prior means that we have been consulted before the activity begins. Informed means we are given all of the available information and informed when that information changes or when there is new information. If our peoples don't understand this information then we have not been informed.
>
> *(ATSISJC 2011, p. 122)*

The requirements underpinning decision-making are particularly apt when assessing how governments 'consult' (rather than negotiate or engage) with Indigenous peoples, and specifically the process through which various policy initiatives are introduced in Indigenous communities, even those cast as benevolent, such as family group conferencing, child protection interventions or alcohol restrictions.

The principle of non-discrimination and equality is particularly important given the history of racial discrimination against Indigenous people that was entrenched within the colonial project. Systematic regimes of racial discrimination played a fundamental role in creating the current socioeconomic marginalization of Indigenous people. Contemporary Indigenous poverty, ill-health, over-crowded housing and poor educational outcomes did not simply 'fall from the sky' – they were created historically through policies such as forced relocations of Indigenous nations, removal of children, control of wages and denial of social security (Cunneen and Tauri forthcoming). Furthermore, the principle of equality requires the recognition of cultural difference. The Declaration affirms that 'Indigenous peoples are equal to all other peoples, while recognizing the right of all peoples to be different, to consider themselves different, and to be respected as such'. Criminal justice systems have played an important historical role in enforcing racial discrimination through discriminatory legislation and practices, including separate regimes for policing, sentencing and punishment (Cunneen 2001, Cunneen et al. 2013). Today various criminal laws and their enforcement (such as public order legislation and police powers) are often seen as constituting indirect racial discrimination in their application, in effect a repudiation of the right of Indigenous peoples to be 'Indigenous', through the criminalization of Indigeneity.

For a decolonizing criminology, a fundamental understanding is that Indigenous culture is a source of strength and resilience, and cultural safety and cultural security are foundational to restoring and maintaining social order in Indigenous communities (ATSISJC 2011, pp. 123–34). In the health, child protection and criminal justice sectors, evidence shows that participation in decision-making and governance leads to improved outcomes, as do holistic Indigenous programmes aimed at family wellbeing, and culturally informed, Indigenous-designed treatment, rehabilitation and diversionary programmes (Kelaher et al. 2014, AIHW 2013, p. 1, SNAICC 2013, pp. 9–11, SCRGSP 2014, pp. 11.39–40).

Furthermore, respect for Indigenous culture (and the right to self-determination), must include respect for the formulation and practice of Indigenous knowledge. In our view, the lack of respect for Indigenous knowledge and Indigenous culture is one of the hallmarks of contemporary criminology. We return to this point below.

Overall, the four principles underpinning the Declaration have significant implications for state-based criminal justice systems – particularly when narrow definitions of universalism are seen to preclude the potential for the development of differential Indigenous approaches to justice. However, rather than seeing Indigenous claims as a *problem*, a decolonizing and human rights-based criminology might see the potential fragmentation of centralized criminal justice systems as an opportunity for progressive change and development.

## Indigenous self-determination and criminal justice: a short history

A major political impact of criminalization is that it disavows the political status of Indigenous people as 'first peoples', as well as denying the validity of Indigenous methods of governance, social control and knowledge. In place of an inherent, empowered political status, Indigenous people are both racialized and criminalized: in effect, they are 'dehumanized'. 'Race' becomes conflated with criminality and the political right of Indigenous people to control their own lives as legal subjects disappears. It is not surprising then that Indigenous political claims to self-determination often focus on criminal justice (see Jackson 1988), and are thus directly linked to a process of decolonization of criminal justice institutions and a decolonization of the discursive construction of Indigenous people as 'criminal'.

The problem with seeing Indigenous people only through the lens of disadvantage and dysfunction is that it leads to a deficit-based approach to public policy where Indigenous people are invariably cast as a 'problem to be solved', rather than as a people who have been actively oppressed and are demanding meaningful recognition of their human rights. Indigenous peoples are political actors engaged in a variety of activities within and against existing colonizing criminal justice systems. Through resistance, reform and creativity new 'justice' spaces have been opened. We only have to look at what Indigenous peoples are doing: Aboriginal and Torres Strait Islander night patrols, community justice groups and law and justice committees in Australia (Blagg 2008) and similar justice processes developed by Canadian First Nations, such as the Stó:lō First Nation's *Qwí:qwelstóm* process (Palys and Victor 2007), and justice institutions, including courts and police institutions instituted and run by the Navajo, the San Carlos Apache and other American Indian nations (see Newton 1998).

More generally, the rise of the modern Indigenous political movement focused on criminal justice issues, particularly the struggle against police brutality and imprisonment. In 1968, what was to become a leading national organization, the American Indian Movement was formed in Minneapolis. Its early work involved setting-up street patrols in Indigenous housing projects to address the problem of police violence, and the establishment of the Legal Rights Center to provide legal representation to American Indians and African-Americans (Dunbar-Ortiz 2014, pp. 184–5). In inner-city Sydney concern over police brutality and discriminatory arrests of Aboriginal people led to the establishment of the first Aboriginal Legal Service (ALS) in 1970. The ALS was from the beginning much broader than simply a service provider. It was a key advocacy organization for Indigenous self-determination and human rights, and represented, according to one of the founding Aboriginal activists, 'the birth of the modern day Aboriginal political movement' (Foley 1988, p. 109).

During the 1980s and 1990s, as a result of the Indigenous political pressure described above, both the Australian and Canadian governments established judicial inquiries that either focused directly on, or substantially considered, the criminal justice system treatment of Indigenous peoples. These inquiries included the Australian Royal Commission into Aboriginal Deaths in Custody (RCADIC), the Canadian Royal Commission on Aboriginal Peoples (RCAP), the Nova Scotia Royal Commission on the Donald Marshall, Jr., Prosecution and the Aboriginal Justice Inquiry of Manitoba (Johnston 1991, RCAP 1996, Hickman et al. 1989, Hamilton and Sinclair 1991). With the exception of the Marshall Royal Commission, all the inquiries emphasized the central role of Indigenous self-determination (Clark and Cove 1999, Cunneen 2001). For example, the relevant recommendation from the RCADIC reads:

> That Governments negotiate with appropriate Aboriginal organisations and communities to determine guidelines as to the procedures and processes which should be followed to

> ensure that the self determination principle is applied in the design and implementation of any policy or program or the substantial modification of any policy or program which will particularly affect Aboriginal people.
>
> *(Johnston 1991, p. 111)*

This recommendation encompassed the philosophical and political basis of action to implement the 337 recommendations of the RCADIC. The RCAP and the Manitoba Inquiry made similar recommendations in relation to self-determination (RCAP 1996, pp. 54–76, Hamilton and Sinclair 1991, p. 266).

As a response to Indigenous activism, government policy during the 1970s in Australia, Canada, Aotearoa/New Zealand and the US moved away from integration and assimilation (and in the US away from the policy of 'termination' – that is, the withdrawal of federal recognition of Indian tribes) to an official policy of Indigenous self-determination. However, 'self-determination' was to be defined by government not by Indigenous nations. It gave rise to an emphasis on consultation, negotiation and partnerships, but in reality denoting 'nothing more than . . . a promise that local [Indigenous] concerns and wishes will be considered in the design and implementation of [Indigenous] policies' (Fleras and Elliott 1992, p. 165). There was thus a substantial gap in the understanding of self-determination between government *policy* and the political demands of Indigenous organizations for recognition of self-determination as an *inherent right*. These differences have played out in the criminal justice sphere where Indigenous peoples have increasingly argued for greater recognition of their law and ability to develop their own systems of justice. Yet government law and policy continues to override Indigenous concerns. The most dramatic example of this in Australia was the Northern Territory Emergency Response (the Intervention) which introduced a range of discriminatory and authoritarian controls over Indigenous people and required the suspension of the Commonwealth *Racial Discrimination Act 1975* to achieve its aims (Cunneen and Rowe 2015). The rights embodied in the UN Declaration have thus far done little to change the way governments do business in the settler colonial states. As Lightfoot (2012, p. 102) argues, these states 'strategically, collectively and unilaterally wrote down the content of the [human rights] norms' to assure current policies and practices comply 'without any intent of further implementation'.

## Indigenous self-determination: where are the criminologists?

There is a significant political disjuncture between the rights embedded in the Declaration and the operation of criminal justice systems. Indigenous people still struggle with the damaging effects of one of the leading institutions of colonial control, and struggle to change the ongoing cycles of marginalization brought about as an outcome of criminalization. Yet with few exceptions (Blagg 2008, Cunneen 2001, Cunneen and Rowe 2014, 2015, Deckert 2014, Tauri 2014), most criminologists proceed with their analysis and prescriptions with the complete absence of any discussion around the importance of the right to self-determination, or indeed of the other core principles found in the Declaration including participation in decision-making, non-discrimination and respect for and protection of culture.

From the rapidly growing field of Indigenous knowledges and methodologies, there are at least five considerations with implications for criminological theory and practice (Cunneen and Rowe 2014, pp. 53–5). First, as the objects of research, Indigenous peoples have been constantly seen as 'research curiosities' and 'problems'. It is not surprising that within the Indigenous lexicon the term 'research' is often linked with colonialism (McIntosh 2011). 'The way in which scientific research has been implicated in the excesses of imperialism remains a powerful remembered history for many of the world's indigenous peoples' (Porsanger 2004, p. 107). Second, an important question raised by the connection between western research structures, philosophies and methods and the colonial process is whether these approaches are fundamentally racialized in their investigation of issues related to colonized peoples. Some have considered these approaches 'racist epistemologies' (Bishop 1998, Tauri 2012). Third, Indigenous perspectives on research represent alternative ways of thinking about the research process. The decolonization of research methods is seen as necessary to develop Indigenous knowledge (Smith 1999, Kovach 2009). There are important epistemological and ontological differences underpinning Indigenous approaches (Cunneen and Rowe 2014). These alternative approaches are not necessarily meant to replace a western research paradigm (Porsanger 2004) but rather to challenge it and to reconfigure Indigenous research as one that is increasingly defined by and responsive to Indigenous needs (Smith 1999). Fourth, Indigenous approaches seek to revalorize Indigenous knowledges as valid ways of understanding and describing the world. Thus, the importance of Indigenous research methodologies has to be understood within the broader valuing and assertion of Indigenous knowledges and cultures. The decolonization *of* research is one strategy emanating from Indigenous approaches, the other is research *for* decolonization. The latter reflects the widely held ethical view among Indigenous scholars that research needs to be for the benefit of Indigenous communities. Finally, Indigenous research is part of the decolonization process, particularly in the struggle for Indigenous self-determination (Porsanger 2004). Criminological research involves relations of power at multiple levels between the researcher and the research participant; in determining the priorities of research agendas; in the broader assumptions that give 'truth' value to certain types of research; and in the social, political and cultural values that underpin our processes of reasoning and understanding of the world (Cunneen and Rowe 2014, p. 54). Yet as Hart (2010, p. 4) notes: 'Eurocentric thought has come to mediate the entire world to the point where worldviews that differ from Eurocentric thought are relegated to the periphery, if they are acknowledged at all' (see also Battiste and Henderson 2000).

At the more extreme level, Indigenous knowledge in understanding Indigenous contexts is actively devalued by mainstream criminology. For example, both Marie (2010) and Weatherburn (2010, 2014) argue that Indigenous knowledge adds little to our understanding of crime and victimization. For instance, Weatherburn (2014, p. 65) claims that the causes of Indigenous violence and crime are 'entirely amenable to explanation in conventional scientific or western terms'. Here, Indigenous ways of knowing are negated, and science remains the preserve of the western intellectual. Alternatively, Indigenous knowledge is silenced by being ignored. We know, for example, the work of successive Aboriginal and Torres Strait Islander Social Justice Commissioners in Australia (ATSISJC 1993, 2006, 2008, 2009, 2011, 2014), of Indigenous scholars in Canada, the US and Aotearoa/New Zealand (including, to name only a handful, Jackson 1988, McIntosh 2011, Monture-Angus 1999, Nielsen and Silverman 2009, Victor 2007), have been fundamental in developing an in-depth Indigenous understanding of a broad range of issues central to contemporary criminological inquiry, including violence against Indigenous women, Indigenous women's experiences of imprisonment and post release, the theoretical and practical development of Indigenous healing, and the role of justice reinvestment in Indigenous peoples drive for self-determination in the justice arena. However, this substantial body of work is often totally ignored in mainstream criminological accounts (see, for example, Weatherburn 2014). In Moreton-Robinson's terms, 'defining Aboriginality continues to be a predominantly white patriarchal knowledge production activity . . . [which] violates our subjectivity by obliterating any trace of our different ontological and epistemological existences' (Moreton-Robinson 2011, p. 414).

The rights of Indigenous peoples to self-determination are given little weight by those charged with reforming criminal justice in settler colonial jurisdictions (Cultural Survival 2013).

Furthermore, Indigenous perspectives on crime control, in particular what causes crime and over-representation, and how best to respond, has little place in the policy formulation processes of the state. One result has been the reinvigorated hegemony of administrative and authoritarian criminology, which arguably has led to a retraction in some of the (slight) gains made by Indigenous peoples in the 1980s and 1990s in the development of community-centred justice initiatives (Tauri 2014). The issue is exemplified through the experiences of the Canadian Stó:lō First Nation being required to *train* to deliver restorative justice conferencing, at the expense of being able to develop a wholly *Stó:lō* approach to youth offending (Palys and Victor 2007). The impact of this reinvigoration of administrative criminology can be seen in the Australian context where some states have begun cutting Indigenous-run programmes, including the discontinuation of the Murri (Aboriginal) sentencing courts programme in 2012 by the former Queensland state government, often on the basis of a failure to meet narrow measures such as recidivism; arguably a 'measure of success' few interventions initiated by the state appear to be able to meet, including the formal courts (Cunneen and Tauri forthcoming).

At a programmatic level, settler colonial states can, and do point to a range of interventions to highlight their concern for, and response to, Indigenous over-representation and Indigenous critiques of the criminal justice system. However, many 'Indigenous' initiatives, such as Family Group Conferencing are best understood as state-centred processes that have been indigenized through the purposeful co-option of what state functionaries determine to be 'acceptable' customary practices. A recent example was the implementation in Aotearoa/New Zealand of Rangatahi (youth) Courts, which entail holding the sentencing phase of the youth court process on *marae* (meeting house). While there is no denying that Māori *tikanga* (philosophies and practices) play an essential part in this process, the sentencing framework and the judicial authority remains very much with the state (Cunneen and Tauri forthcoming).

## Principles of the declaration in practice

Repeatedly, critical and Indigenous writers have called for the implementation and resourcing of many more Indigenous controlled-programmes and mechanisms and the importance of the principle of Indigenous self-determination. This call has been particularly apparent in implementing responses to violence in Indigenous communities (in the Australian context see Blagg 2008, ATSISJC 2011). There are numerous examples where in practice the principles underpinning the Declaration are operationalized by Indigenous people in developing responses to community problems, including, inter alia, Indigenous night patrols (Blagg 2008, pp. 107–25, Blagg and Anthony 2014), various types of Indigenous healing programmes (Cunneen et al. 2013) and Indigenous adaptations of justice reinvestment (Brown et al. 2016). We highlight here the role of night patrols which have been one of the key developments in Indigenous community responses to crime and disorder in Australia.

Indigenous night patrols began in the Northern Territory in the 1980s and subsequently developed in most states of Australia over the next two decades. They are operated by Indigenous people at the local community level and work in a variety of urban, rural and remote locations. They focus on assisting people in need and maintaining social order, and receive varied levels of support from state and federal governments. There is often significant tension between the demands of government (instituted through funding agreements) and the aims and procedures determined by Indigenous communities; there can also be significant tension between Indigenous patrols and state police (Blagg and Anthony 2014, Porter 2015).

Priorities for the night patrols are largely set by local Indigenous need. Blagg (2008, pp. 107–25) describes the services of night patrols as including dispute resolution, removal from danger and safe transportation, connecting people to services, prevention of family violence, assistance and interventions around homelessness, alcohol and substance misuse and anti-social behaviour, keeping the peace at various events such as sports carnivals, and diversion from contact with the criminal justice system. Night patrols are involved in truancy programmes and school breakfast programmes and they transport people to places such as sobering-up shelters, safe houses, women's refuges, men's places, clinics, hostels, family healing and justice groups (Blagg and Anthony 2014, p. 109).

Night patrols operate through developing and maintaining cultural authority. Patrols, unlike state police, do not rely on the use or threat of force. Nor do they rely on the authority of western law. Their legitimacy and authority is held within Aboriginal law and culture. Significantly, Indigenous women have played a substantial role in developing and operating night patrols, and took the initiative in establishing some of the first patrols. Blagg (2008, p. 114) suggests that, perhaps a consequence of the significant involvement of Indigenous women, patrols report 'seeing their work in terms of mediation and persuasion rather than force, and fulfilling a preventative/welfare role, rather than a reactive/controlling one'. Night patrols represent a different vision of policing to that provided by state agencies: external authority is replaced by local cultural authority; bureaucratized state-centred methods of crime control are replaced by an organic approach to community need which focuses on assistance and prevention rather than the use of force. As Porter (2015) suggests, the way night patrols work requires us to rethink the concept of policing as it is understood within western criminological discourses.

## Neoliberalism, risk and Indigenous human rights

The Indigenous search for solutions to social disorder and dislocation lie in enhanced Indigenous authority through self-determination. However, significant barriers exist to the recognition of Indigenous human rights. Not least among these is the tension between Indigenous claims to exercise authority over criminal justice, and settler colonial state demands for tougher law and order responses. The emergence of neoliberalism has coincided with the realignment of approaches in punishment, which emphasize deterrence and retribution. The values and principles of neoliberalism include the individualization of rights and responsibilities; the valorization of individual autonomy; and the denial of cultural values that oppose a market model of social relations. The ascendancy of these values has reinforced a particularly negative view of cultural difference and runs counter to Indigenous claims for self-determination (Cunneen et al. 2013). Indeed, cultural difference itself is used to explain crime and the need for particular types of punishment, with a focus on changing Indigenous culture and promoting greater assimilation (Anthony 2013).

We argue then that neoliberalism has led to less sympathetic attitudes towards Indigenous rights, including self-determination. The politics of insecurity in neoliberal societies like Australia, Canada, the US and Aotearoa/New Zealand have led to a preoccupation with and aversion to risk, uncertainty and dangerousness. Respect for human rights and progressive reform of institutions (particularly criminal justice systems) is more difficult in an environment of paranoia and punitiveness. Along with the politics of insecurity and the ascendancy of neoliberalism, there have been developments in managerialism and risk-thinking that have increasingly permeated criminal justice policy. Criminal justice classification, programme interventions, supervision and indeed incarceration itself is increasingly defined through the management of risk. The assessment of risk in criminal justice involves the identification of statistically generated characteristics drawn from aggregate populations of offenders (such as, drug and alcohol problems, rates of offending and reoffending, domestic violence, prior child abuse and neglect). These characteristics are treated as discrete 'facts' devoid of historical, political and social context (Cunneen et al. 2013). A core problem is the relationship between these 'risk factors', being Indigenous and the outcomes of colonialism.

As we noted previously, the contemporary socioeconomic marginalization of Indigenous people did not magically appear, it was created through colonial dispossession and maintained through ongoing laws and policies of exclusion. Paternalistic and authoritarian government approaches (such as we have seen in Australia and elsewhere) to, for example, school attendance, restrictions on alcohol consumption, access to social security benefits, and so on, reproduce Indigenous people as a highly controlled and criminalized group. The focus on risk management within criminal justice has two significant implications for the human rights of Indigenous people. One is that an understanding of crime and victimization in Indigenous communities is removed from their specific historical and political contexts. Mainstream criminology increasingly understands Indigenous over-representation as the result of individualized risk factors without connection to the social, economic and political relations of colonialism, which lie at the root of contemporary Indigenous marginalization. The second implication is that within the risk paradigm, the human rights of Indigenous peoples (both collective rights such as self-determination, and individual rights as citizens) are seen as secondary to the membership of a risk-defined group. The group's primary definition is centred on the type of risk characteristics they are said to possess. Within criminology these characteristics are invariably negative and represent Indigenous people as collectively dysfunctional. In this context it is difficult to conceive of Indigenous people as bearers of specific Indigenous human rights, or as having their own law and preferred solutions to social problems. Indigenous claims to self-determination are presented as irrelevant to solving the problems of social disorder that are instead defined as a threat of criminality from risk-prone populations. To the extent that Indigenous culture is recognized, it is often seen as criminogenic – as it was, for example, in the Northern Territory Intervention (Cunneen and Rowe 2015). The apparent irrelevance of Indigenous human rights is further entrenched by some criminologists who argue that little or no 'evidence' exists of the efficacy of non-western programmatic responses to crime (see, for example, Weatherburn 2014).

## Conclusion

We have set out in this chapter to consider normative principles and rights within the *Declaration on the Rights of Indigenous Peoples*. It is clear that the exercise of criminal jurisdiction in Indigenous communities is inevitably bound-up with issues of Indigenous human rights including self-determination. These human rights norms have profound implications for the *right* to police, to enforce the law and to maintain order in Indigenous communities. The Indigenous domain of law and culture continues to be defended and where possible extended. Indigenous initiatives (such as night patrols) are practical expressions of sovereignty and self-determination. They are declarations of intent that Indigenous people can and will protect their own people, and deliver Indigenous justice. The success of these programmes has been acknowledged as deriving from active Indigenous community involvement in identifying problems and developing solutions.

In contrast, non-Indigenous governance through the criminal justice system tends to circumscribe and delimit the struggle for Indigenous rights. It is often antithetical and antagonistic towards the principles of self-determination, participation in decision-making and non-discrimination, and so often proceeds in blind ignorance of recognition and respect for Indigenous culture. Unfortunately, there is little better that can be said of criminology. There is almost a total absence of any consideration of Indigenous human rights principles in criminology and how they potentially impact on the discipline. Yet these principles have profound implications for how criminologists might go about their work: the assumptions they employ, their research, and perhaps most importantly, their ethics. Recognition of Indigenous human rights requires us to explore the possibilities of new forms of justice, and a rethinking of existing justice processes. It also requires us to reflexively reconsider our position as criminologists. Indigenous over-representation in the criminal justice system is hardly a peripheral area of special interest. It is one of the most significant human rights issues in settler colonial societies.

## References

Aboriginal and Torres Strait Islander Social Justice Commissioner [ATSISJC], 1993. *Social justice report 1993*. Sydney: Australian Human Rights Commission.

Aboriginal and Torres Strait Islander Social Justice Commissioner [ATSISJC], 2006. *Ending family violence and abuse in Aboriginal and Torres Strait Islander Communities*. Sydney: Australian Human Rights Commission.

Aboriginal and Torres Strait Islander Social Justice Commissioner [ATSISJC], 2008. *Social justice report 2008*. Sydney: Australian Human Rights Commission.

Aboriginal and Torres Strait Islander Social Justice Commissioner [ATSISJC], 2009. *Social justice report 2009*. Sydney: Australian Human Rights Commission.

Aboriginal and Torres Strait Islander Social Justice Commissioner [ATSISJC], 2011. *Social justice report 2011*. Sydney: Australian Human Rights Commission.

Aboriginal and Torres Strait Islander Social Justice Commissioner [ATSISJC], 2014. *Social justice report 2014*. Sydney: Australian Human Rights Commission.

Anthony, T., 2013. *Indigenous people, crime and punishment*. London: Routledge.

Australian Institute of Health and Welfare [AIHW], 2013. *Diverting Indigenous offenders from the criminal justice system*. Resource Sheet No 24. Canberra: AIHW.

Battiste, M. and Henderson, J., 2000. *Protecting Indigenous knowledge and heritage: a global challenge*. Saskatoon: Purich Publications.

Bishop, G., 1998. Freeing ourselves from neo-colonial domination in research: A Māori approach to creating knowledge. *Qualitative Studies in Education*, 11(2), 199–219.

Blagg, H., 2008. *Crime, Aboriginality and the decolonisation of justice*. Leichhardt, NSW: Hawkins Press.

Blagg, H. and Anthony, T., 2014. 'If those old women catch you, you're going to cop it': night patrols, Indigenous women, and place-based sovereignty in outback Australia. *African Journal of Criminology and Justice Studies*, 8(1), 103–24.

Brown, D., Cunneen, C., Schwartz, M., Stubbs, J. and Young, C., 2016. *Justice reinvestment: winding back imprisonment*. Basingstoke: Palgrave Macmillan.

Clark, S. and Cove, J., 1999. Canadian Commissions of Inquiry into Aboriginal Peoples and Criminal Justice. *In*: P. Havemann (ed.), *Indigenous peoples in Australia, Canada and New Zealand*. Auckland: Oxford University Press, 302–15.

Cultural Survival, 2013. Over-representation of Indigenous Peoples in incarceration is a global concern. *The Stringer: Independent News*. 12 July.

Cunneen, C., 2001. *Conflict, politics and crime: Aboriginal communities and the police*. St Leonards: Allen and Unwin.

Cunneen, C., 2012. The race to defraud: state crime and the immiseration of Indigenous people. *In*: J. McCulloch and E. Stanley (eds), *State crime and resistance*. London: Routledge, 99–113.

Cunneen, C. and Rowe, S., 2014. Changing narratives: colonised peoples, criminology and social work. *International Journal for Crime, Justice and Social Democracy*, 3(2), 49–67.

Cunneen, C. and Rowe, S., 2015. Decolonising Indigenous victimisation. *In*: D. Wilson and S. Ross (eds), *Crime, victims and policy*. Basingstoke: Palgrave Macmillan, 10–32.

Cunneen, C. and Tauri, J., forthcoming. *Indigenous criminology*. Bristol: Policy Press.

Cunneen, C., Baldry, E., Brown, D., Brown, M., Schwartz, M. and Steel, A., 2013. *Penal culture and hyperincarceration*. Farnham: Ashgate.

Deckert, A., 2014. Neo-colonial criminology: quantifying the silence. *African Journal of Criminology and Justice Studies*, 8(1), 39–60.

Dunbar-Ortiz, R., 2014. *An Indigenous peoples' history of the United States*. Boston, MA: Beacon Press.

Fleras, A. and Elliott, J.L., 1992. *The nations with In: Aboriginal-state relations in Canada, the United States and New Zealand*. Toronto: Oxford University Press.

Foley, G., 1988. One black life. *Rolling Stone*, 426, 107–111.

Hamilton, A. and Sinclair, M., 1991. *Report of the Aboriginal Justice Inquiry of Manitoba: the justice system and Aboriginal people*. Retrieved on 11 April 2016 from: www.ajic.mb.ca/volumel/toc.html.

Hart, M.A., 2010. Indigenous worldviews, knowledge, and research: the development of an Indigenous research paradigm. *Journal of Indigenous Voices in Social Work*, 1(1), 1–16.

Hickman, A., Poitras L. and Evans G., 1989. *Royal Commission on the Donald Marshall, Jr., prosecution, digest of findings and recommendations*. Halifax: Province of Nova Scotia.

Jackson, M., 1988. *Maori and the criminal justice system: He Whaipaanga Hou – a new perspective*. Wellington: Department of Justice.

Johnston, E., 1991. *Royal Commission into Aboriginal Deaths in Custody National Report*, 5 Vols. Canberra: Australian Government.

Kelaher, M., Sabanovic, H., La Brooy, C., Lock, M., Lusher, D. and Brown, L., 2014. Does more equitable governance lead to more equitable health care? *Social Science and Medicine*, 123(4), 278–86.

Kovach, M., 2009. *Indigenous methodologies: characteristics, conversations, and contexts*. Toronto: University of Toronto Press.

Lightfoot, S., 2012. Selective endorsement without intent to implement: indigenous rights and the Anglosphere. *The International Journal of Human Rights*, 16(1), 100–22.

Marie, D., 2010. Māori and criminal offending: a critical appraisal. *The Australian and New Zealand Journal of Criminology*, 43(2), 283–300.

McIntosh T., 2011. Māori and cross-cultural research: criticality, ethicality and generosity. *New Zealand Sociology*, 26, 61–75.

Monture-Angus, P., 1999. Considering colonialism and oppression: Aboriginal women, justice and the 'theory' of decolonisation. *Native Studies Review*, 12(1), 63–94.

Moreton-Robinson, A., 2011. The white man's burden: patriarchal white epistemic violence and Aboriginal women's knowledges within the academy. *Australian Feminist Studies*, 26(20), 413–31.

National Inquiry into the Separation of Aboriginal and Torres Strait Islander Children from Their Families [NISATSIC], 1997. *Bringing them home: report of the National Inquiry into the Separation of Aboriginal and Torres Strait Islander Children from their Families*. Sydney: Human Rights and Equal Opportunity Commission.

Nielsen, M. and Silverman, R. (eds), 2009. *Criminal justice in Native America*. Tucson, AZ: University of Arizona Press.

Newton, N., 1998. Tribal court praxis: one year in the life of twenty tribal courts. *Indian Law Review*, 22, 285–353.

Palys, T. and Victor, W., 2007. Getting to a better place: Qwí:qwelstóm, the Stó:lō and self-determination. *In*: Law Commission of Canada (ed.), *Indigenous legal traditions*. Vancouver: UBC Press, 12–39.

Porsanger, J., 2004. *An essay about Indigenous methodology*. Retrieved on 15 August 2015 from: http://munin.uit.no/bitstream/handle/10037/906/article.pdf.

Porter, A., 2015. Decolonising policing: Indigenous night patrols, counter-policing and safety. Unpublished paper.

Royal Commission on Aboriginal Peoples [RCAP], 1996. *Bridging the cultural divide*. Ottawa: Minister of Supply and Services Canada.

Secretariat National Aboriginal and Islander Child Care [SNAICC], 2013. *Whose voice counts?* Melbourne: SNAICC.

Smith, L.T., 1999. *Decolonizing methodologies: research and Indigenous peoples*. London: Zed Books.

Steering Committee for the Review of Government Service Provision [SCRGSP], 2014. *Overcoming Indigenous disadvantage: key indicators 2014*. Canberra: Productivity Commission.

Tauri, J., 2012. Indigenous critique of authoritarian criminology. *In*: K. Carrington, M. Ball, E. O'Brien and J. Tauri (eds), *Crime, justice and social democracy: international perspectives*. London: Palgrave Macmillan, 217–33.

Tauri, J., 2014. Settler colonialism, criminal justice and Indigenous peoples. *African Journal of Criminology and Justice Studies*, 8(1), 20–37.

Victor, W., 2007. *Indigenous justice: clearing space and place for Indigenous epistemologies*. National Centre for First Nations Governance.

Weatherburn, D., 2010. Guest editorial: Indigenous violence. *Australian and New Zealand Journal of Criminology*, 3(2), 197–8.

Weatherburn, D., 2014. *Arresting incarceration: pathways out of Indigenous imprisonment*. Canberra: Aboriginal Studies Press.

# 41

# Gender equality, dignity and the right to a fair trial

*Jill Hunter*

## The right to a fair trial and confrontation

The United States (US) Sixth Amendment expressing, as it does, the right to confrontation, sets the international high water mark for the requirement that witnesses be present in court for cross-examination. It does so under US law through the notoriously limited exceptions granted to the rule against hearsay. Long before modern human rights jurisprudence developed, the common law tradition entrenched the importance of testing of witnesses' account by so-called 'confrontation,' placing great store on the deft flair and skills of cross-examiners operating sometimes with crushing effect and typically on a calibrated and exacting game plan. Wigmore's particularly well-known aphorism that cross-examination is 'the greatest legal engine ever invented for the discovery of truth' (Wigmore 1940, p. 29) retains a strong footprint in common lawyers' cultural appreciation of the art of the cross-examiner. Additionally, as Judge Yudkivska in *Y v Slovenia* (2015) observed:

> The . . . crux [of the right to confrontation] lies in a belief that '[i]t is always more difficult to tell a lie about a person "to his face" than "behind his back", and even if the lie is told it will often be told less convincingly'. This was explained by Justice Antonin Scalia in the US Supreme Court's landmark judgment in this respect, *Coy v Iowa* (1988). In that judgment Justice Scalia traced the history of the right to confront as a 'face-to-face encounter', illustrated in Shakespeare's Richard II. . . . He concluded that 'there is something deep in human nature that regards face-to-face confrontation between accused and accuser as "essential to a fair trial in a criminal prosecution"'.

Testing witnesses by cross-examining them is absorbed into the centrality of fair trial norms in numerous human rights instruments and it links, indeed one might say secures, the fair trial requirement that justice be open and public. The right is expressed variously. In Australia it is expressed in terms of permitting the defendant 'to examine prosecution witnesses, or have them examined' (see, for example, *Human Rights Act 2004* [ACT], s. 21; *Charter of Human Rights and Responsibilities Act* 2006 [Vic], 25[2][g]. This language follows closely the expression in the *European Convention on Human Rights* [ECHR], Article 6.3 [d]). In Canada, a jurisdiction where human rights norms have been welded into the common law tradition through its own *Canadian Charter of Rights and Freedoms*, 1982, Cory J in *R v Osolin* [1993], pp. 516–17) noted the link between an accused's right to cross-examine and the presumption of innocence, stating that cross-examination enables 'an accused . . . [to] make full answer and defence . . . [and] is fundamental to providing a fair trial to an accused'. Cory J added that cross-examination is 'the ultimate means of demonstrating truth and of testing veracity' and 'of essential importance in determining whether a witness is credible. Even with the most honest witness, cross-examination can provide the means to explore the frailties of the testimony'. These observations reflect norms accepted in all modern and respected legal traditions. Further, its functionality is acknowledged by psychologists who point to the importance of cross-examination questions drawing out hidden or potential flaws to the scrutiny of decision-makers (Wilson and Sperber 2002, p. 604). Callen, drawing on the psychologist Gilbert also noted an additional benefit of cross-examination in prompting fact-finders who might otherwise 'under-invest cognitive resources in finding facts', to see 'alternative hypotheses and counter-possibilities' (Callen 2013, p. 322). In other words, the very fact that a question is put to a witness can implicitly highlight a topic that a decision-maker might otherwise overlook. In this way cross-examination addresses the danger of decision-maker cognitive overload.

Notably, the public confrontation of witnesses is expressly part of a fair trial in both common law and human rights jurisprudence. Clearly, open testing of prosecution witnesses is preferable to non-transparent processes or the blind acceptance of state evidence put before a tribunal. But what about those caught in the crossfire of confrontation? Lawyers possess a vast repertoire of stratagems for testing witnesses. Their mastery underscores one aspect of the typical power imbalance between questioners and questioned. The other aspect of the disparity between these courtroom protagonists is the vulnerability of certain witnesses. Historically, misogyny-based assumptions caused rape myths to flourish. These permitted demeaning and humiliating cross-examination of sexual assault complainants employed by the defence to unsettle the sexual assault complainant in the witness box – a tactic often perceived as crucial to defeating the prosecution case in the classic 'she says, he says' trial, where the rape complainant's credibility is pivotal. The impact of these bad old days is graphically described by Henning and Hunter (2013, pp. 364–5). The authors recast metaphors used by US criminologist Kamisar (1965) referencing the courtroom as a 'mansion' of rights and the police station as a mere 'gatehouse'. Kamisar had used these terms to great effect to highlight the vulnerability of suspects in police custody but, as Henning and Hunter have observed the mansion that was so richly adorned with rights for the accused (at least in comparison to the gatehouse/police station), offered a far different treatment for the rape victim for much of the twentieth century. '[F]or vulnerable witnesses in Kamisar's time, no part of the criminal justice system was a mansion'. At trial:

> they were '"game" to be stalked and cornered', harried, bullied and hemmed in, their credibility, integrity and morality attacked. . . . [F]or such witnesses the trial process was 'ritualised degradation dressed up as court process' and their treatment, 'state sanctioned victimisation'. For vulnerable witnesses the criminal justice process resembled the Roman Circus.

It is not surprising that these witnesses became the epitome of the vulnerable witness. Since the late twentieth century law reform has removed numerous pernicious elements of law and practice. Rape shield protections, testimonial screens and CCTV have all enhanced restraint on the cross-examination of the sexual assault complainant. However, it is important to appreciate two things. First, legal culture does not change overnight and, second, the bar for acceptable lawyers' trial tactics was set low.

In the twenty-first century to what extent do human rights instruments ensure courts protect the rights of female witnesses from the over-reach of the cross-examiner? This chapter explores this question through two case studies. The first is the 2015 case of *Y v Slovenia*. It illustrates the potential for Articles 3 and 8 of the ECHR to protect witnesses from inhuman or degrading treatment and from incursions into their personal integrity and privacy. The second case study is taken from a 2012 Canadian case in which the witness attempted unsuccessfully to assert her right to religious expression by wearing a niqab, an Islamic veil, that covered her face (but not her eyes) while testifying. In other words, both cases involve women sexual assault complainants in the witness box.

## Re-traumatization in the courtroom

### *The ECHR provides:*

Article 3
No one shall be subjected to torture or to inhuman or degrading treatment or punishment.

Article 8

1 Everyone has the right to respect for his private and family life, his home and his correspondence.
2 There shall be no interference by a public authority with the exercise of this right except such as is in accordance with the law and is necessary in a democratic society in the interests of national security, public safety or the economic wellbeing of the country, for the prevention of disorder or crime, for the protection of health or morals, or for the protection of the rights and freedoms of others.

## The rape victim

The gravity and debasing qualities of the crime of rape are recognized by the European Court of Human Rights (ECtHR) (*SW v United Kingdom* [1995]) in which it was made clear that the state has an obligation to thoroughly investigate and prosecute those reasonably suspected of sexual assault. *Y v Slovenia* concerned an appeal from a sexual assault prosecution brought against X concerning actual and attempted sexual assaults upon Y who was aged 15 at the relevant time. The nature of the alleged assaults meant physical proof was non-existent. Further Y testified that she had not violently resisted X. The significance of *Y v Slovenia* is threefold. First, is the fact that the trial court gave almost unfettered license to the accused's flagrant tactics of delay, intimidation and manipulation. Second, is the retention of narrow and unsatisfactory assumptions with respect to rape law in Slovenia (and it seems, elsewhere), and thirdly, Strasbourg court's finding that the State had breached Y's rights in failing to protect Y from the traumatic experiences to which she was exposed during the trial.

The prosecution was marked by tardy and lack lustre police investigation and an attenuated trial process. Y's complaint to police was first made in mid-2002. It was not until late 2006 that an indictment was lodged. A significant feature of *Y v Slovenia* is the footprint of 'the continental legal tradition [where] the definition of rape contains references to the use of violence or threats of violence by the perpetrator' (*MC v Bulgaria* 2003). Indeed the case shares much in common with the findings from *MC v Bulgaria*. There the Strasbourg court found that in Bulgaria it was a predominant practice to only prosecute rape perpetrators where significant physical resistance could be proved. Little or no physical force and resistance tended to mean the claims of the complainant were not taken seriously. The Court in *Y v Slovenia* held that the delays by police and of the investigating judge (approximately 12 months and then another 21 months), followed by an additional 18 months before the first trial hearing commenced added to the actual times taken to investigate the allegations, meant that more than seven years elapsed between complaint and judgement. The Court observed that:

> While it is not possible to speculate whether these delays, for which no justification has been put forward by the Government, prejudiced in any way the outcome of the proceedings, in the Court's opinion they cannot be reconciled with the procedural requirement of promptness. . . . Accordingly, there has been a violation of the respondent State's procedural obligations under Article 3 of the Convention.

The trial took place over 12 hearings. Y was questioned over four hearings and at the fourth hearing X, *despite being legally represented,* personally cross-examined Y, asking her over 100 questions. The judgement of the Strasbourg court describes it in the following manner:

> 34. On 26 September 2008 the court held the fourth hearing in the absence of the public at which X personally asked the applicant over a hundred questions, starting with a comment in the form of a question 'Is it true that you have told and showed me that you could cry on cue and then everybody believed you'. It does not appear from the record of the hearing that the applicant made any reply. X then asked the applicant a series of questions aimed at proving that they had seen each other mainly at gatherings of their families or when the applicant, in need of transportation or other assistance, had actively sought his company. Among the questions asked by X were the following: 'Is it true that I could not have abused you on the evening of the event, as you stated on 14 April', 'Is it true that if I had wished to satisfy my sexual needs, I would have called you at least once', 'Why did you call me in September and ask me take you out of town if I had already raped you five times before that date', 'Why were you calling me, because I certainly never called you', or 'Is it true that you specifically asked that we drive out of the town alone, because you wished to talk to me and to celebrate your success at a beauty pageant'. The applicant insisted that she had not been calling X or initiated any outings with him, but that he had called her. X also asked the applicant whether she had told him that, once she had a boyfriend, she would always be on top, as she wanted to be the mistress.
>
> . . .
>
> 37. On three occasions the court ordered a short recess due to the applicant's agitation and crying. After one of these recesses X asked the applicant whether she would feel better if they all went to dinner, just as they used to, and maybe then she would not cry so much.
>
> 38. At one point the applicant requested the court to adjourn the hearing as the questions were too stressful for her. However, after being told by X that the next hearing could not be held until after 19 November 2008 when he would return from a business trip, the applicant said, while crying, that he should continue with his questioning as she wanted to get it over with. Eventually, after four hours of cross-examination of the applicant, the presiding judge adjourned the hearing . . .

The first court hearing was scheduled for mid-2007 but X claimed he was too ill, changed attorneys and had business trips delaying the completion of the trial. The 12 hearings were not completed until September 2009. X was ultimately acquitted on the basis of medical evidence supporting the defence that his congenitally weak arm made Y's accounts of events doubtful.

An unsuccessful appeal lodged in late 2009 criticized the court for not considering X's power over Y through his age, size, gender, social and economic status, such that force was not required. It was also noted that X operated manual transmission vehicles which required him to use both his arms. Expert evidence had been led from a clinical psychologist confirming that Y displayed clear symptoms of sexual abuse. However, a confounding element was the fact that Y's psychological trauma indicative of possible sexual abuse could potentially be explained by 'inappropriate conduct' of her mother's former husband. The Court also noted the risk of re-traumatization where an accused directly confronts his alleged victim such that personal cross-examination 'should be subject to a most careful assessment by the national courts, all the more so the more intimate the questions'. The Court noted that:

> 108. ... cross-examination should not be used as a means of intimidating or humiliating witnesses. In this connection, the Court is of the view that some of X's questions and remarks suggesting, without any evidentiary basis, that the applicant could cry on cue in order to manipulate people, that her distress might be eased by having dinner with him or that she had confided in him her desire to dominate men were not aimed only at attacking the applicant's credibility, but were also meant to degrade her character.

The Court concluded that 'X's offensive insinuations about the applicant equally exceeded the limits of what could be tolerated for the purpose of enabling him to mount an effective defence'. It noted that curtailing X's personal remarks would not have 'unduly restricted his right to defence' and would have mitigated Y's distress in the witness box. Y was also subjected to an additional level of brutality. The state-ordered medical examination of her was conducted by a gynaecologist who confronted Y seeking an explanation as to why she had not resisted X more rigorously. The Court noted it was not for the doctor to undertake such inquiries which unnecessarily added to Ys' stress. In all, the Court concluded that in affording X his defence rights the State had failed to strike the appropriate balance in protecting Y's Article 8 rights and interests.

Despite all of the above findings regarding Y's re-traumatization, the Court fell short of finding that Y had suffered inhuman or degrading treatment breaching Article 3 of the Convention. Thus, while appearing to be a Strasbourg decision strengthening the rights of witnesses, *Y v Slovenia* achieves its goal with a depressing degree of tentativeness in not applying Article 3 to conduct which reveals a high level of entrenched misogyny embedded in the investigation, prosecution and adjudication of sexual assault offences.

The second dimension to the severe compromising of witness's rights in the courtroom is illustrated by cases where the sexual assault complainant has been required to remove her Islamic veil before she can testify. As we see below, also in this context the clash between testing the prosecution case by cross-examination and protecting witness rights is deeply contested.

## Religious freedom and the Islamic veil

A notable backdrop to this topic is that the topic of religious freedom for those of the Islamic faith has been swept up in concern about threats to security in the post-9/11 hysteria of terrorism. It manifested in Australia with respect to the wearing of an Islamic veil in late 2014 following the issuing of a parliamentary memorandum that '[p]ersons with facial coverings entering the galleries of the House of Representatives and Senate will be seated in the enclosed galleries. This will ensure that persons with facial coverings can continue to enter the chamber galleries without needing to be identifiable' (www.abc.net.au/news/2014-10-02/parliament-burka-rules-introduced/5786132). Women wearing Islamic veils were directed to sit in places usually designated for school children, immediately sending messages with multiple meanings to the public. As Human Rights Commissioner Tim Wilson observed segregating people on the basis of their apparel was described by as 'ill-considered'. Australia's Race Discrimination Commissioner Dr Tim Soutphommasane described the decision as 'baffling' and made references to 'reckless rhetoric'. He cautioned against the danger of anti-Muslim bigotry and mixing of messages of terrorism with any form of religious difference. He concluded that Australia's foremost law-making institution was imposing segregation on the basis of religion and gender. Within a week the rule was reversed. This political backdrop may seem a far cry from criminal courts, but it is not. Common law courts internationally have struggled with the issue of the facial coverings and Islamic witnesses. In this context it is not security that has raised concerns. It is the right to a fair trial.

## In the witness box: looks can be deceiving

The remainder of this chapter explores the rights of women of Islamic faith who wish to testify whilst fully veiled. Unlike the sexual assault complainant Y, the witness's rights and interests said to be at odds with the defendant's fair trial rights, are located in the right to religious freedom. As Article 9.2 of the ECHR indicates:

> the freedom to manifest one's religion or beliefs shall be subject only to such limitations as ... are necessary in a democratic society in the interests of public safety ... or for the protection of the rights and freedoms of others.

Within the courtroom, the wearing of the burqa has been held in England, the US, Canada, Scotland, Australia and New Zealand as offending the right to a fair trial. This is because, it is said, a prosecution witness's face should be subject to scrutiny when she testifies. The authorities are generally relatively consistent, but, it is suggested, they are uncompelling. For example, in the English case it is reported that the veiled participant was the criminal accused. Thus in that case, their right to a fair trial presents no argument in favour of unveiling. The court, in a decision that has not received appellate consideration, noted Article 9 of the ECHR regarding the right to manifest one's religious beliefs but held that the veil should be removed to ensure proceedings were conducted 'in accordance with the rule of law, open justice, and the adversarial process' (Kirk 2013, p. 460). In the US in 2008 in *Muhammad v Paruk*, a civil action was dismissed because the plaintiff Ms Muhammad, refused to remove her veil. Similarly in Australia, in the Western Australian District Court fraud prosecution of Anwar Sayed in August 2010, Judge Deane ruled that the Muslim witness, known only as Tasneem, would need to remove her burqa to testify. But, if some witnesses can testify remotely without the court seeing or hearing them clearly, why is it otherwise for women who wish to testify wearing a full veil? In the New Zealand case of *Police v Razamjoo* (2005) the judge permitted women found to hold sincere religious beliefs to testify behind a screen, but with the veil removed from their faces (Griffiths 2011). As Griffiths notes, the case involved no greater latitude than had occurred in other totally unrelated instances. He cited as comparison the case involving witnesses who testified remotely by way of closed circuit TV (including with the picture and sound distorted to avoid identifying them) in a trial involving a gang-related killing. Griffiths also noted that both child and adult witnesses in sexual assault prosecutions had been permitted to testify behind screens on other occasions.

This brings us to the 2012 Canadian Supreme Court case of *R v NS* where the court held by majority (McLachlin CJ, Deschamps, Fish and Cromwell JJ) that even where a witness, a sexual assault complainant, has a sincere religious commitment that requires her to wear a niqab (described as only permitting NS's eyes to be seen) while testifying, NS would be nevertheless required to remove her veil in court. In other words, trial fairness trumped freedom of religion. There was no compromise. Justices LeBel and Rothstein agreed with the majority but added an additional dimension based on the openness of courts, citing Bingham *The Rule of Law* (2010, p. 8). Their Honours observed that courts are:

> part of the complex web of institutions, rules and values embraced by the notion of the rule of law, of a state and a society living under and within the law. Such a system is critical to the maintenance of the rule of law, a fundamental Canadian value.

As such, 'the trial becomes an act of communication with the public at large' and:

> Wearing a niqab ... does not facilitate acts of communication. Rather, it restricts them. It removes the witness from the scope of certain elements of those acts on the basis of the assertion of a religious belief in circumstances in which the sincerity and strength of the belief are difficult to assess or even to question. The niqab shields the witness from interacting fully with the parties, their counsel, the judge and, where applicable, the jurors.

It is in the dissent of Justice Abella in *NS* that one finds close scrutiny of the fair trial claims favouring the removal of the veil. Her Honour points to the claimed benefit of viewing witnesses' faces to assess their demeanour, encompassing 'every visible or audible form of self-expression manifested by a witness whether fixed or variable, voluntary or involuntary, simple or complex' (quoting from Morrison et al. 2007, p. 179). Justice Abella adds that '[t]rial judges often rely on many indicators *other than* facial cues in finding a witness credible', including:

> certitude in speaking, dignity while on the stand, exhibition of disability, exhibition of anger, exhibition of frustration, articulate speaking, thoughtful presentation, enthusiastic language, direct non-evasive answering, non-glib answering, exhibition of modesty, exhibition of flexibility, normal (as in as expected) body movement, cheerful attitude, kind manner, normal exhalation, normal inhalation.

Justice Abella thus introduces one of a number of major flaws in the fair trial requirement of unveiling, noting 'that relying on the appearance of sincerity [would lead to] a purely arbitrary finding and justice would then depend upon the best actors in the witness box'. Justice Abella notes that evaluating credibility in fact demands consideration of other factors such as the witness's opportunity to observe, judge and remember and her ability to describe clearly what he or she has seen and heard. Her Honour quoted from the Court of Appeal for Alberta in *R v Pelletier* (1995):

> I question whether the respect given to our findings of fact based on the demeanour of the witnesses is always deserved. I doubt my own ability, and sometimes that of other judges, to discern from a witness's demeanour, or the tone of his voice, whether he is telling the truth. He speaks hesitantly. Is it the mark of a cautious man, whose statements are for that reason to be respected, or is he taking time to fabricate? Is the emphatic witness putting on an act to deceive me, or is he speaking from the fullness of his heart, knowing that he is right? Is he likely to be more truthful if he looks me straight in the face than if he casts his eyes on the ground, perhaps from shyness or a natural timidity? For my part I rely on these considerations as little as I can help.

> ... I judge a witness to be unreliable if his evidence is, in any serious respect, inconsistent with these undisputed or indisputable facts, or of course if he contradicts himself on important points. I rely as little as possible on such deceptive matters as his demeanour.

Justice Abella also quoted from Acting Chief Justice Morden in the Ontario Court of Appeal case of *R v Levogiannis* (1990) regarding the non-absolute right to face-to-face confrontation:

> The reason underlying the right is said to be that it is more difficult not to tell the truth about a person when looking at that person eye to eye.... [B]ut ... it is difficult to dogmatize about this – and in some cases ... eye to eye contact may frustrate the obtaining of as true an account from the witness as is possible. This is why I think the right is more accurately considered to be one that is subject to exceptions or qualifications rather than a fundamental or absolute one.

A feature of the equation relevant to both demeanour assessment and the notion that witnesses participate in a public communication, not addressed by the majority, is the vast array of occasions where documentary evidence or the reporting by one witness of another's accounts is permitted before the court instead of direct witness testimony. On these occasions no face is observable, no demeanour can be assessed, communication and openness is compromised, but the law permits the evidence without engaging an inflexible rule such as we see with respect to the Islamic veil. Indeed, for witnesses such as NS, the court can see how she expresses herself through her eyes, her body language, by gestures, by her language, tone, inflection and cadence of her speech and by the substance of her evidence. All of these elements are observable to the court, the accused, the public and the cross-examiner.

Why is confrontation or communication held to be at a premium where it is partially disturbed because a female Islamic witness claims her religious right to wear a full veil, but not where the witness is deceased, or is viewed through pixelated CCTV, or whose words are communicated by another? No answer has been given by any of the courts who have ruled against the veiled witness.

## Conclusion

> To those affected, this is like hanging a sign over the courtroom door saying 'Religious minorities not welcome'.
>
> *(Abella J, [94])*

This chapter has used two cases to critically scrutinize courts' willingness to give full expression to recognized human rights in the face of traditional and outdated reticence. While the interplay of gender, the rights of the accused and religion is complex, it is suggested that the cases of *Y v Slovenia* and *NS* are two sides of the same coin where gender and women's rights may not expressly define the issues in question, but in practice are at the heart of the decisions.

Trial fairness may be defined in human rights instruments and by the common law through defence rights, but it should not be assessed in a vacuum disengaged from democratic and communitarian values. These values apply to all, not just to those whose values are reflected in historically shaped traditions. Further, access to justice and the openness of courts includes those who seek justice, including those who testify in court. Public confidence in courts includes protecting those who claim to be victims of crime as well as those who wish to see defence rights properly protected. As Justice Abella reveals, these rights are not necessarily in tension. The historic expression of the ideals of the fair trial are not without persuasive force, but where they cannot be justified without exacting a cost to other protected rights and interests, they have no place in the modern trial. Indeed, they make the trial unfair in the broader sense, that is, in the sense that all trial protagonists have rights that must be protected.

At one level, one might view human rights instruments' expression of dignitarian rights for all people as central to their rationale. Dignitarian rights for witnesses are not, as might be said of the common law conception of trial fairness, merely an afterthought, tacked on to assuage feminist-led criticism of abusive cross-examination practices. Case law reveals however that the full expression of witness rights, fairly balanced against those of the criminal accused, remains on a long journey. The process of reconciling traditional assumptions with contemporary values is ongoing, and must meet tenacious opposition of the unspoken kind. This requires courts to dig far deeper in its conception of the fair trial than reflecting that 'there is something deep in human nature' that makes confrontation essential.

## References


Bingham, T., 2010. *The rule of law*. London: Allen Lane.

Callen, C., 2013. Human deliberation in fact-finding. *In*: P. Roberts and J. Hunter (eds), *Criminal evidence and human rights: reimagining common law procedural traditions*. London: Hart Publishing, 309–26.

Griffiths, D.H., 2011. Defining the secular in the New Zealand Bill of Rights era: some cases and controversies. *Otago Law Review*, 497.

Henning, T. and Hunter, J., 2013. Finessing the fair trial: complainants and the accused – mansions of justice or castles in the air? *In*: P. Roberts and J. Hunter (eds), *Criminal evidence and human rights: reimagining common law procedural traditions*. London: Hart Publishing, 347–68.

Kamisar, Y., 1965. Equal justice in the gatehouse and the mansions of American criminal procedure. *In*: A. Howard (ed.), *Criminal justice in our time*. Virginia University Press, 3–95.

Kirk, D., 2013. Appearance in court: veiled threats. *Journal of Criminal Law*, 77, 459–61.

Morrison, B.R., Porter, L.L. and Fraser, I.H., 2007. The role of demeanour in assessing the credibility of witnesses. *Advocates' Quarterly*, 33, 170.

Wigmore, J.H., 1940. *A treatise on the Anglo-American system of evidence in trials at common law*. Vol. 5. London: Little, Brown & Co.

Wilson, D. and Sperber, D., 2002. Truthfulness and relevance. *Mind*, 111, 583–632.


## *Cases*

*Coy v Iowa* 487 US 1012 (1988).

*MC v Bulgaria* (Application no 39272/98), 4 December 2003.

*Muhammad v Paruk 553* F Supp 2d 893 (Mich 2008).

*Police v Razamjoo* [2005] DCR 408.

*R v NS* [2012] 3SCR 726.

*R v Osolin* (1993) 86 CCC (3d) 481.

*R v Pelletier* (1995) 165 AR 138.

*R v Levogiannis* (1990) 1 OR (3d) 351.

*R v Sayed* [2010] WADC.

*SW v United Kingdom* [1995] 21 EHRR 363.

*Y v Slovenia* (Application no 41107/10), 28 May 2015.

## *Statutes*

*Canadian Charter of Rights and Freedoms*, ss 2, 7, 11

*Charter of Human Rights and Responsibilities Act* 2006 (Vic), ss 14, 25

*Constitution* (US), 6th Amendment

*European Convention on Human Rights*, Articles 1, 6, 8, 9

*Human Rights Act 2004* (ACT), ss 14, 21

# 42

# China's criminal response to domestic violence against women

## Private prosecution and a human rights approach

*Sanzhuan Guo*

## Introduction

The problem of domestic violence in China is serious, but the term 'domestic violence' has become known to China only very recently. After the United Nations (UN) passed the *Declaration on the Elimination of Violence against Women* (DEVAW) in 1993, and at a time when China was looking for opportunities after the 1989 incident to show the world its achievements in human rights, the country successfully hosted the World Conference on Women in 1995 in Beijing. Since 1995, domestic violence against women has become an increasingly important human rights topic in China.

Along with its active participation in the international arena regarding domestic violence against women, China has been undergoing a process of reforming its domestic legislation to address the issues. China's *Amendment to Marriage Law* in 2001 is the first legislation in the country to prohibit domestic violence (Article 3). On 25 December 2001, the Supreme People's Court issued the *Interpretation No. 1 on Several Issues in the Application of Marriage Law of the People's Republic of China* (or the *2001 No.1 Marriage Law Interpretation*), which includes important parts on domestic violence. In 2008, the Chinese Institute for Applied Jurisprudence of the Supreme People's Court issued the *Guide for Handling Matrimonial Cases Involving Domestic Violence* (or the *2008 Guide on Domestic Violence*). More importantly, after several decades of lobbying, particularly through the efforts of All-China Women's Federation (ACWF), on 25 November 2014 the Chinese government's law-drafting body announced the *Anti Domestic Violence Law (Draft for Comments)* (or the *2014 Draft Anti Domestic Violence Law*). This draft legislation is currently open for general comments and paves an important pathway for the People's Republic of China (PRC) to finally develop a national law that specifically addresses domestic violence.

Compared to the civil law response to domestic violence in China, in particular under the Marriage Law, the development of a criminal justice response to domestic violence has been limited. At this stage there is no crime of 'domestic violence' in the PRC's *1979 Criminal Law* (hereafter, the Criminal Law). Instead, domestic violence can be prosecuted under other crimes, such as the crime of 'intentional injury', 'rape' or 'murder' if the harm reaches the level prescribed by the Criminal Law. In addition, domestic violence against women can be and is mainly prosecuted under the crime of 'maltreatment' (Criminal Law, Article 260). While the crimes of intentional injury, murder and rape are prosecuted only by the procuratorate, maltreatment in China is a criminal offence partly based on private prosecution (minor maltreatment) and partly based on public prosecution (serious maltreatment). In practice, due to the nature of domestic violence, unless intentional injury or murder is involved, domestic violence criminal cases are handled only on the basis of private prosecution.

A recent development with respect to the criminal justice response to domestic violence in China is the *Opinion on Handling Criminal Cases of Domestic Violence in Accordance with Law* (or the '2015 Opinion on Criminal Cases of Domestic Violence') issued on 2 March 2015. Among other things, the opinion recognizes the proxy complaint for certain specially protected groups including minors, the elderly, disabled persons, pregnant women and women who are breastfeeding (Article 2[9]).

The question remains as to whether the current justice criminal response in China, in particular private prosecution, is sufficient to protect women's rights in the context of domestic violence. Indeed, whether private prosecution is doing more harm than good for victims in domestic violence criminal cases has been a point of controversy.

In seeking to answer the above question, this chapter consists of three key sections. The first section explores the definition of domestic violence against women in China and lays down a clear foundation for the ensuing discussion. In particular, how we understand the terms 'domestic' and 'violence' in this context is examined. The second section addresses the question of how private prosecution works to fight domestic violence, including consideration of the subject and scope of private prosecution. The third section evaluates the problems and prospects of private prosecution in addressing domestic violence.

## Defining 'domestic violence against women' in China

DEVAW defines the term 'violence against women' as 'any act of gender-based violence that results in, or is likely to result in, physical, sexual or psychological harm or suffering to women, including threats of such acts, coercion or arbitrary deprivation of liberty, whether occurring in public or in private life' (Article 1). Obviously the definition of violence against women under DEVAW is not limited to domestic violence.

In China, different legislative instruments have adopted their own definitions of domestic violence. For example, the *2008 Guide on Domestic Violence* defines domestic violence as 'a behaviour occurring among family members, primarily between husband and wife, whereby one party causes another physical, sexual, mental or other harm through violence, coercion, insults, economic control or other means, with the purpose of controlling another party' (Article 2). Under the *2014 Draft Anti Domestic Violence Law*, domestic violence means 'physical, mental or other harm done by a family member', where 'family member' includes a 'spouse, parents, children or any other close relatives living together' (Article 2).

The existence of different definitions of domestic violence can create some confusion around our understanding of violence against women. Two key issues relating to the above definitions of domestic violence against women are discussed in turn below: (1) the scope of the term 'domestic', and (2) the scope of the term 'violence'.

### *Scope of the term 'domestic'*

DEVAW uses the term 'violence in the family' rather than domestic violence, where the scope of 'family' is very broad. Specifically, according to the 15 Years of United Nations Special Rapporteur on Violence against Women:

> [t]he definition of the family has been expanded by the mandate to encompass intimate-partner and interpersonal relationships, including non-cohabitating partners, previous partners and domestic workers. This has allowed inclusion of 'wives, live-in partners, former wives or partners, girl-friends (including girl-friends not living in the same house), female relatives (including but not restricted to sisters, daughters, mothers) and female household workers' to be recipients of State protection.

In China's legislation regarding domestic violence, all Acts use or partly use the term 'family members'. However, the definition of 'family members' varies across the legislation. For the specific purpose of applying the Marriage Law, the *2001 No.1 Marriage Law Interpretation* and *2008 Guide on Domestic Violence* limit domestic violence to the family relationship, particularly that between husband and wife. This is a very narrow understanding of a 'domestic' relationship. On the other hand, under the *2015 Opinion on Criminal Cases of Domestic Violence*, criminal cases of domestic violence occur 'between family members', as well as 'between persons with guardianship, support, foster care, cohabitation or similar relationships'. This represents another spectrum of 'domestic' violence, in that it extends the law to cover other relationships such as guardianship and foster care. 'Similar relationship' in the *2015 Opinion on Criminal Cases of Domestic Violence* also leaves wide room for statutory interpretation. However, there is no definition of 'family members' under either the Marriage Law or the *2015 Opinion on Criminal Cases of Domestic Violence.*

Under the *2014 Draft Anti Domestic Violence Law*, 'family members' are defined as including a 'spouse, parents, children or any other close relatives living together', and domestic violence extends to cover 'the violence among people who have a foster relationship' (Article 2).

Compared with the *2015 Opinion on Criminal Cases of Domestic Violence*, the definition of domestic violence in the *2014 Draft Anti Domestic Violence Law* does not mention 'guardianship, support, cohabitation or similar relationships' but only foster relationships. However, the definition of 'family members' in the *2014 Draft Anti Domestic Violence Law* includes 'any other close relatives living together' and may be interpreted broadly to cover some 'guardianship, support, cohabitation or similar relationships'.

Clearly, to understand the scope of 'domestic' under the *2014 Draft Anti Domestic Violence Law*, the definition of 'close relatives' must be explored. As pointed out by Chunbin Li (2011, pp. 18–19), the term 'close relatives' has a range of meanings in Chinese civil law, administrative law and criminal law.

According to Article 12 of the *Opinions of the Supreme People's Court on Several Issues concerning the Implementation of the General Principles of the Civil Law of the People's Republic of China (For Trial Implementation)*, 'close relatives' under the *General Principles of the Civil Law* shall include a 'spouse, parents, children, brothers and sisters, paternal or maternal grandparent, grandchildren, and maternal grandchildren'. Under Article 10 of the *Law of Succession 1985*, 'children' include 'legitimate children, illegitimate children and adopted children, as well as step children who supported or were supported by the decedent'; 'parents' include 'natural parents and adoptive parents, as well as step-parents who supported or were supported by the decedent'; and 'brothers and sisters' include 'blood brothers and sisters, brothers and sisters of half-blood, adopted brothers and sisters, as well as step-brothers and step-sisters who supported or were supported by the decedent'.

In criminal law, pursuant to Article 106(6) of the *Criminal Procedure Law of People's Republic of China (2012 Amendment)*, the term 'close relatives' refers to 'a person's husband or wife, father, mother, sons, daughters, and full siblings'. Thus, it is clear that the definition of 'close relatives' in criminal law is much narrower than that provided in civil law. Under criminal law only full siblings are included and no grandparents and grandchildren are covered by the law.

According to Article 11 of the *Interpretation on Several Issues concerning the Implementation of the Administrative Procedure Law of the People's Republic of China* in 2000, the scope of 'close relatives' under administrative law is even broader than that given under civil law as they include 'other relatives who has support or foster relationship' in addition to a 'spouse, parents, children, brothers and sisters, paternal or maternal grandparent, grandchildren, and maternal grandchildren'.

Based on the above discussion of China's legislation, the following observations can be made regarding the scope of 'domestic' in domestic violence. First, it definitely includes core family relationships of spouse, parents and children. Parents and children can be biological, adoptive or step if a support relationship exists. Second, siblings or grandparents living together, in particular those who have a guardianship, support or foster relationship, fall within the scope of 'domestic'. But if siblings or grandparents do not live with the victim, they do not fall within the scope of 'domestic'. Third, the relationship of uncle/aunt and niece/nephew does not fall within the scope of domestic violence unless they have a guardianship, support or foster relationship, as uncle/aunt and niece/nephew do not come under any legal definition of 'close relatives'. However, Case I of the *2014 Ten Domestic Violence Model Cases* includes such a relationship. In that case, 'daughter Luo was frequently beaten and abused when living together with her grandmother and elder uncle', and the court made a ruling to prohibit the grandmother and elder uncle from 'beating, threatening, abusing, harassing and following the daughter Luo, effective for 6 months'. Fourth, whether domestic violence should cover a de facto relationship, girlfriends and boyfriends or former spouses requires further exploration (Xia 2015, pp. 15–17). According to the *Statements of the State Council on the 2014 Draft Anti Domestic Violence Law*, violence that occurs between persons living together as boyfriends and girlfriends, former spouses and any other non-marriage situation does not fall within the scope of domestic violence (Section 1). Legally, China does not recognize de facto relationships; girlfriends and former spouses are not part of the 'family'. All cohabitation outside marriage has been regarded as 'illegal cohabitation' for a long time. However, social moral standards and the context within which cohabitation outside marriage exists in China are rapidly changing at the present time. Pursuant to the *2015 Opinion on Criminal Cases of Domestic Violence*, a de facto relationship should fall within the scope of 'domestic' as there is a cohabitation relationship. In addition, the *2015 Domestic Violence Criminal Model Cases* includes a case concerning a former spouse relationship. In that case, the defendant and the victim divorced in 2007 but lived together after the divorce. The male defendant beat the female victim frequently, which led to the victim's suicide. The defendant was found guilty of maltreatment. On the other hand, we note that no case relating to a de facto relationship has been found in the model cases. Fifth, although domestic violence no doubt exists within homosexual relationships, China keeps silent on domestic violence issues in relation to homosexual people because it does not recognize the legal status of homosexual relationships and any legal recognition of domestic violence among homosexual groups would imply such recognition of homosexuality. And finally, in summary and in comparison with DEVAW, the scope of China's 'domestic' violence is limited and does not yet include 'live-in partners, former wives or partners, girl-friends (including girlfriends not living in the same house)' and certainly not 'female household workers'.

## *Scope of the term 'violence'*

It has been widely accepted internationally that domestic violence should include physical, sexual, psychological and economic violence. For example, the *UN's Good Practices in Legislation on Violence against Women* recommends that the legislation regarding domestic violence should include 'a comprehensive definition of domestic violence, including physical, sexual, psychological and economic violence' (at 26).

In China, all legislation on domestic violence includes physical violence and mental violence. For example, the *2001 No.1 Marriage Law Interpretation* speaks of 'physical or mental injuries' (Article 1); the *2008 Guide on Domestic Violence* includes four types of violence – physical, sexual, mental and economic control (Article 3); and the 2014 *Draft Anti Domestic Violence Law* refers to 'physical, mental or other harm' (Article 2).

In addition, although the term 'mental harm' rather than 'psychological harm' is used in Chinese legislation, the two refer to the same thing. The *2008 Guide on Domestic Violence* defines mental violence as an 'act or omission of perpetrators, by way of insulting, abusing, ignoring it, giving no medical treatment, refusing to divorce and other means, to mentally torture victims in order for victims to produce humiliation, fear, or worthlessness' (Article 3).

With respect to sexual violence, DEVAW's definition uses the term 'sexual abuse' and refers to marital rape. Although China's *2014 Draft Anti Domestic Violence Law* and *2001 No.1 Marriage Law Interpretation* do not use the term 'sexual' and only mention 'mental or other harm' (*Draft Anti Domestic Violence Law*, Article 2) and 'mental injuries' (*2001 No.1 Marriage Law Interpretation*, Article 1), the *2008 Guide on Domestic Violence* separates 'sexual violence' from 'mental violence' and expressly lists 'sexual violence' as one of the four types of domestic violence (physical, mental, sexual violence and economic control) (Article 3). However, none of the above legal documents refers to 'marital rape'.

In practice, it is still difficult to establish marital rape in China, especially when the marriage still exists. According to scholars, only under three circumstances might marital rape be supported by Chinese legislation: (1) within forced or purchased marriage, (2) during a period of separation, or (3) during divorce proceedings (Zhao 2000, p. 218, Luo 2003, p. 8). The so-called first marital rape case in Shanghai occurred on 24 December 1999 when the defendant Weiming Wang forced his ex-wife to have sex with him after his petition for divorce was granted (October 1999) but not effective. The Shanghai Qingpu District People's Court ruled that the defendant was guilty of rape (*R v Wang Weiming*, Qing Xing Chu Zi Di 36 Hao).

In terms of economic control, DEVAW's definition of violence against women includes 'dowry-related violence' and 'violence related to exploitation' (Article 2). Outside China, advocates for battered women contend that financial abuse and property abuse are forms of domestic violence perpetrated against women (Zhao 2000, p. 213). The *2008 Guide on Domestic Violence* recognizes economic control, like sexual violence, as one of four types of violence, but no other legislation expressly states this. According to the *2008 Guide on Domestic Violence*, economic violence means that a 'perpetrator destroys the victim's self-respect, confidence and self-esteem, through strict control of family or joint property and income, and achieves the purpose of controlling the victim' (Article 3).

## Domestic violence and right of the private prosecution: subject and scope

As Heather Douglas has pointed out, western feminist scholars and activists have argued that criminal punishment of domestic violence advances the protection of women as it encourages public condemnation of domestic violence and increases women's sense of entitlement to safety and quality of life (Douglas 2008, p. 443, Lewis 2004, pp. 205, 221).

Based on similar arguments, domestic violence has been gradually recognized in Chinese legislation as a form of criminal assault, and not merely a private or civil matter. Pursuant to Article 45 of the *Marriage Law of PRC (amended in 2001)*, criminal liability shall apply to 'those who have committed domestic violence or maltreated or deserted any family members so seriously as to have constituted a crime', and 'the victim may file a private prosecution at the People's Court according to the provisions of the *Criminal Procedure Law*; the relevant public security organ shall make investigations and the people's procuratorate concerned shall make a public prosecution according to the provisions of law'.

Although the Marriage Law treats domestic violence and maltreatment separately, there is no crime of 'domestic violence' in the Criminal Law. As discussed earlier, most criminal domestic violence cases in China would be dealt with under Article 260 the crime of maltreatment, which provides:

> Those maltreating their family members, if the case is serious, are to be sentenced to 2 years or less in prison, or put under criminal detention or control.
>
> Those committing crimes stipulated in the above paragraph and causing the victims to suffer severe injuries or death are to be sentenced to 2 to 7 years in prison.
>
> Those committing crime stipulated in the first paragraph of this article are to be investigated only if they are sued.

As we can see, maltreatment without severe injuries or death falls within the scope of private prosecution, which means that in such cases a female victim of domestic violence has the right to decide whether or not to bring a criminal complaint against the male defendant.

Private prosecution in the context of domestic violence against women includes consideration of both the subject of the right and the scope of the right, which are discussed in turn below.

### *Subject of the right: who can bring a complaint?*

Private prosecution is a right of the victim of domestic violence. However, some other people may also have the right to bring a criminal complaint on behalf of the victim. In addition, the right to bring a complaint is different from the right to intervene in a domestic violence case.

In China, private prosecution is more commonly called 'to be handled only upon complaint'. According to Article 98 of the Criminal Law, it refers to 'handling a case only when the victim files a complaint', and 'if the victim is unable to file a complaint because of coercion or intimidation, a people's procuratorate and the victim's close relatives may also file the complaint'.

It is not uncommon for the female victim of domestic violence not to bring a criminal complaint at all because of the pressure they face from family or society. Yet it can be difficult to argue that such pressure falls under the category of 'coercion' or 'intimidation' as per Article 98 of the Criminal Law. Sometimes victims simply cannot make a complaint as they may have limited capacity or their freedom may have been restricted. To some extent, the *2015 Opinion on Criminal Cases of Domestic Violence* considers the above factors and stipulates that:

> In private prosecution of domestic violence crimes where the victims are unable to make a complaint or cannot personally make the complaint, their legal representative or close relatives may make a complaint or complain on their behalf. Where victims have no capacity or limited capacity, and their legal representative and close relatives have not made a complaint, the people's procuratorate may make a complaint. For crimes that are only handled upon a complaint, such as humiliation or violent interference with freedom of marriage, where victims are unable to make a complaint due to compulsion or intimidation, the people's procuratorate may also make a complaint. People's courts shall lawfully accept complaints or complaints made on others' behalf. (Article 9)

As discussed earlier, in the criminal law, the term 'close relatives' refers to 'a person's husband or wife, father, mother, sons, daughters, and full siblings' (*Criminal Procedure Law*, Article 106[6]). This means only a limited range of people can make a complaint, whether for themselves or on behalf of the victim, even when other conditions for private prosecution are met.

In terms of the role of the public organizations in the private prosecution of domestic violence, it is important to understand the relationship between victims and their close relatives, on the one hand, and the public organizations such as the police office and the procuratorate, on the other. Under the *2014 Draft Anti Domestic Violence Law*, the police office has the obligation to inform victims and their legal representative and close relatives of the right to file a criminal complaint where domestic violence has occurred, which should be punished through private prosecution (Article 20). Some scholars have recommended that when victims seek the assistance of the police office to collect evidence, the case should be changed from a private to a public prosecution (Li and Cui 2009, p. 93).

In terms of the public procuratorate's role of bringing a complaint for a private prosecution case, the *2014 Draft Anti Domestic Violence Law* only provides one situation where victims have no capacity or limited capacity and their legal representative and close relatives have not made a complaint (Article 20). However, the *2015 Opinion on Criminal Cases of Domestic Violence* has broadened the role of the public procuratorate to cover an additional situation for 'crimes that are only handled upon a complaint . . . where victims are unable to make a complaint due to compulsion or intimidation, the people's procuratorate may also make a complaint' (Article 9).

In addition, the persons who can bring a criminal complaint are different from those who can take action to stop domestic violence, which is also crucial in combatting domestic violence. Under the *Draft Anti Domestic Violence Law*, any organization or citizen can dissuade, stop or report domestic violence to the police office (Article 13). Article 46 of the *Law on Protection of the Rights and Interests of Women (amended in 2005)* prohibits domestic violence against women, and stipulates that:

> The State takes measures to prevent and stop domestic violence.The departments of public security, civil affairs, judicial administration, etc., as well as urban and rural mass organizations of self-government at the grass roots level and public organizations shall, within the scope of their respective duties, prevent and stop domestic violence, and provide assistance to female victims.

Timely and effective intervention in criminal domestic violence has been listed as a basic principle in the *2015 Opinion on Criminal Cases of Domestic Violence*. In the Marriage Law, 'neighbourhood or villager committees' have been given the right to intervene to mediate in domestic violence cases, but these bodies are not given the right to bring a criminal complaint on their own or on the behalf of victims. As scholars have reflected, such community-level intervention, or even intervention by the ACWF, has not been effective as they are controlled by the government and victims are reluctant to use the service (Tam et al. 2013, p. 115).

Intervention is important to protect victims' rights and freedom, but it must be balanced with victims' right to choose whether they wish to be assisted. As the protection of victims' safety and privacy and respect of victims' wishes are also basic principles, which reflect a human rights approach in domestic violence cases, it is important to know the line between intervention and the right of victims. The *2015 Opinion on Criminal Cases of Domestic Violence* states that 'victims must be fully heard when filing a case, adopting criminal compulsory measures, making an indictment, giving criminal punishments, or giving communication or parole', and 'a reasonable and rational disposition made within the range provided by law' (Article 3).

### *Scope of the right: what can victims complain about?*

The application of private prosecution depends on the distinction between the crimes of maltreatment and domestic violence under civil and administrative laws, and the distinction between two different types of maltreatment, one of which applies to private prosecution and the other to public prosecution.

The line between public and private prosecution for the crime of maltreatment is relatively clear because public prosecution is focused on physical injury. In practice, whether severe injury or death has occurred will decide whether the prosecution is private or public. Article 95 of the Criminal Law defines the term 'severe injury' as:

1 injuries resulting in loss of the use of a person's limbs or disfigurement;
2 injuries resulting in loss of the use of a person's hearing, sight, or functions of any other organ; or
3 other injuries that cause grave harm to a person's physical health.

However, it is more difficult to distinguish between criminal and non-criminal domestic violence as only durative and frequent occurrences of domestic violence constitute a crime (*2001 No.1 Marriage Law Interpretation*, Article 1) but the standard for 'durative and frequent occurrences' is not fully clear.

If a physical injury is involved, there are more detailed rules to determine the level of seriousness of the injury. According to the *Standards for Assessing the Extent of Bodily Injuries*, jointly issued in 2013 by the Supreme People's Court, the Supreme People's Procuratorate, the Ministry of Public Security, the Ministry of State Security and the Ministry of Justice, there are three levels of injury: severe injury (including critical and serious injury) (Zhong Shang), minor injury (Qing Shang) and slight injury (Qing Wei Shang). The basic rule is that slight injury does not lead to criminal but only administrative justice while minor injury can trigger criminal responsibilities. Severe injury is generally an aggravating factor for sentencing and will lead to public prosecution in the crime of maltreatment.

However, there is no such clear standard for non-physical harm. Questions remain around whether psychological, sexual and economic harm can ever lead to public prosecution in domestic violence cases and when those harms fall under the scope of criminal law rather than civil or administrative law as the case must be 'serious' in order to meet the requirement of the crime of maltreatment. The *2015 Opinion on Criminal Cases of Domestic Violence* provides some guidance about what kinds of cases are serious. It provides that 'circumstances such as abuse continuing over a long time or occurring many times; the means of abuse being cruel; the abuse causing minor injuries or serious illness in the victim, and severe abuse of minors, the elderly, persons with disabilities, pregnant women, nursing women or persons with serious illness, are all "serious (or heinous) circumstances", as per paragraph 1 of Article 260 of the Criminal Law, and shall be convicted and punished as the crime of maltreatment' (*2015 Opinion on Criminal Cases of Domestic Violence*, Article 17).

## Domestic violence and private prosecution: problems and prospects

Two questions are addressed under this section. One is why victims of domestic violence are unable or unwilling to bring a private prosecution complaint and how to solve the problem. The second is whether private prosecution is effective to protect women against domestic violence.

## Evidence and willingness

One crucial factor that may prevent victims from pursuing private prosecution is a lack of evidence. Evidence is difficult to obtain in all domestic violence cases. This is partly because of the nature of the crime but also because victims may not know how to collect evidence. Under the *2015 Opinion on Criminal Cases of Domestic Violence*, courts should guide victims in a timely manner on how to collect evidence and inform victims of what evidence is required and the method by which it must be collected. If victims cannot obtain certain evidence for reasons beyond their control, they can apply to the people's court to collect it; the court should then hear and review the case carefully and, where a genuine need is found, the court should collect the evidence (Article 14).

In addition to guidance on evidence collection, legal aid assistance to victims should be strengthened. Interestingly, although the *2015 Opinion on Criminal Cases of Domestic Violence* emphasizes the importance of legal aid provided by the people's procuratorate to the victim in public prosecution cases (Article 15), it does not refer to legal aid in private prosecution cases. However, if domestic violence is regarded as a serious human right issue, the state should have an obligation to provide assistance to fight domestic violence.

In relation to the willingness of women to bring a private prosecution in response to domestic violence, according to surveys, women do not want to sue their husbands often because of the fear of retaliation or financial dependence (Zhao 2000, p. 227). Financial aid may assist battered women for a short period, but in the long term, they may prefer to stay with their husbands due to the lack of resources available to them were their husbands to be sent to prison. Sometimes, even if victims have filed a case, they may regret their decision to do so, and then seek to minimize the penalty, or even withdraw the complaint. The data shows that some 40 per cent of domestic violence cases are withdrawn (Chen and Duan 2012, p. 34).

More importantly, women may be unwilling to file a private prosecution because of the influence of the cultural and social environment. According to the research, women in China, particularly in rural areas, believe that husbands are entitled to beat their wives if the wives do something wrong, and even police officers would not intervene (Liu and Chan 1999, p. 1477). In addition, the systematic inequality between men and women and stereotypical views of the role of women in the family and in society are the true causes of domestic violence against women. On this point, there is no better way to change the culture than through education and increasing awareness of a human rights approach to fight domestic violence against women. As reflected in China's State Report to the CEDAW in 2004, 'enhancing the role of the media to create a social environment conducive to the elimination of violence against women' is an important measure that China has undertaken (CEDAW/C/CHN/5-6, 18–23). For example, the first Chinese TV show on domestic violence – 'Do not speak to strangers' (2001), in which Yuanzheng Feng played the part of a famous surgeon who consistently abused his wife – attracted great attention from the public and played an important role in opening up the discussion of domestic violence in China. Another example is that of Kim Lee, an American national and the ex-wife of Chinese celebrity Yang Li, known for his 'Crazy English' teaching. Kim Lee publicized her husband's domestic violence behaviours through Weibo, a popular social network in China, and got a divorce in 2013. Even though Kim Lee did not bring a private prosecution under criminal law, her disclosure of a celebrity's domestic violence behaviours set a good example for other Chinese women to follow.

## Effectiveness and prospects of private prosecution

To evaluate the effectiveness and the prospects of private prosecution in combatting domestic violence, it is important to strike a balance between respecting women's right of autonomy in choosing private prosecution and the state's obligation to protect women from domestic violence.

Women's right to autonomy is part of their human rights. Although criminalizing domestic violence is important to protect women's rights, identifying what women really want from the criminal justice system regarding domestic violence is essential to evaluate the value of private prosecution. Although sometimes victims' interest and wishes may not be the same, it is true that victims have a greater need for a court's intervention and protection (such as a restraining order) rather than criminal punishment (Zhao 2000, p. 231).

On the other hand, domestic violence violates women's human rights, including the right to equality, the right to liberty and security of person, the right to equal protection under the law, and the right to be free from all forms of discrimination (DEVAW, Article 3). DEVAW provides that states should 'refrain from engaging in violence against women' and 'exercise due diligence to prevent, investigate and, in accordance with national legislation, punish acts of violence against women, whether those acts are perpetrated by the State or by private persons' (Articles 4 [b] and [c]). Furthermore, according to CEDAW's General Recommendation No. 19, domestic violence has been recognized as a form of discrimination against women under CEDAW (Article 1) and the state should 'take appropriate and effective measures to overcome all forms of gender-based violence, whether by public or private act' (Article 24). That is to say, states cannot leave the response to domestic violence fully in the hands of individuals.

The *2015 Opinion on Criminal Cases of Domestic Violence* recognizes and reconciles the tensions between private prosecution and the roles of police officers and public prosecutors. The role of the police and procurator should be strengthened. Respecting women's autonomy does not equate to leaving them alone and the police and procurator not intervening in the private family situation. If private prosecution is not effective, the state should intervene and prosecutors should take a more active role in stepping in to bring a complaint where victims and their close relatives are unable or unwilling to do so. As China's recent state report to CEDAW revealed, cross-departmental cooperation on intervention has been further enhanced, such as the National Coordination Group for Safeguarding the Rights and Interests of Women and Children and for Creating the 'Safe Family', which was established by the relevant government ministries in 2001 (CEDAW/C/CHN/7-8, 2013, para. 98). However, due to the reluctance of the police and prosecutors to intervene in domestic violence cases in reality, it is important to maintain the right of the victim to bring a case. The autonomy of women and the right of the victim to bring a criminal case must be respected.

In addition, when we evaluate the effectiveness of private prosecution in domestic violence cases, it should be noted that the problem may not originate in private prosecution itself, but may lie in other areas. For example, the sentence for the crime of maltreatment under private prosecution is lenient as it is only up to a fixed-term imprisonment of two years. Thus, such lenient sentencing can make victims more hesitant to bring a private prosecution case.

## Concluding remarks

Criminal law is one legal pathway to prevent and punish domestic violence and private prosecution is only one part of the criminal justice response to the issue. This chapter was not intended to analyse domestic violence in China as a whole, but to highlight a particular related issue (that is, private prosecution) in the hope of opening a door for broader discussion.

In a nutshell, the key issues regarding domestic violence against women in the context of private prosecution are the need to clarify the subject and scope of private prosecution and balance women's right of autonomy with the state's obligations to intervene and protect, by strengthening the current law and practice and passing the *Anti Domestic Violence Law* in a timely manner, and assisting women with evidence collection, legal aid, shelter and financial assistance, as well as utilizing protection orders wisely.

## Note

This chapter was finalized before the PRC's new Anti Domestic Violence Law came into effect, on 1 March 2016.

## References

Chen, W. and Duan, W., 2012. Empirical studies on roles of courts in combating domestic violence cases. *Hebei Law Science*, 30(8), 28–38.
Douglas, H., 2008. The criminal law's responses to domestic violence: What is going on? *Sydney Law Review*, 30, 439–69.
Lewis, R. 2004. Making justice work: effective legal interventions for domestic violence. *British Journal of Criminology*, 44, 204–24.
Li, C., 2011. Defining 'family member' in the legislation of prevention against domestic violence. *Journal of China Women's University*, 2011(5), 18–22.
Li, G. and Cui, L., 2009. Brief review on shortcomings of Chinese criminal responses to domestic violence. *Legal System and Society*, 92–3.
Liu, M. and Chan, C., 1999. Enduring violence and staying in marriage: stories of battered women in rural China. *Violence Against Women*, 5, 1469–92.
Luo, C., 2003. Looking at domestic violence by criminal law. *Journal of Hubei Police Officer College*, 75, 5–8.
Tam, D.M.Y. et al., 2013. Comparing criminal justice responses to violence against women in Canada and China. *Asia Pacific Journal of Social Work and Development*, 23(2), 106–20.
Xia, Y., 2015. Study on the definition of domestic violence in China: Anti-Domestic Violence Law (Draft for Soliciting Suggestions). *Journal of China Women's University*, 2015(2), 12–19.
Zhao, Y., 2000. Domestic violence in China: in search of legal and social responses. *Pacific Basin Law Journal*, 18, 211–51.

# 43

# Human rights law and juvenile justice

## Emerging law and practice

*Ursula Kilkelly and Louise Forde*

### Introduction

International human rights law provides strong and clear protection to children in conflict with the law. Protections enshrined in the United Nations (UN) *Convention on the Rights of the Child* (CRC) are matched by a range of instruments adopted at international and regional levels that set out the rights to which children are entitled when they are involved in the criminal justice system. These instruments make clear that children, like adults, have the right to a fair trial as a fundamental right although they also recognize that children require additional protections if their rights are to be protected in this sphere. In recent times, the law has developed to elaborate the elements of a fair trial that are particular to children. Key here is the right to participate effectively in the criminal trial process, developed by the case law of the European Court of Human Rights (ECtHR) and the *European Guidelines on Child-friendly Justice*, which articulate how the justice system must be adapted to enable children to access and enjoy justice that is consistent with their rights, needs and circumstances.

The aim of this chapter is to examine what human rights law contributes to our understanding of the rights of child defendants in the criminal justice system. It aims to interrogate how rights for child defendants in the criminal process are interpreted and protected in various contexts, and to consider how these rights are implemented through the criminal procedure in place for child defendants in a number of jurisdictions. It begins with an outline of the rights of children in the criminal justice system under the UN *Convention on the Rights of the Child* (CRC). It then goes on to consider the interpretation of children's rights in the criminal process before the ECtHR. Consideration will then be given to the protection given to these rights in a number of jurisdictions, including Ireland, England and Wales, Scotland and Australia.

### The UN CRC

International law on children's rights provides a wealth of standards and guidance in the area of youth justice (Kilkelly 2008a). The CRC contains two specific and detailed provisions on youth justice and detention, which provide that children in conflict with the law have the right to be treated:

> in a manner consistent with the promotion of the child's sense of dignity and worth, which reinforces the child's respect for the human rights and fundamental freedoms of others and which takes into account the child's age and the desirability of promoting the child's reintegration and the child's assuming a constructive role in society.

Significantly, the Convention recognizes the child's rights of due process, including the right to a fair and public hearing, the right to be presumed innocent until proven guilty, the right to free translation and not to be compelled to give testimony. In addition to these general due process rights, the Convention contains special protections for children. For example, Article 40(2)(b)(vii) provides that children have the right to have their privacy respected at all stages of their proceedings and Article 40(3) makes provision for the establishment of laws, institutions and procedures specifically applicable to children in conflict with the law. States must both establish an age of criminal responsibility below which children will be presumed not to have the capacity to infringe the criminal law and they are required under the Convention to provide for the development of measures for dealing with children without resorting to judicial proceedings, provided that human rights and safeguards are fully respected. Under Article 40(4), states must make a variety of dispositions – including care, probation, guidance, foster care, educational and vocational training – available to ensure that children are dealt with in a manner appropriate to their wellbeing and proportionate both to their circumstances and the offence. Taken together, these provisions reinforce the importance of human rights and due process to children in conflict with the law, while also making clear that to protect the rights of the child, criminal justice systems must be adapted to children's particular circumstances.

Further guidance on the implementation of these obligations can be found in the General Comment on Juvenile Justice adopted by the Committee on the Rights of the Child in 2007 (Committee on the Rights of the Child 2007). This is an elaborate and comprehensive document that advises states about the application of the Convention in the area of youth justice. Although the General Comment reinforces the Convention's core principles in relation to the treatment of children in conflict with the law, it also seeks to address some of the gaps in the Convention. One such gap is that the child does not have an unequivocal right to a lawyer; rather, Article 40(2)(b)(ii) makes provision for the child's entitlement to legal 'and other appropriate assistance'. Clearly, according to the Convention, the child does not always have to be represented by a lawyer, but he/she must have 'appropriate' assistance. According to the Committee, states should provide as much as possible for 'adequate trained legal assistance, such as expert lawyers or paralegal professionals' and whereas other appropriate assistance is possible . . . that person must have sufficient knowledge and understanding of the various legal aspects of the process of juvenile justice and must be trained to work with children in conflict with the law'. More generally, the General Comment elaborates on how the trial process should be adapted to take into account children's particular circumstances. Based on Article 14 of the Beijing Rules (on the Administration of Juvenile Justice), the General Comment highlights that 'the proceedings should be conducted in an atmosphere of understanding to allow the child to participate and to express himself/herself freely' and that taking the child's age and maturity into account may also require 'modified courtroom procedures and practices'.

Overall, the Convention and the Committee's General Comment reinforce the rights-based approach to juvenile justice. They provide important guidance as to how best to secure the rights of children in conflict with the law, notably their rights as children and not simply as offenders.

## The case law of the ECtHR

Although the *European Convention on Human Rights* (ECHR) is a general rather than a child-specific human rights treaty, Article 6 contains special protection for children. In particular, Article 6(1) which guarantees the right to a fair and public hearing provides for an exception to this rule where the protection of juveniles so requires. The sense of this provision is that children's interests are harmed by the public nature of the trial process and this provision has been applied in children's cases to underscore that under the ECHR children in conflict with the law not only have the right to the same procedural guarantees as adult defendants, they also have the right to the benefit of special procedures which take into account their age, maturity, and level of vulnerability.

Breaches of children's rights under Article 6 have been found where a report by the judge rapporteur which had been communicated to the advocate general had not been communicated on an equal basis to the defendant, as occurred in the case of *De Sousa v France* [2005] ECHR App. No. 61328/00, and in *Çobanoglu and Budak v Turkey* [2007] App. No. 45977/99 and *Yesilyurt v Turkey* [2010] ECHR App. No. 15649/05, where it was considered that the time it took to complete the proceedings was unduly lengthy. While these are rights that apply equally to both adult and child defendants, it is also apparent that more will be required where the case concerns children, and that special principles apply. In relation to the right to have the charges determined within a reasonable length of time, the ECtHR has acknowledged that the court may have regard to the age of the defendant in its assessment of whether the time taken is reasonable. In the case of *Oblov v Russia* [2009] ECHR App. No. 22674/02, the court observed that a case involving a minor defendant should be conducted with 'special diligence', in order to ensure that those charged with criminal offences should not remain in a state of uncertainty about his or her state for too long a time (*Oblov v Russia*, para. 24).

The differing capacities and vulnerabilities of children as compared to adults have made it necessary to consider how particular elements of the criminal process need to be adapted when children are accused of a crime, and this has been a particular issue in respect of the trial process. According to the ECtHR, special provisions and procedures must be put in place for child defendants in order to ensure that they can participate effectively in the trial process. In the cases of *T.* and *V. v the United Kingdom* (1999) 30 EHRR 121, the ECtHR found that there had been a breach of Article 6 where two young defendants were tried in public in the Crown (adult) Court on the ground that they had not been able to participate effectively in the proceedings. In this regard, a number of aspects of the procedure were problematic including the huge level of publicity that surrounded the trial process, the raised dock on which the defendants were seated, and the formality of the courtroom proceedings. Taken together, these created conditions under which the defendants could not follow the proceedings or participate effectively, and had the effect of denying them a fair hearing as required by Article 6.

This concept of effective participation as it relates to child defendants has been developed by the ECtHR in subsequent cases. In *S.C. v the United Kingdom* (2005) 40 EHRR 10 it considered what this would mean for a young person with limited intellectual capacities. The defendant in *S.C.* was 11 years old but had been assessed as having a mental age of an 8-year-old, at best. He was tried in the Crown Court, however, a number of changes had been made to the trial process by the United Kingdom (UK) authorities, in line with the Practice Direction for young defendants which had been introduced in the wake of the *T* and *V* cases. The court here reiterated the requirement that children be dealt with in criminal proceedings 'in a manner which takes full account of his age, level of maturity and intellectual and emotional capacities', and which required positive steps to be taken to promote understanding and participation (*S.C. v the United Kingdom*, para. 28). The court found that, despite the steps which had been taken to modify the procedures in line with the Practice Direction, this had not been sufficient to ensure that the applicant in this case had understood the significance or nature of the proceedings in order to enable him to give directions and to participate effectively in the proceedings, resulting in a breach of his rights under Article 6. The ECtHR elaborated further on the principle of effective participation in coming to this decision, holding that it was not required that a child defendant be able to understand every technical detail of the trial, such as points of law or evidential detail. Rather, it held that 'effective participation' required a 'broad understanding of the nature of the trial process and of what is at stake for him or her, including the significance of any penalty which may be imposed' (*S.C. v the United Kingdom*, para. 29). The ECtHR emphasized that if a state chose to prosecute a young person with limited intellectual capacities using criminal procedures rather than some other form of disposal, it would be essential to make use of special tribunals with adapted procedures which would be able to consider fully and make allowances for any limitations experienced by the defendant (*S.C. v the United Kingdom*, para. 35).

It is apparent from these judgements that states must take positive steps to ensure that child defendants are supported adequately to ensure that they understand the nature and significance of criminal proceedings and are able to participate in them. Moreover, the ECtHR has said that this requirement of effective participation applies not only at the trial stage, but at all stages of the criminal process. In *Martin v Estonia* [2013] ECHR App. No. 35985/09 the ECtHR held that the right to effective participation applied from the earliest stages of the criminal investigation, and in particular, covered questioning by the police. In this context, the requirements of effective participation were said to be as follows:

> The right of an accused minor to effective participation in his criminal trial requires that the authorities deal with him with due regard to his vulnerability and capacities from the first stages of his involvement in a criminal investigation and, in particular, during any questioning by the police. The authorities must take steps to reduce as far as possible his feelings of intimidation and inhibition . . . and ensure that the accused minor has a broad understanding of the nature of the investigation, of what is at stake for him, including the significance of any penalty which may be imposed as well as of his rights of defence and, in particular, of his right to remain silent.
>
> *(Martin v Estonia, para. 92)*

This right to effective participation at all stages of the criminal proceedings, including at the point where the young person is being questioned by police, was reaffirmed more recently in the case of *Blokhin v Russia* [2013] ECHR App. No. 47152/06, although this decision is not yet final and has been referred to the Grand Chamber.

The jurisprudence of the ECtHR, therefore, requires that young people in conflict with the law have the same rights as adult defendants, however, the special vulnerabilities and lesser maturity and capacities of young people oblige States to take positive steps to ensure that young people are able to effectively participate at all stages of the criminal proceedings. The implementation of this, particularly during the trial process, require adjustments and modifications to be made to procedure to take account of this.

## The European Guidelines on Child-friendly Justice

Adopted by the Committee of Ministers of the Council of Europe in October 2010, the European Guidelines on Child-friendly Justice built on the case law of the ECtHR, practice of

European states and the provisions of the Convention on the Rights of the Child. According to the Guidelines, child-friendly justice systems are those that guarantee:

> the respect and the effective implementation of all children's rights at the highest attainable level, bearing in mind the principles listed below and giving due consideration to the child's level of maturity and understanding and the circumstances of the case. It is, in particular, justice that is accessible, age appropriate, speedy, diligent, adapted to and focused on the needs and rights of the child, respecting the rights of the child including the rights to due process, to participate in and to understand the proceedings, to respect for private and family life and to integrity and dignity.

Although they clearly articulate how justice systems need to be adapted to account for children's particular circumstances, the Guidelines are firmly grounded in the values of human rights and due process. For instance, according to the Guidelines:

> Children should be treated with care, sensitivity, fairness and respect throughout any procedure or case, with special attention for their personal situation, well-being and specific needs, and with full respect for their physical and psychological integrity. This treatment should be given to them, in whichever way they have come into contact with judicial or non-judicial proceedings or other interventions, and regardless of their legal status and capacity in any procedure or case.

Significantly, the Guidelines address the contradiction between the requirement to act in the child's best interests (as required by Article 3 of the CRC) and the duty to respect the child's due process rights by emphasizing the importance of the rule of law as a fundamental principle. In this regard, the Guidelines note that:

> Elements of due process such as the principles of legality and proportionality, the presumption of innocence, the right to a fair trial, the right to legal advice, the right to access to courts and the right to appeal, should be guaranteed for children as they are for adults and should not be minimised or denied under the pretext of the child's best interests. This applies to all judicial and non-judicial and administrative proceedings.

In this way, the Guidelines make clear that respect for the child's human rights should not give way to paternalistic considerations as to what is in the child's best interests. Indeed, they reinforce the importance of the child's due process rights, reflecting the principle in Article 40(3) of the CRC that alternatives to judicial proceedings should only be used where the child's human rights and legal safeguards are fully respected.

The Guidelines are divided into sections that cover child-friendly justice in the three stages of 'before', 'during' and 'after judicial proceedings'. They address the general elements of child-friendly justice, including particularly detailed sections on access to information, the importance of a multidisciplinary approach, the need to protect children from harm and the importance of ensuring proceedings respect children's private and family life. In these areas, the Guidelines add considerably to existing international standards, providing precise and detailed guidance as to the application of children's rights to the specific context of judicial and administrative proceedings. The Guidelines do not generate new standards but focus, importantly, on implementation. For instance, they require that all 'professionals working with and for children receive interdisciplinary training on the rights and needs of children while also specifying that professionals having direct contact with children should be trained in communicating with them at all ages and stages of development'.

Throughout the remainder of the Guidelines, the emphasis is placed on the importance of ensuring that children have the supports and information to access, participate in and understand the formal decision-making processes that determine their lives. The Guidelines combine practical recommendations with important points of principle. Examples of the former are that court rulings are explained to children in a manner they can understand, children should be familiarized with the courtroom setting before the proceedings begin and interviews of children should be carried out by trained professionals. In relation to the latter, the Guidelines assert that children should be considered as fully fledged clients with their own rights and that exceptional diligence is required to prevent the negative effects of delay in proceedings. Other common themes flow through the Guidelines including the importance of specialization among those who work with and for children, the need to adapt the accessibility and operation of the structures of justice for children and the need to ensure that the justice system is oriented towards and informed by the needs, circumstances and rights of children.

## National implementation of international principles

Subsequent to the judgements in the cases of *T.* and *V.* against the UK, a Practice Direction concerning the trial of children and young persons in the Crown Court (2000) was issued by Lord Bingham which applies to all children tried in the Crown Court in England and Wales. This set out a number of modifications to apply to the procedures of the adult court in order to allow young people to participate effectively and it evolved into a further Practice Direction (Criminal Proceedings: Consolidation) issued in 2007. Para III.30 of this Practice Direction applies to children being tried or sentenced in either the Crown Courts or the magistrates' court, with clear overriding principles that should apply in such cases. It recognizes that the understanding of the proceedings and the participation of young people may be inhibited in the case of a child or young person, and requires that 'all possible steps should be taken to assist a vulnerable defendant to understand and participate' in the proceedings. It also requires that trial procedures be adapted as far as necessary to meet these ends and stipulates that regard should be had to the welfare of the young person in this process.

Practical guidance is given on a number of points in order to facilitate the participation of the young person. It recognizes that, in some cases, it may be appropriate that the defendant should visit the venue for the trial before the hearing takes place, in order to allow him or her to become familiar with the setting. It also requires that the assistance of the police be sought in situations where widespread public or media interest has been attracted to try to ensure that the defendant is not subjected to intimidation or abuse. During the course of the trial itself, the Practice Direction stipulates that all participants should be on the same or almost the same level, that the child defendant should normally be allowed to sit with members of his family or another supportive adult and in a position which 'permits easy, informal communication with his legal representatives', and that the trial should take place according to a schedule which takes sufficient account of the defendant's ability to concentrate on and follow the proceedings. Other requirements, aimed at ensuring the full understanding of the child defendant are included. These include a requirement on the part of the court to explain the trial process, the role of the jury and the possible consequences of a guilty verdict, and to ensure as far as practicable 'that the trial is conducted in simple, clear language that the defendant can understand and that cross-examination is conducted by questions that are short and clear'. Provision is also made to enable the child to apply to give evidence by video link in certain circumstances.

Restrictions should be put in place on the attendance of the trial by members of the public, and efforts to reduce the formality of the court setting are evident in the guideline that robes and wigs should generally not be worn in court, and that there should be no recognizable police presence in the courtroom save for good reason.

A Youth Court Bench Book was issued in the UK in 2013 (Judicial College January 2013). This sets out a number of guidelines on issues such as those who should be entitled to attend the court, and on engagement with the young person, as well as setting out the procedural considerations that should apply. It stipulates that children under the age of 16 must be accompanied by a parent or guardian unless the court considers this unreasonable. In addition, only members of the court, those connected to the case, lawyers and bona fide members of the press, and any others given permission by the youth court should be present in youth court. It encourages magistrates to sit on the same level as others in the courtroom, and stipulates that the young person should be allowed to sit with their parent or guardian during the proceedings. The issue of engagement is given special attention in the Bench Book, and it highlights that both children and the parents or guardians should be involved at all stages of the proceedings. It advises that magistrates should introduce themselves and those present in court at the beginning of proceedings and give a brief explanation of their roles. Direct engagement between the court and the young person is also encouraged after the young person has been convicted, and at all stages it stipulates that questions should be posed in plain language that the child can understand, and that legal jargon should be avoided.

Judicial guidance has been issued elsewhere in Europe too. In Ireland, for instance, the law (*Children Act* 2001, as amended) recognizes that children who appear before the criminal courts must have equal rights to adults, and particular recognition is given to the right to be heard and to participate in any proceedings of the court that can affect the child (Kilkelly 2008b). In 2007, the President of the District Court issued a Practice Direction in relation to the operation of the Children Court in the Dublin Metropolitan region (District Court, January 2007). Its purpose is to ensure compliance with the constitutional rights of the young person, as well as with the relevant international standards in the area. It sets out as a key principle that the trial process 'should not itself expose the young defendant to avoidable intimidation, humiliation or distress' and requires that the trial process be adapted in order to ensure this happens, as well as to ensure the welfare of the young person as appropriate.

It also contains guidance on what kind of modifications and adjustments should be made. In particular, it limits the attendance in the Children Court to officers of the court, the parents or guardians of the child or adult relative of the child, a person directly concerned in the proceedings, a bona fide member of the press, or any other person the court allows to attend in its discretion. It makes several directions regarding the courtroom environment and indicates that the child should normally be allowed to sit with members of his family or those supporting him or her, and the guidelines require that there be no recognizable uniformed presence in the courtroom. It provides for arrangements to be made for the child to visit the courtroom outside of court hours before the hearing takes place if he or she so wishes to do so. It also requires the legal representatives for the prosecution and the defence to introduce themselves, the child, any family members and any witnesses to the court before the commencement of proceedings. The Practice Direction stipulates that wigs and robes should not be worn in the children court, requires legal representatives involved in the case to 'take all steps necessary to ensure that young defendants are fully aware of what is in involved in complying with bail conditions and understand the consequences which flow from breach of bail conditions'. It also sets out that it is the duty of the legal representative to bring it to the court's attention if the young person requires any other special arrangements, or translation or other advocacy services in order to participate meaningfully.

In 2015, the Children Court developed a Bench Book to guide the judiciary in the implementation of legislation in light of international law and related instruments (District Court May 2015). It details the way in which the court should function in order to protect the rights of child defendants and takes particular cognizance of international law, including the case law of the ECtHR, the CRC and *European Guidelines on Child-friendly Justice*.

Aside from the issuing of practice guidelines, a number of other developments have attempted to mitigate the harshness of the court environment for child defendants in the law of England and Wales. In particular, a number of special measures exist under the *Youth Justice & Criminal Evidence Act 1999*, and these have the potential to apply to child defendants (Stone 2010). These provisions include the possibility of giving evidence through video link. While these provisions were initially confined to witnesses and victims, and were considered by the UK courts not to apply to child defendants in cases where applications were made to give evidence in this manner, (See further *R. (on the application of S.) v Waltham Forest Youth Court* [2004] EWHC 715 (Admin); 2004 2 Cr. App. R. 21 and *R v SH* [2003] EWCA Crim 1208) an amendment to the legislation introduced by the *Police and Justice Act 2006* to section 33A(4) of the *Youth Justice and Criminal Evidence Act 1999* allows child defendants to given evidence through video link if his ability to participate effectively as a witness giving oral evidence is compromised by his level of intellectual ability or social functioning and it is considered that use of a live link would enable to participate more effectively as a witness.

An additional development in England and Wales has been the possibility of using an intermediary in the court procedure to help mitigate the harshness of the court environment. This can be particularly useful in cases where the young person in question has mental health difficulties or intellectual impairments. In the case of *C. v Sevenoaks Youth Court* (2009) EWHC 2088 (Admin), the court considered the use of an intermediary as part of the supports to be provided to a 12-year-old defendant with learning and behavioural difficulties. The court there held that it was part of the 'duty under its inherent powers and under the Criminal Procedure Rules to take such steps as are necessary to ensure that he has a fair trial, not just during the proceedings, but beforehand as he and his lawyers prepare for trial' (at 17). This duty existed notwithstanding the absence of an express power to that effect under the *Youth Justice & Criminal Evidence Act 1999*. The court here said that it would be necessary for the defendant to meet the intermediary in advance of the trial if he was to know and have confidence in him or her. The acknowledgement of the need for such assistance will be a significant aspect of ensuring that young people, especially those with a cognitive impairment of one type of another are supported to participate effectively in the provisions concerning them.

## Practice in some national courts

Evaluations of practice in criminal proceedings involving child defendants are crucial in determining how well the rights of children in this context are being realized in practice. It also serves to highlight important gaps between the legislation and policy provision and their implementation in practice.

A study of the Irish Children Court in 2007 (Carroll et al. 2007) served to highlight some of these issues. In particular, it was noted that there were significant delays in the completion of proceedings, with young people having to appear on a number of occasions. They also found that a number of the young people involved in the study had significantly lower levels of literacy as compared to their age, and some also had learning or behavioural difficulties or functioning at exceptionally low levels of intelligence. Research suggests that these factors may be significant in how effectively young people presenting with such difficulties can participate in the courtroom processes (Seymour and Butler 2008). In a further study, based on courtroom observation, Kilkelly noted a number of issues with the participation of young people in the Children Court, pointing out that engagement with young people in the Children Court was extremely low, and in 55 per cent of cases no communication whatsoever took place between the judge and the young person, and observations were made which indicated that the young person was not following, was not engaged in or did not understand the procedure (Kilkelly 2008b). This study also highlighted that the courtroom environments were not supportive of the participation of young people generally and it impacted significantly on their ability to do so. Although other jurisdictions have made better strides towards the implementation of the principle of effective participation (Weijers 2004), these observations highlight that not all states are successfully implementing these core human rights principles for children.

Evaluations have also been undertaken of the operation of the Children's Courts in Australia where similar issues which may also have a significant impact on the realization of the rights of child defendants. One particular study that was undertaken in the Australian Capital Territory sought to identify the status of, and the challenges faced by the courts from the perspective of the judicial officers and other professional stakeholders within the system (Camilleri et al. 2011). Particular issues also arose in relation to the understanding of children and young people in this context, with reports of 'marked variability amongst court users in their understanding of court processes and the implications of those processes', with both children and parents reported as seeming to have little comprehension about the significance of court outcomes in many cases. Issues in relation to the court environment, especially the lack of privacy in waiting areas, was also raised as a concern. As in Ireland, the imposition on young people of bail conditions that they struggled to meet in light of their disadvantaged backgrounds were also problematic.

Observations have also been drawn about the trial of child defendants in other regions of Australia. In an assessment of the Victorian courts against the *Victorian Charter of Human Rights and Responsibilities*, it was noted that few modifications are made in criminal proceedings involving children despite an awareness on the part of the judiciary that young people often experience difficulties in understanding the courtroom proceedings fully (Burnard 2008).

## Conclusion

This chapter sought to draw a clear line between human rights law, reflected in the CRC and the case law of the ECtHR, and the very particular standards now found at international level concerning children in conflict with the law. From different sources, the chapter highlights how the evolving law promotes respect for children's human rights when they come into conflict with the law. Even from the small scope of this study, it would appear that those states who employ the adversarial criminal justice process to children are nonetheless beginning to develop child-friendly approaches that respond to children's particular circumstances as outlined in these international standards. Although much wider research is required to justify a stronger conclusion, initial indications are positive as to the nature of these developments.

## References

Burnard, A., 2008. The right to a fair trial: young offenders and the Victorian Charter of Human Rights and Responsibilities. *Current Issues in Criminal Justice*, 20(2), 173.

Camilleri, P., McArthur, M. and Thomson, L., 2011. *Challenges, possibilities and future directions: an assessment of Australia's Children Court, ACT Report*. Canberra: Institute of Child Protection.

Carroll, J., Meehan, E. and McPhillips, S., 2007. *The Children Court: a national study*. Dublin: Association for Criminal Justice Research and Development.
Committee on the Rights of the Child, 2007. *General Comment No 10 Children's Rights in Juvenile Justice*. CRC/C/GC/10.
Kilkelly, U., 2008a. Youth justice and children's rights: measuring compliance with international standards. *Youth Justice*, 8(3), 187–92.
Kilkelly, U., 2008b. Youth courts and children's rights: the Irish experience. *Youth Justice*, 8(1), 39–52.
Seymour, M. and Butler, M., 2008. *Young people on remand*. Dublin: Department of Children and Youth Affairs.
Stone, N., 2010. Legal commentary: special measures for child defendants – a decade of developments. *Youth Justice*, 10(2), 176.
Weijers, I., 2004. Requirements for communication in the courtroom: a comparative perspective on the Youth Court in England/Wales and the Netherlands. *Youth Justice*, 4(1), 22–31.

## *Practice Directions*

Practice Direction concerning the trial of children and young persons in the Crown Court, 16 December 2000. 1 WLR [2000].
The Practice Direction (Criminal Proceedings: Consolidation), para. III.30 (as inserted by Practice Direction (Criminal Proceedings: Further Directions) [2007] 1 WLR 1790).
Judicial College, *Youth Court Bench Book*, January 2013.
Practice Direction of the President of the District Court, DC04 – Children Court/Dublin Metropolitan Children Court, 17 January 2007.
Children Court. *A Bench Book*, District Court, May 2015.

## *Cases*

### European Court of Human Rights

*De Sousa v France* [2005] ECHR App. No. 61328/00.
*Çobanoglu and Budak v Turkey* [2007] App. No. 45977/99.
*Yesilyurt v Turkey* [2010] ECHR App. No. 15649/05.
*Oblov v Russia* [2009] ECHR App. No. 22674/02.
*T. v the United Kingdom; V. v the United Kingdom* (1999) 30 EHRR 121.
*S.C. v the United Kingdom* (2005) 40 EHRR 10.
*Martin v Estonia* [2013] ECHR App. No. 35985/09.
*Blokhin v Russia* [2013] ECHR App. No. 47152/06.

### United Kingdom

*R. (on the application of S.) v Waltham Forest Youth Court* [2004] EWHC 715 (Admin); 2004 2 Cr. App. R. 21.
*R v SH* [2003] EWCA Crim 1208.
*C. v Sevenoaks Youth Court* (2009) EWHC 2088 (Admin).

# 44

# Legal status of customary criminal justice systems and human rights in Ethiopia

*Wondwossen Demissie Kassa and Muradu Abdo Srur*

## Introduction

Ethiopia is a pluralist society in which customary laws play a significant role in the day-to-day affairs of people, including in settling disputes, both civil and criminal. This chapter examines the legal place of Customary Criminal Justice Systems (CCJSs), their interface with the state criminal justice system, and the implications of their status and interface for human rights in Ethiopia.

Between 1957 and 1965, the Ethiopian Government decided to modernize its laws by importing foreign laws. During this period, the country promulgated several law codes including the 1957 Penal Code and the 1961 Criminal Procedure Code. There is overwhelming consensus that Ethiopia's past state criminal laws tacitly but sweepingly abrogated CCJSs in favour of the principle of legality (Degefa 2013, Lowenstein 1965). While this claim is partly true, it needs qualification. This chapter thus begins by proposing some points that qualify this consensus.

While the *Federal Constitution of Ethiopia* (the Constitution) expressly recognizes custom in certain civil matters, such explicit recognition is missing in relation to criminal cases. However, nor does the Constitution expressly denounce customary practices in criminal cases. The second section of this chapter deals with possible interpretations of this silence, in light of the status of CCJSs in relation to the International Bill of Human Rights, the spirit and some specific provisions of the Constitution, other federal and state laws, and government policy documents. The third section addresses de facto and *de jure* relations between customary and formal criminal justice systems in Ethiopia and their impact on human rights. The conclusion follows.

## The place of CCJSs under Ethiopia's past state criminal law

While Ethiopia's state criminal justice system previously incorporated the principle of legality, it recognized some elements of CCJSs in a nuanced manner. The 1930 Penal Code embraced CCJSs, for example, in relation to 'homicide by revenge or by simple conflict' by permitting *guma* (blood money) as a form of sanction (Penal Code 1930, Articles 406 and 408). And the 1933 Affersata Proclamation accommodated CCJSs by recognizing *Affersata* – a collective inquiry carried out by a community to identify an offender. Ethiopia also recognized the role of assessors (Singer 1970–71, the Administration of Justice Proclamation 1942, Article 19): people drawn from among local elders for the purpose of assisting judges in lower courts in criminal matters by attending hearings, giving their opinion about oral evidence and advising judges in disposing cases (Jembere 1992, Abdo 2010). Moreover, the Administration of Justice Proclamation 1942 authorized 'the hearing and settlement of minor disputes in any manner traditionally recognized in Ethiopian law' (Article 23).

In 1947, Ethiopia introduced the *Atbia Dagna* (local judge), whereby a person who commanded respect in the community and was familiar with local contexts was elected to this position. The local judge had adjudicative jurisdiction and reconciliatory power over criminal cases (Singer 1970–71, Local Judges Establishment Proclamation 1947).

There was also an avenue for CCJSs in the case of criminal offences that can only be prosecuted upon a formal complaint (Penal Code 1957, Article 217).[1] A victim of such offences was at liberty to decide either to file a complaint with a public prosecutor or to initiate CCJS procedures. It is plausible to argue that in a situation where the grip of tradition is tight and in the absence of other alternative means the most realistic outcome would be to set CCJS procedures in motion. Even in cases where the victim files a complaint with a public prosecutor but that prosecutor refuses to take it up, private prosecution is an option. In this scenario, the law provided that 'the court shall attempt to reconcile the parties. Where reconciliation is effected, it shall be recorded by the court and shall have the effect of a judgment' (Criminal Procedure Code Proclamation 1961, Article 151[2]). Besides, the Criminal Procedure Code of 1961 retained the *Atbia Dagna* with its reconciliatory and adjudicatory powers (Articles 223 and 224).

The *Atbia Dagna* was transformed into *Fered Shengo* (judicial tribunals) presided over by popularly elected lay *kebele* (neighbourhood) residents in 1975. In 1989, the judicial tribunals were replaced by social courts that were set up in each *kebele* throughout the country, with the purpose of continuing to promote the 'participation of the people in the direct . . . judicial administration' of the state. Judges of social courts were to 'be elected by a majority vote of the general assembly of residents of the locality in which such court is situated' (Social Courts Proclamation 1989, Article 7) and 'residents of the locality who are respected and held in esteem by the residents for their exemplary activities, hard work and worthy social services' could qualify for election as a judge (ibid., Article 8). And judges 'shall be guided by no other authority than that of the law' (ibid., Articles 2 and 4). The social courts were empowered to handle virtually all petty offences (ibid., Article 15) defined by the 1957 Penal Code and they could warn the offender or order the offender to apologize to the injured person or publicize the offender's shameful act (ibid., Article 16).

In the late 1990s, regions established social courts as grass roots justice forums, which continue to operate to this day (Oromia Social Courts Proclamation 2003). At present, social courts are not considered to be part of the state court system and are accountable to *kebele* council rather than *woreda* (district) courts. Social courts are viewed as informal courts since they are not required to strictly adhere to state law and they reconcile disputants in addition to their adjudicatory functions (Fiseha 2013, Baker 2013a).

## Status of CCJSs

### *Under international and regional human rights instruments*

Neither the *International Bill of Human Rights* nor the *African Charter on Human and People's Rights* (the Charter) explicitly recognizes the right to use custom in resolving disputes. As the

International Council on Human Rights Policy (ICHRP) (2009, p. 27) notes, '[t]he human rights framework does not recognise "plural legal orders" as a distinct area of policy'.

However, the ICHRP does recognize human rights benchmarks pertaining to plural legal orders, which encompass the right to use customary rules to resolve criminal cases. One such benchmark is the right to self-determination, the meaning of which has evolved continuously. This right had been in use since before World War 2 in connection with the protection of minorities (Perry 2011). It was later included under Article 1 of the UN Charter. However, its meaning had been unclear until the Declaration on the Granting of Independence to Colonial Countries and Peoples was adopted in 1960. In the Declaration, it was understood as referring *only* to the 'legal and moral response to the phenomenon of colonialism' (Perry 2011, p. 85), entitling colonized peoples to be free from colonial rule[2] (Xanthaki 2004, Lám 2000). It was then incorporated into Common Article 1 of the two international human rights covenants, and construed to include the right to use customary rules in criminal proceedings (Perry 2011).

As Perry (2011, p. 87) notes, following completion of decolonization, the right was expanded 'beyond its rigid origin as a tool of decolonization' so as to accommodate the right of Indigenous people who, as opposed to people under colonial rule, are citizens of a state dominated by settlers and who maintain an association with that state. On the significance of the right to self-determination to the right of Indigenous people to apply their customary laws, Ahrén (2004, p. 108) affirms that 'an integral part of the right to self-determination is the right to have their own legal system recognised and applied, because legal norms constitute a central part of the system through which a people govern its society'. Perry (2011, p. 82) emphasizes the centrality of customary systems of law to the survival of Indigenous people as follows:

> The processes and purposes of regulating communal activity and resolving disputes in accordance with customary norms are inseparable elements of the general cultural life of indigenous communities making it an integral part of their right to self-determination.

Article 20(1) of the Charter incorporates the right to self-determination. The subsequent sub-articles refer to the right of colonized or oppressed people to be free from the bonds of domination and to seek assistance from other states in their struggle against foreign domination. Moreover, by virtue of its Article 60, which provides for the rights that it recognizes to be interpreted in the light of pertinent international law, the right to self-determination referred to under Article 20 can be construed as sharing the same definition as that under Article 1 of the Twin Covenants cited above.

While there is no explicit reference to the right to apply CCJSs in the binding international and regional human rights instruments, different non-binding documents envision recognition of customary rules in resolving criminal matters at the national level. For example, the way the UN Human Rights Committee (HRC) (General Comment No. 23 1994, para. 7) has interpreted 'culture' under Article 27 of the *International Covenant on Civil and Political Rights* (ICCPR) is claimed to be broad enough to 'arguably encompass [a] Customary System of Laws' (Perry 2011, p. 89). In 2006, the UN General Assembly (General Assembly Resolution 60/167) called on states 'to ensure that their political and legal systems reflect the multicultural diversity within their societies'.

More specifically, the UN HRC in its General Comment No. 32 (2007) has included statements that envision the application of customary rules in criminal proceedings. One of the statements indicates that Article 14 of the ICCPR (on the right to a fair trial) applies 'where a State, in its legal order, recognizes courts based on customary law . . . to carry out or entrusts them with judicial tasks'. The phrase 'where a State . . . recognizes' implies that there is no obligation on the state to recognize customary courts; rather, it rests on its discretion. The committee also lists important standards that compulsory judgements of such courts need to fulfil and calls on states to give binding effect to such judgements only upon the fulfilment of those standards. The matters that the committee envisions to be treated by customary courts include criminal matters. The first requirement limits the jurisdiction of customary courts 'to . . . minor . . . criminal matters'. Other requirements include due process and fairness of the trial, which, as the ICHRP (2009, p. 32) notes, 'have been shaped largely to address criminal cases'.

Similarly, by holding that 'traditional courts are not exempt from the provisions of the African Charter relating to fair trial' (Mungoven 2001, p. 22), the African Commission on Human and People's Rights has implied that the Charter envisions a customary dispute settlement mechanism. The commission's 2003 declaration that 'traditional courts, where they exist, are required to respect international standards on the right to a fair trial' reinforces this interpretation.

## *Under Ethiopian law*

### At the federal level

In determining what status a country accords to customary practices, consideration of its constitution is relevant. The ICHRP (2009, p. 92) notes that constitutions are vital in understanding the recognition given to plurality of legal orders for, among others, 'they indicate how far the state has recognised the "laws" or *outputs* of a non-state legal order, as well as the authority and autonomy of the *processes* by which the non-state legal order produces its laws' (emphasis in the original).

The Ethiopian Constitution unequivocally recognizes the Ethiopian people's diversity. As the upshot of this recognition, the Constitution (Article 8[1]) bestows all sovereign power upon the Nations, Nationalities and Peoples (NNPs) of Ethiopia. Moreover, the Constitution recognizes an unconditional right to self-determination, including the right to secession, of every NNP in the country. However, it does not include a provision that expressly deals with the status of CCJSs, which makes their status open to interpretation. On the one hand, one may argue that the monopoly of the state over criminal justice has been established under the Constitution. As provided under its Article 37, 'everyone has the right to bring a justiciable matter to, and to obtain a decision or judgment by, a court of law or any other competent body with judicial power'.[3] This provision seems to refer to regular state courts or customary or religious courts, the establishment and jurisdiction of which are stipulated under the Constitution. Article 79(1) indicates that judicial powers, at both the federal and state levels, are vested in the courts. Article 79(2) instructs judges to be directed solely by the law. Besides, without prejudice to the possibility that concerned law-making bodies may establish religious and customary courts, the jurisdictions of which are confined to specific civil matters under Article 78(5), the establishment of special or ad hoc courts that take judicial powers away from the regular courts or institutions is prohibited under Article 78(4) of the Constitution.

On the other hand, one may contend that the Constitution's silence on the status of CCJSs, while envisaging the applicability of custom in specific civil cases (Articles 34 [4 & 5] and 78[5]), is not conclusive evidence of non-recognition. In this regard, Mengiste (quoted in Enyew 2014) has argued that the absence of express recognition of the application of customary laws to criminal matters does not necessarily mean that they are totally excluded from application. And it could be argued that the Constitution would have expressly excluded the application of customary laws to criminal matters had that been its position. More broadly, it could be contended that reading a lack of intent to accommodate customary laws over criminal matters into the Constitution's silence would defeat the overall objective of cultural plurality embodied in the Constitution. Indeed, the Constitution's explicit reference to specific civil cases might have been an attempt to address the concern triggered by the 1960 Civil Code that explicitly repealed customary practices on civil matters. There would not be similar concern relating to customary laws pertaining to criminal matters since, as discussed above, state criminal laws have never repealed CCJSs so explicitly and sweepingly.

Donovan and Assefa (2003) emphasize the Ethiopian Government's real commitment to the preservation of the country's customary heritage. Indeed, the prominence given to cultural diversity under the Constitution, as pointed out above, is clear. Thus, it would make sense to argue that a constitution that elevates its recognition of the right to self-determination of NNPs to the level of secession for stronger reasons would provide space for them to apply their dispute settlement mechanisms while they are still within the federation. As argued by Xanthaki (2004), the core of the right to self-determination is recognition of customary systems of law. Washburn (2005–06) goes even further in asserting the centrality of regulating criminal cases for the meaningful exercise of the right to self-determination. Similarly, Weber et al. (2014) note the link between alternative justice practices and self-determination.

Furthermore, a glance at the Constitution's Article 9(1) seems to support this interpretation. By stipulating that 'any law, customary practice or . . . which contravenes this Constitution shall be of no effect', the Constitution appears to imply that any customary law, including those relating to criminal matters, can be applied insofar as it is compatible with the Constitution. Moreover, Article 91(1) imposes a responsibility on the government 'to support . . . the growth and enrichment of cultures and traditions that are compatible with fundamental rights, human dignity, democratic norms and ideals'.

However, both constitutional provisions might still be understood as not *recognizing* cultures or customary practices generically as such but referring to those that have been recognized in other provisions of the Constitution. Thus, Article 9, which provides for supremacy of the Constitution, might be interpreted as requiring *recognized* customary laws (such as those envisioned under Articles 34 and 78) to be harmonious with the Constitution. That is, while Articles 34 and 78 of the Constitution stipulate the customary laws that are recognized under the Constitution, Article 9 provides for the limitation on their application. And Article 91(1) stipulates the government's responsibility with respect to cultures and traditions that the Constitution has *recognized*.

While Enyew (2014, p. 140) sees merit in Mengiste's 'broader and holistic interpretation' on the ground that it 'helps to give formal legal status to applying customary laws in criminal matters', he asserts that 'the *acontrario* interpretation of Article 34 (5) of the Constitution may be understood as implying an explicit prohibition of the application of customary dispute resolution mechanisms in criminal matters'. Moreover, an argument for the applicability of CCJSs, in the absence of express recognition by the Constitution, would make Articles 34 and 78 of the Constitution superfluous, which is contrary to one of the canons of legislative interpretation, which requires that legal provisions be construed so as to avoid rendering them redundant.

Be the issue of direct constitutional recognition of CCJSs as it may, the Constitution (Article 39) recognizes the right to self-determination which, as noted above, has been interpreted to encompass people's right to apply their customary rules in general and CCJSs in particular. The Constitution places international human rights instruments at the top in the hierarchy of laws relating to human rights (Article 13[2]). Thus, even if the reading of the five sub-articles under Article 39 does not seem to entitle NNPs to use their customary rules in criminal proceedings, by virtue of Article 13(2) of the Constitution, it might be interpreted to include this right as does Article 1 in each of the Twin Covenants. However, as noted earlier, the right to self-determination under the two covenants is interpreted to subsume the right to use customary rules in criminal proceedings in the context where customary rules refer to the traditional rules of Indigenous people or of the people who had been under European colonization.

Even though the interpretation that extends the scope of the right to self-determination to include customary rules of colonized countries is more relevant to no continent than Africa, the colonization and Indigenous population thesis ill suits Ethiopia. Ethiopia has never been under European colonization, save the five years of Italian occupation. Thus, the applicability of the right to self-determination to include the collective right to apply customary rules cannot be taken for granted in the Ethiopian context.

The Criminal Justice Policy of Ethiopia stipulates that 'in cases of crimes that are punishable by simple imprisonment or upon complaint, the investigation or trial can be interrupted if the disputing parties have settled their differences through reconciliation and upon the initiation or request of the parties'. Wada (2012, p. 291), citing the policy, goes to the extent of contending that charges may not be pressed because of public interest 'if the prosecution is of the opinion that the conflict between the accused and the victim can be better handled through customary laws and institutions than the formal justice system even in serious crimes such as aggravated homicide'. The Criminal Justice Policy (2011) hence appears to give discretion to prosecutors to withdraw charges in the public interest which may, among other things, mean referring a matter for consideration by customary authorities. And while this is merely a policy, which may or may not be reflected in the law, the policy direction is clear, as these elements relating to CCJSs have been incorporated into Ethiopia's Draft Criminal Procedure Code, which is currently underway. This policy acknowledges CCJSs that emphasize:

> letting the criminal accept his guilt and regret about his wrongdoing instead of prosecuting him . . . where, in view of the nature of the crime and the behavior of the suspect, [these] better serve the interest of the public than a formal prosecution would.
>
> *(Kassa 2012, p. 241)*

## At the state level

The Constitution adopts a federal arrangement with nine federal units called states to accommodate the diversified interests of the NNPs of Ethiopia.[4] Thus, the Constitution allocates matters over which there is a shared value to the federal government, while it leaves other matters to the states. The division of power between the federal and state governments is provided under Articles 50–52. A criminal matter is not included in the list of matters over which the federal government has exclusive power, nor is it a matter over which both the federal government and states can exercise concurrent powers, which implies that it is within the legislative jurisdiction of the states.[5] Thus, it is up to each state to decide whether to regulate a criminal matter over which it has legislative jurisdiction, through formal criminal legislation or customary rules, which makes a reference to state constitutions important.

Two states have given a role to elders in governance. The Afar State Constitution (Article 63) allows the State Council to establish a council of elders. Similarly, the Somali State Constitution (Article 52) recognizes *Gurtii* (council of elders). These constitutions do not explicitly authorize a council of elders to resolve criminal matters, nor have statutes to this effect been issued. However, both states have actually established councils of elders with the mandate to settle inter-clan disputes, including in relation to homicide (Fiseha 2014).

## Interface between state law and CCJSs

While the preceding sections have discussed the past and present legal standing of CCJSs in Ethiopia, this section sheds some light on their interface with the state legal order. In many parts of the country, citizens resort to local justice providers who utilize informal methods of justice (Baker 2013a, Enyew 2014). The state has been unable to deal with criminal cases according to formal mechanisms for practical reasons such as a shortage of resources (Donovan and Assefa 2003, Baker 2013a). As Baker (2013a, p. 205) indicates, 'in practice, local communities across Ethiopia rely heavily on informal justice for dispute settlement'. People resort to customary dispute resolution mechanisms for reconciliation even after a case has been dealt with through the formal criminal justice system (Zeleke 2010). As Baker (2013b, p. 300) emphatically notes:

> The reality is that for the most part neither the federal and regional police nor the formal courts reach . . . into the village/town neighbourhoods (*kebele*).Thus, . . . it is the elders and traditional leaders who provide most of the protection from crime and disorder and the resolution of it through mediation and compensation when it occurs.

Similarly, Fiseha (2013, p. 9) indicates that 'the [formal] criminal justice process has little impact on the majority of the population, who prefer their own village and tribal processes of dispute resolution'.

Customary authorities assert power over cases using different methods. They pressurize victims not to report a crime to the state authorities; where the police are informed of a crime, they pressurize the police not to undertake an investigation; where the crime is investigated by the police, the customary authorities request the public prosecutor not to frame a charge; where a charge is framed, they ask the court to order that the charge be dropped; where the court refuses to do so, the customary authorities may even cause the disappearance of witnesses or instruct the witnesses to lie; or, where the court convicts and sentences the offender, the elders subject him/her to the traditional criminal justice process upon the completion of his/her term. Customary authorities justify these measures on the grounds that the disputants are ready to reconcile or they have already reconciled, or that the state cannot solve the problem as revenge will continue or conflict will escalate in the community (Abdo 2014). Put differently, customary authorities claim that they handle cases in a manner that promotes the 'welfare of all involved in it' (Focus Group Discussion Summary, 23 July 2013).

> When the government punishes a wrongdoer, he rots in prison instead of being allowed to support himself, his family, tender his farm and animals and compensate the victim. His family misses him; his family also suffers. When he finishes his punishment, he cannot mingle automatically with his family for fear of revenge and thus we are forced to initiate and complete the reconciliation process before he resumes normal life.
>
> *(Focus Group Discussion Summary, 22 July 2013)*

State justice actors sometimes deny that they allow elders to handle serious crimes, even suggesting that involvement in that type of referral constitutes a criminal act. But there is an unstated state policy of referring criminal cases to customary institutions when state authorities believe that doing so will advance local stability and security, especially in Lowland Ethiopia. At times, elders handle serious crimes such as homicide and arson; and in some cases where crime incidents have already been reported to the justice actors, officials allow elders to handle such serious offences (Focus Group Discussion Summary, 23 July 2013). At other times, the authorities even encourage elders to settle serious crimes through reconciliation which is taken into consideration in suspending or mitigating punishment (ibid.). 'People are frequently hit by a car on a highway. Elders handle all these deaths. I do not recall a single case of this kind going to the court. Both sides consider it sensible to complete the process through tradition' (Interview with Mr Tsegaye Tabor, 21 July 2013).

Some regions even offer institutional mechanisms to elders to entertain criminal jurisdiction. For example, the Tigray State and the Afar State have jointly established *Abo Gereb* (a council of elders), which they have permitted to adjudicate serious crimes such as homicide and cattle raiding in their borders (Fiseha 2014). The Oromia State has also set up a council of *Aba Gada* (chief elders) to handle, inter alia, crimes that have inter-tribal significance (Shiferaw 2015).

The actual practices of the state criminal justice authorities, some criminal provisions and the Criminal Justice Policy, therefore, reveal Ethiopia's tendency to offer space to CCJSs even in respect of serious crimes, despite constitutional silence on the matter. This suggests that:

> constitutional silence on the issue of customary law does not mean that customary law does not exist or is unimportant or irrelevant in a country. As long as there is no provision expressly excluding or limiting the application of customary law, there is potential scope to develop the relationship between customary and statutory law.
>
> *(Cuskelly 2011, p. 27)*

While this positive gesture towards CCJSs is sound on account of legitimacy, practicality and cherishing diversity, the ambiguity on the legal status of CCJSs and the absence of a clear, principled approach to and legal framework governing their relationship with the state criminal justice system are sources of significant concern. Though adoption of customary practices exemplify the right to self-determination in the criminal justice context in Ethiopia (Weber et al. 2014), owing to the equivocal nature of the legal status of such practices, parties to a criminal case cannot confidently assert their right to resolve their disputes through CCJSs. It is only with the blessing of state agents that they can resort to CCJSs. On the other hand, because the state officials themselves have no clear idea of the applicability of customary practices in criminal matters, they prefer to shy away from CCJSs instead of adopting a mechanism to ensure their compatibility with constitutional and human rights principles.

The existing application of CCJS procedures and their interface with human rights are founded upon pragmatic considerations of stability and security rather than on rights enshrined in the Constitution and international human rights documents. This approach can undermine Ethiopia's commitment to human rights by working to the detriment of the weak and disempowered members of communities, especially women. Broadly, the state's inability to provide a normative and institutional framework that ensures due process requirements and other principles of fair trial in the course of handling criminal matters through CCJSs makes it complicit in the human rights violations associated with the application of CCJSs (Donovan and Assefa 2003).

## Conclusion

The International Bill of Human Rights does not seem to recognize the individual or collective right to apply customary laws in resolving disputes, especially in a non-colonization context. That makes the legal status of CCJSs dependent on the extent of recognition in each country's formal legal system or constitution. Though the legal status of customary law is a subject that needs to be addressed in a constitution, none of the previous constitutions of Ethiopia deals with the matter. Except where it refers to areas in which customary laws are applicable in civil matters, the current Constitution does not address the issue either.

However, the legal status of customary laws in relation to civil cases has been addressed by the 1960 Civil Code of Ethiopia, which expressly repeals customary laws pertaining to civil matters. While Ethiopia's modern criminal law has been in place since 1930, there has never been a similar provision pertaining to the status of customary laws relating to criminal cases. This absence makes the status of CCJSs in Ethiopia unclear.

While the literature acknowledges that CCJSs play a pivotal role in practice, there seems to be a consensus that the law does not give them any place. However, a close look at the matter does not seem to warrant this radical view. True, the principle of legality, which is closely related to this issue, is part and parcel of the Ethiopian legal system. This principle prohibits treating conduct as criminal and imposing punishment other than that provided under formal criminal law. However, it does not preclude administration of the criminal law in accordance with customary procedures insofar as the latter are compatible with the constitutional standards of the time. This makes it difficult to equate the adoption of the principle of legality with a wholesale repeal of CCJSs.

The absence of any specific provision repealing pre-existing customary criminal justice systems coupled with the central place that the Constitution gives to NNPs and their culture, and provisions of the substantive and procedural criminal codes that envisage out-of-court settlement of minor offences, tend to imply that, at least in minor cases, the law envisions a place for CCJSs. The recently adopted Criminal Justice Policy, the abundant application of CCJSs in resolving disputes on the ground, and the 2010–11 Draft Criminal Procedure Code give credence to this approach.

The equivocal nature of the legal status of CCJSs and the absence of a legal framework regulating their interplay with the state system have impacted human rights in the context of criminal justice in two ways. First, citizens do not have a firm ground on which to claim their right to resolve criminal disputes in accordance with CCJSs. Second, while in reality citizens predominantly rely on CCJSs, state institutions have avoided monitoring the compatibility of the CCJSs with human rights provisions, including those that require fairness of criminal proceedings.

## Notes

1 These offences include insulting behaviour and outrage, defamation and calumny, injury to the honour of deceased persons, adultery, failure to maintain, abstraction of things jointly owned, misappropriation of lost property and simple intentional destruction and damage to the property of another.

2 The rules that the people under colony apply are referred as customary or traditional in comparison with the rules that the European colonizers had brought (Tamanaha 2008, p. 397).

3 However, having a *right* does not mean that one cannot waive this right and resort to other alternatives.

4 However, not all NNPs have their own states.

5 Article 52(1) of the FDRE Constitution provides 'all powers not given expressly to the Federal Government alone, or concurrently to the Federal Government and the States are reserved to the States'. Article 55(5) of the Constitution which empowers the House of Peoples Representatives to enact the Penal Code could only refer to a penal code the subject matter of which should not be broader than safeguarding federal matters as listed under Article 51 of the Constitution. Article 55 cannot give legislative power to the federal government over a matter over which it does not have jurisdiction based on the division of power provided under Articles 50–52. By virtue of Articles 52(1) and 55(5), states have legislative jurisdiction over criminal matters not related to the federal matters listed under Article 51 of the Constitution. However, the federal government has proclaimed an all-inclusive Criminal Code leaving almost no space for state legislation on criminal matters.

## References

Abdo, M., 2010. *Introduction to Legal History and Traditions*. Addis Ababa: Bahir Dar and Jimma Universities.

Abdo, M., 2014. *The Gordenna Sera of Kistane Guraghe*. Unpublished, on file with the authors.

Ahrén, M. 2004. Indigenous peoples' culture, customs and traditions and customary law: the Saami people's perspective. *Arizona Journal of International and Comparative Law*, 21, 63–112.

Baker, B., 2013a. Where formal and informal justice meet: Ethiopia's justice pluralism. *African Society of International and Comparative Law*, 21(1), 202–18.

Baker, B., 2013b. Hybridity in policing: the case of Ethiopia. *The Journal of Legal Pluralism and Unofficial Law*, 45(3), 296–313.

Cuskelly, K., 2011. *Customs and constitutions: state recognition of customary law around the world*. Bangkok: International Union for Conservation of Nature and Natural Resources.

Degefa, A., 2013. Legal pluralism in multicultural setting: legal appraisal of Ethiopia's monist criminal justice system. *In*: E.N. Stebek and M. Abdo (eds), *Law and development, and legal pluralism: law and development series No. 1*. Addis Ababa: Justice and Legal Systems Research Institute.

Donovan, D. and Assefa, G., 2003. Homicide in Ethiopia: human rights, federalism, and legal pluralism. *American Journal of Comparative Law*, 51(3), 505–52.

Enyew, E.L., 2014. Ethiopian customary dispute resolution mechanisms: forms of restorative justice? *AJCR*, 14(1), 125–54.

Fiseha, A., 2013. Customary dispute resolution mechanisms and the rule of law: areas of convergence, divergence and implications. *In*: E.N. Stebek and M. Abdo (eds), *Law and development, and legal pluralism: law and development series No. 1*. Addis Ababa: Justice and Legal Systems Research Institute, 111–40.

Fiseha, A., 2014. Improving access to justice through harmonization of formal and customary dispute resolution mechanisms. *In*: Pietro Toggia et al. (eds), *Access to justice in Ethiopia: towards an inventory of issues*. Addis Ababa: Addis Ababa University Center for Human Rights, 99–122.

International Council on Human Rights Policy, 2009. *When legal worlds overlap: human rights, state and non-state law*. Geneva, Switzerland. Retrieved on 11 April 2016 from: http://www.ichrp.org/files/reports/50/135_report_en.pdf.

Jembere, A., 1992. *Yatatayaq Muget*: the traditional Ethiopian mode of litigation. *Journal of Ethiopian Law*, 15, 82–93.

Kassa, W.D., 2012. *Ethiopian criminal procedure text-book*. Addis Ababa: American Bar Association.

Lâm, M.C., 2000. *At the edge of the state: indigenous peoples and self-determination*. Leiden, the Netherlands: Martinus Nijhoff Publishers.

Lowenstein, S., 1965. The penal system of Ethiopia. *Journal of Ethiopian Law*, 2(2), 383–424.

Mungoven, R., 2001. Beyond the courts: developing Amnesty International's position on non-judicial mechanisms for accountability and redress. AI Index POL 30/003/2001.

Perry, R., 2011. Balancing rights or building rights? Reconciling the right to use customary systems of law with competing human rights in pursuit of indigenous sovereignty. *Harvard Human Rights Journal*, 24, 71–114.

Shiferaw, A., 2015. Customary laws and self-determination in Ethiopia. Unpublished, on file with the authors.

Singer, N., 1970–71. A traditional legal institution in a modern legal setting: the Atbia Dagnia of Ethiopia. *UCLA Law Review*, 18, 308–34.

Tamanaha, B.Z., 2008. Understanding legal pluralism: past to present, local and global. *Sydney Law Review*, 30, 375–411.

Wada, T., 2012. Coexistence between the formal and informal justice systems in Ethiopia: challenges and prospects. *African Journal of Legal Studies*, 5, 269–93.

Washburn, K.K., 2005–06. Federal criminal law and tribal self-determination. *North Carolina Law Review*, 84, 779–856.

Weber, L., Fishwick, E. and Marmo, M., 2014. *Crime, justice and human rights*. London: Palgrave Macmillan.

Xanthaki, A., 2004. The right to self-determination: meaning and scope, in minorities. *In*: Nazila Ghanea and Alexandra Xanthaki (eds), *Minorities, peoples and self-determination – essays in honour of Patrick Thornberry*. Leiden, the Netherlands: Martinus Nijhoff Publishers, Chapter 12.

Zeleke, M., 2010. *Ye Shakoch Chilot* (the court of the sheikhs): a traditional institution of conflict resolution in Oromiya zone of Amhara regional state, Ethiopia. *African Journal on Conflict Resolution*, 10(1), 63–84.

## Laws

Administration of Justice Proclamation, 1942.
Affersata Proclamation, 1933.
Consolidation of Peasant Associations Proclamation, 1982.
Criminal Code Proclamation, 2004.
Criminal Justice Policy of Ethiopia, 2011.
Criminal Procedure Code Proclamation, 1961.
Draft Criminal Procedure Code of Ethiopia, 2011.
FDRE Constitution, 1995.
Local Judges Establishment Proclamation, 1947.
Oromia Regional State Social Courts Re-establishment Proclamation, 2003.
Penal Code Proclamation, 1957.
Penal Code, 1930.
Social Courts Proclamation, 1989.

# 45

# *Daiyou kangoku*

## Systemic human rights violations in pre-indictment detention in Japan

*Saul Takahashi*

*Under the country's criminal procedure, suspects can be held by the police before being formally charged for up to 23 days. During these 23 days, the detainee is subject to heavy-handed interrogation techniques that sometimes amount to torture, such as sustained sleep deprivation, refusal of contact with family members, and standing or sitting still for long periods in extremely uncomfortable positions. Access to legal counsel is prohibited during interrogation sessions, and criminal suspects are often convicted by the courts on the basis of confessions obtained through these means.*

One might assume that the above is describing the criminal justice process in a dictatorship, or a country under military occupation. Or perhaps it describes a special procedure for dealing only with particularly serious types of crimes, such as terrorism. Such systemic human rights violations would surely not be part of the routine procedure for dealing with everyday criminal acts, and surely not in an advanced democracy.

Unfortunately, one would be wrong. The above is a description of the criminal procedure in Japan, an advanced democracy internationally renowned as a peace-loving country. Described by international experts as something resembling the Middle Ages,[1] criminal justice in Japan has inadequate safeguards for the rights of criminal suspects and is characterized by systemic human rights violations. And the problems are not exhibited in practice alone: they form an integral part of the relevant Japanese legislation, which is exploited to the fullest extent by law enforcement officials with the acquiescence of the judiciary. A Bill that is, at the time of writing, at the final stages of adoption in the Japanese parliament is a lost opportunity at reform, and could even lead to more violations.

### *Daiyou kangoku*: substitute prisons

Japan operates a unique system known commonly as *daiyou kangoku*, or 'substitute prisons'. Under *daiyou kangoku*, police can detain criminal suspects in police lock-ups during the initial stage of investigation and interrogation, before the suspect is formally charged with an offence. Detention at police facilities was a common practice during the early years of industrialization, in the Meiji period of the late nineteenth century, and the practice was institutionalized in the Prison Law of 1908. The government made clear at the time that it recognized the potential for abuse, and that *daiyou kangoku* was intended only as a stopgap measure while an adequate number of facilities were being built. Indeed, government statements suggest that *daiyou kangoku* was only foreseen as something to be applied in a limited number of rural areas with inadequate infrastructure (Keiji Rippou Kenkyuu-kai 2007, p. 37).

However, as the oppression of socialist and other popular movements grew, police power expanded, and *daiyou kangoku* changed from being an exception to the norm. Police lock-ups became notorious for torture during the pre-war period – a reputation they continued to earn through the end of World War 2 (Keiji Rippou Kenkyuu-kai 2007, p. 38). Although many abusive laws were discarded immediately after the war, the overall framework of *daiyou kangoku* has been maintained to the present day. In 2006, the Prison Law was revised, and while this appeared to be an opportunity for reform, *daiyou kangoku* was solidified, from an ostensibly temporary arrangement to a semi-permanent feature.[2]

The Japanese Criminal Procedure Code stipulates that a suspect can be detained in *daiyou kangoku* for interrogation for up to 72 hours (three days), after which time the prosecutor must present the suspect to a judge in a habeas corpus procedure. The judge may allow the suspect's continued detention for an additional 10 days for further interrogation, at the end of which the prosecutor may request the judiciary for an additional, final 10 days (Amnesty International Japan 1 n.d.). It is virtually unheard of for the judge to refuse these extensions: 2006 data published by the National Police Agency shows that the police requested the first 10-day extension for an overwhelming 93 per cent of suspects, with judges releasing only 570 out of 136,110 detainees – 0.004 per cent. The percentage of detainees released at the outset of the second 10-day period is even more infinitesimal. Over 50 per cent of criminal suspects arrested end up in *daiyou kangoku* for the maximum of 23 days (Keisatsu-chou n.d.).

In reality, even the above safeguards are often circumvented by law enforcement, through the common tactic of what is known in Japanese as *bekken taiho*, or arrest for an unrelated offence. The police arrest the suspect, and at the end of the 23 days arrest them again on another charge, thereby keeping the suspect in detention. Evidence gathered through this method is in principle inadmissible in court; but *bekken taiho* remains common, and detainees are sometimes kept for months before indictment. A system of regular release on bail pending indictment does not exist (Toukyou Bengoshi-kai 1, n.d.).

Access to lawyers during *daiyou kangoku* is severely restricted, to the point that the detainee's right to representation cannot be exercised in any meaningful manner. Lawyers are barred from attending the interrogations, and can only visit the detainee outside the sessions to provide advice. The law allows for law enforcement officials to restrict even those meetings if 'necessary for the investigation' – a provision that in practice allows police officers to arbitrarily prevent access. In practice, requests by lawyers to meet their clients, if accepted at all, are often allowed only after some days. Meetings are routinely restricted to visits of 15 minutes, and sometimes only during normal working hours (Amnesty International Japan 1). Correspondence with the suspect is, as a rule, opened, examined and even censored by the police (Kuzuno 2014, pp. 364–72). Even these meagre provisions for access only apply to detainees who possess the resources required to secure private representation; while public defenders (who are allowed in only narrowly defined categories of cases) are barred from visiting suspects during the entire period of *daiyou kangoku* (Toukyou Bengoshi-kai 1, n.d.). The violations are not confined to the interrogation sessions: for example, 'uncooperative' suspects (that is, those claiming innocence) are routinely denied family visits (Toukyou Bengoshi-kai 2, n.d.).

The interrogation sessions during *daiyou kangoku* are rife with abusive practices that meet the international definition of torture.[3] Subjects are subject to extremely long (for example, over 12 hours) interrogation sessions, with the aim of wearing them down and forcing them to 'confess' to their crimes (JFBA 2012, p. 3). Deprivation of sleep and adequate food is routine, as are various methods of mental intimidation; and, through a torture technique utilized by security forces the world over, suspects are sometimes made to stand or sit still in uncomfortable positions for hours on end. Although relatively rare, beatings have also been known to take place (Amnesty International 2014a, p. 14, JFBA 2008).

Unsurprisingly, miscarriages of justice are a defining feature of Japanese criminal justice. The criminal conviction rate can only be described as astounding: over 99 per cent of criminal defendants have been found guilty every year since 1957 (Houmu-shou 2007, 2014).[4] This figure may not necessarily be evidence of malfeasance, but advocates are unanimous in claiming that Japanese courts are often quick to convict defendants on the basis of very limited evidence, with the confession forming the bulk of the prosecution's case. Although the law does prohibit convictions on the basis of a confession alone, the Japan Federation of Bar Associations (JFBA) notes that these safeguards have been interpreted excessively narrowly: 'The provision is interpreted to mean that evidence other than the confession is not required . . . it is clear that the confession is the decisive evidence in reality' (JFBA 2015, p. 9).

The recent case of Iwao Hakamada is a prominent example. Hakamada was arrested for murder in 1966 and sentenced to execution two years later. He had spent 23 days in *daiyou kangoku*, during which time he was subject to beatings, deprivation of food and water, and was often not allowed to use the toilet. During these 23 days, he was allowed only three brief meetings with his lawyers. Even the court in 1968 found that only one of the 45 'confessions' submitted by the prosecution was admissible as evidence – yet he was still found guilty. Like all death row prisoners, Hakamada was in solitary confinement until his release in March 2014, after a court found that the prosecution might have fabricated the (very limited) evidence that had been used in his conviction. Now 79 years old, Hakamada is frail, of ill health, and suffers from a range of mental disorders as a result of his prolonged detention and isolation. The decision to release Hakamada pending his retrial is in itself extremely unusual – most prisoners (death row or otherwise) remain incarcerated during any appeal. The prosecution has indicated that it will continue to argue his guilt at a retrial (Amnesty International 2014b, 2015).

While it is internationally prominent, the Hakamada case is but the tip of the iceberg. The list of miscarriages of justice, confirmed or strongly suspected by experts, is a long one, and common to them all is the issue of *daiyou kangoku* and forced confessions. For example, in a 2003 case pertaining to alleged crimes during a local election in the Japanese city of Shibushi, one suspect was held in *daiyou kangoku* for a total of 185 days, finally 'confessing' after day upon day of interrogation sessions lasting up to 14 hours each. He was eventually found not guilty (JFBA 2011, p. 3). In the same year in a different region, Hiroshi Yanagihara was convicted of rape largely on the basis of his 'confession', though the physical evidence clearly indicated that he could not have committed the crime. He served over two years of his three-year sentence before being released (JFBA 2011, p. 5). In 2012, four men were arrested on suspicion of being behind high-profile computer hacking incidents. Two of the men 'confessed' while in *daiyou kangoku*, but days later the police found evidence of their innocence in their respective personal computers (Sankei 2012).

## International criticism

Due to the efforts of Japanese advocates and non-government organizations (NGOs), *daiyou kangoku* has come under sustained international criticism. Besides longstanding reporting on the issue by prominent international NGOs such as Amnesty International, *daiyou kangoku* has come under intense scrutiny by international human rights treaty bodies, in particular the Human Rights Committee (the HRC, which monitors application of the *International Covenant on Civil and Political Rights*, or ICCPR) and the Committee against Torture (the CmmteAT, which monitors application of the *Convention against Torture*, or CAT). Japan became state party to the ICCPR in 1979 and to CAT in 1999, and, upon the occasion of their respective reviews of Japan's treaty implementation, both of these bodies have urged Japan several times to either abolish *daiyou kangoku* or reform it fundamentally. After the most recent review of Japan's implementation of the ICCPR, in July of 2014, the HRC stated that Japan should 'take all measures to abolish the substitute detention system or ensure that it is fully compliant with all guarantees in [the ICCPR], inter alia, by guaranteeing: (a) That alternatives to detention, such as bail, are duly considered during pre-indictment detention; (b) That all suspects are guaranteed the right to counsel from the moment of apprehension and that defence counsel is present during interrogations; (c) Legislative measures setting strict time limits for the duration and methods of interrogation, which should be entirely video-recorded; (d) A complaint review mechanism that is independent of the prefectural public safety commissions and has the authority to promptly, impartially and effectively investigate allegations of torture and ill-treatment during interrogation' (HRC 2014a, para. 18).

Over the years, Japan has essentially recycled the same, somewhat simplistic arguments to justify the country's retention of *daiyou kangoku*. The argument is summed up in the government's response to the HRC's list of questions on this issue:

> In Japan, the number of penal institutions is smaller than that of detention facilities, and increasing the number of penal institutions would require a larger budget which would not be easy to achieve. Therefore, the substitute detention system is being used as an alternative that contributes to the prompt and proper performance of criminal investigations and is convenient for the lawyers and family members to visit and meet with the suspect.
>
> *(HRC 2014b, para. 135)*

In this regard there are, therefore, several elements which, though presented as if they are intertwined, are in fact easily separated: (1) there are insufficient resources to reform the system, (2) *daiyou kangoku* provides an effective means for conducting criminal investigations, and (3) having detainees in local police lock-ups is more convenient for visitors.

The reality, of course, only reflects the second point above: that law enforcement officials in Japan see the free hand offered during *daiyou kangoku* as an effective tool to obtain confessions and increase the rate of convictions. The other points are wholly unconvincing: the notion that one of the largest economies in the world is unable to fund the building of adequate detention facilities strains credibility, as noted by one member of the HRC during the recent review of the country.[5] Advocates also point out the fallacy of this: the JFBA stated in 2015 that 'crime in Japan is decreasing noticeably . . . the police have recently been building large detention facilities in many districts, and [*daiyou kangoku*] can be easily abolished simply by transferring the jurisdiction over these facilities to the Ministry of Justice' (JFBA 2015, p. 7).

The third claim made by the government – namely, that the government wishes to maintain *daiyou kangoku* because it is beneficial for lawyers and family members who want to visit detainees – is almost laughable: as noted in this chapter, visits are heavily restricted or prohibited in practice. Nevertheless, such notions of benevolent official intentions appear in other sections of the report to the HRC (and other international bodies) as well. Indicative is what the government has to say about the restrictions on lawyers' access during *daiyou kangoku*:

> if the presence of a defence counsel at the place of interrogation were mandatory, it could be likely to have [sic] serious adverse effect on investigations . . . the primary function of

> an interrogation is to find out the truth of the case in the course of an interrogator's face-to-face communication to gain the trust of the suspect and persuade the suspect, and such function would be likely to be considerably disturbed . . . as evidence or information brought to the place of an interrogation would be observed or heard by the defence counsel firsthand, this could sometimes make it difficult to use the interrogation methods generally adopted in Japan.
>
> (*HRC 2012, para. 180*)

The idea that *daiyou kangoku* contributes to building trust between the interrogator and the detainee – and that this process will be hampered by the presence of a lawyer – is somewhat ludicrous. It is, however, a prominent feature of the approach of Japanese law enforcement in this area. For example, a manual on interrogation techniques published in 2012 by the National Police Agency (apparently prepared with the assistance of a psychologist from Hokkaido University) is full of references to 'building rapport' with the suspect and the need to 'show empathy' (Keisatsu-chou Keiji-kyoku Keijikikaku-ka 2012). The general attitude here is that the criminal is essentially the same as a wayward child: the role of the investigator, the representative of authority, is to show the child the folly of their ways, and encourage, or indeed force, them to repent through the confession process. The lawyer is seen as nothing but a selfish troublemaker; a sophist who takes pleasure in making things difficult for both the suspect and interrogator, and preventing the truth from coming to light. Authority is, of course, infallible in this worldview, and it is the weak who need to make adjustments – not the powerful.

In any case, the failure of Japan to comply with the successive recommendations of international human rights bodies goes far beyond the issues surrounding *daiyou kangoku*; the country has not taken any serious action on many of the human rights issues raised over the years, including the creation of a national human rights institution that would function as an independent ombudsman, the abolition of the death penalty and the treatment of refugees, amongst other issues. In successive reports, both the HRC and CmmtteeAT have been forced to express their disappointment at Japan's general recalcitrance (HRC 2014a, para. 4). Of course, the pronouncements of the treaty bodies are not legally binding as such, but they are authoritative interpretations of the provisions of the relevant treaties, and as such states party are expected to treat them with respect and deference. These appear to be lacking in the case of Japan. When opposition parliamentarians raise the criticisms of international bodies, the approach of successive governments has simply been to dismiss the recommendations as not binding (JFBA 2013, p. 20).

## Lost opportunity for reform

In recent years there has been a glimmer of hope for reform. The trigger was the case of Atsuko Muraki, a 'fast-track' career civil servant serving in senior positions in the Health Ministry. Muraki was accused of corruption-related charges and arrested in Osaka in 2009. However, unlike the down-and-outs who are often the victims of miscarriages of justice in Japan, Muraki was a member of the elite class: educated and eloquent, her case attracted wide-ranging media attention and public sympathy. The court found her not guilty the following year, soon after which a newspaper reported that several prosecutors in Osaka had fabricated the evidence against her. These officials were subsequently arrested, and one was eventually sentenced to imprisonment.

The Muraki case involved the usual elements seen in the Japanese criminal justice system, including *daiyou kangoku* and forced confessions (JFBA 2012, p. 3). At the same time, the public reaction to the case was arguably indicative of the power relations in Japan. As a member of the establishment, Muraki had access to various avenues to pursue her claim – avenues that many other criminal suspects from lower rungs of the social ladder cannot access. Journalists in Japan were also sympathetic to her cause, in stark contrast to their usual treatment of criminal suspects. In any case, the result was widespread outrage at police and prosecutorial excesses, and eventually the establishment of a government panel, the 'Special Task Force on Criminal Justice in the New Era', to review criminal procedure and make recommendations for legal revisions.

Reform seemed inevitable; however, much to the chagrin of many human rights advocates, truly meaningful measures (primarily the complete abolition of *daiyou kangoku*) were never on the table. Rather, from the outset the public debate centred on the issue of video recording the interrogation sessions – a measure that had been urged for some time. Although video recording would go some length towards preventing abusive police practices, as envisaged it does not depart from the *daiyou kangoku* framework. Suspects could still be detained for up to 23 days and interrogated without their lawyer – and thus such a move could never be but an adjustment (albeit a significant one). In this regard the reform debate was arguably doomed from the outset.

Pilots of video recording interrogation sessions had been undertaken by the Prosecutor's office since 2006, and by the police since 2008, but these were extremely limited, generally including only one, final, somewhat Orwellian session where the suspect would read out his 'confession' before the camera (Amnesty International Japan 2 n.d.). After the Muraki case, there were repeated calls for video taping to be extended to all interrogation sessions – a measure that, unsurprisingly, was met with fierce resistance by law enforcement, in particular officials of the politically powerful National Police Agency (Sekiguchi 2015, p. 70). Opponents of reform repeated essentially the same arguments, with the interrogation process being presented as an 'essential method of discovering the truth', and an approach 'supported by the people of Japan' as an 'important factor behind the low rate of crime in the country'. These opponents were successful in framing the terms of reference for the New Era task force so as to exclude discussion of fundamental reform, ensuring that only minor tweaks would be made (Housei Shingi-kai shin-jidai no keiji-shihou seido tokubetsu-bukai 2013, pp. 2, 8).

In the end, the panel's 2014 recommendations for video recording were meagre at best, recommending that it be implemented only for narrowly defined categories of crime that would amount to a total of 2–3 per cent of criminal cases. The panel also recommended extremely vague exceptions, such as when the investigating officer believes that 'the suspect would not be able to give adequate testimony if recorded' or that the recording 'could cause harm, intimidation, or confusion to the suspect, the suspect's family, or the suspect's property' (Housei Shingi-kai shin-jidai no keiji-shihou seido tokubetsu-bukai 2014, p. 2). Clearly, these provisions leave wide latitude for law enforcement officers to prevent recording. Regarding *daiyou kangoku*, advocates for abolition at the panel were essentially shouted down or ignored as irrelevant to the discussion (Kawasaki and Mishima 2014, p. 177), and the final report of the panel makes no mention of the subject. No serious debate seems to have even been conducted on increasing lawyers' access to interrogation sessions.

Equally problematic is the fact that law enforcement officials were able to take the opportunity presented by the panel to increase the weapons in their arsenal, including the long-sought-after broad expansion of wiretapping and surveillance powers, and the introduction of a system of plea bargaining for informants.

In particular, the plea bargaining system for informants is extremely problematic: while the suspect's lawyer must be present for any formal discussions regarding the terms of an agreement, the lawyer is of course still barred from attending the interrogations during which the detainee would have 'offered cooperation'. With *daiyou kangoku* as it is, therefore, the potential for abuse can only be described as enormous, and even proponents of plea bargaining had based their arguments on the assumption that all interrogations would be video recorded (Itou 2015, p. 77). Thus, a government panel that was formed to rein in police powers ironically resulted in the opposite outcome.

It is worth stressing that the inability of Japanese law enforcement to utilize methods such as wide-ranging electronic surveillance and plea bargaining has also been used to justify their arguments for retaining *daiyou kangoku*. The notion that law enforcement in Japan has no choice but to rely on interrogations to obtain evidence was advanced explicitly in Japan's report to the HRC: 'Under the criminal justice system of Japan, interrogating a suspect is the most important investigation method to discover the whole truth of the case and plays an extremely important function in the investigation, since unlike in other countries, most of the powerful methods for evidence collection, including plea bargains and electronic surveillance, are not allowed in Japan' (HRC 2012, para. 140).

As self-serving and questionable as this argument may be, should (as seems likely) the current Bill become law, these techniques will be added to the investigator's arsenal. This means that there should be a corresponding de-emphasis on the interrogation process, and, by extension, abolition of *daiyou kangoku*. However, given the entrenched nature of the system (and the corresponding abuses), there appears little prospect for this to occur in the foreseeable future.

## Draft constitution: sweeping restrictions on rights and the misquoting of international law

It is also worth noting the broader political context in which the current debate has been taking place. In 2012, the ruling Liberal Democratic Party (LDP) published a draft revised Japanese Constitution, intended to replace the current one.[6] The current Constitution of Japan was adopted in 1948, while the country was under American military occupation, and conservative politicians (including the current Prime Minister, Shinzo Abe) have long stated their desire to revise the document. Given that the LDP has been the ruling party in Japan continuously since its formation in 1955, aside from two brief periods of a couple of years each, its policy pronouncements require particular attention.

First and foremost on the list of constitutional changes would be the discarding of the pacifist Article 9, which 'forever renounce[s] war as a sovereign right of the nation and the threat or use of force as means of settling international disputes'. The ambitions of the LDP (and of the conservative wing in general) to do away with this Article have been reported extensively by the international media. What is less well known (not only abroad but also in Japan) is that the draft Constitution also makes fundamental (and problematic) revisions to the human rights provisions of the current Constitution, weakening them considerably.

Most relevant for the issue of criminal procedure is the draft revision of the current Article 36, which contains an absolute prohibition on torture. The current Article reads: 'The infliction of torture by any public officer and cruel punishments are absolutely forbidden.' The draft Constitution deletes the words 'absolutely', seemingly indicating that there are circumstances in which torture may be justified.[7] In addition, the draft Constitution introduces a sweeping restriction on the exercise of all rights, stating that the people 'must understand that freedom and rights are accompanied by responsibilities and obligations' and that the exercise of rights 'must never oppose the public interest or public order' (Jiyuuminshu-tou 2012a).

The current Constitution also contains a blanket restriction, requiring that exercise of rights be 'for the public welfare': however, promotional material issued by the LDP appears to confirm that public interest or public order would be a much broader concept than this, stating that '"Public order" means the "social order", and refers to a peaceful social life. It is obvious that individuals claiming their rights should not cause inconveniences for the social life of others' (Jiyuuminshu-tou 2012b, p. 14).

What defines a 'peaceful social life' is of course open to question, especially since senior LDP politicians have been known to call peaceful demonstrations against government policy 'a form of terrorism'.[8] Other LDP material calls the current Constitution 'individualistic' and states that 'just because you have fundamental human rights doesn't mean you can do whatever you want . . . if everybody acted selfishly, society would fall apart' (Jiyuuminshu-tou 2015, p. 22).

Equally of concern, LDP material misquotes the international human rights conventions, stating incorrectly that they allow the restriction of rights for the purposes of 'national security, public order, and the protection of public health and morals' (Jiyuuminshu-tou 2012b, p. 14). This is blatantly misleading: while international human rights standards do allow for restrictions on some rights for some of the stated grounds, there is no provision for an overarching, blanket restriction on all rights, as is suggested by the LDP.

## Conclusion

*Daiyou kangoku* is a hotbed for human rights violations, enabling widespread and systemic violations by law enforcement officials. This is abundantly clear, not only on the basis of analysis conducted by national and international human rights experts, but also by the simple fact that miscarriages of justice continue in Japan as a result of its criminal procedure. The common thread running through practically every case of a wrong conviction (or near conviction) is obvious: prolonged pre-indictment detention at the hands of the police, severely limited access to legal representation, ill-treatment and a forced confession.

In some ways, what is surprising is not that the system exists, but that it has managed to prevail for so long. Although subject to strong criticism, in particular internationally, *daiyou kangoku* has been sustained, and even strengthened. The current Bill before parliament will accomplish little in the way of fundamental reform, and could even lead to greater rights violations. And while it is an open question as to whether constitutional revision will actually take place, the prospect of legalized torture in Japan is a chilling one.

The limited video recording of interrogations foreseen in the current Bill may provide safeguards in some cases. Nevertheless, it is submitted that, as things stand now, the prospects for improving the overall state of criminal justice in Japan are grim.

## Postscript

The government was unable to steer the aforementioned criminal justice bill through parliament in September 2015, due mainly to time having been taken by other, even more controversial bills. The government has announced its intention to re-submit the bill to parliament at the earliest opportunity.

## Notes

1 One member of the Committee against Torture made this remark at the review of Japan's second periodic report by the Committee in May 2013, referring to the heavy reliance on confessions in Japanese

criminal procedure. In response, the head of the Japanese delegation reportedly screamed that the member (and those in the audience agreeing with him) should 'shut up'. See, for example, Huffington Post, 'Ueda Hideaki Taishi, kokuren de "sharappu!"' ['Ambassador Ueda tells the UN to "Shut Up!"'], 11 June 2011.

2 The 2006 law, inter alia, provides a legal framework for *daiyou kangoku*, and institutionalizes the practice of maintaining a separate branch within the police department responsible for managing the lock-up facilities.

3 The *Convention against Torture* defines torture in Article 1 as 'any act by which severe pain or suffering, whether physical or mental, is intentionally inflicted on a person for such purposes as obtaining from him or a third person information or a confession . . . or intimidating or coercing him or a third person . . . when such pain or suffering is inflicted by . . . a public official'.

4 In 2014, the last year for which data is available, 122 persons were found not guilty by Japanese courts, compared to 364,824 persons found guilty. Houmu-shou (2014), at 14.

5 See Human Rights Committee, Summary record of the 3080th meeting, 11 August 2014, CCPR/C/SR.3080 at para. 17.

6 Constitutional reform is not a given: amendments would require the votes of 2/3 of parliamentarians in both houses of the Japanese parliament, and ratification in a national referendum. This has never been attempted in post-war Japan.

7 The LDP has not made any comment clarifying this language.

8 In November 2013, Shigeru Ishiba, then LDP Chief Whip and still widely recognized as a future contender for premiership, made this comment referring to people demonstrating peacefully against the widely criticized Designated Secrets Bill. See, for example, Asahi Shimbun, '"Zekkyou demo, tero to kawaranu", Ishiba Kanjichou, burogu de' ['"Screaming demonstrators are the same as terrorists" says Ishiba in his blog'] 29 November 2013. In 2014, LDP politicians tried to compare demonstrations in front of parliament with extremist marches against racial minorities. See, for example, Toukyou Shimbun, 'Jimin, kokkai demo kisei kentou seiken hihan fuuji no kenen' ['LDP considers restricting demonstrations in front of parliament, concerns raised about clamping down on opposing views'], 29 August 2014.

## References

(This chapter builds on, develops, and adds to a short article previously published by the author, 'Japan's authoritarian criminal justice system: a system that breeds human rights violations'. *CounterPunch*, 2 June 2014.)


Amnesty International, 2014a. *Submission to the Human Rights Committee on Japan.*

Amnesty International, 2014b. *Japan: appeal adds to 'psychological torture' of freed death row inmate Hakamada.* 31 March.

Amnesty International, 2015. *One year since Hakamada's release, how much has really changed for Japan's death row inmates?* 26 March.

Amnesty International Japanese Section (Amnesty International Japan 1), n.d. 'Tori-shirabe no kashika: "taiho" sareru to dou naru no?' ['Making interrogations transparent: what happens when you are "under arrest"'?]. Retrieved on 12 April 2016 from: www.amnesty.or.jp/human-rights/topic/visualization/flow_of_taiho.html.

Amnesty International Japanese Section (Amnesty International Japan 2), n.d. 'Tori-shirabe no kashika ni kansuru Q&A' [Transparency of interrogations: Q&A]. Retrieved on 12 April 2016 from: www.amnesty.or.jp/human-rights/topic/visualization/faq.html.

Houmu-shou [Ministry of Justice], 2007. *Hanzai Hakusho heisei 19 nendo-ban [White Paper on Crime 2007].* Retrieved on 12 April 2016 from: http://hakusyo1.moj.go.jp/jp/54/nfm/mokuji.html.

Houmu-shou [Ministry of Justice], 2014. *Hanzai Hakusho heisei 26 nendo-ban [White Paper on Crime 2015].*

Housei Shingi-kai shin-jidai no keiji-shihou seido tokubetsu-bukai [Legislative Council Special Task Force for Criminal Justice in the New Era], 2013. 'Jidai ni souk-shita aratana keiji-shihou seido no kihon kousou' ['Basic elements of a new criminal justice system adapted to the current times'], January.

Housei Shingi-kai shin-jidai no keiji-shihou seido tokubetsu-bukai [Legislative Council Special Task Force for Criminal Justice in the New Era], 2014. 'Arata na keiji-shihou seido no kouchiku ni tsuite no chousa shingi no kekka' ['Creation of a new criminal justice system: result of debate'], July.

Human Rights Committee [HRC], 2012. *Sixth Periodic Report of Japan*, 9 October, CCPR/C/JPN/6.

Human Rights Committee [HRC], 2014a. *Concluding Observations on the sixth periodic report of Japan*, 20 August, CCPR/C/JPN/CO/6.

Human Rights Committee [HRC], 2014b. *Replies of Japan to the list of issues in relation to the sixth periodic report of Japan*, 19 May, CCPR/C/JPN/Q/6/Add.1.

Itou, Mutsumi, 2015. 'Sousa, kouhan kryouryoku-gata kyougi, goui seido' ['System for consultation and agreement within investigation and trials'], 82 *Criminal Defence*, at 75–80.

Japan Federation of Bar Associations [JFBA], 2008. 'Kokusai jinken kijun ni kanatta miketsu koukin seido kaikaku to daiyou kangoku no haishi ni mukete' ['Towards pre-trial detention reform in accordance with international human rights standards and the abolition of Daiyou Kangoku']. Retrieved on 12 April 2016 from: www.nichibenren.or.jp/activity/criminal/detention/haishi.html.

Japan Federation of Bar Associations [JFBA], 2011. 'Enzai gen'in chousa kyuumei i'inkai no secchi wo motomeru iken-sho' ['Position paper calling for establishment of committee to investigate miscarriages of justice'].

Japan Federation of Bar Associations [JFBA], 2012. *Bengoshi haku-sho 2011-do ban [Attorney White Paper 2011]*.

Japan Federation of Bar Associations [JFBA], 2013. 'Kokuren goumon kinshi-i'inkai wa nihon seifu ni nani wo motometaka' ['What did the Committee against Torture Ask from the Japanese Government'].

Japan Federation of Bar Associations [JFBA], 2015. Report of the Japan Federation of Bar Associations in response to the Comments by the Government of Japan concerning the conclusions and recommendations of the Committee against Torture. 16 July.

Jiyuuminshu-tou [Liberal Democratic Party], 2012a. 'Kaike'an' ['Draft Revised Constitution'].

Jiyuuminshu-tou [Liberal Democratic Party], 2012b. 'Nippon-koku kenpou kaisei souan Q&A' ['Draft Revised Constitution of Japan Q&A'].

Jiyuuminshu-tou [Liberal Democratic Party], 2015. 'Hono-bono katei no kenpou kaisei-tte na-ni?' ['the heartwarming family: what is revising the constitution about?'].

Kawasaki, Hideaki and Satoshi Mishima (eds), 2014. *Keisji-shihou Kaikaku to ha Nani ka [What are the Criminal Justice Reforms]*, Gendai Jinbun-sha.

Keiji Rippou Kenkyuu-kai [Criminal Legislation Research Association] (ed.), 2007. *Daiyou kangoku, kouchi-sho kaikaku no yukue [Reform of Daiyou Kangoku and Detention Facilities: the Way Forward]*, Gendai Jinbun-sha.

Keisatsu-chou [National Police Agency], n.d. 'Keisatsu no ryuuchi gyoumu' ['Pre-trial detention by the police']. Retrieved on 12 April 2016 from: www.npa.go.jp/syokai/ryuchi/Detention_house-J_080415-3.pdf.

Keisatsu-chou Keiji-kyoku Keijikikaku-ka [National Police Agency Criminal Division Planning Section], 2012. 'Tori-shirabe (kiso-hen)' ['Investigation (The Basics)'], December.

Kuzuno, Hiroyuki, 2014. *Miketsu Koukin-hou to Jinken [Pre-trial Detention Laws and Human Rights]*, Gendai Jinbun-sha.

*Sankei, Shimbun*, 2012. 'PC enkaku souse no kyoufu (ue)' ['The danger of remote PC control'], 19 October.

Sekiguchi, Kazunori, 2015. 'Tori-shirabe no roku-on, rokuga seido' ['Procedures for audio or videotaping interrogations'], 82 *Criminal Defence*, at 70–74.

Toukyou Bengoshi-kai [Tokyo Bar Association] (Toukyou Bengoshi-kai 1), n.d. 'Daiyou kangoku Q&A' ['Daiyou kangoku Q&A']. Retrieved on 12 April 2016 from: www.toben.or.jp/know/iinkai/keiji/qa/.

Toukyou Bengoshi-kai [Tokyo Bar Association] (Toukyou Bengoshi-kai 2), n.d. 'Kazoku ni dekiru koto' ['What the family can do']. Retrieved on 12 April 2016 from: www.toben.or.jp/bengoshi/soudan/taihokeiji/kazoku.html.

# 46

# The International Criminal Court, human rights and intervention narratives

*Nerida Chazal*

## Introduction

This chapter explores how the International Criminal Court (herein, the ICC or Court) is constructed as the judicial arm of humanitarian intervention measures and the enforcer of human rights on a global scale. The ICC's narratives of prevention, which are used as justification for judicial intervention, significantly extend and buttress human rights discourses making them an even more prominent part of international relations and the structure of international society. Discourses of preventing human rights abuses through the threat of judicial investigation, prosecution and punishment fuse human rights to processes of criminalization as human rights abusers are labelled as criminal and pursued via an international criminal justice process. Through this process of criminalization and labelling the ICC legitimates other, more 'muscular' (Orford 1999) forms of intervention, such as military intervention. This chapter explores how criminal justice investigations and prosecutions conducted by the ICC are operationalized alongside military interventions using the case study of Libya. This international militarization of justice (Degenhardt 2015) is problematic as powerful countries and entities can construct themselves as heroes (Orford 1999) or saviours (Mutua 2001) who intervene in conflicts under the guise of protecting human rights, while being driven by less altruistic motives such as realpolitik and geopolitics.

## The evolution towards international human rights enforcement

In the decades post-World War 2 human rights discourses have gained significant traction and have become a dominant ordering force for international society. The spread of human rights has been driven by the creation of documents such as the *Universal Declaration of Human Rights*, the *International Covenant on Economic, Social and Cultural Rights*, and the *International Covenant on Civil and Political Rights* which codify human rights standards. The growing number of treaties and conventions that seek to protect human rights at an international level reflects a paradigm shift in the way we consider human rights protection. Traditionally, the role of protecting human rights has fallen on the state. Founding human rights documents, such as the American Declaration of Independence (1776), The Constitution of the United States of America (1787) and the American Bill of Rights (1791), the French *Déclaration des droits de l'homme et du citoyen* (1799), and the UK Bill of Rights (1688), were created following periods of violence and revolution with the goal of redeining the role of government and placing limits on state power in order to protect the rights of its citizens. In this era of rights, the state was seen as the foremost protector of human rights.

However, the world wars clearly demonstrated that the state simultaneously carries the potential to be the premier abusers of human rights. The recognition of the ambivalent role of the state as human rights protector/abuser, coupled with the rapid growth of an 'international community' of civil society organizations (including human rights organizations) has created the desire for human rights standards to be enforced at an international level. Now, individuals are viewed as cosmopolitan citizens of the world, citizens who belong to a universal humanity. This position justifies intervention in human rights abuses (often committed by the state) at an international level. Following World War 2, the enforcement of human rights was achieved in a fairly 'soft' manner through negotiation, diplomacy, and the development of treaties and conventions as well as by placing pressure on errant states. Increasingly, however, the international community has seen this approach as too weak and there have been calls from civil society organizations to increase enforcement mechanisms in a bid to uphold human rights standards around the world.

These calls have seen two major developments: the intensification of judicial options for investigating and prosecuting human rights abusers (the development of universal jurisdiction and the creation of ad hoc tribunals and international criminal courts), and the justification of military interventions in conflict situations for humanitarian reasons (that is, where the human rights of non-combatants are being severely abused). Progressively, these the two initiatives of military and judicial intervention have overlapped. For example, in response to ethnic conflict in the Yugoslav Wars (1991–2001), conflict that involved crimes against humanity and war crimes, the North Atlantic Treaty Organization (NATO) carried out several bombing campaigns in attempt to halt violence. These military operations also killed several hundred civilians. At the same time, the United Nations (UN) Security Council also created the ad hoc tribunal known as the International Criminal Tribunal for the Former Yugoslavia in 1993. The creation of trials to investigate and prosecute human rights abuses criminalizes human rights abuses and their perpetrators. Military intervention is then more readily justified due to the crimes that are occurring in conflict situations. The labelling of human rights abusers as criminal also validates military action to stop criminals.

The justification for military responses to protect human rights abuses (humanitarian military intervention) has been growing. This is reflected in the development of the principle of the responsibility to protect, which was established by the UN in 2005 to reflect the emerging norm that sovereignty is not a right, but a responsibility and that if a state abuses its responsibility to protect the rights of citizens, the international community may intervene. The responsibility to protect norms seeks to prevent or stop international crimes and human rights abuses by invoking a range of tools including economic sanctions, military intervention, and mediation (Stahn 2012). The development of international norms, courts and justification for military intervention in state conflict gives greater power to the international community to enforce human rights standards. This enforcement power has led to a strong preventative paradigm in which the international community has constructed a responsibility to curb conflict and stop human rights abuses from occurring or escalating. This preventative paradigm is clearly reflected in the development of the International Criminal Court, which is explored in the following section.

## The preventative aims of the International Criminal Court (ICC)

The preventative paradigm of the ICC stems from the impetus for its creation within the existing culture of international criminal justice in the 1990s. The ICC was developed after the establishment of ad hoc tribunals, such as the International Criminal Tribunal for the Former Yugoslavia and the International Criminal Tribunal for Rwanda, proved time consuming and resource intensive. The premise of the ICC was thus significantly different to the ad hoc tribunals. Whereas these tribunals were established in the aftermath of conflict and were largely focused on providing justice and redress in times of transition and relative peace, the ICC was established to act in the midst of violence and conflict. The tribunals were designed to respond to discrete events, often located in the past. In contrast, the ICC exists permanently to respond to crimes as they unfold across the world. In this sense, the ICC is not limited to the past or to geographical boundaries as such, and it is this position that constructs the Court as a future-orientated intuition that must be able to adapt to capricious situations and a range of unpredictable conflicts as they develop.

The future-orientated focus of the ICC significantly shapes its aims and objectives. The Court's aims need to be sufficiently flexible to allow it to intervene in many different situations in an unpredictable international environment. At the same time, the aims of the Court also need to reflect the forward looking nature of the court and the spirit of 'never again' that drove the creation of the ICC (Chazal 2013). Originating in responses to the horrors of Auschwitz and Nazi Germany, and reiterated following the genocide in Rwanda in 1994, discourses of 'never again' were prominent in negotiations around the creation of the Rome Statute (UN 1999). For example, Kofi Annan (cited in UN Information Service 2002) declared that the message from the international community in negotiating the ICC was clear:

> Never again would it stand aside and let the fabric of humanity be torn asunder by those who commit genocide, crimes against humanity, war crimes and the crime of aggression.

The first Chief Prosecutor of the ICC, Louis Moreno-Ocampo (2010), echoes these sentiments, stating:

> The Rome Statute ... transformed the words 'never again' from a moral promise to the victims, into a legal duty. ... Never again will victims of atrocities be ignored. This is the time of action, to show how the law is implemented.

The rhetoric of 'never again' results in a strong preventative paradigm for the Court. Preventing future international crimes from occurring and stopping unfolding crimes from escalating is a core aim of the ICC. This preventative ideal is often expressed through the mantra of 'ending impunity' and is evident in the focus on deterrence as a primary aim of the ICC (Rothe and Shoultz 2013).

The aims of prevention and deterrence are reflected in the prosecutorial strategy of the Office of the Prosecutor (OTP) of the ICC. The Chief Prosecutor has frequently cited the aim of prevention as a core aim. To achieve this aim the OTP has adopted the strategy of pursuing the 'big fish' (Takemura 2007), which entails focusing 'on those who bear the greatest responsibility, such as the leaders of the State or organisation allegedly responsible for those crimes' (ICC OTP 2003, p. 7) in order to achieve deterrence and prevention. The strategy of prosecuting 'those most responsible' uses highly visible cases as symbolic exemplars to demonstrate potential punishments for international crimes and thus achieve general deterrence. The OTP argues that high-ranking officials act in a calculated and rational manner when orchestrating and commanding international crimes and thus the threat of punishment can be an effective deterrent for rogue leaders (Akhavan 2001).

Through this strategy the ICC seeks to help end conflict and contribute to peace by incapacitating leaders in the midst of ongoing conflict and by achieving specific deterrence. The ICC also uses the principle of general deterrence to contribute to peace by undertaking highly visible and symbolic prosecutions in order to deter other individuals from perpetrating similar violence (Human Rights Watch 2009, Mullins and Rothe 2010). For example, when the ICC focused on Thomas Lubanga's use of child soldiers in the Democratic Republic of Congo in its first successful case there were claims of a 'Lubanga effect'. Radhika Coomaraswamy, UN special envoy for children and armed conflict, stated that the ICC indictment sent a message around the world that recruiting child soldiers is a serious offence (IRIN 2011). However, these claims are anecdotal and the deterrent effect is notoriously difficult to measure or prove (Mennecke 2007).

In a similar bid to stop violence and contribute to peace, the ICC has issued early warnings or threats in its preliminary investigation stage to countries where violence has threatened to escalate (Human Rights Watch 2011). The Prosecutor also used this strategy following election violence in Kenya in 2007–08. In 2008 the Prosecutor reminded Kenya that they were under the jurisdiction of the ICC and that the ICC and, specifically, the OTP carefully monitors such situations (ICC OTP 2008) in an effort to curb further incitement to violence (International Crisis Group 2012). In 2009 the Prosecutor stated, 'the OTP continues to follow-up whether national proceedings into the post-election violence in Kenya in early 2008 are being conducted' (ICC OTP 2009, p. 1).

These types of strategies highlight the importance of deterrence for the Court and construct the ICC as a 'threat' that can be invoked to warn individuals from committing further crimes. There are, however, several limitations for the ICC in achieving its preventative aims of deterrence and ending impunity. One of the major barriers for the Court is its reliance on state support to enforce its arrest warrants, conduct investigations and collect evidence, a situation which has seen the ICC perceived as a 'paper tiger' (Human Rights Watch 2011).

The ICC's reliance on state support means that the Court has been unsuccessful in situations where it does not have the support of a situation country, as demonstrated by the indictment of Sudanese president Omar Al-Bashir. In this case the ICC attempted to enforce a symbolic, highly visible prosecution of a sitting head of state with the aim of achieving both general and specific deterrence. However, this strategy failed and instead illustrated the weakness of the Court: Al-Bashir remains free even though his location is known and he has travelled to other African nations, and around the world (Strydom 2015). Following the UN Security Council's referral of the situation in Darfur to the ICC, Sudan characterized the Court as just another instrument in the toolbox of the US and its allies to topple an Islamic regime of which they do not approve (Dealy 2009). The Court's involvement in Sudan also caused the African Union to express hostility towards the ICC for its exclusive focus on African countries and leaders (Kegoro 2011, Stearns 2011). In this situation the ICC is depicted as a weapon that can be used by powerful countries against weaker countries or longstanding opponents (Dealy 2009, Nouwen and Werner 2011).

As this illustrates, the necessity of state support and support from the international community makes the ICC vulnerable to being used as a tool to leverage political divides. The ICC's reliance on external support means that it will often align itself with powerful countries and their military interventions, instead of targeting soldiers or leaders from powerful countries as they participate in humanitarian interventions. The need for support and the use of the ICC as a tool explains why the ICC is often used in conjunction with military intervention, making the ICC the judicial arm of the emerging norm of the responsibility to protect human rights around the world. This is particularly illustrated by the recent case of Libya, explored in the following section.

## The merging of judicial and military intervention: the case of Libya

In Libya, the ICC was mobilized by international actors to dispose of a problematic leader and achieve favourable political outcomes, while also justifying military intervention. Forming part of the Arab Spring movement the violence in Libya was sparked by civilian uprisings against the Libyan regime and escalated as president Muammar Gaddafi struggled to maintain power. The Arab Spring was a movement that spread across numerous Middle Eastern countries, including Tunisia, Egypt, Libya, Syria, Yemen and Bahrain, in 2011 (Goldstein 2012). In each country mass protests were sparked by brutal acts of repression: in the case of Libya it was the arrest of Fathi Terbil, the lawyer for the victims of the 1996 Abu Salim prison massacre that sparked the demonstrations (Roth 2012). In an attempt to control the uprisings in Libya, Gaddafi used excessive force against protesters and committed gross and systematic human rights violations, including indiscriminate armed attacks against civilians, extrajudicial killings, arbitrary arrests, and detention and torture of peaceful demonstrators (United Nations Human Rights Council 2011).

The international community quickly became involved as the situation in Libya unfolded. On 26 February 2011, the UN Security Council unanimously adopted resolution 1970 referring the unrest and violence in Libya to the International Criminal Court (UN Security Council 2011). The referral of the situation to the ICC for investigation was one of a range of measures taken by the Security Council in response to the violence. Other measures included travel bans and asset freezes for Gaddafi and his associates and arms embargos (du Plessis and Louw 2011). In response to the referral, the ICC Prosecutor swiftly commenced an investigation of the situation in Libya on 3 March 2011 (ICC 2011a). Soon after, the Prosecutor requested the Pre-Trial Chamber of the ICC to issue arrest warrants for Gaddafi, as well as his son Saif Al Islam Gaddafi, and de facto prime minister and Head of the Military Intelligence Abdualla Al-Senussi (ICC 2011b). In announcing the request for the arrest warrants the Prosecutor declared:

> Most of the victims are Libyans, but the widespread and systematic attacks against them are affecting the international community as a whole. The crimes are crimes against humanity. . . . The execution of the warrants will have a deterrent impact for other leaders who are thinking of using violence to gain or retain power.
>
> *(ICC 2011b)*

This statement clearly demonstrates that the preventative goal of general deterrence drives the ICC's investigations. On 27 June 2011, the Pre-Trial Chamber of the ICC issued the arrest warrants for all three suspects (ICC 2011c).

Closely following the initial referral of the situation to the ICC the UN Security Council took further actions, outlined in Resolution 1973, ordering a cease-fire, authorizing a no-fly zone and sanctioning the use of 'all means necessary', short of foreign occupation to protect civilians in Libya (United Nations Security Council 2011). Military intervention in Libya began on 19 March with the French Air Force and a coalition of 10 European and Middle-Eastern states, notably Qatar and the United Arab Emirates, participating in the intervention with US support (du Plessis and Louw 2011, Norton-Taylor 2011, Voice of America 2011). This was followed by sustained airstrikes by NATO and non-stop patrols by armed US drones and other surveillance missions in an effort to curb violence and hamper Gaddafi loyalists (Borger 2011), using a narrative of protecting citizens from further human rights abuses.

The NATO air combat missions were criticized for causing unnecessary civilian deaths (Amnesty International 2012, BBC 2012) with Human Rights Watch (2012a) estimating that at least 72 civilians, one-third of them children under 18, were killed by the attacks. As Roth (2012) highlights, the decisive interventions in the Libyan crisis were disproportionate to the international responses in other countries experiencing similar violence as part of the Arab Spring, such as Tunisia and Egypt. The focused intervention in Libya can be explained by the west's desire to depose Gaddafi (Coughlin 2011). As Johnstone (2011) explains, the west has had a hostile relationship with Gaddafi over the past two decades, particularly since the Lockerbie bombings in 1988.

Viewed within this wider framework of international intervention, the ICC is constructed as just one tool in a range of measures taken by the international community in reaction to the violence in Libya. Through its association with UN sanctioned measures, the ICC was constructed as the 'judicial arm' of the international responsibility to protect in Libya (Stahn 2012). The preamble of Resolution 1970 invoked the responsibility to protect stating, 'recalling the Libyan authorities' responsibility to protect its population'. The invocation of the responsibility to protect in the UN's resolution positions the Court as one of many existing tools, such as economic sanctions and military interventions, which are used by the UN in response to violence and conflict. The construction of the ICC as a tool in wider responses to violence was reinforced in a later debate in the Security Council which explored 'how the Court, as a tool of preventive diplomacy, can assist the council in carrying out its mandate to uphold the rule of law, maintain peace and security, and combat impunity while ensuring accountability for mass atrocities' (Coalition for the International Criminal Court [CICC] 2012). Through these discourses, the ICC is given a broad role and criminal investigations are positioned alongside military intervention to protect and enforce human rights standards.

The UN mobilization of the ICC in early responses to the Libyan violence established the ICC as a key actor in international interventions in unfolding violence. However, the UN referral was problematic for several reasons, primarily as Libya is not a State Party to the ICC. Although the ICC's jurisdiction is limited to states that have signed the Rome Statute, the UN Security Council has the power to refer situations to the Court for investigation. Despite these powers of referral it is problematic to see many core actors using the Court while simultaneously refusing to be bound by its jurisdiction. The US, Russia and China, three out of the five permanent members of the UN Security Council, are not parties to the ICC. Despite this, the UN referral was unanimous. This means that numerous actors who are not parties of the Court are either mobilizing the ICC or being investigated by the ICC. The African nations who were parties to the Security Council, Gabon, South Africa and Nigeria also supported the referral despite ongoing tensions between the ICC and African states (du Plessis and Louw 2011).

The ambivalent interactions with the Court evidenced in the Libya situation further construct the ICC as a tool to be used selectively to achieve broader, strategic aims, such as getting rid of antagonistic leaders of particular countries. Smith (2012, p. 2) emphasizes this use of the Court as a 'tool of coercive diplomacy'. By invoking the ICC in accordance with a range of other military measures, the ICC is instrumentalized to achieve certain outcomes. Despite the death and destruction caused by NATO airstrikes there has been no attempt by the ICC to prosecute these crimes (Human Rights Watch 2012a). Similarly, the ICC's prosecutions focus solely on crimes committed by Gaddafi's regime and ignore the violence perpetrated by rebel forces (Human Rights Watch 2012b).

For the ICC, its engagement as a tool in the Libyan situation provided it with much visibility and credibility. The inclusion of the ICC at the early stages of intervention was particularly beneficial for the ICC as it reinforced the identity of the Court as a preventative and persuasive institution with a future-oriented focus and a desire to be involved in events as they unfold. The Court capitalized on the UN's early engagement by promptly conducting investigations and issuing arrest warrants. However, this swift response was, in itself, problematic as the case was driven by political expediency rather than 'objective consideration of the situation or of whether the ICC may be in a position to successfully prosecute the cases' (Schaefer and Groves 2011, pp. 2–3). Another issue with the politically expedient use of the ICC is that investigations may not proceed to successful prosecutions. This was the case with Libya. As highlighted, the ICC only issued three arrest warrants in the Libyan situation. The warrant for Muammar Gaddafi was terminated after he was killed. The transitional Libyan authorities later refused to surrender the other two suspects (Saif Al Islam Gaddafi and Abdualla Al-Senussi) to the ICC, preferring instead to prosecute and punish these individuals in national courts. This lack of cooperation with the ICC caused controversy as the international community, and the ICC, raised concerns that the Libyan justice system would not respect the rights of these individuals or provide them with a fair trial. Thus, further human rights concerns were raised, including the use of torture and the death penalty by Libya. As this wrangling demonstrates, although the ICC may be a step forward in the development of the enforcement of human rights on an international level, the ICC is still a limited and relatively powerless enforcement mechanism.

## Conclusion: human rights and intervention

Both the positive and negative perceptions of the ICC construct the Court as a threat. The ICC is a threat in the positive sense as it exists to warn and deter unaccountable perpetrators of mass atrocities with the possibility of punishment and the enforcement of the rule of law. At the same time, the ICC can also be seen as a negative encroachment on sovereign powers and a form of lawfare, where the threat of law and prosecution is used in place of the threat of war (Scheffer 2010). Despite this potential threat, during its first decade of existence, the Court has given no indication that it will prosecute crimes associated with military interventions in humanitarian crises. As highlighted, although NATO operations in Libya reportedly killed up to 80 civilians (Human Rights Watch 2011), the ICC's Libyan prosecutions have centred solely on key leaders of the Gaddafi regime. Indeed, UN Security Council Resolution 1970 which referred the Libyan situation to the Court limited the ICC investigations to Libyan nationals, effectively protecting the interests of those states and organizations who participated in military interventions in Libya (Jose 2013).

As this illustrates, the 'threat' of the ICC has been used in a highly selective manner, meaning that the Court has been aligned with the strategic interests of more powerful countries and the political will of the international community. Thus, instead of being used against those who participate in military interventions, the ICC has been used as a tool of coercive diplomacy alongside military interventions. In this sense, ICC investigations and prosecutions bolster a range of other measures, such as political, economic and military interventions that are taken in response to ongoing conflicts and justified by humanitarian concerns and the responsibility to protect doctrine (Stahn 2012). The merging of judicial and military paradigms was again seen in 2013 when the ICC swiftly responded to the escalating situation in Mali, coinciding with French military interventions (Cole 2013).

As the ICC is instrumentalized in political and diplomatic manoeuvres that support state interests justice becomes a tool of coercive diplomacy. For the ICC, its use as a tool is beneficial as it allows the Court to obtain the support of states and international organizations such as the UN, support that is vitally important for an institution lacking enforcement power. The Court's involvement in numerous situations also positions it as part of real-time international responses to conflict, an image that constructs the Court as constantly relevant in a changing and fast-paced world. The 'dark side' (Kennedy 2004) of this situation is that only certain human rights abuses are criminalized and subject to potential military intervention and judicial investigation. Other human rights abuses, committed by more powerful leaders and countries remain invisible, legal, or ignored by international instruments designed to enforce human rights on a global scale.

## References

Akhavan, P., 2001. Beyond impunity: can international criminal justice prevent future atrocities? *The American Journal of International Law*, 95 (7), 7–31.

Amnesty International, 2012. Libya: civilian deaths from NATO airstrikes must be properly investigated. *Amnesty International News*. Retrieved on 20 August 2012 from: www.amnesty.org/en/news/libya-civilian-deaths-nato-airstrikes-must-be-properly-investigated-2012-03-19.

BBC, 2012. NATO urged to investigate civilian deaths in Libya. *BBC News*. Retrieved on 20 May 2012 from: www.bbc.co.uk/news/world-africa-18053488.

Borger, J., 2011. NATO may end Libya air strikes. *The Sydney Morning Herald*. Retrieved on 15 November 2012 from: www.smh.com.au/world/nato-may-end-libya-air-strikes-20111006-1lbnu.html.

Chazal, N., 2013. The rationale of international criminal justice: idealpolitik, realpolitik and the ICC. *In*: W. de Lint, M. Marmo and N. Chazal (eds), *Criminal justice in international society*. New York, NY: Routledge, 19–36.

Coalition for the International Criminal Court [CICC], 2012. *CICC website*. Retrieved on 12 December 2012 from: www.coalitionfortheicc.org/?mod=coalition.

Cole, A., 2013. Mali and the ICC: what lessons can be learned from previous investigations? *The Guardian*. Retrieved on 17 January 2013 from: www.guardian.co.uk/law/2013/jan/17/mali-icc-lessons-learned-investigations.

Coughlin, C., 2011. Libya: the west wants to get rid of Gaddafi, but doesn't know how. *The Telegraph*. Retrieved on 5 November 2011 from: www.telegraph.co.uk/comment/columnists/concoughlin/8381739/Libya-The-West-wants-to-get-rid-of-Gaddafi-but-doesnt-know-how.html.

Dealy, S., 2009. Interview; Sudan's President Omar al-Bashir. *Public Broadcasting Service*. Transcript. Retrieved on 20 June 2010 from: www.pbs.org/newshour/bb/africa/july-dec09/bashir-full_08-13.htm.

Degenhardt, T., 2015. Crime, justice and the legitimacy of military power in the international sphere. *Punishment & Society*, 17(2), 139–62.

du Plessis, M. and Louw, A., 2011. Justice and the Libyan crisis: the ICC's role under Security Council Resolution 1970. *Institute for Security Studies*. Briefing paper. Retrieved on 21 December 2011 from: www.issafrica.org/pgcontent.php?UID=30878.

Goldstein, E., 2012. Before the Arab Spring, the unseen thaw. Human Rights Watch World Report 2012. Retrieved on 12 November 2013 from: www.hrw.org/world-report-2012/arab-spring-unseen-thaw.

Human Rights Watch, 2009. *Selling justice short: why accountability matters for peace*. Retrieved on 19 January 2010 from: www.hrw.org/sites/default/files/reports/ij0709webwcover_3.pdf.

Human Rights Watch, 2011. *International justice: unfinished business closing gaps in the selection of ICC cases*. Retrieved on 20 December 2011 from: www.hrw.org/sites/default/files/reports/icc0911webwcover.pdf.

Human Rights Watch, 2012a. *Unacknowledged deaths: civilian casualties in NATO's air campaign in Libya*. Retrieved on 15 November 2012 from: http://www.hrw.org/sites/default/files/reports/libya0512webwcover_0.pdf.

Human Rights Watch, 2012b. *Death of a dictator: bloody vengeance in Sirte*. Retrieved on 20 December 2012 from: www.hrw.org/reports/2012/10/16/death-dictator-0.

ICC, 2011a. ICC Prosecutor to open an investigation in Libya. *ICC Press Release*. Retrieved on 3 March 2011 from: www.icc-cpi.int/en_menus/icc/situations%20and%20cases/situations/icc0111/press%20releases/Pages/statement%20020311.aspx.

ICC, 2011b. Statement ICC Prosecutor press conference on Libya 16 May 2011. *ICC Press Release*. Retrieved on 17 May 2011 from: www.icc-cpi.int/en_menus/icc/structure%20of%20the%20court/office%20of%20the%20prosecutor/reports%20and%20statements/statement/Pages/statement%20icc%20prosecutor%20press%20conference%20on%20libya%2016%20may%202011.aspx.

ICC, 2011c. Pre-Trial Chamber 1 issues three warrants of arrest for Muammar Gaddafi, Saif Al-Islam Gaddafi and Abdualla Al-Senussi. *Press Release*. CC-CPI-20110627-PR689. Retrieved on 28 June 2011 from: www.icc-cpi.int/en_menus/icc/situations%20and%20cases/situations/icc0111/press%20releases/Pages/pre_trial%20chamber%20i%20issues%20three%20warrants%20of%20arrest%20for%20muammar%20gaddafi_%20saif%20al.aspx.

ICC OTP, 2003. *Paper on some policy issues before the Office of the Prosecutor*. Retrieved on 12 December 2012 from: www.icc-cpi.int/NR/rdonlyres/1FA7C4C6-DE5F-42B7-8B25-60AA962ED8B6/143594/030905_Policy_Paper.pdf.

ICC OTP, 2008. *OTP statement in relation to events in Kenya*. The Hague. Retrieved on 4 November 2012 from: www.icc-cpi.int/NR/rdonlyres/1BB89202-16AE-4D95-ABBB-4597C416045D/0/ICCOTPST20080205ENG.pdf.

ICC OTP, 2009. *ICC Prosecutor reaffirms that the situation in Kenya is Monitored by his Office.* Retrieved on 4 November 2012 from: www.icc-cpi.int/NR/rdonlyres/06455318-783E-403B-8C9F-8E2056720C15/279793/KenyaOTPpubliccommunication20090211.pdf.

International Crisis Group, 2012. Kenya: impact of the ICC proceedings. *Africa Briefing*, No.84. Retrieved on 3 August 2015 from: www.crisisgroup.org/en/regions/africa/horn-of-africa/kenya/b084-kenya-impact-of-the-icc-proceedings.aspx.

IRIN, 2011. Jury still out on the ICC trials in DRC. *News From Africa.* Retrieved on 6 February 2011 from: www.newsfromafrica.org/newsfromafrica/articles/art_12244.html.

Johnstone, D., 2011. Gaddafi's Libya as demon. *CounterPunch.* Retrieved on 15 October 2012 from: www.counterpunch.org/2011/08/31/gaddafis-libya-as-demon/.

Jose, B., 2013. The case for restraint: Syria and the International Criminal Court. AlJazeera, 21 March. Retrieved on 10 December 2015 from: www.aljazeera.com/indepth/opinion/2013/03/2013320164619306786.html.

Kegoro, G., 2011. AU hostility threatens international justice. *The Kenyan Section of the International Commission of Jurists, Commentary.* Retrieved on 15 October 2012 from: www.icj-kenya.org/index.php/media-centre/press-releases/commentary.

Kennedy, D., 2004. *The dark sides of virtue.* Oxford: Princeton University Press.

Mennecke, M., 2007. Punishing genocidaires: a deterrent effect or not?. *Human Rights Review*, 8(4), 319–39.

Moreno-Ocampo, L., 2010. Prosecutor of the ICC, statement. *Review Conference: General Debate.* Kampala, English version. Retrieved on 19 November 2010 from: www.icc-cpi.int/iccdocs/asp_docs/RC2010/Statements/ICC-RC-statements-LuisMorenoOcampo-ENG.pdf.

Mullins, C. and Rothe, D., 2010. The ability of the International Criminal Court to deter violations of international criminal law: a theoretical assessment. *International Criminal Law Review*, 10, 771–86.

Mutua, M., 2001. Savages, victims, and saviours: the metaphor of human rights. *Harvard International Law Journal*, 42(1), 201–45.

Norton-Taylor, R., 2011. Libya: a new breed of military intervention. *The Guardian.* Retrieved on 23 September 2012 from: www.guardian.co.uk/commentisfree/2011/aug/25/libya-military-intervention.

Nouwen, S. and Werner, G., 2011. Doing justice to the political: the International Criminal Court in Uganda and Sudan – a rejoinder to Bas Schotel. *European Journal of International Law*, 22(4), 1161–4.

Orford, A., 1999. Muscular humanitarianism: reading the narratives of the new interventionism. *European Journal of International Law*, 10(4), 679–711.

Roth, K., 2012. Time to abandon the autocrats and embrace rights: the international response to the Arab Spring. *Human Rights Watch World Report.* Retrieved on 16 December 2012 from: www.hrw.org/world-report-2012/time-abandon-autocrats-and-embrace-rights.

Rothe, D. and Shoultz, I., 2013. International criminal justice: law, courts and punishment as deterrent mechanisms. *In:* W. de Lint, M. Marmo and N. Chazal (eds), *Criminal justice in international society.* New York, NY: Routledge, 151–65.

Schaefer, B. and Groves, S., 2011. The motivation for the referral of Libya to the ICC: political pressure or justice? *The Heritage Foundation Web Memo.* No. 3180. Retrieved on 29 November 2012 from: www.heritage.org/research/reports/2011/03/the-motivation-for-the-referral-of-libya-to-the-icc-political-pressure-or-justice.

Scheffer, D., 2010. Whose lawfare is it, anyway? *Case Western Reserve Journal of International Law*, 43, 215–28.

Smith, A., 2012. The emergence of international justice as coercive diplomacy: challenges and prospects. *Harvard Human Rights Program Research Working Paper Series*, May.

Stahn, C., 2012. Libya, the International Criminal Court and complementarity: a test for 'shared responsibility'. *Journal of International Criminal Justice*, 10, 325–49.

Stearns, S., 2011. African Union says ICC prosecutions are discriminatory. *Voice of America News.* Africa. Retrieved on 1 May 2012 from: www.voanews.com/english/news/africa/-African-Union-Says-ICC-Prosecutions-Are-Discriminatory-125012734.html.

Strydom, H., 2015. Why al-Bashir's visit to the UN presents the US with a diplomatic challenge. *The Conversation.* Retrieved on 15 October 2015 from: https://theconversation.com/why-al-bashirs-visit-to-the-un-presents-the-us-with-a-diplomatic-challenge-46898.

Takemura, H., 2007. Big fish and small fish debate: an examination of the prosecutorial discretion. *International Criminal Law Review*, 7, 667–85.

United Nations (UN), 1999. *Rome Statute of the International Criminal Court overview.* Retrieved on 1 December 2014 from: http://untreaty.un.org/cod/icc/general/overview.htm.

United Nations Human Rights Council, 2011. *Report of the International Commission of Inquiry to investigate all alleged violations of international human rights law in the Libyan Arab Jamahiriya*, A/HRC/17/441. Retrieved on 8 August 2012 from: www2.ohchr.org/english/bodies/hrcouncil/docs/17session/A.HRC.17.44_AUV.pdf.

United Nations Information Service (UNIS), 2002. Exciting but challenging journey lies ahead, says Secretary-General on fourth anniversary of adoption of ICC statute. *Press Release*. SG/SM/8309 L/3011. Retrieved on 26 September 2009 from: www.unis.unvienna.org/unis/pressrels/2002/sgsm8309.html.

United Nations Security Council, 2011. *Resolution 1970*. Retrieved on 26 July 2012 from: www.icc-cpi.int/NR/rdonlyres/081A9013-B03D-4859-9D61-5D0B0F2F5EFA/0/1970Eng.pdf.

Voice of America, 2011. World powers agree to military intervention in Libya. *Voice of America*. Retrieved on 19 December 2012 from: www.voanews.com/content/world-powers-agree-to-military-intervention-in-libya-118298724/157707.html.

# Part VI
# Human rights and penality

This final section of the collection examines the adoption and expansion of new and adapted forms of penality in custodial and non-custodial settings, and the impact, not only on people in conflict with the law, but also on society more broadly. Chapters in this section consider whether human rights informed principles have the capacity to reshape contemporary penal policies and practices and mitigate the worst excesses of the exercise of power in community based supervision and closed environments. In so doing, the authors question whether politicians, policy-makers, practitioners and the public are ready to embrace human rights discourse as a basis for reform, and if so, on what basis that would occur. The chapters also remind us that despite claims to universalism and the importance of non-derogation of states from human rights principles, in many countries human rights claims are contingent, especially for populations who are deemed to be undeserving such as criminalized, or otherwise marginalized populations, including refugees, asylum seekers and others who are hidden from the public gaze and are detained in closed institutions.

The section opens with a reflective, thought provoking piece by Elizabeth Stanley on overcoming the challenges presented by human rights violations. She argues that the promise of human rights as a protective force is always a work in progress and uses the example of the shifting nature of human rights protections in relation to prisoners and asylum seekers to illustrate her argument. Stanley argues that there are two key sites that present challenges to human rights protections: the first, the human rights bureaucratic apparatus of law and monitoring; and the second, the need to achieve the kinds of sociocultural changes that integrate a broader positive vision of human rights. Stanley argues that we need determination to pursue a human rights agenda but that ultimately human rights as a protective force is worth fighting for.

Loraine Gelsthorpe and Madeline-Sophie Abbas, extend the discussion of penality and human rights beyond the institutional walls to include those offenders who exist in the liminal, regulated space of community supervision and non-custodial sentences. In their chapter, they explore the potential for human rights discourse to guide the development of probation policies and practices in the United Kingdom (UK) at a time when managerialism, austerity measures, and concerns with risk management have led to the fragmentation and privatization of many aspects of the Probation Service, and have challenged its pre-existing social work ethos. In so doing, the authors examine the changes in probation in the UK over the recent years, and outline the challenges and the potential benefits of adopting a human rights framework for practitioners, offenders, victims, and the general public.

The section then turns to focus on key issues facing people in both criminal and administrative detention. Peter Scharff-Smith documents the history of the philosophical underpinnings of penal policies from the nineteenth century onwards and their relationship to prisoners' human rights, and international and regional human rights mechanisms. Scharff-Smith also highlights contemporary challenges and tensions in penal policy and human rights that have occurred as a result of governmental concerns with terrorism and security, as well as from the mass incarceration trends in countries like the United States. The chapter concludes by examining how human rights informed policies do have the capacity to adapt to emerging issues such as the use of digital technologies and the rights of children with a parent in prison.

Bronwyn Naylor also discusses the rights of detainees and the specific situations that they face in closed institutions with a particular focus on those in prisons, police cells, and forensic psychiatric institutions. Naylor compares and contrasts the practices and cultures of different conceptual frameworks underpinning closed environments – punitive, therapeutic and administrative – and proposes that there needs to be a more sophisticated and informed debate about penal policies that moves beyond the populist appeal of the punitive. From their ethnographic research with older prisoners in a Belgian prison, Diete Humblet and Sonja Snacken provide us with insights into the particular difficulties faced in detention by ageing prison populations and the failure by prison authorities on the whole, to specifically address their needs and rights. The chapter examines compliance with the standards associated with the human rights principle of human dignity, and provides us with theoretical and empirical insights into an underexplored issue in criminology.

In the following chapter Lorana Bartels and Jeremy Boland critically evaluate the potential for a human rights framework to inform the architecture, policies and practices of places of detention in their exploration of the philosophy and practice of the Alexander Maconochie Centre in Australia, an institution often purported to be a model of a human rights compliant prison. The authors argue that the *Human Rights Act 2004* (ACT), the *Corrections Management Act 2007* (ACT), and the establishment of the prison itself, despite a number of shortcomings, represents a significant international development in the recognition of the human rights of prisoners.

Despite what many might see as the innate legitimacy of their claims, progress towards human rights informed policies depends on support from politicians, policy-makers, and the general public. This final chapter by Des McNulty, Nicholas Watson and Gregory Philo explores how fluid that support can be. Based on an original content analysis of five major newspapers in the UK, their audiences and relevant political policy statements the chapter examines how recent discussions of human rights of prisoners, refugees and other marginalized groups have been framed in the UK, especially in the lead up to the 2015 general election. The authors interrogate the relationship between dominant human rights narratives expressed in sections of the media, which present the rulings of the European Court of Human Rights as an attack on British sovereignty and democracy, and the policy agenda of the Conservative government to repeal the *Human Rights Act 1998* and replace it with an independent British Bill of Rights. The chapter raises important issues about how human rights discourse is used and abused instrumentally by governments and the media, for garnering populist credentials and political capital, especially when applied to certain groups who, despite the universality of human rights protections, are deemed to be undeserving in some way.

Each chapter highlights the precarious nature of support for human rights principles in politics, policy and practice especially in relation to particular populations deemed to be undeserving, or 'other'. As each of the authors demonstrates, human rights protections for those deemed in conflict with the law need to be monitored and fought for as they are easily abused or removed, especially for those people in closed environments, marginalized from mainstream society. No matter one's philosophical take on human rights, it is clear that the protections that they offer cannot be taken for granted and human rights defenders need to be ever vigilant.

# 47

# Human rights as a protective force

*Elizabeth Stanley*

## Introduction

Human rights are values that deepen the chance of a better life. With 'an agenda' for individual and social improvement, they herald opportunities for freedom, dignity, respect, peace and social justice. These hopeful 'principles of social protection . . . provoke action' towards a world that has not yet emerged (Moyn 2010, p. 1). Human rights are, and will always be, a work in progress. Their promise as a source of protection has to be continually articulated, enacted, remembered and fought over.

This chapter considers human rights in relation to the detention of prisoners and asylum seekers. Rights relating to detention have a long history within Anglophone states but detainees regularly experience an extensive loss of rights. This chapter reflects upon how this occurs and how the erosion of protections might be prevented. In particular, it explores two principal sites of challenge: first, within the bureaucratic apparatus of law and monitoring; and, second, within sociocultural change. In doing so, the chapter outlines some of the challenges of attaining human rights when dominant structural, institutional and sociocultural relations are arranged to inhibit human rights standards. It also demonstrates that both reformism and visionary endeavours are necessary to the protection of all humans in the twenty-first century.

## Human rights and detention

The demand that individuals are not subject to unlawful detention, *habeas corpus*, is one of the oldest liberal rights – practised in thirteenth century England, it was legally established there in 1679. More recently, over the last century, the United Nations (UN) has developed laws, rules and principles to provide for the fair treatment and dignity of detainees across all countries, and they have established a corresponding network of mechanisms for oversight and accountability.[1] Similarly, regional bodies have established human rights agreements that are backed by administrative and legal processes.[2] Protections for those made vulnerable through state confinement are promised across the world.

And yet, despite these activities, detainees regularly endure human rights violations on account of their representational difference from the rest of 'us'. Bauman (1989, p. 192) illustrated how violations are more likely to happen when distancing takes place: when we lose sight of other humans, when we have moral indifference or when our 'responsibility for the other shrivels'. Such distancing has been directed to numerous groups over time – from colonized populations to women, children or welfare claimants, among others – however, it is practised in extreme ways for those detained on account of their 'threats' (Bauman 1995, Malloch and Stanley 2005).

Detainees are commonly 'put out of sight or below the threshold of moral vision' (Humphrey 2002, p. 32). For example, in their study of European immigration policing and detention practices, Aas and Gundhus (2015) demonstrate how professionals 'on the front line' focus on 'crime-fighting' and administrative tasks that allows them to distance themselves from the humans they encounter. Notwithstanding the risks from which asylum seekers flee and their victimization, they are dealt with 'as "the risk" that other citizens need to be secured against' (McCulloch 2005). The end result is that these migrants are generally regarded as suspicious, and their traumatic experiences remain obscured under collected statistics that favour institutional entry, apprehension or detention processing.

Similarly, criminologists have observed how the objectification of prisoners makes them appear 'deserving' of disregard and harm. Within Anglophone countries, the label of 'prisoner' has become shorthand for those who must be 'expelled', socially outcast or placed outside the boundaries of citizenship (Drake and Henley 2014, p. 154). The notion of universal rights is replaced by the idea that human rights can only be accorded to citizens who are virtuous (Brown 2008, Genders and Player 2014). Prisoners are viewed as implicitly to blame for their situation and, in their position of less-eligibility for human rights, 'they fall outside any moral relationship of care or responsibility' (Humphrey 2002, pp. 32–3).

One product of this exclusion includes a common Anglophone perception that human rights for prisoners are a societal affront. Commentators propose that protecting their rights will undermine human rights for victims, as if there is only a limited supply of human rights to go around or as if prisoners are a mutually exclusive category from victims (Stanley 2011). For some, this exclusion from rights is made permanent. Prisoners can become 'zombies', the 'living dead' who pose an ever-lasting inescapable threat (Simon 2014, p. 50). Under these conditions, anything goes. Prisons in the United States (US) state of California institutionalize a 'war model' that aims to 'neutralize' this 'permanent enemy' through state-organized violence involving tasers, gas guns, military-grade body armour and psychological torture (Simon 2014, pp. 60–1). In many other countries, pre-emptive punishments – including detention without trial, 'three strikes', or the use of 'civil detention' to imprison specific offenders without end on account of their potential criminality – thrive (Pratt and Eriksson 2013). Prisoners also find that basic human rights are denied or subject to constant attack – for example, rights to vote, healthcare, family life, education, work, or personal safety are all deeply precarious or non-existent within prisons in liberal democracies.

We should not necessarily be surprised at the vitriol and violence aimed at detainees. The state has always relied upon a certain level of violence as a means to build and sustain power. Through human rights violations, states shape and regulate social, economic, legal and political life, and they derive legitimacy in doing so (Green and Ward 2004, Weber 1970). That is, human rights violations allow states to symbolically 'flex their muscles', or to practically assert their power. Governments can rigorously pursue violations, especially when they sense a voter or nationalist surge. For example, in the United Kingdom, the recent wrangling of the government on the right to vote for prisoners barely touched on the substantive human rights arguments. The media led the charge, exposing 'unelected', 'arrogant' 'foreign' judges who dictated law and interfered in British affairs. With media commentators vilifying those who progressed 'moral or legal arguments for enfranchisement', the *Sun* newspaper called for the government to stand 'up to Europe over human rights madness' (cited in McNulty et al. 2014, pp. 368–72). The prime minister duly obliged. Setting out his vision, David Cameron (2014) declared that the European Court of Human Rights needed 'sorting out'. He rallied against any judicial incursion into 'the country that wrote Magna Carta' and rather headily promised to 'scrap' the *Human Rights Act 1998* that codifies the *European Convention on Human Rights* into national law. The erosion of a fundamental human right transformed into a point of state sovereignty.

The application of 'national interests' to trump human protection is also clearly demonstrated in debates on borders. The fear invoked through discourses that emphasize national belonging or common identity invigorates exclusionary practices directed to those who do not or cannot belong (McCulloch 2005). In an era of human insecurities, linked to advanced global capitalist economies that have embedded dramatic inequalities between and within states, the identification of problem groups becomes a point of pride. Burgeoning, and self-serving, border control and crime industries soak up finances previously directed to education, housing, employment, health, pensions, welfare or development (Giroux 2004). We are all subsequently made less secure (McCulloch 2005). Yet, amidst fear-based stories of 'boat people' or 'Calais migrants', we are 'expected to express gratitude' as we endure ever-increasing administrative and technological processing for an aspiration of national protection (Davis 2001, p. 45). This is an 'unwinnable' but permanent crisis that requires human rights violations as a matter of course. Contemporary border controls funnel desperate populations into hopeless situations: a life as a criminal, and often no life at all (Weber and Pickering 2011). And so, between 1993 and 2010, almost '14,000 people are known to have died . . . trying to enter Europe, or while in detention or during forcible deportation' (Weber and Pickering 2011, p. 1) while, from 1 January to 24 August 2015, a recorded 2,373 individuals died in Mediterranean waters (International Organization for Migration 2015). Innumerable children, women and men have also suffered the gross violations and indignities of national and offshore processing centres in Europe, Australasia and elsewhere. In their attempts to find safer, better lives across territorial borders, their damaged lives become little more than unsavoury but accepted symbols of a state's 'rightful' power (Reus-Smit 2001, p. 526). With the state as the 'protector . . . of good citizens', human rights violations against those 'who have contravened the law or proven themselves as threatening' are made legitimate as a condition for 'our collective safety and security and the very foundations for social order' (Drake 2012, p. 149).

There is, therefore, a chasm between human rights laws or values and the experiences of those detained (or those being propelled into detention). Part of the problem, as Moyn (2010) shows, is that the rise of human rights discourse, slowly through the 1970s and then more rapidly from the early 1990s, came at a time when political conditions undermined opportunities for 'the good life' of human security. Human rights consolidated as a 'moral utopia when political utopias died' (ibid., p. 214) and neoliberal economies kicked in. Under these circumstances, it is difficult to see how rights-conscious shifts can occur. The next sections reflect on how this might be achieved – first, through legal or administrative action; and, second, through socio-cultural shifts.

## Protection through bureaucracy

A key means by which human rights are protected is through courts and international bodies that provide restraint on harmful state behaviours. States can be legally challenged or shamed into providing human rights standards within places of detention. Often, this requires an external force to intervene. For example, in 2013, the UN Subcommittee on Prevention of Torture (UNSPT) undertook a visit to New Zealand. Across just ten days, the six members visited 35 places of detention including police stations, courts, prisons, defence force facilities, youth justice residences and immigration detention centres. They also held meetings with government authorities, local organizations and members of civil society. Their subsequent report outlined numerous concerns about conditions and treatment, including: the long (19-hour) lockdowns of young prisoners; the use of collective punishments; 'deplorable', 'tin-can' cell conditions; the use of 'a small cage' for an 'exercise yard'; limited prisoner safety; poor food standards; the lack of prisoner access to sunlight; as well as problems around transparency, oversight and complaints processes. This bleak picture pinpoints how the New Zealand state, and the private provider Serco, fail to treat humans with dignity and care (UNSPT 2014). In a country that has no independent inspectorate and an overloaded Ombudsman's Office, the UNSPT plays a valuable role.

One part of this external scrutiny is that the UNSPT and civil society organizations are able to uncover the 'fantasies of goodness' often propounded by states or their contractors (Aas and Gundhus 2015, p. 13). After all, states increasingly strengthen their 'legitimacy and reputation' through the use of human rights language and through their self-presentation as 'humanitarian' entities (ibid.). External review, to expose the gaps between stated laws or policies and actual practice, is a vital challenge to the lived realities of detention, including to conditions that are 'deeply inhumane' (ibid., p. 14). With the above example, New Zealand, currently on the UN Security Council with a self-defined mandate to achieve 'peace and security for all people', will now have to demonstrate how it will put its own 'big houses' in order.

Of course, the UNSPT has no remit to force change. In the legal realm, there can however be significant 'wins'. For example, Simon (2014) illustrates how mass-imprisonment in California, US, has been directly challenged by court decisions. Judges found that state prisons were so overcrowded that they constituted 'cruel and inhuman' conditions. And, in the face of extreme mental health and medical problems for prisoners, they upheld a 'systemwide population-reduction order, as opposed to relief for particular prisoners with recognized illnesses' (Simon 2014, p. 134). This was a significant response, as it went beyond individual suffering and, instead, provoked deep changes: a drop in the Californian prison population, from 156,000 in 2009 to 120,000 in 2014 (Simon 2014). Simon (2014, p. 137) argues that such decisions represent a new 'dignity cascade' in which 'society recognizes that it has profoundly violated human dignity and in response expands its very understanding of what humanity includes and requires of the law'. It reflects an optimistic shift from the previous limits of legal protection for prisoners in the US.

At certain junctures, legal and administrative actors can therefore intervene in detention practices and create real change (Scott 2013a). The impact of these interventions may be significant at a local level – if nothing else, they remind us that states oppress but they can provide protection (Scott 2013b) – but they can also have international resonance. New international jurisprudence or guidelines can affect populations across the world, as applications in one state create ripple effects across multiple states (Barbaret 2014). Strategies to secure progressive rights-conscious change can inspire widespread hopeful action.

## *The limits of bureaucratic protections*

Nonetheless, we have to be mindful of the protective limits of these bureaucracies. Part of their problem is that they *are* professional bureaucracies – their operations are 'bound up with the power of the powerful' (Moyn 2010, p. 227). To circumnavigate human rights claims, one increasingly needs to be, or have access to, an expert with knowledge of particular laws, regulations, language and mechanisms, as these processes operate along 'alienating, exploitative and disempowering' lines

(Scott 2013a, p. 238). For example, legal processes can be less than helpful – legal language, exclusionary practices, discrimination, cultural silencing, limited legal aid and political interference can all prevent protection (Weber et al. 2014). Further, in many countries, rights laws are viewed as 'charters for villains, career criminals, and terrorists' (Easton 2013, p. 487). Claimants often need courage to bring a case, and have to prepare themselves for reputational attacks.

Many groups can, then, be squeezed out of official mechanisms intended to protect their rights. This is exacerbated when human rights reforms 'fall short of those already low in social status by virtue of their race or color, gender, class, and/or queerness' (Simon 2014, p. 151). For example, while there are a host of international instruments, 'Standard Minimum Rules' and 'Principles' concerning the treatment of prisoners, most 'barely mention women and girl prisoners. If anything, they discuss women's biological needs' (Barbaret 2014, p. 173). In 2010, the UN adopted the (Bangkok) 'Rules for the Treatment of Women Prisoners and Non-Custodial Measures for Women Offenders'. This has helped to recognize the different needs and backgrounds of women, but it remains 'soft law' that can be quickly dismissed (Barbaret 2014). Under these conditions, women are more likely to be disregarded as rights-bearers.

However, these legal and administrative processes are limited in other ways, particularly in their individualized focus. For example, judges concentrate on the facts of particular cases, and their decisions are specifically directed, meaning they have relatively limited application (Scott 2013a, Simon 2014). In this respect, legal rights for detainees are like 'sandbags against . . . the rising tide' (Sparks 2010, p. 522). They offer narrow respite or gains. Indeed, courts have failed to challenge numerous problems, including 'neglect, assaults, inadequate treatments, facilities and inappropriate allocation of resources' as well as deteriorating 'food, exercise, education, work, and cell occupancy levels' (Scott 2013a, p. 246). In turn, states will often rely on past legal decisions 'to preserve the status quo' and 'avoid . . . positive obligations' that might 'enhance the scope of protection' (Gilbert 2011, p. 23). In the same way, while the UNSPT helpfully outlines wide-ranging deficiencies, they remain focused on narrow conceptions of human rights. UN monitoring agencies have had little impact on structural violations – for example, the mass imprisonment of Indigenous or poor populations has not faced substantive challenge. Similarly, when the UNSPT (2014, s. 91) noticed that youth justice residences in New Zealand were becoming increasingly crowded, their concern focused on the 'lack of overall capacity'; the fundamental fact that such residences are developmentally damaging for young people, was not subject to scrutiny. In short, these protective mechanisms hold 'considerable tolerance' for 'profoundly unhealthy, and perhaps even dangerous, living environments' (Scott 2013a, p. 246). The boundaries of detention, who is placed there and its impact on them are not examined. These mechanisms reflect 'the extraordinary powers' of states to 'absorb, co-opt, and neutralize' challenges (Cohen 1988, p. 8).

Another issue relates to how states respond to compliance demands. After all, even the most apparent progressive human rights reforms can be detrimental to detainees. As Malloch (2013, p. 37) identifies, reforms can even 'become part of the problem' as they increase the 'carceral network' or take our attention away from harmful practice. We may feel some ease when correctional departments talk about their focus on 'rehabilitation services', or 'gender responsive approaches' or 'culturally appropriate programmes'. It is enticing to accept them as human-rights conscious changes yet critical examinations remind us that they often lead to expanding prison populations, increasingly repressive conditions as well as social discrimination (Carlton and Segrave 2013, Cohen 1988, Hannah-Moffat 2010, Mihaere 2015). In short, apparently progressive reforms can just maintain or worsen the status quo.

The notion of compliance must also, in current circumstances, be reflected upon in relation to 'risk-management'. Under a risk-averse strategy, detention facility officials view human rights claims as 'organizational risks' that they wish to avoid – publicity about bad treatment of detainees can undermine an institution's reputation but it can also lead to costly legal battles (Whitty 2011, p. 124). In these circumstances, compliance efforts can produce distorted approaches to human rights. For example, consider the 'right to life'. In a bid to prevent prisoner deaths, prisons have introduced various 'initiatives', including: solitary confinement, anti-ligature gowns, CCTV, and the removal of hanging points. The architecture is modified, clothing is changed, communications are decreased and surveillance intensified. The result is that the person does not die, or they may be less likely to die. But, along the way, any semblance of humanity or dignity for individuals suffering in extreme circumstances is removed (Moore and Scraton 2013). It is a stretch to consider this a human-rights approach.

In the same way, institutions engage numerous techniques to avoid condemnation for human rights violations. At an extreme level, we know that stealth techniques in torture (the use of forced standing, electric shocks or psychological tortures) have developed as human rights monitoring has increased (Rejali 2007, Stanley 2009). Criminologists have also tracked how violations increasingly revolve around the psychological control of prisoners (such as the use of isolation) that leave few physical signs but take a heavy psychological toll. Forcible restraints, segregations or punishment cells all have their place in this new human rights aware environment (Crewe 2011). One paradox of human rights talk and monitoring is that state violence emerges in less obvious ways. Further, these new approaches are often legally accepted, making it almost impossible for detainees to stop harms or gain redress.

Similarly, while private companies might feature human rights in their brochures and training manuals, they will inevitably prioritize corporate standing or profit over these values (Aas and Gundhus 2015). This has been readily demonstrated by Serco, a company that runs two prisons in New Zealand. In July 2015, the Department of Corrections resumed control of 'Mt Eden', a Serco prison in Auckland (Department of Corrections 2015). While described as 'exceptional' in the Department's 'prison performance table' (Department of Corrections 2015), reports have emerged of prisoner violence and organized 'fight clubs', a situation that has led to the death of a prisoner. A Labour MP, Kelvin Davis, has asserted that Serco transferred prisoners with serious or grave injuries to public prisons so that the company would retain a high standing on 'performance indicators' for assaults (Davison 2015). By meeting their performance indicators for 'prisoner safety' the company would avoid financial penalties from state authorities.

Clearly, private companies and public institutions can work hard to avoid blame for human rights failings. In the same way, states also circumnavigate monitoring – when they have limited political will for human rights, they can devote limited resources to oversight bodies. For instance, in New Zealand, the UNSPT (2014, s. 12) reported that oversight organizations, like the Human Rights Commission and the Children's Commissioner, only play a tokenistic oversight role as they are 'severely impeded' by inadequate resources.

Overall, legal and administrative mechanisms for human rights protections offer useful but limited scope for change. Part of their problem is that they are 'avowedly state-centric' and work within the boundaries of the definitions, structures and processes established by states as a response to social problems (Weber and Pickering 2011, p. 213). They raise few questions about the current use of imprisonment or the current policing of borders; nor do they offer challenge to the social, cultural or economic conditions that make some populations intensely vulnerable to detention, and that magnify their harms within detention. Instead, this dominant response to human rights problems has been one that has strengthened '*the legitimacy of the state and of a society*' that has been '*highly productive*' of violations in the first place (Mathiesen 2004, p. 68, emphasis in original). The 'orthodox' debates and responses 'keep inside the circle of officially accepted and acceptable disagreements' rather than digging deeper into structures (ibid., p. 104). In this way, legal and official bureaucracies prioritize reform but generally ignore the 'pathologies of power' that underpin violations (Farmer 2003).

## Protection through sociocultural change

To provoke deeper change, we require action on different levels. Here, two strategies are outlined: (1) contesting the state-led discourse on human rights; (2) nurturing cultures of solidarity. Human rights cannot remain static principles and, whilst short-term reforms are useful, we must always be attentive to the long-termer utopian prospects of peaceful action and social justice.

### *Contesting the limited version of human rights*

The most limited observation of detainees tells us that there are identifiable 'drivers' of detention. Detained populations are generally those who have endured disadvantage and discrimination: Indigenous people, minority populations, the poor, those who are badly educated, those in poor physical and mental health, those who have been unemployed or underemployed, or those who have faced violence, trauma and harm (Scraton and McCulloch 2009, Scott 2008, Stanley 2011). Prisons and immigration detention facilities are dramatic indictors of the erosion of social, economic or cultural rights for vast numbers of people.

It is also worth registering that our overuse of detention shifts attention away from these wider violations. In our criminalizing focus on the 'actions or inactions of relatively powerless individuals' we obscure the institutional, societal and structural conditions that paved their 'pathway' to detention (Slapper and Tombs 1999, p. 145); we avoid examination of routine negligence, institutionalized harms and discrimination. In our acceptance of detention, we simultaneously accept and normalize social, economic or cultural disadvantages.

Given this, it is important to consider how a critical engagement with a 'full' human rights remit might be undertaken to challenge detention practices as well as wider social injustices. Central to this endeavour is the contestation of the falsely imposed disconnection between 'civil and political rights' and 'economic, social and cultural rights'. The mainstream human rights approach concentrates almost exclusively upon the former while ignoring latter violations associated with the 'normal' inequitable workings of the market-led state system (Herman 2002, Moyn 2010, Weber and Pickering 2011).

This distorted approach obscures the reality that such rights are intertwined. As just one example, a person's secure economic status has dramatic implications on their ability to secure effective legal representation to avoid detention; however, their status can also mean that others view them as less suitable for detention in the first place (Smart 1989). Many civil or political rights – the right to life, right to liberty and security, right to liberty of movement, right to equal treatment in the courts or right to freedom of expression – are also made more secure when a person holds a positive economic, social or cultural standing. It is imperative, then, that these human rights disconnections are more clearly articulated and acted upon.

### *Nurturing cultures of solidarity*

Another crucial element to human rights protection relates to the removal of distance, and the development of empathy and solidarity between populations. After all, at their core, human rights emerge through relationships, participation and interaction (Genders and Player 2014); collective trust and 'mutual dependence' are vital to their protection (Scott 2013b). At a basic level, as UN guidelines and conventions envision, a human rights approach prioritizes the dignity of human beings. Within detention facilities, this requires institutional action to ensure that detainees have access to everything they need to flourish (such as education or employment, healthcare, counselling, access to family or social life, and leisure opportunities). No doubt, implementing such provisions requires a degree of state imagination yet international guidelines provide a significant 'springboard' from which rights practices can be launched.

The development of dignity is also dependent on a staff culture that is supportive, kind and that operates on the basis of equal standing. In this respect, it is important to recognize that, even in the most difficult of circumstances, workers may undertake 'small humanitarian gestures' to alleviate suffering (Aas and Gundhus 2015, p. 6). Further, states regularly have to work very hard to maintain staff compliance to violatory regimes. For example, in June 2015, the Australian government introduced the 'Border Force Act' which, among other things, allows the imprisonment of 'entrusted persons' who speak out about events within immigration detention centres. As over 40 workers from Nauru and Manus Island reported in their open letter:

> standing by and watching sub-standard and harmful care, child abuse and gross violations of human rights is not ethically justifiable. If we witness child abuse in Australia we are legally obliged to report it to child protection authorities. If we witness child abuse in detention centres, we can go to prison [for up to two years] for attempting to advocate for them effectively.
>
> *(The Guardian 2015)*

In releasing this letter, they challenged the state to prosecute them 'so that the issues may be discussed in open courts and in the full view of the Australian public' (ibid.). While the Australian state has attempted to force workers to comply with state violence, these workers have demonstrated the power of solidarity with humans in the most degrading circumstances.

Social empathy develops further when bystanders have access to the stories of those victimized by the state – this is precisely why human rights organizations often focus on individual case studies to build a connection between 'us' and 'them' (Cohen 2001). Visual images are also important to develop 'humanitarian anxiety' (Simon 2014, p. 150). In the successful legal challenge to mass imprisonment in California, lawyers included photographs of the horrific 'dry cages' used to hold prisoners. Revolted at the image, 'powerful legal elites' became increasingly motivated to act 'in the name of decency', and avoid further litigation (ibid.). As Simon continues, 'the circuit between image, revulsion, anxiety, and moral resolve' can be 'self-sustaining for a time' (ibid.).

To achieve longer-term shifts, there has to be fundamental cultural changes in how governments, institutions and communities respond to harms or insecurities. There is a need, then, to promote enduring cultures that reduce social distance. This can seem a daunting task. However, recent work by Pratt and Eriksson (2013) has exposed how human rights values can be built upon accessible democratic values. In their analysis of how Scandinavian countries approach imprisonment, they show how social norms of community, inclusion, egalitarianism, education and human security have led to a dominant perspective that all people have equal eligibility to human rights. They note how the adherence to professional expertise and evidence has also underpinned a rehabilitative approach to punishment. In these countries, the state role is directed to protect people and 'to develop social policies that would reduce the criminogenic features of the criminal's environment' (ibid., p. 131). This includes the provision of a democratic welfare system but it also facilitates the more limited use of detention as a response to harms.

## The value of human rights

The above discussions demonstrate the deeply precariousness nature of human rights protection. Despite the growth of laws and regulations, states and their institutional representatives have become increasingly adept at managing the risks of human rights compliance while ensuring that structural and socio cultural inequalities remain in place. This does not mean, however, that the vision of human rights should be disbanded; rather, it requires active reinvigoration through bureaucratic and sociocultural means. After all, human rights thinking allows us to recognize vital values for peaceful and socially just lives. A sense of shared humanity, dignity, respect, care, engagement and compassion are all prioritized through human rights. Moreover, pursuing a human rights path inevitably requires renewed determination to develop humane responses to the social problems of 'crimes', harms and mass inequalities. New solutions that emphasize engagement, redress and care would reduce the scope and nature of detention. The protective gains would be substantial; they are worth fighting for.

## Notes

1 Including the Standard Minimum Rules for the Treatment of Prisoners 1955/1977 (currently being updated); International Covenant on Civil and Political Rights 1966; Convention against Torture and Other Cruel, Inhuman or Degrading Treatment or Punishment 1984; Body of Principles for the Protection of All Persons Under Any Form of Detention or Imprisonment 1988; Rules for the Protection of Juveniles Deprived of Their Liberty 1990; and the Basic Principles for the Treatment of Prisoners 1990. These link to other laws and declarations that address detention issues in relation to specific groups such as children, women, refugees as well as Indigenous populations.

2 Such as the European Convention on Human Rights 1950, the European Prison Rules 1973 and the European Court of Human Rights.

## References


Aas, K. and Gundhus, H., 2015. Policing humanitarian borderlands. *British Journal of Criminology*, 55, 1–18.

Barbaret, R., 2014. *Women, crime and criminal justice.* London: Routledge.

Bauman, Z., 1989. *Modernity and the Holocaust.* Cambridge: Polity Press.

Bauman, Z., 1995. The strangers of consumer era. *Tijdschrift voor Criminologie*, 3(3), 210–18.

Brown, D., 2008. Giving voice: the prisoner and discursive citizenship. *In*: T. Anthony and C. Cunneen (eds), *The critical criminology companion.* Sydney: Hawkins Press, 228–39.

Cameron, D., 2014. Speech to Conservative Party Conference. 1 October 2014. Retrieved on 12 April 2016 from: http://press.conservatives.com/post/98882674910/david-cameron-speech-to-conservative-party.

Carlton, B. and Segrave, M., 2013 (eds), *Women exiting prison.* London: Routledge.

Cohen, S., 1988. *Against criminology.* London: Transaction Publishers.

Cohen, S., 2001. *States of denial.* Cambridge: Polity.

Crewe, B., 2011. Depth, weight, tightness: revisiting the pains of imprisonment. *Punishment and Society*, 13(5), 509–29.

Davis, M., 2001. The flames of New York. *New Left Review*, 12, Nov–Dec, 34–50.

Davison, I., 2015. MP: 'ill' prisoner died after 'dropping'. *New Zealand Herald*, 21 July. Retrieved on 12 April 2016 from: http://m.nzherald.co.nz/nz/news/article.cfm?c_id=1&objectid=11484604.

Department of Corrections, 2015. *Prison Performance Table for 12 Months to March 2015.* Retrieved on 12 April 2016 from: www.corrections.govt.nz/__data/assets/pdf_file/0003/793263/PPT_Q3_2014_15.pdf.

Drake, D., 2012. *Prisons, punishment and the pursuit of security.* Basingstoke: Palgrave Macmillan.

Drake, D. and Henley, A., 2014. 'Victims' versus 'offenders' in British political discourse. *The Howard Journal of Criminal Justice*, 53(2), 141–57.

Easton, S., 2013. Protecting prisoners. *The Prison Journal*, 93(4), 475–92.

Farmer, P., 2003. *Pathologies of power.* Berkeley, CA: University of California Press.

Genders, E. and Player, E., 2014. Rehabilitation, risk management and prisoners' rights. *Criminology and Criminal Justice*, 14(4), 434–57.

Gilbert, G., 2011. Law and human rights rather than international human rights law. *In*: G. Gilbert, F. Hampson and C. Sandoval (eds), *Strategic visions for human rights*. Abingdon: Routledge, 19–33.

Giroux, H., 2004. *The terror of neoliberalism*. Boulder, CO: Paradigm Publishers.

Green, P. and Ward, T., 2004. *State crime*. London: Pluto Press.

*The Guardian*, 2015. Open letter on the Border Force Act. 1 July. Retrieved on 12 April 2016 from: www.theguardian.com/australia-news/2015/jul/01/open-letter-on-the-border-force-act-we-challengethe-department-to-prosecute.

Hannah-Moffat, K., 2010. Sacrosanct or flawed. *Current Issues in Criminal Justice*, 22(2), 193–216.

Herman, E., 2002. Foreword. *In*: D. Chandler (ed.), *From Kosovo to Kabul: human rights and international intervention*. London: Pluto Press, vii–xv.

Humphrey, M., 2002. *The politics of atrocity and reconciliation*. London: Routledge.

International Organization for Migration, 2015. *IOM Continues to Monitor Mediterranean Migrant Arrivals and Deaths*. Missing Migrants Project, 24 August. Retrieved on 12 April 2016 from: http://missingmigrants.iom.int/.

Malloch, M., 2013. Crime, critique and utopian alternatives. *In*: M. Malloch and B. Munro (eds), *Crime, critique and utopia*. Basingstoke: Palgrave Macmillan, 21–43.

Malloch, M. and Stanley, E., 2005. The detention of asylum seekers in the UK. *Punishment and Society*, 7(1), 53–71.

Mathiesen, T., 2004. *Silently silenced: essays on the creation of acquiescence in modern society*. Winchester: Waterside Press.

McCulloch, J., 2005. (In)security in the age of globalisation. *Just Policy*, 37, 18–23.

McNulty, D., Watson, N. and Philo, G., 2014. Human rights and prisoners' rights. *The Howard Journal of Criminal Justice*, 53(4), 360–76.

Mihaere, R., 2015. *A Kaupapa Māori analysis of the use of Māori cultural identity in the prison system*. Unpublished thesis (PhD). Wellington: VUW.

Moore, L. and Scraton, P., 2013. *The incarceration of women*. Basingstoke: Palgrave Macmillan.

Moyn, S., 2010. *The last utopia*. Cambridge, MA: Belknap/Harvard University Press.

Pratt, J. and Eriksson, A., 2013. *Contrasts in punishment*. London: Routledge.

Rejali, D., 2007. *Torture and democracy*. Princeton, NJ: Princeton University Press.

Reus-Smit, C., 2001. Human rights and the social construction of sovereignty. *Review of International Studies*, 27, 519–38.

Scott, D., 2008. Thinking about detention. *Criminal Justice Matters*, 71, 11–13.

Scott, D., 2013a. The politics of prisoner legal rights. *The Howard Journal of Criminal Justice*, 52(3), 233–50.

Scott, D., 2013b. Visualising an abolitionist real utopia. *In*: M. Malloch and B. Munro (eds), *Crime, critique and utopia*. Basingstoke: Palgrave Macmillan, 90–113.

Scraton, P. and McCulloch, J. (eds), 2009. *The violence of incarceration*. London: Routledge.

Simon, J., 2014. *Mass incarceration on trial*. NY/London: The New Press.

Slapper, G. and Tombs, S., 1999. *Corporate crime*. Harlow: Pearson/Longman.

Smart, C., 1989. *Feminism and the power of the law*. London: Routledge.

Sparks, R., 2010. Review of principles of European prison law and policy. *Edinburgh Law Review*, 14, 520–22.

Stanley, E., 2009. *Torture, truth and justice*. London: Routledge.

Stanley, E., 2011. *Human rights and prisons*. Wellington: Human Rights Commission.

UN Subcommittee on the Prevention of Torture [UNSPT], 2014. *Report on the visit of the Subcommittee on Prevention of Torture and Other Cruel, Inhuman or Degrading Treatment or Punishment to New Zealand*. 25 August, CAT/OP/NZL/1.

Weber, L. and Pickering, S., 2011. *Globalization and borders*. Basingstoke: Palgrave.

Weber, L., Fishwick, E. and Marmo, M., 2014. *Crime, justice and human rights*. Basingstoke: Palgrave.

Weber, M., 1970. *From Max Weber* (translated and edited by H.J.H. Gerth and C.W. Mills). London: Routledge.

Whitty, N., 2011. Human rights as risk. *Punishment and Society*, 13(2), 123–48.

# 48

# Supervising offenders in the community

## Vision, values and human rights

*Loraine Gelsthorpe and Madeline-Sophie Abbas*

## Introduction

It seems rather odd to be writing a chapter about human rights and community penalties at a point where the British Government is contemplating scrapping the *Human Rights Act 1998* (hereafter the HRA),[1] and when the delivery of community penalties has itself been subject to major overhaul to a point where elements of the community supervision of offenders in England and Wales are hardly recognizable (Robinson et al. 2015). This said, it is perhaps both fitting and timely to revisit some of the relevant issues precisely because of the British government's intentions. Indeed, worldwide, there has been a renaissance of interest in both 'helping relationships' in the community and in making supervision in the community from probation officers, parole officers and others (bearing in mind different titles for supervisors of offenders in the community in different contexts) more effective. Such renewed interest, with concomitant practical developments, raises important questions about human rights. Certainly, such developments need to be placed in a context of attempts to legitimize community penalties as 'real sentences' as well as the fact that in times of austerity budgeting they cost less than imprisonment. Focusing on developments in England and Wales, by way of illustration, it is clear that moves towards the privatization of community penalties highlight questions as to whether professional values (including commitment to human rights) can help guard against the worst effects of fragmentation and inconsistency in service delivery as more organizations enter the offender management market. Fiscal austerity in the post-2007 period in England and Wales has supported a qualitatively different era in which the predominance of marketized logic has reformulated contemporary organizations, both within government and the third sector. The opening up of the provision of community-based supervision and rehabilitative services to diverse providers within private and voluntary sectors and the development of 'payment by results' in reducing reoffending re-casts the role and values of probation and community supervision (Fox and Albertson 2011, Burke and Collett 2015). Indeed, it is suggested that shifting community supervision into the matrix of market expansion and capital accumulation severs the lineaments of a moral economy based on justice, truth and fairness (Whitehead and Crawshaw 2013). Whilst the Probation Service in the United Kingdom (UK) has traditionally symbolized humanitarian values based around social work (Gelsthorpe 2007, p. 485), the rise of the third and private sectors as providers competes as proponents of 'care' for offenders. The creeping marketization of criminal justice thus nudges concerns about values and human rights to the periphery in the treatment of offenders within a context of fiscal realignments and 'punitive and bureaucratic expansion' which have arguably contributed to the undermining of a moral economy within criminal justice.

Again, drawing on developments in England and Wales to illustrate some of the debates, beyond this, we need to consider the 2015 Conservative Party Manifesto (Conservative Party Manifesto 2015) which outlines moves to 'scrap' the HRA and introduce a British Bill of Rights instead. The effect of this would be to formally break links between British courts and the European Court of Human Rights. Such proposals are located within an increasingly stringent 'culture of control' (Garland 2001) that encompasses the complete removal of any notion that prisoners ought to be able to vote, widespread random drug testing in prisons, the use of new body scanners, and greater use of mobile 'phone blocking technology' (Conservative Party Manifesto 2015, pp. 59–60). Importantly, it is envisaged in the Manifesto that such technologies are to be used to 'monitor offenders in the community' for example extending the existing use of technology in regard to tracking and monitoring offenders via electronic ankle bracelets and similar, as a way of ensuring that curfew hours are kept (Nellis et al. 2013).

In the first part of the chapter we consider changing values and sensibilities in the supervision of offenders in the community and the normative values which might inform practice. In the second part of the chapter we consider some of the more recent developments and challenges in regard to competing and contextual factors in relation to modern community penalties practice and the prospect of a discourse imbued with human rights.

## Changes in penal practices, values and sensibilities

Penal practices, values and sensibilities have undergone enormous transformation since the early 1990s and it follows that we should ask some searching questions about the moral dimensions of what probation officers now do in their everyday practice with offenders and victims, and more particularly what they are guided to do by national directives. In contrast to the prison service, which has been frequently challenged to display its humanitarian and civilized values (Liebling and Arnold 2004), the Probation Service itself has perhaps symbolized a particular humanitarian value base revolving around social work. As Nellis (2007) describes, from its inception the Probation Service has epitomized 'care' for offenders in the community. The popular story is that the Probation Service's roots lay in the activities of police court missionaries who would offer 'five bob' and a bible to miscreants identified by the court. Nellis (2007) offers a revisionist history to show that whilst politicians, policy-makers, practitioners and academic commentators alike recognized the importance of the introduction of probation in 1907, the aim was to both 'toughen up' established mechanisms to impose recognizances on offenders (convicted and unconvicted offenders alike if the courts so chose) by creating a condition that they be supervised by a person named in a probation order, and at the same time, emphasize the non-punitive nature of the order through the notion that such a person might serve to 'advise, assist, and befriend' the offender.

But if the history of probation is more complicated than has been presupposed, it is fair to say that the value base for probation is arguably even less clear now than it was then, over a hundred years ago. The notion that supervising probation officers might serve to 'advise, assist and befriend' offenders no longer has currency at all. The *broad* social values relating to the 'humanization' of the individual offender and his or her treatment, to which the Probation Service laid claim from its inception in 1907 right through to the *Criminal Justice Act 1991*, seem to have disappeared. The new strapline in relation to community penalties revolves around 'enforcement, rehabilitation, and public protection'. These three themes do not easily meld into a single value position in relation to offenders – the key clientele of the probation service.[2]

Combined with a managerial thrust which refers not to 'values' but to 'commitments' and 'responsibilities' and emphasized that the purpose of probation was broadly to be of 'service to the courts and the public by supervising offenders in the community, helping offenders to lead law-abiding lives' (Home Office 1992), the new discourse for the supervision of offenders in the community has been distinctly managerial. The credos of efficiency and punishment have been seen to displace any social work 'caring' or 'humanity' credo which prioritizes liberal and humanitarian values in relation to offenders (Rutherford 1993). The managerialist movement, as such, has arguably been inextricably bound up in the reconstruction of public services in the UK from the 1980s onwards (Clarke et al. 2000), which has itself involved the development of processes designed to scrutinize, evaluate and regulate the performance of agencies and organizations involved in service provision.

It is partly as a result of this managerialist movement that there have been a number of attempts to address the changing values that inform probation practice. The 'values' of probation were identified by the National Probation Service in 2001 (NPS 2001) as: valuing probation staff and partnership colleagues; victim awareness and empathy; paramountcy of public protection; law enforcement; rehabilitation of offenders; empiricism, continuous improvement; openness and transparency; responding and learning to work positively with difference; problem solving; partnership; better quality services. But they read more like an operational methodology and promote an eclectic mix of moral commitments (victim awareness, rehabilitation of offenders), scientific aspirations (empiricism) and organizational imperatives (partnership, continuous improvement) (Hoy 2005–6, Nellis and Gelsthorpe 2003).

Anti-custodialism (Senior 1989), community safety (Nellis 1995), community justice (Harding 2000), restorative justice (Nellis 1995, 2001), relational justice/reintegrative shaming (Spencer 1995), and humanity and mercy (Glover 1999, Lacey 2002) all feature in the quest for a new value base. But none are straightforward, carry widespread favour, or foster 'legitimacy' (Christie 1993, Gelsthorpe 2007, Hilder 2007, Gelsthorpe and McIvor 2007, Canton 2011). Diversity and anti-discrimination have also been considered as a potential value base, but there is little to suggest positive change on the ground (Hilder 2007, Gelsthorpe and McIvor 2007, Canton 2011).

The 'what works' movement might also be considered as a key element of a new credo, given a resurgence of interest in 'helping relationships' and in making community penalties more effective (Canton 2011, Craig et al. 2013) although one of the limitations here is that unless there are explicit statements about the intended purposes or outcomes of probation practice, questions about 'what works' are arguably problematic, if not meaningless (Robinson and McNeill 2004, Burke and Collett 2015). This said, the supervision of offenders in the community today is shaped by an understanding of the importance of relational aspects of supervision in encouraging desistance (McNeill and Weaver 2010), and concerns about risk assessment and public protection (Kemshall and Hilder 2013), and evidence about the effectiveness of interventions drawing on the risk/needs/responsivity model (Bonta and Andrews 2010). These concerns can be seen as complementary and new insights from research add empirical weight to the moral and practical argument that the supervision of offenders in the community requires an atmosphere and occupational culture in which people are valued and supported (Robinson et al. 2013) – there are clear links with human rights perspectives in this which we address later.

It has been suggested by some critics that traditional values of probation came under attack because of their 'seeming inability' to respond to a changing conceptualization of the criminal justice system and the associated policy agenda (Raynor and Vanstone 2007).

The emerging vision for the supervision of offenders in the community has revolved around an eclectic mix of the managerial and the moral, with a strong tilt towards enforcement, and with some resilience regarding traditional values of 'caring', but it is worth asking what values *should* guide probation practice and where do more recent developments take us in terms of a value base for the supervision of offenders in the community? Moreover, what prospect is there for a new human rights discourse which, in some ways, might be seen as emblematic of 'care'?

## The Coalition government: transforming rehabilitation in an age of austerity

When the coalition government came to power in the UK in May 2010 it announced a rehabilitation revolution – thought to be necessary given reoffending rates, the size of the prison population and an over-reliance on centrally set targets at the expense of outcome orientated innovation (Ministry of Justice 2010). Proposals for the future were also set in the context of economic austerity and the need for the Ministry of Justice to make financial cuts. The government argued that competition, moving to a mixed provider market and a system of payment by results would help secure the desired change. This was not a new idea of course, the electronic monitoring of offenders supervised in the community under curfew orders, having being privatized from the outset (Nellis and Gelsthorpe 2003).

The 'competition strategy' included a split between work that would remain the business of public sector and work that would be opened up to competition. In the event, local Probation Trusts were replaced by a new National Probation Service (NPS) responsible for the public sector duties and by private or voluntary sector organizations (called Community Rehabilitation Companies [CRCs]) commissioned by the National Offender Management Service to work in 21 'contract package areas'. The Transforming Rehabilitation (TR) proposals maintained the commitment to 'payment by results' as the means of ensuring that services successfully reduced reoffending. The proposals also extended statutory post-release supervision to short sentence prisoners (those serving less than 12 months in custody) (Burke and Collett 2015). The successful bidders for the CRCs (Ministry of Justice 2014) were, with one exception,[3] consortia led by private sector companies working with voluntary agencies, and included a few agencies formed by staff from probation trusts. Notwithstanding the unpopularity of the changes, and a seeming lack of logic, given that some aspects of the TR proposals do not follow inevitably from the decision to move work to the private sector the reforms went ahead. For example, extending post-release supervision to short sentence prisoners is a task that could have been allocated to a public sector probation service. Similarly, payment by results mechanisms could have been introduced into the funding arrangements for Probation Trusts; there are a number of different financial models that aim to reward outcomes judged successful and they can operate in public, voluntary and private sectors (Fox and Albertson 2011). Moreover, the government's funding proposals have been criticized from a number of angles. An independent analysis of the initial payment by results mechanism concluded that it was likely to reward providers who allowed a small increase in reoffending and would discourage them from investing in rehabilitation (Mulheirn 2013). Those familiar with the practice challenges of working with offenders questioned whether success can sensibly be measured by looking for the presence or absence of a further offence in a short follow-up period. They also argued that a simple binary measure of offending fails to take account of the diversity of people on the probation caseload (Gelsthorpe and Hedderman 2012).

In sum, recent developments suggest that those responsible for the supervision of offenders in the community are working in a much changed world where a preoccupation with risk, managerialism, competition, market forces and so on might overshadow any residual attempts to hold on to 'traditional probation values'. Writing just before the TR agenda was fully put into effect, Mawby and Worrall (2013) suggested that probation workers find creative ways of resisting narratives of decline and maintain a positive work identity in the present. But the dismantling of probation as a strong occupational culture, staffed by highly intelligent, skilled and deeply motivated people and parcelling it out to the lowest bidders may end up being counter-productive, notwithstanding efforts to keep values and ethics in mind (Probation Institute 2014). Can a human rights discourse bring further solution?

## Some general issues regarding human rights and criminal justice

There is certainly evidence of a wish to champion human rights. Indeed, the late twentieth century has been described as the 'age of rights' (Bobbio 1995). A number of factors have conspired to put the concept of rights high on the social and political agenda. These range from human rights as an offspring of the post-war expansion of international conventions, human rights as part of the development of regional systems of protection, the emergence of human rights as a platform from which to resist some of the worst features of capitalist globalization, and human rights as new ideals of equality and justice (Freeman 2002, Turner 2006) and dignity (Carozza 2013) (see Tomuschat 2014 and particularly Weber et al. 2014 for an overview of different perspectives). To these perspectives we might add the notion of human rights as a solution to the problems of a fragmentary society. As Klug (2002) has put it, human rights might be seen as providing 'values for a godless age'.

Human rights may also be presented as resistance to the oppressive culture of control which Garland (2001), amongst others, has described. Thus there is an idea of 'human rights' as a new criminal justice discourse. Suffice to say that whether or not human rights law can help us reconstruct a normative theory of crime control and justice is an extremely difficult question. There is the hard question as to whether the HRA is necessarily limited to a constraining influence rather than serving as a normative one (Cheney et al. 1999, c.f. Hudson 2001).

The European Convention does not specifically include a right to proportionate punishment. Nevertheless, there is a principle of proportionality contained in the Convention and similar ordinances. It is suggested that other rights, such as the right to respect for private and family life, should be considered when imposing and carrying out measures for the sake of prevention of further crimes. Whether considered as part of the principle of proportionality, as freedom from degrading punishment, or as rights in their own regard, respect for private and family life and religious freedom should arguably restrict the intrusiveness of community-based supervision and programmes. Curfews, electronic tagging, attendance at treatment centres, should be planned carefully to interfere as little as possible with family and intimate life, just as they should be planned so as not to restrict the right of religious observance.

One concern about offenders being supervised in the community revolves around risk. A rights-balance approach suggests that what needs to be achieved is *risk management*, rather than *risk elimination* (Clear and Cadora 2001).[4] Risk management is the strategy of trying to reduce risks by better assessments, better programming, better decision-making; risk elimination attempts to remove any possibility of the risked event occurring by removing the possibility of carrying out the action from the potential offender. Risk-management tries to minimize bad events from occurring but nevertheless accepts that risky events cannot be eliminated altogether without unacceptable levels of restriction of liberty and other rights. Indeterminate sentences which disregard proportionality and community programmes where the deleterious effects on offenders' rights are disproportionate to the salutary effects on crime prevention and offender rehabilitation are examples of risk control policies which approach the model of risk elimination. Achievement of a rights-balance rather than the zero-sum approach to rights is most likely if those responsible for the supervision of offenders in the community, and more particularly the NPS which has responsibility for preparing pre-sentence reports and risk assessment, keeps in mind the principles of proportionality, least intrusion and least restriction, so that gains in public protection will not be at the expense of offenders' human rights.

## A human rights discourse in probation?

So what might be the best way forward? Some commentators have suggested that a human rights discourse and the idea of a 'human rights culture' is a way of invigorating the early anti-discriminatory discourses, facilitating a respect for difference (at the heart of diversity), avoiding the worst excesses of managerialism (understood as an expression of state power and the application of market forces) and a way of holding on to 'respect' for offenders as people. Moreover, a 'language of human rights' is shared across the criminal justice system, which the earlier probation 'social work' discourse was not. John Scott (2002), the Chief Officer of Probation most involved in charting the implications of the HRA for the Probation Service, expressed early enthusiasm for the transformative potential of the legislation. Building on foundational work on civil liberties and ways in which they should inform probation practice, Scott (2002) suggested that a human rights discourse can give impetus and legitimacy to existing forms of good practice. Community involvement, the recognition that offenders are citizens, and partnerships with statutory and voluntary agencies as a bridge to helping offenders, can all be seen as ways of taking the human rights agenda forward.

The HRA came into full effect across the UK in October 2000, bringing the *European Convention on Human Rights* into British law. The substance of the Convention can be found within its first 18 Articles and additional protocols. As Cheney et al. (1999) describe, the rights and freedoms the states each undertake to secure include the right: without discrimination, to life, liberty and security of the person; not to be subjected to torture, or to inhumane or degrading treatment or punishment; to a fair trial and the presumption of innocence; to respect for private life, home and correspondence; to freedom of expression, freedom of thought, conscience and religion; to freedom of assembly and association, and to the peaceful enjoyment of personal possessions. The HRA places an obligation on public bodies to ensure they respect human rights in everything they do (section 6 duty). This obligation is intended to make litigation through the courts a last resort. This duty also provides individuals with an important framework for holding public bodies to account when things go wrong and helps services to do their job better. In this way the Act was intended to develop a culture of respect for human rights within the public services, making litigation in the courts a last resort. Through this section 6 duty the HRA can influence the way public services are developed and delivered, ensuring that people are treated with dignity and respect. How far private providers (CRCs) can be held to account in this way has still to be tested; they are commissioned by public bodies, but also function as private companies.

Article 3 of the European Convention, which guarantees protection against inhuman or degrading punishment is of particular interest. One can imagine that, if those undertaking unpaid work in the community as part of a Community Order under the *Criminal Justice Act*

*2003*, were required to wear leg-irons and humiliating clothing, this might be judged a breach of Article 3. The Prison Reform Trust (1997) and other bodies have taken a close interest in electronic monitoring and have collected relevant case studies – for example, the man who cut off his tag and threw it into a pond because he claimed that it made him feel like a dog, or the man wearing a tag who was assaulted by youths because they believed he was a sex offender. At the same time, there have been concerns that as a consequence of electronic monitoring of offenders there may be a breach of Article 8 which guarantees respect for private and family life. If an offender's life is disrupted to a sufficient degree and the family breaks down as a result, it is arguable that the punishment and control mechanism of electronic monitoring would breach Article 8. But the issues are complicated, not least by the fact that 'tagging' has been welcomed by some offenders, and particularly when it facilitates early release from prison for example (Mortimer and May 1997). The human rights implications of GPS technology, increasingly popular to enforce community penalties, and which can be used for anytime and everywhere tracking and/or the monitoring of exclusion zone perimeters, and combined with traditional curfew technologies, have perhaps been underexplored thus far (but see, for example, http://technologyandhumanrights.org).[5]

## Towards a conclusion: developing a rights culture?

Developing a 'rights culture' rather than 'rights fire-watching' is arguably consistent with probation values, and is contained in some of the best rationales and descriptions of 'what works' programmes and of restorative justice projects. Both approaches stress that the offender is a person, not just the personification of a criminal act; both approaches stress the importance of treating offenders *and* victims with respect. Achieving a 'rights balance' is the goal of restorative justice, and it is also the goal of rehabilitative programmes which aim to enhance offenders' capacity to enjoy the rights and privileges of citizenship and at the same to behave responsibly towards their communities. Adoption of a positive rights agenda and of the rights balance approach – the key elements of developing a rights culture – would arguably help to protect the best of contemporary supervision practice from the managerialist impulse and culture of control.

Thus in conclusion, ideally, criminal justice systems should balance the aspirations to deal justly with offenders, to contribute to crime reduction and public safety, and to provide redress and reassurance for victims. Although real, existing criminal justice systems must serve these different objectives and values, the balance between them changes from time to time. These criminal justice orientations have been described as *crime control* and *due process* models (Packer 1969), and although their objectives are necessarily combined in actual penal policy and practice, looking at them as conceptually separate models highlights the fact that there are tensions between the two sets of goals and values. In the UK and other western jurisdictions, we can observe pendulum swings between the two models.

Whatever the strengths and limitations of the HRA and convention/legislative approaches to rights in general, the idea of human rights is held to be a way of keeping the two criminal justice models – crime control and due process – in balance (Ashworth 1995). Human rights means that criminal justice must pay attention to the rights of victims not to be re-victimized and the rights of the general public to live their lives in security and freedom from fear, but it also must care about the rights of offenders to have their liberty restricted only to the degree that is strictly and demonstrably necessary to prevent harms to others. Furthermore, restriction of liberty, however necessary, should not involve lack of care for offenders' rights to family life, freedom of religious observance, freedom from degrading treatment, and participation in civil/political rights. One way of achieving this is to develop a criminal justice ethic in which crime control goals are pursued within due process restraints (Braithwaite and Pettit 1990). Whether seeing a rights culture in these terms, drawing on existing criminal justice models, or whether seen in terms of new concepts and models, adopting human rights as the value base for criminal justice means developing a rights culture, and, moreover, a rights-balance value commitment.

Turning to probation practice again, in practical terms, human rights protection should be built in to supervision practice at every level. New polices and practices should be subjected to a rights audit whenever and wherever they are introduced. This does not mean a bland, generalized statement of compliance; it means going through each innovation one by one, looking at whose rights might be augmented or curtailed, assessing which rights are strengthened or threatened, and to what degree (Hudson 2001).

A body of UK judgements is beginning to emerge with regard to the protection of offenders' rights in the HRA era, although these judgements give rather mixed messages about the impact of the HRA on the administration of punishment.[6] Those now responsible for the supervision of offenders in the community (including new providers) could view human rights as a basic value for the management of offenders in the twenty-first century. As intimated earlier, a human rights approach incorporates values of equality, respect for diversity, concern for community, victims and offenders (Canton 2011, 2012). Prioritizing rights entails managing risk, because it involves the duty of seeing that all are enabled to live their lives freely and securely. Risk control – over-emphasizing risk, dividing people into the risked and the risky – would leave the criminal justice system mired in the zero-sum approach. Although it might seem obvious that victims' and the public's rights to safety are more important than offenders' rights to as much liberty as possible and to respectful treatment, it would be a mistake to think that the former are everything and the latter are but nothing. If both sets of views and needs are 'rights', then they are the same category of thing, and must be held in careful balance, rather than the one being everything and the other nothing (Dworkin 1986).

It would be a mistake to pin *all* hopes and desires for a new system of values on human rights; whilst a rights culture provides a basis for supervision activities, it does not itself provide the 'transparent statement of values' that might inspire practitioners. We have also to question whether the credibility of human rights depends on a prior sensibility which expresses why and how they matter, or whether the legislation itself creates and sustains the sensibility. Important as it is, an abstract commitment to rights is perhaps not enough to kindle and sustain respect, decency, and a moral agenda within probation practice. Ignatieff suggests that we view the human rights discourse as something on the 'outermost arc of our obligations, but which are only as strong as our innermost commitments' in essence (Ignatieff 2000, p. 41).

In this sense a culture of human rights might serve as much more than 'a dry enumeration of entitlements in constitutional codes . . . and as more than a set of instruments that individuals use to defend themselves', as Ignatieff once put it (2000, p. 125). But it will not pay to be confident that the notion of a culture of human rights *alone* will be able to provide ethical salvation for the new Probation Service and Community Rehabilitation Companies; rather it can serve as a resource for sustaining ethical ideal and moral sensibilities. A 'rights-culture' need not be the simple 'back-stop' that many have assumed it to be: it can also be a galvanizer of good practice. At the same time there is arguably need for another kind of 'viable post-managerialist vision' too, as McLaughlin (2001) has suggested, so that the dangers of managerialism in everyday supervision practice can be attended to. A culture of human rights should arguably be accepted *sine qua non*, with the HRA welcomed as a legal lowest common denominator, but there needs to be professional practice and commitment which embodies more than the 'mechanistic' adherence to policy. Nellis and Gelsthorpe (2003) have framed this in terms of practitioners needing to be equipped to draw on 'overarching knowledge'; to know *when* and *how* to exercise intelligent discretion is better than hidden discretion and discretion as resistance to the excesses of managerialism for example.

In terms of the *aims* of work with offenders in the community, the notion of 'responsibility' captures much of the intention of rehabilitating and reintegrating offenders; there appears to be shared sense of purpose which revolves around encouraging the 'responsible offender' (working alongside offenders to identify their problems, promoting self-diagnosis, encouraging voluntary mentoring support, and so on). Indeed, one might view the central aims and values of supervision as being to engage in problem-solving so as to *facilitate compliance*. A respectful professional relationship is indispensible to this. In this sense, a culture of human rights can provide an important basis for probation practice, but probation values need also to be conceptualized and articulated as forward looking normative statements to help those working within different agencies to address contemporary penal challenges. The creation of a human rights culture is thus a necessary but not a sufficient condition in this context.

Finally, at the beginning of this chapter, we indicated that it seems rather odd to be writing about human rights at a time when the British government is intent on replacing the HRA with a bill of rights instead. There is claim that there is no intention to dilute the central principles of the HRA, but the aim in the 1998 legislation was to 'bring rights home', allowing UK nationals to rely on rights contained in the *European Convention on Human Rights* before the domestic courts. Numerous myths and muddles have surrounded the interpretation and implementation of the Act and thus it has been subject to sustained criticism. The notion of a bill of rights is not sufficiently developed to know how it would impact on the criminal justice system and more particularly on the supervision of offenders in the community, although we might worry that offenders would not be seen as a priority given that some criticisms in the popular tabloid press have branded the Act as a 'criminals charter'. Of particular concern here relates to foreign nationals and migrants who have committed crimes. Would a bill of rights be a 'citizens' convention', for instance, with only certain people counted as citizens and others excluded? Moreover, if the HRA were repealed and Convention rights no longer contained in UK law, aggrieved parties might once again have to take their case to the Strasbourg court for determination – a long journey, and at great cost. For the moment, the human rights as enshrined in the HRA are worth holding on to as scaffolding for normative values and ethics in work with offenders in the community.

## Notes

1 'The Tory plan to scrap the Human Rights Act just moved one step closer' Jon Stone, *Independent*, 8 September 2015 although with some delay 'Plans to scrap Human Rights Act delayed until 2016 – Michael Gove'. Agnes Chambre, *Politics Home*, 3 December 2015.

2 Probation work in Scotland survived within the remit of social work for much longer than in England and Wales, but as McIvor and McNeill (2007) show, in the early years of the twenty-first century this situation was changing.

3 The successful bidder in the Durham Tees Valley area was a joint venture without private sector company involvement.

4 Clear and Cadora use the term 'risk control' rather than risk elimination, but it is arguable that 'risk elimination' makes the distinction clearer (see Rutherford, 1996).

5 Note also that the Confederation of European Probation 9th European Electronic Monitoring Conference focused specifically on Electronic Monitoring, Probation and Human Rights in its December 2014 conference. Retrieved on 17 October 2015 from: http://cep-probation.org/wp-content/uploads/2015/03/Final-report-EM-2014.pdf.

6 The European Rules on community sanctions are also ambiguous, both expressing commitment to human rights, but also encouraging interventions in offenders' lives that may limit their freedom more than is strictly necessary (see van Zyl Smit et al., 2015).

## References


Ashworth, A., 1995. Principles, practice and criminal justice. *In*: P. Birks (ed.), *Pressing problems in the law, Vol.1: criminal justice and human rights*. Oxford: Oxford University Press, 43–48.

Bobbio, N., 1995. *The age of rights*. Cambridge: Polity Press.

Bonta, J. and Andrews, D., 2010. Viewing offender assessment and rehabilitation through the lens of the risk-needs-responsivity model. *In*: F. McNeill, P. Raynor and C. Trotter (eds), *Offender supervision*. Cullompton: Willan, 19–40.

Braithwaite, J. and Pettit, P., 1990. *Not just deserts: a Republican theory of criminal justice*. Oxford: Oxford University Press.

Burke, L. and Collett, S., 2015. *Delivering rehabilitation: the politics, governance and control of probation*. Abingdon: Routledge.

Canton, R., 2011. *Probation: working with offenders*. Abingdon: Routledge.

Canton, R., 2012. The point of probation: on effectiveness, human rights and the virtues of obliquity. *Criminology & Criminal Justice*, 13(5), 577–93.

Carozza, P., 2013. Human dignity. *In*: D. Shelton (ed.), *The Oxford handbook of international human rights law*. Oxford: Oxford University Press, 345–59.

Cheney, D., Dickson, L., Fitzpatrick, J. and Uglow, S. et al., 1999. *Criminal justice and the Human Rights Act 1998*. Bristol: Jordon.

Christie, N., 1993. *Crime control as industry*. London: Routledge.

Clarke, J., Gewirtz, S., Hughes, G. and Humphrey, J., 2000. Guarding the public interest? Auditing public services. In: J. Clarke, S. Gewirtz and E. McLaughlin (eds), *New managerialism: new welfare?* London: Sage, in association with the Open University, 250–66.

Clear, T. and Cadora, E., 2001. Risk and community practice. *In*: K. Stenson and R.R. Sullivan (eds), *Crime, risk and justice: the politics of crime control in liberal democracies*. Cullompton: Willan Publishing, 51–67.

Conservative Party Manifesto, 2015. Retrieved on 17 June 2015 from: www.conservatives.com/manifesto.

Craig, L., Dixon, L. and Gannon, T., 2013. *What works in offender rehabilitation: an evidence-based approach to assessment and treatment*. London: Wiley-Blackwell.

Dworkin, R., 1986. *A matter of principle*. Oxford: Clarendon Press.

Fox, C. and Albertson, K., 2011. Payment by results and social impact bonds in the criminal justice sector: new challenges for the concept of evidence-based policy. *Criminology & Criminal Justice*, 11(5), 395–413.

Freeman, M., 2002. *Human rights: an interdisciplinary approach – key concepts*. Cambridge: Polity Press.

Garland, D., 2001. *Culture of control: crime and social order in contemporary society*. Oxford: Clarendon Press.

Gelsthorpe, L., 2007. Probation values and human rights. *In*: L. Gelsthorpe and R. Morgan (eds), *Handbook of probation*. Cullompton: Willan Publishing, 485–517.

Gelsthorpe, L. and Hedderman, C., 2012. Providing for women offenders: the risks of adopting a payment by results approach. *Probation Journal*, 59(4), 374–90.

Gelsthorpe, L. and McIvor, G., 2007. Difference and diversity in probation. *In*: L. Gelsthorpe and R. Morgan (eds), *Handbook of probation*. Cullompton: Willan Publishing, 322–51.

Glover, J., 1999. *Humanity: a moral history of the twentieth century*. London: Jonathan Cape.

Harding, J., 2000. A community justice dimension to effective probation practice. *Howard Journal of Criminal Justice*, 39, 132–49.

Hilder, S., 2007. Anti-discriminatory practice. *In*: R. Canton and D. Hancock (eds), *Dictionary of probation and offender management*. Cullompton: Willan Publishing, 9–11.

Home Office, 1992. *Three year plan for the probation service 1993–96*. London: HMSO.

Hoy, C., 2005–6. Probation one hundred years on. *VISTA*, 10(3), 138–45.

Hudson, B., 2001. Human rights, public safety and the probation service: defending justice in the risk society. *Howard Journal of Criminal Justice*, 40(2), 103–13.

Ignatieff, M., 2000. *The rights revolution*. Toronto: House of Anansi Press.

Kemshall, H. and Hilder, S., 2013. Multi-agency approaches to effective risk management in the community in England and Wales. *In*: L. Craig, L. Dixon and T. Gannon (eds), *What works in offender rehabilitation: an evidence based approach to assessment and treatment*. Chichester: Wiley-Blackwell, 436–51.

Klug, F., 2002. Human rights: a common standard for all peoples? *In*: P. Griffith and M. Leonard (eds), *Reclaiming Britishness*. London: Foreign Policy Centre, 20–35.

Lacey, M., 2002. Justice, humanity and mercy. *In*: D. Ward, J. Scott and M. Lacey (eds), *Probation: working for justice*, 2nd edn. Oxford: Oxford University Press, 25–38.

Liebling, A. and Arnold, H., 2004. *Prisons and their moral performance: a study of values, quality and prison life*. Oxford: Oxford University Press.

Mawby, R.C. and Worrall, A., 2013. *Doing probation work: identity in a criminal justice occupation*. Abingdon: Routledge.

McIvor, G. and McNeill, F., 2007. Probation in Scotland: past, present and future. *In*: L. Gelsthorpe and R. Morgan (eds), *Handbook of probation*. Cullompton: Willan Publishing, 131–54.

McLaughlin, E., 2001. Managerialism. *In*: E. McLaughlin and J. Muncie (eds), *The Sage dictionary of criminology*. London: Sage, 260–1.

McNeill, F. and Weaver, B., 2010. *Changing lives? Desistance research and offender management*. Glasgow: Scottish Centre for Crime and Justice Research.

Ministry of Justice, 2010. *Breaking the cycle: effective punishment, rehabilitation and sentencing of offenders*. Cm 7972, London: Ministry of Justice.

Ministry of Justice, 2014. *The Transforming Rehabilitation Programme: the preferred bidders for the community rehabilitation companies*. Retrieved on 23 December 2015 from: www.gov.uk/government/uploads/system/uploads/attachment_data/file/368266/table-of-preferred-bidders.pdf.

Mortimer, E. and May, C., 1997. *Electronic monitoring in practice: the second year of the trials of curfew orders*. Home Office Research Study No. 177, London: Home Office.

Mulheirn, I., 2013. *Paying for results? Rethinking probation reform*. London: Social Market Foundation.

National Probation Service [NPS], 2001. *A new choreography*. London: National Probation Service.

Nellis, M., 1995. Probation values for the 1990s. *Howard Journal of Criminal Justice*, 34(1), 19–44.

Nellis, M., 2001. Community values and community justice. *Probation Journal*, 48(1), 34–8.

Nellis, M., 2007. Humanising justice: the English Probation Service up to 1972. *In*: L. Gelsthorpe and R. Morgan (eds), *Handbook of probation*. Cullompton: Willan Publishing, 25–58.

Nellis, M. and Gelsthorpe, L., 2003. Human rights and the probation values debate. *In*: W.H. Chui and M. Nellis (eds), *Moving probation forward: evidence, arguments and practice*. Harlow: Pearson Education, 227–44.

Nellis, M., Beyens, K. and Kaminski, D. (eds), 2013. *Electronically monitored punishment: international and critical perspectives*. Abingdon: Routledge.

Packer, H., 1969. *The limits of the criminal sanction*. Stanford, CA: Stanford University Press.

Prison Reform Trust, 1997. *Electronic tagging: viable option or expensive diversion?* London: Prison Reform Trust.

Probation Institute, 2014. *Code of ethics: core values and ethical principles*. London: Probation Institute.

Raynor, P. and Vanstone, M., 2007. Towards a correctional service. *In*: L. Gelsthorpe and R. Morgan (eds), *Handbook of probation*. Cullompton: Willan, 59–89.

Robinson, G. and McNeill, F., 2004. Purposes matter: examining the 'ends' of probation. *In*: G. Mair (ed.), *What matters in probation*. Cullompton: Willan, 277–304.

Robinson, G., Burke, L. and Millings, 2015. Criminal justice identities in transition: the case of devolved probation services in England and Wales. *British Journal of Criminology*, Advance Access published 19 May 2015. doi:10.1093/bjc/azv036.

Robinson, G., McNeill, F. and Maruna, S., 2013. Punishment in society: the improbable persistence of probation and other community sanctions and measures. *In*: J. Simon and R. Sparks (eds), *The Sage handbook of punishment and society*. London: Sage, 321–40.

Rutherford, A., 1993. *Criminal justice and the pursuit of decency*. Winchester: Waterside Press.

Rutherford, A., 1996. *Criminal policy and the eliminative ideal*. Inaugural Lecture. Institute of Criminal Justice, University of Southampton.

Scott, J., 2002. Human rights: a challenge to culture and practice. *In*: M. Lacey, J. Scott and D. Ward (eds), *Probation: working for justice*. Oxford: Oxford University Press, 3–24.

Senior, P., 1989. Radical probation: surviving in a hostile climate. *In*: M. Langan and P. Lee (eds), *Radical social work now*. London: Unwin Hyman, 292–319.

Spencer, J., 1995. A response to Mike Nellis: probation values for the 1990s. *Howard Journal of Criminal Justice*, 34(4), 344–9.

Tomuschat, C., 2014. *Human rights: between idealism and realism*. Oxford: Oxford University Press.

Turner, B., 2006. *Vulnerability and human rights*. University Park, PA: Pennsylvania State University Press.

van Zyl Smit, D., Snacken, S. and Hayes, D., 2015. 'One cannot legislate kindness': ambiguities in European legal instruments on non-custodial sanctions. *Punishment & Society*, 17(1), 3–26.

Weber, L., Fishwick, E. and Marmo, M., 2014. *Crime, justice and human rights*. Basingstoke: Palgrave Macmillan.

Whitehead, P. and Crawshaw, P., 2013. Shaking the foundations: on the moral economy of criminal justice. *British Journal of Criminology*, 53, 588–604.

# 49

# Prisons and human rights

## Past, present and future challenges

*Peter Scharff-Smith*

## Introduction

A free citizen in a democratic society can demand a long list of rights, but what happens when a citizen is taken into state custody and locked in a cell? In the western world, this question has been the subject of intense debate over the last more than 200 years. In the pre-modern prisons of the sixteenth and seventeenth centuries prisoner rights were not a consideration, but in the eighteenth century, and in the spirit of the Enlightenment, a process of reform began and the use of torture, the death penalty and corporal punishment was criticized. Very gradually this led to an increased use of imprisonment and shifted focus from corporal public punishment towards a utilitarian rehabilitative agenda focusing on the individual lawbreaker – illustrated, for example, by Jeremy Bentham's famous panopticon and later by the modern penitentiary and its ideology of rehabilitation through isolation.

While the construction of prisons and the treatment of prisoners began to change significantly from the late eighteenth century and onwards this group of citizens were not granted any rights as such. Furthermore, as described in the literature on the modern penitentiaries of the nineteenth century and in the theoretical literature on the sociology of punishment, the new prisons were not simply utilitarian nor were they necessarily more humane than their predecessors – in reality these institutions produced a modern technology of power through which knowledge of the individual became an instrument of control (Foucault 1995).

It was not until after World War 2 that any serious development of prisoner rights took place. After 1945 an international human rights framework was gradually established and many of the principles and concrete rights underpinning today's human rights standards for prisons were agreed upon in the early aftermath of the war and with the unravelling of the Holocaust still fresh in mind. Nevertheless, the introduction of legally enforceable prisoner rights generally had to wait until the 1960s and 1970s and was mainly a product of national courts and reform processes. A later important addition to the international human rights framework came with the development of human rights prison inspections, which were introduced as part of the international and regional systems of torture prevention.

In recent years, however, the framework for human rights protection of prisoners has been challenged in a number of ways. The most important of these challenges include: the phenomenon of penal populism, 'tough on crime' policies and punitive legislation; the terrorism and security agenda following 9/11; and the broader processes of globalization and migration which have caused, among other things, a significant rise in the number of foreigners in many prison systems. In addition, the international human rights framework and the associated values have in themselves come increasingly under fire, especially in this millennium, and some claim that the 'Endtimes of Human Rights' are now fast approaching (Hopgood 2013).

Despite these developments, human rights continue to develop and sometimes their application is still broadened and strengthened. Two topical and future challenges include the question of prisoners' children and the way in which they and their rights are affected by the use of imprisonment, and the revolution in communications technology and the question of how this will affect prisons and punishment. Both these cases reveal how the use of imprisonment relates to society in very broad and significant ways which clearly have an important human rights dimension.

## Prison reform in the wake of the age of enlightenment

There will always be tension between the power of the State and the rights of its individual citizens and at the root of this conflict lies a centuries-old dilemma between an individual's natural freedom and his or her security in a society of law and order (Hobbes 1998, Locke 1997). Cesare Beccaria, in his 1766 book *On crimes and punishments*, found that every individual should only give up the smallest possible amount of freedom which then gave the state a certain power to punish. According to Beccaria, a use of force above and beyond that was a misuse of state power and hence unjustified (Beccaria 1998, p. 56). But principles are one thing and practice another. One can argue that the big philanthropic prison reformers of the late eighteenth century and early nineteenth century were some of the first to look empirically at the possible practical implications of Enlightenment philosophy in the context of prisons. Especially renowned was John Howard, who visited prisons all over Europe and summed up his observations and critique in his book *The state of prisons* in 1777 (Howard 1929 [1777]). Howard highlighted problems relating to health, religion, and order of the prisons that he visited and his empirical fieldwork created and supported actual reforms. Others undertook similar projects often with the ambition of bringing about comprehensive change in prisons (Smith 2003, p. 79 ff). In 1831, the famous, religious English prison reformer, Elizabeth Fry, for example, brought about changes in Danish prisons after reporting on conditions to the Danish royal family. Concrete outcomes were that heating was introduced in Copenhagen's prisons during the winters and that prisoners received a considerable increase in food rations (Smith 2003, p. 144 ff.).

Considered from today's perspective, Fry, Howard and their philanthropic contemporaries performed a monitoring role that anticipated the much later human rights developments in this area. Agencies, such as the European Committee for the Prevention of Torture (CPT) are based on the philosophy that systematic monitoring and documentation of States' actual prison practice can prevent torture and ill-treatment. However, it can be difficult to assess to what extent prisoners in nineteenth-century Europe were treated better as a result of prison reforms. With the modern prisons the physical health of prisoners generally improved and the mortality rate fell in many prisons but implementation of isolation practices and often-strict solitary confinement led to severe problems with the mental health of prisoners (Smith 2004). In any case, prisoners did not receive individual rights and were still entirely in the hands of the prison management.

## The development of prisoners' rights and the principle of normalization

In 1871, the Supreme Court of Virginia determined that imprisoned citizens were 'slaves of the State' (*Ruffin v The Commonwealth 1871*). This and other judgements helped lay the groundwork for the 'hands-off' doctrine, which characterized American jurisprudence for the next nearly 100 years (Morris 1998, p. 219). According to this doctrine, prisoners had no rights and courts should not interfere in internal prison matters whereby prisoners were left 'to the unchecked power of the administration' (Rotman 1998, p. 171). Nevertheless, prison practice developed through international forums. Three international prison conferences were held between 1846 and 1857 where concrete standards for prison practices were adopted and the International Prison Commission (IPC) held further conferences from 1872 onwards. The work within the IPC was oriented towards prison practice and was up until the 1930 congress in Prague unpolitical. In 1935, the penitentiary congress in Berlin became heavily influenced by the Nazi regime and Dr Goebbels was among the official speakers. The IPC was transformed into the IPPC which continued to cooperate with the Nazis during the war and consequently it was dissolved by the UN General Assembly in 1950. Thereafter, the international work with prison standards continued within the UN and resulted in, for example, the adoption of the UN 'Standard Minimum Rules for the Treatment of Prisoners' during the First United Nations Congress on the Prevention of Crime and the Treatment of Offenders in 1955 (Teeters 1972).

In the meantime, and as I will return to below, an international human rights system had begun to take shape after World War 2. Nevertheless, it was not until the 1960s and 1970s that a proper national and international reform process began whereby prisoners' rights were secured in several countries through a number of ground-breaking decisions and judgements.[1] In 1974, the United States (US) Supreme Court declared that there 'is no iron curtain drawn between the Constitution and the prisons of this country' (*Wolff v McDonnell 1974*). Prisoners' rights were further highlighted in a Canadian judgement in 1969, according to which, 'an inmate of an institution continues to enjoy all the civil rights of a person save those that are taken away or interfered with by having been lawfully sentenced to imprisonment' (*R. v Institutional Head of Beaver Creek Correctional Camp 1969*). Arguably, these judgements were also based on the principle that the deprivation of liberty is punishment enough in and of itself. In the words of prison reformer Alexander Paterson: 'Men come to prison *as* a punishment, not *for* punishment' (Stern 1998, p. 197). In Denmark a comprehensive penal reform was introduced in 1973, which led to the formal adoption of the principle of normalization (Engbo and Smith 2012). The principle of normalization is also reflected in the European prison rules and hence part of the regional European human rights framework and consists of two related key elements:

1 Prisoners retain all their rights when imprisoned except those which are taken away by necessary implication of the deprivation of liberty; and
2 Conditions in prison should resemble conditions in the free community as much as possible. (Smith 2012, p. 461).

While the principle of normalization features quite prominently, for example, in the Scandinavian prison systems this is not always the case. Even the principle that prisoners generally retain their rights is still very controversial and the question of what rights are 'taken away by necessary implication' is interpreted very differently also within Council of Europe (CoE) Member States.

## The international human rights framework: a brief outline

Some of the most fundamental human rights principles relevant to the deprivation of liberty were included in the *Universal Declaration of Human Rights* in 1948, which, for example, prohibited slavery and torture (Articles 4 and 5). In the UN *International Covenant on Civil and Political Rights* (ICCPR), adopted in 1966, some of these principles were linked even more explicitly to prisons in Article 10, according to which 'All persons deprived of their liberty shall be treated with humanity and with respect for the inherent dignity of the human person'. Furthermore, and unlike most other human rights mechanisms, Article 10(3) of the ICCPR defines that the 'essential aim' of the treatment of prisoners 'shall be their reformation and social rehabilitation'. The Convention further confirms a range of other basic human rights relevant to prisoners, including: the prohibition of torture (Article 7), the right to life (Article 6), the right to liberty and security of person (Article 9), freedom of expression (Article 19), freedom of religion (Article 18), the rights to privacy (Article 17) and the right to respect for the family (Article 23). Finally, Article 26 ensures equal protection before the law, regardless of gender, race, colour, and so on.

The UN Human Rights Committee (HRC), which monitors compliance with the ICCPR, has stated that prisoners may not:

> be subjected to any hardship or constraint other than that resulting from the deprivation of liberty; respect for the dignity of such persons must be guaranteed under the same conditions as for that of free persons. Persons deprived of their liberty enjoy all the rights set forth in the Covenant, subject to the restrictions that are unavoidable in a closed environment.
>
> *(General Comment No. 21[44] regarding Article 10, 3 April 1992)*

This interpretation does not copy but nevertheless lies quite close to the principle of normalization. A wealth of human rights soft law instruments and rules that are highly relevant to prisons and prisoners have also been drafted and adopted by numerous states, not least of which include the UN prison rules which were introduced in 1955 and revised in 1977. A new and quite extensively revised version of these rules has recently been adopted by the UN and entitled the 'Mandela rules' (UN, E/CN.15/2015/L.6/Rev.1, 21. May 2015).

To sum up, if we today consider the history of prisoner rights as well as the overall international human rights approach to the deprivation of liberty, then the following three principles appear as fundamental:

1 The principle of a natural human dignity.
2 The absolute prohibition of torture, inhuman and degrading treatment.
3 Recognition that prisoners, by default, retain their rights except those which are taken away by necessary implication of the deprivation of liberty.

## Regional mechanisms: the European human rights framework

Prison practice is also regulated by regional human rights conventions and instruments. One can argue that the European human rights mechanism demand particular attention because it has been equipped with a court, complaint and monitoring system unrivalled by the other regional models. The *European Convention on Human Rights* (ECHR) entered into force in 1953 and established the European Court of Human Rights (ECtHR), which applies to all of the Council of Europe's 47 Member States. Interestingly, although the ECtHR had a powerful mandate right from the start its judicial role was very limited for the first two to three decades of its existence. During this period the cases were relatively few and most of these were decided by the European Commission of Human Rights which, until it was abolished in 1998, screened and dealt with cases before they reached court. In its first 30 years the ECtHR only delivered 72 judgements, of which approximately 15 dealt with prisons. Furthermore, the ECtHR and the Commission of Human Rights adopted a very conservative approach to a number of prison cases and chose to see a range of potential violations as natural consequences of imprisonment lying within the doctrine of 'implied limitations' (Van and Snacken 2009, p. 10). However, in 1975, in the case *Golder v the United Kingdom*, the ECtHR took the first step in a more progressive direction in this area and concluded that prisoners generally retain their rights. The ECtHR has since repeatedly confirmed this approach and underlined 'that prisoners in general continue to enjoy all the fundamental rights and freedoms guaranteed under the Convention save for the right to liberty' (*Hirst v the United Kingdom 2005*, para. 69).

Among the human rights principles that have gained support, especially within the European system, the principle of normalization is arguably very important as well as the principle that imprisonment should only be used as a last resort. The latter has been included in a range of recommendations from the CoE's Committee of Ministers over a number of years and along with comprehensive practical guidelines. As the Committee of Ministers stated in 1999: 'deprivation of liberty should be regarded as a sanction or measure of last resort and should therefore be provided only when the seriousness of the offence would make any other sanction or measure clearly inadequate' (CoE Recommendation No. R [99] 22). In reality this means that a human rights approach to prisons also becomes a question of choosing an overall penal policy that ensures minimal use of the deprivation of liberty. Accordingly, recommendations from the CoE in this area includes, for example, that a range of offences are decriminalized, that alternatives to prison sentences are increasingly adopted, and that the legal requirements for pre-trial imprisonment become more strict (Van and Snacken 2009, p. 86 ff).

## From human rights principles to prison practice

There is obviously not a direct link between the ratification of human rights conventions and the improvement of prison conditions and prisoner rights. There are large variations in how states and legal systems interpret and relate to human rights soft law as well as hard law. One study of English prisoners' rights, for example, concluded that English judges were 'disinclined to intervene in many areas of prison life, notwithstanding the introduction of the Human Rights Act [in] 1998' (Lazarus 2004, p. 3).

In Europe, a major disagreement on the interpretation of what rights are 'taken away by necessary implication' of the deprivation of liberty has played out between the United Kingdom (UK) and the ECtHR. In the Hirst case, the UK was found in violation of the ECHR for not allowing prisoners to vote (*Hirst v UK*). This led to a national debate in England, including criticism of the ECtHR and in 2011, the influential English Policy Exchange think tank, for example, argued that it was time to consider an English withdrawal from the jurisdiction of the ECtHR. At the same time, English Prime Minister David Cameron declared that 'giving prisoners the vote makes him feel "physically ill"' (*Daily Telegraph*, 7 February 2011). From a human rights point of view, the issue has still not been settled and in February 2015 the UK was again found in violation of the ECHR (Article 3 of Protocol No. 1) for not allowing a prisoner to vote (*McHugh and Others v the UK*). In Denmark, several politicians including previous ministers of justice have also argued in favour of creating harsher prison conditions in order to intensify the punitive element of the deprivation of liberty (Engbo and Smith 2012). Some politicians in other words perceive the potentially damaging effects of prisons as a useful element of penalties and not something that should be curtailed to protect prisoners. Accordingly, while:

> many Western European Countries officially adhere to a reductionist policy and have introduced new forms of non-custodial sanctions and measures . . . their actual policies remain bifurcated . . . and "serious" offenders, especially those involved in drugs, violent or sexual delinquency, are dealt with by increasingly severe terms of incarceration.
>
> *(Van and Snacken 2009, p. 61)*

A different question, which in a sense problematizes the whole idea of a human rights approach to prisons, is whether it makes sense at all to argue that the punitive element of imprisonment can be limited to the deprivation of liberty (the loss of freedom of movement) if prisons by their very nature are 'designed to deliberately create human suffering, hurt and injury', as some argue (Scott 2013, p. 301).

On a general note, it is clear that the reform process of the 1960s and 70s has now faded out and in addition, a number of authoritarian regimes apparently continue to ignore prisoners' rights to a greater or lesser extent. According to Amnesty International, torture and arbitrary detention was, for example, widespread in China and Saudi Arabia in 2014 (Amnesty International 2015, p. 107 f. and 313 ff). At the same time, however, there has also been an expansion and consolidation of human rights bodies, standards and especially monitoring mechanisms in recent years, which in some ways has strengthened the protection of prisoners.

## Monitoring and prevention

The UN *Convention against Torture and other Cruel, Inhuman or Degrading Treatment or Punishment* (CAT) was introduced in 1987 and monitors the relevant activities of the countries which have signed and ratified the CAT, and the UN Special Rapporteur on Torture also has a mandate to conduct visits to institutions in all membership states where people are deprived of their liberty. Furthermore, the *Optional Protocol to the Convention against Torture and other Cruel, Inhuman or Degrading Treatment or Punishment* (OPCAT) entered into force on 22 June 2006 and created a sub-committee that can undertake country visits with the aim of strengthening national systems for the prevention of torture. According to this Protocol, individual states also have to establish national preventive mechanisms that undertake prison inspections.

In the CoE Member States, monitoring of prisons was introduced with the *European Convention for the Prevention of Torture and Inhuman or Degrading Treatment or Punishment* in 1987, which established the European Committee for the Prevention of Torture and Inhuman or Degrading Treatment or Punishment (CPT). The CPT has a very strong mandate, visits Member States regularly, and has free access to prisons and other places of detention. The work of the CPT has been used increasingly by the ECtHR and has, thereby, influenced legally binding standards (Van and Snacken 2009, p. 375). Furthermore, visit reports from monitoring mechanisms have created insight into local practices and raised awareness about prison conditions. The CPT has created an impressive catalogue of empirical data on national prison practices collected during numerous visits in all membership countries – a material which has been surprisingly neglected in comparative criminology and in criminological prison research. The effects of monitoring and torture prevention are still debated but according to Jonathan Simon, who approaches the matter from a US perspective, 'the reach of human rights norms as a counterweight to punitive populism in Europe owes much to the development of specialized governmental organs that support this mission' such as especially the CPT and the CoE Committee of Ministers (Simon 2014, p. 140 f.).

## Current human rights challenges

While a human rights approach to prison practice has been strengthened through the development of monitoring mechanisms and national inspection units there are certainly also other contradictory signs on the horizon. One of these has to do with the role of human rights as a legal, political and moral force. Historian Samuel Moyn argues that, during the 1970s, human rights began to appeal to broad communities as a cause of justice and across the western world 'came to define people's hopes for the future as the foundation of an international movement and a utopia of international law' (Moyn 2010, p. 7). As already shown, this was also the period when the rights of prisoners began to be acknowledged by national courts as well as the ECtHR. However, according to Moyn, human rights have since followed a path 'from morality to politics' and today 'stand for an exploding variety of political schemes', and the prominence of human rights may turn out to be short lived (Moyn 2010, p. 227). According to Stephen Hopgood, the 'Endtimes' of what he calls universal 'Human Rights' (with capital letters) are in fact fast approaching as the 'vast superstructure of international human rights law and organization is no longer "fit for purpose"'(Hopgood 2013, p. 2).

To what extent these developments have been correctly analysed and whether the above prophecies are correct is still very much discussed – but there is little doubt that the concept of human rights is questioned and lack the broad political support that it did in democratic states just a few decades ago. In addition, a number of developments specifically challenge prison and punishment standards and threaten to roll back or eliminate a human rights approach to this area. These challenges include the phenomenon of penal populism, the terrorism and security agenda following 9/11, and the broader processes of globalization and migration.

To start with the first, there is little doubt that recent decades have witnessed an increased focus on retribution and the introduction of more punitive sentencing and penal practices in several jurisdictions. The US has for the last three or four decades inspired and led this international trend and in doing so reached an unprecedented level of imprisonment. During the early 1990s, this wave of punitive policies reached Europe and prison populations grew significantly in, for example, England, Spain and Holland. This tendency has been termed a new 'culture of control' and 'penal populism' (Garland 2001, Tonry 2004, Pratt 2007) and has clearly influenced penal policy in ways that are very problematic from a human rights point of view. In some places, prisoner rights have been directly influenced by this trend, and in the US, legislation introduced in the mid-1990s means that it is now more difficult for prisoners to assert their rights in court (Jacobs 2003, p. 185). The new punitive penal policies are also reflected in the design of increasingly restrictive and harsh prisons – the American Supermax being prime examples in this regard as 'political symbols of how "tough" a jurisdiction has become' (Riveland 1999, p. 5). In Europe, penal populism has also influenced prison conditions directly including in a Scandinavian country like Denmark (Engbo and Smith 2012).

Furthermore, it is well-known how the anti-terror legislation introduced since 2001 has challenged due process and rule of law principles in many parts of the world, by giving states increased power to control and monitor their citizens (International Commission of Jurists 2009). Within the framework of the War on Terror this security agenda has also had a specific impact on prison conditions and prison standards as the former international leader of the human rights movement, the US, created and upheld inhumane and degrading prison and interrogation practices on a large scale in, for example, Afghanistan and at Guantanamo and various 'Black' sites around the world. By doing this, and by officially and legally redefining torture, the US administration arguably ridiculed international law, prisoner rights and the entire human rights movement. Post-9/11 security policies have also impacted prison and human rights issues in many other parts of the world (Weber et al. 2014, p. 172 f.).

Thirdly, the broader processes of globalization and migration have caused a significant rise in the number of foreigners in many prison systems along with political initiatives aimed at getting rid of these prisoners (Ugelvik 2014). In some places, including Denmark, there has also been political pressure towards treating such prisoners worse than their national counterparts. Novel methods to lessen the pressure on prison systems are also discussed and the Norwegian state has recently begun to send prisoners to the Netherlands where they have rented prison space (something which Belgium is also doing). The result looks like an experiment with international human rights law and the Norwegian National Preventive Mechanism under the OPCAT has voiced serious concern that the Norwegian state will have trouble living up to the CAT.

## Prison and society: the case of prisoners' children and families

Despite the serious challenges described in the above, human rights continue to develop and as a result standards are sometimes strengthened and broadened in scope in ways that can clearly enhance protection of rights holders. One interesting case in that regard is the question of prisoner's children. Traditionally, discussions, research and court judgements within the field of prisons and human rights have almost exclusively been a matter of balancing the state's legitimate use of power and security concerns against the individual prisoners' rights. The question of whether and to what degree the use of imprisonment has also affected the rights of people living outside of prison has for many years been left out of consideration.

There is however currently a very interesting development in this area and in 2011, the UN Committee on the Rights of the Child produced a detailed set of recommendations, urging:

> that States parties ensure that the rights of children with a parent in prison are taken into account from the moment of the arrest of their parent(s) and by all actors involved in the process and at all its stages, including law enforcement, prison service professionals, and the judiciary.
>
> *(Smith 2014, p. 85)*

Furthermore, there are now examples of how courts in some jurisdictions have begun to take prisoners children and their rights into account when passing sentences and while the ECtHR for many years treated prisoner family rights cases without referring to the rights of the child this has now also changed (*Horych v Poland 2012*). Norway has taken an important step towards recognizing the rights of prisoners children by legally requiring that children of prisoners 'shall receive special attention' during the imprisonment (Smith 2014, p. 107). This means that some of the wider societal effects of imprisonment are now being acknowledged and gradually incorporated into the human rights, and sometimes national legal, framework.

## Modern communications technology and the future of prisons and punishment

The development of digital information and communications technology (ICT) has during a remarkably short time span changed our societies and the way we live. Internet access is today, in many countries, almost a requirement for people who want to actively participate in some of the basic aspects of life and as a result such access is increasingly becoming a human rights issue, meaning that it requires specific, democratically legitimate and lawful reasons to enforce any kind of restrictions (Jørgensen 2013).

There are, however, groups in society who risk becoming excluded from accessing the Internet and this is certainly the case for prisoners. There are several good reasons for not allowing unrestricted Internet access for all prisoners, some of which have to do with protecting public order, inhibiting the spread of crime as well as protecting victims of crime. There are, however, also several reasons why lack of prisoner Internet access can cause serious problems and further exclude an already marginalized group of citizens. Internet access can be used to educate prisoners; uphold well-functioning family ties; and become indispensable when it comes to maintaining effective contact with public authorities.

It seems that we today stand at a threshold where prison administrators and lawmakers have begun to realize that they must relate much more to ICTs not only from a security point of view but also from a prisoner point of view as well as from a broader societal perspective involving reintegration of offenders. But what will happen when the Internet will clash with the whole concept of deprivation of liberty as a punishment? While the Internet community has been described as being a free 'global social space' which is 'naturally independent' (Barlow 1996) imprisonment is *the* symbol, above any other, of incapacitation and lack of freedom. These two positions and their associated values and ideologies spawn two radically different futures and visions of what imprisonment can come to look like in the age of the Internet. One the one hand, we have a scenario, which in a sense is almost a high-tech revival of the prison abolition movement. In this future, prisoners are always online and although physically inhibited from fleeing their imprisonment they have attained a virtual global freedom where they can communicate with people all over the world – and perhaps offenders will even be diverted away from prison through the use of electronic tagging. At the other end of the scale we have an Orwellian future where ICTs are used to minimize face-to-face contact and where prisons operate with 'prison cloud' systems and in-cell computer terminals, which do not allow any kind of real access to the Internet but offer the most basic services via a secure intranet and a TV screen in the cell. In this scenario prisoners do not have to leave their cells and are even more isolated and excluded than previously. Electronic tagging can also be used in this manner to create high-tech social control, constant monitoring and very restrictive sanctions outside of prisons. We will thereby have created a new Weberian 'iron cage' where a group of people have become completely trapped in rationalized and bureaucratic systems of control (Weber 1995, p. 181). In the words of Zygmunt Bauman, modernity and bureaucratic decision-making have an inherent potential to produce social immorality on a large scale and systems of law and order are particularly vulnerable in that regard (Bauman 1991, 2000).

In reality the future is likely to lie somewhere in between the two scenarios but one can fear that in an age of penal populism the second alternative will appeal more to politicians while the first will be used to create fear, anxiety and 'moral panics' among the public. As this chapter has shown, there is little continuity and no linear progression in human rights over history and across the world. Perhaps this ebb and flow of human rights in prisons illustrate how the symbolism and politics of punishment always carry the potential to undermine the rational nature of the enlightenment project, and equally so the philosophical basis of human rights? In any case the experience of imprisonment is likely to change in the future which in itself might require a redefinition of our human rights standards. It has been argued that ICTs have the potential to change 'the social, technological and legal circumstances in which current definitions of human rights were developed' which can necessitate reinterpretations (Jakubowicz 2011, p. 142).

It is not inconceivable that punishment in the age of the Internet at some point will change the practice and concept of deprivation of liberty to a degree where many of our current human rights standards in the area no longer make much sense.

## Note

1 'The heyday of the prisoners' rights movement roughly spanned the period from 1960 to 1980', according to James B. Jacobs, 'Prison Reform amid the Ruins of Prisoners' Rights' (2004, p. 183). Regarding the US, see also Rotman (1998), and regarding Germany see Lazarus (2004, p. 34 ff.).

## References


Amnesty International, 2015. *The state of the world's human rights: report 2014–15*. Retrieved on 12 April 2016 from: www.amnesty.org.au/features/comments/36642.

Barlow, J.P., 1996. A declaration of the independence of cyberspace. 8 February. Retrieved on 12 April 2016 from: https://www.eff.org/cyberspace-independence.

Bauman, Z., 1991. *Modernity and the Holocaust*. Oxford: Polity Press.

Bauman, Z., 2000. Social issues of law and order. *British Journal of Criminology*, 40, 205–21.

Beccaria, C., 1998. *Om forbrydelse og straf*. Copenhagen: Museum Tusculanums Press.

*Daily Telegraph*, 2011. UK 'should withdraw from European Court of Human Rights'. 7 February. Retrieved on 12 April 2016 from: www.telegraph.co.uk/news/worldnews/europe/8307782/UK-should-withdraw-from-European-Court-of-Human-Rights.html.

Engbo, H.J. and Smith, P.S., 2012. *Fængsler og menneskerettigheder*. Jurist- og Økonomforbundets forlag.

Foucault, M., 1995. *Discipline and punish: the birth of the prison*. New York, NY: Vintage Books.

Garland, D., 2001. *The culture of control*. Oxford: Oxford University Press.

Hobbes, T., 1998. *Leviathan*. Oxford: Oxford University Press.

Hopgood, S., 2013. *The endtimes of human rights*. Ithaca, NY: Cornell University Press.

Howard, J., 1929 [1777]. *The state of prisons*. London: Dent.

International Commission of Jurists, 2009. *Assessing damage, urging action*. Report of the Eminent Jurists Panel on Terrorism, Counter-terrorism and Human Rights. Retrieved on 12 April 2016 from: www.un.org/en/sc/ctc/specialmeetings/2011/docs/icj/icj-2009-ejp-report.pdf.

Jacobs, J.B., 2004. Prison reform amid the ruins of prisoners' rights. *In*: M. Tonry (ed.), *The future of imprisonment*. Oxford: Oxford University Press, 179–98.

Jakubowicz, K., 2011. *Media revolution in Europe: ahead of the curve*. Strasbourg: Council of Europe Publishing.

Jørgensen, R.F., 2013. *Framing the net: the internet and human rights*. Cheltenham: Edward Elgar Publishing.

Lazarus, L., 2004. *Contrasting prisoners' rights: a comparative examination of Germany and England*. Oxford: Oxford University Press.

Locke, J., 1997. The second treatise of the state of nature. *In*: M. Ishay (ed.), *The human rights reader*. New York, NY: Routledge, 93–103.

Morris, N., 1998. The contemporary prison. *In*: N. Morris and D. Rothman (eds), *The Oxford history of the prison*. Oxford: Oxford University Press, 202–34.

Moyn, S., 2010. *The last utopia: human rights in history*. Cambridge, MA: The Belknap Press of Harvard University Press.

Pratt, J., 2007. *Penal populism*. London: Routledge.

Riveland, C., 1999. *Supermax prisons: overview and general considerations*. Washington, DC: National Institute of Corrections.

Rotman, E., 1998. The failure of reform. *In*: N. Morris and D. Rothman (eds), *The Oxford history of the prison*. Oxford: Oxford University Press, 151–77.

Scott, D., 2013. Unequalled in pain. *In*: D. Scott (ed.), *Why prison?* Cambridge: Cambridge University Press, 301–24.

Simon, J., 2014. *Mass incarceration on trial*. New York, NY: The New Press.

Smith, P.S., 2003. *Moralske hospitaler: Det moderne fængselsvæsens gennembrud 1770–1870*. Copenhagen: Forum.

Smith, P.S., 2004. Isolation and mental illness in Vridsløselille 1859–1873: a new perspective on the breakthrough of the modern penitentiary. *Scandinavian Journal of History*, 291, 1–25.

Smith, P.S., 2012. Imprisonment and internet access: human rights, the principle of normalization and the question of prisoners access to digital communications technology. *Nordic Journal of Human Rights*, 4, 454–82.
Smith, P.S., 2014. *When the innocent are punished: the children of imprisoned parents*. London: Palgrave Macmillan.
Stern, V., 1998. *A sin against the future: imprisonment in the world*. Boston, MA: Northeastern University Press.
Teeters, N.K., 1972. *Deliberations of the International Penal and Penitentiary Congresses: Questions and Answers 1872–1935*. Philadelphia, PA: Temple University Book Store.
Tonry, M., 2004. *Thinking about crime: sense and sensibility in American penal culture*. New York, NY: Oxford University Press.
Ugelvik, T., 2014. The incarceration of foreigners in European prisons. *In*: S. Pickering and J. Ham (eds), *The Routledge handbook on crime and international migration*. London and New York: Routledge, 107–20.
Van, D.Z.S and Snacken, S., 2009. *Principles of European prison law and policy: penology and human rights*. Oxford: Oxford University Press.
Weber, L., Fishwick, E. and Marmo, M., 2014. *Crime, justice and human rights*. Basingstoke: Palgrave Macmillan.
Weber, M., 1995. *The Protestant ethic and the spirit of capitalism*. London: Routledge.

## Cases

ECtHR: *Hirst v UK* 2005.
ECtHR: *Horych v Poland* 2012.
ECtHR: *McHugh and Others v the UK* 2015.
*R v Institutional Head of Beaver Creek Correctional Camp* 1969.
*Ruffin v The Commonwealth, Supreme Court of Virginia*, 62 Va. 790; 1871 Va. LEXIS 89; 21 Gratt. 790, November, 1871.
*Wolff v McDonnell* 1974.

# 50

# Human rights, criminal justice and closed environments

*Bronwyn Naylor*

## Introduction

Criminal justice systems can demand the detention of people in closed institutions such as prisons, police cells and forensic psychiatric facilities. Detention, however, introduces heightened risks of rights abuse, given its fundamentally coercive character and relative absence of public scrutiny.

This chapter first outlines briefly the bases on which people can be detained, and rationales for such detention, beginning with a broad analysis and then focusing on Australian jurisdictions. It identifies rights that are challenged by the practice of detention, some of which are common to places of detention and some specific to particular types of detention, and reviews protections provided by formal rights instruments and domestic legislation. It then evaluates the significance of rights-based monitoring for protecting rights.

## Detention within the criminal justice system

Liberty is a basic human right; it is a fundamental principle dating back to the Magna Carta that a person is not to be deprived of their liberty without lawful justification. This chapter will assume that the forms of detention discussed have been lawfully imposed; thus unlawful detention is beyond the scope of this chapter. However, the rationales for such detention must be clearly referable to lawful authority, and are important in determining whether other rights are retained, or can be overridden.

Detention in police cells may be lawful when a person is held for questioning, or for their own or community safety. Detention in prisons is authorized where a person has been convicted of an offence and lawfully sentenced to a term of imprisonment, and where the person has been refused bail. The rationale for the first is the loss of liberty as punishment; the rationale for the second is primarily community safety, to ensure attendance at trial and protect witnesses. International covenants recognize that people on remand require greater protection. For example, Article 10(2)(a) of the 1976 *International Covenant on Civil and Political Rights* (ICCPR) requires that '[a]ccused persons shall, save in exceptional circumstances, be segregated from convicted persons and shall be subject to separate treatment appropriate to their status as unconvicted persons'.

People may also be detained in forensic psychiatric facilities, if found not guilty of an offence on the basis of mental impairment, or if seriously mentally ill whilst imprisoned. Rationales will then include both therapeutic support and community safety.

These forms of detention do not operate in a vacuum. Where the dominant discourse is punitive, public support for the recognition of rights varies: there may be scepticism about whether prisoners have any rights at all, and anxiety about forensic patients. Formal rights protection mechanisms are the focus here but their implementation and support depend on their broader community acceptance, a point that will be returned to later.

### *Rights and detention*

These closed environments are 'total institutions' (Goffman 1961, p. 15). The fundamental feature of the total institution is loss of autonomy: people living in 'total institutions' spend night and day with people they have not chosen, following a structured scheme of activities imposed by a bureaucracy, their every activity controlled by others. Central features of any closed environment, then, are the enforced loss of liberty, the power imbalance between detainees and staff, the dominance of security concerns (that is, sustaining the security of the detention), and the 'closed' nature of the institution. Each of these features heightens the risk of rights violations and abuses.

In the prison context it is now formally accepted that, when people are imprisoned for committing a criminal offence, the loss of liberty is the punishment. They are not to be further punished by harsh conditions, humiliation or violence. This means that people detained within the criminal justice system retain all human rights other than rights the limitation of which is 'demonstrably necessitated by the fact of incarceration' (Principle 5, *UN Basic Principles for the Treatment of Prisoners* [1990]).

People held in secure psychiatric units under mental impairment legislation similarly face impairment of rights when detention and involuntary treatment are statutorily authorized but should otherwise retain their rights, such as rights to consent to treatment and to an equivalent standard of treatment to those in the community (see Mackay 2015).[1]

What this means in practice is much debated. Whilst it varies across closed environments it means, at least, that rights which jeopardize the security of the detention are probably lost or modified. Any additional constraints on rights depend on the environment, and will be considered below.

## Rights issues across the closed environments

Detention raises rights issues about, for example, physical conditions, contact with family members, practices of control and restraint, access to medical care or involuntary treatment, and abuses of power such as disrespect and violence.

Rapid increases in prison incarceration rates have occurred in many countries including Australia, and led to serious overcrowding. Overcrowding exacerbates pressures on all services – accommodation, medical services, education, training – including access to mental healthcare, a serious issue both in prisons and in overstretched forensic psychiatric facilities.

It is widely recognized that the proportion of people in the criminal justice system with mental illnesses is high. For example, 30 per cent of police call-outs in Victoria have been found to involve mental illness (Herrington and Clifford 2012, p. 121) and 38 per cent of prison entrants report having a mental illness (AIHW 2013, p. 35). Imprisonment is itself a source of additional psychological stress and can exacerbate mental illnesses (Hanley and Ross 2013,

Edgar and Rickford 2009). The Victorian Institute of Forensic Mental Health concluded that 'the current system for managing mentally ill offenders in the criminal justice system and the community does not afford adequate protection of the human rights of this group' (quoted in Hanley and Ross 2013, p. 350).

Rights protections for detainees in international instruments will be discussed, followed by a review of domestic legislative schemes, and an evaluation of the protections offered by rights-based monitoring.

## Formal human rights protections

### *International rights*

The main international conventions relevant to rights in these closed environments are the ICCPR, the *Convention against Torture and other Cruel, Inhuman or Degrading Treatment or Punishment* (CAT) and the *Convention on the Rights of Persons with Disabilities* (CRPD). Australia is a signatory to all three treaties.

The most important provisions for people held in detention spelt out in the ICCPR are the negative right not to be subject to 'torture or cruel, inhuman or degrading treatment or punishment' (Article 7; see also the CAT Articles 1 and 16; CRPD Article 15) and the positive right of people deprived of their liberty to be treated 'with humanity and with respect for the inherent dignity of the human person' (Article 10[1]). Other important rights for people held in detention include the right to life, the right to liberty and security of the person, to equality before the law, privacy, and the protection of family and children.

This prohibition has been central to much international litigation around detention. At the same time international jurisdictions have recognized the reality that imprisonment is, simply in itself, likely to be experienced as cruel, inhuman and degrading. The European Court of Human Rights has stated that the prohibition on inhuman or degrading treatment (Article 3 European Convention, equivalent to ICCPR Article 7), is not breached in the prison context by suffering which is simply the 'inevitable' result of legitimate punishment (*Frerot v France* [2007]). It has therefore been necessary to draw a line between what is 'inherent' in detention and what goes further.

The European Court has held, for example, that overcrowded and insanitary conditions *may* amount to inhuman or degrading treatment or punishment, in breach of Article 3 (see, for example, *Badila v Romania* [2011], 79). Whether a breach is found will then depend on whether, for example, there was one or more people in the cell, and the length of time the person was held in the poor conditions (*Grant & Anor v The Ministry of Justice* [2011]).

The total institution controls the physical and mental wellbeing of the detainee, and rights violations can arise from the failure to provide healthcare, or from the imposition of treatment, for example in a forensic psychiatric facility. The bar is again set high for showing that the treatment, or lack of treatment, was inhuman or degrading. In the case of healthcare, a decision whether rights are being violated has been held to depend on '(a) the medical condition of the prisoner; (b) the adequacy of the medical assistance and care provided in detention, and (c) the advisability of maintaining the detention measure in view of the state of health of an applicant' (*Dybeku v Albania* [2007], 42). A breach was found, for example, in the case of a life prisoner in an Italian prison, confined to a wheelchair, despite medical advice that his need for round-the-clock medical care meant he should not be detained in a prison (*Scoppola v Italy* [2008]).

It has been noted that the unavoidable degradation of punitive detention is taken into account when considering whether imprisonment amounts to inhuman or degrading treatment.

The courts considering involuntary treatment similarly weigh up the therapeutic intention, and overall tend to defer to medical opinion about the medical necessity for the treatment. In *Herczegfalvy v Austria* [1993] the ECtHR concluded that extensive restraints employed against a violent psychiatric patient did not amount to inhuman or degrading treatment. It accepted the claim that the treatment was medically justified, saying that, while the Court must be satisfied of the medical necessity:

> [A]s a general rule, a measure which is a therapeutic necessity cannot be regarded as inhuman or degrading.
>
> *(82)*

Whilst it is likely to be difficult to disprove medical necessity, the case nonetheless confirms that the prohibition applies even where the action complained about was intended for the patient's protection. There is currently debate about whether the more recent CRPD right to 'respect for . . . physical and metal integrity on an equal basis with others' (Article 17) prohibits involuntary psychiatric treatment, but according to McSherry it is more likely to be read as requiring limitations rather than total abolition of such practices (McSherry 2013, p. 387). Potentially more challenging to the whole practice of involuntary detention is the right to liberty under the CRPD. The provision that 'the existence of a disability shall in no case justify a deprivation of liberty' (Article 14.1[b]) may mean that 'mental health laws that enable the involuntary detention of those with mental impairments are in breach of Art 14' (McSherry 2013, p. 391).

In addition to the formal conventions, international standards exist to protect people in detention. These are not binding or enforceable, but may influence policy and practice. They include the UN Basic Principles for the Treatment of Prisoners (1990) and the Standard Minimum Rules for the Treatment of Prisoners (SMR) adopted in 1957 and substantially revised as the 'Mandela rules', with reference to human rights and other developments in 2015.[2] The UN Principles for the Protection of Persons with Mental Illness for the Improvement of Mental Health Care (1991) include rights to least restrictive interventions and to independent oversight of involuntary detention and treatment.

There are, however, significant limitations to the application of these instruments in Australia. Rights under international conventions are not directly enforceable unless they have been incorporated into domestic law; the main protections discussed here are not part of Australian law (Naylor 2013, p. 401).

Complaints of violations of the ICCPR can be brought by Australians to the UN Human Rights Committee, to the Committee against Torture for breaches of the CAT, and to the Committee on the Rights of Persons with Disabilities for breaches of the CRPD. These Committees can provide views on the merits of complaints and make recommendations for a remedy. These cannot be enforced, however, and there are obvious practical barriers to accessing a committee in the first place, especially for a person in detention. Australian governments have a history of ignoring views adverse to their actions, and this was the response to the only complaint brought by a prisoner (*Brough* [2003]).[3]

The international instruments and jurisprudence are most directly relevant in Victoria and the Australian Capital Territory (ACT), which have legislated for the same rights. The international case law on, for example, the prohibition on cruel, inhuman and degrading treatment, can therefore be referred to in Victorian and ACT courts in interpreting the application of that right. The application of formal human rights legislation will be discussed next, followed by consideration of the rights protections provided by other domestic legislation governing these closed environments.

## *Domestic human rights legislation*

Only two Australian jurisdictions, Victoria and the ACT, have formal rights instruments. Otherwise Australian jurisdictions have not taken up the internationally recognized human rights in a formal sense. The National Human Rights Consultation in 2009 demonstrated majority support for a formal human rights document, and recommended an enforceable Human Rights Act, but the federal government opted for a non-binding national Human Rights Framework, as well as legislation that introduced a requirement for parliamentary scrutiny of all legislation for human rights compliance (Lynch 2013, pp. 20–4).

The Victorian *Charter of Human Rights and Responsibilities Act 2006* (*Charter*) and the ACT *Human Rights Act* 2004 (HRA) largely incorporate the rights specified in the ICCPR. Public authorities, which include private and public prisons and psychiatric facilities, are required to comply with these human rights obligations (s. 38 Charter; s. 40B HRA), and the courts are required to interpret all statutory provisions in a way that is compatible with protected rights, as far as is possible consistent with the statutory purpose (s. 32 Charter; s. 30 HRA). The HRA includes the right to bring an action for a breach of the legislation (s. 40C), but there is no such power of direct enforcement under the Charter, under which any breach has to be raised along with another pre-existing cause of action.

The only case where this has been successful in the prison context in Victoria was the decision in *Castles* (2010) which upheld a prisoner's request to continue IVF treatment, with reference to the s. 47(1)(f) *Corrections Act* right to 'access to reasonable medical care and treatment necessary for the preservation of health' and to the requirement for 'humane treatment' when detained, under the Charter. Rights principles have, however, been drawn on in a number of cases on prison conditions.[4] They may also be included in private prison contracts, although these are not enforceable by prisoners due to the doctrine of privity of contract.

Australian and international studies emphasize the substantial health needs of prison populations (AIHW 2013, Victorian Ombudsman 2011, 2014). For example, the Victorian Ombudsman and the Office of Police Integrity reported in 2006 that healthcare for prisoners had 'significant deficiencies' (p. 89). As one commentator observed at the time:

> it is imperative that the relevant public authorities review and improve Victorian prison conditions and prisoner health care services if they are to meet the threshold required by s 10 (protection from torture and cruel, inhuman or degrading treatment), s 21 (right to liberty and security of person) and s 22 (humane treatment when deprived of liberty) of the Victorian *Charter.*
>
> *(Lynch 2008)*

Particular challenges are providing appropriate mental healthcare in prisons, and the increasing proportions of prisoners with mental illnesses. The Victorian Supreme Court in the case of *R v White* (2007) was critical of the continued imprisonment of a person found not guilty on the grounds of mental impairment, due to the unavailability of a bed in the mental health facility, noting that 'his continued incarceration in a prison would appear to be contrary to the spirit, if not the letter of the *Charter of Human Rights and Responsibilities*' (p. 4). The Victorian Ombudsman was critical of the continued unmet demand at the facility in his 2014 report (2014, p. 13).

The prohibition on cruel, inhuman and degrading treatment under the Charter was discussed in relation to involuntary treatment in the case of a mentally ill sex offender prescribed the anti-libidinal medication Depo-Provera as part of a community-based order under the

*Mental Health Act 1986* (*Re Appeal of 09-085* [2009]). The medication had led to significant levels of osteoporosis, and the applicant challenged the continued treatment on the basis that it was in breach of the Charter. The Victorian Mental Health Review Board held that therapeutic treatment, being intended to benefit the patient, would not be regarded as cruel, inhuman or degrading unless it reached a certain level of severity. Despite the serious side effects of the medication, it was not seen as reaching this level of severity. However, the board clearly accepted that this treatment *could* reach the point of breaching the patient's rights.

Finally, however, most human rights are subject to limitations. Under s. 7(2) of the Charter a right can be subject to 'such reasonable limits as can be demonstrably justified in a free and democratic society based on human dignity, equality and freedom' (see also HRA s. 28). This means that where a claim is made to the protection of a right, the first question will be whether the right is 'engaged' on the particular facts, and then whether it has in any event been overridden by other competing requirements. This means that for a person held in a closed environment the real question may be, not what rights they retain, but in what circumstances their rights can lawfully be overridden.

## Other domestic rights protections

Rights can be protected in sector-specific legislation such as corrections and mental health acts. These are important but generally not directly enforceable by detainees. Australian states have corrections legislation covering conditions in prisons, which usually addresses access to, for example, visits, correspondence, and religious practice, and regulates uses of restraints, segregation, prison transfers and so on. To the extent that these offer protections they are not enforceable by prisoners. Further, such legislation usually articulates an overriding obligation to maintain the security of the facility, the 'security and good order of the prison and the safe custody and welfare of the prisoners' (Vic s. 21[1]) and the courts have generally accepted the argument of correctional management as to the need for particular restrictive measures in the interests of security (Edney 2001).

For people in the criminal justice system with mental illnesses, legislative protections vary. They may be held in police cells and prisons due to their criminal offending, in which case issues of access to appropriate care may be raised. There are no specific legislative provisions addressing this other than, for example, the Victorian *Corrections Act* right to 'reasonable medical care' (s. 47[1][f]). Pressure of overcrowding and under-resourcing can make this difficult in practice, as noted in the Ombudsman reports mentioned above.

Detention in a secure facility will usually be authorized by mental health legislation that establishes the criteria for lawful detention and incorporates review mechanisms. The recently reformed *Mental Health Act 2014* (Vic) (MHA) is explicitly rights-based with clear criteria for involuntary detention and treatment and notification requirements, and oversight, independent review and complaints avenues. International jurisprudence has emphasized that independent review is vital to protecting rights of people subject to compulsory treatment. The failure to provide the required regular review was found to be a breach of the Charter right to a fair hearing under the previous Victorian mental health legislation (*Kracke v Mental Health Review Board* [2009]).

## Rights-based monitoring

Some sector-specific legislation therefore incorporates human rights principles, but there is limited scope to protect the rights of people in closed environments through the courts in Australia (other than under the HRA).

A separate form of rights protection can, however, be provided through external monitoring of closed environments. The very nature of these facilities – secure and closed off from the community – gives rise to the risk of abuse, irrespective of the purpose of the facility. External monitoring provides a form of oversight, of opening the closed environment to the public gaze. Monitoring involves inspection of the facility, and the presentation of a report and recommendations; there is no separate power of enforcement. Monitoring will ideally prevent rights abuses; it should at least discover and report publicly on abuses.

Monitoring is internationally regarded as a vital part of rights protections, and the international best practice framework will be discussed, followed by consideration of the forms of monitoring currently carried out in Australia.

## *International approaches to monitoring closed environments*

A comprehensive process has been established under the Optional Protocol to the Convention against Torture (OPCAT) to give practical effect to the Convention against Torture. The OPCAT came into force in 2006, covering all places where a person is deprived of liberty, defined as, 'any form of detention or imprisonment or the placement of a person in a public or private custodial setting which that person is not permitted to leave at will by order of any judicial, administrative or other authority' (Article 4[2]). This definition clearly includes the closed environments discussed here.

Countries ratifying OPCAT are agreeing to a two-tiered monitoring framework. At the national level they are to establish effective and robust domestic monitoring bodies to visit places of detention to investigate and report on the treatment and conditions of detention in closed environments (National Preventive Mechanisms, or NPMs). OPCAT specifies that the domestic NPMs must have statutory powers, be functionally independent, have unrestricted access to visit closed environments, have adequate resources to carry out their role, and be able to report publicly (OPCAT Articles 18, 19, 20 and 23).

As a second tier, signatories are also required to provide access for announced and unannounced visits from the international monitoring body the UN Subcommittee for the Prevention of Torture (SPT). The state is required to provide unrestricted access to the selected places of detention, including records and data, and for private interviews with detainees, staff, government officials and anyone else they wish to speak to. The SPT provides reports and recommendations to the state. It only publishes the reports at the request of the state (Part III OPCAT) but to date almost all states have agreed to publication. It therefore has unparalleled opportunity to work with countries collaboratively, bring comparative expertise from other countries and other forms of closed environment.

In other countries concerns have been expressed at failure to fully resource monitoring bodies, in particular (but not only) when they have taken on an NPM role (Nowak 2012, p. 309). There are also limits to the capacity of the SPT to provide comprehensive international oversight for resourcing reasons. A country's participation in the OPCAT process is, however, a significant statement of support for these rights protections, and requires commitment to ensuring that domestic monitoring bodies have the powers for effective oversight.

Australia became a signatory to the OPCAT in May 2009 and has taken some steps towards ratification (Fletcher 2012). The next stages depend on political will, but if ratified and implemented, the OPCAT will provide a significant addition to the oversight of rights in places of detention across Australia.

Eighty-one countries have now ratified OPCAT (according to the Association for the Prevention of Torture database [accessed 24 May 2016]). Most countries have identified one or more existing domestic monitoring bodies to fulfil the role of NPMs. For example, OPCAT was ratified by New Zealand in 2007, and its NPM draws on five existing monitoring agencies, with the NZ Human Rights Commission being the Central NPM. If this was to be the approach taken in Australia it would be necessary to review existing monitoring bodies and to address any deficiencies in their structure and powers.

### *Domestic monitoring bodies*

Australia nonetheless already has a range of formal monitoring bodies whose role – explicitly or implicitly – includes oversight of rights of detainees.

At federal and state levels there are Ombudsman Offices, and Human Rights Commissions, which respond to complaints; most also have powers to inspect places of detention. The Victorian Ombudsman, for example, can receive complaints about prisons and other closed environments (other than police cells), can inspect these closed environments, and can carry out 'own motion' inquiries. The Victorian Ombudsman also has explicit powers to investigate whether a government action is incompatible with a right under the Charter (*Ombudsman Act 1973* [Vic], s. 13[2]), and has examined systemic human rights issues in recent reports on conditions in prisons, in juvenile justice facilities, and on deaths in custody. Most recently the Victorian Ombudsman has reported on an investigation into rehabilitative programmes in Victorian prisons, and the impacts of the unprecedented overcrowding in Victorian prisons on prison conditions.[5]

There are also a number of specialist monitoring bodies in Australian jurisdictions. For example, Western Australia (WA) and New South Wales (NSW) have independent statutory prison inspectorates, modelled on the long-established and highly regarded United Kingdom Inspectorate of Prisons, with powers to carry out announced and unannounced visits to prisons and juvenile detention centres, and to report publicly (pursuant to the *Inspector of Custodial Services Act 2003* [WA] and the *Inspector of Custodial Services Act 2012* [NSW]). In Victoria the MHA provides for oversight by Community Visitors (Pt 9), the Chief Psychiatrist (Pt 7 Div 2) and the Mental Health Tribunal (Pt 8), and for complaints to a separate Mental Health Complaints Commissioner (Pt 10).

To be effective in protecting rights, monitoring bodies need to be independent of government and of the agency, well resourced, and to have unrestricted powers of entry to the closed environment. Some Australian monitoring bodies do have these powers, but others are more limited and there is no overarching monitoring structure for closed environments. Australia has been said to have a 'patchwork' of oversight bodies (Harding and Morgan 2008).

Monitoring regimes are clearly useful mechanisms of transparency and accountability. Many publish their reports, in parliament and on their websites, and achieve public exposure of their critiques of the operation of closed environments, as well as negotiating a range of changes in more low-key ways. Some report high rates of implementation but they are, at the same time, limited by the ultimate unenforceability of their recommendations. Their effectiveness is therefore dependent on political factors such as their reputational credibility and capacity to negotiate change (Naylor 2013, p. 413).

## Conclusion

People can be detained in closed institutions such as prisons, police cells and forensic psychiatric facilities as a result of decisions in the criminal justice system. Detention in any closed facility brings inevitable risks of rights abuse, from the very fact of detention in a 'total institution' or as a result of the punitive, therapeutic or administrative context. In prisons and police cells the concept of 'rights' can be seen by the community as contradicted by the fact of having (even allegedly) committed a crime, and the loss of rights as acceptable as part of punishment. In closed psychiatric facilities therapeutic goals may lawfully lead to controls and treatments for the individual's 'good' and for the safety of the other patients/detainees. Most fundamentally in all closed environments the expectation that escape is prevented means security requirements are likely to take priority over any individual rights.

As outlined above, there are a range of human rights protections articulated in international conventions, in domestic rights instruments, and in domestic legislation more generally, although their practical usefulness to people held in detention may be limited. There are important protections also provided by external monitoring bodies. Some places of detention are more robustly monitored than others. Ratification of OPCAT would drive improvement of monitoring bodies in Australia, to achieve compliance as NPMs. It would also expose Australia to internationally informed oversight.

It is said that a society shows its true values in its places of detention. In the words of Nelson Mandela: 'no one truly knows a nation until one has been inside its jails' (Mandela 1995). The punitive discourses that justify limitations on rights in Australia are at least in part related to the understanding and awareness of rights in the Australian community. The 2009 National Human Rights Consultation found limited knowledge of human rights in Australia and 'complacency about the state of human rights protection, and ignorance about how they are protected' (Dunn 2013, p. 519, Colmar Brunton Social Research 2009). The international treaties spell out the obligation to educate communities about rights, as a prerequisite to democratic citizenship. There is need for a more informed and sophisticated discussion about human rights and detention in the general community, from which detainees, staff, clinicians and management all come.

Managing detention as part of the criminal justice system, in ways that minimize the loss of rights for detainees, reflects political will. More effective and enforceable human rights depend on a community that rejects simplistic punitive discourses and demands a more humane approach to detention.

## Notes

1 'The right of all clients to respect for individual human worth, dignity and privacy is not waived by any circumstance, regardless of an individual's history of offending or their status as a forensic mental health client or a prisoner. The capacity or right to consent is not forfeited as a result of a history of offending or status as a prisoner.' National Statement of Principles for Forensic Mental Health 2006 (Principle 7).
2 The new Rule 1, for example, now embodies the prohibition on torture and cruel, inhuman or degrading treatment or punishment, and specifies that 'All prisoners shall be treated with the respect due to their inherent dignity and value as human beings'.
3 The UN Human Rights Committee found that the prisons conditions in which Brough, a young Indigenous offender, had been kept amounted to inhuman and degrading treatment in contravention of Articles 10(1) and 10(3) of the ICCPR. The Australian Government did not accept that there had been a violation of the ICCPR: see *Response of the Australian Government to the Views of the Committee in Communication No 1184/2003 Brough v Australia.*
4 See, for example, *Dale v DPP* [2009].
5 See Report September 2015 (Victorian Ombudsman 2015).

## References

Australian Institute of Health and Welfare [AIHW], 2013. *The health of Australia's prisoners 2012.* Canberra: AIHW.

Colmar Brunton Social Research, 2009. *National human rights consultation: community research phase.* Sydney: Colmar Brunton Social Research.

Dunn, K., 2013. Do Australians care about human rights? Awareness, hierarchies of sympathy and universality of human rights. *In*: P. Gerber and M. Castan (eds), *Contemporary perspectives on human rights law in Australia*. Pyrmont, NSW: Lawbook Co., 515–30.

Edgar, K. and Rickford, D., 2009. *Too little too late: an independent review of unmet mental health need in prison*. London: Prison Reform Trust.

Edney, R., 2001. Judicial deference to the expertise of correctional administrators: the implications for prisoners' rights. *Australian Journal of Human Rights*, 7, 91.

Fletcher, A., 2012. Australia and the OPCAT. *Alternative Law Journal*, 37(4), 233.

Goffman, E., 1961. On the characteristics of total institutions: staff-inmate relations. *In*: D. Cressey (ed.), *The prison: studies in institutional organization and change*. New York: Holt Reinhart & Winston, 15–67.

Hanley, N. and Ross, S., 2013. Forensic mental health in Australia: charting the gaps. *Current Issues in Criminal Justice*, 24(3), 341–56.

Harding, R. and Morgan, N., 2008. *Implementing the Optional Protocol to the Convention Against Torture: Options for Australia – A report to the Australian Human Rights Commission by Professors Richard Harding and Neil Morgan (Centre for Law and Public Policy, The University of Western Australia)*. Australian Human Rights Commission.

Herrington, V. and Clifford, K., 2012. Policing mental illness: examining the police role in addressing mental ill health. *In*: Isabelle Bartkowiak-Theron and Nicole Asquith (eds), *Policing vulnerabilities*. Annandale, NSW: The Federation Press, 117–31.

Lynch, P., 2008. *Case Note: Fact and Conditions of Detention Must be Appropriate to Detainee's State of Health*. Retrieved on 13 April 2016 from: www.hrlc.org.au/scoppola-v-italy-2008-echr-5055006-10-june-2008.

Lynch, P., 2013. Australia's human rights framework: can there be action without accountability? *In*: P. Gerber and M. Castan (eds), *Contemporary perspectives on human rights law in Australia*. Pyrmont, NSW: Lawbook Co, 17–36.

Mackay, A., 2015. Human rights protections for people with mental health and cognitive disability in prisons. *Psychiatry, Psychology and Law*, 22(6), 842–68.

Mandela, N., 1995. *Long walk to freedom: the autobiography of Nelson Mandela*. Boston, MA: Back Bay Books.

McSherry, B., 2013. Australian mental health laws and human rights. *In*: P. Gerber and M. Castan (eds), *Contemporary perspectives on human rights law in Australia*. Pyrmont, NSW: Lawbook Co., 371–93.

Naylor, B., 2013. Protecting the human rights of prisoners in Australia. *In*: P. Gerber and M. Castan (eds), *Contemporary perspectives on human rights law in Australia*. Pyrmont, NSW: Lawbook Co., 395–416.

Nowak, M., 2012. What's in a name? The prohibitions on torture and ill-treatment today. *In*: C. Gearty and C. Douzinas (eds), *The Cambridge companion to human rights law*. Cambridge: Cambridge University Press, 307–28.

Victorian Ombudsman, 2011. *Investigation into prisoner access to health care*. Melbourne: Victorian Ombudsman.

Victorian Ombudsman, 2014. *Investigation into deaths and harm in custody*. Melbourne: Victorian Ombudsman.

Victorian Ombudsman, 2015. *Investigation into the rehabilitation and reintegration of prisoners in Victoria*. Melbourne: Victorian Ombudsman.

## Cases

*Badila v Romania* [2011] ECHR App No. 31725/04.

*Brough v Australia* (UN Human Rights Committee, Communication No. 1184/2003).

*Castles v Secretary to the Department of Justice & Ors* [2010] VSC 310 (9 July 2010).

*Dale v DPP* [2009] VSCA 212.

*Dybeku v Albania [2007] App no. 41153/06.*

*Frerot v France* [2007] ECHR App No. 70204-01.

*Grant & Anor v The Ministry of Justice* [2011] EWHC 3379 (QB).

*Herczegfalvy v Austria [1993] 25 Eur Court HR 437.*

*Kracke v Mental Health Review Board* [2009] VCAT 646.

*Napier, Re Petition for Judicial Review* [2004] ScotCS 100.

*R v White* [2007] VSC 142 (7 May 2007).

*Re Appeal of 09-085* [2009] VMHRB 1.

*Scoppola v Italy [2008] ECHR App no. 50550/06.*

# 51

# Human rights and imprisonment of older adults

*Diete Humblet and Sonja Snacken*

## Introducing different dimensions of age

The greying of prison populations in western prisons is a relatively recent phenomenon. Older adults seem more adversely affected by imprisonment than their younger counterparts (Mann 2012, Crawley 2005, Crawley and Sparks 2005a, 2005b, 2006, Wahidin and Aday, 2005), indicating that the experience of imprisonment and the struggle to access basic rights and services is age-associated. There is however no agreement as to what constitutes an 'older prisoner': definitions range from 50 to 65 years and above (Maschi et al. 2012, p. 544). We adopt the most common definition in European studies of 65 years and above, linked to the age of retirement (Crawley and Sparks 2006), as the American and Australian definition of 'older prisoners' as aged 50 or over is 'too low to address the distinctive psychological and physiological adjustments and responses to the prison environment of ageing individuals' (Crawley 2005, p. 362). Moreover, there is evidence to suggest that the intra- and inter-individual differences among the older adult population are stronger than intergenerational differences (Westerhof 2013, Hayslip and Panek 1993).

This variation is further enhanced by their different profiles in terms of prison experience. Four main groups of 'elderly' prisoners are recognized (Aday 2003, Goetting 1984), with different experiences of and adaptation to prison life: (1) first timers, incarcerated for a relatively long prison sentence at an older age; (2) prisoners serving a long or life sentence who grow old while incarcerated; (3) ageing recidivist prisoners who enter and exit prison throughout their lifetime; (4) prisoners sentenced to shorter periods of incarceration later in life.

This illustrates the complexity of grasping the process of ageing in a prison context. The different dimensions of age developed in gerontology help us to better understand this complexity and its implications for penological research, human rights concerns and prison policy. We first briefly describe these dimensions. We then scrutinize how European human rights standards, as developed by the European Court of Human Rights (ECtHR), the European Committee for the Prevention of Torture and Inhuman or Degrading Treatment or Punishment (CPT) and Recommendations of the Committee of Ministers of the Council of Europe address various dimensions of age regarding imprisonment of older adults.

## Chronological age

The main distinction within the concept of age is between chronological and non-chronological age. Chronological age refers to the amount of time that has passed since birth, and is closely related to the legal definition of age – that is, at which persons are entitled to access specific goods, services or benefits, such as retirement (Hayslip and Panek 1993).

Although most prison studies use the chronological age, it is criticized for failing to predict other aspects in an individual (Hayslip and Panek 1993). In our own ethnographic study, prison staff and fellow prisoners were often mistaken in designating or omitting certain prisoners as 'older' (+65y). Chronological age should thus be used in combination with other dimensions, as described below.

## Biological, psychological, social, and functional age

*Biological age* can be defined either by (a) the condition of the individual's bodily processes, or (b) as an individual's present position relative to potential lifespan (Hayslip and Panek 1993). Drawing on prison time, O'Donnell (2014) introduced the concept of the 'pain quotient', referring to the ratio of 'time to be served' and 'time to be lived'. The pain quotient is greatest for the prisoner whose life expectancy is shorter than his prison time and for whom the absence of a non-prison future must be confronted (O'Donnell 2014, p. 202). The knowledge that 'time is running out' is what makes the experiences of elderly prisoners distinctive (Crawley and Sparks 2006, Deaton et al. 2009–10). Moreover, international research suggests that prisoners experience 'accelerated ageing', due to factors arising both prior to (lifestyle, drug abuse) and during incarceration (impact of imprisonment) (Fazel et al. 2001, Loeb et al. 2008, Maschi et al. 2012).

*Psychological age* comprises behavioural and perceptual aspects. Behaviourally, psychological age is based on the adaptive capacities and skills that people have and use to adapt to changing biological and environmental demands (such as memory, intelligence, problem-solving, coping, emotions), whereas the perceptual component refers to how old people perceive or feel that they are ('subjective age', 'feel-age') (Hutchison 2011). Both concepts correlate with life satisfaction and wellbeing (Mock and Eibach 2011).

The term *social age* denotes an individual's habits, attitudes, preferences, behaviours, and activities relative to the expectations of society (Hayslip and Panek 1993). Prisoners' social age is important from a human rights perspective considering that older people are often victims of stereotypes ('ageism'): for example, older persons no longer need education or vocational training, have no future expectations. This may result in a lack of meaningful prison activities such as education, work, vocational training, exercise, and recreational activities (Crawley and Sparks 2006, Mann 2012). Conversely, expectations may be too high, such as finding employment as a condition for parole (Scheirs 2014).

Definitions of *functional age* vary greatly, but have in common that they are an index of one's level of capacities (Hayslip and Panek 1993, p. 10). Functional limitations impact the opportunities to engage in prison activities (such as work and physical exercise) and to thrive in the physical prison environment. The specific nature of prison life should be taken into account. Drawing on the traditional literature concerning 'activities of daily living' (ADLs), Williams et al. (2006) coined the term 'prison activities of daily living' (PADLs) in their study on the functional impairment in geriatric (55+) female prisoners. In addition to five traditional ADLs (bathing, eating, toileting, dressing, and transferring in/out of bed), they identified five physical activities that are unique to independent daily functioning in prison: dropping to the floor for alarms, standing for head count, getting to the dining hall, hearing orders from staff, and climbing on/off the top bunk bed. They found that functional impairment is much more common in PADLs measures than in measures of ADLs and argued that individuals who are independent in the community, might be regarded as functionally impaired in a prison environment.

To conclude, the common use of chronological age to delineate who is considered 'old' can be considered as inadequate, whereas other types of age provide a more adequate method to denote a person's ability and to identify those individuals who are in need of, or lacking, support (Rikard and Rosenberg 2007).

## Human dignity

The first question to be raised from a human rights perspective is whether imprisonment at old age is in itself compatible with human dignity (Article 3, *European Convention on Human Rights* [ECHR]). Several cases before the ECtHR challenge the sentencing of elderly offenders to imprisonment as inherently inhuman and degrading (*Sawoniuk v UK* 29 May 2001, *Papon v France* 7 June 2001, *Hasko v Turkey* 17 January 2012). Their advanced age (80, 90 and 80 years respectively: cf. 'chronological age') and the fact that their sentences exceed their expected lifespan (to life imprisonment, 10 years and 4,5 years respectively), are seen as amounting de facto to a death sentence (cf. 'biological age' and high 'pain quotient'). The Court, however, retorts that there is no prohibition in the ECHR or in any of the Council of Europe's Member States against the detention of persons at an advanced age. A sentence to life imprisonment for war crimes imposed on an 80-year-old is not disproportionate due to the seriousness of the crime and the fact that there is still a prospect of release (*Sawoniuk v UK* 29 May 2001). However, where imprisonment is imposed, its implementation must be in accordance with human dignity. Detention of an elderly person over a lengthy period may violate human dignity, but regard is to be had to the particular circumstances of each specific case (*Papon v France* 7 June 2001, *Priebke v Italy* 5 April 2001, *Sawoniuk v UK* 29 May 2001). These relate to the age and state of health of the person concerned as well as the duration and nature of the treatment and its physical or mental effects. The Court consistently emphasizes the duty of care of the authorities for the health and wellbeing of older prisoners, including assessments whether they are fit for continued detention on medical grounds ('biological/physical age').

## Health

Ageing is often accompanied by health concerns; rights regarding their health are hence of paramount importance to older prisoners.

### *Unfit for continued detention*

Advanced age coupled to poor health can become a bar to continued detention (*Papon v France* 7 June 2001). According to the CPT, typical examples of prisoners unsuited for continued detention are:

> those who are the subject of a short-term fatal prognosis, who are suffering from a serious disease which cannot be properly treated in prison conditions, who are severely handicapped or of advanced age. . . . In cases of this type, it lies with the prison doctor to draw

up a report for the responsible authority, with a view to suitable alternative arrangements being made.

*(3rd General Report, CPT/Inf (93) 12 §70)*

The Court systematically looks into three elements: (a) the situation of the prisoner, (b) the quality of medical care, and (c) the continued appropriateness of detention given the person's health status (*Patsos v Greece* 25 September 2012 §53). Advanced age and health problems in themselves are not sufficient to bar continued detention if they cannot be considered as critical for detention purposes and if the prisoner receives adequate medical care (*Papon v France* 7 June 2001, *Haidn v Germany* 13 January 2011). Even the continued detention of an 82-year-old prisoner recognized as 70 per cent invalid, in a dormitory with 50 prisoners, was not found to constitute inhuman and degrading treatment, as his overall condition was found to be 'good' by the prison doctor, he did not suffer from a physical handicap that significantly and permanently affected his sensory and motor skills, and the authorities closely monitored his health through repeated transfers to hospitals (*Patsos v Greece* 25 September 2012). This predominance of the 'functional age' and medical care is confirmed in a case where Article 3 of the ECHR was violated due to continued detention of a paraplegic prisoner who was completely dependent on others for all daily activities; to whom 'medical' care was provided by unqualified fellow prisoners; whose release had been requested by the prison director based on medical reports but had been delayed by the court for one year (*Farbtuhs v Latvia* 2 December 2004). A decision to transfer an 85-year-old prisoner from prison to home detention on medical grounds within three months was, however, found to be satisfactory (*Priebke v Italy* 5 April 2001). The inaction or lack of diligence on the part of the public authorities is hence an important criterion for assessing breaches of Article 3 of the ECHR.

## *Equivalence of medical care*

The right to adequate medical care equivalent to that in the outside society is endorsed by other European human rights instruments (CPT Standards, Recommendation No. R [98] 71) and is of paramount importance to older prisoners in daily prison life. The health of older prisoners is generally described as worse than that of their younger counterparts, and worse than that of community-dwelling older adults (Fazel et al. 2001, Loeb et al. 2008). The (co)morbidity of older prisoners is well documented: hearing and vision impairments, respiratory and heart problems, diabetes, arthritis, bladder problems, hypertension, Alzheimer's, Parkinson's, cancer, and mental health problems, such as depression and anxiety disorders (Aday 2003, Kakoullis et al. 2010, Mann 2012, Fazel et al. 2001, 2004). These health challenges are often *left unaddressed* within prison environments (Aday 2003, Mann 2012, Wahidin 2004, Fazel et al. 2004), despite the existence of their legal status as patients. The stories of some older prisoners bear witness to despair and frustration, caused by wrong or late diagnosis, chaotic dispensation of medication, absence of sufficient resources and prison staff, lengthy waiting times, wrongfully prescribed or lack of medication, degeneration caused by infrequent check-ups, and even death of fellow prisoners attributed to the lack of concern by healthcare staff (Humblet and Decorte 2013, Mann 2012, Fazel et al. 2004). In our own research, a male respondent denounces the lack of adequate prison healthcare as follows:

> You'd better stay healthy in here! In 2009, I received medication for kidney infection for 4 weeks from the doctor. Until I got a burst appendix, and had to have surgery in the hospital the same night! When I asked the doctor why he hadn't noticed anything, and

> nothing was wrong with my kidneys, he said: 'We haven't got the medical equipment to check for this'. The only what you can get in here are pain inhibitors.
>
> *(Male, age 73)*

Experiences stating the contrary are also sometimes present ('they do what they can', 'requested medical treatment is received on time'), representing a more resigned acceptance.

Older inmates appear extremely conscious of their more vulnerable health status. They fear becoming seriously ill, resulting in uncertainty and distress and adding to the general 'pains of imprisonment' (Wahidin 2004, Sykes 1958). They often dwell on the possibility that something might happen to them, especially at night. Many prisons do not provide permanent medical care, and certainly not at night. The fact that the cell doors are locked at night, combined with fewer prison staff who have to follow an elaborate procedure in case of an emergency, is felt as highly threatening. As one older male prisoner wrote: 'If anything goes seriously wrong here at night, you're dead'.

In sum, there appears to be a lack of preventive or proactive attention to the (health) problems, needs, and sensibilities of older prisoners. Mann (2012, p. 106) provides a possible explanation as 'many of the health care professionals are unsure as to what their role within the prison actually is, with many demonstrating a distant and non-empathic attitude which is more akin to the role of custodian than carer'. In addition, prisoners have a 'second-class' status, and thus are not regarded to be in a position to 'make demands' for healthcare (Mann 2011, Wahidin 2004). This exercise of power might in turn lead to forms of resistance, such as refusing healthcare, which undermines the right to adequate prison healthcare. In the wake of the tension between 'control' versus 'care' that has characterized prisons since time immemorial (Sim 2002), it is argued that the older ones are mainly losing out (Mann 2012, Wahidin 2004).

### *Use of restraints*

Power is also exercised by prison officers during transfer to another prison or to an outside hospital in order to receive treatment. Prisoners tell stories of being carried off *handcuffed* for medical care, resulting in strong feelings of humiliation, degradation and stigmatization (Humblet and Decorte 2013, Mann 2012), also termed 'visible signifiers of discipline' (Wahidin 2004, pp. 133–4). Despite several rulings of the ECtHR declaring the practice of restraining prisoners who present no serious risk of escape to constitute humiliating treatment violating Article 3 ECHR (*Henaf v France* 27 November 2003 §§ 56–60, *Mouisel v France* 14 November 2002 § 47, *Tarariyeva v Russia* 14 December 2006 §§ 109–11), shackles and handcuffs are still regularly utilized on older prisoners (cf. Prisons and Probation Ombudsman 2013).

### *End of life*

Older prisoners are at risk of becoming terminally ill or dying in prison. This enhances the need for palliative care and other end-of-life decisions, such as assisted suicide or medically assisted euthanasia in those countries where this is legally possible (Snacken et al. 2015). The rare empirical studies into these situations illustrate the difficulty of introducing palliative care in prisons. Palliative care is 'a comprehensive approach to treating serious illness with a focus on keeping dying patients comfortable through pain control and addressing psychological, social and spiritual concerns, instead of treating the disease or condition' (Crawley 2007, p. 234). Its emphasis on the physical and emotional comfort of the patients and on providing compassionate nursing care is at odds with the 'often rigid concerns and procedures of the prison environment' (ibid., p. 354), with prison staff culture focused on security and with difficult access to medication due to fear of drug misuse (Turner et al. 2011). Release on humanitarian or compassionate grounds seems the most humane solution (van Zyl Smit and Snacken 2009, p. 156). The Council of Europe's Recommendation R (98) 7 on the ethical and organizational aspects of healthcare in prison states (§ 51):

> The decision as to when patients subject to short term fatal prognosis should be transferred to outside hospital units should be taken on medical grounds. While awaiting such transfer, these patients should receive optimum nursing care during the terminal phase of their illness within the prison health care centre. In such cases provision should be made for periodic respite care in an outside hospice. The possibility of a pardon for medical reasons or early release should be examined.

Terminally ill or dying prisoners would normally no longer be a threat to society and should have the possibility to die outside of prison if they so wish (CPT 3rd General Report, CPT/ Inf (93) 12 § 70).

## Safety and wellbeing: 'institutional thoughtlessness', personal resources and human rights

### *'Institutional thoughtlessness'*

National authorities are not only responsible for the health but also for the safety and wellbeing of older prisoners. Prison regimes should be adjusted to meet their special needs (*Papon v France* 7 June 2001). This requirement is at odds with what Crawley and Sparks (2005a, 2005b) have described as the 'institutional thoughtlessness' of prisons towards the older population. This concept comprises two separate but complementary strands, the *physical prison environment* and traditional *prison practice:* it covers 'prisons being poorly adapted to the needs of older prisoners and of staff, consciously or otherwise, failing to mitigate the effects of this when it would be within their power to do so' (Crawley 2005, p. 356). As a result, many older prisoners experience imprisonment as a more severe form of punishment. We now look into major aspects of institutional thoughtlessness.

### *Accommodation*

The ECtHR takes an overall view of conditions of detention when assessing infringements of Article 3 ECHR. In *Papon v France* 7 June 2001, the ECtHR observes:

> that some of the matters raised by the applicant (the absence of grab bars in the shower, the short chain on the fanlight and the steep stairs preventing him from reaching the exercise yard) have now been resolved (a seat has been installed in the shower, the chain has been lengthened and the applicant now has permission to walk on the landing). Some of the other inconveniences he mentioned (such as his light being turned on by the warder in the night in order to carry out a check) form part of the constraints imposed on all prisoners for reasons of surveillance and security.

Prisons may thus require additional facilities or modifications to meet the needs of elderly prisoners (van Zyl Smit and Snacken 2009, p. 140). Institutional thoughtlessness is rooted in the prison practice that every prisoner should be treated the same. As a result, elderly prisoners are often unable to take advantage of facilities that are in principle available but which de facto they cannot access, which may result in human rights violations (Crawley 2005, p. 356; *Farbtuhs v Latvia* 2 December 2004, § 58). The principle of 'normalization' of prison life should prevail here (R 5 EPR), as stated by Recommendation R (98) 7 on ethical and organizational aspects of healthcare in prison (§ 50):

> Prisoners with serious physical handicaps and those of advanced age should be accommodated in such a way as to allow as normal a life as possible. . . . Structural alterations should be effected to assist the wheelchair-bound and handicapped on lines similar to those in the outside environment.

## *Regime, services and activities*

Prison regimes and balanced programmes of activities are essential in determining whether conditions of imprisonment amount to inhuman or degrading treatment (*Alver v Estonia*, 8 November 2005, R 25.1 and 25.2 EPR). For the CPT, this entails at least '8 hours or more outside their cells, engaged in purposeful activity of a varied nature' (2nd General Report, CPT/Inf (92) 3 § 47). In reality, a majority of older prisoners in our study kill most of their time in their cell, mainly as a consequence of their biological, social, psychological or functional age. Virtually no allowances are made for older prisoners in terms of disciplinary rules, work, activities, or timetables. This may lead to more disciplinary sanctions, for example, because of hearing impairments, and to social isolation within prison, for example, when physical ailments prevent older prisoners from participating in prison labour or outdoor exercise. As one older prisoner described: 'Old age is not only a prison, but in itself a punishment'.

Prison studies emphasize the importance of the 'dialectic of control' and forms of 'resistance' by prisoners, 'whose interests and preferences must be taken into account to some extent in order to sustain a fragile, negotiated order' (Crawley and Sparks 2005a, p. 355). Older prisoners, however, are often regarded as a more compliant group, whose acts of resistance do not touch upon fundamental issues of order. 'A structured inability to protest or register complaint in an effective manner' (Crawley and Sparks 2005a, p. 355) may entail that their complaints about prison conditions and breaches of their rights are never heard.

## *Meaning of life: the importance of personal resources*

Imprisonment is a significant life-event which 'by disturbing the orderliness of life, [it] may bring the meaning of life itself into question' (Crawley and Sparks 2006, p. 70). Meaning in life encompasses an explicit existential question as well as meaning in everyday life. Apart from the physical (physical integrity) and functional dimension (capacities), the psychological (autonomy, privacy) and social dimension (social support, social integration) are put forward as significant sources for older adults to live a meaningful life on a day-to-day basis (Westerhof 2013, Kuin and Westerhof 2007). Although all dimensions are important, the right balance between various sources is necessary to counter excessive vulnerability (Westerhof 2013, p. 16). The case law of the ECtHR on older prisoners seems to prioritize the physical and functional dimensions, while paying only scant attention to the psychological and social dimensions (for an exception, see *Papon v France* 7 June 2001: 'It is also clear from the case-file that the applicant keeps up a social life and receives regular visits from his family, friends and lawyers'). Prison studies, on the contrary, describe how losses and deprivations make it increasingly difficult for older prisoners to keep their lives purposeful. On the other hand, the age-associated decline of purpose in life should not be overgeneralized, as some prisoners may find enrichment in positive experiences (Doron and Love 2013) or benefit from intrapsychic ways of coping with previous experiences (Mann 2012, Crawley and Sparks 2005b) or unchangeable losses (Pinquart 2002).

### *Integration or segregation?*

An adequate regime, adapted activities and healthcare, good relationships with staff and fellow inmates, and contacts with the outside world are of pivotal importance for all prisoners, but raise specific challenges for older prisoners. Are these best met through policies of integration or segregation in specific units? Both options have advantages and disadvantages. Specific units are more adapted to their special needs and less focused on security, but may lead to social isolation *intra* and *extra muros*. Integration may result in increased victimization due to their physical weakness, access to medication or because of their offence (such as sex offenders), inadequate prison regimes, and disproportionate levels of security. Several European countries have started organizing special units (including Germany, Switzerland and Belgium) providing more adequate facilities (larger cells accessible by wheelchair; adapted sanitation, activities and outdoor exercise) and reintegration programmes (memory exercises and food instruction rather than vocational training) (Forum Européen de Politique Criminelle Appliquée 2015). In our own research, older prisoners developed adaptation strategies aiming at avoiding transfer to the medical centre or the special unit by posing as more healthy than they were. Keeping in touch with other, younger prisoners and equating special units with 'old people homes' were an important motivation, illustrating the importance of the psychological and social dimensions of age. We advocate that the personal choice of the prisoner should prevail in such decisions.

## Conclusion

The concept of 'age' and grasping the process of ageing in a prison context is a complex matter. We have highlighted some of the inequalities in older prisoners' access to and use of services and basic rights in prison environments. To address issues of dignity and equity, it appears paramount to acknowledge the diversity among the ageing prisoner population. However, prison studies on 'older' prisoners are often based on chronological age, while the case law of the ECtHR on human dignity refers mainly to biological and functional age (health status, dependency) and the quality of medical care. In order to establish infringement of Article 3 of the ECHR, a minimum level of severity must be attained, which does not appear to be easily reached. In current prison practice, however, compliance with other basic penological principles such as 'normalization' of prison life for older prisoners is hardly established. More research is necessary, integrating penological standards on prisons with gerontological insights into the meaning of age.

## References


Aday, R.H., 2003. *Aging prisoners: crisis in American corrections*. Westport, CT: Praeger.

Crawley, E., 2005. Institutional thoughtlessness in prisons and its impacts on the day-to-day prison lives of elderly men. *Journal of Contemporary Criminal Justice*, 21(4), 350–63.

Crawley, E., 2007. Imprisonment in old age. *In*: Y. Jewkes (ed.), *Handbook on prisons*. Cullompton: Willan, 224–44.

Crawley, E. and Sparks, R., 2005a. Hidden injuries? Researching the experiences of older men in English prisons. *Howard Journal of Criminal Justice*, 44(4), 345–56.

Crawley, E. and Sparks, R., 2005b. Older men in prison: survival, coping and identity. *In*: A. Liebling and S. Maruna (eds), *The effects of imprisonment*. Cullompton: Willan Publishing, 343–65.
Crawley, E. and Sparks, R., 2006. Is there life after imprisonment? How elderly men talk about imprisonment and release. *Criminology & Criminal Justice*, 6(1), 63–82.
Deaton, D. Aday, R.H. and Wahidin, A., 2009–10. The effect of health and penal harm on aging female prisoners' views of dying in prison. *Omega*, 60(1), 51–70.
Doron, I.I. and Love, H., 2013. Aging prisoners: a brief report of key legal and policy dilemmas. *International Journal of Criminology and Sociology*, 2, 322–7.
Fazel, S., Hope, T., O'Donnell, I. and Jacoby, R., 2004. Unmet treatment needs of older prisoners: a primary care survey. *Age and Ageing*, 3, 396–8.
Fazel, S., Hope, T., O'Donnell, I., Piper, M. and Jacoby, R., 2001. Health of elderly male prisoners: worse than the general population, worse than younger prisoners. *Age and Ageing*, 30(5), 403–7.
Forum Européen de Politique Criminelle Appliquée, 2015. *Colloque européen: vieillir dans un lieu privatif de liberté – seniors dans un lieu de contrainte,* 4–6 June 2015, Saxerriet – Oberschan (Suisse).
Goetting, A., 1984. The elderly in prison: a profile. *Criminal Justice Review*, 9(2), 14–24.
Hayslip B. and Panek, P.E., 1993. *Adult development and aging*, 2nd edn. New York, NY: Harper Collins College Publishers.
Humblet, D. and Decorte, T., 2013. Detentiebeleving door oudere gevangenen in België: een exploratief onderzoek. *Panopticon*, 34(4), 267–83.
Hutchison, E.D., 2011. A life course perspective. *In*: E.D. Hutchison (ed.), *Dimensions of human behaviour: the changing life course*, 4th edn. Thousand Oaks: Sage Publications, 1–38.
Kakoullis, A., Le Mesurier, N. and Kingston, P., 2010. The mental health of older prisoners. *International Psychogeriatrics*, 22(5), 693–701.
Kuin, Y. and Westerhof, G., 2007. Zingeving. *In*: A.M. Pot, Y. Kuin and M. Vink (eds), *Handboek ouderenpsychologie*. Utrecht: de Tijdstroom, 175–90.
Loeb, S.J., Steffensmeier, D. and Lawrence, F., 2008. Comparing incarcerated and community-dwelling older men's health. *Western Journal of Nursing Research*, 30(2), 234–49.
Mann, N.R., 2011. Ageing prisoners. *In*: B. Crewe and J. Bennett (eds), *The prisoner*. London: Routledge, 92–102.
Mann, N.R., 2012. *Doing harder time? The experiences of an ageing male prison population in England and Wales*. Farnham: Ashgate Publishing, 1–141.
Maschi, T., Viola, D. and Sun, F., 2012. The high cost of the international aging prisoner crisis: well-being as the common denominator for action. *Gerontologist*, 53(4), 543–54.
Mock, S.E. and Eibach, R.P., 2011. Aging attitudes moderate the effect of subjective age on psychological well-being. *Psychology and Aging*, 26(4), 979–86.
O'Donnell, I., 2014. *Prisoners, solitude, and time*. Oxford: Oxford University Press.
Pinquart, M., 2002. Creating and maintaining purpose in life in old age: a meta-analysis. *Ageing International*, 27(2), 90–114.
Prisons and Probation Ombudsman, 2013. *Annual Report 2012–2013*. London: The Stationery Office.
Rikard, R.V. and Rosenberg, E., 2007. Aging inmates: a convergence of trends in the American criminal justice system. *Journal of Correctional Health Care*, 13(3), 150–62.
Scheirs, V. 2014. *De strafuitvoeringsrechtbank aan het werk*. Antwerpen: Maklu.
Sim, J., 2002. The future of prison health care: a critical analysis. *Critical Social Policy*, 22(2), 300–23.
Snacken, S., Devynck, C., Distelmans, W., Gutwirth, S. and Lemmens, C., 2015. Demandes d'euthanasie en prison: souffrance psychique entre dignité humaine et peine de mort? *Criminologie*, 48(1), 101–22.
Sykes, G., 1958. *The society of captives*. Princeton, NJ: Princeton University Press.
Turner, M., Payne, S. and Barbarachild, Z., 2011. Care or custody? An evaluation of palliative care in prisons in North West England. *Palliative Medicine*, 25(4), 370–7.
van Zyl Smit, D. and Snacken, S., 2009. *Principles of European prison law and policy. Penology and human rights*. Oxford: Oxford University Press.
Wahidin, A., 2004. *Older women in the criminal justice system: running out of time*. London: Jessica Kingsley.
Wahidin, A. and Aday, R.H., 2005. The needs of older men and women in the criminal justice system: an international perspective. *Prison Service Journal*, 160, 13–22.
Westerhof, G.J., 2013. Zingeving en ouder worden. *Psychopraktijk*, 5(1), 15–18.
Williams, B.A., Lindquist, K., Sudore, R.L., Strupp, H.M., Willmott, D.J. and Walter, L.C., 2006. Being old and doing time: functional impairment and adverse experiences of geriatric female prisoners. *Journal of the American Geriatrics Society*, 54(4), 702–7.

## *Cases of the European Court of Human Rights*

*Alver v Estonia* App no. 64812/01 (ECtHR 8 November 2005).
*Farbtuhs v Latvia* App no. 4672/02 (ECtHR, 2 December 2004).
*Haidn v Germany* App no. 6587/04 (ECtHR, 13 January 2011).
*Hasko v Turkey* App no. 20578/05 (ECtHR, 17 January 2012).
*Henaf v France* 27 App no. 65436/01 (ECtHR, 27 November 2003).
*Mouisel v France* App no. 67263/01 (ECtHR, 14 November 2002).
*Papon v France* App no. 64666/01 (ECtHR, 7 June 2001).
*Patsos v Greece* App no. 10067/11 (ECtHR, 25 September 2012).
*Priebke v Italy* App no. 48799/99 (ECtHR, 5 April 2001).
*Sawoniuk v UK* App no. 63716/00 (ECtHR, 29 May 2001).
*Tarariyeva v Russia* App no. 4353/03 (ECtHR, 14 December 2006).

## *European prison standards*

Committee for the Prevention of Torture, General Reports on the CPT's activities. Retrieved on 13 April 2016 from: www.cpt.coe.int/en/annual/rep-03.htm.
Committee of Ministers, Council of Europe, 1952. *Convention for the Protection of Human Rights and Fundamental Freedoms* (CETS no. 177) 20 March 1952.
Committee of Ministers, Council of Europe, 1998. *Recommendation R (98) 7 concerning the ethical and organisational aspects of health care in prison (adopted on 8 April 1998).* Strasbourg: Council of Europe.
Committee of Ministers, Council of Europe, 2006. *European Prison Rules.* Strasbourg: Council of Europe.

# 52

# Human rights and prison

## A case study from the Australian Capital Territory

*Lorana Bartels and Jeremy Boland*

### Introduction

This chapter examines human rights standards in the prison context. It presents an overview of the international framework governing the treatment of prisoners[1] and discusses the extent to which this has been adopted in Australia, as well as considering the relevant Australian guidelines. Australia has a federal government structure and management, with the management of prisoners in Australia governed by the laws of its six states and two territories. The key focus of the chapter is the Australian Capital Territory (ACT), which opened Australia's first 'human rights' prison, the Alexander Maconochie Centre (AMC), in 2009.

We argue that the introduction of the *Human Rights Act 2004* (ACT) (HRA) and the *Corrections Management Act 2007* (ACT) (CMA), together with the establishment of the AMC, are significant developments of international consequence in the recognition, if not protection, of human rights for prisoners. However, we also argue that the principles on which these laws are based have not been effectively implemented in the transition from paper-based ideas to bricks-and-mortar reality, despite significant efforts on the part of the ACT government. There is clearly still a long way to go before the human rights of prisoners in the ACT are adequately realized. Nevertheless, we are optimistic about what other jurisdictions in Australia and overseas can learn from what has been achieved so far.

### International protection of prisoners' human rights

Human rights standards are articulated in formal documents drafted and agreed to by states. The key documents are the *Universal Declaration of Human Rights*, the *International Covenant on Civil and Political Rights* (ICCPR) and the *International Covenant on Economic, Social and Cultural Rights*. Collectively, these documents are known as the *International Bill of Human Rights* (IBHR) (Bailey 2009). Other international agreements relevant to prisoners include the United Nations (UN) *Convention Against Torture and Other Cruel, Inhuman or Degrading Treatment or Punishment*, *International Convention on the Elimination of All Forms of Racial Discrimination*, *Convention on the Elimination of all Forms of Discrimination Against Women* and *Convention on the Rights of the Child*.

Overall, prisoners have the same rights as other citizens. However, given the potential for abuse, some rights, such as the prohibition on torture and cruel, inhuman or degrading treatment or punishment (ICCPR, Article 7), are arguably more relevant for prisoners (see Giffard 2002). However, human rights are not absolute (Naylor 2013). For example, the rights expressed as freedoms, such as freedom of movement (ICCPR, Article 12[1]), expression (ICCPR, Article 19[2]) and assembly (ICCPR, Article 21), are usually restricted in closed environments such as prisons. Similarly, a prisoner can be arrested and detained, despite a right not to be subject to 'arbitrary arrest or detention' (ICCPR, Article 9[1]).

Article 10(1) of the ICCPR provides that '[a]ll persons deprived of their liberty shall be treated with humanity and with respect for the inherent dignity of the human person'. Article 10(3) states that reformation and social rehabilitation is the essential aim of the treatment of prisoners in the penitentiary system. The UN Human Rights Committee (UNHRC), which oversees the ICCPR, has stated that Article 10(1):

> applies to everyone deprived of their liberty under the laws and authority of the State who is held in *prisons* . . . or *correctional institutions*. . . . States parties should ensure that the principle stipulated therein is observed in all institutions and establishments within their jurisdiction where persons are being held.
>
> *(UNHRC 1992, [2], emphasis added. See also Bailey 2009)*

The UNHRC went on to say that Article 10 imposes a 'positive obligation' on states parties because people who are deprived of their liberty are particularly vulnerable. The Committee's comments here are important:

> not only may persons deprived of their liberty not be subjected to treatment that is contrary to article 7 . . . but neither may they be subjected to any hardship or constraint other than that resulting from the deprivation of liberty; respect for the dignity of such persons must be guaranteed under the same conditions as for that of free persons. Persons deprived of their liberty enjoy all the rights set forth in the [ICCPR], subject to the restrictions that are unavoidable in a closed environment.

These comments reinforce the bedrock principle that custodial sentences are imposed *as punishment*, not *for punishment* (see Naylor 2014a). Put another way, persons deprived of their liberty should not be subject to any further punishment, in addition to that already resulting from imprisonment.

This principle is reflected in the *Standard Minimum Rules for the Treatment of Prisoners* (the Rules) (UN 1955), which were approved in 1977. The Rules build on the principles contained in the IBHR (see Bailey 2009) and are designed to apply to offenders placed in prison following a judicial decision, whether sentenced or on remand (Giffard 2002). The Rules are used by many countries to guide the development and implementation of national legislation relating to the treatment of prisoners. They set out a number of minimum conditions that should be observed, including minimum floor space for each prisoner, adequate sanitary facilities, clothing, provision of a separate bed and provision of nutritional value adequate for health and strength. However, it is not expected that the Rules are strictly observed at all times. Indeed, they:

> seek only, on the basis of the general consensus of contemporary thought and the essential elements of the most adequate systems of today, to set out what is generally

> accepted as being good principle and practice in the treatment of prisoners and the management of institutions.
>
> *(UN 1955)*

A revised version, known as the Mandela Rules, was adopted by the UN Commission on Crime Prevention and Criminal Justice in May 2015. The Mandela Rules were unanimously approved by the UN General Assembly in December 2015 (Penal Reform International [PRI] 2015b). The Mandela Rules include a clearer enunciation of the principle that '[a]ll prisoners shall be treated with the respect due to their inherent dignity and value as human beings' (Proposed Rule 1). They also focus on:

- medical and health services;
- disciplinary measures (including strict limitations on the use of solitary confinement);
- investigation of deaths in custody;
- the protection and special needs of vulnerable groups;
- the right of access to legal representation;
- complaints and independent inspection;
- the replacement of outdated terminology; and
- staff training to implement the Rules.

Collectively, the changes strengthen the foundational international human rights statements protecting prisoners' rights. PRI (2015a) has suggested that adoption of the Mandela Rules 'is a historic moment for the treatment of prisoners and improvement of prison conditions'.

## Australian protection of prisoners' human rights

It is beyond the scope of this chapter to exhaustively describe the circumstances of Australian prisoners, but it is well recognized (see, for example, Mackay 2014, Segrave 2015) that they have higher rates of intellectual disability and mental and physical illness than the general population. In addition, Indigenous prisoners are significantly overrepresented in the prison population, and imprisonment rates have increased dramatically in recent years, especially for women (Australian Bureau of Statistics [ABS] 2015a, 2015b, Mackay 2015).

Australia is a signatory to the ICCPR, but the protection afforded is limited. In fact, human rights expert Bronwyn Naylor has described Australia as:

> famously backward in its implementation of the usual internationally-accepted human rights. Australia has ratified all the main treaties – ICCPR, CAT, CROC, CRPD etc. But we have no national human rights legislation and no direct way of enforcing any of the rights in those treaties.
>
> *(Naylor 2014b, p. 5, see also Naylor 2013, 2014a, 2015)*

In addition, the Rules are not formally binding on states, a proposition accepted in the decision of *Collins v State of South Australia* ([1999] 74 SASR 200). However, the Rules were used as a basis for the development of the *Standard Guidelines for Corrections in Australia* (the Guidelines), first published in 1978. The current edition (Australian Corrective Services Ministers' Conference 2012) reflects contemporary issues in corrections in Australia, such as the rise of private prisons, the importance of evidence-based programming to address criminogenic needs, and an increasing focus on 'throughcare' and victim reparation.

Again, the Guidelines do not have the force of law in Australia (Naylor 2013). In fact, they expressly state in the preface that they 'constitute outcomes or goals to be achieved by correctional services rather than a set of absolute standards or laws to be enforced'. Nevertheless, they assist legislatures and government agencies in drafting their own binding rules and operational policies and procedures that recognize the human rights of prisoners. As discussed further below, this is certainly the case in the ACT in respect of the policies and procedures that give effect to those aspects of the CMA that relate to the treatment of prisoners in the AMC.

## ACT protection of prisoners' human rights

Australia is the only common law country not to have a national human rights framework. However, two jurisdictions have specific human rights legislation. Significantly, the ACT was the first jurisdiction to enshrine its citizens' human rights in legislation, with the passage of the HRA in 2004. Victoria followed suit in 2006, with the *Charter of Human Rights and Responsibilities Act 2006* (Vic) (the Charter) (for discussion, see Mackay 2014). As Naylor (2013, p. 405) has noted, the HRA and Charter 'essentially incorporate the ICCPR rights'. This section considers the legal protection of the human rights of prisoners in the ACT.

Section 10 of the HRA replicates Article 7 of the ICCPR, while Article 10(1) is replicated in section 22(1). The HRA also imposes duties on public authorities, including the AMC, making it unlawful to act inconsistently with the human rights prescribed in the HRA, and requiring consideration to be given to these rights when making decisions (ss 40, 40B; for discussion, see Mackay 2014). However, the ACT goes further than Victoria, giving citizens the right to bring legal action in relation to alleged breaches of duty by public authorities to comply with the provisions of the HRA (see ss 40B, 40C, Mackay 2014).

The provisions of the HRA that are mainly relevant to prisoners are those relating to recognition and equality before the law (s. 8), protection from torture and cruel, inhuman or degrading treatment (s. 10), liberty and security of person (s. 18), humane treatment when deprived of liberty (s. 19), the various rights relating to a fair trial (s. 21), criminal proceedings (s. 22), compensation for wrongful conviction (s. 23), and the right not to be tried or punished more than once (s. 24). The ICCPR freedoms discussed above that more often than not become restricted as a consequence of incarceration are also found in the HRA. These freedoms include freedom of movement (s. 13), association (s. 15), and expression (s. 16). However, it should be noted that all of the human rights provided for in the HRA may be subject to reasonable limits set by Territory laws (s. 28).

The CMA also seeks to make a significant contribution to protecting prisoners' human rights in the ACT. Functions under the CMA in relation to prisoners must be exercised in accordance with a list of 'rights' in section 9, namely:

(a) respecting and protecting the detainee's human rights;
(b) ensuring the detainee's decent, humane and just treatment;
(c) precluding torture or cruel, inhuman or degrading treatment;
(d) ensuring the detainee is not subject to further punishment (in addition to the deprivation of liberty) only because of the conditions of detention;
(e) ensuring the detainee's conditions in detention comply with section 12; and
(f) if the detainee is an offender, promoting, as far as practicable, their rehabilitation and reintegration into society.

In addition, the principle that custodial sentences are imposed as punishment – and not for further punishment – is explicitly reflected in the CMA as a general principle (see Preamble [2]).

In relation to the segregation of prisoners specifically, section 89 provides: 'To remove any doubt, segregation under this part must not be used for punishment or disciplinary purposes'.

Section 12 of the CMA, referred to in s. 9(e), provides 11 minimum living conditions 'to protect the human rights of detainees at correctional centres'. The minimum living conditions in section 12 mirror the Rules and Guidelines discussed above. The conditions include: access to sufficient food and drink; access to suitable clothing and facilities for personal hygiene; suitable accommodation and bedding; reasonable access to open air and exercise; reasonable access to telephone, mail and other forms of communication; reasonable access to visits; and reasonable access to health services.

Chapter 6 of the CMA elaborates on these minimum living conditions and covers the matters contained in section 12, as well as such issues as the treatment of convicted and non-convicted detainees (s. 44), transfers to health facilities (s. 54) and religious, spiritual and cultural needs (s. 55). However, many of the rights and minimum living conditions contained in the CMA are expressed in general terms, and leave much to the discretion of prison authorities. For example, although sections 12(1)(d) and 43 of the CMA provide that 'detainees must have suitable accommodation and bedding for sleeping in reasonable privacy and comfort' (ss. 12[1][d], 43), this does not create an entitlement to bedding of a particular quality suitable for a cold climate. Similarly, while 'detainees must have reasonable access to the open air and exercise' (ss 12[1][e], 45), this does not mean that access to an open-air space suitable for more vigorous forms of exercise like running (as opposed to walking up and down a concrete slab) will always be possible in the face of staff shortages and corresponding lockdowns, or operational limitations related to non-associations.

In addition, detainees' right to 'have reasonable opportunities to receive visits from family members, accredited people and others' (ss 12[1][g], 46) does not create an entitlement to a contact visit as opposed to a non-contact visit in a specially designed cubicle. However, we accept that this is certainly justifiable where intelligence suggests visitors may be the source of prison contraband. Under sections 12(1)(i) and 52, 'detainees must have reasonable access to news and education services and facilities to maintain contact with society', but there is no detail about the standard of education programmes, or the regularity or quality of teaching. Finally, although the CMA prescribes in sections 12(1)(j) and 53(1)(a) that detainees must have access to a 'standard of health care equivalent to that available to other people in the ACT', this does not create an entitlement to access health services at the detainee's discretion, or to make choices about the kind of medical professionals they see.

The human rights of prisoners receive significant legal protection in the ACT. The HRA and CMA mirror general human rights principles expressed in the IBHR. They also mirror a wide range of specific protections. Together, they cover a lot of ground, and, in many respects, provide a template – if not the beginnings of an entirely new model – for the administrative and legal protection of prisoners' human rights. However, the protections are limited by, and in many cases contingent on, the operational realities of modern prison administration; after all, despite 50 years of rights consciousness, prisons remain places of strict confinement that exist for the purpose of disciplining certain groups of people, usually poor people, and the core aspects of incarceration have remained unchanged for several centuries. The following section considers the challenges related to translating good intentions to improved human rights outcomes for prisoners.

## Transitioning from paper-based ideas to bricks-and-mortar reality

The foregoing section presented an overview of the formal protection of prisoners' rights in the ACT. In this section,[2] we examine how effectively these principles have translated to practice.

As noted above, the AMC opened in 2009; prior to this, ACT prisoners were housed in New South Wales (NSW). According to the ACT Attorney-General (Corbell 2008), the decision to name the new prison after the nineteenth-century penal reformer Alexander Maconochie reflected the ACT's philosophy of rehabilitating, rather than punishing, prisoners. As has been widely reported, it was (and remains) 'the first prison in the country to be purpose built to meet human rights obligations' (see, for example, *ABC News* 2008). Mackay has likewise acknowledged that there 'was an intention to create a human rights culture in the AMC from its very inception' (Mackay 2014, p. 283; for background, see also Mackay 2012).

All ACT prisoners – sentenced and remand, male and female, minimum, medium and maximum security – are housed at the AMC. Nearly half the accommodation is in five-bedroom cottages, and no female detainees are housed in cells. This model aims to 'enable detainees to develop and practice living skills' and 'facilitates normalisation' (ACT Corrective Services [ACTCS] 2015a). According to the ACTCS website (2015b), the AMC:

> emphasises rehabilitation, compliance with Human Rights principles and adherence to the Healthy Prison Concept. A Healthy Prison is one in which: everyone is and feels safe (detainees, staff and visitors alike); everyone is treated with respect and as a fellow human being (again, all people within the AMC); everyone is encouraged to improve him/herself and is given every opportunity to do so through the provision of purposeful activity; and everyone is enabled to maintain contact with their families and is prepared for release.

There have been a number of positive reports about the AMC. For example, in 2011, the then Official Visitor, Ivan Potas, said he was 'rather impressed' and 'praised the prison's human rights compliance' (*Canberra Times* 2011). In an independent review, the AMC was described as:

> unique in relation to other Australian prisons in the high level of attention paid to detainees' human rights in its Legislation, policies and procedures, in the design of its facilities, in delivery of services to detainees and in the scrutiny applied to its administration.
>
> *(Knowledge Consulting 2011, p. 37)*

As Mackay observed in relation to this quote, however, this 'arguably does not set the bar very high, given the documented conditions in prisons around the country that are inconsistent with human rights' (Mackay 2014, p. 268). On the other hand, respected prison expert David Biles (2014) recently asserted that 'hav[ing] visited just about every prison in Australia . . . the AMC is one of the best designed and equipped correctional institutions in this country'. Similarly, a human rights audit of the treatment of women at the AMC found that 'women detainees at AMC are treated humanely in custody, and that correctional staff and management are respectful of the particular needs and vulnerabilities of women' (Watchirs et al. 2014, p. 5).

It appears, therefore, that substantial progress has been made towards respecting ACT prisoners' human rights. However, the AMC's ability to deliver on its human rights principles has been significantly hampered by overcrowding. Concern has also been expressed about the human rights implications of the lack of purposeful activity for prisoners (ACT Auditor-General 2015, Bartels 2015a) and the number of lockdowns (Knaus 2013a).

### Overcrowding

The ACT has traditionally had Australia's lowest imprisonment rate (for discussion, see Bartels 2015a, 2015b). One of the key arguments against building a prison in the ACT was that this would lead to an increase in the use of prison (see Australian Law Reform Commission 1988). This concern appears to have been justified: the year the AMC opened represented a low point in the ACT imprisonment's rate, at 74 per 100,000, compared with 85, 90 and 93 in 2006, 2007 and 2008 respectively (ABS 2015b, Table 18). By contrast, the rate has since risen each year, to 130 per 100,000 in 2014. This represents a 76 per cent increase over five years, compared with a 5 per cent increase nationally.

Interestingly, these increases have not been accompanied by any significant policy changes, such as reforms to bail in NSW and parole in Victoria (cf. Mackay 2015). However, the ACT Justice Minister, Shane Rattenbury MLA (the Minister), and Human Rights Commissioner, Dr Helen Watchirs OAM, have argued that a number of factors have caused recent increases, including community attitudes, judicial appointments, court delays and improved policing (Mares 2014; see also Australian Capital Territory [ACT] Legislative Assembly Standing Committee on Justice and Community Safety 2015).

It was initially reported that the AMC would house 300 prisoners (*ABC News* 2008). Extra beds were subsequently installed to take its capacity to 366 (Mosley 2013b). At the time of writing, the AMC had a population of 373 (Gorrey 2015), although the most recent ABS data (2015a) reported 355 people in full-time custody in the June 2015 quarter. In 2013–14, the ACT prison operated at 123 per cent of its design capacity – second only to the Northern Territory, at 125 per cent – and much worse than an already concerning national average of 104 per cent (Productivity Commission 2015). According to the Victorian Auditor-General (2012, p. 9), operating at or above 95 per cent utilization 'compromises the ability of prison management to safely and humanely manage prisoners'.

In April 2014, the ACT government announced that it would spend $54 million building a new 56-cell block with 80 beds and a 30-bed special care centre for detainees requiring intensive support (Knaus 2014). In September 2015, it was reported that nearly 30 prisoners would be moving into the special care unit 'in coming days' (Gorrey 2015), with the larger expansion expected to be complete in 2016. Earlier in 2015, the government upgraded the Symonston Correctional Facility (premises near the AMC which house offenders on periodic detention) for use as a temporary full-time prison (Knaus 2015). The first prisoners were moved to Symonston in June 2015 (Gorrey 2015). Additional prisoners were moved over in July (Knaus and Gorrey 2015), bringing the number housed there to 28, nearly 8 per cent of the prison population. Although the Human Rights Commissioner and Official Visitor have been granted access to the temporary facility, it has been suggested that the decision to house prisoners there is 'likely to raise questions on . . . whether it will be human rights compliant, given its comparative lack of services and facilities' (Knaus 2015).

As has been detailed recently (Bartels 2015a; see also Knaus 2013b), the overcrowding pressures at the AMC are due in part to the fact that the government chose to ignore advice on projected prisoner numbers, a matter that has been the subject of significant criticism. Biles (2013) described the government's response to the 'crisis' as 'breathtakingly inept' and 'pathetic'. Even the Minister (who was not part of government at the time of the decisions about the size of the AMC) agreed that 'the overcrowding . . . pose[d] a risk for human rights compliance and rehabilitation at the prison' (Knaus 2013b).

Mackay would doubtless agree, having recently asserted that 'individuals' human rights are being violated on a daily basis in Australian prisons because of overcrowding' (Mackay 2015). Prisoners in Victoria and Western Australia recently raised this is as a key human rights concern (Naylor 2014a). Internationally, overcrowding has been found to amount to a breach of human rights (see Mackay 2015, Naylor 2013, 2014b). The UN Office on Drugs and Crime has described overcrowding as 'the root cause of a range of challenges and human rights violations in prison systems worldwide, threatening, at best, the social reintegration prospects, and at worst, the life of prisoners' (UN Office on Drugs and Crime 2013, p. 14; see also Naylor 2014a).

## Lessons for Australia and overseas

The ACT experience provides a number of lessons for Australia and overseas. The relevance of the relationship between international standards (such as the Mandela Rules), national standards (such as the Guidelines), local legislation (such as the CMA) and operational policies and procedures is becoming increasingly evident in the ACT. The key principles articulated in the Rules are reflected in the Guidelines and the CMA and, to a lesser extent, in the policies and procedures that guide staff in their daily interactions with detainees. High principles therefore permeate daily operations, even if those tasked with maintaining security and good order may not always carry out their tasks with these principles in mind.

As Mackay has noted (2014, p. 276), prison culture poses challenges for human rights implementation because prisons are total and closed institutions that maintain a strictly controlled routine. Since prisoners are unable to leave at will, the prevailing culture permeates every aspect of their lives, and correctional officers wield extensive power over them (see also Naylor 2014b). Embedding international human rights standards in local legislation and operational policies and procedures is therefore an important factor in developing organizational respect for human rights principles and practice.

When it comes to embedding respect for prisoners' human rights, the ACT experience also shows that recruitment and training are important factors. A recent study by Beijersbergen et al. (2015) set out to show why developing a procedurally just prison environment is important. They emphasized that the behaviour and characteristics of custodial officers are critical when it comes to determining a fair and humane prison. Clearly, this has implications for recruitment of new staff. Beijersbergen et al. focused on three types of officer characteristics they considered relevant to how prisoners perceive their treatment: background, work-related attitudes and workload.

With respect to *background*, matters hypothesized to make a difference included gender (a higher proportion of female officers), education (completion of higher education levels), age (older officers) and length of service (new to the job). Perhaps surprisingly, only the proportion of female officers was found to have a significant impact on prisoners' perception of their treatment as fair and humane.

Beijersbergen et al. also suggested that officers with a more positive *attitude* toward prisoners and rehabilitation would approach prisoners in a more fair, respectful and humane manner. The results showed only limited support for this hypothesis, but prisoners did perceive their relationships with officers to be more positive in units where officers held positive attitudes towards rehabilitation.

With respect to *workload*, they assumed that prisoners in units with a higher officer-to-inmate ratio would judge their interactions with officers as more fair, respectful and humane. The results very clearly showed that prisoners in these units perceived their treatment as procedurally fair.

Arguably, this study suggests that ACTCS – and other correctional agencies – ought to recruit more women and officers with a positive attitude towards rehabilitation, and employ more officers overall. Recent recruitment activity suggests ACTCS has given consideration to attracting more women to uniformed roles at the AMC through targeted advertising. In addition, ACTCS has sought to recruit officers with an appreciation of the importance of rehabilitative outcomes through psychometric testing that supports assessment of applicants' attitudes towards prisoner rehabilitation.

Beijersbergen et al. (2015) suggested that prison authorities could encourage officers to adopt a more rehabilitative orientation through training. ACTCS has made significant progress in this regard. For example, all new officers receive human rights training on the provisions of the HRA and CMA that are relevant to prisoners, jointly delivered by ACTCS and the Human Rights Commission. New officers also receive training on the detainee life cycle, giving them a deeper understanding of the detainee journey in, through and out of the criminal justice system, and their role in rehabilitation. Additionally, new officers receive training on working with women detainees, which supports understanding of their particular vulnerabilities (see Bartels and Gaffney 2011, Watchirs et al. 2014).

There are other lessons to be learnt. The Extended Throughcare Program, which links 'prisoners up with everything from housing, employment, transport, health services, and drug and alcohol rehabilitation' for a year following their release from the AMC (Knaus 2013c), demonstrates that prison administrations can appropriately concern themselves with what happens to prisoners after they return to the community. This represents a significant departure from concern only with the security and good order of closed environments. Time will tell whether prison authorities ought to concern themselves with what happens beyond the prison gates. For example, it might be shown that the non-government sector is better placed to support ex-prisoners on their reintegration journey.

## Conclusion

The Human Rights Law Centre (HRLC 2015) observed that Australia has 'a long way to go' in implementing human rights in prison. The HLRC pointed to the Mandela Rules as providing 'a contemporary blueprint to guide prison management in a way which is both safe and humane', and called on all Australian states and territories to commit to implementing them. We likewise hope the Mandela Rules will inspire the humane treatment of prisoners around the world and be adopted by prison administrations in Australia to strengthen existing human rights approaches.

In the interim, there are some important lessons from the ACT experience. There are many positive aspects to the AMC. As discussed above, detainees are treated respectfully and humanely. Recent research has identified being treated with respect and dignity by staff as key human rights themes among prisoners in Victoria and Western Australia (Naylor 2014a, 2014b, 2015). The facilities at the AMC are also pleasant and many detainees live in cottage accommodation designed to foster healthy living skills. In addition, the Extended Throughcare Program is an Australian first (Knaus 2013c). The programme is currently being independently evaluated, but there has been initial success in keeping participants from returning to custody (Bartels 2015b).

Mackay (2014, p. 268) recently stated that 'the ACT has the most comprehensive legislation protecting the human rights of imprisoned people of any Australian jurisdiction'. The HRA and the CMA have a lot to say about the principles that underpin the protection of prisoners' human rights in the ACT, and the mechanisms that ought to enable the protection of those rights, including mechanisms that support the translation of principles and prescriptions about minimum living conditions into operational policies and procedures. In this regard, the ACT is to be commended, and provides a model for other jurisdictions in Australia and overseas to emulate.

The Minister acknowledged in a 2013 Legislative Assembly committee hearing that he did not think that the AMC 'will ever be perfectly human rights compliant' (Mosley 2013a). The editor of the *Canberra Times* recently opined that 'despite expectations that Australia's first "human rights-compliant" prison would break the old correctional mould, the reality has proved different' (*Canberra Times* 2014).

We endorse Mackay's (2014, p. 271) assessment that in spite of 'positive developments' since the HRA, 'there is still evidently cause for concern about the protection of human rights of . . . the people imprisoned in the AMC . . . [and] work to be done to improve human rights compliance'. We are mindful of the fact that correctional agencies must accommodate all prisoners they receive. Clearly, ACTCS has had to adapt to overcrowding issues that are not of their making. Nevertheless, as Naylor (2013, p. 411) has observed, 'human rights instruments do not state that rights can be reduced in response to resource pressures'. The UNHRC has determined that overcrowding may breach Article 10 (see Naylor 2014b). As the ACT Human Rights Commission asserted (2007, p. 26), '[i]nhumane treatment cannot be justified on the grounds of lack of resources or financial difficulties'.

We believe that operationalizing human rights for prisoners at the AMC remains a difficult, often delicate, and sometimes distant, enterprise. It is vital for the ACT government to ensure that the AMC is adequately resourced and supported to enable it to make its bold human rights vision a reality.

## Notes

1 In this chapter, we use the term 'prisoner' to describe people who are incarcerated, whether sentenced or on remand. However, we use the term 'detainee' when referring to provisions in the CMA to reflect the terminology adopted there.

2 This section draws significantly on Bartels 2015a.

## References

*All internet references were correct as at 9 October 2015.*


*ABC News*, 2008. New ACT jail awaits inmates. 11 September. Retrieved on 9 October 2015 from: www.abc.net.au/news/2008-09-11/new-act-jail-awaits-inmates/507128.

Australian Bureau of Statistics [ABS], 2015a. *Corrective services, Australia, June quarter 2015,* Cat. 4512.0, Canberra.

Australian Bureau of Statistics [ABS], 2015b. *Prisoners in Australia,* Cat. 4517.0, Canberra.

Australian Capital Territory [ACT] Auditor-General, 2015. *The rehabilitation of male detainees at the Alexander Maconochie Centre.* Canberra.

Australian Capital Territory Corrective Services [ACTCS], 2015a. *Alexander Maconochie Centre.* Retrieved on 9 October 2015 from: www.cs.act.gov.au/custodial_operations/types_of_detention/alexander_maconochie_centre.

Australian Capital Territory Corrective Services [ACTCS], 2015b. *Custodial Operations.* Retrieved on 9 October 2015 from: www.cs.act.gov.au/custodial_operations.

Australian Capital Territory [ACT] Human Rights Commission, 2007. *Human rights audit on the operation of ACT correctional facilities under Corrections legislation.* Canberra.

Australian Capital Territory [ACT] Legislative Assembly Standing Committee on Justice and Community Safety, 2015. *Inquiry Into Sentencing: Report 4.* Canberra.

Australian Corrective Services Ministers' Conference, 2012. *Standard Guidelines for Corrections in Australia.* Retrieved on 9 October 2015 from: www.aic.gov.au/media_library/aic/research/corrections/standards/aust-stand_2012.pdf.

Australian Law Reform Commission, 1988. *Sentencing,* Report 44. Sydney.

Bailey, P., 2009. *The human rights enterprise in Australia and internationally.* Sydney: LexisNexis Butterworths.

Bartels, L., 2015a. The ACT prison: human rights rhetoric versus crowded and bored reality. *Court of Conscience,* 9, 21–25.

Bartels, L., 2015b. The state of imprisonment in Australia: can the ACT achieve a 'human rights' prison? *The Conversation,* 17 April. Retrieved on 9 October 2015 from: https://theconversation.com/state-of-imprisonment-can-act-achieve-a-human-rights-prison-39119.

Bartels, L. and Gaffney, A., 2011. *Good practice in women's prisons: a literature review*. Technical and Background Paper 41. Canberra: Australian Institute of Criminology.

Beijersbergen, K., Dirkzwager, A., Molleman, T., van der Laan, P. and Nieuwbeerta, P., 2015. Procedural justice in prison: the importance of staff characteristics. *International Journal of Offender Therapy and Comparative Criminology*, 59, 337–58.

Biles, D., 2013. Scales of justice off balance. *Canberra Times,* 7 May. Retrieved on 9 October 2015 from: www.canberratimes.com.au/comment/scales-of-justice-off-balance-20130516-2jp71.html.

Biles, D., 2014. First-rate Alexander Maconochie Centre needs a little work. *Canberra Times,* 12 July. Retrieved on 9 October 2015 from: www.canberratimes.com.au/comment/firstrate-alexander-maconochie-centre-needs-a-little-work-20140712-zt483.html.

*Canberra Times,* 2011. Canberra's holding cells harmful and 'Dickensian'. 28 November. Retrieved on 9 October 2015 from: www.canberratimes.com.au/act-news/canberras-holding-cells-harmful-and-dickensian-20111128-1v14c.html.

*Canberra Times,* 2014. Editorial: growing pains at the Alexander Maconochie Centre. 7 November. Retrieved on 9 October 2015 from: www.canberratimes.com.au/comment/ct-editorial/growing-pains-at-the-alexander-maconochie-centre-20141107-11ijn8.html.

Corbell, S., 2008. The new ACT prison: what is planned and what will be achieved. Christians For An Ethical Society Forum on the ACT Prison, March, Canberra.

Giffard, C., 2002. International human rights law applicable to prisoners. *In*: D. Brown and M. Wilkie (eds), *Prisoners as citizens: human rights in Australian prisons*. Sydney: Federation Press, 177–95.

Gorrey, M., 2015. Prisoner numbers at ACT's overflowing jail jumped 4 per cent in past year. *Canberra Times,* 10 September. Retrieved on 9 October 2015 from: www.canberratimes.com.au/act-news/prisoner-numbers-at-acts-overflowing-jail-jumped-4-per-cent-in-past-year-20150910-gjjf36.html.

Human Rights Law Centre [HLRC], 2015. UN's new 'Mandela Rules' shine a light on sub-standard Australian prison conditions and practices. 14 October. Retrieved on 9 October 2015 from: http://hrlc.org.au/uns-new-mandela-rules-shine-a-light-on-sub-standard-australian-prison-conditions-and-practices/.

Knaus, C., 2013a. Concern inmates' rights breached. *Canberra Times,* 27 May. Retrieved on 9 October 2015 from: www.canberratimes.com.au/act-news/concern-inmates-rights-breached-20130526-2n5mh.html.

Knaus, C., 2013b. Stanhope says he has 'anxiety' over prison management. *Canberra Times,* 11 October. Retrieved on 9 October 2015 from: www.canberratimes.com.au/act-news/stanhope-says-he-has-anxiety-over-prison-management-20131010-2vbro.html.

Knaus, C., 2013c. Prisoner support program a first. *Canberra Times,* 25 March. Retrieved on 9 October 2015 from: www.canberratimes.com.au/act-news/prisoner-support-program-a-first-20130324-2goek.html.

Knaus, C., 2014. $54 million jail expansion to begin soon. *Canberra Times,* 29 April. Retrieved on 9 October 2015 from: www.canberratimes.com.au/act-news/54-million-jail-expansion-to-begin-soon-20140428-37ebr.html.

Knaus, C., 2015. ACT Government set to use second full-time prison to tackle overcrowding crisis. *Canberra Times,* 8 April. Retrieved on 9 October 2015 from: www.canberratimes.com.au/act-news/act-government-set-to-use-second-fulltime-prison-to-tackle-overcrowding-crisis-20150408-1mgthh.html.

Knaus, C. and Gorrey, M., 2015. More detainees sent to temporary Symonston jail from overcrowded prison. *Canberra Times,* 21 July. Retrieved on 9 October 2015 from: www.canberratimes.com.au/act-news/more-detainees-sent-to-temporary-symonston-jail-from-overcrowded-prison-20150721-gih14o.html#ixzz3klItPLlR.

Knowledge Consulting, 2011. *Independent review of operations at the Alexander Maconochie Centre: report for ACT Corrective Services*. Canberra.

Mackay, A., 2012. The road to the ACT's first prison (the Alexander Maconochie Centre) was paved with rehabilitative intentions. *Canberra Law Review*, 11, 33–57.

Mackay, A., 2014. Operationalising human rights law in Australia: establishing a human rights culture in the new Canberra prison and transforming the culture of Victoria Police. *In*: B. Naylor, J. Debeljak and A. Mackay (eds), *Human rights in closed environments*. Sydney: Federation Press, 261–94.

Mackay, A., 2015. Overcrowding in Australian prisons: the human rights implications. *Precedent*, 128, 37–41.

Mares, P., 2014. A view of pale hills. *Insider Story,* 25 February. Retrieved on 9 October 2015 from: http://insidestory.org.au/a-view-of-pale-hills.

Mosley, L., 2013a. Canberra's jail may never be fully human rights compliant. *ABC News,* 13 November. Retrieved on 9 October 2015 from: www.abc.net.au/news/2013-11-13/canberras-jail-may-never-be-fully-human-rights-compliant/5089852.

Mosley, L., 2013b. Canberra prison close to capacity. *ABC News,* 10 October. Retrieved on 9 October 2015 from: www.abc.net.au/news/2013-10-09/canberra-prison-at-capacity/5012024.

Naylor, B., 2013. Protecting the human rights of prisoners in Australia. *In*: P. Gerber and M. Castan (eds), *Contemporary perspectives on human rights law in Australia.* Sydney: Thomson Reuters, 395–416.

Naylor, B., 2014a. Human rights and respect in prisons: the prisoners' perspective. *In*: B. Naylor, J. Debeljak and A. Mackay (eds), *Human rights in closed environments.* Sydney: Federation Press, 84–124.

Naylor, B., 2014b. *Prisons, overcrowding and rights.* Castan Centre Symposium, November, Melbourne.

Naylor, B., 2015. Researching human rights in prison. *International Journal for Crime, Justice and Social Democracy,* 4, 79–95.

PRI, 2015a. *Mandela Rules on prisoner treatment adopted.* 26 May. Retrieved on 9 October 2015 from: www.penalreform.org/news/mandela-rules-on-prisoner-treatment-adopted/.

PRI, 2015b. *UN Standard Minimum Rules for the Treatment of Prisoners (Nelson Mandela Rules).* Retrieved on 17 May 2016 from: www.penalreform.org/resource/standard-minimum-rules-treatment-prisoners-smr/.

Productivity Commission, 2015. *Report on government services.* Canberra.

Segrave, M., 2015. The state of imprisonment in Australia: it's time to take stock. *The Conversation,* 12 April. Retrieved on 9 October 2015 from: https://theconversation.com/the-state-of-imprisonment-in-australia-its-time-to-take-stock-38902.

United Nations [UN], 1955. *Standard Minimum Rules for the Treatment of Prisoners.* New York, NY: United Nations.

UNHRC, 1992, *General Comment No. 21: Article 10 (Humane Treatment of Persons Deprived of Their Liberty).* New York, NY: United Nations.

UN Office on Drugs and Crime, 2013. *Handbook on strategies to reduce overcrowding in prisons.* New York, NY: United Nations.

Victorian Auditor-General, 2012. *Prison capacity planning.* Melbourne.

Watchirs, H., McKinnon, G., Costello, S. and Thomson, J., 2014. *Human rights audit on the conditions of detention of women at the Alexander Maconochie Centre.* Canberra: ACT Human Rights Commission.

53

# Human rights versus citizenship rights

## Media coverage of human rights in the UK

*Des McNulty, Nicholas Watson and Gregory Philo*

### Introduction

Human rights have been high on the United Kingdom (UK) political agenda for a number of years. Debate is intensified by the election of a Conservative government that, in their manifesto, pledged to repeal the *Human Rights Act 1998* (HRA) introduced by the Labour party in 1998, and replace it with a British Bill of Rights.[1] Whilst this move has considerable support in Conservative supporting media, it will be strenuously opposed by the other main political parties, the devolved administrations of Scotland and Wales and by much of the legal profession.

Owners and editors of newspapers such as the *Daily Mail*, *Telegraph* and *Express* have repeatedly expressed concerns about the implications of human rights legislation with a focus, following the 2004 House of Lords ruling in the Naomi Campbell privacy case,[2] on the impact of court interpretation on press freedom. However, our research shows that the most frequent context in which human rights are discussed in the press are cases of 'undeserving' individuals or groups claiming rights under the legislation that the newspapers disagree with.

In an earlier article (McNulty et al. 2014), we showed how the issue of prisoners' right to vote was a proxy for debates on Europe. The focus on Europe is also found in coverage of other human rights topics and with a similar blurring of the roles of different legal and institutional structures.[3]

The evidence presented here, based on a study of how human rights was reported in a selection of newspapers in 2011, shows that Conservative politicians and the Conservative supporting press led and shaped the UK debate about human rights. In the chapter we examine the components of this narrative, including the focus on marginalized 'outsider' groups, the role of Europe and concern about the role of judges, and explore some of the implications of the dominance of such themes in the media discourse about human rights.

### Methods

In collating and collecting the data used in this study we employed a range of different media analysis and audience reception techniques, building on earlier work of the Glasgow Media Group (ESRC 2004, Philo et al. 2015). While the initial focus of the work was the controversy surrounding the ECHR's ruling on prisoner's voting rights early in the life of the 2010–15 coalition, we broadened scope to examine how media coverage of human rights was organized, drawing on coverage of terrorism, immigration, asylum and other issues. The aim of the study was to provide a systematic analysis of the way that human rights were discussed either in the media or in other forms of public discourse.

The data we present below are drawn from a content review of five major UK newspapers: the *Guardian*, *Telegraph*, *Daily Mail*, *Daily Mirror* and *Sun* between January and December 2011. We compared and contrasted how human rights were described using coding categories devised specifically for that purpose. We also examined coverage in the *Daily Express* and *The Times* in the first four months of the research period, online material including BBC News and Sky News and looked at blogs, websites, and other relevant public forums.

Using the database Newsbank we searched for articles using the term 'human rights'. As Figure 53.1 shows, coverage of human rights across the five papers occurred in peaks throughout the period. Each of these peaks was linked to particular controversies – the first peak, for example (see period 2 in Figure 53.1), was generated by debates around rights to vote, in period 6 asylum/migration was the key issue and in period 10 the rights of travellers and Dale Farm dominated human rights discourse. Other prominent topics with a human rights dimension that were distributed more evenly over the research period included the 'Arab Spring', terrorism and the deportation of terror suspects.

The content analysis was supplemented by an audience reception study to determine how reporting of human rights in the media was interpreted by the general public and how this was impacting on their perceptions of human rights. Six focus groups of five or six people were held in England and Scotland in February and March 2012. We used the groups to further examine key trends highlighted during the content analysis. They were organized according to standard audience reception techniques (ESRC 2004) and the topic guide was set by the findings from

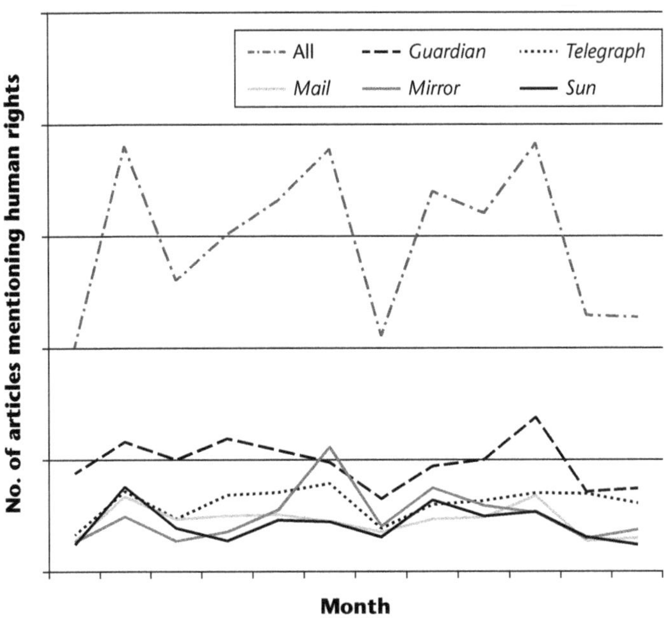


*Figure 53.1* Flows of coverage of human rights across 2011 (articles per month)

the content analysis. All the focus groups were taped for subsequent analysis, which was based on standard qualitative methodologies. Key themes across the groups and the interviews were identified.

Our analysis took the form of a number of case studies in which we: (1) explored the nature of the political discourse around human rights, (2) identified the key media and political spokespersons whose views on human rights issues were reported, (3) examined the language used to discuss human rights, and (4) picked out the common themes developed in the coverage, analysing fault lines between the views of politicians and newspapers in our sample. We sought where relevant to highlight 'gaps' – groups whose rights are not recognized in, or are excluded from, human rights discourse in the media.

Issues of balance and accuracy in the representation of events and viewpoints were considered and, through focus groups, we sought to evaluate the impacts of these processes on the beliefs and understandings of audience members. Our work generated a series of case studies; one on prisoners' rights to vote published as a journal article (McNulty et al. 2014), a second on refuges incorporated in to a wider study (Philo et al. 2013) and another on gypsy travellers is in preparation. The chapter provides an account of the main conclusions drawn from the study as a whole.

## Legal context

International human rights law is derived from the Statute of the International Court of Justice (see ICJ Statute Article 38[1]). Norms around human rights are defined by the *European Convention on Human Rights* and the United Nations (UN) Declaration on Human Rights, rather than by European Union (EU) institutions. The requirement to adhere to the *European Convention on Human Rights* was transcribed into UK law through the HRA[4] the aims of which were:

> To give further effect to rights and freedoms guaranteed under the European Convention on Human Rights.

The UK is also party to a number of other international instruments/treaties that seek to protect and promote human rights such as the Refugee Convention and the *Convention on the Rights of the Child*. Some are not fully binding on signatories – they are intended to define values such as equality, fairness and dignity rather than provide a basis for legal enforcement. The EU Charter of Fundamental Rights has had full legal status since 2009, binding EU institutions and Member States when acting within the field of EU law. Apart from the European Convention, the only specifically international human rights instrument that currently permits an *individual* right of complaint is the *Convention on the Elimination of all Forms of Discrimination against Women*.

Under the HRA, British courts must 'take into account' judgements of the European Court of Human Rights (ECtHR).[5] Repealing the Act would break the formal link between British courts and the European Court on human rights matters, making the UK Supreme Court 'the ultimate arbiter'.[6]

These legal complexities result in, and allow, blurring of distinctions between the remits and responsibilities of the EU and other European institutions in the press and in the public mind. In a speech about the European Union reported in full in the *Daily Telegraph*, David Cameron acknowledged this saying 'people in the UK are angered by some legal judgements made in Europe that impact on life in Britain. Some of this antipathy about Europe in general really relates of course to the European Court of Human Rights, rather than the EU'.[7]

While distinctions between the functions of the ECtHR, the EU and the European Court of Justice are well set out in the academic literature, they are rarely made explicit in mainstream press coverage, where 'Europe' is blamed even where, as in the case of prisoners' right to vote, the EU has played very little part.

Crucially, the simplistic notion that the repeal of the HRA would remove all obligations to abide by EU legal regimes is incorrect – the legal basis of the requirement that UK courts take account of judgements by the ECtHR might be removed but the UK would be still bound by the web of treaties and obligations created within the EU to protect rights. This is a dynamic process as EU law is constantly changing: if the EU were to accede to the *European Convention on Human Rights* by becoming a signatory to the Convention as envisaged in Article 6 of the most recent EU treaty, which stipulates that 'fundamental rights as guaranteed by the ECHR . . . shall constitute general principles of the Union's law', Member States would be required to defer to the rulings of the Strasbourg court. Thus, even if the HRA were repealed, cutting through the knot that links human rights to European law would only be achieved if the UK were to fully withdraw from the EU.

It is also worth noting that issues that in other jurisdictions might have been regarded as human rights matters have mostly been debated in the UK as equality issues. Case law took time to evolve after human rights legislation came into force. Issues of gender inequality, racism or disadvantage experienced by protected groups were, until the passing of the Single Equality Act and the incorporation of human rights into the remit of the Equality and Human Rights Commission (which replaced the group specific equality organizations), typically resolved by recourse to the creation of specific statutory rights. Although that is rapidly changing, especially in relation to rights linked to sexual orientation, the range of uses of human rights legislation has been narrower than it might otherwise have been, potentially impacting on perceived value.

## The political context

The Conservative Party consistently opposed the HRA, passed by the Labour government in 1998.[8] The Conservatives' manifesto in 2010 included a commitment to repeal the HRA – but the 2010 coalition agreement with the Liberal Democrats stipulated its retention and the government's continued adherence to European human rights treaty obligations. But specific controversies – over prisoners' right to vote, gypsy travellers, detention of individuals suspected of terrorist sympathies and deportation of individuals to countries where no guarantee could be given of their safety – all fell within Conservative held cabinet portfolios. So it was Conservatives rather than Liberal Democrat ministers who set the tone and agenda in the government's response to these matters. Discussion of human rights was linked to the question of Britain's relationship with the EU and European institutions, especially where Convention rights, or court rulings based on human rights obligations, prevented actions that backbench MPs and their press supporters were calling for.

However, not all members of the Conservative parliamentary party were inclined or able to adopt an anti-HRA or anti-European stance. Ministers who held a justice or legal brief were obliged to support the legal process, even when the balance of opinion within their own party and its supporters was strongly opposed to particular rulings. This was a particular difficulty in relation to the controversy over the European court ruling that obliged the UK to remove a 'blanket ban' on a prisoner's right to vote. The Ministers most directly affected were Dominic Grieve[9] and Kenneth Clarke[10] who were also liberal Conservatives, regarded with great suspicion by many on the right of their party because of their supposedly pro-European views.

Parliamentarians keen to maintain the primacy of the legislature as against judicial decisions were not confined to the Conservative benches. Labour politicians, including Shadow Justice Secretary Jack Straw, were fierce opponents of change on the question of prisoners' right to vote. Straw joined demands for change from 'Europe' that threatened parliamentary sovereignty (McNulty et al. 2014). More generally, Labour appeared reluctant to speak up in defence of human rights, especially in support of marginalized groups or causes such as terror suspects facing deportation and gypsy travellers. Senior Labour strategists were worried that supporting human rights in such cases would risk losing some sections of the electorate to UKIP, particularly those most concerned about immigration.[11]

Labour's tactical approach and the extent to which the Liberal Democrats were constrained by being in coalition, meant that both in the House of Commons and in the wider political setting, the agenda on human rights was set by those opposed to the HRA rather than those who might have been inclined to defend it. Right-wing Conservatives were able to make the running, backed up – and sometimes egged on – by newspapers whose opposition to the HRA was entrenched.

## Findings

The first finding of our analysis of media coverage is that *the positive case for human rights being relevant to the majority of people in the UK is either ignored or given little credence in much of the press.* Within the coverage examined there were very few articles that discussed the concept and purpose of human rights. British legal experts played a prominent role in framing the UN and European Conventions on human rights. The intention was to set a benchmark, by identifying what constitutes human agency, defining what is needed for a 'good life' and clarifying social entitlements. In principle, both Conventions enshrine a very wide range of protections that apply to everyone. But questions of the origins, scope and validity of human rights – what the rights consist of, the principles involved and how they provide protections for citizens – are very rarely addressed in tabloid and mid-market newspapers.

Across our newspaper sample, there were occasional articles that examine the role of human rights in protecting individuals from the state in the UK. The broadsheet newspapers, the *Guardian*, and the *Telegraph* on occasion, gave space to commentators arguing that the HRA is relevant and important in protecting rights for all. The dominant narrative in the *Telegraph* was, however, critical of both the HRA and the way it was being utilized through the courts, supporting those in the Conservative Party calling for the repatriation of rights through a British Bill of Rights.[12] In the tabloid and mid-market papers, advocates for human rights were either not reported or counterposed to an assumed reader view that citizenship rights are already protected in Britain and therefore an additional layer of protection (via the HRA) is unnecessary and unwelcome. In our audience reception studies, we found this assumption was largely borne out, with most people not placing much value on the HRA.

In the rare examples where human rights were presented in the press in a positive light, for example in commentary on the UK's Equality and Human Rights Commission's report on home care for elderly people, the impact of human rights and the possibilities they afford were rarely discussed. In all the coverage we examined there were very few examples where a positive defence of human rights as a universal principle was made.[13] The emphasis instead was on whether particular people or groups should be allowed to assert their human rights and the implications/threats to the public and the British way of life if they were allowed to do so.

In sharp contrast to the dismissive attitude of much of the press towards human rights in the UK, coverage of demands for human rights in countries with unaccountable governments frequently show human rights in a positive light. This is especially true when demands for human rights come from respectable individuals or legitimate opposition representatives such as Aung San Suu Kyi in Burma. The press defines rights to free speech, to democratically accountable government, to freedom from torture and unjustified imprisonment in terms of values (for example, liberty, freedom and democracy) to which all countries should adhere. This discussion about rights is framed in terms of liberty and freedom and is kept quite separate from discussion about human rights for people living in the UK, although there are some points of intersection. Examples we found where human rights were treated positively included cases where someone living in the UK was being threatened with deportation to a country where human rights are not respected. The *Daily Mail* and the *Telegraph* were strongly opposed to aspects of the Justice and Security Bill and what they saw as proposals for 'secret courts' which in their view negate press freedom. In an editorial, the *Daily Mail* attacks what it refers to as 'the government's chilling secret justice green paper' and links it to the past treatment of the Libyan rebel Abdel Hakim Belhadj. The headline reads:

> MAIL COMMENT: Secret Courts, Libya and Britain's Shame
>
> (Daily Mail *9 April 2012)*

> A key point is that the government proposals mean that in future, 'civil cases such as that being brought by Belhadj . . . will take place behind closed doors'.
>
> (Ibid. *9 April 2012)*

The paper's hostility to 'secret courts' in the Belhadj case and their concern to protect press freedom does not mean that they regard other deportation cases in the same way. Abu Hamza, described in the *Telegraph* as the 'terrorist "recruiting sergeant"', was seen by both the *Mail* and the *Telegraph* as beyond the pale. Both papers were strong supporters of government attempts to deport him and castigated the use of procedures involving human rights legislation to prevent it. This leads clearly to the second major theme to emerge from our analysis: *the dominance of a narrative that links human rights in the UK with 'undeserving' groups and often with illegal or criminal activity*. The focus on the alleged misuse and/or inappropriate application of human rights legislation set much of the content and tenor of political debate about human rights. As highlighted earlier, peaks in coverage of human rights in the press throughout 2011 were media storms centring on matters such as the eviction of travellers, detention of terrorist suspects, deportation of asylum seekers and prisoners right to vote (following on from controversies about prisoners right of access to pornography and slopping out). In the case of prisoners' rights, newspapers repeatedly catalogued the crimes committed by those claiming entitlements using the HRA to undermine the credibility of any argument that their claim to rights could be valid.

Our data shows that the political and media debate in the UK about human rights is inextricably tied up with the labelling and stigmatization of marginalized groups such as criminals, immigrants, gypsy/travellers and terrorists whose claims to rights through human rights law are portrayed as illegitimate.[14] Underneath this discourse are questions about what protections should be extended to certain groups on the margins of society and what rights they are entitled to. But these issues are not dealt with as matters of principle – instead specific cases are used to illustrate where the exercise of these rights or protections are inappropriate and conclusions drawn on the basis of these cases. This can be illustrated by looking at media concerns about immigration and the numbers of people entering Britain, voiced regularly in the media. Philo et al. (2013), who compared the reporting of refugees and asylum seekers in the national media in 2006 and 2011, showed that in both periods, coverage was persistently and overwhelmingly hostile to these groups. In the coverage we looked at, sympathy for refugees and asylum seekers diminishes as they near UK borders. The attitude of much of the press at the time to refugees and asylum seekers who had arrived in the UK was that they were an unwanted burden and in some circumstances could pose a 'threat'.

Those fleeing from violence in Eritrea or Yemen were considered by much of the press as economic migrants rather than as legitimate refugees even when they were given refugee status by the authorities. Those seeking refugee status were particularly vulnerable to the consequences of media hostility since governments seek to defend themselves by pointing to their punitive actions – apprehending 'illegal migrants, and deporting 'failed asylum seekers'.

Repeated and vitriolic attacks, led by the right of centre press, most notably the *Daily Mail*, the *Sun* and the *Daily Telegraph*, aided and abetted by right-wing politicians, forced advocates for human rights legislation onto the defensive – not just politicians but lawyers and organizations representing these groups. The right-wing view is best illustrated by columnists such as Peter Hitchens 'the Human Rights Act has been deployed to reduce the freedoms of the hard-working, the tax-paying and the law-abiding' (*Daily Mail* 28 May 2011) and Richard Littlejohn 'the perverse rulings of Left-wing judges in human rights cases are not only an affront to natural justice but pose a clear and present danger to our national security' (*Daily Mail* 27 September 2011). However, it also permeated stories about human rights legislation elsewhere in the press. The discourse claimed to speak on behalf of the majority, with human rights legislation presented as only being relevant to and invoked by undesirables or criminals. This association was used by columnists to justify the call for removal of the HRA from the statute book where it was presented as a major threat to the safety of the public and traditional British freedoms.

The third theme that emerged from our work was *the depiction of human rights legislation as undermining democracy by giving more power to judges*. Within the media narrative there are two strands: hostility to *Europeanization* – the threat to national sovereignty posed by the overweening power of European institutions; and concern over *juridification* – the creation of law by judges rather than through parliamentary process. These are sometimes combined – for example where the threat to sovereignty[15] is seen to come from the actions of 'foreign judges'.

Although a British judge chaired the ECtHR at the time the research was conducted, analysis of the newspaper coverage of human rights in 2011 shows that enforcement of human rights legislation through rulings based on European court decisions were seen by right of centre newspapers as unwarranted 'interference'. Where judges in a British court upheld the human rights of those the government wanted to deport, they opened themselves to accusations of undermining democracy, parliamentary sovereignty and the wishes of the British people. Backbench MPs such as Andrew Rosindell and Priti Patel expressed their concern/anger about the role of judges and the courts in the pages of the *Mail*, the *Sun* and the *Telegraph*. The strongest reaction from these newspapers came over rulings directly from the European court.

European court judges can rule a country in breach of its treaty obligations if it fails to change the law to meet the requirements of the *European Convention on Human Rights* and admit compensation cases when the Convention has been breached. When the Grand Chamber made its decision over votes for prisoners in May 2012, the *Daily Mail* and the *Sun* loudly castigated judges in the European court for imposing judgements on Britain that ran counter to the wishes of the domestic democratic institutions, undermining parliamentary sovereignty.

The *Daily Mail*'s headline was 'Contempt for Our Democracy':

> European judges rode roughshod over British sovereignty yesterday by ruling that prisoners should be allowed to vote. In a devastating blow, they rejected last year's overwhelming

> vote by MPs for maintaining our historic blanket ban on voting by convicts. The unelected judges instead gave David Cameron six months to obey their dictat or risk having to pay £150million on compensation to killers, rapists and other prisoners.
>
> (Daily Mail *22 May 2012)*

The *Sun*'s headline was 'Porridge Votes: Fury at Euro Judges as Britain forced to give lags election rights':

> The unelected judges in Strasbourg backed a ruling declaring that the UK's blanket ban on lags voting breaches human rights. The decision – overwhelmingly opposed by MPs from all sides – could allow killers, rapists and thugs held in jails like London's Wormwood Scrubs to take part in elections.
>
> (Sun *22 May 2012)*

One of the most persistent themes in press coverage of human rights is the inappropriateness of unelected judges rather than elected representatives deciding what a breach of human rights is. Of course, it is precisely the role of judges to determine how any law should be applied to specific cases before them. The notion of interference, whether by judges, by Europe or by both, as a threat to sovereignty formed a key component of the dominant narrative in the *Mail*, the *Telegraph* and the *Sun* and was reflected in audience perceptions recorded in the focus groups.

It wasn't only judges whose actions were questioned by the press. Lawyers seeking redress for their clients under human rights legislation were claimed to be manipulating the system to the advantage of these undeserving groups. In the context of deportation cases, UK courts are asked to rule whether it is safe for someone to be sent back to their country of origin. Appeals against deportation that involve Article 8, the right to a family life, require judgements be based on family circumstances. The dispute between Kenneth Clarke and Theresa May at the 2011 Tory party conference provides an example where the press alleged a misuse of human rights legislation as a vehicle for bashing the role of judges. A story had featured in the press about a Bolivian who had allegedly been allowed to remain because he had a cat. This was used by Shadow Home Secretary Theresa May in her conference speech to denounce the decision. When Mr Clarke as justice secretary disputed the facts as presented by Mrs May, he was attacked by the *Daily Mail*, the *Sun* and the *Daily Telegraph* on several fronts: his disloyalty to a colleague, his endorsement of a 'crazy' court decision, his support for human rights and for being soft on Europe.

Under pressure over votes for prisoners, David Cameron used a Supreme Court ruling that those convicted of paedophile offences could not be kept on the sex offender's register indefinitely without any right of appeal to call for an overhaul of 'completely offensive' rulings from the ECtHR which he asserted had influenced UK judges. He said, 'It's about time we started making sure decisions are made in this Parliament rather than in the courts' (*Daily Mail* 17 February 2011). The tension between the sovereignty of democratic processes and judicial process is a familiar one in many jurisdictions – it is one of the foundations of the separation of powers in the United States constitution. But in the context of human rights legislation in the UK it is not clear from a legal point of view that sovereignty is attenuated by judicial interpretation of a law that was approved by parliament. But from a political management point of view, in the context of media hostility to human rights legislation, judges, and especially foreign judges, have proved a convenient target.

The fourth theme is *the media's treatment of human rights as a proxy for 'Europe'*. There are genuine disagreements about whether prisoners should have the vote but the dramatization of such rows serves a wider political purpose. Human rights legislation has become a symbol and a rallying point for those wanting to change Britain's relationship with Europe. The argument that Europe is imposing its interpretation of human rights, which conveniently overlooks the fact that Westminster approved the HRA and is signed up to the European Convention, pre-empts discussion about what rights people should have and who should be entitled to them.

The debate is not about whether there should be enforceable rights. Those supporting the abolition of the HRA and its replacement by a British Bill of Rights within the Conservative Party or the right-wing press are principally motivated by opposition to the involvement of European or international bodies as articles in the *Daily Mail* (21 February 2011, 17 April 2011, 28 October 2011) and the *Daily Telegraph* (9 September 2011, 2 October 2011) make clear. Those newspapers, politicians and commentators most hostile to human rights legislation are also those most antagonistic to the EU. Even when there was little discussion in parliament about Europe, campaigns against human rights misuse in the *Sun* and the *Daily Mail* prominently featured stories about 'foreign criminals', 'benefit scroungers' and 'perverts' who escaped jails or deportation through human rights rulings, allowing these newspapers to keep their opposition to Europe high up the political agenda. As we suggested in our earlier article about the prisoner's right to vote:

> The controversy should, therefore, be seen not as an issue in isolation but as a continuing public conversation in which demonisation of human rights is the preferred way for the right of centre press and many Conservative politicians (Ministers as well as back benchers) to express opposition to Europe and support for a particular notion of British legal and constitutional arrangements.

The final theme to which we wish to draw attention is *the importance of the media gaze in shaping public debate about human rights*. The intense pressure brought to bear on politicians by the *Daily Mail*, *Sun* and *Daily Telegraph* over human rights and Europe has arguably shifted the debate onto terrain of their choosing. The proactive stance adopted by the right of centre newspapers led those who support human rights to react rather than adopt a positive stance, promoting the benefits of human rights legislation. Politicians expressing a different view can expect similar treatment to that meted out to Mr Clarke, and understandably, few of them are prepared to speak up in the newspapers in support of human rights other than in the most general terms.

The extent to which the debate on human rights has been shifted is reflected in comments reported in the *Daily Mail* from Trevor Phillips, head of the Equalities and Human Rights Commission, who said the laws had 'fallen into disrepute' and were seen as 'protecting criminals, terror suspects and illegal immigrants at the expense of everyone else'. According to Mr Phillips, human rights laws are being interpreted in a way that is 'thoroughly bonkers'. These rights should not be 'the exclusive property of minorities', they were the 'last line of defence' for elderly, disabled or vulnerable Britons who are mistreated or neglected. He added:

> Human rights should help us better protect vulnerable people who are targeted with violence because of who they are, or who suffer because our police, local councils and courts don't take their calls seriously or provide enough support to get them justice.
>
> . . .
>
> But while we must defend human rights tenaciously, it is also essential that supporters of human rights recognize and address the reasons why these great principles have fallen into disrepute. 'For too many people nowadays human rights have come to mean the defence of the rights of unpopular minorities – of criminals, terror suspects and illegal immigrants – at the expense of everybody else.
>
> (Daily Mail *12 December 2011)*

Our research demonstrates that media coverage has helped create and sustain the perception Mr Phillips describes. We focused mainly on coverage during 2011; further study would be required to look at changes in coverage over time. Some previously marginalized groups whose rights had previously been restricted have gained media acceptance. The rights of gays and lesbians to civil partnerships and to marry are now both accepted and enshrined in legislation in the UK.

As groups win acceptance/gain legitimacy, their rights are not viewed as part of wider human rights – which the media continue to associate mainly with 'outsiders'. Further research is required to explore how, within this discourse, a separation is made between 'them' and 'us' and how these boundaries change over time. Our work shows that the selection of marginalized groups whose claim to human rights is contested is episodic – the focus shifts although there are obvious continuities. Some of the media storms in 2011 were brief eruptions that were resolved, for example the case of Abu Hamza or lost their dramatic force, such as Dale Farm. Others continue to ignite controversy, for example, prisoners' right to vote where no resolution has been found. Other issues have emerged in a new setting; for example, refugees and asylum seekers, which has moved up the political agenda both as a result of the numbers fleeing towards Europe from the conflict in Syria and television as well as press coverage of the plight of children in particular.

## Conclusion

The case for human rights in the UK is largely missing in the media. Those who might have been expected to make the argument have been forced on the defensive, to react to the dominant discourse rather than argue the relevance and importance of human rights to the majority. With few exceptions, human rights have been associated with unpopular groups at the margin of society. The HRA was depicted by sections of the press and government politicians as constraining and even subverting democracy. The positive potential of human rights legislation for protecting individuals or for developing safe and equitable services was rarely discussed. Alleged abuse of human rights legislation was used as part of a wider political agenda about Britain's future relationship with Europe and for short-term political advantage with judges cast as enemies of democracy.

The volume and nature of coverage of human rights in the right of centre newspapers has affected the way in which all newspapers and arguably broadcasters deal with human rights related issues, by forcing a response to the agenda that the *Mail*, *Sun* and *Telegraph*, amongst other papers, have set. In our analysis of the prisoner's right controversy, we argued that the press were not merely reporting the political debate; they were forming, leading and directing its content. Right of centre newspapers not only covered the topic extensively but also actively campaigned against votes for prisoners. In their coverage, any attempt at compromise was seen as a betrayal. As Scott (2012, p. 8) has argued, for many people, prisoner's rights are 'perverse, unnatural, abnormal, or simply wrong'. Prisoners were not, at least according to some section of the media, worthy of human rights.

Following the election of a majority government in 2015 and the removal of the Liberal Democrat veto, the pressure on the Conservatives from their press supporters as well as most of their backbenchers has dramatically intensified. In handling human rights issues, Justice Secretary Michael Gove will have to take into account Euroscepticism within his own party, David Cameron's intention to renegotiate the UK's relationship with the EU in advance of a referendum and contradictory press and public attitudes towards refugees and asylum. The UK government's policy of flying in controlled numbers of refugees with high levels of humanitarian need from refugee camps in Turkey and Jordan, while closing its borders to Syrians who have made their way to Europe is not driven by any economic logic. It is comprehensible only in political terms, in the context of discourses that have built up around human rights and immigration.

There is a framework of understanding, encapsulated in the themes we have identified, that shapes any narrative about human rights in the UK going forward. Those who want to argue strongly in favour of human rights being of relevance to all rather than being a mechanism used by marginalized groups will have to swim against a strong tide. Given the level of dominance that narrative has achieved, the depiction of human rights as a mechanism for Europeanization and juridification, expressed in populist terms, will be very difficult to counter. And even responses to the victims of the conflict in Syria are conditioned by the ways in which human rights are framed by influential sections of the press.

## Notes

1 www.conservatives.com/~/media/files/downloadable/human_rights.pdf.
2 www.publications.parliament.uk/pa/ld200304/ldjudgmt/jd040506/campbe-1.htm.
3 There is more than one legal Europe – but the distinctions between, for example, the European Union and the Council of Europe, or the European Court of Justice and the European Court of Human Rights, are rarely made clear, even in broadsheet newspapers.
4 www.legislation.gov.uk/ukpga/1998/42/contents.
5 www.liberty-human-rights.org.uk/human-rights/what-are-human-rights/human-rights-act/how-human-rights-act-works.
6 https://s3-eu-west-1.amazonaws.com/manifesto2015/ConservativeManifesto2015.pdf.
7 www.telegraph.co.uk/news/worldnews/europe/eu/9820230/David-Camerons-EU-speech-in-full.html.
8 For an account of the passage of the HRA through parliament, see Ewing (1999).
9 Attorney-General May 2010 to July 2014.
10 Lord Chancellor and Secretary of State for Justice, May 2010 to September 2012.
11 www.sheffield.ac.uk/news/nr/ukip-labour-conservatives-research-1.457052.
12 www.telegraph.co.uk/news/politics/11626651/Britain-needs-a-Bill-of-Rights-forthe-individual-and-the-country.html.
13 Rights organizations, aware that the media can play a vital part in mobilization for human rights ends: both in generating public support for human rights and by reporting human rights violations, are trying to exert influence by themselves acting as journalists – see Borer 2012 – but it remains very difficult to get this information into mid-market and tabloid newspapers.
14 Yet despite the media account, of the 297 people winning cases against the UK at the ECtHR, 14 were terrorist cases, 35 were criminals, 45 were prisoners and there were 203 others: see http://rightsinfo.org/infographics/human-rights-uncovered/.
15 Young (2008) illustrates clearly that the challenge posed by the HRA to the sovereignty of parliament is a consistent theme in the legal as well as the political debate.

## References

Borer, T.A. (ed.), 2012. *Media, mobilization and human rights: Mediating Suffering*. London: Zed Books.

ESRC, 2004. *Audience receptions of television news, current affairs and documentary programmes end of award report*. ESRC R/000/23/9669.

European Court of Human Rights [ECtHR], 2012. Case of *Scoppolo* v *Italy* (No. 3). Retrieved on 12 December 2012 from: www.bailii.org/eu/cases/ECHR/2012/868.html.

Ewing, K.D., 1999. *The Human Rights Act and parliamentary democracy. The Modern Law Review*, 62(1), 79–99.

McNulty, D., Watson, N. and Philo, G., 2014. Human rights and prisoners' rights: the British press and the shaping of public debate. *Howard Journal of Criminal Justice*, 53(4), 360–76.

Philo, G., Briant, E. and Donald, P. (2013) *Bad News for Refugees*. London: Pluto.

Philo, G., Miller, D. and Happer, C., 2015. Circuits of communication and structures of power: the sociology of the mass media. Retrieved on 21 April 2016 from: http://www.academia.edu/12813975.
Scott, D., 2012. Sympathy for the devil: human rights and empathetic construction of suffering. *Criminal Justice Matters*, 88(1), 8–9.
Young, A., 2008. *Parliamentary Sovereignty and the Human Rights Act*. Oxford: Hart.

# Index

For Product Safety Concerns and Information please contact our EU representative GPSR@taylorandfrancis.com
Taylor & Francis Verlag GmbH, Kaufingerstraße 24, 80331 München, Germany

www.ingramcontent.com/pod-product-compliance
Ingram Content Group UK Ltd.
Pitfield, Milton Keynes, MK11 3LW, UK
UKHW050755180926
475701UK00007B/1059

*9780367581503*